'WOW! This remarkable volume synthesizes the global and content breadth, offering incredible depth on specific topics, whilst forecasting the future of HRD. It establishes that HRD has become a profession with a legitimate body of knowledge. It will be an invaluable reference for academics and practitioners for years to come.'

Dave Ulrich, Rensis Likert Professor, Ross School of Business, University of Michigan, USA

'This excellent book . . . is a valuable and comprehensive resource for every HR professional, and those in fields that touch and support HRD. Rob Poell, Tonette Rocco, and Gene Roth have sourced and edited a masterful handbook that combines the theoretical and practical. It looks back at the history of the field, delves into current and emerging practices, and asks important questions about the future.'

Tony Bingham President and CEO, ASTD (from the Foreword)

'This text is a significant contribution to contemporary theory and practice in HRD, containing an impressive collection of authoritative treatments from well-established and up-and-coming scholars from 30 countries. I highly recommend it as an invaluable resource for courses on the topic and as an important reference for scholars, public policymakers and practitioners internationally.'

Philip Taylor, Professor of Human Resource Management, Federation University, Australia

'This book is a great guide on Human Resources Development. It is comprehensive and covers all aspects of HRD across the globe. This text is a valuable addition to the HRD literature and gives a macro, micro and a 360 view of HRD.'

Prof. T.V. Rao, Chiarman, TVRao Learning Systems Pvt. Ltd., India

THE ROUTLEDGE COMPANION TO HUMAN RESOURCE DEVELOPMENT

The field of Human Resource Development (HRD) has grown in prominence as an independent discipline from its roots in both management and education since the 1980s. There has been continual debate about the boundaries of HRD ever since.

Drawing on a wide and respected international contributor base and with a focus on international markets, this book provides a thematic overview of current knowledge in HRD across the globe. The text is separated into nine sections which explore the origins of the field, adjacent and related fields, theoretical approaches, policy perspectives, interventions, core issues and concerns, HRD as a profession, HRD around the world, and emerging topics and future trends. An epilogue rounds off the volume by considering the present and future states of the discipline, and suggesting areas for further research.

The Routledge Companion to Human Resource Development is an essential resource for researchers, students and HRD professionals alike.

Rob F. Poell is Professor of Human Resource Development at Tilburg University, the Netherlands. Rob has published widely in leading HRD, management and organization journals. He served as Editor-in-Chief for *Human Resource Development International* from 2010–2012 and was a twice-elected member on the Board of Directors of the Academy of Human Resource Development.

Tonette S. Rocco is Professor and Graduate Program Leader of Adult Education and Human Resource Development at Florida International University, USA. She is a former board member of the HR Certification Institute and the American Society for Training and Development, and is an award-winning author with over 200 publications.

Gene L. Roth is Emeritus Distinguished Teaching Professor of Adult and Higher Education at Northern Illinois University, USA. His research interests include learning to learn, international adult education, workplace learning, and humor and adult learning. He is a past president of the Academy of Human Resource Development.

Routledge Companions in Business, Management and Accounting

Routledge Companions in Business, Management and Accounting are prestige reference works providing an overview of a whole subject area or sub-discipline. These books survey the state of the discipline including emerging and cutting edge areas. Providing a comprehensive, up to date, definitive work of reference, *Routledge Companions* can be cited as an authoritative source on the subject.

A key aspect of these *Routledge Companions* is their international scope and relevance. Edited by an array of highly regarded scholars, these volumes also benefit from teams of contributors which reflect an international range of perspectives.

Individually, *Routledge Companions in Business, Management and Accounting* provide an impactful one-stop-shop resource for each theme covered. Collectively, they represent a comprehensive learning and research resource for researchers, postgraduate students and practitioners.

Published titles in this series include:

The Routledge Companion to Fair Value and Financial Reporting
Edited by Peter Walton

The Routledge Companion to Nonprofit Marketing
Edited by Adrian Sargeant and Walter Wymer Jr

The Routledge Companion to Accounting History
Edited by John Richard Edwards and Stephen P. Walker

The Routledge Companion to Creativity
Edited by Tudor Rickards, Mark A. Runco and Susan Moger

The Routledge Companion to Strategic Human Resource Management
Edited by John Storey, Patrick M. Wright and David Ulrich

The Routledge Companion to International Business Coaching
Edited by Michel Moral and Geoffrey Abbott

The Routledge Companion to Organizational Change
Edited by David M. Boje, Bernard Burnes and John Hassard

The Routledge Companion to Cost Management
Edited by Falconer Mitchell, Hanne Nørreklit and Morten Jakobsen

The Routledge Companion to Digital Consumption
Edited by Russell W. Belk and Rosa Llamas

The Routledge Companion to Identity and Consumption
Edited by Ayalla A. Ruvio and Russell W. Belk

The Routledge Companion to Public-Private Partnerships
Edited by Piet de Vries and Etienne B. Yehoue

The Routledge Companion to Accounting, Reporting and Regulation
Edited by Carien van Mourik and Peter Walton

The Routledge Companion to International Management Education
Edited by Denise Tsang, Hamid H. Kazeroony and Guy Ellis

The Routledge Companion to Accounting Communication
Edited by Lisa Jack, Jane Davison and Russell Craig

The Routledge Companion to Visual Organization
Edited by Emma Bell, Jonathan Schroeder and Samantha Warren

The Routledge Companion to Arts Marketing
Edited by Daragh O'Reilly, Ruth Rentschler and Theresa Kirchner

The Routledge Companion to Alternative Organization
Edited by Martin Parker, George Cheney, Valerie Fournier and Chris Land

The Routledge Companion to the Future of Marketing
Edited by Luiz Moutinho, Enrique Bigne and Ajay K. Manrai

The Routledge Companion to Accounting Education
Edited by Richard M. S. Wilson

The Routledge Companion to Business in Africa
Edited by Sonny Nwankwo and Kevin Ibeh

The Routledge Companion to Human Resource Development
Edited by Rob F. Poell, Tonette S. Rocco and Gene L. Roth

THE ROUTLEDGE COMPANION TO HUMAN RESOURCE DEVELOPMENT

Edited by Rob F. Poell, Tonette S. Rocco and Gene L. Roth

Routledge
Taylor & Francis Group
LONDON AND NEW YORK

First published 2015
by Routledge
2 Park Square, Milton Park, Abingdon, Oxon OX14 4RN

and by Routledge
711 Third Avenue, New York, NY 10017

Routledge is an imprint of the Taylor & Francis Group, an informa business

British Library Cataloguing in Publication Data
A catalogue record for this book is available from the British Library

Library of Congress Cataloging-in-Publication Data
The Routledge companion to human resource development / edited by Rob F. Poell, Tonette S. Rocco, and Gene L. Roth.
pages cm. — (Routledge companions in business, management, and accounting)
Includes bibliographical references and index.
1. Personnel management. 2. Human capital. 3. Organizational learning. 4. Manpower policy. I. Poell, Rob F. (Robert Frans), 1968– II. Rocco, Tonette S., 1954– III. Roth, Gene Leon.
HF5549.R637 2014
658.3—dc23
2014002636

ISBN: 978-0-415-82042-4 (hbk)
ISBN: 978-0-203-38644-6 (ebk)

Typeset in ApexBembo
by Apex CoVantage, LLC

CONTENTS

PREFACE

When we started floating our initial ideas for the *Routledge Companion to Human Resource Development*, it quickly became apparent that all three of us wanted this handbook to be truly international, in terms of content, authorship, and orientation. Most books published by Western publishing houses with Western editors contain chapters with a Western orientation. Although many of this Companion's chapters have a Western orientation, a broad range of other chapters were written by non-Western authors who have given ample description of Human Resource Development (HRD) in their homeland and/or who have included non-Western perspectives on HRD.

HRD means many things to many people and its meanings can differ greatly across geographical and cultural contexts. At the heart of HRD, however, we believe is a sincere concern with furthering the learning, growth, and flourishing of people in the context of organizations and/or nations. The aim of this book is to bring together key authors and core themes that have shaped and will be shaping the field of HRD in all its richness and diversity. We believe the audience for this book is as international as its authors are, and practitioners and scholars alike will find its content relevant and useful.

The section on "HRD around the world" is probably the clearest manifestation of our desire for this book to go beyond the dominant focus on Western conceptions of HRD. It contains eleven chapters that describe the state of (what could be labeled) HRD in, amongst others, Ghana, South Africa, Chile, Panama, Mexico, Canada, India, China, the Middle East, Japan, Taiwan, Australia, New Zealand, Hungary, and Poland. These chapters alone dramatically enrich our view of how human resources are developed across planet Earth.

Also within many of the chapters on core themes, we brought together authors from different countries and cultures to write on a subject relevant to HRD. Hence, the chapter on performance improvement was prepared by authors from South Korea and Argentina. The contribution that deals with social capital theory was authored by Claire Gubbins (Ireland) and Russ Korte (US). Who better to draft a paper on National Human Resource Development (NHRD) than the combination of Gary McLean (Canada) and AAhad Osman-Gani (Malaysia)? The topic of diversity and inclusion was tackled by Martin Kormanik (US) and Peter Nwaoma (Nigeria); that of certification by Canadian and British scholars. The work–life system was described by Sunny Munn (US) and Hae-Young Lee (South Korea). And there are more in this volume, which features authors hailing from some 30 different countries.

Besides those chapters in the "HRD around the world" section, the remaining 42 chapters are loosely organized in eight sections dealing with the origins of the field, adjacent and related fields, theoretical approaches, policy perspectives, interventions, core issues and concerns, HRD as a profession, and emerging topics and future trends. Although the large number of chapters may suggest otherwise, we did not attempt to be complete in presenting the current field of HRD. Even disregarding the definitional difficulties this attempt would have brought with it, we could probably have filled a few more volumes dealing with topics relevant to the HRD field. Simply put, this *Routledge Companion to Human Resource Development* contains those themes and authors that we felt could not be omitted in any internationally relevant HRD handbook.

To deal with the inevitable diversity ensuing from such an attempt, we created an epilogue chapter ("A synopsis of the present, future and intrigue of HRD") with input from our authors. This final contribution to the book consists of their summative comments on three questions related to their respective chapter topics: (1) What is the current state of affairs? (2) What should we be concerned about in future? (3) What intriguing research question needs addressing most? A conceptual matrix was formed on the basis of the answers provided by the authors and its contents provide a fascinating summary of where the HRD field is and where it should go.

Rob F. Poell
Tonette S. Rocco
Gene L. Roth

Tilburg, Netherlands/Miami, FL/St Charles, IL
January, 2014

FOREWORD

Could you run your business without good people working for you? I couldn't. People are every organization's most valuable resource. It doesn't matter what industry you're in, what product you make, or what cause you serve; if you don't have the right people with the right skills working in the right jobs, you cannot achieve your goals. Organizations that are best positioned to grow and succeed have leaders who understand this. These same leaders also understand that it isn't enough to have the right people in the right jobs, there must also be a commitment to developing the talents and skills of those people. Jack Welch, the former CEO of General Electric once said, "My main job was developing talent. I was a gardener providing water and other nourishment to our top 750 people. Of course, I had to pull out some weeds, too."

In a recent column posted on LinkedIn Welch, now Executive Chairman of the Jack Welch Management Institute stated, "Look, HR should be every company's 'killer app'. What could possibly be more important than who gets hired, developed, promoted, or moved out the door? Business is a game, and as with all games, the team that puts the best people on the field and gets them playing together wins. It's that simple."

This is classic Welch, of course, but the truth of his observation is rock solid.

The value of human capital has never been more important. I hear this everywhere I travel as the president and CEO of the Association for Talent Development, formerly ASTD. Finding talent – and keeping talent – is a top priority. And it is challenging. In today's knowledge economy where technology advances in what seems like the blink of an eye, where a dispersed workforce is very often the norm, and where multiple generations and cultures work side by side, the challenges associated with developing human capital are very real. Layer on top of this the demands of the global economy, scalability, economic pressures, regulations, policies, and a variety of other factors and you see why human resource development is a field laced with complexities.

Human resource development (HRD) as a profession has reinvented itself over time. No longer just about hiring, benefits, and a handful of training courses, HRD now intersects with organizational development, career development, performance improvement, and more. The profession has evolved as business has evolved. And yet, if you were to ask five CEOs what "human resource development" means, you'd likely get five different answers. As the editors of this book wisely note, HRD means many things to many people, and those meanings can differ greatly based on geography as well.

So how do you make sense of a vast and complex field like HRD? How do you get a sense of where it should be going or what it could be achieving? Business leaders who want to grow their companies have a vested interest in what the future of HRD looks like.

This excellent book advances the conversation. It is a valuable and comprehensive resource for every HR professional, and those in fields that touch and support HRD. Rob Poell, Tonette Rocco, and Gene Roth have sourced and edited a masterful handbook that combines the theoretical and practical. It looks back at the history of the field, delves into current and emerging practices, and asks important questions about the future.

Most importantly, in my view, it brings valuable international insights. Section VIII, titled "HRD around the world," offers the perspectives of geographically diverse authors. HRD issues in Ghana, South Africa, Central and South America, the Middle East, India, China, Japan, Taiwan, New Zealand, Australia, the European Union, Hungary, and Poland are explored. I cannot think of another book that takes this unique approach to unpacking how geography impacts this field.

These important perspectives are reason enough to read the book. But the authors offer so much more. The scholarly work presented in several chapters is important and informative.

Context is paramount. There is a nice progression from laying the groundwork about the history of the profession and different avenues associated with HRD like technical and vocational learning, and continuing professional development. The ancillary fields, like organizational development and performance improvement, are discussed. This is important to help fully appreciate how HRD influences so many aspects of achieving any organization's full potential.

Understanding how adult learning differs from K-12 (primary) education is important if you want to make sure organizational learning initiatives are effective. In today's world where social media create connections and learning opportunities, understanding social capital theory and the learning-network theory are beneficial for those developing HRD practices. This is equally true for systems, human capital, and screening theories. In short, one of the powerful strengths of this book is providing the depth of research and context that forms and supports the broader HRD profession. The authors brought some of the best and brightest researchers to this effort and we all benefit from their perspective.

I also appreciate the authors' Epilogue which provides an excellent synopsis of all 53 chapters. Each contributor provides summative comments about their chapters, and the editors form a matrix of their answers revealing an intriguing summary of insights on where the field is today and where it's going. This is intriguing from several perspectives. Because of the multiple international and disciplinary perspectives provided in the book we are able to view HRD not only across cultures, but also across disciplines and ideologies. In today's global business environment, a broad perspective is invaluable when considering how best to invest in, and leverage, the talent in an organization.

Poell, Rocco, and Roth also asked each contributor to posit an interesting research question based on the topics they addressed. This singular question holds so much potential for the HRD profession. It is my sincere hope that today's students and researchers in the field will take up the challenge presented here. HRD has evolved over time and our understanding of it will continue to grow and develop, but we need people – like the authors of this book – to probe deeper, ask different questions and . . . learn.

Organizations have no greater resource than the people who work in them. Those of us who are lucky enough to work in roles that support the development of this talent should be grateful to the authors of this book.

Tony Bingham
President and CEO, Association for Talent Development, formerly ASTD

FIGURES

TABLES

CONTRIBUTORS

Mesut Akdere, PhD, is Associate Professor of Human Resource Development in the Department of Administrative Leadership at the University of Wisconsin-Milwaukee, United States, and a visiting professor in the College of Business at Antalya International University. His research focuses on quality management, leadership, and performance improvement through training and organization development. He conducts research both in the US and internationally. He has published in T&D, HRD, organization development, and education journals. He is the recipient of the 2012 Early Career Scholar Award of the Academy of Human Resource Development.

Meera Alagaraja, PhD, is Assistant Professor of Human Resource and Organization Development at the University of Louisville (USA), where she teaches leadership, performance improvement and organizational learning. Her research interests include strategic HRD, employee well-being and international HRD. Her work has appeared in publications such as *Human Resource Development Review, Human Resource Development International, Human Resource Development Quarterly,* and *European Journal of Training and Development.*

Carlos Albornoz, EdD, is Assistant Professor at the Business School, Universidad del Desarrollo in Santiago, Chile. He obtained a degree in Psychology from the Pontificia Universidad Católica de Valparaíso, Chile, an MS in Business and a doctorate in Adult Education from the Florida International University. He has been consultant for the Interamercican Development Bank and national coordinator of policies about HRD for the Chilean Ministry of Economy.

Alexandre Ardichvili, PhD, is Professor of HRD at the University of Minnesota, United States. He has published an edited book and more than 70 peer-reviewed articles and book chapters related to HRD, international education, entrepreneurship, business ethics, and knowledge management. He is Editor-in-Chief of *Human Resource Development International* and Fellow of the Center for Ethical Business Cultures. Alexandre has done consulting and/or applied research at many businesses and nonprofits in the US, Europe, Asia, and Latin America.

Nana K. Arthur-Mensah is PhD candidate in the Educational Leadership and Organizational Development Program at the University of Louisville, United States. Her research interests include the use of work-based learning to improve human resource and economic development. She has presented papers on technical vocational education and training (TVET) in emerging markets, apprenticeships and women in non-traditional occupations. She has degrees from the University of Ghana and the University of Louisville. Her career interest includes policy and academia.

Arup Barman, PhD, is Associate Professor in the Master of Business Administration Program in Jawaharlal Nehru School of Management Studies at Assam University, India. His research aims to explore issues and status of cross-national and national human resource development. He is a visionary researcher and academician for developmental thinking in the context of human resources in developing economics. His work has been published in several peer-reviewed journals, books, and received many celebrated awards.

Kenneth R. Bartlett, PhD, is Professor of Human Resource Development in the Department of Organizational Leadership, Policy, and Development and Associate Dean in the College of Education and Human Development at the University of Minnesota, United States. Originally from New Zealand, his research has focused on many aspects of international HRD. In addition, he conducts ongoing research to explore the links between HRD, organizational commitment, and employee engagement.

Paul Bélanger, PhD, became Director (1989–2000) of the UNESCO Institute for Lifelong Learning in Germany after directing research centers on adult learning in Canada. He is now professor at UQAM in Montreal and director of the Research Center on Lifelong Learning. He is (co-)author of *Lifelong Learning* (1995), *The Emergence of Learning Societies. Who Participates in Adult Education?* (1997), *Transitions toward LLL* (1998), *Transnational Analysis of Adult Learning Policies* (1999), and *Theories of Adult Learning* (2011).

Stephen Billett, PhD, is Professor of Adult and Vocational Education in the School of Education and Professional Studies at Griffith University, Brisbane, Australia and also an Australian Research Council Future Fellow. He has worked as a vocational educator, educational administrator, teacher educator, professional development practitioner and policy developer within the Australian vocational education system. Since 1992, he has researched learning through and for work and in the fields of vocational and professional education.

Travor C. Brown, PhD, is Professor of Human Resource Management and Labor Relations with the Faculty of Business, Memorial University of Newfoundland, Canada. An active HRD and IR scholar, he has published over 20 journal articles and co-authored one of Canada's leading industrial relations textbooks. His research often focuses on issues of employee and management development as well as HR practices in unionized firms.

Saul Carliner, PhD, is Associate Professor, Provost Fellow for e-Learning, and Director of the Education Doctoral Program at Concordia University in Montreal, Canada. His research focuses on the design of materials for workplace learning and communication, the management of groups that produce these materials, and the transfer of research to practice. He has over 175 publications and is a past Chair of the Certification Steering Committee for the Canadian Society for Training and Development.

Bronwyn Cass is a graduate student studying employment relations. She has worked as a research assistant with Dr Travor Brown on topics such as human resource development, training transfer and goal setting. Since beginning her studies at Memorial University, Canada, she has won awards allowing her to do research on employment issues both locally and internationally. Bronwyn has professional experience in the advertising and retail industries.

Ronald M. Cervero, PhD, is the Associate Vice President for Instruction and Professor in the Department Lifelong Education, Administration, and Policy at the University of Georgia. He has published extensively about lifespan professional development and education and two of his books have received the Cyril O. Houle World Award for Literature in Adult Education: *Effective Continuing Education for Professionals* in 1989 and *Working the Planning Table: Negotiating Democratically for Adult, Continuing, and Workplace Education* in 2006.

Yonjoo Cho, PhD, is Associate Professor of Instructional Systems Technology at Indiana University, United States. She worked as an HR professional for more than 10 years in South Korea, both in business and academic sectors. Her research interest centers on action learning in organizations, based on her experience in working as an external facilitator in large companies. Other research interests include learning in organizations and HRD. She received her PhD degree in Instructional Technology from the University of Texas at Austin.

Simone C.O. Conceição, PhD, is Professor for the University of Wisconsin-Milwaukee School of Education Department of Administrative Leadership and holds a PhD in Adult Learning and Distance Education from the University of Wisconsin-Madison and a Master's degree in Administration and Development of Adult and Continuing Education Programs from the University of Wisconsin-Milwaukee, United States. Her research interests include adult learning, online education, impact of technology on teaching and learning, instructional design, staff development, and international education.

Maria Cseh, PhD, is Associate Professor of Human and Organizational Learning at the George Washington University, United States, and Honorary Professor at the University of Pécs, Hungary. Her refereed publications focus on informal learning, change and leadership across cultures, and global mindset and competence. She is a member of journal/non-profit organizations' Editorial and Advisory Boards, was elected to serve for two terms on the AHRD Board of Directors, and serves as advisor and consultant to organizations.

Barbara J. Daley, PhD, is currently Interim Dean for the School of Education at the University of Wisconsin-Milwaukee, United States. Previously Daley served as a faculty member earning the rank of Professor, as well as Department Chair and Associate Dean. Holder of a doctoral degree in adult and continuing education from Cornell University, her research interests surround activities designed to expand the current knowledge base related to the linkages between learning theory, the context of professional practice and adult education.

Alexandra Dehmel, PhD, joined the European Centre for the Development of Vocational Training (Cedefop, Greece) in 2010 and works as an expert in the field of Adult and Work-Based Learning. She holds a Diploma degree in Vocational Education and Training (VET) and Business Studies from the University of Munich, Germany, a Master of Science degree in Comparative and International Education from the University of Oxford, United Kingdom, and a Doctorate in Economic Sciences from the University of Paderborn, Germany. She has over 10 years of experience in VET research.

Maarten de Laat, PhD, is Professor of Professional Development in Social Networks at the Welten Institute, Research Center for Learning, Teaching and Technology at the Open University of the Netherlands. His research concentrates on informal learning in the workplace, lifelong learning, professional development and knowledge creation through (online) social networks and communities. He is also interested in the impact that technology, learning analytics and social design have on the ways in which these networks and communities work, learn and create value.

José Ernesto Rangel Delgado, PhD, is Professor in the Faculty of Economics; Coordinator of the Transpacific Relations PhD; and director of the Pacific Basin Studies Center and APEC Study Center at the University of Colima, Mexico. He got his PhD from the Academy of Sciences of Russia (1991). He was Pacific Circle Consortium President (2007–2009); APEC Study Centers Mexican Consortium Chairman (2009–2011); Korea Foundation Fellowship (2010); and Southern Baja California Autonomous University visiting professor (2012–2013).

Khalil M. Dirani, PhD, is Associate Professor in, and Program Chair of, the Human Resources and Organization Development (HROD) program at the University of Georgia, United States. Khalil's research focuses on testing applicability of Western management and change theories in international contexts and understanding cultural differences and their effect on international HRD and HRM practices. His articles have appeared in both research and professional publications including *HRD International*, *European Journal for T&D*, *Advances in Developing HR*, and *HRM International*.

Toby Egan, PhD, is a tenured Associate Professor in Public Policy at the University of Maryland (UMD) in the United States and Senior Fellow at UMD's Robert H. Smith School of Business. Dr. Egan previously served as associate professor and Director of International HR Programs at Texas A&M University and was also a tenured associate professor at Purdue University, Indianapolis. Toby also served as Vice-President for ProGroup/Korn/Ferry International, facilitating executive coaching and organization development in Fortune 500, multinational, governmental and non-governmental organizations. He is an award winning researcher and doctoral student advisor.

Andrea D. Ellinger, PhD, is Professor of Human Resource Development at The University of Texas at Tyler, United States. She has published and presented her research nationally and internationally. Andrea is the Editor of *Human Resource Development Quarterly* and is the recipient of the 2012 Academy of Human Resource Development Scholar of the Year Award. Her research interests include informal learning in the workplace, organizational learning, evolving managerial roles, managerial coaching, mentoring, and the learning organization concept.

Tara Fenwick, PhD, is Professor of Education at the University of Stirling in the United Kingdom, and Director of ProPEL, international network for research in Professional Practice, Education and Learning (www.propel.stir.ac.uk). Her research focuses on understanding learning, knowledge politics and practice in professional work. Her most recent books include *Reconceptualising Professional Learning: Sociomaterial Knowledges and Practices* (with M. Nerland, Routledge 2014), *Governing Knowledge: Comparison, Knowledge-based Technologies and Expertise in the Regulation of Education* (with E. Mangez and J. Ozga, Routledge 2013) and *Emerging Approaches for Educational Research: Tracing the Sociomaterial* (with R. Edwards and P. Sawchuk, Routledge 2011).

Thomas N. Garavan, EdD, is Research Professor-Leadership at Edinburgh Napier Business School. He has authored or co-authored 14 books and over 100 refereed journal papers and book chapters. Thomas is Editor-in-Chief of the *European Journal of Training and Development* and Associate Editor of *Personnel Review*. He is a member of the editorial board of *Human Resource Development Review*, *Advances in Developing Human Resources*, *Human Resource Management Journal*, *Human Resource Development International* and *Human Resource Development Quarterly*.

Rajashi Ghosh, PhD, is Assistant Professor in the Human Resource Development program with the School of Education at Drexel University, United States. Her research aims to explore different factors (e.g. mentoring, coaching, workplace incivility) that can reinforce or hinder workplace learning and development both in domestic and international contexts. Prior to joining academics, Rajashi worked in the corporate sector on employee development and performance management. Her work has been published in several peer-reviewed journals and has been recognized by many prestigious awards.

Rod P. Githens, PhD, is Associate Professor in Policy, Organization, and Leadership at Drexel University, United States. His interests center around fostering humane, accessible, and diverse workplaces. He has worked and studied extensively in Panama and Mexico. Prior to beginning his faculty career, Rod worked for several years in the corporate sector doing HRM and HRD work. He continues to consult with various types of organizations through his consulting practice, Githens and Associates.

Librado Enrique Gonzalez, PhD, is author of several books on communication and management excellence. He has written several Human Resource Management and Lean Implementation articles in business sections of North Carolina Newspapers. He sits on the Board of Advisors for Stevenson University, United States. He has recently completed a Latin America research project on "Attributes for teaching effectiveness" in collaboration with Tampa University. His new book *Latin America – The New Land of Opportunities* came out in March of 2014.

Claire Gubbins, PhD, is Lecturer of HRM and Organizational Behavior at Dublin City University, Ireland, Deputy Director at LINK Research Centre, and Associate Editor for *Human Resource Development Quarterly*. Research awards include: a Fulbright Scholarship, Government of Ireland Scholarship, a University of Limerick Registrars Scholarship, an Academy of HRD Finalist award for her dissertation. She has published in *Organization Studies*, *Journal of Management Inquiry*, *Advances in Developing Human Resources*, *Human Resource Development Review* and *Journal of European Industrial Training*.

Robert G. (Bob) Hamlin, PhD, is Professor Emeritus and Chair of HRD at the University of Wolverhampton, United Kingdom. His research interests are focused mainly on "perceived managerial and leadership effectiveness" within public and private sector organizations within the UK and a diverse range of other countries around the globe. The results have been published widely in management and HRD-related international journals, and he has contributed over 20 authored and co-authored chapters to numerous HRD-related books.

Roger Harris, PhD, is Professor in the School of Education at the University of South Australia. He has had extensive experience in VET teacher education and VET research, publishing widely on many aspects of national training reform. He has been Vice President of the Australian VET Research Association. Currently, he is Program Leader (Workforce Development) in the CRC for Rail Innovation, serves on academic boards of two private providers, and edits the *International Journal of Training Research*.

Joshua D. Hawley, EdD, is Associate Professor in the John Glenn School of Public Affairs and Director of the Ohio Education Research Center, United States. He teaches courses on education and workforce policy, and conducts research on government efforts to train the workforce for the future. In recent years he has worked extensively on federal and state efforts to develop data systems to monitor educational performance of the workforce.

Linda M. Hite, PhD, is Professor and Chair of Organizational Leadership and Supervision at Indiana University-Purdue University Fort Wayne, United States. Her publications include journals and book chapters primarily focused on career development and workplace diversity. She serves on the editorial boards of *Advances in Developing Human Resources* and *Human Resource Development Quarterly*. Prior to joining the faculty at IPFW, she worked in corporate training and development and in academic administration.

Jian Huang, PhD, is Vice President of the Shanghai Institute for Lifelong Education and Professor of the first graduate program in Adult Education/Human Resource Development of East China Normal University in China. The main interests of her team focus on: workplace learning and HRD, organizational learning and learning organization, continuing professional development, lifelong education policies, learning communities, etc. She is also a Fulbright Scholar and active in promoting international academic exchange in lifelong learning.

Holly M. Hutchins, PhD, is Associate Professor of Human Resource Development at the University of Houston, United States. Her research areas are in transfer of learning, organizational crisis management, and faculty development and leadership. Dr. Hutchins has published work in leading HRD and performance improvement journals, and is a sought out speaker on transfer of learning. She was awarded the Academy of Human Resource Development Early Career Scholar Award in 2011.

Paul Iles, PhD, is Professor of Leadership and HRM at Glasgow School for Business and Society, Glasgow Caledonian University, United Kingdom. A Chartered Psychologist, Associate Fellow of the British Psychological Society, and Chartered Fellow of the Chartered Institute for Personnel and Development, he has a particular interest in leadership development, international HRM and talent management, publishing in *The Journal of World Business* and the *International Journal of Human Resource Management* and designing research and change programs in the UK and China.

Knud Illeris, PhD, is a freelance educational consultant and Emeritus Professor of Lifelong Learning at Aarhus University, Denmark. He has also been professor of educational research, leader of Learning Lab Denmark's consortium for Learning in Working Life, honorable adjunct professor at Columbia University, and member of the International Adult Education Hall of Fame. His most important books are *How We Learn, Contemporary Theories of Learning, The Fundamentals of Workplace Learning*, and *Transformative Learning and Identity*.

Maimunah Ismail, PhD, is Professor at Universiti Putra, Malaysia. Her current research foci include career development of the millennial employees and Malaysian returnees. She has authored twelve books and numerous articles in international journals. She sits on the Editorial Advisory Board of journals such as *Gender in Management, Human Resource Development International*, and *European Journal of Training and Development*. She is a member of the Academy of Human Resource Development and the British Academy of Management.

Ronald L. Jacobs, PhD, is Professor of Human Resource Development and Director of International Programs, College of Education, University of Illinois at Urbana-Champaign, United States. He has written over 100 journal articles and book chapters, and has authored or edited six books that address a range of topics including workplace learning and performance, system theory applied to HRD, and structured on-the-job training. Ron is emeritus professor of workforce development and education at The Ohio State University.

Clare Kelliher, PhD, is Professor of Work and Organization at Cranfield School of Management, Cranfield University, United Kingdom. Her principal research interests are in the organization of work and the management of the employment relationship. She is the author of many published papers and book chapters. Her recent book, *New Ways of Organising Work*, co-edited with Julia Richardson was published by Routledge.

Jennifer Kelly, PhD, is Professor and Department Chair of Educational Policy Studies in the Faculty of Education, University of Alberta, Canada. Her research areas are race, racialization, and the histories of racialized communities. Her current work includes mapping the Alberta history of African Canadian and other racialized workers. Her books include *Work and Learning: An Introduction* 2013 (with Bruce Spencer), *Under the Gaze: Learning to be Black in White Society*, and *Borrowed Identities*.

Joseph W.M. Kessels, PhD, is Professor of Human Resource Development at the University of Twente, Netherlands. His main research interest is in the transformation of the day-to-day workplace into a powerful learning environment, in specific in the context of an emerging knowledge economy. He studied andragology at the University of Amsterdam with a strong focus on emancipation, empowerment and self-directedness.

Heather C. Kissack, PhD, is the Executive Director of Human Resources and Institutional Development at Hill College, United States. Her research interests include sex and gender matters in organizations, critical HRD, and organizational culture. Her work has appeared in the Journal of European Industrial Training, and she has presented at several conferences including the annual conferences hosted by the Academy of Human Resource Development and the University Forum of Human Resource Development.

Ann Kohut, EdD, began her career as a junior high science teacher. She earned an MBA degree in 1994 and her EdD in 2010 (Northern Illinois University, United States). Ann has held a variety of positions in her 22 years with Motorola, including marketing; sales; supply chain, operations and training management. Ann is currently the Chief Learning Officer at Nokia Solutions and Networks. Her research interests include change management, learning organization, and organizational politics.

Martin B. Kormanik, EdD, is President and CEO of OD Systems (www.odsystems.com), providing organizational assessment, consulting, training, facilitation, and coaching services. He has 35 years of experience working with corporations, government agencies, and nonprofits to enhance organizational, work group, and individual learning and performance. His published research focuses on individual and organizational development. He serves as Professorial Lecturer on the graduate faculty of the George Washington University. He earned his doctorate from the same institution.

Russell Korte, PhD, is Associate Professor at Colorado State University, United States. He has been a researcher for the Center for the Advancement of Engineering Education. His research investigates how professionals navigate their education and how they transition into the workplace – specifically studying how they adapt to the social and political systems in organizations. Research interests include theory, philosophy, social science, workplace learning and performance, socialization, adult and professional education, and organization studies.

Andre Kraak, PhD, is Research Associate at the Centre for Researching Education and Labor, University of Witwatersrand, Johannesburg, South Africa, teaching a master's program on "Sectors, skills and the economic evolution of South Africa". Prior to this, he was Executive Director of a Research Program focusing on Human Resources Development at the Human Sciences Research Council (HSRC) in Pretoria. His research interests span further and higher education, skills development, and science and technology policy studies.

Béla Krisztián, PhD, is Professor Emeritus of Adult Education and Human Resource Development at the University of Pécs, Hungary. He is the author of more than 250 Hungarian, Russian and English language publications in the areas of organizational psychology, organization development, risk assessment, ergonomics, curriculum development, transfer of learning and innovation. He is the editor of the journal of *Tudásmenedzsment* (Knowledge Management Journal), a leading Hungarian refereed journal.

K. Peter Kuchinke, PhD, is Professor of Human Resource Development at the University of Illinois at Urbana-Champaign, United States. A native German, he holds a doctoral degree from the University of Minnesota in Human Resource Development and Strategic Management. His current research interests include the role of work in overall life design, self-directed career behaviors, and cross-cultural differences in career preparation and development. He is past editor of *Human Resource Development International.*

Min-Hsun Christine Kuo, PhD, is Assistant Professor at the National Central University in Taiwan. Receiving her degrees in BA in Economics, MA and PhD both in Human Resource Development from the University of Minnesota, she teaches Organization Development, HRD, and Organizational Behavior. Her professional experiences include speeches, lectures, training, and workshops in government agencies, academic institutions, and enterprises. She serves as reviewer and committee member in domestic and international journals. She has been rewarded with various awards.

Sarah Leberman, PhD, is Professor of Leadership at Massey University, New Zealand. Her current research interests are women and leadership in sport and academia, and the transfer of learning. Her research publications have focused on mothers in sport leadership roles, and as elite athletes. In 2008 as a Fulbright Senior Scholar she was based at the Tucker Centre, University of Minnesota, United States. Sarah is Chair of the New Zealand Women in Leadership program steering group.

Hae-Young Lee, EdD, is Researcher at the National Institute for Lifelong Education in South Korea. He has led projects on: job analysis of the "Lifelong Education Consultant", network analysis of literacy instructors, and knowledge management strategies of higher education institutions. He developed a manual for Recognition for Prior Learning, which is designed to link higher educational institutions with various life experiences. Since 2011, he has participated in "AllinHE project", an international research project sponsored by the European Union.

Mimi Miyoung Lee, PhD, is Associate Professor in the Department of Curriculum and Instruction at the University of Houston, United States. She received her doctorate degree in Instructional Systems Technology in 2004 from Indiana University at Bloomington. Her research interests include theories of identity formation, sociological examination of online communities, cross-cultural communication, issues of representation, and critical ethnography.

Monica Lee, PhD, is Visiting Professor at Northumbria University and Life Member of Lancaster University, United Kingdom. She is a Chartered Psychologist, Fellow of CIPD, and Associate Fellow of the British Psychological Society. She is Founding Editor-in-Chief of *Human Resource Development International* (1998–2002), Editor of the Routledge monograph series *Studies in HRD*, and Executive Secretary to the University Forum for HRD. She has worked extensively in Central Europe, CIS and the USA coordinating and collaborating in research and teaching initiatives.

Jessica Li, PhD, is Associate Professor of Human Resource Development, University of Illinois at Urbana-Champaign. She is Associate Editor of *Human Resource Development International* and Senior Research Fellow for The Conference Board. Prior to becoming a professor, she worked for large multinational corporations Motorola, Nokia, and Raytheon as a business executive for ten years. Her current research interest including effective organizational HRD initiatives, changes in employee work related values and attitudes with a focus on China.

Doo Hun Lim, PhD, is Associate Professor of Adult and Higher Education at the University of Oklahoma, United States. He received his PhD in Human Resource Education from the University of Illinois at Urbana-Champaign. He teaches OD, T&D, and evaluation courses at the graduate level. His primary research interests include: cross-cultural HRD curriculum issues, integration of learning and knowledge management, generational studies focusing on knowledge management, and cross-cultural organizational issues impacting workplace performance.

Clíodhna A. MacKenzie is Lecturer in the School of Management and Marketing at University College Cork, Ireland. She holds a degree in Business from the University of Limerick. She has previously worked for both US multinationals and global IT consulting firms. Her academic research focuses on "dark side" organizational behavior such as organizational narcissism, leadership derailment, counterproductive work practices, and organizational personality disorders. Her research interests include risk-taking behavior, corporate governance, ethics, CSR, HRM/D, and leadership and organization development.

Victoria J. Marsick, PhD, is Professor of Adult Learning and Leadership and Co-Director with Martha A. Gephart of the Huber Institute at Teachers College, Columbia University, United States. She holds a PhD in Adult Education from the University of California, Berkeley, and a MIPA from Syracuse University. Victoria's scholarly interests include informal learning, action learning, team and organizational learning. With Karen Watkins, she developed and validated the "Dimensions of the Learning Organization Questionnaire" used in numerous published studies.

Kimberly S. McDonald, EdD, is Professor of Organizational Leadership and Supervision and Associate Dean for the College of Engineering, Technology, and Computer Science at Indiana-Purdue University Fort Wayne, United States. Currently she is also Editor-in-Chief for *Advances in Developing Human Resources*. Prior to joining the faculty at IPFW, she worked in training and development. She has published a variety of book chapters and journal articles, most of which focus on career development.

David McGuire, PhD, is Senior Lecturer in Human Resource Development and Deputy Director of MBA programs at Edinburgh Napier University, United Kingdom. To date, he has published two textbooks and over 30 articles in journals including *European Journal of Training and Development*, *Advances in Developing Human Resources*, *Human Resource Development Review* and *Human Resource Development Quarterly*. David serves as Associate Editor of *Advances in Developing Human Resources* and also sits on the Editorial Boards of *Human Resource Development Quarterly* and *Journal of Change Management*.

Gary N. McLean, EdD (PhD hon.), is President of McLean Global Consulting, Inc., an OD family business. He teaches regularly at graduate programs in Thailand, Mexico, and France. He was formerly a senior professor at Texas A&M University and is professor emeritus at the University of Minnesota, United States. He served as President of the Academy of HRD and the International Management Development Association. His research interests focus on organization development and national and international HRD. He has been appointed as Renowned Scholar at the Graduate School of Business in the International Islamic University, Malaysia, for the second half of 2014.

Sunny L. Munn, PhD, is an Assistant Professor of Leadership Studies in the College of Education at Ashland University, United States. Previously she served as Postdoctoral Associate for the Ohio Education Research Center (OERC) at The Ohio State University (OSU), where she received a PhD in Workforce Development and Education. Her previous experience in higher education includes advising, teaching in corporate training and development, and research on the evaluation of TANF demonstration (welfare-to-work) projects. Current research focuses on the work-life system, the intersection of organizational culture, work-life benefits and organizational performance, non-traditional families including men and sexual minorities, and low-wage workers.

Kyoung-Ah Nam, PhD, is an Assistant Professor of the School of International Service at American University in Washington, DC, United States. As a scholar-practitioner, she has extensive experience working with key international organizations and multi-national corporations. Her research and publications, which draw upon this experience, cover subjects such as intercultural training, cross-cultural communication, international education, and global leadership development. Originally from South Korea, she has worked and traveled in more than 40 countries over the last 16 years.

Zsolt Nemeskéri, PhD, is Dean of the School of Adult Education and Human Resource Development and Associate Professor at the University of Pécs, Hungary. He is the author of more than 50 Hungarian and English language publications in the areas of measurement of HRD activities, and the role of HRD in equal opportunities and corporate social responsibility. As an HRD consultant he works with McDonald's, AVON Cosmetics, Hungarian Post, and Paks Nuclear Power Plant.

Paul L. Nesbit, PhD, is Senior Lecturer at the Graduate School of Management at Macquarie University in Sydney, Australia. He has degrees in Psychology, Sociology, and an MBA and PhD in Organizational Behavior from the University of New South Wales. His current research focuses on self-development and learning processes of managers. He sits on the editorial board of the *Human Resource Development Review* and *Employment Relations Record*.

Femke Nijland, PhD, is Assistant Professor at the Welten Institute, Research Center for Learning, Teaching and Technology at the Open University of the Netherlands. Her research focuses on how educational professionals create knowledge in verbal interaction in informal settings such as networks and communities. In addition she studies how these professionals create value in these processes, both for themselves and for their stakeholders.

Peter Chikwendu Nwaoma is a PhD student in Human Resources Management at Michael Okpara University of Agriculture, Umudike, Nigeria. He was a university planner and manpower analyst previously hired by the National Universities Commission, Nigeria. Since 1993 he has served in various executive capacities as Head, Human Resources, Planning Officer, and ultimately as the Acting Registrar of Michael Okpara University of Agriculture, Umudike in 2011. Peter has been a resource person at various intellectual and professional discourses with interest in public policy and diversity issues. He has 16 years of experience as a part-time lecturer.

AAhad M. Osman-Gani, PhD, is Professor and Director (Dean), Graduate School of Management, IIUM University, Malaysia. He worked at Nanyang Business School of Singapore, and at several organizations/universities in the USA, Bangladesh, China, Saudi Arabia. Published extensively in the fields of HRD and International Management, he was recognized as Outstanding HRD Scholar by the Academy of HRD. He is the Editor of IJTD and Board Member of several journals published from the USA and the UK.

Zhongming Ouyang is affiliated with the College of Humanity and Law at Nanchang Hangkong University, Nanchang, China.

Pascale Peters, PhD, holds a position as Associate Professor at Radboud University Nijmegen (Institute for Management Research), the Netherlands. She received her PhD in 2000 from the Faculty of Social Science, Tilburg University, Netherlands. Her main area of expertise relates to the flexible organization of work, in particular, the adoption of home-based telework, New Ways to Work, and working carer support in organizations, in relation to topics such as (gendered) labor market participation, work–life balance, employability, boundary management values and strategies, and work outcomes, such as work engagement and burn-out.

Rob F. Poell, PhD, is Professor of Human Resource Development in the Department of Human Resource Studies at Tilburg University, Netherlands. His core field of expertise within HRD is workplace learning, especially viewed from the employee perspective. Rob has published widely in leading HRD, management, and organization journals. He served as Editor-in-Chief for *Human Resource Development International* from 2010–2012 and was a twice-elected member on the Board of Directors of the Academy of HRD.

Thomas G. Reio, Jr., PhD, is Associate Dean of Graduate Studies and Professor of Adult Education and Human Resource Development at Florida International University in Miami, United States. He is immediate past editor of *Human Resource Development Review* and co-editor of *New Horizons in Adult Education and Human Resource Development.* His research concerns curiosity and risk-taking motivation, workplace socialization, incivility, and workplace learning. His work has been published in leading journals in education, business, and psychology.

Paul B. Roberts, EdD, is Associate Dean in the College of Business and Technology at The University of Texas at Tyler, United States. He has received more than $980,000 in grants and funded projects. His research focuses on virtual HRD and the demographics of HRD programs.

Paul serves as the editor of the *Directory of HRD Programs in the US*. He has received many honors for teaching, including the Chancellor's Council Outstanding Teaching Award.

Tonette S. Rocco, PhD, is Professor and Graduate Program Leader of Adult Education and Human Resource Development, and Director of the Office of Academic Writing and Publication Support at Florida International University, United States. She is a Houle Scholar, a Kauffman Entrepreneurship Professor, and a former board member of the American Society for Training and Development, Certification Institute Board of Directors. She is an award winning author, co-editor of *The Handbook of Scholarly Writing and Publishing*, and several other books, monographs and special issues. She has over 200 publications, serves on ten editorial boards and is lead editor of *New Horizons in Adult Education and HRD*, published by Wiley online.

Katherine Rosenbusch, EdD, has over ten years of experience in training and development with private and non-profit organizations, including three years living in Indonesia where she served as the regional manager and corporate trainer for a specialty coffee company. It was this international experience that inspired her current academic interests in cross-cultural adjustment, international human resources, and global leadership development. Dr Rosenbusch received her EdD from The George Washington University and is currently Assistant Professor at Towson University, United States.

Gene L. Roth, PhD, is Emeritus Distinguished Teaching Professor of Adult and Higher Education, Northern Illinois University, United States. His research interests include learning to learn, humor and adult learning, HRD, and international adult education. He has been the principal investigator of over 30 research projects with budgets that have totaled over $1.5 million. He is a past president of the Academy of Human Resource Development.

Andrzej Różański, PhD, is Professor of Human Resource Development at the Maria Curie-Skłodowska University in Lublin, Poland, and the CEO and Managing Director of the Institute of Human Resource Development, an organization focused on providing international postgraduate programs and consulting services to individuals and companies in the HRD field. He is the coordinator of the Polish-American postgraduate program and MBA program, has numerous publications and serves on the Editorial Board of the *HRDI Journal.*

Sally Sambrook, PhD, is Professor of Human Resource Development at Bangor Business School, United Kingdom, where she leads the HRM/OB subject group. Sally's research focuses on HRD and links to other areas of HRM, including the psychological contract and employee engagement. She employs a critical and auto-ethnographic approach to management and organizational research, including doctoral supervision. Sally has published widely and holds various editorial roles on leading HRD, Management Education, and Ethnography journals.

Robert J. Schalkoff is Professor of English Education and Director of International Education at Yamaguchi Prefectural University, Japan. He has over 15 years of experience as a teacher educator and has worked extensively as an instructor and consultant in professional development domestically and internationally. His research interests include continuing professional education and the transformative nature of international experiences on higher education faculty members. He is a doctoral candidate in Adult and Higher Education at Northern Illinois University, United States.

Bieke Schreurs is PhD student at the Welten Institute, Research Center for Learning, Teaching and Technology at the Open University of the Netherlands. Her research focuses on how professionals learn in the workplace through (online) networks. More specifically she investigates how people's personalities and the working environment have an impact on the social structure of professionals' learning networks. Her aim is to help organizations strengthen their professional development policies to support learning in the workplace.

Brad Shuck, EdD, is Assistant Professor of Organizational Leadership and Learning at the University of Louisville, United States. He was the 2010–2011 Malcolm Knowles Dissertation of the Year Runner-Up and recipient of the 2011 Advances in Developing Human Resources Issue of the Year Award for the special issue on employee engagement. Shuck's research is focused on the use of employee engagement and positive psychology in HRD.

Bruce Spencer, PhD, is Professor of Labor Relations and Adult Education, and Director of the Human Resources and Labor Relations program in the Faculty of Humanities and Social Science, Athabasca University, Canada. His books include *Work and Learning: An Introduction* (2013, with Jennifer Kelly); *The Purposes of Adult Education: An Introduction*, 3rd edition (2014 ,with Elizabeth Lange); *Contexts of Adult Education: Canadian Perspectives* (2006, co-edited) and *Unions and Learning in a Global Economy: International and Comparative Perspectives* (2002, edited).

Jim Stewart is Professor of HRD at Coventry Business School, United Kingdom. He has previously held similar positions at Leeds Business School and Nottingham Business School. Jim is Chair of the University Forum for HRD and has conducted research funded by UK research councils, UK government departments, the European Union and employers in all sectors of the economy. This work has led to Jim writing and co-editing over 20 books and numerous chapter contributions and journal articles.

Judy Yi Sun, PhD, is Assistant Professor of Human Resource Development at the College of Business and Technology, The University of Texas at Tyler, United States. Prior to her academic appointment, she worked for multinational corporations including Motorola and KPMG for over ten years. Her research interests include career development, management development, HRD theory building, and international HRD.

Kristopher J. Thomas, PhD, is a scholar-practitioner that earned his doctorate in Human Resource Development from the University of Wisconsin-Milwaukee, United States. He currently works as a Leadership Development Manager at MillerCoors in Milwaukee, Wisconsin. His research interests include the use of mobile technology in the workplace, organizational culture, work–life balance, and knowledge management. His prior professional experience includes HR management roles in the technology consulting field and leading HR teams for a Fortune 500 financial services organization.

Richard J. Torraco, PhD, is Associate Professor in the Department of Educational Administration at the University of Nebraska-Lincoln, United States. He is a faculty member in the educational leadership and community college leadership programs. He conducts research and teaching in workforce and HRD. He has served as Vice President of research for the Academy of Human Resource Development and as editor of the journal *Human Resource Development Review*.

Beatrice I.J.M. Van Der Heijden, PhD, is Head of the Department Strategic HRM at the Radboud University Nijmegen, Institute for Management Research, the Netherlands. Moreover, she is Professor of Strategic HRM at the Open Universiteit in the Netherlands and at the University of

Twente, the Netherlands. Her main research areas are: career development, employability, and ageing at work. She is Associate Editor of the European Journal of Work and Organizational Psychology, and has published in, among others, *Journal of Vocational Behavior, HRM, Journal of Occupational and Organizational Psychology, Work & Stress*, and *Career Development International.*

Ferd J. Van Der Krogt, PhD, is Associate Professor Emeritus of Human Resource Development in the Department of Education at the Radboud University Nijmegen, Netherlands. His interest is in the organization of HRD in organizations. He is currently doing action research especially into the HRD strategies of workers, using the learning-network theory (LNT) as a framework.

Jasper B. Van Loo, PhD, is senior expert at Cedefop, the European Centre for the Development of Vocational Training. He works on lifelong learning and skills issues and coordinates Cedefop's monitoring of vocational education and training policies in Europe. Previously, Jasper worked for a national education and labor market research institute. His publications focus on competences and lifelong learning, ageing and skills obsolescence and workplace diversity. Jasper is a reviewer for several HRD journals.

Nor Wahiza Abdul Wahat, PhD, is serving as the head of the Youth Citizenship and Leadership Laboratory in the Institute of Social Science Studies, Universiti Putra, Malaysia. She is also Senior Lecturer at the Department of Professional Development in Continuing Educational and Professional Development. Her research area is organizational psychology and career development. Nor Wahiza Abdul Wahat has also taught career development and organizational psychology undergraduate courses and a leadership development course for graduates.

John Walton, PhD, is Professor Emeritus in Human Resource Development (HRD) in the Business School at London Metropolitan University, United Kingdom, where he was Director of the Management Research Centre. He is a Fellow of the Chartered Institute of Personnel and Development, for which he has been involved for over 15 years in the design and development of advanced national professional qualifications. He is a founder member and former Chair of the University Forum for HRD.

Greg G. Wang, PhD, is Professor of Human Resource Development at the University of Texas at Tyler, United States. He is also the current Editor of the *Journal of Chinese Human Resource Management.*

Karen E. Watkins, PhD, is Professor of Human Resource and Organization Development and Associate Department Head in the Department of Lifelong Education, Administration and Policy at The University of Georgia, United States. She holds a PhD in Educational Administration from The University of Texas at Austin. Karen's scholarly interests include incidental learning, action science, and organizational learning assessment. With Victoria Marsick, she developed and validated the "Dimensions of the Learning Organization Questionnaire" used in numerous published studies.

Jon M. Werner, PhD, is Professor of Management at the University of Wisconsin-Whitewater, United States. His research has covered topics such as training, performance appraisal, and organizational citizenship behavior. He is co-author of *Human Resource Development*, with Randy DeSimone, and *Merit Pay*, second edition, with Robert Heneman. He is an Associate Editor at *Human Resource Development Quarterly*, serves on the Editorial Board of the Academy of Management Learning and Education, and the Case Review Board for Entrepreneurship Theory and Practice.

Christine Wiggins-Romesburg is a doctoral candidate in the Educational Leadership and Organizational Development program at the University of Louisville, United States. Christine's primary research focus is the training and development of immigrant and migratory labor from Latin America, with an emphasis on the international economic patterns to which they are susceptible. Prior to pursuing graduate education, Christine worked for several years in the construction sector where she did HRM, HRD, OD, and project management work.

Pedro A. Willging, PhD, is Professor at the University of La Pampa (Argentina), where he is Director of the Research and Development Group of Educational Innovation (GrIDIE). Pedro has a PhD in Education from the Department of Human Resource Education at the University of Illinois at Urbana-Champaign (United States). His work experience includes development of e-learning training programs and materials. His current research focuses on educational technologies trends and interactions in online environments.

Seung Won Yoon, PhD, is Professor of Instructional Technology/Workplace Learning and Performance at Western Illinois University, United States. He teaches courses in Web development/integration, e-learning, human performance technology, and research methods. His research focuses on connecting technology, leadership, organizational learning/knowledge, and employee behavior. He currently serves on the editorial board of the *Human Resource Development Quarterly*, *Advances in Developing Human Resources*, *Quarterly Review of Distance Education*, and *Korean Human Resource Development Research*.

SECTION I

Origins of the field

1
THE HISTORY, STATUS AND FUTURE OF HRD

Monica Lee

We talk about HRD and we work with it day in and day out – but what do we mean by it? As with many things that we are close to, it is hard to encapsulate. In this chapter I want to step back a bit and take a look at the shape of HRD – to review the field, to contextualize it, locate it and provide a very brief overview.

The history of HRD

HRD has a history. This history helps explain some of the oddities around HRD that can be found today. For example, in the Netherlands HRD is associated more with schools of Education; in the UK, with management; in the US, with both; and in Germany more with organizations – why is this? In order to explore these odd differences we need to look at how HRD came to be in the different countries; in order to do that we need to first look at how "management" developed. People have been "doing" what could have been called HRD for many years, but these activities were not initially conceptualized as HRD – it is only us looking backwards that now call "it" HRD. To trace the path of what "it" might be we first need to explore it through the eyes of "management." "The verb manage comes from the Italian *maneggiare* (to handle, especially tools), which derives from the Latin word *manus* (hand). The French word *mesnagement* (later *ménagement*) influenced the development in meaning of the English word management in the 17th and 18th centuries" (Wikipedia 2013). The manager was part of the domestic staff, and learnt the trade via apprenticeships. In the USA the notion of "management" became widespread during the nineteenth century, alongside the need to organize the development of railroads, mass production and trading. Since this period there has been no single view of management and even less agreement about the form of education appropriate for the needs of industry and the economy, something we might now call HRD. In order to explore the (very) diverse understandings we have of HRD I shall present a quick overview of four main views of management (see also Lee 2005).

Views of management

The classical view

This view of management is derived from the late 1800s (see Fayol 1916). This is associated with the archetypal administrative bureaucracy, with clear hierarchy, chains of command, clarity of procedures, and budgets for resource allocation – in which managers create rules and procedures for others to follow. HRD is about selecting the right people; ensuring that they are fully conversant with past experience and current practice, and that they are committed both to their calling and to the organizations in which they will subsequently work. Most staff development occurs within the organization, in what would be best seen as apprenticeships with a focus on the teaching of good practice through the use of cases as exemplars. To a certain extent, externally accepted qualifications are seen as an inducement to job mobility and hence organizational instability. From this perspective, the role of HRD is to ensure that all members of the organization have the knowledge and skills necessary for the completion of their tasks.

The scientific view

This view came to dominance after the Second World War and is based upon the belief that human behavior is rational, and people are motivated by economic criteria (Taylor 1947), thus there were logical solutions to questions of organizational design and operation. Managerial experience was mistrusted as unscientific practice and the focus turned to the scientific selection of students, managerial staff and academic faculty. This era was marked by the rapid development of functional disciplines, departments within organizations, and compartmentalization within business schools. This was particularly so in the USA, where there was a revolution in management education following Gordon and Howell's (1959) report. It is here that business schools as delineators of distinct knowledge-based areas of expertise and providers of hierarchical qualifications come to the fore, and it is here that HRD (in the form of what we would now call training) came to be labeled and known as a subset of HRM; the development part of what we now know as HRD was seen to be education and outside of the business school remit. This view remains the dominant paradigm, despite many critics (Lincoln 2012). Even Howell was commenting by 1984 that the industry had lost its way in some respects: he felt that specialization had continued too far and that the strength of functional academic disciplines in schools meant that they were not capable of rising to interdisciplinary problems posed by environmental issues or information technology.

The processual view

In the scientific view it is the individuals that are engineered (and engineer themselves) to fit the needs of the organization. In the processual view of management it is the internal processes of the organization that are reengineered. The idea has been around since Henry Ford implemented the assembly line in 1908 (Ponzi and Koenig 2002), but is often associated with Business Process Reengineering (BPR) that came to the fore in the USA where, by the mid-1990s, as many as 60 per cent of the Fortune 500 companies claimed to either have initiated reengineering efforts, or to have plans to do so. The stated aim was to help organizations fundamentally rethink how they do their work in order to dramatically improve customer service, cut operational costs, and become world-class competitors whilst recognizing the complexity of the external environment. However, the strict focus on strategy, efficiency and technology is accused of leading to the dehumanization of the workplace, and an increase in managerial control. Very often, the label BPR was seen as synonymous with downsizing and major workforce reductions (Davenport 1995). The role of HR was to meet the organization's strategic needs via the reworking of the organization's internal processes.

The phenomenological view

This approach also has early roots. Herzberg *et al.* (1959) showed that people are less motivated by economic rationality than by being given recognition and responsibility; and Mintzberg (1973) demonstrated managers spend most of their time talking and dealing with immediate problems, so they rarely have time to do any of the things such as planning and analyzing problems as recommended by the textbooks. In the early 1980s there was a drive to replicate the success of Japanese organizations by replicating their consensual culture (Ouchi 1982). This was known as total quality management (TQM) in the West. TQM assumed that managerial problems are complex and unpredictable so managers need to be able to spot opportunities, to learn rapidly, and to create appropriate commitment amongst colleagues. This approach was linked to complexity theory (Weick 1977) which emphasizes the lack of ability to plan or control organizational development. The manager was seen as a stakeholder in his or her own education and development, alongside both the organization and the provider. This was associated with the vision of multi-disciplinary flexible pathways of development and life-long learning that benefit all the stakeholders, who together shape a learning organization that is able to adapt and change in response to a changing environment. The role of HRD became more that of supporting managers to develop their own ideas through tackling real problems in a work situation (Revans 1971).

The rise of HRD

The way in which we see management feeds directly into our understanding of the HRD that we know today. Naturally, the whole project of tracing links through time and through cultures is much more complicated than I am presenting here, but, nevertheless, there are clear links. HRD rose to the fore as a subset of HRM (at least, from the scientific view) as an academic field of study in the early 1990s. The different views of management outlined above were rooted in different cultures and carried with them different approaches to HRD. For example, in the 1990s there were very few management or HRD courses in German universities, because most managers received a long technical training followed by short bouts of skill-specific training within the organization. Similarly, in Japanese companies on-the-job training was structured and systematized, job rotation was normal for most managers, and managers were expected to act as coaches/tutors for their subordinates (Storey 1991). In both, the onus was on the organization to provide the education, training and development. In the USA the onus was on the individual to progress via the gaining of qualifications, and there was a split in HRD provision between training as a subset of HRM – part of the management function and provided by business schools, and development which was provided through educational qualifications within schools of education. In the UK there was a mixture of different schemes, alongside active government involvement designed to improve that quality of management nationally (Stewart *et al.* 2009). At roughly the same time two groups, the University Forum for HRD (UFHRD) in the UK, and the Academy of HRD (AHRD) in the USA, were formed independently within a couple of years of each other. A separate body also called the Academy of HRD was formed in India at about the same time.

In 1994 the European Council of Ministers decided to adopt measures to establish a common framework of objectives for community action (Lee *et al.* 1996). This influenced a wide range of Europe-wide initiatives, including the development of a system that provided dual qualification (masters-level academic and professional recognition) to students from across Europe. The certificate recognized diverse masters-level HR courses in participating institutions alongside a common framework of professional attainment across all institutions, and was jointly awarded by all the participating institutions. This system was known as Euresform and was the first multinational attempt to establish what HRD might be. It quickly became clear that we could not reach common agreement on what should be taught – but we could agree on what we expected an HR professional to be able to do at the end of the course, and so qualification was based on learning outcomes, not input – a novel approach at the time. This initiative finished in 2000 as European priorities and funding changed. Its influence, however, is still evidenced by the cross-European nature of UFHRD. Since then UFHRD and AHRD have been active in participation and sharing in each other's conferences, publishing activities, research collaborations, teaching initiatives and so on. The AHRD has expanded to support an Asian network, with the first conference in 2002, and a network in the Middle East and North Africa (MENA) whose first conference was in 2010.

The status of HRD

I hope I have shown that as HRD emerged from the mists of the last century it has not done so as a single cohesive concept or field of study. Instead, it might be considered to have several interrelated dimensions. For the purpose of this chapter I will focus on those around its nature, its focus, and its scope.

The nature of HRD: being or becoming?

As the field of HRD emerged, particularly in the USA, it was firmly rooted in a positivist scientific management paradigm – one so predominant that most people did not feel the need to acknowledge it in their work. As Boyacigiller and Adler (1991) point out, the bulk of early management research was done on (and in) white US bureaucratic organizations and our current understandings of management theory and practice are derived from this culturally specific and non-representational sample. Despite this, early research was assumed to apply to all management, and it was assumed that management was a singular global concept without national or situation-specific boundaries, that there were right and wrong ways of managing and that it was possible to derive a single global set of tenets for best practice. It was the right way to do good research and academics sought to establish a clear, tight, and limited definition of what HRD was (Swanson 1995).

This pervasive way of thinking might be described as a Parmenidian view of reality (Lee 2001) in which clear-cut, definite things are deemed to occupy clear-cut definite places in space and time. This being ontology, is a statement of what is, and provides a representationalist epistemology. The need to find out what HRD is, and to define it in some way, has occupied many writers. This includes attempts to establish its roots (McLean 1998, Lee 2005) and underlying theories (Weinberger 1998); to examine its key paradigms (Garavan *et al.* 2001) and beliefs and to compare it with other subject areas. However, despite keen efforts to reach a unitary understanding of HRD, this goal has never been achieved (Rigg *et al.* 2007).

In Lee (2001) I argued that HRD would be better seen through a Heraclitean worldview (which sees reality as emergent and constantly changing), and that to define HRD is to intervene in its process of becoming. Thus we need to "adopt a discursive perspective on HRD by which what we know as HRD is emergent and co-created, negotiated and subject to a variety of interpretations by organisational actors" (Sambrook 2012). Integral to this approach is the personal quality of what might be called hanging loose, or negative capability (Keats 1817). This quality is one of resisting conceptual closure, and thereby creating the necessary space for the formulation of personal insights, and the development of foresight and intuition; a quality that is vital for counseling and other helping professions, and one that should be within the remit of HRD professionals.

This approach carries with it a fundamentally different way of seeing and understanding the world (Whitehead 1929), and thus different ways of researching, of relating to subjects, and to the values, morality and ethics in HRD and HRD research. Methods such as content analysis and discourse analysis allow the flexibility to examine concepts that are complex, ambiguous and lack clarity. As Sambrook (2009) points out, the developing field of critical HRD resonates strongly with the Heraclitean approach in so far as it is concerned with such issues as exploring contested boundaries, emancipation, and ethics, and in the acceptance of methodological plurality, alternative methodologies, and problematizing the concept of HRD.

The focus of HRD: performance or learning?

The focus on performance arose with the scientific view of management in the USA, and is based in the Parmedian approach to reality. It is founded on human capital theory in which people are seen as an organizational resource and the role of HRD is to train and develop them in order to maximize performance, productivity, and profitability (Swanson 1995). It is also closely tied to the processual approach to management, in which performance is defined, measured, and rewarded, and is seen as the key to organizational success (usually as measured by profit). Individual goals, rights and development, as well as ethical considerations, are irrelevant to that key goal. Recent banking crises give examples of this. The overriding focus on performance has been challenged, in the USA by those whose HRD roots spring from the education system, and elsewhere by those whose roots are in classical or phenomenological management. The focus on performance is portrayed as treating people merely as means to an end or as elements of production; in contrast, a focus on the learning and development of employees is portrayed as a way of ensuring their commitment and valued contribution to the achievement of organizational goals and thus leading to competitive advantage (Watkins and Marsick 1995). The wider range of provision in Europe, with its apprenticeships, competencies, mixed qualifications, personal development plans, and multiple stakeholders also moves away from the concentration on performance, though critics point out that despite the different rhetoric, the ultimate aim remains that of competitive advantage as delineated by the organization's hierarchy. HRD remains the tool of those in power to coerce and manipulate (O'Donnell *et al.* 2006).

Initiatives such as the "Learning Organisation" and TQM seek to incorporate learning and development into the core of the organization, promoting a holistic approach to business strategy and evidencing its operation within the organization and as a national strategy (Chiangmai 2012). Although such initiatives are held to involve all aspects of the organization, leadership is seen to play a key role, both in developing the organization and in the development of community social capital (Clarke 2012). As the view of what constitutes an organization widens, so do the alternative forms and understandings of leadership and of learning and development (Poell 2012). Kuchinke (2012) talks of "human flourishing" as a central role for HRD; however, it is only as workers also become "those in power" such as shareholders, or in other innovative power sharing organizational structures, that the emancipatory rhetoric of HRD can start to become more of a reality. As McLean (2012) notes, the pay gap between workers at the top and bottom of an organization indicates how the workers are valued: he describes this gap as enormous in the US, calling for a more balanced share of risk-taking and rewards.

The scope of HRD: global or local?

Whilst rejecting the performative perspective and its ethnocentric approach there was, and still is, a drive to look at the big picture – to explore a global understanding of HRD, International HRD (McLean 2012, Metcalfe and Rees 2005) or multi-level frameworks. Garavan (2012) argues that there is a need to break away from the focus on national culture, which reinforces the traditional values of the country, in order to focus on sector regional and global levels of analysis that incorporate wider values. For example Haworth and Winterton (2012) step outside national HRD to compare HRD in EU and APEC countries in relation to their underlying values, and Chalofsky *et al.* (2013) sets out different perspectives from which HRD can be viewed (humanistic, learning, and performance), each with its own definitions and implications for theory and practice. Changes in our conception of HRD have also included the questioning, weakening or dissolution of boundaries between different fields (Lee 2010). These writers are adopting a macro approach when trying to conceptualize HRD. This is hard to adopt in practice. As demonstrated by the pan-European Euresform initiative described above, we found that it is simply not feasible to seek global standardization or definition based upon current practice. The level of diversity we encountered meant that we had to focus on commonality of learning outcomes, not on inputs or definitions, but we did not see this as a problem. Indeed, the diversity of HRD could be seen as a sign of maturity. This diversity emphasizes a disjunction between theory and practiced, however HRD is defined or designated in research circles; when we try to describe it, to see what it is, we see that HRD practice varies across nations, sectors, organizations, and, indeed, within organizations. We can provide appropriate localized definitions that fit the current practice, and these are of great use for standardization, comparison, and delineation of best practice, but they become less relevant as the diversity within their pool of concern increases.

The picture is different if we adopt the Heraclitean view of HRD as becoming. Ironically, although we cannot define what HRD is, it is because of the emergent nature of HRD that we need to develop an understanding of what HRD might become (in the knowledge that it will never get there). It is the aspirational side of HRD that we need to capture. So what do we aspire to – what is the future of HRD?

The future of HRD

In Lee (2010) I explored the future of HRD in relation to global trends and the changing nature of organizations. I presented a picture of shifting boundaries: geographical, cultural, economic, and social; climate related migration and an ageing population leading to population shift; shifts in personal identity and cultural identity, such that the tensions associated with multiculturalism and change will affect us all. Similarly, as boundaries become more uncertain, so the nature of the traditional organization becomes eroded. In the permeable boundaries of the cyber world the power and economic influence of large multinationals already challenge that of some nation states. Traditional bureaucracies are being replaced by cross-national network organizations and clusters of smaller, innovative, entwined organizations that work for each other providing goods and services to whoever may want them across the world. The profile of the workforce is changing and organizations need to be able to offer flexible work patterns, manage high turnover, attract skilled staff, and retain those already employed (Coyne *et al.* 2003).

HRD practice

These predictions challenge traditional notions of work and organization. "Wherever they are located, skilled individuals can work for several organizations from across the world at the same time, and similarly, wherever they are located, adept organizations can call upon the services of skilled individuals from across the world. Skilled workers need be no longer bounded by geography or loyalty – they can sell their human capital to those that offer the best packages of pay and benefits" (Lee 2007: 163–64). As we develop systems of flexible interrelated organizations that can draw employees from across the globe we also need to establish some global understanding of what we expect such employees to be able to do. We might not be able to develop a global definition of HRD, but we do need to help develop people and places of work in a way that meets future global needs.

I am sure that in the future HRD provision will continue to help support the organization's structures and functions, evaluating, monitoring, and developing. HRD will continue to provide traditional training and development, with greater emphasis on areas such as cross-cultural awareness, diversity, and conflict resolution. HRD will hopefully go further: overseeing alternative forms of employee benefit that might retain staff in a world of high staff turnover where promotion and more pay are not the only drivers; developing the organization's culture in a way that balances the needs of all employees; benchmarking and making sound judgments about the comparability of qualifications, attainment and provision; and, taking a proactive part in the development of strategy, sustainability, and longevity. The role of HRD in SMEs and alternative organizations is less functionally clear (Stewart and Beaver 2003) but the processes involved remain the same. HRD might (I hope) more firmly move from being seen as just training and development to playing an important role at the core of the organizational processes (whatever form they may take).

HRD profession

Professional bodies will play a greater role in the future – individuals are likely to be members of one or more professional bodies all their working life, but may only be with an organization for a few years. As well as offering members a sense of identity at work and greater permanence, it is through these professional bodies and associated collective action that HRD can take a stance that addresses issues that are wider than "what happens in my own organisation." The professional bodies such as UFHRD and AHRD already provide a vehicle for sharing information – whether it is research findings, course outlines, job expectations or best practice. Some, such as the Chartered Institute of Personnel and Development in the UK, also provide systems of accreditation and qualification – supporting methods by which employers and employees can be matched, regardless of background or nationality. They act as think-tanks for decision makers, and have the (potential) power to influence the shape of HRD (and the world of work) to come.

Those acting in HRD roles are regularly (and increasingly) faced with ethical dilemmas. HRD is permeated by emancipatory values. These might differ from group to group, and can be in conflict with organizational values of performance and profit, but professional bodies can play a leading role in establishing and voicing the ethical side of HRD (see AHRD 2009). Perhaps through these bodies we can most easily create the sort of HRD in the future that we want – but first we need to know what it is that we want.

HRD as an aspiration

We need to step into the Heraclitean world of becoming, in the knowledge that we will never get there, and question the path we want to walk along. As boundaries become eroded so will HRD face issues that are about self and other; power and control; identity and ownership; inclusion and exclusion. These issues are an essential part of the human condition, as is HRD (Lee 2005). In our understanding of HRD do we include child labor, the self-employed, NGOs or even virtual organizations? What form of governance and leadership should the organization adopt, and how is that supported by the HRD function? How does HRD strike a balance between the thrust for organizational growth (including year on year increase in profit) and notions of sustainability and concomitant steady-state economy? At what stage does HRD become the mediator (and facilitator?) of exploitation? Where does HRD stand on issues of cultural imperialism – particularly in relation to migrant workers or satellite organizations? How is information about employees managed – does the written information match that which "everyone knows" through rumour, innuendo, and off-record discussions? How transparent are the organizational processes? To what extent are ethical codes really followed? And so on . . .

I don't think we can ever answer these questions in an absolute sense – but by considering them we are engaging Keats's negative capability. Individuals will develop their own resolution on these issues (either by action or inaction) and I cannot speak for you, but personally, I believe that we are doing well if we can foster the development of professionals who are able to think and work independently and ethically within the whirlwind of changing circumstances. We need to be developing alternative forms of education that challenge as well as teach. We need to be proactive in the emergence of a people (and planet) friendly world of work. HRD encompasses considerably more than training and development. If HRD is to be an active and ethical agent in this new world in which the divide between the rich and the poor grows increasingly large, then HRD has to engage in areas such as politics and policy; law and economics; strategy and structures; philosophy and morality. As individuals we cannot change much, but, if we don't try nothing will change, so we can but try!

References

AHRD (2009) *Academy of Human Resource Development Standards on Ethics and Integrity*, Bowling Green, OH: AHRD. Online. Available HTTP: http://www.ahrd.org (accessed July 16, 2009).

Boyacigiller, N. and Adler, N.J. (1991) The parochial dinosaur: organisational science in a global context, *Academy of Management Review* 16: 262–90.

Chalofsky, N., Rocco, T. and Morris, L. (2013) (eds) *The Handbook of HRD: Theory and Application*, San Francisco, CA: Jossey-Bass.

Chiangmai, C.N. (2012) Challenges and issues of HRD in Thailand: seeking holistic and sustainable development, in M. Lee (ed.) *Human Resource Development as We Know It*, New York: Routledge, 83–90.

Clarke, N. (2012) New boundaries in leadership development: the need for a multi-level perspective in evaluation and research, in M. Lee (ed.) *Human Resource Development as We Know It*, New York: Routledge, 168–80.

Coyne, E., Coyne, B. and Lee, M. (2003) (eds) *Human resources, care giving, career progression and gender*, London: Routledge.

Davenport, T. (1995) *Reengineering – the fad that forgot people*, Online. Available HTTP: http://www.fastcompany.com/26310/fad-forgot-people (accessed July 16, 2009).

Fayol, H. (1916) *Administration Industrielle et Générale; Prévoyance, Organisation, Commandement, Coordination, Controle*, Paris: H. Dunod et E. Pinat.

Garavan, T. (2012) International, comparative and cross-cultural HRD: challenges for future research and practice, in M. Lee (ed.) *Human Resource Development as We Know It*, New York: Routledge, 38–49.

Garavan, T., O'Donnell, D., McGuire, D., Murphy, J. (2001) HRD as a social and discursive construct: exploring the significance of culture in HRD discourse, in Jan Streumer (ed.) *Perspectives On Learning at The Workplace: Theoretical Positions, Organisational Factors, Learning Processes and Effects*. Enschede: University of Twente, 381–88.

Gordon, R.A. and Howell, J.E. (1959) *Higher Education for Business*, New York: Columbia University Press.

Haworth, N. and Winterton, J. (2012) HRD policies and the supra-state: a comparative analysis of EU and APEC experience, in M. Lee (ed.) *Human Resource Development as We Know It*, New York: Routledge, 91–101.

Herzberg, F., Mausner, B. and Snyderman, B.B. (1959) *The Motivation to Work*, New York: Wiley.

Keats, J. (1817) *Letter to George and Tom Keats, 21 December 1817 Hampstead*. Online. Available HTTP: http://www.poetryfoundation.org/learning/essay/237836?page=2 (accessed February 16, 2013).

Kuchinke, K.P. (2012) Human flourishing as a core value for HRD in the age of global mobility, in M. Lee (ed.) *Human Resource Development as We Know It*, New York: Routledge, 292–305.

Lee, M.M. (2001) A refusal to define HRD, *Human Resource Development International* 4: 327–41.

— (2005) Complex archetypal structures that underlie the 'Human Condition', *Organisational Transformation and Social Change* 1: 49–70.

— (2007) HRD from a holistic perspective, *Advances in Developing Human Resources* 9: 150–68.

— (2010) Shifting boundaries: the role of HRD in a changing world, *Advances in Developing Human Resources* 12: 524–35.

Lee, M.M., Letiche, H., Crawshaw, R. and Thomas, M. (1996) (eds) *Management Education in the New Europe*, London: Routledge.

Lincoln, Y. (2012) In and out of the "black box": human learning, contextual performance and qualitative research, in M. Lee (ed.) *Human Resource Development as We Know It*, New York: Routledge, 27–37.

McLean, G. (1998) HRD: a three-legged stool, an octopus or a centipede, *Human Resource Development International* 1: 375–77.

— (2012) Human resource development: trends from a global perspective, in M. Lee (ed.) *Human Resource Development as We Know It*, New York: Routledge, 247–60.

Metcalfe, B.D. and Rees, C.J. (2005) Theorizing advances in international human resource development, *Human Resource Development International* 8: 449–65.

Mintzberg, H. (1973) *The Nature of Managerial Work*, London: Harper and Row.

O'Donnell, D., McGuire, D. and Cross, C. (2006) Critically challenging some assumptions in HRD, *International Journal of Training and Development* 10: 4–16.

Ouchi, W.G. (1982) *Theory Z: How American Business Can Meet the Japanese Challenge*, New York: Avon.

Poell, R.F. (2012) Towards a self-conscious, self-critical, and open-minded discipline of HRD, in M. Lee (ed.) *Human Resource Development as We Know It*, New York: Routledge, 261–74.

Ponzi, L. and Koenig, M. (2002) Knowledge management: another management fad?, Online. Available HTTP: http://www.informationr.net/ir/8-1/paper145.html (accessed March 16, 2014).

Revans, R.W. (1971) *Developing Effective Managers: A New Approach to Business Education*, Westport, CT: Praeger.

Rigg, C., Stewart, J. and Trehan, K. (2007) (eds) *Critical Human Resource Development: Beyond Orthodoxy*, Harlow: Pearson Education FT Prentice Hall.

Sambrook, S. (2009) Critical HRD: a concept analysis, *Personnel Review* 38: 61–73.

— (2012) What's so critical about human resource development?, in M. Lee (ed.) *Human Resource Development as We Know It*, New York: Routledge, 67–80.

Stewart, J. and Beaver, G. (2003) (eds) *Human Resource Development in Small Organisations: Research and Practice*, in M. Lee (ed.) *Routledge Studies in Human Resource Development*, London: Routledge.

Stewart, J., Lee, M.M. and Poell, R.F. (2009) The University Forum for Human Resource Development: its history, purpose and activities, *New Horizons in Adult Education and Human Resource Development* 23: 29–33.

Storey, J. (1991) Do the Japanese make better managers?, *Personnel Management* 23(8): 24–8.

Swanson, R.A. (1995) HRD: performance is the key, *Human Resource Development Quarterly* 6: 207–13.

Taylor, F.W. (1947) *Scientific Management*, London: Harper and Row.

Watkins, K.E. and Marsick, V.J. (1995) The case for learning, *Studies in Continuing Education* 14: 115–29.

Weick, K. (1977) Organisational design: organisations as self-organising systems, *Organisational Dynamics* 6: 31–46.

Weinberger, L. (1998) Commonly held theories of Human Resource Development, *Human Resource Development International* 1: 75–94.

Whitehead, A.N. (1929) *Process and Reality*, New York: Free Press.

Wikipedia (2013) *Management.* Online. Available HTTP: http://en.wikipedia.org/wiki/Management (accessed February 12, 2013).

2
ANDRAGOGY

Joseph W. M. Kessels

This chapter offers an overview of the origins and development of andragogy, since the German teacher Kapp (1833) first mentioned the term. This overview explores the close relationships with adult education and addresses some of the major debates that dominated the development of andragogy, in specific its assumptions, the scientific foundations and its critical ambitions. The main focus of andragogy has been: helping adults learn and develop, creating favorable conditions for learning and development in a work environment as well as in their private lives. Several of these topics still play an important role in the current advances in HRD. However, the conceptual elaboration, the empirical evidence and thus the scientific development of andragogy have been rather complicated since it has been a field of study at a number of universities in Europe, the United States and Asia.

The chapter ends with an inventory of research questions for the future development of andragogy. The main question leading this exploration is what andragogy still can contribute to the further advancement of HRD in a knowledge society.

Origins and development of andragogy

Andragogy comes from the Greek *anere* [adult] or *andras* [adult man] and *agein* [leading] or *agogos* [helping others to learn]. Kapp (1833) probably was the first who used the term andragogy in his writings on *Platon's Erziehungslehre* [Plato's Educational Ideas], describing the importance of education in adult life including self-reflection, the development of character and vocational education. It is not clear why he used the new term andragogy for adult education, as in the first half of the nineteenth century there was a growing interest in educating adults in Europe and the United States, offering reading classes, cultural programs and upliftment of the underprivileged. Almost 100 years later the Hohenrodter Bund introduced andragogy in Germany and presented a new direction (*Neue Richtung*) in adult learning (Reischmann 2004). Andragogy was a rather theoretical concept mainly used to denote the development of a free mind as opposed to "demagogy". Lindeman's experiences at the Academy for Labor in Frankfurt, Germany led to the first introduction of andragogy in the United States (Lindeman 1926).

> Pedagogy is the method by which children are taught. Demagogy is the path by which adults are betrayed. Andragogy is the true method of adult learning.
>
> *Anderson and Lindeman 1927: 2–3*

In this introduction we read not only the distinction between the teaching of children and the facilitation of learning of adults, but also the ambition of andragogy to create critical awareness for oppression and the need for emancipation. The concept was strongly influenced by the inter-war period (1918–1939). The social and economic reconstruction was in need of a humanistic approach to democratic development.

These early explorations of andragogy as a concept for adult learning remained largely unnoticed until the 1950s and 1960s when in Europe and in the United States a new interest emerged in adult learning and andragogy in specific. The work on adult learning and andragogy by Malcolm Knowles is regarded as probably the most influential in spreading the popularity of andragogy, especially in the United States (Knowles 1970; 1980; 1990; Knowles *et al.* 2011). In Europe andragogy played a role in several countries spreading from Germany in 1947 (Pöggeler 1994) to the rest of Europe (Savicevic 2006) where in the 1960s and 1970s the term became quite common for adult learning (Henschke 2008; Reischmann 2004).

Andragology in the Netherlands and Flanders

In the Netherlands and Flanders the development of andragogy followed a different path, strongly influenced by the work of Ten Have, professor of social pedagogy at the University of Amsterdam. In 1966 his chair became the first official chair of andragogy (Van Gent 1991). Ten Have (1973) proposed an elaborate system of "agology", distinguishing between the practice of andragogy and specific methods of andragogical work, named "andragogics" and the scientific study of andragogy, named andragology. He placed andragogy – as the study of social work with adults – between pedagogy (educational work with children) and gerontology (the study of guidance of elder people). In the Netherlands andragogy was not restricted to adult learning and adult education. It encompassed the broad domain of "social agology" including community work, social work, counseling, mental health care, social and cultural upliftment, emancipation and social change. This concept of a broad domain of agology and andragology in the Netherlands as it developed in the 1970s was an almost natural result of the long history of the School for Social Work founded in 1899 [*Opleidingsinrichting voor Socialen Arbeid* and later *School voor Maatschappelijk Werk*, and later *Sociale Academie*], which was one of the first professional training institutes in the world for social work (Van Gent 1991). At that time social work and welfare had strong links with cultural development and adult education in view of enrichment and upliftment of deprived people.

During the reconstruction period after World War II the social agology and later andragology were inspired by Lewin's work on "planned change", which Ten Have considered as an acceptable third way between the complete freedom of liberalism and the strong central control of communism. Neither the individual, nor the large masses were an object of study, but the small group and community work in the welfare state became the focal point of study (Van Gent 1991).

Ten Have and Knowles knew each other and respected each other's work. Knowles was impressed by the work of Ten Have, which he saw as an important source of inspiration (Knowles 1970). Nevertheless, the broad interpretation of Dutch andragology as the scientific study of social change and cultural work, guiding adults and their professional development in the context of the civic society and the labor market, soon narrowed down to adult education.

Academic recognition and decline

In 1970 andragology was admitted as an official field of study in the Netherlands and recognized degrees were awarded at several Dutch universities. Initially, the main purpose was providing academic training and research as a scientific support for professionals active in social work, and cultural guidance of adults and community development. On the other hand Ten Have (1986) and his successor Nijk were convinced that a theoretical foundation of andragology underpinning the new academic discipline should be a top priority. This controversy between the theoretical foundation and the relevance for day-to-day practice has not yet been reconciled between academics and practitioners. Fifteen years later in 1985, official status as an academic discipline ended due to several internal university conflicts and influenced by societal changes. The economic crisis of the 1970s speeded up the transformation of the welfare state with trained professionals into "the caring society" run by volunteers. There was no need any more for academically trained professionals in social and cultural community work (Van Gent 1996). The scientific discipline of andragology had not yet reached a recognized international reputation. As in many other countries the study of adult, vocational and corporate education was taken over by the departments of pedagogy, education, psychology and the business schools. The training in the fields of social work, welfare and community development lost its academic background at the university level and continued mainly in institutes for higher vocational education.

The wide domain of "planned social change" offered broad opportunities for diffuse studies and practices, often lacking focus and coherence. As a result, the Dutch andragology never managed to grow towards a mature and respected academic identity. As was the case with andragogy in many other European countries, the lack of empirical research and the sparse research publications in the English language inhibited a growing academic recognition and left interesting local experiments rather unknown to an international readership.

The relatively short history of andragogy in the Netherlands shows many commonalities with discussions and debates on andragogy in the United States, as well as on adult education and HRD more recently. The need for academic recognition, the development of coherent research programs and the normative disputes about object and methods are recurrent issues.

Andragogy as an international concept?

The important influence of Knowles has spread internationally, promoting andragogy as a science of understanding and supporting lifelong learning and lifewide education of adults (Reischmann 2004; Knowles *et al.* 2011). In most publications, andragogy includes a humanistic conception of self-directed and autonomous learners, and the term is used in the Netherlands, Belgium, the United Kingdom, Germany, Switzerland, Finland, Yugoslavia, the Czech Republic, Slovenia and Estonia (Savicevic 2006; Henschke 2008). Outside Europe and North America we find references to andragogy in South Korea, Venezuela and the People's Republic of China where Deng Xiao Ping designated an important role to adult learning and andragogy in the transformation of the planned economy to a socialist market economy (Zang 1996, in Cooper and Henschke 2003). In most countries the concept is closely related to adult learning and the academic support for professional development is in the domain of adult education and lifelong learning. However, it is difficult to make a clear delineation between andragogy, adult education and HRD (St Clair 2002). Today, in the Netherlands and Flanders the concept of andragogy still refers to a much broader field of study, including interventions in the domain of social work, welfare, community work, and mental health care, with a strong emphasis on promoting change for increased well-being of citizens. In the recent manifesto of the alumni of the study of andragology at the University of Amsterdam this broad field of study has been redefined and applied to current developments in society like diversity, urban education, knowledge productivity, integration of immigrants and leadership development (Andragologen Alumni Amsterdam 2012).

However, the expanding interpretation of the object of study, the wide variety of methodologies, diffuse terms and internal disagreements, and the lack of international exchange and cooperation did not contribute to a strong and focused development of andragogy as a respected discipline of academic endeavor.

Discussions and debates on andragogy: self-directedness, critical awareness and emancipation

When we look at the available literature on andragogy (Davenport 1987; Draper 1998; Henschke 2008; Heimstra, no date; Van Gent 1996), many discussions take place on matters of definitions, assumptions and epistemology. Should andragogy be scientifically rooted or mainly practice driven? Is self-direction a viable principle for academic study? Why should small group activities get more attention than individual and mass approaches? Is learning of adults in a society at risk of greater importance than professional development of employees in commercial industries? Is personal growth or performance improvement more important? It seems the fierce debates about the right answers had the most attention at the expense of empirical studies of specific contributions to better understand and solve matters related to learning and development.

The disputes on the academic foundations and viability of andragogy go back to the roots of adult learning theory, focusing on individual learning experiences (Lindeman 1926), the need for critical consciousness and liberation (Freire 1970), the interventions for promoting well-being (Ten Have 1973), emancipatory learning and critical theory (Habermas 1984) and critical, reflective thinking and analysis (Brookfield 1986; Mezirow 1981). These normative laden aspects of emancipation, liberation, critical awareness of oppression, promoting self-directedness and autonomy have always been part of the discussions about adult education (Brookfield 1996) and andragogy (Merriam 2001). Somehow the debates about andragogy reflect the turmoil of the ongoing development in society and economy, and the accompanying political discourses. In a community driven society the plea for self-directedness can be seen as individualistic and even antisocial, whereas mass communication in a post-Nazi period is easily connected to indoctrination and demagogy. In societies with large power distance, segregation, deprived minorities and inequity, the engagement of professionals in performance improvement for the upper class is easily criticized. It looks as if academic disciplines like andragogy, adult education and HRD are very sensitive to these value orientations, as they are closely related to influencing human behavior and development.

The assumptions underlying the direct facilitation of the development of individuals through improving the educative quality of their environment (Knowles 1980; 1990) and the normative aspects of lifelong learning and the new educational order (Field 2000) played an important role in the acceptance of andragogy as a scientific discipline. In combination with weakly developed prestige in the settled academic world, the struggle for recognition of andragogy in a changing and tough output driven academic system has never ended.

The relationship between andragogy and HRD

When we look over the history of andragogy since the first use of the term almost 180 years ago, what does andragogy contribute to current HRD?

When we perceive

> HRD as an organisational process [that] comprises the skilful planning and facilitation of a variety of formal and informal learning and knowledge processes and experiences, primarily but not exclusively in the workplace, in order that organisational progress and individual potential can be enhanced through the competence, adaptability, collaboration and knowledge-creating activity of all who work for the organisation[,]
>
> *Harrison and Kessels 2004: 4–5*

then andragogy can easily be viewed as one of the founding building blocks for HRD. Especially when we take into account the learning and development aspects of adults in the context of their professional work, andragogy has offered valuable principles for organizing meaningful learning environments. Knowles (1980) and Knowles *et al.* (2011) further developed the set of assumptions on which andragogy has been based. Important elements are the facilitators' responsibility to help adults move from dependency towards increasing self-directedness; personal experiences as a rich resource for learning, especially when related to real-life tasks and problems; the development of capabilities and competencies in a meaningful way; and the dominant role of intrinsic motivation and self-esteem. When we consider andragogy as an important foundation for HRD, its historical background strongly contributes to the development of a learning paradigm that inherently values self-efficacy. The critical roots of andragogy favor the idea of the independent and autonomous learner striving for freedom of choice and emancipation. Pre-described performance improvement in the interest of dominating others does not fit with the origins of andragogy.

Andragogy in learning and working

Although the andragogical approach does not provide a clear delineation between what can be considered adult education and what cannot, its set of assumptions stated several decades ago, still offers helpful guidelines in designing a work environment that is conducive for learning and knowledge development. The Nottingham Andragogy Group (1983) has somewhat reinterpreted Knowles' andragogical concepts in terms of their beliefs about adults and adults' abilities to think creatively and critically in learning settings. It is important to become aware of the assumptions that adults have uncritically accepted as governing their conduct and lives. Therefore, the andragogical approach encourages adults to critically reflect and not to accept another's interpretation or meaning on the basis of hierarchy and authority. Facilitators of adult learning should create a climate conducive to learning, including mutual trust and respect, and collaborative activities. It is important that adult learners participate in needs assessment, setting goals, searching for relevant resources, and jointly evaluating their learning processes and outcomes. These design principles directly stem from the contributions of Lindeman to andragogy (Brookfield 1984). Later, the collaborative and communicative design of learning environments has been empirically tested, and became known as the relational approach to corporate education (Kessels and Plomp 1999).

Andragogy and the knowledge economy

HRD plays an important role in an emerging knowledge economy, as human beings are the main knowledge producers. In a knowledge economy, growth is based on improvement and innovation of work processes, products, and services and is a result of knowledge productivity (Kessels 2001; 2004). Knowledge productivity requires personal involvement and individual learning, in a favorable social context. Through the lens of knowledge productivity, the work environment should transform into a supportive learning environment. The development of knowledge and its application to improvement and innovation cannot be managed in a conventional way. Successful innovation is not an industrial production process; it requires personal involvement, dedication and intrinsic challenge of a large proportion of the workforce. Moreover, innovative knowledge work requires creative thinking and critically reflective work behavior of emancipated professionals. This inevitably leads to employees whose shared interests, passion, responsibility, reciprocal appeal, and career awareness will challenge traditional power positions. To better understand these developments, a renewed interest in andragogy will emerge, as it has a long tradition in social, critical and emancipatory learning. Therefore, if HRD is to play a prominent role in an emerging knowledge economy, HRD needs to rediscover andragogy as part of its foundations, as andragogy offers valuable assumptions on self-directed, individual learning in combination with the social network for collective knowledge productivity (Kessels 2004; Kessels and Poell 2004).

Conclusions on a future agenda for andragogy and HRD

Andragogy has a turbulent history when it comes to specific attention for helping adults to learn and develop. This domain of study not only marked the shift from teaching of children towards helping adults in their learning, it also promoted self-directedness, autonomy, emancipation and social cooperation in the wider context of work and living. HRD and andragogy share an interest in the facilitation of adults in their learning and professional development. Due to the lack of official academic recognition of andragogy these important aspects of HRD also seem to get lost. In an emerging knowledge society where lifelong learning, knowledge development and innovation seem to become the license to participate a renewed study of the critical pillars of andragogy will be necessary for the further advancement of HRD. A critical awareness associated with andragogy can also be found in the critical perspectives of HRD (Bierema 2008; Fenwick 2004). Human development in view of a knowledge society, specifically the reciprocal relationships between individual growth, corporate prosperity and community development in a knowledge economy need to be better understood (Kessels and Poell 2004).

In some countries like the Netherlands and Flanders andragogy claimed a broad domain of study including social change, far beyond the primary focus of employees in the world of work as it is generally studied in HRD. Does andragogy inspire HRD to broaden its horizon of inquiry or is such an expansion of the field a potential pitfall and will it burden HRD with the same discussions on the lack of focus and devastating debates about academic rigor that led to the decline of andragogy?

From the current economic crisis another intriguing research question emerges directly related to andragogy. This economic and even ecological crisis has often been ascribed to the perverse financial performance triggers of financial institutions, corporations and even government agencies. What new perspectives does an andragogical lens offer when examining human development and growth in the context of a fair and sustainable society?

Since the German teacher Alexander Kapp (1833) coined the term almost 200 years ago, andragogy still can offer valuable assumptions as building blocks for HRD. Especially when we refer to a humanistic and emancipatory approach promoting critical reflection and awareness, while avoiding merely instrumental methods for facilitating learning, development and growth of adults in the context of their work, andragogy will make a meaningful contribution in an emerging knowledge society.

References

Anderson, M.L. and Lindeman, E.C. (1927) Education through experience: An interpretation of the methods of the academy of labor. *Workers' Education Research Series* 1.

Andragologen Alumni Amsterdam (2012) *Andragologen Alumni Amsterdam* http://www.andragologie.eu. Retrieved November 12, 2013.

Bierema, L.L. (2008) *Critical Human Resource Development Education: A Review of the Literature and Recommendations for Teaching.* Paper presented at the Annual Academy of Human Resource Development Conference, Panama City, Florida, 538–45.

Brookfield, S.D. (1984) The contribution of Eduard Lindeman to the development and philosophy in adult education. *Adult Education Quarterly* 34(4): 185–96.

— (1986) *Understanding and Facilitating Adult Learning.* San Francisco: Jossey-Bass.

— (1996) Adult learning: An overview. In A.C. Tuijnman (ed.) *The International Encyclopedia of Adult Education and Training.* Oxford: Pergamon, 375–80.

Cooper, M.K. and Henschke, J.A. (2003) *Thinking about Andragogy: The International Foundation for its Theory, Research and Practice Linkage in Adult Education and Human Resource Development.* Food 'n' thought session: New linkages for andragogy and human resource development. Academy of Human Resource Development International Research Conference, March 6, 2004.

Davenport, J. III (1987) Is there a way out of the andragogy morass? *Lifelong Learning: An Omnibus of Practice and Research* 11(3): 17–20.

Draper, J.A. (1998) The metamorphoses of andragogy. *The Canadian Journal for the Study of Adult Education* 12(1): 3–26.

Fenwick, T. (2004) Toward a critical HRD in theory and practice. *Adult Education Quarterly* 54(3): 193–209.

Field, J. (2000) *Lifelong Learning and the New Educational Order.* Stoke on Trent: Trentham.

Freire, P. (1970) *Pedagogy of the Oppressed.* New York: Herter and Herter.

Habermas, J. (1984) *The Theory of Communicative Action. Vol. 1: Reason and Rationalization of Society.* Boston: Beacon.

Harrison, R. and Kessels, J.W.M. (2004) *Human Resource Development in a Knowledge Economy: An Organizational View.* Hampshire: Palgrave Macmillan.

Heimstra, R. (no date) *Moving from Pedagogy to Andragogy; With Annotated Bibliography of Sources Related to Andragogy.* http://courses.forum.ncsu.edulcgi-binlnetforumlaee523moore. Retrieved on December 30, 2012.

Henschke, J.A. (2008) A global perspective on andragogy: an update. In *Proceedings of the Commission on International Adult Education* [CIAE] *Pre-Conference*, American Association for Adult and Continuing Education [AAACE] Conference, vol. 1, 43–94.

Kapp, A. (1833) *Die Andragogik oder Bildung im männlichen Alter. Platon's Erziehungslehre, als Paedagogik für die Einzelnen und als Staatspaedagogik* [Andragogy or Education in the Man's Age. Plato's Educational Ideas as Pedagogy for Individuals and as State Pedagogy]. Leipzig: Ferdinand Essmann.

Kessels, J.W.M. (2001) Learning in organizations: a corporate curriculum for the knowledge economy. *Futures* 33: 479–506.

— (2004) The knowledge revolution and the knowledge economy. The challenge for HRD. In J. Woodall, M. Lee and J. Stewart (eds) *New Frontiers in HRD.* London: Routledge, 165–79.

Kessels, J.W.M. and Plomp, T. (1999) A systematic and relational approach to obtaining curriculum consistency in corporate education. *Journal of Curriculum Studies* 31(6): 679–709.

Kessels, J.W.M. and Poell, R.F. (2004) Andragology and social capital theory: the implications for Human Resource Development. *Advances in Developing Human Resources* 6(2): 146–57.

Knowles, M.S. (1970) *The Modern Practice of Adult Education.* New York: Association Press and Cambridge Book Publishers.

— (1980) *The Modern Practice of Adult Education.* Englewood Cliffs, NJ: Prentice Hall.

— (1990) *The Adult Learner: A Neglected Species* (4th edn). Houston, TX: Gulf Publishing.

Knowles, M.S., Holton, E.F. and Swanson, R.A. (2011) *The Adult Learner: The Definitive Classic in Adult Education and Human Resource Development* (7th edn). London: Elsevier.

Lindeman, E.C. (1926) *Andragogik: The Method of Teaching Adults. Workers' Education*, L 4, 38.

Merriam, S.B. (2001) Andragogy and self-directed learning: pillars of adult learning theory. The new update on adult learning theory. *New Directions for Adult and Continuing Education* 89: 3–13.

Mezirow, J. (1981) A critical theory of adult learning and education. *Adult Education* 32(1): 3–24.

Nottingham Andragogy Group (1983) *Toward a Developmental Theory of Andragogy. Adults: Psychological and Educational Perspective* (9). Nottingham: Department of Adult Education, University of Nottingham.

Pöggeler, F. (1994) Introduction: Trends of andragogical research in Europe. In P. Jarvis and F. Pöggeler (eds) *Developments in the Education of Adults in Europe: Studies in Pedagogy, Andragogy and Gerontology* 21: 9–15.

Reischmann, J. (2004) *Andragogy: History, Meaning, Context, Function.* http://www.andragogy.net. Retrieved December 23, 2010.

Savicevic, D. (2006) *Convergence or divergence of ideas on andragogy in different countries.* Paper presented at the 11th Standing International Conference on the History of Adult Education (IESVA), Bamberg, Germany, September 27–30.

St Clair, R. (2002) *Andragogy Revisited: Theory for the 21st Century? Myths and Realities* (ERIC Document Reproduction Service No. ED468612). Columbus, OH: ERIC Clearinghouse on Adult, Career and Vocational Education.

Ten Have, T.T. (1973) *Andragologie in blauwdruk* [Blueprint of Andragology]. Deventer: Tjeenk Willink.

— (1986) *Andragologie in ontwikkeling; van sociale psychologie/sociale pedagogiek naar een wetenschap van de andragogie van 1947 tot 1975. Verzameld werk* [Andragology in Development; From Social Psychology/Social Pedagogy to a Science of Andragogy from 1947 to 1975. Collected Works]. Lisse: Swets and Zeitlinger.

Van Gent, B. (1991) *Basisboek andragologie. Een inleiding in de studie van het sociaal en educatief werk met volwassenen* [Handbook on Andragology. An Introduction to the Study of Social and Educational Work with Adults]. Amsterdam: Boom.

— (1996) Andragogy. In A.C. Tuijnman (ed) *The International Encyclopedia of Adult Education and Training.* Oxford: Pergamon, 114–17.

3

ADULT LEARNING

Knud Illeris

The purpose of this chapter is to give a short up-to-date account on adult learning in relation to learning in general and to children's learning. Adult learning has been part of my focus for over forty years. My research and developmental work has been on what characterizes human learning, especially learning in youth and adulthood with a specific interest in less educated learners (e.g. Illeris 2004, 2006a, 2007, 2009).

Adult learning did not emerge as a special area of interest before about 1970. Prior to 1970 there was, in the industrialized countries, a kind of general understanding that studies of learning should be related mainly to children and youth. Of course there would also be some learning in adulthood, but this would either be for updating, minor issues, or new matters. The age of important and organized learning was considered with few exceptions to be over when one had finished an education and/or got a permanent job. For example, the great names in personality psychology in the 1950s and 1960s launched the ideals and concepts of "the mature personality" (Allport 1961) and "the fully functioning person" (Rogers 1961), i.e. the adult person who had reached a level of integrity and needed no further learning or development, and Erikson saw youth as the age of identity development, whereas adulthood was the age of stabilization of what had already been learned (Erikson 1968). For adults stability was both the norm and the ideal, and changes were related to disruptions and weakness.

Around the 1970s changes in the world were more frequent and the ideal of stability was supplemented by an ideal of flexibility. Adults needed to be able to change, which implies a need to reject earlier learning and engage in new learning. Gradually adult learning became a very important issue. These new tendencies followed two main courses, learning for work and learning for social change.

In the trades and industries interest in adult learning was mainly related to the movement of human resource development (see e.g. Swanson and Holton 2001), and in practice seemed to be realized according to the so-called "Matthew effect" that "for whoever has to him shall be given and he shall be caused to be in abundance" (Matthew 13:12), i.e. that those who already have learned most also get the best opportunities to learn more, both in practice at work and by further educational activities – which as a side-effect inevitably will lead to an increased social imbalance.

But adult learning also became a focal point in social movements which involved the uneducated, poor, and oppressed people in a combination of basic education and personal consciousness raising, often related to political objectives. The most famous and widespread of these movements was, no doubt, initiated by Brazilian Paulo Freire, who combined the teaching of reading and writing with so-called "generative themes," and whose book *Pedagogy of the Oppressed* has been translated into a great number of languages and sold more than 700,000 copies (Freire 1970). Another similar, but in the English speaking world not so well-known example, was started by German trade union courses, in which the sociologist Oskar Negt introduced exemplary learning, similar to Freire's generative themes (Negt 1968). The idea of transformative learning, introduced in the USA by Jack Mezirow (and to which I shall return later in this chapter), was similarly inspired by the women's liberation movement (Mezirow 1978).

Somewhere between these two trends the United Nations published the book *Learning to Be* (Faure *et al.* 1972) which introduced the catchphrase or slogan of "lifelong learning." Lifelong learning gained a central position in international politics and was adopted by many countries although it has often had a stronger impact as a slogan than in consequent learning arrangements for ordinary people.

Adult learning versus children's learning

American Malcolm Knowles claimed that adults' and children's ways of learning differ and that an increasing focus on adult education should be accompanied by an increased interest in researching and understanding of what characterized adult learning to inform adult education. He proposed the term of "andragogy" in relation to adult education and as a counter play to "pedagogy" for children (e.g. Knowles 1970), but this raised a veritable storm of protest and rejection from learning theorists and educational scholars, who claimed that learning is the same for all people and would certainly not let the up and coming adult education field be overtaken by the "andragogy morass" (Davenport 1987, see also Hartree 1984). More recently, British Alan Rogers has deliberately maintained "that there is nothing distinctive about the kind of learning undertaken by adults" (Rogers 2003: 7).

This question, however, needs a closer elucidation to avoid such unprofitable discussion covering an underlying power struggle. For the traditional psychology of learning, there are no age-conditioned differences, because learning has been studied as a common phenomenon of which researchers endeavored to discover the basic and decisive characteristics. Therefore research often involved animals and humans in constructed and simple laboratory situations. And in relation to adult education the researchers claimed that adults' learning as a psychological function is basically of the same kind as children's learning.

This depends, however, on which definition of learning is used. If learning is defined as only the internal psychological function of acquisition of new knowledge, skills and attitudes, as traditional learning psychology tends to do, it is to some extent possible to claim that, independent of the concrete conditions such as age differences or social background, learning processes are fundamentally the same.

But if the emotional dimension and social interaction processes are also seen as necessary and integrated elements of learning, the picture changes. The majority of modern learning theorists have accepted this, and some have even considered learning as mainly or only a social process (e.g. Lave and Wenger 1991, Gergen 1994). In relation to age it is obvious that the nature of our relationships to the social and societal environment changes during the life course from the new-born child's total dependence to a striving for independence in youth and adulthood and, eventually, a new sort of dependence at old age. These changes strongly influence the character of the social and emotional dimensions of learning. In order to see what is characteristic of adult learning, I shall therefore start by pointing out some basic features of children's learning.

In general, learning in childhood could be described as a continuous campaign to capture the world. The child is born into an unknown world and learning is about acquiring this world and finding out how to deal with it. In this connection, two learning-related features are prominent, especially for the small child. First, children's learning is comprehensive and uncensored. The child learns everything within its grasp, throws itself into everything, and is limited only by its biological development and the nature of its surroundings. Second, the child places utter confidence in the adults around it because it has no criteria to evaluate their behavior. Children must, for example, learn the language these adults speak and practice the culture they practice.

Throughout childhood, the child's capturing of its surroundings is fundamentally uncensored and trusting as it endeavors, in an unlimited and indiscriminate way, to make use of the opportunities that present themselves. Of course, late modern society has led to growing complexity and even confusion of this situation as older children receive impressions from their pals and especially from the mass media, which go far beyond the borders of their own environment. But still the open and confident approach must be recognized as the starting point.

Opposite of childhood learning stands learning during adulthood. Being an adult essentially means that an individual is able and willing to assume responsibility for his/her own life and actions. Formally, our society ascribes such "adulthood" to individuals when they attain the age of 18. In reality, it is a gradual process that takes place throughout the period of youth, may last well into the 20s or be entirely incomplete if the formation of a relatively stable identity is chosen as the criterion for its completion (which is the classical description of this transition provided by Erik Erikson, 1968).

As concerns learning, however, being an adult also means, in principle, that the individual accepts responsibility for his/her own learning, i.e. more or less consciously sorts information and decides what he/she wants and does not want to learn. The situation in today's complicated modern society is that the volume of what may be learned by far exceeds the ability of any single individual. This is immediately true concerning content in a narrow sense, but it also applies to views and attitudes, perceptions, communications options, behavioral patterns, lifestyle, etc. So input must always be sorted.

As a general conclusion, however, children's uncensored and confident learning is in contrast to adults' selective and self-directed learning, or to put it in more concrete terms:

- adults learn what they want to learn and what is meaningful for them to learn
- adults draw on the resources they already have in their learning
- adults take as much responsibility for their learning as they want to take (if they are allowed to)
- and adults are not very inclined to learn something they are not interested in, or in which they cannot see the meaning or importance. At any rate, typically, they only learn it partially, in a distorted way or with a lack of motivation that makes what is learned extremely vulnerable to oblivion and difficult to apply in situations not subjectively related to the learning context (Illeris 2006a: 17).

These conditions imply that learning incentives or adult education options, consciously or subconsciously are met by skeptical questions and considerations such as: Why do "they" want me to learn this? What can I use it for? How does it fit into my personal life perspectives?

Finally learning in youth in this connection can be seen as a transition in which the uncensored learning of children is gradually replaced by the selective learning of adults, and the identity is developed as a kind of scale or yardstick of the selectivity.

Common adults' attitudes to learning

It is not only researchers, administrators and teachers who traditionally have had the idea that learning is mainly related to childhood and youth. Also among adult learners this understanding is widespread. When adults have to involve themselves in ordinary learning courses, they will often talk about it as "having to go back to school" and this is certainly not meant positively. On the contrary adults experience the situation as if they are forced to return to an artificial kind of childhood, something that is degrading or even humiliating – because returning to school indirectly means not being good enough for the tasks in which one is involved.

In what we call free and democratic societies adults are in principle regarded as people of majority who can and must take responsibility for themselves and what they do and say. But at the same time they are subject to risks and situations which they cannot control. In relation to learning and education, anyone can suddenly and without having any responsibility for it themselves realize that their qualifications have become worthless and no longer can be sold on the (labor) market. This may happen, for example, if the owners and stakeholders of their workplace decide to move it to a country far away in which labor is cheaper, or if a new management undertakes a reorganization which makes certain departments and persons unnecessary. But there may also be other and more personal reasons as for example, a bad relationship to a leader, low concentration because of too many problems at home, too many days lost through illness, etc.

A considerable number of adult learners do not participate in adult education because they want to do so, but because for some reason outside their control they have to do so. The central condition is that these adult learners are not in control of the situation. Therefore they are ambivalent – and the slogan of lifelong learning may in such situations become very ambiguous. Reality seems quite different from the 'maybe' good intentions of powerful organizations like UNESCO, OECD, EU or the World Bank. Adult education today is usually far from the emancipating projects of the folk high schools or public enlightenment – in relation to which the idea of lifelong learning was originally launched.

Therefore not only the concrete learning content, but also the general learning situation and the messages and influence it contains, will often be met with skeptical attitudes, and will be seen and dealt with in the light of the individual's own experience and perspectives, whether it is communicated in the form of conversation, guidance, persuasion, pressure or compulsion. If the possibilities for learning shall be turned in a positive direction, the adults must accept them psychologically, they must be able to understand the meaning of the learning activities in relation to themselves and their life situations (see e.g. Illeris 1998, 2003, 2006b).

Adult learning possibilities

Whereas questions of the specific character of adult learning were neglected by traditional learning psychology and also by most adult educational research, there has been some often indirect discussion concerning adults' possibilities for learning.

The cognitive learning theory put forward by Jean Piaget in the 1930s on the basis of extensive empirical studies, focused on the development of learning possibilities in childhood through a number of cognitive stages and sub-stages and thus maintained that there is a highly specific developmental course. This development ends between the ages of 11–13 when the "formal operational" level is reached. The formal operational level makes logical-deductive thinking possible as a supplement to the forms of thinking and learning acquired at earlier stages (see e.g. Flavell 1963).

However, Piaget's perception of this process has been questioned from several quarters. On the one hand, it has been pointed out that far from all adults are actually able to think at a formal operational level. Empirical research indicates that in England in about 1980 actually less than 30 per cent of adults could think at this level, even though at the beginning of puberty a decisive development occurs in the possibilities for learning and thinking in abstract terms, so that distinguishing a new cognitive phase extending beyond the formal operational level is justified (Shayer and Adey 1981, Commons *et al.* 1984). American adult education researcher Stephen Brookfield has pointed to four possibilities for learning which, in his opinion, may only be developed in the course of adulthood: the capacity for dialectical thinking, the capacity for applying practical logic, the capacity for realizing how one may know what one knows, and the capacity for critical reflection (Brookfield 2000).

Recent brain research seems indirectly to support Brookfield's claims. A well-established understanding today, psychologically as well as neurologically, is that the brain matures for formal logical thinking in early puberty. But evidence has been found that the brain centres of the frontal lobe that conduct such functions as rational planning, prioritization and making well-founded choices, do not mature until the late teenage years (Gogtay *et al.* 2004) or perhaps even later. This finding seems to provide some clarification of the differences between the capacity of formal logical and practical logical thinking and learning as well as between ordinary cognition and meta-cognition in adolescence and early adulthood.

The general conclusion must be that during puberty and youth a physiological and neurological maturing process takes place that makes possible new forms of abstract and strictly logical thinking and learning. An individual acquires the potential to operate context-independently with coherent concept systems and manage balanced and goal-directed behavior (whether or not this potential is actually applied is, as mentioned, a different question). Teenagers' determination to find out how things are structured and to use such understanding in relation to their own situation could be seen as a cognitive developmental bridge signifying the difference between children's and adults' ways of learning.

The longing for independence and the longing for coherent understanding of how they themselves and their environment function and why things are the way they are, in a decisive way, separates adult learning from the learning of childhood. Up through the period of youth, individuals will increasingly assume responsibility for their own learning and non-learning, make choices and rejections, and in this context understand what they are dealing with and their own roles and possibilities.

However, all this has been enormously complicated by the duality of late modernity between the apparently limitless degrees of freedom and reams of information, and the far-reaching and often indirect pressure for control from parents, teachers, youth cultures, mass media, and authorities. The transition from child to adult has thus, in the area of learning, become an extended, ambiguous and complicated process, with blurred outlines and unclear conditions and goals.

Barriers towards learning

In our complicated modern society the amount one can learn far outstrips what any person can manage, and this applies to the content of learning as well as the options for attitudes, modes of understanding, communication possibilities, patterns of action, lifestyles etc. Selection becomes a necessity, and in principle adults would like to carry out and take responsibility for this selection themselves.

Thus, adults' basic desire to learn and to direct and take responsibility for their own learning are strongly modified, first by the impact of their school experiences, and second by the inevitable selection which is necessarily developed into the kind of semi-automatic defense system which has been described as "everyday consciousness" (Illeris 2004: 113ff., 2007: 160ff.).

The way this works is that one develops some general pre-understandings within certain thematic areas. When one meets with influences within such an area, these pre-understandings are activated so that if elements in the influences do not correspond to the pre-understandings, they are either rejected or distorted to make them agree. In both cases, the result is not new learning but, on the contrary, the cementing of already existing understanding.

This is also part of the reason why adults are skeptical and often reluctant vis-à-vis everything that others want them to learn and they themselves do not feel an urge to learn. Consciously or unconsciously, they want to decide for themselves. But, at the same time, it is easier to leave the decisions to others, to see what happens, and retain the right to protest, resist or drop out if one is not satisfied. In sum, the attitude is thus very often ambiguous and contradictory.

However, the very widespread and important mechanisms of learning defense should not be confused with learning resistance, which is a much more active and usually also conscious kind of general learning barrier. Whereas the system of learning defense is gradually built up during youth and exists in advance of the situations in which it works, resistance is provoked by elements in the learning situation and content which are unacceptable to the learner. There may be many reasons for learning resistance, of which some are unconscious and may be anchored in traumatic experiences in childhood, whereas others are conscious and may, for instance, have to do with political, moral, or religious convictions.

Teachers and educators need to realize that learners are excited and sensitive in situations of learning resistance. Often, when adults are asked when they have really learned something of personal importance, they refer to situations of learning resistance. Therefore, in such situations learners should not just be turned down or neglected, but the teacher should try to find an opportunity for a personal talk, so the learner can be helped to find the reason for the reaction, determine what was at stake, and the consequences for different actions.

Identity, life projects and transformative learning

The main thread here is that adult learning may be subjectively meaningful or not and this outcome is determined by the learner's life course and life projects.

The essence of the life course has resulted in the building up of an identity, i.e. a central mental instance containing the understanding of who one is, who one wants to be, and how one experiences oneself and is experienced by others. While the concept of identity was originally a psychological construction, mainly elaborated by Erikson (1968), it has been further explained by modern sociologists, such as German Ulrich Beck (1997) [1986]), British Anthony Giddens (1991) and Polish-British Zygmunt Bauman (2000). The central understanding which has been developed, as least as I see it (Illeris 2014), is what Bauman has termed the age of "liquid modernity" (Bauman 2000). In order to cope with the ever-changing world we have to develop identities which are so stable that we have a coherent experience of ourselves, and at the same time so flexible that we can transform ourselves in accordance with changes in our life situations. In this regard Jack Mezirow's concept of transformative learning gains new meaning and importance, because it can be seen as the kind of adult learning which deals with the necessary transformations of the identity.

In relation to identity, the role of life projects in relation to adult learning has relevance. Adults usually have life projects that are relatively stable and long-term, for example, a family project that concerns creating and being part of a family, a work project that concerns a personally and financially satisfying job, perhaps a leisure-time project concerning a hobby, a life project to do with fulfillment, or a conviction project that may be religious or political in nature.

These life projects are embedded in the life history, present situation and possible future perspectives of the individual and are closely related to identity. We design our defenses on this basis so that we usually let what is relevant for our projects come through and reject the rest. Also on this basis, as the central core of our defenses, we develop defense mechanisms to counter influences that could threaten the experience of who we are and would like to be.

These matters typically comprise the fundamental premises for school-based or course-based adult learning seen from the perspective of the learners. These premises make the learners' initial motivation quite crucial and influence how they regard the study course in relation to their life projects.

In some cases, adult learning can lead to extensive, enriching development for the participants if they arrive with positive motivation and the study programs live up to or exceed their expectations. But in many adult education activities a considerable proportion of the participants only become positively engaged if they meet a challenge that "turns them on" at the beginning or along the way. Quite often, in current adult education situations, participants are only engaged superficially and do not learn very much, leading to the waste of human and financial resources.

What we all must realize is that the adult's way of learning is very different from the child's and that adult education must, therefore, be based on fundamentally different premises. The basic requirement is that the adult must take, and must be allowed to take, responsibility for his or her own learning. Adult learning activities should be designed out of respect, support and even demand for this basic requirement. We all have a great deal to learn in order to fully understand these fundamental conditions of adult learning.

Current adult learning theory

Efforts to work out a theoretical basis for adult learning came late and have been rather sparse until the 1980s. However, since then quite a few important contributions have been launched of which the most important shall be taken up here.

I have already mentioned Jack Mezirow's contribution on transformative learning, which was launched in 1978 and has been further developed (e.g. Mezirow 1991, 2000, 2006, 2009). Seen from a theoretical point of view the most important innovation in Mezirow's approach has been his attention to adults' possibilities of involving themselves in a type of learning that implies changes of a broader and further-reaching kind than what is comprised in Piaget's concept of accommodation (cf. Illeris 2007, 2014).

American Robert Kegan's constructive-developmental theory of human development refers to broad personal learning at different levels and can be understood as partly a support and partly a critique of Mezirow's approach as being too narrowly cognitively oriented (Kegan 1982, 1994, 2000).

The most comprehensive contribution has, however, been delivered by the British sociologist Peter Jarvis, who since the middle of the 1980s has published books and articles on adult and lifelong learning and at the same time has edited the *International Journal of Lifelong Education* and a number of international handbooks. His first important book was *Adult Education and Lifelong Learning* (Jarvis 1983), which has later been revised twice. Then came two more exceptional books which strongly introduced the social dimension of adult learning (Jarvis 1987, 1992). After many other publications in 2006–2008 he published a trilogy on *Lifelong Learning and the Learning Society*, covering his full theoretical understanding (Jarvis 2006, 2007, 2008) and finally he has edited two important international handbooks (Jarvis 2009, Jarvis and Watts 2012). In general his theory can be said to be founded in the philosophical and social dimensions, whereas the psychological dimension is less comprehensive. Jarvis' contribution has supplied a comprehensive and coherent theoretical understanding of adult learning.

Other theories from later years have helped to complete the picture. Some of the most specific contributions have been made by the Finnish psychologist Yrjö Engeström (e.g. Engeström 1987, 2009 [2001]) building on the Russian activity-theoretical approach from the mid-war period (Lev Vygotsky, Aleksei Leontjev), the American organizational theorists Chris Argyris and Donald Schön's contributions on organizational learning (e.g. Argyris and Schön 1996), the German sociologist Peter Alheit (e.g. Alheit 2009) who has been a driving force of the so-called biographical approach, seeing adult learning in the perspective of the life course in interaction with important external events – and, finally, I hope it will not be too presumptuous to mention by own contribution in this connection (e.g. Illeris 2004, 2007, 2011, 2014).

Seen in relation to the concept and issue of human resource development I hope that this chapter has contributed to making it clear that such development is not just a practical matter of following various more or less detailed recommendations or prescriptions. The human mind is not an automatically functioning construction following certain rules or directions but an extremely complex, unpredictable and personal creation following its own ways or ideas and sometimes also unconscious patterns – and that all of this has become particularly distinct in the present ever-changing world. In relation to adult learning the point of HRD must therefore be to encourage and make space for the manifold potentials offered by the available human resources.

References

Alheit, P. (2009) Biographical learning – within the new lifelong learning discourse, in K. Illeris (ed.) *Contemporary Theories of Learning*, London: Routledge.

Allport, G.W. (1961) *Pattern and Growth in Personality*, New York: Holt, Rineholt and Winston.

Argyris, C. and Schön, D. (1996) *Organizational Learning II – Theory, Method, Practice*, Reading, MA: Addison-Wesley.

Bauman, Z. (2000) *Liquid Modernity*, Cambridge, UK: Polity Press.

Beck, U. (1997 [1986]) *Risk Society: Towards a New Modernity*, London: SAGE.

Brookfield, S.D. (2000) Adult cognition as a dimension of lifelong learning, in J. Field and M. Leicester (eds) *Lifelong Learning – Education Across the Lifespan*, London: Routledge-Falmer.

Commons, M.L., Richards, F.A. and Armon, C. (eds) (1984) *Beyond Formal Operations: Late Adolescent and Adult Cognitive Development*, New York: Praeger.

Davenport, J. (1987) Is there any way out of the andragogy morass?, *Lifelong Learning: An Omnibus of Practice and Research* 11(3): 17–20.

Engeström, Y. (1987) *Learning by Expanding: An Activity-Theoretical Approach to Developmental Research*, Helsinki: Orienta-Kunsultit.

— (2009 [2001]) Expansive learning: toward an activity-theoretical reconceptualization, in K. Illeris (ed.) *Contemporary Theories of Learning*, London: Routledge.

Erikson, E.H. (1968) *Identity, Youth and Crisis*, New York: Norton.

Faure, E., Herrera, F., Kaddoura, A.R., Lopes, H., Petrovsky, A.V., Rhanema, M., and Ward, F.C. (1972) *Learning to Be: The World of Education Today and Tomorrow*, Paris: UNESCO.

Flavell, J.H. (1963) *The Developmental Psychology of Jean Piaget*, New York: Van Nostrand.

Freire, P. (1970) *Pedagogy of the Oppressed*, New York: Seabury.

Gergen, K.J. (1994) *Realities and Relationships*, Cambridge, MA: Harvard University Press.

Giddens, A. (1991) *Modernity and Self-Identity*, Cambridge, UK: Polity Press.

Gogtay, N., Giedd, J.N., Lusk, L., Hayashi, K.M., Greenstein, D., Vaituzis, A.C., Nugent, T.F. III, Herman, D.H., Clasen, L.S., Toga, A.W., Rapoport, J.L. and Thompson, P.M. (2004) Dynamic mapping of human cortical development during childhood through early adulthood, *Proceedings of the National Academy of Sciences of the USA* 101(21): 8174–9.

Hartree, A. (1984) Malcolm Knowles' theory of andragogy: a critique, *International Journal of Lifelong Education* 3: 203–10.

Illeris, K. (1998) Adult learning and responsibility, in K. Illeris (ed.) *Adult Education in a Transforming Society*, Copenhagen: Roskilde University Press.
— (2003) Adult education as experienced by the learners, *International Journal of Lifelong Education* 22: 13–23.
— (2004) *Adult Education and Adult Learning*, Malabar, FL: Krieger.
— (2006a) What is special about adult learning, in P. Sutherland and J. Crowther (eds) *Lifelong Learning – Concepts and Contexts*, London: Routledge.
— (2006b) Lifelong learning and the low-skilled, *International Journal of Lifelong Education* 25: 15–28.
— (2007) *How We Learn: Learning and Non-Learning in School and Beyond*, London: Routledge.
— (ed.) (2009) *Contemporary Theories of Learning: Learning Theorists ... In Their Own Words*, London: Routledge.
— (2011) *The Fundamentals of Workplace Learning: Understanding How People Learn in Working Life*, London: Routledge.
— (2014) *Transformative Learning and Identity*, London: Routledge.
Jarvis, P. (1983) *Adult Education and Lifelong Learning: Theory and Practice*, New York: Croom Helm.
— (1987) *Adult Learning in the Social Context*, New York: Croom Helm.
— (1992) *Paradoxes of Learning: On Becoming an Individual in Society*, San Francisco: Jossey-Bass.
— (2006) *Towards a Comprehensive Theory of Human Learning*, London: Routledge.
— (2007) *Globalisation, Lifelong Learning and the Learning Society: Sociological Perspectives*, London: Routledge.
— (2008) *Democracy, Lifelong Learning and the Learning Society: Active Citizenship in a Late Modern Age*, London: Routledge.
— (ed.) (2009) *The Routledge International Handbook of Lifelong Learning*, London: Routledge.
Jarvis, P. and Watts, M. (eds) (2012) *The Routledge International Handbook of Learning*, London: Routledge.
Kegan, R. (1982) *The Evolving Self: Problem and Process in Human Development*, Cambridge, MA: Harvard University Press.
— (1994) *In Over Our Heads: The Mental Demands of Ordinary Life*, Cambridge, MA: Harvard University Press.
— (2000) Which "form" transforms? A constructive-developmental approach to transformative learning, in J. Mezirow and Associates *Learning as Transformation: Critical Perspectives on a Theory in Progress*, San Francisco: Jossey-Bass.
Knowles, M.S. (1970) *The Modern Practice of Adult Education – Andragogy Versus Pedagogy*, New York: Association Press.
Lave, J. and Wenger, E. (1991) *Situated Learning: Legitimate Peripheral Participation*, New York: Cambridge University Press.
Mezirow, J. (1978) *Education for Perspective Transformation: Women's Reentry Programs in Community Colleges*, New York: Teachers College, Columbia University.
— (1991) *Transformative Dimensions of Adult Learning*, San Francisco: Jossey-Bass.
— (2000) Learning to think like an adult: core conceptions of transformative theory, in J. Mezirow and Associates *Learning as Transformation: Critical Perspectives on a Theory in Progress*, San Francisco: Jossey-Bass.
— (2006) An overview on transformative learning, in P. Sutherland and J. Crowther (eds) *Lifelong Learning – Concepts and Contexts*, London: Routledge.
— (2009) Transformative learning theory, in J. Mezirow, E.W. Taylor and Associates *Transformative Learning in Practice: Insights from Community, Workplace and Higher Education*, San Francisco: Jossey-Bass.
Negt, O. (1968) *Sociologische Phantasie und Exemplarisches Lernen* [Sociological imagination and exemplary learning], Frankfurt: Europäische Verlagsanstalt.
Rogers, A. (2003) *What is the Difference? A New Critique of Adult Learning and Teaching*, Leicester, UK: NIACE.
Rogers, C.R. (1961) *On Becoming a Person*, Boston: Haughton Mifflin.
Shayer, M. and Adey, P. (1981) *Towards a Science of Science Teaching*, London: Heinemann Educational.
Swanson, R.A. and Holton, E.F. (2001) *Foundations of Human Resource Development*, San Francisco: Berrett-Koehler.

4

TECHNICAL AND VOCATIONAL LEARNING

Stephen Billett

A growing concern for tertiary education students (including those in technical and vocational education) in many countries with advanced industrial economies is for them to move smoothly into practicing their selected occupations upon graduation (Department of Education, Science and Training 2002, Silverberg *et al.* 2004, Department of Innovation, Universities and Skills 2008). That is, for them to be "job ready" (Organisation for Economic Co-operation and Development 2010). Yet, securing job readiness is a tough educational goal, because it is not often known which jobs students will obtain upon graduation. Given that work requirements differ across workplaces even when the same occupation is being enacted (Billett 2001), ensuring job readiness will always be problematic. Yet, the imperative of job readiness means that work-based experiences are now increasingly becoming elements of tertiary education provisions. Some occupations have well established traditions of including work experiences in their preparatory processes (e.g. medicine, law, nursing, teaching, trades) as do some countries. The cooperative education movement in North America (Ricks 1996) and German dual apprenticeship systems (Deissinger and Hellwig 2005) are well-entrenched examples of these arrangements. However, work-based experiences are now being widely included in occupation-specific tertiary education programs (Billett 2009). These experiences can be directed towards quite distinct educational purposes (e.g. work readiness, occupational preparation, refinement of skills, etc) and take particular forms (e.g. internships, day-release, practicums, clinical experiences, work experience programs). Hence, education-focused interactions and engagements are increasing between tertiary education institutions and workplaces, involving supervisors, managers and, where they exist, human resource development (HRD) practitioners.

These interactions, potentially, can lead to significant opportunities and roles for HRD practitioners. Realizing this potential is the focus of this chapter. That is, how can HRD practitioners support work-based provisions of vocational and technical education? Opportunities include the possibility to engage with tertiary education students as potential employees through providing experiences that assist them to become aware of and effective in their chosen occupations. Building productive and ongoing interactions between workplaces and vocational and technical education institutions can also lead to effective working relationships that can build companies' human resources. These relationships can influence and shape the educational goals to be achieved, course content, and students' activities in their course work and workplace-based experiences and projects. Such relationships are essential for effective cooperative education (Eames and

Coll 2010) and dual system (Deissinger and Hellwig 2005) provisions. The potential of such relations extends to enriching students' learning through advising how best they can be prepared for workplace experiences, how that learning might be advanced in workplaces, and how these experiences can be effectively integrated into their educational programs at both individual and collective levels. In countries where mature relations between tertiary education institutions and local enterprises are cultivated and maintained (e.g. Germany, Switzerland, Austria) (Deissinger 2000), workplace-based HRD practitioners or their equivalents often develop and sustain such working relationships. These engagements can include identifying and fostering students as potential employees, and assisting their induction into and progression within the workplace. Hence, the shift to provide tertiary students with work-related experiences potentially expands, in productive ways, the roles and reach of HRD practitioners.

However, the expansion of these roles may not be universally welcomed by workplaces or workplace-based HRD practitioners (Slotte *et al.* 2004). The demands can include engaging with large numbers of students, negotiating around educational institutions' program requirements, and content and stipulations of professional or licensing bodies, teachers', supervisors' and managers' schedules, and meeting students' expectations. Also, where relations between educational institutions and workplaces are underdeveloped and processes for engagement are immature, the demands made upon HRD practitioners may be greater (Billett *et al.* 2007). Here, these practitioners may need to develop and sustain these relationships. These responsibilities will also likely need to be fulfilled whilst undertaking other roles and responsibilities, thereby presenting significant challenges for HRD practitioners.

This chapter, therefore, focuses on how HRD practitioners might come to understand more about the purposes and practices of workplace-based tertiary education experiences, participate effectively in them, build workplace capacities to support tertiary education students' learning, and develop and sustain effective relations with tertiary educational institutions. The discussions extend to how these practitioners might advance their workplaces' HRD goals for inducting staff and supporting ongoing development across their employment. The case commences by outlining a range of educational purposes to be achieved through work-based experiences for technical and vocational students. Next, the qualities of these experiences are discussed including how they can be enriched by HRD practitioners seeking to secure particular purposes. How the HRD function and practitioners can build mature and constructive relations with technical and vocational education institutions is briefly discussed in conclusion. The conceptual and empirical bases advancing the case here are drawn from studies of workplace learning, vocational education, social partnerships and tertiary teaching.

Educational purposes associated with workplace experiences

Educational programs and processes should be intentional. That is, there should be clear purposes for what is to be achieved through their enactment (Marsh 2004). This maxim extends to experiences in workplaces that are part of educational provisions. That is, there need to be particular purposes that are to be attained by providing such experiences. Therefore, experiences provided need to be aligned with particular intended purposes. Hence, these purposes guide bases for identifying the kinds of experiences provided for students, and how they are enacted and evaluated. A range of distinct educational purposes may be realized by providing technical and vocational education students with workplace experiences. These include:

- learning about their selected occupations;
- learning about variations in occupational practice;

- building capacities to engage in and be effective professional practitioners;
- extending the knowledge learned in university settings;
- being oriented to circumstances of the occupation's practice, their requirements; and
- meeting occupational or professional licensing requirements (Billett 2011).

Each of these purposes is also important for the HRD function. Firstly, given the high attrition rate within initial programs of occupational preparation in many countries and immediately after them, students' understanding about their chosen occupation needs to be developed early in that preparation. Students also need to learn the requirements for competently performing their selected occupation to assist employability (i.e. job readiness). Understanding these requirements can guide and direct students' effort in how and what they learn (Newton *et al.* 2011). This understanding can also instantiate what constitutes the goals for students' learning in their tertiary education programs. Therefore, having opportunities to observe and experience that occupation in practice and participate in its enactment is salient for students to identify with and develop capacities required for effective occupational practice.

Secondly, learning about variations in the enactment of occupations can assist students' adaptability. Students need to understand that the requirements for occupational performance differ across workplaces and time, so they appreciate the diversity of procedures and practices that are adopted across workplaces. Consequently, exposing students to variations of occupational practice or arranging for the sharing of experiences of those differences with other students can assist the development of these understandings and capacities. Doctors' and nurses' practices of major metropolitan hospitals can differ from those in medical centers in regional, small or remote communities, just as the work of motor mechanics, teachers, carpenters and hairdressers is similarly shaped by the particular circumstances of their practice (Billett 2001). Those conceptions are important as graduates find employment in particular workplaces with their norms and practices, and come to move across or within workplaces, and as work requirements change. Importantly, processes of human adaptability (or transfer) are increasingly held to be premised on understandings and practices about variations in different reasons for how the occupation is practiced (Barsalou 2009).

Thirdly, learning the capacities required for effective occupational performance is central to being able to practice. Many such capacities arise from opportunities to engage in specific kinds of experiences. For workers to become competent with specific occupational procedures such as putting dressings on patients, cutting hair, fixing motors, or talking to patients requires opportunities to initially develop, practice and refine those capacities. Often, but not always, workplace settings can provide access to such experiences, particularly when ordered to effectively develop these capacities (Eraut 2007, Colin 2004). Consequently, the role of the HRD practitioner can be to assist the organization of these experiences which incrementally exposes students to specific procedures, and then provides opportunities for practicing and honing them.

Fourthly, extending the knowledge students learn in educational settings is useful for subsequently grounding it in the practice in which they are employed. Links between what is taught in vocational education programs and what occurs in workplace activities are not always apparent. Workplace experiences provide opportunities for making, reinforcing and refining those links. Certainly, developing causal links and responses between concepts and practices is central to developing robust occupational knowledge of the kind possessed by expert practitioners (Ericsson 2006, Groen and Patel 1988). There is also a role for making explicit the knowledge taught within educational institutions and its applicability to practice. That role may involve making explicit the alignments between propositional (i.e. factual) knowledge learned through classroom experiences and building links and causal associations that are central to effective work performance.

Fifthly, orientations to workplaces are important, as occupational requirements are shaped situationally (Billett 2001, Newton *et al.* 2011). Occupation-specific courses are usually guided by national standards and these are often the bases against which graduates are assessed in educational programs. Yet, ultimately their capacities are judged on how they perform *in situ*, where the actual practices may be quite distinct from what they have experienced in their courses. Consequently, to assist students' understandings and graduates' successful transitions to particular work settings, orientations to their particular practices, emphases, and requirements are valuable. In particular, opportunities to engage in one or more instances of practice can assist students understand those important situated qualities.

Sixthly, meeting occupational certification or compliance requirements is increasingly important for both individuals and workplaces. Many occupations now require significant periods of work experience before graduates are certified to practice the occupation as stipulated by professional and occupational bodies. Therefore, HRD practitioners can assist students and graduates access the kind and quantum of required experiences through workplace activities or probationary periods as part of productive workplace activities.

HRD practitioners can provide and enrich experiences that meet these purposes, and through which enterprises can benefit from a productive engagement with these students.

The range of experiences which might be undertaken

Particular kinds of learning experiences are aligned with the educational purposes set out above. For instance, experiences permitting students to understand more about their chosen occupation, any specializations within it and orientations to particular work settings are quite different to those for developing and honing specific occupational capacities (Molloy and Keating 2011). Then, experiences aiming to be aligned with and make explicit what has recently been taught to or learned by students are different again (Grubb and Badway 1998). The kinds and duration of experiences required by licensing authorities may be of a different kind again through stipulating number of hours of experience, or particular kinds of experiences (e.g. X number of hours of direct teaching, the witnessing of X number of births, etc.) (Billett 2011). So, particular kinds of experiences may be required which can make demands upon HRD practitioners. Here, workplace considerations extend to the duration of experiences (i.e. short or longer term), whether or not particular sequencing of experiences is needed and what if any rotations of experiences through particular work areas are required.

A common form of tertiary student engagement in workplaces is through supervised placements. These placements usually comprise students being assigned mentors, preceptors, buddies who guide and supervise, and sometimes work alongside or collaboratively with them in workplaces. This arrangement is commonly used where particular kinds of risks exist (e.g. patients in hospitals or children in schools). When these processes of support and guidance work well, they are very effective. They seem to work best when workplace supervisors:

- have expertise in the occupation and work area;
- are viewed as credible by learners;
- understand what is required for successful performance in the workplace;
- value mentoring – see a need for it and the knowledge to be learned by mentees;
- are willing to share knowledge with learners; and
- are guides for learners rather than teaching them (e.g. making learners do the thinking and acting) (Billett 2000).

In some occupations and workplace settings, this support for learning is available as part of everyday practice. However, more likely, the capacities for effective learning support need to be developed within workplaces and sustained over time. This role often falls to HRD practitioners. Beyond engaging with developing students' occupational competence, developing such capacities in workplaces also has benefits. These benefits include using these capacities to orientate new employees and sustaining existing employees' occupational currency through everyday work activities across lengthening working lives. Hence, because HRD practitioners may be unable to undertake mentoring roles themselves, as they lack competence in occupational fields, this expert guidance requires to be developed (Slotte *et al.* 2004). So, their roles could be to develop supervisors' and experienced workers' capacities to support students, graduates and other employees. Yet, supervised placements are resource intensive and not always available in numbers to meet the increasing requests for student workplace experiences. Therefore, other ways, such as internships or practicums, are needed to support students seeking long-term placements to develop and hone occupational capacities. Such approaches can also benefit those who are being inducted into workplaces either before or after they graduate from tertiary education programs. Some students can draw on their current or previous work experience when coming to understand the requirements for work performance. These understandings include non-specific capacities such as working together and interacting with other workers. Some workplace learning experiences do not require close supervision and guidance. For instance, students may engage in activities such as observing others' work activities to understand how occupations are practiced and how requirements impact particular workplaces. These processes can be supported by HRD practitioners who can arrange such experiences and facilitate the sharing and augmentation of students' experiences. These practitioners can engage students in dialogue about how their observations relate to particular practices in workplaces.

Students can also come to understand more about workplaces and occupational practices through processes such as report writing, observing, and shadowing other employees. Opportunities exist in some occupations for engaging students in part-time employment aligned with their career learning needs. These experiences allow students to observe the workplace and gain understanding of the occupational practice and how work is enacted in workplaces. Particular kinds of workplace experiences can provide rich insights and learning. Often, these occur when occupational practitioners come together to articulate, discuss, and make decisions about their work. For students, observance of and involvement in these meetings can be richly informative. For instance, a common practice in health care is the "hand-over" meetings in which a shift of incoming workers (i.e. doctors, nurses) are briefed about their patients by those completing the shift. In these meetings, the patients, their conditions, treatments, progress and prognoses are described and discussed by the healthcare workers. These handovers afford opportunities for novices and students to observe and listen, engage personally or interactively and with likely different kinds of outcomes for students depending upon their level of knowledge or readiness to engage. Importantly, more than just making the process of healthcare accessible, these meetings provide forums through which the occupational knowledge is richly embedded and grounded in experiences that can be made accessible to students. These experiences involve bases for comparisons and contrasts and the formation of causal associations of the kind that experts effectively utilize. In short, these meetings represent potentially effective learning experiences, particularly if students engage fully in them.

So, particular kinds of learning experiences can be aligned with achieving particular educational goals. Some of these experiences are well-known and practiced, including supervised practicums or internships. However, students can engage in other ways to develop particular capacities. When the purpose is to understand what constitutes the occupation in practice, requirements for particular workplaces or some variations across them, opportunities to observe either passively or through some form of work activity or engagement can be organized to realize these kinds of goals. Nevertheless, a key consideration with all of these suggestions is the degree to which a workplace's resources can and will be utilized for these purposes. Situations that involve the greatest risk to clients or critical processes are conditions in which supervision is required to be close, and costs and restrictions are key considerations. Workers who supervise, mentor or guide students and novices in workplaces need to be properly prepared to be effective in the roles set out above. These important tasks may fall to HRD practitioners. However, the benefits from such preparation are not restricted to engaging students and newcomers, as they can contribute to other HRD functions such as sustaining workers' competence and other ongoing developments of the workforce, such as those required to manage change, including those providing mentoring and guidance.

The enrichment of workplace experiences

A key finding from a national project focusing on how to integrate experiences in work and educational settings (Billett 2011) was that merely providing students with workplace experiences is not sufficient. Instead, to realize the potential of these experiences requires the use of particular activities, including specific pedagogic practices. Many of these activities are undertaken within educational institutions and are outside the scope of HRD practitioners' roles. However, some have direct relevance to their roles and to the HRD processes in workplaces, albeit variously for employees' orientation, initial occupational preparation, and professional development activities. Identified was also a set of considerations to guide pedagogic practice: (1) in preparing students for engaging in workplaces as learning environments, (2) whilst in workplaces, and (3) after those experiences had been completed. Overall, the concern here is to propose pedagogic practices that can augment students' learning experiences and be enacted by busy tertiary teachers. However, the same concern of time availability will be applicable to HRD practitioners.

The findings from the range of projects across a range of occupations identify particular pedagogic practices likely to be most helpful at different times in students' development. These practices can be categorized as those informing how that learning might best be assisted (1) before, (2) during, and (3) after tertiary students' participation in workplace-based experiences. In overview, these pedagogic considerations are as follows.

Pedagogic practices before workplace experiences

Firstly, before students engage in workplace experiences it is helpful to:

- establish bases for those experiences, including identifying what happens in those settings;
- clarify expectations about purposes, support, responsibilities, etc. (i.e. goals for learning);
- inform about purposes, roles, and expectations of different parties;
- prepare students to be active learners – including the importance of observations, interactions, and activities through which they learn;
- develop procedural capacities required for engaging productively; and
- prepare students for contestations they may encounter.

In all, students need to be advised about what they might learn in those workplaces and how they are to be engaged. This advice includes their roles as active learners, what expectations others might have of them, being clear of the kinds of educational purposes intended to be achieved, and having the capacities to participate successfully in workplace activities. The last three key points emphasize orientation or preparation, not only to the workplace, but also for students to be prepared as active and engaged learners, and not to expect what they learn to arise from being taught. In short, these practices emphasize students' responsibility to engage and learn productively in workplaces, including through interactions with other workers, albeit in considered and reflective ways when constructing the knowledge they need to learn. However, some preparatory work may be needed so students can participate productively, even as peripheral participants (Lave and Wenger 1991). In healthcare, for instance, students often engage in clinical laboratories in tertiary educational institutions to develop specific procedural capacities before practicing on patients. So, simulations in making sutures, inserting cannulas and taking temperatures, and applying and removing dressings are practiced in these laboratories to develop procedural competence before they engage directly with patients. Students also need to be able to negotiate difficult interpersonal interactions with other workers or their mentor. In busy everyday work activities, some coworkers may not be able to be helpful and may even unnecessarily test students. Hence, students need a preparation that provides an orientation to the workplace, others, and expectations. They may need assistance developing appropriate procedures to be effective – even in relatively routine workplace activities. They may also need to learn to know how best to interact with others in the workplace, so that those involved can come to engage with them productively. Although this kind of preparatory work needs to be undertaken in education institutions, HRD practitioners can make a difference in preparing students, graduates, or new employees to effectively participate in the workplace.

Pedagogic practices during workplace experiences

Secondly, during workplace-based experiences it is helpful for technical and vocational education students to access forms of support or to engage actively themselves in their learning. Students may require support characterized by:

- direct guidance by more experienced practitioners (i.e. close guidance);
- sequencing of activities in which they engage (i.e. "learning curriculum", (Lave 1990);
- active engagement by students in pedagogically rich work activities or interactions (e.g. nurses' handovers);
- effective peer interactions (i.e. collaborative learning) (Newton *et al.* 2011); and
- active and purposeful engagement by learners in workplace settings (Billett and Pavlova 2005).

Again, the need for students to be actively engaged in the learning process predominates here. Even when guided by workplace experts or more experienced workers, they will need to engage effortfully when learning the kinds of knowledge (e.g. conceptual, procedural) that cannot easily be learned alone. In addition, HRD practitioners might organize group activities amongst the students so that they can develop peer support and peer networks thereby reducing the reliance on supervisors, mentors, and the HRD practitioners. Moreover, these kinds of peer-assisted forms of learning support are reported as helping students to support each other, share common goals and concerns, and also make links to their educational programs (Billett 2011).

Pedagogic practices after workplace experiences

Thirdly, after students have had workplace-based experiences, it is helpful to:

- facilitate the sharing and drawing out of their experiences (i.e. articulating and comparing commonalities and distinctiveness (e.g. occupational and situational requirements for practice);
- explicitly make links to what is taught in the college and what is experienced in practice settings;
- emphasize the agentic and selective qualities of learning through practice; and
- generate critical perspectives on work and learning processes in students.

The goals here are to utilize and maximize students' workplace learning experiences. This sharing can be used as the basis for extending what individuals have experienced and learned, and then extending and enriching their collective learning. In many ways, this sharing is probably the most potentially rich opportunity. By this time, students can reflect on their learning from particular experiences. Hence, they can engage with other students in comparing and contrasting experiences, and take their understandings forward. Early in the North American cooperative education movement, co-op seminars were introduced for these purposes (Grubb and Badway 1998). One particularly important outcome of these kinds of shared activities is for students to identify practices and understandings that are both broadly applicable with an occupation (i.e. the canonical knowledge and qualities expected of anybody practicing that occupation) and those that are specific to a particular workplace (i.e. situational requirements – "what we do here is"). Identifying and making distinctions between the canonical knowledge of occupations and situational requirements can be helpful for the development of adaptable or transferable occupational knowledge. Through developing these capacities in students an understanding of situational specific requirements of occupational capacities opens up the possibility of their understanding the differences in the requirements for and ways of applying canonical knowledge. Moreover, when these experiences are augmented through being shared with others, the platform of what is required at the occupational level, and particular instances of practice can come to be better understood. Practitioners need such adaptable knowledge across their working lives as performance requirements change.

The degree to which HRD practitioners want to or can enact these kinds of augmenting experiences will depend upon whether the learners are students gaining experience, being prepared for an occupation, or novice or experienced employees. However, to different degrees, and for distinct purposes, these kinds of practices can be helpful for occupational skill development. These practices can be central to the HRD role within organizations that are seeking to orientate workers to the requirements of workplaces, develop further employees' occupational capacities, and generate the kinds of capacities in workers that will allow them to be adaptable in responding to changes arising across working lives. The kinds of processes and practices outlined above are not necessarily resource intensive, can occur as part of work practice in many workplaces, and can be engaged with through work or in work-related activities such as meetings. However, they allow workplace experiences to be utilized individually and collectively in workers' initial preparation and ongoing development.

Importantly, these processes prompt for a broader consideration of HRD practitioner roles and practices. There is a continuing tendency to see HRD practices as being delivered through the offering of taught courses where the content is predetermined, the learning process is premised upon didactic presentations and the intended outcomes pre-specified (Fenwick 2005). Certainly, there is a need to go beyond seeing HRD provisions as being through courses. Here, the emphasis is on developing students' and workers' capacities to be more self-directed and engaged in ongoing learning. Furthermore, workplace activities and support must be utilized to achieve goals associated with individuals' learning and development and workplace continuity. However, these processes and outcomes arising from them will likely best be achieved with appropriate guidance and support. Assistance is particularly needed for introducing and initiating learners into workplaces, making accessible to them knowledge which they might not otherwise learn and engaging with them as coworkers, rather than as students to be taught.

Building and sustaining partnerships

Finally, a central consideration for the enactment of these kinds of processes is establishing mature working relations between workplaces and educational institutions (Cardini 2006). As noted, in some situations (e.g. German dual system, North American co-op education) cultural privileging and support for such relationships occurs, but this privileging is far from universal. Where these beliefs exist, the task for the HRD practitioner is likely to be easier, with fewer barriers to be negotiated and less justification required. However, some principles associated with building partnerships across tertiary education institutions and local enterprises have been identified that warrant consideration. Arising from an evaluation of such partnerships, five sets of principles were identified as being central for developing and sustaining effective partnerships associated with technical and vocational education (Billett *et al.* 2007). These principles comprise building and maintaining: (1) shared purposes and goals; (2) relations with partners; (3) capacities for partnership work; (4) partnership governance and leadership; and (5) trust and trustworthiness. Again, the degree by which it is possible for individual HRD practitioners to engage in these kinds of arrangements will depend on the size, scope, and interests of their employing organization. However, some important considerations arising from such principles and practices are that these qualities characterize mature vocational and technical education systems. That is, such systems engage with their communities to identify the requirements for programs and enact those programs, and do not merely react to prescriptive national measures and mandates. Instead, systems that feature localized negotiations and engagements seem to be central to what constitutes effective and mature vocational education provisions. HRD practitioners are often well-placed to contribute to the development and longevity of such mature relationships. Yet, such partnerships need to be developed in the first instance, and then sustained through shared intent, interests, and the building of trust in these working relationships. Roles that HRD practitioners establish in both the provisions of support and building such relationships can be central to influencing the integrating experiences in the workplace and the technical and vocational education institutions.

HRD practitioners and vocational and technical education

This chapter has focused on and discussed how HRD practitioners can engage in the provision of vocational and technical education and with its students, teachers and administrations for mutually beneficial purposes and outcomes. The key premises and vehicles for this engagement are the increased emphasis on providing these students with workplace-based learning experiences. It is in the interests of hosting workplaces, students and overall education provisions if HRD practitioners are able to support and augment these experiences. In doing so, this role extends the scope and perhaps activities of many HRD practitioners, so understandings about and ways in which this support might be provided have been outlined and discussed here drawing on empirical research and appropriate literature.

References

Barsalou, L.W. (2009) Simulation, situated conceptualisation, and prediction, *Philosophical Transactions of the Royal Society B* 364: 1281–89.

Billett, S. (2000) Guided learning at work, *Journal of Workplace Learning* 12: 272–85.

— (2001) Knowing in practice: re-conceptualising vocational expertise, *Learning and Instruction* 11: 431–52.

— (2009) Realising the educational worth of integrating work experiences in higher education, *Studies in Higher Education* 34: 827–43.

— (2011) *Curriculum and Pedagogic Bases for Effectively Integrating Practice-Based Experiences*, Sydney: Australian Learning and Teaching Council.

Billett, S. and Pavlova, M. (2005) Learning through working life: self and individuals' agentic action, *International Journal of Lifelong Education* 24: 195–211.

Billett, S., Ovens, C., Clemans, A. and Seddon, T. (2007) Collaborative working and contested practices: forming, developing and sustaining social partnerships in education, *Journal of Education Policy* 22: 637–56.

Cardini, A. (2006) An analysis of the rhetoric and practice of educational partnerships in the UK: an arena of complexities, tensions and power, *Journal of Education Policy* 21: 393–415.

Colin, K. (2004) Workplace's learning and life, *International Journal of Lifelong Learning* 4: 24–38.

Deissinger, T. (2000) The German "philosophy" of linking academic and work-based learning in higher education: the case for vocational academies, *Journal of Vocational Education and Training* 52: 605–25.

Deissinger, T. and Hellwig, S. (2005) Apprenticeships in Germany: modernising the dual system, *Education and Training* 47: 312–24.

Department of Education, Science and Training (2002) *Employability Skills for the Future*, Canberra: Department of Education, Science and Training, Commonwealth of Australia.

Department of Innovation, Universities and Skills (2008) *Higher education at work: high skills, high value*, Sheffield: Department of Innovation, Universities and Skills.

Eames, C. and Coll, R. (2010) Cooperative education: integrating classroom and workplace learning, in S. Billett (ed.) *Learning Through Practice: Models, Traditions, Orientations and Approaches*, Dordrecht, Netherlands: Springer, 180–96.

Eraut, M. (2007) Learning from other people in the workplace, *Oxford Review of Education* 33: 403–22.

Ericsson, K.A. (2006) The influence of experience and deliberate practice on the development of superior expert performance, in K.A. Ericsson, N. Charness, P.J. Feltowich and R.R. Hoffmann (eds) *The Cambridge Handbook of Expertise and Expert Performance*, Cambridge, UK: Cambridge University Press, 685–705.

Fenwick, T. (2005) Conceptions of critical HRD: dilemmas for theory and practice, *Human Resource Development International* 8: 225–38.

Groen, G.J. and Patel, P. (1988) The relationship between comprehension and reasoning in medical expertise, in M.T.H. Chi, R. Glaser and R. Farr (eds) *The Nature of Expertise*, New York: Erlbaum, 287–310.

Grubb, W.N. and Badway, N. (1998) *Linking School-Based and Work-Based Learning: The Implications of LaGuardia's Co-op Seminars for School-to-Work Programs*, Berkeley, CA: National Center for Research in Vocational Education.

Lave, J. (1990) The culture of acquisition and the practice of understanding, in J.W. Stigler, R.A. Shweder and G. Herdt (eds) *Cultural Psychology*, Cambridge, UK: Cambridge University Press, 259–86.

Lave, J. and Wenger, E. (1991) *Situated Learning – Legitimate Peripheral Participation*, Cambridge, UK: Cambridge University Press.

Marsh, C.J. (2004) *Key Concepts for Understanding Curriculum*, London: RoutledgeFalmer.

Molloy, L. and Keating, J. (2011) Targeted preparation for clinical practice, in S. Billett and A. Henderson (eds) *Developing Learning Professionals: Integrating Experiences in University and Practice Settings*, Dordrecht, Netherlands: Springer, 59–82.

Newton, J., Billett, S., Jolly, B. and Ockerby, C. (2011) Preparing nurses and engaging preceptors, in S. Billett and A. Henderson (eds) *Developing Learning Professionals: Integrating Experiences in University and Practice Settings*, Dordrecht, Netherlands: Springer, 43–58.

Organisation for Economic Co-operation and Development (2010) *Learning For Jobs*, Paris: OECD.

Ricks, F. (1996) Principles for structuring cooperative education programs, *Journal of Cooperative Education* 31: 8–22.

Silverberg, M., Warner, E., Fong, M. and Goodwin, D. (2004) *National Assessment of Vocational Education: Final Report to Congress*, Washington, DC: Department of Education.

Slotte, V., Tynjälä, P. and Hytönen, T. (2004) How do HRD practitioners describe learning at work?, *Human Resource Development International* 7: 481–99.

5

CONTINUING PROFESSIONAL EDUCATION, DEVELOPMENT AND LEARNING

Barbara J. Daley and Ronald M. Cervero

Continuing professional education (CPE) and systems of continuing professional development (CPD) are being challenged to change dramatically across many contexts. Over the last two decades, CPE has moved from a focus on episodic delivery to a planned/sustained delivery, from a focus on the adult learner to a focus on patient and client outcomes, and from education at remote locations to job embedded training (Day and Sachs 2004). These changes are reflected in the broader conception of CPD, as opposed to continuing education. This chapter will provide a rationale for this broader conception, analyze CPD within social and global contexts, and discuss the movement towards developing systems of lifelong professional development and learning. The chapter will conclude by examining trends in professional practice that have implications for the future of CPE.

Social and global contexts for CPE

A central feature of societies in the twentieth century was the professionalization of their workforces with nearly 25 per cent of the American workforce, for example, being classified as professionals (Cervero 1988, Noordegraaf 2007). These professionals include teachers, physicians, clergy, lawyers, social workers, nurses, business managers, psychologists, and accountants. Educational systems have been a key feature of this professionalization project (Larson 1977) and consequently, substantial financial and human resources have been deployed to support three to six years of professionals' initial education. Until the 1960s many leaders in the professions believed that these years of pre-service professional education, along with some refreshers, were sufficient for a lifetime of work. However, with the rapid social changes, the explosion of research-based knowledge, the growing emphasis of evidence-based practice and spiraling technological innovations, many of these leaders now understand the need to continually prepare people for 40 years of professional practice through continuing education (Houle 1980, Cervero and Daley 2010). Beginning in the 1960s, embryonic evidence emerged for systems of CPE. Perhaps the first clear signal of this new view was the publication in 1962 of a conceptual scheme for the lifelong education of physicians in the United States (Dryer 1962). The 1970s saw the beginning of what is now a widespread use of continuing education as a basis for relicensure and recertification. By the 1980s organized and comprehensive programs of continuing education were developed in engineering, accounting, law, medicine, pharmacy, veterinary medicine, social work, librarianship, architecture, nursing, management, public school education, and many other professions (Cervero 1988). During that decade, many professions also developed their systems of accreditation for providers of continuing education.

In the rapid growth of continuing education, educational leaders have generally relied for guidance and models on the distinctive knowledge base and structure of their own profession. However, observers (Houle 1980, Cervero 1988) noted the similarities of the continuing education efforts of individual professions in terms of goals, processes, and structures. Thus, the concept of CPE began to be used in the late 1960s. Various terms are used throughout the world referring to this concept, including CPD (Fraser *et al.* 2007) and professional learning (Cervero and Daley 2010). The rationale for this movement to a cross-professional conception is that the understanding of similarities across the professions would yield a fresh exchange of ideas, practices, and solutions to common problems.

Formal continuing education programs are offered by a variety of providers, with the major types being universities and professional schools, professional associations, the workplace, and a collection of independent, governmental, and for-profit organizations (Cervero and Daley 2010). Although there is no national repository of statistics, a consensus in the literature is that the workplace provides by far the largest amount of formal CPE programs (Cervero 2001, Cervero and Daley 2010). With the vast majority of professionals now employed by organizations, as opposed to solo practice, the workplace has increasingly become the focal point for these employees' ongoing professional development. Goals have shifted from merely updating professionals on the newest knowledge to goals that focus on improving practice (Cervero 2012). As the workplace has become the major provider, a greater intersection has occurred between the fields of CPE and HRD (Bierema and Eraut 2004). Whereas CPE is defined by the individual participating (e.g. the professional) in multiple professionals contexts, HRD is defined by the individual in the workplace context. For example, Nadler and Nadler (1989: 6) define HRD as "organized learning experiences provided by employers within a specified period of time to bring about the possibility of performance improvement and/or personal growth." With the focus on performance improvement in HRD programs and the move towards practice-based education in CPE, goals, educational methods, and evaluation approaches are converging and research is being shared across these two fields.

Although the growth of continuing education is a worldwide phenomenon, the most articulated systems exist in the nations of the global North, such as Canada, Europe, Australia and New Zealand, and the United States. In these regions specifically, there has been an emergence of global organizations focused on CPD and an increasing interest in both international comparisons of practice and research across countries and professions (Institute of Medicine 2010). Continuing education and training have been addressed in such global contexts as the World Trade Organization and the General Agreement on Tariffs and Trade because of the implications of the transportability of professional licenses and services across borders (Lenn and Campos 1997). Global institutions are now setting standards for the accreditation of educational programs across the continuum in medicine with the World Federation for Medical Education/World Health Organization partnership (Karle 2006). In the past 10 years, the pharmacy profession has produced a *Statement of Professional Standards on Continuing Professional Development* (International Pharmaceutical Federation 2002) and *A Global Framework for Quality Assurance of Pharmacy Education* (Rouse 2008). Finally, there are now global professional associations focusing on continuing education in specific professions, such as the Global Alliance for Medical Education.

Alongside the emergence of global institutions, the field of continuing education has witnessed an increased interest in international comparisons of practice and in the research literature. The most common comparative analyses are those focused across countries within professions, such as in teaching (Coolahan 2002), nursing (Robinson and Griffiths 2007), and medicine (Merkur *et al.* 2008). The most prominent cross-professional comparative analysis is the chapter on "International Comparison of Continuing Education and Continuing Professional Development" in the Institute of Medicine's (IOM) landmark book (2010) on redesigning continuing education in the health professions. Based upon a comprehensive analysis of literature across the professions, the book argued: "Cross-fertilization of innovative education models provides comparative formative and summative evaluations to validate and improve best practices while leading the way towards international coherence on the training, registration, and continual assessment of health professionals" (IOM 2010: 233). This review of literature found a move towards the broader focus on CPD in contrast to continuing education, which is consistent with trends in teacher education (Muijs and Lindsay 2008) and other professions. The distinction is that continuing education is generally focused on updating and reinforcing knowledge and is counted by accumulating credits, whereas CPD is an umbrella for all sorts of interventions, including CPE, and deals with a variety of skills that professionals need in addition to content. The report also found that many countries are reforming their systems of CPD to focus on improving competence and performance. While differences exist in these systems, core similarities include reliance on professional self-regulation, lack of financial resources for improving CE systems, and an increasing use of peer review and practice audit (IOM 2010). As argued in reference to British teacher education, the needs of individuals (through CPE) and of employers (through HRD) will continue to converge as the workplace becomes more prominent as a location for education: "Continuing professional development is increasingly seen, then, as a key part of the career development of all professionals, which is a shared responsibility with their employers because it serves the interests of both" (Muijs and Lindsay 2008: 196).

Moving towards systems of lifespan professional development

We are now entering a transformational era in which professions are constructing systems of CPD. The professions are in a transitional stage, experimenting with many different purposes, forms, and institutional locations for the delivery of CPD (Day and Sachs 2004, IOM 2010). These systems are incredibly primitive and can be characterized as:

- Devoted mainly to updating practitioners about the newest developments,
- Transmitted in a didactic fashion,
- Offered by a pluralistic group of providers (workplaces, for-profits, associations, and universities) that do not coordinate their work together,
- Using "seat time" to re-credential practitioners, and
- Often paid for by vendors who stand to benefit from the learning.

Although the emerging systems of CPD have many dimensions, their four fundamental changes involve moving from: 1) a pre-service to a lifespan focus, 2) content updates to practice-based education, 3) un-coordinated events to a curriculum, and 4) re-credentialing based on participation to re-credentialing based on learning and practice.

In building these systems of CPD we can expect to see clearer connections to the entire continuum of professional development, including the stage of pre-service education as well as the critically important induction/residency stage. These connections are likely to include an alignment of curricula across the lifespan, a better coordination of providers for all three stages, a more seamless credentialing system across the lifespan, and a more transparent portfolio of learning opportunities for learners. Education in the third stage of the continuum of professional education has a great advantage over the other two stages in promoting effective practice because it occurs in a place and time when professionals are most likely to have a need for better ways to practice. But to exploit this natural advantage, the emerging systems must integrate CPD, both in its content and educational design, into professionals' ongoing individual and collective practice. Practice-based education across the continuum of professionals' education offers a strategy that will define the systems of CPD (Hager *et al.* 2008). For example, this strategy is recognized globally in teacher education (Fraser *et al.* 2007) and practice-based learning models are also now at the center of reform proposals in the first two stages in the continuum of medical education (Association of American Medical Colleges [AAMC] 2004, Accreditation Council for Graduate Medical Education 2007). The past 40 years have seen an incredible elaboration and extension of this practice-based educational model and this movement is now at the forefront of educational agendas throughout the professions (Cervero 2012, Institute of Medicine 2010, Thorpe *et al.* 2004).

The professions' pre-service and induction/residency programs have fixed curricula, courses, and timeframes. These educational programs are highly regulated by accrediting bodies in order to assure competence upon entry to practice. This feature is true universally for both the classroom and clinical portions of these first two stages of professional education. Once professionals enter into practice, however, the locus of responsibility for the curriculum of professional development shifts almost entirely to the individual. A small number of organizations require participation in a formal course that covers a specific topic as part of the requirements for re-credentialing, usually related to the ethics of professional practice. However, medicine is at the forefront of developing a curriculum of professional development across the lifespan. There is a movement towards using general competencies that would structure the re-credentialing of medical specialties in the United States (Spivey 2005). The six general competencies, which have been accepted by all the major stakeholder groups across the continuum in medical education, are focused on developing knowledge and skills related to patient care, medical knowledge, practice-based learning and improvement, interpersonal communication skills, professionalism, and systems-based practice (Miller 2005). These competencies, however, do not constitute a comprehensive curriculum because no course content is prescribed. Rather, the processes of "self-directed learning" and "directed self-learning" are used to determine the curriculum. In the self-directed learning process, the American Board of Medical Specialties states that "physicians should evaluate their practice and their need to learn and define and receive help in defining areas of learning need as well as methods and resources to assure satisfaction of those needs in the process of improvement" (Miller 2005: 154). What is new, however, comes from the process of "directed self-learning" that requires the specialty boards to help physicians "in identifying those areas of need and also to direct learners towards improvement mechanisms, taking care to make sure there is a balance established between self-directed learning and learning that is other directed. Both must be addressed" (154). Thus, both self-directed learning and directed self-learning are key dynamics in the proposal for a professional development curriculum.

Policymakers responsible for licensing and certification will develop systems that move from accumulating credits based on participation in CPD to rewarding effective individual and system learning (Davis and Willis 2004). Looking across the professions globally, existing re-credentialing programs are based on the central premise articulated by Houle over 25 years ago: "To achieve its greatest potential, continuing education must fulfill the promise of its name and be truly continuing – not casual, sporadic, or opportunistic . . . This fact means essentially that it must be self-directed" (1980: 12). Houle, however, recognizes that "reliance cannot be solely based on self-direction" (12) because adult learners are not always in the best position to know what they do not know in terms of maintaining competency. The emerging recertification scheme that calls for the active involvement of medical specialty boards is the first example in which other stakeholders help practitioners construct their own professional development curriculum. There are many substantive reasons for not prescribing a standard curriculum for professional development across the lifespan. Thus, the involvement of professional bodies and employing organizations in partnering with individual practitioners to develop curricula for re-credentialing may become the model across the professions over the next 20 years.

Relatively speaking, these systems of CPD are in their infancy. By way of analogy, the field is in the same state of development as pre-service education was 100 years ago. Medical education serves a useful point of comparison. In his report on medical schools in Canada and the United States, Flexner (1910) found that only 16 of 155 schools expected their incoming students would have any previous college education and he recommended closing the ones that did not. It is unlikely that anyone in 1910 would have predicted the structure of medical education today. Likewise, systems of continuing education are likely to grow through this transitional period to achieve an equivalent coherence, size, and stature as the pre-service stage of professional education. As Houle (1980: 302) explained:

> The plans to establish basic educational programs for those entering the professions were thought in the first quarter of this century to be visionary, but they have now been realized at levels far beyond those of the original dreams. Continuing education will follow the same pattern of growth; what we hardly dare prophesy today will be seen by later generations as efforts to achieve a manifest necessity.

Perspectives on Continuing Professional Learning (CPL)

As new systems of CPD are created within changing global contexts, a central issue to be addressed is what type of learning will be most effective in these new systems? Learning in and for professional practice is central to whatever systems are created, and yet, most often discussions of CPD focus on creating programs, deciding content, determining instructional strategies, and planning evaluations. The manner in which professionals learn is an area that needs attention within systems of CPD. As Eraut (1994: 40) explained, behind "professional education lies a remarkable ignorance about professional learning."

According to the IOM report (2010: 4) discussing the redesign of continuing education for the health professions, "the scientific literature offers guidance about general principles for CE but provides little specific information about how to best support learning." This same report advocates that new systems of CPD take "a holistic view of health professionals' learning, with opportunities stretching from the classroom to the point of care" (5). What is important to note is that the control of learning in this view is shifted to the individual professionals so that the professionals, in cooperation with specialists, can create the kind of learning opportunities for themselves that will best support the development of their professional practice. Finally, the IOM report (2010) recognizes that adult education research and theory are sources for understanding and developing better learning methods for CPD.

Early models of learning in professional practice focused on technical rationality (Houle 1980), adoption of innovation (Rogers 1995) and transfer of learning (Broad and Newstrom

1992). In these views new information learned in one setting, most often the classroom, was assumed to be transferred to professional practice. Other models of learning (Benner 1984, Cervero 1988, Dreyfus and Dreyfus 1985, Schön 1983, 1987) have shifted to include how professionals develop knowledge for practice through reflection and the development of expertise. In these models (Cervero 1988) both technical and practice knowledge is integrated into the professional's practice.

Adult education research (Daley 2001a, 2001b) indicates that fostering learning within professional practice is a complex endeavor and relies on multiple interrelated components. Learning for professional practice requires that knowledge, context and professional practice are integrated into a complex web of understanding (Daley 2000). Professionals learn as they create a knowledge base for themselves by integrating new information with previous experience. This type of learning is evident in the constructivist (Brunner 1990) frameworks that professionals use to create meaning for their professional work. Professionals take pieces of information from many areas, including classes, client interactions, colleague conversations, readings and webinars, merging these into a sophisticated knowledge base that supports their practice. This knowledge is not only created in a complex interactive way, but it is also transformed as professionals develop relationships with clients that may challenge the assumptions on which this learning was based (Daley 2000). Learning for professionals involves constructing and transforming a knowledge base for their practice.

In addition, the context in which professionals work provides the practice-based learning arena that is important to the development of their knowledge base. Context for professionals means the area in which they work with their clients. For example, nurses may practice in long term care, acute care or community care agencies. Each of these contexts demands that the learning in which they engage will be different. Each context will have different factors that support or hinder learning in different ways. Professionals learn within each of these various contexts by developing an understanding of the diverse elements in the context and how each element impacts their practice. For example, Bolman and Deal (2008) identify four organizational frames that foster understanding of different contexts. Each of these frames, structural, human resources, political and symbolic, serves as a lens through which professionals understand their work context. The professional's interpretation and understanding of these organizational frames fosters the way in which new information is integrated into the professional's practice. Since the context of professional practice is most often the workplace, HRD strategies and performance improvement strategies tend to be integrated with professional learning.

Finally, the nature of the professional practice determines how a professional learns. Different professionals (e.g. lawyers, physicians, nurses, social workers) do different work and, as such, they provide different services to their clients. The nature of the services provided and the thinking patterns that are required to do this work determine in many ways how professionals learn. Individuals within different professions fundamentally think in distinctive ways (Donaldson 2002). For example, previous research (Daley 2001b) indicates that lawyers often see their work as providing the best possible legal outcome for a client. As such, they collect the facts of the case, and compare these facts with the law to determine the best strategy for the services they provide. For lawyers, learning in practice means searching out the newest or most up-to-date changes in the law so they can incorporate the new information in their practice. Social workers on the other hand, tend to see themselves as an advocate for their client. With that in mind social workers will learn information and incorporate it into their practice as it matches with their advocacy role. In both of these examples, the nature of the professional work drives the learning. It drives how professionals search out information, how they incorporate it in their practice and how they use it for the benefit of their client. This process of constructing knowledge and transforming knowledge for practice is much more active compared with transferring information learned in the classroom to the practice setting.

The three concepts of knowledge, context and professional practice discussed above are essential components of a model for professional learning that supports CPD. In addition, consideration must be given to the level of expertise of the professional. Professionals enter practice from pre-service education with a particular group of competencies that often lead to safe and dependable practice. However, as professionals continue to work they develop higher levels of expertise in their professional field. Research (Dreyfus and Dreyfus 1985) indicates that professionals move through stages (novice, advanced beginner, competent, proficient, expert) as they develop this expertise. Additionally, novice practitioners tend to learn differently than expert practitioners (Daley 1999). Novices tend to learn in a more contingent fashion, in other words, depending on others to assist them, trying to memorize actions to take, and relying on standards along with rules of practice to guide their actions. Experts, on the other hand, seem to be much more aware of their own learning processes and tend to learn in a more constructivist fashion. Experts can identify what they need to know and determine how to search out that knowledge. They are much more confident in their learning and practice ability and, as such, will engage in conversations with many people to assist in their learning. At formal conferences for example, one often sees the experts in the hall conversing with others about professional practice situations and different ways to handle those versus listening to formal didactic presentations. Professionals who have developed a certain level of expertise commonly use practice-based discussions to foster the type of learning that they need.

CPE has attempted to develop this in-depth focus on learning as the field moves to a focus on CPD. Yet, the vast majority of CPE or CPD programs still rely on traditional modes of delivery. Webster-Wright (2009) critiques the move to CPD indicating that the field should instead be focused on developing CPL. She indicates this focus is far more than a simple change in language but a shift in assumptions of CPE providers. Webster-Wright (2009) indicates that the provision of CPE has not changed because CPE providers tend to hold the following often undiscussed assumptions:

- Knowledge is a commodity that is transferable to practice,
- Within the workplace context, outcomes can be standardized and controlled leading to a greater certainty in professional practice, and
- Professionals need to be "developed" because they are deficient in areas of their practice.

Webster-Wright (2009) specifies that before the practice of CPE can be systemically changed, providers need to acknowledge and alter their assumptions about CPE practice. In addition, she advocates that research in community education, adult education, workplace learning, and professional education needs to be combined to develop systems for what she terms "authentic professional learning" that is focused on "holistic situated experiences of learning" (711).

At this point research in CPE has demonstrated that professionals learn from experience, that reflection on this experience is an important part of the learning cycle as it gives meaning to the experience, that new information needs to be integrated with experience, and finally, that professional learning is mediated by the context of professional work and the nature of professional practice itself. The challenge is how to incorporate this knowledge into the development of systems for professional learning.

Implications for CPD and CPE

As indicated in this chapter the field of CPE is moving towards the development of systems of CPD. Systems of authentic CPL are being increasingly situated in the context of professional practice. Even though the development of these systems is relatively new we believe three trends are converging that will push this development forward.

First, the foci of CPD and learning are shifting away from time spent in educational activities to the demonstration of learning outcomes and competencies achieved. This shift is evident, for example, in the IOM (2010) report that recommends that practitioners be able to demonstrate how they provide patient-centered care, work in an interdisciplinary fashion, use evidence-based practice, incorporate quality improvement and utilize informatics. Demonstrating these competencies will be a major emphasis for the healthcare professions, and we anticipate that other professions will move in this direction as well. The implications for continuing education providers are that systems of professional learning will need to be developed that foster the professional's ability to demonstrate these competencies. Considering Webster-Wright's (2009) critique of CPE, the question is how can these expectations be met while at the same time providing learning experiences that are holistic and situated in practice? We believe that these systems will need to provide learning that is experiential, self-directed, reflective, based on simulated cases, is interactive and provides timely feedback to learners. In addition, for this to be accomplished CPE providers will need to assist professionals in understanding their own learning processes, so that a new approach to learning can be realized. Even though these ideas have existed previously, we believe that a greater emphasis on learning and learning outcomes can be used to frame systems that are authentic and situated within the context of professional practice.

Second, evidence-based practice is becoming prevalent for both individuals in professional practice and continuing education providers. According to Melnyk and Fineout-Overholt (2011: 4) evidence-based practice "takes into consideration synthesis of evidence from multiple studies and combines it with the expertise of the practitioner as well as patient preferences and values." Practice decisions for the professional and the CPE provider need to link research evidence with their individual expertise so that the best decisions are made for the benefit of the client. To implement this type of change, CPE providers will need to develop programs that rely on evidence from research in learning, program planning, evaluation, and translation to practice.

Third, increasing use of technology will impact the development of new learning systems. Educational technology and e-learning systems have the potential to accelerate both the competency movement and the evidence-base practice movement. E-learning systems are available that can assist professionals to create self-directed learning projects and to document the learning in e-learning portfolios. Additionally, technology and informatics infrastructures can assist professionals in obtaining research information needed for an evidence-based practice approach.

Conclusion

New systems of CPE, development, and learning are needed across professions, contexts, organizations and in most countries around the globe. For all professionals to function in the workforce at the highest levels of professional practice, CPE and HRD providers will need to work collaboratively to develop new systems that focus on the integration of learning, context and professional practice. Additionally, providers of CPE will need to integrate methods in which professionals can demonstrate learning outcomes and competencies, create evidenced based practices and learn with technology.

Finally, CPE providers will need to create a research agenda that evaluates and substantiates the changes advocated in this chapter. For example, how does the demonstration of competencies impact client outcomes? What types of evidence are needed to create professional practice improvements? Can high fidelity technology based simulations lead to more in-depth professional learning? As Webster-Wright (2009) indicates the time is right to create the shift from CPE, to CPD, to authentic professional learning.

References

Accreditation Council for Graduate Medical Education (2007) *Common Program Requirements: General Competencies*. Online. Available HTTP: https://www.acgme.org/acgmeweb/Portals/O/dh_dutyhours CommonPR07012007.pdf (accessed September 18, 2008).

Association of American Medical Colleges (AAMC) (2004) *Educating Doctors to Provide High Quality Medical Care: A Vision for Medical Education in the United States*, Washington, DC.

Benner, P. (1984) *From Novice to Expert: Excellence and Power in Clinical Nursing Practice*, Menlo Park, CA: Addison-Wesley.

Bierema, L.L. and Eraut, M. (2004) Workplace-focused learning: perspective on continuing professional education and human resource development, *Advances in Developing Human Resources* 6: 52–68.

Bolman, L. and Deal, T. (2008) *Reframing Organizations: Artistry, Choice and Leadership*, San Francisco, CA: Jossey-Bass.

Broad, M.L. and Newstrom, J.W. (1992) *Transfer of Training*, Reading, MA: Addison-Wesley.

Brunner, J. (1990) *Acts of Meaning*, Cambridge, MA: Harvard University Press.

Cervero, R.M. (1988) *Effective Continuing Education for Professionals*, San Francisco, CA: Jossey-Bass.

— (2001) Continuing professional education in transition, 1981–2000, *International Journal of Lifelong Education* 20(1/2): 16–30.

— (2012) Lifespan professional development through practice-based education: implications for the health professions, in G.J. Neimeyer and J.M. Taylor (eds) *Continuing Professional Development and Lifelong Learning: Issues, Impacts, and Outcomes*, New York: Nova Science Publishers, 265–76.

Cervero, R.M. and Daley, B.J. (2010) Continuing professional education: multiple stakeholders and agendas, in P. Peterson, E. Baker and B. McGaw (eds) *International Encyclopedia of Education* 3rd edn, Oxford: Elsevier, 127–32.

Coolahan, J. (2002) *Teacher education and the teaching career in an era of lifelong learning*, OECD working paper 2, Paris: Education Directorate, OECD.

— (1999) Novice to expert: an exploration of how professionals learn, *Adult Education Quarterly* 49: 133–47.

— (2000) Learning in professional practice, in V. Mott and B. Daley (eds) *Charting a Course for Continuing Professional Education: Reframing Professional Practice*, New Directions in Adult and Continuing Education 86, San Francisco, CA: Jossey-Bass, 33–42.

Daley, B. (2001a) Learning in clinical nursing practice, *Journal of Holistic Nursing* 16(1): 43–54.

— (2001b) Learning and professional practice: a study of four professions, *Adult Education Quarterly* 52: 39–54.

Davis, N.L. and Willis, C.E. (2004) A new metric for continuing medical education credit, *The Journal of Continuing Education in the Health Professions* 24: 139–44.

Day, C. and Sachs, J. (2004) *International Handbook on the Continuing Professional Development of Teachers*, Columbus, OH: The Open University Press.

— (2004) *Professionalism, Performativity and Empowerment: Discources in the Politics, Policies and Purposes of Continuing Professional Development*, Maidenhead, UK: Open University Press.

Donaldson, J. (2002) *Learning to Think: Disciplinary Perspectives*, San Francisco: Jossey-Bass.

Dreyfus, H., and Dreyfus, S. (1985) *Mind over Machine: The Power of Human Intuition and Expertise in the Era of the Computer*, New York: Free Press.

Dryer, B.V. (1962) Lifetime learning for physicians: principles, practices and proposals, *Journal of Medical Education* 37: 1–134.

Eraut, M. (1994) *Developing Professional Knowledge and Competence*, Washington, DC: Falmer.

Flexner, A. (1910) *Medical Education in the United States and Canada*, New York: Carnegie Foundation for the Advancement of Teaching.

Fraser, C., Kennedy, A., Reid, L. and McKinney, S. (2007) Teachers' continuing professional development: contested concepts, understandings and models, *Journal of In-service Education* 33: 153–69.

Hager, M., Russell, S. and Fletcher, S.W. (2008). *Continuing Education in the Health Professions: Improving Healthcare Through Lifelong Learning*, New York: Josiah Macy Jr. Foundation.

Houle, C.O. (1980) *Continuing Learning in the Professions*, San Francisco, CA: Jossey-Bass.

Institute of Medicine (2010) *Redesigning Continuing Education in the Health Professions*, Washington, DC: The National Academies Press.

International Pharmaceutical Federation (2002) *FIP statement of professional standards: continuing professional development*, The Hague: International Pharmaceutical Federation.

Karle, H. (2006) Global standards and accreditation in medical education: a view from the WFME, *Academic Medicine* 8: S43–S48.

Larson, M.S. (1977) *The Rise of Professionalism: A Sociological Analysis*, Berkeley, CA: University of California Press.

Lenn, M.P. and Campos, L. (1997) *Globalization of the Professions and the Quality Imperative: Professional Accreditation, Certification, and Licensure*, Madison, WI: Magna.

Melnyk, B.M. and Fineout-Overholt, E. (2011) *Evidence-based Practice in Nursing and Health Care: A Guide to Best Practice*, 2nd edn, Philadelphia, PA: Lippincott Williams & Wilkins.

Merkur, S.E., Mossialos, E., Long, M. and McKee, M. (2008) Physician revalidation in Europe, *Clinical Medicine* 8: 371–6.

Miller, S.H. (2005) American Board of Medical Specialties and repositioning for excellence in lifelong learning: maintenance of certification, *The Journal of Continuing Education in the Health Professions* 25: 151–6.

Muijs, D. and Lindsay, G. (2008) Where are we at? An empirical study of levels and methods of evaluating continuing professional development, *British Educational Research Journal* 3: 195–211.

Nadler, L. and Nadler, Z. (1989) *Developing Human Resources: Concepts and a Model*, 3rd edn, San Francisco, CA: Jossey-Bass.

Noordegraaf, M. (2007) From "pure" to "hybrid" professionalism, *Administration & Society* 39: 761–85.

Robinson, S. and Griffiths, P. (2007) *Nursing Education and Regulation: International Profiles and Perspectives*, London: Nursing Research Unit, King's College.

Rogers, E.M. (1995) *Diffusion of Innovations*, New York: MacMillan Publishing, The Free Press, A Division Simon and Schuster.

Rouse, M.J. (2008) *A Global Framework for Quality Assurance of Pharmacy Education*, The Hague: International Forum for Quality Assurance of Pharmacy Education.

Schön, D.A. (1983) *The Reflective Practitioner*, New York: Basic Books.

— (1987) *Educating the Reflective Practitioner: Toward a New Design for Teaching and Learning in the Professions*, San Francisco, CA: Jossey-Bass.

Spivey, B.E. (2005) Continuing medical education in the United States: why it needs reform and how we propose to accomplish it, *The Journal of Continuing Education in the Health Professions* 25: 134–43.

Thorpe, R., Woodall, J., Sadler-Smith, E. and Gold, J. (2004) Studying CPD in professional life, *British Journal of Occupational Learning* 2(2): 3–20.

Webster-Wright, A. (2009) Reframing professional development through understanding authentic professional learning, *Review of Educational Research* 79(2): 702–39.

SECTION II

Adjacent and related fields

6

ORGANIZATION DEVELOPMENT IN THE CONTEXT OF HRD

From diagnostic to dialogic perspectives

Toby Egan

Since the rapid growth period of the 1980s and 1990s, in which HRD was firmly assembled as a defined area of practice and scholarship, organization development (OD) has been integrated into the definition of HRD. Compared with OD, HRD is a relatively youthful field of practice and scholarship; yet OD and HRD share many of the same roots and dispositions. OD was born out of the formation of the human relations related exploration and scholarship that began in the 1930s. This early work led to important observations and assumptions that are now well integrated into everyday modern life – that organizational processes and structures shape employee motivation, behavior and work-related mindsets. The work of Lewin and Trist and Bamforth in the 1940s and 1950s demonstrated the value of feedback in clarifying and addressing organizational social processes. "More recently, work on OD has expanded to focus on aligning organizations with their rapidly changing and complex environments through organizational learning, knowledge management and transformation of organizational norms and values" (Shull *et al.* 2013: 1).

Framing OD

One of the challenges to exploring, researching, and implementing HRD is in demarcating its boundaries. HRD is often described in terms of levels or frames of interaction. Certainly one of the most commonly used HRD-related frameworks has been McLagan's (1989) "HR Wheel". In it, OD is featured as one of three elements of HRD. According to McLagan, HR may be segmented into 11 key elements, including three areas described as HRD: OD, Training and Development (T&D), and Career Development.

Regardless of its positioning, those defining OD share overlapping vantage points. French and Bell (1999: 25–6), defined OD as:

> a long-term effort, led and supported by top management, to improve an organization's visioning, empowerment, learning and problem-solving processes, through an ongoing, collaborative management of organization culture – with special emphasis on the culture of intact work teams and other team configurations – using the consultant-facilitator

role and the theory and technology of applied behavioural science, including action research.

French and Bell's definition reflects both the early and enduring aspects of OD. Since then, organizations have evolved as a result of the influence of organizational complexity, an understanding of the influence of systems on the scope of OD, and the influence of multicultural and global perspectives. The OD professional role and central processes used to facilitate OD are key elements that extend OD from a behavioral science approach to a profession and action-oriented practice. The aims of OD are key aspects in terms of desired results. In an earlier review of multiple definitions of OD, ten key outcomes were identified, including:

- Advancing organizational renewal
- Engaging organization culture change
- Enhancing profitability and competitiveness
- Ensuring health and well-being of organizations and employees
- Facilitating learning and development
- Improving problem solving
- Increasing effectiveness
- Initiating and/or managing change
- Strengthening system and process improvement
- Supporting adaptation to change (Egan 2002: 67).

More recent overviews of OD definitions support these ten OD outcomes (Cummings and Worley 2014, Rothwell and Sullivan 2005, Rothwell *et al.* 2009).

A brief history of OD

To a great degree, OD can be viewed as involving application of and influences from some of the major social science thought leaders of the twentieth century. Psychologists from Freud, Adler and Jung to Skinner and Rogers heavily influenced the ways in which OD is framed. In particular, these psychologists informed understanding of human motivation, attitudes, behavior change, performance, and ways in which individual, group and organizational outcomes could be predicted, directed, explained and supported. Economists Keynes, Malthus, Shepherd, Coase, Bain, Mason and, later, Becker and anthropologists and management scholars, such as Hall and Hall, Hofstede, Mead, Schein and, more recently, Drucker, Argyris and Schön provided key insights regarding organizations and the larger cultural contexts in which they are situated. In addition, Deming, Juran and Ishikawa provided important contributions to organization quality and productivity making the quality movement a central period in the history of OD-related interventions. Of course there are many more contributors who, either directly or indirectly, impacted OD-related research, theory and practice.

As OD has grown and expanded internationally, records of related happenings, changes and insights have also dispersed. However, many OD authors emphasize and reemphasize similar key events leading to the current state of OD as a field and professional practice. Kurt Lewin was an early influencer regarding the formation, theoretical development, and practice approaches to change – including work in communities and organizations. Strongly influenced earliest by Elton Mayo, the human relations movements, that spanned much of the past century, influenced thinking about the potential for change in organizational contexts. Tavistock and National Training Lab work on groups and group dynamics (Hall and Williams 1970) informed social scientific understanding regarding power and authority, and shared decision making informed the potential for group facilitation and organizational change. Data driven approaches to understanding organizations was influenced by Rensis Likert's formation of relatively easy to use scales of measurement that allowed for assessment of individual perceptions in a variety of contexts including, most importantly for OD, organization members.

More recently, a number of scholars and practitioners have strived to define and assess quality of work life. This issue has become especially important in societies allowing for employee mobility across organizations – when, during periods of economic growth, employees are free to choose organizations based on organizational climate, policies and opportunities. Clarification of values and ethics in OD, such as those developed by the National Training Lab, OD Network, and others, have informed organizations about the importance of values-driven organizations and OD practices.

Broad application of systems theory has influenced OD as well. Learning organization concepts, advanced in practice literature by Peter Senge (1990), and Watkins and Marsick (1993, and 1996), led to further broadening of how OD was framed, heightening sensitivity not only to internal-to-organization systems perspectives, but to the potential impact of larger systems on the organization or area of focus for OD. Employee knowledge, learning and development have emerged as essential for organizational contexts. Application of systems thinking can also be attributed to supply chain management and the increasingly overt influence of complex exchanges in the global marketplace. Most importantly for HRD, systems thinking formed the rationale for HRD being seen as the more complete framework to describe organizational learning and development – thus, for those favoring HRD, subordinating OD within the HRD framework. It must also be noted that some OD scholars and practitioners have subjugated HRD beneath the OD framework, while still others situate OD and HRD beneath human resources (HR) or human resources management (HRM). Ironically, HRD scholars and practitioners point to McLagan's (1989) model, "The HR Wheel" as validation for their approach; however, it overtly subjugates HRD and OD under HR.

Increased use and application of coaching, particularly executive coaching, has impacted the ways in which OD and HRD practitioners think about their work and their skill development (Ellinger *et al.* 2014). For many OD practitioners, executive coaching has become an important part of their OD practice. In a recent survey of 388 OD practitioners, 87 per cent identified coaching as "an integral part of OD today" (Shull *et al.* 2013: 19). Such coaching serves to support the executive during a large-scale OD effort and/or can support individual executives in the refinement of their individual knowledge and skills.

Workforce diversity and globalization has also led to some rejecting OD as a historically, male, European/European-American frame, with calls for new perspectives (Cox 1993, Greene 2007, Griffith *et al.* 2007, Holvino 2010). Non-OD practitioners and scholars, as well as some members and leaders involved in OD-focused professional associations, have critiqued and deconstructed the history of OD, and related current practices. However, while HRD and OD have involved increasing numbers of women and professionals from a variety of non-European backgrounds, few novel notions regarding the reframing of OD research, theory and practice have emerged. At the same time, the embracing of diversity and inclusion as an essential aspect of OD has been affirming to the array of professionals currently involved in and new to OD. And, it can certainly be argued that many early contributors to OD applied their humanistic viewpoints in a manner intended to be broadly inclusive of practitioners and organization members. The grassroots, participatory and humanistic traditions of OD contribute to the longstanding potential for OD to be viewed and deployed as a critical action research approach. OD-related professional organizations strive to communicate an openness and inclusivity towards new perspectives and approaches (Adler 2008, Shull *et al.* 2013).

Over time, the organization as machine metaphor was infused with more naturalistic considerations; this transition was concurrent with evolutions in collective thinking about scientific inquiry and behavioral sciences. Social constructivism contributed to new thinking about organizations and diminished the fully positivistic ambitions of early behavioral scientists to a more constrained, post-positivistic perspective. Key elements contributing to the formation of classical approaches to OD are associated with this values shift – including emphases on systems thinking, employee feedback, T&D, action research, diversity and inclusion, and facilitation of organizational change. And, consistent with evolutions in philosophies of research in social science, many OD scholars and practitioners have been influenced by postmodern and critical theory oriented perspectives (Bierema 2010, Bushe and Marshak 2008). While these philosophical paradigm shifts created disorientation among some scholars and researchers, constructivism and participatory research contributed to an interactive mode of inquiry and action. Learning and performance began to be organized in far more humane ways than approaches found in large, post-war organizations. Participatory OD approaches, which truly engage stakeholders at all levels (including "frontline" and underrepresented individuals in whatever context OD is being implemented), often reflect critical and postmodern perspectives.

OD interventions

OD interventions can take on a variety of forms and foci. Similar to medicine or psychology, the instigation of OD interventions is often due to emergent "symptoms," which may take the form of needs for learning or performance improvement, pain or ongoing disputes, or in reaction to environmental or organizational change or felt need for change. McLean (2005: 26) developed the following list of situations in which OD could be deployed. In utilizing OD organizations may desire:

- To develop or enhance the organization's mission statement (statement of purpose) or vision statement for what it wants to be
- To help align functional structures in an organization so they are working together for a common purpose
- To create a strategic plan for how the organization is going to make decisions about its future and achieving that future
- To manage conflict that exists among individuals, groups, functions, sites, and so on, when such conflicts disrupt the ability of the organization to function in a healthy way
- To put in place processes that will help improve the ongoing operations of the organization on a continuous basis
- To create a collaborative environment that helps the organization be more effective and efficient
- To create reward systems that are compatible with the goals of the organization
- To assist in the development of policies and procedures that will improve the ongoing operation of the organization
- To assess the working environment, to identify strengths on which to build and areas in which change and improvement are needed
- To provide help and support for employees, especially those in senior positions, who need an opportunity to be coached in how to do their jobs better

- To assist in creating systems for providing feedback on individual performance and, on occasion, conducting studies to give individuals feedback and coaching to help them in their individual development.

Although not exhaustive, McLean's list provides insight into the broad spectrum of interventions that OD practitioners may undertake with the use of OD-related tools and frameworks.

OD as a values-based applied behavioral science

OD has long been characterized as a humanistic, values-based applied social science intervention. This includes careful reflection by OD practitioners on their behavior and actions in a manner consistent with the values of the field and their own, careful interpretation of the appropriate course of action. In an effort to establish the values of the field, the OD Network formed values-based principles of practice, including: (1) Respect and Inclusion – equitably values the perspective and opinions of everyone; (2) Collaboration – builds collaborative relationships between the practitioner and the client while encouraging collaboration throughout the client system; (3) Authenticity – strives for authenticity and congruence and encourages these qualities in their clients; (4) Self-awareness – commits to developing self-awareness and interpersonal skills. OD practitioners engage in personal and professional development through lifelong learning; and (5) Empowerment – focuses efforts on helping everyone in the client organization or community increase their autonomy and empowerment to levels that make the workplace and/or community satisfying and productive (OD Network 2013).

This values set is intended to guide the development, discussion and focus of OD practitioners and OD-related interventions. Similarly, Margulies and Raia (1972) articulated several humanistic values for OD practitioners including the respect for each human being as an individual person with a set of complex needs, all of which are important to work and in life. These OD humanistic values also emphasize an expansion of opportunities for exciting and challenging individual work while maximizing the potential of each employee. Additionally, the effectiveness of the organization in terms of the workplace environment and accomplishment of shared organizational goals is also identified as a central value for OD practitioners.

Together, these types of humanistic values present a framework for the reflective OD consultant that is intended to communicate, in broad terms, the aims of OD, while at the same time, provide meaningful challenges for OD practitioners and those participating in OD. The challenges that any statement of values present to OD practitioners are the need to continuously revisit the ideals of the field and to carefully tend to interpretations of their professional actions. Because many organizations often frame values primarily in legal terms, practitioners must embrace the notion that a values-based field does more than establish the legality of their actions. Meeting professional standards and striving to respect individuals entail a more expansive commitment than handling legalities alone.

Confusion and dilemmas are generated within any attempt to organize a profession around its values. Bradford (2005: xxvi) provided the following elaboration:

> *OD is confused about its values.* On the one hand, OD claims that it is firmly based in the applied behavioural sciences. But on the other hand, it stresses its humanistic roots. What happens when the latter is not supported by the former? Unfortunately for many OD consultants, it is the humanistic values, not the applied behavioural sciences, that dominate . . . What OD has lost is its commitment to rigorous, objective analysis of

what truly is effective and instead has replaced that with a view of what it thinks the world should be.

A closer look at any professional field of practice would reveal the presence of dilemmas and confusion regarding how to align values statements in practice. Regular dialogue and exchange among peers is a key aspect in the evolution and enactment of professional values statements. Perhaps one of the potentially greatest negative impacts of the lack of professionalization of OD and HRD is the absence of systematic renewal regarding the values of the field. The best of counselling and clinical psychology professionals, and their associations, participate in supervision, team reviews of professional cases, mandatory continuing education, and ongoing renewal and development of ethical standards – all within the structured and managed guidelines of their profession. Without professionalization, OD and HRD practitioners are commonly on their own in terms of reflection and peer-support regarding their ethical obligations and practices. However, thoughtful OD practitioners can access available support resources and work collaboratively to determine the best ways to enact and maintain the values and professional aspirations of the field. Such intentions are made more complex in multicultural or multinational contexts.

From an organization environment standpoint, OD practitioners may be faced with the need to challenge the status quo regarding the treatment of employees, unfair treatment and workplace justice issues (Bierema 2010, Cobb *et al.* 1995, Cox 1993, Greenberg and Colquitt 2013, Greene 2007). Additionally, intersections between multinational stakeholders and individuals within the organization from a variety of national, racial, and culture backgrounds demand OD practitioners extend themselves regarding their cultural awareness and capacity for intercultural exchange. This is equally true regarding gender, as organizations largely struggle to support women's participation and advancement in the workplace.

OD practitioner roles and competencies

OD practitioners are commonly referred to as "change agents." While OD practitioners may have specific technical or industry knowledge emphasized in their practice roles, they most commonly have expertise in social science or human systems and must have strong analytic, facilitation, and interpersonal communication skills. A key focus is the OD practitioner's capacity to support organizational involvement towards collective problem solving. The change agent combines social science knowledge with multiple intervention techniques and action research. The OD Network provided a list of 141 competencies commonly needed by OD practitioners (Sullivan *et al.* 2001). Although not a comprehensive list, details regarding the extensive capabilities needed by an OD practitioner are provided.

One common comparison within OD practice is the internal versus external OD consultant. Differences between internal OD practitioners (employed by the organization as a standing member of the firm) and external OD practitioners (contracted as consultants to the organization) have been outlined in many ways. The focus of attention by an internal OD consultant is often more relationship network oriented, as the maintenance of ongoing relationships with organization members is important, beyond any single OD project. External OD consultants are frequently most concerned with their success as perceived by their main organizational contacts/clients, as opposed to specific organization members. Because of the relatively short-term nature of the relationship, the success of each individual OD project is often of highest importance to the external OD consultant. Because internal consultants are often motivated by longevity and rewards within the organization, they may be far more aware and sensitive to the impact of social networks and internal political issues impacted by a proposed OD intervention.

While internal OD practitioners benefit from inside knowledge and subject matter expertise, seasoned external OD practitioners bring an array of experiences from across organizations and industries. Many organization leaders and members may prefer external consultants, as they are often perceived to bring a fresh view and novel ideas/perspectives, over an internal consultant who is viewed as an immersed stakeholder/contributor to the current set of issues or problems. However, internal consultants have the advantage of historical and specific knowledge of the organization, its systems and policies. The external consultant's lack of specific knowledge, given the complexity of many organizational systems, can be a liability. An advantage internal consultants may have over external consultants, in terms of OD project deployment, is the utilization of internal resources. While external consultants are largely constrained to organizational resources provided within their contracts, internal consultants can utilize organizational assets available to them or internal OD stakeholders throughout the course of an OD intervention. External OD consultants commonly have options to depart from an OD intervention at any time. But, internal OD practitioners must wade through the challenges of a stagnant or failing OD effort, while maintaining their internal role. Some internal OD practitioners develop internal-to-organization service contracts as a way to avoid entrenchment; however, there are commonly greater complications for consultants seeking to depart from their internally led interventions.

Internal versus external is one of many ways to describe OD-related roles; however, one may have OD-related obligations or opportunities as part of a larger managerial or executive role. Although OD practitioners are often characterized as advanced degree holders with specialized training, there have been many instances where frontline employees have been taught OD-related skills. In fact, the classic total quality management approach often involved training of employees and managers on OD-related skills and tools. Beckard (1969) provided several examples whereby employees were trained to use OD intervention techniques and who successfully led impactful change processes. This type of synergy between OD/HRD practitioners and organizations seems to be ideal, as is the combined use of internal and external OD practitioners. And, this type of knowledge transfer differentiates the facilitative approach commonly described in OD literature – whereby OD consultants spread OD knowledge, rather than maintaining autonomy as "the expert." This compares with other types of consultants who are interested in keeping information from clients in order to maintain their "expert" status or who may be focused more on their proprietary or "off-the-shelf" approaches than the clients' specific needs.

OD as Action Research

Any credible approach to applying social science related knowledge should involve use of data collection and analysis towards some eventual intervention or approach to change (Egan and Lancaster 2005). Action research (AR) is the best developed approach for such applications. In fact, one would be hard pressed to identify a model or application of OD that could not be framed within AR. At the same time, action research is also used by schools, teachers and employees in a way that may not frame a particular issue or problem at the larger systems level that is commonly used in OD. A key example of alignment of OD and AR from the "action research side" of the applied social science literature is Shani and Pasmore's (1985: 439) definition of AR:

> an emergent inquiry process in which applied behavioral science knowledge is integrated with existing organizational knowledge and applied to solve real organizational problems. It is simultaneously concerned with bringing about change in organizations,

> in developing self-help competencies in organizational members and adding to scientific knowledge. Finally, it is an evolving process that is undertaken in a spirit of collaboration and co-inquiry.

Although deeper discussions about differences between AR and OD often lead to more differentiation, it would seem that most OD practitioners would embrace Shani and Pasmore's definition as relevant for OD – if not a reasonable OD definition. For AR experts Coghlan and Brannick (2009) AR is (1) research *in* action, rather than research *about* action; (2) a collaborative democratic partnership; (3) concurrent with problem solving; and (4) a sequence of events and an approach to problem solving. These features are also well aligned with OD-specific literature and definitions. The overlap between AR and OD is important for the understanding of the central processes of OD.

Because of the complexity involved in OD, models are helpful representations of potential actions in OD practice. In reviewing the history of change processes, most identify Shewhart's (1939) cycle as an original expression of the AR process. Shewhart's Plan-Do-Check-Act cycle is a model depicting a repeatable process involving planned action, assessment, and realigned action (see Figure 6.1).

From the perspective of changing habits or patterns of behavior, Lewin (1947) suggested AR involved unfreezing the current practices and related habits in response to needed change; changing the current situation through data collection, analysis and plans for new action; and, finally, refreezing new behaviors and approaches after appropriate exploration and testing of the actions planned in the previous step. Together Shewhart's and Lewin's approaches contain the most common features described by AR authors and implementers.

Similarly, OD practitioners who map their consultative process are likely to present an AR-related model. McLean (2005) formed an AR model framed in the context of OD (see Figure 6.2).

Different from a model co-developed earlier in his academic and practitioner career, McLean's current 8-step model – entry, start-up, assessment and feedback, action plan, intervention, evaluation, adoption, and separation – is not only more complex than Shewhart's in terms of the number of steps, but it interrupts the ordinal step process, common to such models, in favor of a more realistic depiction of steps that may be repeated or reengaged. While reconsidering the stepwise approach commonly depicted in AR, McLean embraces the importance of each step in

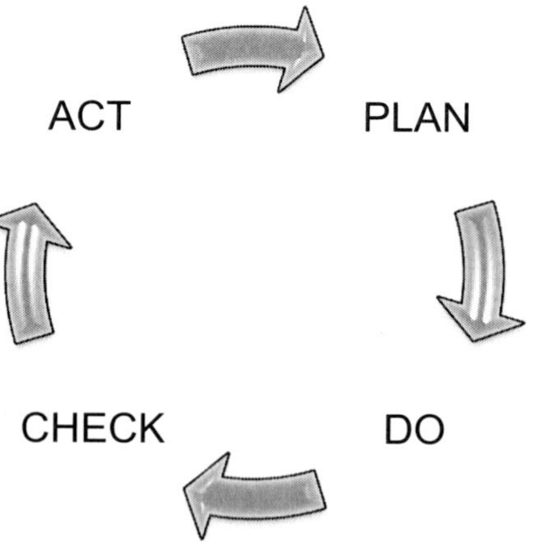

Figure 6.1 The Shewhart cycle

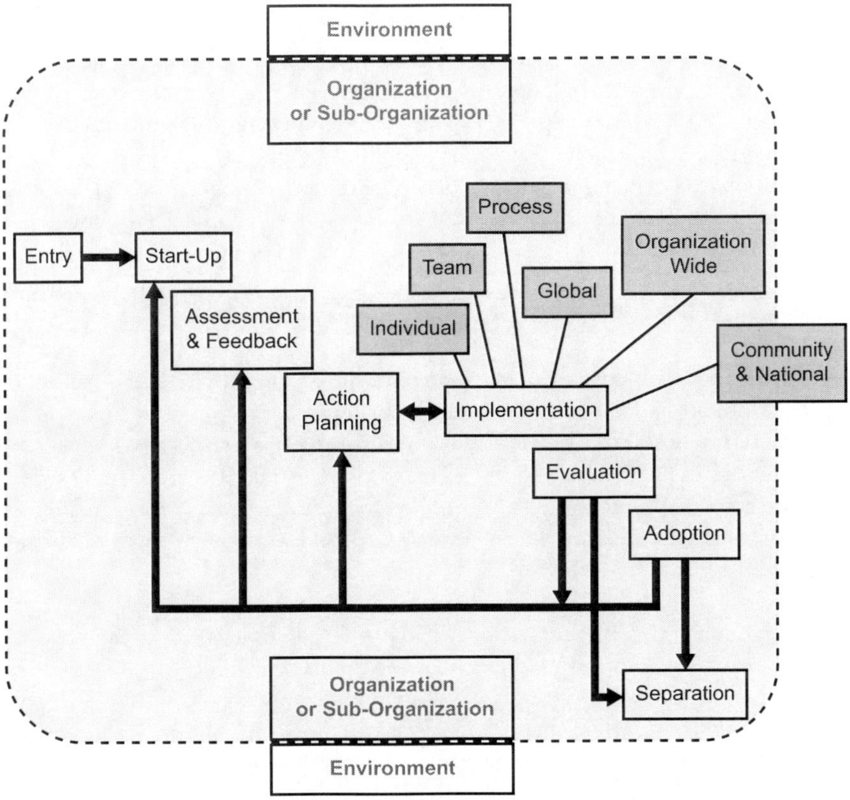

Figure 6.2 McLean's (2005) model of Action Research in OD

the process. At the same time, experienced OD practitioners recognize they may need to reengage assessment, reexamine the contractual relationship, or return to the action planning phase in order to fully implement an intervention. This more flexible AR model depicts a realistic, OD-specific context.

While the AR models in OD may seem straightforward, even simple, they are often misused or underutilized. OD practitioners (and/or those desiring to implement OD approaches) are vulnerable to criticism if they skip or underutilize assessment and feedback and evaluation in OD. It is common for organization members and clients of OD to report OD interventions that did not effectively utilize assessment and feedback and/or evaluation. If OD was a licensed practice, this would amount to OD malpractice. However, conditions such as client demands, timelines, internal pressures, and impatience by leaders not familiar with the time needed to deploy a proper assessment, may undercut OD practitioner plans to engage in a thorough examination of the OD area of focus.

Probably most challenging for any OD approach is the OD practitioner's management of a collaborative AR approach, which involves multiple stakeholders and complex issues. And, OD practitioners may face additional challenges when organization members are, for the first time through the collaborative AR process, experiencing authentic involvement in assessment and decision making. Individual opportunity presented in high power distance structures, can evoke excitement and anticipation by AR participants. However, process outcomes may not always meet anticipated expectations from all organization members.

Appreciative inquiry in OD

Nearly in tandem with the emergence of Positive Psychology, Appreciative Inquiry (AI) was principally developed by David Cooperrider, a professor at Case Western Reserve University. Central to AI is the rejection of the traditional problem-solving approach in change management and OD. AI and related approaches have expanded over the past 20 years and are an important, novel contribution to OD literature and practice. According to Cooperrider and Srivastva (1987: 159), AI "refers to both a search for knowledge and a theory of intentional collective action, which are designed to help evolve the normative vision and will of a group, organization or society as a whole." Bushe (1999) identified AI as one of the most significant new OD interventions. Cooperrider and Whitney (1999: 10) describe the merits of AI:

> Appreciative inquiry is the cooperative search for the best in people, their organizations, and the world around them. It involves systematic discovery of what gives a system "life" when it is most effective and capable in economic, ecological, and human terms. AI involves the art and practice of asking questions that strengthen a system's capability to heighten positive potential . . . In AI, intervention gives way to imagination and innovation; instead of negation, criticism, and spiralling diagnosis there is discovery, dream and design.

The AI process emphasizes the importance of the first question asked at the start of the AI intervention – the discovery step in Cooperrider and Whitney's (1999) AI 4-D cycle. Discovery emphasizes the appreciation of "what gives life" followed by dream, or "what might be." Similar to AR, the next step is to explore the ideal of what could be or might be done to enact action, or design. Design is followed by an approach to sustainability, or destiny, which involves "how to empower, learn and improvise" (see Figure 6.3).

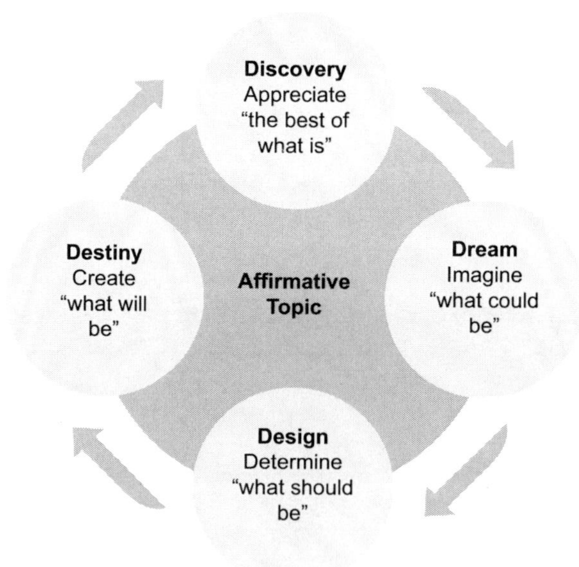

Figure 6.3 Appreciative inquiry 4-D cycle (Cooperrider and Whitney 1999)

Although AI has some distinctive differences from AR, Egan and Lancaster (2005) identified some key similarities between the two approaches. Each model was founded by individuals interested in theory-building and is applicable to a variety of human systems, from individuals to organizations and even larger frameworks. Both AI and AR engage real social systems and are values-based. Both tend to be iterative, cyclical processes emphasizing reflection and action. Additionally, these approaches are change-oriented processes focused on making improvements beyond the current organizational state by involving organizational stakeholders in an interactive, real change process.

Using a qualitative research process, Egan and Lancaster asked OD practitioners who use AI to identify the strengths and weaknesses of AI and AR overall. One key conclusion by OD practitioners was that a challenge of AI, which maintains a relentlessly positive perspective regarding the organization and the AI process itself, has some potential weaknesses that may block its successful use in OD. Four key limitations identified by experienced OD practitioners using AI included: (1) difficult interpersonal situations may be overlooked, (2) feelings of anger or frustration not voiced, (3) dissatisfied organization members retreat and withdraw, and (4) managers may avoid challenges by focusing exclusively on "the positive" (Egan and Lancaster 2005: 43). Although AI was endorsed by each interviewee in Egan and Lancaster's study, these AI oriented OD practitioners all voiced concerns or shared experiences where situational and data analysis within the AI 4-D process may have overlooked opportunities for critical thinking or analysis in favor of positive framing.

In response to the strengths and weaknesses of AI and AR identified, and in acknowledgment of the potentially transformative contributions of AI, Egan (2004) formed an Appreciative Action Research approach (see Figure 6.4).

Entry	The need for change and the leadership for the change process are identified.
Start-Up	A change agent clarifies general approach to change and clarifies commitment to a change process.
Discovery	An appreciative interview process is undertaken involving all stakeholders, if possible. Organizational capacities are clarified.
Dream	Results from the Discovery phase are reviewed by stakeholders and a mission, vision, and goal statement is created.
Design	Provocative questions or propositions are developed and elaborated upon leading to clarity regarding the organizational goals.
Assessment & Feedback	Multiple data collection activities are engaged in regard to fulfillment of the Design goals and are forwarded to stakeholders/decision makers—includes evaluation of both strengths and challenges faced by the organization.
Action Planning	The change agent works with stakeholders to develop an Action Plan addressing challenges and opportunities identified.
Intervention	The Action Plan is enacted.
Evaluation	Multiple data collection activities leading to an understanding of changes that have/have not occurred as a result of the Intervention.
Adoption	Stakeholders embrace the change and it is extended throughout the organization.
Separation	The change agent undertakes appropriate steps to disengage from the organization and/or change process (Returning to Start-up of ongoing change efforts is also possible depending on the need).

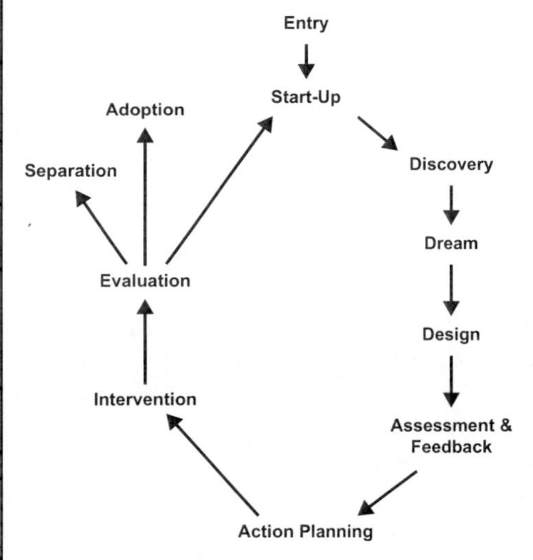

Figure 6.4 Appreciative Action Research model (Egan 2004)

Appreciative Action Research (AAR) "emphasizes that OD begins with the appreciative development of an understanding of collective capacity, mission, vision, goals, and steps that could be taken to accomplish those goals" (Egan 2004: 46). In AAR, Egan emphasized disciplined focus by OD practitioners to the positive questioning orientation outlined by the founders of AI, followed by assessment and feedback that provides a balanced perspective regarding the positive visions and promising action steps developed during the discovery, dream and design steps in the AAR process. As Cady and Caster (2000: 90) noted, the blending of "the humanistic side of OD with the empirically driven data collection is needed to add rigor to our field . . . [and] allows for seemingly polar opposite theories, such as the problem approach and the appreciative approach, to exist in a synchronous relationship." This may be one of the most important next steps advancing the future of OD and HRD professional practice.

The future of OD

The dynamic and seemingly unpredictable world economy, our growing international interdependence, and growth in technology leading to the transformation of human interaction are some, among many, forces contributing to uncertainty regarding the nature of OD in the future. Shull *et al.*'s aforementioned (2013) study explored perspectives regarding OD by contrasting survey data gathered over a 20-year period (data collection occurred in 1993 and 2013). The 388 responding OD professionals indicated that while they perceived continued weakening of traditional OD values, they were very optimistic about the future of OD. At the same time, these researchers and others have found blurring boundaries between OD and other areas of HR – along with less emphasis on group dynamics and process consultation. Overall, OD practitioners appear more focused on key organizational results and business outcomes and they tend to utilize quantitative research and topic areas focused on improving organizational results. Shull *et al.* (2013) found younger, newer OD practitioners tend to emphasize traditional OD frameworks and values less, while (as a group) they indicated greater optimism about OD than their more senior counterparts. Therefore, it would seem that a large number of practitioners are likely to continue actively working in and promoting OD practices.

The original framing of OD was *diagnostic* and strongly situated within a positivistic perspective that dominated social sciences during the first seventy years of the last century (and which still does today in economics and industrial/organization psychology). This classical approach assumes an objective organizational reality and the collection of valid data. According to Bushe and Marshak (2010: 350) "This commitment to empirical, scientific inquiry may well be why OD is one of the few fields of consulting practice to also be recognized as a scholarly discipline." Diagnostic approaches to OD include sociotechnical systems analysis, task-oriented team development, survey feedback, and SWOT (strengths, weaknesses, opportunities and threats).

Bushe and Marshak note that newer, *dialogic* OD perspectives have begun to be positioned in new ways. Although the epistemological assumptions related to dialogic OD have been delineated for some time, dialogic OD practice is still exploring and developing. In addition to including AI as a dialogic approach to OD interventions, Bush and Marshak identified *search conferences* and *future search* both of which engage large groups in collective identification and elaboration of their desired future. These dialogic perspectives aim towards the identification and presentation of multiple perspectives, versus providing an objective diagnosis. Another large group approach, called *technology of participation*, helps groups to develop common ground, to plan together, and to enact planned action together. These participants engage in discussion that elaborates on the current organizational system and emphasizes participants' beliefs, stories, and assumptions. The intended outcome of this process is an agreed upon vision. Additionally, *open space* and *world café* approaches also involve large groups. Open space involves bottom-up identification of shared interests and motivations that lead to formations of agreements about future shared enterprises (new idea development, projects and more) on a variety of scales, from dyadic to team and large-scale collaborations. Although much more structured, world café is also a bottom-up process that helps participants to discover latent mental models through a facilitated process and solid coaching skills (Shull *et al.* 2013).

As noted by the majority of participants in the Shull *et al.* study, there are reasons to believe that OD has been responsive to dynamic organizational environments much different from those experienced by the founders of the field. Including the placement of OD within the context of HRD, OD practitioners and scholars remain engaged and responsive with an eye on the next dynamic changes that may well have an impact on HRD overall.

References

Adler, N.J. (2008) *International Dimensions of Organisational Behavior*, 5th edn, Mason, OH: Thomson South-Western Corporation.

Beckard, R. (1969) *Organization Development: Strategies and Models*, London: Addison-Wesley.

Bierema, L. (2010) *Implementing a Critical Approach to Organization Development*, Malibar, FL: Krieger.

Bradford, D.L. (2005) OD a promise yet to be realized. In W.J. Rothwell and R.L. Sullivan (eds) *Organization Development: A Guide for Consultants*, San Francisco: Pfeiffer, xxii–xxvii.

Bushe, G. (1999) Advances of appreciative inquiry as an organization development intervention, *Organization Development Journal* 17(2): 61–68.

Bushe, G. and Marshak, R. (2008) The postmodern turn in OD, *OD Practitioner* 40(4), 9–11.

— (2010) Revisioning organization development: diagnostic and dialogic premises and patterns of practice, *Journal of Applied Behavioral Science* 45: 348–68.

Cady, S.H. and Caster, M.A. (2000). A diet for action research: an integrated problem and appreciative focuses approach to organization development, *Organization Development Journal* 18(4): 79–93.

Cobb, A.T., Folger, R. and Wooten, K.C. (1995) The role justice plays in organizational change, *Public Administration Quarterly* 19: 135–51.

Coghlan, D. and Brannick, T. (2009) *Doing Action Research in Your Own Organisation*, London: SAGE.

Cooperrider, D.L. and Srivastva, S. (1987) Appreciative inquiry in organizational life, in R. Woodman and W. Pasmore (eds) *Research in Organizational Change and Development*, vol. 1, Greenwich, CT: JAI Press, 126–69.

Cooperrider, D.L. and Whitney, D. (1999) *Collaborating for Change: Appreciative Inquiry*, San Francisco: Berrett-Koehler.

Cox, T. (1993) *Cultural Diversity in Organisations: Theory, Research and Practice*, San Francisco: Berrett-Koehler.

Cummings, T.G. and Worley, C.G. (2014) *Organization Development and Change*, 10th edn, Mason, OH: Cengage.

Egan, T.M. (2002) Organization development: an examination of definitions and dependent variables, *Organization Development Journal* 20(2): 59–70.

— (2004) An appreciative action research model, *unpublished manuscript.*

Egan, T.M. and Lancaster, C.M. (2005) Comparing appreciative inquiry to action research: OD practitioner perspectives, *Organization Development Journal* 23(2): 29–49.

Ellinger, A., Egan, T. and Kim, S. (eds) (2014) Coaching and HRD, *Advances in Developing Human Resources* 16(2).

French, W. and Bell, C. (1999) *Organization Development: Behavioural Science Interventions for Organization Improvement*, New York: Prentice Hall.

Greenberg, J. and Colquitt, J.A. (eds) (2013) *Handbook of Organizational Justice*, Mahwah, NJ: Lawrence Erlbaum.

Greene, M.P. (2007) Beyond diversity and multiculturalism: towards the development of anti-racist institutions and leaders, *Journal for Nonprofit Management* 11: 9–17.

Griffith, D.M., Mason, M., Yonas, M., Eng, E., Jefferies, V., Plihcik, S. and Parks, B. (2007) Dismantling institutional racism: theory and action, *American Journal of Community Psychology* 39: 381–92.

Hall, J. and Williams, S. (1970) Group dynamics training and group decision making, *Journal of Applied Behavioral Science* 6(1): 39–68.

Holvino, E. (2010) Intersections: the simultaneity of race, gender and class in organization studies, *Gender, Work & Organization* 17: 248–77.

Lewin, K. (1947) Frontiers in group dynamics, in D. Cartwright (ed.) *Field Theory in Social Science*, London: Social Science, 188–237.

Margulies, N. and Raia, A.P. (1972) *Organizational Development: Values, Process and Technology*, New York: McGraw-Hill.

McLagan, P. (1989) *Models of Human Resource Development Practice*, Alexandria, VA: ASTD Press.

McLean, G.N. (2005) *Organization Development. Principles, Processes, Performance*, San Francisco: Berrett-Koehler.

OD Network (2013) Principles of OD practice. Online. Available HTTP: http://www.odnetwork.org/?page=PrinciplesOfODPracti (accessed November 20, 2013).

Rothwell, W.J. and Sullivan, R.L. (eds) (2005) *Organization Development: A Guide for Consultants*, San Francisco: Pfeiffer.

Rothwell, W.J., Stavros, J.M., Sullivan, R.L. and Sullivan, A. (2009) *Practicing Organization Development: A Guide for Leading Change*, 3rd edn, San Francisco: Pfeiffer.

Senge, P. (1990) *The Fifth Discipline: The Art and Practice of the Learning Organization*, London: Century Business.

Shani, A.B. and Pasmore, W.A. (1985) Organization inquiry: towards a new model of the action research process, in D.D. Warrick (ed.) *Contemporary Organization Development: Current Thinking and Applications*. Glenview: Scott, Foresman, 438–48.

Shewhart, W.A. (1939) *Statistical Method from the Viewpoint of Quality Control*, Washington, DC: The Graduate School, Department of Agriculture.

Shull, A.C., Church, A.H. and Burke, W.W. (2013) Attitudes about the field of organization development 20 years later: the more things change, the more they stay the same, *Research in Organizational Change and Development* 21: 1–28.

Sullivan, R.L., Rothwell, W.J. and Worley, C.G. (2001) 20th edition of *Organization Change and Development Competency Effort*. Online. Available HTTP: http://odnetwork.org/?page=ODCompetencies (accessed November 20, 2013).

Watkins, K. and Marsick, V. (1993) *Sculpting the Learning Organization: The Art and Science of Systemic Change*, San Francisco: Jossey-Bass.

— (1996) *In Action: Creating the Learning Organization*, Alexandria, VA: ASTD.

7

CAREER DEVELOPMENT IN THE CONTEXT OF HRD

Challenges and considerations

Kimberly S. McDonald and Linda M. Hite

Career development in the twenty-first century is facing what might be described as an identity crisis. While evolving over time to meet the needs of each new decade, it is now beset with challenges that will require a higher level of reinvention and resiliency to persevere. This chapter will begin with a brief historical perspective; then move to an examination of three current challenges and how they can be addressed through HRD.

Brief historical perspective

The history of career development is rich and varied and began long before it was identified as one of the original three functional areas assigned to HRD by McLagan in 1989. Beginning in the twelfth century, European trade guilds were early providers of vocational education (Wollschlager and Guggenheim 2004). However, interest in the development of careers has its origins in the late 1800s and early 1900s (Herr 2001; Moore *et al.* 2007; Pope 2000). The economic and societal changes brought on by the industrial revolution prompted the rise of vocational guidance in the US and in Europe (Brewer 1942). In the US, this movement also was fueled by demographic changes: immigration of those seeking better opportunities in a new country and migration as rural residents moved to the cities for more plentiful pay (Pope 2000). While books on occupations were available prior to Parsons' 1909 *Choosing a Vocation*, he is credited with being the founding father of vocational guidance, a phrase he coined, because of the model he detailed in that publication. He suggested basing vocational choice on a combination of self-understanding, knowledge of job requirements and consideration of how those fit together. However, Parsons was not a theorist and the three-step model attributed to him was based on his own experience and exposure to others' writings on occupational choice rather than on a sturdy foundation of research (Moore *et al.* 2007; Pope 2000).

Parsons' approach was focused on the individual but other social scientists; primarily those representing sociology, often looked at careers in the context of social and work systems. Moore *et al.* (2007) particularly noted the work of sociologists Durkheim, Weber and Hughes as relevant to careers. Durkheim's thoughts on the interconnectedness of division of labor to identity in organizations and society and his insights into work status and job decision making were not focused on career theory, but play out in subsequent career research. Weber's recognition of the opposing interests between the system benefits of routinized work and the risks it imposes on the creative contribution of the individual can be viewed as a prelude to current attempts to devise career development practices that can promote both organizational and individual gain. Weber's delineation separating socioeconomic class from status of occupation also factors into contemporary discussions about career opportunity. Hughes built upon the foundation of both Durkheim and Weber but applied his work particularly to career theory, leading to influential ethnographic studies of various occupations.

The individual focus on careers also transitioned with time. Although Parsons' devotees relied upon one-on-one techniques such as guided reflection, individual observation and coaching (Herr 2001), the process became more mechanized with the development of instruments designed to gather information about individuals that could be used to guide them towards vocations. Early efforts produced intelligence and aptitude tests, employed by the military in World War I to determine efficient placement of personnel. This so-called "scientific approach to vocational guidance" (Moore *et al.* 2007: 23) prompted a third type of instrument, interest tests. Despite their reported scientific foundation, interest tests have been criticized for relying on stereotypical gender work roles and for their Western perspective (Einarsdottir and Rounds 2009; Watson *et al.* 2005). Initially, interest inventories were part of the directive trait-and-factor approach to counseling, sometimes characterized as "test them and tell them" for its extreme dependence on test results to determine one's career destiny (Hansen 2005: 295). Over time, this was replaced by the person-environment (P-E) fit approach that continued to rely on testing but included more constructs in an effort to identify the best fit between an individual's "ability, personality, needs and values" and work (Hansen 2005: 295).

The history of career development is characterized by the dichotomy between individual and organizational career development; with the former focused on one's personal quest for a career; and the latter concentrating instead on maximizing human resources within systems (Patton and McMahon 2006). Pope (2000) has suggested that the growth of organizational career development in the US was at least partially the result of high unemployment rates coupled with the idealism of the 1960s. Government agencies were mobilized to encourage more career development in organizations, including business and industry, leading some (e.g. IBM) to establish corporate career centers. Organizations of varied sizes and types began to see career development as a way to build a cadre of qualified workers; succession plans were put into place and employees bought into the process because it seemed to ensure job security. Interestingly, a government-initiated career development project was also being initiated in Taiwan in the 1960s, resulting in vocational centers to bring together potential employees and employers.

More recently, corporations in Taiwan have instituted their own career centers to "enhance human resources" (Chang 2002: 221). Arthur (2008: 166) has proposed that the study of "how individuals and organizations interact over time" attracted the interest of management schools in the 1970s, delineating their focus on career development as separate from the educational tradition of emphasizing individual career choice. Until the late twentieth century, those two traditions coexisted with little difficulty, but economic and societal changes that affected the workplace in the 1980s appeared to highlight their differences, with researchers and practitioners taking sides rather than working to integrate the two (Arthur 2008), creating a contested terrain. This is not just a US phenomenon. Global economic downturns have made career development a more complex and contentious process in the East as well as the West (Chang 2002; Pope *et al.* 2002).

Three challenges

We will focus on three major challenges facing career development: the turbulent economic environment, the increasingly diverse workforce with varied career needs and the contested terrain, which refers to the tension between individuals' career needs and interests and the organization's priorities and goals.

Turbulent economic environment

The first issue, the turbulent economic environment, has been discussed in the career literature for several years (see for example Arthur 2008; Herr 2000; Savickas *et al.* 2009). The indicators of this turbulence are many; some of the most prevalent include a lack of employment security, continuous organizational restructuring and, often, dramatic changes in the nature of work itself (Arthur 2008; Savickas *et al.* 2009). According to Arthur (2008: 174): "The knowledge economy makes a habit of introducing new ways of working, condemning old ways of working, and thereby triggering changing career arrangements around the globe." Some of these changes include: technological innovations that have altered jobs, created jobs and made many jobs obsolete; project driven jobs that cease to exist once the project is over resulting in more temporary or contract workers; and the globalization of the economy causing jobs to move to other locations in the world, creating more market competition and more interaction with individuals in various locations around the globe (Savickas 2011; Savickas *et al.* 2009).

This volatility has been heightened in the past five years as many parts of the world have experienced high unemployment, governmental debt crises and high profile financial institution failures due to "excessive risk-taking behavior" (MacKenzie *et al.* 2012: 353). Rae (2008: 749) suggested we are in an "economic storm":

> there is a mix of economic, environmental, political and technological factors, which together produce a rapidly changing and turbulent context. It can be suggested that this is a more complex set of circumstances than have existed previously, and the level of interdependence between these factors is leading to, and will continue to result in, unpredictable economic changes.
>
> *Rae 2008: 753–754*

In the past, career theorists have responded to turbulent economic environments with new approaches to career development. Two of the most well-known are the boundaryless career and the protean career. The boundaryless career is conceived as not being constrained by "traditional organizational career arrangements" (Arthur and Rousseau 1996: 6), but rather as one that "involves physical and/or psychological career mobility" (Sullivan and Arthur 2006: 22). The protean career is described as being self-driven rather than being driven by organizational structures, norms or policies (Briscoe *et al.* 2012). There have been several criticisms of these approaches, particularly the concept of the boundaryless career (see for example, Inkson *et al.* 2012; Rodrigues and Guest 2010). However, Briscoe *et al.* (2012: 315) found that having a protean and boundaryless mindset may be helpful as individuals navigate their careers in these turbulent environments. They wrote:

> The value of protean and boundaryless attitudes has primarily been demonstrated in relatively healthy economic contexts. The positive outcomes these attitudes produced

in a more challenging context suggest all the more that greater knowledge about how to identify and inculcate them is in order.

The field of career counseling has also responded to this changing environment by developing new techniques and practices to help individuals navigate their careers (Savickas 2011). For many working in the field, constructivist approaches to counseling have replaced more positivistic methods such as person-environment (P-E) fit. The notion of matching individual interests or traits with jobs, usually done through standardized instruments, has been criticized as not reflecting the current career and workplace landscape and for superseding individual realities and experiences with "aggregate career information" (Sampson 2009: 92). At the heart of constructivism is the idea that "individuals are active agents in the production of their careers" (McMahon and Watson 2008: 280). Savickas *et al.* (2009: 246) explained the difference in these approaches in this way: "Positivist research on careers concentrates on decision making and declaring a choice. The comparable process for the social constructionist perspective is articulating intentions and anticipations regarding possible selves and life in the future."

A variety of counseling theories have emerged with a foundation based in constructivism (e.g. Patton and McMahon's Systems Theory Framework, Savickas' Theory of Career Construction and Pryor and Bright's Chaos Theory of Careers). Central to constructivist theories is the importance of narratives which focus on an individual's subjective perspective of his/her experiences, interests and beliefs (Russell 2011; Savickas 2011). The data emerges from the individual, rather than imposing a career perspective on the person, which is more likely when test results supply lists of potential careers or categorize individuals into job clusters. Russell (2011) found the use of narratives to be beneficial to unemployed, underemployed and displaced workers in that counselors and clients collaborated in the process, resulting in a greater understanding of each client's unique situation.

Diversity

A global economy and changing demographics worldwide have resulted in a workforce that is more diverse than most organizations have experienced to date. The responsibility to address this wider range of individual needs and interests has left many organizations uncertain about how to proceed with career development and perhaps overwhelmed at the challenge it presents. This dilemma is exacerbated both by the changes brought on by economic turmoil, as noted in the previous section, and by research indicating individuals from under-represented groups have historically faced more hurdles than their majority counterparts in career development.

In 2003, a diverse workforce and diverse teams were listed among future trends for HRD (Chermack *et al.* 2003). Yet, seven years later, Bierema (2010) asserted that the field of HRD has been resistant to address diversity in the workplace in research as well as in practice. Not surprisingly, if there is a dearth of HRD research on diversity in general, the amount devoted to career development for non-majority group members is even more limited. As in many other fields, HRD career development and diversity research focuses most on the career needs of women, but that attention in the literature does not equate to resolution of gender issues and careers in practice, as evidenced by two recent issues of *Advances in Human Resource Development* that discuss hurdles facing women in higher education leadership (Madsen 2012a, 2012b) or Al-Ahmadi's (2011) article on challenges for Saudi Arabian women leaders in *Human Resource Development International*.

Other under-represented groups fare even less well in the literature, with a smattering of articles addressing their career progress. These examples highlight some of the concerns. One study observed few Black managers compared with their White counterparts and surmised it was partially the result of "comfort hiring and mentoring" (Bristol and Tisdell 2010: 232) that prompts majority executives to choose those most like themselves. The authors concluded that under-represented group members need additional assistance (e.g. formal or informal learning, mentoring) to learn cultural expectations if they aspire to career success (Bristol and Tisdell 2010). Barrett *et al.* (2003: 117) reported that "lack of promotion and glass ceiling issues" hindered the career progress of Black human resource developers in their qualitative study. Another under-represented group, lesbian employees find they must overcome biases in the workplace that can derail their career progression (Gedro 2010). Similarly, Nafukho *et al.* (2010) cited discrimination as a career barrier for people with disabilities. Aware of generational issues in institutions, Van Veldhoven and Dorenbosch (2008: 125) reported that despite organizations often touting the value of keeping an older workforce engaged, "age was negatively associated with career opportunities." These are not new issues, but their persistence and the variety of employees affected by them indicate a pressing challenge for career development in HRD.

A weakened global economy and the protean career mindset have prompted an increase in another type of workforce diversity, temporary, part-time and stop-out workers (Esteban-Pretel *et al.* 2011). The wide-ranging impact of this phenomenon on developed countries is evidenced through articles like De Cuyper *et al.*'s (2007) review of the literature, which included studies from North America, Australia and Europe. Despite the prominence of contingent workers, there has not been commensurate growth in research regarding their career development possibilities. One exception is Connell and Burgess' (2006) study of Australian temporary workers and career development. A few other studies have explored how part-time or temporary full-time work influences promotion opportunities (Zeytinoglu and Cooke 2008), affects chances for full-time employment (Esteban-Pretel *et al.* 2011) and impacts perceptions of career success (Allen 2011). Career development issues for these members of the workforce include questions of skill building for future employability.

Another variation of non-standard work will require yet a different approach to career development. Less a function of economics and more a reflection of the protean approach, employees seeking to balance life and work may choose unique career trajectories. These career paths account for interruptions in the cycle of work or assorted levels of work over time (e.g. part-time, self-employment) as individuals determine what pattern of work and life best fit at different points in their lives (see for example, the kaleidoscope career, Mainiero and Sullivan 2005). Career development for these varied pathways will need to be adaptive and flexible.

Contested terrain

Economist Richard Edwards (1979: 16) argued that the "workplace becomes a contested terrain" due to the competing interests between employees and employers. "Conflict exists because the interests of workers and those of employers collide and what is good for one is frequently costly for the other" (Edwards 1979: 12). Scholars have used the notion of the contested terrain to explain various HRD workplace issues. For example, Jackson and Jordan (2000) wrote about the politicizing of workplace learning in Australia and *Aotearoa*/New Zealand and questioned who benefits from training policies that were adopted in these countries during the 1990s. Folinsbee (2009) described the ethical issues she faced as a workplace literacy practitioner as often hinging on the competing interests and values of managers and employees.

The contested terrain has also been used as a way of describing the tension between individuals' career interests and needs and the goals of the organizations in which individuals are employed. Inkson and King (2011: 39) argued that much of this tension can be understood through an examination of how two academic literatures, the "vocational perspective" and the "strategic human resource management perspective," approach the subject of careers. The vocational perspective, which is grounded in psychology and education, focuses on the individual and how one chooses and develops a career, while the strategic human resource management perspective, with roots in economics, focuses on how the organization benefits from investing in individuals' development. Inkson and King (2011: 41) wrote:

> The disjuncture, and the consequent focus by the vocational perspective on employees and occupations, and by the SHRM perspective on managers and organizations as distinctive foci for careers, appear to represent a major barrier to the development of interdisciplinary theory and research on careers (Arthur 2008), and to hinder attempts to resolve contests for terrain between the parties.

Indeed this strain between what is good for the individual (e.g. developing skills that maximize employability) and what is good for the organization (e.g. keeping a skilled workforce but retaining the flexibility to "downsize" at any time), while not new to the career landscape, seems to be exacerbated during tight economic times when each party is more likely to feel the stress of professional survival. Often this has resulted in the organization maintaining the upper hand in terms of power. According to Thite (2001: 312):

> While employers have the managerial prerogative to change the context and contents of the tasks as the situation demands, the employees are today left in a hapless situation. They can no longer rely on the organization to steer them through the career maze nor can they bargain collectively as effectively as they did before on employment security, promotion, training, health and safety, etc.

Inkson and King (2011) offered a framework and specific suggestions to manage the diverse and often competing interests of the individual (e.g. vocational perspective) and the employer (e.g. the SHRM or economic perspective). First they provided a model which used the psychological contract as the basis for understanding and examining the contested terrain. They offered "various loci of contestation" that can occur between career capital (at the individual level) or organizational knowledge capital and intended outcomes (Inkson and King 2011: 46). To effectively manage the contested terrain Inkson and King (2011: 51) emphasized the importance of communication; suggesting that both parties need to trust one another, engage in open discussions about these competing interests, and be "actively interested in the other's future."

HRD's response to these challenges

The challenges we have outlined here are not new ones, yet they continue to persist in many organizations and nations today. In 2009, Kuchinke called for both HRD scholars and practitioners to increase their relevance in these turbulent times. We echo this request and offer the following recommendations to begin to address these challenges.

Implications for practice

First, HRD as a discipline needs to develop much more awareness of the careers of blue collar, non-exempt, contingent, underemployed and unemployed workers. Both our scholarship and our practice suggest these populations are often ignored (McKee-Ryan and Harvey 2011). For example, Inkson and King (2011) recognized that their focus in considering the contested terrain was on management, professional and technical employees. HRD also must recognize that a "one size fits all" mentality regarding these employees will not suffice. For example, Feldman (2006) pointed out that within the contingent employment population alone there are a multitude of differences.

Second, HRD needs to consider the role counseling may take in helping employees navigate their careers. Through the years, the career counseling field has focused most attention on the young, helping them to make decisions regarding employment and college majors, and on the unemployed (Goodman and Hansen 2005; Patton and McMahon 2006; Verbruggen *et al.* 2007). HRD has largely ignored the research and the practice of career counseling except in those instances where outplacement services are recommended due to downsizing. The turbulent economy, the changing nature of careers (in terms of both content and form) and changing demographics suggest more individuals throughout their lives will need career counseling in some form. Herr (2003: 11) indicated that career counseling in the twenty-first century will increasingly focus on issues other than career choice and decision making. Rather, counselors will be needed to help individuals with work–life balance, stress and anger issues, personal and career identity, or other concerns. Several scholars have argued that career development is about constructing a life, which suggests that career counseling is needed throughout one's life and should be readily available to all (Savickas *et al.* 2005; Watts 2005).

In 2004, individuals from 46 countries met at the Symposium on International Perspectives on Career Development to discuss a variety of career issues. Among the recommendations from this conference was the need for more career services to be provided by employers (Watts 2005). Savickas *et al.* (2005: 83) suggested these types of services are particularly needed for those employees who are "in risk of social exclusion," which they define as those individuals "at risk because they are poor or disabled or are immigrants or the 'wrong' race or sex." While many large organizations offer such services to their employees, many workplaces do not. If this recommendation is to be implemented in organizations around the world, HRD practitioners need to be involved in both the planning and the implementation of such services.

However, as a field, we have not adequately prepared practitioners to take up this charge. For this to become a reality, HRD academic programs need to strengthen their career development component within the curriculum. HRD practitioners will need the skills to help employees seeking guidance and counseling to determine if external counselors are required and how to select them, and to develop a strong knowledge base of resources both within and outside the organization that can assist with employees' career needs. More interdisciplinary collaborations between HRD programs and graduate counseling programs could be one way to help HRD practitioners become prepared to take on career development initiatives in organizations.

These collaborative efforts could potentially help the field of career counseling as well. The training of career counselors has been criticized for several years now. In many parts of the world, very little is required in terms of training and qualifications to become a career counselor (Patton and McMahon 2006). Even countries with a well-developed history of counselor education find their programs susceptible to criticism. Many scholars are concerned that graduate-level counseling programs offer few courses in career counseling and that increasingly, students are more interested in other types of counseling such as marriage and mental health (Savickas *et al.* 2005). Hence the concern is not simply inadequately prepared counselors, but also a shortage of counselors. Dual programs, where individuals would learn about and develop skills in traditional HRD concepts (e.g. organizational systems, learning and program planning and implementation) and also develop career counseling skills could be beneficial to many constituencies.

Third, HRD practitioners are in the unique position to serve as facilitators in helping employers and employees negotiate the contested terrain. We believe they are in a "unique" position in that the HRD function should clearly understand the needs and interests of both parties and be committed to assisting both in achieving their goals. Managers need assistance regarding how to provide career coaching to their employees. They also need to develop strong communication skills so they can effectively listen to their employees, provide feedback and support for their career endeavors, and be honest regarding how the organization can help with their careers (Inkson and King 2011). At the same time employees need to develop employability skills, learn about resources both internal and external to the organization and become more cognizant of the needs of the organization. They too, need to become better communicators so they can articulate their needs and interests, be responsive to feedback and develop strong internal and external networks (Inkson and King 2011).

Implications for research

With a few exceptions, HRD career development research has not kept up with the changing career environment. It has been decades since the protean and boundaryless approaches were proposed and downsizing initiatives altered traditional ideas about job security and single employer careers. During those years, the workforce has become increasingly diverse, knowledge work has continued to eclipse manufacturing, technology has advanced to allow any company to have a global presence and repercussions from worldwide economic woes have prompted higher unemployment and underemployment. Searching the literature leads to the conclusion that HRD has fallen behind in cutting-edge career development research (see for example, Egan *et al.* 2006; McDonald and Hite 2005). Some might argue that HRD's lack of response has been prompted by uncertainty of how to respond. However, research from the counseling/vocational literature can provide ideas of where to begin.

The turbulent career environment is a global phenomenon. Economic conditions vary by geographic region, but the underlying concerns are similar. It is widely acknowledged that the careers of those entering the world of work now will likely be nomadic in nature, as employees negotiate serial working arrangements over their life spans. This will require crafting a different type of career development, focused more on employability and adaptability than on seniority.

> Employability is no longer considered important only for those who are deprived and unemployed, but for the entire active population. It is now mainly considered an alternative to job security. It is not only important to stimulate entry into the labour market, but also to ensure career possibilities within and beyond the borders of organisations
>
> *Forrier and Sels 2003: 104*

It is a reciprocal arrangement where "employees are expected to take responsibility for their own career [sic]" and employers are expected "to offer the necessary support and facilities" (Forrier and Sels 2003: 104). Research on this concept may be hampered from lack of agreement on terms and measurement, but Forrier and Sels (2003) offered a model on the employability process and suggest exploring the process in parts, rather than trying to address all aspects in single massive studies.

Other researchers have suggested that successful employees of the future will need to develop adaptability and the capacity to continue learning. Karaevli and Hall (2006: 360) acknowledged that adaptability, "a key quality that enables a person to manage the process of change and development over the span of her career," is increasingly necessary to thrive in an uncertain work environment, and it is gained through "career variety," taking on varied work responsibilities, particularly early in one's career (ibid: 363). In addition to testing out the framework they proposed, their research recommendations are to further investigate "various individual outcomes of career variety" to help systems determine how best to foster adaptability in future leaders (ibid: 370). On a related theme, Kwakman (2003) pointed out the importance of "professional learning," continued opportunities for gaining skills and knowledge to better prepare for innovative work required for a changing workplace. Research to determine how best to incorporate adaptability and a learning mindset into career development has the potential to benefit both employees and employers, as individuals solidify skills and knowledge and organizations benefit from a workforce prepared to innovate and thrive in a changing environment.

Research on employability and adaptability, while initially posed as a response to the unsettled work environment, could easily also address the challenges of workforce diversity and the contested terrain. The concerns of the unemployed, the underemployed and the cyclically employed are a natural fit. One illustration is an empirical study by McArdle *et al.* (2007: 260) that found "the adaptability and career identity associated with employability are likely to be particularly important in obtaining re-employment." Research on careers and demographic diversity will require adding the complexities of discrimination and access to career development to studies of employability and adaptability. Longitudinal comparison studies may be particularly useful here. Other research might be more directed at how life experience influences careers; for example, since under-represented group members often must adapt to fit into a majority culture, how might those skills transfer to career adaptability? The dearth of research on under-represented groups and career development provides lots of opportunities for HRD to make a contribution.

Employability and adaptability, while essentially giving career responsibility to the individual, may seem to be firmly on only one side of the contested terrain. However, these skills are built within the context of systems and the implementation has the potential to benefit organizations as well. The constructs of employability and adaptability can operate within organizational boundaries as well as outside of them. It remains for research to determine how best to meld these forces so that cooperative efforts yield mutual advantages. Opportunities for research are plentiful and varied. Longitudinal studies that track progress both for individuals and for organizations are large undertakings, but they can provide the empirical foundation needed to redefine career development. International research on career development recognizes the global nature of careers and presents opportunities to share resources and knowledge. Interdisciplinary collaborations between HRD and career counseling researchers have the potential to advance career development theory and practice in both fields. HRD has the capacity to rebuild its reputation in career development, but a key part of the process is fostering research that can help shape the future of careers.

References

Al-Ahmadi, H. (2011) Challenges facing women leaders in Saudi Arabia, *Human Resource Development International* 14: 149–66.

Allen, B.C. (2011) The role of professional identity commitment in understanding the relationship between casual employment and perceptions of career success, *Career Development International* 16: 196–216.

Arthur, M.B. (2008) Examining contemporary careers: A call for interdisciplinary inquiry, *Human Relations* 61: 163–86.

Arthur, M.B. and Rousseau, D.M. (1996) *The Boundaryless Career*, New York: Oxford University Press.

Barrett, I.C., Cervero, R.M. and Johnson-Bailey, J. (2003) Biculturalism-outsiders within: The career development experiences of Black human resource developers, *Journal of Career Development* 30: 109–28.

Bierema, L.L. (2010) Resisting HRD's resistance to diversity, *Journal of European Industrial Training* 34: 565–76.

Brewer, J.M. (1942) *History of Vocational Guidance*, New York: Harper and Brothers.

Briscoe, J.P., Henagan, S.C., Burton, J.P. and Murphy, W.M. (2012) Coping with an insecure employment environment: The differing roles of protean and boundaryless career orientations, *Journal of Vocational Behavior* 80: 308–16.

Bristol, T.L. and Tisdell, E.J. (2010) Leveraging diversity through career development: Social and cultural capital among African-American managers, *International Journal of Human Resources Development and Management* 10: 224–38.

Chang, D.H.F. (2002) The past, present, and future of career counseling in Taiwan, *Career Development Quarterly* 50: 218–25.

Chermack, T.J., Lynham, S.A. and Ruona, W.E.A. (2003) Critical uncertainties confronting human resource development, *Advances in Developing Human Resources* 5: 257–71.

Connell, J. and Burgess, J. (2006) The influence of precarious employment on career development, *Education + Training* 48: 493–507.

De Cuyper, N., De Jong, J., De Witte, H., Isaksson, K., Rigotti, T. and Schalk, R. (2007) Literature review of theory and research on the psychological impact of temporary employment: Towards a conceptual model, *International Journal of Management Reviews* 10: 25–51.

Edwards, R. (1979) *Contested Terrain*, New York: Basic Books.

Egan, T.M., Upton, M.G. and Lynham, S.A. (2006) Career development: Load-bearing wall or window dressing? Exploring definitions, theories, and prospects for HRD-related theory building, *Human Resource Development Review* 5: 442–77.

Einarsdottir, S. and Rounds, J. (2009) Gender bias and construct validity in vocational interest measurement: Differential item functioning in the Strong Interest Inventory, *Journal of Vocational Behavior* 74(3): 295–307.

Esteban-Pretel, J., Nakajima, R. and Tanaka, R. (2011) Are contingent jobs dead ends or stepping stones to regular jobs? Evidence from a structural estimation, *Labour Economics* 18: 513–26.

Feldman, D.C. (2006) Toward a new taxonomy for understanding the nature and consequences of contingent employment, *Career Development International* 11: 28–47.

Folinsbee, S. (2009) Workplace literacy: Ethical issues through the lens of experience, *New Directions for Adult and Continuing Education* 123: 33–42.

Forrier, A. and Sels, L. (2003) The concept employability: A complex mosaic, *International Journal of Human Resources Development and Management* 3: 102–24.

Gedro, J. (2010) The lavender ceiling atop the global closet: Human resource development and lesbian expatriates, *Human Resource Development Review* 9: 385–404.

Goodman, J. and Hansen, S. (2005) Career development and guidance programs across cultures: The gap between policies and practices, *Career Development Quarterly* 54: 57–65.

Hansen, J.C. (2005) Assessment of interests, in Brown, S. and Lent, R. (eds) *Career Development and Counseling: Putting Theory and Research to Work*, Hoboken, NJ: Wiley.

Herr, E.L. (2000) Collaboration, partnership, policy, and practice in career development, *Journal of Employment Counseling* 37: 53–61.

— (2001) Career development and its practice: A historical perspective, *Career Development Quarterly* 49: 196–211.

— (2003) The future of career counseling as an instrument of public policy, *Career Development Quarterly* 52: 8–17.

Inkson, K. and King, Z. (2011) Contested terrain in careers: A psychological contract model, *Human Relations* 64: 37–57.

Inkson, K., Gunz, H., Ganesh, S. and Roper, J. (2012) Boundaryless careers: Bringing back boundaries, *Organization Studies* 33: 323–40.

Jackson, N. and Jordan, S. (2000) Learning for work: Contested terrain?, *Studies in the Education of Adults* 32: 195–211.

Karaevli, A. and Hall, D.T. (2006) How career variety promotes the adaptability of managers: A theoretical model, *Journal of Vocational Behavior* 69: 359–73.

Kuchinke, K.P. (2009) HRD in turbulent times, *Human Resource Development International* 12: 115–16.

Kwakman, K. (2003) Professional learning throughout the career, *International Journal of Human Resources Development and Management* 3: 180–90.

MacKenzie, C.A., Garavan, T.N. and Carbery, R. (2012) Through the looking glass: Challenges for human resource development (HRD) post the global financial crises – Business as usual?, *Human Resource Development International* 16: 353–64.

Madsen, S.R. (ed.) (2012a) Women and leadership in higher education: Learning and advancement in leadership programs [Special issue], *Advances in Developing Human Resources* 14: 3–128.

— (ed.) (2012b) Women and leadership in higher education: Current realities, challenges, and future directions [Special issue], *Advances in Developing Human Resources* 14: 131–236.

Mainiero, L. and Sullivan, S. (2005) Kaleidoscope careers: An alternate explanation for the opt-out revolution, *Academy of Management Executive* 19: 106–23.

McArdle, S., Waters, L., Briscoe, J.P. and Hall, D.T. (2007) Employability during unemployment: Adaptability, career identity and human and social capital, *Journal of Vocational Behavior* 71: 247–64.

McDonald, K.S. and Hite, L.M. (2005) Reviving the relevance of career development in human resource development, *Human Resource Development Review* 4: 418–39.

McKee-Ryan, F.M. and Harvey, J. (2011) I have a job, but . . . A review of underemployment, *Journal of Management* 37: 962–96.

McMahon, M.L. and Watson, M.B. (2008) Systemic influences on career development: Assisting clients to tell their career stories, *Career Development Quarterly* 56: 280–88.

Moore, C., Gunz, H. and Hall, D.T. (2007) Tracing the historical roots of career theory in management and organizations studies, in Gunz, H. and Peiperl, M. (eds) *Handbook of Career Studies*, Thousand Oaks, CA: SAGE.

Nafukho, F.M., Roessler, R.T. and Kacirek, K. (2010) Disability as a diversity factor: Implications for human resource practices, *Advances in Developing Human Resources* 12: 395–406.

Patton, W. and McMahon, M. (2006) *Career Development and Systems Theory* (2nd edn), Rotterdam: Sense.

Pope, M. (2000) A brief history of career counseling in the United States, *Career Development Quarterly* 48: 194–211.

Pope, M., Musa, M., Singaravelu, H., Bringaze, T. and Russell, M. (2002) From colonialism to ultranationalism: History and development of career counseling in Malaysia, *Career Development Quarterly* 50(3): 264–76.

Rae, D. (2008) Riding out the storm: Graduates, enterprise and careers in turbulent economic times, *Education + Training* 50: 748–63.

Rodrigues, R. and Guest, D. (2010) Have careers become boundaryless?, *Human Relations* 63: 1157–75.

Russell, J.C. (2011) The use of narratives to contextualize the experiences and needs of unemployed, underemployed, and displaced workers, *Journal of Employment Counseling* 48: 50–62.

Sampson, J.P. Jr (2009) Modern and postmodern career theories: The unnecessary divorce, *Career Development Quarterly* 58: 91–96.

Savickas, M.L (2011) New questions for vocational psychology: Premises, paradigms, and practices, *Journal of Career Assessment* 19: 251–58.

Savickas, M.L., Van Esbroeck, R. and Herr, E.L. (2005) The internationalization of educational and vocational guidance, *Career Development Quarterly* 54: 77–85.

Savickas, M.L., Nota, L., Rossier, J., Dauwalder, J., Duarte, M.E., Guichard, J., Soresi, S., Esbroeck, R.V. and Van Vianen, A.E.M. (2009) Life designing: A paradigm for career construction in the 21st century, *Journal of Vocational Behavior* 75: 239–50.

Sullivan, S.E. and Arthur, M.B. (2006) The evolution of the boundaryless career concept: Examining physical and psychological mobility, *Journal of Vocational Behavior* 69: 19–29.

Thite, M. (2001) Help us but help yourself: The paradox of contemporary career management, *Career Development International* 6: 312–17.

Van Veldhoven, M. and Dorenbosch, L. (2008) Age, proactivity and career development, *Career Development International* 13(2): 112–31.

Verbruggen, M., Sels, L. and Forrier, A. (2007) Unraveling the relationship between organizational career management and the need for external career counseling, *Journal of Vocational Behavior* 71: 69–83.

Watson, M.B., Duarte, M.E. and Glavin, K. (2005) Cross-cultural perspectives on career assessment, *Career Development Quarterly* 54(1): 29–35.

Watts, A.G. (2005) Career guidance policy: An international review, *Career Development Quarterly* 54: 66–76.

Wollschlager, N. and Guggenheim, E.F. (2004) From divergence to convergence: A history of vocational education and training in Europe, *European Journal of Vocational Training* 32: 6–17.

Zeytinoglu, I.U. and Cooke, G.B. (2008) Non-standard employment and promotions: A within genders analysis, *Journal of Industrial Relations* 50: 319–37.

8

WORKERS AND UNION HRD

Seeking employee voice and empowerment[1]

Bruce Spencer and Jennifer Kelly

It could be argued that referring to employees as human resources – another input in the production process – dehumanizes workers (Schied 1995) and that human resource development (HRD) is essentially about how to improve that input in order to extract additional value (surplus labor) from that resource. The idea that increased learning and education results in increased labor productivity has been argued as the keystone of human capital theory (HCT) for some time (for a critique of HCT see Bouchard 2006). The role that unions have historically played in educating members, including skills development, has been overlooked in the recent literature much of which has become exclusively focused on HRD in the service of the work organization/corporation – reflecting a unitarist perspective adopted by researchers either consciously or unconsciously.

This contribution to the handbook on current HRD opens with a brief outline "understanding unions" followed by a discussion of workers' and unions' learning at work, before moving on to a longer exposition of what constitutes labor education – another key area of HRD that is under-reported. This is followed by an examination of employee development schemes (EDS) and a brief review of empowerment HRD/Learning and EDS.

Understanding unions

This discussion of the role of labor unions accepts the contradictory nature of unionism (as both a force for opposition and accommodation to organizations and society); the tendency towards union incorporation into managerial goals (at both local and national levels of the union); towards bureaucratization and oligarchic structures and so on: but also argues that independent active unionism may provide the best chance to democratize the corporate workplace (to paraphrase Hugh Clegg [1978], collective bargaining *is* a form of industrial democracy).

With the decline of union influence in many developed economies other forms of representation, participation, and worker-initiated learning have emerged – bolstered in Europe by EU legislation favoring worker participation – but the results are mixed, "in most cases, employee representatives (in the participatory structures) are merely informed of upcoming changes by management with no input into decision making" (Freeman *et al.* 2007: 177). While implementing new participation and learning organization strategies may be successful in helping employers fight off unions (particularly in the US and the UK) the evidence supports the view that much higher levels of participation are found in organizations that *do* recognize unions; supporting a view that unionization and employee involvement may be complementary (ibid: 196). It is also noteworthy that union membership in the US would treble immediately if workers were *free* to choose union membership (confirmed again by the USA survey presented in Freeman *et al.* 2007).

Too many writers on HRD fail to recognize the importance of power relations at work and how unions can provide a countervailing power to the concentration of power wielded by management and owners when discussing workplace learning issues. There should be no place for the kind of open hostility towards unions displayed in the media and in much of the HRD literature. Of course unions must be subject to critical analysis along with other organizations, but to challenge the right of workers to organize and collectively bargain is to not only deny a key element of democracy at work but also a key component of liberal democracy (note the International Labour Office was set up in 1919 after the devastation of the First World War to promote workers' rights; it became the first agency established by the UN in 1946). This attitude stems from an elitist belief that the workplace should be beyond societal democratic goals and under the sole control of owners/management. This reflects a belief that it is legitimate for workers to be treated as "resources" not as citizens – citizens with democratic rights *even* when at work.

Productivity revisited

The importance of labor productivity in growth, competitiveness and trade is often asserted and is closely allied to the HRD agenda in the literature but it is very rarely examined. Productivity in different sectors of the economy can vary enormously and, as a generalization, the more "capital" a worker has to work with the more productive she or he will appear to be. Manufacturing jobs are the most "productive" because the machinery and technology (capital in economic terms) that support each job result in high value output, particularly compared with service jobs: close down manufacturing plants and a country's "productivity" falls – the fall in productivity has little to do with "investments in human capital" or "workers' skills." If companies maintain technology investments workers' productivity can rise; if they run down a plant, move processes overseas and/or close plants, labor productivity falls. Countries that follow an active industry policy, not just a supply-side economic approach of training and re-training, have higher overall productivity.

Perhaps the reason why the productivity-linked workplace learning argument is so important to HRD writers is because of the central role it gives to HRM/HRD via HCT. The argument here is that if workers can increase their own human capital via training, workplace learning and, as argued more recently, investments in emotional labor, then productivity can rise. HRM is then key not peripheral, as it once was, in the corporate world. The HRM/HRD Director can sit on the top table with the other CEOs! For example the 2007 Conference Board of Canada publication, *Learning and Development Outlook: Are We Learning Enough?* (Hughes and Grant 2007: 1), argues:

> Canada's productivity is lagging behind that of its competitors. One strategy Canadian organizations are using to meet these challenges is the renewal and upgrading of their workers' skills. By spending on TLD [Training, Learning and Development] to build workers' skills, organizations seek to create enough additional human capital to make themselves more competitive.

But they also report on low spending rates on TLD by Canadian organizations because most companies' training needs are modest – which is a reflection of the nature of most work and capital investment in Canada: few skilled workers need apply!

Workers' and unions' learning at work

Workers have always learned at work; learning at work is not a new phenomenon. What they have learned has always been diverse; for example, it ranges from learning about the job and how to do the work to how to relate to fellow workers, supervisors and bosses (the social relations of work) to gaining understandings about the nature of work itself and how work impacts on society. Workers, generally speaking, have always tried to make meaning out of their work experience. It's difficult for someone to spend 8 hours a day, 5 days a week, doing something in a totally detached way, and even more difficult if a person hates every minute of it. Read most accounts of workers describing their work and this need to make meaning is clear (Terkel 1977; Sennett 1998). Workers have always wanted to do a good job, even if that job is menial; the new emphasis on workplace learning should not mask that pre-existing situation.

Apart from this obvious day-to-day workplace learning, identifying examples of significant employee-organized learning on-the-job is problematic; many situations describing workers undertaking their own workplace learning are more accurately described as responses to manager and supervisor prompting (for example, Honold 1991). A few studies undertaken with a workers' perspective do throw light on employee knowledge but are often looking at knowledge across the course training/informal learning divide which makes it difficult to sort out which examples of "learning" are genuinely worker-initiated rather than union- or management-initiated. For example, Livingstone and Sawchuk (2004) provide a number of case studies examining learning in different sectors and report on workers' knowledge generation within company training courses, union education, and informal workplace and out-of-work situations. It is not always clear which are employee-initiated; however, we can conclude that opportunities may be greater for the auto and small-parts workers than the largely immigrant female garment workers and that all engage in some forms of employee-initiated learning that is both work and non-work related. Issues of control over on-the-job training, pay for knowledge, gender and ethnic divisions, inequitable access to learning, and the struggles of marginalized workers to secure permanent employment have all been documented at different times and are central to understanding the context of HRD. Nor should we underestimate the importance of workers' informal learning and knowledge-sharing as a key component of workplace learning.

Perhaps we should not be surprised to find union-organized learning at work is concerned with broader issues of worker influence over management policies: workplace insecurity goes hand-in-hand with globalization. Employees are asked to embrace the idea that there are no "permanent" jobs anymore; workers are expected to be flexible, to move from job to job and build a "learning profile" more than a career. An interesting international survey of "employee voice" in six "Anglo-American" countries reports that while workers do engage in learning and knowledge creation activities at work, many would like to have more union representation and more participation in management decision-making processes (Freeman *et al.* 2007). This desire is captured in a quote reproduced in Sawchuk (2001: 347):

> As unionists, we have always struggled for a voice. If we have asked for nothing else, we have asked to be heard, to be part of the process . . . Until now, we have been pounding at the door. Asking for an audience . . .

This lack of representation and access causes workers to be more guarded and less trustful of employers; the data of Freeman *et al.* (2007) revealed that those with most access were found to be most loyal.

A recent development in the UK is the establishment of "union learning representatives" (ULR) and a "union learning fund": the intention is that ULR will help connect workers to learning opportunities, essentially occupational-related training, and help organize workplace employee learning opportunities (Shelley and Calveley 2007). Studies suggest that in a number of situations these representatives can make a difference although major questions remain to be answered: is union involvement in new neo-liberal global economic agendas merely incorporation or can unions and ULR moderate the impact of these policies and guide these resources to meet broader social goals? Are ULR worker representatives or are they primarily agents of government and corporate policy? Also do they threaten, or do they enhance, the tradition of independent union education? What is known is that after the first 4 years of ULR only about 10 per cent of workplace representatives *bargained* about learning provision (Kersley *et al.* 2006: 20, 153). It should also be acknowledged that these developments are taking place at the same time as freely negotiated recognition agreements and collective bargaining structures are being displaced by "partnership agreements" that emphasize employer rights including in some cases denying the rights of work groups to democratically determine their own union representative (Wray 2001).

Labor education

In this section we will focus on what learning opportunities workers are developing for themselves within their own organizations. Labor education refers to education and training offered by labor unions (trade unions) to their members and representatives. The extent to which this education is provided directly by unions or by another agency or educational institution for unions varies from country to country and union to union. A main purpose of labor/union education is to prepare and train union lay members to play an active role in the union. Another purpose is to educate activists and members about union policy, about changes in the union environment such as new management techniques or changes in labor law. Labor education is also used to develop union consciousness, to build common goals and to share organizing and campaigning experience. Unions have a small full-time staff and therefore rely on what is essentially voluntary activity of their members to be effective at work and in society; the labor education program is thus a major contributor to building an effective volunteer force.

Labor education attracts more participants than any other form of non-vocational non-formal adult education in developed countries and is therefore one of the most important forms of non-formal adult education available to working people: but it is most often under-reported and ignored in discussions about adult and workplace learning. The 2003 report on the state of labor education in the US demonstrated that labor education provision had grown since 1968 (the time of the last survey) but that current development was uneven (Byrd and Nissen 2003). One of the reasons for the lack of knowledge about labor education amongst HRD scholars in Canada and the US is that most North American labor education is provided in-house by unions – outside the experience of trainers and adult and community educators in the US and Canada.

Most union members learn about the union while on the job (what is often referred to as informal or incidental learning). They probably will learn more and become most active during negotiations, grievances and disputes, but they also learn from union publications and communications, from attending meetings, conferences and conventions, and from the union's educational programs. Although labor education programs only cater to a small number of representatives in any one year they are designed to benefit a larger number of members because the course participants are expected to share the learning gained with other union members.

Most of the labor education courses provided by unions are *tool* courses (for example, shop steward training, grievance handling, and health and safety representative courses). The next largest category is *issues* courses (for example, sexual harassment or racism or new human resource management strategies), which often seek to link workplace and societal issues. A third group of courses can be labeled *labor studies*, which seek to examine the union context (for example, labor history, economics and politics). (These categories are explored in more detail in Spencer 2002 and ILO 2007.)

Unions are increasingly directly involved in a number of membership education programs some of which have a "basic educational skills" or vocational purpose – what is normally associated with mainstream HRD. In some cases union-run literacy and second language courses are tutored by fellow unionists and act as a bridge linking immigrant or illiterate workers to union concerns and publications as well as workplace issues. Similarly, unions are responsible for a number of worker training programs, which allow the unions to educate workers about union concerns alongside of vocational training. In some countries skilled and professional unions have a long history of union sponsored vocational training and education courses. Unions, including non-craft unions, are becoming much more proactive in responding to company restructuring and deskilling and are arguing for re-skilling, skills recognition and skills profiling, as well as challenging employers to live up to their rhetoric on "pay for knowledge." This is a growing area of union educational work and a number of unions in different countries are increasingly becoming more involved in offering general membership education of all kinds (in some cases running courses in basic literacy skills and vocational training jointly with management, for example in UAW and USW plants and schools).

New developments in labor education

The majority provision of continuing core labor education is targeted at local union representatives. This important work is ever changing, with differing examples evident in all countries where unions are active. More emphasis may be on peer tutoring in one country and significant content changes in another. New specific forms of representative training are occurring, such as that for European Works Council representatives in Europe; and examples of union representative training in difficult circumstances such as those in South Africa where unions are still coming to terms with gaining recognition and bargaining rights after years of opposition under apartheid. We also have reports on more sophisticated educational provision for full-time officers; an under-reported area of representative training.

Training recruiters is another development. The educational components of the US *Organizing Institute*, the Australian *Organising Works*, and the UK *Organising Academy* are important labor education responses to the decline of union influence and to shifting employment patterns. The work undertaken in organizing immigrant workers in Los Angeles is a particular example that has been successful in linking union activity to community groups and community-based organizing with labor education playing a key role. The *Justice for Janitors* campaigns have been most impressive and have relied on educational support to bolster activity, recruitment and contract negotiation – they have also provided a model for similar campaigns in Toronto and elsewhere.[2]

In Brazil, *Programa Integrar* has come to offer relevant vocational training and educational opportunities for the unemployed and the employed. The program illustrates that even in a hostile climate union education can succeed: it provides an example to other countries of how to build community links and to argue for alternative worker cooperative employment for union members in opposition to global corporate power. This example links with others in South America where union members are taking over closed factories and building local economic networks.

Although the use of research circles (workers conducting their own research into workplace or sector problems) has been around for some time, it is clear from Swedish experience that this approach has a bright future in terms of strengthening union activity within the union as well as externally. It represents an important alternative for union members wishing to conduct independent "workplace learning" projects.

Reflections on union education

Most of the examples above are in the tradition of independent workers' education while the development of ULR in the UK and the tradition of joint programs (for example the UAW–Chrysler National Training Center and UAW–Ford University plus others of collaborative union–company schemes) point to another direction in workers' education. Many of the joint programs are concerned with employee development in relation to employment. In some cases these programs have been boosted by the desire to develop workers' skills in order to remain employed (upskilling). In other cases they are designed to provide employment opportunities for workers who have been made redundant; of course, no guarantees are offered that re-skilling and broader educational upgrading will lead to new jobs. An example of a regional joint union–employer–state program is the *Wisconsin Regional Training Partnership* which claims success in creating both new employment opportunities and improvement in existing employment (Bernhardt *et al.* 2001). Another development in the same vein is organized labor's *Working for America Institute*, labor's nonprofit workforce development initiative, by which the AFL-CIO hopes via employer and other partnerships to boost high skills, knowledge work, and good jobs – the so-called "high road" to future employment opportunities.

Overall, unions remain an important and positive social organization for working people: it is the absence of strong independent unions that remains a problem for workers in the "economic south," sometimes referred to as less developed countries (LDCs) (Miller 2012).

Employee development schemes

This section is based on some limited empirical investigation and literature search (mainly relating to the UK) and some thinking about what model or theoretical understanding best describes EDS. This section will review what kinds of EDS have been supported by organizations in the UK. The financial crisis of 2008, and the resulting cuts in public spending over the following five years, and the further loss of jobs in the UK does render some of this data dated – but the issues and arguments remain valid. Similar though more limited schemes are operated by employers in the USA and Canada but as yet these have not been fully documented.

EDS that encourage and fund workers to undertake forms of non-vocational HRD of their own choosing have taken root in Britain. The evidence to date suggests that these progressive EDS are benefiting workers in terms of encouraging learning activities (and benefiting employers in terms of worker confidence to take on new responsibilities). While the public policy framework was an important factor it has arguably been less important than key initiatives undertaken by unions and some employers in promoting these schemes. The early progress on EDS appears to have been spearheaded by Ford and the Ford recognized unions in the private sector and by UNISON (the largest UK public sector union at the time) in the public sector.

From a union perspective an EDS is essentially a fund that fully or partially pays the fees of employees who want to take part in education and learning that is not directly job related. In some schemes paid time off work may also be available. The schemes can fund a range of personal, academic or leisure interests including hobbies or sport, opportunities to improve basic skills, or the pursuit of mainstream academic qualifications including college diplomas and university degrees. EDS are seen as helping employees develop their careers or personal interests; the focus may be on broadening workers' transferable skills or simply encouraging employees to return to learning or develop a learning habit. The union's involvement in negotiating, establishing and monitoring an EDS is considered essential to achieving these broad goals and meeting union members' learning needs.

The Ford scheme known as the *Ford Employee Development and Assistance Programme* (Ford EDAP) was set up in the UK in 1987 and is generally regarded as the forerunner of private employer EDS. It offers employees the range of personal education and training (non-vocational employee development) opportunities, discussed above, outside working hours. Many activities are offered onsite to fit around shift patterns and have included car maintenance, languages and keyboard skills but workers can also go offsite and study a range of adult education programs offered in the community.

A number of other companies have devised their own EDS and they may be grouped into three different categories:

- *Single schemes*: one organization – be it a company, or industry, or industry training body – develops its own scheme for its own group of workers (in a company, geographical area, or industry). These borrow from Ford EDAP.
- *Coordinated schemes*: several companies work together to set up a co-managed scheme to provide opportunities for all their employees.
- *Multi-schemes*: one body – usually the local Learning and Skills Council – helps smaller organizations design their own schemes, and provides them with support perhaps linking them to other small employers' schemes: networked more than coordinated.

The main features of EDS include: access to education and training (not usually job related); workplace-based (or nearby) provision often delivered by a local college or other educational/training institution; voluntary participation – although participation is encouraged and programs and courses are promoted; learning normally takes place outside of working hours in the workers' own time; and employers fund the cost of the learning within an agreed or negotiated range, which sometimes will be expressed as a yearly entitlement and can typically vary between as low as $200 or as high as $2,000 per employee.

The EDS can offer a "second chance" for members who may have missed out on previous school or college or community learning opportunities. EDS is also seen by unions as offering their members a chance to gain additional, more diverse transferable skills that can offer greater job security and improved career prospects. They also increase self-confidence, morale and motivation which can pay off not only at work (and therefore for the employer) but also in increased union activity.

Union action on EDS

Most of the major UK unions have become involved with EDS to a greater or lesser extent. They seek to be a participant from the outset in establishing workplace schemes and regard the most successful as those jointly managed by trade unions and employers. They argue for a commitment to the EDS by senior management and for the learning opportunities to be focused on what members want, not on business priorities. Unions are well aware of the educational biases favoring the most privileged and therefore argue for the entire workforce to have access to the EDS with a particular emphasis on access for the less privileged. Unions recognize that members will need advice and guidance as to what is available and how to take advantage of the opportunities. All this and course promotion too need to be included within the scheme. In some cases promotion is shared with the new union learning representatives (Forrester 2004).

The leading example of union action on learning is Britain's *UNISON Open College* concept, which includes labor education, basic skills, return to learn, recognition of prior learning and non-vocational and vocational training opportunities for all union members. This concept connects with members' immediate needs for education, learning and training opportunities and in time feeds into strengthening union activity and presence in society. It can also provide critical approaches to current issues, something which is lacking from more homogenized adult education and training. UNISON has recognized the failure of much basic adult education to reach workers in the lower socio-economic strata and stepped in with a Return to Learn (R2L) program. Further, they laddered that introductory course up through their Open College to other programs, even to the attainment of college degrees. It takes the "learning society" rhetoric seriously and accesses employer and state funding and claims time off work for its members. The R2L courses are based on UNISON/Workers' Educational Association (WEA) developed educational material. UNISON's link with the WEA for tutoring of R2L assures an adult education focus, with materials centered on collective understandings. This educational initiative benefited the members and the union; as a result of increased confidence and understanding gained through the courses, members volunteered for union representative positions and argued for policies to benefit their local membership (Kennedy 1995). It also should be noted that 80 per cent of participants in the R2L programs are women and overall approximately 25 per cent of members enrolled in R2L programs (Terry 2001: 190). (It should be noted that some of the above has been undermined by legislated ULR and a renewed focus on vocational training along with cuts in WEA funding.)

Other unions also developed these more comprehensive programs, linking basic union education to graduate courses for union members focused on critical social science perspectives but have been stymied by recent economic developments and government policies – it will be interesting to see if the newly merged union "Unite" can rescue some of the more progressive EDS practices of the former now merged unions (MSF/AMICUS and TGWU).

UNISON's Open College concept has also served as a key example of what unions can achieve in a hostile environment; it was able to sell itself as a major component of the government desired "learning society." Speakers from UNISON have addressed a number of union gatherings in the USA and Canada.

The impact of EDS

Evidence to date shows that employers who support non-vocational learning can benefit from their modest support for EDS; the learning spills over into increased participation in workplace training which together with the EDS can provide a more "adaptable and skilled" workforce. The boost in self-confidence, morale and motivation noted above can result in a more positive attitude to training and learning and to a greater commitment to work resulting in lower turnover and absenteeism. The first major study supporting these arguments was conducted on Ford EDAP (Beattie 1997) – it should be noted however that these studies are generally looking to encourage EDS and therefore can be expected to accentuate the positives. The concrete benefits to employers seem to be real but may also be overstated.

In Beattie's study it was found that employees felt better about their work and their employer and returned from their educational activities with greater loyalty and respect for the organization. With the push from EDAP (42 per cent of manual workers took advantage of EDAP) worker involvement in adult education leapt to more than three times the national average for this socio-economic group of adults, a clear benefit for the workers involved. Research has suggested that private sector EDS covered 20 per cent of the private sector workforce (Berry-Loud *et al.* 2001). This coverage is significant for schemes that increase payroll costs but are not at first glance financially beneficial to employers. The data provided in this paragraph, particularly Beattie's study, may be interpreted as lending support to the view that EDS operates as a sophisticated and subtle extension of employer control but it also points to greater employee confidence and learning that could result in more independent worker and union actions.

A number of reports have been produced in the UK documenting aspects of EDS (Berry-Loud *et al.* 2001; Lee 1999; Parsons *et al.* 1998). It should be noted however that the move to ULR discussed above and the institutionalization of "learning representatives" operating within a state-determined learning framework and union learning fund, may be pushing unions away from the more generic EDS towards narrower job-related training and has also undermined some of the independence of union schemes such as that of UNISON (and its link with the WEA).

Approaches to empowerment, HRD/learning and EDS

Empowerment has become a readily used descriptor of the impact of workplace learning and new HRD/HRM practices – the learning organization is said to *empower* workers to take control of their own work and learning – to improve their contribution to company performance. It is clear that the term "empowerment" is often being used to mask the basic corporate desire to improve employee productivity (this analysis is similar to many others: see for example Argyris 1998). It does not result in any increase in *power* to the workers vis-à-vis the power of employers and as Wilkinson has commented, based on his study of the hospitality sector, "empowerment as currently practiced is less empowering than employee participation of earlier times" (1998: 49).

This investigation of EDS has focused on UK literature, partly because of the availability of data and partly because of the government support that was given to EDS (that support in turn helped make data more available – more surveys, reports, etc.). Similar schemes operating under different names can be found in US and Canadian workplaces, both public and private. In some cases the small amount of funds made available to employees to pursue educational endeavors are limited to "workplace specific" training/knowledge but in others this can be quite open, similar to some training discussed above.

The case supporting EDS may be argued in terms of the advantages to both employers and workers but it is a mistake to argue that it is best depicted as "learning for and within capitalism" concerned with the "problem of credentializing learning" (Livingstone and Sawchuk 2004: 281), for in the case of many union negotiated and provided schemes, EDS *is* linked to all kinds of non-credential (i.e. non-formal) learning opportunities and in some cases to collective union education provision that *is* intended to be *empowering*. These schemes can provide a reawakening in individual learning that can be described as individually empowering in a way that can lead to other union education and to independent worker and union actions, not just to greater employer control.

Conclusion

Finally it should be recognized that unions can also find themselves promoting a different vision of work that goes beyond collective bargaining towards a greater empowerment. On October 27, 2009 the United Steelworkers (USW) announced a framework agreement for collaboration in establishing Mondragon-styled cooperatives in the manufacturing sector within the United States and Canada:

> The USW and MONDRAGON will work to establish manufacturing co-operatives that adapt collective bargaining principles to the MONDRAGON worker ownership model of "one worker, one vote."

> "We see today's agreement as a historic first step towards making union co-ops a viable business model that can create good jobs, empower workers, and support communities in the United States and Canada," said USW International President Leo W. Gerard. "Too often we have seen Wall Street hollow out companies by draining their cash and assets and hollowing out communities by shedding jobs and shuttering plants. We need a new business model that invests in workers and invests in communities."
>
> *Sturr 2009*

Unions are taking notice of Mondragon's success but it will be instructive to review what progress the Steelworkers and others make over the next decade not only in developing worker-owned cooperative enterprises but also in establishing union-influenced progressive EDS. Mondragon and other worker-owned cooperatives have demonstrated that ownership and control are important if the work, wealth, and HRD are to belong to employees. The question remains: what can labor unions do with that knowledge?

Notes

1 This chapter draws on Spencer and Kelly (2013) *Work and Learning: An Introduction*, Toronto: Thompson Educational Press.

2 Ken Loach's film *Bread and Roses* dramatically represents the story of a group of immigrant laborers struggling with the issues as part of the *Justice for Janitors* campaign.

References

Argyris, C. (1998) Empowerment: The emperor's new clothes. *Harvard Business Review* 76, 5: 98–105.

Beattie, A. (1997) *Working People and Lifelong Learning: A Study of the Impact of an Employee Development Scheme.* Leicester: NIACE.

Bernhardt, A., Dresser, L. and Rogers, J. (2001) Taking the high road in Milwaukee: The Wisconsin Regional Training Partnership. *WorkingUSA* 5, 3: 109–30.

Berry-Loud, D., Rowe, V. and Parsons, D. (2001) *Recent Developments in Employee Development Schemes* (Report RR310). London: DfES.

Bouchard, P. (2006) Human capital and the knowledge economy. In Fenwick, T., Nesbit, T. and Spencer, B. (eds) *The Contexts of Adult Education: Canadian Perspectives.* Toronto: Thompson Educational, 164–72.

Byrd, B. and Nissen, B. (2003) *Report on the State of Labor Education in the United States.* Berkeley, CA: Center for Labor Research and Education.

Clegg, H. (1978) *Trade Unions Under Collective Bargaining.* Oxford: Basil Blackwell.

Forrester, K. (2004) Workplace learning. In Foley, G. (ed) *Dimensions of Adult Learning: Adult Education and Training in a Global Era.* Sydney: Allen & Unwin, 219–25.

Freeman, R., Boxall, P. and Haynes, P. (eds) (2007) *What Workers Say: Employee Voice in the Anglo-American Workplace.* New York: Cornell University.

Honold, L. (1991) The power of learning at Johnsonville foods. *Training* 28, 4: 55–8.

Hughes, P. and Grant, M. (2007) *Learning and Development Outlook: Are We Learning Enough?* Toronto: Conference Board of Canada.

International Labour Organization (2007) Strengthening the trade unions: The key role of labour education. *Labour Education* 1–2: 146–47.

Kennedy, H. (1995) *Return to Learn: UNISON's Fresh Approach to Trade Union Education.* London: UNISON.

Kersley, B., Alpin, C., Forth, J., Bryson, A., Bewley, H., Dix, G. and Oxenbridge, S. (2006) *Inside the Workplace: Findings from the 2004 Workplace Employment Relations Survey.* London: Routledge.

Lee, C. (1999) *Learning from Employee Development Schemes* (Employment Brief no. 41). London: Institute for Employment Studies.

Livingstone, D. and Sawchuk, P. (2004) *Adult Learning and Technology in Working-class Life.* Cambridge: Cambridge University Press.

Miller, D. (2012) *Last Nightshift in Savar: The Story of the Spectrum Sweater Factory Collapse.* Alnwick: McNidder & Grace.

Parsons, D., Cocks, N. and Rowe, V. (1998) *The Role of Employee Development Schemes in Increasing Learning at Work*. London: DfEE.
Sawchuk, P. (2001) Trade unions-based workplace learning: A case study in workplace reorganization and worker knowledge production. *Journal of Workplace Learning* 13(7/8): 344–51.
Schied, F. (1995) *How did humans become resources anyway? HRD and the politics of learning in the workplace*. Proceedings of the 36th Annual Adult Education Research Conference. Edmonton: University of Alberta.
Sennett, R. (1998) *The Corrosion of Character: The Personal Consequences of Work in the New Capitalism*. New York: Norton.
Shelley, S. and Calveley, M. (eds) (2007) *Learning With Trade Unions: A Contemporary Agenda in Employment Relations*. Aldershot: Ashgate.
Spencer, B. (ed) (2002) *Unions and Learning in a Global Economy: International and Comparative Perspectives*. Toronto: Thompson Educational Press.
Spencer, B. and Kelly, J. (2013) *Work and Learning: An Introduction*. Toronto: Thompson Educational Press.
Sturr, C. (2009, October 27). *Steelworkers Form Collaboration with Mondragon*. Online. Available HTTP: http://www.dollarsandsense.org/blog/2009/10/steelworkers-form-collaboration-with.html.
Terkel, S. (1977 [1974]) *Working: People Talk About What They Do and How They Feel About What They Do*. New York: New Press.
Terry, M. (2001) *Redefining Public Sector Unionism: Unison and the Future of Trade Unions*. New York: Routledge.
Wilkinson, A. (1998) Empowerment: theory and practice. *Personnel Review* 27(1): 40–56.
Wray, D. (2001) What price partnership? Paper presented at the Work, Employment and Society Conference held September 11–13, 2001 at the University of Nottingham, UK.

9

HUMAN RESOURCE MANAGEMENT AND HRD

Connecting the dots or ships passing in the night?

Jon M. Werner

To the casual observer, little seems to distinguish the terms human resource management and human resource development. For many workers, both may be subsumed within their understanding of "HR," that is, the place in their organization that specifically deals with "people stuff." This "stuff" might include proper forms and legal documents signed at the start of a new job, the orientation program on the first day of work, registration for a training program, making sure that pay and benefit issues are handled properly, or conducting the organization's holiday party. Within academic circles, however, many have attempted to distinguish these terms, as well as to point out areas of overlap (e.g. Chalofsky 2007, Hamlin and Stewart 2011, Ruona and Gibson 2004, Swanson and Holton 2009, Thurston *et al.* 2012). An uneasy tension seems to exist between the two fields. For example, most HRM scholars would consider the Academy of Management (and the HR Division within it) to be their primary professional association. The majority of HRD scholars, on the other hand, look first to the Academy of Human Resource Development, though they may also be involved with the larger, and more diverse conferences held by other organizations.

Both human resource management (HRM) and human resource development (HRD) are multidisciplinary fields, bringing together research and writing from various disciplines such as economics, industrial/organizational psychology, industrial relations, management, education and adult learning, as well as other fields (Campbell 1971, Kaufman 2002, Mankin 2001, McGuire and Jørgensen 2011, Ruona and Gibson 2004, Swanson and Holton 2009). Monica Lee (2001) has referred to HRD as in a state of becoming, and this apt description fits well for both HRM and HRD.

How do HRM and HRD define themselves? How do they connect? Where do they diverge? The purpose of this chapter is threefold: (1) to describe the related fields of human resource management (HRM) and human resource development (HRD), (2) to clarify both what sets them apart, as well as the overlap between the fields, and (3) to suggest a synergistic way forward, where the growth and development of humans in workplaces is addressed holistically and from multiple perspectives. Oscar Wilde once humorously described the wife of an American minister living in England in the following terms: "Indeed, in many respects, she was quite English, and was an excellent example of the fact that we have really everything in common with America nowadays, except, of course, language" (Wilde 1887: 5). HRM and HRD seem to have much in common, except, of course, language. Some of these variances come from different academic and cultural backgrounds. Some of these variances come from geographic differences, especially between North America and Europe, though increasingly with new voices appearing from Asia, Africa, and South America.

In this chapter, I will first briefly address historical underpinnings for both HRM and HRD. I will then highlight some commonalities across the fields, i.e. areas of common interest. Next, I will emphasize the contributions across the fields, i.e. how both HRM and HRD have contributed to the broader study of individuals at work. I will then address prospects for the future, seeking to promote a healthy rapprochement between the disciplines. Although inevitable tensions and differences may affect HRM and HRD, the hope for synergistic efforts is evident – even in the inclusion of the present chapter within this larger volume on human resource development.

History lesson #1: from personnel management to HR management (HRM)

In the United States, personnel administration sprang up in the 1900s, primarily in large organizations (Kaufman 2008). With the surge in union membership in the 1930s and 1940s, labor relations grew as a related field of research and practice. In some manufacturing settings, labor relations staff dealt with the unionized workers, while personnel staff handled the non-union workers. Authors such as Kaufman have documented the significant impact that labor relations (and economics) had on the growing field of personnel administration, or personnel management (Kaufman 2002). Krell (2009) maintains that because of the declining union density in the United States, there is a dearth of labor relations expertise amongst current HR professionals.

In 1948, a small group of personnel administrators founded the American Society for Personnel Administration (ASPA). This group changed its name to the Society for Human Resource Management in 1989 (SHRM 2013). With its headquarters in Alexandria, Virginia, SHRM has a global membership of over 250,000, making it the largest professional organization for HR professionals in the world. SHRM publishes a monthly magazine called *HRMagazine*, which is geared towards the interests and needs of HR professionals. According to its website, "SHRM is committed to advancing the human resource profession to ensure that HR is an essential and effective partner in developing and executing organizational strategy" (SHRM 2013).

SHRM has led an effort to increase the credibility and professionalism of individuals working in human resource management, in conjunction with an organization called the Human Resource Certification Institute (HRCI). HRCI now offers various certifications, with the largest and most common one being the Professional in Human Resources, or PHR. In the PHR "body of knowledge," HRM is broken down into six main topic areas, i.e. business management and strategy, workforce planning and employment, human resource development, compensation and benefits, employee and labor relations, and risk management (HR Certification Institute 2013a). The greatest number of questions on the PHR exam has to do with workforce planning and employment (24 per cent), with 18 per cent of the questions pertaining to human resource development. As of August 2012 over 70,000 individuals had obtained the PHR certification, with a separate group of over 50,000 individuals who had obtained the Senior Professional in Human Resources (SPHR) designation (HR Certification Institute 2013b). It can be seen that SHRM, as well as most current HR professionals, would view human resource development as one central element – among others – that defines the field of human resource management. To state it more bluntly, the dominant view in HRM is that HRD is a subset within the larger field of human resource management. If there was a "big four" in terms of critical HRM functions, most in the field would list staffing, training, compensating, and appraising employee performance.

In terms of the SHRM/HRCI body of knowledge, HRD would include training, coaching, performance management, and organization development. There is clearly overlap with HRD definitions of human resource development (described in more detail below); however, there remains a tension here as to both what human resource development is, as well as concerning what the proper relationship is to the practice of human resource management. This leads to the second mini-history lesson.

History lesson #2: from training to HRD

One of the ironies of the field of training in the United States is that two of the greatest causes of growth for the profession were World War I and World War II. As one example, the US Government ran the Training Within Industry (TWI) service from 1940–1945 to address the job training needs of war-related industries (Dinero 2005). Over 1.6 million US workers were estimated to have completed TWI training programs. Further, Dinero (2005) cites the TWI training as the foundation for modern lean or quality efforts in manufacturing.

A parallel and related occurrence was the forming of the American Society for Training and Development (ASTD) in 1943, some five years before the forming of ASPA. The group was originally called the American Society for Training Directors, and was formed by a small group of trainers who worked in the petrochemical industry (ASTD 2011, Werner and DeSimone 2012). This group grew and expanded, and in the 1980s, it was ASTD that formally approved the use of the broader term human resource development to indicate that the field included more than classroom training (Nadler and Nadler 1989). Today ASTD has over 38,000 members in over 100 countries (ASTD 2011).

In an ASTD-sponsored study in the 1980s, McLagan (1989) presented a wheel illustration, in which HRD was depicted with three primary parts: training and development, career development, and organization development. Training and development included both classroom training as well as coaching. Career development was the means to prepare workers for future jobs and responsibilities, and organization development was the means of addressing issues of organizational structure and change. This breakdown served as a primary means of delineating major HRD domains for over two decades (Werner and DeSimone 2012).

In a follow-up ASTD-sponsored study, Bernthal and colleagues presented an expanded HRD wheel (Bernthal *et al.* 2004, Davis *et al.* 2004). In this depiction of workplace learning and performance, the HRD domain is expanded out to 10 topical areas: (1) designing training, (2) delivering training, (3) coaching, (4) career planning and talent management, (5) facilitating organizational change, (6) improving human performance, (7) managing organizational knowledge, (8) managing the learning function, (9) sales, and (10) measuring and evaluating. As can be seen, the three main areas from McLagan – training and development, career development, and organizational development – are all incorporated within this expanded wheel. Primarily, finer distinctions are made in the expanded wheel, especially concerning various aspects of training and development. Further, this breakdown is consistent with the systems or process model of training/HRD used in most textbooks in this area (e.g. Goldstein and Ford 2002, Noe 2013, Werner and DeSimone 2012, Wexley and Latham 2002, Yorks 2005).

An additional element of the 2004 expanded learning and performance wheel is the inclusion of two other sets of spokes, namely one set for traditional human resource disciplines, and a second set for other organizational disciplines (Davis *et al.* 2004). The HR disciplines include: staffing and job design, compensation and benefits, information systems, labor and employment relations, and rewards and recognition. The other organizational disciplines include operations/production, distribution, marketing/public relations, customer services, finance, legal, and research and development. All three sets of spokes (HRD, HRM, and other) are meant to revolve around business strategy at the hub, as supported by technology. What is most noteworthy for this present discussion is that HRD is seen as parallel or alongside HR and other organizational disciplines in promoting workplace learning and performance. The core elements of HRM overlap highly between the SHRM/HRCI definition presented above and that given by the 2004 ASTD authors. Bernthal and colleagues (2004) provide a valuable breakdown concerning the various domains of HRD, and then link this to roles and competencies needed by HRD professionals. This delineation is useful, as HRD as a field of study continues to define the parameters of the field, as well as the value added by research in this area (cf. Jacobs and Park 2009, Mankin 2001, McLean 2010, Ruona and Gilley 2009). This leads to the next sections on commonalities and contributions across the fields of HRM and HRD.

Commonalities across the fields of HRM and HRD

Even in this brief survey of the fields of HRM and HRD, it should be evident that both areas have very applied backgrounds. Both fields have strong links to "people initiatives" within business and the military. Further, neither field features strong or well-defined theoretical underpinnings. In reviewing 50 years of publications for the American journal, *Human Resource Management*, Hayton *et al.* (2011) documented the following dominant themes by time period:

- 1961–1971: Practice-focused
- 1971–1982: Theory development
- 1983–1999: Strategic HRM
- 2000–2010: Globalization.

Although exceptions occurred across the decades, this leading bridge journal for HRM academic and practitioner audiences experienced an increase in the number of both empirical and theory-based articles published. Within this journal, and by extrapolation to research on HRM topics in general, growing trends include greater use of theory and empirical research, and greater focus on strategic issues, as well as on international and global issues (Hayton *et al.* 2011).

Turning towards the field of human resource development, Yorks (2005) depicts the HRD field as undergoing a similar progression. Yorks discusses the early roots of HRD from adult education, behaviorism, and organization development, and then presents ways that HRD has become increasingly linked to both strategy and theory. Yorks (2005) closes his work by discussing the impacts of technology, globalization, and the challenges of maintaining a strategic focus on workforce issues. Other authors have made similar points concerning the field of human resource development, e.g. Jacobs and Park (2009), Streumer and Kommers (2002), Swanson and Holton (2009), Van Woerkom and Poell (2010).

Implied in this path from a primary focus on practice towards a greater focus on theory, strategy, and global/international issues is the notion that both HRM and HRD have often been criticized for their relative lack of theory, lack of strategy, and lack of particular concern or interest in international and global issues (e.g. Grieves 2003, Keegan and Boselie 2006, McLean and McLean 2001, Wright and Boswell 2002, Yawson 2013). Indeed, while both leading professional organizations, i.e. SHRM and ASTD, currently address the importance of strategic issues, a viewer of the websites of either organization might wonder where, in fact, this supposed emphasis on the strategic can be found, i.e. where is the content, or where are the initiatives, to back up the rhetoric?

Both HRM and HRD continue to address definitional and even existential issues concerning what defines them as a field and discipline (Carliner 2012, Chalofsky 2007, Hamlin and Stewart

2011, Kaufman 2008, Keegan and Boselie 2006, Lee 2001, Mankin 2001, Welbourne 2011). While progress is evident, both fields are obviously still in process in terms of becoming more theoretically and empirically grounded. In addressing this issue concerning training and development, Kozlowski and Salas (2010: 1) write that a hallmark of training and development research

> has been the shift from simplistic atheoretical research (e.g. "Is A training better than B training?") to theoretically driven research that endeavors to elucidate learning processes and to understand the effects of interventions, individual differences, and their interaction – via learning processes – on a range of multidimensional training outcomes.

Wright and Boswell (2002) address a similar theme as this pertains to research on strategic HRM.

Contributions across the fields of HRM and HRD

Both HRM and HRD have been heavily influenced by myriad psychological theories, as well as psychologists writing on topics such as training and development, career development, and organization development. A good portion of this influence (though far from all) comes from the subfield of industrial/organizational (I/O) psychology. One of the more prestigious annals in psychology is the *Annual Review of Psychology*, and the first chapter devoted to personnel training and development was written by Campbell in 1971. This has led to periodic updates over the years, with the most recent one written by Aguinis and Kraiger (2009). Two early research-based books written on the topic of training and development were by industrial psychologists, i.e. Goldstein (1974, cf. Goldstein and Ford 2002) and Wexley and Latham (1981, 2002).

The title of Goldstein's 1974 volume is instructive, i.e. *Training: Program Development and Evaluation*. A hallmark of I/O psychology is measurement and evaluation, and this is evident in this seminal work, as well as in much of the writing and research that has followed. Some variation of a systems model, i.e. assess-design-implement-evaluate, is now widely espoused in scholarly writing on training and development, and this process model can be seen in both early books (Goldstein 1974, Wexley and Latham 1981), as well as in subsequent work (Noe 2013, Werner and DeSimone 2012).

Kirkpatrick (1967, see also Kirkpatrick and Kirkpatrick 2007) created one of the more enduring evaluation frameworks in training and development, namely that good evaluation will look at trainee reactions, learning, behavior change, as well as tangible results or outcomes. This framework has also been heavily criticized – by I/O psychologists, HRM, and HRD scholars alike (see Werner and DeSimone 2012 for a review). A positive impact of Kirkpatrick's four levels has been the ongoing challenge to move beyond "smiles sheets," and "did you like the training?" forms of evaluation, towards measures that capture changes in learning, behavior, and measurable outcomes. The heavy emphasis on training transfer (i.e. is there meaningful change in workplace behavior after training?) can be seen as a logical follow-up to Kirkpatrick's approach to evaluation (e.g. Werner *et al.* 1994). In short, the calls for strong (or at least, appropriate) research design, as well as strengthening the quality and rigor of empirical research have been contributions to both fields, often driven by researchers with a psychological/measurement focus (Goldstein and Ford 2002, Kraiger *et al.* 2004). The relatively low levels of high quality, rigorous evaluation have been an ongoing concern (e.g. Campbell 1971, Kozlowski and Salas 2010, Salas and Kosarzycki 2003, Salas *et al.* 2012).

With its primary emphasis on workplace learning and performance, HRD scholars have often emphasized topics such as adult learning, lifelong learning, and the impact of learning style differences on learning and workplace performance outcomes (e.g. Bennett and Bierema 2010,

Knowles *et al.* 2011, McGuire and Jørgensen 2011, Swanson and Holton 2009, Watkins *et al.* 2011, Yorks 2005). This has clearly enriched the broader study of workplace issues, including HRM (Crouse *et al.* 2011, Vance and Paik 2011). Further, at least to this observer, it seems that there is a greater openness to – and appreciation of – qualitative research within journals that are more HRD- than HRM-oriented (e.g. Rocco 2010, Storberg-Walker 2012). While both HRD and HRM research has grown in the amount of theory-based and strong quantitative research now published, there appears to be greater acceptance for well-done case-based and other qualitative research within HRD circles. Similarly, while there are HRM researchers pursuing a critical/dialectical research approach (e.g. Keegan and Boselie 2006), such approaches are perhaps more visible in HRD circles (e.g. Lee 2001, McGuire and Jørgensen 2011). Finally, while both HRM and HRD researchers have addressed diversity issues – and thankfully moved beyond "diversity training for training's sake" approaches – HRD authors frequently address broader aspects of diversity, as well as their implications, e.g. Marques (2010), Schmidt *et al.* (2012).

Prospects for the future

Prospects are encouraging for the future of both HRM and HRD, as well as for the continued positive commingling of the two fields. For starters, both major practitioner groups, SHRM and ASTD, are more global, as well as more focused on strategic issues than ever before. Whether or not one always agrees with their viewpoints, both groups are seeking to exert more influence on public policy decisions relating to workplace topics. Next, the two largest academic groups, i.e. the Academy of Management and the Academy of Human Resource Development, are strong and growing, both in numbers and in visibility. An interesting recent development is the increasing collaboration between SHRM and the HR Division of the Academy of Management, with joint sessions and initiatives undertaken by both groups.

In the past, most of the "best" HRM research could be found in outlets such as the *Journal of Applied Psychology* or *Personnel Psychology*. For HRD, the first journal to focus exclusively on HRD topics, i.e. *Human Resource Development Quarterly*, began publication in 1990, under the editorship of Richard Swanson. One of the more encouraging developments of this century concerning HRD research is the addition of both *Human Resource Development Review* and *Human Resource Development International* as sources for scholarly HRD research. In addition, the journal *Advances in Developing Human Resources* has grown as a bridge journal between HRD academics and practitioners, in much the same manner that the journal *Human Resource Management* has served as a link between academics and HRM practitioners.

Further, there are now three journals in particular that connect scholars from psychology, management, education, and other fields, with topics pertaining to learning and education, namely, the *Academy of Management Learning & Education*, the *Journal of Management Education*, and *Management Learning*. Such journals have made remarkable strides in promoting the notion that pedagogical, or learning-related, research is worth conducting with the same rigor and standards as other more discipline-specific forms of research. This development bodes well for a growing rapprochement between HRM and HRD scholars wishing to pursue common topics and interests across the two fields.

Hopefully more efforts will bring together HRM and HRD perspectives and approaches in the future. As Theresa Welbourne (2011: 659) wrote in looking to the future of the journal *Human Resource Management*, the essence of HRM is "creating opportunities for people at work to be successful." A good portion of those opportunities will include HRD efforts or initiatives. Included within such efforts is a need to create stronger linkages between scholarship and practice (Cascio 2008, Ruona and Gilley 2009, Short 2006, Van de Ven 2007). Some of these linkages are occurring in journals such as *Human Resource Management* and *Advances in Developing Human Resources*, but more are needed. Some final thoughts are offered in the final section of this chapter.

Conclusion

Yorks (2005: 20–1) has written that:

> The fundamental purpose of HRD is to contribute to both long-term strategic performance and more immediate performance improvement through ensuring that organizational members have access to resources for developing their capacity for performance and for making meaning of their experience in the context of the organization's strategic needs and the requirements of their jobs.

This strategically focused statement concerning the purpose of HRD seems broad enough to fit many aspects of human resource management as well. Furthermore, Yorks (2005) mentions the importance of HRM systems being attuned to strategic HRD. In an effort to further delineate how HRM and HRD might work together side-by-side, a framework by Mankin (2001) will be utilized. Mankin's (2001) HRD model brings together ideas discussed above, and provides a visualization concerning how HRM and HRD might work together to address "people issues" at work. An adaptation of this model can be seen in Figure 9.1.

Mankin (2001) begins with the basic HRD components discussed above, i.e. training and development, career development, and organization development. He then brings in Ogbanna's (1994) depiction of the need to link organizational strategy/structure, culture, and human

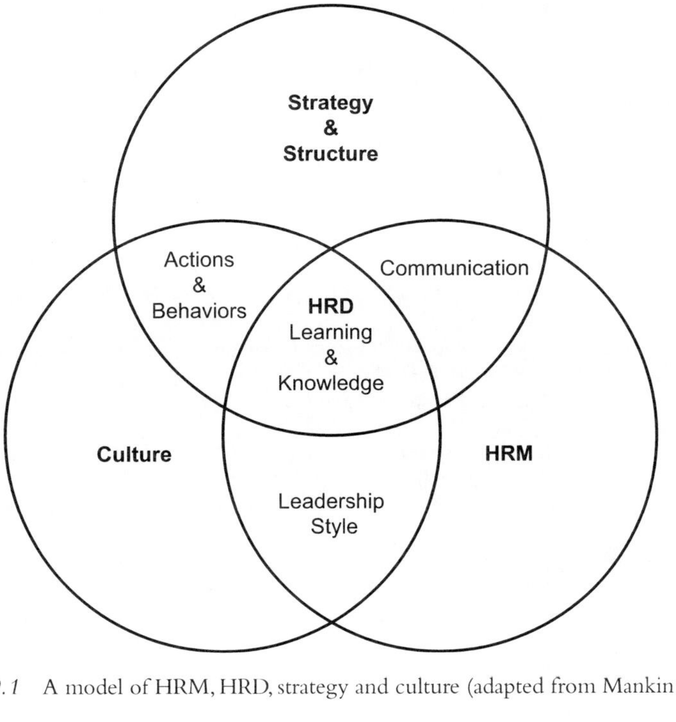

Figure 9.1 A model of HRM, HRD, strategy and culture (adapted from Mankin 2001)

resource management. Mankin (2001) then describes overlaps between the three circles (see Figure 9.1). The overlap between strategy and HRM emphasizes organizational communications and information, whereas the overlap between strategy and culture emphasizes individual actions and behaviors. The overlap between culture and HRM emphasizes leadership style, whereas the central overlap – the intersection of all three circles – is the emphasis on HRD, i.e. individual learning and knowledge.

This view of HRM as broader than HRD is consistent with the discussion presented above from both HRM and HRD sources. Topics such as staffing, compensation, and employee relations/communications are generally viewed as HRM topics that do not directly overlap with HRD. As such, communications and information systems depict the overlap between organizational strategy and HRM. The types of employee actions and behaviors should hopefully be influenced by both HRM practices (e.g. staffing, appraisal, rewards) as well as HRD practices (e.g. training and career development). However, the emphasis of this model is on the influence of both organizational strategy and culture on these employee actions and behaviors. Similarly, the overlap between organizational culture and HRM emphasizes leadership style, and captures the notion of different leadership styles to fit different situations and employees.

HRD can be viewed as the center point or core of Figure 9.1, i.e. that place where strategy, culture, and HRM overlap. The hope is that as the three circles converge in greater alignment, the degree of overlap increases, and thus the need for and centrality of strong HRD principles and practices increases (Alagaraja 2013). While all organizational leaders (and HRM professionals) will care about individual and organizational learning, HRD professionals will have these areas as their particular focus or *raison d'être*. This distinction can also address the branding issue for HRD and HRM raised by authors such as Carliner (2012) and Love and Singh (2011).

What will the future hold? Predicting the future developments in one area of study is hard enough, let alone across fields or national borders (Calver *et al.* 2013, Kim and McLean 2012, Welbourne 2011). Although differences of perspective and emphasis will continue, the future should see a closer alignment between the two fields, with commonality in maintaining a dual focus on the performance and well-being of individuals in organizations, while still maintaining a strategic focus on organizational survival and growth (Van Woerkom and Poell 2010). When individuals from HRD and HRM backgrounds dialogue and work together, let us hope that the common view is (to change the phrase from Oscar Wilde), "We have really everything in common with one another nowadays – *including* language." Work such as the current edited volume should further this process. May the future bring more "connected dots" between HRM and HRD, and fewer ships passing in the night!

References

Aguinis, H. and Kraiger, K. (2009) Benefits of training and development for individuals and teams, organizations, and society, *Annual Review of Psychology* 60: 451–74.

Alagaraja, M. (2013) Mobilizing organizational alignment through strategic human resource development, *Human Resource Development International* 16: 74–93.

ASTD (2011) *ASTD 2011 Annual Report*. Online. Available HTTP: http://www.astd.org/~/media/Files/About%20ASTD/2011%20annual%20report.pdf (accessed January 20, 2013).

Bennett, E.E. and Bierema, L.L. (2010) The ecology of virtual human resource development, *Advances in Developing Human Resources* 12: 632–47.

Bernthal, P.R., Colteryahn, K., Davis, P., Naughton, J., Rothwell, W.J. and Wellins, R. (2004) *Mapping the Future: Shaping New Workplace Learning and Performance Competencies*, Alexandria, VA: ASTD.

Calver, J., Cuthbert, G., Davison, S., Devins, D., Gold, J., Hughes, I. and Tosey, P. (2013) HRD in 2020: a hop-on, hop-off city tour, *Human Resource Development International* 16: 94–105.

Campbell, J.P. (1971) Personnel training and development, *Annual Review of Psychology* 22: 565–602.

Carliner, S. (2012) Certification and the branding of HRD, *Human Resource Development Quarterly* 23: 411–19.

Cascio, W.F. (2008) To prosper, organizational psychology should . . . bridge application and scholarship, *Journal of Organizational Behavior* 29: 455–68.

Chalofsky, N. (2007) The seminal foundation of the discipline of HRD: people, learning, and organizations, *Human Resource Development Quarterly* 18: 431–42.

Crouse, P., Doyle, W. and Young, J.D. (2011) Workplace learning strategies, barriers, facilitators and outcomes: a qualitative study among human resource management practitioners, *Human Resource Development International* 14: 39–55.

Davis, P., Naughton, J. and Rothwell, W.J. (2004) New roles and competencies for the profession, *T&D* 58(4): 26–36.

Dinero, D. (2005) *Training Within Industry: The Foundation of Lean*, Portland, OR: Productivity Press.

Goldstein, I.L. (1974) *Training: Program Development and Evaluation*, Monterey, CA: Brooks/Cole.

Goldstein, I.L. and Ford, K. (2002) *Training in Organizations: Needs Assessment, Development, and Evaluation*, 4th edition, Belmont, CA: Wadsworth.

Grieves, J. (2003) *Strategic Human Resource Development*, London: SAGE.

Hamlin, B. and Stewart, J. (2011) What is HRD? A definitional review and synthesis of the HRD domain, *Journal of European Industrial Training* 35: 199–220.

Hayton, J.C., Piperopoulos, P. and Welbourne, T.M. (2011) Celebrating 50 years: 50 years of knowledge sharing: learning from a field moving forward', *Human Resource Management* 50: 697–714.

HR Certification Institute (2013a) PHR. Online. Available HTTP: http://www.hrci.org/our-programs/our-hr-certifications/phr (accessed January 20, 2013).

— (2013b) *Statistics*. Online. Available HTTP: http://www.hrci.org/our-programs/who-is-certified-/exam-statistics (accessed January 20, 2013).

Jacobs, R.L. and Park, Y. (2009) A proposed conceptual framework of workplace learning: implications for theory development and research in human resource development, *Human Resource Development Review* 8: 133–50.

Kaufman, B.E. (2002) The role of economics and industrial relations in the development of the field of personnel/human resource management, *Management Decision* 40: 962–79.

— (2008) *Managing the Human Factor: The Early Years of Human Resource Management in American Industry*, Ithaca, NY: Cornell University Press.

Keegan, A. and Boselie, P. (2006) The lack of impact of dissensus inspired analysis on developments in the field of human resource management, *Journal of Management Studies* 43: 1491–511.

Kim, S. and McLean, G.N. (2012) Global talent management: necessity, challenges, and the roles of HRD, *Advances in Developing Human Resources* 14: 566–85.

Kirkpatrick, D.L. (1967) Evaluation, in Craig, R.L. and Bittel, L.R. (eds) *Training and Development Handbook*, New York: McGraw-Hill, 87–112.

Kirkpatrick, D.L. and Kirkpatrick, J.D. (2007) *Implementing the Four Levels: A Practical Guide for Effective Evaluation of Training Programs*, San Francisco: Berrett-Koehler.

Knowles, M.S., Holton, E.F. III and Swanson, R.A. (2011) *The Adult Learner: The Definitive Classic in Adult Education and Human Resource Development*, 7th edition, Burlington, MA: Elsevier.

Kozlowski, S.W.J. and Salas, E. (eds) (2010) *Learning, Training, and Development in Organizations*, New York: Routledge.

Kraiger, K., McLinden, D. and Casper, W.J. (2004) Collaborative planning for training impact, *Human Resource Management* 43: 337–51.

Krell, E. (2009) The rebirth of labor relations, *HRMagazine* 54(2): 57–60.

Lee, M. (2001) A refusal to define HRD, *Human Resource Development International* 4: 327–41.

Love, L.F. and Singh, P. (2011) Workplace branding: leveraging human resource management practices for competitive advantage through "Best Employer" surveys, *Journal of Business & Psychology* 26: 175–81.

Mankin, D.P. (2001) A model for human resource development, *Human Resource Development International* 4, 65–85.

Marques, J.F. (2010) Colorful window dressing: a critical review of workplace diversity in three major American corporations, *Human Resource Development Quarterly* 4: 435–46.

McGuire, D. and Jørgensen, K.M. (2011) *Human Resource Development: Theory & Practice*, London: SAGE.

McLagan, P.A. (1989) Models for HRD practice, *Training and Development Journal* 41(9): 49–59.

McLean, G.N. (2010) Human resource development scholar as rebel, *Human Resource Development Quarterly* 21: 317–20.

McLean, G.N. and McLean, L. (2001) If we can't define HRD in one country, how can we define it in an international context?, *Human Resource Development International* 4: 313–26.

Nadler, L. and Nadler, Z. (1989) *Developing Human Resources*, San Francisco: Jossey-Bass.

Noe, R. (2013) *Employee Training and Development*, 6th edition, New York: McGraw-Hill/Irwin.

Ogbanna, E. (1994) *Integrating strategy, culture and human resource management: a case study of the UK food retailing sector*, Paper presented at the Ninth Workshop on Strategic Human Resource Management, St Gallen, Switzerland, March 1994.

Rocco, T.S. (2010) Criteria for evaluating qualitative studies, *Human Resource Development International* 13: 375–78.

Ruona, W.E.A. and Gibson, S.K. (2004) The making of twenty-first-century HR: an analysis of the convergence of HRM, HRD, and OD, *Human Resource Management* 43: 49–66.

Ruona, W.E.A. and Gilley, J.W. (2009) Practitioners in applied professions: a model applied to human resource development, *Advances in Developing Human Resources* 11: 438–53.

Salas, E. and Kosarzycki, M.P. (2003) Why don't organizations pay attention to (and use) findings from the science of training?, *Human Resource Development Quarterly* 14: 487–91.

Salas, E., Tannenbaum, S.I., Kraiger, K. and Smith-Jentsch, K.A. (2012) The science of training and development in organizations, *Psychological Science in the Public Interest* 13: 74–101.

Schmidt, S.W., Githens, R.P., Rocco, T.S. and Kormanik, M.B. (2012) Lesbians, gays, bisexuals, and transgendered people and human resource development: an examination of the literature in adult education and human resource development, *Human Resource Development Review* 11: 326–48.

Short, D.C. (2006) Closing the gap between research and practice in HRD, *Human Resource Development Quarterly* 17: 343–50.

SHRM (2013) *About SHRM, mission and history*, Online. Available HTTP: http://www.shrm.org/about/history/Pages/default.aspx (accessed January 4, 2013).

Storberg-Walker, J. (2012) Instructor's corner: tips for publishing and reviewing qualitative studies in applied disciplines, *Human Resource Development Review* 11: 254–61.

Streumer, J.N. and Kommers, P.A.M. (2002) Developments in the emerging human resource development discipline, *International Journal of Human Resources Development and Management* 2: 1–16.

Swanson, R.A. and Holton, E.F. (2009) *Foundations of Human Resource Development*, 2nd edition, San Francisco: Berrett-Koehler.

Thurston, P.W., Jr, D'Abate, C.P. and Eddy, E.R. (2012) Mentoring as an HRD approach: effects on employee attitudes and contributions independent of core self-evaluation, *Human Resource Development Quarterly* 23: 139–65.

Vance, C.M. and Paik, Y. (2011) *Managing a Global Workforce: Challenges and Opportunities in International Human Resource Management*, Armonk, NY: Sharpe.

Van de Ven, A.H. (2007) *Engaged Scholarship: A Guide for Organizational and Social Research*, Oxford: Oxford University Press.

Van Woerkom, M. and Poell, R.F. (eds) (2010) *Workplace Learning: Concepts, Measurement, and Application*, New York: Routledge.

Watkins, K.E., Marsick, V. and Kim, Y.S. (2011) 'The impact of lifelong learning on organizations', in D.N. Aspin *et al.* (eds) *International Handbook of Lifelong Learning*, 2nd edition, Berlin: Springer-Verlag, 859–73.

Welbourne, T.M. (2011) Editor-in-chief's note: the next 50 years of Human Resource Management: moving forward faster and together, *Human Resource Management* 50: 695–96.

Werner, J.M. and DeSimone, R.L. (2012) *Human Resource Development*, 6th edition, Mason, OH: Cengage/South-Western.

Werner, J.M., O'Leary-Kelly, A.M., Baldwin, T.T. and Wexley, K.N. (1994) Augmenting behavior modeling training: testing the effects of pre- and post-training interventions, *Human Resource Development Quarterly* 5: 169–83.

Wexley, K.N. and Latham, G.P. (1981) *Developing and Training Human Resources in Organizations*, Englewood Cliffs, NJ: Prentice-Hall.

— (2002) *Developing and Training Human Resources in Organizations*, 3rd edition, Englewood Cliffs, NJ: Pearson/Prentice-Hall.

Wilde, O. (1887) *The Canterville Ghost*, London: John W. Luce.

Wright, P.M. and Boswell, W.R. (2002) Desegregating HRM: a review and synthesis of micro and macro human resource management research, *Journal of Management* 28(3): 247–76.

Yawson, R.M. (2013) Systems theory and thinking as a foundational theory in human resource development: A myth or reality?, *Human Resource Development Review* 12(1): 53–85.

Yorks, L. (2005) *Strategic Human Resource Development*, Mason, OH: Thomson/South-Western.

10
PERFORMANCE IMPROVEMENT
Goals and means for HRD

Seung Won Yoon, Doo Hun Lim and Pedro A. Willging

Performance improvement (PI) is commonly understood as (1) a concept (improving individual, group, or organizational performance), (2) a practical framework (models or processes with steps to follow), or (3) scholarly discipline (the International Society for Performance Improvement [ISPI] is the primary association among PI scholars). Often, the term PI is confused with other similar terms, particularly performance technology, human performance technology (HPT), and human performance improvement (HPI) (Stolovitch and Beresford 2012). For the purpose of this chapter, PI's meaning and relevance to HRD must be clarified.

We believe that PI offers useful conceptual frameworks and practical tools for HRD. In addition, concepts and interventions grounded in HRD can advance PI tools and frameworks; thus, HRD and PI must further converge (Cho and Yoon 2010). To this end, a clear understanding of the term and trends in PI research and practice is important. Therefore, we clarify relevant terms and review scholarly efforts to identify the core of PI research and then introduce widely practiced PI analysis/process frameworks, adding our insights.

Furthermore, effectively applying PI frameworks is not complete without technologies. One of the most pressing demands facing organizations today is to leverage technologies wisely to create and evolve a system that balances growth, equity, and environmental health. Roles that technologies play within the PI literature have continuously grown, but few frameworks exist to systematically incorporate emerging technologies into PI processes. Readers interested in technologies are also suggested to read the Virtual HRD chapter from the Emerging Topics and Future Trends section. In searching for a viable framework, our discussion will focus on how selected trends in technologies will impact workplace learning and performance.

Performance improvement: clarifying terms and relevance

One reason that PI sounds simple yet is difficult to grasp is because the goal and scope of PI can vary greatly depending on how one defines it. Clark (2008) synthesized the work of Robert Gagné and David Merrill to propose that almost all training (and also *performance*, italics added) content can be framed according to the following five content types: fact, concept, procedure, process, and principle/rules. These five content types vary in scope and usage, but when applied to designing HRD interventions, a concrete, targeted, and systematic solution can be created based on the identification or combination of task-matching content types (Clark 2008). For instance, when charged with a task to improve engineers' performance in technical writing, a standardized procedure with steps to follow can be created while facts (e.g. unique product specifications) and concepts (good or poor examples) are incorporated into relevant steps. PI is a fact given that any HRD work must improve the client's performance. PI is also a concept that has examples and non-examples (e.g. solutions that attempt to improve learning or development only). More importantly, some consultants sell PI as a procedure (more efficient and easy-to-follow steps). Yet for effectiveness, a procedure requires one to identify the demanding situation correctly; if the context changes, its applicability suffers. Performing CPR on adults compared with children is an example. Others present PI as a process that attempts to explain or utilize how a system works (processes are common in natural, technical, or business systems). A process can be created as the primary goal or as a backdrop of an intervention/solution and is essential for individuals who perform managerial or diagnostic functions. PI frameworks that we review later are exemplary processes. Finally, a principle or rule consists of causal relationships between concepts and, compared with procedures (which focus on efficiency and how-to), a set of rules and principles as a guideline enables individuals to align what and why with how (to make informed decisions based on the pros and cons of consequences). The ten principles of HPT from the ISPI, such as focusing on outcomes, taking a systems view, and establishing partnerships, are examples (ISPI 2012). As seen above, PI defies a single-dimensional definition.

Clarifying terms

One's understanding and use of PI greatly vary based on the individual's affiliation with the primary professional association, academic training, or job title. The most commonly used terms in the literature are PI, Performance Technology (PT), HPT, and HPI. More HRD professionals adopt PI as a fact or concept, or a principle, whereas consultants and individuals associated with the ISPI and those who take university courses or obtain a higher education degree in PI consider the term to be a procedure or process. ISPI on its website (2012) defines HPT as:

> A systematic approach to improving productivity and competence, uses a set of methods and procedures – and a strategy for solving problems – for realizing opportunities related to the performance of people. More specifically, it is a process of selection, analysis, design, development, implementation, and evaluation of programs to most cost-effectively influence human behavior and accomplishment. It is a systematic combination of three fundamental processes: performance analysis, cause analysis, and intervention selection, and can be applied to individuals, small groups, and large organizations.

Stolovitch and Beresford (2012) instead proposed the term human performance improvement (HPI), stating that HPI communicates the vision, concept, and desired end better than any other term (i.e. achieving successful accomplishments through people that are valued by all organizational members) (Kaufman 2006 cited in Stolovitch and Beresford 2012). They also noted that HPI is "what we wish to achieve and HPT is the means we use to achieve it . . . In a strict sense, it is a euphemism . . . It emerged in the 1990s, most likely because of its softer sound than HPT" (2012: 137). Stolovitch and Beresford further claimed that these two terms can be used interchangeably because both are an approach to accomplishing desired results from human performers by determining gaps in performance and designing efficient and effective interventions.

We refer readers who would like to know more about the growth of PI as a scholarly discipline to Part one: Foundations of HPT, particularly the chapters on definitions, origins, and history from the two edited volumes by Pershing (2006) and Stolovitch and Keeps (1999), respectively.

Our review of terms shows that PI is an inclusive term that can be interchangeably used with PT, HPT, or HPI. Stolovitch and Beresford's (2012) chapter, 'The Development and Evolution of Human Performance Improvement', is included in the section entitled "Performance Improvement" in a fundamental book of instructional technology edited by Reiser and Dempsey (2012). The other three chapters within the PI section include performance support, knowledge management, and informal learning. The term PI is also found within the name of the association ISPI, indicating that PI is clearly both the goals and means to be managed.

Clarifying relevance between PI and HRD

The evolving emphasis on intangible assets for organizational competitiveness, particularly human capital (Ulrich 1997), organizational knowledge/capacity (Nonaka 1994, Grant 1996), and social capital (Nahapiet and Ghoshal 1998), has been instrumental to the growth of PI and HRD. These frameworks provide the theoretical backings for investing in human behaviors and interactions. Our review undoubtedly indicates that PI scholars and practitioners have keen interests in identifying and utilizing practical procedures or methods. In comparison, the HRD literature shows that PI has been primarily used as a concept to determine the role and value of HRD. In the following, we review related studies and discuss PI's conceptual relevance to HRD.

Most ISPI publications recognize Thomas H. Gilbert (1927–1995) as the founding father of PI as a scholarly discipline (Pershing 2006). Gilbert's work started from the basis that formal training or instruction alone was largely ineffective in addressing various workplace issues. Huglin examined the citation patterns of articles, books, and authors within ISPI journals (2009a, 2009b, 2010) between 1962 (Gilbert's first publication year) and 2007, reporting that the core body of PI research is founded upon the fields of psychology, business, education, and sociology (HRD scholars have identified psychology, economics, systems theory, and adult learning as its foundations, Swanson and Holton 2009) and that the field's most frequently cited sources were the ISPI's own journals and books with the exception of the most cited authors (6 of 20 top cited authors were not from ISPI, and the top 10 most cited authors were Thomas Gilbert, Roger Kaufman, Robert Mager, Robert Gagné, Geary Rummler, Harold Stolovitch, Donald Kirkpatrick, Alan Brache, Walter Dick, and Joe Harless). Although Huglin did not analyze major subject domains of PI research, findings from most cited authors and journal articles indicate that major topics of PI research have focused on training, instructional design, performance analysis, educational technology, organizational effectiveness, and business process engineering. Interestingly, key PI scholars pointed out the lack of theory-building efforts and consultant-driven advancement of the field as critical barriers to the future growth (Rummler 2007).

Over the years, the role of HRD has changed from transactional functions towards strategic partners contributing to improving organizational performance and competitiveness (Gilley *et al.* 2002). The adoption of PI as a concept to determine the role and value of HRD is strongly felt when key books and HRD publications are examined. Swanson and Holton's (2009) popular HRD foundation book identified learning and performance as two major HRD paradigms. In their book, they put HRD's work in training and expertise development under the learning perspective while associating organizational development and change management with the performance perspective. They also claimed that the performance paradigm (more than learning) will more likely lead HRD to more strategic roles in organizations because the HRD value is to connect employee expertise with the strategic goals of the organization. Kuchinke (1998) also noted that, in the 1990s, whether HRD should focus more on learning or performance was a frequent debate, but the field must move beyond this dualism because, whether it is training or culture change, HRD's ultimate value is the degree to which it contributes to the organization's overarching goal. Using performance as a search term within the journals of *Advances in Developing Human Resources* and *Human Resource Development Review* (two AHRD journals that focus on HRD themes and theories) shows that various HRD interventions have been examined against the goal of improving the performance of individual employees, work group/business units, organizations, and occasionally, larger systems (e.g. communities, cities, and nations).

More research on the symbiotic relationships between the PI and HR fields (including HRD) is warranted. McLagan's (1989) HR wheel popularized many people's understanding of what HR does within organizations. The wheel identified HRD as consisting of organizational, training, and career development and Human Resource Management (HRM) as addressing HR planning, compensation/benefits, selection/staffing, performance management/appraisal, HR information systems, and employee relations. Ruona and Gibson (2004) noted that distinctions among these HR functions (e.g. HRD's focus on developing workforce skills versus HRM's focus on employee relations) have become blurry over the years to emphasize HR's strategic roles to create high-performing and learning organizations. In their study, they mentioned only HPT as an emerging field that HR professionals should note.

Within the PI literature, PI's relevance to other disciplines is only briefly mentioned. Such relevance includes: (1) PI uses core concepts and principles from behavioral psychology, instructional systems design, HRM, and OD (Rosenberg *et al.* 1999); (2) systems and communication theories are cognate fields to be further leveraged (Huglin 2009b); and (3) convergence among PI, HRD, OD, and organizational effectiveness is conceivable as these fields should deliver valued organizational results primarily through people (Stolovitch and Beresford 2012). Recently, Cho and Yoon (2010) discussed the implication of HR convergence to HPT and stated that HPT's use of instructional design, HRM, and OD as main solutions reflects how HR fields – particularly HRD – are closely related to HPT. HRD scholars have also performed citation network analyses with AHRD and ISPI journals and found that research on workplace learning (training, training transfer, instructional design) and performance (performance systems and support) comprised the core body of HRD's and PI's research networks (Cho *et al.* 2011, Jo *et al.* 2009).

Major PI frameworks: insights, benefits and issues to consider

The preceding section has established a solid backdrop to understand the meaning and scope of PI as well as its relevance to HRD. PI's rapid past growth can be attributed to the availability of practical models for consulting. For HR professionals whose primary work is not performance consulting, distinctions among popular PI frameworks might not be apparent. Therefore, this section introduces major PI frameworks followed by sharing our lessons learned. Perhaps the most popular and comprehensive PI framework is Van Tiem *et al.*'s (2012) HPT model (Figure 10.1), which has been officially adopted by the ISPI (we will henceforth refer to it as the ISPI model).

Figure 10.1 shows that the ISPI model consists of five components: (a) performance analysis, (b) intervention selection and design, (c) intervention implementation/maintenance, (d) evaluation, and (e) change management (most recently added). The ISPI model shows that (1) a PI process begins with sets of analyses (particularly about workers, workplaces, and environments) to determine performance gaps; (2) solutions are selected based on two factors: (a) alignment with

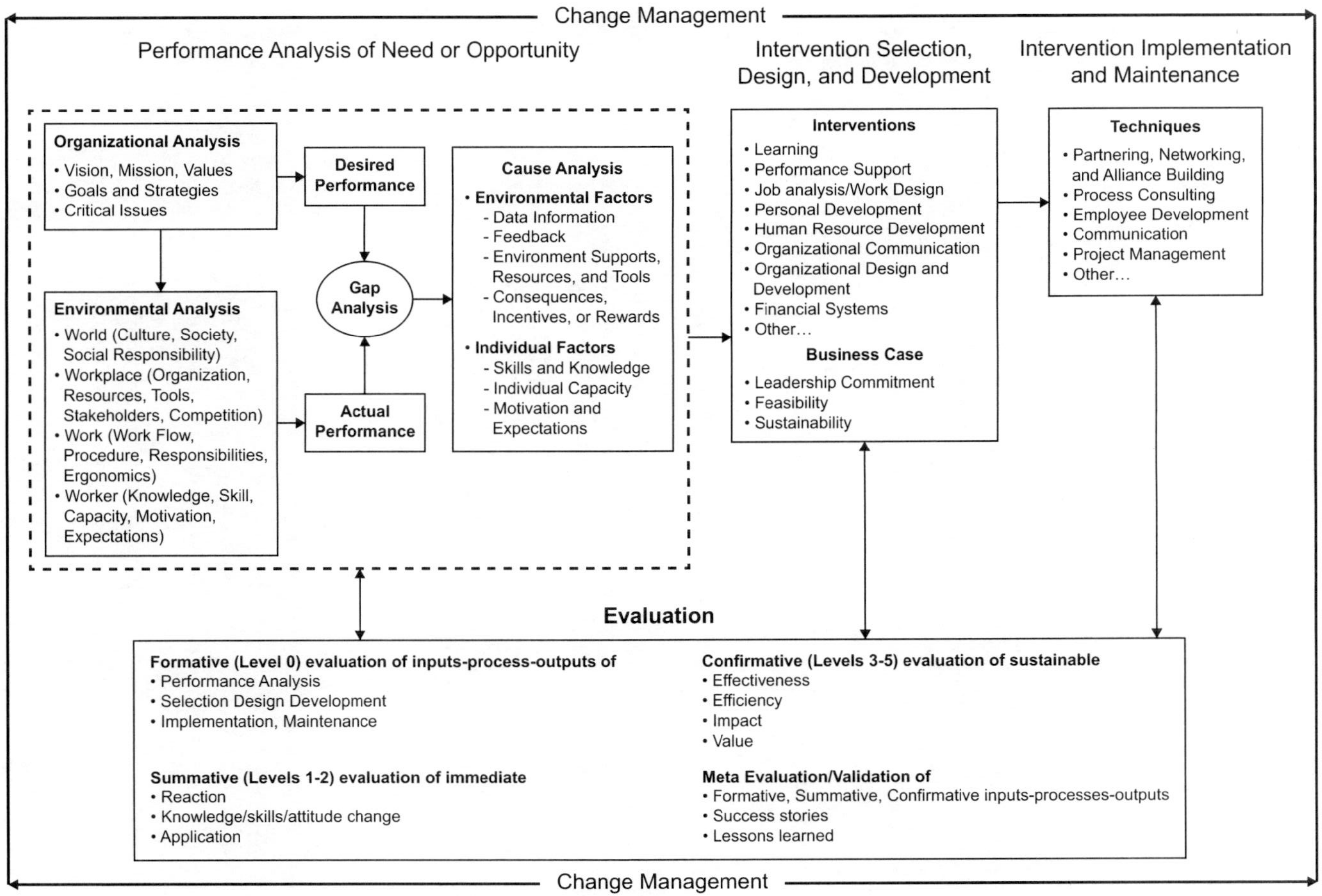

Figure 10.1 ISPI's performance improvement/HPT model (Van Tiem *et al.* 2012, used with permission)

major individual and environmental causes of client-agreed performance gaps and (b) practicality (i.e. business cases in the intervention box); (3) solutions are then implemented; (4) changes are managed; and (5) throughout the process, an evaluation follows each phase to examine the results formatively (to ensure the efficacy of each phase) and summatively (to measure the improvement of employee performance and business outcomes). Those who are familiar with instructional systems design (ISD)will find that the PI process from the ISPI model is akin to the familiar Analysis, Design, Development, Implement, and Evaluate (ADDIE) model. The major difference between ISD and PI is that the former is used to design instructional solutions to improve knowledge, skills, or attitudes (KSA) of employees while the latter considers KSA deficiency and instructional solutions as part of the performance problems and solutions.

ISPI has been publishing books and resources, such as newsletters and webinars, in order to expand the body of knowledge for each phase of the ISPI model. Due to the limited space, Figure 10.1 only mentions that others exist for selecting/designing/developing and implementing/maintaining PI interventions. What those additional interventions and techniques entail is best captured by ISPI's HPT handbook series (Pershing 2006, Stolovitch and Keeps 1999) and three edited volume series of (a) Instructional Design and Training Delivery, (b) Selecting and Implementing Performance Interventions, and (c) Measurement and Evaluation (Silber *et al.* 2010).

Swanson (1999) noted that the analysis phase is the most critical yet most poorly managed phase for the PI process. We agree with this statement because results of performance analyses determine the goal, scope, selection, and direction of solutions. Rossett's (2009) framework is very useful at the analysis phase. It proposed that four situations – (1) a roll out (of a product or service), (2) problem fix, (3) people development, and (4) strategy – present the most common performance analysis opportunities within organizations. She further stated that having a clear focus of any PI project and then examining ideals, drivers, and barriers from key sources (e.g. model/target performers, documents, service records) help prioritize critical performance issues. Mager and Pipe (1997) also proposed a useful seven-step decision-making process for analyzing performance problems (i.e. problem identification, value decision, work environment analysis, consequences analysis, skill deficiencies analysis, causes analysis, and solution decision).

Alternatives

Other popular PI frameworks emphasize different perspectives, particularly organizational development or systems theory. Rummler and Brache's (1990) PI model is very popular in the OD literature and utilizes two core concepts: the three levels of performance (organization, process, and performer levels) and the three dimensions of performance (goals and measures, design, and management). Using these two axial concepts of performance improvement (a three-by-three matrix of performance analysis), they developed the Nine-Performance-Model comprising the nine areas of PI in (1) organizational goals and measures, (2) process goals and measures, (3) job performer goals and measures, (4) organizational design and implementation, (5) process design and implementation, (6) job performance design and implementation, (7) organizational management, (8) process management, and (9) job performer management. Over the years, this model has been expanded to redefine organizational purpose as creating and delivering valuable goods and services to its market (Rummler *et al.* 2010).

Swanson's (1999) Systems Model of Performance Improvement defined PI as a process that parallels and enhances core organizational tasks (e.g. product development, customer acquisition, production, and order fulfillment) by aligning environmental factors (economic, political, and cultural forces) and organizational factors (mission and strategy, organizational structure, technology, and human resources) with the enhancement of core performance variables (mission/goal, design, capacity, motivation, and expertise) at the individual, process, and organizational levels. Last but not least, Gilbert's (1996) Behavioral Engineering Model (BEM, originally created in the mid-1970s), which is still popular and regarded as the first PI model, proposed six categories of environmental and individual variables as determinants of workplace performance (information, resources, and incentives at the environmental level and motives, knowledge/skills, and capacity at the individual level). These variables work together as stimuli, responses, and consequences.

Benefits and lessons learned

In practicing PI frameworks, our experiences tell us that PI approaches profoundly affect the culture, work routines, and behaviors that are rewarded and discouraged in great magnitudes; thus, we would like to emphasize that an event- or occasion-driven approach to PI should be avoided at all costs. We taught graduate-level HPT courses and supervised PI projects in various contexts, including faculty development in higher education, undergraduate admission, a local Salvation Army office, a learning and development support unit within a global insurance company, and test score improvement in a K–12 school. Some of them began as a reaction to explicit demands/requests (i.e. can you help with our issue of . . .?) whereas others started more proactively based on felt desires (e.g. we want to improve . . .). Regardless, projects were more successful and sustainable when strong support and commitment from the leadership were present. We saw varying degrees of resistance and enthusiasm when leadership/personnel changes were expected or employees preferred the status quo.

PI projects present many opportunities and challenges at different phases, but perhaps one of the more common and most pressing challenges is to clarify the primary focus of performance needs or opportunities. Most PI projects can manifest multiple possibilities (compared with the narrower focus of training needs analysis to determine knowledge/skill gaps). For instance, a program or software rollout can have people development needs/opportunities, but its primary goal is still an effective rollout; thus, determining and prioritizing primary performance opportunities together with the client are critical (performance focus and scope also set the boundary for subsequent phases of designing, implementing, and evaluating interventions). Another suggestion is that the results of performance gap analyses rarely indicate that performance ideals will be sufficiently addressed by a single intervention, and one will rarely possess expertise in all major areas of PI interventions. This is where we find that popular PI models can incorporate knowledge and tools from other disciplines more (topics recognized as important in HRD research, such as workplace incivility/violence, crisis management, or corporate social responsibility are cases in point). Last but not least, the widespread use of social media and web-enabled mobile devices are not about media or learning, but they are about the community in which organizations do business in today's environments; thus, understanding what these emerging technologies really mean to the organization and how to incorporate everyday-use technologies into PI processes is becoming essential.

Technologies: drivers of change

The PI literature has been at the forefront in adopting computer technologies for improving performance. For instance, electronic performance support systems (EPSS) find their root in the PI literature as technological solutions to improve productivity and work performance while countering the high cost and low transfer of training (Gery 1991). Rosenberg (2006) aptly noted that, as more knowledge management (KM), collaboration, performance support, and coaching solutions are blended into strategies and then implemented into work, work disruptions will be reduced while work productivity (and conceivably learning too) can increase. Pershing's (2006) latest HPT handbook places EPSS and e-learning under the individual and team-level performance interventions while putting KM as an intervention at the organizational level. Currently, technologies are discussed in PI frameworks as interventions (Pershing 2006, Silber *et al.* 2010) and resources for data collection/analysis (Rossett 2009, see also Rothwell and Whiteford's chapter in Moseley and Dessinger 2010). We feel that major emerging technologies must be further integrated into PI processes. For instance, greater knowledge about cloud computing and web application architecture (Shklar and Rosen 2009) can improve the effectiveness of the intervention implementation phase, while analytics (Fitz-enz 2010) strengthen the analysis of determining and measuring performance goals. To explore what roles technologies can play in PI, this section reviews key sources and technologies relevant to workplace learning and performance.

Waddill and Marquardt (2011) recently identified four major areas of technologies as essential for HR professionals: (1) learning technologies, (2) human resource information systems (HRIS), (3) communication technologies, and (4) knowledge management. Although their categorization of technologies seems to be based on different functional areas of HR work, included technologies highlight that HR professionals must be knowledgeable not only in traditional and more familiar domains of e-learning and HRIS, but also in areas of emerging technologies, particularly mobile learning, groupware, social media, and online communities, which are essential for more frequent virtual communication and collaboration. Similarly, Yoon (2008) pointed out that HRD professionals must understand how major technologies for learning, performance (KM, EPSS, portals, and dashboards [graphical displays of key performance indicators]), and even daily communications and information acquisition are converging to improve workplace learning and performance at individual and network levels.

Core trends: mobile, analytics, sensory recognition and web-enabled objects

New technological developments that promise to make our life easier and richer and our work more efficient are so frequent that identifying core trends can be daunting. Smart devices, high-tech gadgets, innovative software, and web applications continuously arrive in the mainstream population. Some achieve a successful adoption, while others quickly disappear or phase out. What seems to be clear is an increasing number of options. In education, an international community of educational technologists called the New Media Consortium has been releasing upcoming key trends in higher education, museum education, and K–12 education. Its 2012 *Horizon Report* (Higher Education Edition) identified six key technologies as significant over the coming several years: mobile apps, learning analytics, games, gesture-based learning, tablet computing, and The Internet of Things (Johnson *et al.* 2012). Although no direct equivalent research has been done in organizational settings, we see that those technologies are shaping workplace learning and performance in similar directions (companies releasing 3D simulations to mobile-accessible iTunes to introduce new products while gathering user experiences for market research and future changes is one good example).

Web-enabled phones and tablets – namely, mobile devices – are becoming increasingly powerful, affordable, and feature rich (through the explosion of mobile apps), making them the first choice for many people accessing the Internet. Mobile devices are contributing to ubiquitous access to data, microlearning/contents (Schmidt 2007), and greater use of social media/networks (Kerpen 2011). The vast explosion of connectivity and digital usage trails has led to an extensive analysis and use of a large amount of data, called analytics. Performance goals are becoming more knowledge centric in today's connected and networked environments. Identifying context-sensitive customer needs, forecasting product needs based on market performance, and analyzing environmental risks are no longer effective without large-data-driven business analytics. Transaction databases, discussion boards, social network spaces, e-learning platforms, and other forms of web-based communication/collaboration tools are generating unprecedented amounts of data, and analytics are used to identify interaction patterns and concentrations to uncover trends and relevant statistics to help in decision making. Big data lead to a challenge in storing and accessing information in a cost-effective manner. The technology related to scaling the infrastructure is cloud computing, which is the manifestation of the utility model of computing, where computing is seen as water or electricity – namely, commodities that users should be able to access without regard to where the services are hosted or how they are delivered. Examples of cloud computing include web-based email, collaborative writing (Wiki, Google Drive), software as a service (SaaS), file storage (DropBox), and file synchronization and backup, among others. New technologies such as cloud computing and business analytics that utilize distributed systems and unstructured text data reflect the growing importance in leveraging technologies for business performance.

Sensory recognitions and web-enabled objects refer more to how our interactions with machines, products, and environments will change. Our discussion of sensory recognitions incorporates game-based learning, gesture-based computing, and augmented reality (building upon 3D representations and virtual reality). When we review submission entries for e-learning or technology awards, we observe various 3D models in use for product marketing, salesforce training, and customer education. What used to be only a fantasy in science fiction movies, gesture-based computing is now getting close to reality in everyday life thanks to improvements in interface technologies. In gesture-based applications, the control of digital devices moves from a keyboard, a mouse, or a joystick to the movements of the body or face. Video games are already making use of these features that can be experienced through the Wii or similar gadgets by means of Kinect, SixthSense (a wearable gestural interface from the MIT lab), or software that can translate players' body movements into actions on a screen.

Augmented reality (AR) relates to virtual reality, sharing the use of 3D representations. Unlike virtual reality, in AR, the real world is not replaced, but supplemented with additional layers of virtual information. The augmentation is typically done in real time and in semantic context with environmental elements (Furht 2011). Through AR, real and virtual worlds can be blended, providing users with immersive experiences by means of a variety of devices. The combination of augmented reality, mobile devices, and global positioning system (GPS) technologies allows for location-based information, computer simulations with onsite data, and the manipulation of 3D virtual objects. The Internet of Things refers to the evolution of smart objects that embed contextual information, such as product details as well as environmental data. When such smart objects interact with web-enabled devices, users' computing devices become more effective learning, knowledge, and performance support tools, and their usage trails are fed back into the cloud for ongoing analytics and business decision making.

Implications for future research

In this chapter, we reviewed how PI is understood differently as (1) a goal (HRD's outcome) and concept (that contrasts with or complements learning) or (2) a methodical/practical framework (to conduct performance analysis and manage performance projects). By reviewing terms, core research streams, major PI frameworks, and trends in technologies, we attempted to show that

(1) PI is both ends (goals) and means (processes/principles) for HRD work and, equally important, (2) HRD and PI have symbiotic relationships and convergence potentials. In consulting situations, PI processes provide methodical and practical frameworks for conducting gap analyses, selecting/designing and implementing interventions, and evaluating the efficacy of decisions and results.

Our review of PI frameworks and trends in technologies also indicated that technologies such as EPSS and KM as well as some emerging technologies (web-enabled mobile devices, analytics, sensory recognition, and web-enabled consumer objects) affect workplace learning and performance in significant ways; thus, major technologies should be further incorporated into PI processes (e.g. analytics at the analysis and the evaluation phase). HRD research has been keen on factors affecting successful technology adoption. Waddill and Marquardt (2011) properly noted that, for the successful adoption of new technologies, organizations must address other important factors, including culture and environments, user skills or readiness, laws and regulations, technology standards and reusability, and cost and benefits. Although many recognize the growing importance of digital literacy in the modern workplace, what it entails and how it should be taught need more research as well. Other promising and important research areas also include the impact of interface design and the ethical use of personal information.

References

Cho, Y. and Yoon, S.W. (2010) Theory development and convergence of human resource fields: implications for human performance technology, *Performance Improvement Quarterly* 23: 39–56.

Cho, Y., Jo, S.J., Park, S., Kang, I. and Chen, Z. (2011) The current state of human performance technology: a citation network analysis of *Performance Improvement Quarterly*, 1988–2010, *Performance Improvement Quarterly* 24: 69–95.

Clark, R.C. (2008) *Developing Technical Training: A Structured Approach for Developing Classroom and Computer-Based Instructional Materials*, 3rd edn, San Francisco: Pfeiffer.

Fitz-enz, J. (2010) *The New HR Analytics: Predicting the Economic Value of Your Company's Human Capital Investments*, New York: AMACOM.

Furht, B. (2011) *Handbook of Augmented Reality*, New York: Springer.

Gery, G. (1991) *Electronic Performance Support Systems*, Boston: Weingarten.

Gilbert, T. (1996) *Human Competence: Engineering Worthy Performance*, tribute edn, Washington, DC: ISPI.

Gilley, J.W., Maycunich Gilley, A. and Quatro, S.A. (2002) Comparing the roles, responsibilities, and activities of transactional vs. transformational roles in HRD, *Performance Improvement Quarterly* 15(4): 23–44.

Grant, R.M. (1996) Toward a knowledge-based theory of the firm, *Strategic Management Journal* 17: 109–22.

Huglin, L. (2009a) HPT roots and branches: analyzing over 45 years of the field's own citations. Part 1: journal citations, *Performance Improvement Quarterly* 2: 95–115.

— (2009b) HPT roots and branches: analyzing over 45 years of the field's own citations. Part 2: book citations, *Performance Improvement Quarterly* 22: 95–104.

— (2010) HPT roots and branches: analyzing over 45 years of the field's own citations. Part 3: author citations, *Performance Improvement Quarterly* 23(3): 5–13.

ISPI (2012) *What is HPT?* Online. Available HTTP: http://ispi.org/content.aspx?id=54 (accessed November 28, 2012).

Jo, S.J., Jeung, C., Park, S. and Yoon, H. (2009) Who is citing whom: citation network analysis among HRD publications from 1990 to 2007, *Human Resource Development Quarterly* 20: 503–37.

Johnson, L., Adams, S. and Cummins, M. (2012) *The NMC Horizon Report: 2012 Higher Education Edition*, Austin, TX: The New Media Consortium, Online. Available HTTP: http://www.nmc.org/publications/horizon-report-2012-higher-ed-edition (accessed November 28, 2012).

Kerpen, D. (2011) *Likeable Social Media*, New York: McGraw-Hill.

Kuchinke, K.P. (1998) Moving beyond the dualism of performance versus learning, *Human Resource Development Quarterly* 9: 377–84.

Mager, R.F. and Pipe, P. (1997) *Analyzing Performance Problems or You Really Oughta Wanna*, 3rd edn, Belmont, CA: Lake Publishers.

McLagan, P.A. (1989) Models for HRD practice, *Training & Development Journal* 43(9): 49–59.

Nahapiet, J. and Ghoshal, S. (1998) Social capital, intellectual capital and the organizational advantage, *Academy of Management Review* 23: 242–66.

Nonaka, I. (1994) A dynamic theory of organizational knowledge creation, *Organization Science* 5: 14–37.

Pershing, J.A. (ed.) (2006) *Handbook of Human Performance Technology*, 3rd edn, San Francisco: Pfeiffer.

Reiser, R.A. and Dempsey, J.V. (eds) (2012) *Trends and Issues in Instructional Design and Technology*, 3rd edn, Saddle River, NJ: Pearson Education.

Rosenberg, M. (2006) *Beyond E-Learning: Approaches and Technologies to Enhance Organizational Knowledge, Learning, and Performance*, New York: Pfeiffer.

Rosenberg, M.J., Coscarelli, W.C. and Hutchison, C.S. (1999) The origins and evolution of the field, in H.D. Stolovitch and E.J. Keeps (eds) *Handbook of Human Performance Technology*, 2nd edn, San Francisco: Jossey-Bass/Pfeiffer, 24–46.

Rossett, A. (2009) *First Things Fast: A Handbook for Performance Analysis*, 2nd edn, San Francisco: Jossey-Bass/Pfeiffer.

Rothwell, W.J. and Whiteford, A.P. (2010) Using new technology to create a user-friendly evaluation process, in J.L. Moseley and J.C. Desinger (eds) *Handbook of Improving Performance in the Workplace, Measurement and Evaluation*, San Francisco: Jossey-Bass/Pfeiffer, 296–313.

Rummler, G.A. (2007) The past is prologue: an eyewitness account of HPT, *Performance Improvement* 46(10): 5–9.

Rummler, G. and Brache, A. (1990) *Improving Performance: How to Manage the White Space on the Organization Chart*, San Francisco: Jossey-Bass.

Rummler, G.A., Ramias, A.J. and Rummler, R.A. (2010) *White Space Revisited: Creating Value Through Process*, San Francisco: Jossey-Bass.

Ruona, W.E.A. and Gibson, S.K. (2004) The making of twenty-first-century HR: an analysis of the convergence of HRM, HRD, and OD, *Human Resource Management* 43: 49–66.

Schmidt, A. (2007) Microlearning and the knowledge maturing process: towards conceptual foundations for work-integrated microlearning support, in M. Lindner and P.A. Bruck (eds) *Micromedia and Corporate Learning, Proceedings of the 3rd International Microlearning*, Innsbruck, Austria: Innsbruck University Press, 99–105.

Shklar, L. and Rosen, R. (2009) *Web Application: Principles, Protocols and Practices*, 2nd edn, Glasgow, UK: Wiley.

Silber, K.H., Foshay, W.R., Watkins, R., Leigh, D., Moseley, J.L. and Dessinger, J.C. (eds) (2010) *Handbook of Improving Performance in the Workplace* 1–3, San Francisco: Pfeiffer.

Stolovitch, H.D. and Beresford, B. (2012) The development and evolution of human performance improvement, in R. Reiser and J. Dempsey (eds) *Trends and Issues in Instructional Design and Technology*, 3rd edn, Boston, MA: Pearson, 135–46.

Stolovitch, H. and Keeps, E. (1999) *Handbook of Human Performance Technology: Improving Individual and Organizational Performance Worldwide*, 2nd edn, San Francisco: Jossey-Bass.

Swanson, R.A. (1999) The foundations of performance improvement and implications for practice, in R. Torraco (ed.) *The Theory and Practice of Performance Improvement*, San Francisco: Berrett-Koehler, 1–25.

Swanson, R.A. and Holton, E.F. III (2009) *Foundations of Human Resource Development*, 2nd edn, San Francisco: Berrett-Koehler.

Ulrich, D. (1997) *Human Resource Champions: The Next Agenda for Adding Value and Delivering Results*, Boston, MA: Harvard Business School Press.

Van Tiem, D.M., Moseley, J.L. and Dessinger, J.C. (2012) *Fundamentals of Performance Improvement: A Guide to Optimizing Results Through People, Process, and Organizations*, 3rd edn, San Francisco: Pfeiffer/ISPI.

Waddill, D.D. and Marquardt, M.J. (2011) *The e-HR Advantage: The Complete Handbook for Technology-Based Human Resources*, Boston, MA: Nicholas Brealey.

Yoon, S.W. (2008) Technologies for learning and performance, in A. Rozanski, K.P. Kuchinke and E. Boyar (eds) *Human Resource Development Theory and Practice*, Lublin, Poland: Lublin Technical University, 245–62.

SECTION III

Theoretical approaches

11

CONCEPTUALIZING CRITICAL HRD (CHRD)

Tensions, dilemmas and possibilities[1]

Tara Fenwick

Critical modes of enquiry and practice in HRD have been taken up relatively recently in the field. It wasn't until 2002–2003 that prominent conferences began to feature sessions exploring critical viewpoints. However, interest seems to have mobilized quickly in the years immediately following, and by 2007 CHRD scholarship had burgeoned to the point where Callahan (2007) claimed that it represented "a" future of HRD research. Critical human resource development is by now, argue McGuire and Garavan (2011:5), "playing an important role in changing how HRD sees itself and identifying whom it serves . . . bringing clarity to the field and helping it secure a sustainable future". Critical HRD also, as evidenced in the collection edited by Stewart *et al.* (2006), is a diffuse association of critical perspectives, pedagogies, and declarations of what critical HRD means.

These diverse perspectives may be argued to share two commitments. First, CHRD generally promotes *critical analysis of power relations* in work organizations, particularly in the many taken-for-granted work practices that can reduce human knowledge, relationships and identity to the dictates of productivity. Second, CHRD tends to be *oriented towards action* that aims to address unfair inequities and improve life and well being in work organizations. Naturally tensions and dilemmas about what precisely is "critical" and how to engage critical learning flourish within CHRD as energetically as they do in the critical social sciences more broadly. This chapter takes up a broad discussion of these tensions, particularly around critiques of "emancipation" and empowerment leveled at the more zealous, less reflexive enunciations of critical learning and development. The aim is to offer a more diffuse and perhaps less morally strident orientation to CHRD.

The first section of the chapter outlines the tensions embedded in what comprises "critical" in critical HRD. The second offers three dimensions as a departure point to consider critical human resource development. Section three discusses a series of dilemmas inherent in these principles and in the general project of CHRD, both theoretical and practical. The final section suggests approaches to educating for CHRD that attempt to navigate these dilemmas without losing central critical principles.

The beginnings of CHRD: what is "critical"?

Although feminist HRD work was being published in the late 1990s, and a groundbreaking volume applying Foucauldian analysis to HRD practices appeared back in 1994 (Barbara Townley's *Reframing Human Resource Management: Power, ethics and the subject at work*), HRD literature in the main avoided the engagement with critical social theory that exploded in the critical management studies movement of the 1990s. In their review of 600 papers presented to the Academy of Human Resource Development (AHRD) 1996–2000, Bierema and Cseh (2003: 23–4) concluded that:

> HRD focuses little on issues of social justice in the workplace or larger social context. Women's experiences as well as those of other diverse groups is ignored, as are asymmetrical power arrangements. Gender/race/ethnicity is not used as a category of analysis – even when data are collected by gender. Organizational "undiscussables" such as sexism, racism, patriarchy, and violence receive little attention in the literature yet have considerable impact on organizational dynamics. Finally, HRD research has only weakly advocated change.

Bierema and Cseh ended with a call for critical perspectives in HRD practice and research: for greater focus on how HRD might reproduce power relations in organizations, for questions about "who benefits" from HRD, and for strategies that address gender and equity issues. The first explicitly "critical" session at an AHRD conference was held in 2002, with the intent of unpicking assumptions and challenging "the predominantly performative and learning-outcome focus of the HRD field" (Elliott and Turnbull 2002: 971). The UK Critical Management Studies Conference inaugurated a Human Resources Management stream in its 2003 annual conference: the call for papers expressed puzzlement that HRD "has largely slipped outside the gaze of critical management analysts (CMS 2002). Presenting at that conference, Sambrook (2004) argued the importance of bringing discourses of "being critical" to bear *among* current conflicting eclectic discourses of HRD, without privileging the critical iconoclast pitted against the HRD "other".

But what exactly is it to "be critical"? Theoretical notions are wide-ranging in critical studies of management, education, accounting, law, and health care as well as, increasingly, HRD. Common aims in all of these critical professional studies are to challenge taken-for-granted configurations of power and control that determine de facto knowledge authorities, limit identities, create exclusions, reinforce repressive practices, and generally conceal their own tactics of consolidating resources for the few. The general goal tends to be organizational and broader societal reform in terms of justice, democracy and equity. What constitutes such reform is broadly debated, of course, and subject to dynamics in particular contexts. Activities of challenging ideology, recognizing hegemony, and unmasking power figure prominently in critical management as well as CHRD studies.

However, caution is advised to avoid conflating the positional distinctions of various critical views taking up these themes. Most of these assert very different, even incommensurable, views about the nature of organizations, power, and ways forward. For example, some Marxist views (Brookfield and Holst 2010) argue that anything short of revolutionary action for worker control of the means of production is not emancipatory. Others focus on recognition of sexual orientation, race and gender politics beyond class. Post-structural views tend to focus upon understanding how flows of discursive practices produce particular subjects and regimes of knowledge in work.

To show patterns amidst this pluralism, Fournier and Grey (2000) suggest two main "lines of tension" in critical management studies. One concerns the nature of power, with tension between those arguing from a structural Marxist understanding of exploitation and contradiction, and those who understand power as continually circulating among heterogeneous assemblages of people and things. Another tension concerns critical engagement with practice. Some CMS writers argue that a pragmatic orientation dilutes critical integrity, and others that a purist academic stance is elitist and insular. Meanwhile practitioners juggle uncomfortably with both pragmatism and purism. In any case, a complicating factor in critical management studies is the quick slide that can occur from analysis to prescription for particular practices, sometimes blurring ontological arguments with normative assertions about desirable conditions and virtuous behaviors. Appeals for social justice and liberation can obscure what exactly is the object of inquiry and what assumptions are being made in the selection and analysis of particular organizing processes.

The potential here for problems is neatly summarized by Perriton and Reynolds (2004), whose focus was management development but pertinent to HRD more broadly. They trace the emergence of the "critical approach" in management development, showing that it was mostly influenced by ideas of the educator Paulo Freire who of course was writing for a very different context than twenty-first-century human resource developers: his 1970 book *Pedagogy of the Oppressed* was about liberation of poverty-stricken peasants in mid-twentieth-century Brazil through collective literacy education. Freirian-based pedagogies were borrowed to "conscientize" students in management schools; that is, to develop students' political agency to challenge those individual and collective oppressions embedded in conventional managerialist ideologies, such as techno-rational control, unitarism, and worker subjection to profit and productivity. Critical pedagogy developed largely for public school education further influenced the uptake of what became an emancipatory focus in critical management development. That is, not only are the processes of power and ideology foregrounded along with inequalities they produce, but the fundamental aim of critical management education has been to realize "a more just society based on fairness, democracy and 'empowerment'" (Perriton and Reynolds 2004: 63) largely by contesting inequities and by liberating the voices of the marginalized.

The problems of such critical approaches to development and learning have been widely addressed by feminist and post-structural writers, most notably by Ellsworth (1989). The notion of emancipation remains a very hierarchical and presumptive intrusion of the enlightened into the lives of those dupes who are considered less fortunate. The desirable end point is usually determined by the gaze of the critical educator, as argued elsewhere (Fenwick 2005b). Such essentialist binaries between dominant and oppressed groups hardly reflect the complex blurriness and continual negotiations and subversions of power among multiple networks and sub-groups in contemporary organizations (Fenwick 2005b). Nor do they map persuasively onto the diversity and hybrid identities of organizational members and groups that are continually produced by complex intersections of gender, race, sexuality, generation and language. Overall, Perriton and Reynolds (2004: 69) call for a general re-envisioning of critical development that presents:

> a challenge to the rationalist assumptions that underpin critical reflection as the core pedagogical practice [of CHRD], the charge that it is not only gender blind in its pedagogical practices but that it also lacks reflexivity.

In summary, the meanings of "critical" in CHRD are diffuse and contested, emanating as they do from widely different philosophical bases. These histories and purposes of different critical trajectories that influence CHRD need careful analysis to highlight their particular assumptions and obsessions, and to map their fit with HRD. Finally, the problems of emancipatory intents, and the importance of self-reflexivity, are worth close attention in critical HRD.

Dimensions of CHRD

Because of this eclectic terrain of critical ideas associated with CHRD, any argument in this field needs to declare its own particular critical position, particularly when critical treatises can quickly become normative and then prescriptive. For purposes of this chapter, therefore, three dimensions first introduced in Fenwick (2005a) are described as a point of departure for dialogue. These are intended neither to provide a heuristic device for CHRD writers and practitioners, nor to totalize diverse critical positions. Rather, these three dimensions aim to recognize similarities across selected critical perspectives to draw forth certain shared values. They draw largely from critical HRD and management studies (Alvesson and Willmott 1996, Bierema 2008, McGuire and Garavan 2011, Sambrook 2009, Townley 1994) that focus on questions of interests served by the organization of work, exclusions from the construction of knowledge, effects of economic ideologies, power relations underpinning organizational structures, and discursive practices that regulate individuals within these structures. These dimensions also draw from feminist and anti-racist pedagogies the injunction to engage people in critical analysis of social practices, texts and environments to examine the inequities produced and the possibility for alternate subject positions and more just and generative practices (e.g. Alfred and Chlup 2010, Brookfield and Holst 2010, Metcalfe 2008). This framework is not intended to eliminate the vibrant pluralism now flourishing in the general field of critical human resource development studies, but rather to offer a starting point for investigating their nuances.

As noted in the introduction, two principles appear to underpin these dimensions. First, CHRD promotes *critical analysis of power relations*, commonly focused on inequities. In context of work organizations, this analysis challenges the subjugation of human knowledge, skills, relationships and education to orthodoxies of organizational and management knowledge, goals and practices. Second, CHRD tends to be *oriented towards action* that that will improve life and well being in work organizations. CHRD assumes that HRD practitioners, managers and employees can learn, for example, to notice and question the ways organizational structures can compromise human dignity and health, ethical engagements with stakeholders, and ecological and social responsibility. It assumes that practitioners can learn to envision and help bring about reform of organizations and management practice to enable, in Kincheloe's (1999) words, more just, equitable, life-giving and sustainable workplaces.

Working from these two principles, the following three dimensions are proposed for critical human resource development as a site of practice.

- ***Purposes of critical human resource development*** are primarily to promote practitioners' critical awareness of power relations and their effects, as well as their capacity to act towards particular projects within these power relations. That is, CHRD opens spaces and directions for practitioners' critical questioning of key organizational practices and discourses that influence their own and others' thinking, identities, and behaviors. Opening spaces implies unpicking the complex power relations that hold together what appear to be stable and immutable routines, texts and goals, and questioning the central contradictions embedded within them. Opening spaces is also about making available alternate spaces, which means introducing people to theoretical tools that provide various critical entry points and angles of questioning, while exposing these tools themselves to critical questioning. For example, students can be introduced to projects such as organizational reform in directions aligned with justice, equity, sustainability and democratic participation. But they are also encouraged to examine the internal tensions and the practical difficulties in such projects.

- ***Assumptions of critical human resource development*** include understanding both management and human resource knowledge and skill as contested, within the contested relations of organizations. No monolithic body of knowledge and no orthodoxy of procedure can address these contestations adequately. Further, these relations are fluid. Tools, texts, policies and people are brought together and translated into practices, institutions and knowledge in ways that appear stable, and whose construction is concealed by a-historical illusions of homogeneity and alignment. CHRD assumes, however, that the circulations of power and the various negotiations that have created and are holding together all of these practices and identities can in fact be traced and exposed. This exposure reveals important differences in the organizational landscape. This exposure can also dissolve or at least weaken the apparent power of certain orthodoxies, and ultimately can lead to expansion: expansion of possibilities and capacities, of individuals as well as of objectives, processes and structures. CHRD also assumes that when individuals become aware and, ideally, appreciative of difference, a practice of HRD can be devised that acknowledges and even works productively with difference.
- ***Practices of critical human resource development*** engage practitioners as well as educators in a critical reading of their worlds. Activities push people to problematize taken-for-granted conditions, representations, practices and policies. Managers are engaged in inquiry about the justice and equity of these conditions, and encouraged to see links between personally experienced struggles and larger economic, socio-cultural and political forces. CHRD also creates uncomfortable spaces for people to question whose interests are served by their practices, how knowledge is constructed, what knowledge counts and who influences its assessment. CHRD challenges people to truly acknowledge human difference and how difference is treated in organizations. People are encouraged to question their own positionality, their investments and desires, and their (often) contradictory implications in sustaining particular ideologies, interests and power relations in communities of difference – both in organizations and in the classroom. Reflexivity, both philosophical and methodological, is central in CHRD to challenge not only orthodoxies of "managerial" regulation, but also the imposition of emancipatory efforts. The main orientation of CHRD is towards practice: exploring approaches practitioners might adopt in organizations to interrupt unreasonable inequity, promote inclusion, and encourage critical questioning of the way-things-are towards more productive processes.

In this framework, the central purpose and approach of CHRD remains political: engaging new managers in recognizing relations of power, locating undesirable effects of these power relations for oneself and others touched by the organization's work, and envisioning action that can be taken or encouraged by managers. Determining just what comprises desirable action is rife with moral assumptions. Virtuous ideals like justice, equity and democracy bear a complex relationship to organizational action in a global capitalist economy, leading to tensions in critical human resource development.

Tensions and dilemmas of CHRD

As was intimated earlier, some dilemmas emerge when trying to graft ideals of critical theory and pedagogy onto human resource development. These critical principles of justice, democracy, equity and participation take what Perriton and Reynolds (2004) call the moral high ground. But practices of exposure, iconoclasm and reflexivity inevitably produce conflict when inserted into the complex everyday worlds of HRD practice and organizational life.

Critical practice in capitalist structures?

Some critical theorists (e.g. Brookfield and Holst 2010) might argue that emancipatory educative practice within capitalist institutions, particularly in the hands of HRD or management, is completely untenable: what emerges would always be a domesticated shadow of critical struggles against oppression, exploitation and inequity. It is all very well to say that critical studies and organizational practice should be married. However, without further theorizing of fundamental contradictions and their political play in workplace organizations, little may be gained beyond further disillusion or duplicity. Critical human resource development needs to address these very contradictions, perhaps linking itself more explicitly to critical studies already flourishing in professional fields of accounting, law, and medicine as well as education and management. At the same time, an effective CHRD will be grounded in people's actual needs and experiences working in organizations. To disengage from practice is to confine critique to research and theory, risking hermetic scientism or naïve prescriptions.

Sustaining radical purpose amidst managerialism?

Another dilemma concerns the feasibility of critical practice in organizations. Some argue that human resource development is becoming increasingly aligned with management and managerialism (Bierema 2009). Conventional expectations for managers are held in place by prevailing organizational structures of authority, systems of reward and accountability, and divisions of labor. Critical human resource practice is difficult to sustain without either system change or sophisticated strategies to work through such complexities. Both workers and managers are usually quite constrained in terms of the actions they could take, the decisions they could make and the influence they could have, despite organizational resolves for empowered, self-directed teams and thinking workforce. Further, as argued elsewhere (Fenwick 2003, 2005a), empowerment as a concept has long been co-opted in popular management literature for purposes of promoting productivity and organizational gain rather than organizational reform. There is by now healthy suspicion of management declarations of support for non-hierarchical structures, collaborative management approaches, and continuous learning. All of these have been used to introduce reengineering efforts that in fact have sedimented inequities and undemocratic power relations.

Developing resources critically?

The contradiction of purporting commitments to human equity and empowerment while calling people "resources" has been recognized for some time (Stewart *et al.* 2006). Furthermore, "development" can often be enacted as a hierarchical rather than cooperative relation, where the "other" is constituted in the developer's gaze as progressing from incompleteness to wholeness. In the tradition of HRD this process has been driven by organizational performance needs and conducted through "technologies of control", as Townley (1994) describes HRD practices such as performance appraisal and classification. Radical commitments challenge this hierarchical management of human learning and subjugation of human lives to organizational productivity, and seek to explore a range of more worker-centered definitions of meaningful work and growth. Furthermore, radical educative approaches aim not to increase humans' exchange value, but to liberate human beings and their knowledge from this commodification. Contemporary critical orientations tend to seek a reframing of historic conceptions of production and exchange. This reframing is not conducted through imposed "technologies" but through participatory dialogues in dialectic with collective action. Thus there appear to be ideological contradictions between the radical orientation of critical dimensions and the performance-development orientation of much mainstream HRD practice.

Fallibility of critical perspectives?

A further dilemma inheres simplistic conceptualizations of domination/oppression presented by certain Marxian critiques. To view managers and workers as separate groups in unitary and fixed positions is to ignore today's shifting and often networked organizations and identities. Similarly, assumptions that singular groups in the workplace intentionally wield domination and control over others are insupportable amidst complex and overlapping interests and power circulations. These dynamics are linked with a host of affiliations and identifications related not just to class but to language, race, gender, sexual orientation, generation, and knowledge in particular cultural contexts. It is difficult to point to clear centers and peripheries in organizations, or to power situated unambiguously in any one position. Too often managers are portrayed as homogenous, or unproblematically as the oppressors. But emancipatory approaches can present an equally insalubrious rescue. As Alvesson and Deetz (1996: 195) point out, "the irony of an advocate of greater equality pronouncing what others should want or how they should perceive the world 'better' is not lost on either dominant or dominated groups".

Diluting critique?

In critical management studies as well as CHRD, this dilemma is voiced in debate between those advocating for developing a practical critical agenda, and those worried that such engagement dilutes the critical project. Alvesson and Willmott (1996) argued some time ago that engaging critical theory *within* organizations helps avoid replacing "old" instrumental management dogma with "new" critical ideology. Critical projects worked through messy organizational realities also avoid, write Alvesson and Willmott, a theoretical tendency towards simplistic iron cage depictions of organizations, or broad utopian visions that ignore micro-problems and possibilities persisting in organizations.

Practical difficulties?

However, the question of *how* to integrate critical theory with workplace practice continues to trouble. As McGuire and Garavan (2011) point out, a key problem dogging critical writings in HRD is their tendency to focus on problematizing what *is* rather than providing alternative practices for what *could be*. Feasible practical strategies are needed perhaps more than extended debates about critical social theories in work. McGuire and Garavan suggest that strategies for change, as well as analysis, be developed simultaneously in a multi-leveled approach: individual, organizational, and community/societal. The next section offers some beginning ideas towards the first two levels.

Educating for CHRD

In the dimensions offered earlier, the practice of CHRD is about creating spaces for people to question whose interests are served by their practices, how knowledge is constructed, what knowledge counts and who influences its assessment. The point of these critical spaces is, first, to engage people in recognizing how everyday processes of work organizations generally and HRD specifically shape people's identities and activities in particular ways. Second, dialogue in these spaces helps people to inquire into the justice and equity of these processes, and to recognize links between their own personal struggles and the larger forces affecting practice. Third, these spaces should help generate strategies, both to create more democratic practices and to engage others in productive critical questioning. As Valentin (2006) has argued, a good starting point is education: using critical pedagogy to promote critical HRD.

Good critical educators have been practicing in the workplace for some decades (Simon *et al.* 1991). They often begin by introducing people to critical theoretical perspectives, then design activities where students apply these perspectives to actual cases to identify issues of equity, exclusion, and interests, contradictions embedded within the organization, and so on. Some educators also guide students through critical analyses of popular management texts and media stories fortify a-political management assumptions. But beyond these rational analyses, how are people to be engaged in a critical reading of the world that is sustainable beyond the classroom and even converted into their everyday practices? If a radical view is simply presented alongside other views, argue Brookfield (2004) and others, it is vulnerable to being domesticated or dismissed as irrelevant by students. Therefore, the critical educator is often challenged to take up a clear critical position as an orientation to both organizations and education – while surviving in conservative academies and avoiding the hubris of heroic emancipator.

Reflexivity is one of three core dimensions for critical development of organizations proposed by Fournier and Grey (2000). That is, the reflexive critique of voice, positionality and knowledge is refracted on to the classroom activities and procedures whenever possible. In particular, the teacher's own authoritarianism is confronted. The assumptions circulating in the classroom about knowledge authority and the power ascribed to procedural norms (such as grades) can be challenged continually. An entire course might be framed within a critical perspective if students are continually encouraged to raise dimensions of voice, positionality, and the politics of knowledge legitimation unfolding in the different texts and perspectives examined throughout the course. The critical perspective thus is not presented solely as ideological content, but more as a tool for exposing and assessing the ideologies implicit in all voices, including those presenting themselves as neutral, as all-inclusive and tolerant, or as empowering – including, perhaps especially, itself.

Working from individual experience

Personal change begins with learners' own experiences of inequity – naming these and analyzing them in ways that link their origins to particular relations of power and positioning. The educator's challenge is to balance deconstructive critique with hopeful reconstruction of alternate visions. These visions need to be formulated as authentic alternatives, not illusory transformations that in effect do nothing to challenge existing conditions and relations except to proclaim empowerment and democratic improvement.

As discussed elsewhere (Fenwick 2005b), students often welcome tools of critical cultural analysis for their own organizational experiences. Many find critical language and concepts useful for examining contradictions, everyday politics, accelerating pressures, disciplinary HRD technologies (e.g. performance appraisals, classification schemes, "confessional" dialogues, and remediation by training), ineffectual procedures that appear immutable – and various acts of resistance. They can analyze their own stories to examine organizational structures (reward mechanisms, knowledge most valued, activities dependent on perpetual disablers), as well as larger cultural discourses and accepted imperatives (such as performance, measurement, continuous change and innovation). Dialogue in small groups and plenary is useful for analyzing personal experience, although it often needs critical mediation to sustain a collective commitment to reflexivity. There are always some voices, sometimes very aggressive, espousing dominant assumptions, discriminatory sentiments, intolerance for others' views, or refusal to recognize experiences outside their own. Some students may have difficulty problematizing their own workplace structures and practices in terms of what *they* do and why, but most can engage critically to analyze what they have experienced as *done to them*. Overall the critical educator keeps moving the analysis outwards, examining the interacting systems of practices, people and objects which constitute power relations. The general movement is towards action, involving students in experiments to devise a critical practice of HRD.

Linking individual to organization-based projects

Action is particularly important for human resource development education where students are preparing not for careers of inquiry, but for the difficult work of enacting change in complex and uncertain situations. If CHRD is to actually help prospective practitioners not only to internalize critical insights but also to enact them in organizations, practice should be integrated with critical analysis. At this theory/practice nexus, all of the dilemmas emerge that were discussed earlier.

However, serious engagement of CHRD with work-based practitioners can help sidestep this old theory/practice polarity, and avoid dualisms between organizations as simplistic iron cages and broad utopian visions that ignore nuanced actualities. One approach is work-based education, where Boud and Solomon (2001) argue for classroom critical inquiry linked to organizational internships. Critical action learning projects within organizations are another approach that have been widely explored (Alvesson and Willmott 1996, Fenwick 2003). Loosely based on a combination of critical problem-posing and "Action Learning" (AL), groups undertake collaborative problem-solving processes of naming, analyzing, exploring action-based solutions, and critically reflecting on an organizational condition or management practice. Critical AL projects can be undertaken by individual students mobilizing employees in their own organizations, or adopted as class field projects conducted by individual or small groups of students in volunteering organizations, supported by discussion back in class. A third approach is organizational narrative, facilitating employees' construction and critical analysis of a change event. Students can even facilitate the development of alternative scenarios with an organizational group. Finally, Meyerson's (2001) work on "small wins" and "tempered radicalism" suggests more modest activities that are adaptable for student projects, such as timing the challenge of one exclusionary meeting protocol and analyzing what happens. There are problems in such approaches (Fenwick 2003), although the critical educational environment can help draw forth the complex micropolitics and contradictions that are enacted. Perhaps the key is fostering, as Brookfield (2004) suggests, a flexible and above all, a reflexive approach to critical learning, through experiments and various collaborations.

Conclusion

Critical human resource development sets out to promote critical practice, among HRD practitioners as well as the wider organization. While this is far from well-defined or even feasibly conceptualized, it can be characterized as a fundamentally political project. From the injunctions of Fournier and Grey (2000), CHRD promotes non-performativity, de-naturalization, and reflexivity in organizations by developing managers' critical insights about organizational power relations, interests and inequity, and by exploring alternative possibilities and opportunities for action. Many dilemmas are inherent in the project itself of critical management development. This chapter discussed tensions between notions of "management development" and critical learning, potential subversion or appropriation of radical purpose, incommensurable assumptions, inadequacies of certain critical conceptualizations, potential dilution of critique in practice, and practical difficulties of implementation. The practical strategies for CMD suggested in this chapter emphasize reflexivity, working from students' experience, and linking classroom to action: both through organization-based projects and to deep critical consideration of the classroom dynamics themselves, following Reynolds and Trehan's (2001) argument for a pedagogy of difference. Perriton and Reynolds (2004) remind us of the educator's complex position in all of this, with their recommendation for a pedagogy of refusal.

Overall, CHRD sets out to negotiate difficult links between the amorphous traditions of critical thought and the complexities of practice in organizations, at a time when both managing and organizing are highly contested and rapidly shifting domains of activity. To further link all of this with notions of pedagogy and development, particularly within formal institutions, is to invite debate around interests, contradiction and the educative project. These ongoing dilemmas need not be viewed as problems requiring solution, but as open questions to return to again and again as various new models and prescriptions for CHRD to emerge.

Note

1 This chapter draws from material published in Fenwick (2005a,b) which has been substantially modified and updated here.

References

Alfred, M.A. and Chlup, D.T. (2010) Making the invisible, visible: Race matters in human resource development, *Advances in Developing Human Resources* 12: 332–51.

Alvesson, M. and Deetz, C. (1996) Critical theory and postmodernism: Approaches to organisational studies, in Clegg, S., Hardy, C. and Nord, W. (eds) *The SAGE Handbook of Organization Studies*, London: SAGE.

Alvesson, M. and Willmott, H.S. (1996) *Making Sense of Management: A Critical Introduction*, London: SAGE.

Bierema, L.L. (2008) Critical human resource development education: A review of the literature and recommendations for teaching, *Proceedings of the Annual Academy of Human Resource Development Conference*, Panama City, Florida, 538–45.

— (2009) Critiquing human resource development's dominant masculine rationality and evaluating its impact, *Human Resource Development Review* 8(1): 68–96.

Bierema, L.L. and Cseh, M. (2003) Evaluating AHRD research using a feminist research framework, *Human Resource Development Quarterly* 14(1): 5–26.

Boud, D. and Solomon, N. (2001) *Work-Based Learning: A New Higher Education*, Berkshire: Open University Press.

Brookfield, S.D. (2004) *The Power of Critical Theory: Liberating Adult Learning and Teaching*, San Francisco: Jossey-Bass.

Brookfield, S.D. and Holst, J.D. (2010) *Radicalising Learning: Adult Education for a Just World*, San Francisco: John Wiley/Jossey-Bass.

Callahan, J.L. (2007) Gazing into the crystal ball: Critical HRD as a future of research in the field, *Human Resource Development International* 10(1): 77–82.

CMS (2002) *Critical Management Studies Conference 2003, Human Resources Stream: Call for Proposals.* Available at http://criticalmanagement.org/.

Elliott, C.J. and Turnbull, R.S. (2002), *Critical Thinking in Human Resources Development*, London: Routledge.

Ellsworth, E. (1989) Why doesn't this feel empowering? Working through the repressive myths of critical pedagogy, *Harvard Educational Review* 59: 297–324.

Fenwick, T. (2003) Emancipatory potential of action research: A critical analysis, *Journal of Organizational Change Management* 16(6): 619–32.

— (2005a) Conceptions of critical HRD: Dilemmas for theory and practice, *Human Resource Development International* 8(2): 225–38.

— (2005b) Ethical dilemmas of critical management education, *Management Learning* 36(1): 31–48.

Fournier, V. and Grey, C. (2000) At the critical moment: Conditions and prospects for critical management studies, *Human Relations* 53(1):7–32.

Kincheloe, J.L. (1999) *How Do We Tell the Workers? The Socioeconomic Foundations of Work and Vocational Education*, Boulder, CO: Westview Press.

McGuire, D. and Garavan, T.N. (2011) *Critical human resource development: A levels of analysis approach*, Paper presented at 12th UFHRD/AHRD Conference on HRD Research and Practice across Europe, University of Gloucestershire, May, 25–27.

Metcalfe, B.D. (2008) A feminist poststructuralist analysis of HRD: Why bodies, power and reflexivity matter, *Human Resource Development International* 11(5): 447–63.

Meyerson, D. (2001) *Tempered Radicals: How people Use Difference To Inspire Change At Work*, Boston, MA: Harvard Business School Press.

Perriton, L. and Reynolds, M. (2004) Critical management education: From pedagogy of possibility to pedagogy of refusal? *Management Learning* 35(1): 61–77.

Reynolds, M. and Trehan, K. (2001) Classroom as real world: Propositions for a pedagogy of difference, *Gender and Education* 13(4): 91–109.

Sambrook, S. (2004) A critical time for HRD, *Journal of European Industrial Training* 28(8/9): 611–24.

— (2009) Critical HRD: A concept analysis, *Personnel Review* 38(1): 61–73.

Simon, R.I., Dippo, D. and Schenke, A. (1991) *Learning Work: A Critical Pedagogy of Work Education*, Toronto: OISE.

Stewart, J., Rigg, C. and Trehan, K. (2006) *Critical Human Resource Development: Beyond Orthodoxy*, Essex: Financial Times/Prentice Hall.

Townley, B. (1994) *Reframing Human Resource Management: Power, ethics and the subject at work*, London: SAGE.

Valentin, C. (2006) How can I teach critical management in this place? A critical pedagogy for HRD: Possibilities, contradictions and compromises, in Stewart, J., Rigg, C. and Trehan, K. (eds) *Critical Human Resource Development: Beyond orthodoxy*, Harlow: Pearson Education, 169–80.

12

SOCIAL CAPITAL THEORY AND HRD

Debates, perspectives and opportunities

Claire Gubbins and Russell Korte

It is now recognized within management, organizational behavior and human resource management literatures that the *relational* component is key to understanding individual, collective and societal behavior. Individuals, groups, processes, and organizations always exist in a relational system and artificially separating a thing (person, process, or group) from its system will produce a flawed understanding (Oshry 1996). The HRD field also recognizes the importance of relationships for HRD research and practice, though the extent of research is still limited (Gubbins and Garavan 2005; Korte 2012; Morton *et al.* 2004; Storberg-Walker and Gubbins 2007). The emerging challenges facing HRD include developing not only the *human* capital of organizations, but also the *social* capital, or the "asset value of human relationships" embedded in the informal structure of the organization (Harrison and Kessels 2004:88).

A social capital perspective generates research questions that focus on the *relations between*, rather than an exclusive focus on the *characteristics of*, individuals, groups, processes, or organizations (Storberg-Walker and Gubbins 2007). For example, team performance is often investigated in terms of the characteristics of team members. As an alternative, the social capital perspective finds that interventions to develop teams could focus on the social networks of team members (Reagans *et al.* 2004). Also, while learning occurs first at the individual level (Sadler-Smith 2006), a social capital view facilitates understanding of collective learning which is key to organizational survival (Gubbins and MacCurtain 2008).

In this chapter we discuss the various conceptualizations of social capital. We review the theoretical underpinnings and scope of social capital theories. This includes consideration of the economic and/or social orientations on social capital and the social capital or social network perspectives. We conduct a review of empirical research on topics within the HRD field which are studied from a social capital and network perspective at the collective and individual levels. The chapter concludes with a presentation of the resultant implications and directions for future HRD research.

Defining social capital

The concept of social capital is grounded in social relations (Coleman 1988)—in contrast to human capital, which refers to individual knowledge and skills. Generally, scholars describe social capital as resources or goodwill that can facilitate action, which are derived from relationships among people (Adler and Kwon 2002; Bourdieu 1997; Coleman 1988). However, there is notable variation in the enumerable definitions of social capital that exist.

Structurally, the concept of social capital is considered from the perspective of whether the social relations are internal or external. Definitions that focus on the internal relations are referred to as 'bonding' or 'linking' forms of social capital and those that focus on the external relations have been referred to as 'bridging' or 'communal' (Adler and Kwon 2002; Oh *et al.* 1999) forms of social capital. Those definitions that are neutral consider that the distinctions between the views are a matter of perspective and unit of analysis and they are not mutually exclusive.

In terms of the content of social capital, there is debate about definitions encompassing reference to the structure of relations and the social resources available in the network. Leenders and Gabbay (1999) specify that social capital comprises the beneficial resources actors draw from their social networks, rather than the relationships that constitute those social networks. Burt (1992) states that social capital is, at once, the resources that contacts hold and the structure of contacts in a network. He posits that the resources describe 'who' you reach and the structure describes 'how' you reach.

Still other definitions add further complexity by incorporating characteristics about the relationships. Putnam (2000) argues that trust is fundamental to all definitions of social capital as it would appear that without trust, cooperation is limited to activities that are easy to monitor. Adler and Kwon (2002) suggest that goodwill is the substance of social capital. Others argue that these characteristics are antecedents to and/or effects of or outcomes of social capital (Leana and Van Buren 1999; Lin 2002).

Definitions also vary based on the chosen level of analysis. In the macro sense, social capital is an attribute of nations or geographic regions (Fukuyama 1995) and communities (Putnam 1993). In the micro sense, it is defined in terms of individual networks (Burt 1992), firms in their interactions with other firms (Baker 1990) and individual actors (Belliveau *et al.* 1996). The public good perspective focuses on the macro or meso level of social capital and emphasizes the secondary nature of individual benefits. The private good perspective focuses explicitly on the individual and his/her accrued social assets, such as prestige, educational credentials and social clubs. The private good model has been applied at individual, group, organizational and industry levels.

It is argued that one reason for the diverse conceptualizations of social capital is due to there being two major paradigms on social capital: the economic or capital perspective and the sociological or social perspective (Storberg-Walker 2007). The economic rational-objective paradigm led to perceiving social capital from the perspective of economic theories of rational instrumentalism. Coleman (1988) evolved his notion of social capital from sociology and the construct of social exchange and individuals' interactions in the pursuit of self-interest. However, Fine and Lapavitsas (2000) argue that exchange as a market concept and social exchange as a non-market concept are completely different and therefore are not two forms of interaction in an exchange category. The former is impersonal and quantifiable, and the latter is personal and qualitative. In a similar vein, it is argued that social capital has not achieved 'capital' status alongside economic and human capital (Herreros 2004), as in terms of the traditional, economic characteristics of 'capital', social capital is weakly conceptualized (Fine 2001). Evaluations of the concept of social 'capital' against the properties of 'capital' (Robison *et al.* 2002; Adler and Kwon 2002) reveal that social capital in part adheres to and in part differs from the properties of capital.

Debate and differences in the definition of social capital have led to concern that the social capital concept will have limited value as an analytical construct due to a lack of precision and comparability (Castle 1998). Woolcock (1998) argues that it is necessary to recognize that there are different types or dimensions of social capital that respond differently to various situations and can be combined in different configurations for different purposes. Andriessen and Gubbins (2009) argue that critics who ask for a precise definition of social capital assume that social capital is something that is objectively 'out there' instead of a human construct created by metaphorical conceptualization and thus there is no single definition of social capital. They argue that it is legitimate for social capital to possess certain characteristics of capital (that it is valuable) and not others (such as the existence of a social capital market). Despite all the problems with the concept, many (Fine 2001; Schuller *et al.* 2000) look positively on the use of the concept as a valuable heuristic for research on social phenomena that helps to open up complex issues, rather than provide definitive answers.

Theories of social capital

It is not surprising to note that there are also multiple theories or models of social capital (see Payne *et al.* 2011). Within the field of social capital the extent to which theories contrast or complement can be seen by classifying the theories based on their orientation: (a) economic or sociological; (b) social resources or social network; or (c) macro or micro perspective.

Social capital: economic and sociological paradigms

In the 1980s, sociology began to examine how value was created from social relations (Portes 1998), with the result that social capital is now investigated at micro and macro levels such as communities, nations and organizations in terms of understanding and nurturing economic performance at these levels (e.g. Cohen and Prusak 2001; Cross and Cummings 2003; Dess and Shaw 2001; Leana and Rousseau 2000; Reagans and Zuckerman 2001). Consequently, the economic, rational or capital accumulating perspective assumes a dominant position in empirical studies on social capital. In contrast, the sociological orientation is more concerned with such factors as changing inequitable distribution of resources, quality of life, health, building *civil* society, community engagement; essentially more humanistic outcomes. Work by authors such as Hanifan (1916), Putnam (1995, 2000) and Bourdieu (1984) are most notable here. Hanifan (1916) refers to social capital as goodwill, fellowship, mutual sympathy and social intercourse, which addresses individuals' social needs as well as improving the living conditions in a social unit or community. Putnam (1995) framed social capital as a producer of civic engagement and a measure of communal health. Bourdieu (1984) focused on inequality in communities.

Adler and Kwon (2002) integrated these paradigms. They proposed that social structure, such as market, social and hierarchical relations, determine the network content in the form of opportunity, ability, and motivation. Thus an individual who is connected to others needs: the opportunity to act through a network of connections in which s/he is positioned; the ability (competencies and resources) to act, and to be motivated to act (instrumentally or consummatorally or based on norms [Portes 1998]). Despite some criticisms (Storberg-Walker 2007) this theory recognizes the value and role of both the economic and humanist paradigms and possibly provides encouragement for further theory development which is integrative rather than disparate. However, the choice of paradigm will be based on HRD research goals. Storberg-Walker (2007) presents an analysis of how different paradigms on social capital theory may inform economic/social, objective/subjective, structuralist/humanist HRD research goals.

Social capital and social network theory

The fields of social capital and social networks substantively address the same topics (Glanville and Bienenstock 2009; Moody and Paxton 2009). The literature on social networks is focused on the *structure of networks*. This includes research on the methods and theory about network structure (Moody and Paxton 2009), how structural characteristics determine outcomes such as power, exchange or formal models of network structure, and issues about social support, family, migration and community. Research from this perspective is most frequently grounded in two theories focused on the structural properties of networks, namely Granovetter's (1973) weak tie theory and Burt's (1992) structural hole theory. Granovetter's (1973) weak tie theory argues that individuals in a social group have two types of ties to individuals within and external to their social group. Strong ties are likely to exist between individuals within the social group and weak ties enable individuals to reach beyond their small defined social group in order to make connections with parts of the internal and external social structure not directly accessible. Burt (1992) defines a structural hole as that which exists between two individuals who are not connected to each other and who circulate in different flows of information. The fundamental difference between structural hole theory and weak tie theory is that weak tie theory addresses the strength of the ties and structural hole theory addresses the existence or non-existence of ties.

On the other hand, the literature on social capital is focused on the *content* of social relationships. This literature addresses issues about defining social capital, topics on community, health, getting a job, economic development, social support and more specifically the bulk of the research is on the relationship between social capital and concepts and outcomes such as trust, civil society, community and social-problem applications such as that on schools and finding a job (see Moody and Paxton 2009). The fundamental difference in these fields of research is that research on social capital which does not focus on network *structure* and connections refers to relations, feelings or norms that are a generalized result of social embeddedness. Conversely, research on social networks which does not focus on *content* refers to connection without reference to what type of connection it is, such as friendship or support.

Despite the social network and social capital literatures possessing fundamentally differing starting points, Moody and Paxton's (2009) review argues that research at the intersection of the two literatures will yield better theory, better predictions and better measurement. Content from the social network field possess opportunity to address some of the criticisms (Castle 1998) levelled at the concept of social capital and its measurement, as there exists substantial, clearly defined, mathematically rigorous measurements of network properties (Wasserman and Faust 1994). Equally, conceptual and theoretical developments in areas such as connectivity, structural equivalence, homophily, social balance, generalized exchange and hierarchy, social processes of networks, network formation and network change, can provide deeper insight into social network studies. Thus, greater integration between the social capital and social network fields has additive potential. Social network models which present relationships as present or absent can be richer with the addition of distinctions made in the social capital literature between connections based on trust, friendship, support, etc. (Moody and Paxton 2009). Similarly, where social capital researchers investigate membership as social capital, social network literature enables identification of how the benefits obtained by different sub-groups and individuals, such as information access, power and influence, differ as a consequence of their position within the network structure.

Theories which are integrative of both network structure and content perspectives include Lin *et al.*'s (1981) social resource theory and Nahapiet and Ghoshal's (1998) social capital theory. Lin *et al.* (1981) argue that it is not the weakness of the tie per se nor the bridging properties that are important, but the fact that such ties are more likely to reach an individual with the resources or information that the focal individual requires to fulfill his/her objectives. Nahapiet and Ghoshal (1998) propose that social capital is composed of structural, relational and cognitive dimensions. Research which integrates these perspectives illustrates the value for investigating outcomes. Podolny and Baron's (1997) study found that network ties (social network perspective) conveying resources (social capital perspective) were positively related to promotion but network ties conveying identity and expectations were negatively related. Levin and Cross (2004) found that trusted (social capital perspective) weak ties (social network perspective) over and above trusted strong ties and untrusted weak ties yielded the most useful knowledge of all. They argue for more research which integrates the structural and relational components of social capital. Efforts at developing integrative social network structure and resource models can be seen in work by Seibert *et al.* (2001), Gubbins and Garavan (2005) and Wong (2008).

HRD and the contribution of social capital

As the broader economic and social environments have changed so have the roles and expectations of HRD practitioners. Gubbins and Garavan (2005) claimed that important shifts in HRD work included: (a) placing greater emphasis on the distributed nature of expertise in organizations, (b) being more responsive to a broader and more diverse network of stakeholders, and (c) the need to solve increasingly novel and complex problems. Developing a more multilevel and socially oriented approach to HRD requires a shift in focus from the narrow individualistic view of learning and development (e.g. developing human capital) to a broader social systems view that encompasses the teams and organizations within which individuals work (developing social capital). Social capital is a powerful heuristic for developing a deeper and more systemic understanding of important drivers of learning and performance in organizational settings. The following sections look more closely at the contributions of social capital to learning and performance in organizational and communal settings.

Learning and the contribution of social capital

Learning is in part a social process (Bandura 2001; Billett 2004; Illeris 2003). Individuals can learn from others, and share what they learn with others (Edmondson 2012). This exchange of information, knowledge, and expertise among members of a group is enabled by the social capital embedded in the relationships among the members of a group. Studies of learning in professional and organizational settings found that learning was highly dependent on the social and historical contexts in which learners worked (Dall'Alba and Sandberg 2010; Eraut 2004; Edmondson 2002). Knowledge is perceived as a group resource shared among coworkers to various degrees depending on the quality of the relational structure of the group (Edmondson 2012; Korte 2009). Generally, the learning required to effectively manage and work in complex systems and solve complex problems is a collective effort beyond the capabilities of any one individual (Edmondson 2012; Eraut 2004).

In a line of work on the effectiveness of learning, Holton and others (Laird *et al.* 2003) developed a model on the transfer of training in organizations. Social context is one of the key factors for transfer of learning to the workplace. Specifically, the climate of the workplace and the support of managers and coworkers are important. These factors provide indicators as to the influence of social capital in the group for training transfer.

Learning is especially crucial for socializing newcomers into an organization. In the realm of organizational socialization, recent studies (Korte 2009; Korte and Lin 2013; Saks and Gruman 2011) find that the quality of newcomer learning in the workplace is largely dependent on the quality of work relationships in the newcomers' work groups. The better the relations and support available in the group—the better the learning. Successful socialization also includes the quality of newcomer integration into the social structure of the group. The characteristics of the existing social structure and the resources afforded to newcomers influenced the quality of integration into the group. Thus, social capital is an important resource to help newcomers learn their new jobs and integrate into their new workplaces.

In related work about team learning, Silberstang and London (2009) described how improving the quality of communication among members of a group facilitated learning. The quality of communication in a group is largely influenced by the quality of the relationships among members of teams. Knapp (2010), and McCarthy and Garavan (2008) synthesized various views on team or collective learning highlighting the importance of positive relational activity in the group for enabling learning. In addition, Yorks *et al.* (2003) stated that trust (a relational attribute) is an important requirement for team learning.

Performance and the contribution of social capital

As with learning, performance in organizations and communities is not just an individual endeavor (Edmondson 2012). Research on performance in the workplace highlights the importance of work groups, often conceptualized as social structures or networks, in which individuals work (Edmondson 2002; Sparrowe *et al.* 2001). More specifically, studies report positive relationships between social capital and performance (Andrews 2010; Ellinger 2005; Ellinger *et al.* 2011). Senge (1990) and others (Edmondson 2012) advocate that the abilities of a group can exceed the aggregated abilities of the individuals in the group. This speaks to the power of collective learning and collective intelligence for solving complex problems and innovating breakthrough ideas.

Positive social relations also increase trust among members of a group, which promotes knowledge creation and sharing, collaboration, coordination, creativity, and lower monitoring costs (Andrews 2010). Thus, social capital has strategic value, which derives from the increased effectiveness of high-performing relational structures (especially informal networks) through which the work of organizations and communities gets done (Burt 1997; Lengnick-Hall and Lengnick-Hall 2003). Edmondson (2002) found empirical support for the effects of team relations on team learning and performance. Across 12 teams in the study, the enabling or constraining effects of varying levels of psychological safety in teams affected their ability to learn and act. Psychological safety could be perceived as a form of relational social capital that affords members of a team greater freedom to learn and perform.

Many of the large-system methods used in organization development have been applied beyond the confines of industrial organizations to the needs of various communities and societies at large. The presence of multiple stakeholders and the need for high levels of participant collaboration rely on the powers of relational networks and social resources that are often described as the social capital of a community or society. McLean *et al.* (2012) recounted the results of several case studies in which the methods of HRD have been applied to improving the education, health, safety, culture, and productivity of communities and societies. Action learning and collaboration were core processes in these efforts. These methods depend on social conditions that foster knowledge creation and sharing, coordination, and trust.

Conclusion

The social capital perspective provides an alternative way to investigate factors that affect HRD. As a complement to the individualist focus on human capital, social capital focuses on the collectivist elements of organizational and communal life. For example, the cooperation or conflict between groups; the cultural and social norms that govern thought and behavior in group settings; the social and professional identities of individuals as members of a group; the interpersonal and inter-subjective dynamics affecting learning and performance among individuals in and across groups; and the resources embedded in social networks and collectives. Social capital is a critical factor influencing the effectiveness of learning, the development of expertise, the quality or effectiveness of work performed, and the well-being of members of a community.

However, there is also a downside associated with the concept that is not often addressed. An important consideration is the tension between fostering human capital (investments in learning and development) and fostering social capital (investments in community and networks) as the two concepts tend to compete with each other. The dominant emphasis on individual learning and performance tends to negate the social emphasis on equality and equity (Brown and Lauder 2000). This is exemplified in the widespread practice of promoting teamwork while primarily rewarding individual effort in organizations. In addition, Portes (1998) cautioned that the strong ties that are a benefit to members of a group also tend to exclude others, which increases inter-group conflict, negative stereotyping, and discrimination. There are pressures for conformity and group-think within a group, which negatively affect cooperation, collaboration, and innovation potentially reducing the levels of organizational or communal performance. Finding the right balance between individual and collectivist practices is important. The performance of the workforce and the community becomes more crucial as problem solving, work tasks, and innovation become more complex, interdependent, and unpredictable. Collaboration is an essential condition for performing complex tasks. It is essential for sharing information, solving problems, and developing new knowledge. It is essential for the common good in communities. The cache of resources embedded in a group and the ability to access and share these resources depend on the quality of the relational structures of the group. In many ways, learning, performance, and well-being are intimately tied to the quality of social capital existing in a group.

Social capital is important for the management of talent in organizations and the development of communities and societies. Having high levels of human capital has marginal value without the means to apply the knowledge and skills of individuals in the service of organizational or communal goals (Burt 2000). Dess and Shaw (2001) claimed that social capital was just as valuable as, if not more so than, human capital because of the interdependencies of work in organizations and communities. Thus, it is critical for HRD practitioners to design and support positive relational structures and processes in and among groups to better foster the learning, performance, and well-being required in highly complex, interdependent, and competitive organizations and communities.

References

Adler, P.S. and Kwon, S.W. (2002) Social capital: Prospects for a new concept. *Academy of Management Review* 27(1): 17–40.

Andrews, R. (2010) Organizational social capital, structure and performance. *Human Relations* 63(5): 583–608.

Andriessen, D. and Gubbins, C. (2009) Metaphor analysis as an approach for exploring theoretical concepts: The case of social capital. *Organization Studies* 30(8): 845–63.

Baker, W. (1990) Market networks and corporate behaviour. *American Journal of Sociology* 96(3): 589–625.

Bandura, A. (2001) Social cognitive theory: An agentic perspective. *Annual Review of Psychology* 52(1): 1–26.

Belliveau, M.A., O'Reilly, C.A.I. and Wade, J.B. (1996) Social capital at the top: Effects of social similarity and status on CEO compensation. *Academy of Management Journal* 39(6): 1568–93.

Billett, S. (2004) Co-participation at work: Learning through work and throughout working lives. *Studies in the Education of Adults* 36(2): 190–205.

Bourdieu P. (1984) *Homo Academicus.* Translated by P. Collier (1988) Stanford, CA: Stanford University Press.

— (1997) The forms of capital. In Halsey, A.H., Lauder, H., Brown, P. and Stuart Wells, A. (eds) *Education: Culture, economy, society* (46–58). Oxford: Oxford University Press.

Brown, P. and Lauder, H. (2000) Human capital, social capital, and collective intelligence. In Baron, S., Field, J. and Schuller, T. (eds) *Social Capital: Critical Perspectives* (226–42). Oxford: Oxford University Press.

Burt, R.S. (1992) *Structural Holes: The Social Structure of Competition.* Cambridge, MA: Harvard University Press.

— (1997) The contingent value of social capital. *Administrative Science Quarterly* 42(2): 339–65.

— (2000) The network structure of social capital. In Sutton, R.I. and Staw, B.M. (eds) *Research in Organizational Behavior* (345–423), Greenwich, CN: JAI Press.

Castle, E.N. (1998) A conceptual framework for the study of rural places. *American Journal of Agricultural Economics* 80(3): 621–31.

Cohen, D. and Prusak, L. (2001) *In Good Company: How Social Capital Makes Organizations Work.* Boston, MA: Harvard Business School.

Coleman, J.S. (1988) Social capital in the creation of human capital. *American Journal of Sociology* 94(5): 95–120.

Cross, R. and Cummings, J.N. (2003) Relational and structural network correlates of individual performance in knowledge intensive work. *Academy of Management 2003 Annual Conference Best Papers.*

Dall'Alba, G. and Sandberg, J. (2010) Learning through and about practice: A lifeworld perspective. In Billett, S. (ed) *Learning through Practice: Professional and Practice-based Learning.* Dordrecht: Springer.

Dess, G.G. and Shaw, J.D. (2001) Voluntary turnover, social capital, and organizational performance. *Academy of Management Review* 26(3): 446–56.

Edmondson, A.C. (2002) The local and variegated nature of learning in organizations: A group-level perspective. *Organization Science* 13(2): 128–46.

— (2012) *Teaming: How organizations learn, innovate, and compete in the knowledge economy.* San Francisco: Jossey-Bass.

Ellinger, A.D. (2005) Contextual factors influencing informal learning in a workplace setting: The case of "Reinventing Itself Company". *Human Resource Development Quarterly* 16(3): 389–415.

Ellinger, A.D. Ellinger, A.E., Bachrach, D.G., Wang, Y. and Elmadag, A.B. (2011) Organizational investments in social capital, managerial coaching, and employee work-related performance. *Management Learning* 42(1): 67–85.

Eraut, M. (2004) Informal learning in the workplace. *Studies in Continuing Education* 26(2): 247–73.

Fine, B. (2001) *Social Capital Versus Social Theory: Political Economy and Social Science at the Turn of the Millennium.* New York: Routledge.

Fine, B. and Lapavitsas, C. (2000) Markets and money in social theory: What role for economics? *Economy and Society* 29(3): 357–82.

Fukuyama, F. (1995) *Trust: The Social Virtues and the Creation of Prosperity.* New York: Free Press.

Glanville, J.L. and Bienenstock, E.J., (2009) A typology for understanding the connections among different forms of social capital. *American Behavioral Scientist* 52(11): 1507–30.

Granovetter, M.S. (1973) The strength of weak ties. *American Journal of Sociology* 78(6): 1360–80.

Gubbins, C. and Garavan, T.N. (2005) Studying HRD practitioners: A social capital model. *Human Resource Development Review* 4(2): 189–218.

Gubbins, C. and MacCurtain, S. (2008) Understanding the dynamics of collective learning: The role of trust and social capital. *Advances in Developing Human Resources* 10(4): 578–99.

Hanifan, L.J. (1916) The rural school community center. *Annals of the American Academy of Political and Social Science* 67(1): 130–38.

Harrison, R. and Kessels, J. (2004) *Human Resource Development in a Knowledge Economy: An Organisational View.* New York: Palgrave Macmillan.

Herreros, F. (2004) *The Problem of Forming Social Capital: Why Trust?* New York: Palgrave Macmillan.

Illeris, K. (2003) Towards a contemporary and comprehensive theory of learning. *International Journal of Lifelong Education* 22(4): 396–406.

Knapp, R. (2010) Collective (team) learning process models: A conceptual review. *Human Resource Development Review* 9(3): 285–99.

Korte, R. (2009) How newcomers learn the social norms of an organization: A case study of the socialization of newly hired engineers. *Human Resource Development Quarterly* 20(3): 285–306.

— (2012) Exploring the social foundations of human resource development: A theoretical framework for research and practice. *Human Resource Development Review* 11(1): 6–30.

Korte, R. and Lin, S. (2013) Getting on board: Organizational socialization and the contribution of social capital. *Human Relations* 66(3): 407–28.

Laird, D., Naquin, S.S. and Holton, E.F. (2003) *Approaches to Training and Development* (3rd edition). Cambridge, MA: Perseus.

Leana, C.R. and Van Buren, H.J. III (1999) Organizational social capital and employment practices. *Academy of Management Review* 24(3): 34–59.

Leana, C.R. and Rousseau, D.M. (2000) Relational wealth: The advantages of stability in a changing economy. In Leana, C.R. and Rousseau, D.M. (eds) *Relational Wealth: The Advantages of Stability in a Changing Economy* (3–24). Oxford: Oxford University Press.

Leenders, R.T.A.J. and Gabbay, S.M. (eds) (1999) *Corporate Social Capital and Liability*. London: Kluwer.

Lengnick-Hall, M.L. and Lengnick-Hall, C.A. (2003) *Human Resource Management in the Knowledge Economy: New Challenges, New Roles, New Capabilities*. San Francisco: Berrett-Koehler.

Levin, D.Z. and Cross, R. (2004) The strength of weak ties you can trust: The mediating role of trust in effective knowledge transfer. *Management Science* 50(11): 1477–90.

Lin, N. (2002) *Social Capital: A Theory of Social Structure and Action*. Cambridge: Cambridge University Press.

Lin, N., Ensel, W.M. and Vaughn, J.C. (1981) Social resources and strength of ties: Structural factors in occupational status attainment. *American Sociological Review* 46(4): 393–405.

McCarthy, A. and Garavan, T.N. (2008) Collective learning processes and human resource development. *Advances in Developing Human Resources* 10(4): 451–71.

McLean, G.N., Kuo, M., Budhwani, N.N., Yamnill, S. and Virakul, B. (2012) Capacity building for societal development: Case studies in human resource development. *Advances in Developing Human Resources* 14(3): 251–63.

Moody, J. and Paxton, P. (2009) Building bridges linking social capital and social networks to improve theory and research. *American Behavioral Scientist* 52(11): 1491–506.

Morton, S.C., Brookes, N.J., Smart, P.K., Blackhouse, C.J. and Burns, N.D. (2004) Managing the informal organization: Conceptual model. *International Journal of Productivity and Performance Management* 53(3): 214–32.

Nahapiet, J. and Ghoshal, S. (1998) Social capital, intellectual capital, and the organizational advantage. *Academy of Management Review* 23(2): 242–66.

Oh, H., Kilduff, M. and Brass, D.J. (1999) Communal social capital: Linking social capital, and economic outcomes. Paper presented at the Annual Meeting of the Academy of Management, held in Chicago.

Oshry, B. (1996) *Seeing Systems: Unlocking the Mysteries of Organizational Life*. San Francisco: Berrett-Koehler.

Payne, G.T., Moore, C.B., Griffis, S.E. and Autry, C.W. (2011) Multilevel challenges and opportunities in social capital research. *Journal of Management* 37(2): 491–520.

Podolny, J.M. and Baron, J.N. (1997) Resources and relationships: Social networks and mobility in the workplace. *American Sociological Review* 62(5): 673–93.

Portes, A. (1998) Social capital: Its origins and applications in modern sociology. *Annual Review of Sociology* 24(1): 1–24.

Putnam, R.D. (1993) *Making Democracy Work: Civic Traditions in Modern Italy*. Princeton, NJ: Princeton University Press.

— (1995) Bowling alone: America's declining social capital. *Journal of Democracy* 6(1): 65–78.

— (2000) *Bowling Alone: The Collapse and Revival of American Community*. New York: Simon and Schuster.

Reagans, R. and Zuckerman, E.W. (2001) Networks, diversity, and productivity: The social capital of corporate R&D teams. *Organization Science* 12(4): 502–17.

Reagans, R., Zuckerman, E. and McEvily, B. (2004) How to make the team: Social networks vs. demography as criteria for designing effective teams. *Administrative Science Quarterly* 49(1): 101–33.

Robison, L.J., Schmid, A.A. and Siles, M.E. (2002) Is social capital really capital?, *Review of Social Economy* 60(1): 1–21.

Sadler-Smith, E. (2006) *Learning and Development for Managers*. Oxford: Blackwell.

Saks, A.M. and Gruman, J.A. (2011) Getting newcomers engaged: The role of socialization tactics. *Journal of Managerial Psychology* 26(5): 383–402.

Schuller, T., Baron, S. and Field, J. (2000) Social capital: A review and critique. In Baron, S., Field, J. and Schuller, T. (eds) *Social Capital: Critical Perspectives* (1–38). Oxford: Oxford University Press.

Seibert, S.E., Kraimer, M.L. and Liden, R.C. (2001) A social capital theory of career success. *Academy of Management Journal* 44(2): 219–37.

Senge, P.M. (1990) *The Fifth Discipline: The Art and Practice of the Learning Organization.* New York: Doubleday.

Silberstang, J. and London, M. (2009) How groups learn: The role of communication patterns, cue recognition, context facility, and cultural intelligence. *Human Resource Development Review* 8(3): 327–49.

Sparrowe, R.T., Liden, R.C., Wayne, S.J. and Kraimer, M.L. (2001) Social networks and the performance of individuals and groups. *Academy of Management Journal* 44(2): 316–25.

Storberg-Walker, J. (2007) Borrowing from others: Appropriating social capital theories for "doing" HRD. *Advances in Developing Human Resources* 9(3): 312–40.

Storberg-Walker, J. and Gubbins, C. (2007) Social networks as a conceptual and empirical tool to understand and "do" HRD. *Advances in Developing Human Resources* 9(3): 291–311.

Wasserman, S. and Faust, K. (1994) *Social Network Analysis: Methods and Applications.* Cambridge: Cambridge University Press.

Wong, S.S. (2008). Task knowledge overlap and knowledge variety: The role of advice network structures and impact on group effectiveness. *Journal of Organizational Behavior* 29(5): 591–614.

Woolcock, M. (1998) Social capital and economic development: Toward a theoretical synthesis and policy framework. *Theory and Society* 27(2): 151–208.

Yorks, L., Marsick, V.J., Kasl, E. and Dechant, K. (2003) Contextualizing team learning: Implications for research and practice. *Advances in Developing Human Resources* 5(1): 103–17.

13
THE LEARNING-NETWORK THEORY
Actors organize dynamic HRD networks

Rob F. Poell and Ferd J. Van Der Krogt

Human resource development (HRD) serves important functions in organizations and there is increasing interest in the question of how HRD should be organized. Organizing HRD, however, has turned out to be a difficult task in practice. This difficulty is due in part to a limited conceptualization of what it means to organize HRD, which has dominated the field and will be referred to here as the structure approach. This approach focuses on designing learning structures (e.g. HRD-policy plans) intended to direct various organizational actors in giving rise to HRD processes. The Learning-Network Theory (LNT), which this chapter will summarize, offers a broader perspective on organizing HRD so that it is better capable of analyzing and improving HRD processes. The LNT is a dynamic-network theory focusing on the interactions among actors in creating several HRD processes.

The LNT was first published in the mid-1990s (Van Der Krogt 1995; 1998) and has gone through a number of modifications since then. Initially, its focus was on the organizational learning networks themselves, their different types, and how these were likely to occur in various types of work and organizations (e.g. Poell *et al.* 2000; Poell *et al.* 2001). Gradually, however, the emphasis shifted to the group and individual level, addressing the issue of how various actors (i.e. stakeholders such as employees, educators, managers, HR, trade unions, professional associations, and so forth) created learning programs in different organizational contexts (e.g. Poell and Van Der Krogt 2002; 2003). Most recently, the LNT has focused on the issue of employee strategies in organizing HRD processes (e.g. Van Der Krogt 2007; Poell and Van Der Krogt 2007; 2010; 2014). Elements of all three 'stages' in the development of the LNT are part of its current make-up and featured in the present chapter.

The chapter explains two major reasons why organizing HRD processes is such a difficult task in practice: its dualistic and its strategic nature. It then proceeds to show how the traditional (structure) approach to organizing HRD deals with those issues. The chapter goes on to present a broader, LNT inspired, perspective on HRD: the dynamic-network approach. The latter approach is compared with the structure approach and investigated for its merits in doing justice to the dualistic and strategic nature of organizing HRD.

The dualistic and strategic nature of organizing HRD

There are two main reasons why organizing HRD in organizations tends to be a troublesome affair: its dualistic and its strategic nature.

HRD's dualistic nature: work experiences and explicit learning experiences as its basis

The workplace has always been of major importance in employee development practice. In recent years, workplace learning has gained prominence in HRD research and theory building as well (Van Woerkom and Poell 2010). Various settings of learning (e.g. informal, non-formal and incidental) have been distinguished to gain insight in employees' learning experiences in settings other than education and training. Workplace experiences doubtless form a crucial element in their professional development; however, taking them in uncritically leads to serious problems in organizing HRD, which is predominantly based on ideas about organizing educational programs. Notions about curriculum design and delivery in schools and training institutes are widely used for organizing HRD. How, then, is HRD to be organized so that it combines workplace experiences and explicit learning settings?

HRD's strategic nature: an instrument for all actors

Individual employees need to ensure that they possess the necessary qualities to get a job, keep it and do it well. To that end most of them have always gained relevant experiences as well as taken training courses offered by institutes outside of the organization. In recent decades, however, it has become understood that other actors, too, have major interests in employees' professional development and should not leave it to its own devices. Management in organizations, for instance, started putting effort into personnel development, attempting to align it with development in and around the organization, such as changes in the internal and external labor market, technological and organizational changes and market developments. Still other actors started attempts to use HRD to support their own agendas, including governments, trade unions and employers' organizations. Organizing HRD has thus become a complex interplay of different actors, including employees themselves, each with their own views of and interests in professional development. It has turned into a strategic issue.

The structure approach to HRD: planning and structuring

Planning and structuring are dominant activities in HRD theory and practice related to organizing employees' professional development in organizations (Anderson 2009; Swanson and Holton 2009; Jacobs 2003). In this approach, organizing is viewed as designing structures as well as designing and executing plans. Managers and HRD practitioners emphasize the designing of learning structures intended to direct employees' development: they create guidelines (procedures, protocols) for other organizational actors (employees, trainers, supervisors) to act upon and pay ample attention to the design of the learning infrastructure (training programs and techniques).

Four HRD processes

The structure approach usually distinguishes among three HRD processes: learning-policy making, learning programs and learning processes. A fourth one has been added in recent years: designing personal development plans (PDPs), also referred to as learning-path creation (Poell and Van Der Krogt 2014). The structure approach gives center stage to learning-policy making in directing HRD, thus forming the framework within which the other three processes should take shape.

Learning-policy making

Learning-policy making is a process, usually initiated by HRD managers and supported by line management, in which the main features of the organization's HRD are established. Attempts are made to align HRD to the issues and development occurring in and around the organization. Making the learning policy explicit serves two purposes here: better (external) alignment of HRD to the organization and better (internal) alignment of various HRD processes. The aim of learning-policy making is that employees and other actors will act more in accordance with the policies developed. This process is usually initiated by HRD managers, who want to bring more clarity to the diversity of learning activities and programs.

Learning programs

In the second HRD process, learning programs, HRD practitioners (often assigned by management) create learning plans and structures suited to develop specific qualities in employees. Usually a group is involved in organizing a learning program, which may consist of employees, HRD practitioners, managers, supervisors, and content experts, among others. This group analyzes the opportunities, in view of the learning theme selected and the composition of the group, to use elements from the existing learning structure (learning opportunities) in the organization and to adapt it if needed. Elaborating the learning theme and selecting and/or developing suitable learning activities are key elements in this process.

Learning paths

In recent years many organizations have encouraged (or even forced) their employees to draw up a PDP. This plan should contain the qualities that the employee wants to develop in the near future and how to go about that. The key activity is for the employee to make a plan to create his or her own individual learning path (Poell and Van Der Krogt 2014). Such PDPs can be integrated into the annual appraisal cycle that many larger organizations have put into place.

Learning processes

In organizing learning processes, the employee participates in learning-relevant activities that can lead to a change in his or her action repertoire. Such activities are usually conducted together with other HRD actors, such as a trainer, educator, coach or instructor. These actors make use of all available elements from the existing learning structure (tools, techniques, procedures). The learning structure, explicitly or implicitly, also comprises the tasks and responsibilities of the learning employee and the other HRD actors.

Learning structures

In the structure approach, managers and HRD practitioners emphasize the designing of learning structures intended to direct employees' development. They create descriptions of tasks and responsibilities for course designers, management consultants, HRD managers, trainers, personal coaches, and other HRD actors. They draw up guidelines (procedures, protocols) for these HRD actors to act upon. Much emphasis is placed on designing the learning infrastructure, including learning programs (e.g. training courses, seminars, workshops) and tools (e.g. learning-style instruments, study materials, ICT support, learning-needs analysis, evaluation criteria, tests).

Designing these learning structures happens mostly in the processes of leaning-policy making and learning-program creation. The expectation is that employees and HRD practitioners in the other processes (organizing learning paths and learning processes) will act in accordance with the structures that have been designed previously. As the chances of this compliance occurring increase when these actors participate in the design process, they are usually involved in policy making and program creation as informants in some way or other. This involvement helps to attune the policies and programs that are being designed to their needs and problems (cf. Kessels 2000).

Dualistic nature: workplace learning as a separate issue?

Work is an important point of orientation for HRD in the structure approach. Learning-policy making and learning-program creation explicitly take into account the developments in work and the opportunities that (doing and improving) work offers to gain experiences relevant to learning. There is much consideration in the structure approach for those work characteristics that can influence learning.

Although work experiences are taken into account in the structure approach, such consideration seldom occurs in relation to explicit learning experiences. In studying transfer problems, for instance, aligning HRD to work is an important issue as well; however, minimal consideration is given to the possibility that work can offer opportunities that are not necessarily in line with the explicit learning experiences (cf. Holton and Baldwin 2003).

Strategic nature: HRD limited to a tool of management

The structure approach views HRD as a tool of management only. The key idea is that by designing HRD policies the other HRD processes can be directed. To increase the chances of this occurring, (HRD) managers involve other actors in learning-policy making. Employees and HRD practitioners contribute to the designing and planning of learning structures (especially policies and programs) in the expectation (of managers) that they will then act in accordance with these structures as they participate in the ensuing learning activities. Strategic interests of actors other than managers are taken into account to a very limited extent (Walton 1999; Yorks 2005).

Empirical research shows little support for the basic idea underlying the structure approach, that is, the notion that HRD processes are executed according to the structures and plans that have been designed beforehand. This minimal support applies to learning-policy making (Anderson 2009; Harrison and Kessels 2004; Mulder 2002; Sels *et al.* 2002; Sterck 2004), to learning programs (Wognum 1999; Overduin *et al.* 2002; Poell and Van Der Krogt 2005; 2007), and to PDPs (Seegers 2008; Janssen 2008; Doornbos and Phaff 2007; Beausaert 2011). Actors do make learning (policy) plans occasionally with a view to acquiring facilities (e.g. if HRD managers are assigned by funding bodies to draw up a policy plan, if educators are assigned by line (or HR) managers to design a learning program, if employees are assigned to fill out their PDP by their supervisor); however, the execution of these plans often turns out rather differently. Many times the policy plans do not materialize and if they do their ability to direct other HRD processes is found to be limited.

Empirical research rather presents an image of HRD in organizations being conducted with little planning and not very systematic at all. Actors (especially supervisors, employees) seem to initiate HRD processes in response to problems experienced in work or in the labor market rather than contribute to building a broader policy plan for the organization (Van Der Waals 2001; Smith and Hayton 1999; Sikkema and Witziers 2007). These actions are probably also an important reason why policy planning and designing structures contribute little to systematically organizing HRD processes: other actors' views and qualities as well as their room to operate accordingly are not taken into account enough. The structure approach is too narrowly focused on managers attempting to direct HRD processes through designing learning structures and takes too little account of other relevant actors and their interrelationships. The LNT-inspired dynamic-network approach to HRD that will be presented in the remainder of this chapter broadens the structure approach and places the emphasis more clearly on all relevant actors in learning networks as the driving forces for HRD processes.

The dynamic-network approach: actors organize HRD processes from learning networks

Actors are the driving forces of HRD in the dynamic-network approach. HRD emerges in an organization along the way, as actors tackle problems using employees' work and (explicit) learning experiences. For instance, managers may use employee training to solve internal labor market shortages; educators may design a learning program to help implement a new working method on the shop floor; employees may use budgets and other facilities to create a PDP. Thus, over time an HRD structure emerges, which clarifies who has which authority in HRD, how external support for HRD may be utilized, which learning programs and facilities are effective and so forth. In turn, this HRD structure will start to influence the ways in which actors develop new initiatives using HRD activities. Actors gain experiences organizing HRD and learn about doing so at the same time.

HRD structures in different organizations

How HRD develops is different from one organization to the next. Table 13.1 shows how specific learning networks emerge in different organizational types (Mintzberg 1989; see also Bergenhenegouwen 2007; Van Der Krogt 1995; Van Woerkom 2003).

Table 13.1 Four types of organizations and their learning network structures

Organizational Type		*Learning-Network Structure*
Bureaucratic organization - centrally governed network - by line managers and staff	⟷	*Vertical learning network* - hierarchical relations - between line, staff and shop-floor employees
Organic unit organization - organic network of organic units connected through linking pins - with tight work teams	⟷	*Horizontal learning network* - organic and collegial relations within work teams - direct supervisor as process facilitator
Professional organization - collegial network of professionals within and outside the organization - with many external connections	⟷	*External learning network* - profession governs initial and continuing education - external support
Entrepreneurial organization - loosely coupled network - of independent agents	⟷	*Loosely coupled learning network* - contractual relations - employees are self-managed

In *bureaucratic organizations* (e.g. a traditional manufacturing plant or a government agency) a vertical learning network is expected to emerge. In a vertical learning-network structure, the relationships between managers and employees are dominant; (HRD) managers have wide authority and easy access to various learning facilities. Organizations based on self-managed teams, *organic unit organizations*, are likely to develop a horizontal learning network. This structure sees strong relationships among employees who make decisions about HRD processes based on mutual consultation. In *professional organizations* (e.g. a hospital, research institute or law firm) an external learning network is expected to come into being over time. In this structure a substantial influence of external actors is characteristic, for instance, of professional colleagues from other organizations and of professional institutes providing (continuing) education. *Entrepreneurial organizations* (e.g. a partnership of real-estate agents) bring together employees who resemble independent entrepreneurs. The loosely coupled learning-network structure allows them individually to exert ample influence when it comes to their professional development and the facilities that they want to use.

Thus organizations develop learning-network structures. Actors hold certain positions in these learning networks, which determine their opportunities to shape HRD processes in interaction with each other. These HRD processes, however, create new learning structures and thus change the existing learning network. This cycle is, at its core, the dynamic nature of the network approach put forward in this chapter.

The dynamic-network approach views organizing HRD as a cycle (depicted in Figure 13.1). Actors in learning networks are the drivers of HRD processes; from their positions in the existing learning network they shape HRD processes in interaction with one another and, in doing so, they develop themselves as well as that learning-network structure. Their positions and mutual relationships in the learning-network determine their opportunities to participate in HRD processes and to use the existing learning structures to their own benefit.

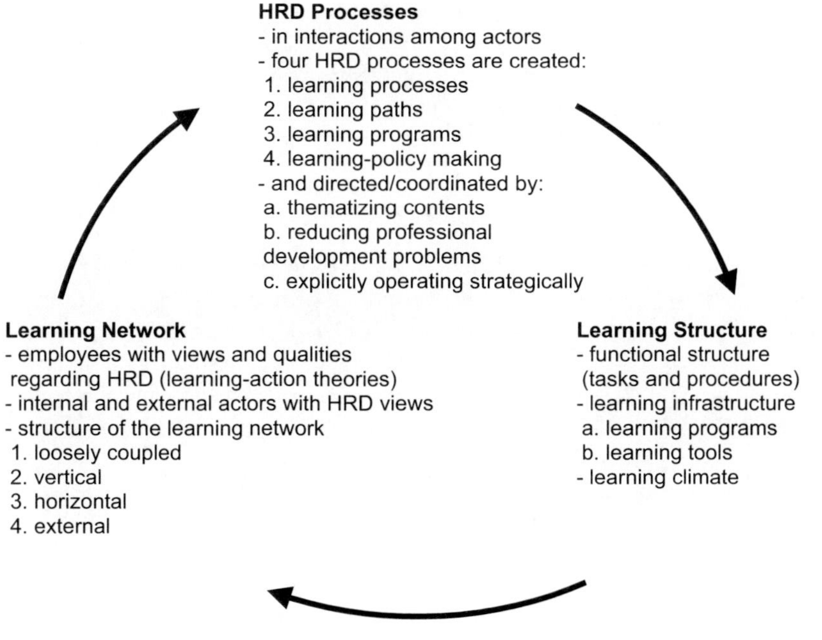

Figure 13.1 Organizing HRD according to the dynamic network approach

Compared with the structure approach, the dynamic-network approach emphasizes two elements much more strongly, namely, the learning networks and the directing of HRD processes.

Learning networks

The key difference with the structure approach lies in the actors in learning networks. Learning networks are the connection between the learning structures and the HRD processes.

The network approach has its roots in theories about inter-organizational networks (Gössling *et al.* 2007). In inter-organizational networks, actors from different organizations come together to give rise to a specific process, for example, to develop a new product or to conduct a complex research project. Employees who possess specific qualities and hold specific positions in their 'home organization,' which give them access to other actors and facilities, participate in these projects or processes. These various actors interact with each other, develop plans and execute them, discuss problems and solve them; thus along the way they create a network structure (lines of authority, consultation and communication) and other structures (procedures, infrastructural facilities, a climate), which give direction to their activities in the project or process.

In recent years similar network concepts have been used also to analyze and shape processes within an organization (Kilduff and Tsai 2003). Actors in the organization shape processes from their positions in the organizational network, for example, the primary work process, the HRM process (personnel selection, employment and outflow) and also the HRD process. Their positions in the network determine actors' opportunities to participate in these processes in accordance with their views and qualities.

In a similar vein, the relationships among the actors in the learning network determine their opportunities to reach, directly and indirectly, other actors (with their qualities and access to still other actors), and also their opportunities to use particular facilities (infrastructure, money, other material tools). How they make use of these opportunities in turn depends on their own views and qualities; for instance, which facilities and actors they deem suitable for deployment in the process, what they could do themselves and what they could leave to others to do.

The learning networks determine to what extent actors can operate in HRD processes in line with their own views and qualities; however, the actors are also the connection between the learning structures and the HRD processes. There are no directs links between learning structure and HRD processes; they both impact one another through the perceptions and interpretations of the actors.

Directing the HRD processes

A second difference with the structure approach is that the dynamic-network approach introduces three important steering mechanisms: by thematizing, problematizing and explicitly operating strategically, actors together can direct the HRD processes. Directing the HRD processes occurs not only by creating learning structures and plans (like in the structure approach) but also by making adjustments along the way. Actors form images of the present situation and the opportunities to change it during the process. The three mechanisms by which they can do this are elaborated below.

Thematizing the contents of the HRD process

Thematizing involves directing the HRD process in terms of its contents. Problems that actors experience in the organization are commonly the contents of the HRD process; problems that they think can be reduced by using HRD efforts. Sometimes they attempt to determine beforehand what should be learned and formulate learning goals (like in learning programs and learning processes). However, actors are often trying to clarify the theme at hand, adapt it to circumstances or change it along the way. They will also need to try and get their views on the theme more or less aligned. This process of clarification and adaptation is referred to here as thematizing.

Problematizing the HRD process

As the HRD process and its outcomes unfold, actors will experience problems, that is, they will find discrepancies between their own views and qualities, on the one hand, and the HRD process and outcomes, on the other hand. Actors can adjust the HRD process by solving these problems. Two types of problems are relevant in this connection.

First, and best known, are problems concerning the effectiveness of HRD processes. Actors have ideas about the outcomes that HRD processes should yield. When they experience discrepancies between their intended and achieved outcomes, there is an effectiveness problem. For example, this problem occurs when they have participated in a learning program that did not offer them relevant learning experiences; or when they have engaged in learning processes that did not provide them with the right knowledge or allowed them to develop useful skills. What they can do is try to solve these problems and thereby adjust the HRD process in line with their views and qualities.

Second, and at least as important (certainly for employees) to adjust HRD processes, are problems associated with the quality of that process. These problems occur during an HRD process, as actors become aware of discrepancies between the actual way in which the process is going and their own ideas about an appropriate way of conducting it. For instance, employees can feel that the learning groups are wrongly established or that they receive too little feedback on their individual progress. Actors can attempt to reduce such quality problems and adapt the HRD process by doing so.

Explicitly operating strategically

The third mechanism through which actors can direct HRD processes is by explicitly operating strategically. Actors have more or less explicit ideas about the ways in which they can organize HRD processes and about the elements that they deem important in the action of organizing. These ideas can lead their (inter)actions in HRD processes. This impact of actors' ideas about organizing HRD is not just the case for HRD practitioners (although their ideas will be relatively explicit) but also for the other actors engaged in the HRD process at hand. As employees (or managers) make their existing ideas more explicit, they become more aware of the strategic roles of their activities and how these are related to one another. This awareness will allow them to develop a more comprehensive strategic plan for their own professional development, guiding the activities they undertake in their learning paths. The plan will be informed by their own views and interests regarding professional development and how it should be organized in the present situation, taking into account their own position in the learning network and organizational structure (Poell and Van Der Krogt 2011).

The dual and strategic nature of HRD in the dynamic-network approach: organizing learning paths

As we showed earlier in this chapter, the structure approach takes into account the dual and strategic nature of HRD in a rather limited way, with management taking a dominant position. This section addresses how the dynamic-network approach takes into account the dual and strategic nature of HRD. The best opportunities to do so are offered by employees organizing learning paths. Learning paths enable employees to combine work, career and explicit learning experiences with a view to realizing their strategic interests in professional development, in interaction with managers, educators and external actors.

Learning-path creation

The creation of a learning path is one of the four HRD processes in the network cycle (Figure 13.1). Employees shape their learning paths by interacting with other actors in the learning network and through the use of available learning structures.

Employees' experiences form the base for their professional development (Fenwick 2003; Illeris 2007). They gain experiences as they are doing their job, changing their work, furthering their labor market and career opportunities, participating in explicit learning activities, and so forth. The challenge for employees is to pave their way amidst this array of work, career and learning experiences; to link them together in a meaningful way. This sense-making is what an employee does (with other actors and using the available learning structures) in the process of creating a learning path (see Figure 13.2).

A learning path is *not* a marked route. It unfolds as the employee integrates his or her experiences with other actors in various processes, in ways that are meaningful to him or her, and gives direction to new experiences possibly relevant for learning. Hence, learning-path creation comprises two types of activities: 1) creating experiences, actualizing previous experiences, and gaining new experiences in three processes; and 2) directing and coordinating these various experiences. These activities are undertaken, more or less intensively, in interaction with other actors.

Creating experiences in three processes: work, career and HRD processes

Three processes enable employees to gain experiences that are relevant to their professional development. First of all, the experiences happen in the primary work process, where the production and/or service take place. Employees can, for instance, run into problems conducting their job and attempt to reduce these obstacles; they can work on innovations; they can use new equipment, they can observe their colleagues working on a task and use some elements in their own job. The second process relevant for professional development is HRM, especially the allocation and employability of employees. Employees gain various types of experiences as they acquire and fulfil different jobs. They can try to integrate other tasks into their jobs, participate in specific projects, negotiate with their supervisors about the work conditions and list their strengths during the process. HRD processes are the third context in which professional development takes place. There are four types of HRD processes (learning-policy making, learning programs, learning-path

Interacting with other actors:	*Gaining experiences in:*	*Directed and coordinated by:*
• internal and external colleagues • supervisors and managers • HR practitioners, educators • and so forth	• the primary process (work experiences) • career development (employability) • HRD processes (explicit learning programs)	• thematizing contents • problematizing • explicitly operating strategically

Figure 13.2 Employees create learning paths with other actors (based on Poell and Van der Krogt 2014)

creation and individual learning processes), all of which are aimed explicitly at professional development of employees in the organization. Examples include participating in study circles, workshops, training courses, self-study, self-reflection, conferences and so forth.

Directing and coordinating experiences

For employees to be able to use these experiences for their professional development, they need to bring some order and coherence to them. Together with other actors they thus need to direct and coordinate their experiences in the three processes. This organizing can be done in three ways: by thematizing, by reducing professional-development problems and by operating according to their own explicit professional-development strategy.

Thematizing in the context of learning-path creation

Thematizing involves clarifying and further developing the contents or theme central to the learning path. Employees are then able to bring coherence and direction to their various experiences. A theme can emerge from everyday experiences, such as a problem with a client, a casual remark from a colleague or a change in the job. A theme may also be recognized more systematically, for example, through appraisal interviews, quality improvement meetings, career building sessions, and also through HRD (e.g. coaching) activities. Thematizing is a broader and more general activity than formulating learning goals.

Problematizing in the context of learning-path creation

Actors can adjust the process of learning-path creation as it unfolds. They can make changes and/or solve problems that occur on the basis of preliminary outcomes. For instance, they may notice that the learning path contains too many work experiences, that it focuses too little on explicit training courses, that the expertise it draws on is not quite appropriate, or that the qualities of external colleagues remain under employed in the learning path. It is also possible that employees reinforce the elements in their learning paths that are going well.

Explicitly operating strategically in the context of learning-path creation

Employees have more or less crystallized ideas about how they can organize their own professional development. Over the course of their career they have noticed to what extent and how they can realize these ideas in their jobs. The more aware they are of these ideas and possibilities, the easier it is for them to create an explicit professional-development strategy. This strategy may take the shape of a PDP that gives coherence and direction to their learning path.

The dual and strategic nature of learning paths: integrated in learning-path creation

The various actors together create learning paths; both the gaining of experiences and their direction and coordination occur in interaction with other actors. Managers, educators and especially employees themselves can thus exert influence on learning paths. The dual and strategic nature is integral to learning-path creation, as the different actors try to realize their strategic interests throughout the process.

Actors can determine together which experiences an employee can gain in his or her job, career and HRD processes. Interactions among employees and with their supervisors determine how the primary work process flows; HR officers, line managers and employees are core actors in career development; and educators place a major mark on the HRD activities. Each of these actors can thus impact the experiences that employees gain and contribute to their coordination. However, all actors do not necessarily have equal opportunities to affect which experiences are gained in all three processes. Managers probably have most influence on work processes; HR officers have some impact on the HRM process as well; and educators can put their emphasis on the explicit learning experiences that employees gain in HRD processes. Most importantly, the employee plays a more or less influential role in each of the processes, too!

Directing and coordinating the learning path can also occur along the way. Especially the employee plays a major role here. Employees can choose to involve other actors in doing so, for example, in solving professional-development problems and in thematizing the contents of his or her learning path. When it comes to thematizing, the ambitions and problems of the different actors play a crucial role. Each of the actors will try to incorporate particular themes or contents in the learning path and also solve problems in their own way. Managers will probably be inclined to direct a learning path by suggesting concrete themes rather than by solving problems during its creation. Many employees are likely to base a learning theme on their career ambitions. Educators will be inclined to deploy explicit learning experiences (e.g. in training programs) as a basis for employee learning paths and use problems that occur along the way to direct and coordinate them (Poell and Van der Krogt 2003).

Conclusion

The LNT-inspired dynamic-network approach of HRD offers a broader set of mechanisms for organizing HRD processes than the structure approach. In that sense the dynamic-network approach described in this chapter broadens the structure approach to HRD. In addition to designing learning structures, which the structure approach emphasizes, the dynamic-network approach strongly takes into account the opportunities of all actors (i.e. not just managers) to influence HRD processes in interaction. Moreover, adjusting HRD processes along the way (through thematizing, problematizing and explicitly operating strategically) is another important mechanism to direct and coordinate these processes; one that is much more feasible and effective in many situations than drawing up learning (policy) plans.

The dynamic-network approach also offers better opportunities to do justice to the dual and strategic nature of HRD. Especially the process of learning-path creation allows actors (employees and others) to combine work, career and explicit learning experiences with a view to employees' professional development according to their own views and qualities. It takes into account that each of the actors (both internal and external) will want to impact the experiences of employees as well as the coordination of those experiences. The dynamic-network approach views HRD not just as a tool of management but as an instrument that all actors can use to reduce their problems and realize their ideas.

A key condition for doing justice to the dual and strategic nature of HRD processes lies in taking into account the relationships among the actors in and outside the organization. These relations determine to a large extent the unfolding of HRD processes and their respective outcomes. HRD is the product of internal and external actors, and the same is true for learning paths. Relations between managers and employees determine the opportunities that the latter have to gain particular experiences in the primary work process. Employees in strongly bureaucratic organizations, for instance, will not be able to gain the same array of experiences as employees in entrepreneurial or professional organizations (Bergenhenegouwen 2007; Van Woerkom 2003). In a similar vein, the career experiences that employees gain in the HRM process will be heavily influenced by the relations among managers, employees and HR officers (Admiraal-Hilgeman 2009). And the explicit learning experiences that employees gain in HRD processes are determined by the relations among managers, educators and employees; educators are dominant actors in learning programs, whereas managers can exert considerable influence in learning-policy making (Poell *et al.* 1999).

Learning paths probably offer actors the best opportunities to organize employees' professional development in ways that do justice to the dual and strategic nature of HRD; they allow the various actors, especially employees themselves, to gain experiences in three relevant processes and to contribute to directing and coordinating these at the same time.

References

Admiraal-Hilgeman, T.J. (2009) *Loopbaanontwikkeling als middel om competent te leren omgaan met organisatieontwikkeling in het onderwijs* [Career development as a means to learn to handle organization development competently in education]. PhD dissertation, Tilburg University.

Anderson, V. (2009) Desperately seeking alignment: reflections of senior line managers and HRD executives. *Human Resource Development International* 12: 263–77.

Beausaert, S.A.J. (2011) The use of personal development plans in the workplace: effects, purposes and supporting conditions. PhD dissertation, Maastricht University.

Bergenhenegouwen, G.J. (2007) *Situationeel opleiden en leren* [Training and learning situationally]. Alphen aan den Rijn: Kluwer.

Doornbos, A. and Phaff, J. (2007) De verborgen kracht van POP's [The hidden power of PDPs]. *Develop* 3: 58–67.

Fenwick, T.J. (2003) Reclaiming and re-embodying experiential learning through complexity science. *Studies in the Education of Adults* 35(2): 123–41.

Gössling, T., Oerlemans, L.A.G. and Jansen, R.J.G. (2007) *Inside networks: A process view on inter-organisational relationships and networks*, Cheltenham: Edward Elgar.

Harrison, R. and Kessels, J.W.M. (2004) *Human resource development in a knowledge economy: An organizational view*, Hampshire: Palgrave Macmillan.

Holton, E.F. and Baldwin, T.T. (eds) (2003) *Improving learning transfer in organizations.* San Francisco: Jossey-Bass.

Illeris, K. (2007) What do we actually mean by experiential learning? *Human Resource Development Review* 6(1): 84–95.

Jacobs, R.L. (2003) *Structured on-the-job training: Unleashing employee expertise in the workplace* (2nd edition). San Francisco: Berrett-Koehler.

Janssen, S. (2008) *Guidance and the quality of professional development plans.* Heerlen: Ruud de Moor Centrum.

Kessels, J.W.M. (2000) Het ontwerpproces als leerproces [The design process as a learning process]. In Nieveen, N. (ed) Het ontwerpen van leertrajecten. *HRD Thema* 1(1): 16–21.

Kilduff, M. and Tsai, W. (2003) *Social networks and organizations.* London: SAGE.

Mintzberg, H. (1989) *Mintzberg on management.* New York: Free Press.

Mulder, M. (2002) *Competentieontwikkeling in organisaties: Perspectieven en praktijk* [Competence development in organizations: Perspectives and practice]. The Hague: Elsevier Bedrijfsinformatie.

Overduin, B., Kwakman, F. and Metz, B.J. (2002) De performancebenadering in Nederland: Een onderzoek onder HRD-afdelingen [The performance approach in the Netherlands: A study among HRD departments]. *M&O Tijdschrift voor Organisatiekunde en Sociaal Beleid* 56(2): 36–51.

Poell, R.F. and Van Der Krogt, F.J. (2002) Using social networks in organisations to facilitate individual development. In Pearn, M. (ed.) *Individual differences and development in organisations* (285–304). London: Wiley.

— (2003) Learning-program creation in work organizations. *Human Resource Development Review* 2(3): 252–72.

— (2005) Customizing learning programs to the organization and its employees: How HRD practitioners create tailored learning programs. *International Journal of Learning and Intellectual Capital* 2(3): 288–304.

— (2007) Tailoring learning programmes to every-day employee learning: Customisation strategies of HRD practitioners in health care. In: Sambrook, S. and Stewart, J. (eds) *Human resource development in the public sector: The case of health and social care* (239–52). London: Routledge.

— (2010) Individual learning paths of employees in the context of social networks. In Billett, S. (ed.) *Learning through practice: Models, traditions, orientations and approaches* (197–221). Dordrecht: Springer.

— (2011) Professionaliseringsstrategieën van werknemers: Hoe kunnen werknemers strategisch opereren bij het organiseren van hun professionele ontwikkeling? [Professional-development strategies of employees: How can employees operate strategically in organizing their professional development?]. In Kessels, J.W.M. and Poell, R.F. (eds) *Handboek human resource development: Organiseren van het leren* (2nd edition) (197–214). Houten: Bohn Stafleu Van Loghum.

— (2014) The role of human resource development in organizational change: Professional development strategies of employees, managers and HRD practitioners. In Billett, S., Harteis, C. and Gruber, H. (eds) *International handbook of research in professional and practice-based learning*. Dordrecht: Springer.

Poell, R.F., Van Der Krogt, F.J. and Wildemeersch, D.A. (1999) Strategies in organizing work-related learning projects. *Human Resource Development Quarterly* 10(1): 43–61.

— (2001) Constructing a research methodology to develop models for work-related learning: Social science in action. *International Journal of Qualitative Studies in Education* 14: 1, 55–70.

Poell, R.F., Chivers, G.E., Van Der Krogt, F.J. and Wildemeersch, D.A. (2000) Learning-network theory: Organizing the dynamic relationships between learning and work. *Management Learning* 31(1): 25–49.

Seegers, J. (2008) *Leiders leren* [Leaders learning]. PhD dissertation, Free University Amsterdam.

Sels, L., Delmotte, J. Lamberts, M. and Van Hootegem, G. (2002) *Personeelsbeleid in KMO's* [HRM in SMEs]. Leuven: Catholic University.

Sikkema, M. and Witziers, B. (2007) Effectmeting van HRD-interventies: De stand van zaken [Measuring the effect of HRD interventions: State of the art]. *Develop* 3(1): 9–19.

Smith, A. and Hayton, G. (1999) What drives enterprise training? Evidence from Australia. *International Journal of Human Resource Management* 10(2): 251–72.

Sterck, G. (2004) *Leerbeleid en leerpatronen in kennisintensieve arbeidsorganisaties: Concepten en praktijken* [Learning policy and learning patterns in knowledge-intensive organizations: Concepts and practices]. PhD dissertation, Catholic University Leuven.

Swanson, R.A. and Holton, E.F. (2009) *Foundations of human resource development* (2nd edition). San Francisco: Berrett-Koehler.

Van Der Krogt, F.J. (1995) *Leren in netwerken: Veelzijdig organiseren van leernetwerken met het oog op humaniteit en arbeidsrelevantie* [Learning in networks: The many-faceted job of organizing learning networks with a view to humanity and work relevance]. Utrecht: Lemma.

— (1998) Learning network theory: The tension between learning systems and work systems in organizations. *Human Resource Development Quarterly* 9(2): 157–78.

— (2007) *Organiseren van leerwegen: Strategieën van werknemers, managers en leeradviseurs in dienstverlenende organisaties* [Organizing learning paths: Strategies of workers, managers, and consultants in service organizations]. Rotterdam: Performa.

Van Der Waals, J. (2001) *Op eigen kracht: Over facilitaire diensten en hun veranderende rol in de primaire bedrijfsprocessen* [On their own: Facilities services and their changing roles in primary business processes]. PhD dissertation, Twente University.

Van Woerkom, M. (2003) *Critical reflection at work. Bridging individual and organizational learning*. PhD dissertation, Twente University.

Van Woerkom, M. and Poell, R.F. (eds) (2010) *Workplace learning: Concepts, measurement and application*. London: Routledge.

Walton, J. (1999) *Strategic human resource development*. Harlow: Pearson Education.

Wognum, A.A.M. (1999) *Strategische afstemming en de effectiviteit van bedrijfsopleidingen* [Strategic alignment and corporate training effectiveness]. PhD dissertation, Twente University.

Yorks, L. (2005) *Strategic human resource development*. Mason, OH: Thomson South-Western.

14

SYSTEMS THEORY

Relevance to HRD theory, research and practice

Richard J. Torraco

Since systems theory provides a common conception of organizations or any system, it can serve as a conceptual framework or organizer through which the field of HRD can ensure a holistic understanding of its work. Systems are viewed as unitary wholes composed of parts or subsystems; the system serves to integrate the parts into a functioning unit (Boulding 1956). Although systems vary in different ways – in size and complexity, for example – they have a number of common characteristics by virtue of being systems, and those properties can be applied to systems as any level.

Problem statement

Systems theory is often dismissed by some as irrelevant because it is associated with the terms "theoretical" and "impractical," and is considered too abstract for everyday use. Few people, other than some scholars and theorists, seem to get excited about systems theory. So it's left to do its job – explaining the behavior of dynamic systems – quietly behind the scenes. But systems theory deserves more credit than this. Although rarely acknowledged by those who think "outside-the-box" and are capable of seeing "the big picture," systems theory enables boundary spanning, broader perspectives, and its applied derivation – systems thinking. Without systems theory we risk overlooking dimensions of human and organizational phenomena marginalized or omitted by our disciplinary and ideological perspectives. However, despite the wide application of systems theory to human and organizational systems, and the large bodies of literature on systems theory (Boulding 1956; Jacobs 1989; Kast and Rosenzweig 1972; Mele *et al.* 2010; Ruona 2009; von Bertalanffy 1968; Yawson 2013) and systems thinking (Senge 1990; Senge and Sterman 1992; Sterman 2001; Watkins and Marsick 1993; Yawson 2013), limited work has been done on the relationship of systems theory to HRD. In addition, little research to date has examined the purpose and application of systems theory to all aspects of HRD – theory, research, and practice.

This chapter discusses systems theory and its applications to human resource development, and is organized into four sections. First, systems theory and its basic components are described. Then, literature on the use of systems theory in HRD is reviewed. Third, the purposes and applications of systems theory to HRD are discussed in three parts – applications of systems theory to HRD research, theory, and practice. Finally, implications for further HRD research and practice related to systems theory are offered. A glossary of systems theory terms and definitions is provided in Table 14.1.

Table 14.1 Systems theory – a glossary of terms

Term	*Definition*	*Reference Sources*
Inputs	Inputs are the resources and/or information converted by system processes into outputs.	McLagan (1989)
Process	A process converts inputs into outputs. Through a dynamic relationship with the environment, the system transforms resources and/or information into products, services, information, and/or programs as outputs. Biological and social systems use multiple processes.	Boulding (1956)
Outputs	Outputs are the products, services, information, and/or programs processed and exported by the system.	McLagan (1989)
Environment	The environment is everything outside the system that affects or is affected by the system's behavior.	McLagan (1989)
Subsystem	A subsystem is a component or part of the system that is interconnected with the system. In higher order biological and social systems, subsystems may possess the basic properties of an intact system.	Boulding (1956)
Open system	An open system has permeable boundaries that separate itself from its external environment.	Kast and Rosenzweig (1972)
Closed system	A closed system has rigid, impenetrable boundaries between itself and its external environment.	Kast and Rosenzweig (1972)
Boundaries	Boundaries separate the system from its environment. A closed system has rigid, impenetrable boundaries; whereas an open system has permeable boundaries between itself and the environment. Boundaries are easily defined in physical and biological systems, but are more difficult to delineate in social systems, such as organizations.	Kast and Rosenzweig (1972)
Feedback	Feedback is information about the outputs or the process of the system that is fed back as an input to the system. The system uses feedback, both positive and negative, to maintain balance among internal components and subsystems, and a steady state within its environment.	Boulding (1956)
Homeostasis	Homeostasis is a state of balance maintained through information exchanges between the system and the environment which allows the system to maintain a state of equilibrium over time.	Mele, Pels and Polese (2010)
Self-regulation	Self-regulation is the adaptive mechanism that allows the system to keep itself in a balanced condition, within the limits of its structure and through information exchange with the external environment.	Mele, Pels and Polese (2010)
Equilibrium/ Balance	Equilibrium/Balance is the ability of a system to maintain a steady state with its environment through the continuous exchange of materials, energy, and information.	Mele, Pels and Polese (2010)

Hierarchy	Hierarchy is a vertical structural relationship among components of a system. A system can be composed of subsystems of a lower hierarchical order and supra-systems of a higher hierarchical order.	Kast and Rosenzweig (1972)
Autopoiesis	Autopoiesis is a distinctive feature of self-organizing systems that stimulate specific mechanisms that align the system's internal functions with external environmental conditions. Autopoiesis is present in social systems such as organizations and communities.	Mele, Pels and Polese (2010)
Equifinality	Equifinality is the principle that open systems have multiple ways of reaching the same end state. Equifinality means that the same results may be achieved from different starting conditions and through different means. This principle suggests that social organizations can accomplish their objectives with diverse inputs and through different processes.	Kast and Rosenzweig (1972)

Basic components of systems theory

A system is a collection of interdependent, organized parts that work together in an environment to achieve the purposes of the whole (Boulding 1956). General systems theory describes the elements of a system, the interactions among a system's elements and subsystems, and the dynamics of the system's operation in its environment (von Bertalanffy 1968). Any system can be viewed as a transformation model which receives inputs, transforms these inputs in some way, and exports outputs. The system's environment is everything outside the system that affects or is affected by the system's behavior. The system uses feedback to maintain balance among internal components and subsystems, and a steady state within its environment. Boundaries separate the system from its environment. Boundaries with the environment can be open or closed one-way or both-ways. A boundary with one-way flow of information into the system exists for military intelligence operations. Political propaganda from a closed culture or country such as North Korea is an example of a boundary with one-way flow of information out of the system. Schools and universities maintain boundaries that are open in both directions. Examples of systems with boundaries closed in both directions are abusive families and dysfunctional communities or cults. Other concepts and properties of systems theory are defined in Table 14.1.

Review of the literature on systems theory and HRD

The first influential application of systems theory to HRD was a theory-to-practice monograph with chapters contributed by twelve leading HRD scholars and practitioners (Gradous 1989). One of the contributors (Jacobs 1989) acknowledged the broad set of skills needed by HRD professionals and characterized their pivotal role in organizations by referring to them as organizational problem solvers. He proposed systems-based human performance technology as a framework for understanding HRD practice (Jacobs 1987). Consistent with this view, providing training programs on request is no longer considered the primary or exclusive responsibility of HRD professionals. HRD is considered broader and more influential than being a source of training programs. Yet without a systems perspective, it is easy for others to adopt this narrow conception of HRD. A broader perspective of HRD as an interdisciplinary body of knowledge was proposed in which HRD is based in five bodies of knowledge: education, psychology, economics, organizational behavior, and systems theory (Jacobs 1990).

System thinking was brought to the forefront of organizational research and practice by Senge's (1990) exposition of the elements of the learning organization: personal mastery, mental models, shared vision, team learning and, as the framework that integrates the other disciplines, systems thinking – "the fifth discipline." Senge's work influenced the development of HRD scholarship on the dynamics of individual and organizational learning (Confessore and Kops 1998; Dixon 1994) and the learning organization (Ellinger *et al.* 2000; Holton and Kaiser 2000; Watkins and Marsick 1993).

System theory has been proposed as one of three disciplinary perspectives for guiding HRD research. Passmore suggested that HRD researchers would benefit by identifying the strong parallels between existing human and organizational systems and HRD systems (Passmore 1997). It has also been suggested that systems theory provides a means of determining the domains and boundaries between and across the related fields of continuing professional education, HRD, and workforce development (Roth 2004). Given the perennial problems faced by organizations of aligning internal integration with external adaptation, systems theory has been discussed as framework for analyzing organizations and providing leadership amid disorder and ambiguity (Yoon and Kuchinke 2005).

Systems theory has been a central part of the debate among HRD scholars as to which theories comprise HRD's theoretical foundation. While several disciplines and theories – adult learning, psychology, anthropology, sociology, activity theory, change theory, human performance technology, and economics – have been proposed as appropriate for HRD, nearly all scholars agree that systems theory is an important theoretical cornerstone of the field (McLean 1999; Roth 2004; Ruona 2009; Swanson 2001; Weinberger 1998). Ruona (2009) examined the contributions of systems theory to HRD by discussing the analytical capabilities systems theory provides to the field, the information about systems it enables the field to use, and the direction systems theory offers for conducting its work and planning its future. Yawson (2013) provided an extensive commentary on the relationship of systems theory and thinking (ST&T) to HRD and, in particular, on the ways in which ST&T has served a foundational role for the field and the areas of disconnect between ST&T and HRD.

Purposes and applications of systems theory

Systems theory can be used at various points along the theory–research–practice cycle to enhance our understanding of human resource development, as Figure 14.1 shows.

Each of the three domains of the theory–research–practice cycle makes a necessary contribution to HRD. The model demonstrates the need for all three domains to inform each other in order to enrich the profession as a whole. Exchange among the domains is multidirectional. Any of the domains can serve as an appropriate starting point for proceeding through the cycle.

If one begins with research, undertaken to create and expand the professional knowledge base, research is expected to yield recommendations for the improvement of practice. This link from research to practice is illustrated by new, innovative models of learning, organizational change, cross-cultural leadership, and other products of research that have led to improvements in professional practice.

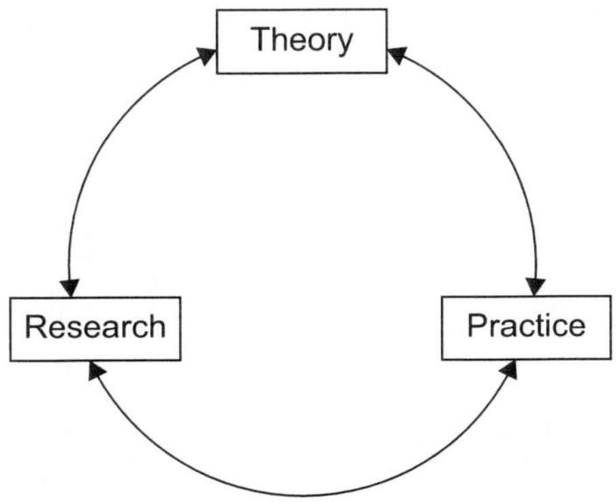

Figure 14.1 The Theory–Research–Practice cycle

Research can also proceed along the cycle to produce theory. Theory building continues to have an important role in HRD as the basis for strengthening research and practice. Additional theory is needed in HRD for greater understanding of the wide range of human and organizational phenomena that influence HRD research and practice. Thus, research serves a dual role in advancing HRD knowledge: it generates knowledge that can be applied to the improvement of practice, and it is used to develop core theories of HRD.

If we enter the cycle at practice, this provides a nearly inexhaustible source of researchable problems and challenges for HRD scholars to explore. Proceeding along the cycle from practice to research traces the familiar path between the organizational problems and the research efforts they stimulate. For example, research is often needed to help organizations with problems of practice such as the adoption of new technology. Problems occur when new technology is implemented before integrative systems are in place and personnel have the expertise to use them. Many HRD research projects are undertaken to address similar important problems of practice.

In addition, practice serves as a crucial real-world test of theories developed to enhance our understanding of organizations. Theories are tested in practice settings to assess how well they model real-world phenomena. This illustrates the link between practice and theory in Figure 14.1. Thus, practice, like each of the domains in the theory–research–practice cycle, serves a dual role in the advancement of HRD knowledge. It is both a catalyst to research and a source of validation for theory.

The cycle frequently starts with theory when it is used to guide the process of research. The variables and relationships to be examined by research are identified by reviewing the literature, which includes relevant theory. For example, if we wish to examine the influence of recent changes in work design on worker motivation, we might start with existing theories of work motivation and identify variables from these theories that are relevant to our research.

In summary, the theory–research–practice cycle provides a unified way of viewing the major domains of HRD. Systems theory is the basis for understanding and applying the theory–research–practice cycle to HRD. The systemic nature of the cycle is itself a manifestation of the integrative properties of systems theory. The roles that systems theory can play at each of the three stages of the cycle are explained in the following sections.

Research applications of systems theory

Even though we may value systems theory, we often engage in subsystems thinking. Each of us and our academic disciplines have a limited perspective of the systems we study. While proclaiming a broad systems viewpoint, we often overlook variables outside our interest or discipline, or dismiss unfamiliar factors as irrelevant, and the scope of our research is limited to those inputs which we can handle with our disciplinary knowledge and techniques. We find comfort in the relative certainty which this creates. However, our research likely presents only part of the potential knowledge offered because we have taken a partial systems view. Systems theory cannot coexist with subsystems thinking.

Torraco (2005) noted the following roles of theory as they apply to HRD: (a) to interpret old data in new ways, (b) to interpret new research findings, (c) to define applied problems, (d) to evaluate solutions to problems, (e) to determine research priorities, (f) to identify new research directions, and (g) to respond to new problems that have no previously identified solutions. The research implications of these roles of theory can be stated in concrete terms. Theory allows us to avoid recreating the wheel in our research (roles a, b, and d); it means we do not have to approach new research opportunities blindly (roles c and g); and theory can open up new intellectual perspectives to catalyze research (roles e and f). Systems theory can serve in each of these roles.

The importance of theory to research, and of systems theory in particular, can be seen in today's troublesome trends in education and employment. Shifts in the U.S. labor market seem to ebb and flow as they always have, but under the surface, transformative change is occurring in the composition and availability of jobs that, if sustained, portends negative consequences for the quality of life and social stability of the United States. The dynamics of job growth, information about jobs, how this information is used, and the responsiveness of our education and training system to labor market needs are critical to future economic and workforce development. However, current education and employment policy seems uninformed by relevant research based on systems theory. Most studies of education and employment examine only part of our workforce development system (Carnevale *et al.* 2010; Kalleberg 2011). Due in part to technological unemployment, fewer new jobs are emerging in which human workers have a comparative advantage over computer-mediated machines and technology. Despite the need for good jobs for a strong economy and prosperous society, the economy is not generating enough jobs to keep pace with the normal expansion of the working-age population. The national emphasis on increasing the proportion of those with a college education is an empty promise if there are too few good jobs available for the working-age population. More integrative studies are needed that combine research on job creation, the dynamics of fluctuating employment levels, and the education and training needed to gain employment, that is, research informed by systems theory.

Systems theory is the basis of a systems approach to thinking that can more effectively foster learning organizations (Watkins and Marsick 1993) and organizational innovation (Nonaka and Takeuchi 1995). To learn more rapidly and increase flexibility in a world of accelerated change and complexity, leaders are exploring new ways of organizing people and resources, for example by widely disseminating information and empowering people for local decision making, and rewarding innovation. But local decision making and individual autonomy can lead to organizational inertia and anarchy unless researchers account for the interconnections and long-term consequences of local decisions amid system-wide change. Consequently, research on organizational learning, innovation, and change should be based on an "organizations as systems" perspective. Researchers are encouraged to use systems theory, and managers to become systems thinkers, if research in organizations is to generate the knowledge associated with thinking globally and acting locally (Senge and Sterman 1992).

Most organizations today, regardless of size, operate within a global context. HRD researchers have been on the forefront in helping organizations to understand the importance of honoring cultural values across national and cultural boundaries if they are to be productive and sustainable. Hansen and Brooks (1994), using systems thinking as a theoretical foundation, reviewed a decade of cross-cultural research to confirm the culturally bound nature of HRD and identify differences in the meaning and purpose of HRD depending on the country or culture in which it occurs.

Systems theory constitutes an important element of the theoretical basis for social network analysis (SNA). Social network analysis is used as a research method for mapping and measuring the relationships between and among people, groups, organizations, computers, URLs, other connected information/knowledge entities, and even nation-states. The nodes in the network are the people and groups, while the links show relationships or flows between the nodes. SNA provides both a visual and a mathematical analysis of human relationships. Management consultants use this methodology, known as organizational network analysis (ONA), to analyze the effectiveness of communications and resource allocations. Systems theory provided a means for determining the environment for SNA, its boundaries and subject populations, and the types of social and material interactions for analysis (Knoke and Yang 2008).

Systems theory in theoretical research

Another important role of systems theory is to provide guidance to HRD scholars conducting theoretical research. Systems theory is widely applicable to theoretical work and is an implicit component of all theory building research methods. Theoretical researchers may choose among several positivistic, naturalistic, or multi-paradigm theory building methods (Torraco 2005), all of which are based, in part, on systems theory. As Weick (1995: 494) maintains, most of what is proffered as theory is "interim theory—an approximation of theory." As theorists work through the research process, theory is initially conceptualized through a review of related literature, through the theorist's hunches and "thought trials," the use of foundational concepts, existing theory, the development of new concepts and conceptual relationships, and finally, a new theoretical framework or model emerges that reflects synthesis of these components into a potentially powerful explanation of the phenomenon. However, systems theory requires that most theoretical research be offered as provisional since few theories are final and definitive. As Torraco (2005) states, authors who do not provide this imply that their work is the final statement on the topic. Few, if any, great contributions to science occur in a single installment; good theory is cumulative.

Systems theory as meta-theory

Moving along the theory–research–practice cycle in Figure 14.1, systems theory serves a role at the "theory" portion of the cycle. Systems theory serves as meta-theory, a framework for organizing related theories and their relationships. A meta-theory explains or elaborates on a body of theory (Ritzer 1992). Synthesis of a body of literature can provide the basis for developing meta-theory across theoretical domains, as demonstrated by Wilson's (1998) meta-theory of knowledge. In addition, systems theory can serve as a meta-theory for HRD, as examined in the monograph edited by Gradous (1989). As a meta-theory for the field, systems theory was proposed as an effective way to organize and integrate all aspects of HRD theory, research, and practice.

Systems theory and professional practice

Systems theory also serves an important role at the "practice" stage of the theory–research–practice cycle. Researchers and practitioners share responsibility for developing good theory that eventually serves to guide professional practice. Reflecting the challenges and opportunities inherent in the theory-to-practice phenomenon, we are reminded of Kurt Lewin's (1951) dictum that "nothing is quite so practical as a good theory." This important message is frequently repeated in the literature of management scholars (Van de Ven 1989) and practitioners (Christensen and Raynor 2003), and in the literatures of human resource development (Holton 2002), psychology (Jensen 1999), sociology (Cohen 1989), and in cross-disciplinary meta-theory (Wilson 1998). Given the apparent desirability of theory, few issues seem more significant to professional practice in HRD than examining areas of practice in need of greater understanding through theoretical research. The following brief illustrations highlight the importance of systems theory to effective HRD practice.

Rummler and Brache (1995) use "organizations as open systems" to show how the presence or absence of a systems perspective can make a major difference in strategic decision making. Using systems theory Rummler and Brache bring together the elements of an organization interacting together with the environment as the blueprint for their strategies for improving organizational performance. They recommend that an organization be viewed as a *processing system* that converts various resource *inputs* into product and service *outputs*, which it provides to receiving systems, or markets. The organization is guided by its own internal criteria and *feedback* from both internal and external sources. Competitor organizations also draw on these resources and provide their own products and services to the market. The entire scenario occurs in the broad context of the social, economic, and political *environment*. Looking inside the organization, there are functions or *subsystems* which exist to convert various inputs into products and services. These internal functions or departments have structural and functional characteristics that are consistent with the organization. Finally, the organization has control mechanisms, management, that interpret and react to the internal and external feedback so that the organization can maintain *balance* with the *external environment*. Rummler and Brache contend that this systems perspective describes every organization and without it, organizations cannot achieve optimal performance.

Another application of systems theory to professional practice is the diagnostic model used for organization development-based change called the "open systems model" (Cummings and Worley 2009). The open systems model acknowledges that organizations exist within a larger environment that affects how well the organization performs. The open systems model suggests that organizations and their subsystems – departments, groups, and individuals – share a number of common features that explain how they are organized and function. Diagnosis is the process of understanding how an organization is currently functioning by collecting pertinent data about current operations and analyzing those data to provide the information necessary to initiate and manage organizational change. When organizations are viewed as systems, the open systems model can be used as a framework for diagnosis that is applicable at three levels – the organization level, the group level, and the individual level. Based on systems theory, each organization level affects the other two levels and, in turn, is affected by them. For example, the external socio-economic environment is a key input to organization strategy and design decisions which, in turn, are inputs to group-level functions and decision making which, in turn, serve as inputs to job performance at the individual level. These cross-level relationships demonstrate the systems theory principle that structure and function at each level must fit together if the organization is to operate effectively. The open systems model is one of the most common frameworks used for organizational diagnosis in OD.

Implications for further HRD research and practice

Although other disciplines and theories have been suggested as a theoretical basis of HRD, nearly all scholars agree that systems theory is an important theoretical foundation for the field. At the same time, however, its application and use by HRD practitioners is rare (Swanson 2001; Yawson 2013). The foregoing discussion demonstrates that systems theory is relevant and applicable to both HRD scholars and practitioners. Systems theory is evident in the systematic relationships among the phases of the theory–research–practice cycle and has been cited in the literature on organization development (Cummings and Worley 2009), human performance improvement (Rummler and Brache 1995), organizational learning (Senge 1990; Watkins and Marsick 1993) and cross-cultural HRD (Hansen and Brooks 1994). Given the relevance of systems theory and systems thinking to these contexts of practice, why is systems theory not more prominent in HRD practice? If systems theory and systems thinking are foundational to HRD, this seems an important issue for further study.

Many new product development initiatives are plagued by unexpected rework and frustrating delays, forcing product development teams to take heroic measures to salvage projects before product launch deadlines. Sterman (2001) shows how the strenuous efforts to keep projects on track, with the long hours and single-minded focus on getting the product out, divert people's attention from pending upstream work on the next-generation product, which, in turn, gets further behind schedule, setting off another crisis and the need for more heroics. Managers react to events by making decisions to correct problems, but which also create side effects and unintended consequences. Why don't senior managers and other intelligent people who operate in dynamic organizational systems learn through experience to overcome these problems? Despite the principles and applications of systems theory, why do crisis management and short-term thinking persist?

Weick and Berlinger (1989) discuss organizations as self-designing systems and describe six properties of self-designing organizations by proposing that such organizations (1) redesign their processes, (2) value impermanence, (3) facilitate learning, (4) encourage meta-level analyses, (5) remove information filters, and (6) focus commitment. Referring to a key characteristic, they state, "Self-designing systems are distinguished by their preoccupation with continuous redesign such that most decisions are made to protect and exercise this capability" (Weick and Berlinger 1989: 320). Self-designing systems face rapidly changing environments with improvisation, generalists rather than specialists, and networks. But today's jobs and careers are slow to evolve, and most people are reluctant to move outside the comfort zones of their past experience and training, to take on the unfamiliar challenges and risks of new jobs and careers. But under such rapidly changing conditions, how do individual goals and aspirations remain aligned with organizational goals? What does systems theory say about reconciling the dynamic features of self-designing organizations with traditional jobs and careers?

Senge (1990) laments the human tendency to regress to linear, cause-and-effect thinking and to misperceive feedback from the environment, especially under conditions of stress and complexity. Are these tendencies for linear and short-term thinking innate or learned? If learned, what types of experience and education facilitate the development of system thinking capabilities? What does systems theory tell us about the mental models people use to make decisions in complex, dynamic situations? Can systems thinking be taught?

Conclusion

Systems theory is a theoretical cornerstone of HRD. Applications of systems theory to HRD theory, research, and practice have been examined. The systemic nature of the theory–research–practice cycle is itself a manifestation of the integrative properties of systems theory. Implications for further HRD research and practice related to systems theory include examining why systems theory is not more prominent in HRD practice and asking if systems thinking can be taught.

References

Boulding, K.E. (1956) General systems theory: The skeleton of science. *Management Science* 2: 197–208.

Carnevale, A.P., Smith, N. and Strohl, J. (2010) *Help wanted: Projections of jobs and education requirements through 2018*. Washington, DC: Center on Education and the Workforce, Georgetown University.

Christensen, C.M. and Raynor, M.E. (2003) Why hard-nosed executives should care about management theory. *Harvard Business Review* 81(9): 66–74.

Cohen, B.P. (1989) A theory and its analysis. In Cohen, B.P. (ed.) *Developing sociological knowledge: Theory and method* (2nd edition, 199–225). Chicago: Nelson-Hall.

Confessore, S.J. and Kops, W.J. (1998) Self-directed learning and the learning organization: Examining the connection between the individual and the learning environment. *Human Resource Development Quarterly* 9(4): 365–75.

Cummings, T.G. and Worley, C.G. (2009) *Organization development and change* (9th edition). Mason, OH: South-Western.

Dixon, N. (1994) *The organizational learning cycle: How we can learn collectively*. New York: McGraw–Hill.

Ellinger, A.D., Ellinger, A.E., Yang, B., and Holton, E.F. (2000) An empirical assessment of the relationship between the learning organization and financial performance. In Kuchinke, K.P. (ed.), *Academy of Human Resource Development Conference Proceeding*. Baton Rouge, LA: Academy of Human Resource Development.

Gradous, D.B. (ed.) (1989) *Systems theory applied to human resource development* (Theory-to-practice monograph). Alexandria, VA: ASTD.

Hansen, C.D. and Brooks, A.K. (1994) A review of cross-cultural research on human resource development. *Human Resource Development Quarterly* 5(1): 55–74.

Holton, E.F. (2002) The mandate for theory in human resource development. *Human Resource Development Review* 1(1): 3–8.

Holton, E.F. and Kaiser, S.M. (2000) Relationship between learning organization strategies and performance driver outcomes. In Kuchinke, K.P. (ed.), *Academy of Human Resource Development Conference Proceeding*. Baton Rouge, LA: Academy of Human Resource Development.

Jacobs, R.L. (1987) *Human performance technology: A systems-based field for the training and development profession*. Columbus, OH: ERIC.

— (1989) Systems theory applied to human resource development. In Gradous, D.B. (ed.) *Systems theory applied to human resource development* (Theory-to-practice monograph). Alexandria, VA: ASTD.

— (1990) Human resource development as an interdisciplinary body of knowledge. *Human Resource Development Quarterly* 1(1): 65–71.

Jensen, P.S. (1999) Links among theory, research, and practice: Cornerstones of clinical scientific progress. *Journal of Clinical Child Psychology* 28(4): 553–57.

Kalleberg, A.L. (2011) *Good jobs, bad jobs: The rise of polarized and precarious employment systems in the United States, 1970 to 2000s*. New York: Russell Sage Foundation.

Kast, F.E. and Rosenzweig, J.E. (1972) General systems theory: Applications for organization and management. *Academy of Management Journal* 15(4): 447–65.

Knoke, D. and Yang, S. (2008) *Social network analysis* (2nd edition). Thousand Oaks, CA: SAGE.

Lewin, K. (1951) *Field theory in social science*. New York: Harper and Row.

McLagan, P.A. (1989) Models for HRD practice. *Training and Development Journal* 41(9): 49–59.

McLean, G.N. (1999) Get out the drill, glue and more legs. *Human Resource Development International* 2(1): 6–7.

Mele, C., Pels, J. and Polese, F. (2010) A brief review of systems theories and their managerial applications. *Service Science* 2(1/2): 126–35.

Nonaka, H. and Takeuchi, K. (1995) *The knowledge creating company: How Japanese companies create the dynamics of innovation*. New York: Oxford University Press.

Passmore, D.L. (1997) Ways of seeing: Disciplinary bases of research in HRD. In Swanson, R.A. and Holton, E.F. (eds) *Human resource development research handbook* (199–214). San Francisco: Berrett-Koehler.

Ritzer, G. (ed.) (1992) *Metatheorizing*. Newbury Park, CA: SAGE.

Roth, G.L. (2004) CPE and HRD: Research and practice within systems and across boundaries. *Advances in Developing Human Resources* 6(1), 9–19.

Rummler, G.A. and Brache, A.P. (1995) *Improving performance: Managing the white space on the organization chart* (2nd edition). San Francisco: Jossey-Bass.

Ruona, W.E.A. (2009) Systems theory as a foundation for human resource development. In Swanson, R.A. and Holton, E.F. (eds) *Foundations of human resource development* (2nd edition, 128–36). San Francisco: Berrett-Koehler.

Senge, P.M. (1990) *The fifth discipline: The art and science of the learning organization*. New York: Doubleday-Currency.

Senge, P.M. and Sterman, J.D. (1992) Systems thinking and organizational learning: Acting locally and thinking globally in the organization of the future, *European Journal of Operational Research* 59(1): 137–50.

Sterman, J.D. (2001) System dynamics modeling: Tools for learning in a complex world. *California Management Review* 43(4): 8–25.

Swanson, R.A. (2001) Human resource development and its underlying theory. *Human Resource Development International* 4(3): 299–312.

Torraco, R.J. (2005) Theory development research methods. In Swanson, R.A. and Holton, E.F. (eds) *Foundations of human resource development* (351–74). San Francisco: Berrett-Koehler.

Van de Ven, A.H. (1989) Nothing is quite so practical as a good theory, *Academy of Management Review* 14(4): 486–9.

von Bertalanffy, L. (1968) *General systems theory: Foundations, development, applications*. New York: Braziller.

Watkins, K.E. and Marsick, V.J. (1993) *Sculpting the learning organization: Lessons in the art and science of systematic change*. San Francisco: Jossey-Bass.

Weick, K.E. (1995) What theory is not, theorizing is. *Administrative Science Quarterly* 40(3): 385–90.

Weick, K.E. and Berlinger, L.R. (1989) Career improvisation in self-designing organizations. In Arthur, M.B., Hall, D.T. and Lawrence, B.S. (eds) *Handbook of career theory*. New York: Cambridge University Press.

Weinberger, L.A. (1998) Commonly held theories of human resource development. *Human Resource Development International* 1(1): 75–93.

Wilson, E.O. (1998) *Consilience: The unity of knowledge*. New York: Knopf.

Yawson, R.M. (2013) Systems theory and thinking as a foundational theory in human resource development – A myth or reality? *Human Resource Development Review* 12(1): 53–85.

Yoon, S.W. and Kuchinke, K.P. (2005) Systems theory and technology: Lenses to analyze an organization, *Performance Improvement* 44(4): 15–20.

15

HUMAN CAPITAL THEORY AND SCREENING THEORY

Relevance to HRD research and practice

Judy Yi Sun and Greg G. Wang

The purpose of this chapter is to review two primary economic theories, human capital theory (HCT) and screening theory, and highlight their relevance to HRD at national, organizational, and individual levels.

Human capital theory

Since Becker's (1962) path-breaking "human capital revolution" (Bowman 1966: 111), HCT has changed the landscape of research in social science disciplines. HCT was conceptualized to explain education and training choices of individuals. It was quickly expanded to cover broader economic decisions by individuals, including occupational choice, migration, health care, and planned family size, such as fertility and mortality (Sobel 1982) as well as national economic development policies (Harbison and Myers 1964). Although HCT is rooted in Adam Smith's early work, analyses of human behaviors were traditionally not part of economic theory.

Approaches to studying HCT

A number of research approaches were used to conduct studies on HCT from the late 1950s to the early 1960s at both macro and micro levels. These different research approaches contributed to findings that led to the establishment of the human capital hypothesis (Bowen 1964).

The correlation approach

Combining data from 75 nations, Harbison and Myers (1964) developed human capital investment indices and classified them into four categories. These indices were correlated with national income within a four-category classification based on the development level of the nations. This study suggested that moving upward into a higher national income category could be achieved by increasing investment in humans. In a separate study, Galenson and Pyatt (1964) adopted an aggregated production function to account for growth in labor productivity in 52 countries between 1951 and 1961. The rate of growth in labor productivity was correlated with the nutritional variable (calories per head), enrollments in higher and secondary education, expenditures on health and housing, and other welfare expenditures. Together, nutrition and higher education, along with physical capital, explained 50 per cent of labor productivity increases. Both studies found that national income and labor productivity were correlated with human capital investment activities. These preceding studies provided strong evidence of the link between investments in human capital and national wealth.

The residual approach

The residual approach adopted a linear production function technique, aimed at relating changes in either national product or per capita income to increases in productive factors. The residual was then attributed to factors not included in the production function (e.g. Denison 1962, Kendrick 1961). Early residual measurements by Solow (1957) included quantitative increases in capital and left a very high residual attributed to labor. Denison (1962) added more variables, including increases in man-hours worked and education and training, with the latter treated as synonymous with improvement in labor quality. The Denison (1962) study inferentially attributed 42 per cent of the growth of per capita income in the US to investment in people.

The return-on-education approach

Several other pioneering studies have shown that the rate of return on education (at the college level), both private and social returns, is significantly higher than the rate of return on investment in physical capital (Becker 1962, Mincer 1962, Schultz 1960). For example, Schultz (1962) estimated that the stock of educational capital in the US tripled from 1930–1957, and the return from investment in educational capital accounted for about 20 per cent of the economic growth during this period.

These three approaches led to the core finding that investment in humans can significantly impact labor productivity gains. These studies created a foundation for helping scholars recognize the economic outcomes of training and education. The studies' findings included variables such as the quality, competence and performance of human resources – topics that were soon to become core areas of HRD research and practice.

The cornerstone of HCT: general versus specific training

Although formal education and firm specific training are both human capital investment activities, they were treated differently under HCT. Becker (1962, 1993) established the cornerstone of HCT by differentiating general skills from specific skills (Acemoglu and Pischke 1999). This differentiation effectively explains human capital investment at both individual and organizational levels. General training increases an individual's skills and competencies which are portable to other organizations (e.g. computer literacy training), whereas specific training is much less portable and may only increase an individual's productivity within his/her respective organization (Becker 1993).

In organizational practice, however, most skills contain both types of skills. The distinction of general skills and specific skills was mostly useful for conceptualization and as an analytical tool (Acemoglu and Pischke 1998). However, the distinction between general versus specific skills training has different policy implications in terms of who pays for, and who benefits from, the respective training investment. Because of the portability of general skills training, business organizations may be less motivated to provide such training, and they may believe that public educational systems should provide general skills training. Business organizations might take the stance that the private sector should limit its investment to specific training for the purpose of pursuing organizational objectives.

In most contemporary organizations, both general skill training and specific skill training are offered to employees, even though some businesses may have reservations about offering general training, as noted in the previous paragraph. These offerings may include training as general as project management and as specific as how to operate organizational-based proprietary software or machinery. General and specific training may also be offered outside the walls of the organization. Increasingly, business organizations offer tuition reimbursement to encourage employees to pursue formal education. These opportunities exist because organizations recognize the value of both specific skills and general skills that are closely embedded in individual employees. All jobs require employees to apply a combination of general and specific skills in order to complete work tasks.

Organizations operate in economic environments (including costs associated with workers' mobility and market imperfections) that often deviate from the theoretically derived assumptions of HCT. For example, economic studies have revealed that an employer may sponsor general skills training under asymmetric information regarding employees' abilities relative to other firms (e.g. Acemoglu and Pischke 1998). Information asymmetry occurs when one party of economic agents retains information that is unknown to the other party, or vice versa. Acemoglu and Pischke (1999) showed that labor market imperfections such as turnover costs or an employer with dominating power in a particular industry can provide organizations with incentives to invest in employees' general skills. Thus, skewed information sources as well as power dynamics can influence when, where or if investments are made in employees' general and/or specific training.

Human capital externalities or spillover

Human capital externalities or human capital spillover are economic phrases related to interactions among workers. Marshall (1890) was among the first to recognize that social interactions among workers create learning opportunities that can enhance productivity. Human capital externalities refer to the phenomenon where the presence of educated and skilled employees makes their coworkers more productive (Moretti 2004). In economics literature, this phenomenon is also referred to as HC spillover. The development of HCT accelerated the research on spillovers. Coworkers can seemingly trade human capital skills, such as communication skills and desirable work behaviors, to mutually raise productivity (Stoyanov and Zubanov 2012). For example, a worker's motivation to acquire human capital is often influenced by the human capital of others in the social network or workplace interactions. Such an effect has been found to influence productivity and individual earnings in the workplace (e.g. Battu *et al.* 2003, Moretti 2004). Economists have long speculated that human capital may generate significant spillovers. Lucas (1988), among others, asserted that human capital externalities are large enough to explain differences between poor and rich countries in long-term growth rates. Studies have found that human capital spillovers are a main engine for economic growth (Lucas 1988, Abel *et al.* 2012) and they also add value to team dynamics in the workplace (Idson and Kahane 2000).

The human capital spillovers research in the economic literature provides a theoretical base to study related HRD mechanisms in organizations. For example, team synergy, on-the-job training, informal learning, workplace socialization and coaching and mentoring are examples of spillovers within the HRD domain. Understanding spillovers and facilitating the mechanisms of spillovers can be beneficial to organizational performance.

Challenges to HCT

Although a case can be made that HCT has revolutionized economic thinking, its challenges are embedded in its neoclassic roots and analytical logic. A strong challenge pertained to HCT's neoclassical roots; that is, markets are in perfect competition with free entry and exit, and that information is perfect and access to it does not involve any cost (Wang and Holton 2005). However, most markets are imperfect, and information is asymmetric. In other words, economic agents often incur substantial costs to access valuable information. Under this condition, a question unaddressed by HCT is: How is private information about potential employees' productivity acquired through training and education transmitted to potential hiring organizations so that the right people can be selected by an organization?

A second challenge is related to HCT's analytical logic. A traditional HCT viewpoint would posit that individuals receive a higher return if they acquire more years of education (degrees, diplomas and/or certifications). In the USA, this viewpoint is linked to the American Dream and the belief that education can lift one toward greater economic success. However, the logic of this belief does not address whether individuals would be more productive if they spent longer time in earning an education. In other words, HCT does not offer sufficient explanation for students who take more time to complete a degree with a higher investment and opportunity costs (Riley 1979). This aspect of HCT has been disillusioning to college graduates in low-demand majors who have invested heavily in their studies only to find very limited possibilities for employment at the conclusion of their studies.

A third challenge to HCT pertains to the assertion that learning increases productivity. This assertion is strictly theoretical. A clearly identified mechanism for measuring changes in productivity brought about by learning does not exist in the economic literature. The connection between learning and productivity is primarily derived from observed quantitative correlations or deductions between education levels and lifetime earning profiles of individuals or nations (e.g. Becker 1962, Harbison and Myers 1964, Mincer 1962). One could argue that HCT treated the process from learning to productivity as a black box and hypothesized that education and training would increase a worker's future productivity (Sobel 1982). In other words, the connection between human capital investment and productivity and between productivity and earnings is an HCT assumption which is difficult to prove (Sobel 1982).

The preceding three challenges associated with HCT create gaps between theory and practice in HRD. Organizations operate with imperfect competition and information asymmetry, yet they must make decisions on identifying and selecting the right employees from the labor pool. Therefore, HCT has limited utility as a tool that can be used to help firms know if job applicants and current employees will be productive and capable of meeting organizational goals.

Screening theory as an alternative to HCT

Individuals may increase their productivity through investment in education and training activities, initially in schools and then continuing in the form of workplace learning. However, the potential productivity of a new hire is difficult to ascertain by those involved in the hiring process. Applicants may have augmented their potential productivity through schooling, but those enhancements may be unrecognizable to employers when individuals enter the labor market. Costs associated with defining and verifying employees' potential for performance can be a large expense for organizations (Bac 2000). If people are hired by an organization and they fail to meet expectations, human and fiscal resources are wasted by an ineffective hiring process. Screening theory was developed to ease the financial burden of making well-informed staffing decisions.

The formulation of screening theory

Screening theory, as an alternative to HCT, argues that a heuristically superior explanation must be able to accommodate the unique institutional characteristics of the labor market. Thus screening theory contends that schooling may have the same apparent effect on earnings, either because the productivity linkage is a valid one, or because it is the instrument through which the effect of some other background variable is transmitted, such as family background, or because it masks an intervening variable other than productivity (Sobel 1982). This contention provides the underlying basis for screening theory.

Building on the analysis of limitations of HCT's theoretical base, Spence (1973a) and Arrow (1973) independently and simultaneously formalized the hypothesis that education served as a credentialing process which signaled high innate productivity to organizations. From organizations' perspectives, screening theory, similar to HCT, considers hiring as an uncertain investment. Organizations are not sure of the productive capabilities of a potential employee at the time of hiring, among other information asymmetries. Nor will this information become available immediately after hiring. The job may take time to learn, and often on-the-job specific training is required. To an extreme, Spence (1973a) compares the organizational process of hiring an employee to buying a lottery ticket. In formulating screening theory, Arrow (1973: 194) proposed the following extreme assumptions:

> Higher education contributes in no way to superior economic performance; it increases neither cognition nor socialization. Instead, higher education serves as a screening device, in that it sorts out individuals of differing abilities, thereby conveying information to the purchasers of labor.

Accordingly, the theory considers the filtering role of education as a value-added one that conveys much needed information by the economic agents in the markets. Productivity and ability of a potential employee cannot be accurately determined, but diplomas are easy to decipher, and such information can be obtained easily by organizations at minimal cost. In the screening model, education is assumed to act as a filter, with successful completion of education signaling higher levels of innate ability. The signaling model has been applied to other economic phenomena from advertising (Nelson 1974) to financial structure (Ross 1977), social phenomena from courtship (Spence 1973b) to gift exchange (Camerer 1988). Nevertheless, screening theory is often contrasted with HCT with respect to education and training related investments.

Although the terms "screening, filtering, and signaling" that are associated with screening theory are often used interchangeably, each has a distinctive connotation in the economic literature. Potential employees use education to "signal" their productivity to employers. Employers "screen" and "filter" out potential employees who possess a minimum level of training and education credentials (Weiss 1995).

Empirical studies comparing educational credentialing to the "sheepskin effect" (e.g. Belman and Heywood 1991, Wang and Holton 2005) have found that the diploma had value apart from the accumulated years of education. Findings indicated that diplomas serve as a proxy for productivity and may play a role in increasing productivity (Hungerford and Solon 1987).

In testing screening theory, Miller and Volker (1984) hypothesized that if returns were strictly related to productivity according to HCT, graduates who took jobs in their own major should be paid more than those who took jobs in an unrelated field of study. Their investigation found no difference in the starting salaries of economics graduates and persons graduating with non-economics majors in jobs related to economics. The same study also examined science majors versus non-science majors in science related jobs and obtained similar results. Diploma-based sheepskin effects attenuate over time with increased years of workforce experience because additional work experience allows more direct observation of individual productivity (Belman and Heywood 1997).

On-the-job screening

In addition to the education screening process, other economic studies have investigated a second layer of the screening process, on-the-job screening (Bac 2000, Pinoli 2008). On-the-job screening is based on the following rationale. After the initial screening based on educational credentials, information about an employee's productivity and performance will be gradually revealed to the organization during an employee's work life. This information is not known to the employer at the time of hiring, but it eventually emerges and the employer becomes better informed about the employee's productivity and performance. On-the-job screening involves using systemic processes to collect multiple sources of data about employees, and employers are then able to make data-based decisions about the organization's human capital.

Employers use a variety of performance appraisal tools and techniques to make judgments about past, present and future job performances of employees. And, these judgments are directly related to decisions about current and future pay for these workers. Some of these tools are used to screen out employees whose performances do not meet organizationally defined performance indicators. Decisions are made as early as possible so that investments in underperforming employees are kept to a minimum, and investments are maximized in higher producing employees in order to develop desired human capital for the organization. Some organizations adopted a forced-ranking strategy to sort out high performers from other performers, although the effects of this strategy are controversial (Gary 2001). Organizations may face a trade-off in pursuing these strategies. The efficiency of on-the-job screening may be sacrificed because of the employer's need to invest in a specific human capital area (specific types of workers or job classifications). Or, alternatively, when the organization has an effective training system, organizations may have to sacrifice employee performance during the on-the-job screening process (Bac 2000).

HRD research based on HCT

During the late 1990s, HRD scholars began to realize HCT's significance and relevance to HRD research (Weinberger 1998). Gradually, HCT's foundational role for HRD research and practice began to gather momentum (Swanson 2001, Swanson and Holton 2001, also see Garavan *et al.* 2001). Since then, HRD research has been engaged in research and theory building around HCT and learning, change and performance (Dobbs *et al.* 2008, Wang and Dobbs 2008). In general, HRD research incorporating economic theories has developed at individual, organizational and national levels.

HRD research at individual and organizational levels

Research at the individual and organizational levels has been focused on individual learning and performance and their impact on overall organizational performance. This impact is represented by research and practice in HRD evaluation and measurement (Wang and Spitzer 2005). Multiple measurement approaches and techniques have been proposed (e.g. Bassi and McMurrer 2008, Fitz-enz 2009, Phillips 2011, Wang *et al.* 2002); however, a central tenet has been consistent. That is, organizations investing in employee learning and performance improvement are expected to recoup the returns in the form of improved organizational performance and competitiveness, represented by increased revenue, profitability, or customer loyalty. The same tenet has been adopted widely by HRD researchers to understand the relationship between HRD interventions and individual and organizational performance (see for example Park and Jacobs 2011).

Although HCT has been applied to HRD research and practice, a few scholars have questioned the relevance of HCT in the new economy. For example, McLean (2007) has posited that HCT's distinction between general and specific skills becomes obsolete and outdated in the new economy, thus losing its interpretive and predictive power. Conversely, a counter argument would assert that the same theory has been adopted as an analytical tool to understand and describe the emerging HRD trend of corporate universities (CUs) in worldwide organizations (e.g. Wang *et al.* 2010). To answer questions concerning the CU practice, Wang *et al.* (2010) applied HCT, from the lens of general versus specific skills, and analyzed the inadequacy of previous literature about CUs. Their analysis further revealed that the key difference between CUs and traditional universities was their different foci on skill specificity based on different contexts of skill requirements; thus, CUs were not predicted to present a threat to traditional universities in shaping individuals' skills.

HRD research at the national level

HCT has been used to analyze national economic development policies and associated education and training investment (Harbison and Myers 1964). With a similar analytical strategy, the international HRD literature has paid close attention to HRD national policies and their influence on economic development. Ashton *et al.* (2000) proposed a conceptualization of national skill formation systems to explain and predict national policies in response to the challenges of globalization. Based on a critical review of literature, Ashton *et al.* (2000) identified four national skill formation process models adopted by different nations. Ashton (2002) further studied national HRD policies and strategies in three Asian "tiger" countries: Singapore, South Korea and Taiwan. A commonality was that control over the education and training system provided the three countries with the ability to quickly recognize and act on workforce needs. HRD national strategy enabled the three nations to build a skill base in one generation as opposed to the three generations necessary in developed countries. Effective HRD strategy allowed the nations' economic growth to proceed without employers experiencing severe skill shortages (Ashton *et al.* 2002).

Future HRD research directions

Research based on HCT has not taken a prominent position in HRD literature. Minimal HRD research has been conducted that uses economics as either a theoretical foundation, or methodological and analytical base. Wright and McMahan (2011: 100) make this observation regarding organizational research: "while the concept of human capital may be 40 years old, its treatment in organizational research is in an infant stage." Ample room exists for future studies that link HRD and HCT.

Future research at individual and organizational levels is likely to focus on human capital's role as a mediator in the relationship between HRD interventions and organizational performance. This role may include continued inquiry on learning transfer and its impact on employee and organizational performance (Holton *et al.* 2000). Another possibility is to explain new HRD phenomena, for example, exploring the nature of CUs, examining their roles in shaping organizational human capital capacity and competitiveness, and speculating how they might inform HRD strategies at the organizational level (Abel and Li 2012).

Future research needs to explore, from a more strategic perspective, where human capital originates, and how and through what process it is created and transformed. Furthermore, future research is needed that examines mechanisms through which individual knowledge, skills and abilities drive organizational performance (Ployhart and Moliterno 2011).

Finally, the HRD domain and its relationship with human capital building at national or international levels need to be clearly articulated to clarify existing confusion and inconsistencies in the literature. A theory can only be judged in relation to its rivals purporting to explain the same range of phenomena. For instance, screening theory accounts for the same evidence used by HCT by a different set of assumptions and equally powerful theoretical framework. In our judgment, screening theory challenged HCT and established its place as complementary to HCT. Future research needs to continue with efforts of theory building that can establish the utility of HCT in HRD research and practice.

References

Abel, A.L. and Li, J. (2012) 'Exploring the corporate university phenomenon: development and implementation of a comprehensive survey', *Human Resource Development Quarterly* 23: 103–28.

Abel, J.R., Dey, I. and Gabe, T.M. (2012) 'Productivity and the density of human capital', *Journal of Regional Science* 52: 562–86.

Acemoglu, D. and Pischke, J. (1998) 'Why firms train? Theory and evidence', *Quarterly Journal of Economics* 113: 79–119.

— (1999) 'Beyond Becker: training in imperfect labor markets', *Economic Journal* 109: 112–42.

Arrow, K.J. (1973) 'Higher education as a filter', *Journal of Public Economics* 2: 193–216.

Ashton, D. (2002) 'Explaining change in national HRD strategies: the case of three Asian Tigers', *European Journal of Development Research* 4: 136–44.

Ashton, D., Sung, J. and Turbin, J. (2000) 'Toward a framework for the comparative analysis of national systems of skill formation', *International Journal of Training and Development* 4: 8–25.

Ashton, D., Green, F., Sung, J. and James, D. (2002) 'The evolution of education and training strategies in Singapore, Taiwan and S. Korea: a development model of skill formation', *Journal of Education and Work* 15: 5–30.

Bac, M. (2000) 'On-the-job specific training and efficient screening', *Journal of Labor Economics* 18: 681–701.

Bassi, L. and McMurrer, D.P. (2008) 'Toward a human capital measurement methodology', *Advances in Developing Human Resources* 10: 863–81.

Battu, H., Belfield, C.R. and Sloane, P.J. (2003) 'Human capital spillovers within the workplace: evidence for the Great Britain', *Oxford Bulletin of Economics and Statistics* 65: 575–94.

Becker, G.S. (1962) 'Investment in human capital: a theoretical analysis', *Journal of Political Economy* 70(Supplement 5, Pt. 2): 9–49.

— (1993) *Human Capital: A Theoretical and Empirical Analysis with Special Reference to Education*, 3rd edn, Chicago: University of Chicago Press.

Belman, D. and Heywood, J.S. (1991) 'Sheepskin effects in the returns to education: an examination of women and minorities', *The Review of Economics and Statistics* 73: 720–24.

— (1997) 'Sheepskin effects by cohort: implications of job matching in a signaling model', *Oxford Economic Papers* 49: 623–37.

Bowen, W.G. (1964) 'Assessing the economic contributions of education: an appraisal of alternative approaches', in S. Harris (ed.) *Economic Aspects of Education*, Paris: OECD, 177–200.

Bowman, M.J. (1966) 'The human capital revolution in economics thought', *Journal of Sociology and Education* 39: 111–37.

Camerer, C. (1988) 'Gifts as economic signals and social symbols', *American Journal of Sociology* 94: S180–S214.

Denison, E.F. (1962) *The Sources of Economic Growth in the United States and the Alternatives Before Us*, Supplementary Paper 13, New York: Committee for Economic Development.

Dobbs, R.L., Sun, J.Y. and Roberts, P.B. (2008) 'Human capital and screening theories: implications for human resource development', *Advances in Developing Human Resources* 10: 788–801.

Fitz-enz, J. (2009) *The ROI of Human Capital: Measuring the Economic Value of Employee Performance*, New York: AMACOM.

Galenson, W. and Pyatt, G. (1964) *The Quality of Labour and Economic Development in Certain Countries*, Geneva: International Labour Office.

Garavan, T.N., Morley, M., Gunnigle, P. and Collins, E. (2001) 'Human capital accumulation: the role of human resource development', *Journal of European Industrial Training* 25: 48–68.

Gary, L. (2001) 'The controversial practice of forced ranking', *Harvard Management Update* 6: 3–4.

Harbison, F. and Myers, C.A. (1964) *Education, Manpower, and Economic Growth: Strategies of Human Resource Development*, New York: McGraw-Hill.

Holton, E.F., Bates, R.A. and Ruona, W.E. (2000) 'Development of a generalized learning transfer system inventory', *Human Resource Development Quarterly* 11: 333–60.

Hungerford, T. and Solon, G. (1987) 'Sheepskin effects in the returns to education', *Review of Economics and Statistics* 69: 175–77.

Idson, T.L. and Kahane, L.H. (2000) 'Team effects on compensation: an application to salary determination in the National Hockey League', *Economic Inquiry* 38: 345–57.

Kendrick, J. (1961) *Productivity Trends in the United States*, Princeton: Princeton University Press.

Lucas, R.E. (1988) 'On the mechanics of economic development', *Journal of Monetary Economics* 22: 3–42.

Marshall, A. (1890) *Principles of Economics*, New York: Macmillan.

McLean, G.N. (2006) 'National human resource development: a focused study in transitioning societies in the developing world', *Advances in Developing Human Resources* 8: 3–11.

— (2007) 'The good, the bad, and the ugly of human capital theory', Paper presented at the 2007 Asia International Research Conference in China, Beijing, November.

Miller, P. and Volker, P. (1984) 'The screening hypothesis: an application of the Wiles Test', *Economic Inquiry* 22: 121–27.

Mincer, J. (1962) 'On-the-job training: costs, returns, and some implications', *Journal of Political Economy* 70: 50–79.

Moretti, E. (2004) 'Workers' education, spillovers and productivity: evidence from plan-level production functions', *American Economic Review* 94: 656–90.

Nelson, P. (1974) 'Advertising as information', *Journal of Political Economy* 82: 729–54.

Park, Y. and Jacobs, R.L. (2011) 'The influence of investment in workplace learning on learning outcomes and organizational performance', *Human Resource Development Quarterly* 22: 437–58.

Phillips, J.J. (2011) *Handbook of Training Evaluation and Measurement Methods*, New York: Routledge.

Pinoli, S. (2008) 'Screening ex-ante or screening on-the-job? The impact of the employment contract', MPRA Paper 11429, Munich Personal RePEc Archive.

Ployhart, R.E. and Moliterno, T.P. (2011) 'Emergence of the human capital resource: a multilevel model', *Academy of Management Review* 36: 127–50.

Riley, J. (1979) 'Testing the educational screening hypothesis', *Journal of Political Economy* 87: S227–52.

Ross, S.A. (1977) 'The determination of financial structure: the incentive-signaling approach', *Bell Journal of Economics* 8: 23–40.

Schultz, T.W. (1960) Capital formation by education, *Journal of Political Economy* 68(6): 571–83.

— (1961) 'Investment in human capital', *American Economic Review* 51(1): 1–17.

— (1962) 'Reflections on investment in man', *Journal of Political Economy* 70, 5(2): 1–8.

Sobel, I. (1982) 'Human capital and institutional theories of the labor market: rivals or complements?', *Journal of Economic Issues* 16: 255–72.

Solow, R.M. (1957) 'Technical change and the aggregate production function', *Review of Economics and Statistics* 39: 312–20.

Spence, M.A. (1973a) 'Job market signaling', *Quarterly Journal of Economics* 87: 355–74.

— (1973b) 'Time and communication in economics and social interaction', *Quarterly Journal of Economics* 87: 651–60.

Stoyanov, A. and Zubanov, N. (2012) 'Productivity spillovers across firms through worker mobility', *American Economic Journal: Applied Economics* 4: 168–98.

Swanson, R.A. (2001) 'Human resource development and its underlying theory', *Human Resource Development International* 4: 299–312.

Swanson, R.A. and Holton, E.F. (2001) *Foundations of Human Resource Development*, San Francisco: Berrett-Koehler.

Wang, G.G. and Holton, E.F. (2005) 'Neoclassical and institutional economics as foundations for human resource development theory', *Human Resource Development Review* 4: 86–108.

Wang, G.G. and Spitzer, D.R. (eds) (2005) Advances in HRD Evaluation and Measurement: Theory and Practice [Special Issue], *Advances in Developing Human Resources* 7(1).

Wang, G.G. and Dobbs, R.L. (2008) 'Institutional economics and human resource development', *Advances in Developing Human Resources* 10: 770–87.

Wang, G.G., Dou, Z., and Li, N. (2002) 'A systems approach to measuring return on investment for HRD interventions', *Human Resource Development Quarterly* 13: 203–24.

Wang, G.G., Li, J., Qiao, X. and Sun, J.Y. (2010) 'Understanding corporate university phenomenon from human capital theory', *International Journal of Human Resources Development and Management* 10: 182–204.

Weinberger, L.A. (1998) 'Commonly held theories of human resource development', *Human Resource Development International* 1(1): 75–93.

Weiss, A. (1995) 'Human capital vs. signaling: explanations of wages', *Journal of Economic Perspectives* 9: 133–54.

Wright, P.M. and McMahan, G.C. (2011) 'Exploring human capital: putting human back into strategic human resource management', *Human Resource Management Journal* 21: 93–104.

SECTION IV

Policy perspectives

16

NATIONAL HUMAN RESOURCE DEVELOPMENT (NHRD)

Gary N. McLean and AAhad M. Osman-Gani

For almost half a century, HRD has focused solely on performance (Swanson 1995) or learning (Watkins 2000), and both have been almost entirely focused on for-profit corporate contexts. Gradually, however, the boundaries of HRD have been expanding, including many foci not originally considered, as generated in the definition of HRD by McLean and McLean (2001: 322):

> Human resource development is any process or activity that, either initially or over the long term, has the potential to develop adults' work-based knowledge, expertise, productivity, and satisfaction, whether for personal or group/team gain, or for the benefit of an organization, community, nation or, ultimately, the whole of humanity.

This chapter focuses on national HRD (NHRD), the use of HRD principles and practices to support the development of countries. Over the years, many terms have been used to reflect concepts similar to what is now known mainly as NHRD: human capital development, national human capital development, national manpower development, national workforce development, human development (now the preferred term for the United Nations), and many others. Throughout this chapter, we will proceed as if all of these concepts contribute to NHRD, though some may use the terms as synonyms. It is still up for discussion as to which term will dominate moving forward.

The development of the concept of NHRD

Human capital was first viewed as personal wealth by early economists, such as Adam Smith, Alfred Marshall, J.B. Mill, and A. Fisher (Sweetland 1996). During the late 1950s and early 1960s, Mincer (1958), Fabricant (1959), Becker (1960), and Schultz (1961) contributed in laying the foundation for empirical studies on Human Capital (HC) by authors such as Denison (1962), Schultz (1963), and Becker (1964), who contributed to explaining the relationship between HC and income growth. Becker (1993: 15–16) explained that "expenditures on education, training, and medical care, etc., are investments in [human] capital."

According to McGuire (2011), from its modern-day origins (Harbison and Myers 1964, Nadler 1970), HRD has evolved with a tripartite agenda of human betterment, organizational enhancement, and societal development. "The transformative power of HRD lies in its capacity to empower the creation of innovative and radical solutions to real world problems. HRD has evolved to meet the changing individual, organizational, and societal environments it inhabits" (McGuire 2011: 1).

To understand the continuing expansion of HRD, McLean *et al.* (2004) provided a platform for exploring NHRD, focusing on macro-level HRD initiatives based on successful organizational-level HRD initiatives being applied within appropriate national contexts. National HRD is an increasingly significant area of inquiry and practice in the field of HRD (Kenzhegaranova 2008, Byrd and Demps 2006, Lynham and Cunningham 2006, Paprock 2006, McLean *et al.* 2004). Lynham and Cunningham (2004: 319) offered an operational definition of NHRD, as "a process or processes of organized capability and competence-based learning experiences . . . to bring about individual and organizational growth and performance improvement, and to enhance national, economic, cultural, and social development." This is consistent with the much earlier observation by Harbison and Myers (1964: 13) that, "If a country is unable to develop its human resources, it cannot develop much else, whether it be a modern political and social structure, a sense of national unity, or higher standards of material welfare." Wang and McLean (2007: 101) also observed that, "As NHRD develops around the world, many nations are including education, health, safety, and other factors in their understanding of NHRD." Some country-level examples of NHRD applied to specific countries follow in this chapter.

Case examples of national HRD

Early in the development of NHRD, examples of countries that are implementing NHRD would have been difficult to find. Now, however, the literature containing case studies is expanding rapidly, with more and more countries having NHRD approaches and having them included in the literature. The number is far too large to include in one chapter. We have picked a few examples to include below, and even their coverage is, of necessity, rather superficial. Because India appears to have been the first to have a ministry named HRD specifically, we will begin with India.

India

NHRD in India can also be termed HRD for the state, with responsibility falling primarily on government organizations, including the Ministry of HRD, established in the mid-1980s. Attempts have been made by scholars to bridge this national approach with organizational HRD but with little success. Though awareness is growing that both streams are dependent on each other, a schism exists in the absence of any policy level mechanism to encourage alignment (Rao and Varghese 2009).

India's comprehensive NHRD policy can be traced to its Education policy, addressing structure, systems, internal processes, implementation issues, and internal review mechanisms. It is targeted to developing children, youth, illiterate adults, out-of school youth, women, teachers, educational administrators, handicapped, and all categories needing education and skills development. It is also focused on institutions at various levels, content and management of education, implementation issues, and monitoring of education. Furthermore, it recognized existing strategic institutions that are doing research and promoting the tools of HRD (Rao and Varghese 2009).

In spite of its early recognition of the importance of NHRD, perhaps the first country to do so, India has not expanded on the concept beyond its recognition of the importance of education for human development. This is not to say that it has not continued to expand and develop other aspects of what would be assumed to be part of NHRD, but these components have not been integrated into its NHRD philosophy.

People's Republic of China

Based on the Cho and McLean (2004) classification system, China clearly used a centralized planning approach to NHRD. However, it is probably now a transitioning society as there is more and more freedom for movement towards a free-market approach.

China faces unique challenges in developing its HC. Chen and Yuan (2004) analyzed the status of HC development and identified five major issues. First, China has a large population with a relatively low education level. China's population increased from 520 million in 1949 to over 1.3 billion at the dawn of the twenty-first century. Compared with this large and yet relatively lower-skilled population, human resources are a limited natural resource. Second, there is a severe shortage of investments in HC. While education and training tend to be the major channels of HC investment, in which many economically developed countries invest 4–6 percent of total GDP on education, China spends only about 3 percent of its GDP on education (Jiang 2007). Further, a recent survey revealed that only 5 percent of Chinese enterprises accelerate HC investment (Yang and Wang 2009). Third, HC allocations are not adequate for modernization. In China, a large portion of human resources is working in primary industries and relatively small portions are working in other sectors of the economy. Such disproportional distribution of human resource tends to constrain the development of new industries, such as hi-tech and service sectors. Fourth, the efficiency of HC utilization tends to be low. For example, many new college graduates fail to learn what is most needed in the market. Finally, like many other developing countries, China faces a serious challenge of brain drain. It is estimated that, yearly, more than 50,000 college graduates (equivalent to the number of all graduates from the top 10 Chinese universities) go to the USA to pursue advanced degrees and that the majority of them remain there (Ke *et al.* 2006, Yang and Wang 2009).

Developing HC has been a national policy priority in China (Yang *et al.* 2004). Systematic and coordinated efforts in developing the workforce at a national level have always been the emphasis since the new China was established. Benson and Zhu (2002) observed that HRD policies in China have changed over time in an attempt to improve the skills of the entire population. In the 1950s and 1960s, key initiatives were taken for making compulsory primary education and in improving the literacy rate. During the ten years of the Cultural Revolution from 1966 to 1976, formal educational systems experienced serious setbacks. The Chinese government paid particular attention to education, science, and technology, since economic reform and modernization were launched in the late 1970s. HRD initiatives such as improving national skill levels have become a national strategy integrated with its overall strategy of economic development and modernization (Yang and Wang 2009). Jiang (2001) further mentioned five concrete measures of the outcomes of HRD: (1) establishing a new perspective of development and strengthening human capacity building; (2) building a lifelong learning system and learning society; (3) utilizing new learning technology; (4) promoting innovation and educating a new generation; and (5) strengthening international communication and collaboration (Yang and Wang 2009: 6).

China's national approach to HC development was reflected in its strategic plan. The strategic plan of education and HRD during the first half of the twenty-first century was outlined by Chen and Zhang (2003). The goal of this plan was to catch up with developed countries within 50 years in three stages.

Stage one of the strategic plan was projected from 2001 to 2010 for establishing a solid foundation for sustainable development. This stage of development could be compared to the period of 1900–1950 in the USA, when its average workforce education had increased from eight to nine years. In the 10th Five-Year Plan (2001–2005), a chapter on human resource development was included (Xie and Wu 2001). The name for the 11th Five-Year Plan was changed to Guideline instead of Plan, as China is moving towards transforming into a free-market-oriented economy; thus, in the 11th Five-Year Guideline (2006–2010), HC development was re-emphasized.

In the second stage from 2011–2020, the main objective is to catch up with developed nations in the areas of HRD and education. This stage of development could be compared to the period of 1950–1970 in USA, when its average workforce education was increased from nine to twelve years.

The third stage is from 2020–2050, and the objective is to catch up and surpass the developed countries. This stage of development could be compared to the period of 1970–1995 in USA, when its average workforce education increased from 12 to more than 13 years.

The major issues and challenges of HC development faced by many state-owned enterprises (SOEs) were analyzed by a number of Chinese scholars, who observed that HC development concepts have been accepted widely in Chinese firms and have a profound influence on managerial practices (Chen 2005, Gu 2004, Zhao 2002).

Several major HRD challenges faced by SOEs in China have been identified by Gu (2004). Some of these challenges include lack of sufficient investment in HC, brain drain, and an imbalance of human talent among sectors. Two major factors constrain HC investment in many SOEs. For a long time, the workforce has not been considered as HC that can yield greater returns when resources are adequately invested in the workforce. Consequently, employees were not viewed as special assets. Further, under the traditional central planning system, not enough attention was paid to the cost and benefit, productivity and efficiency of the workforce, and there was almost no market competition. Although the country was transforming from a central planning economy to a market oriented one, the old mindset and social norms continued to influence managerial behavior in many SOEs (Gu 2004).

Yang and Wang (2009) stated that the underdevelopment of HRD has resulted in four problems: a) labor productivity remains low, b) the application of science to industrial production is low, c) product quality is low with 10 per cent of production being rejected, and d) industrial accidents are frequent with the majority of accidents resulting from inadequate training and job skills.

China is among the most successful countries that have experienced or are experiencing transition from a centrally planned economy to a free-market economy. China has set an example for many developing countries in terms of economic growth and a reference frame in terms of HC development. China's experiences are worthy of analysis, and thus to offer valuable lessons and illuminations for those countries with similar social and cultural contexts (Alagaraja and Wang 2012).

Singapore

Human resources have been identified early as the single most important strategic capital for Singapore (Osman-Gani 2004). A small country with virtually no natural resources, Singapore has become one of the most developed countries in Asia, primarily due to its strong emphasis on developing human resources and continuously making significant investments in its HC. HRD has long been a core element in its strategic economic plans, as reflected in the eight strategic thrusts of its Strategic Economic Plan. As economic growth moved from investment to innovation driven, together with its emphasis on the regionalization and globalization of business, the government has embarked on more sophisticated HRD strategies. The HRD strategies have been continuously revised and adjusted in conjunction with other national strategic economic policies. Singapore is thus a unique case that exemplifies the benefits of NHRD policies and strategies (Osman-Gani and Chan 2009, Osman-Gani and Tan 2000, CIEB 2013).

Recent trends of an ageing workforce, retention of foreign talent, utilization of local talent, and the social impact of a multicultural workforce are impacting economic growth. Singapore's national survival depends on the effective utilization and continuous development of its strategic HC, thereby developing new talents and upgrading of skills for catering to the needs of emerging industries of the future (Osman-Gani and Chan 2009).

The HRD policy arising from the national planning followed the recommendations made in the Manpower 21 Plan (MOM 1999). For example, the focus on R&D in biomedical, pharmaceutical, and digital media sectors was supported by changes made in the science and mathematics curriculum (Boon and Gopinathan 2006). The Ministry of Education (MOE) is empowered to close defaulting schools and colleges that do not adhere to accepted standards of teaching and management (MOE 2008). The description of the education system and HRD at the national level has been discussed by Osman-Gani and Tan (2000), Osman-Gani (2004), Low (2004), Osman-Gani and Chan (2009), and CIEB (2013).

Singapore is one of the few countries in the world that has a well-structured statutory requirement for companies operating in Singapore to contribute a fixed percentage of the payroll for employee development, and to recover those training investments through a claim-back system as part of overall skills development (SDF 2008). In addition, it manages its manpower/personnel deployment through payment of additional incentives for compliance and support. For instance, its workforce development policies provide incentives to companies to train their mature workers. Such policies are well coordinated by ministries and public sector agencies. The fact that many of the large Singapore companies are owned by or linked to the government helps to make some of the training and skills development efforts successful. Because of this connection, HRD is seen to be mostly government-led, unlike many other countries or administrative units of the region, such as Malaysia, Taiwan, and Hong Kong, where HRD is driven more by the private sector, especially by multinational companies. Singapore's HRD policies are founded on developing key competencies in new science and technology areas, such as nanotechnology, environmental services, info communications and e-media, logistics, precision engineering, transport engineering, electronics, multimedia, biotechnology and biomedical sciences, clean energy, educational services and other emerging industries (intellectual property, information and physical security, and photonics). At the same time, it has to develop enough personnel for its chemical, petrochemical and high value added manufacturing industries like wafer fabrication, semiconductor technology and services, like integrated resort and hospitality services, financial services and logistics (Osman-Gani and Chan 2009).

In addition, Singapore is moving more into quality research and development, and into educational services. To do this, it has to attract workers, particularly from the regions of Southeast Asia, India, and China, which will create a more diverse Asian workforce in the future. For the biomedical and biotechnology fields, it is attracting international talents with supporting research grants. Hence, in the universities and polytechnics, courses are currently being taught to develop knowledge and skills in these areas. HRD is taken seriously by the government, leading to developing new skills and attracting foreign talents, developing local talents, and retaining global talents.

United States of America

While Cho and McLean (2004) concluded that the United States was one of the few industrialized countries that did not have an NHRD policy, this conclusion proved to be somewhat misleading. The United States may fit under the decentralized free-market mode identified by Cho and McLean, with HRD policies and practices existing at several levels of government. The US government does not use the term HRD or NHRD for any of its programs. Rather, it is much more likely to refer to workforce development with an emphasis on career and technical education. These emphases are covered in separate chapters of this HRD Companion by Billett and Hawley.

Many of the aspects that we have included in NHRD, such as education and safety, fall under the jurisdiction of states and local communities. Even when broad policies are established at the federal level, their implementation and even policy modifications often take place at local levels, such as state, county, city or town, or regions within states. However, rather than integrating such policies, as envisioned by countries with stated NHRD policies, such practices in the United States often remain disjointed, uncoordinated, duplicative, and lacking in synergy.

As only one example of such decentralization, among many, Ahn and McLean (2010) explored a federal program implemented at a state level for developing personnel. A case study was undertaken of the use of the federal Workforce Investment Act in the state of Texas for the purpose of developing and upgrading HC within the state to reduce unemployment and to increase productivity. This approach reflects the education and training components of NHRD but was not integrated with other components of NHRD such as safety, technology development, economic policy, cultural policy, and so on.

Theoretical underpinnings of NHRD

As a field, HRD has struggled with identifying the foundational theory sets underlying its practices, varying from Swanson's (1995) simplistic three-legged stool model of systems, economics, and psychology; to McLean's (1998) broader but unspecified octopus model, arguing for a broader set of theories. Likewise, given the complexity of NHRD, compared with HRD, no given set of theories has been identified for NHRD, nor is it ever likely to have complete and all-inclusive theory sets. Nevertheless, theory sets for NHRD will likely draw on business/management (and all of its subsets, like marketing, finance, and so on), education, economics, psychology, sociology, anthropology, communications, policy administration, safety and security, and many others.

Without regard to the fact that there is no consensus on the foundational areas of HRD, Wang and Swanson (2008) criticized the concept of NHRD as not having an underlying theory. McLean *et al.* (2008) responded by pointing out that expecting (or demanding) a single theory base for NHRD is unrealistic when we do not have such for HRD, and, further, when NHRD is situational, based on the history, culture, politics, geography, infrastructures, and so on, that are different from country to country, and always will be.

Does NHRD work?

This question is difficult to answer unambiguously because it is not clear what it means for NHRD to work. Clearly, we should not expect all NHRD policies to result in the same outcomes because each country that uses the NHRD concept has different objectives. In some countries, NHRD is solely focused on economic development; other countries, in contrast, have much larger objectives that integrate many components of human development. As a result, NHRD has worked extremely well in some countries; in other countries, it has not worked as well.

Arguments against NHRD

Some countries have not been as successful as others in their NHRD efforts. India, for example, even though it was supposedly the first country to stipulate NHRD as a policy, focused solely on the educational process. After almost 30 years, many problems remain with the educational process in India, and India has still not developed an integrated approach to NHRD.

South Korea undertook a comprehensive approach to NHRD. However, political realities resulted in struggles for power and control among the various ministries. As a result, leadership was removed from the Ministry of Education and HRD and transferred to the Ministry of Science and Technology. This appears not to have worked well, and HRD is no longer a ministry in the national government, although an NHRD focus remains.

What to call national human development efforts is a contested issue. As an example, some countries reference national vocational qualifications (Australia, New Zealand, United Kingdom), workforce or manpower development (Singapore, United States), human development (United Nations), and so on. Are these all forms of NHRD? They appear to be – but clarity is needed.

Arguments for NHRD

One argument that supports the success of NHRD efforts is implicit and intuitive. An exploration of those countries that have NHRD policies indicates that most of the countries with such a national policy are at the top in terms of economic development. No known countries are near the bottom of the economic development rankings that have NHRD policies. At the same time, there is no evidence of the causal relationship between development and the use of NHRD. As richer countries clearly have more resources to invest, it may be that development success leads to the use of NHRD policies.

Explicitly, there are increasing efforts to provide empirical evidence of the success of countries with NHRD policies. Both such sets of studies (Oh *et al.* 2013, Verkhohlyad and McLean u.r.) have verified the implicit connection between development and the use of NHRD, though still without causal evidence.

The existing evidence, whether implicit or explicit, suggests that NHRD approaches have value. NHRD policies have the potential for greater effectiveness and efficiency through an integrated approach to several components of human development that can enrich the lives of those within countries using NHRD.

What's next?

Of course, no one can predict the future. However, in the following sections we have tried to suggest what is needed in the areas of theory development for NHRD, as well as providing implications for practice and for future research.

Theory development

As pointed out in the theories underpinning NHRD sections of this chapter, it is unlikely that there will ever be *a* theory of NHRD, just as it is unlikely that a unanimously accepted theory of HRD will emerge. The pool of theory bases underlying NHRD is vast, and these theory sets will likely continue to expand and improve our understanding of NHRD. To look for one theory of NHRD, however, would be a fool's chase and should not be undertaken. For those desiring a more focused approach to theory development for NHRD, however, attention to the recommended research below is likely to have the greatest impact on our understanding of theories that underlie NHRD.

Implications for practice (implementing NHRD)

McLean (2000) titled an article "It Depends." and noted that no two countries are alike; thus, the implementation process for NHRD will be dependent on the characteristics of a country and its stated objectives. NHRD cannot be implemented with a cookie cutter approach. Those charged with implementing NHRD might do well to consider how other countries have implemented NHRD and their results. They might identify countries similar to their own and explore their approaches, modifying them as necessary to meet their own needs and objectives

A country could also take advantage of the measurement instruments developed by Oh *et al.* (2013) and Verkhohlyad and McLean (2013). Identifying those areas from among the variables used in the two instruments on which the country falls short might help the country involved to strengthen and improve that aspect of its current NHRD implementation.

Implications for future research

In order to accomplish the above, many more regional, country, and community narrative case studies are needed on NHRD, especially research that focuses on the processes used by countries under review. The larger the base of case studies, the greater the number of approaches that will have been used from which to draw. Further, case studies in a particular country of focus will allow that country to understand better what has worked and what has not worked in implementing NHRD in that country. Such indigenous research (McLean 2010) is likely to be much more relevant than research conducted on any other country.

In addition to the narrative case studies recommended above, a need remains for more empirical research based on measurement tools (Oh *et al.* 2013, Verkhohlyad and McLean 2013), both to improve and validate existing instruments and to extend the number of measurement tools with additional variables. Further, both of these existing instruments need to be updated on at least an annual basis, as the input data for the instruments change at least annually. Further, both instruments contain variables for which it is not possible to determine the existing values because some countries do not gather such data. It will become increasingly important for countries to have current data on a broader set of variables to allow for the use of such instruments.

Detailed comparative data, such as found in Alagaraja and Wang's (2012) comparison of NHRD approaches in India and China, are also useful. There are few such studies available in the literature. Most existing case studies are single country only, or comparisons across many countries at a high level rather than a detailed level, such as found in McLean *et al.* (2004) and Lynham *et al.* (2006). Thus, comparisons between major countries pursuing NHRD policies would be a great contribution to the literature.

Conclusion

NHRD is an exciting expansion of the application of the principles and practices of HRD that is still in its infancy, both in its application and in the research helping us to understand NHRD. Because of word limitations, this chapter is in all respects a brief summary of the available literature. As a field, we need a much more comprehensive overview of NHRD. Especially missing from this chapter is an update on NHRD as it applies to regional, community, and societal applications of NHRD.

As a field, we must embrace the concept of NHRD, through our research, our practices, and our theory foundations. We must set aside any remaining resistance that exists related to NHRD. If we can wholeheartedly embrace NHRD, then it is reasonable to assume that we can accomplish the goal of improving all of humanity, as envisioned by McLean and McLean (2001) in their global definition of HRD.

References

Ahn, Y.S. and McLean, G.N. (2010) 'Regional human resource development systems and policies in the USA: focus on the Workforce Investment Act', *Journal of Lifelong Education and HRD* 6: 221–39.

Alagaraja, M. and Wang, J. (2012) 'Development of a national HRD strategy model: cases of India and China', *Human Resource Development Review* 11: 407–29.

Becker, G.S. (1960) 'Underinvestment in college education?', *The American Economic Review* 50: 346–54.

— (1964) *Human Capital: A Theoretical and Empirical Analysis, with Special Reference to Education*, New York: National Bureau of Economic Research.

— (1993) *Human Capital: A Theoretical and Empirical Analysis, with Special Reference to Education* (3rd edn), Chicago: University of Chicago Press.

Benson, J. and Zhu, J. (2002) 'The emerging external labor market and the impact on enterprise's human resource development in China', *Human Resource Development Quarterly* 13: 449–66.

Boon, G.C. and Gopinathan, S. (2006) 'The development of education in Singapore since 1965', background paper presented on Asia education tour for African policy makers, Singapore: Singapore National Institute of Education, Nanyang Technological University.

Byrd, M. and Demps, E. (2006) 'Taking a look at national human resource development (NHRD): interviews with Gary McLean and Susan Lynham', *Human Resource Development International* 9: 553–61.

Chen, G. and Zhang, Z. (2003) 'Strategic outline for education and human resource development in China during next 50 years' [in Chinese], *Studies of Education Development* 23: 29–41.

Chen, R. (2005) 'Reflections on human resource development and management in SOEs' [in Chinese], *Modern Management Science* 6: 105–6.

Chen, Z. and Yuan, L. (2004) 'On the strategy of human capital development in China' [in Chinese], *Technical Economy* 193: 33–35.

Cho, E. and McLean, G.N. (2004) 'What we discovered about NHRD and what it means for HRD', *Advances in Developing Human Resources* 6: 382–93.

CIEB (2013) 'Singapore overview'. Online. Available HTTP: http://www.ncee.org/programs-affiliates/center-on-international-education-benchmarking/top-performing-countries/singapore-overview/ (accessed 11 May 2013).

Denison, E.F. (1962) *The Sources of Economic Growth in the United States and the Alternatives Before Us*, New York: Committee for Economic Development.

Fabricant, S. (1959) *Basic Facts on Productivity Change*, New York: National Bureau of Economic Research.

Gu, Q. (2004) 'A tentative discussion on development of the state-owned enterprise and investment of human resource capital', *Journal of Shanxi Radio & TV University* 3: 100–1.

Harbison, F. and Myers, C.A. (1964) *Education, Manpower and Economic Growth: Strategies of Human Resource Development*, New York: McGraw-Hill.

Jiang, Q. (2007) 'Human capital investment and educational development of China', *Journal of Nanjing University of Posts and Telecommunications (Social Science)* 9: 46–51.

Jiang, Z. (21 June 2001) 'Strengthening human resource capacity building, promoting development and prosperity in Asia-Pacific region', presidential speech presented at the APEC high level meeting on human resource capacity building, Beijing, China.

Ke, K., Chermack, T. J., Lee, Y. and Lin, J. (2006) 'National human resource development in transitioning societies in the developing world: The People's Republic of China', *Advances in Developing Human Resources* 8: 28–45.

Kenzhegaranova, M. (2008) 'National human resource development in the developing world: The Republic of Kazakhstan', unpublished thesis, College Station, TX: Texas A&M University.

Low, A. (2004) 'Education for growth: the premium on education and work experience in Singapore', MAS (Monetary Authority of Singapore) staff paper 26, Singapore.

Lynham, S.A. and Cunningham, P.W. (2004) 'Human resource development: the South African case', *Advances in Developing Human Resources* 6: 315–25.

— (2006) 'National human resource development in transitioning societies in the developing world: concept and challenges', *Advances in Developing Human Resources* 8: 116–35.

Lynham, S.A., Paprock, K.E. and Cunningham, P.W. (eds) (2006) 'National human resource development in transitioning societies in the developing world', *Advances in Developing Human Resources* 8: 116–58.

McGuire, D. (2011) 'Foundations of human resource development', in D. McGuire and K.M. Jorgensen (eds) *Human Resource Development: Theory and Practice*, London: SAGE, 2–11.

McLean, G.N. (1998) 'HRD: a three-legged stool, an octopus, or a centipede?', *Human Resource Development International* 1: 375–77.

— (2000) 'It depends.', *Advances in Developing Human Resources* 7: 39–43.

— (2010) 'The need for indigenous theory and practice in human resource development in Thailand', *NIDA HROD Journal* 1: 1–19.

McLean, G.N. and McLean, L. (2001) 'If we can't define HRD in one country, how can we define it in an international context?', *Human Resource Development International* 4: 313–26.

McLean, G.N., Osman-Gani, A.M. and Cho, E. (2004) 'Human resource development as national policy', *Advances in Developing Human Resources* 6: 269–75.

McLean, G.N., Lynham, S.A., Azevedo, R.E., Lawrence, J.E.S. and Nafukho, F. (2008) 'A response to Wang and Swanson's (2008) article on national HRD and theory development', *Human Resource Development Review* 7: 241–58.

Mincer, J. (1958) 'Investment in human capital and personal income distribution', *The Journal of Political Economy* 66: 281–302.

MOE (2008) 'Ministry of Education, list of external degree programs'. Online. Available HTTP: http://www.moe.gov.sg/education/private-education/ (accessed 5 March 2014).

MOM (1999) 'Ministry of Manpower, launch of Manpower 21 Plan'. Online. Available HTTP: http://www.mom.gov.sg/skills-training-and-development/Pages/default.aspx (accessed 5 March 2014).

Nadler, L. (1970) *Developing Human Resources*, Houston, TX: Gulf Publishing.

Oh, H.S., Ryu, H.H. and Choi, N.W. (2013) 'How can we assess and evaluate the competitive advantage of a country's human resource development system?', *Asia Pacific Education Review*.

Osman-Gani, A.M. (2004) 'Human capital development in Singapore: an analysis of national policy perspectives', *Advances in Developing Human Resources* 6: 1–12.

Osman-Gani, A.M. and Tan, W.L. (2000) 'International briefing: training and development in Singapore', *International Journal of Training and Development* 4: 305–23.

Osman-Gani, A.M. and Chan, T.H. (2009) 'Trends and challenges of developing human capital in Singapore: an analysis of current practices and future trends', *Human Resource Development International* 12: 47–68.

Paprock, K.E. (2006) 'National human resource development in transitioning societies in the developing world: concept and challenges', *Advances in Developing Human Resources* 8: 116–35.

Rao, T.V. and Varghese, S. (2009) 'Trends and challenges of developing human capital in India', *Human Resource Development International* 12: 15–34.

Schultz, T.W. (1961) 'Investment in human capital' [Presidential address delivered at the annual meeting of the American Economic Association, Saint Louis, MO, December, 1960], *The American Economic Review* 51: 1–17.

— (1963) *The Economic Value of Education*, New York: Columbia University Press.

SDF (2008) 'The total training plan scheme and Singapore. Skills development levy (SDL)'. Online. Available HTTP: https://sdl.wda.gov.sg/Default.aspx (accessed 5 March 2014).

Swanson, R.A. (1995) 'Performance is key', *Human Resource Development Quarterly* 6: 207–13.

Sweetland, S.R. (1996) 'Human capital theory: foundations of a field of inquiry', *Review of Educational Research* 66: 341–59.

Verkhohlyad, O. and McLean, G.N. (under review) 'Country-wide human capital portraits: a conceptual framework', *Human Resource Development Review*.

Wang, G. and Swanson, R.A. (2008) 'The idea of national HRD: an analysis based on economic and theory development methodology', *Human Resource Development Review* 7: 79–106.

Wang, X. and McLean, G.N. (2007) 'The dilemma of defining international human resource development', *Human Resource Development Review* 6: 96–108.

Watkins, K. (2000) 'Aims, roles and structures for human resource development', *Advances in Developing Human Resources* 17: 54–59.

Xie, J. and Wu, G. (2001) 'Training and development in the People's Republic of China', *International Journal of Training and Development* 5: 223–32.

Yang, B. and Wang, X. (2009) 'Successes and challenges of developing human capital in the People's Republic of China', *Human Resource Development International* 12: 3–14.

Yang, B., Zhang, D. and Zhang, M. (2004) 'National human resource development in the People's Republic of China', *Advances in Developing Human Resources* 6: 297–306.

Zhao, H. (2002) 'Application of the human capital theory in Chinese enterprises' [in Chinese], *Journal of Wuhan University of Technology* 24: 87–9.

17
WORKFORCE DEVELOPMENT

Joshua D. Hawley

The term workforce development has been increasingly used to describe a range of education and training or development practices. It is generally understood to include all of human resource development, as well as the related fields of career and technical education and adult education (Jacobs and Hawley 2009). Workforce development can often be stretched to cover private sector activities that are generally thought of as the constituent parts of human resource development such as training or organizational development. However, there is a tension between the emphasis on societal outcomes for workforce development and the organizational focus for human resource development (Jacobs 2006; Hawley, forthcoming).

This chapter first provides a definition of the term workforce development, emphasizing the challenges to the definition that the economic recession has brought to light. The chapter reviews common perspectives with HRD, adult education, and career and technical education – as well as focusing on how the term workforce development is distinctive. Secondly, the chapter reviews the way the term has been used in academic scholarship, using a brief review of references and citations from the Social Science Citation Index. Finally, the chapter raises new policy issues that are causing a refocusing of workforce development, including college completion and firm level training, where current government business interests overlap a great deal.

Defining the term and area of practice

Defining workforce development

The term workforce development is commonly understood to represent a range of education and related programs that cater to those entering and already employed in the workforce. Over the last 100 years, workforce development has evolved from a range of narrow nationally funded efforts to a set of policies and programs conducted in collaboration with the private sector. Workforce development is generally understood as either public or private sector interventions that strive to increase individual, organizational or societal outcomes in the workforce.

Starting in the early 2000s, Ohio State University has used the following four issues as a way to conceptualize workforce development.[1] Workforce development has essentially four purposes:

1 To prepare individuals to enter or re-enter the workforce.
2 To enable organizations to provide learning opportunities that improve workplace performance.
3 To help organizations to respond to changes that impact workforce effectiveness.
4 To offer individuals a hand up when the workforce participation suffers.

These four areas have been described in detail elsewhere (Jacobs and Hawley 2009; Jacobs 2006) but provide a framework for helping understand the goals of workforce development. In this framework we define "Workforce development as the coordination of public and private sector policies and programs that provides individuals with the opportunity for a sustainable livelihood and helps organizations achieve exemplary goals, consistent with the societal context" (Jacobs and Hawley 2009). Appendix 17.1 provides a visual representation of the issues.

The balance between different aspects of workforce development means that what is covered by the definition will change. In a period of time (mid-1990s or most of the 2000s) when the economy was hot, workers were in demand, and business competed with extravagant efforts to recruit workers, even those at the bottom of the rungs were able to get a hand up with training or retraining. During that time workforce development focused primarily on issues of retention and workforce performance (purposes 2 and 3) which are focused more on HRD issues. Many firms were concerned with retaining highly qualified employees because individual workers had many options in a rapidly growing labor market. During the 1990s boom workforce development focused on regional or sectoral programs (Giloth 2004) in order to help finance and health sectors meet the need for workers. This is also true in current day Germany or Japan, where regional governments struggle to recruit and train skilled labor for industrial employment, in the face of declines in working population due to demographic shifts.

In contrast, in recent years under the current recession and the tepid recovery many workers were shut out of the labor market, and job searches themselves have become much more difficult. In this environment, the workforce development topics that have been most important are purpose 1 and 4, which focus on improving the access of all workers to jobs and helping people when they cannot find employment. This is also characteristic of Southern European nations, or even places like South Africa, with large numbers of youth who cannot find employment or remain underemployed as a result of both lackluster economic growth and mismatch between education and job development. There have been a range of definitions of workforce development proposed, each of which emerged from a different sub-discipline. The core of workforce development focuses on providing services to help disadvantaged workers re-enter the workforce. Workforce development includes "common functional elements such as recruitment, training and retention" (Giloth 2000). The focus is on disadvantaged workers and emphasizes continuing education or training designed to train people for the workforce. This core definition has also been used internationally. Organisation for Economic Co-operation and Development (OECD) nations all have formal programs designed to help disadvantaged workers reintegrate to the labor market (Carcillo and Grubb 2006). Programs in OECD nations have historically focused on matching individuals to jobs and providing basic training, all with a goal of quick re-employment (Giguère 2008).

This definition focusing on quick employment services and training is operationalized in different ways across the globe. For example, in the United States, workforce development is defined in legislation as a set of core services, including job search assistance and case management. These universal services are supplemented by training if required, which has been provided through a series of voucher programs called Individual Training Accounts (ITAs) since the reauthorization of WIA in 1998 (Eberts 2008; Giloth 1998, 2000). In France, regional government has had greater freedom since 1993 to establish local training and job placement programs (Greffe 2008; Culpepper 2003). Programs were designed at the regional level as a way to provide training for specific jobs that were projected to be in demand at the local level. Germany's program focuses, much as the U.S. does, on the most disadvantaged workers, those on public assistance. As a result of significant policy reform in the 2003–2004, Germany refocused efforts on job placement for unemployed workers, as well as expanding services to employers (Mosley and Bouché 2008).

This focus on job matching and limited training has changed in recent decades as countries emphasize connections between regional development – so-called place-based economic development – and workforce retraining. The specific definition of workforce development has shifted to a more general focus on workforce retraining with an eye towards increased economic development in a specific region. One example of this thinking comes from a series of comparisons between workforce development in Singapore and U.S. metropolitan areas, such as Cleveland. In these comparisons, the definition adopted by the individual area for workforce development focuses not only on the retraining of workers, but on the relationship to industrial development in the region (Berry 1998).

This emphasis on place-based strategies is reflected in changing definitions for workforce development, and has influenced national policies on workforce development throughout the world. For example, in the United States organizations such as the Center for Employment Training (CET) gained a reputation for carrying out high quality workforce training with a specific industrial sector (Meléndez 1996). CET was eventually picked up by the federal Department of Labor, and spread nationally in the 2000s, to mixed results. Other non-governmental efforts, such as the Casey Jobs Initiative led to a series of coordinated responses in major metropolitan areas such as Boston and Seattle, focused on expanding access to workforce training through training and governance improvements (Giloth 2004). This is similar to the focus in EU nations to build infrastructure supporting training and research development in "finance" for London or manufacturing for Germany. In every case, the workforce system is seen as a key part of industrial development, differentiating it from the classic workforce development definitions that focus on job training for the disadvantaged.

The recession and lingering hangover have revealed the gaps in the U.S. public workforce development programs. Total numbers of workforce participation fluctuate, but generally increase for those that are means tested, requiring income verification, in recessionary periods. The Workforce Investment Act covered about 1.8 million people in 2011 (defined as exiters, people who left the system). This is an increase from 1.1 million in 2007 before the recession.

While many people have recovered from the recession, regaining lost jobs or retraining for new careers (Van Horn 2013), many more remain disconnected from economic success. New labor market entrants, youth in particular, face among the highest unemployment rates in living memory. African American youth specifically have unemployment rates over 20–25 per cent over the last few years, and youth as a whole face 17 per cent unemployment in the past year (Bureau of Labor Statistics 2012).

Short history of workforce development practice

Workforce development as a coherent area of practice emerged in the nineteenth and early twentieth century. Workforce development was initially based on European models of apprenticeship training, but individual nations developed national systems to address the needs of unemployed or underskilled workers (Culpepper 2003; Dorn 2007; Kincheloe 1999). Beginning in the nineteenth century the United States was specifically worried about the influx of new immigrants from Europe. Immigrants needed new education and training programs because the individuals lacked the skills in demand for the industrial economy. Adult education and vocational-technical education expanded dramatically in the early decades of the twentieth century to address this need for skills training among new immigrants (Kincheloe 1999). At the same time in Europe we observe the creation of systems to deal with the unemployed in the United Kingdom, while Germany, France, Austria and Italy continued to emphasize apprenticeship development (Arndt 1988). In the United Kingdom, the New Poor Act of 1834 established programs for unemployment, including a way of identifying the truly poor (King 1995). Benefits for training were often reserved for union members in the United Kingdom in the nineteenth century. In Germany and many areas of Austria, Switzerland, and Italy a system of apprenticeships remained largely in force as the primary tool for dealing with skills training in the nineteenth century, although by the early twentieth century there was development of a system of labor exchanges in the United Kingdom to address training needs. The primary focus of early British workforce policy was to serve the truly poor, those without any resources, rather than to intervene.

Around the turn of the twentieth century nations created systems for workforce development focusing on standard benefits like unemployment pay and increased support for training. National governments established programs to deal with unemployment and skills training, including public welfare programs, training to workers fighting or working in war, and established vocational schools for the secondary level (Grubb and Lazerson 2004; Dorn 2007). In a very detailed look at government actions around World War I, Dorn (2007) described the specific efforts made to train technically skilled workers for the war economy. In the UK, the system of labor exchanges was expanded after 1909 and linked placement in work with welfare benefits (King 1995).

The two World Wars and the Great Depression led to a dramatic increase in programs specifically developed for the workforce. As an example I want to note the efforts to pass the Full Employment Act, a piece of legislation first proposed in the 1930s and finally passed in a much reduced form until 1945. The Full Employment Act of 1945 was a far reaching piece of legislation that as initially proposed would have given the government authority to address unemployment for all working age adults, in much the same way that during the Great Depression the government provided targeted employment for artists or skilled trades workers (Weir 1992; Dorn 2007). As it was passed in 1945, it allowed the federal government to promote economic outcomes including employment, but did not generate new efforts to build a federal employment system.

This movement towards vocational education grew out of a century of experimentation with formal training for occupations in Europe and the United States. One of the drivers for early secondary schooling in Europe was to systematize the previously decentralized apprenticeship training structures (Anderson 2004). The central reason, however, for the emergence of a vocational education system had to do with economic development, and the sense that nations needed to explicitly train workers for new occupations (Benavot 1983; Grubb and Lazerson 2004). In the United States, therefore, the Smith-Hughes Act of 1917 established state level funding for vocational education in specific fields.

Despite this attention to workforce programs, most nations created disparate systems of workforce development that duplicated services and had conflicted missions. A comparison of the criticisms in workforce development programs in the U.S. and Europe shows both regions created many specific programs to train workers, while also attempting to support the dislocated or unemployed. These often had little relationship to each other. This lack of a coordinated system relates to the federal governance structures of the U.S. and Europe, where national

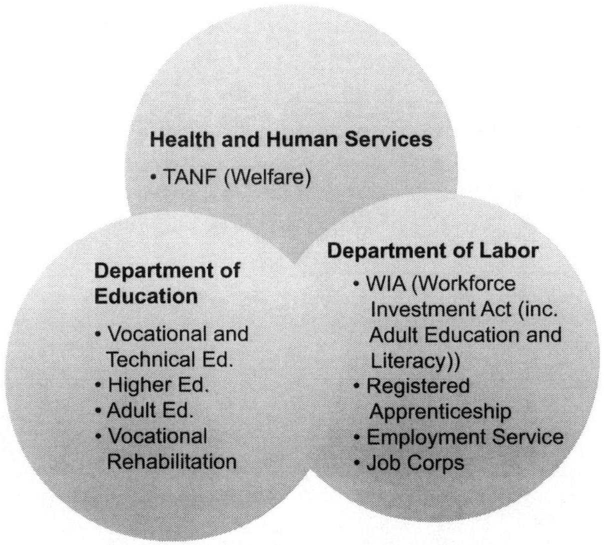

Figure 17.1 Workforce development programs in the U.S. federal government (2009)

Note: Other agencies include the following: Dept. of the Interior, Dept. of Agriculture, Dept. of Defense, Environmental Protection Agency, Dept. of Justice, Dept. of Veterans Affairs.
Source: GAO (2011).

governments exist with local or regional structures, often with conflicting programs and policies. The fragmentation of governmental services is related to the uncertain missions addressed in the previous section, as governments added programs to address similar issues. It is an end result of the fact that the workforce system exists for uncertain purposes, ranges across most of the federal government, and also includes the state and local efforts that try to cover people left out of programs with very rigid eligibility criteria. Figure 17.1 offers a representation of workforce development programs across key U.S. federal agencies (a reality that is mirrored at the state level).

There are many criticisms of the workforce systems as they have evolved. These include:

- There is no system that integrates education/training for work.
- The amount of funding for the "system" is inadequate.
- The evidence that programs have been successful is weak at best, and realistically raises major questions about the designs federal grants have supported.
- There is no attempt to involve firms in training/education.

Moreover, as opposed to career and technical schooling or adult education, workforce development is not traditionally applied to either youth or adults (Gray and Herr 1998). Government programs such as the Workforce Investment Act in the United States or the Leonardo da Vinci program in the European Union cover everything from sixteen-year-old high school dropouts to retirement age workers attempting to re-enter the labor market. In the United States, adult programs are much larger, however, serving up to 5 million people annually, while the youth program includes 200,000 or so on an annual basis (Rankin *et al.* 2012). In the EU, while each nation funds its own vocational and technical education system, the da Vinci program also tries to link nations together to learn from each other in the broad area of workforce development (Arndt 1988; Rouhiainen and Valjus 2003).

Overview of research in workforce development

Workforce development is not a discipline, but is an area of practice that crosses from the public to private sector. Researchers have continued to study the implementation of workforce programs. In order to better describe the state of research in workforce development this literature review identifies trends in terms of disciplinary differences and topic of study. A keyword search of the Social Science Citation Index for workforce development and related keywords was completed. Terms included workforce development or the more general term of "workforce." Using these terms a total of 5,174 articles were tabulated from the Social Science Citation Index database.

The term workforce development started to be used in the late 1960s, in conjunction with federal policies no doubt, such as the Manpower Demonstration and Training Act (1962) and the Comprehensive Employment and Training Act (1973). Both explicitly worked to create systems of federal and state support for workers and firms facing skills gaps (Dorn 2007; Mangum 2000). The earliest articles, such as those from the mid-1970s, focus on descriptions of economic conditions for the workforce. Earlier pieces reference workforce needs of colonies in Asia or Africa.

Overall, the number of citations using workforce or related terms doesn't grow significantly until the mid-1990s (Figure 17.2). After a decade or more of under 100 citations on a specific year, and since 1995 there has been a rapidly growing literature on workforce topics. While earlier years of workforce development research were generally about describing the labor force, after the mid-1990s we start to see the development of sub-literatures workforce development, specifically those focusing on health care or public health. Of the citations in every year after 1995, health care is the most important topic. Fifteen to twenty per cent of all articles in these years are on the larger topic of the medical workforce. In contrast, by the late 2000s (2008–2010), Occupational Health or Management have replaced health care as the most common areas for research. For the most recent complete year in SSCI (2012), the most common topics are Public Environmental Occupational Health and Medicine General Internal. They account for 25 per cent of all of the citations (103 of 394).

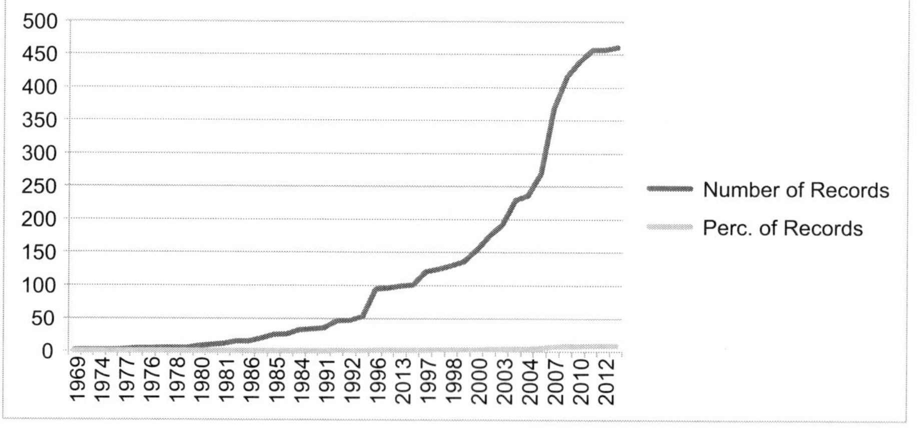

Figure 17.2 Number of workforce development publications in Social Science Citation Index (1969–2012), n = 5,174

Using the terms workforce development, adult education, human resource development, human performance, development, or welfare we identified a total of 2,981 citations with these code words in the abstract fields. The majority of the papers came from the term workforce alone.

Evolution of scholarship in workforce development

Because workforce development is not a theory in and of itself, there is no consensus on the key scholarship. There are core readings in the field, but not a general acceptance of a conceptual framework governing workforce outcomes or even a general agreement about the kinds of outcomes that should be counted. The earliest scholarship that might be explicitly labeled "workforce development" grew out of the debate following World War II surrounding the rebuilding of Europe (Arndt 1988; Schultz 1961). The primary point being made in these early works was that human capital, like physical capital, could be a resource for nations to use in expanding economic growth. There were many well-known papers written during this time, often from the economics discipline (Blaug 1976; Becker 1993).

In the period following World War II, as the nations of Europe rebuilt and Asia exploded, workforce development began to be seen as the critical reason for the growth of Asia specifically. The classical view, as articulated by publications from the World Bank and scholars who work on Asia, was that lacking significant natural resources, nations such as South Korea, Japan, and Taiwan were able to develop quickly because they invested in schooling or had a population with a strong support for education (World Bank 1993). Of course, it isn't this simple and subsequently economic crises in the late 1990s and further scholarship led to a significant understanding that government institutions can both influence economic growth and address skills shortages in the labor market. The specific industrial structure of South Korea or Japan, for example, led to massive state directed development in education and economic development (World Bank 2000; Williamson 1993; Pernia 1993; Pasuk 1992; Berry and Aram 2002; Ashton *et al.* 2002; Hawley and Paek 2005).

Singapore is an important case of how government used its power to address skills shortages. The success of Singapore is specifically attributed to a series of political and economic decisions taken by a relatively autocratic regime. This regime was able to increase economic development by a combination of setting economic targets and tax rules, controlling wages and worker inflows, and education policies. These efforts in combination led to a sustained growth in a relatively small colonial protectorate, turning it into a regional hub for western industry (Ashton *et al.* 1999, 2002).

The situation in Germany after the fall of the Wall in 1989 forced Western Germany to absorb the Eastern half of the nation. While the West had a very evolved workforce training system that has been well described (Broadbent *et al.* 1994; Rauner 1998; Brand 1998; Knoke 1998), Eastern German training and education was based on the system in the Soviet Union. This system in Germany was based on a social order – a formal agreement at the Länder level (state or province) which required firms, associations, and schools to train and hire workers. As Culpepper (2003) has described in great detail, as this system was placed under strain by exporting it to Eastern Germany, the whole system of workforce development in Germany was forced to adapt. In regions that had strong ties between firms that allowed for trusting relationships to be built, training and education could be done efficiently. In contrast, in those regions where firms competed but did not trust each other, government had to develop a substantial infrastructure to make the system work (Culpepper and Finegold 2000; Culpepper 2003). There are similar debates in other European nations like France and Italy (Capecchi 1994;

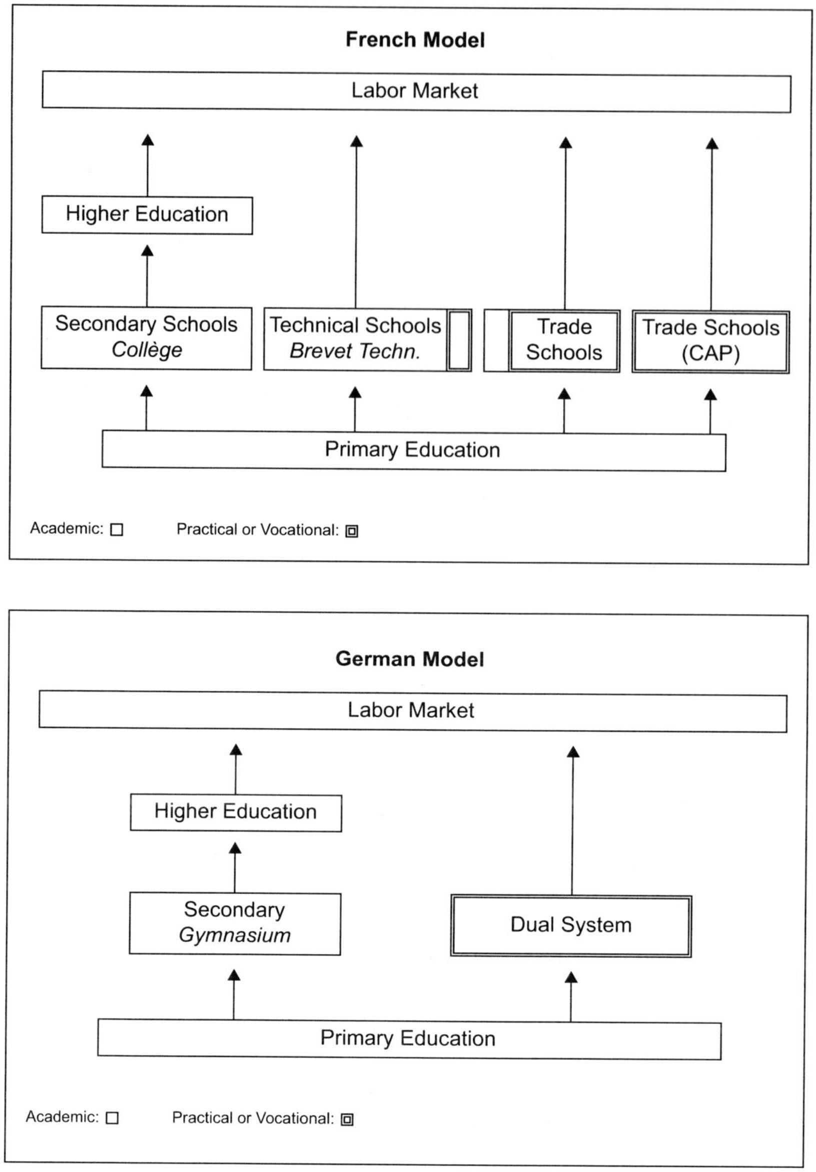

Figure 17.3 French and German educational systems (based on Castro *et al.* 2000)

Culpepper 2003). Figure 17.3 illustrates the structure of how school to workforce patterns have generally existed for France and Germany.

Workforce development as theory and scholarship in Africa and South America has received less attention, although there exist some efforts to compare governance systems in these nations with those in East Asia or Europe (di Gropello 2006; Johanson and Adams 2004).

In general, the literature on developing nations has shown us nations can use the governmental institutions to develop workforce development systems. There is a core set of understandings about workforce development and nations which might be stated as such: *workforce development programs serve to educate workers and ensure that firms can respond to changes in demand for skilled workers.*

Conclusion: linking workforce development to HRD

The term workforce development is difficult to pin down. It stands somewhere between education, government and business. As authors have described in the past, business level outcomes such as profit or productivity can be linked to workforce inputs, and this is what allows workforce development and HRD to share common purposes. Firms have organizational outcomes that can be considered part of workforce development. However, workforce development is bigger than HRD in that it includes societal outcomes, such as the skill level of the whole labor force. Therefore, the education system creates the conditions for business investment.

This chapter has provided an overview of workforce development, both as a term and as an emerging area of scholarship. As a term, workforce development is rooted in the historical experience of European and American states, which developed standardized secondary education and post-secondary systems only in the late nineteenth and early twentieth centuries. As nation states developed grade schools and universities, businesses and other interest groups pushed to develop training programs to help the unemployed or underskilled workers. While there is some history in nations like the United Kingdom or Germany of helping the poor or destitute, the workforce development efforts in the last hundred years are distinctive.

The formal institutional structure of workforce development that exists currently was built in the post World War II era when nations such as the United States and European Union states not only had to address poverty but simultaneously had to deal with significant skills gaps between workers that wanted to gain employment and the demands of the increasingly complex jobs in the service and manufacturing sectors. The key public policies that led to the workforce development infrastructure in the United States include the Job Training Partnership Act from 1982.

The primary emphasis of workforce development has changed over the last hundred years. Current efforts in workforce development employ "place-based" strategies to address skills shortages. These efforts ensure that workforce development programs can meet the need of a specific locale, instead of addressing perceived national or regional problems that may in fact have substantial geographic variation. Government and business leaders have increasingly been involved in these new workforce strategies as collaborative models for service delivery have overtaken government only delivery mechanisms (McCormick *et al.* 2008).

The future of workforce development is in new efforts to 1) increase college completion for adults, 2) focus on Science, Technology, Engineering and Math (STEM) training for youth, and 3) ensure that firms have access to skilled workers through increased training. College completion is a major concern as adults who have completed high school or secondary level qualifications are faced with increasing skills demands in many industrialized nations (Hawley and Chiang 2013). Secondly, STEM has been pushed by nations as a primary route to building economic competitiveness. Finally, there is a realization that as demands for high-level skills in jobs have increased that countries not only need to develop the infrastructure to lessen the burden of poverty, but also need to work actively with firms to meet the changing demand for skills. This is currently accomplished through state or national level training programs. In the United States state level training efforts exist in most states, with the largest in California's Employment and Training Panel (Gorman *et al.* 2004).

Note

1 The original author of this precise set of issues is lost in the mists of time, although Ron Jacobs, David Stein and Josh Hawley helped fill out the definitions.

References

Anderson, R. (2004) The idea of the secondary school in nineteenth-century Europe. *Paedagogica Historica* 40: 93–106.

Arndt, H.W. (1988) *Economic Development: The History of an Idea.* Chicago: University of Chicago Press.

Ashton, D., Green, F., James, D. and Sung, J. (1999) *Education and Training for Development in East Asia: The Political Economy of Skill Formation in Newly Industrialized Economies.* London: Routledge.

Ashton, D., Green, F., Sung, J. and James, D. (2002) The evolution of education and training strategies in Singapore, Taiwan, and S. Korea: A developmental model of skill formation. *Journal of Education and Work* 15: 5–30.

Becker, G.S. (1993) *Human Capital.* New York: Columbia University Press.

Benavot, A. (1983) The rise and decline of vocational education. *Sociology of Education* 56: 63–76.

Berry, D.E. (1998) The Jobs and Workforce Initiative: Northeast Ohio employers' plan for workforce development. *Economic Development Quarterly* 12: 41–53.

Berry, D.E. and Aram, J.D. (2002) Lessons for regional workforce development: East Asian experiences. *Economic Development Quarterly* 16: 155–66.

Blaug, M. (1976) Human capital theory: A slightly jaundiced view. *Journal of Economic Literature* 14: 827–55.

Brand, W. (1998) Change and Consensus in Vocational Education and Training: The Case of Germany's Dual System. In: Finlay, I., Niven, S. and Young, S. (eds) *Changing Vocational Education and Training: An International Comparative Perspective.* London: Routledge.

Broadbent, J.P., Knoke, D., Pappi, F. and Tsujinaka, Y. (1994) *Patterns of Policy-Making: Comparing Japan, Germany and the U.S.* Paper presented at the International Sociological Association XIII World Congress, Bielefeld, Germany, July 18–23.

Bureau of Labor Statistics (2012) *Labor Force Characteristics by Race and Ethnicity.* Washington DC: US Bureau of Labor Statistics.

Capecchi, V. (1994) Case 4: Emilia-Romagna, Italy: Labour Standards and Flexible Industrialization. In: Sengenberger, W. and Campbell, D. (eds) *Creating Economic Opportunities: The Role of Labour Standards in Industrial Restructuring.* Geneva: International Institute For Labour Studies.

Carcillo, S. and Grubb, D. (2006) *From Inactivity to Work: The Role of Active Labour Market Policies.* OECD Social, Employment and Migration Working Papers 36.

Castro, C., Carnoy, M. and Wolff, L. (2000) *Secondary Schools and the Transition to Work in Latin America and the Caribbean*, Washington. D.C.: Government Accountability Office.

Culpepper, P.D. (2003) *Creating Cooperation: How States Develop Human Capital in Europe.* Ithaca: Cornell University Press.

Culpepper, P. and Finegold, D. (eds) (2000) *The German Skills Machine: Sustaining Comparative Advantage in a Global Economy.* New York: Berghahn Books.

Di Gropello, E. (2006) *Meeting the Challenges of Secondary Education in Latin America and East Asia: Improving Efficiency and Resource Mobilization.* Washington, DC: World Bank.

Dorn, R.D. (2007) *Investing in Human Capital: The Origins of Federal Job Training Programs 1900 to 1945.* Columbus, OH: Ohio State University.

Eberts, R.W. (2008) The United States: How Partnerships Can Overcome Policy Gaps. In: Giguère, S. (ed.) *More than Just Jobs: Workforce Development in a Skills-Based Economy.* Paris: Organisation for Economic Co-operation and Development (OECD).

Giguère, S. (ed.)(2008) *More than Just Jobs: Workforce Development in a Skills-Based Economy.* Paris: Organisation for Economic Co-operation and Development (OECD).

Giloth, R.P. (1998) *Jobs and Economic Development: Strategies and Practice.* Newberry Park, CA: SAGE.

— (2000) Learning from the field: Economic growth and workforce development in the 1990s. *Economic Development Quarterly* 14: 340–59.

— (2004) *Workforce Development Politics: Civic Capacity and Performance.* Philadelphia: Temple University Press.

Gorman, P., Moore, R., Blake, D. and Phillips, M. (2004) An empirical study of the effectiveness of publicly-funded structured on-site training: Implications for policy and practice. *Journal of Vocational Education and Training* 56: 387–408.

Government Accountability Office (2011) *Multiple Employment and Training Programs: Providing Information on Collocating Services and Consolidating Administrative Structures Could Improve Efficiencies*, Washington, D.C.: Government Accountability Office.

Gray, K. and Herr, E. (1998) *Workforce Education: The Basics.* Boston: Allyn and Bacon.

Greffe, X. (2008) France: Bridging Regional Training and Local Employment. In: Giguère, S. (ed.) *More than Just Jobs: Workforce Development in a Skills-Based Economy.* Paris: Organisation for Economic Co-operation and Development (OECD).

Grubb, W.N. and Lazerson, M. (2004) *The Education Gospel: The Economic Power of Schooling.* Cambridge, MA: Harvard University Press.

Hawley, J.D. (forthcoming) Human Resource Development Policy. In: Chalofsky, N., Rocco, T. and Morris, L. (eds) *Handbook of Human Resource Development.* San Francisco, CA: Jossey-Bass.

Hawley, J.D. and Paek, J. (2005) Developing human resources for the technical workforce: A comparative study of Korea and Thailand. *International Journal of Training and Development* 9: 79–94.

Hawley, J.D. and Chiang, S.-C. (2013) Developmental Education for Adults and Academic Achievement. In: Hattie, J. and Anderman, E.M. (eds) *International Guide to Student Achievement.* Florence, KY: Taylor and Francis.

Jacobs, R.L. (2006) Perspectives on Adult Education, Human Resource Development, and the Emergence of Workforce Development. *New Horizons in Adult Education & Human Resource Development* 20: 21–31.

Jacobs, R.L. and Hawley, J.D. (2009) Emergence of Workforce Development: Definition, Conceptual Boundaries, and Future Perspectives. In: Maclean, R. and Wilson, D. (eds) *International Handbook of Education for the Changing World of Work.* Bonn: Springer.

Johanson, R.K. and Adams, A.V. (2004) *Skills Development In Sub-Saharan Africa.* Washington, DC: World Bank.

Kincheloe, J.L. (1999) *How Do We Tell the Workers? The Socioeconomic Foundations of Work and Vocational Education.* Boulder, CO: Westview Press.

King, D. (1995) *Actively Seeking Work? The Politics of Unemployment and Welfare Policy in the United States and Britain.* Chicago: University of Chicago Press.

Knoke, D. (1998) The organizational state: Origins and prospects. *Research in Political Sociology* 8: 147–63.

Mangum, G.L. (2000) Reflections on Training Policies and Programs. In: Barnow, B.S. and King, C.T. (eds) *Improving the Odds: Increasing the Effectiveness of Publicly Funded Training.* Washington, DC: The Urban Institute Press.

McCormick, L.E., Hawley, J.D. and Meléndez, E. (2008) The Economic and Workforce Development Activities of American Business Associations. *Economic Development Quarterly* 22: 213–27.

Meléndez, E. (1996) *Working on Jobs: The Center for Employment and Training.* Boston, MA: The Mauricio Gaston Institute, University of Massachusetts.

Mosley, H. and Bouché, P. (2008) Germany: The Local Impact of Labour Market Reforms. In: Giguère, S. (ed.) *More than Just Jobs: Workforce Development in a Skills-Based Economy.* Paris: Organisation for Economic Co-operation and Development (OECD).

Pasuk, P. (1992) Technocrats, Businessmen, and Generals: Democracy and Economic Policy-Making in Thailand. In: Macintyre, A.J. and Jayasuriya, K. (eds) *The Dynamics of Economic Policy Reform in South-East Asia and the South-West Pacific.* Singapore: Oxford University Press.

Pernia, E.M. (1993) Economic Growth Performance of Indonesia, the Philippines, and Thailand: The Human Resource Dimension. In: Ogawa, N., Jones, G.W. and Williamson, J. (eds) *Human Resources in Development along the Asia-Pacific Rim.* Singapore: Oxford University Press.

Rankin, K.M., Kroelinger, C.D., Rosenberg, D. and Barfield, W.D. (2012) Building analytic capacity, facilitating partnerships, and promoting data use in state health agencies: A distance-based workforce development initiative applied to maternal and child health epidemiology. *Maternal and Child Health Journal* 16(19): 6–202.

Rauner, F. (1998) School-to-Work Transition: The Example of Germany. In: Stern, D. and Wagner, D.A. (eds) *International Perspectives on the School-to-Work Transition.* Cresskill, NJ: Hampton Press.

Rouhiainen, P. and Valjus, S. (2003) *Towards Closer European Cooperation in Vocational Education and Training: The Leonardo Da Vinci Programme Supporting the Copenhagen Declaration – Case Finland.* Helsinki: Finnish Education Authority, Leonardo Centre and Centre for International Mobility CIMO, Leonardo unit.

Schultz, T.W. (1961) Investment in human capital. *American Economic Review* 51: 1–17.

Van Horn, C. (2013) *Working Scared (Or Not at All): The Lost Decade, Great Recession, and Restoring the Shattered American Dream.* Lanham, MD: Rowman & Littlefield Publishers.

Weir, M. (1992) *Politics and Jobs: The Boundaries of Employment Policy in the United States.* Princeton, NJ: Princeton University Press.
Williamson, J.G. (1993) Human Capital Deepening, Inequality, and Demographic Events along the Asia-Pacific Rim. In: Ogawa, N., Jones, G.W. and Williamson, J. (eds) *Human Resources in Development along the Asia-Pacific Rim.* Singapore: Oxford University Press.
World Bank (1993) *East Asian Miracle: Economic Growth and Public Policy.* Washington, DC: World Bank.
— (2000) *East Asia: Recovery and Beyond.* Washington, DC: World Bank.

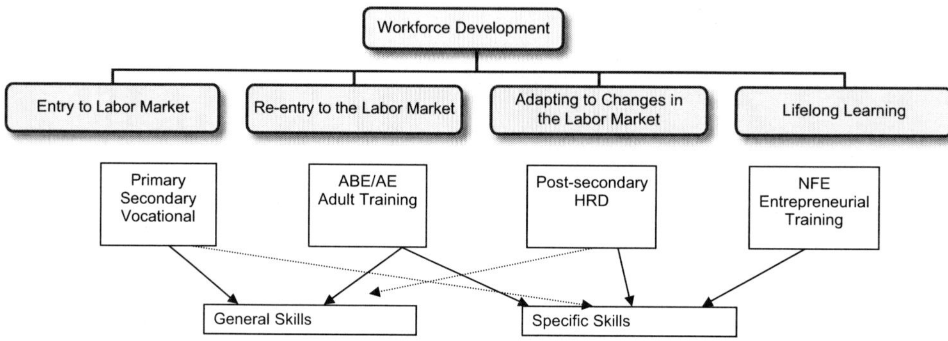

Appendix 17.1 Visualization of the four issues

18

LIFELONG LEARNING AS A LIFE-LARGE AND LIFE-DEEP REALITY

Paul Bélanger

The world of work is undergoing a transformation that can be seen not only in the places where goods and services are actually produced, but also in the career paths that people follow and steer. Changes in production methods and technologies and the globalization of the economy are altering both the individual's relationship to work and the individual's life course. Major debates are also going on about the economic demand for greater flexibility and about how work should be organized. Keeping the same job for life is becoming more difficult. How then can we ensure that individuals, in spite of job mobility, could exercise their right to work? And if jobs cease to be permanent, then shouldn't adult learning and education become a continuing component of people's biography? In some European countries, there is talk of "flexicurity" policy—not external flexibility based on deregulation, but internal flexibility based on continuously enhancing the qualifications and versatility of the active population and implementing programs to achieve these goals (Rubenson 2009, 2006).

In the workplace itself, the transition from Taylorism ("scientific management") and assembly-line production methods to more team-based production methods is altering the content of jobs and demanding greater versatility from workers. In addition, new technologies are being introduced that not only make work more abstract, but also make workstations more complex, enabling and requiring workers to make frequent changes in the current operation to meet increasingly diverse production requirements. In Europe, 80 per cent of the technologies now in use were introduced within the past 10 years, but 80 per cent of the workers in the labor force completed their initial vocational education more than 10 years ago (Pedersen, cited by Rubenson 2009). And in the service sector of the new economy, the increasing number of relational jobs is creating a growing demand for increasingly complex interpersonal skills based on both cognitive and affective capabilities (Field and Malcolm 2008).

In the traditional employment model based on the Fordist alliance between capital and labor, workers were expected to follow a well-defined three-phase career path: initial training, leading to a specific and stable job at that company, followed by a regulated transition to retirement at a specified age. Now this model applies in only a minority of cases, or has even become the exception rather than the rule, and the three phases often overlap in confusing ways (Lowe 2002; Guillemard 2003). Some workers will have a career path that consists of a succession of different jobs, interspersed with phases of intensive training. But for other workers—many others—the path will always remain uncertain. For them, the labor market has become a high-risk society, with a high likelihood of job losses or being limited to jobs that are precarious, part-time, or seasonal.

This dual transformation, in the world of work and in personal career paths, is altering the relationship between the worker and his or her work.

Prescribed work versus actual work

Work activity can no longer be reduced to executing the prescribed task, not even on an assembly line. The action, even if it is a repetitive one, is always performed by a knowing agent. Ergonomists in the French tradition (Chatigny and Montreuil 2003; Noulin 2002; Teiger and Montreuil 1996; Wisner 1995) have shown that the prescribed roles are only one dimension of the actual observed roles. An individual's actual work does of course include following instructions that set out the production objectives and procedures. But the worker must also make adjustments every day in the targets to be achieved and the methods of achieving them. To make these adjustments, workers must consider varying contingencies and conditions, including random events and unforeseen circumstances, such as equipment failures (Beckett and Hager 2010). And to do that, workers must rely on their experience, their practical intelligence, and their initiative. In fact, work activity requires workers to mediate constantly between their assigned tasks, on the one hand, and the conditions under which they are performing these tasks and the ways in which they are performing them, on the other. To perform their functions and control their situation, workers must intervene and become agents who can interpret what is happening, draw on their experience, and manage shifting contexts.

We cannot ignore the myriad challenges that individuals face in their work. They must foresee hazards, and thereby avoid them. They must observe and develop intuition through experience and apply them to new situations. They must improvise workaround methods, manage fatigue, remain alert for signs of equipment malfunctions, and maintain contact with other people on the shop floor. In addition, individuals will react and interact differently, depending on their cultural and educational backgrounds, their personal aspirations, and their private assumptions and concerns, which do not simply vanish when they walk in the shop door.

Workers attempt to "[translation] make the operating method conform to the needs of their mental structures"; they need a certain "[translation] freedom in production" to experience the "[translation] pleasure of functioning" (Dejours 2000: 158, 164 and 168). "Work activity is not something to endure, but rather something to construct" (Daniellou and Garrigou 1995). Thus this gap reveals nothing less than the creative aspect of any work activity (Dejours 2000), the capacity for independent action and continuing experiential learning that it requires—in short, the personal component of work. In this inevitable distance between the prescribed and the real, the distinctive contribution of the individual becomes essential. In the space that this distance creates, employees are more than a work force: they are agents who build knowledge and seek to define themselves individually and collectively. The singular production of tacit knowledge and the invention or adaptation of tricks of the trade—in short, the day-to-day improvisations in which workers engage to give themselves some room for maneuver and forge their skills on the job—all express an intelligence in action that sadly too often remains the hidden face of work.

And if this constant mental engagement is necessary even in the most routine work (Teiger 1993), then it is all the more so in the new work settings described earlier and characterized by quantitative and qualitative variations in production, variability in tasks and teams, and rotation of roles within teams. In this context, the barrier between designing work and executing work is becoming slimmer and slimmer. First, there is a growing demand for co-operation and feedback from workers when innovations are being tested. There is also a demand not only for prescribed skills but also for open, unsaturated skills (Aneesh, quoted by Sawchuk 2006), that is, for workers to learn, to learn from one another, and to create, even if the product of this intimate activity often remains tacit. Individual workers' use of their practical and strategic intelligence to diagnose and solve the problems of their daily work produces an internally driven quest to continue developing their inner capacities.

The effect of radically separating manual work from intellectual work, beyond being wrong from a bio-paleontological perspective, is, as in the Taylorist model, to limit the space for mental activity, if not shut it out entirely. When workers are treated as nothing but a blind force that performs prescribed, fragmented tasks repeatedly, their intelligence is denied (Dejours 1993), as are their professional skills (Friedmann 1950). But their "shrewd intelligence" persists nonetheless. Even in such "[translation] unconscious, fragmented work" (Friedmann 1950: 337), their senses remain alert; their collective and professional awareness does not disappear. By reacting intelligently, by improvising individually and collectively (Dejours 1993), workers invent and share procedures by which they can keep workplace accidents from recurring.

This subjective relationship to productive activity, as revealed by the tension between the prescribed tasks and the actual work, leads individuals to seek not only exchange value but also use value in their work.

Exchange value versus use value

Of course, the exchange value of work, such as the wages paid or demanded in compensation for the work done, is just as decisive a factor for society, for the national economy, and for businesses as it is for individuals. It constitutes the main mechanism for distributing collective wealth and resources and hence tends to be regulated. The same holds true for the exchange value of education. Formal recognition of qualifications is one of the non-arbitrary criteria for allocating jobs and pay; it is also an objective reference when adults register to return to school—hence the importance of recognized certifications.

However, the reality both of work and of learning and education cannot be limited to their exchange value. They also, and first of all, have a use value, for society and organizations as well as for individuals. Socially, the use value of work comes primarily from the goods and services that it produces and from the collective and individual needs that it thereby satisfies. Similarly, the use social value of education comes from its distributing knowledge more widely throughout the population and enhancing the population's capacity for action. Individually, the use value of work comes from the quality of the activity, from its meaning for the worker, from the self-actualization that the worker derives from it, and from each worker's need to be consulted before performing it and to be regarded as a "colleague" by his or her peers. In this context, Field and Malcolm (2008) speak of the "sense of agency" and "personal authenticity." In education, beyond the degrees and diplomas, the use value of work for individuals consists in its contribution to their personal development and their gradual self-actualization, due to the cognitive development and emotional maturity that it engenders. Although these use values have no immediate price in the marketplace, they are no less real.

When work and education are cut off from the individual's contribution and the individual's capacity for action, they lose their intrinsic value. In the new organization of work, which calls for workers to participate actively, it is less and less possible for an organization to maximize the productive contribution of its labor force without recognizing the individual workers' aspirations to find a subjective use value in their work as well. Otherwise, work and learning activities become commodities, reduced to their market value, activities with no intrinsic motivation, devoid of any opportunities for inner creativity.

Now—and this is a societal issue—individual workers cannot participate in a productive activity in any true sense unless it provides a concrete way of at least partially satisfying their legitimate aspirations to develop their potential, to exercise it every day, and to take pleasure in doing so. For the individuals who perform the work, it is not just an instrumental activity; it is also a reflective one. Individuals cannot be active agents unless their personal contribution is recognized and a context is created in which this can happen. Individual workers can be nothing but passive consumers of the training they receive, unless they find that it not only gives them the knowledge and skills they need to stay employed, but also meets their personally felt need to increase their knowledge and their capacity for action.

The social implications of recognizing the individual use value of work and education include enhanced efficiency of productive activities, but go well beyond it. This search for use value in work and a positive relationship with work is many-faceted. It of course includes individuals' quest for meaning in their work and the recognition of a zone of autonomy needed for reflective participation. But this search also involves the demand for working conditions that allow for individual needs and a balance between work and private life. Examples of such conditions include arrangements that help to reconcile the conflicting demands of work and family (often difficult, especially for women, who may work one shift during the day and then go home to work a "second shift" in the evening); parental leave (Tremblay 2008; Philipson 2002); time off to pursue education or training; permission to work at home; flexible retirement arrangements, etc.

That said, the use value of work is not unrelated to its exchange value. Workers cannot be expected to contribute to productivity unless they participate in the benefits that it generates. In today's globalized economy, increasing productivity is a major concern. But there is productivity and productivity. The negative approach to raising productivity ("la productivité sèche") is to cut production costs, wages, staff, and pension benefits—in other words, to increase productivity on the backs of workers. A more positive approach is to make the workers active participants in research and development and enlist their help in introducing innovations. In exchange for their active participation in raising productivity, workers demand a redistribution of the benefits thus achieved. But first and foremost, they demand, as noted earlier, *decent work*—a concept that, according to the International Labour Organization (2011: n.p.) "sums up the aspirations of people in their working lives (Bonnechère 2008). It involves opportunities for work that is productive and delivers a fair income, security in the workplace and social protection for families, better prospects for personal development and social integration, freedom for people to express their concerns, organize and participate in the decisions that affect their lives and equality of opportunity and treatment for all women and men."

The point is not to deny that work has exchange value, but rather to link it to its use value, which should have primacy. The same is true of workplace-based learning, whose transformation is not solely quantitative and morphological.

The transformation of learning in the workplace

The demand for learning and education in the workplace, like any demand, has two sides. On the one hand, organizations seek to develop their workers' skills to meet the growing demand to modify their productive activities and make them more efficient. The competitiveness of national economies is, indeed, more and more closely tied to the ongoing development of the knowledge and skills of their personnel. This involves more than just a demand to increase skills continuously. Organizations that are evolving and attempting to innovate recognize that they must take the risk of leaving more room for individual initiative in an increasingly reflective organization of work (Brown *et al.* 2001; Bélanger and Federighi 2000; Lash and Urry 1987).

On the other hand, individuals, in their actual work activities, which are in constant tension with their prescribed tasks, have their own demands as well. They also want their work to have a personally meaningful use value and let them enhance their ability to act independently on the job. They are demanding recognition not only of the tension between their prescribed tasks and their actual work, but also of the gap between their prescribed learning and their actual learning.

This dual demand explains the growth of adult learning and education in advanced industrial countries over the past 30 years. On average, one out of every three workers now participates in structured learning activities, and in northern Europe, the figure is one out of two (Rubenson 2009).

The demand for education in the workplace is not only growing, but also becoming more complex. It extends to all levels of qualifications and takes many guises, both formal and informal. Examples include attending a set of education and training activities inside or outside the organization, formal or informal mentoring, assisted self-study, and possible recognition of experiential learning. However, surveys show that adults' participation in adult learning and education is not evenly distributed (Bélanger and Tuijnman 1997; OECD 2003; Doray and Bélanger 2005; Rubenson and Desjardins 2009). It varies with age, initial level of education, occupational status, industry, organization size, access to educational institutions, and individuals' propensity to take the training offered. It also varies by country, because of the mechanisms and policies put in place to alter the unequal development of these activities (Bélanger and Federighi 2011).

Workers, says Sawchuk (2006), are "knowing and acting subjects." In that perspective, not from the standpoint of the organization, but from that of the individuals, the distinction between formal and informal learning remains formal because, regardless of what form it takes, learning always remains the act of an individual learner (Billett 2002). It is the learner who interacts with the sources of knowledge. By verifying its relevance to the questions that triggered the learning process, learners interpret new knowledge so that they can then make it their own. Only after comparing new concepts with previously encoded knowledge can learners absorb them successfully. And they will succeed in applying their newly acquired expertise to productive activity only if they successfully experiment with it and thus organize it and internalize it in their own individually distinctive manner. In fact, over an individual's lifetime, formal and informal learning are inter-related in many ways (Livingstone 1999): with formal and non-formal education, individuals learn the words to state and define the tacit knowledge that they have developed informally, which in turn enables them to initiate further self-education and experiential learning (Eraut 2004; Evans *et al.* 2004).

Workers' demand is not limited to the subjective conditions for effective and significant learning. It also comprises individuals' plans—articulated to varying degrees—for "self-construction." It relates to *self-image* (the way that individuals perceive themselves and see others as perceiving them), *self-esteem* (what value they place on these perceptions), *self-confidence* (how they act on the basis of this self-evaluation), and *self-worth* (the importance that they accord to their capacity to create) (Billett 2002). The importance of this intimate dimension is also seen in inter-learning relations (Billett 2007; Candy 1991). In his studies on the role of emotions in the workplace and their impact on training, Field (2006) offers a complex analysis showing how individuals draw on their affective and cognitive resources to position themselves in their workplaces and negotiate their working lives.

In this regard, we cannot ignore the doubts that individuals often have about their ability to master and perform the particular tasks required of them. Though individuals often sacrifice their dreams of self-actualizing work in order simply to stay employed, those dreams never die.

Difficulties in negotiating or mediating this transformed demand

The work-related learning demand is thus complex and its expression even more. For example, in France, after the mass student/worker protests of May 1968, the Grenelle Agreements signed by government, labor, and business led to the Law of July 1971 on Continuing Occupational Training and Education, opened access to education and training, and achieved a historic breakthrough by recognizing workers' right to "paid education leave." But this legislation still left management the right to determine unilaterally the content of such learning activities. As one writer has put it, "[translation] the unions secured the right to education and training, but the employers secured the right to control it" (Rodary 1980: 15).

The expression of the learning demand and the mediation between the organization's requirements and the employees' aspirations and expectations, cannot be taken for granted. On both sides, such demand comprises two dimensions: first, the perception of the usefulness of the learning activity ("valence"), and second, the perception of its feasibility and potential success ("expectancy") (Rubenson 1977; Rubenson and Xu 1997).

From the organization's perspective, even though more and more studies are showing the economic value of providing education and training for employees and the positive returns that such investments can provide (Chochard and Davoine 2008; Dunberry 2006; Phillips 2003), the perception of such need is not always obvious in day-to-day operations. Often, the demand emerges and becomes operative only when the organization faces a specific problem and sees that certain special skills have to be developed to deal with it—for example, when new equipment or a new work-organization method is introduced, or when a new quality-control requirement is identified. But even once convinced that such a need exists ("valence"), an organization may well question the feasibility of providing the learning activities in question ("expectancy"), for all sorts of reasons—trouble in scheduling time for employees to attend training sessions, lack of appropriate training options, lack of funds, etc. Thus, even when employers are convinced of the need for education and training, they may defer a decision.

From the employees' perspective, the perceived value of the foreseen activities depends on how much they believe it will help them to operate more autonomously, or improve their working conditions, or simply keep their jobs. Second, employees' needs and interests not directly related to their work may also be involved. The possible motivations are manifold. And even when individuals perceive a definite benefit in taking part in such activities ("valence"), they may worry about whether they can do so successfully and may hesitate because of the risk to their self-esteem ("expectancy"). They also simply may not have the conditions that they would need to participate effectively; they may have scheduling conflicts, or lack the necessary physical resources, or have trouble in reconciling the demands of training with those of work and family (Tremblay 2008), especially if they are women. People may even perceive the value in the proposed education and training, but if they doubt their chances of success, they will still resist getting involved. I will always remember the case of a Montreal firm, that, back in 2000, had replaced all of its workstations and offered the 50 affected employees the choice of either taking six months of training and having guaranteed jobs at the new workstations when they were done, or else taking early retirement. Only 12 per cent of these employees opted for the proposed training. The vast majority, out of fear of failing the course and thus being publicly humiliated, had not even dared to accept the challenge. Yet every one of the six employees who did take the training succeeded, with no problems!

Of course, as Rubenson (1977) underscores, individuals' perceptions of the need for a given training program and the feasibility of participating in it are influenced by their immediate work situations and by their past learning experiences, which are themselves marked by the settings in which they took place and the cultural attitudes that the individuals absorbed in them. But the fact remains that if individual expectations are not expressed, then the effectiveness and the subjective meaning of the proposed learning activity will be severely compromised. On-the-job learning is a relational transaction between the individuals and the organization. If this transaction is not mediated in a structured way ahead of time, then the problem of reconciling the two components of the demand (from employer and employees) may resurface while the training is in progress and hinder its successful completion. Our observations also show that though the demands of workers and employers are different, they are also potentially complementary and hence negotiable. Workers want the assurance that the increased capacity for action that they are going to have to acquire personally will improve their personal situations. Employers will want their investment in education and training to provide a return: the desired improvement in their production activities.

An organized expression and a contextualized analysis of this dual demand is thus essential both for planning an appropriate response to the organization's contextualized needs and for ensuring that the learning will be meaningful for the learners. Such expression of the learning demand can be effective only if it is proactive, involves all of the stakeholders on the ground, and recognizes that the demand for continuous professional development emerges at every level of the jobs pyramid (Schuller and Watson 2009; Goldenberg 2006; Anderson 1994). On-the-job learning and education no longer is and no longer can be the sole prerogative of management (Teiger 1993: 185).

Indeed, education and training is increasingly the subject of discussions and agreements in labor–management negotiations (Haipeter and Lehndorff 2009). However, the expression and mediation of these two aspects of any demand for on-the-job training requires special mechanisms both at the company or even sectorial level and at the more immediate level of day-to-day work.

Such mechanisms are now being negotiated for expressing and negotiating demands. In France and Germany, there is a growing trend to expand the mandate of company works councils to include education and training or, in companies that do not have works councils, to establish labor–management education and training committees. Issues such as work force flexibility, continuing learning and education, productivity-related ergonomics, and work/training rotation are subjects of negotiations. Unions are negotiating increases in training budgets and are demanding to negotiate company education and training plans (Glassner and Keune 2010; Haipeter and Lehndorff 2009). In Quebec, over half of all collective agreements contain clauses that deal with education and training. One quarter of these agreements provide for labor–management education and training committees, and half of these committees are not merely consultative but have decision-making authority shared by the two parties.

In the United Kingdom, business and labor organizations, working with government, have established a special fund to pay for legally recognized Union Learning Representatives (ULRs). Their role is to provide employees with information, advice, and support regarding all kinds of education and training—basic, technical, and cultural, for professional purposes or personal ones. Such union representatives also operate in other countries, such as New Zealand (where they are referred to by the same title); Denmark (where they are known as educational ambassadors); Finland (union competence pilots); and Sweden (union learning counsellors) (Hart 2011; Lee and Cassell 2009).

Until recently, these negotiation and mediation processes tended to deal chiefly with access to and recognition of education and training. But these learning brokers, operating in the immediate, local context (Hart 2011) tend more and more to facilitate expression of the learning demand of workers.

Expressing learning demand related to career transitions

On-the-job education and training, along with policies and mechanisms for regulating the labor market, are indispensable for meeting the changing demand for a qualified labor force, but can no longer suffice to do so on their own. In today's increasingly uncertain labor market, in which career paths are less and less continuous, individuals have also to take their own initiatives to develop their skills or qualify for new professions. Cumulatively, such individual initiatives contribute greatly to self-regulation of the labor market. Some countries have introduced mechanisms to facilitate such personal initiatives. Examples of such mechanisms include individual learning accounts, in Scotland; paid educational leave, in France and Germany; individual training entitlements, in France; training vouchers, in Belgium; and training accounts, in Italy. All of these mechanisms, which focus on the individual, complement policies that focus on the organization (Cedefop 2009). It has even been proposed that some of the funds allocated for initial occupational training be redirected to help people, who are currently employed, train for new occupations (Schuller and Watson 2009). These personal decisions are usually made at key junctures in individuals' work lives, when they are seeking promotions or planning to change careers. But to plan and carry out these intensive periods of substantial learning, workers need access not only to information, advice, and guidance services, but also to financial support. Only then will the number of workers who take such personal initiatives become large enough to actually facilitate the continuous adjustment of labor supply and demand that has become necessary now that medium- and long-range workforce planning has become so difficult (Brown *et al.* 2010).

Conclusion

As the discrepancy between prescribed work and actual work is more and more recognized, the personal contributions that workers make are increasingly revealed. In striking a new balance between the exchange value of their work and its use value, people are more and more openly seeking a sense of meaning not only in their work, but also in the learning that they are expected to do in relation to it. Collectively, workers are helping to change the culture of their organizations so that individuality gains more recognition and productive activity becomes more reflective (Field and Malcolm 2008). Indeed, knowledge can be put to active use by the organization only once it has been appropriated by people.

The expression and mediation of learning demand are becoming an issue for individuals as well as for organizations, which, if they are going to grow, will have to risk distributing the capacity for initiative more widely. There can be no sustainable productivity unless individuals' capacity for action is mobilized. The intelligence of work is being rediscovered. Workers are increasingly recognized as "knowing subjects." The intimacy of learning is being acknowledged.

Working women and working men are more than just human resources to be managed. They are agents who are developing their own capabilities. The knowledge-intensive economy cannot exist without an organization of work that is "actor-intensive" as well. But even though the new organization of work can create spaces for expressing one's self in one's actual work, and even though enhanced mobility can enable individuals to change career directions and negotiate career transitions more effectively, certain conditions must be present to make all this possible. The concept of human capital does identify human labor as a key resource, but results in a reductive, one-dimensional perspective in which the individual is not seen as a sentient actor who can observe, reflect, solve problems, communicate—in short, change and evolve. As Indian economist and philosopher Amartya Sen (2000) asserts, human beings are more than a means of production or a passive force that performs work; they are the agents and the ultimate end of production.

What is at stake is human capacity and its continuing social and personal development, as well as the continuing capacity for occupational mobility that ensures both the right to work and endogenous flexibility. Individuals cannot enhance their performance and their autonomy unless there is recognition of their individual and collective demand for a type of learning that has personal meaning for them not just now, in their workplaces, but also throughout their lives. The expression of this complex learning demand transforms the meaning of work-related lifelong learning education which, to be significant for individuals and productive for organizations, needs also to become life-large and life-deep.

References

Anderson, G. (1994) "A proactive model for training needs analysis" *Journal of European Industrial Training* 18(3): 23–38.

Beckett, D. and Hager, P. (2010) "Making judgments as the basis for workplace learning: Towards an epistemology of practice" *International Journal of Lifelong Education* 19(4): 300–11.

Bélanger, P. and Federighi, P. (2000) *La Libération difficile des forces créatrices. Analyse transnationale des politiques d'éducation des adultes*, Montréal: CIRDEP-UQAM; Paris: L'Harmattan.

Bélanger, P. and Tuijnman, A.C. (eds) (1997) *New Patterns of Adult Learning: A Six-Country Comparative Study*, London: Pergamon.

Billett, S. (2002) "Critiquing workplace learning discourses: Participation and continuity at work" *Studies in the Education of Adults* 34(1): 56–67.

— (2007) "Exercising self through working life: Learning, work and identity" In Brown, A., Kirpal, S. and Rauner, F. (eds) *Identities at Work*, Dordrecht: Springer, 183–210.

Bonnechère, M. (2008) "Travail décent et modernisation du droit du travail" *Travail et Emploi* 113: 91–101.

Brown, P., Green, A. and Lauder, H. (2001) *High Skills: Globalization, Competitiveness and Skill Formation*, Oxford: Oxford University Press.

Brown, A., Bimrose, J., Barnes, S.A., Kirpal, S. and Gronning, T. (2010) *Changing Patterns of Working, Learning and Career Development across Europe*, Warwick.: Warwick Institute for Employment Research.

Candy, P.C. (1991) *Self-direction for Lifelong Learning. A Comprehensive Guide to Theory and Practice*, San Francisco: Jossey-Bass.

Cedefop (2009) *Individual Learning Account*, Luxemburg: European Community Publication Office.

Chatigny, C. and Montreuil, S. (2003) "Apprenticeship in a work setting: The contribution and limits of operational resources constructed by workers" *Safety Science* 41: 377–91.

Chochard, Y. and Davoine, E. (2008) "À quoi sert la formation managériale et comment évaluer son retour sur investissement? Analyse d'un cas d'évaluation dans une entreprise suisse" XIXe congrès AGRH 2008, Reims (France).

Daniellou, F. and Garrigou, A. (1995) "L'Ergonome, l'activité et la parole des travailleurs" In Boutet, J. (ed.) *Paroles au Travail*, Paris: L'Harmattan.

Dejours, C. (1993) "Intelligence pratique et sagesse pratique: Deux dimensions méconnues du travail réel" *Éducation Permanente* 116: 47–70.

— (2000) *Travail et usure mental* (nouvelle édition augmentée), Paris: Bayard.

Doray, P. and Bélanger, P. (2005) "Société du savoir, éducation et formation des adultes" *Éducation et Société* 15: 119–36.

Dunberry, A. (2006) *Analyse des pratiques d'évaluation de la formation et de son rendement dans des entreprises performantes*, UQAM: CIRDEP.

Eraut, M. (2004) "Informal learning in the workplace" *Studies in Continuing Education* 26(2): 173–247.

Evans, K., Kersh, N. and Sakamoto, A. (2004) "Learner biographies: Exploring tacit dimensions of knowledge and skills" In Rainbird, H., Fuller, A. and Munro, A. (eds) *Workplace Learning in Context*, London: Routledge, 222–41.

Field, J. (2006) *Lifelong Learning and the New Educational Order* (2nd edn), Stoke on Trent, UK: Trentham.

Field, J. and Malcolm, I. (2008) *Learning working lives: A working paper* (3), Stirling: Stirling University.

Friedmann, G. (1950) *Où va le travail humain?*, Paris: Gallimard.

Glassner, V. and Keune., M. (2010) *Negotiating the Crisis? Collective Bargaining in Europe During the Economic Downturn*, Geneva: Industrial and Employment Relations Department, International Labour Office.

Goldenberg, M. (2006) *Employer Investment in Workplace Learning in Canada*, Ottawa: Canadian Council for Lifelong Learning.

Guillemard, A.M. (2003) *L'Âge de l'emploi: Les sociétés à l'épreuve du vieillissement*, Paris: Armand Colin.
Haipeter, T. and Lehndorff, S. (2009) *Collective Bargaining on Employment*, Geneva: Industrial and Employment Relations Department, ILO.
Hart, S.A. (2011) "Les Union Learning Reps du Royaume-Uni: Lorsque des représentants syndicaux deviennent des learning brokers" *Bulletin OCE* 2:1.
International Labour Organization (2011) *Decent Work*. Retrieved 20 June 2014 from http://www.ilo.org/global/topics/decent-work/lang--en/index.htm.
Lash, S. and Urry, J. (1987) *The End of Organized Capitalism*, Cambridge: Polity Press.
Lee, B. and Cassell, C. (2009) "Learning organisations, employee development and learning representative schemes in the UK and New Zealand" *Journal of Workplace Learning* 21(1): 5–22.
Livingstone, D. (1999) "Exploring the icebergs of adult learning: Findings of the first Canadian survey of informal learning practices" *Canadian Journal for Studies in Adult Education* 13(2): 49–72.
Lowe, G. (2002) "Employment relationships as the centrepiece of a new labour policy paradigm" *Canadian Public Policy/Analyse de Politiques* 28(1): 93–104.
Noulin, M. (2002) *Ergonomie*, Toulouse: Éd. Octares.
OECD (2003) *Literacy Skills for the World of Tomorrow*, Paris: OCDE-PISA.
Philipson, I. (2002) *Bringing the Second Shift* (Working paper 50), Berkeley, CA: Center for Working Family.
Phillips, J.J. (2003) *Return on Investment in Training and Performance Improvement Programs*, Second Edition. Amsterdam; Boston: Butterworth-Heinemann.
Rodary, J.F. (1980) "L'Éducation populaire en France témoin de deux traditions" *Revue internationale d'action communautaire* 43(3): 7–16.
Rubenson, K. (1977) *Participation in Recurrent Education*, Paris: OCDE-CERI.
— (2006) "The Nordic model of lifelong learning" *Compare* 36(3): 327–41.
— (2009) "Lifelong Learning for All in the Context of Flexicurity" Paper presented at the Global HR Forum, Seoul, 3–5 November 2009.
Rubenson K. and Xu, G. (1997) "Barriers to participation in adult education and training: Towards a new understanding" In Bélanger, P. and Tuijnman, A.C. (eds) *New Patterns of Adult Learning: A Six-Country Comparative Study*, London: Pergamon.
Rubenson, K. and Desjardins, R. (2009) "The impact of welfare state regimes on barriers to participation in adult education. A bounded agency model" *Adult Education Quarterly* 59(3): 187–207.
Sawchuk, P. (2006) "'Use-value' and the re-thinking of skills, learning and the labour process" *Journal of Industrial Relations* 48(4): 238–62.
Schuller, T. and Watson, D. (2009) *Learning Through Life: Inquiry into the Future for Lifelong Learning*, Leicester: NIACE.
Sen, A. (2000) *Un nouveau modèle économique: Développement, Justice, Liberté*, Paris: Éditions Odile Jacob.
Teiger, C. (1993) "L'Approche ergonomique: Du travail humain à l'activité des hommes et des femmes au travail" *Éducation Permanente* 116: 71–96.
Teiger, C. and Montreuil, S. (1996) "The foundations and contributions of ergonomics work analysis in training programmes" *Safety Science* 23(3): 81–95.
Tremblay, D.G. (2008) *Conciliation emploi-famille et temps sociaux*, Québec: Presses de l'Université du Québec.
Wisner, A. (1995) "Understanding problem-solving building: Ergonomic work analysis" *Ergonomics* 38(3): 595–605.

19
STRATEGIC HRD

Jim Stewart

This chapter is concerned with what is termed 'strategic human resource development' (SHRD). This might be assumed to be an unproblematic term which refers to HRD policy and practice at the strategic level. But, that is not necessarily the case as we shall see as the chapter develops. For example, what exactly is the 'strategic level' and, conversely, what is not? These are not straightforward questions. So, the chapter will proceed from a different assumption, which is that the meaning of 'strategic' is more complex than commonly assumed. That assumption will also inform an exploration of attaching the term to the concept of HRD and the implications of doing so for HRD practice. The purposes of the chapter can be summarized as follows:

- To examine and critique the meaning of the term 'strategic'
- To explore the implications of this critique for understanding the term 'strategic HRD'
- To explore applications of 'strategic HRD' in the policy and practice of organization based HRD.

Achieving these purposes will be met by first examining the key concepts. 'Strategic' is often confused with 'strategy' but they can be argued to be distinct and so, having established some understanding of terms the chapter will look at this distinction through some examples of HRD strategies. The penultimate section will extend this by exploring the links between strategic HRD and the HRD function. A section with a conclusion and summarizing points will close the chapter.

Strategic HRD is similar to strategic anything else – finance, marketing, information management for example – in that it attempts to distinguish certain approaches to the function from others. The distinction is usually with operations. This also suggests a time scale as at least one distinguishing factor (Johnson *et al.* 2011). Operations are concerned with day-to-day activities while strategic is concerned with longer term activities and/or impact. So, the context of SHRD is application within, mostly but not exclusively, work organizations. It is not a foundation of HRD; each emerged separately from the other. It is not a theory of HRD; the concept has too wide an application for that and in any case 'strategic' as we have already seen is not HRD specific. It is not a current concern or issue as it is too well established, and neither is it an HRD intervention since it is too general a concept to fit that term (see Garavan 2007 for example). Strategic HRD fits into this book as one way of understanding the formulation and implementation of policy. Strategy and policy are often used as synonyms by writers in organization and management studies (Johnson *et al.* 2011) and so that is an acceptable rationale for the placing of the chapter. But, strategic HRD has many connections with other parts of the book. For example, core and emerging issues such as ethics and employability have implications for strategic HRD. So too do theories such as human capital and critical HRD. It is therefore important not to read this chapter or to think about strategic HRD as separate or in isolation from the other topics dealt with in other parts and other chapters of this book. Any of those topics can and will have implications for strategic HRD, and vice versa.

The notion of strategic

Attaching the word 'strategic' to organization functions is now so common that the concept has lost its original meaning. The history and development of the concept in business management are mainly the application of economic theory to long-range planning and the long-term survival and prosperity in economic terms of business and commercial organizations (Whittington 2000). This original meaning was associated with its own function of strategic management, which in turn is the duty of general and senior management; for example a function of chief executives, managing directors, chief operating officers and other similar titles. The purpose of strategic management was to ensure at least the continued survival, and at best the growth, of an organization (Johnson *et al.* 2011). Given that purpose, the function and concept are also associated with the specialist and non-specialist contributions to organization management by top and senior functional managers, especially those with responsibility for operations and finance. These are the two functions which in most organizations are concerned with generating income and controlling expenditure respectively. The relative levels of income and expenditure commonly and in most organizations determine survival and prosperity.

In conventional terms, strategic management is concerned with managing an organization's relationships and connections with its business environment and the key actors which constitute that environment; investors, customers and competitors for example. The main outcome of strategic management in these terms is a set of strategies that are themselves plans, programmes and activities to be undertaken by the organization and the resource allocations to support those activities (Johnson *et al.* 2011). Still in conventional terms, strategies are derived from an analysis of external and internal factors and a 'matching' process to ensure that the organization continues to be successful, especially in relation to formulating and achieving appropriate organizational-level performance goals and objectives.

This conventional view is of limited value. This is for a number of reasons, one being the limitations placed on the plans of senior managers being implemented by the vagaries of human behavior both within and outside of an organization. An additional reason is that this conventional view implies that, once the overall corporate and business strategy is decided and set by say the Chief Executive and Board, functions such as HRD then formulate functional strategies to support implementation and achievement of the business strategy. This scenario further implies a linear and static process, where fixed plans for HRD are formulated to contribute to the achievement of the business strategy, which in turn contributes to the achievement of the corporate strategy. But, 'linear', 'static' and 'fixed' are not concepts which accurately represent the possible, actual or desired behavior of organizations (see for example Watson 2000).

The logic of the conventional understanding of strategic management and strategy is that a functional strategy for finance or IT or HRD is impossible in the absence of corporate and business strategy and that the purpose of functional strategies is to support, or serve, business strategy. This view has been questioned by many writers (see Watson 2000). Specifically in relation to

HRD, Stewart and McGoldrick (1996) adopted a different view of the strategic management process. This view sees strategic management as an emergent rather than planned process and one which is ad hoc in nature rather than systematic and controlled by top managers (Mintzberg *et al.* 2009). This view allows for a more proactive and processual contribution from specialist functions, including HRD. In Stewart and McGoldrick's (1996) nonlinear model of the strategy process, the focus is first on what they refer to as the 'strategic direction' of a given organization. This suggests the possibility of differences in relation to long-term survival between what is determined and planned by top and senior managers and what actually happens in practice. Stewart and McGoldrick go on to argue that strategic direction is the result of the interplay of a number of internal factors, the most significant of which are culture, leadership, the commitment of employees and the responses to changed and changing internal and external conditions. They further argued that HRD in theory and practice has a major influence on each of these factors through:

- shaping organizational culture
- developing current and future leaders
- building commitment among organization members
- anticipating and managing responses to changed conditions.

Thus, HRD is of itself a strategic function as it has a significant impact on long-term survival. This view was supported by the work of Fredericks and Stewart (1996), who examined the connection between strategy and HRD from a processual rather than a functional perspective and argue that there are clear and mutually influencing relationships between organization structure (internally facing), organization strategy (externally facing), the actions and behaviors of organization members, management/leadership style and HRD policies and practices. So, both pieces of work suggest that HRD is in and of itself strategic, since its practices have an impact on long-term survival and prosperity. What then are the implications of this processual view of strategic for the notion of strategic HRD?

The notion of strategic HRD (SHRD)

An obvious implication of the arguments of Stewart and McGoldrick is that the notion of strategic HRD is redundant. If HRD itself is strategic then there is no distinction to be drawn between HRD and strategic HRD. But other writers such as Walton (1999), Garavan (1991, 2007), Wilson (2005) and McCracken and Wallace (2000) argue such a distinction can and should be drawn. Early work on SHRD (e.g. Garavan 1991) adopted the conventional view of strategic management as being a long-term planning function and responsibility of top and senior managers. More recent writing on the subject, summarized and applied by Garavan (2007), attempts to integrate both functional and processual perspectives on strategy to justify a meaning for SHRD. Garavan defines SHRD as a 'coherent, vertically aligned and horizontally integrated set of learning and development activities which contribute to the achievement of strategic goals' (Garavan 2007: 25). This view of SHRD suggests responsiveness to organizational strategy and various components of it, including the strategies and goals of business units or departments, and problems and issues that emerge and which require an HRD response (Mayo 2004). Thus SHRD means HRD which creates value by being business-led (see Krohn 2000, Montesino 2002, and Wang *et al.* 2009 for examples of this view being applied).

This view of strategic HRD can be characterized as HRD that is 'aligned' with business goals. This is also termed 'strategic alignment'. However, research by Anderson (2009) found that alignment requires a great deal of iteration between managers and HRD practitioners requiring both formal and informal discussions. HRD practitioners need to involve themselves in 'dialogue and bartering' (Anderson 2009: 275) and, while this could enable an influence on strategic thinking, it is not always easy to achieve in practice. A related view of SHRD applies what is known as the resource-based view of strategy. This perspective focuses on how an organization's internal capabilities enable it to compete. Such capabilities can lead to superior performance and are based in part on what people learn through their work and interactions with each other, customers and suppliers. Over time, these capabilities become core competencies. Clardy (2008) argues that HRD practitioners are well placed to identify such competencies through their work with employees on skills, attitudes, knowledge and actions. HRD practitioners can thus contribute more significantly to strategic plans as illustrated in the work of Alagaraja (2013) and so practice SHRD.

Including emergent aspects of HRD practices in SHRD provides significant opportunities. Defining an organization as a site for workplace learning means it is possible that new ideas for action can come from many sources. This is most sharply evident where work is knowledge-intensive such as in professional firms. However, as Watson and Harmel-Law (2010) found in a Scottish law firm, there is a need for support from managers and senior staff. In addition, contextual factors such as income generation targets are always a possible constraint.

SHRD strategy

While debates continue on the distinguishing characteristics of SHRD, there is value in applying the concept of 'strategy' to HRD practice. The work of Stewart (1999) and Stewart and Rigg (2011) suggest a meaning which is commonly understood and accepted. This defines an HRD strategy as a course of action intended to have long-term rather than short-term impact on significant rather than marginal areas of performance at organizational rather than individual levels.

Particular impacts and courses of action to achieve them, i.e. the HRD strategy, will have been arrived at from analysis of external as well as internal factors. They will be intended to directly contribute to matching organizational capability to changed and changing market conditions in order to achieve competitive advantage, or whatever conditions affect long-term survival. In the case of public or quasi-public sector organizations for example, satisfying the expectations of funding and political stakeholders could well be the intended impact.

Common examples of HRD strategies include culture focused change programmes and leadership and/or talent development programmes designed and intended to ensure a sufficient quantity and quality of future senior and top managers (Stewart and Rigg 2011). Programmes to support the development of particular organizational forms, such as a 'learning organization' can also be described as an HRD strategy. The use of the word 'support' here is significant. HRD strategies are commonly components in a range of programmes and activities designed and intended to bring about the kinds of changes implicit in these examples. Other components will usually include related HR strategies in, for example, employer branding, job and work design, employee reward and performance management.

HRD strategy is thus distinguished from other HRD activities by factors such as time scale, scope and significance for organizational survival and prosperity. But HRD practice encompasses other activities. These may be linked to and have connections and contributions to strategies but they are primarily aimed at ensuring that the day-to-day work of the organization can be accomplished, which is also of course both necessary and important. Such activities are commonly referred to as 'operational' plans as opposed to 'strategies' and will include for example programmes to train new starters, programmes to develop knowledge and skills associated with some new technology or system and programmes of supervisory or management development to prepare individuals for promotion.

An additional way of distinguishing between HRD strategies and operational plans is to apply the notions of 'maintenance' and 'change' (Fredericks and Stewart 1996). The basic idea here is that HRD 'maintenance' programmes and activities are intended to keep the organization as it is, and effective and efficient at what it currently does. This is achieved by HRD operational plans. In contrast to this, HRD 'change' programmes are designed and intended to make the organization different and develop it to be able to do new and different things effectively and efficiently. This is achieved by HRD strategies. In the same vein as Fredericks and Stewart, it has been argued more recently (MacKenzie *et al.* 2012) that HRD can and should play a more proactive strategic role by helping managers and leaders critically reflect on assumptions that underpin the status quo through a process of strategic learning which will lead to beneficial change. It is relatedly argued that it is important to focus on critique to avoid simply reinforcing assumptions that maintain the status quo (Starbuck *et al.* 2008).

This discussion of HRD strategies and the distinction between those and other HRD activities provides a useful way of conceptualizing a difference between HRD and SHRD. This is simply to say that operational activities – maintenance in the language of Fredericks and Stewart (1996) – constitute HRD. Activities which can be characterized as strategies – change orientated activities in the language of Fredericks and Stewart – constitute SHRD. Thus, HRD is aimed at short-term day-to-day operations and SHRD is aimed at longer term change initiatives. This difference in focus has implications for organizational arrangements for the HRD function and the role of HRD professionals to be examined in the next section.

Strategic HRD and the HRD function

This penultimate section considers the question of relating SHRD and HRD strategy to the HRD function. The latter term refers to the organizational structural arrangements for ensuring provision of HRD expertise and services. The common answer to this is to have an HRD department, but that is not the only answer. This in part explains why, just as with SHRD as a concept, there remains debate about how best to ensure provision of HRD expertise and services (Stewart and Rigg 2011).

Over the last decade, there have been signs that the HRD function has shifted in significance. In 2005, Sloman talked about a shift from 'training' to 'learning'. Since then, survey data (e.g. CIPD 2012) suggests that with continuing pressure on reducing costs, the function is expected to be more organization- and business-focused. This brings change management and organization development into more prominence as a skill set for the function (Cheung-Judge and Holbeche 2011). Like any part of an organization, the HRD function has always had to operate with respect to forces both within and external to the organization (see for example Hendry *et al.* 1988; Gold and Smith 2003). During turbulent and difficult times, it is important that the HRD function attempt to enhance its position in organizations as a strategic player. One approach to achieving that is the business partner model.

The business partner model

The idea of a business partner is simple, perhaps deceptively so. The HRD function and HRD professionals operate as a 'partner' alongside the various business units and as an agent to facilitate change in the organization. This enables engagement with the strategic development of the organization. The word 'partner' is crucial, implying that HRD has an equal, credible and legitimate role to play in relation to the most important business decisions taken within the organization. The function becomes responsible for aligning HRD with the business strategy and ensuring that HRD can add value at any level within the organization. In this model, HRD has a key leadership role, working in collaboration with other senior figures to help determine the vision and direction of the organization (Ulrich 1997). Gubbins and Garavan (2007) add the word 'Strategic' and position the 'Strategic Business Partner' model as professional roles moving from the traditional role – training intervention, or operational and maintenance focused – to one of 'transformational strategic partner'; a change orientation and focus. This is not exactly a neat continuum but it does usefully suggest that the journey away from this traditional role may well involve a range of different pathways and configurations. Recently Ulrich *et al.* (2009) outlined the opportunity for business partners in HRM more generally to take an active role in business-focused transformation (see Analoui 1994 for further discussion of the more 'traditional' and 'transactional' roles, and Gilley and Maycunich Gilley 2003 for discussion of the more 'transformational' roles).

It is important to note that the business partner model may well seek to integrate a number of subfunctions. Three such subfunctions are likely to be shared services, centres of excellence and strategic partners. This partnering model has not been without criticism. Firstly, it is argued that if most focus is given to business issues, this can lead to a neglect of staff issues (Francis and Keegan 2006). Secondly, the model can result in divisions among HR staff and a loss of trust by employees. In addition, HR managers, including those in the HRD function, may not have the right skills for business partnering nor to make the HR strategy–business strategy linkage (Griffin *et al.* 2009; Caldwell 2010). There could be a tendency for HR practitioners to exaggerate the effectiveness of their partnering abilities, which would not enhance their position against other organization functions.

Positioning and managing the HRD function

Two important sets of questions arise when considering positioning the HRD function: first in relation to a centralizing–decentralizing tension and second in relation to the capabilities of those aspiring to purportedly 'new' HRD/SHRD roles. The research of Hirsh and Tamkin (2005) sought to ascertain how organizations align their HRD activity with business needs. Their findings uncover some underlying 'dilemmas'. They note that business needs can be both corporate and local, but which of these should influence what happens in terms of HRD or SHRD practice? If line managers are taking greater responsibility for the training and development of their teams, this will act as a force towards devolvement including devolved budgets. A desire for 'just in time training' and tailored learning closer to the job reinforces such pressures. However, Hirsh and Tamkin's research shows that, for large organizations in particular, a perceived need to measure and control expenditure 'and to focus on corporate priorities' creates a powerful 'centralizing effect' (Hirsh and Tamkin 2005: 33). Shared service initiatives associated with the business partner model and operating a call centre-type role, further reinforce centralizing tendencies and plans.

Hirsh and Tamkin (2005) report the case of Diageo, one of the world's leading drinks businesses. Diageo provides an interesting example of how a company has sought to deal with the corporate–local tension. The corporate policy is to devolve and embed training and learning throughout the business. However, Diageo differentiates between resources for strategic, company-wide priorities and those for more local and operational needs. A process called the 'organization and people review' aims to join and integrate the top-down view with the bottom-up view. HRD operates with local managers to identify capability issues. This information is then 'amalgamated upwards' and a corporate perspective added at group level.

The second set of questions concerns capability. One of the challenges associated with the business partner model concerns the role and contribution of line management. A consequence of engagement with strategy by HRD practitioners is that line management take on board a much greater responsibility for the day-to-day, week-by-week development of their staff. The question then is: have they the capability to fulfill such a responsibility effectively? A recurrent concern flagged by the UK Chartered Institute of Personnel and Development (CIPD) as a result of its annual learning and development survey work has been this very theme. For example, while coaching has become a crucial HRD activity in organizations, usually enacted by line managers, it is seldom evaluated so it is difficult to show if this activity is adding value (CIPD 2012).

An additional question concerns the capability of HRD practitioners to provide a leadership role at the strategic centre of the organization. Two capabilities are considered critical: first, power and influence, and second, learning expertise. Stewart and McGoldrick (1996) argue that a strategy for augmenting influence is imperative if the HRD department is to survive; we have been discussing a role that is much more than mere 'survival'. However, as Caldwell (2010) notes, some organizations appoint managers without HR expertise or credentials to senior HR roles, because those with credentials cannot make the link to business strategy. Thus, at least one capability, that of learning expertise, may be absent. Research by Holden and Griggs (2011) illustrates that the second capability, that of power and influence, may not come naturally or easily to HRD practitioners. In addition, the issue of gendered power relations in HRD raises some important questions (Hanscome and Cervero 2003) since the majority of HRD professionals in the UK at least are women. In relation to learning, the necessary expertise goes beyond a technical proficiency in identifying and managing learning needs and provision. The strategic HRD role requires an understanding of knowledge management and organizational learning and, increasingly, an appreciation of how technology may be utilized as a strategic learning tool.

Conclusion

In summary, it is clear that SHRD is neither a simple concept nor a simple approach to HRD practice. The meaning of the term remains debated and debatable and applying it in practice produces many challenges for practitioners. However, as conceptualized by academics and as applied by many professionals, the idea presents important opportunities for changing and improving work organizations as places of work and as essential components of and contributors to societies. Achieving these possibilities will require connections and engagement with many of the other concepts examined in this book. SHRD or HRD strategies of themselves will not produce beneficial change. At the very least they need to be informed by sound theoretical foundations and take account of core issues such as CSR and ethics, as well as respond to emerging issues such as work–life balance as well as to varying national contexts. All of this of course adds to the challenge. But, the work of HRD can produce and is producing beneficial change whether or not its labeled 'strategic'.

References

Alagaraja, M. (2013) Mobilizing organizational alignment through strategic human resource development, *Human Resource Development International*, 16(1): 74–93.

Analoui, F. (1994) Training and development: the role of trainers, *Journal of Management Development*, 13(9): 61–72.

Anderson, V. (2009) Desperately seeking alignment: reflections of senior line managers and HRD executives, *Human Resource Development International*, 12(3): 263–77.

Caldwell, R. (2010) Are HR business partner competency models effective?, *Applied HRM Research*, 12(1): 40–58.

Cheung-Judge, M.Y. and Holbeche, L. (2011) *Organization Development: A Practitioner's Guide for OD and HR*, London: Kogan Page.
CIPD (2012) *Learning and Talent Development Survey*, London: Chartered Institute of Personnel and Development.
Clardy, A. (2008) The strategic role of human resource development in managing core competencies, *Human Resource Development International*, 11(2): 183–97.
Francis, H. and Keegan, A. (2006) The changing face of HRM: in search of balance, *Human Resource Management Journal*, 16(3): 231–49.
Fredericks, J. and Stewart, J. (1996) The strategy–HRD connection, in Stewart, J. and McGoldrick, J. (eds) *Human Resource Development: Perspectives, Strategies and Practice*, London: Pitman.
Garavan, T.N. (1991) Strategic human resource development, *Journal of European Industrial Training*, 15(1): 17–31.
Garavan, T. (2007) A strategic perspective on human resource development, *Advances in Developing Human Resources*, 9(1): 11–30.
Gilley, J.W. and Maycunich Gilley, A. (2003) *Strategically Integrated HRD: Six Transformational Roles in Creating Results-driven Programmes* (2nd edition), Cambridge: Perseus.
Gold, J. and Smith, V. (2003) Advances towards a learning movement: translations at work, *Human Resource Development International*, 6(2): 139–52.
Griffin, E., Finney, L., Hennessy, J. and Boury, D. (2009) *Maximising the Value of HR Business Partnering*, Horsham: Roffey Park.
Gubbins, C. and Garavan, T. (2007) The changing context and role of the HRD professional, 8th International Conference on HRD Research and Practice across Europe, held in Oxford.
Hanscome, L. and Cervero, R. (2003) The impact of gendered power relations in HRD, *Human Resource Development International*, 6(4): 509–25.
Hendry, C., Pettigrew, A. and Sparrow, P.R. (1988) The forces that trigger training, *Personnel Management*, 20(12): 28–32.
Hirsh, W. and Tamkin, P. (2005) *Planning Training for Your Business* (Report no. 422), Brighton: Institute of Employment Studies.
Holden, R. and Griggs, V. (2011) Teaching the politics of HRD: a journey in critical curriculum development, *International Journal of Management Education*, 9(2): 71–82.
Johnson, G., Scholes, K. and Whittington, R. (2011) *Exploring Corporate Strategy: Text and Cases* (9th edition), Harlow: FT Prentice-Hall.
Krohn, R.A. (2000) Training as a strategic investment, *Advances in Developing Human Resources*, 2(1): 63–75.
MacKenzie, C., Garavan, T. and Carbery, R. (2012), Through the looking glass: challenges for human resource development (HRD) post the global financial crisis – business as usual?, *Human Resource Development International*, 15(3): 353–64.
Mayo, A. (2004) *Creating a Learning and Development Strategy*, London: Chartered Institute of Personnel and Development.
McCracken, M. and Wallace, M. (2000) Towards a redefinition of strategic HRD, *Journal of European Industrial Training*, 24(5): 281–90.
Mintzberg, H., Ahlstrand, B. and Lampel, J. (2009) *Strategy Safari* (2nd edition), London: Prentice-Hall.
Montesino, M.U. (2002) Strategic alignment of training, transfer-enhancing behaviors and training usage: a post-training study, *Human Resource Development Quarterly*, 13(1): 89–108.
Sloman, M. (2005) *Training to Learning: Change Agenda*, London: Chartered Institute of Personnel and Development.
Starbuck, W., Barnett, M. and Baumard, P. (2008) Payoffs and pitfalls of strategic learning, *Journal of Economic Behavior & Organization*, 66(1): 7–21.
Stewart J. (1999) *Employee Development Practice*, London: FT/Pitman.
Stewart, J. and McGoldrick, J.A. (1996) *Human Resource Development: Perspectives, Strategies and Practice*, London: Pitman.
Stewart, J. and Rigg, C. (2011) *Learning and Talent Development*, London: Chartered Institute of Personnel and Development.
Ulrich, D. (1997) *Human Resource Champions: The Next Agenda for Adding Value and Delivering Results*, Boston, MA: Harvard Business School Press.
Ulrich, D., Alenn, J., Brockbank, W., Younger, J. and Nyman, M. (2009) *HR Transformation: Building Human Resources From the Outside In*, New York: McGraw-Hill.
Walton, J. (1999) *Strategic Human Resource Development*, Harlow: FT Prentice-Hall.
Wang, J., Hutchins, H.M. and Garavan, T.N. (2009) Organizational crisis management: exploring the strategic role of human resource development, *Human Resource Development Review*, 8(1): 22–53.

Watson, S. and Harmel-Law, A. (2010) Exploring the contribution of workplace learning to an HRD strategy in the Scottish legal profession, *Journal of European Industrial Training*, 34(1): 7–22.
Watson, T.J. (2000) *In Search of Management: Culture, Chaos and Control in Managerial Work* (revised edition), Andover: Cengage Learning.
Whittington, R. (2000) *What is Strategy and Does it Matter?* (2nd edition), Andover: Cengage Learning.
Wilson, J.P. (ed) (2005) *Human Resource Development* (2nd edition), London: Kogan Page.

20

TALENT MANAGEMENT AND LEADERSHIP DEVELOPMENT

Paul Iles

Talent management (TM) and leadership development (LD) are two inter-related, emerging topics in HRD. This chapter will discuss similarities and differences between the two in a global context in relation to the following questions and issues:

- How are talent and leadership defined?
- Inclusive or exclusive approach?
- Performance or potential?
- Born or made?
- Person, position or process?
- Individual or collective?
- Are TM and LD fashions?
- Are TM and LD ethical?
- Are global LD/TM different from domestic LD/TM?
- How can we develop talent and leadership?
- Where next?

How are leadership and talent defined?

TM and LD both present similar issues of construct definition and ambiguity over conceptual boundaries. With respect to LD, the main arena of contestation has been over how leaders differ from followers and managers; managers may have formal authority over subordinates but are leaders different? Kotter (1990) claims that organizations need both stability and change, requiring both leaders and managers, whilst Mabey and Finch-Lees (2008) argue that de-layering, workforce fragmentation and greater flexibility mean that both leadership and followership are now necessary for most staff at all levels, especially for knowledge workers.

Similarly, with respect to TM, talent is often contrasted with untalented or less talented, but as Lewis and Heckman (2006: 140) claim: 'the terms in the debate are not clear and confuse outcomes with processes with decision alternatives.' TM is defined variously as a combination of standard HR practices, the creation of talent pools to ensure employee flow, and 'as an unqualified good and a resource to be managed primarily according to performance levels' (Lewis and Heckman 2006: 141). A boundary issue (Vaiman and Collings 2013) exists here over who or what is to be considered as talent and why; how does talent differ from longer-established terms in the HRD literature, like skills, human capital or competence? Many organizations use organization-specific definitions, influenced by sector or type (CIPD 2007), and often companies do not know how to define talent, let alone how to manage it (*The Economist* 2006). For Tansley (2011: 266), 'people are rarely precise about what they mean by the term "talent" in organizations and the implications of defining talent for talent management practice.' CIPD (2007) found talent mainly focused on individual attributes, with great variations over definition. In many organizations, talent may be equated with leadership or leadership potential, but in health, it may refer to clinical excellence; in IT, technical skills; in restaurants, chef creativity.

Does talent refer to people (*subjects*) or to characteristics/attributes (*objects*)? Contemporary TM discourse uses the term in both ways. Talent as object refers to characteristics such as natural ability, mastery, skills, competence, potential or commitment, often vaguely defined. Talent first entered English as object, denoting biblical units for measuring silver (Tansley 2011, Matthew 25: 14–30, Luke 19: 12–28); other terms denote valued personal attributes, such as 'light' or 'gift'. Not to 'hide your light under a bushel' (Matthew 5: 15, Matthew 5: 14–16) is often interpreted as advice not to be too modest, but to use the talents/gifts God has given. This interpretation has normative connotations: a moral imperative to develop, apply and use one's talents, with condemnation of those who throw away, fritter, squander or waste them.

Talent subsequently evolved to refer to personal aptitudes and abilities; in the early nineteenth century Sir Walter Scott (1826) praised Jane Austen for 'a talent for describing the involvements of feelings and characters of ordinary life', whilst in *Pride and Prejudice* (Austen 1813/2003) Mr. Bennet claims 'it is happy for you that you possess the talent of flattering with delicacy.' Darcy protests 'I certainly have not the talent . . . of conversing easily with those I have never seen before.' Talent here denotes a natural, easy fluency or social skill, operating narrowly, and specific to a particular field or *domain* – a talent for something specific, not a general ability.

A fundamental distinction here is between talent as inborn, natural ability and talent as mastery of systematically developed skills and knowledge. Austen (1813/2003) and others used 'accomplishments' for skills acquired through practice; Bingley (Austen 1813/2003: 38) is amazed 'how young ladies can have patience to be so very accomplished, as they all are.' Essential for marriage, these are not the exceptional abilities of gifted (mostly male) elites, reminding us of the contextualized, gendered nature of talent. That talent can be identified is therefore a problematic, not value-free activity. The gendered nature of leadership (Appelbaum *et al.* 2003) and the impact of personal attractiveness/appearance (Watkins and Johnston 2000), popularity, likeability and the manipulation of reputation (Martin and Hetrick 2006) all show how talent is socially constructed.

Talent as subject sees talent as embodied in people: the talent of the entertainment industries (e.g. the 1914 Huddersfield rugby league 'Team of all Talents', the 1880s Sunderland football 'Team of All the Talents'). Are object/subject approaches complementary or contradictory? The next section discusses 'subject' approaches.

Inclusive or exclusive approach?

Similar debates have occurred over whether leadership/talent should be seen narrowly/exclusively or widely/inclusively. Calling for leadership competencies redefines people, their expectations, how they see themselves and how they are seen by others, differentiating them from mere followers or managers (Mabey and Finch-Lees 2008). Many LD theories focus on the *individual* as leader, rather than leadership as a collective or shared responsibility, differentiating leaders sharply from followers; in contrast, *distributed leadership* or shared leadership theories blur boundaries between leader and followers, include more people within leadership acts and practices, and share power/influence among individuals. Such leadership may be distributed within small teams (for example, between co-leaders such as chair and chief executive, or more widely among team/organizational members) (Thorpe *et al.* 2011).

In terms of talent as people, how widely should this group be defined? Thunissen *et al.* (2013) and CIPD (2007) both note that talent can be seen inclusively (all people/*complete* definition) or exclusively (some people/*elite* definition). Exclusivity is the most common approach taken in practice, and most common in companies in Beijing (Iles *et al.* 2010a) and in the UK (CIPD 2007).

Performance or potential?

Are subject-based LD and TM focused on people's performance, or their potential? With respect to LD, many organizational efforts focus on high potentials deemed to have leadership potential. High performance and/or high potential also underpin most subject definitions of talent/TM (e.g. CIPD 2007, Iles *et al.* 2010b). Talents are often grouped into different pools to be talent managed (Tansley and Tietze 2013). A box matrix of performance against potential may be used, with talent reserved for high-value staff, a small percentage based on appraisals or qualitative assessments of current capability/future potential to deliver exceptional performance, often associated with talent pipeline metaphors (CIPD 2007, Tansley 2011, Cappelli 2008).

Born or made?

Closely linked to this issue is whether leaders or talents are born or made. Within LD, some leadership theories (e.g. trait theory) are often linked to views that leaders are born; others such as leadership style theories emphasize that leaders can be made. The widespread use of LD programs implies some faith that leadership can be developed. Similarly, if talent is perceived as fixed, early talent assessment and buying, not building, talent will be stressed. A fundamental distinction in object approaches is whether talent is inborn, or developed through practice. Innate talent is often stressed in sport, education and the arts; here gifted pupils showing early signs of talent are identified by trained people – talent spotters/scouts – before exceptional levels of mature performance have been demonstrated. Early indications of talent therefore provide a basis for predicting who is likely to excel. Gagné (1999) stresses that talent emerges as 'the superior mastery of systematically developed abilities and knowledge in at least one field of human endeavor, rather than mere "potential"' (cited in Heller *et al.* 2000: 67), clearly differentiating gifts (natural abilities) from talents (systematically developed abilities). Talent may be seen in terms of packages of personal characteristics accelerating acquisition of expertise; whether a unique package counts as a talent depends on the domain, as 'people can mix and match their own unique package of characteristics in various ways to express the same talent' (Kaufman 2013a: 20).

Recent developments here also stress the importance of intensive practice in developing talents (Kaufman 2013b), as well as prior expectations; deep, well-connected databases of domain-specific expertise contribute to elite performance, and breadth/depth of expertise is typically acquired over years of deliberate practice. Motivated individuals constantly look to learn from feedback through targeted exercises provided by experienced, supportive mentors and coaches, challenging them to go beyond their limits and get better faster, suggesting key roles for motivation and learning ability/trainability or absorptive capacity. Talents may be present but unrecognized and undeveloped, as with late bloomers.

Person, position or process?

Within LD there is ongoing debate over whether leadership is associated with people, positions or processes; is it a property of the formally appointed leader, or can it emerge from any position? Perspectives on TM also often differentiate not just people, but also positions (Huselid *et al.* 2005). For Collings and Mellahi (2009: 304), pivotal positions carrying disproportionate influence are starting points for TM, with high performers pooled and segmented through a 'differentiated human resource architecture.' Concepts from marketing (e.g. employer branding, Jiang and Iles 2011), labor segmentation, and logistics/supply-chain management (Cappelli 2008) are often used to develop this concept. Gallardo-Gallardo *et al.* (2012) usefully relate workforce differentiation (inclusive/exclusive) and subject/object distinctions to generate a fourfold typology.

One theoretical rationale for segmentation is provided by resource-based theories of the firm, as human capital provides pools of resources for sustained competitive advantage (Wright *et al.* 2001). For Purcell (1999: 35–36), 'the ability to identify a distinctive group of employees who, for whatever reason, constitute this intangible strength' is important, involving both 'the identification of a core group of employees, sometimes small in number' and 'distinctive policies and practices to maximize their performance . . . a simultaneous differentiation with non-core, peripheral workers.' Purcell (1999) does not use the terms TM or talent but provides one rationale for adopting such terms.

Individual or collective?

An individualistic orientation to leadership is often adopted in LD, often involving initial assessments of individuals against competency profiles, perhaps involving psychometric tests of ability, personality or emotional intelligence. Diagnosis of strengths and development needs; construction of a personal development plan; and provision of training and development experiences to address these needs may follow, including coaching and mentoring, training, projects and perhaps outdoor development. Here, participants experience unfamiliar leadership challenges outside their comfort zone in a mountain, forest or marine environment (Iles and Preece 2006). Such processes may be very useful for personal and human capital development; however, are they sufficient to develop *leadership*, developing social as well as human capital (Day 2000)?

Within TM, an individualistic focus on talent is also often adopted; however, TM can also be explored in more collective, team-based ways, focusing attention on social capital, teamwork, leadership, and networks (Iles *et al.* 2010a). Oltra and Vivas-Lopez (2013) show how Spanish firms employ team-based TM to enhance organizational learning; individual talent needs direction, opportunity and stimulation for potential to be developed and consolidated. Groysberg *et al.* (2004) demonstrate that organizational performance is not solely produced by a few exceptional individual talents; they found that 'star' analyst performance often declined when changing jobs, depending on firm-specific resources. This finding was less common when individuals moved with their team, or where receiving systems and culture were similar (cited in Minbaeva and Collings 2013).

Are talent management and leadership development fashions?

How new and/or substantial is the contribution of TM/LD to HRM? Leadership as an explanatory concept declined in popularity after World War II, given the Fascist/Communist stress on 'great leaders' (Iles 2011). Management was stressed in contrast, but leadership has come back into fashion in recent years. In the 1980s, interest in management development was linked to expansion of business schools and proliferation of management courses such as the MBA. Management was presented as a rational, technical activity with underpinning skills, knowledge and competencies, learned and applied through business education courses at universities and management development programs in companies; relatively poor economic performance, as in the UK, was often attributed to poor management, lack of modern management skills, and the low quantity and quality of management education and development. Since the 1990s, whether management/management development were enough to drive organizational success has been questioned, with renewed emphasis on leadership/LD (Grint 2005, Storey 2004).

Is TM also just another management fad, given bibliometric similarities to other fashions (Iles *et al.* 2010b, Preece *et al.* 2011)? Valverde *et al.* (2013) found little awareness of TM in Spanish medium-sized companies, even when applying TM techniques; it was often seen as a fancy/faddish concept. Many TM techniques are not new (Cappelli 2008); is TM merely a re-labelling of HRM, 'old wine in new bottles' (Iles *et al.* 2010b)? If so, it has lasted longer than many other fads; many companies in China denied that they were fashion followers of fashion-setters like academics and consultancies, but were adopting TM to win the war for talent. However, they did concede that they may be fashion leaders for local companies, especially small and medium-sized enterprises (Preece *et al.* 2011).

Are leadership development and talent management ethical?

LD is often seen as rooted in a strong US, male and private sector view of the heroic leader (Alimo-Metcalfe and Alban-Metcalfe 2001), neglecting issues of ethics, integrity and external networks. Leadership is however inevitably concerned with 'ought', ethical questions. Many examples of unethical behavior are related to a lack of ethical leadership. Leaders may foster unethical behavior among others through their own lack of ethics, promulgating it as normal business practice. Whilst ethical leadership has most commonly been associated with transformational models of leadership, for Bass (1985) some leaders could become so transformational as to breed unethical behavior; excessive charisma may lead followers to commit morally reprehensible acts. Two types of transformational leadership exist: authentic, concerned with follower development and organizational needs; and pseudo-transformational, focusing on self-interest, glory, and personal power/reward.

Ethical leadership involves 'the demonstration of normatively appropriate conduct through personal actions and interpersonal relationships and the promotion of such conduct to followers through two-way communication, reinforcement and decision-making' (Brown *et al.* 2005: 120, Treviño *et al.* 2003). Ethical leadership is thus both similar to, and different from, other influential LD perspectives like authentic leadership – not just emphasizing transformational behaviors but also transactional behaviors such as setting ethical standards and holding followers accountable. Though ethical leadership may be universal, the importance attached to key elements of it varies across cultures (Endrissat *et al.* 2007).

Similar ethical issues occur in TM. Assumptions and metaphors often stress talent rarity and conflicts over sourcing it (e.g. the war for talent, Beechler and Woodward 2009). Selecting a minority on the basis of differential contribution can be de-motivating for the majority; exclusion from talent pools can be interpreted as signaling inferiority. Talent is a relative term; the talented exist only in relation to the less talented/untalented, just as leaders only exist relative to followers or the led. Many staff may not be included in TM programs: those in low-skilled roles, older workers and those with deep knowledge in specific fields or functions. Concepts like strengths from positive psychology or capabilities from development economics (Nussbaum 2011, Sen 1999) may enhance the role of ethics in TM (Downs and Swailes 2013).

Are global LD/TM different from domestic LD/TM?

Are 'global' LD/TM different from domestic or local LD/TM? Models of 'global leadership' also often focus on individual 'leader competencies'. For Mendenhall *et al.* (2008), 'global' LD methods require modification to include coaching/mentoring by those with international experience, international job assignments, and reflections on feedback from intercultural survey instruments. Processes of contrast, confrontation and replacement/remapping in a transformational process of letting go/taking on new constructs and models are needed, requiring experiential rather than didactic methods (such as travel, seminars, project teams, outdoor learning and inpatriation/ expatriation assignments). These help participants confront 'normal' ways of behaving; simulations, field trips, and global development centers carry higher potential for 'remapping' than lectures or seminars, as well as helping build global networks and social capital. McDonnell *et al.* (2010) found many MNCs in Ireland did not engage in global TM/LD practices such as succession planning and formal programs; large MNCs were more likely to undertake TM, but curiously companies in low-tech, low-cost sectors were most likely to have formal global systems to identify and develop high potentials.

Corporate mobility/cross-functional moves can broaden perspectives in global TM/LD; but 'if a company is to get out of its dependence on home-country expatriates . . . talented locals need experience in challenging line positions at headquarters that will provide them with the matrix perspective, the global mindset and the social networks to equip them for senior leadership positions' (Evans *et al.* 2011: 218–19). This may lead to conflicts with high-potential expatriates competing for the same positions. An alternative program to develop 'worldly leadership' (Turnbull 2010) involves the 'managerial exchange': managers pair up and spend time at each other's workplaces to facilitate authentic sharing of unique life biographies and insights. Participants move between concept-based training and real-life experiences, alongside an emphasis on responsibility, conviction, stewardship, sustainability and a cosmopolitan mindset.

Global TM has been driven by greater recognition of the importance of global talent and increasing global competition for such talent (Beechler and Woodward 2009, Scullion and Collings 2011). There is considerable variation according to firm structure and strategy and national context; as with TM generally, a major issue is how talent is defined, and who among the internal pool is defined as talented. Cultural and institutional distance between MNE decision-makers and employees, homophily between individuals and decision-makers, and network position all influenced whether 'talents' were included in or excluded from organizational talent pools (Mäkelä *et al.* 2010).

More collectivist societies like Spain (Valverde *et al.* 2013) or Poland (Skuza *et al.* 2013) seem uncomfortable with highly segmented approaches often advocated in US models of TM; egalitarian countries like Finland may avoid the term in favor of less differentiating terms such as competence (Kabwe 2011). Festing *et al.* (2013) found most German firms preferred inclusive/ developmental approaches to TM, characteristic of a coordinated market economy (Hall and Soskice 2001).

Cooke (2011) highlights the significance of institutional, cultural and sectoral challenges in China, e.g. the legacies of the state planning system, emphasis on theory and knowledge reproduction in education, and involvement of the state (not employers) in management education. Globalization and the international migration of local talent have affected talent supply, exacerbated by an ageing workforce. High turnover, poaching by competitors, and staff leaving due to relationship problems are also issues; the importance of relationships and team-building activities such as social and sports events to Chinese employees is stressed by Hartmann *et al.* (2010). Companies used more collective TM practices than in Europe, reflecting the importance of greater collectivism. Performance appraisal is becoming a key TM practice, with less attention to talent/leadership development, partly due to fears of poaching. Iles *et al.* (2010) and Preece *et al.* (2011) found that TM did seem to promise new and rather different approaches to Chinese people management, emphasizing segmentation and people rather than the former focus on egalitarianism and functions.

How can we develop talent and leadership?

Approaches to LD can be explored using the axes 'individual-collective' and 'emergent-prescriptive'; most current approaches are individual/prescriptive, but other approaches are not just possible, but often appropriate, including more emergent and collective approaches like OD, search conferences and action learning (Iles and Preece 2006). Exclusive approaches to TM are often linked to LD as TM pools often include 'high potentials' for leadership. Inclusive approaches resonate more with collective approaches based on the development of social capital, such as distributed and shared leadership (e.g. Iles and Feng 2011, Thorpe *et al.* 2011).

Organizational LD/TM involves a choice of formal or informal methods targeted at an inclusive or exclusive talent pool. Formal methods may enhance the attraction and retention of staff through formal externally recognized qualifications, demonstrate a clear, staged learning strategy, and support the tracking and career progression of individuals; however, they may be inflexible and fail to recognize diversity of talent needs (CIPD 2007). Standard Chartered (CIPD 2007) used a mix of formal and informal methods, whilst an English NHS Trust employing an inclusive strategy mixed qualifications-based education, in-house programs, projects, Project Teams, one-to-one coaching, mentoring and supervision, local Learning Resources and Learning Zones, shadowing, visits, networking, professional contacts, and reading.

PwC in contrast used an exclusive strategy of four-year education and training mixing projects and work assignments with formal and informal mentoring and coaching for more senior staff. Talent was grouped into different talent pools associated with leadership potential: exceptional talent for executive-level roles, rising stars, emerging leaders and local talent (CIPD 2007). Tansley and Tietze (2013) found separation and liminality (threshold) to be important features: experiencing stretch projects, passing assessments, and making appropriate career choices. Appropriate identities were required for senior managers in ambiguous, ongoing and fluid relationship contexts. Talent development involved collective, structured stage-based processes in communal as well as individual experiences. At initial Rising Talent levels, training and education in core technical/professional skills and preparation for accountancy qualifications predominated. At the Emerging Leader stage, training and education for management with assessment of role/capability fit and interventions by sponsors and mentors were emphasized. At the subsequent Next Generation level, LD through a corporate academy was arranged, with some employees taking Masters/MBA courses. A company-agreed 'seven competencies framework' was employed in an individualized, structured Performance Management process with feedback to enhance mobility through businesses and roles/tasks, strengthening identities as consultants. At the Corporate Next Generation Leader level, one-to-one development by coaches/mentors briefed on corporate governance and strategy was important.

An issue in both talent and LD is striking the balance between top-down or organizationally driven initiatives and bottom-up or open-market, individually driven ones. Open job resourcing initiatives for internal staff, accelerated by global standardization of HR processes through intranet e-HR technology and self-help/self-service technologies like e-learning and transparent career track management may help people look for openings themselves (Evans *et al.* 2011). Senior level leadership roles may still be managed top-down, leaving open how far down or up to cascade these two approaches.

Multinational Enterprise structures influence how to capture and develop specific regional managerial/leadership skills. For Evans *et al.* (2011: 207) 'rapid growth combined with a small pool of experienced leaders means that the lack of global leadership skills has been the primary workforce challenge for enterprises.' Leadership here shows great intransitivity: 'the difficulties of translating leadership capability at one level to capable accomplishment at the next level' (ibid.). Before globalization, managers moved upwards into more extended managerial roles. However, people performing well in operational leadership roles today may find difficulty adjusting to more ambiguous roles as lateral coordinators and integrators in business areas or regions. Individuals with the potential to master such transitions need to be identified, and appropriate developmental experiences provided, as noted below by Evans *et al.* (2011: 208):

> senior managers heading up businesses and countries/regions, to whom these entrepreneurs report, need to be integrative coaches with strong skills in lateral co-ordination, able to cope with the complexity of vertical and horizontal responsibilities simultaneously . . . able to stretch, and at the same time to support, the local units; facilitate cross-border learning; and to build strategy out of entrepreneurial initiatives. Finally, top managers need to be institutional leaders with a longer time horizon, nurturing strategic development opportunities, managing organizational cohesion through global processes and normative integration, and creating an overarching sense of purpose and ambition.

Evans *et al.* (2011: 208) further explain the significant implications here for TM/LD: 'if the skill requirements at one level of responsibility are different from those at the next level of leadership . . . the process of identification and development of high-potential individuals should be managed by the corporation or region, not by the business or country.' How to get local companies to pay attention to LD at early career stages is an issue, as operationally oriented local HR managers may not cope with recruiting, developing and retaining such individuals, and subsidiary managers often act in their own interests, hiding their best employees.

Where next?

We have seen that TM and LD can be compared across a range of dimensions and in relation to a range of questions. In terms of further research, the HR architecture literature on the value and uniqueness of human capital (Lepak and Snell 2002) may help analyze segmentation processes for both TM and LD. De Vos and Dries (2013: 1818) claim that talent 'refers to human capital in an organization that is both valuable and unique', generating four quadrants: low-value/high uniqueness (partners); high-value/low uniqueness (traditionals); high-value/high uniqueness (core creatives); and low-value/low uniqueness (contractors). In addition, further research into the validity of talent/leadership constructs and the reliability/validity of talent/leadership identification and assessment is needed, as well as evidence of the relationships of TM/LD with organizational outcomes. Both TM/LD need to be studied in contexts where 'industry and organizational factors interact with institutional and cultural forces in shaping talent management in practice' (Scullion and Collings 2011: 4), such as in regional structures (Preece *et al.* 2013), different organizational structures, and different national/cultural contexts (Hartmann *et al.* 2010, Iles *et al.* 2010a). Preece *et al.* (2013) identified several challenges involved in a Japanese car company setting up a regional Asia-Pacific headquarters in Thailand, including establishing and operating a regional headquarters, its rationale, staffing, role and legitimacy, as well as how talent and leadership are identified, assessed and developed. The balance between regional centralization versus decentralization in relation to talent mobility, staffing, and LD is also a key issue.

References

Alimo-Metcalfe, B. and Alban-Metcalfe, J. (2001) 'The construction of a new transformational leadership questionnaire', *Journal of Occupational and Organizational Psychology* 79: 1–27.

Appelbaum, S.H., Audet, L. and Miller, J.C. (2003) 'Gender and leadership? Leadership and gender? A journey through the landscape of theories', *Leadership and Organization Development Journal* 24: 43–51.

Austen, J. (1813/2003) *Pride and Prejudice*, London: Penguin Group.

Bass, B.M. (1985) *Leadership and Performance Beyond Expectations*, New York: Free Press.

Beechler, S. and Woodward, I. (2009) 'The global war for talent', *Journal of International Management* 15: 273–85.

Brown, M.E., Treviño, L.K. and Harrison, D.A. (2005) 'Ethical leadership: a social learning perspective for construct development and testing', *Organizational Behavior and Human Decision Processes* 97: 117–34.

Cappelli, P. (2008) *Talent on Demand: Managing Talent in an Age of Uncertainty*, Boston, MA: Harvard Business School Press.

CIPD (2007) *Talent: Strategy, Management, Measurement*, London: CIPD.

Collings, D.G. and Mellahi, K. (2009) 'Strategic talent management: a review and research agenda', *Human Resource Management Review* 19: 304–13.

Cooke, F.L. (2011) 'Talent management in China', in Scullion, H. and Collings, D.G. (eds) *Global Talent Management*, a volume in the *Global Human Resource Management* series edited by R. Schuler, S. Jackson, P. Sparrow and M. Poole, London: Routledge, 132–54.

Day, D. (2000) 'Leadership development: a review in context', *Leadership Quarterly* 11: 581–611.

De Vos, A. and Dries, N. (2013) 'Applying a talent management lens to career management: the role of human capital composition and continuity', *International Journal of Human Resource Management* 24: 1816–31.

Downs, Y. and Swailes, S. (2013) 'A capability approach to talent management', *Human Resource Development International* 16: 267–81.

Endrissat, N., Müller, W.R. and Kaudela-Baum, S. (2007) 'En route to an empirically-based understanding of authentic leadership', *European Management Journal* 25: 207–20.

Evans, P., Smale, A., Björkman, I. and Pucik, V. (2011) 'Leadership development in multinational firms', in Storey, J. (ed.) *Leadership in Organizations: Current Issues and Key Trends*, Abingdon: Routledge, 207–22.

Festing, M., Schafer, L. and Scullion, H. (2013) 'Talent management in medium-sized German companies: an explorative study and agenda for future research', *International Journal of Human Resource Management* 24: 1872–93.

Gagné, F. (1999) 'My convictions about the nature of abilities, gifts, and talents', *Journal for the Education of the Gifted* 22: 109–36.

Gallardo-Gallardo, E., Dries, N. and Gonzalez-Cruz, T. (2012) 'What do we actually mean by talent in business?', Paper presented at the First EIASM Workshop on Talent Management, held 16–17 April 2012, Brussels.

Grint, K. (2005) *Leadership: Limits and Possibilities*, Basingstoke: Palgrave Macmillan.

Groysberg, B., Nanda, A. and Nohria, N. (2004) 'The risky business of hiring stars', *Harvard Business Review* 93–101.

Hall, P.A. and Soskice, D. (eds) (2001) *Varieties of Capitalism: The Institutional Foundations of Comparative Advantage*, New York: Oxford University Press.

Hartmann, E., Feisel, E. and Schober, H. (2010) 'Talent management of western MNCs in China: balancing global integration and local responsiveness', *Journal of World Business* 45: 169–78.

Heller, K.A., Mönks, F.J. and Passow, A.H. (2000) (eds) *International Handbook of Research and Development of Giftedness and Talent*, Oxford: Pergamon.

Huselid, M., Beatty, R. and Becker, B. (2005) ' "A Players" or "A Positions"? The strategic logic of workforce management', *Harvard Business Review* 83: 110–17.

Iles, P. (2011) 'Leadership development and talent management: fashion statement or fruitful direction?', in Lee, M. (ed.) *HRD as We Know It: Speeches that Have Shaped and Developed the Field of HRD*, New York: Routledge, 50–66.

Iles, P. and Preece, D. (2006) 'Developing leaders or developing leadership? The Academy of Chief Executives' programmes in the North-East of England', *Leadership* 2: 317–40.

Iles, P. and Feng, Y. (2011) 'Distributed leadership, knowledge and information management and team performance in Chinese and Western groups', *Journal of Technology Management in China* 6: 26–42.

Iles, P., Chuai, X. and Preece, D. (2010a) 'Talent management and HRM in multinational companies in Beijing: definitions, differences and drivers', *Journal of World Business* 45: 179–89.

Iles, P., Preece, D. and Chuai, X. (2010b) 'Is talent management a management fashion in HRD? Towards a research agenda', *Human Resource Development International* 13: 125–45.

Jiang, T.T. and Iles P.A. (2011) 'Employer brand equity, organizational attractiveness and talent management in the Zhejiang private sector', *Journal of Technology Management in China* 6: 97–110.

Kabwe, C. (2011) *The Conceptualisation and Operationalisation of Talent Management: The Case of European Internationally Operating Business*, PhD dissertation, University of Central Lancashire.

Kaufman, S.B. (2013a) 'The science of talent: can we pinpoint what we will be best at?', *The Observer/The New Review*, 7 July, 20–21.

— (2013b) *Ungifted*, Philadelphia, PA: Basic Books.

Kotter, J.P. (1990) 'What leaders really do', *Harvard Business Review* 68: 103–11.

Lepak, D.P. and Snell, S.A. (2002) 'Examining the human resource architecture: the relationships among human capital, employment, and human resource configurations', *Journal of Management* 28: 517–43.

Lewis, R. and Heckman, R. (2006) 'Talent management: a critical review', *Human Resource Management Review* 16: 139–54.

Mabey, C. and Finch-Lees, T. (2008) *Management and Leadership Development*, London: SAGE.

Mäkelä, K., Björkman, I. and Ehrnrooth, M. (2010) 'How do MNCs establish their talent pools? Influences on individuals' likelihood of being labelled as talent', *Journal of World Business* 45: 134–42.

Martin, G. and Hetrick, S. (2006) *Corporate Reputations, Branding and People Management: A Strategic Approach to HRM*, Oxford: Butterworth-Heinemann.

McDonnell, A., Lamare, R., Gunnigle, P. and Lavelle, J. (2010) 'Developing tomorrow's leaders – evidence of global talent management in multinational enterprises', *Journal of World Business* 45: 150–60.

Mendenhall, M., Osland, J.S., Bird, A., Oddou, G.R. and Maznevski, M. (eds) (2008) *Global Leadership: Research, Practice and Development*, London: Routledge.

Minbaeva, D. and Collings, D.G. (2013) 'Seven myths of global talent management', *The International Journal of Human Resource Management* 24: 1762–76.

Nussbaum, M. (2011) *Creating Capabilities: The Human Development Approach*, Cambridge, MA: Harvard University Press.

Oltra, V. and Vivas-Lopez, S. (2013) 'Boosting organizational learning through team-based talent management: what is the evidence from large Spanish firms?', *The International Journal of Human Resource Management* 24: 1853–71.

Preece, D., Iles, P. and Chuai, X. (2011) 'Talent management and management fashion in Chinese enterprise: exploring case studies in Beijing', *International Journal of Human Resource Management* 22: 3413–28.

Preece, D., Iles, P. and Jones, R. (2013) 'MNE regional head offices and their affiliates: talent management practices and challenges in the Asia Pacific', *International Journal of Human Resource Management* 24: 3457–77.

Purcell, J. (1999) 'The search for "best practice" and "best fit": chimera or cul-de-sac?', *Human Resource Management Journal*, 9: 26–41.

Scott, W. (1826) *Diary*, entry 14 March.

Scullion, H. and Collings, D.G. (eds) (2011) *Global Talent Management*, Abingdon: Routledge.

Sen, A. (1999) *Development as Freedom*, Oxford: Oxford University Press.

Skuza, A., Scullion, H. and McDonnell, A. (2013) 'An analysis of the talent management challenges in a post-communist country: the case of Poland', *International Journal of Human Resource Management* 24: 453–70.

Storey, J. (ed) (2004) *Leadership in Organizations: Current Issues and Key Trends*, London: Routledge.

Tansley, C. (2011) 'What do we mean by the term "talent" in talent management?', *Industrial and Commercial Training* 43: 266–74.

Tansley, C. and Tietze, S. (2013) 'Rites of passage through TM progression stages: an identity work perspective', *International Journal of Human Resource Management* 24: 1799–815.

The Economist (2006) *Survey: talent.* Online. Available HTTP: http: //www.economist.com (5 October: accessed 20, September 2013).

Thorpe, R., Gold, J. and Lawler, J. (2011) 'Locating distributed leadership', *International Journal of Management Reviews* 13: 239–50.

Thunissen, M., Boselie, P. and Fruytier, B. (2013) 'A review of talent management: "infancy or adolescence"?', *International Journal of Human Resource Management* 24: 1744–61.

Treviño, L.K., Brown, M. and Hartman, L.P. (2003) 'A qualitative investigation of perceived executive ethical leadership: perceptions from inside and outside the executive suite', *Human Relations* 56: 5–37.

Turnbull, S. (2010) 'Looking beyond the West for leadership', *EFMD Global Focus* 4(3): 38–42.

Vaiman, V. and Collings, D.G. (2013) 'Talent management: advancing the field', *International Journal of Human Resource Management* 24: 1737–43.

Valverde, M., Scullion, H. and Ryan, G. (2013) 'Talent management in Spanish medium-sized organizations', *International Journal of Human Resource Management* 24: 1832–52.

Watkins, L.M. and Johnston, L. (2000) 'Screening job applicants: the impact of physical attractiveness and application quality', *International Journal of Selection and Assessment* 8: 76–84.

Wright, P.M., Dunford, B.B. and Snell, S.A. (2001) 'Human resources and the resource based view of the firm, *Journal of Management* 27: 701–21.

SECTION V

Interventions

21
CHANGE MANAGEMENT

Ann Kohut and Gene L. Roth

The perspectives through which I (the lead author) have encountered change are multidimensional: as an individual negotiating challenges of daily life in family, community, and church; as an employee in a corporation; and as a senior manager of a Fortune 50 company. Specifically, as a senior level manager I am faced with the challenges of predicting, communicating, facilitating, and accommodating change on a daily basis. My company operates in a technology industry; thus, the speed and complexity of the changes seem to be exacerbated. In my workplace, we change to survive.

As a manager, over time I became more concerned with how individuals experience change. This focus began as I was tasked with my first downsizing experience as a manager over a decade ago. While this was the beginning of a deeper downsizing by this Fortune 50 company, I remember being surprised that employees didn't seem to see the signs. Since then, I have had to lay off multiple employees in major downsizing efforts. Again, people did not seem prepared. I began to question why this phenomenon occurred. I was asking these questions from an individual employee perspective instead of a management perspective because I was fearful that my own job would be eliminated. As a practitioner I was living the complexities of change management.

Most recently, my business was acquired by a struggling European joint venture. I liken this experience to being transported to the middle of a game board. I do not know what game I landed in; I do not know the rules, the players, or the criteria to win. Though frustrating, these practitioner experiences have provided rich opportunities for observation of how individuals and organizations experience change. While these observations have been informal and unstructured, more questions surfaced around change management. The topic of change is so complex that the first order of business is to determine a structure that makes sense for the audience, in this case HRD scholars and practitioners. Toward that end, this chapter begins with an overview of the literature that highlights select models and theories on change management. We then examine prominent issues in the change management literature as well as tensions of change management that are relevant to HRD research and practice. The chapter concludes with implications for HRD practitioners and suggestions for future research.

What is change management? A sampling of models and theories

The literature base on change management has considerable depth and breadth. A worthy starting point is the seminal work of Kurt Lewin. The 3-step model of unfreezing, moving, refreezing is often cited as Kurt Lewin's key contribution to organizational change (Armenakis and Bedeian 1999, Burnes 2004, Dent and Goldberg 1999, Schein 1996). As a psychologist and social scientist, Lewin uses the analogy of changing the shape of a block of ice to explain organizational change. Unfreezing is characterized by creating the motivation to change; the change process in the move phase occurs by promoting effective communications and empowering people to embrace new ways of working; and the process ends when the organization is returned to a sense of stability in the refreeze stage (Lewin 1947). Burnes (2004) clarifies that Lewin saw all four elements of his planned approach to change (3-step model, field theory, group dynamics, and action research) as forming an integrated approach to analyzing, understanding, and bringing about change at the group, organizational, and societal levels. Elements of Lewin's theorizing can be found in much of the research that followed on change management.

Van de Ven and Poole (1995) introduce four theories intended for use as building blocks to explain change processes in organizations: life cycle, teleology, dialectics, and evolution. These four theories are contextualized in terms of the attributes of members (related theories), pioneers (researchers of the related theories), key metaphor, logic, event progression, and generating force. Of the six attributes, key metaphor and event progression provide the best description of the essence of the theory. Van de Ven and Poole's framework can serve as a heuristic for critique and reformulation of future research as well as a foundation for empirical research because it encourages scholars to identify aspects of motors or relationships that are incompletely described in a given theory.

Launching from the work of Lewin (1947) whereby the three distinct processes of unfreezing, moving, and freezing were identified, Armenakis and Bedeian (1999) investigate four models of implementing change and two models of understanding change in their process research. Armenakis and Bedeian (1999) developed a new process map by combining the models, beginning with the integration of Lewin's three phase change process. This new model matches recommended phase/steps for change agents to follow in implementing change (i.e. phases within which change agents act) with the stages in understanding change (i.e. stages through which change targets progress). The development of this new model for understanding the various facets of organizational change advances the previous research by simultaneously considering multiple dimensions of process issues. Armenakis and Bedeian (1999) acknowledge that their organizing scheme parallels that of Van de Ven and Poole's (1995) typology and Weick and Quinn's (1999) distinction between episodic and continuous change.

Whereas Van de Ven and Poole's four theories are intended to be building blocks for future theory building, Armenakis and Bedeian's model is comprehensive in its consolidation of Lewin's previous work and inclusive of the interactions between change agents and change targets. The contribution of Armenakis and Bedeian is that their schemata are revised to include considerations of content and context. Huy (2001) contributes to the development of planned-change theory by focusing on the previously unexplored constructs of time and content of change. In doing so, Huy proposes four ideal types of intervention approaches: commanding (to change formal structures), engineering (to change work processes), teaching (to change beliefs), and socializing (to change social relationships). Huy defines each ideal type as a specific intervention process.

While Huy's model takes a distinctive perspective of the change agent, Fisher reminds HRD professionals that 'for an organization to change, individuals within that organization must change' (2005: 257). Tension associated with the individual employee and change is addressed later in this chapter (see Choi and Ruona 2011). Huy's meta-model for managing the overall change process along a time dimension provides change management practitioners with guidance by addressing issues related to the past, creating a viable future vision, and identifying what is needed in the present to move to the desired state.

Fisher offers a contested model based on his assertion that most change management models either focus on the present or reflect an assumption that the past should be dismissed. This foundational belief is questioned in the literature (Albert 1995, Huy 2001, Lewin 1947). Fisher attempts to focus on the individual and his or her perception of the change process. In fact, Fisher (2005) urges HRD practitioners to consider the situational and environmental past, present, and future as separate elements in the change process when designing interventions focused on employee needs.

Using a longitudinal case study approach, Manz *et al.* (2002) develop a process model of executive leadership under conditions of ongoing organizational change. Manz *et al.* identify three leadership perspectives as being especially relevant to effective executive leadership of major change: visionary, participative, and transactional leadership. They combine these perspectives into a single process model, the bicycle model, graphically depicted as a bicycle. The visionary process is the source of energy represented by the bicycle pedals which keep the participative and transactional supporting mechanisms, or bicycle wheels, in motion (Manz *et al.* 2002). The two wheels of the participative and transactional cycles provide the support that carries the leadership process and enables energy to be transformed into movement and momentum for change. To maintain progress, the bicycle requires that each part, pedals and wheels, needs to cycle repeatedly. Similarly, the leadership perspectives for effective change management must cycle repeatedly by further refining the vision and facilitating identification, internalization, and compliance to achieve forward movement and momentum. The model has utility because it deals with a prominent theme in the literature – the noted problem of the relative ineffectiveness of leaders and managers who are charged with implementing change (Maycunich Gilley *et al.* 2011).

Leaders, managers, and HRD practitioners play various roles as agents of change in organizations. Change agents have been characterized several ways in the literature, but Caldwell (2003) outlines a useful fourfold classification: leadership, management, consultancy, and team models. This classification is a heuristic research tool used to synthesize and reconceptualize the nature of change agency. It emphasizes that there is no universal model of change agency or a single type of change agent with a fixed set of competencies. Within each of the four classifications, a variety of change agent roles or types can be explored (Caldwell 2003). The interplay of these various elements of change agency and change management illustrate the complexities of organizational change, and the importance of attending to both hard and soft aspects of change management, as noted by Sirkin *et al.* (2005). As a result of their longitudinal study whereby change projects in 225 companies in various industries and countries were examined over a two-year period, the researchers identify correlations between the outcomes of change programs and the four hard factors of duration, integrity, commitment, and effort (collectively referred to as the DICE framework) (Sirkin *et al.* 2005). Sirkin *et al.* claim that over an 11-year period, the Boston Consulting Group has used the DICE framework to predict the outcomes and guide execution of more than 1,000 change management initiatives worldwide in which the correlation of the four factors for a successful outcome has held, and no other combination of factors has predicted outcomes as well as the DICE framework. Their contribution to the literature is noteworthy because the DICE framework is a simple, quantitative tool which provides a common language for managing change.

A sampling of prevailing issues in change management

Several prominent themes of change management literature are highlighted in the following sections. Issues that are addressed include resistance to change, change ownership, utility of mental models; importance of communication; and role of organizational politics in change management.

Resistance, change ownership, and new mental models

Clegg and Walsh (2004) tackle core issues in the field of change management by identifying some mindsets dominating the practice of change management and suggesting alternatives that are primarily drawn from operations management and socio-technical frameworks. Using this framework, Clegg and Walsh (2004: 220) argue that,

> all changes comprise a systemic rearrangement, which crosses the perceived divide between the technical and the social . . . The literature on technical innovation reveals the political and systemic nature of change . . . One implication is that we should consider such changes over their life cycle (i.e. from strategy through to use and adaptation)

Clegg and Walsh view approaches to change management as being fragmented because of the lack of continuity among people involved in establishing strategy, and others who might be involved in designing the new way of working, implementing, using, and then maintaining or adapting the strategy. Instead, they argue for a continuous and process-based view they term 'pull' systems whereby the users of the new way of working are responsible for pulling through the changes that they need to undertake their work effectively.

In exploring the role of user in this context, Clegg and Walsh (2004) express concern with the common notions of user participation and resistance to change. They recommend a new mindset that moves the debate from the common concerns and arguments regarding user participation to where new ways of working (involving new technologies, techniques, social systems, etc.) are pulled through and owned by the people who will manage and use them. In this context, resistance to change becomes resistance to ownership. Employees' perspectives toward organizational change are commonly portrayed as that of resistance in the literature. However, Choi and Ruona propose a different construct – that of individual readiness for organizational change. They suggest, 'in order for organizational members' involvement and participation in the change process to have successful outcomes, they must be knowledgeable, capable, and motivated to make a genuine contribution' (2011: 63).

Clegg and Walsh (2004) recommend that we reject some of the old mindsets and language that dominate the field of change management and replace them with new ones. They suggest that a logical corollary of adopting a systemic view of change is that we work with other groups and communities to design better ways of working, thus embracing opportunities for multidisciplinary working (for example, with engineers, computer scientists, strategists, and others), and develop expertise in such collaborations. Clegg and Walsh see an opportunity to develop and use methods and tools which foster the inclusion of social science ideas in the design process, thereby encouraging and facilitating new mindsets. These ideas are consistent with Lehner's (2011) recommendation for understanding mental models as they impact change initiatives. Lehner explains, 'While many factors influence the change process, addressing the differing perceptions of senior leadership and hourly employees is one key' (2011: 4301). Surfacing mental models of leaders and employees can identify differences among them, and provide a starting point for working toward common ground. 'Recognizing and exploring differences in mental models may facilitate the adoption of changes' (Lehner 2011: 4316).

Lehner's contention that intentions behind change initiatives should be transparent has merit. Du Gay and Vikkelso (2012) point out that change is commonly conceived of and represented as a generic entity. More often than not change is presented as a desirable and manageable movement – depending upon one's point of view. Employees are more apt to be ready for change and be willing participants in change initiatives when the impetus behind these forces has been clearly communicated to them.

Communication in leading, managing, and facilitating change

The importance of effective communication in leading, managing, and facilitating change is well documented (Axley 2000, Leitzel *et al.* 2004, Levick 1996, Miles 2001, Rogers *et al.* 2003, Schneider and Goldwasser 1998, Skalik *et al.* 2002). Axley advocates a back-to-basics approach when communicating about change by returning to the basic questions of why, what, who, how, and when. Specifically, the following needs to be addressed: what processes, structures, goals, and standards will change; who among the organization's internal and external stakeholders will be affected; when will key changes take place; and how and when should messages about the change be communicated.

Miles (2001) describes the 'age of the employee' which is characterized by the need for management to find new ways to engage employees so that they can lead the organization in new directions at all levels. Miles purports an all-employee supercharger cascade methodology which is an employee-focused process for communicating change immediately following the corporate transformation planning effort. 'Leaders supercharge the launch of well-articulated plans for corporate transformation by rapidly and intensively involving *all* employees in high-engagement cascades that create understanding, dialogue, feedback, and accountability' (Miles 2001: 315). This strategy appears to have substantial alignment with Choi and Ruona's (2011) construct of employee readiness for organizational change, and the caveat by Maycunich Gilley *et al.* (2011) that management must understand that change has a deeply personal impact on employees.

Although organizational change can create significant stressors in the workplace, employee attitudes toward change can be strongly influenced by support that is communicated by immediate supervisors (Meaker and Wang 2010). Whereas the change process is influenced by numerous variables, an important element is open communication regarding differing viewpoints of senior leadership compared with lower level employees (Lehner 2011). Lehner stresses the surfacing of mental models of both leaders and employees as a communication tool for mediating differences and gaining a collective commitment to change initiatives.

Toward this end, the HRD professional is uniquely positioned as a conduit for translating the business need for change to the employee and correspondingly to represent the employee impact of the change back to management. Ning and Jing (2012) acknowledge that a continuous barrage of change has resulted in high levels of stress to organizations and employees. Change initiatives can benefit from managers and HRD professionals openly communicating with employees about motivations and commitments to change. Ning and Jing offer, 'It is crucial for managers and HRD professionals to understand the antecedents and consequences of employees' commitment to change' (2012: 478). Their roles in facilitating change can be crucial to its success.

Yet understanding the antecedents and consequences of employees' commitment to change is but one aspect of understanding the total context of change. The following section addresses how organizational politics as a context has relevance to HRD practitioners and change management.

Change management and elements of organizational politics

Kohut (2011) emphasizes the important role of organizational politics in successful adaptation to significant workplace change. Reading the organizational environment, interpreting change cues correctly, and resolving conflicts affecting organizational position and job scope are important aspects of political skill necessary to survivorship of workplace change. Yet, organizations do not formally teach political skill to their employees so that they might be better prepared for change scenarios.

A change agent's ability to understand organizational politics and build political skill can be vital to the advancement of both the change objectives and the change agent's career (Ferris *et al.* 2000, Valle 2006). The effective use of political skill has been identified as a key coping mechanism to reduce the stressors associated with a rapidly changing environment (Perrewe *et al.* 2000). Thus, the effective use of political skill by organizational members can advance an organization's capacity for success in an increasingly competitive and fast-changing environment.

Political skill influences performance and success in all types of jobs throughout levels within organizations (Ferris *et al.* 2000). Yet, in a survey of 250 British managers exploring their perceptions of politics, Buchanan (2007) determined that 80% of managers studied did not have any training in the area of organizational politics. Vredenburgh and Shea-VanFossen (2010) explain that organizational politics is a fact of organizational life that influences the types of problems with which HRD practitioners become embroiled. They identify the need for HRD practitioners to play a role in lessening the occurrence of dysfunctional organizational politics. Vredenburgh and Shea-VanFossen (2010: 35–36) contend that,

> in contemporary organization environments genetic predispositions such as aggressiveness, power need, manipulativeness, control orientation, status competiveness, and narcissism can emerge in response to common organizational conditions of uncertainty, resource scarcity, and conflict. The ubiquitous presence of these organizational conditions and the prevalence of these individual attributes make the frequency of organizational politics understandable.

Change management involves scarce resources, and when resources are scarce the aforementioned predispositions can surface in the wake of power struggles. Not only do HRD practitioners need to develop political savvy and sensibilities for their own survival during change initiatives, but they can take lead roles in developing a functional political culture within the organization (Vredenburgh and Shea-VanFossen 2010).

HRD and change management: remaining tensions

Tensions involving HRD and change management are outlined below.

Change management: foundational differences

Change management has arrived as a force for research and practice. It is not merely a peripheral topic; Du Gay and Vikkelso (2012: 121) assert that change management is center stage:

> Because change is regarded both as omnipresent and omnipotent, the ability of organizations to adapt to its imperatives is deemed pivotal. Managing change is therefore seen as a, if not the, crucial feature of the business of organizing, and it is from this basic premise that organizational theory and practice must depart.

However, although the significance of change management has been acknowledged by scholars, consensus regarding its essence remains elusive. Literature highlighted in this chapter provides evidence of the array of viewpoints and strategies for examining change management. An observation by the authors of this chapter is that many of the researchers who write about change management tend to embrace the notion of change itself when making assertions about change management. That is to say, scholars have encouraged other scholars to change the way they conceptualize change management. For example, Coates (2012) questions the functionality of theories about change in organizations when those theories were crafted at a time when workplaces were much different than they are today. Aligned with this concern by Coates is the encouragement by Clegg and Walsh (2004) to discard old mindsets and language that dominate the field of change management and move toward new ones. They suggest a systemic view of change in which disparate groups and communities come together to design better ways of working.

Du Gay and Vikkelso (2012) seem to be of a different mindset, and they are unimpressed by recent generalizations about change and change management. They assert that phenomena found under the contemporary heading of 'change' are not exactly new, but instead they can be found in the traditions of organization theory. In the traditions of organization design, they explain change was not considered to be a general norm (either good or bad), but a guiding force for altering the organization's key features: 'its core tasks, its work roles, its authority structure or its allocation of resources, for example' (2012: 133). They contend that in such cases, attention was paid to detail in the ways that actions were forged to counteract environmental influences. Du Gay and Vikkelso assert that contemporary theories of change management are distanced from classic pragmatism and place change on the outskirts as a generic entity.

HRD positionality and change management

In our view, HRD practitioners and scholars need to enter into the fray of the discussion on change management. A common finding in HRD research is that HR practitioners are not at the strategic planning table for early discussions that involve significant organizational change (Shook and Roth 2011, Anderson 2009). As a field of practice and an area of scholarly inquiry, HRD struggles with its positioning in regard to change management. Strategic HRD is a needed and important component for an organization's response to change (Wang *et al.* 2009). However, HRD practitioners have an uphill battle as change agents because of their limited levels of influence. MacKenzie *et al.* describe the problematic nature of HRD being such a contested concept and HRD practitioners functioning in a 'complex and compromised context' (2012: 354). They describe this milieu (ibid: 362):

> Accepting that organizational life is contentious, ugly and prone to negative outcomes is a challenge and only one half of the problem. The willingness to question the assumptions and challenge the status quo is a more difficult task for both scholars and practitioners – *difficult but not impossible.*

Questioning assumptions and challenging the status quo are important aspects of change management. Not only do HRD practitioners need to have the courage to ask difficult questions and seek out meaningful roles as change agents, but they also need to refine their own skills in organizational politics in order to survive those risky actions. HRD practitioners need to develop political sensitivities so they can bypass and/or effectively negotiate the negative political quagmire described by Vredenburgh and Shea-VanFossen (2010). That is to say, HRD practitioners must be able to recognize and make wise decisions regarding the negativity (e.g. power need, manipulation, narcissism) that can boil over from common problems in organizations linked to uncertainty, scarce resources, and tensions. As noted in the previous section of this chapter, Kohut (2011) found that HRD practitioners struggled with recognizing cues in the workplace that indicated significant workplace changes which were on the horizon. Furthermore, she linked this finding with their inabilities to effectively deal with organizational politics.

Change management and disparate lenses

Researchers pose different opinions regarding the degree to which leaders of change management should focus on the past, present, and future. Viewpoints vary regarding how much leaders should manage change based on organizational precedents, or shift their existing paradigm to seek out new courses of direction. For example, Boje explains that 'change management is often more about future-making than [cognitive] sensemaking of the past' (2012: 256). But Buchanan appears to see change management through a different lens than Boje. Buchanan (2011: 273) explains the need for reflection on the details of implementing change strategies and assurance of their follow-through:

> The aim of this reflection is to identify a set of puzzles which have not been explored by change management researchers, have not been resolved by other approaches and where a change management perspective may be particularly valuable. These puzzles derive from the observation that, following an accident, crisis, disaster, or other extreme event, the recommendations from investigation and inquiries are often not implemented.

If follow-through does not occur with recommendations, then history can repeat itself and the undesirable state of affairs can occur again. However, as previously noted in this chapter, employees may have resistance to change, even if the change recommendations are intended to prevent calamity. Buchanan refers to 'organization learning difficulties' (2011: 273) as a contributing cause to employee resistance to change when the change initiatives are supposedly for the good of the organization.

Weick appears to focus greatly on present and past, and he aligns change management with assessing organizational reliability. He directs the change management discussion toward characteristics of high-reliability organizations. He asserts that these high-reliability organizations 'pay more attention to failures than success, avoid simplicity rather than cultivate it, are just as sensitive to operations as they are to strategy, organize for reliance rather than anticipation, and allow decisions to migrate to experts wherever they are located' (2011: 15). He explains that these types of organizations focus on making sense of ongoing flux and directing order back to their experiences, and thus, touching back and forth between flux and order.

Yorks and Nicolaides provide an intriguing connection to these past and future perspectives. They acknowledge the intense complexities that individuals and organizations face, fueled by technology innovation and globalization; then, they caution HRD practitioners and managers about the use of organizational experiences as a basis for future directions (2012: 185):

> One consequence of complexity is that experience is both an asset and liability; although it provides a basis for action, it potentially blocks awareness of the range of potential real-time responses and inhibits insight into possibilities.

These authors describe the difficulties in making judgments about possible future actions while current conditions are in a state of flux. They explain that making decisions based on past experiences has limitations when unexpected surprises are occurring.

Change management: insights for moving forward

We conclude this chapter with two concepts that we believe have considerable value for HRD scholars and practitioners. For us, these concepts share considerable common ground across the research and practice of HRD and change management.

First, the notion of strategic insight as described by Yorks and Nicolaides is well aligned with the skills HRD practitioners need to develop to be successful players in change management. 'Broadly defined strategic insight involves an increased awareness of new possibilities derived through engaging with diverse perspectives, assessing trends in divergent domains, making assumptions explicit, and challenging those assumptions' (2012: 186). As a construct, strategic insight relates to the types of skills highlighted in the change management literature, such as political sensibilities, change readiness, and future-making. Yorks and Nicolaides describe the importance of early recognition of disruptive trends that are on the horizon and the repercussions of 'the intensifying impact of uncertainty and ambiguity' (2012: 195). We see the construct of strategic insight as a useful link between the literature bases of HRD and change management.

Finally, the second construct that we would like to emphasize from the change management literature is a focus on context. Du Gay and Vikkelso (2012) urge us to pay particular attention to the differences between organizations when considering the construct of change. They explain that organizations have unique missions, distinct obligations, specific constituencies, and their own approaches for dealing with ethical questions. Du Gay and Vikkelso explain that 'It is unlikely that they will experience "change" in an identical manner – as an abstract phenomenon – but rather as a particular matter of concern, with distinctive characteristics and practical implications related to the conduct of concrete aspects of their activities' (2012: 133). If proper attention is not given to context, they caution practitioners and researchers that a generic approach and generalizations toward change can be inappropriate and can lead to undesirable consequences.

Our concluding thoughts bring the preceding two constructs together as the central message regarding change management and the field of HRD. When it comes to successfully managing change, HRD practitioners must (1) be attentive to the unique characteristics of the context and (2) develop and refine their political and communication skills with strategic insight as a means of preparing for and dealing with change. Furthermore, we see these two constructs as important considerations for future research that links HRD and change management.

References

Albert, S. (1995) 'Towards a theory of timing: An archival study of timing decisions in the Persian Gulf War', *Research in Organizational Behavior* 17: 1–70.

Anderson, V. (2009) 'Desperately seeking alignment: reflections of senior line managers and HRD executives', *Human Resource Development International* 12: 263–77.

Armenakis, A.A. and Bedeian, A.G., (1999) 'Organizational change: a review of theory and research in the 1990s', *Journal of Management* 25: 293–315.

Axley, S.R. (2000) 'Communicating change: questions to consider', *Industrial Management* 42(4): 18–22.

Boje, D. (2012) 'Reflections: what does quantum physics of storytelling mean for change management?', *Journal of Change Management* 12: 253–71.

Buchanan, D.A. (2007) 'You stab my back, I'll stab yours: management experience and perceptions of organization political behaviour', *British Journal of Management* 19: 49–64.

— (2011) 'Reflections: good practice, not rocket science – understanding failures to change after extreme events', *Journal of Change Management* 11: 273–88.

Burnes, B. (2004) 'Kurt Lewin and the planned approach to change: a re-appraisal', *Journal of Management Studies* 41: 977–1002.

Caldwell, R. (2003) 'Models of change agency: a fourfold classification', *British Journal of Management* 14: 131–42.

Choi, M. and Ruona, W. (2011) 'Individual readiness for change and its implications for human resource development', *Human Resource Development Review* 10: 46–73.

Clegg, C. and Walsh, S. (2004) 'Change management: time for a change!', *European Journal of Work and Organizational Psychology* 13: 217–39.

Coates, T. (2012) 'A review and critique of foundational change theories and implications for the modern workforce', in Wang, J. and Gedro, J. (eds) *Conference Proceedings, AHRD International Research Conference in the Americas*, Denver, CO: Academy of Human Resource Development, 3151–77.

Dent, E.B. and Goldberg, S.G. (1999) 'Challenging resistance to change', *Journal of Applied Behavioral Science* 35: 25–41.

Du Gay, P. and Vikkelso, S. (2012) 'Reflections: on the lost specification of "change"', *Journal of Change Management* 12: 121–43.

Ferris, G.R., Perrewe, P.L., Anthony, W.P. and Gilmore, D.C. (2000) 'Political skill at work', *Organizational Dynamics* 28(4): 25–37.

Fisher, J.M. (2005) 'A time for a change?', *Human Resource Development International* 8: 257–63.

Huy, Q.N.H. (2001) 'Time, temporal capability, and planned change', *Academy of Management Review* 26: 601–23.

Kohut, A. (2011) 'Survivorship of significant workplace change: change influencers model (CIM)', in Dirani, K., Wang, J. and Doshy, P. (eds) *Conference Proceedings, AHRD International Research Conference in the Americas*, Schaumburg, IL: Academy of Human Resource Development, 2404–43.

Lehner, R. (2011) 'Perceptions, intent, and change initiatives: how do they fit together?' in Dirani, K., Wang, J. and Doshy, P. (eds) *Conference Proceedings, AHRD International Research Conference in the Americas*, Schaumburg, IL: Academy of Human Resource Development, 4298–323.

Leitzel, J., Corvey, C. and Hiley, D. (2004) 'Integrated planning and change management at a research university', *Change*, 36(1): 36–43.

Levick, D. (1996) 'How do you communicate? Managing the change process', *Physician Executive* 22(7): 26–29.

Lewin, K. (1947) 'Frontiers in group dynamics', *Human Relations* 1: 5–41.

MacKenzie, C., Garavan, T. and Carbery, R. (2012) 'Through the looking glass: challenges for human resource development (HRD) post the global financial crisis – business as usual?', *Human Resource Development International* 15: 353–64.

Manz, C., Bastien, D. and Hostager, T. (2002) 'Executive leadership during organizational change: a bicycle model', *Human Resource Planning* 14: 275–87.

Maycunich Gilley, A., Gilley, J. and Heames, J. (2011) 'Leaders and change: make it personal', in Dirani, K., Wang, J. and Doshy, P. (eds) *Conference Proceedings, AHRD International Research Conference in the Americas*, Schaumburg, IL: Academy of Human Resource Development, 2109–18.

Meaker, S. and Wang, J. (2010) 'Employee experience with organizational change: a phenomenological study', in Graham, C. and Dirani, K. (eds) *Conference Proceedings, AHRD International Research Conference in the Americas*, Knoxville, TN: Academy of Human Resource Development, 4002–29.

Miles, R.H. (2001) 'Beyond the age of Dilbert: accelerating corporate transformations by rapidly engaging all employees', *Organizational Dynamics* 29: 313–21.

Ning, J. and Jing, R. (2012) 'Commitment to change: its role in the relationship between expectation of change outcome and emotional exhaustion', *Human Resource Development Quarterly* 23: 461–85.

Perrewe, P.L., Ferris, G.R., Frink, D.D. and Anthony, W.P. (2000) 'Political skill: an antidote for workplace stressors', *Academy of Management Executive* 14: 115–23.

Rogers, P., Shannon, T. and Gent, S. (2003) 'Leading successful change', *European Business Journal* 15: 104–11.

Schein, E.H. (1996) 'Kurt Lewin's change theory in the field and in the classroom: notes towards a model of management learning', *Systems Practice* 9: 27–47.

Schneider, D.M. and Goldwasser, C. (1998) 'Be a model leader of change', *Management Review* 87(3): 41–45.

Shook, L. and Roth, G. (2011) 'Downsizings, mergers, and acquisitions: perspectives of human resource development practitioners', *European Journal of Industrial Training and Development* 35: 135–53.

Sirkin, H.L., Keenan, P. and Jackson, A. (2005) 'The hard side of change management', *Harvard Business Review* 83(10): 109–18.

Skalik, J., Barabasz, A. and Belz, G. (2002) 'Polish managers and the change management process: a management learning perspective', *Human Resource Development International* 5: 377–82.

Valle, M. (2006) 'The power of politics: why leaders need to learn the art of influence', *LIA* 26(2): 8–12.

Van de Ven, A. and Poole, M. (1995) 'Explaining development and change in organizations', *Academy of Management Review* 20: 510–40.

Vredenburgh, D. and Shea-VanFossen, R. (2010) 'Human nature, organizational politics, and human resource development', *Human Resource Development Review* 9: 26–47.

Wang, J., Hutchins, H. and Garavan, T. (2009) 'Exploring the strategic role of human resource development in organizational crisis management', *Human Resource Development Review* 8: 22–53.

Weick, K. (2011) 'Reflections: change agents as change poets – on reconnecting flux and hunches', *Journal of Change Management* 11: 7–20.

Weick, K. and Quinn, R. (1999) 'Organizational change and development', *Annual Review of Psychology* 50: 361–86.

Yorks, L. and Nicolaides, A. (2012) 'A conceptual model for developing mindsets for strategic insight under conditions of complexity and high uncertainty', *Human Resource Development Review* 11: 182–202.

22

INFORMAL LEARNING IN LEARNING ORGANIZATIONS

Victoria J. Marsick and Karen E. Watkins

In recent years, HRD scholars and practitioners have acknowledged the ways in which informal learning is central to strategic organization learning. This chapter defines informal learning and examines ways it is being put into practice as part of creating a learning-rich culture. Learning and development must shape the learning environment and weave learning effectively into a learning architecture.

The workplace is so fast-paced, knowledge-rich, global, and technologically driven, that it has catalyzed a shift in how learning is conceived. HRD is moving from a primary reliance on event-driven organized training, to integrated work and learning architectures that rely on better leveraging of informal learning (Perrin and Marsick 2012). In fact, informal learning has become a primary learning strategy. The proportion of informal-to-formal learning in organizations is now estimated at 70–80 per cent informal learning to 20–30 per cent formal learning and training, a ratio confirmed by several studies (e.g. Cross 2007; Leslie *et al.* 1998; Lowenstein and Spletzer 1994; McCall *et al.* 1988).

There is some evidence that informal learning adds to performance results although research is sparse and its quality uneven. An ASTD survey (Bingham 2009: 60) conducted with the Institute for Corporate Productivity found that 98 per cent of those surveyed say that informal learning enhances employee performance, and 39 per cent of respondents said it is enhancing employee performance to a high extent. A survey by Bersin (2009) (n = 1,050) rated learning approaches which are perceived to drive greatest business value: 60 per cent cited on-the-job experience; 36 per cent cited on-the-job mentoring, projects and rotation; and 33 per cent cited coaching by one's supervisor; all informal learning strategies. In comparison, 28 per cent cited in-company training and 8 per cent cited outside-provider training as approaches that drive business value.

Even though informal learning has grown in importance in today's organizations, many do not know what it looks like and how it can best be supported. The purpose of this chapter is to shed light on what organizations can do to support and facilitate informal learning and in particular, how, in so doing, organizations create a learning-rich culture. We seek to answer the following questions:

- How is informal learning defined?
- What does research say about how to support informal learning?

Informal learning is driven by learner interests as much as, or more than, employer mandates, and by the nature of work itself. Informal learning thus cannot be delivered, managed, or supported in the same way as formal learning because the choices surrounding the pursuit of such learning are not directly in the hands of HRD and the organization. Research and practice suggest that organizations focus, instead, on cultivating a learning culture and environment that, in turn, motivates and incentivizes integrated work and learning architectures. This trend is consistent with a view of learning organizations that emphasizes the learning culture as key to strategic goal achievement (Watkins and Marsick 1993; Marsick and Watkins 2003).

How informal learning is defined and understood

Informal learning definitions share many commonalties. Definitions on informal learning tend to differ in terms of how it happens: organically, arising from the nature and context of work itself or who drives the learning: learners themselves, in their own preferred ways, rather than outside experts or representatives of organizations/institutions. For example, Fuller *et al.* (2003: 5) said that "the term informal . . . draws attention to the workplace as a site for learning in which people learn both with and without structured and specialist support . . . learning is not the primary goal of the workplace but a by-product of workplace activity in general." Similarly, Marsick and Watkins (1990) and Marsick *et al.* (2009: 6–7) state that informal learning is:

> Learning through experience "outside of formally structured, institutionally sponsored, classroom-based activities" that "often takes place under non-routine circumstances, that is, when the procedures and responses that people normally use fail" leading to greater attention to "tacit, hidden, taken-for-granted assumptions." Incidental learning is "a byproduct of some other activity, such as task accomplishment, interpersonal interactions, sensing the organizational culture, or trial-and-error experimentation" and is often semi-conscious.

By contrast, the European Commission (2001, as cited in Colardyn and Bjornavold 2004: 71) frames informal learning as "learning resulting from daily life activities . . . often referred to as experiential learning . . . not structured . . . Does not lead to certification . . . may be intentional but in most cases, it is non-intentional (or 'incidental'/random)." Livingstone (2001: 4) defined informal learning as "any activity involving the pursuit of understanding, knowledge or skill which occurs without the presence of externally imposed curricular criteria."

There are tensions inherent in the concept of informal learning: In what ways is informal learning purposeful or intentional, and in what ways is it less conscious and incidental? When it is less conscious, what drives and shapes that learning? What is the role of the individual as agent of learning vs. the workplace as socializing force? In the next part of this chapter, we look at how informal learning has been conceptualized in order to shed light on these tensions and identify leverage points for understanding practice.

Theoretical bases of informal learning

Three different theory bases help shape our understanding of informal learning. These conceptualizations shed light on the role played by individuals as agents of learning and the way learning is shaped by environment: (1) Dewey-based learning from experience, (2) learning-network theory, and (3) socio-cultural theory.

Dewey-based theories

Pragmatic views of learning from and through experience rest on John Dewey (1938) who applied the scientific method to problem solving and everyday living. Dewey showed how people learn by information gathering and experimentation when framing and solving problems. Dewey's theory focuses on explicit, rational steps involved in learning from experience, but is less helpful in focusing on intuitive or less conscious factors that shape learning.

Dewey-based theories of informal learning emphasize conscious reflection in and on experience. Schön (1983) is best known for his theory of reflective practice engaged by professionals at work. He distinguished between reflection in and reflection-on action, and adapted action science tools to learning at and through work. Dewey-based theories of informal learning emphasize the agency of the individual in intentionally driving learning, but do not account for its social, collaborative nature. We turn next to theories that do.

Learning-network theory

Poell *et al.* (2000) offer a view of learning that is social, interactive, constructivist and contextual in nature. Learners are conceptualized as "actors" or agents who organize their own learning within different social contexts that shape the way they develop learning policies and programs and the way they learn based on existing work and learning structures. Four ideal types of learning networks result from this mix: liberal (designed and executed in a self-directed manner), vertical (guided in design and execution by management), horizontal (in an egalitarian way among people joined together to pursue common interests) or external (linked to professions outside the organization that influence new directions taken up within an organization).

Informal learning varies with the ideal type. Through liberal learning networks, individuals act as their own agents for learning within the social context. The horizontal network functions through collaborative work interest groups with shared motivation and interest. Vertical networks and external networks are guided by mandates or visions developed outside oneself, as represented by power brokers designated as authorities or credible because of their knowledge and expertise. Informal learning occurs if there is buy-in by participating individuals to the goals and directions of either management or external professions or other knowledge-creating groups.

In learning-network theory (see also Chapter 13 in this volume), actors retain control of their learning programs, even when external forces push in different directions. This theory accounts, descriptively, for the interaction of the individual and the social context. Individual actors have learning preferences that shape what and how they learn in collaboration with others in response to interests and challenges that arise, in part, from who takes primary charge for the direction of the learning: oneself, management, collaborative work communities, or external professional and credentialing sources. While descriptive of how learning is negotiated by actors at work, learning-network theory does not fully account for socio-cultural forces. Socio-cultural theory sheds additional light on these factors.

Socio-cultural theory

Billett (2001, 2002, 2004) builds a theory of workplace pedagogy on socio-cultural theory (Vygotsky 1978), situated cognition (e.g. Lave and Wenger 1991), social psychology (Mead 1913), and on Piaget's (1976) cognitive development theory, among others. Taking a socio-cultural perspective, Billett explains that all learning takes place within social organizations or communities that have formalized structures, and hence is structured by these work arrangements. People learn through socialization, e.g. by observing and interacting with significant others with power or credibility to regulate access to knowledge, skill and resources. Through participation at work, they both apply what they know to routine practices, using acquired cognitive frameworks (Piaget's concept of assimilation); and potentially approach work, even when routine, in new ways, thereby creating new frameworks (Piaget's concept of accommodation).

Individuals make choices as agents of their learning, but choices are also guided by work affordances controlled in part by powerful others and are thus contested. Billett notes that some work environments better scaffold informal learning through the nature of work tasks and resources. He shows how individuals retain agency over what and how they learn no matter how rich or poor the environment. Learning depends on the nature of participatory processes at work that regulate access to learning-rich work and resources. Because of the social nature of work and learning, one worker's gains could be another's losses. For this and other reasons, access to learning-rich work is to some extent a negotiated process. Billett's work puts the nature of the job front and central to understanding how informal learning is structured by the work itself. As is also the case in learning-network theory, he demonstrates the key role that organizations play through the power dynamics that are put into play by their representatives.

Marsick and Watkins (1990): theory of informal and incidental learning

Our theory of informal and incidental learning (Marsick and Watkins 1990; Marsick *et al.* 2009) is based in a Dewey-influenced problem framing/problem solving cycle with an additional emphasis on how the context shapes interpretation and action. In the model, we emphasized triggers to informal and incidental learning; what learners selectively attend to or leave out in their interpretations; how they consider alternatives; whether and how they examine consequences or learn from errors; and how they take observations into account in planning next steps. Over time we adapted our conceptualization to acknowledge the central role of context (Cseh *et al.* 2000); and the fact that learning is much more holistic and emotional than the original model depicted. Figure 22.1 presents the Marsick and Watkins model of informal and incidental learning.

In reviewing research we and others conducted on our model (Marsick *et al.* 2009: 580) we found, for example, that "trial-and-error (also referred to as learning from mistakes or from experience) was the most often cited" learning method used in studies we reviewed. Knowledge and skills were often gained through self-directed learning projects. In consonance with this model, the review confirmed that "the ability to critically reflect on one's experience and mental models . . . enhanced learning." Research using learning-network theory, according to Poell *et al.* (2000: 42) fleshes out "a descriptive and interpretive model of how learning *can* be organized rather than a prescriptive model of how learning *should* be organized." Billett's (2002: 29) studies confirm the value of "everyday participation in work activities . . . to develop many of the capacities required for effective work practice"; show that "the use of intentional guided learning strategies has demonstrated a capacity to augment the contributions of this everyday experience"; and shed light on access to resources as inequitable, contested, and negotiable.

Informal learning is challenging to study because it takes place anywhere and anytime, but also because it is not highly conscious and not easily observable or accessible at the point of learning. Nonetheless, a good deal of early research on informal learning focused on describing what *can* be seen, particularly learning practices and processes. For example, Marsick and Watkins (1990) described learning from experience, mentoring, coaching, and self-directed learning. Dale *et al.* (1999: 1) found that "informal learning forms part of everyday activities, and everyday activities support learning." Their study of 15 leading-edge training practice companies highlighted pedagogical practices (instruction, demonstration, shadowing, role modeling, feedback) and a

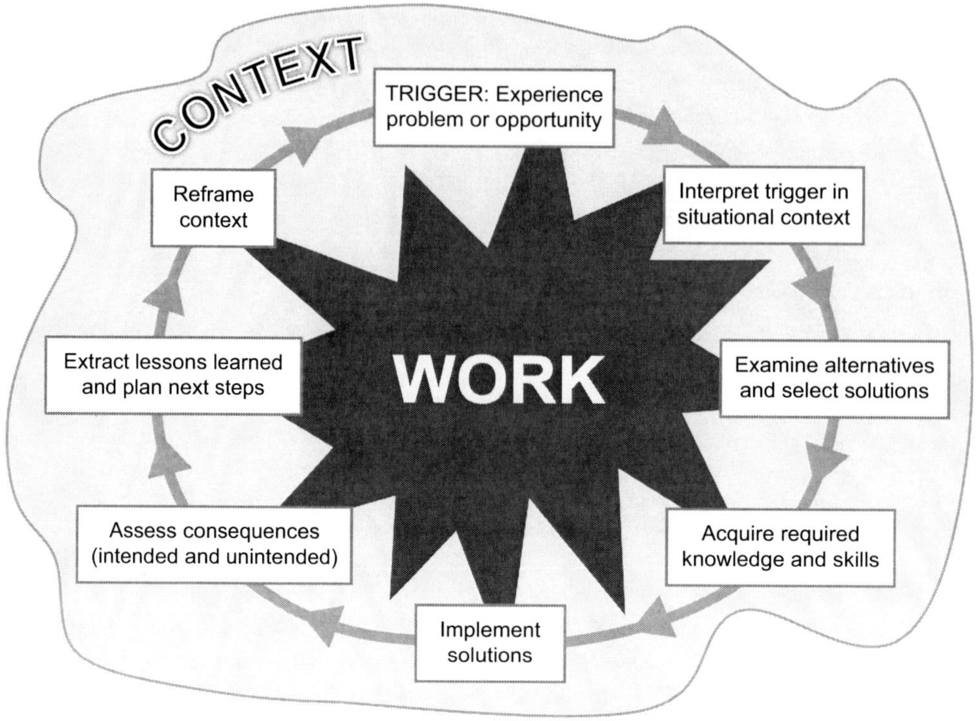

Figure 22.1 Marsick and Watkins' informal and incidental learning model

Note: From Marsick, V.J., Nicolaides, A. and Watkins, K.E. (2014). Adult Learning Theory and Application in Human Resource and Organization Development, in Chalofsky, N., Rocco, T.S. and Morris, M.L. (eds) *Handbook of human resource development*. San Francisco, CA: Jossey-Bass. Adapted from "Informal and incidental learning in the workplace," in Smith, M.C. and DeFrates-Densch, N. (eds). *Handbook of research on adult development and learning*, by Marsick, V.J., Watkins, K.E., Callahan, M.W. and Volpe, M. (2009). This material is reproduced with permission of John Wiley & Sons, Inc.

supportive learning climate. EDC's work on the predominance of informal learning led them to develop the idea of a Teaching Firm based on case studies and centered around informal practices and a climate supportive of teaching and learning on the job (Leslie *et al.* 1998).

A challenge in conducting field research on informal learning is generating a broad enough database that enables comparison across cases and settings. Two sets of studies, however, do offer such depth and, as such, provide further insight into how informal learning is best supported in practice. Both originate in England: Eraut's research on professional practice and Felstead *et al.*'s (2009) body of work in the Teaching and Learning Research Programme.

Professional practice studies

Eraut's (2004) research focused primarily on professionals – e.g. teachers, healthcare and social workers, engineers, accountants. He deconstructs learning that takes place via "Thinking" during professional work that involves: (1) assessing clients and situations; (2) deciding what, if any, action to take; (3) pursuing that action, and modifying along the way as needed; and (4) managing one-self while balancing time, resources, priorities and relationships.

Eraut (2004) developed a typology as a heuristic concerning what can be learned informally at work: task performance, awareness and understanding, personal development, teamwork, role performance, academic knowledge and skills, decision making and problem solving, and judgment. Four main types of work activity accounted for a high proportion of reported learning: (1) participation in group activities, (2) working alongside others, (3) tackling challenging tasks, and (4) working with clients. He identified learning and workplace factors that influence success. Learning factors include: (1) challenge and value of the work, (2) feedback and support, and (3) confidence and commitment to learning. Work-based factors include: (1) allocation and structuring of work, (2) expectations, and (3) the shifting terrain of encounters and relationships with important others at work.

Eraut's framework shares characteristics of Dewey-based models of informal learning, to which have been added elements of the social context, work affordances, and the way personal work histories and life experiences shape professional work. Professionals learn through testing and expanding their knowledge when they confront challenges that require adaptation or the development of new competencies. Individuals draw upon accumulated "personal knowledge" in socially situated workplace learning "that enables them to think, interact and perform" (Eraut 2004: 263).

Work systems studies

Felstead *et al.* (2009) are part of a long-term Teaching and Learning Research Programme funded by the British government to better understand workplace learning. The Teaching and Learning Research Programme engaged an interdisciplinary team over a number of years to investigate workplace learning in light of policy initiatives focused on lifelong learning. This interdisciplinary team conducted a series of studies focused on sectors with "different histories, trajectories, product markets and driving forces" (ibid: 8). They included the public and private sectors, education, healthcare, and industries and firms of different sizes (e.g. construction, manufacturing, high-tech industries, retailers, restaurant chains, hairdressing salons, fitness clubs). Data were collected through hundreds of interviews with different stakeholders; work shadowing and participant observation; examination of photographs, learning logs, artifacts, and documents; and new items added to the National Institute of Adult Continuing Education's Survey on Adult Participation in Learning (ibid: 8–12).

These researchers developed a system-level Working as Learning Framework (WALF) built on three concepts: (1) productive systems, (2) work organization, and (3) learning environments. Learning is situated within a vertical and horizontal, cross-industry, cross-level, cross-job view: "Productive systems comprise the *totality* of social relationships entailed in processes of commodity production. They are constituted by the multiple, interlinked social networks through which economic activity is organized" (Felstead *et al.* 2009: 18). The nature of work and learning is affected by the position of a job (and worker) within the entire interacting environment of the workplace. WALF's authors emphasize three kinds of "discretion" as key to learning on the job – in how work is conceived, in how it is executed, and in how outcomes are evaluated (ibid: 24). When workers are empowered to exercise discretion, they need to calculate risks and take responsibility for consequences in ways that require and reward learning. Taking a socio-cultural view, workplace learning is defined by a person's learning history and the workplace learning environment, that is, "bounded networks of social relationships in which people interact with artifacts and devices that are intrinsic to the performance of their work tasks and roles" (ibid: 27). WALF grows out of case examples of practice that provide a grounded view of informal learning consistent with conceptualizations that privilege work as a vehicle for informal learning that is not highly conscious and structured.

How informal learning is best supported

How is informal learning best supported? Some answers to this may come from pioneering organizations that have found new ways to better support informal learning. Other answers can be derived from what research says about individual, group, and organizational support. It is clear that learning and development must be differently designed and supported, because direct control of conditions and processes for informal learning is not in the hands of HRD. We turn next to a description of practice and research on how to best support informal learning.

Practice-initiated support for informal learning

Informal learning practices rely a good deal on role modeling, mentoring and other apprentice-like, personalized, contextualized "Go Sit By Nellie" approaches found in on-the-job training. These practices are often mediated by technology that enables organizations to target learning to individual needs without the abstractness or complexities of fixed time, fixed place, trainer or Subject-Matter-Expert (SME)-reliant approaches. An extended example is IBM Learning Solutions' emerging Learning on Demand system, consisting of Work Apart Learning, Work Embedded Learning and Work Enabled Learning (Robert 2006). Work Apart Learning is enhanced formal training linked to just-in-time learning that is increasingly self-directed. Modules are available online to enable self-study when new capabilities are needed. Work Embedded Learning embeds knowledge in work roles and makes it available during action. For example, sales professionals can access databases of information, short tutorials linked to job tasks, or experts who can help with non-routine questions as they negotiate sales with customers through an enhanced electronic performance support system linked to electronic work tools. Work Enabled Learning involves coaching and self-initiated learning reviews. Bersin (2009), like IBM, sees three categories of informal learning: on demand, socially enabled, or embedded in the work itself. An adaptation of a framework from Bersin illustrates the range of options organizations might offer using these categories of informal learning. The framework is shown in Table 22.1.

The IBM and Bersin architectures suggest different roles and purposes for training which has been redefined to take advantage of new technologies. Although informal learning has often been contraposed to formal learning, scholars conclude that informal and formal learning should

Table 22.1 Elements of a learning infrastructure

Formal	*Informal: On-Demand*	*Informal: Social*	*Informal: Embedded*
Instructor Led Training	E-Learning	Wikis, Blogs	Performance Support
Virtual Classroom	Internet Search	Communities of Practice	Feedback
Games	Books, Articles Videos	Forums	Rotational Assignments
Simulations	Podcasts	Expert Directories	Quality Circles
Testing and Evaluation	Learning/Knowledge Portals	Social Networks	After Action Reviews
E-Learning	Learning Libraries	Coaching and Mentoring	Development Planning
Self-directed learning	Best Practice Archives	Conferences and Colloquia	Action Learning Teams

Note: Adapted from Bersin, J. (2009) *Formalize informal learning:* The Bersin and Associates Enterprise Learning Framework. Saba-Bersin Associates Webcast, retrieved on 19 March 2010 from www.saba.com.

be considered as complementary parts of the whole. Research conducted as early as 1999 suggests that informal learning, while pervasive, is only one part of a total learning solution (Dale *et al.* 1999).

Learning and development practitioners increasingly follow a guideline recommending a mix of 70 per cent on-the-job learning, 20 per cent learning through relationships, and only 10 per cent training. This heuristic is based on studies originally conducted by the Center for Creative Leadership (Corporate Leadership Council 2004). GE adapted this for its own organizational use, and other organizations have followed GE guidelines. Perrin and Marsick (2012) argue that this guideline is more descriptive of *where* people learn than *how* they learn, i.e. on the job (70 per cent), during mentoring or coaching (20 per cent) or in the classroom (10 per cent). AchieveGlobal has instead opted to think of a 20 per cent formal + 80 per cent informal mix, and redesigned its formal-informal learning delivery system to support that mix. One component of this has been to develop an "i-2-i Continuum™ [that] organizes the many ways that participants in formal training (the 20) can continue learning informally (the 80) in the context of their jobs" (ibid: 5). The continuum maps learning activities beginning with those that are intentional, structured and yet informal, and may be negotiated and tailored to explicitly meet learner goals; and ending with others that are increasingly less structured or planned and more spontaneous and incidental. AchieveGlobal redesigned training to build capabilities needed to learn informally on the job – for example, reflection and skills needed to learn from experience – and to strengthen links between training modules and work back on the job, including involvement of managers and supervisors.

Individual factors that support informal learning

Countries with individualistic national cultures may have a bias toward putting the individual actor at the center of workplace learning solutions. In such cases, support for informal learning is perceived to begin with what people bring to work and learning. A number of studies emphasize the control that individuals have over their own learning.

Lohman (2006, 2009) identified through survey research a number of personal characteristics that support informal learning success: (a) initiative; (b) self-efficacy; (c) love of learning; (d) interest in the profession; (e) integrity; (f) outgoing personality; (g) teamwork ethic; (h) curiosity; and (i) open-mindedness. Critical also are feelings of competence, confidence and commitment to learning – some of which the learner brings to the job, or can be cultivated at work depending on climate, structure, and colleagues and supervisors. Doornbos *et al.* (2008: 133), for example, identified "perceived level of competence and the individual's value of work-related learning" as critical to the successful informal learning of Dutch policemen.

In a study of more than 400 mobile phone users in IBM, Ahmad and Orton (2010) show how sales people in the field used mobile devices to contact experts within the company to get advice that could not otherwise be accessed. The study "findings suggest a direct, positive relationship between employee confidence level and self-perception of job performance" because locating expertise at their point of need helped employees better serve their clients (Ahmad and Orton 2010: 50). So, personal characteristics matter, as does the ability to be self-directed and self-regulating (Deci and Ryan 1997).

Resources also matter, but more important than money or equipment are time and access to the right people at the right time. Eraut's (2004) longitudinal work with professionals in many settings suggests that consultation with someone at the time of need – even if not an expert – is more important than visits with mentors, coaches, or managers scheduled when need is not immediate. Time to consult with others may be more a question of knowing what to do and how to do it than a question of additional funding.

Workplace as a learning environment

Other sources of support reside in the workplace as a resource and shaper of learning embedded in work. Scheeres *et al.* (2010: 14), for example, use the lens of "organisationally-sanctioned and named practices that are initiated explicitly to enhance organizational effectiveness." They call these "integrated development practices" (IDPs) and define them as practices that: "facilitate learning in a way that is embedded in work; are independent of formal training programs and are not typically described in terms of training or education; and are managed or implemented by people whose primary job function is not training or learning" (ibid: 14). Scheeres *et al.* (ibid.) analyze the role of IDPs in two organizations, the first with a mission that legitimizes learning for students – and yet did not value learning for employees, nor use IDPs to embed employee learning – with an organization whose mission was to deliver electricity, yet that valued learning about safety and embedded it in IDP as part of everyday work. This work moves the burden of supporting informal learning away from primarily *fixing the learner* to understanding and enhancing work practices that can be motivating and learning-rich.

Skule (2004: 10) sought "to identify the factors most conducive to informal learning at work" by looking at jobs and the work/learning environment. Skule interviewed up to eight workers, managers or stewards for occupational groups in each of 11 different private and public sector enterprises in Norway, followed by a survey of 1,300 employees in private sector and 200 public sector employees in Norway. He developed a measure of the learning intensity of work based on three factors (ibid: 11):

- "Subjective judgement of how learning intensive/educational the job is"
- "Length of job-specific learning required to master the job"
- "Durability of acquired skills, measured by how long it is possible to be away from work, and still remain professionally updated".

Skule (2004) found that seven job-related factors (labeled "learning conditions") significantly affect learning intensity of a job – (1) "high degree of exposure to changes," (2) "high degree of exposure to demands," (3) "managerial responsibilities," (4) "extensive professional contacts," (5) "superior feedback," (6) "management support for learning," and (7) "rewarding of proficiency" (p. 14). Informal learning is more feasible when jobs are more learning intensive.

Learning organization factors

Integrated system frameworks, such as Working as Learning Framework (Felstead *et al.* 2009), point to the importance of a rich learning environment as the best support for informal workplace learning. In other words, when people are highly motivated whether motivation is intrinsic or extrinsic, the best results are obtained when organizations get out of the way and let people take charge of their own learning. But to do so, organizations need to offer resources (e.g. time, people, technology), identify organizational supports, and help to remove barriers that stand in the way of optimizing informal learning and performance.

Organizational factors that consistently show up as conducive to creating a rich learning environment are: (1) trust, (2) culture, (3) structure and communication, and (4) leadership/ management practices. There is no single prescription as to how a particular organization should optimally operationalize these four factors, but research emphasizes their importance, and shows that they interact with one another (Gephart and Marsick, forthcoming).

Trust is needed in order to ask candid questions, get and give feedback, communicate freely, and build learning relationships. Much informal learning is tacit and acquired while talking with, or observing, others. Informal learning promotes capabilities needed to develop and exercise tacit knowledge through understanding context, problem solving, decision making, and communication. High Performance Work literature emphasizes trust as a pre-condition for effective learning (Fuller *et al.* 2003).

Leaders and managers have the most influence over trust, learning culture, structure and communication. Ellinger (2005) and Ellinger and Cseh (2007) underscore that managers must model learning. Immediate supervisors and the work climate they set are the most important factors for success of an initiative, including informal learning, as they provide feedback, coach, develop, influence job design, arrange resources, or reward success.

An extensive body of research on learning culture, using the Dimensions of the Learning Organization Questionnaire (DLOQ), shows that, to lead to improved results, organizational variables, especially leaders who model learning, and effective strategic interaction with the organization's environment, matter significantly for informal learning at the system level (Marsick and Watkins 2003; Watkins and Dirani, in press; Watkins and Marsick 2003; Watkins and O'Neil 2013). Empowering people toward a collective vision and establishing systems that capture and share learning mediate these outcomes. Factors more easily shaped by HRD, e.g. encouraging collaboration and group or team learning, promoting dialogue and inquiry, and creating continuous learning opportunities are helpful, but not sufficient, factors for achieving best results.

This is particularly important since there is a significant relationship between a learning culture and organizational performance. It is the organizational infrastructure for learning, particularly strategic learning, that drives changes in organizational performance (Watkins and Marsick 2003; Watkins and Dirani, in press; Watkins and O'Neil 2013). Knowledge management systems, environmental scanning, empowering people toward a collective vision, and leaders who mentor and coach those they lead are means through which the organization can translate what individuals learn into organizational performance.

Implications for practice, theory, and research

There is increasing agreement about what informal learning is, that it plays an important role as a partner to structured training and to knowledge management, and that it may help individuals and organizations improve performance. However, formal instruction needs to be redesigned with informal learning capabilities (during and after training) in mind. As argued in this chapter, informal learning is often driven by learner interests and motivation as much as, or more than, those of employers. Informal learning thus cannot be delivered, managed, or supported in the same way because the choices surrounding the pursuit of such learning are not directly in the hands of HRD or even, at times, the organization. What HRD and the organization can provide is *access* to the learning resources that enable individual exploration.

Moreover, challenges persist in how informal learning can be managed and supported because it is diffuse, pervasive, and not tied to organizationally managed events. Informal learning is thus best defined, understood, and supported from an integrated system-level perspective. At this level, the organization can shape learning environments and learning-intensive jobs so that people who are motivated to learn, grow, and improve their performance, can better do so through challenging work assignments. Expectations for performance can be established that exceed current capacities, and then give individuals the time and resources to acquire the needed capacities. This might include job rotations, job shadowing, university courses, etc.

HRD needs to work closely with business clients and partners to advocate for, and conceptualize, system-level support for informal learning. Leaders and managers need help so they can better support informal learning, build their own and employees' capabilities to learn from experience on the job, and optimize work climate for learning success. HRD can support informal learning practice in a number of ways.

Through individual development:

- Integrated development practices (Scheeres *et al.* 2010) can be identified, understood, and leveraged
- Learning environment audits (Watkins and Cervero 2000) can be used to raise individuals' awareness and map more intentional use of informal learning through work opportunities
- Resources (people, time, information, technology, funds, etc.) can be identified (Lohman 2006, 2009) and made available to support learning through work practices
- Managers and supervisors can be helped to increase their own capabilities in developing, coaching, mentoring, and supporting others through and at work (Ellinger 2005).

Through organization development:

- Work can be mapped to understand the extent to which jobs are learning intensive (Skule 2004) and identify ways to enhance learning intensity
- Feedback-intensive learning environments can be created to support the natural motivation, curiosity, and interests of individuals who are already committed to learning.
- Learning architectures can be designed to recognize, identify, and support a range of complementary informal and formal learning activities, both face-to-face and virtual (Perrin and Marsick 2012)
- Organizations can better support mentoring, coaching, networking, communities of practice and other social learning environments
- Integrated system frameworks can be used to identify barriers to address as well as supports to leverage.

A wealth of knowledge about how to facilitate informal workplace learning can be drawn from designed but highly flexible, tailored practices that support intentional learning controlled by the learner. This review suggests that it is wise to keep the focus on the work itself and help individuals, groups, and the organization see how learning helps them reach strategic goals that are intrinsically energizing. Learning must be authentic and organic. Practices that are natural in one context may not work in another.

There is still much to learn about informal learning in the workplace. Perhaps because it is so ubiquitous and multi-faceted, it is unlikely we will be able to fully codify its nature, structure and facilitation. We have identified means of supporting and of eliciting this learning in the workplace, but traditional means of evaluating it such as by looking at transfer will not suffice. Future research is needed to continue to explore organizational support for informal learning, the role of technology in supporting and triggering this learning, strategies for assessing and evaluating informal learning, and cultures that promote informal learning. We have learned a great deal since our earlier exploration of this topic (Marsick and Watkins 1990), and yet have only discovered how much more there is to learn.

References

Ahmad, N. and Orton, P. (2010) "Smartphones make IBM smarter, but not as expected", *T+D* 64(1): 46–50.

Bersin, J. (2009) *Formalize informal learning: The Bersin and Associates Enterprise Learning Framework.* Saba-Bersin Associates Webcast, retrieved on 19 March 2010 from www.saba.com.

Billett, S. (2001) "Workplace affordances and individual engagement at work", *Journal of Workplace Learning* 31(5): 209–14.

— (2002) "Toward a workplace pedagogy: guidance, participation and engagement", *Adult Education Quarterly* 53(1): 27–43.

— (2004) "Workplace participatory practices: conceptualising workplaces as learning environments", *Journal of Workplace Learning* 16(6): 312–24.

Bingham, T. (2009) "Learning gets social", *T+D* 63(8): 56–61.

Colardyn, D. and Bjornavold, J. (2004) "Validation of formal, non-formal and informal learning: policy and practices in EU member states", *European Journal of Education* 39(1): 69–89.

Corporate Leadership Council (2004) "Global Leadership Development Programs", catalogue no. CLCI-IKEAZN, retrieved from http://www.corporateleadershipcouncil.com.

Cross, J. (2007) *Informal learning: Rediscovering the natural pathways that inspire innovation and performance*, San Francisco: Pfeiffer/Wiley.

Cseh, M., Watkins, K., and Marsick, V. (2000) "Informal and incidental learning in the workplace", in Straka, G. (ed.) *Concepts of self-directed learning*, Bremen: Waxmann, 59–74.

Dale, M., Bell, J. and Britain, G. (1999) *Informal learning in the workplace*, London: Department for Education and Employment.

Deci, E. and Ryan, R. (1997) "What is the self in self-directed learning? Findings from recent motivational research", in Straka, G.A. (ed.) *European views of self-directed learning: Historical, conceptual, empirical, practical, vocational*, Münster and New York: Waxmann.

Dewey, J. (1938) *Education and experience*, New York: Macmillan.

Doornbos, A.J., Simons, P.R.J. and Denessen, E. (2008) "Relations between characteristics of workplace practices and types of informal work-related learning: A survey study among Dutch police", *Human Resource Development Quarterly* 19(2): 129–51.

Ellinger, A.D. (2005) "Contextual factors influencing informal learning in a workplace setting: The case of 'reinventing itself company' ", *Human Resource Development Quarterly* 16(3): 389–415.

Ellinger, A.D. and Cseh, M. (2007) "Contextual factors influencing the facilitation of others' learning through everyday work experiences", *Journal of Workplace Learning* 19(7): 435–52.

Eraut, M. (2004) "Informal learning in the workplace", *Studies in Continuing Education* 26(2): 247–73.

European Commission (2001) *Making a European area of lifelong learning a reality*, Brussels: European Commission.

Felstead, A., Fuller, A., Jewson, N., and Unwin, L. (2009) *Improving working as learning*, London: Routledge.

Fuller, A., Ashton, D., Felstead, A., Unwin, L., Walters, S. and Quinn, M. (2003) *The impact of informal learning for work on business productivity*, Leicester: Center for Labour Market Studies, University of Leicester.

Gephart, M.A. and Marsick, V.J. (forthcoming) *Strategic Organizational Learning*, Berlin: Springer Verlag.

Lave, J. and Wenger, E. (1991) *Situated learning: Legitimate peripheral participation*, Boston, MA: Cambridge University Press.

Leslie, B., Aring, M.K. and Brand, B. (1998) "Informal learning: The new frontier of employee development and organizational development", *Economic Development Review* 15(4): 12–18.

Livingstone, D.W. (2001) *Adults' informal learning: Definitions, findings, gaps and future research*, Toronto: OISE.

Lohman, M.C. (2006) "Factors influencing teachers' engagement in informal learning activities", *Journal of Workplace Learning* 18(3): 141–56.

— (2009) "A survey of factors influencing the engagement of information technology professionals in informal learning activities", *Information Technology, Learning and Performance Journal* 25(1): 43–53.

Lowenstein, M. and Spletzer, J. (1994) *Informal training: A review of existing data and some new evidence*, Washington, DC: US Department of Labor, Bureau of Labor Statistics. http://www.bls.gov/ore/pdf/ec94009a.pdf.

Marsick, V.J. and Watkins, K.E. (1990) *Informal and incidental learning in the workplace*, London: Routledge.

— (2003) "Demonstrating the value of an organization's learning culture: the Dimensions of the Learning Organization Questionnaire", *Advances in Developing Human Resources* 5(2): 132–51.

Marsick, V., Watkins, K., Callahan, M. and Volpe, M. (2009) "Informal and incidental learning in the workplace", in Smith, M.C. and DeFrates-Densch, N. (eds) *Handbook of research on adult development and learning*, London: Routledge Press.

McCall, M.W., Lombardo, M. and Morrison, A. (1988) *Lessons of experience: How successful executives develop on the job*, New York: Free Press.

Mead, G.H. (1913) "The social self", *The Journal of Philosophy, Psychology and Scientific Methods* 10(14): 374–80.

Perrin, C. and Marsick, V. (2012) "The reinforcement revolution: How informal learning makes training real", Tampa, FL: AchieveGlobal.

Piaget, J. (1976) *Behaviour and Evolution* (trans. D. Nicholson Smith), New York: Pantheon Books.

Poell, R.F., Chivers, G.E., Van der Krogt, F.J. and Wildemeersch, D.A. (2000) "Learning-network theory: organizing the dynamic relationships between learning and work", *Management Learning* 31(1): 25–49.

Robert, S. (2006) *On demand learning: Blended learning for today's evolving workforce* (Presentation based on IBM white paper).

Scheeres, H., Solomon, N., Boud, D., and Rooney, D. (2010) "When is it OK to learn at work? The learning work of organizational practices", *Journal of Workplace Learning* 22(1/2): 13–26.

Schön, D.A. (1983) *The reflective practitioner: How professionals think in action*, New York: Basic Books.

Skule, S. (2004) "Learning conditions at work: a framework to understand and assess informal learning in the workplace", *International Journal of Training and Development* 8(1): 8–20.

Vygotsky, L.S. (1978) *Mind as action*, New York: Oxford University Press.

Watkins, K.E. and Marsick, V.J. (1993) *Sculpting the learning organization*, San Francisco: Jossey-Bass.

Watkins, K.E. and Cervero, R.M. (2000) "Organizations as contexts for learning: A case study in certified public accountancy", *Journal of Workplace Learning* 12(5): 187–94.

Watkins, K.E. and Marsick, V.J. (2003) "Summing up: demonstrating the value of an organization's learning culture", *Advances in Developing Human Resources* 5(2): 129–31.

Watkins, K.E. and O'Neil, J.A. (2013) "The Dimensions of the Learning Organization Questionnaire (the DLOQ): A nontechnical manual", *Advances in Developing Human Resources* 15(2): 1–15.

Watkins, K.E. and Dirani, K. (in press) "A meta-analysis of The Dimensions of the Learning Organization Questionnaire: Looking across cultures, ranks, and industries", in Watkins, K.E., Dirani, K. and Marsick, V.J. (eds) *Advances in Developing Human Resources.*

23

COMMUNITIES OF PRACTICE AND VALUE CREATION IN NETWORKS

Maarten de Laat, Bieke Schreurs and Femke Nijland

In this chapter we will focus on communities of practice (CoPs) and their impact on the appreciation of informal professional development in organizations. Our perspective on informal professional development is participation-based, situated in shared work practices. We will first explain how this perspective is rooted in the idea of CoPs. We will then discuss how recent organizational developments such as 'new ways of working' (NWOW – see Chapter 47 in this volume) and the use of social media change the organizational landscape into open practices where professionals work, learn and innovate. These emerging open practices stimulate critical reflections about the meaning of CoPs, shifting our ideas to a more dynamic perspective coined as networks of practice (NoPs). In light of these developments we will reflect on the challenges that communities face and how they balance dealing with increased openness, networking and demonstrating the value they create.

Communities of practice

The concept of CoP is perceived by many as one of the most influential and most quoted concepts in social sciences since Jean Lave and Etienne Wenger's book on situated learning (1991). In this book Lave and Wenger (1991) described a CoP as a group of people who share a craft or a profession. Wenger (1998) states that members of a community are informally bound by what they do together and by what they have learned through their mutual engagement in these activities. The shared activities are embedded in a historical and social context that gives structure and meaning to what they do. These people do not necessarily work together every day, but they meet regularly. They learn informally from each other through a process of Legitimate Peripheral Participation (LPP). LPP refers to a learning process where communities offer new members the opportunity to participate in community activities and thereby gradually become a core member. The central issue of LPP is about becoming a practitioner, not about learning about practice.

This approach draws attention away from taught abstract knowledge, transferred through formal education or refreshment courses, and situates knowledge into the practices of informal communities. Wenger (1998) argues that, despite the variety in forms of CoPs, they all share a basic structure. A CoP can be viewed as a unique combination of three fundamental elements: a *domain* of knowledge, which defines a set of issues, creates a common ground and a sense of common identity; a *community* of people who foster interactions and relationships based on mutual respect and trust, and who care about this domain; and a shared *practice* they are developing with a set of frameworks, ideas, tools, styles, language, stories, and documents that community members share.

CoPs fulfill a number of functions with respect to the creation, accumulation, and diffusion of knowledge in organizations (Wenger *et al.* 2002):

- They are nodes for the *exchange and interpretation of information.* Because members have a shared understanding, they know what is relevant to communicate and how to present information in useful ways. Because of the shared understanding and the interpersonal relationships, they feel trusted and valued. The members also know precisely which person in the group has the expertise that they need in case of a specific problem.
- They can *retain knowledge* in 'living' ways, unlike a database or a manual. A CoP preserves the tacit aspects of knowledge that formal systems cannot capture. For this reason, they are ideal for initiating newcomers into a practice.
- They can *steward competencies* to keep the organization at the cutting edge. Members of these groups discuss novel ideas, work together on problems, and keep up with developments inside and outside a firm. They can easily keep up with or push new developments.
- They provide *homes for identities.* Identity is important because, in a sea of information, it helps us sort out what we pay attention to, what to participate in, and what to avoid. Having a sense of identity is a crucial aspect of learning in organizations, and it entails a sense of belonging. This identity also specifies the boundaries of the community.

The CoP theory of learning informally through participation, apprenticeship and shared practices had a huge impact, both as a conceptual lens to perceive situated learning, and to refer to communities as a social structure that facilitates professional development (Cox 2005).

Communities of practice and professional development

Theory on CoPs influenced the approach to professional development in organizations. The concept of CoP, which was intended as a description of a phenomenon that occurred in everyday practice, became a medium to organize professional development and was treated as such in organizations (Davenport and Prusak 1998; Van Winkelen and Ramsell 2003; Lee and Oh 2013). The benefits of CoPs were discussed in Wenger *et al.*'s (2002) second book on the subject, making the shift from describing to prescribing. They argued that CoPs can be a medium for generating, developing, and distributing new knowledge throughout an organization because they create a safe environment for their members.

These ideas have been developed further resulting in a growing body of research and a wide range of managerial tools and consultancy websites (cf. Barton and Tusting 2005; Blackmore 2010; Hughes *et al.* 2013). In a review study on the implications of CoPs on professional development Lee and Oh (2013) claim that many researchers concluded that CoPs can be very beneficial for organizational performance. At the same time researchers start to criticize the implementation of CoPs as a medium for professional development (Hughes *et al.* 2013). They argue that the concept is under pressure by new developments that organizations face. Professionals and organizations, in the current climate of the knowledge and network society, need to adapt and develop quickly. This means that they need to operate in a constantly changing and evolving setting, which requires flexibility, networking and ad hoc collaboration. Based on these reflections we will discuss a number of critical assumptions about CoPs below.

Are CoPs too semi-formal?

Theory on CoPs had a big influence on research investigating and understanding how to enable professional development in organizations. But it also challenged ideas on how to manage professional development. If we place professional development in the midst of professional practice, we assume that the professional has enough autonomy to regulate his or her own learning. CoPs provide professionals with an informal space where they can meet their peers who share a similar interest and passion for their work.

Although the concept of CoPs challenged the general top-down approach towards professional development, the culture of learning and knowledge management styles within organizations usually did not change. This situation resulted in CoPs often becoming an addition to the organization's array of more formal forms of stimulating professional development (Zboralski *et al.* 2004). In these semi-formal CoPs, management decides which communities are allowed, who should join, how often face-to-face meetings should occur, what technology should be used, and what the criteria of success should be (Cox 2005).

To give way to CoPs in organizations we need an improved theory of professional development by changing its metaphors (Büchel and Raub 2002; Hodkinson and Hodkinson 2005; Hargreaves and Fullan 2012). Boud and Hager (2012) put emphasis on the fact that professional development is an on-going process driven by needs that emerge in daily practice. They emphasize terms like organic growth, evolution, gradual unfolding, and see professional development as a process of becoming, where professionals continuously develop their own identity and abilities in response to events in their professional environment. In their view (Boud and Hager 2012: 22):

> Learning is a normal part of working, and indeed, of most other social activities. It occurs through practice in work settings from addressing the challenges and problems that arise. Most learning takes place not through formalized activities but through the exigencies of practice with peers and others, drawing on expertise that is accessed in response to need. Problem-solving in which participants tackle challenges that progressively extend their existing capabilities and where they learn with and from each other appears to be a common and frequent form of naturalistic development.

Boud and Hager's statement reads as a strong plea for placing professional development in a social context where professionals work and learn together, changing and innovating both their professional practice as well as who they are. Enabling this perspective on professional development involves being in touch with one's professional colleagues, building the networked connections needed to participate in constructive professional dialogues about what it means to become a professional.

Professionals in demanding jobs especially are often faced with complex issues and Lohman (2006) found that they rely on others to a great extent to solve work-related problems. Although professionals may be informed about new approaches individually during training workshops, it is through their informal social networks with colleagues that they learn how to interpret, embrace, share, compile, contextualize and sustain this new knowledge (Rikowski 2007; Baker-Doyle and Yoon 2010). These ideas require organizations to review their approach to informal professional development and to try not to plan and control semi-formal CoPs but provide enough professional autonomy for CoPs and networks to develop and produce value.

Are communities too robust to cope with increased openness?

Recent developments in our networked society take the need to stimulate professionals to participate in social networks even further. Organizations today are realizing that opportunities for growth, development and innovation lie outside the boundaries of their own organization. To tap into this productive potential they are looking for ways to integrate these ideas into their core processes. One strategy is setting up competitions where people can win a prize for submitting their ideas. Another approach for generating ideas is crowdsourcing, where the services of a large group of people are sought. Another recent development is NWOW: promoting open workspaces to improve interaction and to increase flexibility and professional autonomy (cf. Chapter 47). These developments in combination with the use of social media have given rise to more openness in organizational practices, making employees less constrained by boundaries that would otherwise impede knowledge sharing. Open practices have always occurred informally, used by freelancers as well as employees; however, nowadays technological platforms and NWOW enable professionals to connect with their peers with greater ease, at a larger scale and on a continual basis.

Open practices consist of networks that are collections of individuals who come together across organizational, spatial and disciplinary boundaries to create and share a body of knowledge. The focus of such networks is usually on developing, distributing and applying knowledge (Pugh and Prusak 2013). According to Pugh and Prusak (2013), organizations of all sizes are seizing on this model to learn more quickly and collaborate productively. Network members come together around a common goal and share social and operational norms. Members typically participate out of common interest and shared purpose rather than because of contract, quid pro quo or hierarchy. They are not bound by shared identities and do not retain knowledge and meaning in the way that CoPs do. The relationship between the different members is much more loose and dynamic, yet is effective in the creation of new ideas.

These new patterns of social relationships are not well maintained by CoPs according to Engeström (2013). His critique on CoPs is based on the fact that CoP theory failed to include a historical perspective on the development of organizations and professional development strategies. He argues that CoPs could be established in earlier conditions where groups were more local, closer and directed centrally, but that these conditions are increasingly less present in today's work practices.

Wenger (1998) shows how professionals organize their lives with their immediate colleagues, peers and customers in CoPs to get their jobs done, and how within this community the rules of the working game are set: how to do the job and how to do it more efficiently. When these rules about performing a practice are the core business of a CoP, one might however expect that a CoP is reluctant about changing the way things are done in the group, or the practice members work in. We might expect that a CoP does not allow for adaptation that results in a radical change of its routines (Hoeve *et al.* 2003). Therefore, we should take into account the notion that CoPs are by nature conservative and therefore could obstruct the innovation or organizational learning needed in current open practices. Much of the research and practice around CoPs has focused on establishing the core of these communities and developing skills and competencies to participate in them (Admiraal *et al.* 2012). While the focus has been on the community building efforts, Wenger's (1998) important notion on boundary crossing and the ability of CoPs to constantly negotiate their practices has largely been ignored.

Participation in open practices is increasingly seen by professionals as a requirement for professional development. Current research in career development (Van den Born and Van Witteloostuijn 2013) stresses that for professional freelancers the ability to join networks is critical to their own development as well as to make the most of intellectual and other resources people have to 'offer' (McMillan and Gunther-McGrath 2000). These open practices offer professionals a more dynamic 'platform' than CoPs do, to stay abreast in a rapidly changing profession by connecting with relevant peers that can help them further. Such NoPs exemplify open practices as they are dispersed across geographical and organizational boundaries, informal and self-directed by nature, and disentangled from hierarchy.

Do CoPs forget the role of the individual professional?

Where CoPs provided a relatively stable social environment, providing access to a shared repertoire and history, open practices behave on a more fluid basis, providing a (temporal) space for collaboration, where professionals come and go, based on their needs. Herein we follow the idea of Billett and Choy (2013), who stress the role of professionals as self-directed agents in responding to the learning affordances they encounter and perceive in the workplace. Individuals bring with them their personal attitudes, experiences and identities that are embedded within their personal NoPs. Therefore Billett and Choy (2013) claim that the nature of the relationship between the individual and the social is symbiotic (mutual). This notion is emphasized by networked individualism (Wellman 2002).

According to Wellman (2002), networked individualism emphasizes the point that professionals have a great ability to act on their own, to solve their problems and organize their lives, but they do this in a networked way, with the help of their friends and other relationships. In other words, our social space has expanded immensely and has opened up to increase social participation by others. The importance of being networked is an aspect that most communities need to emphasize more strongly.

Balancing communities and networks of practice

We should avoid choosing one social structure above the other, as both communities and networks have much to offer for informal professional development. Wenger *et al.* (2011) point out that communities and networks are two aspects of the same social structure. The value of networking lies in having access to a rich web of information sources offering multiple perspectives and dialogues, response to queries, and help from others – whether this access is initiated by the professional or by others. On the one hand, this is because of individual connections; networking helps to target access to resources. On the other hand, it is because information flows can be picked up, interpreted, and propagated in unexpected ways; they traverse networks with a high level of spontaneity and unpredictability.

This potential for spontaneous connections and serendipity is a key aspect of the value of networks for learning and professional development. From a developmental perspective, the coexistence of the community and network aspect suggests two types of cultivation work for those who endeavor to foster professional development. The work of community is to develop the learning partnership that creates an identity around an area for learning as well as to develop a collective sense of trust and commitment. The work of network is to optimize the connectivity among people by strengthening existing connections and enabling new connections. Community and network are distinct as processes of social structuring but they are not opposite; they often develop together (Wenger *et al.* 2011).

Value creation by communities and networks in open practices

We have claimed that CoPs as a medium for professional development need to be revisited based on recent trends changing the organizational landscape. These circumstances are characterized by 'fluidity', implying that membership, interests, social relations and aims are constantly fluctuating and evolving depending on the resources available (Faraj *et al.* 2011). We acknowledge that this new concept could raise tensions for professionals and organizations in the ability to monitor, utilize and integrate the knowledge created in such practices as well as to demonstrate their value. While fluidity ensures alignment to the interests and needs of the professionals involved, learning may also easily dissipate, become fragmented, or even come to a hold (Faraj *et al.* 2011).

Being able to deal with these fluctuations challenges some of the fundamentals of the CoP, that is, the existence of a shared history and repertoire through joint enterprises. Although the social structure and context might be constantly changing, it will be the participants of these open practices who are the carriers of value and it will be their stories that can tie professionals together. Wenger *et al.* (2011) developed a framework that offers room both for structured information sharing and for history and context. They proposed a framework that perceives professional development as a process of value creation. Communities and networks have stories – how they started, what happened since. It is within the context of these stories that we can appreciate the learning that takes place and what value is created. The details of these stories are illustrative of how professionals have learned to question what was taken for granted in their lives, to find patterns and connections, and to think critically and creatively (Beattie 2000).

The value creation framework (Wenger *et al.* 2011) is a means to appreciate value created in communities and networks. As every storytelling genre, this framework follows a particular format. In order to appreciate the richness of these stories the value creation framework introduces several cycles each with its own description of value and a set of indicators. The concept 'cycle' stresses the absence of hierarchy between the types of value.

- Cycle 1, *Immediate* value: Activities can have value in and of themselves. They can be fun and inspiring. But value can also include meeting someone, getting an address, connecting, asking a question to the network, passing a piece of information along or giving input.
- Cycle 2, *Potential* value: Not all value is immediately realized. Activities and interactions can produce 'knowledge capital', whose value lies in its potential to be realized later. This knowledge capital can consist of personal assets, like a piece of information or a skill, relationships and connections as social capital, resources like documents and tools, collective intangible assets like the reputation of the network, and finally, transformed ability to learn, the learning capital.
- Cycle 3, *Applied* value: Looking at applied value means identifying the ways in which practice has changed in the process of leveraging knowledge capital, like re-using a previously developed plan or a piece of code or changing a procedure.
- Cycle 4, *Realized* value: In some cases changed practice can lead to improved performance. Reflecting on what effects the application of knowledge is having on the achievement of what matters to stakeholders can lead to the distinguishing of realized value.
- Cycle 5, *Reframing* value: When social learning causes a reconsideration of the learning imperatives and the criteria by which success is defined, value is reframed.

The following provides an example of a value creation story as proposed by Wenger *et al.* (2011). It is the story of Wendy (cf. Nijland and Van Amersfoort 2013), a 6th grade teacher and school leader who was in search of a new method for teaching English as a foreign language (EFL) for her pupils. The story illustrates how learning can be perceived as a process of value creation, in which the learning not only benefits the professional involved, but also the stakeholders in her organization.

The story of Wendy and her English teaching method

Wendy was searching for a new EFL teaching method, when she joined a bi-monthly meeting with other school leaders from different schools in her region. These meetings were originally installed by its members to discuss matters that concerned running schools and their own personal development. Wendy always enjoys these meetings and usually leaves energized and inspired. To Wendy, this time the meeting was also a nice opportunity to ask around which methods were used at other schools. Her colleagues were happy to help and shared their experiences with different methods. One of the network members even mentioned that he heard there was an EFL method that started in kindergarten.

That remark was the start of a debate on the pros and cons of teaching English to very young children. On the one hand the teachers argued that students learn new languages much easier from an early age on; on the other hand, however, they argued that the pressure on young children was already quite large. Wendy: 'I tended to agree with the latter. However, I was intrigued by the idea. I decided to study the matter further.'

Wendy searched for more information on the internet and found studies on English for young children which changed her perspective radically. The studies indicated that learning a second language at an early age usually does not pressure children; rather, their age provides them with the ability to learn quite naturally, saving them from pressure later on. Wendy got convinced that EFL in kindergarten would be an excellent method for her school. She introduced her idea at the board meeting of her school. And, after reading the articles she found, her colleagues got as excited as Wendy. A few months later, the new method was introduced, resulting in 200 children learning English in a new way, costing them less effort and providing them with more fluency than otherwise would have been the case.

This story shows that Wendy is not just a teacher and a school leader, she is an educational professional. She participates in a network of people with the same interests, who come together across organizational and spatial boundaries to discuss what it means to be a professional and in this dialogue share and construct knowledge. Her network of colleagues can therefore be perceived as an open practice: the members join together voluntarily out of shared interest, work together and solve problems. When Wendy met with her colleagues, asking around to find a solution to her problem was the obvious thing to do, the way professionals rely on others to resolve work-related problems (Lohman 2006). And as the story of Wendy shows, the members were more than happy to discuss a topic contributed by one of them, simply because it interested them.

The story of Wendy is a value creation story, and as such illustrates the five cycles of value. The fact that Wendy experiences her network meetings as energizing and inspiring, realizes *immediate value*. The fact that Wendy felt she could ask around for experiences with teaching methods illustrates the *potential value* of her network. Her connections were social capital: a source of information ready to be tapped when needed. The discussion that followed after she asked for experiences can also be considered *potential value*, as could the remark concerning EFL in kindergarten. That key remark resulted in Wendy's search for more information through other channels, realizing more *potential value*, which eventually led to her changed perspective on the matter: *reframing value*. This changed perspective sparked Wendy to discuss the new method in the board meeting of her school, hereby changing a practice in the school, realizing *applied value*. With their agreement, the new method was installed, again realizing *applied value*. And finally, the students who experience an improved performance feel the *realized value*.

It is interesting to see how value is created in these open practices. In many respects it is a very serendipitous process. Wendy's story shows how information flows traverse unpredictably: a casual remark made by someone in her network resulted in a new perspective on student learning for Wendy and a new method that benefitted the entire school. However, from another perspective it was not coincidental at all. The fact that Wendy made her question explicit in the open practice she engaged in and the fact that her colleagues made their experiences and knowledge explicit, resulted in the creation of value. Making experiences, knowledge and therefore stories explicit is a crucial element in creating value among professionals in open practices.

Future research

The approach to informal professional development presented here encourages participation where learning is seen as open, situated, embedded, and maintained in the daily culture of open practices (Lave and Wenger 1991). These practices concern not only the practice within the organization. Participation also means involvement with a larger, perhaps even global landscape of connected NoPs (Teigland 2003). This perspective gives rise to a more bottom-up, self-governing culture of learning in organizations where informal networks have experiences, knowledge, and contacts, providing each other with access to new and alternative resources. We believe that in organizations these communities and networks are connected and encouraged to grow only to a limited extent. Innovative professional development policies can increase opportunities for professionals to share their expertise, learn from their peers, and collaborate in open practices (Price 2013). An important issue that needs to be investigated is the tension that will arise concerning the term openness. Increasingly organizations are discovering that many of the very best ideas lie outside their organizations, in an ecosystem of potential innovations that possess wide-ranging skills and knowledge. Instead of doing everything in-house, organizations can tap into the ideas cloud of external expertise to develop new products and services. To discover and attract these contributors, organizations are launching competitions and offering prizes. But how will organizations cope with the tension between openness, copyright and privacy and what attitudes and competencies steward productive networking in open practices? The success of open practices is also dependent on raising awareness about the existence of these informal communities and networks and an appreciation of their value. To get more insight into them and how they cross organizational boundaries, more research is needed to understand how they are used by professionals and how they change over time. Finally, although we have already presented an example of a framework to tap into the value of communities and networks, more research is needed to understand how value creation stories function in open practices and how they can be utilized by professionals and organizations.

References

Admiraal, W., Lockhorst, D. and Van der Pol, J. (2012) An expert study of a descriptive model of teacher communities. *Learning Environments Research 15*(3): 345–61.

Baker-Doyle, K.J. and Yoon, S.A. (2010) Making expertise transparent: Using technology to strengthen social networks in teacher professional development. In Daly, A.J. (ed.) *Social Network Theory and Educational Change* (115–27). Cambridge, MA: Harvard Education Press.

Barton, D. and Tusting, K. (eds) (2005) *Beyond Communities of Practice: Language Power and Social Context.* Cambridge, MA: Cambridge University Press.

Beattie, V.A. (2000) The future of corporate reporting: A review article. *Irish Accounting Review* 7(1): 1–36.

Billett, S. and Choy, S. (2013) Learning through work: Emerging perspectives and new challenges. *Journal of Workplace Learning* 25(4): 264–76.

Blackmore, C. (ed.) (2010) *Social Learning Systems and Communities of Practice.* Dordrecht: Springer.

Boud, D. and Hager, P. (2012) Re-thinking continuing professional development through changing metaphors and location in professional practices. *Studies in Continuing Education* 34(1): 17–30.

Büchel, B. and Raub, S. (2002) Building knowledge-creating value networks. *European Management Journal* 20(6): 587–96.

Cox, A.M. (2005) What are communities of practice? A comparative review of four seminal works. *Journal of Information Science* 31(6): 527–40.

Davenport, T.H. and Prusak, L. (1998) *Working Knowledge: Managing What Your Organization Knows.* Boston, MA: Harvard Business School Press.

Engeström, Y. (2013) From communities of practice to mycorrhizae. In Hughes, J., Jewson, N. and Unwin, L. (eds) *Communities of Practice: Critical Perspectives* (52–66). London: Routledge.

Faraj, S., Jarvenpaa, S.L. and Majchrzak, A. (2011) Knowledge collaboration in online communities. *Organization Science* 22(5): 1224–39.

Hargreaves, A. and Fullan, M. (2012) *Professional Capital: Transforming Teaching in Every School.* New York: Teachers College Press.

Hodkinson, H. and Hodkinson, P. (2005) Improving schoolteachers' workplace learning. *Research Papers in Education* 20(2): 109–31.

Hoeve, A., Mittendorf, K. and Nieuwenhuis, A.F.M. (2003) *The interface between learning and innovation: Building a conceptual model.* Paper presented at the Third International Conference of Researching Work and Learning, held in Tampere, Finland, 1 January 2003.

Hughes, J., Jewson, N. and Unwin, L. (eds) (2013) *Communities of Practice: Critical Perspectives.* London: Routledge.

Lave, J. and Wenger, E. (1991) *Situated Learning: Legitimate Peripheral Participation.* Cambridge, MA: Cambridge University Press.

Lee, H.S. and Oh, J.R. (2013) A conceptual model for community of practice and its implications for human resource development practice. *Learning and Performance Quarterly* 2(1): 14–29.

Lohman, M.C. (2006) Factors influencing teachers' engagement in informal learning activities. *Journal of Workplace Learning* 18(3): 141–56.

McMillan, I.C. and Gunther-McGrath, R. (2000) *The Entrepreneurial Mindset: Strategies for Continuously Creating Opportunity in an Age of Uncertainty.* Cambridge, MA: Harvard Business School Press.

Nijland, F. and Van Amersfoort, D. (2013) Waardecreatieverhalen: wat levert netwerkleren op? [Value creation stories: What does networked learning yield?] In De Kruif, R., De Laat, M., Simons, R.J. and Zuylen, J. (eds) *Netwerkleren, de stille kracht achter een leven lang professionaliseren* [Networked learning: The silent force behind lifelong professionalization]. Tilburg: MesoConsult.

Price, D. (2013) *Open: How We'll Work, Live and Learn in the Future.* Kindle Edition.

Pugh, K. and Prusak, L. (2013) *Designing Effective Knowledge Networks.* Retrieved 24 October 2013 from http://sloanreview.mit.edu/article/designing-effective-knowledge-networks.

Rikowski, R. (ed.) (2007) *Knowledge Management: Social, Cultural and Theoretical Perspectives.* Oxford: Chandos.

Teigland, R. (2003) *Knowledge Networking: Structure and Performance in Networks of Practice* (Doctoral dissertation). Retrieved 24 October 2013 from http://hhs.diva-portal.org/smash/get/diva2:573817/FULLTEXT01.

Van den Born, A. and Van Witteloostuijn, A. (2013) Drivers of freelance career success. *Journal of Organizational Behavior* 34(1): 24–46.

Van Winkelen, C. and Ramsell, P. (2003) Why aligning value is key to designing communities. *Knowledge Management Review* 5(6): 12–15.

Wellman, B. (2002) Little boxes, glocalization, and networked individualism. In Tanabe, M., Van den Besselaar, P. and Ishida, T. (eds) *Digital Cities II. Computational and Sociological Approaches* (10–25). Berlin: Springer.

Wenger, E. (1998) *Communities of Practice: Learning, Meaning and Identity.* Cambridge, MA: Cambridge University Press.

Wenger, E., McDermott, R. and Snyder, W.M. (2002) *Cultivating Communities of Practice.* Boston, MA: Harvard Business School Press.

Wenger, E., Trayner, B. and De Laat, M. (2011) *Promoting and Assessing Value Creation in Communities and Networks: A Conceptual Framework.* Retrieved 24 October 2013 from http://www.bevtrayner.com/base/docs/Wenger_Trayner_DeLaat_Value_creation.pdf.

Zboralski, K., Gemuenden, H.G. and Lettl, C. (2004) *A Member's Perspective on the Success of Communities of Practice: Preliminary Empirical Results.* Paper presented at the Fifth European Conference on Organizational Knowledge, Learning and Capabilities, held in Innsbruck, Austria.

24
COACHING AND MENTORING[1]

Andrea D. Ellinger

Coaching and mentoring are powerful developmental interventions that have become increasingly prevalent in workplace contexts. An expansive and growing base of practitioner and academic literature on these two concepts exists across many fields such as business, nursing, and education suggesting their multidisciplinary nature (Cox 2012, Eby *et al.* 2007, Ghosh 2012, Haggard *et al.* 2011, Hezlett and Gibson 2005). These concepts began appearing in the literature in the 1950s, 1970s and 1980s respectively (Evered and Selman 1989, Hezlett and Gibson 2005). However, with regard to coaching, Cox (2012: 1) has acknowledged that "the research underpinning it is notably sparse." Similarly, while knowledge on mentoring is maturing, "the literature on mentoring is still fairly young" (Hezlett and Gibson 2005: 447) and "workplace mentoring is a relatively new focus of study" (Allen *et al.* 2008).

The International Coach Federation's global coaching study (2012) suggests that coaching is a 1.9 million USD industry with over 47,000 professional coaches operating worldwide. Further, the Chartered Institute of Personnel and Development (CIPD) surveys of learning and development (2006, 2007) have reported considerable activity being undertaken in organizations to build internal coaching capability. Thurston *et al.* (2012) acknowledge that more than one-third of major US corporations offer formal mentoring programs and Egan and Song (2008: 351) note that "findings from studies on mentoring participation indicate that up to two-thirds of employees have engaged in some type of mentoring relationship."

Several trends within work organizations are influencing the demand for coaching and mentoring and placing them in the forefront in terms of research and practice in the HRD field. Increasingly, individuals are being challenged to assume responsibility for and ownership of their learning and development at work. This suggests the importance of identifying learning partners that can help them grow and develop. The composition of the multigenerational workforce, employment contracts, conceptions of careers, and mobility underscore the need for individuals to remain current with their skills, knowledge, and abilities within a competitive and turbulent global economy. Lastly, the infusion of technology is changing the nature of learning and work and how such learning and work can be accomplished.

Therefore, given the considerable growth and importance of coaching and mentoring in the workplace, the purpose of this chapter is to define and overview these concepts. The chapter highlights some of the relevant research on coaching, managerial coaching, and mentoring. It specifically discusses trends, issues, and global perspectives related to managerial coaching and mentoring. Lastly, directions for future research on these concepts relative to HRD are offered.

Coaching

Within the context of HRD, McLagan (1996) considered coaching to be an important competency and role of human resource professionals. Similarly, ASTD identified coaching as an area of expertise among workplace learning and performance specialists in their 2004 competency framework and it remains a foundational competency in the 2013 framework. However, with frontline supervisors and managers becoming increasingly responsible for performing many human resource management (HRM) and HRD functions, exploring the concept of the manager as coach is both relevant and necessary within the HRD field.

Defining coaching and types of coaching

There is currently no universally accepted definition of coaching with over 36 definitions identified in the literature (Cox 2012, Hamlin *et al.* 2009). Some definitions refer to coaching in general, whereas other definitions are more specifically labeled as executive, business, and life coaching (Hamlin *et al.* 2009). Similarly, Grant (2008) identifies three types of coaching: executive, workplace, and life coaching. Maycunich Gilley *et al.* (2010) suggest that coaching might be an activity, a function, or a process. A traditional orientation of coaching, to remedy poor performance, is focused on improving problem work performance (Fournies 1987). In contrast, current conceptualizations of coaching embrace developmental and empowerment perspectives and suggest that coaching is a process "by which one individual, the coach, creates enabling relationships with others that make it easier for them to learn" (Mink *et al.* 1993: 2). Sue-Chan *et al.* (2012) consider coaching to be a developmental practice that is a goal-directed interaction between the coach and coachee, a way of relating and communicating with others, and reflects what leaders, managers and others do when interacting with employees on a daily basis to enhance their performance. Ellinger *et al.* (2011: 73) define coaching as "a helping and facilitative process that enables individuals, groups/teams and organisations to acquire new skills, to improve existing skills, competence and performance, and to enhance their personal effectiveness or personal development or personal growth." More recently, Cox (2012: 1) defines coaching as "a facilitated, dialogic, reflective learning process."

Based upon the types of coaching identified, it is evident that coaching can be delivered by "coaches who work in the organization as either line managers or human resource professionals (internal coaches) or by coaches/consultants brought in from the outside (external coaches)" (Gray and Goregaokar 2010: 526). The process of coaching, depending upon the delivery mechanism, can be formal and contractual or highly informal and woven into the daily jobs of managers as they interact with their employees to develop them, facilitate their learning, and improve their performance.

Managerial coaching skills, behaviors, and outcomes

The skills often associated with coaching include listening, analyzing, interviewing, effective questioning, and observing (Graham *et al.* 1993, 1994, Orth *et al.* 1987). Maycunich Gilley *et al.* (2010) suggest that effective coaches have highly developed interpersonal skills. McLean *et al.*'s (2005) model of a self-assessment of coaching skills for managers indicates that managers should communicate openly, take a team approach with tasks, value people over tasks, and should embrace the often ambiguous nature of the work setting. Responding to Peterson and Little's (2005) critique about coaching reflecting a typically one-on-one intervention and the other skills that are considered necessary for coaching, Park *et al.* (2008) added a component related to facilitating development. A growing number of empirical studies have used this assessment and have found that managerial coaching skills positively influence employees' personal learning, organizational learning, and turnover intentions (Park *et al.* 2008). Hagen's (2010) and Hagen and Aguilar's (2012) research has linked managerial coaching skill with project management outcomes in a Six Sigma context, as well as team learning outcomes within a work team context respectively.

Behaviors

While possessing skills to coach is important, translating such skills into behaviors that enable one to coach is necessary. A number of empirical studies have identified the behaviors that are often associated with managers who coach their employees including the provision of feedback, setting clear expectations, and creating trusting relationships (Graham *et al.* 1993). Ellinger (1997) and Ellinger and Bostrom's (1999) research resulted in a taxonomy of behaviors that included 13 empowering and facilitating behaviors. Empowering behaviors include: question framing to promote critical thinking among employees, being a resource, transferring ownership to employees, holding back and not providing answers to employees. Facilitating behaviors include: providing feedback, soliciting feedback, working it out together and talking things through, creating and promoting learning. Similarly, Beattie's (2002) research identified 22 effective facilitative behaviors that she subsequently classified into nine behavioral categories: thinking, informing, empowering, assessing, advising, being professional, caring, developing others, and challenging employees. Additionally, comparisons among these two taxonomies have revealed congruency among these managerial coaching behaviors (see Hamlin *et al.* 2006). Other research has offered support for these behaviors (Amy 2005, Longenecker and Neubert 2005, Noer 2005).

Outcomes

Many positive outcomes have been associated with coaching that include learning, improved performance, higher levels of motivation, job satisfaction, enhanced working relationships, and organization commitment (Anonymous 2001). Although research on managerial coaching is considered under-developed, a growing base of empirical research has begun to examine the impact of managerial coaching (Agarwal *et al.* 2009, Hagen 2012).

For example, Ellinger *et al.* (2003) found that supervisors' coaching behaviors, even at low to moderate levels were significantly related to employees' job satisfaction and performance. Hannah's (2004) study in the British Rail context, found that employees who received coaching experienced improvement in their competency, which also had impacts on increased customer service satisfaction among passengers. In Elmadag *et al.*'s (2008) research, coaching had a stronger influence on employees' commitment to service quality than formal training or rewarding interventions.

Agarwal *et al.*'s (2009) multilevel examination of the effects of managers' coaching intensity on employee performance found significant positive relationships suggesting support for this type of developmental approach. More recently, Wang's research in the Taiwanese context (2012) found that managerial coaching and specific HRM approaches moderated relationships between R and D employees' characteristics and innovative behavior. Kim *et al.* (2013) examined employees' perceptions of managerial coaching behavior and several work-related outcomes in a South Korean public organization. Findings indicate that managerial coaching had a direct impact on employees' satisfaction with their work and their role clarity, and an indirect impact on career and organization commitment and performance. Although they do acknowledge culture-based concerns about managerial coaching in this high power distance culture, coaching behavior was apparently practiced by managers and enhanced employee outcomes.

Trends, issues, and global perspectives

Despite the potential benefits identified, and the trends suggesting that managers will assume roles as coaches, managerial coaching occurs infrequently because challenges accompany embracing this important developmental role (Maycunich Gilley *et al.* 2010). Managers often lack the skills needed to coach their employees, may not have the time, be recognized, rewarded or compensated, or may not find that the culture of the organization supports coaching. Hutchinson and Purcell (2007) suggest that organizational leaders need to ensure that an infrastructure is created that supports managers serving as coaches. Their research also suggests that supportive conditions should include building a language of learning and development and creating a culture that values development, along with ensuring that managers are sufficiently developed to be effective coaches.

Although a predominantly Western construct, a more comprehensive understanding of managerial coaching in other cultural contexts is needed given the vital role that managers play in work organizations (Kim *et al.* 2013). Lastly, managers may also be recipients of coaching from their employees when engaged in this dyadic process. Therefore the notion of upward or reverse managerial coaching and the exploration of managers' development through coaching are additional areas that warrant attention (Gomez and Gunn 2012).

Mentoring

Hezlett and Gibson (2005) acknowledge that few mentoring articles have appeared within the HRD literature. Their review sought to examine mentoring through the core domains of HRD (training and development, career development, and organization development) and to provide directions for future research and practice for HRD professionals. The Gibson and Hezlett (2005) special issue on mentoring has stimulated research and has situated mentoring more firmly within the HRD field. Mentoring has more recently been conceived as "a human resource development (HRD) tool in organizations" (Ghosh 2012: 1), as "a widely used HRD program in the corporate world" (Thurston *et al.* 2012: 139), and an organization development intervention (Cummings and Worley 2009).

Defining mentoring, core functions, and types of mentoring

Like coaching, more than 40 definitions of mentoring exist which has created conceptual confusion in research (Ghosh 2012, Higgins and Kram 2001, Haggard *et al.* 2011). Traditional forms of mentoring represent an intense one-on-one relationship between a more senior, experienced, and knowledgeable person (mentor) and a lesser experienced person (the protégé or mentee) which is focused on providing guidance, support and development within the career context (Chao *et al.* 1992, Eby *et al.* 2007, Horvath *et al.* 2008, Kram 1985, Wanberg *et al.* 2003). More recent conceptions of mentoring draw upon a developmental network perspective and suggest that there are multiple relationship constellations (Higgins and Kram 2001).

Mentors can be peers, supervisors, and more senior leaders either within or outside of the protégé's organization. Core functions provided by mentors typically include career development and psychosocial assistance. Within these functions, sponsorship, exposure, visibility, coaching, challenging assignments and role modeling, confirmation, counseling and friendship have been identified respectively (Chao *et al.* 1992). Scandura (1992) conceived of role modeling as a third function. Ghosh's (2012) review also included protecting, parenting, and motivation/inspiration as mentoring functions provided within a business context.

Informal and formal mentoring have been identified as mentoring types, along with an array of alternative forms of mentoring (Eby 1997, Egan and Song 2008). Informal mentoring often refers to those relationships that develop spontaneously, are not managed, structured or sanctioned by organizations (Chao *et al.* 1992). In contrast, formal mentoring relationships are planned, sponsored and sanctioned by organizations and have been described as "blind dates" or "arranged marriages" (Chao *et al.* 1992). These mentoring relationships can be internal or external. Internal mentors, those within the same organization as the protégé, may be more accessible and able to protect the protégé whereas external mentors, those employed outside of the protégé's organization, may provide long-range and lateral career assistance (Ragins 1997b).

Most mentoring research focuses on mentors who are not direct supervisors (nonhierarchical relationships), but a stream of research has examined hierarchical mentoring relationships. Findings suggest that when direct supervisors mentor their employee protégés, they provide more mentoring functions and communicate more than nonsupervisory mentors (Fagenson-Eland *et al.* 1997, Scandura and Williams 2004). Eby (1997) has also highlighted peer or lateral mentoring and has suggested that lateral, job-related skill development may also be accomplished with other forms of lateral mentoring including: intrateam, interteam, coworker, survivor mentoring and peer mentoring for domestic and international relocators. For lateral, career-related skill development, Eby suggests that internal collegial and external collegial peer mentoring may be appropriate. Eby indicates that internal sponsor–protégé, manager–subordinate and hierarchical domestic and international relocators' relationships might be appropriate for hierarchical mentoring that is focused on job-related skill development. Mentoring that is career-related but hierarchical might be accomplished through group professional associations or external sponsor–protégé relationships.

Research streams on mentoring

More than three decades of scholarly attention has been focused on mentoring, yet, much of the empirical research on mentoring has been conducted within the past 20 to 25 years (Allen *et al.* 2008, Higgins and Kram 2001, Kammeyer-Mueller and Judge 2008). Several comprehensive reviews of the literature have been conducted (see for example, Allen *et al.* 2004, Noe *et al.* 2002, Wanberg *et al.* 2003). Meta-analyses and comprehensive reviews of the methods and contents of published research on mentoring, along with definitional examinations have been done (see for example, Allen *et al.* 2008, Haggard *et al.* 2011 and Kammeyer-Mueller and Judge 2008) along with special issues on mentoring (see for example, *Advances in Developing Human Resources* (2005) and the *Journal of Vocational Behavior* (1997, 2008)). The *Journal of Vocational Behavior* has been considered "the leading journal in publishing workplace mentoring research" (Allen *et al.* 2008: 345).

Haggard *et al.* (2011) recently examined topics and developments in mentoring research across the time period of 1980–2009. They consolidated the topics into five overlapping streams suggesting that the base of literature has been focused on: the construct of mentoring, its dimensions and outcomes for protégés, mentor perspectives (1980–89), dyad composition, gender and racial composition, supervisory mentoring (1989–95), phases of mentoring, expansion of variables examined in terms of outcomes (1994–2003), negative mentoring experiences, mentor selection of protégés and relationship quality (1999–2006), and formal mentoring programs, characteristics, mediating variables, developmental relationships and e-mentoring (2003–09).

They noted considerable variation in the detail provided about mentoring and indicate that level of specificity of the mentoring definition, from broad to specific, and mentoring functions examined, along with four boundary conditions (the mentor's place within the organizational hierarchy, supervisory status as a mentor or nonsupervisory mentor, inside versus outside, and level of intimacy), could produce different results and suggest that such awareness is needed for conducting mentoring research. While they do not advocate for a single definition, they do propose three core attributes that should be considered by researchers to ensure that mentoring is distinguished from other work-related relationships: reciprocity/mutual exchange, developmental benefits, and regular/consistent interaction.

Similar to Haggard *et al.*, other scholars' reviews of mentoring research also indicate that research on mentoring has typically focused on: examining the effectiveness of informal and formal mentoring, characteristics of protégés and mentors, the process, functions, antecedents, outcomes, and diversified and marginal mentoring relationships (Ellinger 2002, Hansman 2002, Hezlett and Gibson 2005). In many of these studies, mentoring has been conceived more traditionally and much of this research has focused on the perspective of the protégé (Higgins and Kram 2001). In fact, Allen *et al.* (2008) indicated that the protégé was the focus in 80.2 per cent of the published mentoring studies, the mentor was the focus in 30.9 per cent of the studies with 27.5 per cent of the studies attending to the dyadic processes. Allen *et al.* (2008) acknowledge that only 7.2 per cent of the studies in their review focused on the organization. Based upon a previous classification for reviewing the literature on mentoring in the workplace (Ellinger 2002), some seminal research in the major areas is highlighted below.

The mentored versus the non-mentored

Research suggests that mentoring is largely beneficial to protégés when comparisons are made between those who are mentored and those non-mentored. Such benefits include psychosocial, career advancement and success, job satisfaction, commitment to the organization and retention (Ragins *et al.* 2000, Scandura 1992, Fagenson-Eland *et al.* 1997). More recently, Eby *et al.* (2008) examined the overall effect size associated with mentoring outcomes for protégés across three areas of mentoring research (youth, academic and workplace mentoring). They found that mentoring is significantly correlated in a positive direction with a range of protégé outcomes including behavioral, attitudinal, health-related, interpersonal, motivational and career outcomes. Research has also examined dispositional distinctions between protégés and non-protégés suggesting that protégés tend to be higher in their needs for achievement and power than non-protégés; however, no differences were found in their needs for autonomy or affiliation (Scandura 1992).

Informal versus formal mentoring and formal mentoring programs

Research suggests that informal mentoring may be more prevalent and beneficial to protégés (Chao *et al.* 1992). Until recently, there has been a lack of empirical research on the effects and outcomes of formal mentoring (Egan and Song 2008, Raabe and Beehr 2003, Wanberg *et al.* 2003). Orpen (1997) examined formal mentoring and confirmed the importance of quality of the mentoring relationship which can impact work motivation and organizational commitment among protégés. Orpen's research also identified barriers to effective mentoring relationships which include conflicting work schedules, lack of physical proximity and time demands. Hegstad and Wentling's (2004) study of exemplary formal mentoring programs found that retention, diversity initiatives and career management or development were the primary reasons why such programs were initiated. Their study offers insights into the design, development, implementation and evaluation of such programs. Allen *et al.* (2006) indicate that input into the pairing process along with training before the formal mentoring relationships commenced were significantly related to perceptions of mentoring effectiveness. Egan and Song (2008) examined formal mentoring program facilitation and their findings suggest greater levels of job satisfaction, organizational commitment, and manager performance ratings were found among those participating in the high-level facilitated mentoring program than in the low-level facilitation group. Their research also has design implications for formal mentoring programs suggesting that orientation to mentoring and ongoing facilitation during the mentoring program can enhance the outcomes of the program for protégés.

Characteristics and factors influencing protégés and mentors

Research has also examined the characteristics and personality traits that influence the selection process for protégés and mentors. Research has suggested that mentors' intentions to mentor have been associated with: internal locus of control and upward striving, past mentoring experience, and a desire to help others as well as personal gratification, pride, learning, and prosocial dispositions that may influence a mentor to mentor others (Allen 2003, 2004, Allen *et al.* 1997, Aryee *et al.* 1996).

Research on the factors that influence mentors' selection of protégés suggests that some mentors consider the protégé a reflection of themselves; personality indicators, such as good people skills, confidence, and dependability, were among those mentioned by mentors; how motivated the protégé appeared to be; competency indicators; mentors felt they could help the protégé; and learning orientation that included a willingness to learn and accept constructive feedback (Allen *et al.* 1997). Allen *et al.* (2001) suggest that mentors are more likely to choose a protégé based upon perceptions regarding the protégé's potential and ability as opposed to the perceptions of the protégé's need for help. Similarly, Allen's (2003) research suggests that mentors are more receptive to mentoring high ability protégés who are willing to learn.

Value similarity between mentors and protégés has also been influential to mentor–protégé dyads. Research by Egan (2005) in a formal mentoring context established that learning goal orientation is an important individual attribute that shapes mentor–protégé dyads and the findings from this study largely support previous research in an informal mentoring context. Kalbfleisch (2000) suggests that gender also affects the selection process and found that same sex mentoring relationships occur more frequently than cross-sex relationships, and that the sex of the mentor or protégé was the best predictor of the sex of the corresponding partner. Overall, Allen (2003: 481) acknowledges that "a combination of mentor and protégé characteristics and the organizational context influence protégé selection."

Benefits and drawbacks of mentoring

The benefits reported for mentoring are numerous for protégés. Hezlett's (2005: 520) study also suggests that protégés' "cognitive, skill-based, and affective learning is enhanced by mentoring." Perceived benefits to mentors identified by Allen *et al.* (1997) include: the development of a support network; satisfaction in seeing others grow; job-related benefits to the mentor that help the mentor to do his/her job or increase knowledge; and, increased visibility of the mentor within the organization as well as increased recognition. Mentors also report the notion of passing on knowledge and building a competent workforce that represented benefits extending beyond themselves. Allen *et al.*'s findings also support previous research.

Negative consequences of mentoring identified by Allen *et al.* include: the time required for mentoring, perceived favoritism to the protégé, potential abuse of the relationship by the protégé, and feelings of failure. Additionally, jealousy, over dependence, unwanted romantic or sexual involvement have been acknowledged (Darwin 2000). Similarly, Eby *et al.* (2000) identified negative mentoring experiences and subsequent research by Eby *et al.* (2004) confirmed the grouping of the experiences into five meta-themes: mismatches within dyads, distancing behavior, manipulative behavior, lack of mentor expertise and general dysfunctionality.

Facilitators and inhibitors of mentoring in organizations

Allen *et al.* (1997) have identified the following facilitators of mentoring: organizational support for employee learning and development, company training programs, manager and coworker support, a team approach to work, mentor empowerment, a comfortable work environment and a structured work environment. The inhibiting factors they found included time and work demands, organizational structure, a competitive and political environment, and unclear expectations of the organization about mentoring and expectations of mentors.

Trends, issues, and global perspectives

Much of the mentoring literature refers to traditional face-to-face and one-on-one mentoring relationships, yet, the pervasiveness of technology has introduced the concept of virtual mentoring, also referred to as e-mentoring, computer-mediated mentoring, tele-mentoring, e-mail mentoring, internet mentoring, online mentoring and cybermentoring (Bierema and Hill 2005). This form of mentoring may augment accessibility to a wide variety of mentors, alter the dynamics of the relationship such that experience and seniority may not be necessary, can promote immediate development given the any-time/any-where nature of this form of mentoring, and may facilitate cross-cultural connection. The challenges identified with this form of mentoring include the availability of technology and associated costs, issues of privacy and sustaining the relationship (Bierema and Hill 2005).

Reverse mentoring has recently emerged given the multigenerational nature of the workforce and the challenges that employees have with remaining current in their skills and competencies. Chaudhuri and Ghosh (2012: 56) suggest that reverse mentoring is an "inverted type of mentoring relationship whereby new junior employees are paired up with more experienced managers to help the experienced worker acquire new learning. They contend that this approach to mentoring may be very valuable given the changing generational demographics in the workplace.

Lastly, the global context has spurred the need to examine the concept of mentoring and its application within other countries (Gong *et al.* 2011, Ramaswami and Dreher 2010). Mentoring is considered a Western concept and much of the research on mentoring has been conducted in the US using established mentoring scales. Yet, Hu *et al.* (2011: 274) acknowledge "workplace mentoring in the international context is an emerging area with increasing number of studies conducted beyond the US context." Because cultural norms vary between individualistic and collectivist cultures and relationship expectations may also differ, "ensuring measurement equivalence/invariance (ME/I) of the measures reflecting mentoring functions should be established prior to studying mentoring across diverse cultural contexts" (Hu *et al.* 2011: 274). Accordingly, the findings from Hu *et al.*'s study examining the measurement equivalence of the Mentoring Functions Questionnaire (MFQ-9) within Taiwan and the US offer preliminary support for the similar conceptualizations of mentoring functions across individuals with varied cultural backgrounds. Lui *et al.* (2009) suggest that mentoring is consistent with Confucian values and a collectivist culture and the findings from their study on mentor benefits in China reveal two major benefits for mentors: in-role job performance and social status through the mediators of personal learning and social interaction quality. Gong *et al.*'s (2011) study was designed to explore the mediation effect of mentoring on the relationship between personal learning and career development in the Chinese context. They conclude that personal learning can be catalyzed by mentoring which enhances career development. Their findings are consistent with existing Western literature.

Ramaswami and Dreher (2010: 515) conducted a qualitative study of Indian MBA students studying within a US university to better understand conceptualizations of mentoring and the dynamics of such relationships. Their comprehensive analysis revealed that "Indian and Western descriptions of 'mentor' and 'preferred ideal mentor' characteristics are similar." Findings regarding the benefits associated with mentoring were also similar along with the notion of having multiple mentoring relationships. Yet, in this context, the researchers found that informal supervisory mentors were the primary mentors which is consistent with more of a paternalistic culture. If unavailable, relatives and peers played such roles. Ramaswami and Dreher (2010: 516, 525) acknowledge that their findings also "suggest the influence of career practices and cultural values, norms, and expectations in mentoring relationships." They indicate that "a global concept such as mentoring, however, also melds with local norms to form a 'glocal' type of mentoring."

Conclusion and implications for practice and future research

This chapter has provided an overview of coaching, managerial coaching, and mentoring concepts, highlighted relevant research, albeit not as comprehensively as existing reviews, and has identified some issues, trends, and global perspectives that require thoughtful attention relative to practice and research.

Implications for practice

Coaching in general, managerial coaching more specifically, and mentoring are widely used developmental interventions and they will likely continue to grow and evolve in work organizations given the aforementioned trends. This review has articulated the requisite coaching skills necessary for effective coaching and has acknowledged the importance of creating a context for coaching, along with the provision of coaching training to managers. The skills and coaching behaviors identified can be integrated into training and management development programs developed and facilitated by HRD professionals for managers to augment coaching practice within organizations.

Informal mentoring and developmental networks and constellations of relationships exist for some employees, which can influence their career success and advancement. Yet, unfortunately, it is evident that those who may benefit most from mentoring may not necessarily receive it. Therefore, the use of formal mentoring programs designed to promote diversity and inclusion, focus on career aspirations, and prevent turnover will continue to become more prevalent. Organizational leaders and HRD professionals should work toward creating infrastructures that support formal mentoring programs, much like managerial coaching. Creating a culture that supports development through mentoring, and appreciates the predispositions of mentors and their propensity to mentor may enable HRD professionals to solicit and recruit mentors to participate in such programs. Further, understanding such attributes of mentors and protégés may enable more appropriate matching among such dyads. Lastly, in terms of design, orientation, pre-training, and active engagement through facilitation processes by HRD professionals can result in more impactful programs as the research suggests.

Future research directions

This review has established that more comprehensive research is needed that examines the antecedents and factors that influence managerial coaching, the skills and behaviors that managers enact, the propensity for managers to engage as coaches, the potential benefits that they receive as a result of developing their employees, and the mediating or moderating variables that may influence the process and the outcomes associated with managerial coaching (Ellinger *et al.*, forthcoming, Hagen 2012, Kim *et al.* 2013). The impact of managerial coaching for the organization also needs attention. Additionally, the cross-cultural implications associated with managerial coaching need to be more thoroughly examined. In some cultural contexts, the more egalitarian nature of developmental coaching, the learning partnership that is formed between managers and their employees and the importance of trust in that relationship may not be cultural norms. Existing instruments assessing coaching skills and managerial coaching behaviors may need to be examined for their measurement equivalence/invariance in such cultural contexts. Lastly, the drawbacks associated with managerial coaching need attention, along with a more robust understanding of how organizational contextual factors influence or inhibit managerial coaching practice.

The literature on mentoring is voluminous, multidisciplinary, but also siloed (Eby *et al.* 2007, Ghosh 2012). While considerable progress has been made in terms of research and practice, Allen *et al.* (2008: 355) acknowledge that their review characterizes "mentoring research as primarily adopting quantitative, correlational, cross-sectional research designs in field settings where data are collected from a single source (typically the protégé) using a single method of data collection" (ibid: 355). Therefore, several avenues for future research need to be undertaken. Scholars contend that caution and attention are needed when defining mentoring, its functions and the use of measurement instruments in the research process (Haggard *et al.* 2011).

Mentoring has been linked to individual and organizational outcomes; however, developing a deeper understanding of how mentoring impacts organizational performance and competitiveness is needed (Thurston *et al.* 2012). Focusing on the learning outcomes associated with mentoring for protégés and mentors is a topic that has garnered attention and also needs further inquiry (Hezlett 2005). The longitudinal effects of mentoring on mentors, protégés and the organization are also needed (Allen *et al.* 2008). Additionally, alternative approaches to mentoring as articulated by Eby (1997) and Higgins and Kram (2001) warrant further attention. Focusing on the distinctions between these different developmental approaches and their respective outcomes is another avenue for research. Haggard *et al.* (2011) indicate that, since mentoring occurs in occupational settings or contexts, more attention to the variation that may be present in such settings or contexts is needed. And, given that "career patterns and organizational experiences have changed dramatically in the last few decades" (Allen *et al.* 2008: 352), more attention to the changing organizational landscape relative to mentoring is also needed.

Additionally, much like coaching and managerial coaching, examining the negative consequences of workplace mentoring along with generating more comprehensive understandings of it in the global context are areas of research and considerably more work needs to be undertaken in other non-Western countries (Hu *et al.* 2011). Research should continue to examine gender and ethnic differences including: cross-gender, cross-racial, cross-cultural mentorship relationships (Ragins 1997a, 1997b, Ragins *et al.* 2000). Lastly, Haggard *et al.* (2011) acknowledge that more research is needed on e-mentoring, mentor motivation for mentoring, reverse mentoring, learning and information sharing within mentoring relationships.

Note

1 Acknowledgements: The author would like to thank Casey Uscanga and Afton Barber, students at The University of Texas at Tyler, for their assistance in identifying some of the literature featured in this chapter.

References

Agarwal, R., Angst, C.M. and Magni, M. (2009) 'The performance effects of coaching: a multilevel analysis using hierarchical linear modelling', *International Journal of Human Resource Management* 20: 2110–34.

Allen, T.D. (2003) 'Mentoring others: a dispositional and motivational approach', *Journal of Vocational Behavior* 62: 134–54.

— (2004) 'Protégé selection by mentors: contributing individual and organizational factors', *Journal of Vocational Behavior* 65: 469–83.

Allen, T.D., Poteet, M.L. and Burroughs, S.M. (1997) 'The mentor's perspective: a qualitative inquiry and future research agenda', *Journal of Vocational Behavior* 51: 70–89.

Allen, T.D., Poteet, M.L. and Russell, J.E.A. (2001) 'Protégé selection by mentors: what makes the difference?', *Journal of Organizational Behavior* 21: 271–82.

Allen, T.D., Eby, L.T., Poteet, M.L., Lentz, E. and Lima, L. (2004) 'Career benefits associated with mentoring for protégés: a meta-analysis', *Journal of Applied Psychology* 89: 127–36.

Allen, T.D., Eby, L.T. and Lentz, E. (2006) 'Mentorship behaviors and mentorship quality associated with formal mentoring programs: closing the gap between research and practice', *Journal of Applied Psychology* 91(3): 567–78.

Allen, T.D., Eby, L.T., O'Brien, K.E. and Lentz, E. (2008) 'The state of mentoring research: a qualitative review of current research methods and future research implications', *Journal of Vocational Behavior* 73: 343–57.

Amy, A.H. (2005) 'Leaders as facilitators of organizational learning', unpublished doctoral dissertation, Regent University at Virginia Beach, VA.

Anonymous (2001) 'Mentoring and coaching help employees grow', *HR Focus* 78(9): 1–6.

Aryee, S., Chay, U.W. and Chew, J. (1996) 'The motivation to mentor among managerial employees', *Group and Organization Management* 21: 261–77.

Beattie, R.S. (2002) 'Line managers as facilitators of learning: empirical evidence from voluntary sector', *Proceedings of 2002 Human Resource Development Research and Practice Across Europe Conference*, Edinburgh: Napier University, January.

Bierema, L.L. and Hill, J.R. (2005) 'Virtual mentoring and HRD', *Advances in Developing Human Resources* 7: 556–68.

Chao, G.T., Waltz, P.M. and Gardner, P.D. (1992) 'Formal and informal mentorships: a comparison on mentoring functions and contrast with nonmentored counterparts', *Personnel Psychology* 45: 619–36.

Chartered Institute of Personnel and Development (2006) *Learning and Development Survey*, London: CIPD.

— (2007) *Learning and Development Survey*, London: CIPD.

Chaudhuri, S. and Ghosh, R. (2012) 'Reverse mentoring: a social exchange took for keeping the boomers engaged and the millennials committed', *Human Resource Development Review* 11: 55–76.

Cox, E. (2012) *Coaching Understood: A Pragmatic Inquiry into the Coaching Process*, London: SAGE.

Cummings, T.G. and Worley, C.G. (2009) *Organization Development and Change*, Mason, OH: South-Western Cengage Learning.

Darwin, A. (2000) 'Critical reflections on mentoring in work settings', *Adult Education Quarterly* 50: 197–211.

Eby, L.T. (1997) 'Alternative forms of mentoring in changing organizational environments: a conceptual extension of the mentoring literature', *Journal of Vocational Behavior* 51: 125–44.

Eby, L.T., McManus, S.E., Simon, S.A. and Russell, J.E.A. (2000) 'The protégé's perspective regarding negative mentoring experiences: the development of a taxonomy', *Journal of Vocational Behavior* 57: 1–21.

Eby, L.T., Butts, M., Lockwood, A. and Simon, S. (2004) 'Protégés' negative mentoring experiences: construct development and nomological validation', *Personnel Psychology* 57: 411–47.

Eby, L.T., Rhodes, J. and Allen, T.D. (2007) 'Definition and evolution of mentoring', in Allen, T.D. and Eby, L.T. (eds) *Blackwell Handbook of Mentoring*, Oxford: Blackwell Publishing, 7–20.

Eby, L.T., Allen, T.D., Evans, S.C., Ng, T. and DuBois, D.L. (2008) 'Does mentoring matter? A multidisciplinary meta-analysis comparing mentored and non-mentored individuals', *Journal of Vocational Behavior* 72: 254–67.

Egan, T.M. (2005) 'The impact of learning goal orientation similarity on formal mentoring relationship outcomes', *Advances in Developing Human Resources* 7(4): 489–504.

Egan, T.M. and Song, Z. (2008) 'Are facilitated mentoring programs beneficial? A randomized experimental field study', *Journal of Vocational Behavior* 72: 351–62.

Ellinger, A.D. (1997) 'Managers as facilitators of learning in learning organizations', unpublished doctoral dissertation, University of Georgia at Athens, GA.

— (2002) 'Mentoring in contexts: the workplace and educational institutions', in Hansman, C.A. (ed.) *Critical Perspectives on Mentoring*, ERIC Document, 15–26.

Ellinger, A.D. and Bostrom, R.P. (1999) 'Managerial coaching behaviors in learning organizations', *Journal of Management Development* 18: 752–71.

Ellinger, A.D., Ellinger, A.E. and Keller, S.B. (2003) 'Supervisory coaching behavior, employee satisfaction, and warehouse employee performance: a dyadic perspective in the distribution industry', *Human Resource Development Quarterly* 14: 435–58.

Ellinger, A.D. Hamlin, R.G., Beattie, R.S., Wang, Y. and McVicar, O. (2011) 'Managerial coaching as an informal workplace learning strategy', in Poell, R.F. and Van Woerkom, M. (eds) *Supporting Workplace Learning: Towards Evidence-Based Practice*, Dordrecht: Springer, 71–87.

Ellinger, A.D., Beattie, R.S. and Hamlin, R.G. (forthcoming) 'The "manager as coach": an update', in Cox, E., Bachkirova, T. and Clutterbuck, D. (eds) *The Complete Handbook of Coaching*, London: SAGE.

Elmadag, A.B., Ellinger, A.E. and Franke, G.R. (2008) 'Antecedents and consequences of frontline service employee commitment to service quality', *Journal of Marketing Theory and Practice* 16: 95–110.

Evered, R.D. and Selman, J.C. (1989) 'Coaching and the art of management', *Organizational Dynamics* 18: 16–32.

Fagenson-Eland, E.A., Marks, M.A. and Amendola, K.L. (1997) 'Perceptions of mentoring relationships', *Journal of Vocational Behavior* 51: 29–42.

Fournies, F.F. (1987) *Coaching for Improved Work Performance*, Kansas, MO: Liberty Hall.

Ghosh, R. (2012) 'Mentors providing challenge and support: integrating concepts from teacher mentoring in education and organizational mentoring in business', *Human Resource Development Review* 12: 1–33.

Gibson, S.K. and Hezlett, S.A. (eds) (2005) 'Mentoring and human resource development: perspectives and innovations', *Advances in Developing Human Resources* 7: 444–586.

Gomez, E. and Gunn, R. (2012) 'Do managers that coach become better leaders? An exploration into the relationship between managerial coaching and leader development', unpublished master's thesis, School of Management, Blekinge Institute of Technology, Sweden.

Gong, R., Chen, S.Y. and Lee, S.L (2011) 'Does mentoring work? The mediating effect of mentoring in China', *Social Behavior and Personality* 39: 807–24.

Graham, S., Wedman, J.F. and Garvin-Kester, B. (1993) 'Manager coaching skills: development and application', *Performance Improvement Quarterly* 6: 2–13.

— (1994) 'Manager coaching skills: what makes a good coach?' *Performance Improvement Quarterly* 7: 81–94.

Grant, A.M. (2008) 'Workplace, executive and life coaching: an annotated bibliography from the behavioural science literature' (July 2008), Coaching Psychology Unit, University of Sydney, Australia.

Gray, D.E. and Goregaokar, H. (2010) 'Choosing an executive coach: the influence of gender on the coach–coachee matching process', *Management Learning* 41(5): 525–44.

Hagen, M.S. (2010) 'Black belt coaching and project outcomes: an empirical investigation', *Quality Management Journal* 17: 54–67.

— (2012) 'Managerial coaching: a review of the literature', *Performance Improvement Quarterly* 24: 17–39.

Hagen, M. and Aguilar, M.G. (2012) 'The impact of managerial coaching on learning outcomes within a team context: an analysis', *Human Resource Development Quarterly* 23: 363–88.

Haggard, D.L., Dougherty, T.W., Turban, D.B. and Wilbanks, J.E. (2011) 'Who is a mentor? A review of evolving definitions and implications for research', *Journal of Management* 37: 280–304.

Hamlin, R.G., Ellinger, A.D. and Beattie, R.S. (2006) 'Coaching at the heart of managerial effectiveness: a cross-cultural study of managerial behaviours', *Human Resource Development International* 9: 305–31.

— (2009) 'Toward a process of coaching? A definitional examination of "coaching," "organization development," and "human resource development"', *International Journal of Evidence Based Coaching and Mentoring* 7(1): 13–38.

Hannah, C. (2004) 'Improving intermediate skills through workplace coaching: a case study within the UK rail industry', *International Journal of Evidence Based Coaching and Mentoring* 2(1): 17–45.

Hansman, C.A. (ed.) (2002) *Critical Perspectives on Mentoring*, ERIC Document.

Hegstad, C.D. and Wentling, R.M. (2004) 'The development and maintenance of exemplary formal mentoring programs in Fortune 500 companies', *Human Resource Development Quarterly* 15: 421–48.

Hezlett, S.A. (2005) 'Protégés' learning in mentoring relationships: a review of the literature and an exploratory case study', *Advances in Developing Human Resources* 7: 505–26.

Hezlett, S.A. and Gibson, S.K. (2005) 'Mentoring and human resource development: where we are and where we need to go', *Advances in Developing Human Resources* 7: 446–69.

Higgins, M.C. and Kram, K.E. (2001) 'Reconceptualizing mentoring at work: a developmental network perspective', *Academy of Management Review* 26: 264–88.

Horvath, M., Wasko, L.E. and Bradley, J. (2008) 'The effect of formal mentoring characteristics on organization attraction', *Human Resource Development Quarterly* 9: 323–49.

Hu, C., Pellegrini, E.K. and Scandura, T.A. (2011) 'Measurement invariance in mentoring research: a cross-cultural examination across Taiwan and the US', *Journal of Vocational Behavior* 78: 274–82.

Hutchinson, S. and Purcell, J. (2007) *Learning and the Line: The Role of Line Managers in Training, Learning and Development*, London: CIPD.

International Coach Federation (2012) *ICF Releases Results of 2012 ICF Global Coaching Study*. Online. Available HTTP: http: //www.ereleases.com/pr/international-coach-federation-releases-results-2012-icf-global-coaching-study-82236 (accessed 11 November 2013).

Kalbfleisch, P.J. (2000) 'Similarity and attraction in business and academic environments: same and cross-sex mentoring relationships', *Review of Business* 21: 58.

Kammeyer-Mueller, J.D. and Judge, T.A. (2008) 'A quantitative review of mentoring research: test of a model', *Journal of Vocational Behavior* 72: 269–83.

Kim, S., Egan, T., Kim, W. and Kim, J. (2013) 'The impact of managerial coaching behaviour on employee work-related reactions', *Journal of Business Psychology* 28(3): 315–330.

Kram, K.E. (1985) *Mentoring at Work: Developmental Relationships in Organizational Life*, Glenview, IL: Scott Foresman.

Longenecker, C.O. and Neubert, M.J. (2005) 'The practices of effective managerial coaches', *Business Horizons* 48: 493–500.

Lui, D., Lui, J., Kwan, H. K. and Mao, Y. (2009) 'What can I gain as a mentor? The effect of mentoring on the job performance and social status of mentors in China', *Journal of Occupational and Organizational Psychology* 82: 871–95.

McLagan, P. (1996) 'Great ideas revisited', *Training and Development* 50(1): 60–5.

McLean, G.N., Yang, B., Kuo, M.C., Tolbert, A.S. and Larkin, C. (2005) 'Development and initial validation of an instrument measuring managerial coaching skill', *Human Resource Development Quarterly* 16: 157–78.

Maycunich Gilley, A., Gilley, J.W. and Kouider, E. (2010) 'Characteristics of managerial coaching', *Performance Improvement Quarterly* 23: 53–70.

Mink, O.G., Owen, K.Q. and Mink, B.P. (1993) *Developing High-Performance People: The Art of Coaching*, Reading, MA: Addison-Wesley.

Noe, R.A., Greenberger, D.B. and Wang, S. (2002) 'Mentoring: what we know and where we might go', in Ferris, G.R. (ed.) *Research in Personnel and Human Resources Management*, Oxford: Elsevier Science, 129–74.

Noer, D. (2005) 'Behaviorally based coaching: a cross-cultural case study', *International Journal of Coaching in Organizations* 3: 14–23.

Orpen, C. (1997) 'The effects of formal mentoring on employee work motivation, organizational commitment and job performance', *Learning Organization* 4(2): 53–60.

Orth, C.D., Wilkinson, H.E. and Benfari, R.C. (1987) 'The manager's role as coach and mentor', *Organizational Dynamics* 15(4): 66–74.

Park, S., McLean, G.N. and Yang, B. (2008) 'Revision and validation of an instrument measuring managerial coaching skills in organizations', in Chermack, T.J., Storberg-Walker, J. and Graham, C.M. (eds) *Proceedings of 2008 Academy of Human Resource Development Conference* (CD-ROM). Panama City Beach, FL, February.

Peterson, D.B. and Little, B. (2005) 'Invited reaction: development and initial validation of an instrument measuring managerial coaching skill', *Human Resource Development Quarterly* 16: 179–83.

Raabe, B. and Beehr, T.A. (2003) 'Formal mentoring versus supervisor and coworker relationships: differences in perceptions and impact', *Journal of Organizational Behavior* 24: 271–93.

Ragins, B.R. (1997a) 'Antecedents of diversified mentoring relationships', *Journal of Vocational Behavior* 51: 90–109.

— (1997b) 'Diversified mentoring relationships in organizations: a power perspective', *Academy of Management* 22: 482–521.

Ragins, B.R., Cotton, J.L. and Miller, J.S. (2000) 'Marginal mentoring: the effects of type of mentor, quality of relationship, and program design on work and career attitudes', *Academy of Management Journal* 43: 1177–94.

Ramaswami, A. and Dreher, G.F. (2010) 'Dynamics of mentoring relationships in India: a qualitative, exploratory study', *Human Resource Management* 49: 501–30.

Scandura, T.A. (1992) 'Mentorship and career mobility: an empirical investigation', *Journal of Organizational Behavior* 13: 169–74.

Scandura, T.A. and Williams, E.A. (2004) 'Mentoring and transformational leadership: the role of supervisory career mentoring', *Journal of Vocational Behavior* 65: 448–68.

Sue-Chan, C., Wood, R.E. and Latham, G.P. (2012) 'Effect of a coach's regulatory focus and an individual's implicit person theory on individual performance', *Journal of Management* 38: 809–35.

Thurston, P.W., D'Abate, C.P. and Eddy, E.R. (2012) 'Mentoring as an HRD approach: effects on employee attitudes and contributions independent of core self-evaluation', *Human Resource Development Quarterly* 23: 139–65.

Wanberg, C.R., Welsh, E.T. and Hezlett, S.A. (2003) 'Mentoring research: a review and dynamic process model', in Martocchio, J.J. and Ferris, G.R. (eds) *Research in Personnel and Human Resources Management*, Oxford: Elsevier Science, 39–124.

Wang, Y. (2012) 'R and D employees' innovative behaviors in Taiwan: HRM and managerial coaching as moderators', *Asia Pacific Journal of Human Resources* 50: 491–515.

25

STRUCTURED ON-THE-JOB TRAINING

Ronald L. Jacobs

How do people learn to do their jobs? Most informed observers suggest that employees learn most of what they know and can do based on their experiences while on the job, not in a corporate classroom or other off-the-job training setting. Research has shown that on-the-job training (OJT) can be especially effective in helping employees learn new job-related knowledge and skills (Lave and Wenger 1991; Hart-Landsberg *et al.* 1992). However, much of the learning that occurs on the job tends to be unplanned, or unstructured, in its nature often resulting in unpredictable and unreliable learning outcomes. That is, having employees acquire job information simply by observing what others are doing or being trained by someone else on an ad hoc basis. Structured on-the-job training (S-OJT) was first introduced in response to the issues inherent in using unstructured forms of OJT (Jacobs and McGiffin 1987). Now, S-OJT is being used in many organizations globally.

S-OJT has been defined as the planned process of having an experienced employee train a novice employee on specific units of work in the actual work setting or a setting that closely resembles the work setting (Jacobs 2003). The definition affirms the underlying desirability of having individuals learn in the same location in which they will be expected to perform their work later on. No other training approach combines the use of a planned process, the active engagement of a trainer, and the delivery of the training in the actual work setting (Jacobs and Park 2009).

Current forms of S-OJT have their roots in the much-discussed Training within Industry (TWI) program that was established by the federal government in 1941 to support the war production efforts. A final report written by its director, Channing Rice Dooley (1945), described in depth how the Job Instruction Training program (JIT) in particular, was used to train hundreds of thousands of new-hires, many of them women, in US production plants. JIT featured the use of supervisors as trainers who used detailed job instruction sheets and a four-step delivery process to deliver the training. The other major TWI programs – Job Relations Training and Job Methods Training – also were discussed in the final report and featured learning in the work setting, but those programs did not have the same overall influence on the productivity of organizations as JIT.

The TWI programs ended at the close of World War II and, as a result, there was limited discussion about the virtues of OJT training in the management and human resources literature afterwards. It was not until the 1980s that OJT began to receive renewed attention as concerns were expressed about the ability of organizations to successfully compete in the emerging global economy.

In general, this chapter presents information that reflects the growing maturity of what is known about the topic of S-OJT. Specifically, the chapter first discusses how the ongoing shifts in employee competence form the underlying impetus for using S-OJT. Next, the chapter discusses what is meant by S-OJT and distinguishes it from other forms of workplace learning. Then, the chapter discusses how S-OJT has been used and presents illustrative case study examples of how the training approach has been used in organizations and as part of public policy initiatives. Finally, the chapter concludes with a brief discussion about issues related to the future use of S-OJT.

Employee competence and S-OJT

It is generally agreed that S-OJT should be used only when individuals lack the knowledge and skills to perform what is expected of them. Such situations arise when one of the following might occur: individuals are new to the work, the work has changed in some way, the work is especially complex with a high likelihood of error, or there may be undesirable consequences when errors are made, among other situations. All of these situations challenge employees to acquire new knowledge and skills, or areas of competence. Competence describes an individual's possession and use of the behaviors required to achieve specific outcomes. In this sense, competence can be considered relative to what task should be performed and the ability of the individual to perform the task (Gilbert 2007).

How well an individual actually performs on a particular task can depend on several different system factors, such as whether the job expectations are made explicit, whether there are appropriate incentives, or whether there is sufficient feedback (Gilbert 2007; Jacobs 1992). Arguably, whether the individual possesses the skill to perform the task in the first place seems the most prominent determining factor among the others. A number of authors have identified models of skills acquisition, ranging from the novice to the expert levels, such as Dreyfus and Dreyfus (1986) and Benner (1984).

As shown in Table 25.1, Jacobs (2003) introduced levels of employee competence: novice, specialist, experienced specialist, expert, and master. The novice represents the lowest level of employee competence, which means that the individual has little or no capacity to perform a given task. The specialist level represents the level achieved as a result of most training programs, providing them the ability to perform most instances of the task. The experienced specialist represents the added benefit of knowing how to perform the task and prolonged contact that provides opportunities to learn from those experiences. Many individuals achieve the experienced specialist level over time, since this level may be sufficient to meet the demands of their work.

Beyond the experienced specialist level are the expert and master levels. The literature makes clear that achieving the expert level of competence requires more than extended experience with

Table 25.1 Levels of employee competence

Category	*Description*
Master	The real expert among experts, teaches others, shares new knowledge
Expert	One who can do both the routine and non-routine instances of the work
Experienced Specialist	One who has performed the work repeatedly and can do it with ease
Specialist	One who can perform the work, but the range is limited
Novice	One who is new to the work and lacks the ability to perform

performing a task alone. Becoming an expert represents a significant leap from the other levels by having individuals become more reflective in their actions through informal learning, engaging in formal learning experiences, and even having some innate talents and abilities that might be required for the task (Davenport 1999). Experts are able to perform procedural behaviors to a high standard and then engage in sophisticated problem solving to develop new procedures. In addition, experts often seek out ways of improving their knowledge base through informal hypothesis testing and experimentation with tasks. The master level is unique in that it implies that the expert is interested in and effective in teaching others what they know and can do.

Logically, everyone starts out as a novice when learning a task. But not everyone will eventually become an expert on the task. The learning progression depends primarily on whether individuals have sufficient time to learn all the possible nuances and variations of a task over time, a possibility that is becoming more and more difficult in today's workplace.

Figure 25.1 illustrates this point by illustrating the major changes that have occurred in the occupation of machine tool operator. Information about the major changes in this occupation and the impact of the changes on individuals were identified through interviews with a panel of subject-matter experts and a review of the literature. The resulting profile shows that for many years, the technology associated with individuals functioning as a machine tool operator had remained relatively stable. That is, individuals starting their career in the 1950s most probably learned on equipment that featured hand controls on the machine itself and they used an array of hand tools, such as calipers, wrenches, and micrometers. In fact, individuals starting at this time might have used the same technology throughout their careers, giving them the opportunity to progress to the expert level and to train others on what they had practiced for many years.

Beginning in the 1960s, however, the machine tool occupation experienced much change, especially in the integration of electronic technology. Indeed, six major changes have been identified for this occupation. Individuals who had previously used hand controls to adjust a lathe – that is, making adjustments by manually turning wheels or tightening screws to raise or lower

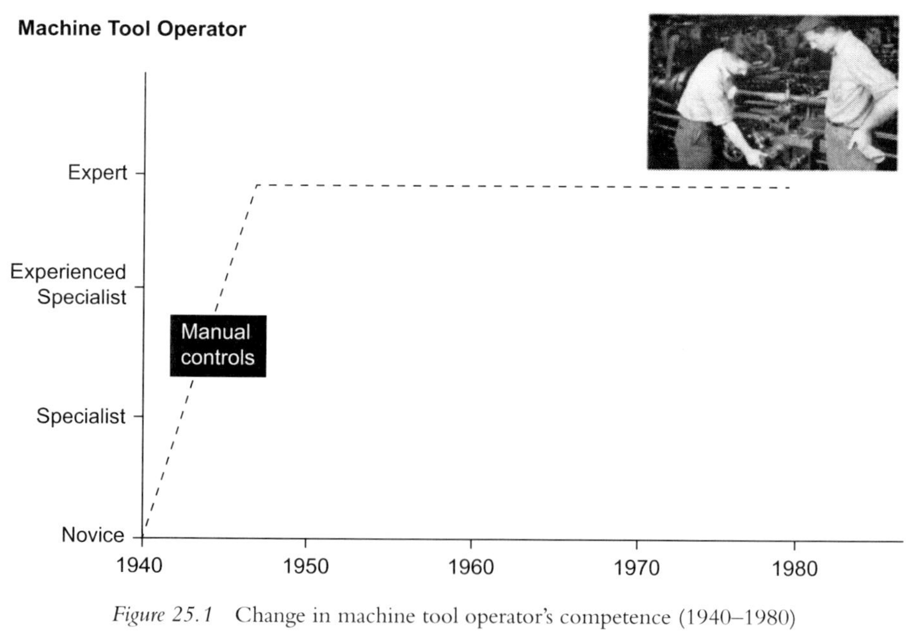

Figure 25.1 Change in machine tool operator's competence (1940–1980)

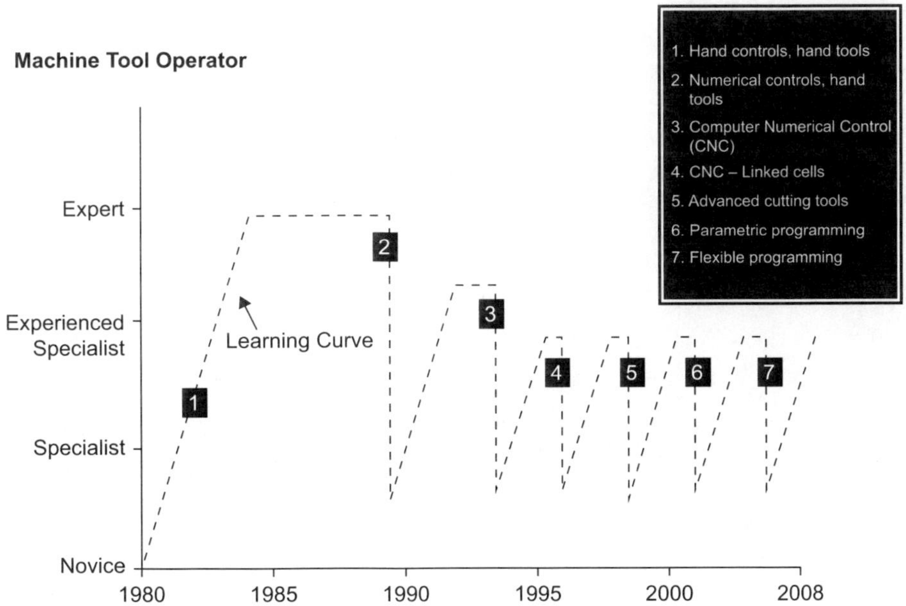

Figure 25.2 Change in machine tool operator's competence (1980–2008)

holding fixtures – were now required to make the adjustments by entering information on a keyboard, which then appeared on an attached computer screen. From that point onward, changes in the occupation involved the increased integration of technology to gain greater precision and flexibility. Perhaps machine tool operators did not literally become novices every time a major advancement was introduced. But it is likely that they were required to engage in both formal and informal learning activities to acquire the new knowledge and skills. Figure 25.2 suggests that as technological changes become more bunched together, individuals usually find it more and more difficult to achieve the highest levels of competence, simply because they likely do not have the same opportunity for prolonged experience with the task.

Similar profiles have been generated for other occupations that have undergone significant changes in their requirements, such as nurses, managers, and engineers. The continuous nature of these changes suggests the relative volatility – or continuous movement up and down – of the overall levels of employee competence. Given the shortened life cycle of job content, being an expert on something today does not guarantee the same status tomorrow. Changes in employee competence and the subsequent demands on employees to respond to those changes suggest the underlying relationship with S-OJT.

Structured on-the-job training defined

As stated, S-OJT is fundamentally about having individuals learn in the same location in which they will perform later on, but with the benefit of having reliable and predictable learning outcomes. Unfortunately, most of the learning that occurs in the work setting is unplanned, or *unstructured*, in nature. Most of us have experienced some form of unstructured OJT during our working experiences, referring to unstructured OJT as "Follow Joe training" or "Sit by Sally training." This means that the employee will try to learn what is expected by watching someone else perform the work and hope this will be sufficient or receiving the training from another individual who may not really know all the training content or know how best to convey it to others. In practice, unstructured OJT typically results in the following outcomes:

- The training rarely achieves the desired learning outcomes.
- The training often includes inaccurate or incomplete content.
- Individuals who serve as trainers are uncertain how to be effective in this role.
- Certain trainers might be wary about how much to share with their trainees, possibly jeopardizing their own job security.

Jacobs (2003) suggests that the following characteristics distinguish S-OJT from unstructured OJT:

- The content to be learned must be systematically documented for use by the trainer and made available to the trainee during the training.
- Trainers should have been selected based on specific criteria, have received some formal instruction and qualification on how to be a trainer, and are required to use specific steps to deliver the training.
- Trainees should be prepared to learn the content and understand what is expected of them before the start of the training.
- The training occurs in the actual work setting, or a setting that closely resembles the actual work setting as much as possible.

As a planned form of training, S-OJT draws upon two interrelated implications from system theory. As shown in Figure 25.3, S-OJT can be represented as a system, containing a set of training inputs, training processes, training outputs, and a context that is comprised of the work setting. Specifically, the inputs of the S-OJT system consist of the novice employee, or the individual who will receive the training. The experienced employee serves as the trainer and should have appropriate knowledge of the task and qualifications to serve in this role. The location is a place in the work setting where the training will actually occur. The work to be learned is the identified units of work, which are packaged in some easy to use way, such as an S-OJT module. Finally, the inputs include the communications technologies that might be used to help manage and deliver the training. Increasingly, communications technology has been used to link trainers and trainees during the training, who might be at different locations (Bennett and Calvin 2002). Each of these inputs should be carefully understood and designed to fit the specific situation on hand.

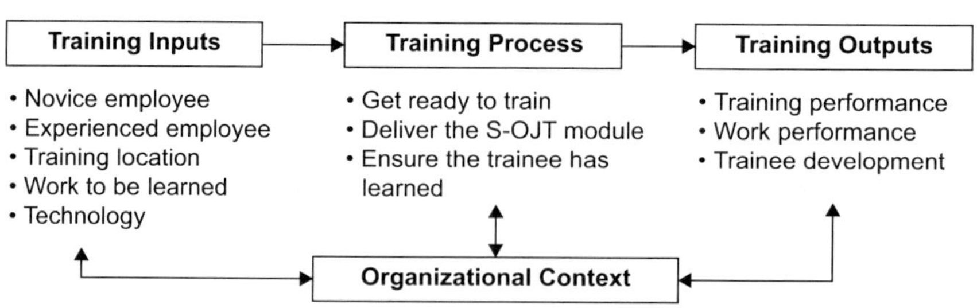

Figure 25.3 S-OJT system

The process component of the S-OJT system includes the activities required for the trainer to get ready to train, the delivery of the training content by the trainer to the trainee, and the performance check to ensure that the trainee has learned. The outputs are the results that occur as a result of the S-OJT program, such as the impacts on the trainees and their development, the impacts on the work, and any longer-term impacts. Finally, the context includes factors in the work setting that might facilitate or constrain the effectiveness of the training. For instance, one of the continuing practical issues in using S-OJT is the potential conflict between using time during the work day to conduct training, all the while there may be production or service delivery schedules to be met at the same time. The context of S-OJT often determines the relative effectiveness of the training.

Viewing S-OJT as a system assists in understanding what components should be present to ensure its effectiveness when developing the system. Further, viewing S-OJT as a system helps identify which components might be deficient when troubleshooting or improving the system. From a research perspective, viewing S-OJT as a system also helps identify what variables might be important to study and what questions to ask.

As shown in Figure 25.4, the second implication of a system theory perspective is the S-OJT design process, which is composed of six phases (Jacobs 2003). The S-OJT process is used to design, deliver, and evaluate S-OJT systems, and should be considered a subset of the broader performance improvement process. The S-OJT process should be used only after a thorough analysis of the performance issue has been conducted. As stated, S-OJT is appropriate only when the cause of the performance issue is caused by a lack of the required employee knowledge and skills, or competence. The first phase of the S-OJT process logically asks the question whether S-OJT is the most appropriate training approach to use given the situation at hand. A series of questions can be asked related to its appropriateness, pertaining to the following categories: the nature of the task, the availability of resources, the constraints in the work setting, financial considerations, and individual or cultural differences (Jacobs 2003).

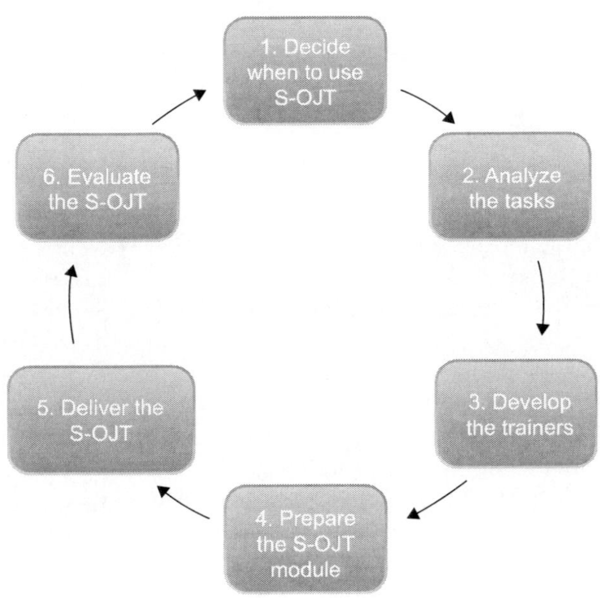

Figure 25.4 S-OJT design process

Next, the process requires that the work in question be analyzed, since this information forms the content of the training program. Task analysis is a critical skill for this phase to be completed. S-OJT has been used for delivering certain types of managerial training, technical training, and awareness training. Developing experienced employees as trainers ensures that these individuals, when called upon, are knowledgeable about the content and are able to deliver S-OJT appropriately. The next phase requires that the S-OJT program is presented to trainees in the form of complete sets of information, called modules. The delivery of the S-OJT requires that the trainer use specific steps, such as the five steps as recommended by Jacobs (2003):

1. Prepare the trainee.
2. Present the training.
3. Require a response.
4. Provide feedback.
5. Evaluate performance.

Finally, the process calls for the S-OJT programs to be evaluated. As will be discussed in the following section of the chapter, most reports of the impacts of S-OJT have focused on the financial benefits of using S-OJT in contrast to some other training option.

As proposed by Jacobs and Park (2009), S-OJT can be considered a unique form of workplace learning because no other approach combines the following attributes: makes use of a planned systematic process, requires the active involvement of a trainer, and the training occurs in the actual work setting. This combination of these variables is derived from their conceptual framework that they had proposed which is comprised of three dimensions for understanding workplace learning: (1) the location of the learning; (2) the degree of planning undertaken to design the learning experience; and (3) the role of a trainer or facilitator during the learning experience.

The location of the training can be either on the job or off the job. That is, whether the learning occurs at the actual work setting or away from the work setting, such as a classroom setting. The degree of planning can vary from the training being unstructured, or unplanned and happenstance, to structured in which a systems approach is used. The role of the trainer or facilitator varies from that person either being passively involved or being active in that a person is formally designated to interact with the trainee in some way.

Use of S-OJT

Arguably, the first research study related to the effectiveness of OJT was the Lens Grinder Study (Dooley 1945; reprinted in Jacobs 2003) that was conducted in 1941. The study sought to establish the effectiveness of a planned approach to training on the job. The results showed that the length of time to train apprentice lens grinders could be reduced from five years to six months, and subsequently to two months. The Lens Grinder Study was reported as part of the final report authored by Channing Rice Dooley, as he was closing the TWI project during the last months of World War II. Most observers suggest that the TWI project influenced much of current understandings of S-OJT.

A review of the literature has shown numerous individual case studies about S-OJT or learning in the work setting (for example, Jacobs 1994; Jacobs and Bu-Rahmah 2012), two edited volumes of case studies (Jacobs 2002a: Jacobs and Osman-Gani 2005), and one edited monograph that introduced issues related to planned learning in the work setting (Jacobs 2001). Jacobs and Osman-Gani (2004) collected case studies with an emphasis on how organizations in international situations have used different forms of S-OJT. The cases illustrate both the similarities and differences based on cross-cultural considerations.

In addition, the author of this chapter and his research associates have begun to document and offer critical analyses of unpublished case studies on learning in the work setting and are making them available at this website location on the Internet: http://publish.illinois.edu/s-ojtglobalcommunity/. The case studies summarized in this chapter were selected to represent a range of the situations in which S-OJT has been used. Specifically, the following criteria were used in selecting the case studies:

- The case study must be available as a publication in the literature or from a reliable website, such as a government source.
- The nature of the training intervention should meet the following minimum criteria: the training had been developed using a systems approach, the training occurred in the work setting or in a setting that resembled the work setting, and there was active involvement of a qualified trainer.
- The case study included sufficient information about what was done and what results were obtained.
- The case study was judged to add in some unique way to the body of knowledge related to S-OJT.

As shown in Table 25.2, five case studies have been categorized at the organization level and four case studies were categorized at the societal level. Not unexpectedly, the most frequently occurring case studies have been found to be within organization settings. An analysis of these case studies suggests that S-OJT is being used across a range of business sectors, but mostly within industrial and production settings. The analysis also shows that the most commonly reported organizational reasons for using S-OJT have been to reduce training time and to increase the consistency of the

Table 25.2 S-OJT case studies

Level	*Case*	*Organization*	*Purpose of training*	*Results*
Organization	Jacobs and McGiffin (1987)	Quality Control Laboratory	• Training time reduction • Consistent training outcomes	• Improved quality of product • Reduced time for training
	Jacobs (2002b)	Truck Assembly and Production Facility	• Lowering repair or replacing windshield	• Reduced time for production • Reduced cost of repairing
	Jacobs and Bu-Rahmah (2012)	Petroleum Refinery	• Higher-order tasks learning	• Professional level employee training by using extensive S-OJT system
	Mafi and Jacobs (2001)	Large Hospital	• Core value training for supervisors	• Awareness training using an inductive instructional strategy
	Gorman, Moore, Blake and Phillips (2004)	California Manufacturing Companies	• Better training practices in organizations	• Increased trainee's competitiveness • Received public funding for training in private sector

(*Continued*)

Table 25.2 (Continued)

Level	*Case*	*Organization*	*Purpose of training*	*Results*
Society	Workforce Investment Act (WIA)	Department of Labor, USA	• Future employment preparation for dislocated and unemployed workers	• N/A
	National Emergency Grants (NEGs)	Department of Labor, USA	• Occupational skill training for quickly re-employing laid-off workers	• N/A
	Skill Development Fund (SDF)	Workforce Development Administration, Singapore	• Future employment preparation for dislocated and unemployed workers	• N/A
	S-OJT Pilot Program for SMEs	Ministry of Employment and Labor, Republic of Korea	• National competitiveness improvement	• Reduced time to learn • Reduced number of defects

training outcomes. Many of the case studies reported using S-OJT to deliver technical training for frontline employees in production environments or service delivery environments.

S-OJT in organizations

The first organization-based case study listed represents the first contemporary reported use of S-OJT (Jacobs and McGiffin 1987). In this instance, S-OJT was used to reduce training times and achieve more consistent training outcomes among lab technicians who were required to perform 18 quality control tests. These outcomes were subsequently linked to measures of product quality and delivery schedule.

Jacobs (2002b) reported the use of S-OJT in a truck assembly and production facility, including the financial outcomes of its use across three different work areas. In all three instances, the results showed that the time to learn, when compared with unstructured OJT, was reduced by one third and that S-OJT provided twice the financial benefits in contrast to unstructured OJT. In addition, the results showed that the implementation of S-OJT had a dramatic effect in lowering the costs of repairing or replacing windshields that leaked at the end of the production process. Of importance in this case study was the point made that even when employees have a relatively short stay in their jobs, it makes financial sense to use S-OJT. The issue of whether it makes financial sense to invest in training for those employees who will likely stay in their positions only a relatively short time is a question posed by many managers.

Jacobs and Bu-Rahmah (2012) described what was done and the results of using S-OJT to develop new-hire engineers in a petroleum refinery setting. In the case study, the authors reported that the organization used an extensive S-OJT system to help the engineers learn to perform critical engineering tasks, such as making design decisions, planning maintenance events, and preparing reports to management. The case study appears unique in that no other S-OJT case study has been found that involves the learning of higher-order tasks that entail the facilitation of processes among professional-level employees.

Mafi and Jacobs (2001) described how S-OJT was used to inform recently promoted first-line supervisors about the four core values of their organization. The supervisors were non-medical personnel in a large regional hospital setting, who would usually receive the information through a classroom-based training program. The S-OJT version was used to ensure that new supervisors received the information no more than two months from the time of their promotions. The hospital's training in core values was an example of using structured OJT for awareness training, a use that has never before been reported. In addition, the training was unique in that it was delivered using an inductive instructional strategy instead of a deductive one.

In general, many of the case studies reporting the use of S-OJT have also provided information about its financial benefits (Jacobs and McGiffin 1987; Jacobs and Hruby-Moore 1998; Jacobs 2005). Two areas of focus seem to emerge from these case studies: training efficiency and training effectiveness. Training efficiency addresses the question of whether learning a unit of work through S-OJT took less time and whether the investment made to reduce the training time was more or less than the value of the outcome of the training. In general, the results related to training efficiency suggest that S-OJT usually takes less time to conduct and it achieves the training objectives when compared with unstructured OJT, classroom training, and blended versions of the training. In addition, the results suggest that the reduction in training time is accompanied by greater financial benefits. The proportion of the time savings and the financial benefits depend on the individual situations.

Training effectiveness addresses the question of whether S-OJT leads to better training outcomes when compared with other training approaches, and whether the investment to achieve those training outcomes results in financial benefits in terms of improved work outcomes. Whereas training efficiency focuses on time as the primary variable, training effectiveness focuses on quality of outcome and the consequences of the outcomes in terms of time for re-work, replacement parts, and labor overtime, among other measures.

S-OJT in public initiatives

S-OJT has also been used as part of publicly funded initiatives. S-OJT has been used in at least two major ways: (1) to provide training for individuals who have experienced job loss and are learning new skills, and (2) to encourage organizations to improve their training practices through S-OJT as a means to improve employer competitiveness.

For individuals, OJT continues to be a prominent component of the Workforce Investment Act (WIA) of the Department of Labor. Specifically, the wages of unemployed or dislocated adults are partially subsidized by the state government, using federal flow-through funding, when a company or some other skills provider offers the training to an individual. The purpose of the training is to prepare the individual for future employment, either with the OJT provider or with some other company that might require the same skills.

The National Emergency Grants (NEGs) from the Department of Labor, temporarily expanded the Workforce Investment Act OJT programs for dislocated workers, and seeks to address the needs of states and communities by providing special funding assistance in response to large, unexpected economic events that cause significant job losses. NEGs generally provide resources to states and local workforce investment boards to quickly re-employ laid-off workers by offering training to increase occupational skills. In spite of efforts otherwise, the nature of the OJT in these instances is of uncertain quality, primarily because the training is offered by private-sector companies. Federal guidelines specify the amount of time that individuals might be eligible for the training, but not the quality of the training experience.

In Singapore, the Workforce Development Administration subsidizes the training of dislocated and unemployed workers, much like the WIA. However, to be an OJT provider, companies must have employees who have undergone a government-sponsored certificate program and met the requirements established for the training materials. These programs are subsidized through the Skills Development Fund (SDF) (Workforce Development Administration 2012 www.wda.gov.sg).

S-OJT has also been used to promote better training practices in organizations. Gorman *et al.* (2004) reported the results of a comprehensive assessment of the effectiveness of publicly funded structured on-site training programs in California manufacturing companies. In general, the results showed that the use of structured on-site training increased trainees' competitiveness to enter both internal and external labor markets. In addition, the use of structured on-site training suggests that there were benefits for private-sector organizations that receive public funding for the training. In this sense, trainees found increased opportunity for advancement in their companies when supervisors observed whether trainees were actually using the skills and completed a formal evaluation.

A somewhat lesser known use of S-OJT to improve national competitiveness is the pilot program in the Republic of Korea, sponsored by the Human Resource Development Service of the Ministry of Employment and Labor (MOEL) (Ministry of Employment and Labor, Republic of Korea 2013). Established in 2006, the initiative encourages small and medium sized enterprises to apply for a governmental subsidy to support the use of S-OJT. Based on MOEL reports, the subsidy has been increasing every year, leading to a reported reduced time to learn on how to accomplish a task and a reduced number of defects by 27.6 per cent and 40.3 per cent respectively. The initiative provides support to develop S-OJT programs and to develop employees as instructors in the companies. Once selected as a participant in this project, companies may receive governmental funds up to a maximum of $7,000.

Future of S-OJT

In spite of increased discussions about the use of electronic media to deliver training and share information, the necessity remains for people to learn in the actual work context in which they are expected to perform later on. While electronic media may allow greater access to expert and peer sources, no communication device alone replaces the human need for a hands-on, face-to-face sensory learning experience. As one HRD director from Motorola University in Asia once remarked to me, "You can't email a warm handshake." These comments are not meant to suggest the overall superiority or lack of effectiveness of one training approach over another. Instead, the comment suggests the limitations of most training approaches when there is an expectation to acquire skills that relate to job expectations. Simply put, no other training approach provides the same level of effectiveness, if that outcome is desired.

Given this perspective, some form of S-OJT will likely remain as one of the most frequently used training approaches in organizations. How it is designed and implemented will continue to challenge managers and HRD professionals alike, primarily because of the additional effort required upfront to use the systems approach. After all, it can be said that people also learn through unstructured forms of OJT as well, but it eventually takes them much longer and the consequences of error are considerably higher. But those undesirable effects are usually only realized after the fact.

S-OJT will also likely remain as part of societal initiatives to assist the unemployed find new employment. Doing some productive work and learning new job skills at the same time seems a practical and attractive approach to helping individuals acquire new job skills. As a tool to help the unemployed and influence training practices, S-OJT can be very effective. Again, the critical issue is whether the nature of the training is stipulated in such initiatives. That is, the most generous programs to help unemployed individuals would be stymied if the companies involved were not assisted in designing and delivering the most effective training possible. This decision involves the commitment and understanding of public policy makers, such as the pilot program in the Republic of Korea.

Finally, in spite of recent economic variations, the generation and transfer of work-related knowledge and skills will continue to loom large in organizations. How to ensure that individuals know and can do what is expected of them is an ongoing challenge.

References

Benner, P. (1984) *From novice to expert: Excellence and power in clinical nursing practice.* Menlo Park, CA: Addison-Wesley Publishing.

Bennett, T. and Calvin, J. (2002) Structured on-the-job training of field service engineers. In Jacobs, R. (ed.) *Implementing on-the-job learning.* Alexandria, VA: American Society for Training and Development, 97–110.

Davenport, T. (1999) *Human capital: What it is and why people invest in it.* San Francisco: Jossey-Bass.

Dooley, C.R. (1945) *The Training within Industry report (1940–1945): A record of the development of supervision—Their use and the results.* Washington, DC: War Manpower Commission, Bureau of Training, Training within Industry Service.

Dreyfus, H.L. and Dreyfus, S.E. (1986) *Mind over machine: The power of human intuition and expertise in the age of the computer.* New York: The Free Press.

Gilbert, T.F. (2007) *Human competence: Engineering worthy performance* (Tribute edition). Silver Spring, MD: The International Society for Performance Improvement.

Gorman, P., Moore, R., Blake, D. and Phillips, M.G. (2004) An empirical study of the effectiveness of publicly-funded 'structured on-site training': Implications for policy and practice. *Journal of Vocational Education and Training* 56(3): 387–408.

Hart-Landsberg, S., Braunger, J., Reder, S. and Cross, M. (1992) *Learning the ropes: The social constructions of work-based learning.* Berkeley, CA: National Center for Research in Vocational Education.

Jacobs, R. (1992) Structured on-the-job-training. In Stolovitch, H. and Keeps, E. (eds) *Handbook of human performance technology: A comprehensive guide for analyzing and solving performance problems in organizations.* San Francisco: Jossey-Bass, 499–512.

— (1994) Comparing the training efficiency and product quality of unstructured and structured OJT. In Phillips, J. (ed.) *The return on investment in human resource development: Cases on the economic benefits of HRD.* Alexandria, VA: American Society for Training and Development.

— (ed.) (2001) *Planned training on the job. Advances in Developing Human Resources* 3(4). Thousand Oaks, CA: SAGE Publications.

— (2002a) Using structured on-the-job training to inform new supervisors of the organization's core values. In Jacobs, R. (ed.) *Implementing on-the-job learning.* Alexandria, VA: American Society for Training and Development, 97–110.

— (2002b) Unstructured versus structured on-the-job training. In Phillips, J. (ed.) *Measuring return on investment.* Alexandria, VA: American Society for Training and Development, 123–32.

— (2003) *Structured on-the-job training: Unleashing employee expertise in the workplace.* San Francisco, CA: Berrett-Koehler Publishers.

— (2005, June) *Comparing the forecasted financial benefits of blended training, classroom training, and structured on-the-job training.* Presented at the American Society for Training and Development, Orlando, Florida.

Jacobs, R. and McGiffin, T. (1987) A human performance system using a structured on-the-job training approach. *Performance and Instruction* 25(7): 8–11.

Jacobs R. and Hruby-Moore, M. (1998) Comparing the forecasted and actual financial benefits of human resource development programs: Learning from failure. *Performance Improvement Quarterly* 11(2): 93–100.

Jacobs, R. and Osman-Gani, A. (2004) Institutionalization of organizational change: a study of HRD interventions in Singaporean, US, Japanese, and German companies. In T. Egan (ed.), *Proceedings of the Annual Conference of the Academy of Human Resource Development.* Bowling Green, OH: Academy of Human Resource Development.

— (2005) *Workplace training and learning: Cases from cross-cultural perspectives.* Singapore: Pearson Prentice Hall.

Jacobs, R. and Park, Y. (2009) A proposed conceptual framework of workplace learning: Implications for theory development and research in human resource development. *Human Resource Development Review* 8(2): 133–50.

Jacobs, R. and Bu-Rahmah, M. (2012) Developing employee expertise through structured on-the-job training (S-OJT): An introduction to this training approach and the KNPC experience. *Industrial and Commercial Training* 44(2):75–84.

Lave, J. and Wenger, E. (1991) *Situated learning: Legitimate peripheral participation.* Cambridge, MA: Harvard University Press.

Mafi, S. and Jacobs, R. (2001, March) Using the gap service-management model to the human resource development function in organizations. In Aliaga, O. (ed.) *Proceedings of the Annual Conference of the Academy of Human Resource Development.* Baton Rouge, LA: Academy of Human Resource Development.

Ministry of Employment and Labor, Republic of Korea (2013) *Learning organization and structured on-the-job training project.* Available at http://news.molab.go.kr/newshome/mtnmain.php?mtnkey=articleviewandmkey=scatelistandmkey2=33andaid=3328.

Workforce Development Administration, Singapore (2012) *Skills development fund (SDF).* Available at http://www.wda.gov.sg/content/dam/wda/pdf/L223E/Information_on_SDF.pdf.

SECTION VI

Core issues and concerns

26

WORK AND ITS PERSONAL, SOCIAL, AND CROSS-CULTURAL MEANINGS

K. Peter Kuchinke

Work is central to human existence. It provides the necessities for life, offers opportunities for service and achievement, and determines social standing and reputation. Work is also linked to personal identity and offers the full range of existential experiences. This may include pride in a job well done, satisfaction with one's efforts, joy in accomplishing a valued goal, and hope for achievement and progress in the future. At other times, the experience of work can be characterized by disappointment, anger, despair, and a sense of failure and futility. The range of experiences can be understood through its extremes. The United States military offers potential recruits the opportunity to "be all that you can be", while the term "going postal" has become part of the US vernacular in reference to the tragic events of disgruntled employees of the US Postal Service engaging in shooting sprees in their former places of work. Aside from these extreme examples, however, it is through work that all individuals participate in the wider society and come to know its good and bad sides. Through work, individuals experience themselves in relation to others, and learn about their strengths and weaknesses, preferences and dislikes, and resources and limitations. As John Dewey observed, work is the primary means by which individuals connect with the broader society though contributing effort and receiving benefits in various forms (Dewey 1938).

In countries around the world work is valued highly. In North America, for example, the inquiry "what do you do for work?" is often an opening question when meeting strangers and serves to assess compatibility and promise of further contact. Valuations of character and moral and ethical worth are closely linked to work. The justification for the development of vocational and workforce education in early German educational thought, for example, was expressed by Georg Kerschensteiner (in Gonon 2009: 84) by noting that the 'path to the "ideal individual" is only attained via the path to the "useful individual". But the useful person is one who knows his work . . . and possesses the will and the strength to do that work (quotation marks in the original). An old proverb dating back to Calvinistic times considers an idle mind to be the "devil's workshop" (Ciulla 2000: 36), and unemployment is often attributed, in part or entirely, to a lack of personal discipline, perseverance, motivation, or even character (Bernstein 1997). Work salience, the perceived importance and value placed on work and career for an individual's sense of self and identity, increases with country-level economic development, trends towards modernity, and individualism as a cultural value (MOW International Research Team 1987). Reflecting these trends, the field of career studies has grown in volume, depth, and breadth over the past 20 years and now includes a wide range of paradigmatic approaches and perspectives (Schein 2007). A central turn in the study of work and career has been the shift from "the economic and societal importance of work . . . to its personal meaning [and] crucial role in the formation of self-esteem, identity, and sense of order" (Super 1982: 95)

HRD is, of course, centrally focused on work: on the role of learning and training *for* work, *at* work, *through* work, and *about* work, to use a prominent domain statement for vocational education (Copa and Tebbenhoff 1990). Work, as a process and a social institution, is the constant that links together the various dimensions and application areas for HRD, ranging from individual to global, as is shown in McLean's typology of HRD performance contexts (Cho and McLean 2004). Yet despite the essential role of work for the profession, there is a lack of theoretical and conceptual writing on the topic in the HRD domain literature, and this is perhaps because most HRD research is so proximally involved in organizational settings and projects that the dramatic changes in the wider world of work are not immediately obvious. This chapter aims to take a step back and provide perspectives on the understandings of the meaning of work. Current formulations suggest kaleidoscopic variety rather than a single or unitary construct. Work carries personal meaning as a project occupying the majority of time and energy of individuals from young age to adulthood often well into the later years of life. Work is also a social institution undergoing massive change and restructuring. Work takes place in a large variety of settings and under various conditions. Work, finally, is as an expression of culture-specific traditions, norms, and values in a dynamic globalizing environment. In this chapter, we will limit the review to work in firms and organizations of various types, sizes, purposes, and forms. These structures provide official positions and roles, but the relationship between role and role taker is reciprocal: individuals act within the expectations and provisions of a defined job but also influence and often change the formal rules over time (see Giddens 1984).

This chapter excludes work as a primarily personal pursuit, such as tending one's vegetable garden or improving one's guitar technique, a restriction that is to some extent artificial. Much learning, development, and training can be involved in private endeavors. Improvisation in jazz music, for example, has been used to illustrate the complexities and interactions in leadership and organizational analysis (Weick 1998), and private work is important to balance out otherwise intense professional engagements. With the literature on meaning of work and the broader scholarship on career studies focused on formal work in institutional settings, this limitation will be maintained here. The study of work, then, to paraphrase Van Maanen's (1977: 8) observation of career research, is the study of individual and organizational change taking place within the context of societal transformation in its many interrelated dimensions, such as economic, demographic, technological, and social.

Work at the intersection of the social and the personal

Current understandings of social phenomena have roots in the past. This chapter, therefore, begins with a short historical review of work in the context of three eras bounded by the transformational effects of industrial revolutions followed by a discussion of contemporary work and alternative work patterns.

Work in pre-industrial times, as explored in a previous publication (Kuchinke 2009), should be imagined as radically different from contemporary understandings. There was minimal division of labor, work processes were performed in a holistic manner, products were produced on demand, and production processes and product features varied widely (Volti 2008). With the exception of the subject matter of liberal arts, philosophy, religion, and medicine taught at medieval universities in Italy, France, Spain, and England to a small elite (Clark 1983), skills and knowledge for the vast majority of jobs were handed down from one generation to the next through on-the-job training. The boundaries between work and non-work were fluid or non-existent as individuals lived on small farms, above the artisan workshop, or close to the places that provided their livelihood. The pace of the seasons dictated demands and flows of rural work and affiliated crafts. Child labor, year-around work, long workdays, and lifelong work were the norm, and so was the lack of protection against illness, injury, or exploitation (Ciulla 2000). Pre-industrial work took place in the context of highly rigid social structures without opportunities for occupational mobility or choice. Social background determined the type of work, standards of living, income, and standing in the community, and occupational roles for women were severely restricted.

Religious institutions and belief systems asserted strong influences over the understanding of work in pre-industrial societies. In Korea, for example, the influence of Confucianism provided the normative framework for working (Kim and Lee 1978). In Germany, the Christian traditions in the various denominations arising from the Protestant Reformation exercised their impact on the meaning of working. As Placher (2005) chronicles, the view of work as religious duty to God during the early centuries of the current era was transferred to the landlord or sovereign in the feudal system of the middle ages and later still to the state. Especially in nineteenth century Prussia and the German Reich founded in 1871, the growing middle class of military officers, civil administrators, and public servants adopted the notion of work as obligation towards the state, and this influence has persisted in Germany to the current day (Wever 2001). Work in colonial America carried many of the characteristics of feudal continental Europe. In the newly formed republic, the democratic foundation of the country with its limited influence of a landed gentry and without influence of an aristocracy provided opportunity and, indeed, the need for an active life. With amazement and admiration, for example, an early observer of the political and civic system of the United States, Alexis de Tocqueville (1956: 215) wrote in 1835 that the

> whole population are [*sic*] engaged in productive industry, and . . . the poorest as well as the most opulent members of the commonwealth are ready to combine their efforts. . . . The Americans arrived but as yesterday on the territory . . . and they have already changed the whole order of nature for their own advantage.

Following Martin Luther's idea that "work was the will of God and even ceaseless 'dumb toil' sufficed to please him [*sic*]" (Gini 2001: 21), work in early America was ideologically grounded in the Protestant belief in the sanctity of labor as a secular calling and a means of serving God. Bestselling books in the early 1800s built on this notion and extolled the lives of self-made men such as Andrew Carnegie and P.T. Barnum, and so did the rags-to-riches stories, such as the popular Ragged Dick novels by Horatio Alger (Wilms 1979). The iconic image of the person from humble origins overcoming hardship through diligence, hard work, courage, ambition, and tough-minded pragmatism is firmly grounded in US American culture to the present day – notwithstanding the fact that opportunities for advancement and success are, in fact, far from evenly distributed.

Industrialization and modernization of work ushered in qualitative shifts in the institution of work and the subjective experience of working. The availability of work for hire in the rapidly industrializing settings, factories, and early corporations of the late nineteenth century in North America and Western Europe provided an alternative to the limitations and often deprivations of life in small rural communities. Whether by desire or necessity, mass migration to the cities ensued at a scale not rivaled until contemporary labor migration in China. Trading membership in poor yet stable rural communities with strong religious traditions and strict family and community hierarchies for factory work in the cities provided choice and opportunity for self-direction, but also increased physical and emotional demands to an extent unknown in the earlier era. As Ciulla (2000) narrates, the rise of the factory system in the United States around the turn of the twentieth century meant that work was now under the control of the clock, which determined the speed of work on the production line, the length of the work day and week, and amount of pay under the piece-rate system. The alienation of mechanized and employment-based work under scientific management, the image of the employee as a cog in the wheel of production, and the – by today's standards – appalling working conditions in the early factories gave rise to the labor unions and collective bargaining. It also ushered in the brief but influential role of the Socialist Party of America, periods of strike and labor unrest in the year prior to the Great Depression of 1929, and the passage of federal laws, economic programs, and social security provisions under President Roosevelt's New Deal in the 1930s.

The human relations movement – focused on the individual's work attitudes and their effects on productivity – emerged from a series of experiments at the Western Electric plant in Hawthorne, Illinois during the mid-1920s. The Hawthorne experiments and the values subsequently adopted by humanistic psychology focused on individual agency, worth, and dignity. The possibility of work as a means of realizing higher aspirations should be seen as a key aspect of the US American idea of work that developed during the middle part of the twentieth century and has become an enduring part of the meaning of work in North America and, indeed, countries around the world as they move from agrarian to industrial to post-industrial stages of economic development. By mid-century, work in large corporations in the US and elsewhere was said to be characterized by its strict hierarchies, large bureaucracies, and anonymous work settings. Their potential to provide the setting for meaningful work proved to be limited, as depicted vividly in, for example, Arthur Miller's play *Death of a Salesman* (Miller 1949/1976), Sloan Wilson's novel *The Man in the Gray Flannel Suit* (Wilson1955/2002), and Hochschild's sociological analysis of the prevalence of emotional labor in contemporary organizations in *The Managed Heart* (Hochschild 1983/2003). The romantic vision of work of the human potentials movement as a place of pride, belonging, satisfaction, and commitment stood in stark contrast to the experience of work as *toil and trouble*, the title of Joe Kincheloe's (1995) book on the integration of academic and vocational education. Employment settings and contemporary organizations remain to be characterized by a tension between the realities of everyday work and the dream of an integration or harmonization of the self and the workplace, expressed today as employee involvement and engagement in the quality and strategic human resource management literatures. This tension, caused by the highly increased expectations for the experience of work, has become a significant characteristic of industrialized work and modern society. It is well expressed in the opening page of the late Studs Terkel bestselling book *Working* which contains first person narratives from individuals in a wide range of occupations:

> This book, being about work, is, by its very nature, about violence—to the spirit as well as to the body. It is about ulcers as well as accidents, about shouting matches as well as fistfights, about nervous breakdowns as well as kicking the dog around. It is, above all (or beneath all), about daily humiliations. To survive the day is triumph enough for the walking wounded among the great many of us.
>
> *Terkel 1984: xiii*

Over the past 30 years, economists, management scholars, and political scientists have suggested a break from the industrial model and a shift towards a post-industrial, new economy based on the decline of the farming/extractive and industrial sectors and the rise of a service and knowledge economy. "(K)nowledge has rapidly become the principal economic resource, replacing capital, natural resources, and labour. . . . [T]here exists [now] a weightless, or dematerialized economy, in which intangible services are increasingly replacing physical goods as the driving force" (Baldry *et al.* 2007: 28–29). Intellectual and cognitive demands are increasing and creating opportunities for advancement and rewards for knowledge work, while decreasing the value of routine operations and personal services (Reich 1992). While many observers warn of an overly simplistic portrayal of the new economy – many facets of work in the industrial age continue to date – dramatic changes have occurred in the world of work since the 1980s and the rate of change continues unabated. Globalization, perhaps the central force of the current era, includes several trajectories. These include rapidly growing economic modernization in many parts of the world; spread of management models and organizational forms originated in Western Europe and North America; rapid growth in the availability of information from and about developed countries through the Internet and social media; preference for western-style consumption, fashions, and other life style choices; and, in general, spread of individualism and associated life politics around the world (Giddens 1991).

At the same time, the disenchantment with the possibilities and ethics of large organizational bureaucracies continues, be they US style multi-national corporations, Korean family-owned *chebol*, or non-governmental organizations of the United Nations. In the North American context, the philosophical tenets of total quality management of the 1980s have given way to the reality of harsher employment regimes. Where, for example, W.E. Deming insisted on progressive employment practices including long term employment security, information sharing, participatory decision making, and inverted organizational pyramids, the corporate landscape is now characterized by down-sizing, restructuring, outsourcing, and off-shoring of jobs. A solid degree of skepticism with respect to the ability of large corporations to fulfill the promises of good work pervades much contemporary writing by management scholars, such as Leavitt (2007) who opined that work in large corporations might, indeed, be unhealthy for individuals. Work in modern organizations is described as increasingly complex, ambiguous, and uncertain (Baldry *et al.* 2007). This has altered the nexus between work and identity in the current volatile and shifting economic and societal moment where

> the catchword is flexibility, and this increasingly fashionable notion stands for a game of hire and fire with very few rules attached, but with the power to change the rules unilaterally . . . [T]he prospect of constructing a lifelong identity on the foundation of work is, for the great majority of people . . . dead and buried.
>
> *Bauman 2000: 316–17*

The betrayal of promising work, to use Ciulla's (2000) characterization, is accompanied by a chasm between an employee-centered rhetoric in the human resource literature and the reality of the work environment. "Employers wanted trust, loyalty, and commitment from employees, but many employees know that their employers are no longer willing or able to reciprocate" (Ciulla 2001: 153). Professional work, still considered by Reich (1992) as secure and full of promise for intrinsic and extrinsic rewards, has intensified both cognitively and emotionally; it has also increased with respect to workload and the time required to complete urgent tasks. The global financial crises of the recent decades have resulted in increased job insecurity, pressures to work hard and long in order to keep one's job, non-standard work schedules, and stagnant wages (Kelly 2000). Economic recoveries have failed to reduce unemployment rates, and part-time work, outsourcing, off-shoring, and automatization of work tasks by computers and robots have replaced work and career patterns of an older era (Sweet and Meiksins 2012).

The increase in work intensity, work duration, and work stress has changed the psychological contract between employees and employers implied by the traditional career. The concept of the protean career (Hall and Moss 1998) is used to denote the untethering of the individual from the social. Self-directed work patterns are characterized by an orientation towards self-selected goals rather than those of the organization, periodic changes in job and career direction, frequent skill and knowledge upgrading, and a search for congruence between personal values and work activities (Hall 1996). While some are undoubtedly able to benefit from the increased choice and opportunity of a free agency work model, a majority appears to lack the necessary personal, social, and economic prerequisites. Cappelli (1999), for example, identified the personality traits required for self-directed career behavior, namely tolerance for ambiguity, openness to new experience, adaptability, and flexibility. In addition, strong professional networks, specialized knowledge, in-demand skills and expertise, and, arguably, financial resources are required. Edgar Schein's work on career anchors provides additional insight into the conditions for self-directed careers. Career anchors consist of a person's assessment of his or her talents and abilities, basic values and motives and needs pertaining to work (Schein 1996). Entrepreneurship, a prominent type of self-directed career behavior, is based upon a person's self-concept as being independent and autonomous, requiring little security or stability, and being able to weather set-backs and failures. Entrepreneurs also require well developed levels of emotional intelligence, creativity, and technical and managerial competence. While it is not known to what degree these career anchors are distributed in a population at large, there is reason to assume that they are the exception rather than the rule. Briscoe and Hall (2006), for example, showed in a large-scale survey that self-directed career behavior was preferred by the young, by men, and by those with higher levels of education. Respondents in affluent countries were more likely to embrace self-directed career behavior. In addition, developmental psychologist Kegan (1982) showed that well developed levels of identity strengths and personality integration are prerequisites for independent career behavior. Less than one-half of the surveyed population in his research showed sufficient levels of psychological maturity to succeed in protean career patterns.

Cross-cultural perspectives on the meaning of work

Much empirical work over the past 30 years has been focused on the variety of meanings attributed to work and the salience of the work role in relation to other areas of engagement. As Greer and Egan (2012: 463–4) summarized in a recent review article, "role salience is a reflection of the importance and value that people place on those roles they determine to be central to their lives and identities. One pivotal aspect of role salience is its influence on how people will fulfill their responsibilities in organizational roles." Characteristic of meaning of work research (MOW) has been the measurement of work in absolute and in relative terms, namely in terms of its overall importance and in relation to other life roles in the family, community, and other areas of life. Meaning of work is

> the set of general beliefs about work held by the individual, who acquires them through interaction with the social environment. It is generally assumed that these beliefs are related to the person's career orientation and behavior in the work situation, including job performance, turnover, absenteeism and job satisfaction.
>
> *Sverko and Vizek-Vidovic 1995: 3*

The first large-scale cross-cultural studies were initiated by England and colleagues (MOW International Research Team 1987) with participants from eight industrialized nations. The MOW project and its follow-up studies and replications (for example Ardichvili 2005) concentrate on five domains: work centrality, desired working conditions, work outcomes, work role identifications, and social norms about working. *Work centrality* is measured by the absolute value of working as a life role, and by the importance of work relative to other life pursuits, namely involvement with family, religion, community, and leisure. In addition, work centrality is often assessed through the lottery question, a hypothetical scenario of winning the lottery and having enough money to live comfortably for the rest of one's life without having to work for a living. Work meaning is affected by the conditions under which work takes place, and thus a second dimension of the construct, *desired working conditions*, assesses the degree to which different aspects of the work process are viewed as important. A third dimension of the meaning of working, *work outcomes*, relates to the intrinsic and extrinsic results that individuals seek from working. This dimension provides insight into the question of why people expend more or less effort at work, why they intend to remain or consider leaving their job, and why they may or may not go beyond the call of duty and display organizational citizenship behaviors. Fourth, the research project measures *work role identification*, namely how people assess work in terms of congruence between personal expectations and perceived reality with respect to tasks, their employing company, products or services produced, co-workers, occupational affiliation, and monetary compensation. The final dimension, *social norms about working*, taps into a collective set of values related to work in the broader societal context. Here, the core distinction is between an entitlement orientation where it is society's responsibility to provide meaningful work and a personal obligation orientation that put the onus on the individual. In the former, it is viewed as society's role to provide education and training for work, satisfying work settings, and decent work tasks for everyone. In the latter, the obligation to find good work is with the individual.

The most recent findings on the meaning of work in international contexts were obtained in a series of studies of mid-level professionals in eight countries in the Americas, Europe, and Asia (Kuchinke *et al.* 2011). Mid-level managers and professionals are individuals with potentially high impact on their organization's success because of their education, experience, and skills levels. They often emerge as future senior leaders in their organizations and are viewed as the winners of globalization: their career prospects with the current employers are high, and their skills are in demand and portable to other organizations. They tend to be well compensated but also often experience high workloads, face intense time pressures, and work long hours (Shor 1991).

When reviewing country-level commonalities and differences, a first observation was the high work centrality in each country. High levels of identity salience of work have been consistent themes in the meaning of work literature in several studies in a dozen countries during periods of economic expansion and contraction over the past 30 years. This suggests that high work centrality can be assumed to be a near universal characteristic among professional employees. It also counters claims about the diminishing role of work in establishing and maintaining personal identity as expressed by sociologists such as Bauman (2000) and Gini (2001). While the institution of work is changing over time, the role of working in people's lives does not appear to diminish. Individuals are navigating the altered landscape of work to meet a complex and interconnected set of instrumental and non-instrumental needs across time and in diverse cultural environments without surrendering high levels of work salience as a central aspect of what provides meaning to their lives.

Individuals, however, cannot be reduced to vocational categories. With John Dewey (1938: 307) "no one is just an artist and nothing else, and in so far as one approximates that condition he [*sic*] is so much the less developed human being; he is a kind of monstrosity." In line with Dewey's assertion is a second broad conclusion from existing MOW research, namely the importance accorded to involvement with family, which was rated higher than work in each country. Among well-educated and successful mid-level managers and professionals who can be assumed to face no shortage of long work hours, demanding tasks, and tight deadlines, there remains the valuation of family as central and as more important than work. In the samples from all eight countries, there was a clear preference ordering – and low degree of variation in responses – of the primacy of family as a second and near-universal characteristic of the meaning of work in developed countries. The private focus on family as a central life anchor has not been supplanted by professional work. This finding suggests the active meaning-making role of individuals when navigating the tensions between work and non-work domains of life. Rather than passively fulfilling static role expectations, individuals actively construct and enact differentiated and highly personalized understandings of themselves with clear importance rankings for work and family. Follow-up research is needed to more clearly understand the behavioral consequences of this preference in light of the lengthening workweek and the intensification of work, where it can be assumed that individuals set boundaries on work demands that intrude overly on family commitment provided that occupational choices are available. Such choices may include seeking different employment, stepping off of the career ladder, withdrawing from certain assignments and duties, shirking and loafing, or otherwise reducing the compliance with work demands in order to maintain the primary allegiance to the private sphere. The research on job crafting opens up an interesting perspective here. Individuals across a wide range of occupations and professional roles have been shown to exercise substantial amounts of discretion about many elements of their jobs, pursuing some tasks with vigor and energy, delaying others, and even shirking unpleasant aspects of the job (Wrzesniewski and Dutton 2001). It would not be surprising to see individuals using job crafting in order to maintain a level of control over their working life when work demands threaten to intrude upon family commitment. In addition, gender, age, and career ladder effects can be expected to moderate the relationship between work and family salience.

It was surprising to see the role of leisure rated far lower than family and work in the current study (Kuchinke *et al.* 2011). While the average age of the samples in the eight countries places the respondents into the post baby boomer generation who reportedly eschew the values of hard work in favor of leisure and enjoyment, participants in this study exhibited traditional work and family-oriented rather than hedonistic sets of values. This finding runs counter to other research suggesting that a generational shift has occurred in work ethic and attitudes towards work and career. In the Korean research literature, for example, Han (2002) points to the clear distinction between the "make money" and the "spend money" generations, constituting the generation that led the transformation of the Korean economy to join the world's leaders in industrial performance in the aftermath of the Korean War and their off-spring respectively. In Germany, Borchert and Landherr (2009) described the decline in values of duty towards employers and countries in the life orientation of Germans, a decline in the once so highly praised German work ethic, and the gradual increase of self-realization values. The German federation of labor unions, for example, published a large-scale investigation on work in multiple industries and observed a declining sense of belonging and identification with work. Germans appeared quite content to seek sources of identity and life satisfaction in areas unrelated to work, such as family, community involvement, travel, and other non-work related dimensions of life. Fewer than 45 per cent of respondents indicated that they were willing to work longer or harder for a higher salary, and 44 per cent answered that they had not done anything over the past three years to improve their job prospects (Deutscher Gewerkschaftsbund 2008). Although suggesting the need for further research, a possible explanation of the lack of generational differences found in the Kuchinke *et al.* study is the fact that survey participants were invited at their place of work. In contrast to the Korean and German studies, where responses were solicited from samples of the working age population in each country at large, the choice of approaching survey participants at their place of work might have primed the response pattern. Even where surveys are conducted anonymously and with full assurance of confidentiality, as in Kuchinke *et al.*, survey responses represent complex socio-emotional events that are influenced by a host of factors rather than objective data collection instruments.

The analysis of the three items in the lottery question added further interesting detail to the question about the centrality of work in the work lives of mid-level professionals in the study. For the entire sample, the majority of respondents (56 per cent) indicated the preference to continue working under changed conditions, and only 12 per cent selected the choice to stop working altogether if the necessity to earn a living was removed because of a large lottery win. When comparing the responses for each country, a more differentiated picture emerged. Respondents from the USA indicated a greater preference for the stop working option than those from the other countries. In light of the much-heralded Protestant work ethic and the high value placed on material wealth and middle-class membership, the researchers expected stronger internal commitment to the idea of continuing to work rather than stopping to work.

Conclusion

Work and career are played out in the context of multiple, often contradictory, and complex forces in the lives of individuals, and in tension between the demands of the work organization and the desire for leisure, free time, and engagement with family, community, and friends. As individuals navigate through the current era, the guide posts of the past appear to vanish: organizations and institutions, long viewed as stable providers of occupational roles, are increasingly unable or unwilling to ensure stable, engaging, and rewarding work. The shift towards individual responsibility of work and career provides promises and increasing options, but comes at the price of instability and material and emotional insecurity.

What then has an investigation into the meaning of working to tell the field of human resource development? For one, developing a basic understanding of the history of one's profession or chosen field is central to professional education and allows to understand the traditions and current trends in light of those of the past (Peters 1973). Given the central role of work, gaining an understanding of the trajectories, trends, and developments in work as a process and work as an institution provides the basis for contemporary research and application. The tendency to view previous eras as homogeneous, unitary, and simpler than the current era, should be avoided. Literary accounts of the plight of working men, women, and children as vividly displayed in Charles Dickens' and Thomas Hardy's novels, accounts of child labor in the cotton mills of the North of England, and German playwright Schiller's plays about the weavers' revolt in the nineteenth-century Silesian mountains are only a few examples that provide insight into the complex array of forces, choices, opportunities and constraints of those days. In contemporary research, too little attention is placed on manual work, the work of immigrants, of transient workers, or other underprivileged groups. Far deeper understanding of the impact of national, regional, and local cultural norms on the evolution of work meaning is needed to guide human resource development and organizations in work design, organization development, leadership and management development, and other forms of learning and change. As the rate of change is increasing and organizations are faced with the challenge of transformation and adaptation, the focus on the meaning of working around the world and in many detailed settings should be given much attention. It is the hope of this author, that this chapter can provide a first orientation and direction for future study in this important area.

References

Ardichvili, A. (2005) 'The meaning of working and professional development needs of employees in a post-communist country', *International Journal of Cross-Cultural Management* 5(1): 105–19.

Baldry, C., Bain, P., Taylor, P., Hyman, J., Scholarios, D., Marks, A., Watson, A., Gilbert, K., Gall, G. and Bunzel, D. (2007) *The Meaning of Work in the New Economy*, New York: Palgrave/Macmillan.

Bauman, Z. (2000) 'On glocalization: or globalization for some, locatization for some others', in Beilharz, P. (ed.) *The Bauman Reader*, Oxford: Blackwell.

Bernstein, P. (1997) *American Work Values: Their Origin and Development*, Albany, NY: State University of New York.

Borchert, M. and Landherr, G. (2009) 'The changing meaning of work in Germany', *Advances in Developing Human Resources* 11(2): 204–17.

Briscoe, J.P. and Hall, D.T. (2006) 'The interplay of boundaryless and protean careers: Combinations and implications', *Journal of Vocational Behavior* 69(1): 4–18.

Cappelli, P. (1999) *The New Deal at Work: Managing the Market-Driven Workforce*, Boston, MA: Harvard Business School.

Cho, E. and McLean, G.N. (2004) 'What we discovered about NHRD and what it means for HRD', *Advances in Developing Human Resource* 6(3): 382–93.

Ciulla, J.B. (2000) *The Working Life: The Promise and Betrayal of Modern Work*, New York: Three Rivers.

Clark, B. (1983) *The Higher Education System: Academic Organizations in Cross-National Perspective*, Berkeley, CA: University of California.

Copa, G.H. and Tebbenhoff, E. (1990) *Subject Matter of Vocational Education: In Pursuit of Foundations* (Report No. MDS-094), Berkeley, CA: National Center for Research in Vocational Education.

de Tocqueville, A. (1956) *Democracy in America*, New York: Mentor.

Deutscher Gewerkschaftsbund (2008) *DGB-Index Gute Arbeit 2008. Wie die Beschäftigten die Arbeitswelt beurteilen, was sie sich von einer guten Arbeit erwarten* [DGB-Index Good Work 2008. How the employees assess the working environment, what do they expect of good work]. Online available http: //www.dgb-index-gute-arbeit.de (accessed May 13, 2013).

Dewey, J. (1938) *Education and Experience*, New York: McMillan.

Giddens, A. (1984) *The Constitution of Society: Outline of the Theory of Structuration*, Cambridge: Polity Press.

— (1991) *Modernity and Self-Identity: Self and Society in Late Modern Age*, Stanford, CA: Stanford University.

Gini, A. (2001) *My Job, My Self: Work and the Creation of the Modern Individual*, New York: Routlege.

Gonon, P. (2009) *The Quest for Modern Vocational Education – Georg Kerschensteiner Between Dewey, Weber and Simmel*, Bern: Peter Lang.

Greer, T.W. and Egan, T.M. (2012) 'Inspecting the hierarchy of life roles: A systematic review of role salience literature', *Human Resource Development Review* 11(4): 464–99.

Hall, D.T. (1996) *The Career is Dead, Long Live the Career. A Relational Approach to Careers*, San Francisco: Jossey-Bass.

Hall, D.T., and Moss, J.E. (1998) 'The new protean career contract: Helping organizations and employees adapt', *Organizational Dynamics* 26(1): 22–37.

Han, S.K. (2002) *Research for Job Perception of Korean (II)*, Seoul: Korean Research Institute for Vocational Education and Training, Korea.

Hochschild, A.R. (1983/2003) *The Managed Heart: Commercialisation of Human Feelings*, Berkeley, CA: University of California.

Kegan, R. (1982) *The Evolving Self: Problem and Process in Human Development*, Boston, MA: Harvard University.

Kelly, G.M. (2000) 'Employment and concepts of work in the new global economy', *International Labor Review* 139(1): 5–32.

Kim, K.D. and Lee, J.Y. (1978) 'The meaning of work and labor commitment in Korea', *Korean Social Science Journal* 5(1): 74–84.

Kincheloe, J. (1995) *Toil and Trouble*, New York: Peter Lang.

Kuchinke, K.P. (2009) 'Changing meanings of work in Germany, Korea, and the United States in historical perspectives', *Advances in Developing Human Resources* 11(2): 168–88.

Kuchinke, K.P., Ardichvili, A., Borchert, M., Cornachione, E., Cseh, M., Kang, H., Oh, S., Rozanski, A., Tynaliev, U. and Zavyalova, E. (2011) 'Work meaning among mid-level professional employees: A study of the importance of work centrality and extrinsic and intrinsic work goals in eight countries', *Asia Pacific Journal of Human Resources* 49(3): 264–84.

Leavitt, H.J. (2007) 'Big organizations are unhealthy environments for human beings', *Academy of Management Learning & Education* 6(2): 253–63.

Miller, A. (1949/1976) *Death of a Salesman*, New York: Penguin.

MOW International Research Team (1987) *The Meaning of Working*, London: Academic Press.

Peters, R.S. (1973) *Philosophy of Education*, Oxford: Oxford University Press.

Placher, W.C. (2005) *Callings: Twenty Centuries of Christian Wisdom on Vocation*, Grand Rapids, MI: Eerdmans.

Reich, R.B. (1992) *The Work of Nations: Preparing Ourselves for 21st Century Capitalism*, New York: Vintage.

Schein, E.H. (1996) 'Career anchors revisited: Implications for career development in the 21st century', *Academy of Management Executive* 10(4): 80–8.

— (2007) 'Foreword: Career Research – Some Personal Perspectives', in Gunz, H.P. and Peiperl, M., (eds) *Handbook of Career Studies*, Thousand Oaks, CA: SAGE, x–xiii.

Shor, J. (1991) *The Overworked American: The Unexpected Decline of Leisure*, New York: Basic Books.

Super, D.E. (1982) 'The relative importance of work: Models and measures for meaningful data', *Counseling Psychologist* 10(4): 95–103.

Sverko, B. and Vizek-Vidovic, V. (1995) 'Studies of the meaning of work: Approaches, models, and some of the findings', in Super, D.E. (ed.) *Life Roles, Values, and Careers: International Findings of the Work Importance Study*, San Francisco: Jossey-Bass.

Sweet, S.A. and Meiksins, P. (2012) *Changing Contours of Work: Jobs And Opportunities in the New Economy*, Thousand Oaks, CA: Pine Forges.

Terkel, S. (1974) *Working*, New York: Pantheon.

Van Maanen, J. (1977) *Organizational Careers: Some New Perspectives*, New York: Wiley.

Volti, R. (2008) *An Introduction to the Sociology of Work and Occupations*, Los Angeles: Pine Forge.

Weick, K.E. (1998) 'Improvisation as a mindset for organizational analysis', *Organization Science* 9(5): 543–55.

Wever, K.S. (2001) *Labor, Business, and Change in Germany and the United States*, Kalamazoo, MI: W.E. Upjohn Institute.

Wilms, W. (1979) 'New meanings for vocational education', *UCLA Educator* 21(1): 5–11.

Wilson, S. (1955/2002) *The Man in the Gray Flannel Suit*, New York: Da Capo.

Wrzesniewski, A. and Dutton, J. (2001) 'Crafting a job: Employees as active crafters of their work', *Academy of Management Review* 26(2): 179–201.

27

ORGANIZATIONAL SUSTAINABILITY, CORPORATE SOCIAL RESPONSIBILITY AND BUSINESS ETHICS

Alexandre Ardichvili

The goal of this chapter is to illuminate the role of HRD in enabling Corporate Social Responsibility (CSR), Organizational sustainability (OS), and ethics in business organizations. Specifically, this chapter will discuss: the importance of CSR, sustainability and business ethics in today's business organizations; definitions of key terms; the role of HRD in embedding OS, CSR, and ethics in organizational practices and cultures; associated learning and development approaches; and critical views of HRD's role and practices.

Consensus is growing among HRD academics that the issues of sustainability, CSR, and business ethics are closely inter-related and that discussions of HRD's role should be addressing all three issues as part of the same conversation (Ardichvili 2011; Becker 2011; Garavan and McGuire 2010; MacKenzie *et al.* 2011; Tomé 2011). To better understand how these three concepts are related, we need to consider first definitions of the key terms. Hopkins (2003: 1) argued that CSR is "treating the stakeholders of the firm ethically or in a responsible manner". According to McWilliams and Siegel (2001: 117), CSR comprises "actions that appear to further some social good, beyond the interests of the firms and that which is required by law". Garavan and McGuire (2010), drawing on Maignan and Ralston's (2002) work, pointed out that CSR can be defined in terms of either underlying principles (e.g. focus on stakeholder's values or performance), or processes. The latter could include, among other things, "programs and activities such as sponsorships, codes of ethics, philanthropic activities, and stakeholder issues related to the community, customer employee, suppliers, and stakeholders" (Garavan and McGuire 2010: 489).

Speaking about *sustainability*, one of the most often cited definitions of this term was offered by the World Commission on Environment and Development (WCED). According to WCED, sustainability is a "development that meets the needs of the present without compromising the ability of future generations to meet their own needs" (WCED 1987: 8). Docherty *et al.* (2002: 12) argued that "Sustainability . . . encompasses three levels: the individual, the organizational and the societal. Sustainability at one level cannot be built on the exploitation of the others . . .". Focusing on the societal level, Cavagnaro and Curiel (2012: 1) argued that "the ultimate goal of sustainable development is securing better quality of life for all, both now and for future generations, by pursuing responsible economic growth, equitable social progress, and effective environmental protection". The emphasis on social, environmental and economic outcomes is based on the Triple Bottom Line model (Elkington 2006; Wikström 2010), which postulates that sustainable development can be achieved only when there is a balanced attention to all three main elements of the system. Pfeffer (2010: 35) extended the discussion of corporate sustainability beyond the emphasis on environmental and economic impacts of corporate policies, and highlighted the importance of human and social sustainability: "Just as physical sustainability considers the consequences of organizational activity for material, physical resources; social sustainability might consider how organizational activities affect people's physical and mental health and well-being – the stress of work practices on the human system."

Finally, defining *ethics* as it applies to business settings, Carroll and Buchholtz (2008: 242) argued that it "is the discipline that deals with what is good and bad and with moral duty and obligation" and can "be regarded as a set of moral principles or values". The definition focuses on two issues: an understanding of what is perceived as good and bad, and an individual's or group's moral duty and obligation. Therefore, business ethics is a discipline that deals with what is perceived as good or bad behavior in a business organization's interaction with its multiple stakeholders and what the business' obligations are to its stakeholders, the society, and, ultimately, to the world and the environment. It follows that a business organization cannot be ethical if it does not behave in socially responsible ways, and it cannot be socially responsible if it is not striving to incorporate principles of sustainability in all its business processes and outcomes.

OS, CSR, ethics, and HRD: three themes

What is the role of HRD in promoting OS, CSR, and ethical business behavior? And what should this role be? In this section we will first discuss the role of HRD in embedding OS, CSR, and ethics in business organizations. Then we will consider related training and education methods and organization development approaches. Finally, we will turn to a discussion of critical perspectives on the role of HRD in organizations and society (including the need for an introspective look at how sustainable, responsible, and ethical are HRD's own practices).

Embedding OS, CSR and ethics in organizations: the role of HRD

According to Garavan and McGuire (2010: 489), HRD can play a significant role in embedding OS, CSR, and ethics in business organizations. It can not only "raise the awareness of employees and develop positive attitudes toward sustainability", but also "can contribute to the development of a culture that supports sustainability, CSR, and ethics". Likewise, Rimanoczy and Pearson (2010), discussing the role of HRD in developing sustainable organizations, argued that the main goal of HRD should be to change organizational cultures. Therefore, developing and delivering ethics or CSR-related training programs is only one of the roles for HRD. An equally important role is to develop organizational cultures that embrace and support business ethics, CSR and sustainability (Liebowitz 2010; Sackmann *et al.* 2009; Sroufe *et al.* 2010).

Among strategies for promoting sustainability and ethical behavior one of the most successful approaches is to influence key organizational players: executives and senior managers. Raising leaders' awareness of ethics and sustainability issues, changing leaders' mindsets and equipping them with necessary tools and models is a necessary step in ensuring that the whole organization will be ready for the needed change (Ardichvili and Jondle 2009; Gond *et al.* 2011; Knights and O'Leary 2006).

A comparison of articles on institutionalizing ethical business cultures (Ardichvili and Jondle 2009; Foote and Ruona 2008) and embedding sustainability in organizational cultures (Garavan and McGuire 2010; Garavan *et al.* 2010) shows that in both cases the ultimate goal is to achieve lasting changes in employee attitudes and behavior, as well as in organizational value systems. HRD can influence these changes through a system of coordinated efforts and programs, which can include, among other things, action learning, experiential learning, encouraging and promoting informal learning and communities of practice, and fostering programs and behaviors, characteristic of learning organizations.

A question is often asked: is it realistic to assume that HRD can play a significant role in changing organizational cultures and influencing organizational leadership's attitudes and behaviors, leading to more ethical and sustainable practices? Skeptics point out that HRD does not have a place at the table when discussions of ethics or CSR-related strategies take place. Thus, an empirical investigation, conducted by Fenwick and Bierema (2008), found a disconnect between HRD and CSR in organizations, and in many cases HRD managers are not allowed to play a central role in CSR programs. Indeed, in many cases HRD executives are not invited to participate in ethics and CSR-related discussions and decision making. Recently I participated in a year-long series of meetings among executives of Fortune 500 and other large business organizations, focused on discussions of current practices and future directions for developing ethical business cultures and CSR. It was symptomatic that the meetings were attended by corporate compliance and ethics officers, top executives in HR, new business development, and strategy areas, and yet the HRD function was not represented. Does this mean, however, that we should accept what seems to be a predominant trend in today's organizations? I would argue that, to the contrary, HRD executives need to be proactive in educating other executives in their organizations about the importance of the role of HRD, demonstrating what specifically HRD can do to promote ethics, CSR, and OS. In this respect, the information discussed in the following section is especially important.

Learning and development strategies

Various learning and development strategies that can be used to cultivate ethical, responsible, and sustainable organizations and individuals are discussed in HRD and management learning literatures. Among most well-known and often practiced HRD interventions are ethical awareness training, corporate environmental education and awareness programs, and ethical leadership programs (Garavan *et al.* 2010: 599).

In addition to compliance and ethics training, an important prescription for developing ethical and responsible human resources is to foster reflection, creativity, and continuous learning on the individual level and learning culture on the organizational level (Boud *et al.* 2006). According to Haugh and Talwar (2010), learning and development strategies used for embedding sustainability and corporate responsibility in organizations include action learning, field projects, and knowledge management. Pless and Maak (2011) described global service learning projects which involved sending participant teams to developing countries to work with NGOs or local social entrepreneurs on resolving sustainability-related issues. These projects were addressing developmental needs on three levels: individual, organizational, and larger community. The authors argued that these experiences had deep individual effect on cognitive, affective, and behavioral levels and helped participants modify their mindsets, by developing more socially responsible attitudes.

A similar approach was advocated by Bradbury *et al.* (2008), who described action research-based global community building projects at Unilever. In these projects, hundreds of leaders from the Asian division of the company worked in communities of learning and practice with managers from Western countries, visiting local villages, schools and temples in various Asian countries, and completing community develoment projects. In addition to hands-on activities and community engagement work, projects included time for self-reflection and journaling, small group discussions of lessons learned, and storytelling, all aimed at generating and sharing individual and group insights.

A range of other related organization development activities could be implemented. For example, an organization could issue communications about its CSR/OS commitments and performance; organize meetings and discussions, aimed at uncovering and clarifying corporate values/norms; and conduct interventions, focused on creating responsible and sustainable learning organization strategies. In addition, organizations could promote stakeholder engagement and creation of opportunities for social learning (Garavan *et al.* 2010: 599), and integration of CSR/OS/ethics considerations into strategic HRD work (Garavan and McGuire 2010). As mentioned earlier, among specific strategies for promoting OS, CSR, and ethical business culture in organizations, leadership development is perceived as an important approach. Part of this strategy is to raise leaders' awareness of related issues, and part is equipping them with necessary tools and models (Gond *et al.* 2011).

Various authors have argued that the key to insuring ethical, responsible, and sustainable behavior in organizations in the long run is establishing an ethical culture that creates a business with a conscience, where decisions are made taking into consideration all stakeholders that are impacted in some way by the business (Ardichvili and Jondle 2009; Goodpaster 2007), and where morally developed individuals are able to act according to their convictions (Feldman 2007).

A model, developed at the Center for Ethical Business Cultures at the University of St Thomas (USA), describes five characteristics of ethical business cultures: Values-Driven, Stakeholder Balance, Leadership Effectiveness, Process Integrity, and Long-term Perspective (Ardichvili *et al.* 2009; Ardichvili and Jondle 2012). *Values* are the core of the model, providing needed structural integrity, a clear focus for organizational strategy and day-to-day activities. There are two types of organizational values: espoused (formal, stated) values and values-in-action (actually practiced, informal, often unstated values) (Goodpaster 2007; Schein 2004). An organization is functioning as an ethical and responsible entity only if espoused values and values-in-action are aligned. Formal values should be carefully formulated, clearly explained, and actively promoted by the organization's executive team. At the same time, culture change interventions need to be designed to ensure that the organizational culture is supportive of responsible and ethical informal values and behaviors. Organizational culture needs to be shielded against proliferation of irresponsible behaviors, often resulting from the lack of focus on clearly articulated corporate values, and a misalignment between espoused and practiced values. When these two sets of values come into conflict, the latter usually prevails (Goodpaster 2007: 153). It follows from the above discussion that one of HRD's roles in establishing and supporting ethical and responsible cultures is to ensure the alignment between stated and practiced values.

The second characteristic of the model, *Leadership Effectiveness*, is closely linked to the *Values-Driven* dimension. Ethical leaders lead by personal example of integrity. Employees learn about organizations' "values in-use" by observing leaders' everyday behavior, and by gauging whether leaders' statements about their values align with their practices. At the same time, leaders need to be proactive in demanding ethical and responsible conduct from all employees at every level of the organization. To support organizational leadership, HRD can position ethics, CSR, and OS topics among some of the central topics of corporate leadership development programs. However, this positioning is not enough. To demonstrate their alignment between espoused and practiced values, leaders need to be invited to play an active role in delivering related training programs for all employees (Collier and Esteban 2007).

The third characteristic, *Stakeholder Balance*, suggests that an organization has responsibility to numerous stakeholders. It is assumed that a tension always exists between interests of multiple stakeholders. Privileging any one stakeholder group could result in serious distortions and, potentially, ethical problems. It is not suggested that the tensions between stakeholders could completely disappear. However, HRD could help to manage these tensions by creating a forum for discussion of interests of various stakeholder groups (e.g. customers, supplier, employees, stockholders, and larger community).

The *Process Integrity* characteristic of the model suggests that ethical, sustainable, and responsible business cultures evolve gradually as a result of the institutionalization of companies' values in all business functions and processes. The key to process integrity is reinforcing company values in all everyday operations.

The final characteristic, the *Long-term Perspective*, implies a balance between the short-term and the long-term outlook, and avoiding making short-term decisions that could cause harm in the long term. A key feature of this dimension is concern for the environment and long-term sustainability not only of the business but also of the larger community. Long-term perspective means that organizations must be environmentally sustainable, socially responsible, as well as profitable in the long run.

In summary, to promote sustainability, responsibility, and ethical behavior in an organization, a range of HRD activities may be needed. Some of these activities include: the clarification of organizational values and related changes in mission and vision statements; development of corporate codes of ethics and related procedures; provision of ethics and CSR-related training at all levels of the organizational hierarchy; and incorporation of ethical and responsible thinking in decision making and in organizational change and leadership development initiatives.

While HRD can play a role in all these activities, its role is likely to be larger in some and less significant in others. For example, the development of codes of ethics is usually managed by a team that includes general HR and legal and compliance officers of the organization. However, to ensure that HRD professionals are able to assist with the dissemination of the information about these codes and principles through training and corporate communication channels, they should be able to participate and provide their input at the stage of the development of relevant documents and processes.

Ethics- or CSR-related training is, on the other hand, an area where HRD's leading role is largely unchallenged. Here the HRD professionals, in their turn, need to be mindful of the need for a systems view of training, and involved in the development and delivery of such training not only with the compliance officers, but also with the line management and C-suite executives. Among other things, such involvement will provide leaders with an opportunity to set an example and demonstrate their commitment to OS and CSR, and to communicate their vision and values.

The role of HRD: critical perspectives

Our third theme is related to the societal role and impact of HRD, and a critical look at HRD's own practices. A number of authors criticize HRD for abandoning its original mission of advancing the well-being of people in organizations through developing human potential, and becoming an instrument of achieving profit maximization goals of corporations; and for being focused on short-term financial results instead of long-term and holistic human development (Fenwick and Bierema 2008; Garavan and McGuire 2010; Kuchinke 2010). Fenwick and Bierema (2008) argued that HRD can contribute to long-term sustainability of organizations and society only if it will pay equal attention to individual and organizational development. Kuchinke (2010) pointed out that human development should be a key concern of HRD, while this concern needs to be viewed in light of HRD's contribution to organizational effectiveness and long-term sustainability.

To be able to provide adequate support for organizational ethics initiatives, the HRD function needs to adhere to its own internal standards of ethics and integrity. Bierema and D'Abundo (2004: 444) stated: "We contend that HRD, as a profession, as well as a managerial practice, has a social responsibility to question performative practices and rediscover human development in the process", and "HRD has a responsibility to create a socially conscious work environment that benefits individuals and the social system they inhabit, not just the organization". Tomé (2011), Garavan and McGuire (2010), Bierema and D'Abundo (2004), and Fenwick and Bierema (2008) all pointed out that HRD needs to focus not only on changing organizational practices and developing individuals, but also on reflecting on its own practices to make sure that they are ethical, sustainable, and socially responsible. Ethical considerations should play a central role in any organization change interventions, implemented by HRD professionals. Are these interventions likely to result in layoffs, and thus lead to the loss of valuable talent and cause distress in local communities? What are the consequences for various stakeholders, including communities in other parts of the country or in other countries, where the organization is sourcing its raw materials and supplies? Is the change initiative strengthening the organization's determination to conduct its business with a long-term sustainability and stakeholder balance in mind, or is it just mindlessly serving the dictates of short-term profit maximization? These and other questions need to inform all decisions that are made in conjunction with new change initiatives (Ardichvili 2012).

Power differentials in organizations must be considered when analyzing the ethics and sustainability dimensions of HRD practices. Foucault (1980) asserted that power exists in the society through multiple and constantly shifting networks of relationships, and is closely intertwined with and reinforced by knowledge. Bourdieu (1998: 32) perceived organizations as "fields of power": "All societies appear as social spaces, that is, as structures of differences that can be only understood by constructing the generative principle which objectively grounds those differences. This principle is none other than the structure of the distribution of the forms of power or the kinds of capital which are effective in the social universe under consideration – and which vary according to the specific place and moment at hand." Further, Bourdieu (ibid: 34) explained that the field of power "is the space of the relations of force between the different kinds of capital, or, more precisely, between the agents who possess a sufficient amount of one of the different kinds of capital".

Organizational cultures are a bundle of negotiated meanings, and organizational members who possess more power can exercise a stronger influence on the emerging culture (Hallett 2003). None of these players, even those endowed with most power, can fully define the organizational culture and shape it according to their goals and vision: even these most powerful players have to give concessions to demands of the other players and of the structures of the organizational field (Bourdieu 1998).

Likewise, Stacey (2003: 329), using Elias's (1991) theory of power asserted that "Instead of thinking of power as the possession of some and not of others . . . power [is] a characteristic of . . . all human relating. In human relating some are more constrained than others . . . As they interact, the power relations, the pattern of enabling constraints, emerges, shifts and evolves." Therefore, "organizations are patterns of power relations sustained by ideological themes of communicative interaction and patterns of inclusion and exclusion in which human identities emerge" (Stacey 2003: 330).

To summarize the above argument: organizational cultures are patterns of relations and interactions between individuals and interest groups and are constantly re-shaped by these interactions; power is the main driving force behind actions and emerging configurations of relationships. The implication of this analysis of power relationships is that HRD can play multiple roles in this process, among them that of power broker, advocate, and shaper of the configurations of the field. Thus, Bierema and D'Abundo (2004: 449) suggested that socially conscious HRD can be "advocating for stakeholders … challenging and revising socially 'unconscious' policies and practices, analyzing and negotiating power relations". Furthermore, Bierema and D'Abundo suggested that the analysis of power relationships, conducted in the field of adult education (e.g. Cervero and Wilson 2001), can be applied to HRD. Elaborating on this application, they point out that HRD interventions may provide power to some groups at the exclusion of others. For example, by making a decision who will participate in a specific training program, HRD professionals could serve as political activists or, alternatively, confine themselves to the role of servants of the established power system (cf. the chapter by Spencer and Kelly in this volume). According to Bierema and D'Abundo (2004: 542), HRD practitioners "must recognize the multiple interests of all stakeholders in any practice with attention to conflicting agendas regarding the production and reproduction of power". To address the issues of power, Fenwick and Bierema (2008: 33) propose that HRD activities "might include ensuring that internal issues of employee rights are on the firm's CSR agenda, that HRD activities are measured in CSR audits and included in CSR reports, and that HRD representatives are included in advisory or design roles in creating processes for CSR implementation".

So far we have been concerned with what HRD professionals can do to promote equitable, ethical, and sustainable practices in organizations. However, we also need to take a critical look at HRD's own practices. Social learning theory suggests that values develop in interactions and through observing behavior of others (Bandura 1986). Therefore, HRD practitioners, as some of the most visible promoters of organizational values, must act as role models of ethical, responsible, and sustainable behavior within their organizations. In addition, HRD needs to carefully examine models and frameworks used in our day-to-day practice. Hatcher (2002) pointed out that the majority of current HRD models are not based on considerations of social responsibility and ethics. Therefore, HRD's ability to create ethical and responsible business organizations is limited by the tools we use. According to Hatcher, most HRD models are "noticeably silent on the impact at both the societal and environmental levels" (2000: 18). Therefore, new models, used in HRD work, should incorporate not only considerations of performance, efficiency, and return on investment, but also outcomes, related to business organizations' impact on society, community, and the environment (Hatcher 2002).

Conclusion

In this chapter I argued that CSR, OS, and ethics in business organizations can be viewed as integral parts of a system that is shaped by a complex interaction between individual knowledge, practice, and moral development, and organizational practices, power relationships, and culture. HRD can play a key role in shaping organizational cultures of ethics, sustainability, and responsibility, by pursuing a range of activities that include culture change efforts and ethics and responsibility-related education and training for employees on all levels. HRD practitioners, being among the most visible carriers and promoters of organizational values, must act as role models of ethical behavior within their organizations, take into account organizational power differentials, and question and re-examine their own practices and models.

References

Ardichvili, A. (2011) Sustainability of nations, communities, organizations, and individuals: The role of HRD. *Human Resource Development International* 14(4): 371–4.

— (2012) Sustainability or limitless expansion: paradigm shift in HRD practice and teaching. *European Journal of Training and Development* 36(9): 873–87.

Ardichvili, A. and Jondle, D. (2009) Ethical business cultures: A literature review and implications for HRD. *Human Resource Development Review* 8(2): 223–44.
— (2012) HRD and business ethics. In Wilson, J. (ed.) *International Human Resource Development*. London: Kogan Page.
Ardichvili, A., Jondle, D. and Mitchell, J. (2009) Characteristics of ethical business cultures. *Journal of Business Ethics* 85(4): 445–52.
Bandura, A. (1986) *Social foundations of thought and action*. Englewood Cliffs, NJ: Prentice-Hall.
Becker, W. (2011) Are you leading a socially responsible and sustainable human resource function? *People and Strategy* 34(1): 18–23.
Bierema, L.L. and D'Abundo, M. (2004) HRD with a conscience: practicing socially responsible HRD. *International Journal of Lifelong Education* 23(5): 443–58.
Boud, D., Cressey, P. and Docherty, P. (eds) (2006) *Productive reflection at work: Learning for changing organizations*. London: Routledge.
Bourdieu, P. (1998) *Practical reason: On the theory of action*. Stanford, CA: Stanford University Press.
Bradbury, H., Mirvis, P., Neilsen, E. and Pasmore, W. (2008) Action research at work: Creating the future following the path from Lewin. In Reason, P. and Bradbury, H. (eds) *The SAGE handbook of action research* (2nd edition). London: SAGE.
Carroll, A.B. and Buchholtz, A.K. (2008) *Business and society: Ethics and stakeholder management* (7th edition). Mason, OH: South-Western Cengage Learning.
Cavagnaro, E. and Curiel, G. (2012) *Three levels of sustainability*. Sheffield: Greenleaf.
Cervero, R.M. and Wilson, A.L. (2001) *Power in practice: Adult education and the struggle for knowledge and power in society*. San Francisco: Jossey-Bass.
Collier, J. and Esteban, R. (2007) Corporate social responsibility and employee commitment. *Business Ethics: A European Review* 16(1): 19–33.
Docherty, P., Forslin, J., Shani, A.B. (Rami) and Kira, M. (2002) Emerging work systems: From intensive to sustainable. In Docherty, P., Forslin, J., Shani, A.B. (Rami) (eds) *Creating Sustainable Work Systems: Emerging Perspectives and Practice* (3–14). London: Routledge.
Elias, N. (1991) *The Society of Individuals*. Oxford: Blackwell.
Elkington, J. (2006) Governance for sustainability. *Corporate Governance* 14(6): 522–29.
Feldman, S. (2007) Moral business cultures: the keys to creating and maintaining them. *Organizational Dynamics* 36(2): 156–70.
Fenwick, T. and Bierema, L.L. (2008) Corporate social responsibility: Issues for human resource development professionals. *International Journal of Training and Development* 12(1): 24–35.
Foote, M. and Ruona, W. (2008) Institutionalizing ethics: A synthesis of frameworks and implications for HRD. *Human Resource Development Review* 7(3): 292–308.
Foucault, M. (1980) *Power and Knowledge*. New York: Vintage.
Garavan, T.N. and McGuire, D. (2010) Human resource development and society: Human resource development's role in embedding corporate social responsibility, sustainability, and ethics in organizations. *Advances in Developing Human Resources* 12(5): 487–507.
Garavan, T.N., Heraty, N., Rock, A. and Dalton, E. (2010) Conceptualizing the behavioral barriers to CSR and CS in organizations: A typology of HRD interventions. *Advances in Developing Human Resources* 12(5): 587–613.
Gond, J., Igalens, J., Swaen, V. and Akremi, A.E. (2011) The human resources contribution to responsible leadership: An exploration of the CSR-HR interface. *Journal of Business Ethics* 98(1): 115–32.
Goodpaster, K.E. (2007) *Conscience and corporate culture*. Malden, MA: Blackwell.
Hallett, T. (2003) Symbolic power and organizational culture. *Sociological Theory* 21(2): 128–49.
Hatcher, T. (2000) The social responsibility performance outcomes model: Building socially responsible companies through performance improvement outcomes. *Performance Improvement* 39(7): 18–22.
— (2002) *Ethics and HRD: A new approach to leading responsible organizations*. Cambridge, MA: Basic Books.
Haugh, H.M. and Talwar, A. (2010) How do corporations embed sustainability across the organization? *Academy of Management Learning and Education* 9(3): 384–96.
Hopkins, M. (2003) *The planetary bargain: Corporate Social Responsibility matters*. London: Earthscan.
Knights, D. and O'Leary, M. (2006) Leadership, ethics and responsibility to the other. *Journal of Business Ethics* 67(2): 125–37.
Kuchinke, K.P. (2010) Human development as a central goal for human resource development. *Human Resource Development International* 13(5): 575–85.

Liebowitz, J. (2010) The role of HR in achieving a sustainability culture. *Journal of Sustainable Development* 3(4): 50–57.

MacKenzie, C., Garavan, T.N. and Carbery, R. (2011) *Corporate Social Responsibility: HRD as a mediator of organizational ethical behavior.* Paper presented at the 12th International HRD conference, University of Gloucestershire: Cheltenham, UK.

Maignan, I. and Ralston, D.A. (2002) Corporate social responsibility in Europe and the US: Insights from businesses self-presentations. *Journal of International Business Studies* 33(3): 497–514.

McWilliams, A. and Siegel, D. (2001) Corporate social responsibility: A theory of the firm perspective. *Academy of Management Review* 26(1): 117–27.

Pfeffer, J. (2010) Building sustainable organizations: The human factor. *Academy of Management Perspectives* 24(1): 34–45.

Pless, N.M. and Maak, T. (2011) Developing responsible global leaders through international service-learning programs: The Ulysses experience. *Journal of Management Learning and Education* 10(2): 237–60.

Rimanoczy, I. and Pearson, T. (2010) Role of HR in the new world of sustainability. *Industrial and Commercial Training* 42(1): 11–17.

Sackmann, S.A., Eggenhofer-Rehart, P.M. and Friesl, M. (2009) Sustainable change: Long-term efforts toward developing a learning organization. *Journal of Applied Behavioral Science* 45(4): 521–49.

Schein, E.H. (2004) *Organizational culture and leadership* (3rd edition). San Francisco: Jossey-Bass.

Sroufe, R., Liebowitz, J. and Sivasubramaniam, N. (2010) Are you a leader or a laggard? HR's role in creating a sustainability culture. *People and Strategy* 33(1): 34–42.

Stacey, R. (2003) Learning as an activity of interdependent people. *Learning Organization* 10(6): 325–31.

Tomé, E. (2011) *Human Resource Development for sustainability and social responsibility: The economic perspective.* Paper presented at the 12th International HRD conference, University of Gloucestershire: Cheltenham, UK.

WCED (World Commission on Environment and Development) (1987) *Our common future.* Oxford: Oxford University Press.

Wikström, P. (2010) Sustainability and organizational activities: Three approaches. *Sustainable Development* 18(2): 99–107.

28

DIVERSITY AND INCLUSION INITIATIVES IN ORGANIZATIONS

Martin B. Kormanik and Peter Chikwendu Nwaoma

The purpose of this chapter is to link workforce diversity and inclusion (D&I) initiatives to human resource development (HRD). The narrative highlights the evolution of diversity management and identifies best practices for D&I. The best practices are drawn from the literature, as well as each author's 25 years of conducting research and providing organization development (OD) assessment, consulting, training, facilitation, and coaching services in support of D&I initiatives.

The nature and meaning of diversity

Multiculturalism. Managing diversity. Valuing diversity. Cultural diversity. Diversity is a hot topic and a major focus area for HRD. The Society for Human Resource Management (SHRM), a worldwide professional association with 250,000 members in 140 countries, shows 68 percent of organizations having D&I practices in place (SHRM 2010a). Organizations see a strategic imperative for effectively managing diversity, realizing that having a proactive policy on diversity enhances competitive advantage (Jayne and Dipboye 2004).

The definition and understanding of workforce diversity have evolved (Kapoor 2011). Initial definitions focused narrowly on race, gender, and age (French *et al.* 2012; Olsen and Martins 2012), and certain populations (e.g. women, minorities, older workers). Ironically, much of the inequity in organizations occurs because employees are treated the same and differences are ignored (Wilson 1997). Aspects of individual diversity have been categorized into two levels: primary, innate factors (e.g. personality, age, race, gender, sexuality, physical abilities) and secondary, nurtured factors (e.g. socio-economic level, education, family/marital status, faith beliefs) (Gardenswartz and Rowe 1994; Loden and Rosener 1991).

Effectively managing diversity means acknowledging differences, including "acknowledging individual employee needs and then accommodating these needs" (Loden 1996: 18). Today, "an organization holding diversity as an instrumental value recognizes workforce diversity as a resource to be leveraged toward the achievement of business objectives" (Olsen and Martins 2012: 1173). Effectively managing workforce diversity requires recognizing the diversity of every employee and attending to all aspects of diversity. Diversity is considered to be inclusive of everyone, rather than limited to certain groups. Moreover, focusing on some groups while ignoring others can send confusing messages to employees and result in opposition to diversity efforts (Loden 1996). Managers, executives, business owners, and employees push to leverage aspects of individual diversity, as well as aspects of organizational diversity (e.g. culture, function, component). "Diversity therefore can be understood as contextually specific and linked to the demographic and socio-political features of a particular population and its workforce" (French *et al.* 2012: 3), resulting in a broad and inclusive conception of diversity.

In practice, HRD provides training, OD, and career development to improve individual and collective effectiveness (McLagan 1989). HRD supports management, often leading D&I efforts, with 62 per cent of organizations giving the human resources (HR) function responsibility for diversity initiatives (SHRM 2010a). "Within the field of HRD, the interest in diversity has primarily focused on the benefits and challenges of successfully managing a diverse workforce" (Ross-Gordon and Brooks 2004: 69). Effectively managing diversity goes beyond coercive pressure vis-à-vis compliance with equal opportunity statutes. "It will also bring in extra talent, new perspectives, learning, and limitless opportunities for innovation" (Bagshaw 2004: 153).

Diversity as a social construct

Three key changes have shaped the diversity movement: government regulatory and policy influences; bottom-line business implications; and evolving demographics, societal concerns, attitudes, and lifestyles. Employment legislation resulting from the US civil and women's rights movements in the 1960s and 1970s laid the foundation for formally addressing demographic diversity in the workforce (Laudicina 1995). New statutes prohibited employment discrimination and harassment around the diversity factors of race, national origin, gender, color, religion, age, and disability. During the 1980s, corporate focus on the customer added to the attention paid to diversity in national, multinational, and international organizations. Enhanced understanding of the external customer involved considering additional diversity factors like culture, education, socioeconomic level, and occupation. Product and service changes were targeted to customer diversity, and focused on profit.

Organizations expanded the philosophy to internal customers, with a focus on service. The search for service excellence was one way organizations fostered their own survival by using best-run corporations' lessons learned on staying close to the customer (Peters and Waterman 1982). The search for excellence proved a galvanizing force for nonprofits and government agencies as well. Organizations began undertaking systematic analyses of their business processes to ensure continuous process improvement. From these movements, the concept of maximizing resources emerged. This included maximizing the use of employees as corporate assets (i.e. "human" resources) (Caudron 1990).

Two late 1980s studies forecasting the work and the workers in the US highlighted trends, such as an increase in women and minorities, an aging workforce, and an increased need for highly skilled workers (Johnston 1988; Johnston and Packer 1987). Although both studies caused heated debate, they renewed the public and private sector focus on the workforce as an asset in need of effective management. Subsequent forecasts showed the workforce becoming even more diverse (Naisbitt and Aburdene 1990), making it increasingly difficult to manage the workplace impact of lifestyle and societal changes. The "increasing awareness of how our melting pot society affects business has increased the demand for diversity" management to help organizations deal with the changes (Caudron 1993: 51).

In summary, diversity is a social construct. "Diversity is a geographically and culturally contingent phenomenon, and needs to be understood as such" (Prasad *et al.* 2006: 3). Consistent with the multidisciplinary nature of HRD, conceptualization of the diversity construct has borrowed from the language of psychology, sociology, and economics.

Effects of diversity in the organizational setting

From the social scientist's perspective, every manifestation in the social system is bound to have its own effects. Research shows that diversity can influence an organization's objectives in both positive and negative ways (Janssens and Steyaert 2003), and diversity research has focused on identifying the conditions under which the potential advantages of diversity can best be exploited while minimizing the negative effects. "An organization's success and competitiveness depends upon its ability to embrace diversity and realize the benefits" (Greenberg 2004: 1). Organizations employing a diverse workforce can supply a variety of solutions to problems in service, sourcing, and allocation of resources. Employees from diverse backgrounds bring individual talents and experiences in suggesting ideas that are flexible in adapting to fluctuating markets and customer demands. A diverse collection of skills and experiences, like languages and cultural understanding, allows a company to provide service to customers on a global basis. A diverse workforce that feels comfortable communicating varying points of view provides a larger pool of ideas and experiences. Such organizations can draw from that pool to more effectively meet business strategy needs and the needs of customers. Multicultural organizations have an advantage in attracting and retaining top talent (Mazur 2010). Companies that foster diversity in the workforce encourage creativity and inspire employees to perform to their highest ability. Thus, company-wide strategies can then be executed, yielding higher productivity, profit, and return on investment.

Diversity in the global context can have negative effects, including ineffective communication, resistance to change, confusion in mission, lack of teamwork, lower levels of psychological identification, higher absenteeism and turnover (Greenberg 2004; Mazur 2010).

> In problem-solving situations, extraordinary costs in time and financial resources can negate the benefits of synergy, and can even degenerate into dysfunctional conflicts. Diversity does not fare well under conditions of uncertainty and complexity which may lead to confusion and frustration. Diversity can make it harder to arrive at an agreement on a particular course of action, and can result in negative dynamics and cultural clashes that can create work disadvantages for women and minorities.
>
> *Mazur 2010: 9*

Managing diversity in the workplace

It is important to acknowledge the evolution in defining diversity within the organizational context. Managing diversity initially referred to "the systematic and planned commitment by organizations to recruit, retain, reward, and promote a heterogeneous mix of employees" (Ivancevich and Gilbert 2000: 75). Early efforts focused largely on race and gender, based on affirmative action mandates. The definition of diversity has expanded to represent the collective *differences* brought to the workplace, based on individual and group characteristics, attributes, values, beliefs, backgrounds, socialization, life experiences, and power dynamics (Bagshaw 2004; Konrad 2006). The struggle for a universal definition is ongoing (Olsen and Martins 2012; Simons and Rowland 2011), though it has evolved to acknowledge *similarity* as well as difference. Managing diversity now includes a focus on the environment, defining *workplace* diversity as "an inclusive corporate culture that strives to respect variations in employee personality, work style, age, ethnicity, gender, religion, socioeconomics, education and other dimensions in the workplace" (SHRM 2010b: 2).

Initially, diversity was largely a human resource management (HRM) function; limited to increasing the workforce representation of historically underrepresented groups (e.g. women, minorities) via recruitment and hiring practices. Today, managing workforce diversity is a topic of increasing concern in HRD (Chermack *et al.* 2003; Ross-Gordon and Brooks 2004). Managing diversity centers on the premise that harnessing diversity will create a productive workplace in which employees feel valued and their talents used in the process of accomplishing organizational goals (Bagshaw 2004). The focus is organizational effectiveness. Managing diversity entails managing in a way designed to fully realize the benefits that diversity can bring. Diversity management means being aware of behavior, leveraging strengths, acknowledging biases, avoiding assumptions, and focusing on merit. For organizations, "diversity is no longer limited to an affirmative action programme, a training intervention, or something 'nice to do'" (SHRM 2008: 9). It makes bottom-line sense.

Expansion to the global context

Although in 2007, only 20 per cent of organizations reported using the term "D&I" to describe diversity efforts (SHRM 2008), the nomenclature appears to have been adopted worldwide by 2011 (SHRM 2011). In the US, the Obama (2011) administration significantly raised the D&I profile with a government-wide mandate to establish a coordinated initiative to promote D&I. Also, the US Office of Personnel Management's (OPM) Leadership Competencies Model identified "leading people" as one of six core qualifications (OPM n.d.), with "leveraging (i.e. managing) diversity" as an enabling competency. Most US government agencies use OPM's model as a framework for HRD. Since 1979, the Nigerian government has brought diversity management to a prominent height through constitutional and administrative mechanisms (Nwaoma 2012). Research has examined D&I initiatives worldwide (Holladay and Quinones 2005; Wentling and Palma-Rivas 2000), and in Europe (Ball and Wicks 2002; Egan and Bendick 2003; Nishii and Özbilgin 2007), Africa (Mengisteab 2010; Ogedengbe *et al.* 2012), the United Kingdom (Pendry *et al.* 2007), Australia (Schneider and Northcraft 1999), India (Benschop 2001; Kundu 2003), and Canada (Jain and Verma 1996).

International and multinational firms expanded D&I initiatives to include the global context. "Increasingly, firms are now known to employ people from different nations with different cultural backgrounds" (Ogedengbe *et al.* 2012: 1049). Best practices in D&I show that firm leadership needs to develop a global perspective to management, as a parochial view is inappropriate (Barak 2014; Kapoor 2011; Ogedengbe *et al.* 2012). A manager who wants global presence should place strong emphases on the external environment. Because the world is increasingly becoming the corporate environment, no organization can position itself in isolation.

> Many people in the United States connect issues of diversity to human rights and civil liberty; Europeans may connect them to cultural heritage and language differences; many in Latin countries focus their diversity dialogues around the innate dignity of the individual; and many Asian societies interpret diversity in terms of collective accountability.
>
> *Gardenswartz and Rowe 1994: 90*

In conducting a D&I needs assessment, setting D&I goals, or developing a global D&I initiative, it is important to understand local cultural nuances and the organization's stage of globalization.

Although not all organizations are global and not all will become global, diversity is still relevant. All organizations can benefit from understanding the different patterns of social and professional behaviors expected from potential international customers, global peers, transnational alliance partners, or the national workforce employed by the organization. Managers in such organizations also need cross-cultural knowledge to understand international opportunities and threats to their markets (Adler 2000; Gardenswartz *et al.* 2003). This is also applicable to organizations that primarily focus on domestic markets, yet buy or sell in other countries. This is in contrast to international enterprises that generally have production and sales activities both in the home country and outside their national borders which are highly influenced by the corporate culture of the home-country headquarters. This type of organization will no doubt demonstrate a strong bias to create a diversity program peculiar to the home country while paying minimal attention to redefining diversity to address the new trans-border(s) context. Although there is a gap in existing theory, in practice, global enterprises having planning, production, and sales operations in multiple countries are more effective via an integrated attempt to use national, cultural, and personal diversity to run their operations. They consciously create mechanisms and processes that allow them to become globally diverse. D&I efforts by global corporations, more so than those of government and nongovernmental organizations, have a substantive opportunity to influence global interactions (Gardenswartz *et al.* 2003).

While domestic diversity efforts traditionally focused on primary and secondary levels of diversity within a specific organizational context, a global approach requires more layers. The Six Spheres of Inclusion (SSI) model provides a helpful framework for considering additional factors at play in any global D&I initiative (Gardenswartz and Rowe 1994; Loden and Rosener 1991). Considering interpersonal and organizational factors, this model supports increasing awareness and breaking free of any domestic diversity bias that might thwart the broader development of employees and the organization itself. The first sphere, civilizational orientation, highlights eight civilizations that are most prevalent globally. These civilizational heritages shape the ways people understand life and how they relate with others, especially those they perceive as different. The second sphere, national identification, represents the geopolitical and natural boundaries that define nations and, sometimes, create artificial, yet very real, barriers between people who share a common civilizational orientation. National identity still matters, even in a global environment. The third sphere, organizational factors, looks at the impact of ways diversity is used (or not used) in organizational structuring. These diversity factors include management status, work location, union affiliation, division/department/work unit, function/level/classification, seniority, and work content or field. The fourth sphere, societal formation, examines the way people are socialized in comparatively mono-cultural institutions that both unconsciously and consciously shape their values, attitudes, beliefs, and behaviors about how to live in the world. Societal formation shapes the way societal members perceive themselves, how they perceive and deal with others, how they believe that others perceive them, and the tolerance others have for accepting (or rejecting) different values and beliefs. These external socialization factors (e.g. economic class, caste systems, literacy levels, education standards, leisure, recreation, personal habits, the balance between work and life, language, religion, spirituality, location, family marital roles and responsibilities) make a difference in the workplace. Bias and exclusion are built into socialization processes (Sidanius and Pratto 1999). The fifth sphere, individual identification, highlights the internal dimensions of diversity that relate to how individuals are socialized (e.g. sexual orientation, age, gender, physical ability). Core to global diversity work is the ability for individuals to affirm their own identity and core assumptions while not being threatened by the presence of another individual who has a different identity. The sixth sphere, personality/style, is the deepest and most intangible level of diversity within the SSI model. This element supports the interpersonal relationships identified with behavioral patterns such as flexibility, adaptability, tolerance, and risk taking.

Global diversity has been shaped from domestic diversity models that examine exclusion and inclusion in terms of who has and who does not have access or opportunity. At the global level, encompassing the national identification sphere, each nation's historical context shapes reactions to diversity and helps determine what constitutes an injustice, a violation, or an affront

(Gardenswartz *et al.* 2003). Behaviors considered discriminatory in one nation may be seen as a national cultural preference in another. For example, at one point, an Italian court approved pinching a female's behind, a behavior that might be illegal in other nations (presidio9 2003).

D&I initiatives in contemporary organizations

Organizations undertake D&I initiatives for many reasons, including coercive pressure from statute and mandate, normative pressure exerted by community and professional associations, and mimetic pressure to adopt competitors' practices (Yang 2005). These pressures have shaped D&I goals to include increasing workforce representation of underrepresented groups, eliminating discrimination, preventing harassment, and promoting inclusion. Initially, coercive pressure resulted in focusing primarily on compliance with legislation and governmental policy. It appears the focus has shifted to normative and mimetic pressures, with improved public image and competitive advantage being top reported outcomes of D&I efforts (SHRM 2010b). Additional reasons for undertaking D&I initiatives include: the tie to enhancing mission accomplishment; avoiding the potential for lost productivity; cost savings that yield bottom-line impact; increasing awareness of self and others; teambuilding; managing conflict due to difference; as a proactive action to preempt inappropriate behaviors (e.g. harassment, discrimination); preempting complaints, grievances, and lawsuits; mitigating liability and financial costs; and, as part of a conciliation agreement.

Despite the many benefits of D&I initiatives, experience reveals three obstacles to success: lack of visible management commitment, lack of positive leadership at all levels, and lack of personal responsibility and accountability. Additional barriers include unclear program objectives (e.g. representation of certain groups versus inclusion of all), the gap between employee and management expectations (Caudron 1993), narrowly defining diversity by factor (e.g. race and gender only) or population (e.g. women and minorities only), backlash from some White males (Kormanik 2000), and lack of integration into the organization's culture and structures (Ferdman and Brody 1996).

Best practices to address the obstacles include: a systematic and systemic approach, visible commitment from senior leadership, clear objectives and strategy aligned with business objectives and core values, reinforcing infrastructure, broad representation within committees and advisory groups, active participation at all levels, institutionalization of a corporate culture that supports positive morale and collaboration, and monitoring and evaluation of progress.

HRD practitioners' roles in D&I initiatives

Sensemaking – developing understanding and a subsequent course of action – about aspects of workforce diversity is difficult (Roberson and Stevens 2006). Managers and supervisors, along with nonsupervisory employees, need HRD practitioners' help. The following discussion highlights HRD practitioners' central role in D&I initiatives.

HRD practitioners should be prepared to play a substantial role in the development of management competencies used for D&I. Top management's genuine commitment is crucial. "Champions for diversity are needed – people who will take strong personal stands on the need for change, role model the behaviours required for change, and assist with the work of moving the organization forward" (Cox and Blake 1991: 52). The competencies for taking a strong personal stand, role modeling behaviors required for change and moving the organization forward are not limited in application to just D&I. They are well established as general management competencies.

HRD practitioners should be able to guide D&I communications using the broad definition of diversity. Optimally framing or reframing training (Holladay *et al.* 2003) may help address any negative perceptions associated with the term "diversity." Because resistance to diversity training may stem from the term, it would be useful to review the training marketing and other messages to ensure inclusivity, eliminate misperceptions, and reduce resistance. In particular, when trying to convey the business case for diversity, it is important for HRD practitioners – both training and diversity specialists – to "learn management-speak. Find out what managers and work organizations value and learn to speak their particular language" (Ross-Gordon and Brooks 2004: 76).

HRD practitioners should be able to sponsor D&I training customized to meet participants' specific challenges related to D&I issues. Although the design of every instructional module might not explicitly link diversity to non-diversity topics, training delivery, given the expanded diversity definition, must help learners make the connection between diversity and each content issue (e.g. interpersonal communication, goal setting, teambuilding, decision making, negotiation, conflict dynamics). The training should help the learner make the link.

HRD practitioners should be able to support D&I training transfer with coaching. All too often participants do not transfer training by reinforcing, supporting, and modeling the behaviors taught in the training (Rynes and Rosen 1995). Practitioners can routinely coach and challenge managers to actively and visibly support D&I via the managers' actions and decision making. Practitioners can assist in the creation and maintenance of social support systems that promote a positive environment (e.g. a workplace that welcomes rather than excludes those who are "other").

HRD practitioners should be able to develop targeted strategies for raising individuals' awareness. Central to awareness development is change in perspective or meaning schema (Kormanik 1999; 2002). Some employees will need additional help in developing awareness around some aspects of diversity (e.g. sexual orientation and gender identity versus sex discrimination and harassment) (Kormanik 2009). Structured dialogue is a targeted strategy that practitioners can use to develop awareness (Schein 1993). The practitioner should be cautious about single loop learning, where cognitive development using existing routines and mental models causing self-reinforcing patterns (Argyris 1982) may inhibit awareness. Facilitated dialogue can help distinguish facts from myths held by employees. First-line supervisors may not be knowledgeable enough to ensure that the dialogue is effectively handled and the work environment remains productive without hostility. HRD practitioners can design D&I initiatives to encourage double-loop learning that provides new solutions for coping with the dynamic.

Considerations for HRD practitioners' professional development

Given HRD practitioners' multiple roles in leading and supporting D&I initiatives, here are three considerations for future professional development. First, it would seem that HRD academic programs should include courses on D&I or, similar to the trend in management training, aspects of D&I could be integrated throughout program curricula. HRD programs could "address D&I within four areas: alignment of diversity with the organizational business strategy; organizational communications using the expanded, inclusive definition of diversity; training design using the emergent integrative strategy for diversity content delivery; and, coaching to support training transfer" (Kormanik and Rajan 2010: 380). Second, D&I certification may be in order. Cornell University started the first such program in 2008, offering the Diversity Management Certificate and the Certified Diversity Professional/Advanced Practitioner. In 2013, there are dozens of programs from which to choose. Third, the American National Standards Institute and SHRM have partnered in developing D&I standards, including definition, measures, and minimum qualifications in key competencies, experience, and education for a top diversity professional. Perhaps the standards can be used to guide development of HRD academic programme curricula. The standards will also help increase the value of certification and differentiate among certification programmes.

Conclusion

The purpose of this chapter was to link HRD to contemporary D&I initiatives. The narrative highlighted the origins of diversity management and identified best practices for D&I. The literature shows a shift in the way organizations operationalize workforce diversity, moving from the narrowly focused rhetoric (e.g. race, gender) to a more inclusive definition. This reflects an evolution in diversity philosophy, from compliance to systemic action to organizational transformation. In the global context, the challenge for any organization is to add a D&I dimension to all current HR activities and communicate the goals and strategy in a transparent way (SHRM 2009).

Diversity has become "a premier business issue" (Avery and Thomas 2004: 380). Lack of understanding of diversity can be stressful and distracting for everyone, has the potential for creating workplace misunderstandings and tension, and may lead to allegations of unfair treatment and/or a hostile work environment. D&I initiatives take careful forethought and, with a similarly thoughtful implementation, can yield positive results when there is organizational commitment and appreciation for the contributions of diversity. Identifying organizational needs, developing a D&I strategy that includes rather than alienates employees, and integrating D&I into the business objectives are key steps in ensuring success.

Managing workforce diversity is a topic of increasing concern in HRD. Because diversity is emergent and complex, ways to convey knowledge and build skills are not straightforward, easy, or static. Managing diversity has evolved beyond compliance with nondiscrimination statutes and efforts to increase representation of historically underrepresented groups. It entails managing in a way designed to fully realize the potential benefits that differences can bring. It means being aware of behavior, leveraging strengths, acknowledging biases/prejudices, avoiding assumptions, and focusing on job performance and conduct. HRD practitioners' professional development must prepare them to support and, in many instances, lead the D&I effort.

The many exploratory studies on D&I provide opportunity for future research, posing hypotheses and collecting quantitative data. This would allow generalizability and, perhaps, leverage the lessons learned into additional D&I best practices. Future research could focus on: correlation among D&I competencies, management effectiveness, and organizational performance; requisite time for completing culture change; impact of the relationship between the training and diversity functions; and, correlation between mandatory participation in D&I activities and the level of negative perception and resistance to D&I.

Globally, attention to diversity will continue to increase, evidenced by the upward trend in organizations' D&I efforts. HRD professionals will emerge as D&I experts in organizations that want to remain relevant in a fast changing global environment. The global community, however, may have to rethink existing notions of citizenship and nationality. For example, democracy and freedom may be elusive in nations without shared values of justice and equality for the rights of all groups (Banks 2007).

Finally, "strategic HRD conceptualizes planned learning and development of individuals and groups to be of benefit to the business as well as individual learners. It advocates aligning the format of organization strategy and HRD activities so that they drive strategic objectives" (Garavan *et al.* 1999: 191). If diversity is a strategic organizational objective, every substantive

HRD activity should include some explicit alignment to D&I. It is, therefore, important for all HRD professionals – theorists, researchers, practitioners – to strategically consider the D&I best practices discussed in this chapter.

Bibliography

Adler, N.J. (2000) *International dimensions of organizational behaviour*, 4th edn, Cincinnati, OH: South-Western.

Argyris, C. (1982) 'The executive mind and double-loop learning', *Organizational Dynamics* 11: 5–22.

Avery, D.R. and Thomas, K.M. (2004) 'Blending content and contact: The roles of diversity curriculum and campus heterogeneity in fostering diversity management competency', *Academy of Management Learning and Education* 7: 380–96.

Bagshaw, M. (2004) 'Is diversity divisive? A positive training approach', *Industrial and Commercial Training* 36: 153–7.

Ball, K. and Wicks, D. (2002) 'Editorial: Power, representation and voice', *Gender, Work and Organization* 9: 239–43.

Banks, J. A. (ed) (2007) *Diversity and citizenship education: Global perspectives*, Indianapolis, IN: Jossey-Bass.

Barak, M.E.M. (2014) *Managing diversity: Toward a globally inclusive workplace*, 3rd edn, Los Angeles: SAGE.

Benschop, Y. (2001) 'Pride, prejudice and performance: Relations between HRM, diversity, and performance', *International Journal of Human Resource Management* 12: 1166–81.

Caudron, S. (1990, November) 'Monsanto responds to diversity: Monsanto Agricultural Co. is actively reshaping its culture to ensure that all employees reach their potential', *Personnel Journal* 69: 72–80.

— (1993) 'Training can damage diversity efforts', *Personnel Journal* 72: 51–62.

Chermack, T.J., Lynham, S.A. and Ruona, W.E.A. (2003) 'Critical uncertainties confronting human resource development', *Advances in Developing Human Resources* 5: 257–71.

Cox, T.H. and Blake, S. (1991) 'Managing cultural diversity: Implications for organizational competitiveness', *Academy of Management Executive* 5: 45–56.

Egan, M.L. and Bendick, M. (2003) 'Workforce diversity initiatives of US multinational corporations in Europe', *Thunderbird International Business Review* 45: 701–27.

Ferdman, B. and Brody, S.E. (1996) 'Models of diversity training', in Landis, D. and Bhagat, R.S. (eds) *Handbook of intercultural training*, 2nd edn, Thousand Oaks, CA: SAGE.

French, E.L., Strachan, G. and Burgess, J. (2012) *The challenges in developing a strategic approach to managing diversity*, 9th Equality, Diversity and Inclusion 2012 Conference: Country and Comparative Perspectives on Equality, Diversity and Inclusion. Online. Available HTTP: http://eprints.qut.edu.au/55424/4/55424.pdf (accessed 27 December 2012).

Garavan, T.N., Barnicle, B. and O'Suilleabhain, F. (1999) 'Management development: Contemporary trends, issues, and strategies', *Journal of European Industrial Training* 23: 191–207.

Gardenswartz, L. and Rowe, A. (1994) *Diverse teams at work*, Homewood, IL: Business One Irwin.

Gardenswartz, L., Rowe, A., Digh, P. and Bennett, M. (2003) *The global diversity desk reference: Managing an international workforce*, New York: Pfeiffer.

Greenberg, J. (2004) *Diversity in the workplace: Benefits, challenges, and solutions*. Online. Available HTTP: http://ezinearticles.com/?Diversity-in-the-Workplace:-Benefits,-Challenges-and-Solutions&id=11053 (accessed 15 June 2013).

Holladay, C.L. and Quinones, M.A. (2005) 'Reactions to diversity training: An international comparison', *Human Resource Development Quarterly* 16: 529–45.

Holladay, C.L., Knight, J.L., Paige, D.L. and Quinones, M.A. (2003) 'The influence of framing on attitudes toward diversity training', *Human Resource Development Quarterly* 14: 245–63.

Ivancevich, J.M. and Gilbert, J.A. (2000) 'Diversity management: Time for a new approach', *Public Personnel Management* 29: 75–92.

Jain, H.C. and Verma, A. (1996) 'Managing workforce diversity for competitiveness: The Canadian experience', *International Journal of Manpower* 17: 14–29.

Janssens, M. and Steyaert, C. (2003) *Theories of diversity within organization studies: Debates and future trajectories*, Fondazione Eni Enrico Mattei. Online. Available HTTP: http://www.feem.it/userfiles/attach/publication/ndl2003/ndl2003-014.pdf (accessed 16 June 2013).

Jayne, M.A. and Dipboye, R.L. (2004) 'Leveraging diversity to improve business performance: Research findings and recommendations for organizations', *Human Resource Management* 43: 409–24.

Johnston, W.B. (1988) *Civil Service 2000*, Indianapolis, IN: Hudson Institute.

Johnston, W.B. and Packer, A.E. (1987) *Workforce 2000: Work and workers for the 21st century*, Indianapolis, IN: Hudson Institute.

Kapoor, C. (2011) 'Defining diversity: The evolution of diversity', *Worldwide Hospitality and Tourism Themes* 3: 284–93.

Konrad, A.M. (2006) 'Leveraging workplace diversity in organizations', *Organization Management Journal* 3: 164–89.

Kormanik, M.B. (1999) 'The Cycle of Awareness Development: A cognitive and psychosocial theory of adult development', in Kuchinke, K.P. (ed.) *1999 AHRD Conference Proceedings*, vol. 2, Baton Rouge, LA: Academy of Human Resource Development.

— (2000) 'White male backlash: Practitioner perspectives on the phenomenon', in Kuchinke, K.P. (ed.) *2000 AHRD Conference Proceedings*, vol. 1, Baton Rouge, LA: Academy of Human Resource Development.

— (2002) 'Developing organizational awareness: Gaining a distributed view of organization-level change in workforce diversity awareness', in Egan, T.M. (ed.) *2002 AHRD Conference Proceedings*, vol. 1, Bowling Green, OH: Academy of Human Resource Development.

— (2009) 'Sexuality as a diversity factor: An examination of awareness', *Advances in Developing Human Resources* 11: 24–36.

Kormanik, M.B. and Rajan, H.C. (2010) 'Implications for diversity in the HRD curriculum drawn from current organizational practices on addressing workforce diversity in management training', *Advances in Developing Human Resources* 12: 367–84.

Kundu, S.C. (2003) 'Workforce diversity status: A study of employees' reactions', *Industrial Management and Data Systems* 103: 215–26.

Laudicina, E.V. (1995, Summer) 'Managing workforce diversity in government', *Public Administration Quarterly* 19: 170–92.

Loden, M. (1996) *Implementing diversity*, New York: McGraw-Hill.

Loden, M. and Rosener, J. (1991) *Workforce America!*, Homewood, IL: Business One Irwin.

Mazur, B. (2010) 'Cultural diversity in organisational theory and practice', *Journal of Intercultural Management* 2: 5–15.

McLagan, P. (1989) 'Models for HRD practice', *Training and Development Journal* 43: 49–59.

Mengisteab, K. (2010) *Diversity management in Africa: Findings from the African peer review mechanism and a framework for analysis and policy-making*, New York: United Nations Economic Commission for Africa.

Naisbitt, J. and Aburdene, P. (1990) *Megatrends 2000: Ten new directions for the 1990's*, New York: William Morrow.

Nishii, L.H. and Özbilgin, M.F. (2007) 'Global diversity management: Towards a conceptual framework', *International Journal of Human Resource Management* 18: 1883–94.

Nwaoma, P.C. (2012) 'Managing cultural diversity in the public sector through the constitutional/administrative imperative: Outcomes and lessons from Nigeria', in Wang, J. (ed.) *Proceedings AHRD 2012 International Research Conference in the Americas*, Schaumburg, IL: Academy of Human Resource Development.

Obama, B. (2011, August 18) *Executive Order 13583 – Establishing a coordinated government-wide initiative to promote diversity and inclusion in the Federal workforce*. Online. Available HTTP: http://www.whitehouse.gov/the-press-office/2011/08/18/executive-order-establishing-coordinated-government-wide-initiative-prom (accessed 26 December 2012).

Ogedengbe, F.A., Ewanlen, O.D., Rebman, C.M., Jr. and Atoe, M.S.O. (2012) 'Achieving unity in diversity through cross-cultural management of resources', *Journal of US–China Public Administration* 9: 1048–56.

Olsen, J.E., and Martins, L.L. (2012) 'Understanding organizational diversity management programs: A theoretical framework and directions for future research', *Journal of Organizational Behavior* 33: 1168–87.

OPM (Office of Personnel Management) (n.d.) *Proficiency levels for leadership competencies*. Online. Available HTTP: http://apps.opm.gov/ADT/ContentFiles/LeadershipCompProficiencyLevels.pdf (accessed 15 December 2009).

Pendry, L.F., Driscoll, D.M. and Field, S.C. (2007) 'Diversity training: Putting theory into practice', *Journal of Occupational and Organizational Psychology* 80: 27–50.

Peters, T.J. and Waterman, R.H., Jr. (1982) *In search of excellence: Lessons from America's best-run companies*, New York: Harper and Row.

Prasad, P., Pringle, J.K. and Konrad, A.M. (2006) 'Examining the contours of workplace diversity: Concepts, contexts, and challenges', in Konrad, A.M., Prasad, P. and Pringle, J.K. (eds) *Handbook of workplace diversity*, Thousand Oaks, CA: SAGE.

presidio9 (2003) *Italy overturns controversial bottom-pinching ruling*, Free Republic. Online. Available HTTP: http://www.freerepublic.com/focus/f-news/941804/posts (accessed 30 November 2013).

Roberson, Q.M. and Stevens, C.K. (2006) 'Making sense of diversity in the workplace: Organizational justice and language abstraction in employees' accounts of diversity-related incidents', *Journal of Applied Psychology* 91: 379–91.

Ross-Gordon, J.M. and Brooks, A.K. (2004) 'Diversity in Human Resource Development and continuing professional education: What does it mean for the workforce, clients, and professionals?' *Advances in Developing Human Resources* 6: 69–85.

Rynes, S. and Rosen, B. (1995) 'A field study of factors affecting the adoption and perceived success of diversity training', *Personnel Psychology* 48: 247–70.

Schein, E.H. (1993) 'On dialogue, culture, and organizational learning', *Organizational Dynamics* 22: 40–51.

— (2010) *Organizational culture and leadership*, 4th edn, San Francisco: Jossey-Bass.

Schneider, S.K. and Northcraft, G.B. (1999) 'Three social dilemmas of workforce diversity in organizations: A social identity perspective', *Human Relations* 52: 1445–67.

Sidanius, J. and Pratto, F. (1999) *Social dominance: An intergroup theory of social hierarchy and oppression*, New York: Cambridge University Press.

Simons, S.M. and Rowland, K.M. (2011) 'Diversity and its impact on organizational performance: The influence of diversity constructions on expectations and outcomes', *Journal of Technology Management and Innovation* 6: 171–82.

Society for Human Resource Management (2008) *2007 State of workplace diversity management*, Alexandria, VA: Society for Human Resource Management.

— (2009) *Global diversity and inclusion: Perceptions, practices and attitudes*, Alexandria, VA: Society for Human Resource Management.

— (2010a) *SHRM research spotlight: Workplace diversity practices poll*, Alexandria, VA: Society for Human Resource Management.

— (2010b) *Workplace diversity practices: How has diversity and inclusion changed over time?*, Alexandria, VA: Society for Human Resource Management.

— (2011) *SHRM research spotlight: An examination of organizational commitment to diversity and inclusion*, Alexandria, VA: Society for Human Resource Management.

Wentling, R.M. and Palma-Rivas, N. (1999) 'Components of effective diversity training programmes', *International Journal of Training and Development* 3: 215–26.

— (2000) 'Current status of diversity initiatives in selected multinational corporations', *Human Resource Development Quarterly* 11: 35–60.

Wilson, T. (1997) *Diversity at work: The business case for equity*, Toronto: Wiley.

Yang, Y. (2005) 'Developing cultural diversity advantage: The impact of diversity management structures', in Weaver, K.M. (ed.) *Academy of Management 2005 Annual Meeting Proceedings*, Briarcliff Manor, NY: Academy of Management.

29

WORKING CONDITIONS OF CHILD LABOR AND MIGRANT WORKERS

Maimunah Ismail and Nor Wahiza Abdul Wahat

This chapter specifically aims to: (1) define the meaning of working conditions, (2) explore the global perspectives of working conditions across selected employed populations such as child labor and migrant workers in terms of statistical occurrence and working conditions, and (3) delineate roles of human resource development (HRD) in dealing with the relevant issues of working conditions of the two segments of population. Particularly relevant resources for this chapter are documents from the United Nations' (2009) survey reports on flexible working arrangements, United Nations' Human Development Report (2010, 2011), several sources from International Labour Organizations (ILO 2012, 2013, Dávalos 2002) and specific countries' studies on the working conditions and employment of selected populations. The next section presents the meaning of work conditions, and statistics from selected countries on migrants and child labor employment, working conditions and problems of the two population segments (namely child labor and migrant workers). Thus, the discussion within this chapter shall highlight how migrants and child labor employment significantly contribute to the HRD and nation building of the selected countries.

Meaning of working conditions

Working conditions refers to the situations in which a person works and aspects of an employee's terms and reference of employment. This topic covers matters such as: pay; the organization of work and work activities; training, skills and employability; health, safety and well-being; as well as work–life balance (The Global Compact 2013). In this chapter, concerns regarding working conditions are addressed with specific segments of populations such as child labor and migrant workers. The need for focussing on these selected population groups, which The Global Compact (2013) classified as "forced or involuntary labour", arises from the principle of human rights that every citizen in any country should be given opportunities for employment regardless of his/her socio-economic status.

The electronics sector of Thailand (Table 29.1) is used here as a frame of reference. The table provides examples of work conditions in several multinational corporations (MNCs), of which the workers are locals and migrants in various compositions (Schipper and de Haan 2007). Although these data are specific to Thailand, they are presented here because variations on the specific work conditions of the same sector may exist in other countries. The types of work conditions and their

Table 29.1 Work conditions in electronics sector, Thailand

Work Conditions	*Description*
Working hours	• Non-hazardous work i.e. 8 hours a day or 48 hours a week in total. • Hazardous work is a maximum of 7 hours a day or 42 hours per week. • The employer may request workers to work longer as deemed necessary.
Forced overtime	• Employees have the choice whether to work overtime or take holiday; consent must be first obtained from the employers. • Maximum overtime hours are limited to not more than 36 hours a week.
Overtime compensation	• The rates vary and range from 1.5 times to 3 times the normal wage rate.
Daily rest period	• At least 1 hour after working 5 consecutive hours and not less than 1 hour a day in total. Not less than 20 minutes before the employee starts working overtime longer than 2 hours. • A weekly holiday: At least one day per week at intervals of a 6-day period must be arranged by the employer.
National holidays	• Workers are entitled to no fewer than 13 days per year, and a minimum of 6 days annual vacation after working consecutively for one full year.
Sick leave	• As many days as necessary, but maximum of 1 month of paid leave. Maternity leave: 90 days including holidays but paid leave should not exceed 45 days.

descriptions delineated in Table 29.1 provide considerations regarding quality of working conditions in an organization.

In the European context, a description on working conditions and recent changes are found in the Article 151 TFEU (European Industrial Relations Dictionary 2011: 1). The article states that: "The European Union and the Member States shall have as their objectives the promotion of employment, improved living and working conditions, so as to make possible their harmonization while the improvement is being maintained." The article further indicates that the Union shall support and complement the activities of the Member States in a range of social policy fields including working conditions. Generally, as applied in other countries, changes in working conditions and other aspects of the employment relationship can generate serious industrial relations problems. One issue is that workers may not have precise information about their working conditions in the first place. Employers are obliged to inform employees of the conditions applicable to the contract or employment relationship. The directive stipulates that the employer must provide information covering all "essential aspects" of the employment relationship. The employer is obliged to prepare a document with the requisite information, and give it to the employee not later than two months after the commencement of employment. Further, a new document that reflects any changes in core working conditions must be issued.

Child labor

The definition of child labor is derived from ILO Convention 138 on minimum age for labor and ILO Convention 182 on the worst forms of child labor. Child labor refers to work that is mentally, physically, socially or morally dangerous and harmful to children; and interferes with their schooling by depriving them of the opportunity to attend school; obliging them to leave school prematurely; or requiring them to attempt to combine school with excessively long and heavy work (ILO 2012). The ILO document establishes the ultimate goal for the effective abolition of child labor and provides for the setting of a minimum age for employment as the yardstick; particularly for hazardous industries, the age limit specified is all children below age 18. In this chapter child labor is referred to children from 5–17 or 18 years of age, working full time (≥ 6 hrs/day) or part time (6 hrs/day) in their respective employment sectors.

However, not all work done by children should be classified as child labor that is to be targeted for elimination. Children's or adolescents' participation in work that does not affect their health and personal development or interfere with their effective schooling is generally regarded as being something positive (ILO 2012). This includes activities such as helping their parents around the home, or earning pocket money outside school hours and during school holidays. Such activities contribute to children's development and the welfare of their families; furthermore, such activities provide them skills and experiences, in the process of becoming future, productive members of society. Whether or not particular forms of "work" can be called "child labor" depends on the child's age, the type and hours of work performed, the conditions under which it is performed and the objectives pursued by individual countries. Appropriateness of the work varies from country to country, as well as among sectors within countries.

The worst forms of child labor as defined by Article 3 of ILO Convention No. 182 (ILO 2012: 1) are as follows:

(a) all forms of slavery or practices similar to slavery, such as the sale and trafficking of children, debt bondage and serfdom and forced or compulsory labor, including forced or compulsory recruitment of children for use in armed conflict;
(b) the use, procuring or offering of a child for prostitution, for the production of pornography or for pornographic performances;
(c) the use, procuring or offering of a child for illicit activities, in particular for the production and trafficking of drugs as defined in the relevant international treaties;
(d) work which, by its nature or the circumstances in which it is carried out, is likely to harm the health, safety or morals of children.

ILO (2013) defined a hazard as potential harm that could lead to a risk or risks. Thus, child labor is a hazardous work because it jeopardizes the physical, mental or moral well-being of a child, either because of its nature or because of the conditions in which it is carried out.

Child labor statistics, working conditions and problems

This section presents the occurrence of child labor and its dilemmas in selected countries. Table 29.2 presents the percentage of child labor based on the Human Development Index (HDI) rank (UNDP 2010). Child labor is one of the indicators in the description of decent work and has a direct relationship with mean years of schooling and gross national income per capita. The table also shows data on the country's population, and the employment to population ratio based on those in the ages of 15–64 years. The table shows a noticeable trend in which the percentage of child labor increases with the decrease in the rank based on the HDI. Bahrain and Portugal are the only two countries with a very high HDI that reported having child labor of 5 per cent and 3 per cent, respectively. Countries with the highest occurrence of child labor are predominantly in Africa such as Uganda (36 per cent), Burkina Faso (47 per cent) and Somalia (49 per cent). The higher percentage of child labor in the lower ranking countries based on HDI could be explained by factors such as poverty in the family and the community, and less access to education. These factors are generally attributed to the lower socio-economic status of the population resulting from the lower gross national income per capita in the respective countries.

Table 29.2 Percentage of child labor in selected countries based on HDI* rank, 2010

Country and Human Development Index (HDI) rank	*Population (millions, 2010)*	*Employment to Population Ratio (per cent of population ages 15–64, 2008)*	*Child Labor (per cent of children ages 5–14, 1999–2007)*
Very High Human Development			
Bahrain (39)	0.8	61.0	5
Portugal (40)	10.7	55.7	3
High Human Development			
Mexico (56)	110.6	57.1	16
Malaysia (57)	27.9	60.4	1**
Peru (63)	29.5	68.8	19
Albania (64)	3.2	46.2	12
Georgia (74)	4.2	54.3	18
Medium Human Development			
Sri Lanka (91)	20.4	54.7	8
Thailand (92)	68.1	71.5	8
Paraguay (96)	6.5	72.8	15
Philippines (97)	93.6	60.1	12
Egypt (101)	84.5	43.2	7
Uzbekistan (102)	27.8	57.5	7
Honduras (106)	7.6	56.3	16
Vietnam (113)	89.0	69.4	16
Guatemala (116)	14.4	62.4	29
India (119)	1,214.5	55.6	12
Pakistan (125)	184.8	51.5	9
Low Human Development			
Kenya (128)	40.9	73.0	26
Ghana (130)	24.3	65.2	34
Nepal (138)	29.9	61.5	31
Uganda (143)	33.8	83.0	36
Burkina Faso (161)	16.3	81.9	47
Somalia (189)	9.4	66.5	49

*Other indicators governing the HDI are life expectancy at birth, mean years of schooling, and gross national income per capita.
**The Malaysian Constitution prohibits child labor. However, the International Confederation of Free Trade Unions estimates that 75,000 children are engaged as laborers in Malaysia making the figure to 0.0027% (or 1%) in 2013, which is considered very low.

Source: Extracted and computed from UNDP (2010).

A recent report on child labor (ILO 2012) indicates that the number of children working in agriculture is nearly ten times more than children involved in factory work such as garment manufacturing, carpet-weaving, or soccer-ball stitching. Investigations by the Human Rights Watch in countries such as Ecuador, Egypt, Pakistan and Uzbekistan, found that children working in agriculture are endangered and exploited on a daily basis. The Human Rights Watch also found that despite the vast differences among these countries, many of the risks and abuses faced by child agricultural workers were strikingly similar (cited in ILO 2012). The following sections present evidence on the working conditions in the above four countries.

Child labor exists in horticulture in Ecuador (Castelnuovo *et al.* 2000). The flower-growing industries in the country have adopted a hacienda or feudal style approach to production and labor. This approach has enabled them to take advantage of the concept of on-the-job training, which has become deeply ingrained in workers. If children considered as helpers are included, the number of minors working during the school year would approach 80 per cent of the adult workers, or approximately 48,000 individuals. Child labor in the flower-growing sector is, in many cases, formal and open; in others, it is clandestine and concealed as help to parents or siblings who work. The incorporation of children in the production of flowers, in addition to providing low-cost or free labor, also trains them as future employees.

On its negative side, child labor in agriculture often leads children to be exposed to too much responsibility from a very early age, given the domestic and formal work they perform. This labor is in conflict with their formal learning and it leads to academic underachievement. They are also exposed to hazards. For example, Ecuadorian children as young as eight work in banana fields and packing plants where they are exposed to toxic pesticides and other unsafe working conditions in violation of their rights.

In Egypt, the working situations of the underage and unprotected child labor in the country's cotton fields (Whitman *et al.* 2001) show that each year over one million children between the ages of seven and twelve are hired by Egypt's agricultural cooperatives to take part in cotton pest management. Employed under the authority of Egypt's Agriculture Ministry, most are well below national minimum age of twelve for seasonal agricultural work. They work eleven hours a day, including a one to two-hour break, seven days a week, which is far in excess of limits set by the Egyptian Child Law. They also face routine beatings by their foremen, exposure to heat and pesticides. These conditions violate Egypt's obligations under the Convention on the Rights of the Child to protect children from ill-treatment and hazardous employment. They are similar to the worst forms of child labor, as defined in the International Labour Organization's Convention 182, which Egypt has not yet ratified.

Pakistan is another country with a high percentage of child labor (9 per cent) in the medium HDI group. Based on action research conducted in the surgical instrument manufacturing industry in Sialkot, Lahore, Pakistan (AKIDA Management Consultants 2004), several reasons were identified for the occurrence of child labor in the country: (a) children of poor parents or large families were forced to increase or supplement household income; (b) inherent weaknesses regarding the definition of child labor, such as the exemption granted to children working alongside their families in hazardous occupations; (c) the mild penalties imposed for breaking of law and neglect of children working in the informal sector; and (d) the high percentage of dropped-out school children. The root of the problem is again poverty. These factors may be similarly applied to other countries with a high percentage of child labor.

Another important reason for child labor is poor families who often fall victim to market forces present in a globalized economy (Baradaran and Barclay 2011). Child labor is often in high demand in the unorganized, informal sectors of the economy where profits are low. Employers in developing nations are driven by low profit margins and a necessity to compete in the globalized market place. Thus, farmers or employers in poor countries turn to child labor in order to lower costs and compete with fluctuating commodity prices.

In Uzbekistan, large retailing companies, including multinational corporations (MNCs) such as Tesco, Walmart-Asda, H&M and Zara, were identified as being complicit in purchasing products made from Uzbek cotton, which is picked by child laborers (The Global Compact 2013). An estimated two million children between the ages of 11–17 harvest cotton in Uzbekistan under conditions described as forced labor. Unlike cases where children work on family farms, the Uzbek case is different in scale involving institutions and government. Each year, for example, the government closes schools, hospitals and offices for three months in order to boost the workforce available for the annual cotton harvest with students, teachers and government employees participating in the process. In relation to working conditions of the child labor it was reported that in extreme cases some school administrators have used physical abuse to ensure that the government-imposed quota of 30–60 kilograms of cotton is picked per child per day, depending on their age. Children receive little pay for their work, and are often provided with food. Uzbekistan is the world's third largest cotton exporter and earns approximately US$1 billion annually.

Migrant workers

Rising economic and demographic differences between countries contribute to an increase of migrant workers. In other words, people movement over borders is seen as a natural phenomenon in the era of globalization. Migrant workers refer to individuals who are lured into working in other countries to meet the shortage of labor in the fast-industrializing and developed nations. Migrant workers can be considered a type of forced labor because of limited choices the workers have in their own country or region. Migrant workers pose many problems not only to the employers (such as MNCs) but also to the countries of origin and their families that rely on their remittances.

Migrant worker statistics, working conditions and problems

Table 29.3 presents data on migrant workers based on country and HDI rank (UNDP 2011). More migrant workers are in countries within the very high HDI rank category such as Norway (13.37 per cent), the United States (10.25 per cent), France (10.26 per cent), the United Kingdom (8.67 per cent) and Finland (2.89 per cent) than countries in the lower ranks of HDI. Reasons for this trend are shortages of labor in the higher HDI rank countries as well as the attraction of the countries to international migrant workers because of greater employment opportunities. Better policies and working conditions in the industrialized countries are other reasons for the high percentages of migrant workers in the aforementioned countries.

The Asia and Pacific regions are estimated to have 29 million migrant workers that include men, women, youth and children. These migrant workers are pursuing their dreams for a better life and searching for better working conditions in foreign lands. In doing so, the workers inevitably face formidable challenges such as restricted legal channels of work, escalating fees and expenses related to their job search and hostile public attitudes in host countries (ILO/SKILLS-AP-KOREA 2010). The Asia and Pacific regions face challenges as they shift towards higher skills and knowledge-based economies to ensure sustainable competitive advantage. This shift has resulted in limited choices for the unskilled and uneducated migrant workers.

Working conditions and problems faced by migrant workers are described in the following section. However, it is noticeable that the problems of migrant workers are more felt in the fast-industrializing countries where many MNCs from the developed countries are operating their businesses. A study in Brazil on an MNC, Zara (The Global Compact 2013) found that the company exercised sub-standard working conditions. The investigation found that in several workshops workers were forced to work 16-hour shifts in windowless rooms and were prohibited from leaving unless it was an emergency. Exposed wiring, faulty equipment and unsanitary living conditions constituted severe health and safety risks. Labor inspectors also found that 15 immigrants from Bolivia and Peru, who had been trafficked into the country, were illegally employed in the workshops where they were struggling to earn enough to pay off their debts to the traffickers. The workers were earning below the 2011 minimum wage.

Table 29.3 Percentage of migrant workers in selected countries (2012)

Country and HDI Category and Rank	*Population (millions, 2011/2012)*	*Total Inflow of Foreign Population (thousands, 2012)*	*Percentage of Migrant Workers by Population*
Very High Human Development			
Norway (1)	4.9	655	13.37
United States (4)	313.1	38,355	12.25
France (20)	63.1	6,471	10.26
Finland (22)	5.4	156	2.89
United Kingdom (28)	62.4	5,408	8.67
High Human Development			
Mexico (57)	114.8	644	0.56
Malaysia (61)	28.9	1,639	5.67
Albania (70)	3.2	83	2.60
Georgia (75)	4.3	191	4.44
Peru (80)	29.4	42	0.14
Medium Human Development			
Sri Lanka (97)	21.0	368	1.75
Thailand (103)	69.5	1,050	1.51
Paraguay (107)	6.6	168	2.55
Philippines (112)	94.9	374	0.39
Honduras (121)	7.8	26	0.03
Vietnam (128)	88.8	21	0.02
Guatemala (131)	14.8	53	0.36
Ghana (135)	25.0	1,669	6.68
Low Human Development			
Kenya (143)	41.6	345	0.83
Nepal (157)	30.5	819	2.69
Uganda (161)	34.5	518	1.50
Burkina Faso (181)	17.0	773	4.55
Somalia (193)	9.6	282	2.94

Sources: Extracted and computed from UNDP (2011); and NationMaster (2013). Accessed February 27, 2013 from http://www.nationmaster.com/index.php.

The Human Rights Watch (HRW) (The Global Compact 2013) also reported on sub-standard working conditions for migrant laborers in the Russian construction industry. They are often not paid the salaries initially promised, are forced to work excessively long hours and are threatened or physically abused by their employers. They are often not protected by the authorities and HRW has recorded instances of police officials extorting money from these workers. Russia has one of the largest migrant populations in the world, with approximately four to nine million migrant workers. Approximately 80 per cent of migrants originate from the nine countries of the former Soviet Union with which Russia maintains a visa-free policy. Approximately 40 per cent of migrant workers are employed in the highly unregulated construction sector.

The inflow of migrant workers to Malaysia is due to rapid expansion in the past three decades of all sectors of the economy especially manufacturing and services sectors. This expansion led in turn to better wages and rapidly improving working conditions. The higher wages and better working conditions attract large numbers of temporary workers from neighbouring Indonesia, Bangladesh, Thailand, and the Philippines. Many of these workers are hired in the low-skill and low-wage construction and service sectors and on agricultural plantations. However, Malaysia has also experienced an inflow of illegal foreign workers, prompting the government to implement harsh detention measures and mass deportation of unauthorized arrivals. Malaysian law does not allow foreign workers to join trade unions. The working conditions of illegal workers are generally inferior to those enjoyed by legally contracted workers.

An Australian television channel investigation uncovered exploitation of migrants at Hytex, a Nike supplier in Malaysia. In July 2009, it was alleged that approximately 1,200 migrant workers were exploited at Hytex, an apparel factory in Kuala Lumpur, Malaysia. According to reports, workers were employed via agents in Myanmar, Bangladesh and Vietnam. The factory makes t-shirts for major apparel companies such as Nike. Although the factory met minimum wage requirements, workers were housed in sub-standard accommodations (with around 26 workers per bedroom and generally poor sanitation and hygiene conditions), had their passports withheld and were subject to excessive and unfair monthly wage deductions. Passports were allegedly retained to compel workers to pay their own employment-permit fees, which otherwise should be paid by the company (Encyclopedia of the Nations 2013).

Bangladesh is one of the major countries of origin of migrant workers. With workers specifically skilled in the garment industry, many Bangladeshi women migrate for work in textile and garment manufacturing in Mauritius or Jordan. Whereas migrant workers in general represent a contribution of 13 per cent of the Bangladeshi GDP in remittances, they largely remain unprotected and often face serious exploitation and abuse throughout their entire migration experience. Little is being done to protect or prevent them from being deceived throughout the process of recruitment or exploited when employed at the final destination. Most are unduly, unfairly and exorbitantly charged for recruitment, transportation and essential needs such as food and accommodation (Institute of Human Rights and Business 2013).

HRD implications

HRD implications in dealing with working conditions of the two groups of employees are highlighted as follows. These implications deserve the attention of responsible groups such as families, society, government, the MNCs and organizations at the international level such as ILO, the United Nations and others.

Child labor

Partnerships that involve HRD practitioners, organizations and appropriate government agencies are needed to impact on child labor elimination. These partnerships should include effective global legislative measures, awareness enhancement geared by the Human Resource Ministry, Labor Department, and media in every country. Furthermore, emphasis must be placed on education as the key to better income and income generating projects for poor families.

ILO Convention 182 requires changes in the legal definition of age for child labor to be raised to 18 years, instead of 14 years. However, the implementation should be time bounded carefully, so that the labor market in certain countries is not disturbed due to abrupt changes. Prudent steps ought to be taken to develop relevant legislative measures based on regulatory and punitive measures, to effectively prevent employment of children in all industries for different age groups: 5–9 years, 10–14 years and 15–18 years.

Proper enforcement of existing child labor laws must be enacted. Until the incidence of child labor is completely eliminated, increased protection to child workers should be provided against violation of their rights and against unsafe industrial practices involving children.

Awareness seminars, advocacy workshops, and counselling sessions geared by Human Resource Ministry or Labor Department ought to be arranged for gaining parents' confidence and awareness about the ill-effects of child labor concerning their children. These counselling services should highlight the alternatives to child labor, including formal or non-formal education, and apprenticeship. Parents should be educated about the benefits of schooling in terms of increased efficiency and income.

The problem of child labor can be managed effectively if poverty problems are alleviated, for example through income generation projects for parents as well as through fair and equitable access to safety nets of the countries concerned. Particularly in Muslim countries the issues of *zakat* funds, *baitulmal*, and other benevolent programs should be capitalized on efficiently in the poverty alleviation efforts of federal and state governments. These actions involve financial institutions which are established to administer taxes, personal finances and government expenditures. They manage the distribution of wealth for the usage of public work and persons in need.

Education for all should be a core policy in countries in which child labor occurs. Such education should be affordable, particularly for the children from poor families. Related to this issue, quality of education should be enhanced and education should be made attractive to help reduce the tendency of children to drop out of school.

Non-formal education (NFE) schools and vocational institutes for children should be established adjacent to locations of industries that employ child labor. NFE schools are particularly essential to stop the supply of labor at the hiring source as well as to offer alternative options of productive engagement and learning for children.

Various media must be involved in creating public awareness regarding child labor issues, including partnerships with non-vocational and vocational education. In addition to workshops and conferences, effective educational materials using information communication technology need to be disseminated to educate society on the damages caused by child labor.

MNCs should adhere to the principles of corporate social responsibility (CSR) in which their involvement in business is not only for economic motives but also with ethical, legal and philanthropic orientations. As such MNCs should avoid actions that are harmful to the society, including the involvement of child labor in the supply chain.

Migrant workers

Mutual cooperation among relative agencies in both parental and host countries of migrant workers are essential to ensure fair benefits for migrant workers and employers. Based on this research, we offer the following suggestions.

Community based organizations such as migrants' rights, faith-based and diaspora organizations sometimes have direct access to migrant communities and could increase the trade unions' capacity to reach out to the most vulnerable groups. Trade unions' strong international networks, bilateral partnerships, expertise in labor market and labor rights related issues, and experience with settling labor disputes offer considerable benefits for migrant organizations in terms of protection of their beneficiaries.

Mutually beneficial cooperation agreements could thus be developed between different civil society organizations, in reaching the mutual goal of better protection of migrant workers. Terms and conditions remain to be explored on national and/or local levels regarding the needs, opportunities and capacities of respective organizations and migrant workers. The agreements should consider the potential to organize the collective voice of migrant workers by addressing their needs and defending their rights and interests.

Pre-departure training should include assessment and collecting evidence of existing competencies and work experience. For instance, training programs are required to prepare prospective female domestic migrant workers from Asian countries to the Middle East and elsewhere. The programs should cover topics such as safety and use of electrical appliances, remittance management and family economy, family well-being and health, foreign language and cultural skills. Similarly, the receiving countries should specify the skills required of migrant workers. This approach should be incorporated into the employment contracts and the contents of the pre-departure training.

Information should be provided by the employers about the receiving country, including information on labor laws, safety, required equipment, health care, job security, social benefits and medical leave. The employers in the receiving country should assist workers in recording skills and experiences they obtain during their assignment.

The host country should maintain a database on the returnees in terms of skills they have acquired abroad which can be mobilized in the home countries. By doing so, the workers' skills are recognized, and their stint abroad is an investment to them and the country.

Conclusion

This chapter has given insights on an aspect of workforce diversity, characterized by child labor and migrant workers, specifically on their numerical occurrences and working conditions across country contexts. Child labor issues are practically absent from most developed countries but they increase in countries with low HDI ranks. The opposite is observed for migrant workers in which the number is higher in the developed and fast-industrializing countries compared with the under developed countries. Market forces seem to influence the occurrences of the two groups of forced labor resulting from the spread of capitalism by the MNCs in the globalized economy.

This dimension of workforce diversity has brought challenges to many, specifically to HRD managers within the entire supply chain in the specific countries and at the international level. An important conclusion for HRD is that companies or employers of the above employed populations should comply with the principles of responsible business in terms of providing appropriate working conditions for workers within the entire supply chain as well as giving protection to them as a worker and a member in the family. The managers and company personnel in the various countries should adhere to ILO standards of socially responsible business and good industrial relations practices involving working conditions for these groups of the labor force, the ultimate aim of which is to produce a healthy and sustainable work force.

References

AKIDA Management Consultants (2004) *Baseline Survey Report on Child Labour in Surgical Instruments Manufacturing Industry Sialkot*, Lahore, Pakistan: ILO.

Baradaran, S. and Barclay, S.H. (2011) *Fair Trade and Child Labor*, Social Science Research Network. Online. Available HTTP: http://ssrn.com/abstract=1823546 (accessed 22 July 2013).

Castelnuovo, C., Castelnuovo, A., Oviedo, J., Santacruz, X. (2000) *Investigating the Worst Form of Child Labour*, Geneva: International Labour Organization. Online. Available HTTP: http://www.ilo.org/ipecinfo/product/download.do?type=document&id=1308 (accessed 2 February 2013).

Dávalos, G. (2002) *Child Labour*, Geneva: International Labour Organization. Online. Available HTTP: http://www.ilo.org/ipecinfo/product/download.do?type=document&id=380 (accessed 2 February 2013).

Encyclopedia of the Nations (2013) *Malaysia – Migration*. Online, Available HTTP: http://www.nationsencyclopedia.com/Asia-and-Oceania/Malaysia-MIGRATION.html (accessed 22 July 2013).

European Industrial Relations Dictionary (2011) Online. Available HTTP: http://www.eurofound.europa.eu/areas/industrialrelations/dictionary/definitions/workingconditions.htm (accessed 3 January 2013).

ILO (International Labour Organization) (2012) 'What is child labour'. Online. Available HTTP: http://www.ilo.org/ipec/facts/lang--en/index.htm (accessed 12 October 2012.

— (2013) *Hazardous Child Labour.* Online. Available HTTP: http://www.ilo.org/ipec/facts/WorstFormsofChildLabour/Hazardouschildlabour/lang--en/index.htm (accessed 3 February 2013).

ILO/SKILLS-AP/KOREA (15–16 September, 2010) 'Regional training workshop on skills assessment of returning migrant workers', Bangkok: ILO.

Institute of Human Rights and Business (2013) 'Business and migration roundtable 3'. Online. Available HTTP: http://www.ihrb.org/pdf/June_2011_IHRB_Business_and_Migration_Roundtable_3_Report.pdf (accessed 3 February 2013).

Schipper, I. and de Haan, E. (2007) *Labour Research Report on Labour Conditions in the Thai Electronics Sector*, Amsterdam: Centre for Research on Multinational Corporations (SOMO). Online. Available HTTP: http://www.somo.nl/html/paginas/pdf/Hard_disk_labour_NL.pdf (accessed 3 February 2013).

The Global Compact (2013) 'Human rights and business dilemmas forum: forced labour'. Online. Available HTTP: http://human-rights.unglobalcompact.org/dilemmas/forced-labour/ (accessed 28 February 2013).

UNDP (United Nations Development Programme) (2009) *Flexible Working Arrangements at the United Nations*, New York: UNDP.

— (2010) *Human Development Report. The Real Wealth of Nations: Pathways to Human Development*, New York: UNDP.

— (2011) *Human Development Report. Sustainability and Equity: A Better Future for All*, New York: UNDP.

Whitman, L., Megally, H. and Parekh, V. (2001) *Underage and Unprotected: Child Labor in Egypt's Cotton Fields*, 13(1E), Human Right Watch: New York.

30

TRANSFER OF LEARNING

Holly M. Hutchins and Sarah Leberman

With rising pressure on global organizations to account for learning and development expenditures, supporting and assessing transfer of learning has never been more important. Transfer of learning has long received important consideration in the study and practice of human resource development (HRD), resulting in the development of several conceptual models, outcome measures, and integrative reviews (Grossman and Salas 2011). Despite these advances, transfer of learning continues to challenge scholars and practitioners given the complexity of factors found to influence positive transfer and the limited application of research findings to practice (Hutchins *et al.* 2010). In this chapter, we review how transfer of learning has been conceptualized and studied, common assessment measures, and transfer interventions that have received empirical support. Although the study of transfer of learning has been primarily grounded in US-based models and practices until the last few years, we highlight the need for work in multinational organizations and with non-US samples. We also highlight "transfer in practice" exemplars from two organizations (US, New Zealand) recognized for their strategic support of employees' learning transfer. In our final section, we synthesize major findings and trends, and offer implications for continuing research and practices in transfer of learning.

Defining transfer

For our discussion and consistent with prior major review studies (cf. Blume *et al.* 2010), we define transfer of learning as *generalizing* (acquiring and applying) and *maintaining* (persisting) knowledge and skills from a learning experience to a relevant setting. Before moving on to the review of transfer concepts, we want to first clarify what has typically been an uneven use of terms pertaining to transfer: transfer of *learning* or transfer of *training.* Although both terms are used interchangeably in the literature and by practitioners, we choose transfer of *learning* to describe the application of knowledge and skills from any learning experience, not just from training. This approach is consistent with current approaches to studying learning that emerges from non-training events such as coaching, mentoring, and informal learning. That is, the extent to which individuals transfer (or not) focuses on how they apply what they learn (rather that what they have been trained on), thus making transfer of *learning* the more accurate term to describe this process. A second reason is that assessing the impact from a training event is rarely based on that experience alone, rather a myriad of factors that include learners' motivation and efficacy, their previous experience, manager support, and opportunity to use the new learning to improve performance (Brinkerhoff 2005). Thus, using transfer of "learning" (rather than training) better describes the process by which learners actualize new knowledge and skills to enhance performance regardless of the event/intervention (e.g. coaching, mentoring, communities of practice, or other learning experiences). Although we urge readers to consider this broader understanding in reading this chapter, please note that much of the research we review primarily examines "training" as the intervention and is consistent with how researchers and practitioners have traditionally thought of and measured transfer.

Guiding models and perspectives

Although early work on transfer of learning focused on students in educational settings (cf. Thorndike and Woodworth 1901) by elucidating the cognitive elements and conditions that influenced knowledge and skills application, Goldstein (1974, 1980) was one of the first to extend and study transfer of learning in organizational settings. A major outcome of Goldstein's work was in describing the training design process (sometimes described as instructional design process) and noting the influence of individual traits and attitudes, training design, and workplace climate characteristics on transfer success. These factors became the primary areas through which transfer of learning was explored and the basis for the guiding models of transfer that are currently used in HRD research.

Researchers have taken great strides in elucidating the factors that influence transfer resulting in several comprehensive review articles published in the last three decades. Although numerous studies have examined specific aspects of transfer of learning, we selected the major review articles (see Table 30.1) that identified factors influencing training transfer based on meta-analysis or integrative literature reviews (that included specific selection and interpretive criteria) to present here. Our intent was to provide readers a condensed review of the literature that has significantly influenced transfer of training research in general, but especially as it has been used in HRD research and practice.

With the exception of the early writings of Thorndike and Goldstein on the conditions of transfer, Baldwin and Ford's (1988) seminal review is the transfer model most cited in the contemporary transfer literature, and likely set the stage for the rise of studies on the transfer of learning. Although the authors grounded their work in Goldstein's three major concepts, the major contribution of Baldwin and Ford's model was in identifying *input* factors of trainee characteristics (ability, motivation, personality), *training design* (principles of learning, sequencing and content), and *work environment* (support, opportunity to use) and *training outputs and conditions* (generalization and maintenance). Modeling these relationships provided a framework through which researchers and practitioners could study transfer and derive interventions to influence successful learning retention and thus individual and organizational performance.

Almost a decade later, Ford and Weissbein (1997) reviewed how well researchers were acknowledging Baldwin and Ford's many suggestions around how to improve the conceptualizing and modeling of transfer. The authors found that researchers had indeed used more diverse samples, had included multiple non-self report measures, and explored transfer of increasingly complex tasks. They also noted that researchers were broadening the study of trainee characteristics to include motivation and attitudinal factors (e.g. motivation to learn, incentives, career alignment) and the effect of the work environment on transfer of learning. Over the next decade, research dramatically increased on both the predictive and relational effects of trainee motivational factors (goal orientation, motivation to transfer, motivation to learn) on the transfer of learning. This work was highlighted by Colquitt *et al.*'s (2000) oft cited meta-analytic work on training motivation

Table 30.1 Major transfer reviews (1988–2012)

Authors/Year	*Review Method, Sample*	*Results and Major Contribution*
Baldwin and Ford (1988)	LR (63 studies, 1907–1987)	Developed a commonly cited model of training transfer that included input (trainee characteristics, training design, work environment), output (learning, retention) and conditions (generalization and maintenance) of transfer.
Ford and Weissbein (1997)	LR (20 studies, 1988–1998)	Found increased variety of measures, theoretical models, time intervals, task complexity, diverse samples and longer intervals used in transfer research since 1988 review. Suggested future research on individual and work environment factors.
Holton, Bates and Ruona (2000)	LR and Factor Analysis (n = 1,616)	Developed and validated the first transfer system diagnostic measure (Learning Transfer System Inventory) that assesses individual, training and environment factors influencing transfer of learning.
Colquitt, LePine and Noe (2000)	MA (106 studies, 1957–2000)	Found moderate and strong correlations between individual factors (ability, personality, traits, motivation and attitudes) and transfer of learning.
Burke and Hutchins (2007)	LR (170 articles, 1979–2006)	Major review of transfer research based on empirical evidence since Ford and Weissbein (1997). Recognized additional individual (e.g. motivation to transfer), training design (e.g. self-management strategies) and work environment factors (e.g. accountability, strategic link) found to influence transfer.
Cheng and Hampson (2008)	LR (NA, 1988–2007)	Proposed theory of planned behavior to explain trainee choice (and intentions) on transfer of learning and highlighted areas of conflicting results among individual differences (locus of control, efficacy and personality) and transfer.
Baldwin, Ford and Blume (2009)	LR (140 articles, 1988–2008)	Described conceptual and methodological advancements since their 1988 review: increased studies of transfer in authentic settings, expanded research that tests transfer interventions and pre- and post-training influences, and varied use of outcomes measures. Called for research examining transfer decisions, increasing influence of contextual factors, and the role of technology (i.e. e-learning).
Blume, Ford, Baldwin and Huang (2010)	MA (89 studies)	Results confirmed positive relationships between transfer and predictors such as cognitive ability, conscientiousness, motivation, and a supportive work environment, but noted inconsistent findings in transfer interventions on transfer of learning. Most predictor variables examined (e.g. motivation, work environment) had stronger relationships to transfer when the focus of training was on open as opposed to closed skills. Noted inflated transfer outcomes of studies using same source or same method measures.

Notes: MA: meta-analysis; LR: literature review; NA: not available that noted several strong to moderate correlations between cognitive ability, personality and traits (anxiety, conscientiousness, locus of control) and attitudinal factors (career-planning, organizational commitment) on the transfer of learning. These factors are also highlighted in the reviews (Table 30.1) conducted between 2001 to present thus demonstrating that transfer researchers were beginning to look more closely at the influence of individual differences in the transfer process and how these influenced learning and retention.

Scholarly inquiry into transfer of learning antecedents, conditions and models flourished over the next two decades likely sparked by the increased pressure on organizations to demonstrate a return on investment. Noting the increased number of comprehensive reviews as one indication of this resurgence (see Table 30.1), researchers may have also felt pressure from the emergence of industry reports on training benchmarks, analytics, and overall spending that increased the discussion of trainer accountability and return on investment to stakeholders. Examples include (from the US) the American Society of Training & Development's (ASTD) *State of the Industry Report* (which will soon include China and India Training Reports) and the *Corporate Learning Factbook* (Bersin and Associates) that served as a comprehensive description of the US training profession. Similar reports were also produced by the European Training and Development Federation and numerous other country-specific training reports (e.g. Australia, New Zealand, China, India, Canada).

In addition to a focus on trainee characteristics, the role of the work environment (i.e. supervisor and peer support, opportunity to perform) also gained more attention from researchers and emerged as one of the more reliable predictors of learning transfer (Blume *et al.* 2010). Reviews conducted by Burke and Hutchins (2007) and Cheng and Hampson (2008) highlighted the importance of work environment factors and renewed the discussion of transfer climate (Rouiller and Goldstein 1993), a concept that describes how workplace cues (situational and consequence) can influence learning transfer. Transfer climate included more factors, expanding on past manager support and opportunities to practice (cf. Tracey *et al.* 1995) adding significantly to the explained variance in post-training job performance; however, researchers were unable to validate the construct structure of the transfer climate factors. The situation changed when Holton *et al.* (2000) developed the Learning Transfer System Inventory (LTSI). This diagnostic assessment of 16 training-specific and general training factors was grounded in the extant transfer literature, and through its usage transfer climate factors were validated as a part of a larger set of "system" of learning transfer factors grounded in the literature. Climate factors were expanded to include feedback, openness to change, personal outcome (positive and negative) and supervisor sanctions. Holton *et al.*'s work (cf. Bates *et al.* 2012, for a current review of LTSI research) was the first to coalesce the emerging research in psychology, management and in HRD around the critical factors influencing the transfer of learning into an internationally validated (translated into eight languages) diagnostic tool widely used by industry as a post-training assessment of trainee perceptions.

Finally, Baldwin and colleagues rounded out the comprehensive inquiries into the transfer of leaning research with two important works. Similar to Ford and Weissbein (1997), Baldwin *et al.*'s (2009) literature review marked the progress of transfer researchers since 1988 to address the criterion and measurement issues that had limited previous work. The authors acknowledged significant advances had been made in studying more complex behaviors in authentic training settings, testing of actual transfer interventions, increased attention on pre and post-training factors that influence transfer and the triangulation of outcomes measures and time intervals to assess transfer. Similarly, Blume *et al.*'s (2010) meta-analysis provided a more statistical synthesis (n = 89 studies) of the transfer literature, and offered support for the predictive strength of individual factors (ability, personality, motivation) and transfer climate factors on the transfer of learning. In fact, they found that transfer climate had the strongest relationship with transfer (.27) within the general environmental construct (which also included peer/supervisor peer and supervisor, and constraints: lack of autonomy, situational constraints). A key finding of their work concerned response bias commensurate with the overwhelming use of self-reports in assessing transfer. When controlling for common method bias in their meta-analysis of reviewed studies, Blume *et al.* (2010) found that studies using the same-source and/or same measurement (SS/SMC) consistently inflated predictors' (i.e. the effect size increased from .23–.36) effect on transfer outcomes. This finding aligned with an earlier meta-analysis exploring differences among rating sources across training outcomes (cf. Taylor *et al.* 2009) noting that transfer effects based on trainees' self-ratings, and to a lesser extent ratings from their superiors, were largest and most varied across studies.

In sum, researchers have made significant strides in conceptualizing the enablers and barriers to the transfer of learning within organizational settings. Considerable advances were made in expanding the individual and work/climate factors found to influence transfer of learning and in increasing the methodological precision and study of transfer variables. However, a glaring gap in transfer studies was the limited number of non-US samples and researchers. In our review of transfer research, we found increasing numbers of researchers, samples and perspectives from UK, Australian, and Chinese scholars emerging only in the last few years.

Transfer of learning interventions

As researchers continued to refine the transfer of learning model, practitioners were equally concerned about interventions that influenced the factors resulting in sustained impact to employee performance. Many of the transfer interventions and practices discussed stem from Broad and Newstrom's (1992), and more recently Broad's (2005) transfer matrix, from empirical reviews of transfer interventions, and from emerging work on action learning.

Broad and Newstrom's transfer matrix

From a pragmatic view, Broad and Newstrom's (1992) transfer matrix provided one of the first approaches to planning out the *temporal* (when the intervention occurs) and *stakeholder* (who is involved in the intervention) components implicit in supporting transfer interventions in the workplace (see Figure 30.1).

The temporal dimension was identified as occurring before, during or after the training event, and the stakeholders included trainees, trainers, and supervisors as the three primary stakeholders

Stakeholders	Before Intervention	During Intervention	After Intervention
Executives			
Supervisors, Team Leaders			
Trainers			
Trainee/Learner			
Peer			
Customers			

Figure 30.1 Transfer matrix (based on Broad and Newstrom 1992, Broad 2005)

affecting training transfer. They identified a number of strategies which participants can employ during the transfer process, in the before, during and after phases of training. Examples of these strategies include demonstrating support and value of transfer by organizational leaders (executives), building transfer into learner performance standards (manager), and aligning the HRD program with the organization's strategic plan (trainer). A primary contribution of their work was in arguing for more consultation between trainer, trainee and manager and that the role of transfer manager should be taken on by HRD professionals. This notion is important, as it highlights that "the training event" is only part of the performance management process of learning transfer and not an end in itself and multiple stakeholders were influential in supporting transfer not just the trainee (Broad 2005). Whilst Broad and Newstrom (1992) accept that "trainees must be encouraged to take greater responsibility for their own development of new knowledge, skills and abilities" (Broad 2005: 14), they also identify that the dominant barriers to transfer come from the work organization and management. Empirical support in organizations using the transfer matrix as a transfer planning and management tool has been represented in a collection of case studies of cross disciplinary organizations (e.g. Texas Instruments, US Central Intelligence, Honda of America) that noted specific outcomes to enhancing learning application and maintenance (cf. Broad 2005, Phillips and Broad 1997).

Empirical reviews of transfer interventions

Bolstered by review findings that transfer interventions, while increasingly included in transfer studies, had inconsistent and sparse findings, studies by Saks and Belcourt (2006) and Hutchins (2009) highlighted specific interventions found by training professionals to influence transfer before, during, and after training. Specifically, Saks and Belcourt (2006) found that activities during the pre- and post-training phases explained 25 per cent of the variance in training transfer, with activities within the training design phase explaining an additional 6 per cent. The authors also found that organizations which provided training activities and support pre-, during and post-training reported higher levels of transfer. Similarly, in a recent review of empirical support for transfer interventions (Burke *et al.* 2013), the most frequently cited evidence-based transfer interventions included the *training design* factors (opportunities for practice, modeling, interactive learning activities, feedback on transfer application, and including diverse delivery methods to enhance learning in training) and *work environment factors* (opportunities to practice, manager reinforcement and support, and the cues and support from the larger organizational climate). The climate factors included having language about the organization's commitment to training/ development in the mission statement, including relevant materials and support available, and ongoing accountability for performance. Many of the organizational climate factors are commensurate with Holton *et al.*'s (2000) LTSI diagnostic measure of an organization's learning transfer system. Each of the transfer interventions noted spans Broad and Newstrom's (1992) temporal and stakeholder dimensions, as well as appearing in multiple categories simultaneously (e.g. feedback on performance), thus supporting Burke and Hutchins' (2008) finding that some transfer interventions were not bound by time and could be used across the dimensions.

Action learning

Another intervention that is gaining increasing support as a transfer intervention is action learning. Developed by Revans (1982), action learning is based on the perspective that learning and taking action in the real world are inextricably linked, whereby the learning gained from any experience would be dependent on the setting and the task of the action learning program.

Bunning (1994: 3) regards the ultimate goal of action learning as developing "a way of functioning so that learning is a natural consequence of your taking action in the real world." He furthermore advocates action learning as a means of integrating knowing (what I know), doing (what I do) and being (who I am). By learning from their experiences, he argues, learners will be empowered to manage their own learning, which will in turn result in more self-directed learning and performance. Action learning helps people develop critical questioning and become reflective practitioners, with a capacity and commitment to life-long learning (Bunning 1992, 1994).

General consensus exists in the literature regarding the outcomes of action learning including personal and professional development; increased confidence and self-esteem and self-awareness; learning to relate to, and communicate with, others more effectively; increased readiness to take responsibility and initiative; and the development of networks (Inglis 1994, Raelin 1997, Weinstein 1995). Specifically, Weinstein (1995: 293) states that action learning "helps people focus on the practicalities of their everyday working lives and gives them an opportunity to do something about the issues that concern them – and learn from that experience. It brings learning to the workplace, rather than separating the two."

Action learning has a long history in the European context, but adoption in the North American context and multinational companies has been more recent (Cho and Egan 2010, Leonard and Lang 2010). It is particularly helpful in the arena of leadership development because of its application in authentic settings, working on organizational issues, and is often longitudinal in nature. In addition, because action learning is tied to real company issues, accountability and relevance to individual and organizational leaning is amplified. Many transfer interventions, as previously noted, are "one-off" learning opportunities and not directly linked to an individual's work environment. Action learning, however, focuses on actual organizational issues that are worked on by staff from across the organization in action learning teams or "sets." Not only does this approach provide opportunities for leveraging strengths across the organization, it also ensures that many leadership qualities and competencies considered difficult to teach in a classroom setting are developed – such as adaptability and innovative thinking.

Action learning is a holistic approach, which rather than separating out pre-, during and post-training phases integrates them all into one approach and therefore maximizes the opportunity to transfer learning. Action learning has been used in developing students' entrepreneurship skills in capstone business classes taught in Asian and Pacific islands settings (cf. Mueller *et al.* 2006), as well as used in developing leaders in government and multinational organizations. For example, Leonard and Lang (2010) describe multiple case examples from government organizations in the US including the Department of Commerce and Agriculture, as well the multinational corporation Boeing, where action learning has been successfully used for participants in leadership development programs. The authors compared action learning with other leadership development interventions (i.e. 360 feedback, assessment centers, simulations) and found action learning was better for developing leaders' skill development, accountability, motivation, insight, and practice which was realized in each of the cases. Most of these, with the exception of insight, have been empirically linked as correlates or predictors of the transfer of learning.

Evaluating transfer of learning

While advances were made in conceptual models and developing interventions, the more challenging area of transfer research and practice continues to be how to easily and effectively measure the transfer of learning (Blume *et al.* 2010). Several approaches on how to measure transfer emerged shortly after Baldwin and Ford's (1988) seminal work, noting advances in how to measure proximal and distal outcomes of the transfer of learning. These measurement approaches ranged from a pre- and post-test of knowledge and skill use, experimental design (where the treatment group receives a transfer intervention), transfer surveys and questionnaires administered at two to four months after training, and some longitudinal designs that assessed transfer at noted intervals (e.g. 6, 9, 12 months). Sample items of a common transfer measure developed by Chiaburu and Lindsey (2008) include "I can accomplish the job tasks better by using new knowledge acquired from the training course" and "I am able to transfer the skills learned in training back to my job." However, the majority of transfer outcome measures were and still are self-reported transfer scores (with few having undergone psychometric validation), an issue that Blume *et al.* (2010) noted in their call for additional measures to offset the response bias implicit in single source measurement. Despite modest improvements in studies including multi-source measures – mostly from a supervisor or peer – to help triangulate transfer assessments over the last decade, researchers still struggle with how to best capture transfer outcomes that directly and indirectly influence job performance.

Two approaches that include more of a pragmatic approach to transfer measurement are from Jack Phillips and Robert Brinkerhoff. Phillips (2009) is best known for his work on assessing the return-on-investment of learning and development interventions. He suggests examining multiple forms of data to describe a more accurate picture of transfer performance that can include objective performance records (i.e. completion rate, processing time, program costs, corrections), work group and quality reports, and sales records together with more subjective self-reports of transfer of learning. In contrast, Brinkerhoff's (2005) Success Case Method (SCM) approach provides more of an embedded approach to assessing transfer of learning. The SCM approach involves comparing successful and unsuccessful cases (or instances) from the training program that includes identifying potential success cases (by reviewing usage records and reports, performance data, or simply by asking people) and collecting stories and evidence of success. SCM also engages stakeholders to explicate what "success" looks like by determining the outcome measure(s) that the trainees' experiences are evaluated against, thus providing data about how the training event, in addition to other performance system factors, influenced the transfer of learning.

Transfer of learning in practice

To further demonstrate how organizations are supporting transfer of their employee learning and development interventions, we include two short descriptions of organizations recognized for their learning transfer located in the United States and New Zealand.

Jiffy Lube International, Houston, Texas (United States)

Jiffy Lube International is a $1.4 billion automotive preventative maintenance organization founded in 1979 and owned by Shell Oil. Jiffy Lube has 22 million customers, and has been recognized for its commitment to learning and development by ASTD and other major learning and development organizations (cf. N.A. 2011). The learning and development is centered in Jiffy Lube University (JLU), a program for service center employees that combines computer-based instruction, supervised on-the-job training, and competency-based testing to help ensure Jiffy Lube technicians are equipped with the requisite skills to provide quality service to customers.

In 2011, Jiffy Lube garnered the first place slot in ASTD's annual BEST award competition, which recognizes organizations that demonstrate enterprise-wide success or achievement as a result of employee learning. The BEST Awards criteria include evidence of an "enterprise-wide" role of the learning function, evidence that learning is valued in the organization's culture, significant learning investments, and an established link between learning and performance (i.e. business alignment, measurement, effectiveness, non-training solutions). A few highlights of Jiffy Lube's success include having an online learning portal, the "Certification Dashboard Report" (where employees and managers can track their own training completion), a Daily Training Observation Guide to assist trainers in recording trainees' on-the-job performance during the training period, and a video message communication system, "JLU Tube," which broadcasts learning updates, best practices and programs to the 20,000 and more technicians working at the independently owned franchised locations.

Jiffy Lube also demonstrates quality through program accreditation from the American Council on Education (ACE). The ACE accreditation, which only two other major service providers have (McDonalds and Starbucks), designates that employees who earn all 10 JLU certifications would have the equivalent of seven hours of college credit. Jiffy Lube also has an agreement with the University of Maryland University to accept the ACE credits and provide a discounted tuition rate for any Jiffy Lube franchise employee and members of the employee's immediate family. Other indicators of support for transfer include management mentoring and coaching (for new managers in the stores), a franchise-wide training committee that standardizes training design and implementation, assessment and follow-up, and a boot-camp for training facilitators (to ensure all trainers have the same expectations and competencies for training delivery). Similar to studies supporting specific interventions and the influence of system factors (i.e. value of learning, alignment, accountability, openness to change) on transfer of learning, Jiffy Lube represents an exemplar of an organization that draws upon multiple facets to support and sustain learning transfer.

FINCO (adapted from Young 2011)

FINCO is a major Australian-owned New Zealand financial service organization recognized for the learning transfer support specifically resulting from a leadership development program. The results discussed here were from a longitudinal in-depth qualitative case study based on the Insight Leadership Development program. The objective of the Insight program was to develop and enhance the attitudes, knowledge and skills of senior FINCO leaders to deliver sustainable high performance. The program consisted of two residential modules (focused on leadership and corporate strategy) followed by a third session, which included group presentations to a panel of the organization's executives. The research involved forty-four people, course participants (11), their managers (7), peers (10), subordinates (10), course trainers/facilitators (4) and executive team members (2). Following Broad and Newstrom (1992), course participants were interviewed at three points to explore the inhibitors and barriers to transfer that occurred before, during and after (9 months) the training course. The other participants were interviewed at various time points.

The findings suggested that inhibitors to transfer were more easily identifiable than facilitating factors. These inhibitors included the lack of managerial and organizational support, as well as a lack of social processes. Peers and subordinate support had very little influence on transfer. In much of the literature, the role of formal training has been viewed separately to other forms of workplace learning; however, in the case of FINCO, these two were complementary with the formal training assisting with socialization and the transfer of tacit knowledge. In addition, the findings suggested that formal training has a role to play in developing communities of practice by facilitating participation, identity development and practice, as well as providing the basis for the creation of new communities of practice. This role was possible because of the formation of networks resulting from the Insight course and therefore challenges traditional notions, which suggest that communities of practice do not develop from formal training courses. Given that communities of practice are seen as facilitators of the transfer, being able to link formal training with the development of communities of practice provides a useful bridge between two areas, which historically have been considered in isolation.

Perspectives and suggestions for future research

Given the increased attention to the transfer of learning evidenced in the literature and by practitioners, we offer several suggestions to further inquiry and improve the practice of learning transfer. First, and as we previously mentioned, researchers need to broaden their study of transfer from just training programs to other non-training interventions. Given the rise of informal learning events such as coaching, mentoring, communities of practice, and action learning, researchers should explore if the same enablers and barriers exist when transfer is examined within these experiences. Almost all of the studies included in the comprehensive literature reviews and meta-analyses (Table 30.1) have focused on training as the intervention, eliminating any non-training intervention as a potential source of transfer. In fact, US organizations doubled their investments for informal learning in 2011 from the previous year (Bersin 2012) suggesting that HRD professionals will need to account for the transfer of learning in these interventions and the impact to job performance.

A second suggestion is to explore the expanding role of technology in supporting and assessing the transfer of learning. Electronic support software offers assessment, analysis and support tools related to performance. Examples include the LTSI availability in an online format (cf. http://ltsglobal.com/index.html) that includes a tracking and reporting feature. The Fort Hill Company (cf. http://www.forthillcompany.com/products/) also has an electronic dashboard that offers reminders and tracking software that cue managers to support trainees on their action plans. Leveraging technology to assess transfer factors and offering targeted support tools greatly enhances the ability of an organization to minimize the perennial diminishing return between learning investments and on-the-job performance improvements. We also suggest that leveraging technology could expand gathering transfer assessments from multiple sources, thus addressing the persistent call to reduce same-source/method bias and to increase objective methods of assessing transfer outcomes in transfer research (Blume *et al.* 2010, Taylor *et al.* 2009).

Finally, research has shown that the transfer of learning (from training) to the work environment continues to be an area where more research is warranted where employees are required to adapt very quickly to changing job requirements. We know that factors such as employee motivation, program design and supervisor support are important, but research exploring transfer of learning interventions is still lacking empirical validity. Interventions such as relapse prevention, and approaches such as action planning, have inconsistent and sparse empirical evidence, thus limiting the application in practice. Because soft skills development such as communication, conflict management and creativity require more than one-off training interventions, practitioners must consider a suite of learning interventions and opportunities embedded in the workplace to provide ongoing development. Many of these skills are developed over time and therefore require continuous engagement with learning rather than necessarily specific training interventions. Action learning programs are one way of achieving not just personal and professional development of individuals, but also wider organizational change, as the learning is very much driven by organizational imperatives. Traditionally, most training has been provided by outside "experts"; however, the emerging research on action learning would suggest that most organizations have the knowledge they need within, but often have not provided learning opportunities to realize this knowledge. Although action learning is most commonly used to explore organizational development, Cho and Egan (2010) recommend that taking a more balanced action learning approach (with an equal focus on learning and action that influences performance) could improve our understanding of the transfer of learning from both training and non-training interventions. Action learning is also an example of a transfer intervention with the majority of empirical evidence represented in UK organizations and samples, thus making it an attractive source of inquiry for US-based researchers and practitioners.

In summary, transfer of learning continues to attract and elude researchers attempting to capture all influences that explain the application of learning to increase job performance. Learning transfer research is best studied from a holistic, yet personalized perspective (Baldwin *et al.* 2009, Brinkerhoff 2005, Broad 2005) that explores the experience of learners in a given setting, rather than merely examining models that are custom-fitted onto a learning program. While there have been several research advances in the study of transfer, our review points to specific opportunities to expand inquiry on better ways to conceptualize, practice and support, and assess transfer of learning.

References

Baldwin, T.T. and Ford, K.J. (1988) 'Transfer of training: a review and directions for future research', *Personnel Psychology* 41: 63–105.

Baldwin, T.T., Ford, K.J. and Blume, B.D. (2009) 'Transfer of training 1988–2008: an updated review and agenda for future research', *International Review of Industrial and Organizational Psychology* 24: 41–70.

Bates, R.A., Holton, E.F., III and Hatala, J.P. (2012) 'A revised learning transfer system inventory: factorial replication and validation', *Human Resource Development International* 15: 549–69.

Bersin, J. (2012) *The Corporate Learning Factbook 2012*, Bersin and Associates. Online. Available HTTP: http://marketing.bersin.com/rs/bersin/images/011112_ES_CLFB2012_Final.pdf (accessed 12 December 2012).

Blume, B.D., Ford, J.K., Baldwin, T.T. and Huang, J.L. (2010) 'Transfer of training: a meta-analytic review', *Journal of Management* 36: 1065–105.

Brinkerhoff, R.O. (2005) 'The success case method: a strategic evaluation approach to increasing the value and effect of training', *Advances in Developing Human Resources* 7: 86–101.

Broad, M.L. (2005) *Beyond Transfer of Training: Engaging Systems to Improve Performance*, San Francisco, CA: John Wiley and Sons.

Broad, M.L. and Newstrom, J.W. (1992) *Transfer of Training: Action Packed Strategies to Ensure High Payoff from Training Investments*, Reading, MA: Addison-Wesley.

Bunning, C. (1992) 'The reflective practitioner: a case study', *Journal of Management Development* 11(1): 25–38.

— (1994) *Action Research: An Emerging Paradigm*, Occasional Papers Series 4, Brisbane: The Tertiary Institute, The University of Queensland.

Burke, L.A. and Hutchins, H. (2007) 'Training transfer: an integrative literature review', *Human Resource Development Review* 6: 263–96.

— (2008) 'A study of best practices in training transfer and proposed model of transfer', *Human Resource Development Quarterly* 19: 107–28.

Burke, L.A., Hutchins, H. and Saks, A. (2013) 'Best practices in training transfer', in M. Paludi (ed.) *The Psychology for Business Success*, Oxford: Praeger Publishing, 115–32.

Cheng, E., and Hampson, I. (2008) 'Transfer of training: a review and new insights', *International Journal of Management Reviews* 10(4): 327–341.

Chiaburu, D.S. and Lindsey, D.R. (2008) 'Can do or will do? The importance of self-efficacy and instrumentality for training transfer', *Human Resource Development International* 11: 199–206.

Cho, Y. and Egan, T.M. (2010) 'The state of the art of action research', *Advances in Developing Human Resources* 12: 163–80.

Colquitt, J.A., LePine, J.A. and Noe, R.A. (2000) 'Toward an integrative theory of training motivation: a meta-analytic path analysis of 20 years of research', *Journal of Applied Psychology* 85: 678–707.

Ford, J.K. and Weissbein, D.A. (1997) 'Transfer of training: an updated review and analysis', *Performance Improvement Quarterly* 10: 22–41.

Goldstein, I.L. (1974) *Training: Program Development and Evaluation*, Monteray, CA: Brooks/Cole.

Goldstein, I.L. (1980) 'Training in work organizations', *Annual Review of Psychology* 31: 229–72.

Grossman, R. and Salas, E. (2011) 'The transfer of training: what really matters', *International Journal of Training and Development* 15(2): 102–20.

Holton, E.F., Bates, R. and Ruona, W.E.A. (2000) 'Development of a generalized learning transfer system inventory', *Human Resource Development Quarterly* 11: 333–60.

Hutchins, H.M. (2009) 'In the trainer's voice: a study of training transfer practices', *Performance Improvement Quarterly* 22(1): 69–93.

Hutchins, H., Burke, L.A., and Berthelsen, A.M. (2010) 'A missing link in the transfer problem? Understanding how trainers learn about training transfer', *Human Resource Management* 49(4): 599–618.

Inglis, S. (1994) *Making the Most of Action Learning*, Aldershot: Gower.

Leonard, H.S. and Lang, F. (2010) 'Leadership development via action learning', *Advances in Developing Human Resource Development* 12: 225–40.

Mueller, J., Liang, T.E., Hanjun, H. and Thorton, J. (2006) 'Where should the action be – inside the classroom or outside the classroom? A comparison of the action-learning outcomes in Singapore, China, Korea, New Zealand and Australia', *Action Learning: Research and Practice* 3: 161–73.

N.A. (2011) 'Training top 125: Jiffy Lube', *Training*. Online. Available HTTP: http://www.nxtbook.com/nxtbooks/lakewood/training_20110102/index.php#/56 (accessed 22 December 2012).

Phillips, J.J. (2009) 'Achieving business alignment with the V-Model', *Proven: Beyond the Process* 2: 8–14.

Phillips, J.J. and Broad, M.L. (eds) (1997) *Transfering Learning to the Workplace*, Alexandria, VA: ASTD Press.

Raelin, J.A. (1997) 'Individual and situational precursors of successful action learning', *Journal of Management Education* 21: 368–94.

Revans, R.W. (1982) 'What is action learning?', *Journal of Management Development* 3: 15–26.

Rouiller, J.Z. and Goldstein, I.L. (1993) 'The relationship between organizational transfer climate and positive transfer of training', *Human Resources Development Quarterly* 4: 377–90.

Saks, A.M. and Belcourt, M. (2006) 'An investigation of training activities and transfer of training in organizations', *Human Resource Management* 45: 629–48.

Taylor, P.J., Russ-Eft, D.F. and Taylor, H. (2009) 'Transfer of management training from alternative perspectives', *Journal of Applied Psychology* 94: 104–21.

Thorndike, E.L. and Woodworth, R.S. (1901) 'The influence of improvement in one mental function upon the efficiency of other functions', *Psychological Review* 8: 247–61.

Tracey, J.B., Tannenbaum, S.I. and Kavanagh, M.J. (1995) 'Applying trained skills on the job: the importance of the work environment', *Journal of Applied Psychology* 80: 239–52.

Weinstein, K. (1995) *Action Learning: A Journey in Discovery and Development*, London: HarperCollins.

Young, A. (2011) *Insight: Leadership Training, Organizational Context and Transfer of Learning – A Case Study*, unpublished PhD thesis, Massey University, New Zealand.

SECTION VII

HRD as a profession

31

CERTIFICATION OF HRD PROFESSIONALS

Saul Carliner and Bob Hamlin

Our chapter focuses on the certification of HRD professionals and considers its potential impact on the field. Certification is a process in which a professional demonstrates competence in a field (Carliner 2012) by "fulfill[ing] a set of requirements or satisfy[ing] a set of standards" (Hale 2012: 1). Although actual certification processes vary, they often include one or more of these components: fulfilling an educational requirement (such as completing a certain vocational, or professionally related degree in a particular area), successfully passing a knowledge exam that tests familiarity with a body of knowledge, successfully demonstrating skill in the field through an annotated work sample or responding to a scenario, agreeing to maintain the certification through continuing professional development and active participation in the profession, and agreeing to adhere to a code of ethics (ICE 2013; Fisher 2011). The code of ethics usually includes a provision to remove the professional should he or she violate the code.

Certification plays two distinct roles in HRD. One is as a job assignment. Many HRD professionals work on delivering programs that prepare workers for certification exams and, in some instances, prepare the certification exams. Some of these certifications are internal to the organization where the workers are trained and developed. For example, some large corporations such as IBM internally certify key, strategic job categories. Other certifications are external to the organizations. For example, many organizations offer accredited training for Project Management Professional certification. The other distinct role for certification in HRD is as a qualification for HRD-related jobs. While academics in the field advocate for the establishment of certification in HRD (such as Kahnweiler 2009; McLean 2013) to distinguish competent professionals from "charlatans" (Swanson and Holton 2009: 457), several organizations have established certifications, some as early as the 1960s. However, none have used the name HRD (Carliner 2012) and most only certify some of the domain of skills in HRD: either training and development (T&D), organizational development (OD), or coaching. The first credentials emerged in the United Kingdom (UK), where the field originally known as *industrial training and development* professionalized in the early part of the twentieth century with the formation of the Institute of Training Officers which, in the 1960s, was re-named as the Institute of Training and Development (ITD). ITD catered to "professional" training officers employed by private, public and nonprofit (third-sector) organizations, as well as external T&D consultants.

As noted earlier, our chapter focuses on the type of certifications that lead to professional recognition and it also considers their potential impact on the field – that is, whether certification has had or will have an impact and, if it has or does, what that impact has or will be. Before considering that issue, the chapter first provides a background on certification in HRD-related fields.

A couple of notes about terminology: We use the term *professional* in a general sense: someone who works in the field of HRD, either as a practicing professional or in academe. We prefer this term to *practitioner* because some of our readers might otherwise imply that we are excluding people in the academic community from those in the field of practice. Similarly, we use the term profession in a general sense to refer to the work of HRD. We do not use it in its most narrow sense, as a field of work that requires a license. Trice and Beyer (1993) refer to such work as an occupation.

A background on certification in HRD-related fields

This section provides a foundation for exploring the potential impact of certification: certification is contrasted with other types of credentials; certifications are listed; and efforts to ensure the quality of certifications are described.

Contrasting certification with other credentials

To make themselves the most attractive candidates in the market for jobs and services, as well as provide external validation of their competence, many professionals seek *transferrable credentials.* Transferrable credentials are forms of recognition granted by independent third parties and recognized by some or all employers, not merely the current employer. Holders of these credentials hope they weigh favorably in hiring, selection, promotion and reward decisions.

General interest in acquiring transferrable credentials has grown with the implicit shift in talent management strategies over the past 2 to 3 decades. In the past, employers sought career-long relationships with their workers, as long as workers' performance was satisfactory. Under such approaches, workers were valued and rewarded for their seniority (Hall 1996). In the late 1980s, talent management strategies started to emphasize skills over seniority (Cappelli 2000). Employers sought relationships with workers as long as those workers had relevant skills to offer the organization. That focus on skills, in turn, drove interest in transferrable credentials, as witnessed by the rise in certification programs since the 1990s (Carter 2005).

Several types of transferrable credentials are available to help professionals demonstrate their qualifications for work in a field. Each type of credential communicates a different message about the qualifications of the candidate and some carry more weight than others with employers. The following describes the most commonly sought credentials.

Licensure

Carrying the most weight with both employers and professionals is *licensure.* In those fields that have it licensure is compulsory to practice. Governments require licenses to practice certain professions, especially those in which the potential for physical, financial, or intellectual risk to the recipient of the service is high. Medicine and law require licenses, but so does cosmetology (hair styling) because, as a stylist once commented, "I can do some serious damage with these scissors." Closer to our field, many jurisdictions require a license to practice as a teacher. For example, most US states require that teachers have a teacher's license. Licenses are also required in some jurisdictions for teaching in other contexts. Peru, for example, requires teaching licenses for instructors in higher education and other jurisdictions. For some professional practitioners licensure is the distinguishing characteristic of an occupation (or, as some call it, a "true" profession).

The process for receiving licenses varies among professions and in different legal jurisdictions: not only countries but also states or provinces as they control licensing in some countries. In fields like law and accounting, for example, licensure involves a test, usually taken soon after completing an approved academic program in the field. In medicine, the process also involves completion of a period of closely supervised work, called an *internship* or *residency* in some jurisdictions, or by a trainee job title in others. The residency alone is sufficient for licensure in other healthcare-related professions. Architecture requires both a test and a residency.

The education and assessment processes are both regulated by the profession. Professional organizations develop the curriculum requirements for programs that prepare people to work in the field and conduct periodic inspections to verify that programs meet these requirements. Professional organizations also develop and validate the tests and other assessments used for licensing, and manage any disputes that arise.

Licensed professionals must maintain their license. For most professions, maintaining their license involves completing a certain number of hours of training within a given time period, such as 30 hours of training every 2 years. Licensed professionals agree to adhere to a code of professional ethics (also established by the professional organization). Should someone accuse a licensed professional of violating the code, the profession has procedures in place for verifying the claim and, if it is valid, sanctioning the person found guilty.

As a result of these processes, licensed professionals also carry full legal liability for their professional decisions. That is, should a licensed professional make an error in judgment in his or her work, the injured party can sue the professional and receive compensation for the resulting damage. That legal liability discourages some professionals from seeking licensure in those professions in which a license is optional. For example, many engineers in the United States practice without a license. In most licensed occupations, however, practicing without a license is not a viable option. As a result, the license acts as a barrier to entry. Licensing is not available to HRD professionals at this time, nor do any active efforts exist to license professionals in the field.

Certification

Many people confuse certification with licensure, but one key characteristic distinguishes the two: licensing is required to practice an occupation; certification is voluntary. At its most basic, certification is the validation of competence by a third party. Certification candidates demonstrate competence through one or more of these means: passing examinations that demonstrate familiarity with a body of knowledge central to the field of certification, skills demonstrations and evaluations of work portfolios (which usually require that candidates certify that the work in the portfolio is their own) (Hale 2012). Some certification programs also require a residency, although residency requirements may merely refer to a minimum number of years of full-time employment in the field or a period of time of working under close supervision by an experienced professional, as is the case of medicine and many allied health professions. Most certification programs do not require that candidates complete an academic program, but many do provide credit towards the residency requirement to people who have completed formal academic degrees. For example, one certification program provides a year of residency for people who have academic degrees in the field.

Like candidates for licensing, candidates who successfully complete a certification process are required to adhere to the code of ethics for their profession. Also like licensing, most certification programs also require that professionals maintain their certification either by participating in ongoing professional development activities or re-taking the certification exam. All certifications are voluntary; candidates can choose whether or not to seek it and employers can choose whether or not to recognize it as a credential when hiring or promoting individuals. The more people who seek certification, the more credibility the credential has. When a program reaches a certain critical mass, it becomes a *de facto* standard. For example, the Project Management Professional certification administered by the Project Management Institute (PMI) has become a *de facto* standard in business. Similarly, the Professional in Human Resources (HR) and Senior Professional in HR offered by the HR Certification Institute (HRCI) are increasingly becoming *de facto* standards for HR professionals in many countries. As noted earlier, although no certifications specifically exist under the name HRD, several exist in the field of T&D. Later sections of this chapter describe each of the HRD-related certifications available in Canada, the USA, the UK and various other countries.

Academic degrees

Academic degrees indicate successful completion of a program of study from an accredited academic institution. In general, academic programs are available at the Bachelor's, Master's and doctoral levels.

Although specific qualifications vary by institution, in many academic systems, completing a Bachelor's degree in the Americas typically suggests that the graduate has completed 10 or more courses in the major, a series of general educational courses required of all students for the degree and maintained a grade point average of 2.0 or better on a 4.0 scale. A Master's degree typically suggests that the graduate completed 8 or more courses in the major, maintained a grade point average of 3.0 or better and might have completed a capstone requirement such as a qualifying examination, a thesis or similar paper, or portfolio presentation. (Requirements often differ on other continents.) A doctoral degree always suggests that the graduate has successfully completed a research dissertation or thesis. To do so, the candidate would have successfully passed qualifying examinations, defended a research proposal, or both. Curricula vary widely among programs and PhDs in T&D and in other components of the HRD domain, and individuals can earn their doctorates in a variety of fields. Completing a PhD in this or a related field provides no guarantee of familiarity with a specified body of knowledge despite the presence of common components in many programs.

In addition to doctoral degrees and Master's degrees, academic institutions also offer certificates and diplomas at the undergraduate and graduate levels. Certificates represent completion of a short program of study in a particular subject area. Postgraduate certificates are awarded to people who already have at least an undergraduate degree and typically complete 4 or 5 courses in a particular area, fewer than required for a full Master's or PhD degree. Some institutions also award undergraduate certificates; these typically involve ten courses in a focused area of study, about the number of courses required for an undergraduate major subject but without all of the other general educational requirements of a Bachelor's degree.

More basic degrees also exist. For example, the community college system in the US offers an associate's degree, which represents at least two years of post-secondary study, with the majority of that study in the major. The Canadian system calls these *diplomas*, but they differ from undergraduate or graduate diplomas.

HRD professionals typically earn degrees in the fields of Adult Education, Educational Leadership, Educational (Instructional) Technology, Management (with a concentration in HR) and HRD. Programs exist at all levels, from post-secondary diplomas offered by community colleges to doctoral degrees offered by public, nonprofit and for-profit universities.

Accreditation

Although sometimes used as a synonym for certification (for example, the Public Relations Society of America (PRSA) calls its certification program "accreditation" (PRSA 2012), accreditation primarily refers to the review and formal recognition of programs of study in academic and vocational institutions (ICE 2013). Within the context of professional education, accreditation is intended to promote high standards of preparation and typically starts by specifying standards that institutions and programs should meet. Accreditation exists at both the institutional and program level. To be recognized as an institution of higher education, an institution must receive accreditation that is recognized by the government in the country in which it operates.

For the purpose of this discussion, however, our interest focuses on accreditation of individual programs. Standards for accreditation of programs identify core competencies that programs should develop, bodies of literature to which students should be exposed, resources that should be available to the program and qualifications of academic faculty. "The guiding belief behind the standards is that of unity in the essentials and diversity in the specifics" (Chalofsky *et al.* 2008: 1).

Although primarily focused on academic programs, continuing education and training programs can also be accredited. For example, PMI accredits programs that prepare candidates for its certification in project management (PMI 2013). Because it validates programs rather than individuals, accreditation is, at best, an indirect credential.

For licensure, however, accreditation is essential because only graduates of accredited programs have a right to become licensed. Accreditation also has value to professions that lack licensure as employers might recognize job candidates with degrees from accredited programs over other candidates; some employers might actively focus their recruiting efforts on accredited programs.

On the one hand, in several countries, all HRD-related academic programs are housed in accredited institutions. On the other hand, no processes exist to specifically accredit HRD programs. Some of the disciplines that underlie HRD, however, have standards to provide the development of academic programs. For example, through its Program Excellence Network (PEN), the Academy of Human Resource Development (AHRD) provides standards in HRD (Chalofsky *et al.* 2008). These standards only address graduate education, however, and several undergraduate programs exist in HRD and related fields. Similarly, the Association for Educational Communications and Technology (AECT) provides lists of competencies and standards to guide development of academic programs in instructional and educational technology, a closely aligned field that develops HRD practitioners (AECT 2012). Note, however, that AECT standards do not specifically focus on T&D and other adult educational contexts.

The UK probably has the most developed accreditation system in HRD, with the Chartered Institute for Personnel and Development (CIPD) and the Institute for Training and Occupational Learning (ITOL). Each offers a certification and recognizes academic programs and private providers that address the key components of their certification programs.

Certificates

Although similar in name to certification, certificates refer to a significantly different accomplishment: completion of a program of study, usually outside of a degree-related context. Certificates are intended to recognize mastery of the content of the program of study and should require both participation in class and successful completion of an assessment (Hale 2000). They also offer many advantages to participants, including easy enrollment (most do not have admissions standards) and quick completion (often a matter of days). In practice, these programs pose many problems.

Certificates vary in format, from a 2- or 3-day workshop, such as those that were offered by the American Society for Training and Development (ASTD) and those offered before the training conferences (sponsored by Lakewood Media) to a 10-course program in a particular field of study, such as the Diploma in Human Resource Management (HRM) available from the continuing education units of the Concordia Universities in St. Paul, Minnesota and Montreal, Quebec. Some certificates require no more than attending a single course without submitting an assessed assignment. Others require as much as earning credits for attending several courses in a program of study and submitting assignments throughout the program. Certificates are offered by a variety of institutions, including the education departments of professional organizations like the Indian Society for Training and Development (ISTD), the continuing education divisions of colleges and universities, and for-profit providers, such as the publishers of *Training* magazine. Some certificates add to the confusion by marketing themselves as "certifications" and suggesting that participants who complete these programs use designators beside their name. Several certificates are available to professionals in HRD; no regulation of certificates exists. Indeed, the number and variety of certificates are so varied that compiling a list of them would be difficult.

Other forms of recognition

In addition to the credentials already listed, other forms of recognition of competence, excellence and commitment exist. The recognition typically comes from peers in the form of awards. Most awards programs are sponsored by professional organizations, including the ASTD Excellence in Practice Awards, the UK-based CIPD People Management Awards and the International Federation of Training and Development's (IFTDO) Global HRD Awards. Some consultancies also offer awards programs, such as the US-based Brandon Hall's awards for excellence in e-learning and the ROI Institute's Awards Program.

The strength of awards is that they demonstrate effective performance. The limitation of some awards is that the standards of performance vary among awards programs and are often not aligned with those of a hiring manager. Furthermore, many awards recognize a work product to which several workers contribute. Such awards neither identify the contributions of individual workers, many of whom do not work in HRD, nor assess that contribution.

Many organizations also recognize career-long contributions to the field, as the Lifetime Membership awarded by the International Society for Performance Improvement (ISPI) and the Fellows program of the Canadian Society for Training and Development (CSTD). *CLO Magazine* recognizes the Chief Learning Officer (CLO) of the Year and *Training* magazine used to induct leaders into its Hall of Fame.

Characteristics of certification programs

In order for the people administering these recognition programs to have the basic guidance they need to administer them and the programs are administered consistently, each program is based on a well-documented set of policies and procedures. The policies and procedures also serve as a form of quality control and provide a context for defining concepts like competence and excellence in concrete ways.

Within the context of certification, policies and procedures specifically provide a means of identifying who can become certified, the means of becoming certified, the standards that the applicant must achieve and the requirements for maintaining certification. Although the specific characteristics of different certification programs vary widely, they share several characteristics (Hale 2012). The first common characteristic is that they are based on an externally defined "body of knowledge" or "competency model" or both. A body of knowledge "represent[s] the complete set of concepts, terms and activities that make up a professional domain, as defined by the relevant professional association" (Wikipedia 2013a). Typically, a committee representing various constituencies within a professional community works together to compile and document the body of knowledge. Some organizations publish their bodies of knowledge (such as PMI), which candidates can review as a means of preparing for the certification process.

A competency model presents the "clusters of interrelated knowledge, skills, attitudes and values necessary for performing effectively in a particular area" (CSTD 2010: vii). A model defines effective performance within a given domain and might also specify the types of deliverables and the standards against which to evaluate them, "but not provide specific 'how to' instructions" (CSTD 2010: viii). The *Handbook of Human Performance Technology* (Pershing 2006) published by the ISPI is an example of a body of knowledge. The competency model published by the ASTD (Rothwell *et al.* 2013; Bernthal *et al.* 2004) and the *Competencies for T&D Professionals* published by the CSTD (2010) are examples of competency models for HRD.

The second common characteristic of certification programs is that they require minimum qualifications to start the certification process. These might involve a minimum amount of work experience (called a *residency requirement*) or completion of an education program. In some cases, additional experience substitutes for a lack of education. Completion of a recognized education program reduces the residency requirement for most HRD-related certifications.

The third common characteristic of certification programs is that the assessment usually involves one or more of the following:

- Test, usually a multiple-choice test administered in a particular testing environment in which test administrators validate the identity of the candidate taking the exam and proctor the exam under strict conditions, such as not having notes or mobile telephones available during the test. Many such tests are conducted online so students can immediately learn whether or not they passed the written exam. Several of the HRD-related certifications involve a test, though none solely bases certification on a test.
- Skill demonstration, in which a candidate submits a work product along with an explanation of the process used to create it. In many instances, candidates must address specific questions in their explanations. Evaluators use explicit criteria to determine the extent to which the work product demonstrates competent performance in the profession. Most HRD-related certifications involve a skill demonstration, though none solely bases certification on the demonstration.
- Portfolio assessment, in which a candidate submits various work samples developed throughout the career to demonstrate particular competencies. The certification committee identifies the competencies that candidates must demonstrate, the type of evidence that they seek and any supporting documentation. Some HRD-related certifications use portfolio-based assessments, and they use them as the primary basis for assessing competence.

As suggested above, certifications often require two or all three of these as part of the certification process. When informing candidates of the result of the tests and reviews, certification committees typically provide limited feedback. If a candidate passes, the individual usually just learns that they passed. If a candidate fails, the individual just learns that they did not pass and, if the process includes several parts, which part they did not pass. In both situations, the candidate does not learn their score, much less which individual test questions and aspects of the portfolio they did not pass.

The fourth common characteristic of certification programs is that they require candidates to adhere to a code of ethics. Admittedly, most professions have a code of ethics whether or not they offer certification. Those that offer certification, however, typically add provisions to their codes of ethics to discipline professionals who violate the code and require that certified professionals sign a statement indicating that they agree to work under the code.

The fifth common characteristic of certification programs is that they require certified professionals to actively maintain their certification as a means of ensuring that certified professionals have the most current skills and knowledge. Although many organizations call this *recertification*, the process rarely involves going through the certification process again. Instead, as noted earlier in this chapter, maintaining certification usually involves completing a certain amount of continuing education during a given time period. HRD-related certifications also let certified professionals receive credit for active involvement in a professional society, publishing articles and other types of informal learning activities.

Certifications available to HRD professionals

As noted several times already, although licensure does not exist for HRD-related fields, several certifications do. This section describes the type of HRD-related certification programs available to HRD practitioners in various countries around the globe.

The designation of a particular grade of membership in a professional organization substantially differs from certifications based in North America where membership in the organization sponsoring the certification is typically not required.

Certified Performance Technologist

This certification, offered by the ISPI, "recognize[s] practitioners who have demonstrated proficiency in the Standards of Performance Technology and . . . promote the adoption of the Standards throughout the profession" (ISPI 2009). Receiving the Certified Performance Technologist (CPT) designation involves evaluation of a portfolio. Candidates submit "a detailed description of work performed in multiple projects in a manner that demonstrates the use of each of the Standards with attestations from internal/external clients or supervisors. A qualified reviewer will review all the documentation received from a candidate and determine if all requirements have been met" (ISPI 2009). Only candidates with at least three years' experience in the field can apply for certification. Upon receiving certification, candidates must formally commit to upholding the ISPI Code of Ethics and to recertify once every three years.

Certified Professional in Learning and Performance

The Certified Professional in Learning and Performance (CPLP) program of the ASTD "equips [practicing professionals] with the tools to be the best in the field and lets employers know that [they] have real world, practical expertise that can be readily applied to the current work environment. CPLP gives [them] the capability, credibility and confidence to be a high performing contributor in [their] organization[s]" (ASTD Certification Institute 2009). Candidates achieve certification by passing a two-part assessment that addresses these areas of competency: designing learning, delivering training, improving human performance, measuring and evaluating, facilitating organizational change and managing the learning function. The first part of the assessment is a computerized knowledge exam that assesses general knowledge of all six areas of competency. The second part is a skills assessment, in which candidates demonstrate their in-depth proficiency with one of the areas of competency. Candidates submit work products that address established criteria as well as a supporting statement that explains particular aspects of the work sample. Certification is valid for three years; the organization offers a recertification process.

Certified Technical Trainer

The Certified Technical Trainer (CTT) program recognizes "that an instructor has attained a standard of excellence in the training industry" (CompTIA n.d.: 3). Specifically, it certifies a competency as both a classroom and virtual classroom instructor. Like the CPLP, receiving the CTT involves a knowledge exam (test) and a skill demonstration. Candidate materials for the certification do not mention an expiration to the certification, or a recertification requirement. CompTIA is a non-profit organization that advocates for the Information Technology (IT) industry. In addition to certification, CompTIA conducts industry research and offers industry-related education.

Certified T&D Professional

The Certified T&D Professional (CTDP) offered by the CSTD "demonstrates [that the candidate has] a thorough understanding of the common body of knowledge of our profession" (CSTD 2009). Certification can be achieved through examination-based or portfolio assessments. Both approaches assess five areas of competency: analysis, design, facilitation, transfer of training and evaluation. Applicants who choose the examination take a two-part exam much like the CPLP and CTT: a knowledge exam, a computerized multiple-choice test that assesses general knowledge of all five competency areas, and a skills demonstration, in which candidates demonstrate their in-depth proficiency with one of the areas of competency. Applicants who choose the portfolio assessment submit a summary of their qualifications and provide work products (along with verification of authenticity) to demonstrate their competencies. Certified professionals must renew their certification every three years. Only applicants with three years or more of work experience are eligible for the examination-based assessment; applicants must have a minimum of 10 years of work experience to apply for a portfolio assessment.

Certified OD Professional

The Certified OD Professional (CODP) program will be launched in December 2013 by the Canadian Organizational Development Institute (CODI). The certification will have two streams of entry. Less experienced professionals require a degree in a related field and must pass a knowledge exam. More experienced professionals must have a degree in a related field and must submit a portfolio for assessment (CODI 2010).

Certified Training Practitioner

The Certified Training Practitioner (CTP) program, a second certification offered by the CSTD, is intended primarily for full- and part-time instructors (as opposed to T&D professionals who, under the CSTD definition, also design, manage, evaluate, coach, or administer training). The certification process is nearly identical to that of the CTDP, with a few differences. The knowledge exam and skills demonstration only address the facilitation competency (the CTDP process assesses the four other competencies).

Member (various levels), CIPD

For several decades, the UK-based CIPD has offered credentials to HR professionals (both HRD and HRM). The credential is a membership in the organization; the level of qualification is indicated by the level of membership. The most current membership scheme, introduced after 2010, guides professionals through various levels of membership. Achieving each level requires completion of designated workshops as well as demonstrating competence through an assignment or exam. That achieving different levels of membership is based partly on completing an educational program, it demonstrates the characteristics of a certificate. That this process also requires that professionals demonstrate competence commensurate with the level, it demonstrates the characteristics of certification. The current membership scheme is also consistent with the Qualifications and Credit Framework (QCF) in England and the European Qualifications Framework (EQF) in other EU countries, which provides a framework for ensuring the *portability* of the credentials (that is, the ability to transfer the credential from the UK to another country that follows the same scheme).

The levels of membership include:

- Associate membership (HRD-related Level 3, foundation qualifications), designed for those aspiring, or embarking on a career in T&D, working in the field in a support role, or who have training responsibilities outside of an HR group. Professionals must complete certain courses of study as well as assignments demonstrating their competence to earn Level 3 membership.
- Associate membership (HRD-related Level 5, intermediate qualifications), designed for those who want to further develop their knowledge and skills in training and similar specializations. Like a Level 3 membership, professionals working towards Level 5 membership must complete certain courses of study as well as assignments demonstrating their competence to earn Level 5 membership. These activities provide professionals with a broader perspective of organizational issues and build analytical and problem solving capabilities.
- Chartered membership (HRD-related Level 7, advanced qualifications) designed for HRD professionals who plan to work as managers and consultants in generalist or specialist roles. Professionals working towards Level 7 membership must complete certain courses of study and pass examinations and assignments demonstrating their competence to earn this level of membership.

Member (various levels), Dutch Association of Personnel Management and Organizational Development (NVP)

Like the CIPD, the credentials offered by the Dutch Association for Personnel Management and Organizational Development (NVP) are levels of membership in the organization. Credentials share characteristics of certificates and certification, because the NVP offers members two routes to full membership:

- An educational route (like a certificate), involving successful completion of a postgraduate qualification in Personnel Policy and HR or a comparable qualification from an institution of higher education.
- A competency-based route (like certification), involving a residency (completion of at least three or more years of work experience in personnel, management, or OD) and demonstration of competence through a review of a work portfolio.

NVP also offers junior Membership of NVP to professionals who meet the requirements for full membership, but are below the age of 28.

All members are expected to adhere to the "Code of Professional and Behavioral Standards" of the organization, running to 24 pages in length which all members are expected to observe and use to govern their professional practice (NVP n.d.).

Member (various levels), ITOL

Like the CIPD, the UK-based ITOL is a professional organization for specialists in training, development and occupational learning, and it offers a membership-based credential for professionals in the field. Based on its *Development Framework for Learning and Development (L&D) Professionals*, the ITOL membership scheme provides various career routes for training professionals. Achieving each level requires completion of designated workshops; most also require demonstrating competence through an assignment or exam. Like the credentialing program offered by the CIPD, the program offered by ITOL displays characteristics of both a certificate (as a result of requiring completion of an educational program) and certification (by requiring, at most levels, demonstration of competence).

The four grades of membership include:

- Associate Member (introductory grade), which only requires completion of two certificate programs. Professionals can complete the programs through self-study that includes open learning, workplace activities, summative checks and self-assessment.
- Member, which involves completion of both certificates of study as well as the demonstration of competence on assignments.
- Licentiate Fellow, which is an advanced qualification. Achieving it involves completion of advanced programs of study in consultancy, design and development, facilitation, organizational learning, as well as the demonstration of competence through project diaries, work-based assignments, assignment presentations and knowledge tests, and students must also complete a reflective learning journal.
- Fellow, which is the highest level qualification, and corresponds to postgraduate diploma or Master's level study. Achieving this level of qualification involves completion of university-level courses accredited by ITOL and the successful completion of academic requirements for the courses.

Coaching certifications

Several certifications focus solely on competency as a coach. A representative sampling of these include: The European Mentoring and Coaching Council (EMCC), which offers a certification program that it calls *accreditation.* The program offers "a rigorous process that represents a valuable investment for mentors and coaches and label of quality excellence for their clients and sponsors" (EMCC n.d.) It offers accreditation (certification) to individual coaches for a period of 5 years, after which individuals must renew the accreditation. Accreditation recognizes competence; professionals become eligible for accreditation after meeting experience requirements. Professionals develop competence by studying with a provider that has been validated through a *quality award*, which provides training that "meet[s] the research-based competence standards presented in the *EMCC Competency Framework*" (EMCC n.d.). A quality award is valid for two years and can be renewed. Accredited individuals can be recognized at one of four levels of development: Foundation, Practitioner, Senior Practitioner and Master Practitioner. The EMCC translates its credentialing materials into several languages.

The International Coach Federation (ICF), a US-based organization, also offers credentials for both individual coaches and organizations that train them. Its programs for individual professionals let them "demonstrate not only knowledge and skill, but also a commitment to high professional standards and a strong code of ethic" (ICF n.d.). Professionals can demonstrate increasing levels of competence through the three levels of certification: Associate Certified Coach, Professional Certified Coach and Master Certified Coach. People can prepare for the certification through Accredited Coach Training Programs, which teach the core competencies of the coaching competency model and Approved Coach Specific Training Hours, for which some hours may be recognized on a case-by-case basis following a review of portfolios of materials compiled during individual learning experience. Coaches maintain their certification through continuing education provided by approved providers. The ICF has conducted surveys to assess the value of its credentials and concluded: "According to the *2012 ICF Global Coaching Study*, credentialed coaches reported a higher-than-average income worldwide compared to non-credentialed-coaches, with the exception of the Middle East and Africa. According to the *2010 ICF Global Consumer Awareness Study*, clients who worked with an ICF Credentialed Coach were more likely to be satisfied with their coaching experience and recommend coaching to others" (ICF n.d.).

People who hold certification from the ICF can go through a simplified process to earn the corresponding certification from the EMCC (n.d.).

OD certifications

The Organizational Development Institute, a US-based organization, offers a series of online OD Certificate Programs. These certificates cover topics such as consulting on OD, advanced consulting, integrated talent management, executive coaching and leadership development. Certificates include several courses, completion of projects in the area of study and successful completion of one or more assessments.

Broader HR certifications

In addition to the certifications available in training and performance, HRD practitioners can also choose to certify in the broader field of HR, whose certification programs cover T&D among other topics. Certifications include the Professional in HR (PHR), Senior Professional in HR (SPHR) and Global Professional in HR (GPHR), sponsored by the US-based HRCI, the certification arm of the Society for Human Resource Management (SHRM), and the Certified HR Professional (CHRP) offered by the Canadian Human Resources Association. Although they cover HRD-related topics, such as training and OD, these certifications primarily focus on other HRM-related topics. (HRD-related issues typically account for fewer than 20 per cent of all test questions.) For example, the HRCI exams cover strategic management, workforce planning and employment, total rewards, employee and labor relations, risk management, and core knowledge, in addition to HRD (HRCI 2010). The Canadian exams cover professional practice in HR; organization effectiveness; staffing; employee and labor relations; total compensation; workplace health and safety; and HR information management (CCHRA 2009).

Certificates in HRD

Numerous certificate programs exist in HRD-related areas and are offered by several types of organizations: community colleges, continuing education units of universities, for-profit providers and professional associations. Although too numerous to catalog here, a few certificates are worth mentioning, because the professional organizations that sponsor them typically promote them as a significant credential; these same organizations do not offer formal certifications. These certificate programs include:

- The ISTD offers a Diploma in T&D. This 18-month correspondence program is intended "to meet the long felt need for skill formation in learning/training skills" (ISTD 2003a). Students take a prescribed set of courses through correspondence, submit several assignments – including theory papers and responses – take examinations and complete an internship (ISTD 2003b). Only those who already meet eligibility criteria (such as a postgraduate degree or another professional designation) can take the course. The Indian Ministry of HRD recognizes this diploma as a qualification to "superior posts" (ISTD 2003c).
- The Irish Institute of Training and Development (IITD) offers a variety of educational programs (IITD n.d.), including a Train the Trainer qualification and an MA in L&D Consultancy. These programs conform to a National Framework of Qualifications scheme established by the Irish government. The framework applies a consistent series of levels corresponding to the complexity of the content and provides formal recognition of the completion of learning. Only programs from recognized "awarding bodies" can have "the power to give . . . a qualification" (National Qualifications Authority of Ireland 2009).

Assuring the quality of certification programs

Because certification validates professional competence, the organizations that offer certification programs have measures in place to ensure that these programs meet quality standards. To ensure that the certification process meaningfully represents practice in the field, they engage experts in certification to guide the process, engage experts in developing competency models or compiling bodies of knowledge, validate those competency models or bodies of knowledge with randomly selected professionals in the field and conduct extensive validation of the resulting program. One significant type of validation is *cut scoring*, in which organizations ask two groups of evaluators to assess several applications. One group uses the criteria to assess it; the other is merely asked to indicate, overall, whether the candidate should receive certification. If the two assessments match, the program is validated. Well-documented evaluation instructions and assessment criteria ensure consistency in evaluations. Furthermore, evaluators receive extensive training and are supervised closely in their first several evaluations before they can evaluate applications independently (Zieky and Perie 2006).

In addition to these individual efforts, two cross-industry organizations offer guidance to assure the quality of certification programs. Through its Standard 1100, the American National Standards Institute (ANSI) establishes guidelines for being a certifying organization. ANSI standards state that the certification must be "based on industry knowledge, independent from training courses or course providers" (Wikipedia 2013c) and only apply for a specific period of time before renewal is required. This is one of the reasons that many North American-based certifications do not require membership in a professional organization (though most of these organizations offer discounts on the certification process and maintenance of certification to members).

The Institute for Credentialing Excellence (ICE) is a US-based organization that develops standards for, and certifies, voluntary certification programs (Wikipedia 2013b). Many of its standards focus on assuring the accuracy and validity of the certification test or assessment process (Wikipedia 2013c).

Critical issues in certification and HRD

With a common foundation of knowledge established, we can now consider the potential impact of certification on the field of HRD and, perhaps of most immediate interest to the readers of this *Handbook*, its potential effect on academic programs in HRD. To consider that, we first consider what the programs actually certify, then consider the impact these credentialing programs have on the profession of HRD and, of interest to the audience of this chapter, on academic programs in HRD.

What do certification programs actually certify?

One of the most basic concerns about certification is the competencies they actually certify and how these competencies relate to those identified for HRD. To start this consideration, let's start with Swanson and Holton's (2009: 5) definition of HRD: the "process of developing and unleashing expertise for the purpose of improving performance . . . performance of the individual, group, process, and organizational systems level."

In spirit, all of the competency models support the general definition of HRD, especially the focus on performance improvement. For example, the first of the CSTD's *Competencies for T&D Professionals* (2010) is assessing performance needs. (Terminology note: Some of the organizations named in this chapter use the term *professional development frameworks* rather than *competency model*; as used in this chapter the term *competency model* applies to both.) This competency model specifically separates performance and training needs assessment. Similarly, in its 2013 competency model, ASTD includes performance improvement as one of its core competencies.

But that is where the support ends. When defining HRD, Swanson and Holton (2009: 5) add that HRD broadly encompasses T&D and OD; its applications include "intellectual and social capital, workforce development, human resources management, organizational effectiveness, leadership and strategy, work system design, change management, process improvement, career development, and quality improvement." Most of the competency models underlying North America-based certifications do not support this more detailed definition. Nearly all of the competency models limit their focus to T&D. OD only appears in the competency models of CIPD (which has a broader focus than HRD) and ITOL; it does not appear in the competency models of ASTD, CSTD, or CompTIA.

ITOL and ASTD list organizational learning in their models, but organizational learning is not the same thing as OD. T&D are viewed somewhat differently on both sides of the Atlantic; the North American-based certifications in T&D do not emphasize the consulting and coaching competencies emphasized in the British and Irish competency models.

In North America, organizations whose primary focus is OD address that competency. In the only OD certification, the tight focus noted with the T&D competency models arises in reverse; the CODI certification only focuses on OD; it does not assess T&D.

The ISPI does not have a competency model *per se*; it lists "standards" (ISPI 2013). The list of standards is unclear about the focus of the attention: individual, organizational, or both. Given other material published by ISPI (such as Pershing 2006), one might assume the organization means both.

Furthermore, except for the ISPI certification, most of the certifications do not assess all of the competencies listed in their models. For example, the ASTD competency model lists a set of competencies called "foundational competencies." These are competencies that every professional is expected to have, are not unique to HRD and, therefore, assumed rather than assessed (Bernthal *et al.* 2004). Furthermore, the skill demonstration section of the ASTD certification exam only addresses some of the competencies, such as analyzing needs, designing programs, facilitating training sessions and evaluating programs; they do not address competencies like integrated talent management and knowledge management. Similarly, CSTD only provides opportunities to demonstrate skills in three of its five competency areas: assessing performance needs, designing programs and facilitating (instructing) programs. The program does not let candidates submit skill demonstrations for transferring or evaluating training. Note, however, that questions on the knowledge exams of both the ASTD and CSTD certifications do cover all of the competency areas.

In fact, a close examination of the different certification schemes suggests that, despite their differences, they share remarkable similarities and fall into these categories:

- Certifications for people who have a broad focus on T&D, including the CPLP (offered by ASTD), CPT (offered by ISPI) and CTDP (offered by CSTD), as well as the CLDP and DLDP programs offered by CIPD and the CTD program offered by ITOL (the latter three lead to particular grades of membership).
- Certifications of instructors, who primarily or exclusively teach, including the CTP (offered by CSTD) and CTT (offered by CompTIA).

The CODI certification is the only one that addresses OD; it is not yet fully launched as of the writing of this chapter and it only focuses on one national context.

Competency models are not necessarily static, however. Two of the certifying organizations have revised their competency models in the past five years. The CSTD competency model was revised and repackaged in a simpler, easier-to-read package (CSTD 2010), but the core model did not substantially change. The only changes were additions to reflect the increased role of technology-based instruction and to add competencies related to project management, which members of CSTD said were missing (CSTD 2010). The revision to the ASTD competency model was more drastic. The original model was *descriptive*; that is, it described the competencies needed by practicing professionals in the field. It included the foundational competencies mentioned earlier, T&D competencies required by anyone working in the field and competencies specific to the role the individual plays in T&D groups, such as a learning strategist or professional specialist (Bernthal *et al.* 2004). The new competency model is *prescriptive*; that is, the competencies reflect a view of the profession that the organization wishes to promote. It includes competencies, such as knowledge management, evaluating learning impact and integrated talent management, to which trainers aspire but that research has not confirmed are actually performed by T&D professionals (Carliner *et al.* 2013; Carliner 2006).

All these certifications only certify "process" skills; none assesses competence in the industry or content area in which the certified professional works. For example, a management trainer would only be certified for training knowledge, not management knowledge. As a practical matter, the organizations that offer HRD-related certifications only have expertise in HRD-related issues; they do not have expertise in every industry or subject area. The issue is possibly significant because research suggests that clients of training services value subject matter and industry expertise (Carliner and Bernard 2011a, 2011b) as much as their platform (or facilitation) skills. However, recognized third-party credentials exist in many industries and trainers that seek validation of their technical expertise might be better served by seeking out these, than for an HRD-related group to offer certification in particular subject matter. For example, someone who trains in the accounting and finance industry might receive more credibility from having their accounting credentials than from a credential from ASTD that certifies the person as a trainer with expertise in accounting.

Only certifications in coaching recognize differing levels of proficiency among professionals. All of the training certifications certify at one level of competence. Although the CSTD offers two certifications, the two overlap one another and represent different jobs rather than different levels of competence within the same job. In contrast, coaching certifications recognize the difference among less experienced and experienced coaches, as well as master coaches.

In other words, HRD professionals seeking validation of all the competencies needed to succeed on the job would need several certifications: one of the training certifications, an OD certification, a coaching certification and a certification in the industry or subject matter in which the professional specializes. Furthermore, although one would need to maintain all of the certifications, only coaching offers a means of receiving formal recognition for greater experience and proficiency.

How might certification affect the profession of HRD?

One of the stated goals of all of the certification programs is to strengthen the profession and most organizations promote their certification programs as a means of individuals demonstrating their competence and commitment to the profession. For example, ASTD notes that its CPLP "provides a way for workplace learning and performance professionals to prove their value to employers and to be confident about their knowledge of the field" (ASTD 2012). Similarly, the CSTD (2013a) invites professionals to "show that you have the knowledge and practical experience to make a difference in your work environment and meet the demands of the future."

Many organizations add that their certifications offer employers a means of distinguishing qualified professionals from others. For example, the ISPI (2013) notes that "Until the development of the CPT designation, anyone could claim that they are professionals in performance improvement and training."

How likely are the current certifications to fulfill these promises? Some of the key measures of the success of a certification program include the following:

- The number of people who have received the credential or are in the process of earning it, expressed both as a number and as a percentage of the total membership of the organization that sponsors the program.
- The number of employers who list the credential as a preferred qualification for jobs, both in actual numbers and as a percentage of total job ads in a given database at a given point in time (for example, X% of all job listings in the ISPI job bank).
- The number of academic programs that align their curricula with the competency model used in a certification process.

As of now, the results are inconclusive at best. Consider the number of people holding the credential. CIPD, which has one of the oldest credentials, has the largest number of credentialed professionals. Although fewer people hold its designation than ASTD or ISPI, as a percentage of membership, CSTD has the second largest percentage of members with its credentials; about 30 per cent of its members hold one of its two designations (Feher-Watters 2013). Other organizations have significantly lower percentages of their memberships with their credentials and most do not publicly report this information.

As a job requirement, some of the incentives offered to employers for listing their jobs in job banks offered by organizations might skew the numbers. For example, CSTD offers free listing to employers who include its credential as a preferred qualification in a job listing (CSTD 2013a).

But a recent analysis of job descriptions for learning consultants suggested that few employers seek the credential without that incentive; fewer than 5 per cent of the job descriptions requested a credential in T&D (Carliner *et al.* 2013).

In terms of the number of academic programs that align with competency models for certification, the results differ by country. Because of the longevity of the CIPD program as well as work and higher education policies that encourage alignment, many universities in the UK that teach HRD, align their curricula with the CIPD professional standards. The North American-based CSTD recognizes programs in 27 colleges and universities that align with its competency model. Only four are Bachelor's or Master's degree programs, however; the rest are either academic certificates or programs offered through continuing education units (CSTD 2013b). Although they have encouraged programs to align their curricula with their competency models, none of the US-based programs has a means of recognizing this alignment.

At this time, then, the goal of strengthening the profession is not fulfilled. That programs established in the 1990s or before seem to have made more progress than those established more recently suggests that time plays a significant role in establishing a credential.

Time alone is not sufficient in establishing a credential. Potential candidates need to perceive that the credential has value to them before they initiate the certification process. Several factors affect this perception. One is whether potential candidates believe that the certification has sufficient rigor. That some applicants fail strengthens perception of this issue. As participants in a focus group that informed one certification process commented, potential applicants do not want to believe that "just anyone" can receive the credential. Another factor affecting the perception of a credential is whether other professionals have it. That's why many organizations show preference for credentialed professionals for their boards and other visible positions. A third factor affecting perceptions of a credential is the likelihood that employers will value it. That's why many promotional pages for certification, such as those of ASTD and CSTD, name the large employers that credentialed professionals work for and the ones that adopted the competency models (ASTD 2012; CSTD 2013c).

But choices within the certifying organizations could affect the extent to which they succeed in strengthening these perceptions. For example, although some failure by applicants does build the perception of rigor in a certification program in theory, in practice, failure creates problems for people who administer certification problems. Extensive failure could build word-of-mouth that the certification is impossible to achieve, which would prevent on-the-fence prospects from applying. So organizations straddle a fine line between rigor and too much rigor, and this might prevent them from building the ranks of the credentialed. Similarly, in situations where large employers want to certify several candidates, including some marginal ones, the temptation exists to adjust standards to please the employer.

The presence of several certifications serving the training market could confuse potential applicants and, rather than building the profession, could prevent any of the certifications from gaining traction. In the UK, for example, duplicate routes to credentialing exist through the CIPD and ITOL professional qualifications schemes. In the United States, ASTD, CompTIA and ISPI offer similar certifications. The ASTD and ISPI certifications are intended for the same professionals who design, develop and sometimes teach programs. Additional confusion comes from partnerships and ownerships of programs. For example, when ISPI launched its CPT program, ASTD participated in the effort before announcing its own credentialing effort. Similarly, although the CompTIA certification distinguishes itself as the only credential available to HRD professionals in the US who primarily teach, the program itself changed ownership several times in its earlier years which affected buy-in by the training community. Initially launched by Chauncey and Associates, the program was sold to Prometric, who later sold it to CompTIA. In

Canada, CSTD offers credentials for designer/developers and instructors, but because of close economic ties with the US, some professionals might seek US credentials, especially those who regularly work across the border.

HRD professionals can look to their counterparts in HRM for a possible solution to this confusion because they have organizations that coordinate certifications across political boundaries. For example, the Canadian Council of HR Associations oversees the development of a Canadian credential in HR and helps provincial HR associations customize the credential to local conditions. The North American HRM Association offers a venue for credentialing organizations in the US, Mexico and Canada to coordinate certifications and the World Federation of People Management Associations provides similar coordination on a global scale.

But HRM organizations represent another source of competition for HRD credentials because all of the HR-related certifications also cover training. The CIPD, for example, includes "developing people," as a mandatory component for its Level 7 program. Similarly, training comprises 16 to 17 per cent of the questions on the exams of the US-based SHRM and Canadian Council of HR Associations (CCHRA) certifications.

HR certification in North America raises additional concerns for HRD professionals. One is that, although some HRD professionals see the field as equal to HRM, the HR certifications clearly indicate that HRD is just a small part of its mandate. Within the SHRM and CCHRA schemes, training represents just a small part of the competency base that professionals must master to receive HR certification. Most HRD professionals work in a limited way, at best, with several of these competency areas, like compensation and benefits.

More fundamentally, many HRD professionals do not work in an HR context. For example, most technical trainers work in product development, information technology and manufacturing groups and play no role in HR. Similarly, other developers of people and organizations such as executive and business coaches do not identify themselves as HRD professionals. Instead, they belong to other professional bodies such as the US-based ICF and the UK-based EMCC.

Although the drive for some of the certifications may have been intended to promote unity among the separate domains of HRD, in reality certification has mainly highlighted divisions within the domain. As suggested already, certification highlights the rivalries among organizations offering certification and also the long-standing tensions between HRD and HRM. But it also highlights tensions among practicing professionals. One type of tension is among those working on different types of programs – such as supervisory training, computer skills training, sales training, manufacturing training and leadership development, and those working in different industries – such as defense and pharmaceutical industries which have their own professional associations. That the certifications focus solely on "T&D" or "OD" skills and do not assess domain or industry expertise helps certifications circumvent these tensions.

Credentialing within the realm of coaching poses its own set of challenges. On the one hand, Grant and Cavanagh (2004: 3) suggest that the coaching industry has reached a point at which it needs to "move from being a service industry to a genuine coaching profession" with its own unique body of underpinning knowledge. On the other hand, it might not be a distinct, separate profession and, therefore, not in need of its own credentials. Hamlin *et al.* (2009) have demonstrated from their definitional examination of the different conceptualizations and definitions of *coaching, OD and HRD*, the respective purposes and processes of these fields are virtually identical. Furthermore, regardless of whether developers self-identify as professional coaches, or as OD or HRD professionals, in practice they all engage to a greater or lesser extent in coaching, OD and HRD activities that are designed to develop and improve the performance of individuals, teams and organizations. Consequently, it is conceivable that all three domains of professional practice could be served by a single credential.

Perhaps more challenging to circumvent, however, are distinctions among those employed as "captive trainers" and those working in the independent sector – firms, contractors, consultants who provide training and related services to corporations. "Captive employees" primarily seek certification for one of two reasons: to fulfill a requirement for their employer or more likely, as a transferable credential that can help these employees should they need to search for a new job. In contrast, "independent" workers seek certification as a sales tool. As a result, captive employees might be more interested in a credential based on a descriptive competency model so they can earn certification based on their current work; independent workers might be more interested in a prescriptive credential that could show the full range of their skills and position them for positions that require skills they do not currently use. Can a single certification meet both of these needs?

How might certification affect academic programs?

Perhaps the most challenging divide faced by certification is in the academic realm. It exposes the divide between academe and industry, but more fundamentally raises questions about the need for academic programs in HRD.

On the surface, organizations that offer certification seek ties with colleges and universities so that the colleges and universities align their programs with the competency models. Many organizations with certification programs have outreach efforts to inform colleges and universities about the competency models, so the schools can include the competencies in their curricula. Some efforts are laissez-faire, like those of ASTD, whose primary outreach efforts have consisted of maintaining ongoing communications with the higher education community and hosting information tables at events aimed at the academic community, like the AHRD Research Conference in the Americas. Some of the efforts are loosely structured, like the effort by CSTD, which provides colleges and universities with an opportunity to formally demonstrate that their programs cover the competencies in their curricula and publish a list of "recognized" programs. Some of these efforts are highly structured. The CIPD and ITOL work closely with universities to offer postgraduate degree programs that address part or all of the competency models adopted by these bodies and link completion of these academic programs to membership in the two institutes.

In North America, especially the US, the efforts have not yet taken hold. Indeed, the academic literature of HRD generally seems unaware of the certifications available, exposing a limited awareness of academe for some major developments in practice. Although the first professional certifications for HRD-related professions were introduced in the 1990s and ASTD, the largest professional organization serving the field, introduced its certification in 2006, in 2009 – three years after ASTD introduced its certification – Kahnweiler (2009: 226) wrote: "If there were a process that certified HRD practitioners, this could provide some assurance to those who employ or engage HRD professionals as consultants that individuals possess at least rudimentary knowledge and skills to practice HRD effectively." The issue does not seem to have made its way into key textbooks either. For example, in the second edition of their landmark *Foundations of Human Resource Development*, Swanson and Holton (2009: 457) suggest that, "The HRD profession is challenged to establish standards for providers and consumers in this realm in order to sort out the HRD charlatans. Certification is one option." But ASTD had published its first competency model five years earlier (Bernthal *et al.* 2004) and CSTD had published its first set of standards for the field over 30 years before Swanson and Holton wrote their book (CSTD 2010). Limited awareness of certification persists as of the publication of this *Handbook*. For example, at the 2013 AHRD Conference, McLean (2013) called for certification or licensing. Although many academics are not aware of certification, however, several have played roles in developing and administering these programs. For example, William Rothwell, a professor at Penn State University, has helped shape the competency model for the ASTD certification program, and past AHRD president Ron Jacobs and HRDQ editorial board member Tonette Rocco have served on the board of the ASTD Certification Institute. Saul Carliner, one of the authors of this chapter, chaired CSTD's certification steering committee and served as a reviewer for the competency model CSTD published in 2010. But these people primarily work in volunteer or consulting roles; the majority of the work on competency models and certification has been conducted by practicing professionals. Each of the organizations has a certification director who works part- or full-time overseeing the development and administration of the credential.

This competency-based approach underlying certification is also the same approach underlying a fundamental re-think of higher education. Although many faculty view the role of higher education as developing critical-thinking citizens, an emerging view among other stakeholders – including the administrators, donors, corporations and the public – is that higher education also serves a role of preparing people for the workforce (Cappelli 2012), especially in professional disciplines, like business, engineering, medicine, law and HRD (Carnevale 2013).

In competency-based education, students "can earn credit by successfully completing assessments that prove their mastery in predetermined competencies or tasks – maybe writing in a business setting or using a spreadsheet to perform calculations" (Fain 2013: n.p.). Competency-based education is in trial phases right now; in some trials of competency-based education, students do not need to take formal courses. Instead, they can develop their own plans of study to master a competency. They can read, take formal courses through the institution, take free Massive Open Online Courses (MOOCs), demonstrate that they can already master some or all of the competency, or any combination of these and similar activities. Students are expected to consult with an instructor to develop these programs of study (Fain 2013). If the trials are successful, adoption is expected to follow. As of the writing of this chapter, university systems in the US states of Arizona and Wisconsin have indicated that they plan to adopt competency-based education (Young 2012) and the US-based Western Governor's University already uses it (Kolowich 2012; Young 2012). This competency-based approach is essentially the same one used by certification.

Given the ever-increasing costs of degrees and that many prospective students seek degrees as a means of earning credentials to work in the field, for some, certification could offer a low-cost alternative to a degree. With preparation classes and resources, certification might cost an applicant between US$ 500 and $2,000 (depending on the resources chosen). Additional preparation, such as the purchase of recommended books, might cost another $200 to $500, for a total of $700 to $2,500. In contrast, one year tuition at a public university (excluding fees, room and board, as well as lost income) hovers between $5,000 and $10,000 (Desigrad 2013). (This is the typical length of many Master's degree programs, though some are two years.)

As a result, the certification programs offer a low-cost alternative to education for some price-conscious applicants. At this time, however, all of the certification programs have an experience requirement, so certification only serves as a viable alternative for those who are already working in the field or can receive a position without any credentials.

At this time, no evidence currently suggests the viability of this scenario. But that's not for lack of efforts to promote it, such as Anya Kamenetz's best-selling book, *DIY U: Cyberpunks, Edupreneurs, and the Coming Transformation of Higher Education* (2010) and entrepreneur Peter Thiel's payments to promising entrepreneurs to drop out of school and begin working to gain credibility in their field (Mac 2013).

Furthermore, universities offer certain services that the do-it-yourself approach lacks. It offers formal feedback and advising, and many programs offer internships that help students gain the experience that is an essential requirement for all certifications. One possible impact of certification and an alternate route to receiving credentials that prepare people for the job market might be that higher education programs sharpen the quality of these services and emphasize them more. Doing so also models the *development* inherent in HRD and uses many of the competencies of coaching.

Other possibilities might emerge if institutions of higher education adopt competency-based education. One is that programs might use the competencies in each of the different areas – T&D, coaching and OD – to forge HRD programs that are more broadly based. Although some programs that serve HRD are called HRD, many others are primarily adult education and educational technology programs. To develop those curricula, some institutions might use the competency models used for the related certifications.

In addition, if education is competency-based, then the temptation might exist to adopt the evaluation processes used by organizations offering certifications as a means of awarding credit to students who want to demonstrate a competency. Universities need to develop and validate these assessments; organizations with certification programs have made large investments devising and developing these assessments and want to see a return on these investments. So even for those students who do complete a degree, certification exams could still play a role.

Conclusion

Although most of this chapter has been focused on the divisions raised or potentially raised by certification, the process of developing and administering certification programs ultimately focuses on what unites the profession, not what divides it. Although readers need to recognize the divisions among the different strands of practice within HRD, what certification ultimately offers is a chance to work past these differences and work together to promote the field of practice, and secure its recognition as a profession.

However, the latter notion will be problematic so long as those developers who label themselves as "OD" or "coaching" professionals choose not to identify or affiliate with the HRD domain. Yet, as Hamlin *et al.* (2009) assert, drawing upon Chalofsky (2004), all three fields of practice rest on three constructs: *people, learning and organizations*, and on a common body of knowledge. Thus, none can claim to have its own unique body of empirically tested knowledge, which is the hallmark of a "true" profession. Thus, this poses a serious challenge for "HRD," "OD" and "coaching," each of which aspires to become recognized as a distinct profession.

In light of the extensive overlap in the purposes and processes as identified by Hamlin *et al.* (2008; 2009), and drawing on their thinking, we also suggest that the three fields of practice should consider converging into a "single unified" domain of practice, with the aim of becoming a new inclusive profession embracing all aspects of people and organization development (POD). But this somewhat provocative proposition would require those academics who educate and train HRD, OD and coaching professionals to consider converging the three fields of study into a "single unified" disciplinary base, albeit containing various specialist bodies of related knowledge.

Yet to date, certification and the drive towards professional recognition have been characterized by limited academic involvement and even less academic research. In many instances it has not been for a lack of effort by those organizations offering certification programs to reach out to the academic community. At the least, the academic community needs to make a more concerted and visible effort to make its members aware of the certification programs and what they entail. At the most, the academic community needs to take a more active role in shaping and developing the existing certification programs, and any practitioner initiatives aimed at creating a "true" HRD (or POD) profession – with an eye towards greater collaboration among them – and conducting research that would inform such work.

References

AECT (2012) *AECT Standards 2012 version.* Retrieved at 21 April 2013 from http://ocw.metu.edu.tr/pluginfile.php/3298/course/section/1171/AECT_Standards_adopted7_16_2.pdf.

ASTD (2012) *Certification.* Retrieved at 25 April 2013 from http://www.astd.org/Certification.

ASTD Certification Institute (2009) *Looking to be the best? CPLP is your ticket to success!* Retrieved at http://www.astd.org/content/ASTDcertification.

Bernthal, P.R., Colteryahn, K., Davis, P., Naughton, J., Rothwell, W. and Wellins, R. (2004) *The 2004 ASTD Competency Study: Mapping the Future.* Alexandria, VA: ASTD.

Cappelli, P. (2000) A market-driven approach to retaining talent. *Harvard Business Review* 78(1): 103–11.

— (2012) *Why Good People Can't Get Good Jobs: The Skills Gap and What Companies Can Do About It.* Philadelphia, PA: Wharton Digital Press.

Carliner, S. (2006) *The limitations of research in performance improvement: Evidence, implications, and suggestions.* Paper presented at the 2006 European HRD Conference held at Tilburg University, Netherlands.

— (2012) Certification and the branding of HRD. *Human Resource Development Quarterly* 23(3): 411–19.

Carliner, S. and Bernard, C. (2011a) *An integrative review of literature on the perceptions of HRD.* Paper presented at the 2011 Academy of HRD Research Conference in the Americas held in Schaumburg, IL.

— (2011b) *A qualitative study of the perceptions of workplace learning professionals.* Paper presented at the Canadian Association for the Study of Adult Education – Adult Education Research Council joint conference held in Toronto, ON.

Carliner, S., Castonguay, C., Ribeiro, O., Sabri, H., Saylor, C., Sheepy, E. and Valle, A. (2013) *What is the job of the performance consultant? An analysis of job descriptions.* Paper presented at the 2013 Academy of HRD Research Conference in the Americas held in Arlington, VA.

Carnevale, A. (2013) *Human capital and American competitiveness.* Keynote presentation at the 2013 Academy of HRD Research Conference in the Americas held in Arlington, VA.

Carter, S.D. (2005) The growth of supply and demand of occupational-based training and certification in the United States, 1990–2003. *Human Resource Development Quarterly* 16(1): 33–54.

CCHRA (2009) *National recertification log.* Retrieved at 1 June, 2014 from http://c.ymcdn.com/sites/www.chrp.ca/resource/resmgr/docs/4.1_-_professional_standards.pdf.

Chalofsky, N. (2004) *Human and organization studies: The discipline of HRD.* Paper presented at the 2004 Academy of HRD Research Conference in the Americas held in Austin, TX.

Chalofsky, N., Ruona, W., Dooley, L., Hatcher, T., Jacobs, R., Kuchinke, K.P., Swanson, R. and Marsick, V. (2008) *Standards for HRD Graduate Program Excellence.* Bowling Green, OH: AHRD.

CODI (2010) *Certification.* Retrieved at 21 April 2013 from http://www.odcanada.org/resources/certification.

CompTIA (n.d.) *CompTIA CTT+ Candidate Handbook of Information Classroom Trainer Certification.* Oakbrook Terrace, IL: CompTIA.

CSTD (2010) *Competencies for Training and Development Professionals.* Toronto, ON: CSTD.

— (2013a) *Certification.* Retrieved at 25 April 2013 from http://www.cstd.ca/?page=Certification.

— (2013b) *Recognized program registry.* Retrieved at 25 April 2013 from https://cstd.site-ym.com/?page=RecognizedPrograms&hhSearchTerms=recognized+and+programs.

— (2013c) *Online store: Career centre.* Retrieved at 25 April 2013 from https://cstd.site-ym.com/store/view_product.asp?id=764682.

— (2014) *Certification.* Retrieved at http: //www.cstd.ca/ProfessionalDevelopment/Certification/tabid/231/Default.aspx.

Desigrad (2013) *Can I afford the graduate school tuition?* Retrieved at 11 May 2013 from http://www.desigrad.com/tuition.php.

EMCC (n.d.) *Setting the standards for mentoring and coaching.* Retrieved at 12 May 2012 from http://www.emccouncil.org/eu/en/accreditation.

Fain, P. (2013) *Credit without teaching.* Retrieved at 23 April 2013 from http://www.insidehighered.com/news/2013/04/22/competency-based-educations-newest-form-creates-promise-and-questions.

Feher-Watters, I. (2013, May 2) *Personal conversation regarding status of the CSTD certification program.*

Fisher, C. (2011) *The Certified Professional Technical Communicator.* Presentation to the 2011 Council of Programs in Scientific and Technical Communication Conference held in Harrisonburg, VA.

Grant, A.M. and Cavanagh, M.J. (2004) Toward a profession of coaching: Sixty-five years of progress and challenge for the future. *International Journal of Evidence-based Coaching and Mentoring* 2(1): 1–16.

Hale, J. (2000) *Performance-Based Certification: How to Design a Valid, Defensible, and Cost Effective Program.* San Francisco: Jossey-Bass.

— (2012) *Performance-Based Certification: How to Design a Valid, Defensible, Cost Effective Program* (2nd edition). San Francisco: Jossey-Bass.

Hall, D.T. (1996) Protean careers of the 21st century. *Academy of Management Executive* 10(4): 8–16.

Hamlin, R.G., Ellinger, A.D. and Beattie, R.S. (2008) The emergent "coaching industry": A wake-up call for HRD professionals. *Human Resource Development International* 11(3): 287–305.

— (2009) Toward a process of coaching? A definitional examination of "Coaching", "Organization Development", and "Human Resource Development". *International Journal of Evidence Based Coaching and Mentoring* 7(1): 13–38.

HRCI (2010) *PHR /SPHR Body of Knowledge, Appendix A – PHR/SPHR Test Specifications.* Retrieved at 2 June 2014 http://www.hrci.org/docs/default-source/media-resources/phr-sphr-body-of-knowledge-.pdf?sfvrsn=0.

ICE (2013) *What is credentialing?* Retrieved at 21 April 2013 from http://www.credentialingexcellence.org/p/cm/ld/fid=32.

ICF (n.d.) *Individual credentialing.* Retrieved at 12 May 2012 from http://www.coachfederation.org/credential/?navItemNumber=502.

IITD (n.d.) *Education and CPD.* Retrieved at 21 April 2013 from http://www.iitd.ie/EducationCPD.aspx.

ISPI (2009) *CPT FAQs.* Retrieved at 2 June 2014 http://www.ispi.org/content.aspx?id=426.

— (2013) *CPT standards and ethics.* Retrieved at 21 April 2013 from http://www.ispi.org/content.aspx?id=418.

ISTD (2003a) *ISTD Diploma: An introduction.* Retrieved at 2 June 2014 http://www.istddiploma.org/diploma.asp.

— (2003b) *ISTD Diploma: Course structure.* Retrieved at 2 June 2014 http://www.istddiploma.org/content.asp.

— (2003c) *ISTD Diploma: Employers and professional recognition.* Retrieved at 2 June 2014 http://www.istddiploma.org/govt.asp.

ITOL (2013) *ITOL Development framework for L&D professionals.* Retrieved at 17 May 2013 from http://itol.org/uploads/images/PDF/framework%20new.pdf.

Kahnweiler, W.M. (2009) HRD as a profession: Current status and future directions. *Human Resource Development Quarterly* 20(2): 219–29.

Kamenetz, A. (2010) *DIY U: Cyberpunks, Edupreneurs, and the Coming Transformation of Higher Education.* White River Junction, VT: Chelsea Green.

Kolowich, S. (2012) *Competency loves company.* Retrieved at 14 December 2013 from http://www.insidehighered.com/news/2012/07/11/northern-arizona-u-partners-pearson-competency-based-degree-programs.

Mac, R. (2013) *Billionaire Facebook investor Peter Thiel backs more students to skip schools, start companies.* Retrieved at 12 May 2013 from http://www.forbes.com/sites/ryanmac/2013/05/09/billionaire-peter-thiel-backs-more-high-schoolers-to-skip-school-start-companies.

McLean, G. (2013) *Remarks at Town Hall Meeting.* Organized at the 2013 Academy of HRD Research Conference in the Americas held in Arlington, VA.

National Qualifications Authority of Ireland (2009) *National framework of qualifications.* Retrieved at 21 April 2013 from http://www.nfq.ie/nfq/en/FanDiagram/nqai_nfq_08.html.

NVP (n.d.) *NVP membership.* Retrieved at 18 May 2013 from http://www.nvp-plaza.nl.

Pershing, J. (ed.) (2006) *Handbook of Human Performance Technology* (3rd edition). San Francisco: Pfeiffer.

PMI (2013) *What is a Registered Education Provider (R.E.P.)?* Retrieved at 21 April 2013 from http://www.pmi.org/Professional-Development/REP-What-is-a-Registered-Education-Provider.aspx.

PRSA (2012) *Accreditation.* Retrieved at 25 June 2013 from http://www.prsa.org/Learning/Accreditation.

Rothwell, W.J., Arneson, J. and Naughton, J. (2013) *ASTD Competency Study: The Training & Development Profession Redefined.* Alexandria, VA: ASTD.

Swanson, R.A. and Holton, E.F. (2009) *Foundations of Human Resource Development* (2nd edition). San Francisco: Berrett-Koehler.

Trice, H.M. and Beyer, J.M. (1993) *The Cultures of Work Organizations.* Upper Saddle River, NJ: Prentice-Hall.

Wikipedia (2013a) *Body of knowledge.* Retrieved at 20 April 2013 from http://en.wikipedia.org/wiki/Body_of_Knowledge.

— (2013b) *Institute for Credentialing Excellence.* Retrieved at 20 April 2013 from http://en.wikipedia.org/wiki/Institute_for_Credentialing_Excellence.

— (2013c) *Professional certification.* Retrieved at 20 April 2013 from http://en.wikipedia.org/wiki/Professional_certification.

Young, E. (2012) *Another state to assess skills.* Retrieved at 19 December 2012 from http://www.insidehighered.com/news/2012/07/09/wisconsin-seeks-competency-based-degree-program-without-help-western-governors.

Zieky, M. and Perie, M. (2006) *A primer on setting cut scores on tests of educational achievement.* Retrieved at 21 April 2013 from http://www.ets.org/Media/Research/pdf/Cut_Scores_Primer.pdf.

32

UNIVERSITY PROGRAMMES IN HRD

Paul B. Roberts, John Walton and Doo Hun Lim

As we examine university programmes in HRD, an understanding of the history and foundation upon which these programmes were built not only provides great insight into where they come from, but also lends guidance into where they are headed. In the United States HRD programmes have taken on many different appearances largely stemming from the focus or points of origin. According to Chalofsky and Larson-Daugherty (1996: 992), "Since there has been no generally accepted body of knowledge or set of accreditation criteria, academic programmes have usually been started by an entrepreneurial faculty member who had some expertise in adult learning and/or experience doing training and recognized the market value of an HRD-related program to the university".

HRD has a long history, but it is generally embedded in other fields under a variety of other names (Knowles 1970). A brief overview of the history of HRD will be presented here; however, there are several sources which include a more detailed history of HRD (Craig 1996; Nadler 1984; Swanson 2009; Werner and DeSimone 2011). In the United States and the United Kingdom, HRD is generally accepted to have developed out of the merchant and craft guilds and then through to the apprenticeship programmes of the Middle Ages. Formal technical and engineering training programmes as well as manual training programmes were introduced in the eighteenth century. Technical and corporate training continued to evolve and the rapid advancements in technology through the twentieth century, bolstered by war efforts, resulted in a large increase in the HRD body of knowledge. Professional societies, such as American Vocational Association (AVA), American Association of Adult Education, American Society of Training and Development (ASTD) and many others made many contributions. Researchers such as Maslow, Dooley, Lewin, Drucker, Skinner, Herzberg, Kirkpatrick, Mager, Becker and Knowles are just a few who extended the knowledge base surrounding HRD. According to Swanson (2009) the term human resource development is first used by Harbison and Myers (1964) in their book *Education, Manpower and Economic Development: Strategies of Human Resource Development*. In 1969 Leonard Nadler is generally credited with first promoting the term *human resource development* for the profession.

The Academy of Human Resource Development (AHRD) evolved out of the Professor's Network of ASTD and the University Council for Research on HRD. In 1993 the combined goal of wanting to advance the profession through research and scholarship realigned the two groups into the newly formed and independent Academy of Human Resource Development. The AHRD has developed significant overseas collaborative links over the years including with the UK based University Forum for HRD (UFHRD) and the AHRD in India.

In the Asian context the origin of HRD is rooted in the ancient apprenticeship systems for educating government officers, craftsmen and artisans in various countries such as China, India, Japan and Korea. It is believed that the flourishing of Confucianism in these countries facilitated the development of the HRD system in a more structured way as the Confucian tradition has historically emphasized the training and development (T&D) of junior scholars (Wang *et al.* 2005). In the modern era, however, many countries have encountered various HRD challenges causing high interest in national-level investment in the HRD field to address national and local demands for skilled human resources and the need for formal educational systems in higher, vocational and workforce development (Gurtoo 2008; Verma *et al.* 1995). One unique finding about a centralized country like China is that its rigidly controlled economy characterized the contexts of HRD that are different from other more "open system" countries such as Korea and Japan between the 1950s and 1970s. While Korea and Japan developed modern HRD systems and practices adapted from the US during this period, those of China and India were more influenced by other countries such as Russia and the UK as major political and economic beneficiaries of these countries (Alagaraja and Wang 2012). As a result, some countries experienced a continual growth of HRD systems and practices (i.e. Korea and Japan) as they kept collaborative partnerships for economic growth and development with the US, whereas other countries (i.e. China and India) had a different path in adopting Western HRD systems and practices as their HRD models did not accommodate the acute economic and societal changes experienced by these countries since the 1970s.

Currently, the high interest in the field of HRD by most Asian countries is noticeable as they have been in great need of competent workers to support rapid economic development of each country. This trend can be illustrated from several phenomena. For example, the numbers of Asian graduate students enrolled in graduate HRD programmes in the US have increased steadily for the past decades indicating a growing need for scholars and practitioners in this field (Lim *et al.* 2013). Also, an analysis of conference participants in the International Conferences on HRD in Asia reveals a great deal of diversity from various Asian countries (see Table 32.1).

The literature related to HRD degree programmes is limited as a result of the relatively young age of the programmes and the lack of a unified definition and consistently agreed upon body of knowledge (how HRD is interpreted across programmes is not the subject of analysis of this chapter). Weinberger (1998) identified 18 unique definitions of HRD, all of which were developed between 1970 and 1995. Lynham *et al.* (2010: 3331) may have expressed it best when they wrote:

> the range of definitional perspectives run the gambit (Hurt, unpublished) from a tightly bounded definition of HRD (Swanson 1995), to a more open and ambiguity accommodating one (McLean and McLean 2001), and a refusal to define HRD (Lee 2001) on the basis of it being in a perpetual state of *becoming*.

Table 32.1 Participants in the International Conferences of HRD in Asia

Year	*Bangladesh*	*China*	*India*	*Japan*	*Korea*	*Malaysia*	*Singapore*	*Sri Lanka*	*Taiwan*	*Thailand*
2002	1	1	50*	0	4	3	1	2	6	1
2003	11	7	18	2	8	7	2	1	1	18*
2004	2	3	11	1	22*	7	5	0	5	5
2008	0	11	7	1	15	7	2	0		19*

*Place of conference: 2002 (India), 2003 (Thailand), 2004 (Korea), 2008 (Thailand)

Within the Asian context, while many Asian countries used a definition of HRD very similar to US definitions, like "the integrated use of training and development, career development, and organizational development to improve individual, group and organizational effectiveness" (McLagan 1989), some countries adopted their independent definitions of HRD influenced by various cultural and social variables such as economy systems, governmental legislation, value systems and cultural traditions (McLean and McLean 2001). For example, the notion of HRD in Japan adopts two perspectives (outcome and process) in defining HRD. According to Harada (1999: 357), the outcome perspective defines HRD as "the development of desirable human resources, characterized by employees who acquire corporate knowledge and a high level of job competencies to use in the improvement of products or services" while the process perspective specifies the notion of HRD as containing "the learning activities and opportunities designed to grow employee job competencies by developing potential human capabilities through their job experiences" (ibid: 357). In Taiwan the concept of HRD is mingled with that of human resource management (HRM), involving personnel, training, manpower planning and industrial relations (Lee and Chen 1998). In mainland China, as indicated by McLean and McLean (2001), there is no clear distinction between HRM, HRD, and Personnel. Due to the effects of Confucianism focusing on the education and holistic development of human beings, Chinese people consider the main purpose of HRD from the perspective of human talent. As such, the Chinese definition of HRD emphasizes educating those who have not developed a talent and on advancing those with talent to higher levels (Yang *et al.* 2004).

University HRD programmes in the United States

History

The first extensive study into HRD programmes was by Gaudet and Vincent in 1993 as they examined Bachelor's, Master's and doctoral degree programmes. They drew on data from the annual ASTD academic directory of programmes in HRD, and their questionnaire was mailed to the 218 identified T&D/HRD programmes. Chalofsky and Larson-Daugherty (1996) also drew on the ASTD database in their chapter on academic programmes for HRD professionals in *The ASTD Training and Development Handbook*. Kuchinke (2002) utilized the ASTD database as he wrote what has become the seminal piece on institutional and curricular characteristics of graduate HRD programmes. Roberts (2008) published the *2008 Human Resource Development Directory of Academic Programs in the United States*. Prior to this, there were no complete or reliable descriptive data on academic programmes preparing HRD professionals in the United States. Roberts continues to publish this directory annually. In the 1980s and early 1990s the ASTD (1996) developed a partial directory. The last directory of HRD academic programmes published by ASTD was in 1996. Li *et al.* (2008) examined Bachelor's programmes and among other things, found that 63 per cent of HRD programmes reside in colleges of education or colleges with education in their name, which is consistent with the findings of Kuchinke (2004, 2007) and of Gaudet and Kotrlik (1995). There have been several other studies looking at various aspects of HRD programmes, for example, their placement within colleges of education (Kuchinke 2004, 2007) and their certificate programmes (Gaudet and Kotrlik 1995; Hatcher 1998; Dare and Leach 1999; Chalofsky and Larson-Daugherty 1996; Henschke 1995; Willis and Kahnweiler 1995; Schwindt 1995; Pace 1988).

Current Bachelor's programmes

The 2011 Human Resource Development Directory of Academic Programmes in the United States (Roberts 2011a) identified 168 degree programmes from the 100 responding institutions, 40 at the Bachelor's level. Thirty-one of these programmes are Bachelor of science degrees, seven are Bachelor of arts, and two are Bachelor of business administration programmes. In fact, of the 100 responding institutions only 37 offer a Bachelor's-level program.

Bachelor's programmes have a wide range of focus, again largely depending upon the location of the host department. Those within colleges of education focus on T&D or instructional design while those in colleges of business have more of an HR focus, often aligning with the Society of Human Resource Management (SHRM) standards. SHRM now produces a directory of "certified" programmes: http://www.shrm.org/Education/hreducation/Pages/HRProgram Directory.aspx. This directory is maintained for programmes that meet the SHRM standards and includes programmes at both the Bachelor's and Master's levels.

Current Master's programmes

The 2011 Human Resource Development Directory of Academic Programs in the United States (Roberts 2011a) identified 168 degree programmes from the 100 responding institutions, 108 of which were at the Master's level. In fact only seven of the 100 responding institutions did not have a Master's-level program. The Master's degree is clearly the heart of HRD programmes in the US Table 32.2 includes a listing of the programme names and the frequency of each. The 100 institutions listed a total of 108 different Master's degrees which was as a result of multiple degrees at a single institution; for example, one institution reported both an MS in Human Resource Development and an MEd in Training and Development.

The most frequently occurring programme names as determined by Gaudet and Vincent (1993), Kuchinke (2002), Roberts (2008) and Roberts (2012) are shown in Table 32.2. This study found that of the 89 Master's-level degrees in Roberts (2009), 46 are Master's of science, 27 are Master's of arts, 14 are Master's of education, one is a Master's of business administration and the final one is a Master's of professional studies degree.

The most commonly occurring word in the programme names is *Development* which occurs in 63 per cent of the names. Programmes with *Human Resource(s)* in the name comprise nearly 51 per cent of the programmes. The next most often occurring word is *Organization(al)*, which is found in 19 per cent of the titles. *Adult Learning* or *Adult Education* is in 13 per cent of the programme names and those with *Work* or *Workforce* make up 11 per cent. Finally, *Training* is found in 10 per cent of the programme names.

Table 32.2 Most frequently occurring Master's programme names in the US

	Gaudet and Vincent 1993 n = 122	*Kuchinke 2002 n = 55*	*Roberts 2008 n = 103*	*Roberts 2012 n = 112*
Human Resource Development	42	18	23	30
Adult Education	22	1	5	8
Instructional (*Systems) Technology	12	*1	*1	*1
Training and Development	7	3	7	5
Human Resource and Organization Development		1	3	2

Current doctoral programmes

The 2011 Human Resource Development Directory of Academic Programmes in the United States (Roberts 2011a) identified 168 degree programmes from the 100 responding institutions, 46 of which were at the doctoral level. These programmes are split between 15 EdD programmes and 31 PhD programmes. Of the 31 PhD granting programmes, 20 reported graduation numbers for 2011. They reported 117 graduates or an average of 5.85 graduates per reporting institution. Of the 15 EdD granting programmes, 8 reported graduation numbers for 2011. They reported 41 graduates or an average of 5.125 graduates per reporting institution.

Table 32.3 compares the average number of graduates across the four studies. There has been a small increase in the average number of graduates over this time. Kuchinke (2002) looked at enrolment numbers, not the number of graduates, and his study also looked at a sample of the 55 leading graduate HRD programmes, while Gaudet and Vincent (1993) and Roberts (2008, 2012) examined the entire population of US programmes. Not all of the responding institutions provided the number of graduates in the Roberts (2008, 2012) studies; the number of reporting institutions are given as a footnote.

Number of faculty

The number of faculty at institutions in the US has also been examined by Roberts (2008, 2009, 2010, 2011b, 2012). The number of faculty is a key metric in programme quality for a number of factors. One of the first measures of quality when examining a programme or institution is

Table 32.3 Average number of Master's students graduating from HRD programmes

Studies	*Number of Programmes Studied*	*Master's Degrees*	*Average Number of Graduates*
Gaudet and Vincent 1993	122	108	20
Kuchinke 2002	55	55	NA
Roberts 2008	103	100	21.12*
Roberts 2012	105	112	21.52*

Note: * In 2008, 59 institutions reported number of graduates and in 2012, 46 did. Adapted from "The current status of human resource development master's programs in the United States," by P.B. Roberts (2011), In K.M. Dirani (ed.) *Proceedings of the Academy of Human Resource Development Conference*. Schaumburg, IL: AHRD.

Table 32.4 Average number of doctoral students graduating from HRD programmes

Studies	*Number of Programmes Studied*	*PhD Degrees Programmes*	*Average Number of Graduates*
Gaudet and Vincent 1993	122	45	4
Kuchinke 2002	55	55	NA
Roberts 2008	103	33	5.78*
Roberts 2012	100	28	7.66*

Note: * In 2008, 19 institutions reported number of graduates; in 2012, 15 did. Adapted from "The current status of human resource development master's programs in the United States," by Roberts, P.B. (2011), In Dirani, K.M. (ed.) *Proceedings of the Academy of Human Resource Development Conference*. Schaumburg, IL: AHRD.

Table 32.5 Number of faculty

Studies	*Number of Programmes Reporting*	*Total Number of Faculty*	*Average Number of Faculty*
Roberts 2008	103	100	3.76
Roberts 2009	84	89	4.44
Roberts 2010	81	352	4.35
Roberts 2011b	100	395	3.95
Roberts 2012	105	412	3.92

the faculty to student ratio. The number of faculty also plays a role in programme sustainability as viewed by accreditation bodies, both regional and programme specific. See Table 32.5 for the average on the number of faculty.

University HRD programmes in Europe

United Kingdom

Bachelor's programmes

There is no tradition in the UK for Bachelor's degrees in the field of HRD. There are none listed with HRD in the title on the most comprehensive website available in early 2013: whatuni.com. Only two relevant programmes were identified, one entitled Professional Development, the other Education in Professional Practice. On the other hand, there were 82 institutions offering degrees that had HRM in the title, the majority based in business schools.

Master's programmes

In the UK the first HRD-oriented Master's programme was the MA in Training initiated in the mid-1980s at the University of Leicester. In the early 1990s there was a trend towards professionally recognized Master's programmes with HRD in the title, the curriculum endorsed by the then Institute of Training and Development (ITD) and following its merger with the Institute of Personnel Management in 1994 by the Chartered Institute of Personnel and Development (CIPD). The first of these professionally recognized HRD Master's programmes was validated at South Bank University, London, in 1991, with others such as at Wolverhampton, Liverpool John Moores and Portsmouth universities following soon thereafter. The University Forum for HRD was established in 1992 as a national network of higher education institutions offering a Master's degree in HRD, and the first UK professor in HRD was appointed at Liverpool John Moores University in 1993 (Walton 2001).

Ten years later this consensus was no longer apparent. Kuchinke (2003) reported considerable heterogeneity among the course titles of the 28 programmes listed as having an HRD orientation. Only eight was he able to identify as having an obvious focus on HRD. He went on to state that "While perhaps the curriculum content reflects HRD proper, the names of the majority of UK courses do no justice to the uniqueness of the field" (Kuchinke 2003: 292). An explanation for this lies in the dominance of the professional body (CIPD) in determining professional standards and its different perspective compared with the ITD. Following the merger it was a requirement that to attain membership status course curricula should cover HRM as well as HRD standards. Furthermore, until recently the CIPD has not used the term HRD in its standards, preferring T&D or learning and development. For career progression reasons the majority of students attending UK Master's level programmes are seeking CIPD membership status, and this is only possible through attending CIPD accredited courses of study. The influence of the CIPD also helps to explain why the majority of programmes in the UK are located in the business school.

Sabine Manning's 2012 European-wide survey revealed a similar situation to that reported by Kuchinke (2003). Only four UK programmes have HRD in the title with an additional two in Training and Development (Manning 2012). On the other hand, she reported six Master's programmes in HRM that had an HRD component.

Doctoral programmes

In the UK there are no formal doctoral programmes devoted to HRD although over the years there have been a number of HRD-oriented theses. In recent years there has been a growth in professional doctorates and currently new route PhDs. A PhD is a research-based doctoral programme which usually involves little or no taught element and is usually academic in nature. Professional doctorate programmes, whilst being equivalent in status and challenge to a PhD, are designed for those pursuing professional, rather than academic, careers. They retain the core research elements of the traditional UK PhD but supplement research with a structured programme of advanced learning in discipline specific and generic skills. Assessment of the taught element is often at Master's level.

Continental Europe

HRD programmes across Europe vary in accordance with the structural system influencing academic qualifications in the country in question. In much of continental Europe, the higher education system has been modelled on the German system – as opposed to the Anglo-American approach – in which there is a clear difference between vocational and academic higher education, with a Master's degree being a continuation of the subject studied for the first degree. Under this tradition Master's awards in HRD or other vocation fields are not common and have lower status than those obtained through a conventional academic route. In the UK on the other hand, the boundaries between academic and vocational qualifications are blurred, and Master's level qualifications in fields unrelated to one's first degree are recognized and valued.

The Bologna Process initiated in 1999 by the European Union is an attempt to harmonize degree qualification frameworks across Europe in terms of similarity between first degree, Master's award, and doctorate in terms of length of study, level and standard of awards. It has still not been fully implemented in a number of countries.

The current situation is still very complicated and diverse because of the various national traditions and different ways of trying to meet the Bologna requirements. However, there is evidence that greater opportunities for vocational Master's qualifications are emerging. For example, in French universities after the advent of the Bologna Process and since 2006, the traditional Master's degrees of Diplôme d'études approfondies (DEA) and Diplôme d'études superieures spécialisées (DESS) have been replaced by degrees of Research Master (Master Recherche) and Professional Master (Master Professionnel). The first degree programme prepares students for PhD studies, while the second type is for professional life.

A new introduction in German speaking countries is the Master in Advanced studies (MAS). Admission criteria are often more flexible than in traditional Master programmes that follow on from first degrees and tend to recognize work experience and non-formal education in addition to formal education. A MAS usually consists of course work, independent study and a Master's thesis. Germany does not offer a Master of Advanced Studies as an academic title but German universities are allowed to offer a Master of Advanced Studies programme as "Post-graduate study opportunities".

Sabine Manning (2012) provides the most comprehensive analysis of university HRD-oriented programmes across Europe, presenting in her Directory 110 examples of current Master's programmes in 23 European countries. The programmes selected for the Directory cover the interrelated field of learning and work, with a particular focus on the areas of HRD and vocational education and training (VET). The data are based on the following sources:

- Questionnaires sent to about 1000 professionals across Europe between 2006 and 2011;
- University research and teaching websites related to the field of learning and work;
- European and national directories of Master's or higher education programmes.

The two main aims of the Directory are (a) to trace the evolution of Master's programmes as part of the Bologna Process, and (b) to identify and map the themes of Master's programmes against the general background of European research activities related to learning and work. She identifies only two Master's programmes in mainland Europe with HRD in the title. One is based in the Netherlands and one in Denmark. The latter is concerned with education and learning in formal and informal settings, learning processes, and learning environments. There were three programmes in HRM with an HRD component. The course titles of themselves do not give an insight into the curriculum. For example, the Master's in International Vocational Education at the University of Magdeburg in Germany is concerned with both international comparative vocational education and training and HRD.

Universities offering vocationally oriented Master's level HRD programmes have a key role to play in the development and assessment of international standards and practices for the profession. One method of establishing some data on convergence or divergence of HRD practice is through analysis of university programmes in the HRD area. Following on from this, one way of facilitating convergence is for university course designers to share ideas on programme inputs and outcomes, incorporating features from other programmes as appropriate. This was initiated in the UK at the national level in the early 1990s as reported above. It is far less common at an international level. Indeed, taking European universities as an example, there is no agreed set of HRD programme outcomes which meet the following conditions:

1. They can be demonstrated by individuals successfully achieving Master's level qualifications taken in different European countries.
2. They are recognized as professionally relevant across the national boundaries of European Union member states.
3. They satisfy the needs of employers looking for high-level practitioners with the breadth and depth of knowledge to operate transnationally as well as domestically.

Walton (1997) reports on a three year research project (1993–1996) to try to resolve this situation and develop a set of common core learning outcomes applicable to Master's programmes in HRD across Europe. It was undertaken through the auspices of EURESFORM, a European network of universities and other Higher Education Institutions providing post-graduate qualifications for HRD practitioners. UK members included London Guildhall University and South Bank University (both located in London); the University of Wolverhampton; and Lancaster University. Other members included the University of Barcelona (Spain); the University of Tilburg (Netherlands); the Conservatoire National des Arts et Métiers (CNAM) (France); the Irish National College of Industrial Relations (Eire); and the Technological University of Helsinki (Finland). Although a number of EURESFORM Certificates were awarded over the years the initiative died out as universities changed their priorities towards Master's awards.

University HRD programmes in Asia (specifically South Korea)

While there are many HRD programmes in existence in different countries in Asia, rare studies have been conducted to identify the specifics of those programmes. Recently, Lim *et al.* (2013) have completed an extensive study about HRD graduate programmes in South Korea. We are including the findings of the study with an intention to illustrate an example of how an Asian country's HRD system has been influenced by various factors and developed into modern HRD programmes at the university level.

Graduate HRD programmes in South Korea have evolved from education and instructional systems fields. The rapid growth of HRD programmes in South Korea echoed the rapid economic development and modernization of society that has occurred since the 1980s (Lee *et al.* 2011). For example, there were only two graduate HRD programmes in the early 1990s in South Korea. As the need for graduate HRD programmes has been growing, the number of universities offering HRD programmes has increased to a significant degree. In 2011 there were 15 institutions offering graduate HRD programmes in South Korea. Among them, all 15 universities offer Master's degree and 7 universities offer doctoral degrees in HRD.

As for the names of graduate HRD programmes in South Korea, some of them are very similar to those in the US while other programme names contain national emphasis areas of HRD. The names of graduate HRD programmes are Educational Administration and Lifelong Education (1), Educational Technology (4), Human Resource Development (1), HRD Policy (1), HRD Strategy (1), Lifelong Education (4), Lifelong Education and HRD (2), Sociology of Education and Adult and Continuing Education (1), and Women Resource Development (1) (numbers in parentheses indicate frequencies). One interesting finding about the names of graduate HRD programmes is that many South Korean institutions used "Lifelong Education" in naming the graduate HRD programmes. It is observed that this trend is shaped by the traditional influence of Confucianism that emphasizes education and holistic development of human beings throughout their whole life span.

When the perceptions about the important content areas of HRD programmes were investigated among the audiences of HRD programmes composed of South Korean HRD professors, graduate students and practitioners, they indicated change management, organizational development, adult learning theories, evaluation and project management tools and techniques as the top-five most important content areas to be mastered. Table 32.6 shows the 25 most important HRD content areas as perceived by the South Korean HRD audience.

When the content areas of graduate HRD programmes in South Korean institutions were compared with those of the US, it was found that South Korean graduate HRD programmes seemed to provide more content areas focusing on functional skills and knowledge of HRD required to successfully perform HRD jobs, whereas graduate HRD programmes in the US seemed to provide those content areas related to supervisory or managerial tasks (e.g. organization development, leadership and management development, organizational behaviour, etc.) (Lim *et al.* 2013).

Table 32.6 HRD topics currently important for Work and Studies

Topical Area	*Mean**
Change management	4.09
Organization development	3.98
Adult learning theories	3.98
Evaluation	3.96
Project management tools and techniques	3.96
Organizational learning/learning organization	3.85
Introduction to HRD	3.81
Talent management	3.81
Grant writing/proposal development	3.80
Quantitative Research	3.79
Writing/speaking/reading skills	3.79
Facilitation	3.78
Competencies development of HRD professionals	3.76
HRD/educational policy studies	3.74
Training and Development	3.73
Technology and innovation	3.71
Instructional Design	3.70
Strategic planning	3.69
HRD consulting	3.69
Research method	3.66
Programme planning and development	3.67
Instructional strategy, methods, and delivery	3.68
Systems thinking	3.67
Knowledge management	3.67
Organization/Workforce analysis	3.67
Performance management	3.67

Note: n = 134. * Based on a 5-point Likert scale (1–5). Adapted from "A comparative analysis of graduate HRD curricular content between the United States and South Korea," by Lim, D.H., Song, J.H., Choi, M. and Kim, H.K. (2013) *Human Resource Development International* 16(3): 1–22.

Trends in university HRD programmes

United States

The absence of a single unifying definition of HRD, common programme names, a common body of knowledge and consistent locations within a university, will always be a limiting factor when attempting to identify trends in HRD programme names. The words used in the names of US programmes lead to a couple of interesting observations. The word *Organization(al)* was found in only 7.3 per cent of names of HRD-related programmes in the Kuchinke (2002) study but appeared in 19.1 per cent of the institutions reported by Roberts (2009). The words *work* or *workforce* also increased from 3.6 per cent in Kuchinke (2002) to 11.2 per cent in Roberts (2009); this may be a simple shift from the word *vocational* to *workforce*, which if combined in the Kuchinke (2002) data would bring the percentage up to 9.1 per cent. Finally, the word *adult* decreased from 21.8 per cent in Kuchinke (2002) to 13.5 per cent in Roberts (2009). A more detailed look at name changes by institutions might determine if these shifts indicate trends in programmes or just word substitutions. The average number of students graduating with a Master's degree in HRD has increased at a very small rate.

United Kingdom

On the surface the same points relating to lack of common programme names apply to the UK, but this is somewhat deceptive. As we have seen the same situation does not apply to HRM where the term is common in Business School programmes influenced by the importance of students obtaining a CIPD qualification in parallel with gaining a university award. It is also highly unusual for HRM programmes not to include an HRD component. The relationship between HRM and HRD has been subject to an ongoing debate in the UK (Walton 1999). There is no indication that this will change in the near future. It brings into question why HRM and HRD have gained academic credibility, as reflected in titles of journals, but UK programme designers are seemingly reluctant to incorporate the term 'HRD' in university awards.

Continental Europe

There is evidence that as the Bologna Process gains momentum, there will be an increasing likelihood that universities will introduce vocational-oriented Master's programmes that equip students for professional life. However, there is no evidence that the term HRD will gain currency. As is the situation in the US and the UK, new programmes have to be approved within universities and even gaining agreement on the title is a time-consuming process requiring an academic and business case that will generate political support.

Asian countries

In Asian countries one clear trend is that HRD programmes at the graduate level will grow exponentially as many countries will continue their rapid economic development. However, the developmental pattern of the characteristics and content of HRD programmes might be different between countries as each country can be influenced by various external and internal factors. For example, one distinction that will create differences in HRD programmes between the Asian countries will be how each country defines the notion of HRD mingled with HRM and Personnel. If some countries inherited many of their organizational and managerial systems from the European countries, more integrated approaches with HRM areas will be required for their HRD education and practices. If some countries have kept close economic and cultural partnerships with the US, they may experience a similar developmental pattern of HRD programmes with those of the US. Also, various factors such as the status of economic development, political structure and cultural value systems may influence the future development of HRD programmes for each Asian country. Like India and China, their rapid economic development will necessitate more expansion and diversification of graduate HRD programmes of their countries. Like South Korea and Japan, as they have experienced a relatively slow or static economic development along with a growing aging population recently, a more strategic approach of HRD practices to satisfy their future workforce needs will influence the future direction and content of graduate HRD programmes of their countries.

References

Alagaraja, M. and Wang, J. (2012) Development of a national HRD strategy model: Cases of India and China. *Human Resource Development Review* 11(4): 407–29.

American Society of Training and Development (ASTD) (1996, November) *Academic directory: Programs in human resource development 1997.* Alexandria, VA: American Society for Training and Development.

Chalofsky, N. and Larson-Daugherty, C.A. (1996) Academic programs for HRD professionals. In Craig, R.L. (ed.), *The ASTD Training and Development Handbook* (4th edn) (991–98). New York: McGraw-Hill.

Craig, R.L. (1996) *The ASTD Training and Development Handbook: A guide to human resource development* (4th edn). New York: McGraw-Hill.

Dare, D.E. and Leach, J.A. (1999) Preparing tomorrow's HRD professionals: Perceived relevance of the 1989 competency model. *Journal of Vocational and Technical Education* 15(2): 5–18.

Gaudet, C. and Vincent, A. (1993) Characteristics of training and human resource development degree programs in the United States. *Delta Pi Epsilon* XXXV(3): 138–60.

Gaudet, C.H. and Kotrlik, J.W. (1995) Status of HRD certificate program development. *Human Resource Development Quarterly* 6(1): 91–99.

Gurtoo, A. (2008) A framework for labour policy reforms in India: Balancing economic growth and social development. *International Journal of Sociology and Social Policy* 28(11/12): 472–84.

Harada, K. (1999) The changing Japanese human resource development system: Two models that enhance prediction and reflection of dynamic changes. *Human Resource Development International* 2(4): 355–68.

Harbison, F. and Myers, C.A. (1964) *Education, Manpower and Economic Development: Strategies of Human Resource Development.* New York: McGraw-Hill.

Hatcher, T. (1998) A study of human resource development degree programs in higher education in the United States. *Delta Pi Epsilon* XXXV(3): 138–60.

Henschke, J.E. (1995) *Theory and practice on preparing HRD professionals.* In Holton III, E.F. (ed.) Conference Proceedings (section 7–2). Baton Rouge, LA: Academy of Human Resource Development.

Knowles M. (1970) *The Modern Practice of Adult Education.* New York: Association Press.

Kuchinke, K.P. (2002) Institutional and curricular characteristics of leading graduate HRD programs in the US. *Human Resource Development Quarterly* 13(2): 127–44.

— (2003) Comparing national systems of human resource development: Role and function of post-baccalaureate HRD courses of study in the UK and US. *Human Resource Development International* 6(3): 285–99.

— (2004) Contested domains: Human resource development programs in colleges of education. *Workforce Education Forum* 3(1): 43–60.

— (2007) Birds of a feather? The critique of the North American business school and its implications for educating HRD practitioners. *Human Resource Development Review* 6(2): 111–26.

Lee, E.S., Chang, J.Y. and Kim, H. (2011) The work–family interface in Korea: Can family life enrich work life? *International Journal of Human Resource Management* 22(9): 2032–53.

Lee, L.S. and Chen, Y.Y. (1998) An introduction to human resource development in Taiwan. ERIC Document Reproduction Service No. ED416414.

Lee, M. (2001) A refusal to define HRD. *Human Resource Development International* 4(3): 327–41.

Li, J., Nimon, K. and Allen, J. (2008) *Undergraduate HRD Programs in the United States.* In Chermack T.J., Storberg-Walker, J. and Graham, C.M. (eds) Proceedings of the Academy of Human Resource Development 2008 International Conference. Panama City Beach, FL: AHRD.

Lim, D.H., Song, J.H., Choi, M. and Kim, H.K. (2013) A comparative analysis of graduate HRD curricular content between the United States and Korea. *Human Resource Development International* 16(3): 1–22.

Lynham, S.A., Lincoln, Y.S., Hurt, A.C. and McLean, G.N. (2010) *The HRD cube: A heuristic for understanding, locating and investigating HRD theory, research and practice.* In Graham, C.M. (ed.) Proceedings of the Academy of Human Resource Development Conference. Knoxville, TN: AHRD.

Manning, S. (2012) European research in learning and work: Directory of Masters Programmes (5th edn). Available on www.master.wifo-gate.org.

McLagan, P.A. (1989) *Models for HRD Practice.* Alexandria, VA: ASTD.

McLean, G.N. and McLean, L.D. (2001) If we can't define HRD in one country, how can we define it in an international context? *Human Resource Development International* 4(3): 313–26.

Nadler, L. (1984) *The Handbook of Human Resource Development.* New York: Wiley-Interscience.

Pace, R.W. (1988) *The Content of HRD Academic Programs.* Dallas, TX: American Society for Training and Development.

Roberts, P.B. (ed.) (2008) *Human Resource Development Directory of Academic Programs in the United States*. Tyler, TX: The University of Texas at Tyler.

— (2009) *Human Resource Development Directory of Academic Programs in the United States*. Tyler, TX: The University of Texas at Tyler.

— (2010) *Human Resource Development Directory of Academic Programs in the United States*. Tyler, TX: The University of Texas at Tyler.

— (2011a) *Human Resource Development Directory of Academic Programs in the United States*. Tyler, TX: The University of Texas at Tyler.

— (2011b) *The Current Status of human resource development master's programs in the United States*. In Dirani, K.M. (ed.), Proceedings of the Academy of Human Resource Development Conference. Schaumburg, IL: AHRD.

— (ed.) (2012) *Human Resource Development Directory of Academic Programs in the United States*. Tyler, TX: The University of Texas at Tyler.

Schwindt, R.C. (1995) *Evaluation and evolution of a HRD program*. In Holton III, E.F. (ed.) Conference Proceedings (section 7–4). Baton Rouge, LA: Academy of Human Resource Development.

Swanson, R.A. (1995) Human resource development: Performance is the key. *Human Resource Development Quarterly* 1(1): 1–25.

— (2009) *Foundations of Human Resource Development* (2nd edn). San Francisco: Berrett-Koehler.

Verma, A., Kochan, T.A. and Lansbury, R.D. (1995) *Employment Relations in the Growing Asian Economies*. London: Routledge.

Walton, J. (1997) *The development of common core learning outcomes for HRD professionals which have currency across national boundaries: A European case study*. In Torraco, R.J. (ed.) Conference proceedings (26–34). Atlanta, GA: Academy of Human Resource Development.

— (1999) *Strategic Human Resource Development*. Harlow, UK: Prentice Hall.

— (2001) *UFHRD Annual Chairman's Report for 2001–2002*. London: University Forum for Human Resource Development.

Wang, J., Wang, G.G., Ruona, W.E.A. and Rojewski, J.W. (2005) Confucian values and the implications for international HRD. *Human Resource Development International* 8(3): 311–26.

Weinberger, L.A. (1998) Commonly held theories of human resource development. *Human Resource Development International* 1(1): 75–93.

Werner, J.M. and DeSimone, R.L. (2011) *Human Resource Development* (6th edn). Mason, OH: Cengage Learning.

Willis, V.J. and Kahnweiler, W.M. (1995) *Genesis and continuance of an HRD academic program: A longitudinal study*. In Holton III, E.F. (ed.) Conference Proceedings (section 7–1). Baton Rouge, LA: Academy of Human Resource Development.

Yang, B., Zhang, D. and Zhang, M. (2004) National human resource development in the People's Republic of China. *Advances in Developing Human Resources* 6(3): 297–306.

33

HRD AND THE GLOBAL FINANCIAL CRISIS

Regaining legitimacy and credibility through people not economics

Thomas N. Garavan and Clíodhna A. MacKenzie

The financial crisis has had a fundamental and devastating effect on organizations, societies and global economies. The International Labour Organization (ILO) for example, has projected the total number of unemployed people globally to hit over 207 million in 2013 rising to over 210 million people by 2016 (ILO 2012) – these stark figures put a human cost on the greatest global financial and economic crisis[1] since the Great Depression. The causes of the financial crisis are many and to some degree, highly contested. Unsurprisingly, the commentary both mainstream and academic has pointed to myriad causes of the crisis. Such has been the financial, economic and social impact that establishing its root cause has proven problematic, both for the academic and practitioner community. Nevertheless, prominent streams of inquiry have emerged in the literature to include for example failures of economic and financial theories (Acemoglu 2009, Colander 2011) and associated *laissez-faire* regulatory enforcement and governance failures (Barth *et al.* 2012, Stiglitz 2010). Also featuring prominently in discourse has been the failure of well-established management and leadership theories; this line of inquiry has been the basis for more critical management oriented analyses of the crises (e.g. Board 2010, Davies 2010, Stacey 2010) that highlighted a consensus among more iconoclastic commentators that systemic and pervasive instances of human and intellectual failures (Haiss 2010, Kling 2010, Krugman 2012, Mattingly and Kopecki 2012, Munir 2011, Tett 2010, Whittle and Mueller 2012) played a significant role in the crisis. However, despite divergent perspectives regarding the root cause of the crisis, one aspect at the core of the financial crisis unites the multitude of opinions – human failures: that is, failures of *people, intellect and knowledge*.

These failures are critically important to HRD scholars and practitioners alike. HRD as an area of scholarly debate and practical application is tasked with shaping organizational culture; developing current and future leaders; and building capacity, capability and commitment among organization members and anticipating and managing responses to changed conditions *inter alia* (Garavan 2007, Stewart *et al.* 2010, Stewart and Sambrook 2012). As a result of the crisis, HRD practitioners now face many challenges in regaining credibility and legitimacy within industry and among professional bodies as a direct result of these human, intellectual and knowledge failures. HRD as an area of scholarly research and discourse will play a fundamental role in this new more fragile organizational reality. HRD scholars may now need to refocus their attention on how best to advance the research debate in recognition of the significant responsibility that comes with managing people, developing organizations and preparing future HRD practitioners. These practitioners must be equipped with adequate skills and tools to ensure a balance between sustained competitive advantage and societal sustainability. The applicability of many economic theories that form the basis of HRD's legitimacy and credibility both as a profession and scholarly research field is now under the spotlight. The unchallenged acceptance of economic theories that underscore human behavior reflects many limitations when valuing human capital as one and the same as other forms of organizational capital such as financial and structural capital (e.g. O'Donnell *et al.* 2007, Trehan and Rigg 2011). The impact of the financial crisis has seen HR scholars and practitioners move beyond the "economics" of efficiency and productivity. Factors of production are simply not sentient – only human beings have that capacity and HR scholars and practitioners are the people qualified to do something about it.

While the full economic impact of the global financial crisis is still unknown; the implications for HRD scholars and practitioners are clear. The failure of leaders and managers in banking institutions that engaged in excessive risk-taking behavior was also an HRD failure; the inability of regulators to maintain adequate levels of knowledge and enforce financial regulations was also an HRD failure; the neoclassical centred curriculum of HRD programs in many business schools that promoted human capital as a "factor or production" without considering cognitive or behavioral dimensions was also a failure of HRD (MacKenzie *et al.* 2012). Like it or not, human resource development scholarship and practice has played a central role in the global financial crisis. Understanding and learning from our mistakes is an important first step in rebuilding trust, credibility and the foundation for how HRD re-establishes itself as a critical function of tomorrow's organization.

In this chapter, we discuss the role of borrowed theories (Swanson 2001) that provided legitimacy to HRD as a field of research and practice. We consider the impact of economic based theories that may have facilitated environments which were conducive to pursuit of financial goals and objectives at the cost of organizational and institutional stability (Campbell *et al.* 2011, Fenwick and Bierema 2008, Werbel and Balkin 2010). We critique the challenges faced by HRD practitioners and scholars from a deconstructionist perspective (Derrida 1991, Howells 1999, Norris 1982) as they adjust to a very difficult economic environment and the impact it will have on developing future leaders and organizations. We conclude by discussing where HRD has been, where it currently stands as a profession and research agenda and highlight where it will need to go if it is to not just survive but thrive in a world that has irrevocably changed. HRD as a profession and scholarly agenda is a powerful force in advancing organizations, society and the academic community – unfortunately, as the financial crisis has demonstrated: with great power, comes great responsibility.

Something old, something new, something borrowed, something . . . *old*

The theoretical underpinnings of HRD although frustratingly difficult to define (Lee 2010, McGoldrick *et al.* 2001, McLean and McLean 2001) are understood as derived from three distinct applied philosophical domains. Swanson's (2001: 306) "three legged stool" metaphor describes the economic, systems and psychological genesis of HRD theory and is important for a number of reasons. First, it highlights why there are often tensions inherent in balancing the needs of people, organization and shareholders (Bierema 2009, McGuire *et al.* 2007). While economics provides a sense of credibility to the practice of HRD; that is, the traditional performance-based position that seeks to achieve goals and objectives through utilization of the organization's human capital, it is of limited applicability in understanding "people" issues – the core tenet of HRD. The economics orientation which is primarily concerned with performance and efficiency can and does undermine the people role of HRD practice resulting in tension and a return to shareholder primacy during turbulent times (Bierema 2009, Fenwick and Bierema 2008). Second, the systems theory perspective allows practitioners to utilize their understanding of process and interconnection within the organization so as to shape alternative futures utilizing human resources to do so. Although the systems approach is not without its limitation (see Yawson 2013), it does view the organization as a diverse ecosystem of human behaviors and interactions – in this sense, the whole is certainly greater and more complex than the sum of its parts, capable of incredible feats of ingenuity and at the same time prone to failures of almost unimaginable impact. Finally, the psychological principles help illuminate behavioral intentions and cognitive processes of the organization's human capital so that they can be developed and harmonized to achieve the organization's goals and objectives. Although the psychological principles that underscore HRD theory form only part of the "three legged stool" metaphor, arguably it is the psychological principles that are the most critically important to both the study and practice of HRD. Given that the psychological leg is concerned with the behavioral and cognitive processes of the organization's human interface; understanding this dimension becomes critically important when explored in the context of the financial crisis and the intellectual and knowledge failures central to its emergence.

The traditional orientation of HRD practitioners *and* scholars has been towards aligning human intellectual capital with the organization's goals and objectives to achieve and sustain competitive advantage (Garavan 2007, Hung *et al.* 2009, May *et al.* 2003, Kuchinke 2000, Garavan *et al.* 2004): or perhaps, more specifically – the conversion of human talent and ingenuity into economic and financial output. As seen from a more strategic perspective, HRD has achieved legitimacy through the conversion of human talent into economic and financial returns for the benefit of the organization. The financial crisis, however, has illuminated features of organizational behavior that are often mooted in more circumspect debate and illustrate limitations in economic centric theories of HRD or what can be referred to as the economic asymmetric orientations of HRD scholarship and practice. Whilst a debate about all the theoretical underpinnings of HRD is beyond the scope of this chapter (see sections I, II and II in this volume) it is important to recognize that economic theory has had a significant influence on the practice of HRD and to a lesser degree, the scholarship of HRD (Kuchinke 2000, Wang and Holton 2005). And, while it is fair to say that HRD practice plays a role in the pursuit of sustained competitive advantage, on the whole the HRD profession has consistently faced challenges of legitimacy and credibility (MacKenzie *et al.* 2012, O'Donnell *et al.* 2006) in justifying its worth to the organization.

One theory that has been both extensively utilized by HRD scholars and is recognized by HRD practitioners as a way to contribute to sustaining competitive advantage is the resource-based view (RBV) of the firm (Penrose 1995, Wright *et al.* 2001). The resource-based view of the firm posits that internal [human] resources are considered potential sources of competitive advantage (Wright *et al.* 2001) so the attraction of this theoretical lens to HRD scholars and practitioners is understandable. The RBV then focuses on how the organization [the firm] might develop unique bundles of human and technical resources in an effort to achieve superior performance (Lado *et al.* 2006, Wright *et al.* 2001). The oft cited statement that people are the most important asset in the organization (Boxall and Purcell 2008, Porter 1985) illuminates why the RBV is so attractive to many HR practitioners but perhaps is considered most important to HRD specialists tasked with developing the organization's human intellectual capital.

The appeal of RBV to HRD specialists is borne out in its ability to capture the "capabilities" (Garavan 2007, Peterson 2008) of the organization's intellectual capital for the benefit of its shareholders [assuming a profit seeking orientation]. However, if we consider this "economics" based theory purely on its merits, then its central tenet is that human capital is an organizational resource to be exploited in a means ends manner (O'Donnell *et al.* 2006) thus calling into question the truth about HRD's "people" responsibilities and the rhetoric that people are the organization's most important asset. The RBV from a human resources perspective suggests that individual human capital is embedded within a socially constructed and dynamically complex arrangement, responsive to and reflective of a multitude of human emotions and behaviors. To suggest that human beings can be detached from their emotions, cognitions and behaviors ignores their very human frailties and questions whether HR is developing people or products. As Fenwick (2011) trenchantly asked – for whom and for what are HRD professionals developing resources? The financial crisis might suggest an answer to this probing question.

Of Schumpeterian shocks and creative *de-construction*

Joseph Schumpeter, the Austrian economist, coined the phrase Creative Destruction (Schumpeter 1994: 83) to describe the free market's endless reinvention of itself with the death of one industry and the birth of another. For example, the way in which individuals communicate has seen one metamorphosis after another in the telecommunications industry with each iteration of innovation being of shorter duration but much more disruptive than the previous one. Over the last two decades, the explosive growth of the mobile communications industry has challenged many traditional telecommunications companies such as AT&T, Eircom and BT to become more dynamic and adapt to changing market conditions. Some did and are experiencing resurgence, new found legitimacy and a renewed sense of purpose; others did not and have either been acquired or are in the process of being acquired. Ironically, mobile operators such as Vodafone, Verizon, Orange and Sprint are now under threat themselves from the exponential growth in non-traditional data services such as social media, online gaming, Voice over IP (VoIP) and Apple FaceTime [personal video conferencing] available on mobile devices other than mobile phones, thus bypassing mobile operator tariffs and traditional revenue streams such as average revenue per unit (ARPU). While Schumpeter and many contemporary economists have viewed this Creative Destruction as a means by which the free market delivers progress, it is also appropriate to apply this as a metaphor when considering the future of HRD scholarship and practice and how it might deliver progress and reinvent itself if need be.

The economic landscape in which HRD scholars and practitioners now operate offers significant theory building opportunities as well as a safe domain in which to question the profession's involvement in the financial crisis. Lee's (2001) argument that HRD is in a constant state of becoming perhaps reflects the ill-defined boundary expansion of roles and responsibilities of HRD over the years, from deliverers of learning, training and development interventions (Garavan 1991, Gubbins and MacCurtain 2008, Stewart *et al.* 2010) to developers of human and organizational capital (Boudreau and Ramstad 2007, Ulrich and Beatty 2001, Ulrich and Brockbank 2005), from iconoclasts critically questioning the role of HRD (Fenwick 2004, O'Donnell *et al.* 2006, Sambrook 2004, Trehan and Rigg 2011) to breaking ground on HRD scholarship and practice in tomorrow's world (Garavan and McGuire 2010, Lee 2010, MacKenzie *et al.* 2012). Given our diverse range of roles and responsibilities it is hardly surprising that little has changed since Lee (2001) made her prescient remarks over a decade ago.

The problem with this evolving conceptualization of HRD is of course that we run the risk of expanding the boundary of responsibilities without ever fully understanding where that expansion will take us or indeed, without ever fully understanding the foundation upon which the expansion is built. The financial crisis is one of the key defining moments if not *the* key defining moment in HRD scholarship and practice over the last two decades and as such calls for a reappraisal not just of what HRD offers to the organization but what HRD actually represents. In order to do this, we need to deconstruct the study and practice of HRD beyond merely purveyors of organizational learning, training and development interventions. Deconstruction allows us to unpack the truth (Norris 1982) about HRD in an effort to write anew. Arguably, it is a critical juncture for banking and financial institutions, one in which their ideological underpinnings are questioned and where core values and the role and responsibility banks have to society as well as their shareholders are reassessed. Similarly, it is also a time for scholars to question the utility of HRD's theoretical foundations and practitioners to challenge the veracity of their "people" orientation. Although deconstruction is an approach to unpacking text and language rather than a deconstruction of philosophical, methodological or theoretical structures (Bloom *et al.* 2004, Norris 1982) ethical and political issues often play a central role in the deconstructionist discourse. Given the responsibility of HRD practitioners to develop interventions that operate in environments where ethics, politics and power plays are pervasive (MacKenzie *et al.* 2012) and given the failures of people and organizations considered core tenets of HRD practice it seems appropriate to approach HRD scholarship and practice from a deconstructionist perspective. To understand our failings requires us to peel back the concept of HRD to its very core.

Software developers have an adage: fragile code fails due to untested uses of the system and external changes in the environment. In many ways, HRD scholars can be viewed as the software developers behind people and organizational development practice. This places HRD scholars as central agents in constructing roles for practitioners to adopt through language and philosophical discourse. In essence, we [HRD scholars] have developed the *HRD code* [Lee's boundary expansion] beyond that of its original conceptualization as defined by Swanson (2001: 304): HRD is a process of developing and/or unleashing human expertise through organization development (OD) and personnel training and development (T&D) for the purpose of improving performance.

As we developed this *HRD code*, we may have failed to properly legislate for and separate each section of code. As we expanded the roles and responsibilities of HRD practice beyond learning, training and development to include: management and leadership development; organizational development; organizational culture development; strategic business partnering; as well as talent and succession management, we may not have fully considered the impact of tight-coupling (Bhide 2009, Weick 2009) on the organizational system. Moreover, as these new roles and responsibilities gained traction they also gained a degree of truth about what it is these new boundary expanding roles could achieve. Deconstruction of HRD does not set out to reject these new roles, rather it serves to unsettle from within the heritage (Howells 1999) to which these roles have obtained their legitimacy and credibility. In doing so, deconstruction can emerge as a "vigilant whistle blower" (Meredith 2004: 15) that allows for dismantling of what Derrida refers to as transcendent truth (Derrida 1991: 40) – in essence, these roles are a function of HRD because we as scholars said it was so and wrote it into being. The role HRD has played in the financial crisis should neither come as a surprise nor be taken lightly. Deconstructing HRD is very much like decompiling software – it is done when the code is bad. The financial crisis has illustrated that our *HRD code* was bad, not fundamentally flawed but not working optimally. As such, we are now faced with a decision on how to reposition and regain legitimacy and credibility but we can only do this when we determine how best to fix the bad code. The practice of HRD, like software, is developed to serve a purpose and in order to do that it must be constantly maintained. While we may have been considerably talented in developing the *HRD code*, the execution in any real practical sense lacked contextual and situational awareness and it is this lack of awareness that has rendered HRD post financial crisis delegitimized and lacking in credibility within and beyond the organizational boundary.

At its most fundamental and historical basis, the theory and practice of HRD has been concerned with the performance paradigm (Bierema 2009, O'Donnell *et al.* 2006). This performance paradigm has been focused primarily on resource maximization through the development of skills and increased organizational commitment (Boudreau and Ramstad 2007, Stewart and Sambrook 2012). If we consider this performance paradigm as the building block or base code for all other "roles and responsibilities" the orientation will always be on performance and efficiency. Our conceptual understanding of what HRD can bring to the table will be coloured by that transcendent truth. Leadership and management development interventions will have a performance and efficiency bent, likewise, OD and organizational culture development will be focused on increasing employee engagement and commitment to achieving the organizational goals of wealth maximization. Recruitment and selection, succession and talent management will all orient towards wealth maximization metrics and as we have seen from the impact of the financial crisis, when the performance and efficiency orientation of the firm is focused solely on achieving organizational goals and objectives above all else – destruction is all but inevitable but not in the Creative way that Schumpeter (1994) posits.

From an HRD perspective, the financial crisis while highlighting the failures of people, intellect and knowledge has enabled us to disassemble the component parts that construct the concept thus enabling an exploration of HRD from the inside out rather than from the outside in. Schumpeterian shocks result in organizations and industries failing and new entrepreneurs emerging to form new industries. Like new entrepreneurs, HRD scholars and practitioners are faced with two options: adapt to a very different environment and re-establish credibility and legitimacy through addressing the bad code [performance orientation] and in the process become invigorated and refocused or build people, intellect and knowledge solutions on top of bad code that may ultimately see HRD become irrelevant in the eyes of its stakeholders and never recover from the impact of the financial crisis. Regaining legitimacy and credibility in the eyes of stakeholders cannot be at the cost of the organization's human intellectual capital, it can only be achieved because of it.

Sage, sustainable and social: tomorrow's focus for a new HRD

We conclude by discussing where HRD has been, where it currently stands as a profession and research agenda and highlight where it will need to go if it is to not just survive but thrive in a world that has irrevocably changed. It is clear that HRD has reached a critical point in its evolution both as an academic discipline and as a set of organizational practices. The financial crisis has laid bare many of the key assumptions that underpin a notion of HRD that is organizational focused but overly focused on one bottom line – that of profit maximization. We therefore paradoxically, need to limit our boundary expansion to broaden our conception of what it is that HRD can do for organizations so that they are better positioned to provide a sustainable competitive advantage. In this realistic conception of competitive advantage, HRD scholars and practitioners must see human ingenuity, individuality not just as resources to be utilized to achieve the organization's goals and objectives but as a deep reservoir of intellectual capability that is both incredibly creative and devastatingly destructive – at times simultaneously.

The notion of ecological sustainability is advocated as a potential way forward. This is conceptualized as the capacity of an organization to function and grow within the constraints and limits of the biophysical world (Porritt 2007). The financial crisis has revealed a "fascination with a particular form of finance and economics" (Starkey and Tempest 2005) which in turn has pervaded the language of HRD in organizations. HRD therefore needs to move beyond the unitarist view of its role in organizations, to more effectively embrace its roots which are a concern for people and conceptualize its contribution through a focus on human and societal responsibilities (Kochan 2014). HRD must become both a discipline and set of practices that are sufficiently robust to help all stakeholders including government, businesses and society prepare for a future where there is a focus on ecological sustainability. Francis *et al.* (2012) talk about the need to engage in "conversations for change" that help organizations to become more ethical, socially responsible and sustainable. As the financial crisis has shown, a focus on profitability and efficiency will not realise these outcomes. HRD must work from a strong ethical foundation that focuses on the individual and engages with multiple perspectives, paradoxes, competing tensions and challenge normative approaches to HRD that emphasise best practice ways of doing things. HRD has a significant journey to make to reposition itself to perform these tasks and resist the tensions that will inevitably arise between the need to deliver short-term performance and long-term ecological sustainability.

Note

1 The global financial and economic crisis will be referred to as the financial crisis.

References

Acemoglu, D. (2009) The Crisis of 2008: Lessons for and from economics. *Critical Review* 21: 185–94.

Barth, J.R., Caprio Jr., G. and Levine, R. (2012) *Guardians of Finance*, Cambridge, MA: MIT Press.

Bhide, A. (2009) An accident waiting to happen. *Critical Review* 21: 211–47.

Bierema, L.L. (2009) Critiquing human resource development's dominant masculine rationality and evaluating its impact. *Human Resource Development Review* 8: 68–96.

Bloom, H., De Man, P., Derrida, J., Hartman, G.H. and Miller, J.H. (2004) *Deconstructionism and Criticism*, London: Continuum.

Board, D. (2010) Leadership: The ghost at the trillion dollar crash? *European Management Journal* 28: 269–77.

Boudreau, J.W. and Ramstad, P.M. (2007) *Beyond HR: The New Science of Human Capital*, Boston, MA: Harvard Business School Press.

Boxall, P. and Purcell, J. (2008) *Strategy and Human Resource Management*, New York: Palgrave Macmillan.

Campbell, W.K., Hoffman, B.J., Campbell, S.M. and Marchisio, G. (2011) Narcissism in organizational contexts. *Human Resource Management Review* 21: 268–84.

Colander, D. (2011) How economists got it wrong: A nuanced account. *Critical Review* 23: 1–27.

Davies, H. (2010) *The Financial Crisis: Who is to blame?*, Cambridge: Polity Press.

Derrida, J. (1991) *A Derrida Reader: between the blinds*, New York: Columbia University Press.

Fenwick, T. (2004) Toward a critical HRD in theory and practice. *Adult Education Quarterly* 54: 193–209.

— (2011) Developing who, for what? Notes of caution in rethinking a global H(R)D: A response to Kuchinke. *Human Resource Development International* 14: 83–89.

Fenwick, T. and Bierema, L. (2008) Corporate social responsibility: issues for human resource development professionals. *International Journal of Training and Development* 12: 24–35.

Francis, H., Holbeche, L. and Reddington, M. (2012) *People and Organisational Development: A New Agenda for Organisational Effectiveness*, London: CIPD.

Garavan, T.N. (1991) Strategic human resource development. *Journal of European Industrial Training* 12: 21–34.

— (2007) A strategic perspective on human resource development. *Advances in Developing Human Resources* 9: 11–30.

Garavan, T.N. and McGuire, D. (2010) Human resource development and society: Human resource development's role in embedding corporate social responsibility, sustainability, and ethics in organizations. *Advances in Developing Human Resources* 12: 487–507.

Garavan, T.N., Mcguire, D. and O'Donnell, D. (2004) Exploring human resource development: A levels of analysis approach. *Human Resource Development Review* 3: 417–41.

Gubbins, C. and MacCurtain, S. (2008) Understanding the dynamics of collective learning: The role of trust and social capital. *Advances in Developing Human Resources* 10: 578–99.

Haiss, P. (2010) Bank herding and incentive systems as catalysts for the financial crisis. *IUP Journal of Behavioral Finance* 7: 30–58.

Howells, C. (1999) *Derrida: Deconstruction from Phenomenology to Ethics*, London: Blackwell.

Hung, R.Y., Lien, B.Y. and McLean, G.N. (2009) Knowledge management initiatives, organizational process alignment, social capital, and dynamic capabilities. *Advances in Developing Human Resources* 11: 320–33.

ILO (2012) *Global Employment Outlook, April 2012 projects.* Online. Available: http://www.ilo.org/wcmsp5/groups/public/---ed_emp/---emp_elm/---trends/documents/publication/wcms_179663.pdf (accessed 15 May 2012).

Kling, A. (2010) The financial crisis: Moral failure or cognitive failure? *Harvard Journal for Law and Public Policy* 33: 507–18.

Kochan, D.J. (2014) Corporate social responsibility in a remedy-seeking society, a public choice perspective. *Chapman Law Review* 17(2): 1–64.

Krugman, P. (2012) *End This Depression Now*, New York: North.

Kuchinke, K.P. (2000) Debates over the nature of HRD: An institutional theory perspective. *Human Resource Development International* 3: 279–83.

Lado, A.A., Boyd, N.G., Wright, P. and Kroll, M. (2006) Paradox and theorizing within the resource-based view. *Academy of Management Review* 31: 115–31.

Lee, M. (2001) A refusal to define HRD. *Human Resource Development International* 4: 327–41.

— (2010) Shifting boundaries: The role of HRD in a changing world. *Advances in Developing Human Resources* 12: 524–35.

MacKenzie, C.A., Garavan, T.N. and Carbery, R. (2012) Through the looking glass: challenges for human resource development (HRD) post the global financial crisis – business as usual? *Human Resource Development International* 15: 353–64.

Mattingly, P. and Kopecki, D. (2012) *JPMorgan Traders Took Risks They Didn't Understand, Dimon Says* [Online]. New York: Bloomberg. Available: http://www.bloomberg.com/news/2012-06-13/jpmorgan-traders-took-risks-they-didn-t-understand-dimon-says.html (accessed 13 June 2012).

May, G.L., Sherlock, J.J. and Mabry, C.K. (2003) The future: The drive for shareholder value and implications for HRD. *Advances in Developing Human Resources* 5: 321–31.

McGoldrick, J., Stewart, J. and Watson, S. (2001) Theorizing human resource development. *Human Resource Development International* 4: 343–56.

McGuire, D., Garavan, T.N., O'Donnell, D. and Watson, S. (2007) Metaperspectives and HRD: Lessons for research and practice. *Advances in Developing Human Resources* 9: 120–39.

McLean, G.N. and McLean, L. (2001) If we can't define HRD in one country, how can we define it in an international context? *Human Resource Development International* 4: 313–26.

Meredith, F. (2004) *Experiencing the Postmetaphysical Self: Between Hermeneutics and Deconstruction.* Basingstoke: Palgrave Macmillan.

Munir, K.A. (2011) Financial crisis 2008–2009: What does the silence of institutional theorists tell us? *Journal of Management Inquiry* 20: 114–17.

Norris, C. (1982) *Deconstruction: Theory and Practice*, New York: Chaucer.

O'Donnell, D., McGuire, D. and Cross, C. (2006) Critically challenging some assumptions in HRD. *International Journal of Training and Development* 10: 4–16.

O'Donnell, D., Gubbins, C., McGuire, D., Jørgensen, K.M., Henriksen, L.B. and Garavan, T.N. (2007) Social capital and HRD: Provocative insights from critical management studies. *Advances in Developing Human Resources* 9: 413–35.

Penrose, E.T. (1995) *The Theory of the Growth of the Firm*, New York: Oxford Press.

Peterson, S.L. (2008) Creating and sustaining a strategic partnership: A model for human resource development. *Journal of Leadership Studies* 2: 83–97.

Porritt, J. (2007) *Capitalism as if the World Matters*, New York: Earthscan Publications, 2nd Edition.

Porter, M.E. (1985) *Competitive Advantage: Creating and Sustaining Superior Performance*, New York: Free Press.

Sambrook, S. (2004) A critical time for HRD. *Journal of European Industrial Training* 28: 611–24.

Schumpeter, J.A. (1994) *Capitalism, Socialism and Democracy*, New York: Harper and Row.

Stacey, R.D. (2010) *Complexity and Organizational Reality: Uncertainty and the Need to Rethink Management after the Collapse of Investment Capitalism*, New York: Routledge.

Starkey, K and Tempest, S. (2005) The future of the business school: Knowledge challenges and opportunities. *Human Relations* 58(1): 61–83.

Stewart, J. and Sambrook, S. (2012) The historical development of human resource development in the United Kingdom. *Human Resource Development Review* 11: 443–62.

Stewart, J., Iles, P., Gold, J., Holden, R., Rodgers, H. and Solomon-Kershaw, H. (2010) Strategic HRD and the learning and development function. In Gold, J., Holden, R., Iles, P., Stewart, J. and Beardwell, J. (eds) *Human Resource Development: Theory and Practice*, London: Palgrave Macmillan.

Stiglitz, J. (2010) *Freefall: Free Markets and the Sinking of the Global Economy*, London: Penguin Books.

Swanson, R.A. (2001) Human resource development and its underlying theory. *Human Resource Development International* 4: 299–312.

Tett, G. (2010) *Fool's Gold*, London: Abacus.

Trehan, K. and Rigg, C. (2011) Theorising critical HRD: A paradox of intricacy and discrepancy. *Journal of European Industrial Training* 35: 276–90.

Ulrich, D. and Beatty, D. (2001) From partners to players: Extending the HR playing field. *Human Resource Management* 40: 293–307.

Ulrich, D. and Brockbank, W. (2005) *The HR Value Proposition*, Boston, MA: Harvard Business School Press.

Wang, G.G. and Holton, E.F. (2005) Neoclassical and institutional economics as foundations for human resource development theory. *Human Resource Development Review* 4: 86–108.

Weick, K.E. (2009) *Making Sense of the Organization: The Impermanent Organization*, Chichester: John Wiley and Sons.

Werbel, J. and Balkin, D.B. (2010) Are human resource practices linked to employee misconduct? A rational choice perspective. *Human Resource Management Review* 20: 317–26.

Whittle, A. and Mueller, F. (2012) Bankers in the dock: Moral storytelling in action. *Human Relations* 65: 111–39.

Wright, P.M., Dunford, B.B. and Snell, S.A. (2001) Human resources and the resource based view of the firm. *Journal of Management* 27: 701–21.

Yawson, R.M. (2013) Systems theory and thinking as a foundational theory in human resource development: A myth or reality? *Human Resource Development Review* 12: 53–85.

SECTION VIII

HRD around the world

34

NATIONAL AND ORGANIZATIONAL IMPERATIVES FOR HRD IN GHANA

Meera Alagaraja and Nana K. Arthur-Mensah

Globalization has transformed the economic, social and political priorities of countries. Not surprisingly, emergent national priorities underscore an overwhelming focus on human capital development through education, skill and workforce development as countries ready themselves for a global war for jobs (World Bank 2011). Despite this common focus, countries differ in their approaches in developing human resources. Western countries view HRD primarily as a means for achieving economic growth through the private sector with limited government interference (Cunningham *et al.* 2006). In the western context, HRD efforts thus generally identify and address organizational imperatives. In contrast, non-western nations take for granted the primary role of the state or government for enabling a complementary reconciliation of economic and social development outcomes (Cho and McLean 2004). The latter perspective defines National Human Resource Development (NHRD) and emphasizes the importance of national imperatives as an additional focus of HRD efforts. Examining NHRD is significant as it emphasizes the influences of important but often overlooked political, economic, sociocultural factors that shape HRD systems, policies and practices in organizations. We bring together western and non-western perspectives as a means for identifying organizational and national imperatives concerning HRD in Ghana with implications for theory and practice. Building a national and organizational platform for long term success with a general recognition that both economic and social development outcomes are necessary for sustaining global competitiveness entails a different understanding and focus for HRD scholars and practitioners.

The HRD literature offers a small and growing body of research on the status of NHRD in many countries from Europe, Asia and Latin America. The limited country examples from Africa (e.g. Kenya, South Africa) in the HRD literature call for increased attention to countries from this region (Nafukho 2006). The examination of NHRD in Africa is still limited in scope and depth. Thus, the case of Ghana offers a unique opportunity for examining HRD for two reasons. First, few studies examine human capital development in the national contexts of countries in Africa. Second, there is even less literature examining the influences of NHRD issues, opportunities and challenges in organizational contexts. This chapter complements existing literature on Africa by examining the status of HRD research and practice in Ghana.

The chapter is structured as follows. We first begin by examining the importance of HRD as it relates to knowledge, skills and capacity building in Africa. This analysis to some extent explains the broad context of Ghana's strategy for developing human resources and identifies national imperatives for HRD. We trace the evolution of NHRD strategy development and describe the sociocultural context that influences HRD outcomes in Ghanaian organizations. This sociocultural context is a constitutive aspect of HRD policies and practices, and its consideration enhances managerial effectiveness (Kamoche 2002). Indeed, overlaying all aspects of HRD decisions are the sociocultural values, norms and beliefs of Ghana. HRD managers must not only recognize the dynamics underlying issues concerning multicultural identities, diversity, equity, participation and ethical management in organizations, but also engage in taking action on these issues and contribute towards enhancing organizational effectiveness as well as the betterment of the larger society. Therefore, HRD efforts in Ghana must address organizational as well as societal or national imperatives for developing human resources. We outline our conclusions and implications of examining national and organizational imperatives for HRD. In what follows, we describe HRD challenges and opportunities in the larger context of Africa.

HRD perspectives of Africa

Africa is blessed with an abundance of natural resources, and a rich cultural diversity rooted in a collectivist approach where family, community, and societal connections are strongly valued. Thus, even though globalization influences the economic and political environments of African countries, national and organizational imperatives for HRD must also consider cultural diversity, societal values and norms. We elaborate on these selected areas to offer general similarities that African countries share and lay the groundwork for contextualizing African challenges and opportunities that are relevant for HRD in Ghana. Globalization, government interference, sociocultural factors, authoritarian leadership styles, and ineffective management practices constrain Africa's growth, development and prosperity (Kamoche 2002). The lack of a trained and educated workforce complicates poverty reduction efforts (Sydhagen and Cunningham 2007). Furthermore, the elevated demand for talented workers is aggravated by skills migration and brain drain. These labor market changes pose challenges for capacity and capability building in different regions of Africa. For example, Sydhagen and Cunningham (2007) identified increasing productivity, improving living conditions, and access to basic necessities through the development of human potential as predictive factors for effective NHRD strategy in the sub-Saharan region which is comprised of 48 African countries including Ghana. NHRD strategies therefore, must consider training and development, skill based competency development, and workforce development initiatives to overcome the challenges of globalization, poverty and access to basic necessities that characterize most African countries.

Some scholars advocate multiculturalism as the means for advancing human resources (Abdulai 2000; Amenumey and Yawson 2013). Multiculturalism describes the rich ethnic, racial and linguistic diversity of Africa. Many African countries have begun to incorporate multiculturalism in public policy as a means of legitimizing and integrating all communities. Inasmuch as regions, cultures and people can feature great diversity, western scholars sometimes treat African countries as a homogenous group as they are unsure of the unique national characteristics that define each country (Kamoche 2002; Sydhagen and Cunningham 2007). An important consideration is the need for understanding traditional sociocultural African worldviews and their influence in shaping national cultures. Africans as a whole tend to ascribe to the collectivist worldview, which emphasizes relationships (extended family), networks, and obligations to family (relatives), tribe and community (Beugré and Offodile 2001; Nafukho 2006). Cunningham *et al.* (2006: 64) identify Ubuntu as "a strong binding force" that characterizes a shared cultural view common to many African countries. Ubuntu represents deeply ingrained values of interdependence, where individuals experience self-worth through an active connection with society (Beugré 2002; Beugré and Offodile 2001). This cultural characteristic unique to Africa emphasizes interdependence, where self-identity and worth are developed through an active connection with society (Beugré 2002; Beugré and Offodile 2001). Consensus building opportunities are facilitated through dialogue and voicing of individual opinions between stakeholders (Bangura 2005).

The collectivist view emphasizes group outcomes and the subordination of individual interests. In addition, Beugré (2002) identified two additional cultural patterns – power distance and strength of interpersonal networks – to describe African cultural values of interdependence and interconnections between people. Power distance refers to those cultural values, which create unequal levels of power and acceptance between people based on ethnicity, gender, power, authority, prestige, etc. The implication is that racial, ethnic and tribal identities are likely to remain strong and consequently, integration across these diverse groups can be both challenging and difficult. These characteristics do not represent all of the many facets of the African culture. However, they offer basic conceptions and understanding of the sociocultural context and illustrate the complexity of managing people (Kamoche 2002).

The impact of the external environment mainly through globalization and the prevailing internal environment characterized by historical traditions, economy, and sociocultural patterns exert a strong influence on HRD in Africa. These factors mediate the impact of HRD in fully addressing human capital needs through systematic training and development for generating productivity, economic growth and development (Sydhagen and Cunningham 2007). The historical and political remnants of western colonialism (e.g. British, French, Dutch influences) introduced administrative and labor management practices in many African countries. Furthermore, the indigenizing of national economies in the postcolonial era witnessed the growth of wholly owned subsidiaries, joint venture strategic alliances, licensing and franchising, and independent supplier/channel members (Kamoche 2002). The development of business infrastructure emphasized leadership development, technical and vocational education and training (TVET) and skill development of the workforce thus, placing HRD in the forefront of economic development initiatives (Palmer 2007). HRD practices and activities can include helping governments to enact policies that focus on key areas such as education and vocational training to prepare the workforce for operating in a global economy (Marquardt and Berger 2003). To that end, the chapter considers the broad impact of globalization, historical, political, economic and sociocultural features characterizing Africa to frame HRD issues, challenges, and opportunities in the Ghanaian context.

Ghana: background and context

Ghana, formerly known as the Gold Coast, became a colony of Britain in 1874. In 1957, Ghana became the first country in sub-Saharan Africa to gain independence. A constitutional democracy, Ghana is governed by a President who is elected every four years and the constitution prohibits anyone from being elected to a third term. The main economic sectors are agriculture, industry and services such as banking and tourism. Agriculture and mining are foundational to the economy, with major exports being gold, cocoa and diamonds (Daaku 1972). In addition, remittances from abroad are major sources of foreign exchange. Recent discovery of oil and gas in Ghana is expected to further boost economic growth and increase productivity (CIA 2012). With a population of about 24 million, Ghana is multi-ethnic and multi-lingual with English as the official language. The multi-ethnic social fabric of Ghana mirrors the pluralistic/collectivist African worldview where decisions and behaviors are influenced by cultural and societal norms (Khan and Ackers 2004). In order to manage people and develop successful HRD practices, managers must consider the role of the state with its legal frameworks and institutional arrangements, the role of family clans, and the importance of social and economic security for employees. With this brief description of Ghana, the chapter elaborates on the NHRD agenda as set forth by the government of Ghana. First, the evolution of NHRD strategy considers key political and economic factors from the period Ghana gained independence in 1957 to advance understanding of status of HRD. Using the classification scheme developed by Alagaraja and Wang (2012), the chapter traces NHRD strategy development and evolution of HRD strategies and systems. Second, the sociocultural factors which guide the everyday management of HRD practices and policies of Ghanaian organizations are identified.

National HRD in Ghana

The National Development Planning Commission (NDPC) of Ghana identifies the importance of producing a "well educated, skilled and informed population capable of transforming the key sectors of the economy for wealth creation and poverty reduction" (NDPC 2010: 150). In addition, the NDPC targeted the macroeconomic environment for stabilizing Ghanaian economic growth. NDPC focused on education, productivity, employment, health, poverty reduction, population management and social policy, which are commonly shared NHRD priorities with other sub-Saharan countries (Sydhagen and Cunningham 2007). Consistent with the focus on developing HRD capacity and capability building, the NDPC also identified human development, economic growth, rural development, urban development, and providing an inclusive and enabling environment for all Ghanaians (NDPC 2010: 28). We identify education, training and productivity as significant for developing HRD responses to both national and organizational imperatives. Through the NDPC focus on education, training and productivity, it is possible to simultaneously advance HRD and NHRD goals by increasing skills and knowledge for all members of society. This was identified as the most significant factor for Ghana's national development (Mensa-Bonsu 2008). For example, improving the technical proficiency of the workforce benefits HRD efforts in the organization as well as enhances the competitiveness of the workforce in domestic and global markets. Furthermore, an NHRD strategy emphasizing skill development, and lifelong learning of the workforce is necessary for long term capacity and capability building of the country.

Evolution of NHRD strategy

A tremendous level of complexity characterizes the evolution of Ghanaian NHRD strategy from key historical, political and economic milestones. To better organize these efforts, the chapter utilizes the national HRD strategy model developed by Alagaraja and Wang (2012) to identify and develop NHRD strategy development in Ghana as centralized, transitional, government-initiated and neo-market phases, focusing on the role of the government in shaping national priorities for developing human resources. We recognize that these NHRD phases are often arbitrary and inaccurate. Yet, the four phase distinction aids in tracing and organizing historical, political and economic development that informs NHRD strategy. Each phase offers a contextual understanding of the issues, challenges and opportunities, which shaped NHRD strategy and policy making during a particular time period.

Phase 1: centralized NHRD (1957–late 1960s)

During the early postcolonial period, informal and traditional forms of administrative systems described HRD work in organizations (Debrah 2001). The Ghanaian government established a tightly controlled centralized NHRD strategy focused on gaining economic self-sufficiency as well as removing any vestiges of reliance on the British colonial system, which prior to independence had relied on indigenous officers to exercise authority with Ghanaian workers. The central purpose of these efforts constituted the Africanization programme.

The Africanization programme emphasized education, health and industrialization and supported large scale employment in the public sector. Schools and universities stabilized the labor market by supplying a pipeline of qualified professionals. However, by the close of 1960s, the Africanization programme failed to address declining productivity of public sector enterprises which were the biggest source of employment in the country. Additionally, private sector industries received little encouragement from the state and also failed to stimulate economic growth of the country. These economic challenges led to political instability and ushered in a new era of military rule in the country.

Phase 2: transitional NHRD (early 1970s–late 1980s)

During this phase, the political environment was characterized by a series of coups and military rule in Ghana. Political governance in this period also saw power shift from the military to civilian rule. These transitions led to instability and mismanagement of public and government run industries. The accompanying political uncertainty plunged the nation into economic recession. The political leadership (both civilian and military) began to focus on developing the private sector, for stimulating economic development and growth. Foreign investors were encouraged to invest in Ghana through an Economic Recovery Programme (ERP), which streamlined public services, promoted organizational efficiency and effectively leveraged human resources (Debrah 2001). This adoption resulted in massive unemployment in the formal sectors, as public institutions were the largest employers. Despite the negative fallout of the reforms on employees, the programmes were perceived as a step in the right direction for rebuilding the economy (Baah-Boateng 2004; Appiah-Adu 1999). Vocational education was incorporated into primary and secondary education systems as a pathway for equipping students with career readiness skills (Akyeampong 2002). The promotion of free market enterprise had a significant impact on HRD as the emphasis shifted to training and skill development as well as the effective management of people for enhancing the performance of local firms. Unlike other African countries in the sub-Saharan region, Ghana continued to evolve through experimentation with different political governance structures, enduring periods of political change by focusing on economic growth and prosperity.

Phase 3: government-initiated NHRD (1990s–2000)

During this period, Ghanaian government instituted laws and labor related legislations, which profoundly impacted HRD activities and practices. For example, the Vision 2020 blue print laid the foundation for an ambitious economic and social development programme (Debrah 2001). The emphasis on social development addressed growing unemployment as a result of massive retrenchment of workers from public sector enterprises as well as the decline of key industries in the manufacturing sector (Debrah 2001). Investments in higher education, training and skill development of personnel from the earlier decades which had emphasized liberal education over career readiness were no longer deemed as sustainable in the newly adopted free market system (Abdulai 2000; Baah-Boateng 2004). The introduction of free market enterprise was encouraged by the World Bank and International Monetary Fund (IMF) that helped in restructuring existing public sector enterprises including banking and financial regulatory agencies. Additional reforms in the financial sector offered more access to capital for improving operational capacities and capabilities of local firms in diverse sectors (Appiah-Kubi 2001).

Phase 4: neo-market NHRD (2000–2013)

Ghana continued to grow as a result of economic reforms, which reduced inflation and consolidated fiscal activities. The National Trade Policy was developed in 2005 with the aim of increasing international competitiveness and securing markets for Ghanaian products (African Economic Outlook 2007). This policy resulted in broad based growth across many sectors of the economy such as agriculture, industry, manufacturing, and tourism albeit at varying levels. Gondwe and Walenkamp (2011) reported agriculture, services and the mining industry as key productive sectors in Ghana. Although manufacturing is an important sector in Ghana, robust growth has been hampered by the high cost of production and the influx of cheaper imports. The development of favourable macroeconomic policies was meant to encourage the growth of the public sector (African Economic Outlook 2007). Additional economic reforms included the growth and poverty reduction strategy (GPRS) for 2006–2009, for enabling an environment where different sectors of the economy could flourish. Competitive market forces stipulated the demand for a skilled workforce. Consequently, private, public and small to medium enterprises (SMEs) received government support for meeting these demands (Mankin 2009). The focus on economic growth, poverty reduction, investment in key sectors, and the need for workforce training and development suggest several characteristics of a neo-market NHRD classification.

We examined the evolution of NHRD strategy development in Ghana in four phases. The identification of centralized, transitional, government-initiated and neo-market phases laid the groundwork for examination of Ghana's responses to historical, political and economic challenges with a focus on developing many aspects of human resources. We find that these phases signal the ability and willingness of HRD in Ghana to engage in developing skills, knowledge, education and training of people for advancing economic growth and sustainable development.

Even though NHRD strategy formulation and implementation is an important factor, it does not provide a complete explanation for Ghana's relative success in comparison to other African countries. Other factors also need due consideration to better understand Ghana's success in the African context which are explained as follows. Ghana, unlike most countries in sub-Saharan Africa did not experience civil wars. Thus, an environment of relative stability helped to sustain political changes and economic reforms over time. Even though the country underwent decades of military rule, the political structure matured to a democratic style of governance. Strong, independent media and constitutional support for the peaceful transfer of power from one elected government to the next created an enabling environment for economic growth and prosperity. Historical, political and economic influences are embedded in the sociocultural values, beliefs and norms that contextualize HRD work in Ghana. Only by understanding and integrating the complexity of the sociocultural context can HRD respond to national and organization level imperatives. This belief is elaborated in the next section.

Sociocultural influences on HRD

Sociocultural contexts have the potential to shape HRD and HRM outcomes in relation to training, staffing, compensation, organizational development and change. The principles of free market systems value economic rationality, bureaucratic efficiency and the primacy of the individual. These values often come in conflict with the collectivist values of the Ghanaian social system. For many Ghanaians, society, community and family values are far more important than the work itself (Khan and Ackers 2004). Commitment to family, society and community is significantly valued in comparison to their commitment to work. As a result, networks and relationships often undermine fairness in recruitment and selection practices as employees are pressured to hire family members and relatives. These values create barriers for developing fair and just HRD practices; as well as undermine the efficiency and effectiveness of HRD systems. Organizational practices must integrate indigenous sociocultural values to fully realize the benefits of the free market economic system as advocated by Ghana's NHRD agenda. Instead of a blind replication of western management style of functioning, effective HRD practices and policies relevant to the Ghanaian context must be encouraged to evolve over time. Organizational effectiveness and efficiency as defined by western theory and practice may have to be reconceptualized to yield effective economic development outcomes.

HRD perspectives in Ghana

Ghana, like most African countries borrowed the concept and definition of HRD from the western world. Thus, HRD is viewed in terms of unleashing human expertise and talent for the benefit of the organization (Swanson and Holton 2009). HRD's role in building performance capabilities is enhanced by the nature and content of skills training, professional development, involvement of different stakeholders, management of rewards, career advancement opportunities and positive working environments (Abdulai 2000; Antwi and Analoui 2008). These HRD responses effectively address organizational needs and improve performance. Furthermore, as a response to the NHRD strategy agenda (e.g. privatization of industries), Ghanaian HRD must also address national imperatives concerning long term human resource capacity building through investments in workforce development, technical and vocational education training, and linking secondary and higher secondary education goals to labor market needs. Combined together, the national and organizational imperatives call for HRD to focus on capacity and capability building that has as its primary emphasis education, knowledge development, skills training and competency building for all Ghanaians (Amenumey and Yawson 2013; Franks 1999). The Ghanaian HRD perspective takes a long term view of development with a focus on interpersonal relationships and a collective orientation; therefore, HRD must engage with the national economic agenda, consider the sociocultural context of the organization, and integrate economic outcomes with the social mission of serving the family, community and society.

Status of HRD practices

The HRD role has been limited to medium and large sized enterprises in manufacturing and service industries in both private and public sector organizations. Ahadzie *et al.* (2009) report increasing emphasis on professional certification, competency profiling, curriculum development and credentialing in several industry sectors as a way for sustaining on the job learning and performance. These changes caused a significant shift in perception of the strategic value of the HRD function (Debrah 2001). Some of the major challenges for HRD practices in Ghana include the lack of key personnel in critical areas (leadership in senior positions including the government), unavailability of training and development programs for local staff, mismatch in the supply and demand of skills, and the lack of coordination among key stakeholders in private, public and government organizations for addressing long term educational needs of the society (Abdulai 2000). HRD managers must focus their efforts on reducing discrimination based on gender, ethnicity and regional backgrounds, ensuring fair standards of practice in the administration of salaries and wages, increasing transparency in decision making, maintaining consistency in hiring, compensation and incentive practices. These HRD efforts would be valuable for Ghanaian organizations (Abdulai 2010; Debrah 2001; Turkson 2010). HRD systems fail when managerial decisions are made based on the strength of interpersonal ties or for political expediencies, which in turn lead to corruption, nepotism and other unethical management practices. HRD must focus on leadership training and development so as to align HRD practices to the strategic goals of the organization (Aryee 2004; Debrah 2001).

According to Debrah (2001), the inherent tension between Ghanaian cultural dimensions (e.g. collectivism, masculinity), and western management styles sometimes undermines individual, team and departmental performance in organizations. The sociocultural values influence managerial decisions based on seniority, status, as well as increased power distance and gender differences. For example, disciplinary actions are often not carried out as managers defer to seniority and status. Because of the sensitivity to networks, relationships, seniority, age, and authority, communication tends to be indirect and highly contextual. As a result, responsibility and accountability do not rest with the individual employee or manager. The prevailing high power distance in the Ghanaian culture makes those in power often less accountable to other members of the society. This orientation affects learning and performance in the organization as workers are expected to take directives from superiors without raising questions (Sydhagen and Cunningham 2007). Aryee (2004) offers a different perspective suggesting that employment relations in the Ghanaian and to a larger extent in the African organizational systems can also have some positive impact on organizational effectiveness. When employees perceive that they are being fairly treated through compensation, rewards, incentives and training and development opportunities, they "reciprocate with attitudes and behaviors that promote organizational effectiveness" (Aryee 2004: 131). HRD managers must recognize the inherent differences and divergence of Ghanaian sociocultural values from western business ideologies. In an organizational context, HRD can lean towards a "crossvergence" view that caters to individual and collective interests (Kamoche 2002). Thus, for example, HRD policies and practices can reward and incentivize both teamwork and individual performance to ensure that the full value and contributions of employees are realized.

Implications for HRD practice and research

This chapter identified national and organizational imperatives for HRD in Ghana. The national imperatives relevant for HRD in Ghana will continue to focus on workforce development, technical and vocational education, literacy and basic education for all citizens. These imperatives address the challenges of globalization and place national economic development at the centre of NHRD efforts. The organizational imperatives call for inclusion, access to professional development opportunities, introduction of organization development and change efforts for fostering positive work environments. Both these imperatives call for HRD responses to the ongoing changes involved in bringing together traditional Ghanaian sociocultural values with western management practices and leadership styles. By emphasizing the traditional approaches that are suitable for Ghana and incorporating free market value orientations and systems in organizations, HRD can support "crossvergence with regard to high-performance work practices" (Kamoche 2002: 995). Thus, HRD managers must understand the underlying dynamics of interactions between sociocultural influences and western business ideologies and develop new and unique value systems for improving organizations and society. HRD managers must also anticipate and address confusions arising out of crossvergence of HRD practices, policies and systems for the workforce. HRD research needs to explore the integrative complexity that arises from the implementation of western models of economic development given Ghana's unique historical, political, economic and sociocultural context.

Although western literature has made significant contributions in the management and development of HRD initiatives for economic performance, these theories must consider socio-cultural influences if they are to reflect the reality of the organizations operating in other country contexts (Kamoche 1997; Khan and Ackers 2004). The uniqueness of the organizational context must consider "equity, competence creation with cooperative teamwork, corporate welfarism, traditionalism, community spirit and social harmony" (Kamoche 1997: 547). The formulation and implementation of HRD strategy must be grounded in the national value systems. These influences should be well managed for training and development as well as career management, managing rewards and compensation.

The renewed focus on training and development, TVET, skills training and macroeconomic policies indicates that human resource priorities will continue to dominate Ghanaian NHRD efforts. Furthermore, organizational related HRD strategies require specific interventions to address the lack of skills in critical industry sectors, succession planning, developing a pipeline of talented managers, reducing skilled migration of workforce, attracting Ghanaian expatriates, and reducing political interference in HRD activities. These efforts improve HRD value not only in the organizational context but also at the national level, which are foundational for Ghana's continued success and growth.

References

Abdulai, A.I. (2000) 'Human resource management in Ghana: prescriptions and issues raised by the Fourth Republican Constitution', *International Journal of Public Sector Management* 13(5): 447–66.

African Economic Outlook (2007) Retrieved online at http://www.oecd.org/dev/emea/africaneconomic outlook2007.htm.

Ahadzie, D.K., Proverbs, D.G., Olomolaiye, P.O. and Ankrah, N.A. (2009) 'Competencies required by project managers for housing construction in Ghana', *Engineering, Construction and Architectural Management* 16: 353–75.

Akyeampong, A. (2002) 'Vocationalization of secondary education in Ghana, a case study', paper prepared for the Regional Vocational Skills Development Review. Washington, DC: The World Bank.

Alagaraja, M. and Wang, J. (2012) 'Development of a National HRD strategy model: cases of India and China', *Human Resource Development Review* 11: 407–29.

Amenumey, F. and Yawson, R.M. (2013) 'Conceptualization and description of HRD in Ghana', Proceedings of the 20th Annual AHRD International Research Conference in the Americas. Arlington, VA.

Antwi, K.B. and Analoui, F. (2008) 'Challenges in building the capacity of human resource development in decentralized local governments', *Management Research News* 31: 504–17.

Appiah-Adu, K. (1999) 'The impact of economic reform on business performance: a study of foreign and domestic firms in Ghana', *International Business Review* 8: 463–86.

Appiah-Kubi, K. (2001) 'State-owned enterprises and privatisation in Ghana', *Journal of Modern African Studies* 39: 197–229.

Aryee, S. (2004) 'HRM in Ghana', in Kamoche, K.N., Debrah, Y.A., Horwitz, F.M. and Muuka, G.N. (eds) *Managing Human Resources in Africa*, New York: Routledge.

Baah-Boateng, W. (2004) 'Employment policies for sustainable development: the experience of Ghana', workshop on employment framework for Ghana's poverty reduction strategy. Government of Ghana/ UNDP/ILO. May 7, 2004. Accra, Ghana.

Bangura, A.K. (2005) 'Ubuntugogy: an African educational paradigm that transcends pedagogy, andragogy, ergonagy and heutagogy', *Journal of Third World Studies* 22: 13–53.

Beugré, C.D. (2002) 'Understanding organizational justice and its impact on managing employees: an African perspective', *International Journal of Human Resource Management* 13: 1091–104.

Beugré, C.D. and Offodile, O.F. (2001) 'Managing for organizational effectiveness in sub-Saharan Africa: a culture-fit model', *International Journal of Human Resource Management* 12: 535–50.

Cho, E. and McLean, G.N. (2004) 'What we discovered about NHRD and what it means for HRD', *Advances in Developing Human Resources* 6: 382–93.

CIA (2012) *World Factbook*. Retrieved online at https://www.cia.gov/library/publications/the-world-factbook/geos/gh.html.

Cunningham, P.W., Lynham, S.A. and Weatherly, G. (2006) 'National human resource development in transitioning societies in the developing world: South Africa,' *Advances in Developing Human Resources* 8: 62–83.

Daaku, K.Y. (1972) 'Aspects of pre-colonial Akan economy,' *International Journal of African Historical Studies* 5: 235–47.

Debrah, Y. (2001) 'Human resource management in Ghana', in Budhwar, P.S. and Debrah, Y.A. (eds) *Human Resource Management in Developing Countries*, London: Routledge.

Franks, T. (1999) 'Capacity building and institutional development: reflections on water', *Public Administration and Development* 19: 51–61.

Gondwe, M. and Walenkamp, J. (2011) *Alignment of Higher Professional Education with the Needs of the Local Labour Market: The case of Ghana*, The Hague: NUFFIC and The Hague University of Applied Sciences.

Kamoche, K. (1997) 'Managing human resources in Africa: strategic, organizational and epistemological issues', *International Business Review* 6: 537–58.

Kamoche, K. (2002) 'Introduction: human resource management in Africa', *International Journal of Human Resource Management* 13: 993–97.

Khan, A.S. and Ackers, P. (2004) 'Neo-pluralism as a theoretical framework for understanding HRM in sub-Saharan Africa', *International Journal of Human Resource Management* 15: 1330–53.

Mankin, D. (2009) *Human Resource Development*, New York: Oxford University Press.

Marquardt, M. and Berger, N.O. (2003) 'The future: globalization and new roles for HRD', *Advances in Developing Human Resources* 5: 283–95.

Mensa-Bonsu, I.F. (2008) 'Ghana's development agenda: past and present', paper presented at KOAFEC On-The-Spot Workshop for West Africa. Accra, Ghana.

Nafukho, F.M. (2006) 'Ubuntu worldview: a traditional African view of adult learning in the workplace', *Advances in Developing Human Resources* 8: 408–15.

NDPC (2010) 'The implementation of the Ghana shared growth and development agenda (GSGDA), 2010–2013'. Accra, Ghana: National Development Planning Commission (NDPC). Retrieved online at http://www.ndpc.gov.gh/Downloads.html.

Palmer, R. (2007) 'Skills for work: from skills development to decent livelihoods in Ghana's rural informal economy', *International Journal of Educational Development* 27: 397–420.

Swanson, R.A., and Holton, E.F., III (2009) *Foundations of Human Resource Development*, 2nd edn, San Francisco, CA: Berrett-Koehler.

Sydhagen, K. and Cunningham, P.C. (2007) 'Human resource development in sub-Saharan Africa', *Human Resource Development International* 10: 121–35.

Turkson, J.K. (2010) 'Human resource planning as a tool for managing staff stability in selected institutions in Ghana', *Business Review, Cambridge* 16: 284–91.

World Bank (2011) *Africa Development Indicators*, Washington, DC: World Bank.

35

VOCATIONAL EDUCATION AND TRAINING POLICY ISSUES IN SOUTH AFRICA

Andre Kraak

This chapter examines state policy reform in the Further Education and Training (FET) College sector in South Africa over the past decade. The reforms, intended to make college curricula more responsive to employer needs, have achieved the opposite effect: employer disillusionment. The analysis argues that the reforms have resulted in a supply-led system of vocational education and training (VET) provision in South Africa as has occurred in other Anglo-Saxon countries. More specifically, the FET college sector reforms were centrally imposed with little consultation with employers. The results have been disastrous. College success rates have plummeted and a high percentage of college graduates face unemployment.

Anglo-Saxon traditions

Historically, the skills regimes of most Anglo-Saxon countries – the United Kingdom, South Africa, New Zealand, Australia and Canada – have come to share similar institutional features including those of the education and training system. For example, the FET colleges in each of these countries reflect very similar characteristics. These countries also share many of the same institutional weaknesses.

Convergence of policy reforms intensified in the 1980s and 1990s with the spread of neo-liberal public sector reforms across the globe. Many of the public sector reforms initially introduced in the United Kingdom (UK) were borrowed and copied across the Anglo-Saxon world. In South Africa, this included the introduction of sector skills councils (SSCs), a national qualifications framework (NQF), competitive funding arrangements, 'New Public Management' methods of performance appraisal and target setting, and important for this chapter, a new set of national vocational qualifications (NVQs) introduced in the FET College sector.

The main area of policy convergence – and policy weakness – has been the adoption of 'supply side' interventions in the VET system – for example, increasing the number of people acquiring an NVQ each year. However, this approach has received considerable criticism recently – especially in the UK and South Africa – because the vast investments in building the supply-side architecture (including the SSCs, the NQF and a plethora of NVQs) have not produced an equivalent outcome with respect to increased numbers of skilled people. Nor are countries such as the UK and South

Africa more productive and competitive after nearly two decades of supply-side restructuring. The supply side model is not working.

Keep and James (2012) view this policy orientation as a misdiagnosis of the knowledge-based economy. They identify a range of problems affecting the UK labor market and economy, including:

- Narrow VET qualifications with limited underpinning of academic content, especially in literacy and numeracy
- Low returns to VET qualifications and limited opportunities for progression from NVQs back into further and higher education
- An underlying lack of demand for higher skills from employers
- An ideological opposition to any form of 'hard' or 'soft' industrial policy aimed at steering firms toward higher value-added production

Keep and James 2012: 217–21

Each of the problems listed above is individually a serious cause for concern, but acting together as a mutually reinforcing matrix of forces, they produce pressures on employers to not raise their demand for higher skills. They also contribute to individuals perceiving the incentives to learn in relation to employment as weak and not worth the effort (Keep and James 2012: 222). The solution proposed by governments such as those in the UK and South Africa – of increasing the supply of skilled and semi-skilled labor – is an inappropriate strategy given low employer demand for increased skills.

An alternative approach

The critique of supply-side dominance of education and training policy in the Anglo-Saxon world (but also within the Organization for Economic Cooperation and Development (OECD) community globally) has grown exponentially over the past decade. There is now an emerging consensus from a number of disciplinary fields that demand-side interventions are necessary and that they are most effectively achieved by the integration of 'economic development' and 'work-force development' strategies in regional and local labor market settings. Three of these contributions will be summarized below: the work of the 'Oxford/SKOPE' school, the work of the OECD on upgrading skills, and research on the community college system in the USA.

Low employer demand for skill

A group of 'education and economy' researchers based at Oxford (Keep and James 2012) have played a prominent role in highlighting the flaws of the supply-side route in the UK. In doing so, they have worked closely with the *Skills, Knowledge and Organisational Performance* (SKOPE) research network based at Oxford and Cardiff Universities (Sung *et al.* 2009). These writers have all been prominent critics of the supply-side approach since the 1990s.

The 'Oxford/SKOPE' school argues firstly, that the product market or competitive strategy of a firm determines a firm's demand for skill – and not national government's skills policy. Secondly, the way in which this competitive strategy shapes the utilization of skills on the factory floor is seen to be a result of the choices made by firms in using the skills of its employees (Sung *et al.* 2009: 3). Two important factors reflect employer choice: (1) the technologies used by employers and (2) the management of production systems and the high performance working practices they adopt (Sung *et al.* 2009: 6). Improvements in skill are not sufficient on their own to move a company's product market strategy up the value chain. This movement requires investments in capital equipment, product development and managerial innovation (Sung *et al.* 2009: 8).

Re-shaping employer demand

The OECD has also made a significant contribution to this debate. The OECD work on skills development is led, surprisingly, by its Local Employment and Economic Development (LEED) research directorate and not by its Education research division. LEED has published a number of monographs over the past decade on partnerships, decentralization and skills upgrading. Skills development is increasingly being viewed as a key component of local economic strategies aimed at creating new jobs through the facilitation of firm restructuring to increase productivity as well as through the creation of new jobs in the 'green' economy (OECD 2013: 13).

This more pro-active role will not be accomplished through the traditional passive labor market policy of matching jobseekers with vacancies, training the unemployed and subsidizing employment for the most disadvantaged workers. The OECD argues that this approach should be superseded by a more active labor market intervention where employment and training agencies become major economic players in local and regional settings through interacting with firms to build their competitiveness.

What the OECD is suggesting is that skills upgrading lies at the core of what drives local economies. In many industries, 'learning by doing' within the firm and collectivities of firms is the best way to develop skills. It requires a localized development focus (OECD 2012a: 56).

Partnerships are a core component of this OECD focus. Local partnerships typically involve businesses, NGOs, VET institutions and local and regional government. Partnerships create more opportunities for local innovation, and utilize the skills and tacit knowledge of specific communities – for example, those organized in 'cluster' and other forms of 'agglomeration' economies. The key priority in this environment is the continuous upgrading of skills as product market and production processes change (OECD 2012a: 52).

This alternative insight into the skill needs of employers throws up an entirely different set of intervention practices to those commonly associated with supply-side VET. It requires localized and regional interventions at firm level to support firm-level adaptive learning – strategies to improve value-added and competitiveness through changes to the organization of work and deployment of skills. This approach will require a broader concept of 'business support' to improve competitiveness and not merely skills improvement.

This analysis is congruent with the Oxford/SKOPE approach. It argues that policy makers in the field of workforce development should play a major role in joined-up strategies to help 'shape' employer demand for skills, steering the local economy towards higher value-added production (OECD 2012b: 65).

Breaking down silos

The task of integrating the work of local and regional economic development agencies with that of skills development agencies is not a simple or straightforward one. Much of what the OECD is arguing currently is heavily shaped by the experience of economic and workforce development agencies in the USA – two distinct types of agencies which now work together. This cooperation was not always the case – previously these agencies 'worked in silos and there was not much collaboration' (OECD 2012c: 8).

Generally, in most countries across the globe, policies to support skills and economic development are delivered by separate government departments and ministries. Public officials from education and economic development departments pursue different strategies which involve different actors and the outcomes often contradict one another. For example, employment and skills are often managed in a labor supply perspective, while economic development is run from the demand point of view. The results of this fragmentation on implementation are severe. Intended outcomes are often not achieved while unintended and unforeseen discrepancies emerge, making the policy terrain more complicated and messy (OECD 2008: 25).

Such divisions are often taken for granted, blamed on historical working relationships and organizational cultures. However, the OECD argues that such silos can be reduced through injecting greater flexibility into the management of policies, and through the implementation of effective local governance arrangements (OECD 2011: 3).

The role of the college sector

The community college sector in the USA is cited by the OECD as playing an important role in demand-side upskilling – a role executed in partnership with employers, state-level government departments and NGOs. The American experience is an unlikely inspiration for skills development given that it has no formal VET policy or vocational institutions – other than the community college system itself. However, it is the 'policy integration' of economic and workforce development initiatives in the USA over the past two decades that has been significant – and a source of inspiration for much of the OECD's emphasis on building skills strategies at the local and regional level (OECD 2008: 58, 61; see also Osterman 2010).

The South African college sector

The South African college sector played a central role, historically, in training white workers for artisanal labor in the racially segregated Apartheid economy throughout most of the twentieth century. Originally started as technical institutes to service the mines and manufacturing plants that emerged around Johannesburg in the early 1900s, these institutions grew in number and size and became known as technical colleges after 1923 (Kraak and Perold 2003: 328–29). By 1994, the year in which democracy was established in South Africa, 152 such colleges were spread across the country. However, a number of problems faced the new democratic government when it came into office in 1994. Colleges formerly restricted to white learners were located in the big cities closer to industry, whereas colleges designated for Africans were located in the former 'homelands' and far from sites of employment. The de-racialization of these colleges was the first priority and this occurred relatively quickly. In 1991, a total of 76,435 students were enrolled in technical colleges – two-thirds of these were white. By 2000, the sector had grown to 350,465 headcounts, and this growth was largely due to a 75 per cent increase in African enrolments (Kraak and Perold 2003: 331).

A second problem facing the new government was that of a very outdated curriculum which employers did not support. The apprenticeship system, which had so effectively supported white learners throughout the twentieth century, was now in severe decline, as was the case in other Anglo-Saxon countries during this time. Curriculum reform was urgently needed. Government began to attend to this problem only in 2007 because of other more pressing institutional changes and policy reforms.

The period 2000–2010 was a turbulent time for the FET College sector. National government intervened with at least six major policy initiatives. The first of these occurred in July 2001 with the publication of *A New Institutional Landscape* (DoE 2001), which recommended the establishment of 50 public FET colleges created out of the merger of 152 former technical colleges. Responsibility for implementing the mergers fell to the nine Provincial Education Departments. This difficult process of change was finalized in 2006. A primary aim of these mergers was to create a set of mega-institutions comprising consolidated resources and systems which would be able to overcome some of the historical inequalities which existed between the 152 Apartheid-built former technical colleges.

The passing of the *FET Colleges Act* in 2006 was a second key moment in government attempts to transform the sector. The Act focused primarily on the construction of a new vision for the sector as a 'modern, vibrant FET college system' built on a 'foundation of lifelong learning and responsive to the needs of the twenty-first Century' (DoE 2008: 8). A key component of this modernization was the launching of a new curriculum framework – the National Certificate Vocational (NCV) – but also, a new governance structure with independent college councils granted significant autonomy to steer institutions and employ their own staff.

The national certificate vocational

The launch of the new NCV curriculum in 2007 was by far the most decisive (and third) moment for the FET College sector in terms of institutional change. It had a dramatic impact on the sector, both positive and negative. The NCV represented a major initiative to shift college provision away from past forms of training which had been perceived to be based on a rather narrow trade training model. Government sought through the NCV to focus on 'general vocational programmes which supported the development of vocational skills with a sufficient breadth of knowledge and a strong general education foundation' (DoE 2008: 14).

The NCV curriculum at NQF Levels 2, 3 and 4 (school grades 10, 11 and 12) was developed in 2006, workshopped with stakeholders and finally implemented for the first time in January 2007. Its rollout in the period 2007–2010 had a disruptive impact on the sector, triggering several new problems including a rapid decline in enrolments in the old trade-oriented national 'N' programmes (the theoretical component of the old apprenticeship system). In particular, the change management process around the NCV was problematic, with insufficient institutional support going to train FET College lecturers to cope with the new curricula, and with extremely blunt instruments steering the restructuring. For example, funding norms were introduced which prioritized NCV enrolments at the expense of 'N' enrolments (which received no funding). An 80 per cent cap was also imposed on college enrolments – only 20 per cent of enrolments would be allowed in programmes other than the NCV (DoE 2008: 15). These blunt instruments were not sufficiently sensitive to the difficulties of change and transition.

The fourth change of the decade came in June 2009 with the installation of a new political administration under the leadership of President Jacob Zuma. A number of new government departments were created, including the new integrated, post-school 'Department of Higher Education and Training' (DHET), which was ceded regulatory authority over three critical sub-sectors of the post-school system: FET Colleges, Higher Education and Skills Development.

FET Colleges have for a long period been administered at the provincial government level. Ever since 1994, this responsibility fell to the nine Provincial Departments of Education. However, in June 2009, FET Colleges became a national competence as is the case for higher education. This was a dramatic reversal of steering mechanisms proposed in the *FET Plan* released only 6 months earlier (in December 2008), which focused on the role of the 'Inter-Provincial Committee for FET Colleges'. Prior to June 2009, these provincial bodies were the institutional architecture that drove the implementation of FET policies in the nine provinces (DoE 2008: 18).

The fifth and most recent policy intervention in the FET College sector was the publication of the *Green Paper for Post School Education and Training* released in January 2012 (DHET 2012). The Green Paper commits the DHET to a number of new and ambitious targets to be attained by 2030: the department wants to see university headcount enrolments reach 1.5 million by 2030 (almost double current enrolments) and 4 million headcount enrolments in colleges and other post-school institutions (DHET 2012: 5). It also believes that the integration of education and training functions into a single unified national Department of Higher Education and Training (DHET) will resolve many of the problems previously faced in the VET sector.

The rise and fall of the NCV and 'N' programmes

As indicated in the introduction, the NCV was introduced in 2007 to solve a wide array of problems associated with the N courses. These had to do with poor quality teaching, weak linkages with industry and antiquated technology (DHET 2010: 27). The 'N' courses were trade-oriented and not sufficiently flexible to allow expansion outside of the traditionally narrow confines of engineering. In particular, it was a poor curricula framework for new occupational fields emerging in the services sector.

In its attempt to modernize the curriculum, government stipulated that all fourteen new fields of the NVC incorporate fundamentals such as language and mathematics. Its greater attention to the integration of theory and practice means that the NCV has become more academically challenging than the N programmes (DHET 2009: 1). It requires all students to enroll for a Language, Life Orientation (includes a business computing component) and Mathematics or Mathematical Literacy course over and above their four vocational subjects per NQF level. These additional requirements attempt to compensate for weaknesses evident in the basic education system (DHET 2010: 28). The NCV represents a dramatic shift in curriculum structure and process away from the old 'N' mode of teaching.

In practice, a whole series of problems have emerged in its short lifespan of six years which has undermined its potential impact. The next section will discuss a number of these problems – many of them unexpected and unintended.

NCV and N enrolments

The flat structure of enrolments over the past decade has been a major underpinning problem facing the sector. Enrolments in 2010 comprised 326,898 headcount learners, distributed across the following programmes:

Table 35.1 Total enrolments, FET college sector, 2007–2010

	Total 'N' Enrolments	*Total 'NCV' Enrolments*	*Other Enrolments*	*Total Enrolled*
2007	245 230	31 414	45 449	322 093
2008	178 086	81 742	41 250	301 078
2009	175 999	166 469	42 638	385 106
2010	169 803	122 257	40 520	332 580

Source: Cosser *et al*. (2012).

As is evident in Table 35.1, aggregate enrolment has remained relatively flat during the period 2007–2010 despite government policy which has sought to expand enrolments up to 1 million learners by 2014, and despite extensive financial investments in the sector. In 2007 government introduced bursaries for poor students enrolling for the National NCV to assist with fees but even this intervention has not boosted aggregate enrolments in the sector. Contributing factors to this decline are as yet not determined by research, but one factor of concern is the fairly dramatic decline of the N programmes. Enrolments in the N1–N3 fields have been brutally shut down, including Engineering Studies which comprises a key leg in the training of artisans in South Africa. Most apprenticeship programmes aiming to increase the number of mechanical and electrical artisans require both theoretical training at a college (in this case, the N1–N3 courses in Engineering Studies) and supervised practical work experience at a workplace over a three year period. The primary reason for the reduction in the N1–N3 engineering courses was to make space for the new NCV programmes which were introduced in 2007.

Another factor in this enrolment decline is that government has erroneously acted to restrict the growth of post-N3 enrolments for more than a decade. For example, in 2001 the *New Institutional Landscape* document instructed the sector to focus only on N1–N3 provision rather than the Post-N3 levels. The document suggested reducing Post-N3 delivery to no more than 10 per cent of total provision. In 2006, the *FET Act* capped the provision of NQF Level 5 and 6 (higher education level) courses in FET Colleges, requiring prior Ministerial approval. These programmes must also be managed under the authority of an accredited higher education provider. The *FET Plan* of 2008 suggested that only 20 per cent of provision should be in non-NCV related training programmes – including post-FET courses.

As a consequence of these rather short-sighted directives, Post-N3 provision was reduced from 57 per cent of total enrolments in 1998 to 44 per cent by 2010. This trajectory of restriction poses problems today for those colleges that have the ability to build stronger articulation pathways between the FET colleges and higher education, particularly the universities of technology.

It is a strange irony, therefore, that enrolments in the N4–N6 programmes continue to remain relatively large in 2010, in defiance of the restrictive government policy during the 2007–2009 era. The current composition of the FET College system has become highly distorted because of the 'blunt' instruments used to enforce change over the past decade. Its current programmatic composition is as presented in Table 35.2.

Table 35.2 Programme composition of the FET college system by programme type, 2010

Program	*Total Enrolments*	*Percentage*
1 N1–N3 (FET level provision)	24 939	7
2 N4–N6 (Post-FET provision)	144 864	43
3 NCV	122 257	38
4 'Other'	40 520	12
TOTAL	332 580	100

Source: Cosser *et al*. (2012).

Tough curriculum standards

As indicated earlier, the NCV comprises a far higher curriculum standard than that applied previously to the 'N' programmes. Creating a new curriculum with higher cognitive and pedagogic demands than its precursor has created new problems for the sector. For example, to acquire an NCV certificate, students need to achieve 40 per cent in the two fundamental (compulsory) subjects: the required official language and Life Orientation. They also need to achieve 30 per cent in Mathematics or Mathematical Literacy (another compulsory module). Lastly, they need to achieve 50 per cent in all four vocational subjects (DHET 2009: 5).

It appears as if many learners do not meet these compulsory requirements and are unable to proceed to the next NCV level – from NCV level 2 to NCV Levels 3 and 4. They might have passed a few of the seven modules in each NCV level but they do not attain the full qualification. The department has made an administrative decision that learners can progress to the next NCV level carrying a maximum of three failed subjects which they would need to 'catch up'. This has now created a huge bottle neck in the system which is difficult to clear. This problem has definitely affected completion rates at the NCV Level 4 although the exact scale of these progression problems is not yet known.

Poor completion rates

Accurate data on NCV completion rates are hard to come by. Progression rates at the 'full qualification' level – for example, reporting on those who attained the NCV Level 2, NCV Level 3 and NCV Level 4 – are extremely low. For example, in 2009, 8,216 learners graduated with NCV Level 2 and 789 with NCV Level 3. However, total enrolments in NCV Level 2 in 2009 comprised 93,293 candidates and 24,637 for NCV Level 3 (DHET 2009: 19). This suggests a completion rate of 8.8 per cent for NCV L2 and 3.2 per cent for NCV L3. Cohort progression rates (comprising all three years of the senior secondary school vocational track – NCV2, NCV3, and NCV4) appear to be equally low. For example, of the 26,540 students that enrolled for NCV Level 2 in 2007, only 1,194 passed the Level 4 NCV examinations in 2009 – a 4.4 per cent 'cohort' progression rate. Colleges have not been able to grow new enrolments in 2010 because of the backlog of mature students needing to repeat failed subjects.

Curricula not aligned to industry

Many employers and vocational education specialists claim that the NCV has not been adequately aligned to the needs of industry. In addition, colleges are currently ill-equipped to help students find workplace experience (Kraak 2008). Given all of these problems, the NCV does not represent a huge improvement over the shortcomings of the N courses, which were criticized for precisely the same problem. Colleges have also not succeeded in forging partnerships with other institutions in society such as employers, the sector skills councils, and NGOs working in the youth labor market. In the absence of strong societal linkages, the colleges have become very isolated, failing to help construct pathways for graduates into work.

Conclusion

The past decade has been a period of dramatic change for the FET College sector – change which unfortunately has triggered considerable institutional instability. Key features of this crisis have been described, including many of the unexpected and unintended consequences of poorly implemented change. Many of these policy errors have been acknowledged by the new political administration that came into office in 2009. As a consequence, government has reversed some of the more problematic decisions made earlier in the transition. Firstly, the department decided in December 2009 to delay the phasing out of the N1–3 courses, essentially to allow colleges to continue to register students for N1–3 courses where there is demonstrable industry support (DHET 2010: 30). The Green Paper agreed with this decision to 'extend the life of these artisan-oriented programmes until the N courses are fully reviewed'. The Green Paper notes that 'there will continue to be a need for the colleges to offer programmes which constitute the theoretical component of apprenticeships that are being revived and strengthened' (DHET 2012: 23).

Secondly, the FET Round Table and Summit processes in 2010 noted that the N4–N6 courses provide 'a useful pathway for students from the FET college sector, as well as adult learners only able to study part-time, to enter higher education' (DHET 2010: 30). The DHET has committed to re-looking at ways of establishing linkages for students between FET colleges and higher education programmes (DHET 2010: 30). The Green Paper also acknowledges that 'there is an urgent need to review and replace or improve the N4–N6 programmes' (DHET 2012: 23).

The most significant change of all has been the transfer of administrative control over FET Colleges from provincial to a single unified national government department, DHET. This action has required substantial changes to FET legislation and to the country's constitution. These legislative reforms were formalized on the 15th May 2012 when the Further Education and Training Colleges Amendment Act was signed into law by the President – a move which has effectively put all FET Colleges in the country under the authority of the national Department of Higher Education and Training. It is too soon to tell whether a unified department will make a difference in resolving problems in the college sector.

Administrative silos

The pooling of administrative control over all VET institutions into a single, unified national department (DHET) comprises a major, potentially positive change. Previously, a major cause of policy failure has been the battles over turf between the two national Departments of Education and Labour, with animosity generally characterizing their interactions. Soobrayan and Marock (2007) described this negative dynamic as an on-going '*tug of war*' which weakened coordination efforts around national human resources development.

This animosity also negatively affected the evolution of the FET college system during the 2000s, with policy imposed on FET Colleges from the top. Employers were not consulted in any substantive way, and curriculum experts were ignored. The new NVC policy framework was not piloted, and was imposed on the college system in 2007 with dramatic consequences as described earlier. The restructuring here shares many of the flawed elements of the UK model of VET reform. The following five problems in both countries stand out as particularly severe. They are:

1. **Neglect of the demand-side**: as in the UK, the South African college reforms were founded on a supply-side approach of increasing the output of graduates with vocational qualifications, whilst leaving a low-skill, low-wage employment environment unchanged. This approach has been 'consistently unable to ensure that improved skill supply is matched by greater demand for, and utilization of, skills in the workplace' (Lanning and Lawton 2012: 20). Skills can only make a substantive contribution to productivity performance if they are effectively deployed in the firm. Supply-side skills policies on their own are not sufficient.

2. **Lack of employer 'buy-in'**: Although the FET College reforms in South Africa and the UK were billed as 'employer-led', the reality has been that few or no actual employers were directly involved. This has led to 'disillusionment for both employers and public sector partners and a degree of cynicism about the extent to which real employer views are being captured' (UKCES 2010: 14). This lack of employer buy-in throws up a big gap between the official policy rhetoric about 'employer-led' VET and the actual reality on the ground.
3. **'Statist' models**: In contrast to employer-led approaches, the system which has evolved in the United Kingdom and South Africa is civil servant dominated, with government imposing national skills policy frameworks on employers without their consent and buy-in. The UKCES states this contradictory reality bluntly: 'the public sector is the main driver behind some "employer-led" arrangements so the idea of employer leadership is a misnomer' (2010: 16). Lanning and Lawton (2012: 3) argue that the failure to engage employers has led to an over-reliance on centralized state-led programmes and institutions to fill the gap.
4. **Absence of partnerships with the college sector**: Unlike the American community college system, the South African and UK college sectors have failed to establish strong partnerships with industry in localized or regional settings, meeting employer demand for skills through customized and specifically tailored training packages. The absence of these sorts of partnership strategies signifies the failure of the college sector to attend to the demand-side needs of the economy.
5. **Poor progression from VET to Higher education**: Progression is a major problem for learners who graduate with VET qualifications in Anglo-Saxon countries – including the USA, UK and South Africa. In all contexts, graduates with NVQ qualifications struggle to get access into higher education degree programmes. Tertiary level VET is highly under-developed in all of these countries as compared with the central European and Scandinavian countries. For example, transfer from two-year associate degree qualifications obtained at community colleges in the USA into four-year university degree-awarding colleges is very low – similarly in the UK and South Africa (Osterman 2010; Kraak 2008; Fuller and Unwin 2012).

Continuous institutional instability

An additional problem rooted in the UK system but also evident in the South African FET College system is the never-ending reform of the system, in the UK dating as far back as the Thatcher era of the late 1970s. These constant reforms deprive the VET systems in both countries of stability and continuity. Institutional reforms need at least five years to take effect, yet constant state reforms in structure and legislation continually undo the potential impact that might have been achieved (UKCES 2010: 44).

The irony facing South Africa today is that, whilst it admires the development state capabilities of countries in South East Asia such as Singapore and South Korea – capabilities which are based on the capacity of the state to steer and reshape demand-side conditions – South Africa's 'education and training' reforms mirror far more closely the neo-liberal market-led restructuring of the UK and other Anglo-Saxon countries such as Australia. Here, the faith in the 'education gospel' (Grubb 2006) around supply-side interventions whilst the demand-side is left unchanged and subject to market forces appears naïve given the claim of a misdiagnosis made by Keep and James (2012) earlier in the text. South Africa appears unable to break away from this Anglo-Saxon burden. The ideological influence of the former colonizer and the global belief that the knowledge-based economy requires vast supply-side inputs continues to be the most influential

VET policy idea in former British colonies such as South Africa – to the detriment of vocational learners and their future employability.

References

Cosser, M., Kraak, A. and Reddy, V. (eds) (2012) *Institutional Identity and Operational Success in the Further Education and Training College Sector.* Education and Skills Development Research Programme, Human Sciences Research Council, unpublished monograph, Pretoria.

DHET (2009) *Further Education and Training Colleges National Certificate (Vocational) and Report 190/191: Report on the Conduct of National Examinations*, Pretoria: Government Printers.

DHET (2010) *Document for Discussion: Proposed Way Forward: Towards Finding Resolutions in Partnership with Stakeholders*, Further Education and Training (FET) Round Table, Pretoria: Department of Higher Education and Training (DHET).

DHET (2012) *Green Paper for Post-School Education and Training*, Pretoria: Department of Higher Education and Training (DHET).

DoE (2001) *A New Institutional Landscape for FET*, Pretoria: Department of Education (DoE).

DoE (2008) *National Plan for Further Education and Training Colleges in South Africa*, Pretoria: Department of Education (DoE).

Fuller, A. and Unwin, L. (2012) *Banging on the Door of the University: The Complexities of Progression from Apprenticeship and other Vocational Programmes in England*, Oxford: ESRC Centre on Skills, Knowledge and Organizational Performance (SKOPE), University of Oxford.

Grubb, W.N. (2006) *Vocational Education and Training: Issues for a Thematic Review*, Paris: OECD.

Keep, E. and James, S. (2012) 'A Bermuda triangle of policy? "Bad jobs", skills policy and incentives to learn at the bottom end of the labour market', *Journal of Education Policy* 27(2): 211–30.

Kraak, A. (2008) 'Incoherence in the South African labour market for intermediate skills', *Journal of Education and Work* 21(3): 197–216.

Kraak A. and Perold, H. (eds) (2003) *Human Resources Development Review 2003: Education, Employment, and Skills in South Africa: Review 2003*, Cape Town: HSRC Press and East Lansing, MI: Michigan State University Press.

Lanning, T. and Lawton, K. (2012) *No Train No Gain: Beyond Free-Market and State-Led Skills Policy*, London: Institute for Public Policy Research.

OECD (2008) *More than Just Jobs: Workforce Development in a Skills-Based Economy*, Local Economic and Employment Development (LEED), Paris: OECD.

OECD (2011) *Local Job Creation: How Employment and Training Agencies Can Help*, Local Economic and Employment Development (LEED), Paris: OECD.

OECD (2012a) *Skills Development Pathways in Asia*, Local Economic and Employment Development (LEED), Paris: OECD.

OECD (2012b) *Skills for Competitiveness: A Synthesis Report*, Local Economic and Employment Development (LEED), Paris: OECD.

OECD (2012c) *Career Pathway and Cluster Skill Development: Promising Models from the United States*, Local Economic and Employment Development (LEED), Paris: OECD.

OECD (2013) *Local Job Creation: How Employment and Training Agencies Can Help: Draft Report for the United States*, Paris: OECD Publishing.

Osterman, P. (2010) *Community Colleges: Promise, Performance and Policy*, unpublished mimeo, Boston, MA: Sloan School of Business, Massachusetts Institute of Technology.

Soobrayan, B. and Marock, C. (2007) *Study to Ascertain How Best to Plan, Coordinate, Integrate, Manage, Monitor, Evaluate and Report on the National Human Resource Development Strategy for South Africa.* Unpublished consulting report, Johannesburg: Singizi Consulting.

Sung, J., Ashton, D. and Raddon, A. (2009) *Futureskills Scotland: Product Market Strategies and Workforce Skills*, Edinburgh: Scottish Government.

UKCES (2010) *What's The Deal? The Employer Voice in the Employment and Skills System*, London: UK Commission for Employment and Skills.

36

DEVELOPMENT OF HUMAN RESOURCES IN CENTRAL AND SOUTH AMERICA

Rod P. Githens, Carlos Albornoz, Librado Enrique Gonzalez, Tonette S. Rocco and Christine Wiggins-Romesburg

Central and South American countries have made gains in economic growth, job creation and political stability, which have produced a 50 per cent growth in the middle class in the last decade (World Bank 2013e). As the economies continue to grow and develop, increased attention is being given to Human Resource Development (HRD) throughout the region.

The approaches to developing human resources in Central and South America differ greatly by country depending on the levels of education, infrastructure, wealth and foreign investment. The countries of this region have diverse cultural, historical and political characteristics which affect the ways in which workforce development, organization development (OD) and national HRD (NHRD) are approached. The purpose of this chapter is to present an overview of the unique contextual and cultural issues in this region by examining the workforce development, capacity and policy needs of two countries. The chapter is divided into sections presenting an overview of Central and South America, a discussion of workforce development and policy and an analysis of two cases: Chile and Panama. We conclude with implications for workforce development and policy.

Overview of Central and South America

South America is the fourth largest continent with the fifth largest population, 12 countries and three dependencies speaking five official languages adopted from former colonizing powers (Spanish, Portuguese, English, Dutch, French) and numerous indigenous languages (World Factbook 2013b). The countries have seen some moves towards trade and political integration through the Union of South American Nations (UNASUR) and Southern Common Market (Mercosur) (Unión de Naciones Suramericanas 2013).

Central America has seven countries with two official languages (Spanish, English) and many indigenous languages (World Factbook 2013b, Kaufman *et al.* 2001). During much of the twentieth century, Central America has been working towards integration of the countries by forming the Central American Court of Justice and the Organization of Central American States (ODECA) (Encyclopedia Britannica 2013).

During much of the twentieth century, politics and governments were heavily influenced by the Cold War, making self-determination, real democracies and economic growth difficult to achieve. Emigration, poor education systems, some of the most severe income disparities in the world and inefficient use of labor are examples of some of the issues prevalent in South and Central America. Today, South and Central American countries have distinct economic differences. Brazil is one of the top ten richest countries in the world and Venezuela is one of the top ten fastest growing economies (Aneki 2013d, Aneki 2013a) in the world. On the other hand, Honduras, Bolivia, Gautemala, Paraguay, El Salvador, Guyana and Belize are among the top 100 poorest in the world (Aneki 2013c). In terms of education, Mexico has just over 15 per cent of its population with postsecondary degrees (Aneki 2013b). Access to education is not uniform in any South or Central American country (World Factbook 2013b). Among Ibero-American States, over 50 per cent of students do not reach the minimum levels of math or reading as determined by the Program for International Student Evaluation (Scasso 2012).

Development of workforce capacity

The 'fit' of HRD in various cultural contexts is important to consider. Formal training programs vary widely from learner-centered programs to traditional information transmission sessions. The continuum of training and learning programs can be widely adapted to almost any culture. However, the OD aspect of HRD has been conceptualized and implemented in highly developed countries with cultural values that align most directly with OD (Cummings and Worley 2009). Particularly, many participation-based change programs have been quite dependent upon functioning in large organizations and in cultures that align with ideas of participation and shared decision making. According to Cummings and Worley, Central and South America have some fit with OD, although certainly not as neat of a fit with traditional OD as Scandinavian countries, which are largely seen as being most compatible with OD's values. The primary challenges result from being high-context, having high power distance, and being achievement oriented. However, the tendency in this region towards high levels of collectivism allows for some compatibility with traditional OD. The issues of cultural fit are further complicated in both international and domestic firms wanting to emulate the values of 'Western' business cultures.

In addition to learning and OD being used for the unleashing of human expertise within an organizational context (Swanson and Holton 2009), HRD can also be conceptualized as existing for the betterment of communities and nations (McLean and McLean 2001). NHRD involves the relationship between government and private sector programs (McLean 2003). In particular, within the developing countries of Central and South America, development of human expertise and unleashing of human potential is a central component of fostering stability and economic development. Success stories in the economic development of countries such as Japan, Taiwan, Singapore, and South Korea are all intertwined in a major way to the NHRD policies of those nations (Ardichvili *et al.* 2012). In these countries, economic and political policies worked in a very concerted way to ensure that HRD was not limited to development of internal capacity in private sector firms – HRD was also extended to workforce development.

Workforce development cannot occur in a vacuum, removed from financial and economic development. According to Jacobs and Hawley (2009: 2543), 'Workforce development is the co-ordination of public and private sector policies and programmes that provides individuals with the opportunity for a sustainable livelihood and helps organizations achieve exemplary goals, consistent with the societal context.' The social context includes financial, social and educational systems which create individual capability and national capacity. In countries that are most successful in the development of economic capacity, consideration is given to possible 'bottlenecks' in several areas: financial capacity, manufacturing or industrial capacity and educational or workforce capacity (Al-Zendi and Wilson 2012). True 'capacity development' in each of these areas allows for localized, culturally appropriate and culturally compatible industry to emerge in a way that harnesses and develops capabilities and resources. Al-Zendi and Wilson explain that attention must be paid to the individual level skills and knowledge; organizational policies, frameworks and practices; and national policies, social norms and legislation.

Although the ultimate focus of this chapter is on the development of workforce capacity, we contend that this development exists as a result of financial and industrial capacity. Without financial capacity and industrial capacity, a skilled workforce will not be needed to work in the formal economy. Githens and Alagaraja (2014) created a matrix (Table 36.1 for modified version) to consider how financial, industrial and workforce capacities are developed at the individual, organizational and national levels.

This framework provides a holistic, yet focused, multi-level approach to consider HRD within a national context (Githens and Alagaraja 2014). Development of workforce capacity cannot be conceived within a vacuum (e.g. only within organizational contexts or devoid of larger considerations effecting economic development). At the same time, the framework is focused on factors most directly affecting the workforce, in order to avoid confusion with larger concepts such as human development. In this chapter, we use this multi-faceted framework as a lens for considering HRD in Central and South America, focusing primarily on national policies and social norms, with less emphasis on individual skills and knowledge and organizational policies and practices.

Two countries' experiences: Chile and Panama

Chile and Panama provide relevant case studies illustrating the successes and difficulties of government and market forces in creating economic opportunity and creating NHRD policy. Such policies include purposeful incentives, policies, and practice in developing the workforce. Chile underwent a major economic transformation during the preceding decades and is considered one of the most highly developed countries in Central and South America. On the other hand, Panama has more recently experienced a transformation, beginning with the transfer of the

Table 36.1 Multi-level framework for considering NHRD

	Individual Skills and Knowledge	*Organizational Policies and Practices*	*National Policies and Social Norms*
Financial capacity	Ability to fund or have access to funding for skill development	Access to financial resources to initiate, grow and sustain firm	Government economic development policies and private sector funding capacity
Industrial capacity	Capability and opportunity to align skills and knowledge with employment needs	Approaches to utilizing and/or developing infrastructure, natural resources and the dominant culture	Infrastructure, natural resources and cultural compatibility for encouraging development
Workforce capacity	Capability to align skills and education with industry needs	Practices utilized for developing both current and future employees	Education, training and skill development of the workforce, cultural traits and compatibility with the direction of national policies

Source: Adapted from Githens and Alagaraja (2014)

Panama Canal and exit of US military personnel in 2000. The country has experienced an economic boom placing it among the world's fastest growing economies (World Factbook 2013b).

The approaches to developing financial, industrial and workforce capacity in both countries provides helpful glimpses into the challenges and opportunities to HRD in Central and Latin America.

Chile: anchor of economic strength in Latin America

Chile is one of Latin America's most stable economies; thus, configurations of its financial, industrial, and workforce capacity at the national level are worth examining. The Republic of Chile, with nearly 17 million people, is located in South America and is bordered by the Pacific Ocean to the west and south, and Argentina to the east. Peru and Bolivia border Chile to the north. Chile and Argentina share a border through the high Andes Mountains. The climate is desert in the north, Mediterranean in central regions and cool and damp in the south. Chile is a long and narrow piece of land with 4,020 miles of coastline and 150 miles average width (World Factbook 2013b). Chile's territory is larger than the US state of Texas and has slightly over 20 per cent of its land used for agricultural purposes (National Atlas 2013, World Bank 2013b, World Bank 2013d).

Chile is a major exporter, with exports accounting for approximately 30 per cent of its gross domestic product (GDP), primarily from commodities (World Factbook 2013b). Chile is the world's largest copper producer, which is the principal natural resource of the nation (Trosziewicz 2011). While copper provides 19 per cent of government revenue, Chile is also known for other exports such as fruits, fish and wood (World Factbook 2013b). The country imports close to 98 per cent of the oil consumed internally (International Energy Agency 2012). Chile is the only South American member of the Organization of Economic Co-operation and Development (OECD 2010).

Financial capacity

In the early 1970s, Chile had a socialist government that nationalized all natural resources (British Broadcasting Corporation 2001). During a dictatorship that controlled the country between 1973 and 1990, Chile went through deep economic transformations privatizing all public assets (Pinochet's rule). The transition to a free market system exposed Chile to a considerable amount of business and production turmoil. But the experience taught the nation, the government, and the private sector how to perform in a global competitive environment. Chile built a reputation for strong financial institutions and sound fiscal policy (OECD 2013b, Sebastian and Ledermen 1998). The country has become one of the world's largest beneficiaries of free trade agreements (FTAs), having 24 trade agreements in place that cover 60 countries, that include Europe, the United States, Canada, and Mexico, Central America and Asia (Perales 2012, World Trade Organization 2013). Chile also has FTAs through its participation in MERCOSUR (*Mercado Comúndel Sur* or Southern Common Market). The 2013 Economic Freedom Index (measure of a country's level of free enterprise) places Chile in 7th place in the world, ahead of the United States (Heritage Foundation 2013).

From 2003 through 2012, real GDP growth averaged almost five per cent per year, despite a slight contraction in 2009 that resulted from the global financial crisis (World Bank 2013c). The Chilean economy has remained stable and growing compared with developed and most developing countries worldwide (Ministry of Finance 2013). The International Monetary Fund (2013) reports that Chile recovered rapidly from the global financial crisis and from the February 2010 earthquake, which devastated a large part of central Chile. The country's strategies included deploying a solid policy framework of fiscal rule, effectively targeting inflation, managing exchange rate flexibility and deploying a sound banking system supported by fiscal buffers (Duttagupta and Helbling 2013).

Chile's sound macroeconomic policy has provided financial capacity for economic development. However, despite the economic growth over the years, the competitiveness of the country has declined steadily since 1995 (Economic Commission for Latin America 2012). The macroeconomic reforms that explain most of the Chilean competitiveness between 1985 and 1995 seem to have decreased in impact. The country reached a point in which microeconomic changes were fundamental and one change is related to the productivity of the workforce (Lepeley and Albornoz 2013). The World Economic Forum ranked Chile as the 13th most competitive economy in the world in 1995, but in 2012 Chile fell to 31st place (Lepeley and Albornoz 2013). Although Chile is still the most competitive economy in Latin America, the decrease in national competitiveness is a concern for business corporations, government and scholars (Lepeley and Albornoz 2013, World Economic Forum 1995).

Industrial capacity

Industrial capacity relates to the infrastructure, natural resources and cultural compatibility for economic development. Key factors in this capacity are the income and availability of workers. Income inequality in Chile is the highest in the countries of the OECD, with a Gini coefficient (measure of income distribution) of 0.50, while the OECD average is 0.31 (OECD 2011). This means that 38 per cent of Chileans have difficulties living on their current income (MercoPress 2013). Minimum wage in Chile is about $2.30 (USD) per hour (OECD 2013c). Argentina, Panama, Brazil and Paraguay have a higher minimum wage compared with Chile.

During 2012, the unemployment rate in Chile averaged in the lower 40 per cent of nations (World Bank 2013f). Business owners raised the issue of the shortage of workers and the high turnover rates reported in industry (Long 2012). With low salaries, the strategy of most companies was to slightly increase salaries, creating competition to attract low skilled workers. In the last decade the mining industry has experienced a boom because of increased demand for copper to supply the construction industry in China. Chile sells as much copper as its copper companies can produce (Economist 2013).

These trends have resulted in a shortage of workers in the construction sector in Chile because many workers left to work in the mines (Long 2012). The continued economic growth forecasted for China will continue to affect the construction and mining sectors in Chile (Duttagupta and Helbling 2013). Due to this projected growth, the demand for copper is anticipated to remain stable for the next ten years (Smith and Craze 2010). Similar to the gold rush that occurred in California, Chile has a copper fever with many workers from the south emigrating or flying north to work each month (Craze and Quiroga 2013). Work shifts in the mining industry are fifteen days inside the mine followed by fifteen days of free time. This schedule allows workers to commute from anywhere in Chile. Because workers are willing to leave their homes to work in the mines in the north, employment sectors elsewhere in Chile are facing worker shortages as well as increased pressure on wages (Craze and Quiroga 2013, Fundación Chile 2013). The cost of human resources increased by 20 per cent in the construction sector because workers emigrated north for jobs in the mining sector. Medium size companies in the construction sector could not compete to retain their specialized workers. The shortage of construction workers has consequences for businesses and the housing industry because it became very hard to find workers to complete household or industrial construction projects across the country. Various public policy initiatives have been created to train new construction workers, including adding more women to this workforce.

The ageing population of Chile is also contributing to the shortage of labor in Chile (World Factbook 2013b). The country is in the advanced stages of demographic transition with fertility below replacement level, low mortality rates and life expectancy on par with developed countries (World Factbook, 2013b). Policy experts and business owners envision the shortage of workers can be resolved partially by increasing women's access to the job market (OECD 2013d). As of 2011, 49 per cent of women ages 15 and over reported working or searching for a job (World Bank 2013a). The workforce participation rate of women in high income nations is 11 per cent higher in developed nations than in Latin America (World Bank 2013a). In Chile, the female participation rate is 26 per cent below the male rate (World Bank 2013a). Therefore, Chilean women have room to enter the job market aggressively.

Government policy for developing workforce capacity

For Chile to return to being among the most competitive economies in the world, developing workforce capacity is a key to fostering productivity, especially because the economy is highly dependent on natural resources (OECD 2012). Regaining the competitiveness of 1995 in the complex and interdependent global economy of the twenty-first century requires the synchronized efforts of government, policy makers, universities and corporations, all focused on the skill development needs of the Chilean workforce (Lepeley and Albornoz 2013). We can distinguish three levels of education for developing human resources in Chile. The lower level of education includes 28 per cent of the workforce (OECD 2013a). Second, 44 per cent of the workforce has attained a medium level of vocational or specialized training (OECD 2013a). Third, 29 per cent of the workforce is highly skilled and possesses a professional or technical degree (OECD 2013a).

In 1976, the Chilean government created SENCE (National Service for Training and Employment), a public agency organized to contribute to national productivity by subsidizing occupational training through tax incentives (UNDP 2012). In 2010, SENCE programs accounted for \$226M (USD), or 80 per cent of Chile's public expenditure on training. Under this program, domestic and foreign-owned organizations operating in Chile are eligible to receive a tax exemption of up to one per cent of their total annual payroll for workforce training (Biblioteca del Congreso 1997). For example, if a company has 500 employees with annual average salaries of \$40,000, that company can request a tax exemption of \$200,000 to refund its workforce development expenses. SENCE does not provide this training directly; however, it oversees the Technical Training Agencies (OTEC) that provide certified training services (UNDP 2012). OTEC providers are unique because training is their sole function, which they provide to public and private organizations alike.

A commission organized by Chile's Ministry of Labor and Social Security found that SENCE has not been effective in closing the skills gap in the Chilean workforce (UNDP 2012). Part of the reason is that training programs are relatively short in duration (averaging 19 hours), and are not grounded in front-end assessment or evaluation. A second criticism is that since organizations decide who receives what training, and the amount of the tax credit is tied to trainee salary, tax incentives tend to flow disproportionately to large organizations that employ moderately to highly educated and salaried employees, and therefore add little to the skills or employability of the population over all.

In addition to supporting the training and development of employed individuals, SENCE also targets members of vulnerable populations who may not possess the skills to be successful in the labor market (UNDP 2012). For instance, several SENCE programs target unemployed youth from low-income families. However, the quality of these programs varies greatly. For instance, one of the most successful is the Special Youth Program which offers 450 hours of instruction to be followed by 300 hours of internship and technical assistance. One of the least successful is the Bicentennial Youth Program which has an 84 per cent attrition rate.

In 2005, a special tax of five per cent of mining profits was enacted on firms with 50,000 tons of copper or more (CONICYT 2012, OECD 2013b). The Chilean government provides a fund to drive innovation through science and technology research (CONICYT 2012). As of 2011, this fund was $874M (USD) which is mostly invested in R&D and human capital development (CONICYT 2012). In 2007, 'Becas Chile' was created, which is the national agency that manages scholarships to study abroad. Becas Chile was established with the goal of increasing opportunities for up to 3,300 Chileans to study abroad each year, modernize the government scholarship system and encourage international involvement and cooperation. Despite the fact that Becas Chile is oftentimes lauded for its innovation, the program is also criticized for its rushed implementation.

Panama: newly revitalized country takes advantage of its strategic location

The Republic of Panama, with nearly 3.5 million people coming from different heritages and ethnic mixes, is located in Central America and is bordered by the Caribbean Sea to the north and the Pacific Ocean to the south. The country's climate is mostly tropical; however, it is hurricane/earthquake free unlike neighboring countries (World Factbook 2013a). Panama has been blessed with a strategic geographical position and many call it 'bridge of the world, heart of the universe' by virtue of the Panama Canal, the inter-oceanic waterway that connects the two oceans. The canal is the biggest contributor to the nation's GDP with 13,000 to 14,000 vessels from around the world going through the canal each year (Panama Canal Authority 2013).

Beginning with US support for Panama's independence from Colombia in 1903, the country's identity and history have been intertwined with the US (World Factbook 2013a). Until 2000, the US provided massive investment and had a major presence in the Panama Canal Zone, a sovereign piece of land administered by a US appointed governor. With the transfer of the canal and exit of US military personnel in 2000, Panama began its transformation as a fully independent country, able to forge its own political identity and able to fully control the use of its economic and natural resources.

Financial capacity

The expansion of Panama's financial capacity is mostly attributed to the government's macro-level infrastructure investments, effective management of the Panama Canal and open market policies in an effort to promote free trade and foreign direct investment (Bureau of Economic and Business Affairs 2012). The country's long history of US involvement provided for transfer of substantial infrastructure in 2000 and a continuation of the country's currency, the Balboa (B/), being based on the US dollar (World Factbook 2013a). The dollar-based economy has provided the foundation for a strong and stable banking sector.

In 2012, Panama's GDP recorded an increase of 10.7 per cent in the production of goods and services compared with the previous year. Based on estimates from the National Institute of Statistics and Census (INEC), the country's GDP sums B/ 755.5 million (USD $755.5 million) represent an annual increase of B/ 483.4 million (USD $483.4 million) (Contraloría General

2013). Other improvements include the declining percentage of people living under extreme poverty conditions which fell from 17.6 per cent in 2006 to 10.4 per cent in 2012, according to the Ministry of Economy and Finance. In other words, approximately 34,000 Panamanians left extreme poverty conditions during that time period. Additionally, general poverty rates fell from 27.6 per cent in 2011 to 25.8 per cent in March 2012 (Panama America 2012).

A nation's economic growth does not necessarily imply positive advances in HRD. In the case of Panama, foreigners with greater education levels and more competitive mindsets hold many of the higher-paid positions and create most of the entrepreneurial activity of the country (Lao 2013). This disparity leaves little room for many Panamanians for whom a sustainable livelihood is still a far-fetched reality.

Industrial capacity

The immense growth that Panama has experienced points to the promise of its internal resources. However, much of the growth can be credited to increased foreign investments, be it in the form of multinationals entering, foreign projects, banking or foreign entrepreneurial activity (Mattson and Teran 2011). As the economy continues to improve and grow, a primary question is whether there will be growth in local human resources (Mattson and Teran 2011, Schwab 2013). The success of the economy will require more advanced leadership, management and technical expertise in order to be sustained. Furthermore, opportunities for domestic entrepreneurial activity need to be fostered to sustain the cycle of continued and stable growth.

Ciudad del Saber ('City of Knowledge') is a complex of research, academic, technology and non-governmental organizations located in the redeveloped Fort Clayton (former headquarters of the US Army Southern Command). It is managed by a non-profit organization and affiliated with the national government. This complex was designed as an incubator of innovation and a space for development of businesses in Panama by foreign and domestic firms around communication and information technologies, biosciences, environmental management, human development, business management and entrepreneurship, and global services (Ciudad del Saber 2013). The case of *Ciudad del Saber* is one of several examples of Panama's retooling of US Military installations for developing industrial capacity in the country.

Government policy for developing workforce capacity

The globalization of markets and technological shifts across the world create the need for a greater specialized labor force in Panama. The demand for workers capable of facing and adapting to the emerging digitalized world is significant. Despite being considered the second most competitive economy in Central and South America (behind Chile), Panama has one of the worst education systems in the world for a country so advanced (Schwab 2013). Executives doing business in Panama see an inadequately educated workforce as the most problematic factor for doing business, even greater than government bureaucracy or corruption (Schwab 2013). This lack of education has resulted in Panama losing high tech jobs to other countries and results in many of the country's high-paying jobs being filled by foreigners, particularly from other Latin American countries (Mattson and Teran 2011).

Currently, Panama's development of human resources is stagnated because unequal distribution of wealth, poverty, public transportation, education and access to healthcare are major issues that affect most Panamanians every day. Panama has the second worst income distribution in Latin America and nearly 30 per cent live in poverty and 12 per cent in extreme poverty, although that rate has been decreasing (World Factbook 2013a, International Monetary Fund 2013). Both inflation and increased demand and use of high tech consumer products have been challenges for the average worker in Panama (International Monetary Fund 2013).

National economic growth that has occurred in Panama has not necessarily been tightly connected to domestic development of human resources. Much of Panama's growth has occurred as a result of foreign direct investment and through the use of foreign management; however, for Panama to have long term domestic growth, development of its workforce capacity is essential. For future growth to be sustained, skilled workers and skilled management must be developed from among the Panamanian population.

An underdeveloped education sector in Panama has been a persistent problem. Although Panama generally has wide access to primary, secondary and higher education (Arocena and Sutz 2000), educational quality is relatively low. Panama has been ranked 133 out of 142 countries for quality of education (Bureau of Economic and Business Affairs 2012). Reforms have been challenging to enact due to lack of progressive cooperation between political leaders and powerful teachers' unions (Mattson and Teran 2011). The country also lacks rigorous regulations and quality standards for established and new universities. In 2011, 43 private universities were certified by the University of Panama (UP), which is also the national regulatory body for higher education. Reforms to primary, secondary and higher education have been a priority for the current president; however, the long term effects of those reforms remain to be seen (International Monetary Fund 2013, Mattson and Teran 2011).

When Panamanian graduates enter the labor market, they oftentimes find that they are under skilled and less competitive than candidates who studied abroad. This situation is challenging for a developing country like Panama that strives to be an advanced economy and is growing at such a rapid rate. Corruption and inefficiencies have resulted in an education sector that needs further reform and change in order to help the country continue to increase in competitiveness. Panama's economic growth demands competitive, aggressive and leader-oriented mindsets that can best be attained through a special focus on education and building of workforce capacity.

Implications for HRD practice and research

The two countries discussed in this chapter, Chile and Panama, are different in history and relationships to colonizing powers. Both represent the unique challenges and opportunities for developing human resources in Central and South America. Chile has endured dictatorships and Panama was in many ways an occupied country for a hundred years by hosting a US military presence and US-governed Canal Zone. Currently, both countries enjoy stable democratic governments but neither country has reached the level of being a fully developed country. Both countries have a dominant industrial presence (mining or the canal/transportation) which plays a large role in determining workforce development policy, setting wages and worker shortages. Both countries have very specific and tangible national policies designed to increase economic growth and skill development. However, these efforts seem to be occurring at the macro levels. In Chile, organizations have access to government sponsored trainers who work to enhance skills and competencies of workers. Educational disparities contribute to extreme disparities in income, with both countries leading in huge income gaps compared with other countries. Chile and Panama have similar educational difficulties with large segments of the population being under-educated by inefficient educational systems. In each country basic skills in math and reading are not enjoyed by large segments of the population.

In order to further develop the knowledge, skills and competencies of workers and prepare them for future industrial jobs, each country needs to address its basic educational needs. These needs include securing qualified and capable teachers who encourage real learning in their students, equity in access to good education, implementing real systemic reform to educational systems and lessening social stigma produced by the disparities in income and educational achievement. A strong primary education system where the population learns basic math, reading, writing, and problem solving is necessary to build a foundation for increasing workforce capacity. In Chile, career opportunities and trajectories can be determined by the private primary and secondary school attended (Albornoz and Rocco in press). The attendance at particular schools creates a social network and career opportunities. These social networks are more important to advancement than merit.

Each country needs to establish standards for higher education institutions to increase quality and to ensure consistency in quality between institutions. Until the quality of higher education in each country is consistent and competitive with other countries skilled labor and higher-paid positions will be filled by immigrants. This dilemma is particularly true in Panama. In Chile, the workforce has an oversupply of professional labor and not enough technical workers because technical careers are not valued. In Panama the education system is not producing workers with traditional or technological forms of literacy. Industrial sectors are difficult to strengthen without technical and technology workers.

HRD does not exist as a field in Chile so students cannot choose it as a career option. An HRD-related degree program is being offered by a foreign higher education institution in Panama, which will help the field gain traction in Panama as a discipline; however, this offering is recent. In Chile, people with degrees in psychology and engineering perform some of the HR functions. Training seems to be handled by the government for larger firms leaving workers in smaller firms to encounter skill obsolescence. Organizations and corporations could support workers' learning and education by hiring people to train with credentials, creating training programs to enhance skill development at various levels and encouraging their workers to participate in continuing education. These activities would in some way mirror the development of HRD as a field in developed countries.

The challenges for the field include: how do we make inroads into countries where HRD does not exist or is little known? How can we learn from research on HRD in Central and South American countries when no research exists? And how can we build relationships with scholars in these countries who may have no understanding of the work of HRD? Each one of these challenges presents an opportunity.

References

Albornoz, C. and Rocco, T.S. (in press) 'Moving beyond employability risks and redundancies: new microenterprise and entrepreneurial possibilities in international contexts', in Mizzi, R., Rocco, T.S. and Shore, S. (eds) *Lives on the Periphery: Politics, Practicalities, and Possibilities in a Changing World*, Albany, NY: SUNY Press.

Al-Zendi D. and Wilson, J.P. (2012) 'Capacity development and human resource development', in Wilson, J.P. (ed.) *International Human Resource Development: Learning, Education and Training for Individuals and Organizations*, London: Kogan Page, 215–39.

Aneki (2013a) *Fastest Growing Economies*. Online. Available HTTP: http://www.aneki.com/fastest_growing_economies.html (accessed 3 November 2013).

Aneki (2013b) *Most Educated Countries*. Online. Available HTTP: http://www.aneki.com/most_educated.html?number=all (accessed 23 December 2013).

Aneki (2013c) *Poorest Countries in the World*. Online. Available HTTP: http://www.aneki.com/poorest.html?number=100 (accessed 3 November 2013).

Aneki (2013d) *Richest Countries in the World*. Online. Available HTTP: http://www.aneki.com/richest.html (accessed 3 November 2013).

Ardichvili, A., Zavyalova, E.K. and Minina, V.N. (2012) 'National human resource development strategies: comparing Brazil, Russia, India, and China', in Wilson, J.P. (ed.) *International Human Resource Development: Learning, Education and Training for Individuals and Organizations*, London, Kogan Page, 177–93.

Arocena, R. and Sutz, J. (2000) *La universidad Latinoamericana del futuro: tendencias, escenarios, alternativas*, Unión de Universidades de América Latina y el Caribe. Online. Available HTTP: http://www.oei.es/salactsi/sutzarocena00.htm (accessed 12 December 2013).

Biblioteca del Congreso (1997) *Statute Approved Training and Employment*, Government of Chile. Online. Available HTTP: http://www.leychile.cl/Navegar?idNorma=6618&buscar=19518 (accessed 23 December 2013).

British Broadcasting Corporation (2001) *Pinochet's Rule: Repression and Economic Success*. Online. Available HTTP: http://news.bbc.co.uk/2/hi/americas/63821.stm (accessed 23 December 2013).

Bureau of Economic and Business Affairs, Department of State (2012) *2012 Investment Climate Statement: Panama*. Government of the United States. Online. Available HTTP: http://www.state.gov/e/eb/rls/othr/ics/2012/191215.htm (accessed 1 May 2013).

Ciudad del Saber (2013) *Non-profit Organization that Manages the City of Knowledge*, Government of Panama. Online. Available HTTP: http://ciudaddelsaber.org/en/foundation (accessed 23 December 2013).

CONICYT (Ministry of Education) (2012) *Science, Technology and Innovation for the Development of Chile*, Government of Chile. Online. Available HTTP: http://www.conicyt.cl/wp-content/uploads/2012/07/Brochure-Institucional-2011-Ingl%C3%A9s.pdf (accessed 23 December 2013).

Contraloría General (2013) *Gross Domestic Product of the Republic*, Government of Panama. Online. Available HTTP: http://www.contraloria.gob.pa/index.php?opcion=InfContral (accessed 31 May 2013).

Craze, M. and Quiroga, J. (5 September 2013) 'In Chile's copper boom, miners spread the wealth', *Bloomberg Businessweek*. Online. Available HTTP: http://www.businessweek.com/articles/2013-09-05/in-chiles-copper-boom-miners-spread-the-wealth (accessed 23 December 2013).

Cummings, T.G. and Worley, C.G. (2009) *Organization Development & Change*, 9th edition, Mason, OH: South-Western/Cengage.

Duttagupta, R. and Helbling, T. (2013) *Global Growth Patterns Shifting, Says IMF*, International Monetary Fund. Online. Available HTTP: http://www.imf.org/external/pubs/ft/survey/so/2013/NEW100813A.htm (accessed 23 December 2013).

Economic Commission for Latin America (2012) *Macroeconomic Report: Chile*, Naciones Unidas. Online. Available HTTP: http://www.eclac.org/publicaciones/xml/6/46986/Chile-completo-web-ing.pdf (accessed 23 December 2013).

Economist (2013) *Coppor Solution: The Mining Industry Has Enriched Chile. But its Future is Precarious, 2013*. Online. Available HTTP: http://www.economist.com/news/business/21576714-mining-industry-has-enriched-chile-its-future-precarious-copper-solution (accessed 23 December 2013).

Encyclopedia Britannica (2013) *Organization of Central American States*. Online. Available HTTP: http://www.britannica.com/EBchecked/topic/102269/Organization-of-Central-American-States) (accessed 23 December 2013).

Fundación Chile (2013) *Fuerza laboral en la gran minería Chilena: Diagnóstico y recomendaciones 2012–2020*, Consejo de Competencias Mineras. Online. Available HTTP: http://www.fundacionchile.com/archivos/reporteccm31425187.pdf (accessed 23 December 2013).

Githens, R.P. and Alagaraja, M. (2014) *Capacity Development: A Multi-Dimensional Framework for HRD*, unpublished manuscript.

Heritage Foundation (2013) *Country Rankings*. Online. Available HTTP: http://www.heritage.org/index/ranking (accessed 23 December 2013).

International Energy Agency (2012) *Oil & Gas Security, Chile*. Online. Available HTTP: http://www.iea.org/publications/freepublications/publication/Chile_2012.pdf (accessed 23 December 2013).

International Monetary Fund (2013) *IMF Country Report No. 13/88: Panama*, United Nations. Online. Available HTTP: http://www.imf.org/external/pubs/ft/scr/2013/cr1388.pdf (accessed 12 December 2013).

Jacobs, R.L. and Hawley, J.D. (2009) 'The emergence of workforce development: definition, conceptual boundaries and implications', in Maclean, R. and Wilson, D. (eds) *International Handbook of Education for the Changing World of Work*, Dordrecht: Springer, 2537–52.

Kaufman, T., Justeson, J. and Zavala, R. (2001) *Project for the Documentation of the Languages of Mesoamerica*. Online. Available HTTP: http://www.albany.edu/anthro/maldp/ (accessed 10 December 2013).

Lao, P. (2013) *Profesionales y gerentes en Panamá*, Panama City: Quality Leadership University.

Lepeley, M.T. and Albornoz, C. (2013) 'Business education in Chile: the entrepreneurial innovation mega trend', in Ilan, A., Jones, V. and McIntyre, J. (eds) *Innovation in Business Education in Emerging Markets*, New York: Palgrave Macmillan.

Long, G. (2012) 'Chile's labor shortage: workers needed', *bUSiness CHILE magazine*, 15 June. Online. Available HTTP: http://www.businesschile.cl/en/news/cover-story/chile%E2%80%99s-labor-shortage-workers-needed (accessed 23 December 2013).

Mattson, S. and Teran, A. (2011) *Education Trap Threatens Panama's Economic Boom*. Online. Available HTTP: http://www.reuters.com/article/2011/09/06/us-panama-education-idUSTRE7857D420110906 (accessed 12 December 2013).

McLean, G.N. (2003) 'NHRD: why countries can't do without it', *Proceedings of the Second Asian Conference of the Academy of Human Resource Development*, Bangkok: Academy of Human Resource Development.

McLean, G.N. and McLean, L. (2001) 'If we can't define HRD in one country, how can we define it in an international context?', *Human Resource Development International* 4: 313–26.

MercoPress (2013) *Chile with Some of the Worst Social Indicators Among the 34 OECD Members*. Online. Available HTTP: http://en.mercopress.com/2011/04/13/chile-with-some-of-the-worst-social-indicators-among-the-34-oecd-members (accessed 23 December 2013).

Ministry of Finance (2013) *Why Chile?*, Government of Chile. Online. Available HTTP: http://www.hacienda.cl/english/investor-relations-office/why-chile.html (accessed 23 December 2013).

National Atlas (2013) *Profile of the People and Land of the United States*. Online. Available HTTP: http://nationalatlas.gov/articles/mapping/a_general.html (accessed 23 December 2013).

OECD (2010) *Members and Partners*, Organisation for Economic Co-operation and Development. Online. Available HTTP: http://www.oecd.org/about/membersandpartners/ (accessed 23 December 2013).

OECD (2011) *6. Equity Indicators. 1. Income Inequality*, Organisation for Economic Co-operation and Development. Online. Available HTTP: http://www.oecd.org/berlin/47570121.pdf (accessed 23 December 2013).

OECD (2012) *Better Skills, Better Jobs, Better Lives: A Strategic Approach to Skills Policies*, Organisation for Economic Co-operation and Development. Online. Available HTTP: http://skills.oecd.org/documents/OECDSkillsStrategyFINALENG.pdf (accessed 23 December 2013).

OECD (2013a) *Chile: Education at a Glance*, Organisation for Economic Co-operation and Development. Online. Available HTTP: http://www.oecd.org/edu/Chile_EAG2013%20Country%20Note.pdf (accessed 23 December 2013).

OECD (2013b) *Economic Surveys: Chile*, Organisation for Economic Co-operation and Development. Online. Available HTTP: http://www.oecd-ilibrary.org/economics/oecd-economic-surveys-chile-2013_eco_surveys-chl-2013-en (accessed 23 December 2013).

OECD (2013c) *Real Minimum Wages*, Organisation for Economic Co-operation and Development. Online. Available HTTP: http://stats.oecd.org/Index.aspx?DataSetCode=RMW (accessed 23 December 2013).

OECD (2013d) *Making the Labour Market More Inclusive*, Organisation for Economic Co-operation and Development. Online. Available HTTP: http://www.keepeek.com/Digital-Asset-Management/oecd/economics/oecd-economic-surveys-chile-2013_eco_surveys-chl-2013-en#page11 (accessed 23 December 2013).

Panama America (2012) *Pobreza extrema se redujo a 10.4% en 2012, según el MEF*. Online. Available HTTP: http://www.panamaamerica.com.pa/notas/1203490-pobreza-extrema-se-redujo-104-2012-segun-el-mef- (accessed 30 August, 2012).

Panama Canal Authority (2013) *This is the Canal*, Government of Panama. Online. Available HTTP: http://www.pancanal.com/eng/index.html (accessed 16 May 2013).

Perales, J.R. (2012) 'The hemisphere's spaghetti bowl of free-trade agreements', *Americas Quarterly*, Spring. Online. Available HTTP: http://www.americasquarterly.org/perales (accessed 23 December 2013).

Scasso, L. (2012) 'Latin American case', *Proceedings of the 4th NILE International Conference on Lifelong Learning*, National Institute for Lifelong Education: Daejoen, Korea, 61–94. [22 November 2012].

Schwab, K. (2013) 'The global competitiveness report 2013–2014: full data edition', Geneva: World Economic Forum. Online. Available HTTP: http://www3.weforum.org/docs/WEF_GlobalCompetitivenessReport_2013-14.pdf (accessed 12 December, 2013).

Sebastian, E. and Ledermen, D. (1998) 'The political economy of unilateral trade liberalization: The case of Chile', National Bureau of Economic Research. Online. Available HTTP: http://www.anderson.ucla.edu/faculty/sebastian.edwards/W6510.pdf (accessed 23 December 2013).

Smith, E.B. and Craze, M. (2010) 'Copper rises 50% in red gold rush on China doubling usage', *Bloomberg Businessweek*, 3 November. Online. Available HTTP: http://www.bloomberg.com/news/2010-11-03/copper-rises-50-in-red-gold-rush-on-belief-china-to-double-consumption.html (accessed 23 December 2013).

Swanson, R.A. and Holton III, E.F. (2009) *Foundations of Human Resource Development*, 2nd edition, San Francisco: Berrett-Koehler.

Trosziewicz, A. (2011) 'World's 10 biggest copper-producing countries in 2010', *Bloomberg*, 26 April. Online. Available HTTP: http://www.bloomberg.com/news/2011-04-26/world-s-10-biggest-copper-producing-countries-in-2010-table-.html (accessed 23 December 2013).

UNDP (United Nations Development Programme) (2012) *Informe Final Comisión Revisora del Sistema de Capacitación e Intermediación Laboral*, United Nations. Online. Available HTTP: http://www.pnud.cl/proyectos/Documentos%20de%20proyectos/2012/Informe%20Final%20Comisi%C3%B3n%20Revisora_291111.pdf (accessed 23 December 2013).

Unión de Naciones Suramericanas (2013) *Historia*. Online. Available HTTP: http://www.unasursg.org/inicio/organizacion/historia (accessed 11 December 2013).

World Bank (2013a) *2.2 World Development Indicators: Labor Force Structure*. Online. Available HTTP: http://wdi.worldbank.org/table/2.2# (accessed 23 December 2013).

World Bank (2013b) *Agricultural Land (% of Land Area)*. Online. Available HTTP: http://data.worldbank.org/indicator/ag.lnd.agri.zs/countries?display=default (accessed 23 December 2013).

World Bank (2013c) *GDP Growth (Annual)*. Online. Available HTTP: http://data.worldbank.org/indicator/ny.gdp.mktp.kd.zg (accessed 23 December 2013).

World Bank (2013d) *Land Area (Sq. Km)*. Online. Available HTTP: http://data.worldbank.org/indicator/ag.lnd.totl.k2 (accessed 23 December 2013).

World Bank (2013e) *Latin America: Middle Class Hits Historic High*. Online. Available HTTP: http://www.worldbank.org/en/news/feature/2012/11/13/crecimiento-clase-media-america-latina (accessed 1 July 2013).

World Bank (2013f) *Unemployment, Total (% of Total Labor Force)*. Online. Available HTTP: http://data.worldbank.org/indicator/SL.UEM.TOTL.ZS?order=wbapi_data_value_2012+wbapi_data_value+wbapi_data_value-last&sort=asc (accessed 23 December 2013).

World Factbook, Central Intelligence Agency (2013a) *Central America and Caribbean*, Government of the United States. Online. Available HTTP: https://www.cia.gov/library/publications/the-world-factbook/wfbExt/region_cam.html (accessed 10 December 2013).

World Factbook, Central Intelligence Agency (2013b) *South America*, Government of the United States. Online. Available HTTP: https://www.cia.gov/library/publications/the-world-factbook/wfbExt/region_soa.html (accessed 11 November 2013).

World Trade Organization (2013) *Welcome to the Regional Trade Agreements Information System (RTA-IS)*. Online. Available HTTP: http://rtais.wto.org/UI/PublicSearchByMemberResult.aspx?MemberCode=152&lang=1&redirect=1 (accessed 23 December 2013).

37
HRD IN NORTH AMERICA

Travor C. Brown, José Ernesto Rangel Delgado and Bronwyn Cass

Given that the field of HRD is relatively new, we should not be surprised that there has been considerable debate concerning its definition and purposes. In a recent work, Hamlin and Stewart (2011: 210) defined four core purposes of HRD. In this chapter, we will ground our discussion on these four core purposes in the context of Canada and Mexico:

- Improving individual or group effectiveness and performance;
- Improving organizational effectiveness and performance;
- Developing knowledge, skills and competencies; and
- Enhancing human potential and personal growth.

From a broader North American perspective, the field of HRD is well established. We see academic programs graduating undergraduate, masters and doctoral degrees (take for example, Texas A&M, University of Minnesota, Florida International University – see www.ahrd.org) and a dedicated society (Academy of Human Resource Development [AHRD]) encompassing scholars, students and practitioners. Clearly, these elements show that HRD has a solid foundation in North America.

However, as will be seen in many other chapters in this collection, much of the HRD field has focused on one North American country, namely, the United States. In this chapter, we will focus less on that country and more specifically on the countries of Canada and Mexico. Specifically, the purpose of this chapter is to examine the similarities and differences within Canada and Mexico that are most relevant to HRD students, scholars, and practitioners. Our specific objectives are to:

- Understand the history of HRD in North America outside the United States.
- Learn about the academic HRD programs offered in both Canada and Mexico.
- Gain a comprehensive understanding of the facets of the field of HRD in Canada and Mexico.
- Understand that HRD practices are similar throughout North America, but that Canada and Mexico present unique challenges in the field.

HRD in Canada

History

The history of HRD as an accredited profession in Canada dates back to at least the 1980s; at this time, scholars were appealing to practitioners to organize and align the HRD profession provincially and nationally through better credential options (Kenny 1986). During this period, Latham, a very established Canadian Human Resources Management (HRM) and psychology professor, in his chapter in the *Annual Review of Psychology*, positively noted "the emphasis that organizations place on training originated relatively recently" (Latham 1988: 548). This was in part due to a preceding "philosophical tug-of-war" within organizations concerning whether *selecting* or *training* employees was the preferred method for promoting employees (Latham 1988). While the advancement of theoretical and empirical research on training and development was ongoing, what troubled some scholars was "the extent to which practitioners and practitioner journals appear[ed] to be unaffected by these advancements" in the scholarly literature (Latham 1988: 577).

Today, it is safe to say that there is an ongoing effort to infuse academic findings into the everyday practice of HRD. However, even with the tremendous growth of human resource management and development practices in Canada (Jeung *et al.* 2011; Latham *et al.* 2005; Saks *et al.* 2011), there has been limited focus on HRD as a unique discipline in Canada. Rather in many cases, HRD publications and research projects are presented in the broader organizational and HRM literature. For example, Jeung *et al.* (2011) identified that the HRD field is largely interdisciplinary in nature, as evidenced by the major journals contributing to the HRD literature, and recognized that the interdisciplinary nature of HRD contains key themes such as training transfer and evaluation, learning in organizations, as well as knowledge sharing and knowledge creation (Jeung *et al.* 2011). Within Canada, we have seen several scholars work on such topics (e.g. Brown and Warren 2009; Budworth and Sookhai 2010; Morin and Latham 2000; Saks and Belcourt 2006); however, the scholars producing such publications in HRD-related journals tend to be placed in business schools (often in HRM departments) rather than in separate HRD units.

Academic programs

Given the predominance of HRD research in Canada conducted by academics with appointments in business schools, it is not surprising that we find limited programs solely dedicated to HRD in the country. In fact, we could only find two academic programs specific to HRD in Canada (as listed on the Association of Universities and Colleges of Canada website www.aucc.ca). The first is offered by the University of Prince Edward Island (UPEI) in conjunction with Holland College; the second is offered at the University of Regina. More specifically, UPEI offers a Bachelor of Education (HRD), while Regina offers a non-degree Certificate in Human Resource Development.

In Canada the topics central to the field of HRD tend to be included in other programs (in particular in business schools and HRM programs, of which there are many) but are not often taught in standalone programs. Similarly, we see the Administrative Science Association of Canada (ASAC, see www.asac.ca), with its broad focus lacks a unique HRD division (or stream); however, it does have at least two divisions where work related to HRD would be presented, namely, HRM and management education and development. In fact, a review of the schools listed on Association of Universities and Colleges of Canada website shows that over 1,000 business programs exist in the country, with the vast majority of such programs (if not all) having HRM courses where students would be exposed to HRD topics such as training, learning, development, etc. Similarly, the same website found approximately 40 educational programs in Canada that focused on adult education and learning.

These later results concerning the prevalence of adult education programs versus HRD programs reinforce the findings of Wiesenberg and Peterson (2004), who compared Canadian and US post-secondary faculty members in the fields of adult education (AdEd) and human resource development (HRD). They found that professionals engaged in providing "workplace learning" programs identified more with AdEd in Canada; whereas, the US context exhibited greater perceptions of a linkage between AdEd and HRD. Not surprisingly, they concluded that there is "a need for academics and practitioners in this emerging field of study and practice to build alliances . . . in order to enrich both the theory and practice – as well as facilitate the translation of theory into practice – that comprises the field of 'workplace learning'" (Wiesenberg and Peterson 2004: 234).

Given the interdisciplinary nature of HRD, it is clear that in Canada, we lack a distinct HRD field; rather, we see scholars active in HRD research and teaching, but often residing in non-HRD academic units. In many ways, this juxtaposition reflects the broader debates of the HRD field. While some scholars argue against trying to produce a universal definition of HRD (Lee 2001), others have identified that there is need for a synthesized definition of HRD due to the lack of clarity on the definitional boundaries of HRD (Hamlin and Stewart 2011). We suspect that this debate concerning "definitional boundaries," and the extent HRD is a truly defined field, will continue. Nevertheless, in Canada, for the time being, the answer is consistent with the view of Lee (2001).

Having examined the academic side of HRD in Canada, we now turn our focus to four core HRD purposes as defined by Hamlin and Stewart (2011). A brief summary of research related to each purpose now follows.

Insights related to purpose 1: improving individual or group performance

Research examining individual and group effectiveness is alive and well in Canada. For example, in the context of HRD, individual employee performance has been shown to have a positive relationship with employee engagement (Saks and Gruman 2011). Similarly, Fairlie (2011) showed how HRD professionals could focus on the role of meaningful work to enhance organizational and employee performance and outcomes.

Canadian scholars have also examined the issue of group effectiveness and performance. For example, Brown (2003) found that a psychology-based training intervention improved team performance and efficacy (or task specific confidence). We have also seen Canadian research examining the interplay between individual and group effectiveness such as research examining vertical transfer, or the extent that a trained individual can "transfer" his or her knowledge to untrained group members (Budworth 2008).

Insights related to purpose 2: improving organizational performance

While perhaps less prevalent in Canada, we do see research concerning this second core purpose. For example, in a study examining the effects of HRD practices on improving organizational performance Benabou (1996: 97) found that "well-designed HRD programs do improve business results and are highly profitable." Improving organizational performance improves not only the efficiency of an organization, but also the bottom line.

Insights related to purpose 3: developing knowledge, skills, and competencies

HRD practitioners understand that providing training and development opportunities to employees can help to ensure they have the right knowledge, skills, and abilities (KSAs) to do their job. Clearly, Canadian scholars (e.g. Latham 1988; Saks and Haccoun 2007) have been active in research related to developing employees' and leaders' skills and knowledge. However, extensive literature on training transfer indicates that training is effective only to the extent that it is applied back on the job (Saks and Haccoun 2007). It is perhaps in the area of transfer where Canadians have made their greatest impact as evidenced by the wealth of transfer research and the development of conceptual models (Brown and McCracken 2009), determination of transfer rates (Saks and Belcourt 2006), and interventions to bolster transfer at the individual (Brown and Warren 2009; Budworth and Sookhai 2010; Gaudine and Saks 2004; Morin and Latham 2000) and group levels (Brown 2003; Budworth 2008).

Insights related to purpose 4: enhancing human potential and personal growth

The premise that HRD can enhance human potential and personal growth underlies many scholarly definitions of HRD (Hamlin and Stewart 2011). This core purpose relates to "a process of developing and/or unleashing human expertise through organization development and personnel training and development for the purpose of improving performance" (Swanson 1995: 208). Canadian scholars have identified that participation in corporate university training, as a way of developing staff, has a positive impact on performance (Morin and Renaud 2004). Furthermore, in today's knowledge economy, the practical implication is that "employees want to be able to develop their skills and that a company that offers good training has a better chance of retaining its key employees" (Morin and Renaud 2004: 304).

Unique challenges for HRD in Canada

Many people do not understand the uniqueness of the Canadian culture relative to its much larger neighbor, the United States. Perhaps our large shared border and extensive trade relationships further solidify the "sameness" that many see between the two countries (Joseph 2010). Thus, we only found a single study (Peterson and Wiesenberg 2004) that examined the professional fulfillment and job satisfaction of HRD faculty in Canada relative to the United States. That study revealed few differences between American and Canadian faculty in terms of job satisfaction. Specifically, Canadian and American AdEd and HRD faculty were found to have similar sources of job satisfaction (e.g. teaching and interacting with students) and dissatisfaction (e.g. administrative responsibilities). Minor differences were noted in specific aspects of professional fulfillment and the fields with which the respondents identify themselves.

While Canada and the United States are, in essence, countries of immigrants, with significant roots in Britain, Canada alone had a much larger French influence. Canada was largely populated by two distinct societies: French and English. Today, both English and French are official languages of Canada and are spoken by about 83 per cent of the population (Marquardt *et al.* 2004). However, the Francophone (French-speaking) society of Canada resides predominantly in the province of Quebec, while the Anglophone (English-speaking) society dominates the remaining provinces and territories. In large cities such as Vancouver, Toronto, and Montreal, the influx of multiculturalism and demographic change have created an environment tending to erode the traditional rivalry between the English and the French (Marquardt *et al.* 2004). Marquardt *et al.* (2004: 299) identified that "most Canadians are sensitive to policies, attitudes, or remarks that seem to favor one province or one culture over another." This, inevitably, has an impact on the way HRD practice and scholarship is performed in Canada. For example, one particular challenge for HRD in Canada is that the small academic community of HRD professionals may publish in one of these two languages, and may not read works of other HRD scholars of the "other" language. Moreover, as shown in the handbook in which this chapter appears, the HRD community largely communicates in English, making findings perhaps less salient in the Canadian Francophone community.

Similarly, in the United States there is a dedicated HRD conference and HRD professional community, namely, the AHRD (see www.ahrd.org). While the AHRD organization is international in scope, from a Canadian perspective, it would be seen as "American" not Canadian in nature. Like our educational programs, we do not see uniquely HRD-related organizations (with professional certification programs). Rather, we see HRM professional associations such as Human Resources Professionals Association (HRPA, see www.hrpa.ca) and International Personnel Management Association (IPMA, see http://ipma-aigp.com). In each of these two organizations, we would see many HRD topics.

Conclusion

As we conclude our discussion of Canada, we note the significant efforts dedicated to employee/leadership training and development, as well as transfer of training in Canada. However, it is clear that in Canada, HRD has not yet seen the rise of a truly distinct HRD discipline. At present, we see limited specialized HRD academic programs and no dedicated HRD society or conference. Rather, in Canada, we see that HRD is housed in largely adult education, and in particular, HRM programs. Thus, it seems probable that for Canadians HRD, as it is known elsewhere in the world, will continue to be practiced under many different names.

HRD in Mexico

History

The Mexican economy was characterized by an import substitution model for approximately 40 years from the late 1940s to the early 1980s. During this period, the need to develop human resources was considered something to be resolved between private enterprise and educational institutions. This partnership formed the basis of a comprehensive working relationship geared towards a common goal which was well organized and clearly addressed as a matter of government policy (Malpica 1995). This, however, was possible only due to strict government control which impeded initiative and economic dynamism. In the 1980s, however, Mexico became concerned about developing the human resources it needed to contribute to its evolving export economy in order to better position itself in what was evolving into a globalized economy.

Facing a new century, a new interest flourished in the field of HRD that considered labor competencies and the performance evaluation of individuals and workgroups linked to process certification and organizational processes (Ibarra 2001). This performance evaluation has improved human resources in several important ways, primarily by establishing global quality control schemes, including the International Standards Organization (ISO), responsible for promoting the development of international manufacturing standards (for both electrical appliances and electronics). Conforming to international standards has represented a major challenge for local labor because it has had to organize itself to meet international norms, based primarily on incorporating and making the Mexican economy more competitive in the world market in benefit of businesses and consumers.

Academic programs

At best, HRD in Mexico is a complimentary part of human resource management undergraduate and graduate educational programs. This, however, is inadequate in today's knowledge society. In recent years the government has developed training programs which employ competencies that better link employers and educational institutions. This inadequate perspective is partially because higher learning institutions need to take a multidisciplinary approach that better incorporates psychology, business administration, educational economics and pedagogy.

Developing countries like Mexico have developed a growing interest in the relationship between HRD and economic growth since World War II because of the need for increased participation in the global economy (Powell 1998). Complex econometric models have been developed that have paid particular attention to the strategic nature of training by the educational system. This approach, however, is insufficient to develop human resources in the global era because it lacks a humanistic and more holistic world view. Recognizing human capital solely on the basis of innovation, technological progress, education, and science, along with the generation and application of technology, does not meet the challenge of incorporating it effectively in both national (urban vs. rural) and global collaborative settings.

The role of the state in relation to civil society is in a process of transformation, which has resulted in delaying a more in-depth understanding of HRD as a discipline. Trade liberalization, economic globalization and competitiveness require associating almost all productive sectors with HRD to impact productivity and competitiveness in the international arena.

Consequently, well-balanced and properly oriented educational programs are the foundation of HRD. Often, the absence of an integrative perspective, unfortunately all-too common among educational programs, is the product of intuition, rather than a well-devised and implemented strategy. For example, a national survey conducted especially for this chapter revealed that only two educational programs were explicitly aimed at developing human resources.

Insights related to purpose 1: improving individual or group performance

This section deals with improving performance regardless of development model or whether it is regional or national in nature. It also considers the formation of teachers and necessary changes with regards to financing education in an effort to improve educational outcomes.

Strongly agricultural countries like Mexico, whose traditional economy was based on monoculture and a low technological level of existing industry, only required unskilled manual labor. However, government policy to promote different geographic areas, especially in the case of the Mexico City metropolitan area and other important cities such as Monterrey and Guadalajara or regions such as the Mexico–United States border, resulted in attracting foreign direct investment and technological development.

Suddenly, the job market evolved and grew in sophistication as it underwent substantial changes from a traditional rural, unqualified and labor intensive scheme to an urban, skilled and more industrialized means of production that widely employed computer and communications technologies. The rapid changes in the job market made a degree of improvisation necessary while the country developed strategies to create and stimulate structural and organizational changes so that it could better adapt to the quickly evolving circumstances (Rodriguez 2000).

According to Koonts and O'Donnell (1979) and Byars and Rue (1986), evaluating the performance of individuals and groups should focus on techniques that center on achieving results for the company at the executive, the supervisory, and operational staff levels. Also, in the case of Mexico, there is a growing trend to evaluate the performance of individuals, groups and organizations. For example, in higher education, PROMEP, a program developed by the Ministry of Education, is in charge of teacher certification. Meanwhile, ESDEPED, a program jointly funded by the federal government and public universities, manages incentives for teacher productivity. Additionally, collegial evaluations are carried out by Committees for the Evaluation of Higher Education (CIEES) and Higher Education for Accreditation Council (COPAES), which evaluate educational programs. Additionally, and equally important, the Council for Standardization and Certification of Labor Competencies (CONOCER) and ISO focus either on the process of HRD or the specific local institutions that evaluate or certify human resources.

Insights related to purpose 2: improving organizational performance

Organizations can benefit from recognizing the specific characteristics of the region in which they function and contract their personnel, which do not necessarily conform to national characteristics. Specific regions of Mexico can vary significantly due to very disparate educational levels, economic and industrial activity, rural vs. urban antecedents, access to computer and communications technologies, as well as local ethnicity, language and culture. In this way, the absence of a comprehensive approach to HRD makes studying it more difficult; however, it is possible to draw some generalization from different disciplines, especially in the areas of economics and business administration. The issue of improving the performance and efficiency of organizations in Mexico is significantly influenced by market forces. Consequently, training and education represent two important factors which must be considered when attempting to improve organizational performance.

Insights related to purpose 3: developing knowledge, skills, and competencies

This section presents the training of human resources based on skills development. Currently, every public educational level in Mexico is based on the development of job competencies and skills. The influence of a market strategy that places importance on the needs of the productive sector is apparent in the process of education and training, despite criticism based on market performance, in general, and on the labor market, in particular.

There are countless examples that evidence the changes Mexico's education system is presently undergoing. Institutions, actions, projects and government programs such as the Ministry of Labor and Social Security (STyPS), the CONOCER, the Project for the Modernization of Technical Education and Training (PMETyC), the National Council for Science and Technology (CONACYT), the Secretariat of Economy (SE), the Secretariat of Public Education (SEP), the Distance Education Program (PROCADIST), the National College of Professional Technical Education (CONALEP), the National Act on Science and Technology, the National Award for Work, Bank of Workforce Innovation, the Catalogue of Core Competences for Innovation and Innovation Online, the National Association of Universities and Higher Education Institutes, regional research centers and various universities, are representative examples of the government's interest in developing job competencies.

Significantly, the traditional vision of formal education which opposes recognizing experience as a sufficient basis for employment strongly prevails. To counter this, the Education Department under agreement number 286, published in the Official Journal of the Federation on October 30, 2000, allows for academic recognition of workplace experience in providing a work skills certificate. This agreement provides transparency and equal conditions for experience gained under real-world experiences while also promoting a more flexible continuing education system.

Recently (December 2012), the Mexican government ratified an educational reform initiative. Current president Enrique Peña Nieto highlights four major points: (1) the creation of a career teacher professionalization program, (2) autonomy for the National Institute for Evaluation, (3) a system to operate and administer the educational system and (4) the establishment of more than 40,000 full-time schools. However, this reform does not adequately integrate studies from the preschool to university-level studies, thereby not adequately linking education to the development of human resources.

Insights related to purpose 4: enhancing human potential and personal growth

This section presents a regional approach that characterizes local needs. In Mexico, the enhancement of human potential and personal growth is limited by a short-range vision that does little to support the decision of individuals with respect to their education or training. People's insertion into the labor market is determined by a market vision, which has a negative impact on educational levels. Jobs in the private sector have been impacted by the growth of information and communication technologies in the production process, which require different generic skills (computer, language, technology) as well as different business values. In short, the evolving job market requires persons who have skills and competencies that go beyond more traditional worker profiles. Having a basic educational level used to be sufficient to meet the employment requirements; currently, however, low-level positions are being filled by graduates of higher education institutions. These graduates face a difficult reality as they often cannot be employed because they are considered over qualified (Rangel Delgado and Boncheva 2012). The problem is even more complicated if we consider that public policies are not designed for the unemployed, but rather for those who are already employed.

Consequently, the decision to finance the modernization of education will not have a major impact on the educational system as such, but only at each educational level. The system will remain disjointed with respect to human resource training necessary for the country's development.

Unique challenges for HRD in Mexico

The existence of many Mexicos, in terms of its 60 ethno-linguistic groups, forces one to think about the different ways to develop human resources. This complexity of HRD makes it a difficult question for businesses, government and society to resolve. It is further complicated by the high level of competitiveness required to meet global market challenges. Thus, HRD in Mexico needs to be considered according to its specific ethnographic circumstances.

HRD should be organized to improve the performance of individuals participating in processes related to the production of goods and services in such a way that corporate training and formal education coordinate with each other to meet the same goal. As a result, in recent years, the conceptualization of "job competencies" at work and "academic competencies" in schools has gained importance.

A vision of HRD based on both real-world work experience and theory and knowledge provided by schooling can substantially reduce the distance between schools and businesses. Unfortunately, this paradigm has been very slow to gain acceptance. One major obstacle is the power exercised by traditional schemes of evaluation employed by academic institutions which are reluctant to recognize real-world work experience as relevant for certification purposes, although there are others that are important. Although substantial progress has been achieved and success has been reported, there is still very much that needs to be done. Even more needs to be achieved to bridge the differences between rural and urban populations, where adopting the "American way of life," already widely accepted by urban dwellers, discourages the incorporation of local customs and traditions into the production process. Another example is that of local cultural and ethnic groups, many with their own languages, who strongly resist western acculturation. All of these points need to be considered in HRD because they can affect their sustainable development and subsequent incorporation into organizations.

Mexico only recently began to pay attention to this problem when it created the National Commission for the Development of Indigenous Peoples (CDI), a decentralized agency of the federal government, established on May 21, 2003. Unfortunately, societal and government efforts such as the CDI, including the recently passed educational reform, are not sufficient to establish a more synchronous relationship between ethnicity and HRD. To achieve this, a large number of initiatives to achieve coexistence between modernity and tradition for the benefit of society will be necessary, according to Rockwell (2011), to not only reproduce the concept of human resources, but to also transform it.

Conclusion

In recent years, HRD in Mexico has focused on the development of knowledge, skills and competencies, as well as on improving the efficiency and performance of organizations, individuals and groups by means of performance appraisal processes and certifications. Despite this, however, efforts to improve human potential, promote personal growth and increase the efficiency and performance of organizations do not appear to be sufficient according to national and international standards. Because of this, there is an area of opportunity to develop human resources for both businesses and higher education institutions. Furthermore, the intention of developing human resources on a regional level and, in particular, the inclusion of ethnic groups is a very recent challenge, resulting, as of yet, in very few tangible results.

Human capital makes the difference in a knowledge-based economy. Organizations are what employers and their workers make them, using their combined talents and experience. Consequently, the role of higher education institutions is essential given its role as creator of knowledge to be transferred to society. Unfortunately, only a few programs aim at developing human resources explicitly and are oriented more towards market pressures and actively participating in development strategies for the country and its very diverse regions. Consequently, we see a substantial need to strengthen the development of local human resources while considering the link between education and training, without underestimating the challenges imposed by external conditions.

Implications

The two countries in this chapter border the United States, which has arguably been at the forefront of HRD scholarship. Given the common language between Canada and the United States, it is not surprising that we see full evidence of the four core purposes of HRD identified by

Hamlin and Stewart (2011) in the Canadian context: (1) improving individual or group effectiveness and performance, (2) improving organizational effectiveness and performance, (3) developing knowledge, skills and competencies, and (4) enhancing human potential and personal growth. Of particular note, the Canadian context has emphasized the training and development area of HRD housed in the third purpose. However, unlike in the US, HRD in Canada is not seen as a separate discipline with much of the work in the field taking place in the HRM or even Adult Education fields.

Like the Canadian experience, HRD in Mexico also tends to be embedded in the HRM or Adult Education fields rather than a standalone discipline. While Mexico does not share the same language base as the United States and Canada, it too shows evidence of HRD scholarship and practice in all four core areas. However, at present, because Mexico lacks a strategy for HRD, insufficient work exists to provide a more integral view of how the four core areas complement and interact with each other or how it affects corporations or the economy, in general. Similar to Canada, the Mexican government's strategy regarding HRD largely focuses on developing knowledge, skills and competencies, and therefore emphasizes educational reform, although a significant effort is also made in the area of improving the efficiency and performance of organizations, individuals and groups by means of performance appraisal processes and certifications. In sum, the Mexican academic community needs to redouble its efforts in the other two core areas to better provide the feedback necessary for the government to develop a more integrated and sustainable HRD policy.

In conclusion, while HRD is not seen as a unique discipline in Canada and Mexico, there is ample evidence that the four core purposes of HRD exist in both countries. What remains uncertain is whether we will see HRD emerge as a distinct, interdisciplinary field as has happened in the US or if the field will remain intertwined with HRM and Adult Education.

References

Academy of Human Resource Development (AHRD) (n.d.) Retrieved on January 29, 2013 from http://www.ahrd.org/?academic_programs_hr.

Administrative Science Association of Canada (ASAC) (n.d.) Retrieved on January 30, 2013 from http://www.asac.ca.

Association of Universities and Colleges of Canada (AUCC) (n.d.) Retrieved on January 29, 2013 from http://www.aucc.ca/canadian-universities/study-programs.

Benabou, C. (1996) Assessing the impact of training programs on the bottom line. *National Productivity Review* 15: 91–99.

Brown, T.C. (2003) The effect of verbal self-guidance training on collective efficacy and performance. *Personnel Psychology* 56: 935–64.

Brown, T.C. and McCracken, M. (2009) Building a bridge of understanding: How barriers to training participation become barriers to training transfer. *Journal of European Industrial Training* 33, 6: 492–512.

Brown, T.C. and Warren, A.M. (2009) Distal goal and proximal goal transfer of training interventions in an executive education program. *Human Resource Development Quarterly* 16: 369–87.

Budworth, M. (2008, August) Vertical transfer of training: The role of collective efficacy. In symposium, Latham, G.P. (chair) *Predicting and enhancing training outcomes*. Proceedings from: AOM 2008: The 68th Annual Meeting of the Academy of Management, Anaheim, CA.

Budworth, M. and Sookhai, F. (2010) Enhancing transfer climate through supervisor training. *Human Resource Development Quarterly* 21: 257–72.

Byars, L.L. and Rue, L.W. (1986) *Administración de Recursos Humanos*. Edit. Interamericana, México.

Fairlie, P. (2011) Meaningful work, employee engagement, and other key employee outcomes: Implications for human resource development. *Advances in Developing Human Resources* 13: 508–25.

Gaudine, A.P. and Saks, A.M. (2004) A longitudinal quasi-experiment on the post-training transfer interventions. *Human Resource Development Quarterly* 15: 57–75.

Hamlin, B. and Stewart, J. (2011) What is HRD? A definitional review and synthesis of the HRD domain. *Journal of European Industrial Training* 35, 3: 199–220.

Human Resources Professionals Association (HRPA) (n.d.) Retrieved on January 30, 2013 from http://www.hrpa.ca.

Ibarra, A.A. (2001) *Formación de los Recursos Humanos y Competencia Laboral.* Retrieved on August 20, 2012 from http://www.losrecursoshumanos.com/phpscript/descargar_pdf.php?id=159.

International Personnel Management Association (IPMA) (n.d.) Retrieved on January 30, 2013 from http://ipma-aigp.com.

Jeung, C.W., Yoon, H.J., Park, S. and Jo, S.J. (2011) The contributions of human resource development research across disciplines: A citation and content analysis. *Human Resource Development Quarterly* 22, 1: 87–109.

Joseph, A.M. (2010) US–Canadian economic relations, twenty years after the USA–Canada free trade agreement. *British Journal of Canadian Studies* 23, 2: 233–46.

Kenny, J.B. (1986) HRD: Better service through credentialling? *Public Personnel Management* 15, 4: 451–58.

Koonts, H. and O'Donnell, C.J. (1979) *Curso de administración moderna.* Editorial McGraw Hill, México.

Latham, G.P. (1988) Human resource training and development. *Annual Review of Psychology* 39, 1: 545.

Latham, G.P., Almost, J., Mann, S. and Moore, C. (2005) New developments in performance management. *Organizational Dynamics* 34, 1: 77–87.

Lee, M. (2001) A refusal to define HRD. *Human Resource Development International* 4, 3: 327–41.

Malpica Faustor, C. (1995) *Decentralisation and planning of education: Recent experiences in five Latin American countries*, UNESCO: Paris.

Marquardt, M., Berger, N. and Loan, P. (2004) *HRD in the age of globalization. A practical guide to workplace learning in the third millennium.* New York: Basic Books.

Morin, L. and Latham, G.P. (2000) The effect of mental practice and goal setting as a transfer of training intervention on supervisors' self-efficacy and communication skills: An exploratory study. *Applied Psychology: An International Review* 49, 3: 566–78.

Morin, L. and Renaud, S. (2004) Participation in corporate university training: Its effect on individual job performance. *Canadian Journal of Administrative Sciences* 21, 4: 295–306.

Peterson, S.L. and Wiesenberg, F. (2004) Professional fulfillment and satisfaction of US and Canadian adult education and human resource development faculty. *International Journal of Lifelong Education* 23, 2: 159–78.

Powell, M. (1998) *Economic Restructuring and Human Resource Development: A Discussion of Events in Mexico.* Working Paper 19. Centre for Labor Market Studies, University of Leicester, UK.

Rangel Delgado, J.E. and Boncheva, A.I. (2012) *The Crisis in Two Pacific Rim Economies: Higher Education and Employment in Mexico and Thailand.* WITpress, UK.

Rockwell, E. (2011) *La experiencia etnográfica. Historia y Cultura en los Procesos Educativos.* Paidós, Argentina.

Rodriguez, V.J. (2000) *Administración Moderna de Personal.* ECAFSA, México.

Saks, A.M. and Belcourt, M. (2006) An investigation of training activities and transfer of training in organizations. *Human Resource Management* 45, 4: 629–48.

Saks, A.M. and Haccoun, R.R. (2007) *Managing Performance Through Training and Development* (4th edition). Nelson, Scarborough, ON.

Saks, A.M. and Gruman, J.A. (2011) Manage employee engagement to manage performance. *Industrial and Organizational Psychology* 4, 2: 204–7.

Saks, A.M., Tamkin, P. and Lewis, P. (2011) Management training and development. *International Journal of Training and Development* 15, 3: 179–83.

Swanson, R.A. (1995) Human resource development: Performance is the key. *Human Resource Development Quarterly* 6, 2: 207–13.

Wiesenberg, F.P. and Peterson, S.L. (2004) Workplace learning as a field of inquiry: A Canadian–US comparison. *Journal of Workplace Learning* 16, 4: 219–36.

38

EMERGING TRENDS, CHALLENGES AND OPPORTUNITIES FOR HRD IN INDIA

Rajashi Ghosh and Arup Barman

Over the last decade or so, India has emerged as a major player in the global market and organizations in India have undergone a transformation in their HRD processes and practices. With a headcount of 1.2 billion people, and half of its residents between 20 to 30 years of age, India is being considered an emerging talent powerhouse, predicted to be among the world's five largest economies and viewed by investors, businesses, and tertiary education providers as a land of opportunity (Budhwar and Varma 2011, Pio 2007, Rao and Varghese 2009). Clearly, this transition calls for a closer look at how global competitiveness and the changing Indian economic scenario have interplayed to transform the value of human capital and hence the perception of HRD in India. While the rapid growth of the Indian economy is unparalleled in its scope and impact on HRD in India, a closer look will also inform us about the key HRD challenges and opportunities still needing urgent attention in the current political and economic context of the country.

The main objectives of this chapter are three-fold: first, to provide a historical overview of the key developments in Indian HRD; second, to highlight the central trends defining the current state of HRD in India; and third, to delineate future directions drawing on HRD challenges and opportunities in India. In doing so, we distinguish HRD in India into two separate streams as noted by Rao and Varghese (2009): (1) HRD in organizations, and (2) HRD for the nation. While private industry in India attends to the former, the Ministry of HRD in the Government of India is largely responsible for the latter. Irrespective of the foci being micro at the organizational level or macro at the national level, the development of human capital is central to HRD's true character and hence, the first section of the chapter briefly explains the backdrop of some political and economic changes that transformed the value of human capital in India.

To conduct an in-depth examination of the trends and challenges facing the field of HRD in India, we took a two-pronged approach to this study. First, we reviewed all extant literature on the topic of "HRD in India" published in peer-reviewed journals. Second, we interviewed a distinguished group of 12 individuals who have either published articles on the topic of HRD in India, taught or are teaching HRD related subjects in India, or have worked or are working in HRD functions in organizations in India. Our intent was to understand the current perspectives of both HRD educators and professionals pertaining to the urgent issues needing attention for future progress of HRD in India. The later sections of the chapter focus on explaining the themes that emerged from the review and the interviews and the future directions for HRD in India.

Understanding the context: value of human capital

India gained independence from the British Commonwealth in 1947. Following independence, India adopted a state-controlled economic development strategy that resulted in fewer international linkages (Srinivasan 2004). The movement of capital and labor was coordinated by the state, public sector endeavors were nationalized, and a socialist framework was central to India's economic development model (Alagaraja and Wang 2012). By the beginning of the 1990s, India's economy experienced decelerating industrial production, high inflation, critically low foreign exchange reserves, and increasing government and external debts (Sparrow and Budhwar 1997, Srinivasan 2004). In response, the Government of India introduced its New Industrial Policy (NIP) resolution on 24 July 1991 liberalizing, privatizing, and globalizing the Indian corporate sector. The economy experienced transformational changes as India opened its market to the influence of other countries, notably the United States (Alagaraja and Wang 2012).

Since liberalization, waves of reform brought several sectors of the Indian economy closer to a market-based system and helped the gross domestic product (GDP) per capita growth rate to soar to an average of 7.5 per cent (Rao and Varghese 2009). Specifically, the information technology (IT) and information technology enabled services (ITES) industry boomed and several new segments in the financial services sector opened up starting from investment banking to insurance to wealth management. Opening up these new segments put a different slant to HRD as the balance of supply and demand of human capital tipped to far more demand than supply. Due to the compulsive forces of a newly emerged market-oriented economy, the HRD function began receiving greater recognition and importance at both micro (i.e. organizational) and macro levels (i.e. national) (Yadapadithaya 2001). At the micro level, all private, public, and multinational organizations in India started focusing more on how to develop and engage their employees to reduce attrition. At the macro level, the Government of India started initiating partnerships with different nongovernmental organizations for planning towards promoting national skill development (Alagaraja and Wang 2012). However, the full scope and potential for economic development in India has been tempered by the complex interplay of political, social, and cultural changes that present challenges for growth and development of India's human capital, especially the huge unorganized sector[1] which employs 93 percent of India's workforce (Saini 2005).

Micro-level perspectives on HRD in India

Roots of the term HRD in Indian organizations can be traced back to the efforts of two consultants, Dr Rao and the late Dr Pareek who established the first HRD department in 1975 in Larsen & Toubro, a prominent engineering company in India (Rao *et al.* 2007). Their conceptualization of HRD was unique and was contingent on efficient functioning of other HR subsystems such as the industrial relations (IR) and personnel management (PM) functions (Pareek and Rao 2008). The integrated HRD system designed by Dr Rao and Dr Pareek was envisioned to ensure future growth by focusing on performance appraisal, feedback and coaching, potential identification and development, career development, training and organization development (Pareek and Rao 2008). However, unfortunately the terms HRD, human resource management (HRM), and PM have been used interchangeably in India. Many personnel departments have been renamed to HRD and then to HRM though not extending their function beyond administration of payroll and welfare (Cho and McLean 2004, Pio 2007). Moreover, many organizations in India followed in the footsteps of renowned organizations in the United States such as the American Society of Training and Development (ASTD) and re-titled training as HRD, further diluting the integrated concept proposed by Dr Rao and Dr Pareek. Nevertheless, barring the confusion surrounding the terminology, the long term focus on employee development as represented by the concept of HRD has gained much traction in organizations in India in the last decade. The following sections present certain trends of those advances across different segments.

HRD in Small–Medium Sized Enterprises (SMEs) versus large organizations in India

Size of an organization influences the extent to which HRD practices are valued and implemented in India. For instance, our interview findings indicated that in large organizations such as Wipro, Infosys, Indian Oil Corporation (IOC), Bharat Electronics Limited (BEL), Tata Motors, ICICI and Axis banks to name a few, the senior leaders are committed towards investing in system driven HRD practices and processes. One of the primary reasons behind such top management buy-in is that senior leaders in these organizations have experienced the benefit of well-designed HRD practices and hence, they appreciate how HR processes can support employee growth. This senior level buy-in can be found in a few SMEs in India run by entrepreneurs who previously worked in larger organizations and have seen the relevance of HRD practices; however, small enterprises in general in India neither employ specialists for HR nor do they have well planned HR policies in place (Koch and De Kok 1999, Singh and Vohra 2005).

In a study of 89 small enterprises in India, Singh and Vohra (2005) found that only about 20 per cent of small enterprises had HR policies and that lack of formal policies often led to loss of owner-manager's valuable time in resolving routine issues. Interestingly, HRD professionals we interviewed noted that in the context of Indian small scale industry where the owner is an active member of the organization, conflicts between the owner-manager and professional managers often pose a roadblock for efficient implementation of HRD practices. As suggested by both extant literature and our interviews, such conflicts can be attributed to: (1) the owners of SMEs in India being apprehensive that formal HRD practices may be too inflexible for the high-growth stage of the firm and the highly ambiguous business environment in India; (2) professional managers failing to understand the complexity of a family run Indian firm; and (3) the owner-managers lacking awareness of how HR processes can support efficient management and development of human resources (Singh and Vohra 2009). However, absence of formal HRD systems can result in biased decision making, especially if the owner is the sole decision maker. Thus, SMEs in India would benefit from an optimal blend of formal and informal HRD practices balancing the need for flexibility with the necessity of strategic integration of HRD processes (Singh and Vohra 2005).

HRD across service and manufacturing sectors in India

Another factor that influences the extent and type of implementation of HRD practices in organizations in India is the nature of the industry (e.g. service or manufacturing). Although examples exist of large pharmaceutical and automobile organizations in India having excellent HRD systems, the general consensus seems to be that compared with the IT and ITES industries, manufacturing organizations tend to have more conventional forms of HRD. The HRD professionals in our interviews explained that the services sector in India was the pioneer in recognizing the value of human capital. Unlike most manufacturing organizations where production material is likely to take higher precedence in value, people are considered to be value adding resources in services. Furthermore, the export-focused nature of services and prevalence of multinationals facilitated the adoption of global and strategic HRD practices in services (Budhwar *et al.* 2006).

However, as pointed out by an HRD consultant we interviewed, not all HRD practices are equally applicable to both sectors. For instance, practices such as flexi-work and telecommuting might be more suited to services than manufacturing as most white collar jobs in manufacturing require supervising shop floor workers in person. Further, in services, the workforce is far younger and more mobile compared with manufacturing and hence, organizations in the services sector are not constrained by history or legacy of traditional bureaucracy while implementing progressive HRD practices. Nonetheless, many examples of manufacturing companies (e.g. Tata Motors, IOC, BEL, etc.) have defied these constraints and increased their focus on HRD at both management and worker levels. An example of such progress as indicated by an HRD professional we interviewed is reflected in the improved skill level of machine operators employed in many manufacturing companies in the last decade. Senior leaders from those organizations need to be role models when it comes to adopting progressive HRD practices that are well aligned with the unique needs of the manufacturing industry.

HRD across public and private sectors in India

The gap between HRD practices in the public and private sectors in India is not frequently significant. For example, as in the private sector organizations, HRD practices in the public sector are also structured and rationalized (Budhwar and Boyne 2004). In fact, our interviewees noted that public sector companies need to have well instituted HRD systems in order to satisfy employees who are otherwise dissatisfied with the low pay scale. As for deficiencies, both public and private sector organizations suffer from lack of a well drafted training and development policy, disconnect between industries seeking training provisions and the institutions providing training, and lack of comprehensive training needs assessment and evaluation (Yadapadithaya 2001). In addition, the public sector is riddled with unique challenges such as "high average age of employees, increase in the retiring population levels, high turnover of new recruits, and resistance to change at senior and middle management levels" (Rao and Varghese 2009: 27). Also, unlike the public sector, HRD managers are board members of private sector companies, possibly to address the need to promptly respond to the competitive business environment in India and due to business owners' relatives occupying top positions in the majority of Indian private sector organizations (Budhwar and Boyne 2004). Nevertheless, given that our findings show that HRD practices in private and public sector organizations in India are more similar than different, sharing of best HRD practices across sectors can help.

Macro-level perspectives on HRD in India

At the macro level, Indian HRD initiatives can take two forms: (1) National, State and Regional HRD that includes programs started by the Government of India for shaping basic education, formal and informal education systems, and workforce education initiatives at the national, state, and regional level (Cho and McLean 2004); and (2) International HRD that includes initiatives undertaken by the Government of India for contributing to its neighboring countries as a developmental partner (Barman 2010).

National, state, and regional HRD

India took the lead in the Asia-Pacific region in 1985 by renaming its Ministry of Education as the Ministry of Human Resource Development (Cho and McLean 2004, Pio 2007). "The HRD Ministry consisted of the Department of Education, Youth, Culture and Sports; Women's development; Integrated Child Development; and others" (Rao 2004: 292). The HRD Ministry's key response to India's human capital challenges has primarily focused on the education sector through initiation of a number of noteworthy efforts for strengthening the educational infrastructure of the country (Rao and Varghese 2009). Some examples of such efforts include increasing fund allocation for construction of schools and higher education institutes, emphasizing quality of education, and establishing equity in education access needed to prepare a skilled workforce for the future. Although these efforts have been multi-pronged, the Indian government has fallen short of preparing a comprehensive National Human Resource Development (NHRD) policy by integrating the HRD efforts of all ministries and states. Each ministry has a separate education and training set-up and each ministry in the government operates as an independent entity, reluctant to learn about the other ministries (Rao 2004). This reluctance has also impaired knowledge dissemination from the corporate sector to the National HRD Ministry.

As noted by Rao (2004), educational administrators in the ministry have mostly believed that the principles governing the management of industry are different from those of education and hence, are not applicable to NHRD policy formulation. Consequently, the ministries have failed to consult with the corporate sector to learn from the successes and failures of HRD professionals in organizations. Also, until recently the Indian government has only initiated a few partnerships with private, public, and nongovernmental organizations for implementing policies on national skill development. For example, in 2008–09 "the Indian government instituted the National Skills Development Corporation (NSDC) focusing on skills acquisition for rural and disadvantaged youth" (Alagaraja and Wang 2012: 15). The corporation is a public and private sector initiative with strong investment from corporate investors (Alagaraja 2012). Also according to our interview findings, lately, the Indian government has connected with the National Human Resource Development network (NHRDN) in India to explore possibilities of involving approximately 12,000 companies that are members of NHRDN as partners in national skill development efforts. For example, as articulated by the NHRDN president we interviewed, the Indian government can benefit from the wide outreach that NHRDN can provide for convincing India's corporate sector to undertake the social responsibility of national skill building through various means (e.g. partnering with institutes imparting technical training programs such as the Industrial Training Institutes, undertaking career counseling for India's youth, etc.). This approach will enable the government to learn from the industry perspective on how to increase the employability prospects of India's burgeoning population.

International HRD

The first formal international HRD activities originated in the country with the launching of the Indian Technical and Economic Cooperation (ITEC) program on 15th September, 1964 as a bilateral program of assistance extended by the Government of India.

From the launch, ITEC was a demand-driven and response-oriented program mainly focused on addressing the needs of developing countries. "Under ITEC and its corollary SCAAP (Special Commonwealth Assistance for Africa Program), 158 countries in Asia and the Pacific, Africa, Latin America and the Caribbean, and East and Central Europe were invited to share the Indian development experience, acquired since its independence" (ITEC n.d.). The training programs conducted under the ITEC have been contributing to capacity building and human resource development in many parts of the world. As per the information brochure of ITEC and SCAAP programs for the year 2012–2013, there were 47 Indian institutions for foreign civilian training and during the year 2010–2011, the Government of India sponsored 232 courses through 46 of those participating institutions. The programs were primarily short term, for working professionals, on a wide and diverse range of skills and disciplines.

Wang and McLean (2007) defined international HRD as a field of study and practice that focuses on for-profit, not-for-profit, and/or governmental entities, and individuals, cooperating in some form across national borders. Following this definition, international HRD in India can be classified under three levels of cooperation: bilateral, multilateral, and regional. At a bilateral level, the government of India is fostering several international collaborations with developed and industrialized countries such as the UK, Australia and so on. The UK India Skills Forum (UKISF) established in April 2002 is an initiative led by the UK India Joint Economic and Trade Committee (JETCO) (Barman 2012). It provides a platform for organizations across the technical and vocational education sectors in the UK and India to tap business opportunities through exchanging ideas for delivery of skills training. Also, the India–Australia collaborative initiative to date has included the establishment of the Australia–India Bureau for Vocational Education and Training Collaboration (BVETC), and the Australia–India VET missions of 2010 and 2011 (Barman 2012).

At the multilateral level, the global agencies such as United Nations Educational, Scientific and Cultural Organization (UNESCO), United Nations Development Programme (UNDP), United Nations Children's Fund (UNICEF), United Nations Industrial Development Organization (UNIDO), World Bank, Asian Development Bank (ADB) and International Labour Organization (ILO) etc. are conducting and sponsoring many programs that are facilitating India's global partnership for human resource development. The recent agreement between India and UNESCO to establish the Mahatma Gandhi Institute of Education for Peace and Sustainable Development (MGIEP) as a UNESCO category-1 institute in New Delhi is an age breaking example of collaboration for HRD to face the global challenge (Press Information Bureau, Government of India n.d.).

Finally, at the regional level, India is a strategic partner in Cambodia, Laos and Vietnam (CLV) and Ganga-Mekong Sub-regional (GMS) HRD Programs and a strategic partner of international organizations such as ADB, Association of South East Asian Nations (ASEAN), and GMS institutions (universities and research institutes) (CUTS 2007). Also, India is the key member and partner in the South Asian Association for Regional Cooperation (SAARC) playing a critical role in the process of regional HRD. This partnership has led to the opening of the South Asia University at New Delhi (Barman 2010, 2011a, 2011b).

Challenges, opportunities, and future directions for HRD in India

Although the field of HRD in India has advanced in the last decade as evidenced by the aforementioned trends, the HRD function is not as well structured as originally envisaged in the mid-1970s at both the organizational and national levels (Rao and Varghese 2009). Some key challenges confronting the field of HRD in India and related opportunities and future directions are articulated below.

HRD's role in diversity management

Barring a few young Indian organizations, Indian public sector organizations and private firms tend to lag behind foreign MNCs and Indian MNCs in their diversity management (DM) practices, with the majority of them taking a legal compliance or affirmative action approach (Cooke and Saini 2010). Historically Indian society is a mix of several ethnic, religious, linguistic, caste, and regional collectivities that are further divided by socio-cultural realities (Budhwar and Varma 2011). Given this diversity, Indian organizations in particular perpetuate a dominant belief that since Indian people are accustomed to living and working alongside others with diverse backgrounds, "DM is not an issue" (Cooke and Saini 2010).

This state of denial has not served the progress of HRD well at both organizational and national levels in India. For instance, while the Indian constitution prohibits discrimination and forced labor and abolishes untouchability, the lower castes have hardly benefited from liberalization and continue to be exploited, especially in the huge unorganized sector in India (Pio 2007).

In addition, gender diversity continues to be a particular challenge in India as evident by the dearth of women in senior positions and the lack of infrastructure (e.g. childcare) required to support women in all levels of work, whether in the corporate sector or in the different government ministries. As women still have to shoulder the major share of household chores in a patriarchic Indian society (Haynes and Ghosh 2012), it seems obvious that organizations should adopt supportive HRD practices that help to integrate women into the Indian workforce. Some organizations as noted by our interviewees are taking progressive steps towards that end. For instance, the Tata Group of companies engaged in a campaign specifically to welcome back women who had previously worked in their organizations but who had left because of family responsibilities. Such practices should lead the way for India to optimize its diverse workforce in the future.

HRD's role as a transactional versus a strategic function

HRD in India seems to be in a transitory phase in moving from a bureaucratic and transactional approach towards a strategic one due to perceived connection between HRD activities and organizational productivity (Som 2007). Until recently HRD was primarily perceived as an administrative function governed by top management. However, HRD professionals are now trying to create an identity and advocate that HRD is a neutral mediator between different levels of management. Some emerging trends showing such progress are the increasing use of HRD audits, scorecards, lateral promotion of business heads to senior HRD positions, and HRD managers' representation on the board of directors of organizations (Rao 2008, Rao and Varghese 2009). Also, as noted by an HRD professional we interviewed, business knowledge and strategic thinking are included as critical HRD competencies in the "HR compass," an assessment tool jointly being developed by NHRDN and Chambers of Commerce for accreditation of HRD professionals in India. These trends can be further advanced if myths of HRD being immeasurable are addressed by appropriately measuring its contribution and reporting the results to the top management for necessary action (Srimannarayana 2009).

Srimannarayana (2009) found that attempts in Indian industry to measure HR activities have improved; however, the focus of measurement is largely on traditional (e.g. number of employees trained, training costs, turnover rate, etc.) instead of business impact measures (e.g. performance improvements made because of training received, etc.). Besides, as pointed out by our interviewees, HRD professionals need to reflect on whether continuing in one industry instead of job hopping across industries would add value in terms of their business knowledge. Also, the HRD fraternity needs to understand the strategic value of HRD generalist roles in India. As HRD generalists (mostly known as HR relationship managers) interface with different departments and functions, they can be great mediators linking operational HRD activities to strategic HRD relevant to the organization's business.

Cultural influences on HRD in India

India has a high-context culture where work relationships are personalized rather than contractual and oral communication and face time from HRD professionals are preferred over emails and phone calls. This ensues from many influences such as authoritarian practices within the family, the educational system, society's hierarchical structure, and religious institutions that act together to create a strong sense of dependence (Sinha 2000). Aycan *et al.* (2000) did a ten country comparison on the impact of culture on HRD practices and developed a model of cultural fit. Their research indicates that India scored high on paternalism, power distance, and loyalty towards the community. Due to high power distance, employees seldom challenge leadership and hence, it is difficult for HRD professionals to encourage alternate views that can foster innovation (Nicholson and Sahay 2004). As noted by an HRD director we interviewed, Tata Steel, a renowned manufacturing company in India, had to run a campaign encouraging alternate views and innovative ideas that would contradict conventional wisdom of leaders.

Also, given that Indian society continues to be highly collectivistic, family and group attainments take precedence over work outcomes and ascribed status, and social and political connections matter in decisions of selections and promotions in Indian organizations (Budhwar 2001). However, aspects of power based on caste and nepotism are being increasingly challenged in the current business environment in India and rationalized practices are being instituted (Budhwar and Baruch 2003). Moreover, there is a positive trend towards co-opting Indian cultural traditions into HRD practices and policies to help employees feel more "at home" in their workplaces (Budhwar and Varma 2011). For instance, as noted by some of our interviewees, HRD professionals are making efforts to give cultural examples and proverbs to help employees understand management theories and concepts in training programs, design employee engagement programs to specifically focus on cultural festivals, and translate some training program content to regional languages if required.

Academia–industry–government disconnection about HRD

Our interviews indicate that a general disconnect exists between the curriculum used in educational institutions to develop India's human capital and the skill level desired by both the corporate sector and the Government of India. This disconnect has led to the challenge of manpower shortages despite the sheer volume of students graduating from the Indian education system every year (Narayan 2007, Pio 2007, Rao and Varghese 2009). Ironically, the Indian government's focus on building the educational infrastructure of the country since independence has failed to address the supply–demand mismatch. Although the government has rolled out initiatives to increase equitable access to quality education, standard high quality schooling is still not available to many in the lower socio-economic status and minority groups and out of the relatively well off who are fortunate to graduate, most lack business perspective and soft skills needed for them to be "industry ready."

NHRDN has undertaken some initiatives towards bridging the academia–industry gap to some extent. For instance, NHRDN has partnered with some educational institutes (e.g. MDI Gurgaon, IIM, Ranchi) to align the curriculum with industry needs so as to increase employability skills of Indian graduates. They have started a mentoring initiative of pairing every student in business schools with mentors from the industry at large so that students understand real work issues and how the concepts they learn in classrooms might transfer to work. NHRDN has also introduced student scholarships in 15 business schools where students are required to write papers with industry professionals, thereby allowing them to develop connections with industry folks early on in their career. Further, NHRDN is implementing the concept of National Professor, proposed and advocated by Dr T.V. Rao, one of the forefathers of HRD in India. Under this initiative, NHRDN will identify business schools that are lagging behind and will appoint senior academicians and practitioners to offer guest lectures so that students in those institutions get an opportunity of learning from their insights.

As for the academia–industry–government gap, the discourse on national skill development has to move away from government focus to collaboration between public and private sectors with a renewed emphasis on both the organized and unorganized sectors (Saini 2005). Particularly, HRD professionals in India should be proactive in ensuring that their organizations are engaging in corporate social responsibility (CSR) through participating on boards of educational institutions, and contributing towards shaping curriculum in institutions that educate their future workforce. Similarly, educational institutions should be proactive towards supporting their faculty to consult with government ministries for contributing towards national skill development policies. Lastly, multiple stakeholders and strategic partners including the Indian government, Chambers of Commerce representing business and industry, and global agencies (e.g. UNESCO, UNDP, ADB, BVETC, JETCO, SAARC, etc.) should share the responsibility of developing India's human capital. Such partnerships will help identify how policies and practices at these different levels can interact to impact the state and future of the field of HRD in India.

Conclusion

We have presented a snapshot of the advances, challenges, and opportunities for HRD in India at multiple levels. While the advances are significant and the future challenges and opportunities are complex, the field of HRD in India needs to optimize learning across the organizational, national, and international levels to pave a way for the future. It is time for both HRD scholars and practitioners across sectors and industries in India to reflect on how to support each other and bridge the divide between HRD at different levels. Together, they need to consider and address critical issues such as: how to prepare an industry-ready skilled workforce; how to ensure equitable workforce education and development; how to integrate women in all levels of the workforce; how to prepare the Indian workforce to embrace globalization in all sectors and industries; and how to align both rural and urban educational institutions in India with industry and government needs and vice versa. In doing so, they will instigate paradigm shifts in understanding the fundamental issues relating to diversity, culture, manpower shortage, changing demographics, and globalization facing HRD in India and build India's growing pool of human capital as its distinctive advantage.

Note

1 In the Indian National Accounts Statistics (NAS), the unorganized sector includes all "operating units whose activities are not regulated under any Statutory Act or legal provision and/or those which do not maintain any regular accounts" (Kulshreshtha 2011: 125).

References

Alagaraja, M. (2012) 'National human resource development in practice: an interview with MV Subbiah', *Human Resource Development International*, 15: 515–24.

Alagaraja, M. and Wang, J. (2012) 'Development of a national HRD strategy model: cases of India and China', *Human Resource Development Review*, 11: 407–29.

Aycan, Z., Kanungo, R.N., Mendonca, M., Yu, K., Deller, J., Stahl, G. and Kurshid, A. (2000) 'Impact of culture on human resource management practices: a 10-country comparison', *Applied Psychology*, 49: 192–221.

Barman, A. (2010) *The Vortex of Cross National HRD in Asia – Developing Research Contexts on India–ASEAN HRD Collaboration'*. Online. Available HTTP: http://ssrn.com/abstract=1669481 (accessed 20 November 2012).

— (2011a) 'India–Singapore HRD collaboration through academic partnership: a case based debate', *International Journal of Commerce and Business Management*, 4: 148–58.

— (2011b) *HRD Collaboration in Mekong-Ganga Sub-Region: An Assessment on India-Lao's Collaboration*. Online. Available HTTP: http://ssrn.com/abstract=1855497 or http://dx.doi.org/10.2139/ssrn.1855497 (accessed 23 November 2012).

— (2012) *International HRD in India – Developing Further Research Context*. Online. Available HTTP: http://papers.ssrn.com/sol3/papers.cfm?abstract_id=2087640 (accessed 25 November 2012).

Budhwar, P.S. (2001) 'Human resource management in India', in Budhwar, P.S. and Debrah, Y.A. (eds) *Human Resource Management in Developing Countries*, London: Routledge, 75–90.

Budhwar, P.S. and Baruch, Y. (2003) 'Career management practices in India: an empirical study', *International Journal of Manpower*, 24: 699–719.

Budhwar, P.S. and Boyne, G. (2004) 'Human resource management in the Indian public and private sectors: an empirical comparison', *International Journal of Human Resource Management*, 15: 346–70.

Budhwar, P.S. and Varma, A. (2011) 'Emerging HR management trends in India and the way forward', *Organizational Dynamics*, 40: 317–25.

Budhwar, P.S., Luthar, H.K. and Bhatnagar, J. (2006) 'The dynamics of HRM systems in Indian BPO firms', *Journal of Labor Research*, 27: 339–60.

Cho, E. and McLean, G.N. (2004) 'What we discovered about NHRD and what it means for HRD', *Advances in Developing Human Resources*, 6: 382–93.

Cooke, F.L. and Saini, D.S. (2010) 'Diversity management in India: a study of organizations in different ownership forms and industrial sectors', *Human Resource Management*, 49: 477–500.

CUTS (2007) *South–South Economic Cooperation: Enhancing GMS–India Relationship*, Consumer Unity and Trust Society (CUTS) Centre for International Trade, Economics and Environment, Jaipur: CUTS.

Haynes, R.K. and Ghosh, R. (2012) 'Towards mentoring the Indian organizational woman: propositions, considerations, and first steps', *Journal of World Business*, 47: 186–93.

ITEC (n.d.) *About ITEC*. Online. Available HTTP: http://itec.mea.gov.in/ (accessed 10 November 2012).

Koch, C.L.Y. and De Kok, J.M.P. (1999) 'A human resource based theory of the small firm', Paper no. 9940, Rotterdam: Erasmus University, Rotterdam Institute for Business Economic Studies.

Kulshreshtha, A.C. (2011) 'Measuring the unorganized sector in India', *Review of Income and Wealth*, 57(S1): S123–34.

Narayan, S. (14 January 2007) '15 years after from the editor', *Business Today*, 282.

Nicholson, B. and Sahay, S. (2004) 'Embedded knowledge and offshore software development', *Information and Organization*, 14: 329–65.

Pareek, U. and Rao, T.V. (2008) 'From a sapling to the forest: the saga of the development of HRD in India', *Human Resource Development International*, 11: 555–64.

Pio, E. (2007) 'HRM and Indian epistemologies: a review and avenues for future research', *Human Resource Management Review*, 17: 319–35.

Press Information Bureau, Government of India (n.d.) *Establishment of the Mahatma Institute of Education for Peace and Sustainable Development (MGIEP) at New Delhi*. Online. Available HTTP: http://pib.nic.in/newsite/erelease.aspx?relid=71002 (accessed 5 December 2012).

Rao, T.V. (2004) 'Human resource development as national policy in India', *Advances in Developing Human Resources*, 6: 288–96.

— (2008) *HRD Score Card 2500: Based on HRD Audit*. New Delhi: SAGE Response.

Rao, T.V. and Varghese, S. (2009) 'Trends and challenges of developing human capital in India', *Human Resource Development International*, 12: 15–34.

Rao, T.V., Rao, R. and Yadav, T. (2007) 'A study of HRD concepts, structure of HRD departments, and HRD practices in India', *Vikalpa*, 26: 49–64.

Saini, D.S. (2005) 'HRD through vocational training: the Indian model', *Indian Journal of Industrial Relations*, 40: 529–46.

Singh, M. and Vohra, N. (2005) 'Strategic human resource management in small enterprises', *Journal of Entrepreneurship*, 14: 57–70.

— (2009) 'Level of formalisation of human resource management in small and medium enterprises in India', *Journal of Entrepreneurship*, 18: 95–116.

Sinha, J.B.P. (2000) *Patterns of Work Culture: Cases and Strategies for Culture Building*, New Delhi: SAGE.

Som, A. (2007) 'What drives adoption of innovative SHRM practices in Indian organizations?', *International Journal of Human Resource Management*, 18: 808–28.

Sparrow, P.R. and Budhwar, P.S. (1997) 'Competition and change: mapping the Indian HRM recipe against world-wide patterns', *Journal of World Business*, 32: 224–42.

Srimannarayana, M. (2009) 'Measurement of human resource activities in India', *Indian Journal of Industrial Relations*, 45: 265–76.

Srinivasan, T.N. (2004) 'China and India: economic performance, competition and cooperation: an update', *Journal of Asian Economics*, 15: 613–36.

Wang, X., and McLean, G.N. (2007) 'The dilemma of defining international human resource development', *Human Resource Development Review*, 6: 96–108.

Yadapadithaya, P.S. (2001) 'Evaluating corporate training and development: an Indian experience', *International Journal of Training and Development*, 5: 261–74.

39

HUMAN RESOURCE DEVELOPMENT IN CHINA

Jian Huang, Zhongming Ouyang and Jessica Li

China has experienced rapid economic development over the past several decades. Globalization and technological advancement, coupled with the shortage of a skilled workforce have been challenging for business organizations and for China as a nation. The Chinese government proposed many strategies to develop human resources to face these challenges such as hosting national conferences on talent development, establishing the Ministries of Human Resources and Social Security, and publishing policies to aid the development of human resources. China has also taken steps to recognize HRD as a discipline.

Similarly, business corporations have set up HR departments to replace the old personnel departments, and created HRD positions to facilitate employee training and development (T&D). Meanwhile, the market for HRD certificates, domestic or foreign, is expanding and workshops/forums in the name of HRD are frequent. Novice practitioners are offered a confusing array of professional development possibilities. In response, efforts are underway to define HRD as a profession and academic discipline.

This chapter first provides a brief analysis of the connotation of HRD in China. The development of HRD in China is then described as a national policy, as a practice, and as an academic discipline. Lastly, the future of HRD in China is discussed.

The meaning of HRD

Similar to debates about the essence of HRD in Western literature, consensus has not been reached regarding the meaning of HRD in China (Ouyang 2011a). For example, some Western scholars position HRD primarily within the organization, whereas other scholars explain that HRD should include the development of community, society, and nation (e.g. Wang and McLean 2007). In China, the viewpoints are evenly distributed. Some researchers argue that HRD should focus on individuals (e.g. Pan 1991), some believe that HRD should center on organizations (e.g. Yu 1997, Zheng 1998), and others think broadly that HRD should serve national needs (e.g. Chen and Chen 1995). The focus on national level HRD is prominent because of the influence of government policies.

The function of HRD has two orientations in China. The first orientation pertains to the process of developing human resources (e.g. Chen and Chen 1995, Zhao 2001, Liao 2003, Luo 2003). Scholars who hold this orientation argue that education, formal as well as informal, is the most important form of HRD, and that systematic education is critical in developing basic skills and capabilities of the population. Some scholars who hold this orientation are concerned with workplace HRD (Wangyou 1989, Xiao 2004, Li 2005, Wang and McLean 2007, Huang 2009).

The second orientation views HRD as a process of exploitation (e.g. Pan 1991, Xiao 1994, Wu and Niu 1996). Pan (1991) believes that HRD should develop and tap into people's potential and allocate and utilize human resources to meet certain purposes. This chapter is aligned with the first orientation and places the focus on T&D in the workplace while discussing the development of HRD in China.

The development of HRD as a national policy

Since the beginning of the twenty-first century, HRD has become an important policy discourse and appeared frequently in speeches and reports of Chinese senior national leaders. HRD was used to shape a societal promise and to demonstrate an unshakable determination of the government towards education and learning as an investment priority for the country. HRD provided a broad framework for developing a learning society.

The leading thoughts on HRD from national leaders

The history of China attests that "the future of a nation depends on the strength of its human capital, while the prosperity of the people depends on the strength of a nation" (Research Project on Chinese Education and Human Resource 2003: 14). Since 1949, four generations of national leaders have given top priority to human resource issues and proposed different views on talent development catering to the different stages of development.

The first-generation Chinese leader, Mao Zedong took into consideration value, quality, cultivation, utilization, and many other aspects of talent. For example, he discussed the value of cadres, members of the Communist Party, soldiers, intellectuals and youth when proposing strategies and tactics in leadership succession planning. Deng Xiaoping, the second-generation Chinese leader, proposed respect for knowledge and talent to liberate productivity when initiating economic reform. Jiang Zemin, the third-generation Chinese leader, declared that human resources are the number one resource. Through his leadership, respect for work effort, knowledge, talents and innovation were included in national policy. Jiang Zemin invested heavily in developing science, technology, management talents, and skilled workers.

Hu Jintao, the fourth-generation Chinese leader, has adhered to a Scientific Development Concept aimed at improving socio-economic equality, furthering prosperity and avoiding social conflict. He believes that talent comes from the masses and that those who possess considerable knowledge or skills are able to undertake creative work, make contributions and promote the national agenda. His policy specified that talent selection should follow no set form; and moral character, ability, knowledge and achievements should be viewed as important standards, regardless of education degrees and professional titles (Party Literature Research Center of the CPC Central Committee 2006).

National leaders have laid an ideological foundation for inclusion of HRD in national policy in the new century. HRD has played an important role in the transformation of China from a "country with a large population" to a "country with rich human resources" – a national strategy that is explained more in the following section.

National strategy and policy on HRD

In 2001, the Fourth Session of the Ninth National People's Congress of China passed the 10th Five-year Plan (State Council 2010) and set an important objective of implementing talent strategies and increasing the number of talented workers. In May of 2002, the Central Government of China issued the National Talent Development Plan for 2002–2005, which put forward the "Strategy of Reinvigorating China through Human Resource Development" (hereafter referred to as the Strategy) and included a detailed implementation plan. *From a Country with a Large Population to a Country with Rich Human Resources* (Central Government of China 2002) was a status report of the present situation of HRD in China, including existing problems and possible solutions. This report was an important event for the development of HRD as a discipline in China.

During the *First Talent Work Conference of China* held in December 2003 in Beijing, Hu Jintao reiterated the importance of HRD. The Strategy was treated as an urgent priority to upgrade the core competitiveness and overall strength of the nation. In September 2007, Hu Jintao emphasized in his report for the Seventeenth National Congress of China that an environment is needed that encourages innovation and fosters world-class scientists and leading technical workers so that creativity can be inspired (Hu Jintao 2007).

On March 5, 2010, Mr. Wen Jiabao, Prime Minister of China, pointed out that a strategy for invigorating China through science, technology, and education should be carried out the following year. HRD was expected to emphasize the cultivation of innovative technological talents and professionals with skills demanded by essential sectors for economic and social development. HRD was also expected to bring high-level talent from around the world, and establish a good institutional environment for talented people to shine.

In September 2010, the Office of the State Council of China issued a white paper titled the *Status of Human Resource of China* (Press Office of the State Council 2010). According to the report, the employment situation in China remained stable. A significant number of important types of talented workers were actively involved in the nation's economic development, and education and health systems improved significantly. The market function proved useful in distributing human resources, and pressing institutional reform on the economy, technology, and education, in addition to replacing old personnel systems. In addition, a human resource legislative system was established, based on the Constitution, promoting vocational education and training, and aiming to have all citizens enjoy fair rights of development, equal employment and independent job-seeking. China has carved out its own path of HRD based on its own history and its unique circumstances. For example, its policies have influenced labor mobility to allow all sectors to tap into human resources through a freed up labor market. These actions have resulted in sustainable development of the Chinese economy and society (Huang 2009).

The development of national HRD

The development of national HRD in China includes HRD policies oriented towards establishing a learning culture. Free and compulsory education has been realized in both rural and urban China. Professional education has also developed rapidly and higher education has evolved and become much more accessible. Education in rural areas is strengthened and overall education equality has been improved (Ministry of Education 2009).

Educational systems have improved and contributed to NHRD in several ways: (1) the gross enrollment rate of higher education has increased continuously; (2) non-traditional education for adults has been greatly improved and literacy education has become effective; and (3) large investments have been earmarked for lifelong learning projects for different population groups, including civil servants, professional and technical personnel, managers, teachers, migrant laborers, peasants, and seniors (Shanghai Municipal Institute for Lifelong Education 2013).

Challenges facing national HRD in China

HRD has become an important area of national strategy in China, and on the basis of this strategy, a series of HRD policies have been put forward with intensified implementation efforts coupled with appropriate investment. The effort has benefited a portion of the population more so than other segments of the society. The following paragraphs discuss issues and policies linked to these disparities.

Policies and tools versus individual empowerment

Tools and policies are emphasized considerably in China and not enough emphasis is placed on individual development and empowerment. National policies often dictate the distribution of perceived social values (Quirk 1989). The value orientation underlying national HRD policies is determined by their nature and characteristics. National HRD policies in China tend to ignore individual development, personal empowerment, and individual initiative. Hence, national HRD in China might be perceived as a tool for control based on assigned social values.

Formal education versus workplace learning

Although national HRD has received considerable attention recently in China, implementation of HRD policies is confined to the formal education sector to a large extent. The administration of HRD policies is often located in the department of education, which favors formal education systems while paying little attention to workplace HRD. Although over 1500 HRD-related policies were published by the Central government between 1985 and 2001, only 30 of them are relevant to workplace learning (Xie 2005). This disparity might be the result of the long held traditional belief that the value of intellectuals is much greater than practitioners/laborers. Intellectuals theorize at a national level because the individual level holds no value for them. Therefore, individual learning and training as occupational development has long been underestimated. Hence, future policy makers need to consider systemic approaches for increasing options for employee workplace learning.

Departmental silos versus cross-departmental cooperation

Chinese government agencies use a vertical reporting structure that creates a silo effect among departments. Many government departments are involved in HRD, including the Organization Department of the Central Committee of the Chinese Communist Party (CPC), the State Development Planning Commission, the Ministry of Human Resources and Social Security, the Ministry of Science and Technology, the Ministry of Agriculture, and the Ministry of Health. An oversight committee does not coordinate HRD as a cross-departmental effort; therefore, discrepancies in implementation occur among departments, ministries and commissions. To a certain extent, chaos and disorder result during implementation, which weaken the effectiveness of HRD policies and practices in China. Therefore, a cross-departmental effort among government agencies should be created to enhance overall implementation of HRD policies and practices.

The development of HRD as a field of practice

As the result of NHRD strategies and to sustain competitiveness, organizations are beginning to invest more in developing human resources. HRD is commonly interpreted as T&D and many organizational HRD efforts are focused on providing employees with T&D opportunities. The

Chinese tradition of favoring learning and education has influenced the development of HRD as a field of practice in China.

HRD as a field of practice is becoming a sizable industry

T&D emerged as an HRD intervention in the mid-1990s and it has gradually evolved into a sizable field of practice. The total value of the T&D market grew from 4 billion RMB in 2000 to 400 billion RMB in 2010. At the same time, a large number of consulting and training institutions appeared. In 2011, Chinese enterprises on average spent 1627 RMB per employee in training, which is an increase of slightly over 10 percent compared with 2010 (Shengshi Huayan Enterprise Management Company 2012). Over ten thousand institutions are currently providing T&D services, with over 3000 residing in Shanghai, over 2000 registered in Beijing and another 1000 institutions or so functioning in Guangzhou (China Baogao Company Limited 2012).

The quality of HRD practitioners

Due to increasing salaries for T&D practitioners, T&D has become a sought-after occupation in China (Shengshi Huayan Enterprise Management Company 2012). T&D has been officially listed by appropriate government agencies as a recognized occupation. The qualifications of trainers have become an issue in the HRD field. Hence, an effort to develop certification to ensure occupational qualifications was started in 1999. In May 2002, a pilot version of the *Occupational Standards for Enterprise Trainers* was issued and accredited for initial certification by the China Association of Staff and Workers Education and Vocational Training (2002). The *Standards* detailed the tasks, competencies, technical, and knowledge requirements, and professional code of conduct, for the T&D occupation (Huang and Xiong 2005). Consulting companies offer programs targeted at T&D professionals for qualification purposes.

The development of the HRD department in organizations

As organizations increasingly recognized the value of T&D, organizational learning and knowledge management, they began to establish HRD departments independent of HRM departments. Today, many state-owned and private enterprises have HRD departments or corporate universities (CU). The corporate university has become popular in China as an organizational form often tasked with delivering HRD solutions within the organization. In 1993 the first CU was established at Chunlan College; since then 1200 CUs have been created. CUs have considerable strategic significance in organizations in China, and have become an example of integrating the practices of lifelong learning, learning organization, core competitiveness, and human capital (Wang *et al.* 2010). In the meantime, new positions such as the chief learning officer (CLO), chief knowledge officer (CKO), executive director for learning and development, training manager, instructional designer, learning assessment expert, career consultant, and organizational development consultant have sprung up like bamboo shoots after a spring rain. These developments indicate the progress achieved in the practice of HRD in China.

Challenges confronting HRD practitioners in China

In less than ten years, the market for HRD has expanded and professional recognition has increased drastically in China. The following paragraphs discuss challenges that confront HRD in China.

Consistency is needed with professional standards

Many government departments are involved in creating HRD professional standards and market regulations. These government agencies are in charge of labor, education, civil administration, industry and commerce, and construction; in addition, industry associations have the right to grant approval of training institutions for their own sectors. Professional standards are inconsistent across agencies and collaboration is minimal between agencies. Alliances are needed among relevant agencies, and together they can introduce and administer a common set of professional standards.

Need for professionalized systematic training for HRD practitioners

HRD has not become a specialized academic field in many of the Chinese higher education institutions, and few professional associations offer certificate programs with acceptable credibility. Current HRD practitioners come from three backgrounds: university faculties, experienced senior professionals currently working in large enterprises, and professional trainers working in consulting companies. Most HRD practitioners, however, have not had opportunities for systematic training in HRD as a discipline.

The development of HRD as an academic field

An academic field often evolves along with the growth of the profession to provide systematic knowledge and research to support the profession. Academic programs and the development of the profession are mutually supportive, which further strengthens the field through research and practice. Aligned with these ideas, the rise of HRD as a field of practice has influenced the development of HRD as an academic discipline in China.

HRD as an academic program in higher education institutions in China

Approximately 30 universities have created master degree programs in adult education in China. More than ten of them have established HRD concentrations, for example Shaanxi University and Qufu Normal University. Others, like Renmin University of China and Peking University have included HRD as a special interest area and are being incorporated with the programs of Human Resource Management or Educational Technology to offer enterprise training and instructional design programs. The first HRD program in China was established at East China Normal University in 2007.

The forming of an academic research community

Gradually, a community of scholars began to conduct research on HRD in China and to expand HRD as a specialized educational program. Two major forces contributed to the formation of the HRD research community. First, The HRD Research Society was established as a national level entity. Second, research teams were formed and led by professors from top Chinese universities, such as Tsinghua University, Peking University, Fudan University, Xiamen University, Shanghai International Studies University and East China Normal University. The involvement of scholars from leading universities has contributed to the development of HRD academic studies in China by lending credibility to the field.

HRD academic journals are still rare in China; the only one that carries the name of HRD is the *Journal of China HRD*, hosted by the China Association of Human Resource Research. The journal covers research studies of advanced HRD technology, best practices, and other HRD-related topics. A positive sign is that journals in fields such as HRM, education, and psychology are accepting an increasing number of HRD-related research papers.

Foundational research

Scholars, subject experts, and practitioners of HRD in China started to conduct research on HRD-related issues in the late 1980s. Four categories of research emerged: (a) translation of Western HRD text books; (b) books in Chinese on HRD or HRD-related disciplines; (c) theses and dissertations; and (d) journal publications.

Some of the more influential publications include *Theory and Methods of HRD* by Minzheng Xiao (2004) of Peking University. Xiao proposed a definition for the HRD discipline in China, and provided constructive ideas on areas that are much needed for a new profession and academic field, such as the object of the study, the foundations of the HRD field, and a practical framework. In 2005, Jinyu Xie published a book titled *Introduction to Human Resource Development* in which Xie appealed for the development of HRD as a discipline in China. Wang and Xie (2008) presented their design of a disciplinary system and curriculum design for HRD programs in China. Huang (2009) wrote *Reflections on the Development of the HRD Discipline in China*, in which she presented a review of current HRD developments in China and explored challenges such as the boundary of the discipline, object of study, and legitimacy of the academic discipline. Ouyang (2011b) took an interdisciplinary approach to explore the orientation, the development, and the construction of HRD on the basis of his doctoral dissertation titled *Constructing a House over a Creek: Research on the Building of the HRD Discipline – An Interdisciplinary Perspective.*

Challenges facing HRD as an academic field in China

A unique theoretical system and integrated disciplinary theories are two basic measures of the maturity of a discipline or an academic field. An emerging discipline often tries to construct its own theoretical system with its own unique characteristics. HRD in China is facing many challenges as it seeks to become a mature academic discipline.

Debates on research boundaries

In terms of the research boundaries of HRD, a few orientations are worth noting in China. The first is the macro perspective, which emphasizes using the entire nation as its research scope with a focus on education, learning and development of different groups of people. The second is the micro research perspective, which suggests that the HRD discipline should take the organization as its unit of analysis and focus its research on enterprise training, education and development activities (Xie 2005). The third view argues that HRD should break through the organization boundary by taking HRD activities to regional levels in China (Huang 2009).

Multidisciplinary nature of the HRD academic community

Members of an academic community commonly partake in important discussions regarding ideology, values, professional standards, professional tradition, content, and knowledge framework of the discipline (Zhou 2009). The HRD academic community members in China feature diverse academic backgrounds; for example, economics, pedagogy, management, and psychology. These varied disciplines may result in members of the HRD academic community having different understandings of HRD as a discipline; however, a benefit of varying viewpoints can be healthy debates among members that can energize the community. Conversely, too many debates may mislead outsiders and hinder HRD's recognition in the whole academic community.

HRD academic community members should work together to integrate their diverse academic backgrounds and identify a set of core values of HRD as a discipline. This accomplishment would help the legitimacy of HRD as a discipline in China. In addition, HRD scholars should work to increase the quantity and quality of academic journals in the HRD field in China.

Insufficient professional education

Currently, the number of graduates produced by quality HRD academic programs is far less than the demand for HRD professionals in China. Therefore, the quality and quantity of HRD programs need to be increased among colleges and universities. At present, only a small number of full-time faculty members are in the HRD field across China. Strategies are needed to bolster resources to support the operation and expansion of HRD in China.

Looking towards the future: contributions of HRD to sustaining economic development in China

Rapid economic development and technology advancement have resulted in an ever-changing society in China. Lifelong learning has become one of the critical skills for individual existence, organizational sustainability, and national HRD development. As a conclusion to this chapter, the following paragraphs offer suggestions on how HRD can continue to contribute to sustaining Chinese economic development.

Promoting lifelong learning skills

Chinese leaders and the Chinese education sector have emphasized lifelong learning as a critical skill in order to promote a learning society, in which all the people will learn or pursue lifelong education. In pursuit of such a learning society, both formal education and informal education will be developed in a balanced and interactive way. Pre-service and in-service education will need to be aligned, and the participation rate of continuing education should be significantly increased. For anyone who is willing to learn, proper assistance should be provided to make the learning possible. HRD as a profession that concentrates on continuous learning should play an important role in developing people's lifelong learning skills.

Interaction and collaboration among HRD academicians and practitioners

As a field of practice, HRD research often emerges from the demands of practice, and research outcomes can be used to guide practice. Therefore, HRD scholars need to be attuned to what corporations are doing with their T&D and HRD departments. Alliances with private organizations can benefit university research and also provide internship and employment opportunities for students. For example, in December 2011, the HRD program of East China Normal University hosted the 7th International Conference for Work and Learning. Participants came from over 18 well-known enterprises, such as Bao Steel, Shanghai Automobile Company, IBM, and TCL Group. Representatives of these organizations participated in the conference and shared their current practices and exchanged ideas with participating scholars from many universities.

Advancing HRD theory through interdisciplinary innovation

McLagan (1989) emphasized that HRD is an interdisciplinary field that pays attention to individuals, groups, organizational learning, and improvement of performance. Disciplines such as pedagogy, economics, psychology, ethics, sociology, engineering, human resources, organizational development, organizational behavior and management have all made contributions to HRD as a discipline. As a newly emerging field of academic research and practice, HRD scholars in China should contribute to HRD theoretical development through academic exchanges by utilizing theories of other disciplines, hence encouraging interdisciplinary innovation.

Strengthening international cooperation and promoting localization of HRD

While gaining experience through international cooperation, Chinese scholars must develop indigenous HRD theories that are reflective of the unique tradition, culture, and economic situation of China. To learn from others, Chinese HRD scholars should continue international exchange programs, such as visiting scholars, student exchanges, faculty exchanges, collaborative research aligned with such exchanges, and international conferences to increase multilateral dialogues. At the same time, HRD scholars in China should conduct independent research that focuses on regional HRD issues.

References

Central Government of China (2002) *From a Country with a Large Population to a Country with Rich Human Resources* (National Talent Development Plan 2002–2005), Beijing: Central Government of China.

Chen, Y. and Chen, Q. (1995) *Human Resources Development and Management in Modern Enterprise*, Beijing: China Statistics Press.

China Association of Staff and Workers Education and Vocational Training (2002) *Occupational Standards for Enterprise Trainers* (pilot version, May).

Huang, J. (2009) 'The thinking on the development of China HRD discipline', *Journal of Lan Zhou*, 9.

Huang, J. and Xiong, Y. (2005) 'Trainer: the favorite occupation in the twenty-first century', *Journal of Education Development Research*, 3: 44.

Li, B. (2005) *Human Resource Development in the Modern Learning Organization*, Beijing: Economic Science Press.

Liao, Q. (2003) *Human Resources Management*, Beijing: Higher Education Press.

Luo, T. (2003) 'Similarities and differences between human talent study and human resource development and management', *China Talent*, 5: 34–5.

McLagan, P. (1989) 'Models for HRD practice', *Training and Development Journal*, 43(9): 49–59.

Ouyang, Z. (2011a) 'On explication of concept and philosophical interpretation on human resource development', *Journal of Hansan Normal University* 2: 70–76.

Ouyang, Z. (2011b) *Constructing a House over a Creek: Research on the Building of the HRD Discipline – An Interdisciplinary Perspective*, unpublished dissertation, East China Normal University.

Pan, J. (1991) *The Primary Resource in China: The Development and Utilization of Human Resource*, Beijing: China Machine Press.

Pan, J. (2001) *The First Resource in China: The Development and Utilization of Human Resource*, Beijing: China Machine Press.

Party Literature Research Center of the CPC Central Committee (2006) *The Important Literature Collection Since Sixteenth National Congress*, Online. Available HTTP: www.iciba.com/Party Literature Research Centre of the CPC Central Committee, Beijing: Central Literary Contributions Publishing Bureau, 623.

Press Office of the State Council (2010) *The Situation of China Human Resources*, Beijing: Press Office of the State Council.

Quirk, P.J. (1989) 'The cooperative resolution of policy conflict', *American Political Science Review*, 83: 905–21.

Research Project on the Report of Chinese Education and Human Resource Problems (2003) *From a Country with a Large Population to a Country with Rich Human Resource*, Beijing: High Education Press, 14.

State Council (2010, September) *The National Mid- and Long-Term Talent Development Plan*, Beijing: State Council Office.

Wang, C., Wang, Y. and Chen, C.B. (2010) *Chinese Talents Cultivation and Enterprise University*, Beijing: China Machine Press 2.

Wang, X.H and McLean, G.N. (2007) 'The dilemma of defining international human resource development', *Human Resource Development Review*, 6: 96–108.

Wang X.H. and Xie, X.Q. (2008) 'The building of the human resource development discipline in China', *Journal of China Human Resource Development*, 9: 18–22.

Wangyou, E. (1989) *Research on the Strategies of Human Resources Development*, Beijing: Economic Daily Press.

Wu, W.D. and Niu, Y.S. (1996) *The System of China Human Resource Development*, Beijing: China Building Industry Press.

Xiao, M.Z. (1994) 'The systemic thinking on human resource development', *Journal of China Human Resource Development* 4: 15–20.

Xiao, M.Z. (2004) *Human Resource Development* (2nd edition), Beijing: Higher Education Press.

Xie, J.Y. (2005) *Introduction to Human Resource Development*, Beijing: Tsinghua University Press.

Yu, K.C. (1997) *Human Resource Development and Management*, Beijing: Enterprise Management Press.

Zhao, Q.C. (2001) *Research on Human Resource Development*, Dalian: Dongbei University of Finance and Economics Press.

Zheng, S.L. (1998) *Human Resources Development and Management in Modern Enterprise*, Beijing: China International Business and Economics Press.

Zhou, Z.C. (2009) *The Interdisciplinary Research in the Modern University*, Beijing: China Social Sciences Press, 69.

40
HRD IN THE MIDDLE EAST

Mesut Akdere and Khalil M. Dirani

The Middle East is considered the cradle of civilizations and religions considering many civilizations existed in this region and the three major religions (Judaism, Christianity, and Islam) started here. The Middle East evolved to become the energy center of the world with 56 per cent of the world's oil reserves (Swindell 2013a) and 65 per cent of the world's gas reserves (Swindell 2013b). Recently, there have been a number of political and societal uprisings which are transforming the political, societal, financial, educational, and cultural future of several countries of the region such as Egypt, Libya, Syria, Tunisia, and Yemen to name a few (Dalacoura 2012). These transformations provide HRD practitioners and scholars alike the opportunity to learn and be actively involved in a transformative environment where both traditional HRD functions and emerging National HRD frameworks may be utilized to potentially benefit this evolving region.

As an interdisciplinary field, HRD is more developed in the West in general, and in the United States in particular. The field has been studied both theoretically and empirically. The focus of HRD has been to explore ways in which the relationship between employees and workplace can be developed, enhanced, and improved further (Swanson and Holton 2009). In doing so, various aspects of HRD in the workplace have been taken into account by HRD practitioners and managers, such as learning, performance, culture, and psychology (Garavan *et al.* 2002). However, HRD is approached from Western philosophical and ideological perspectives. This approach of HRD identity formation puts collective identities such as the Middle East region at a disadvantage against dominant, individualistic forms of identity formation (Mizzi and Rocco 2013).

There has been very little work done to understand the practice of HRD in the Middle East. The purpose of this chapter is to explore various factors influencing and impacting the roles, goals, and outcomes of these HRD practices in that region. The chapter first presents an overview of the region in terms of geography, economy, and politics, followed by a discussion on various HRD practices in the region such as Training and Development (T&D), Organization Development (OD), Career Development (CD), and National HRD; followed by an analysis of divergent and convergent factors influencing HRD functions including economy, literacy, political stability, religion, culture, technology, and globalization. The chapter concludes with implications for research and practice.

Overview of the region

Geography

The Middle East is an indeterminate region extending from Turkey in the North to Oman in the South, and from Iraq in the East to Egypt in the West. The region shares some cultural commonalities (such as religion, history, and language) but has several differences as well (such as terrain, weather, wealth, and natural resources). For instance, the moderate climate in poor Yemen is totally opposite to the harsh desert conditions in wealthy Saudi Arabia. The main languages spoken in the region are Arabic (several dialects) and Turkish.

Among different governmental institutions in Europe, in the United States, and in specialized agencies in the United Nations, different operational definitions of the Middle East exist. Specifically, the region includes the Anatolian Peninsula, Mesopotamia, and the Arabian Peninsula. It is also termed the Near East (Encyclopedia Britannica 2012). It is worth noting that many of the borders of the countries in the region were drawn by the Entente Powers of World War I (mainly the UK and France). As a result, these borders do not necessarily reflect historical, ethnic, racial, and national backgrounds of these countries or the people living in the region. Therefore, the definitions of the region are rather ambiguous and vague (Rahme 1999). For the purposes of this chapter, the term Middle East region refers to the countries listed in Table 40.1 and their current population numbers (see also CIA 2011; World Bank 2012).

Economy

The economies in the region include both developed and underdeveloped economies. This region is famous for its oil-based production and exportation economy. However, the region has diverse economies including agriculture, textiles, construction, manufacturing, and tourism. In parallel with the increased oil prices around the world, oil exporters of the region have witnessed significant growth in their economies. Similarly, the gross domestic product (GDP) per capita of the countries in the region has increased in one year to $17,977 (4.1 percent increase, CIA 2011).

Table 40.1 Middle East countries' populations and Gross Domestic Product (GDP)

Country	*Population*	*GDP per Capita*
Bahrain	1,359,000	$21,200
Egypt	83,958,000	$6,000
Iraq	33,703,000	$3,600
Jordan	6,457,000	$5,300
Kuwait	2,892,000	$40,700
Lebanon	4,292,000	$13,100
Oman	2,904,000	$23,900
Qatar	1,939,000	$102,700
Saudi Arabia	28,705,000	$20,400
Syria	21,118,000	$4,600
Turkey	74,509,000	$16,067
United Arab Emirates	8,106,000	$42,000
Yemen	25,569,000	$2,500
The Palestinian Authority	4,271,000	$2,697

Specific GDP per capita figures are illustrated in Table 40.1 (2011). These GDP figures further present the vast differences in terms of economic wealth and life quality among the countries in the region. For example, Qatar, United Arab Emirates, and Kuwait have very high GDP, while countries like Lebanon and Turkey have medium GDP income, and countries like Egypt, Syria, and Yemen suffer from low GDP per capita.

To better comprehend economic structures of the Middle Eastern countries, economic freedoms are compared. "Economic freedom is the condition in which individuals can act with autonomy while in the pursuit of their economic livelihood and greater prosperity" (Miller and Kim 2013: 87). In this regard, the level of economic freedom that exists in Bahrain ranks first in the region and 12th in the world, followed by Qatar, the United Arab Emirates, Kuwait, Turkey, Saudi Arabia, Lebanon, Yemen, and Egypt, respectively (Miller and Kim 2013).

Many of the economies in the region lack the ability to quickly adapt to changing world economic and financial conditions (IMF 2013). In particular, most countries in the region have recently started investing in a knowledge economy, which became a horizon priority of the region's governments as a way to become competitive with other world economies (Obst and Kirk 2010). However, "related investments in education, information infrastructure, research and development (R&D), and innovation have been insufficient or inappropriate" (Aubert and Reiffers 2003: 1). It is important to note that "there is a strong correlation between a country's overall knowledge economy readiness index and its level of development as measured by GDP per capita" (Aubert and Reiffers 2003: 12). Most of the economies in the region are heavily regulated, including the regulation of human resources and their development and management. For example, in the Persian Gulf region (namely Kuwait, Bahrain, Qatar, the UAE, Oman, and Saudi Arabia) a large number of migrant workers from Far Asia and Africa have low level jobs that do not require sophisticated training. Moreover, mid-level jobs are occupied by educated foreigners from neighboring countries and overseas. Most key positions are occupied by local citizens. This workplace model is unique to the region and it affects how HRD functions exist both in private and governmental sectors in the region.

Politics

The overall political picture of the region is diverse; for example, while Turkey has experienced almost a century of democracy, Egypt and Iraq saw dictatorships come in power after military coups. Regional politics have influenced the rest of the world over the past seventy plus years, with Saudi Arabia being the largest oil producer of the world (Lewis 2010); for instance, through the Lebanese civil war and the Palestinian–Israeli conflict.

The majority of the population in the region is Muslim; and Islam has the "Ummah-nation" concept, which connects all followers of Islam as one nation. At the same time, some of the tension and disputes in the region are due to Islamic sects fighting among each other such as in Iraq, Syria, and Lebanon. Other disputes are ethnic and national in nature such as the Iraqi–Kuwaiti war in 1990 and the ongoing Palestinian–Israeli conflict.

However, the latest focus has been on the Arab Spring which started in Tunisia in 2010 as a people's movement and spread to Egypt, Yemen, Bahrain, and Syria. Although such political turmoil caused further suffering and political instability to an already volatile region, it has also paved the way for change in the region for the majority of countries that have been ruled by autocratic governments for decades. While the Western approach and focus is on bringing and establishing Western democracy models in these countries, this has not fared well to this date as seen in the case of Iraq, Egypt, Libya, and Bahrain. More efforts for societal inclusion and tolerance are needed to help navigate in these turbulent times. The latest silent support of both the US and the European Union towards the military coup in Egypt against an officially elected government further begs the questioning of the West's sincerity in helping the region transform through democracy and bringing peace and prosperity (Esposito 2013).

Today, the region is experiencing new challenges and opportunities in terms of development, improvement, and growth. For example, capacity building and skill development are critical for the survival of over two million Syrian citizens who ran away from their country and sought shelter in neighboring countries of Turkey, Lebanon, and Jordan.

HRD in the Middle East

Traditionally, HRD has focused on Training and Development (T&D), Organization Development (OD), and Career Development (CD) (McLagan 1989). It is also considered as "any process or activity that, either initially or over the long term, has the potential to develop adults' work-based knowledge, expertise, productivity and satisfaction, whether for personal or group/team gain, or for the benefit of an organization, community, nation, or ultimately, the whole of humanity" (McLean and McLean 2001: 322). For the purpose of this study, we consider HRD from both definitions in an attempt to provide a broad perspective of HRD activities and reflect on what HRD means in the diverse region under discussion. In addition, it addresses the workplace models that apply in several countries of the region. Furthermore, the external environmental changes at the national level, represented by the emerging global marketplace, have had some important implications for changes in organizational practices within the Middle East region.

Although specific cultural and contextual factors influence the speed of change, the globalization of business has resulted in the diffusion of Western business and management practices to the countries in the Middle East. Leaders in several countries of the Middle East region have made concerted efforts not to live in silos, and decided to open their borders and embrace change as a twenty-first century strategy (e.g. UAE, Qatar). Now these countries are harvesting the success of their politics and policies. Such practices provide evidence of Cummings and Worley's (2009) statement that how effectively countries respond to the global marketplace has implications for HRD at the organizational and individual levels.

The rapid changes of today's economies and societies in the Middle East, along with the constant evolution of technology, global marketplace, and managerial innovations, lead to a great need for HRD functions that can address them proactively. This is evident in the emergence of satellite and virtual colleges that provide HRD programs to address the needs of the market. The Texas A&M University HRD program in Saudi Arabia and George Washington University's HRD program in Qatar are some of the examples of such developments in the region.

HRD activities and programs

Business and trade in the region is versatile in regards to production and services. While some of the countries in the region have high levels of unemployment, others, mainly in the Gulf region, heavily depend on a foreign labor force. Economic development relies on both financial and human resources. Finding and utilizing financial resources have not been as challenging for many Middle Eastern countries as the development of their human resources has been. For example, Qatar, UAE, Saudi Arabia, Oman, and Bahrain, have abundant financial resources but fall short with developing their human resources, while the case is totally the opposite with countries like Lebanon, Egypt, and Turkey. This factor has an influence at the organizational level. Companies attempt to remain competitive through minimizing business costs and using cheap foreign labor where both a skilled and unskilled workforce are available. Larger employment gaps both in the government and private sectors still exist within the technical areas as national labor forces of these countries do not meet the demands of industries for a specific workforce such as the oil and gas, healthcare, and aviation industries (IMF 2013).

The field of HRD in the region traditionally existed in the form of personnel training and apprenticeship. The apprenticeship model in the Middle East often involved sending a young boy to work with a master in a given occupation such as bakery, metal works, and woodshops. To this date, this practice exists particularly in the countries that are not industrialized. The governments of the region develop and implement programs that combine apprenticeships with formal education in vocational education centers. These programs are also aligned with governmental policies of nationalizing the workforce, where several countries are trying to rely more on their citizens and less on foreign human resources. This is particularly true for industries requiring higher levels of technical knowledge and expertise. This supports policies at the national level to reduce reliance on oil and gas through diversification of economies and development of human resources in other areas where they can become global competitors.

With a majority of the population following Islam, "Work-based learning is part of the Islamic perspective mandating and encouraging all Muslims to learn" (Akdere and Salem 2013: 215). However, education and learning is rather problematic in the region with very low literacy rates and little investment in learning. This certainly has immediate and long term effects on HRD practices in the region. HRD activities exist both in governmental organizations and in the private sector. These activities are often in the form of formal classroom training (Dirani 2012). Dirani (2012) found that little emphasis is given to informal training or other forms of learning. He also observed that training efforts usually focus on providing a specific knowledge base and skill set; thus job-specific training is very common. Many of the training programs are tied to various governmental certification and accreditation processes which are required as evidence that workers have the knowledge base and skill set.

Organization development focuses on culture, management and leadership development (Cummings and Worley 2009). Organizational development activities assist with establishing a workplace culture where people from various cultures, ethnic, and religious backgrounds work together as diverse teams in many of the companies that employ foreign workers. Country specific culture plays a strong role in determining every aspect of HRD activities in the region (Dirani 2007). For example, HRD activities in Lebanon take into consideration the education level and industries prevalent in the country, including financial sector and tourism, while HRD activities in Saudi Arabia account for the religious culture from which all business and management policies stem.

This also leads to another important factor for HRD, the gender issue. In this regard, masculinity and femininity play a significant role in terms of genderization of the jobs, performance evaluation, management and leadership development. Particularly, masculinity implies competitiveness and assertiveness whereas femininity is expected to lead to modesty and care (Hofstede 1980). For example, in most Gulf countries in the region, women in the workforce are almost non-existent, especially among citizens, while the glass ceiling is a major barrier to women in other countries like Jordan and Syria. Thus, most management and leadership development training focuses on helping male natives to develop a skill set to become effective managers and successful leaders.

Career development often takes the form of life-time employment in some industries (the banking sector in Lebanon) and nationalization in some countries (the gas and oil sectors in Saudi

Arabia). Little emphasis is given to continuing education and life-long learning (UNESCO 2012). Furthermore, although some countries in the region have a comprehensive National HRD plan or strategy (Turkey, UAE, Kuwait), the educational and technological backgrounds that support HRD activities are scarce. Specifically, the education programs of academic institutions are not generally determined by the national needs of the countries (UNESCO 2012). Finally, there is little coordination among governmental agencies, academic institutions, and the population at large to help assess and identify needs and develop HRD programs and models to address them.

Diversity of the region

In discussions of management and HRD divergence and convergence practices in different regions of the world, several scholars and international experts view different countries within a region as more homogeneous, while others view them as more heterogeneous (Ronen and Shenkar 1985). The countries in the Middle East fall into both these categories. The region has great diversity: geographically, religiously, economically, linguistically, and otherwise. Economy, levels of literacy, political stability, religion, culture, technology, and globalization can all be looked at from a national perspective or can be viewed from an organizational perspective. These factors within the Middle East region include variables that foster and impede HRD, including, but not limited to, human capital, the external factors affecting the organization, communication preferences and styles (e.g. face-to-face versus the Internet), social norms (e.g. gender relations), education (levels of literacy, both traditional and digital), religion, and the meaning of work. At the organizational level, these factors include leadership roles, management styles, employee expectations, and strategic planning. All of these areas need further development and improvement, which HRD can provide.

Factors influencing HRD functions

This section of the chapter will explore three specific divergent and convergent factors influencing HRD functions, namely, research, education, and information technology.

Research

Scientific research in the Middle East, in general, lags that of the West. HRD scholarship is no different. Of course, there are individual scholars from the region who produce world-class research and make significant contributions to the field. But as a region, Middle Eastern scholars underperformed compared with their colleagues in the West (Dirani 2007). It is important to note here, however, that the political and institutional structures in the region (specifically for the countries with autocratic governmental systems) make it very difficult to conduct research and identify existing research problems and explore solutions to them. We should also add the lack of academic freedom in many of these countries, which not only limits the researcher but also presents many ethical issues and dilemmas for them.

Part of the reason for this goes back to colonization and the ruling elite in these countries that resulted in a huge population of illiterate citizens, especially women. In addition, most of the countries in the region looked for help from the West, or recently from the East. All these regimes failed and resulted in frustrated populations missing real opportunities for development and growth; thus lacking hope for a future. HRD research can provide a roadmap at the national level by systematically understanding and providing solutions that help with eliminating illiteracy, improving education and ensuring active participation of women in the society and in the workplace specifically.

One of the major consequences of the lack of government supported and sponsored research in most of the Middle East is the lack of reliable data and evidence based decision making. With no systematic understanding of the needs of their employees, managers, and customers, countries and organizations in the region usually struggle to implement efficient economic and management strategies and adopt HRD designs from the West (Dirani 2012). Thus, in view of the scarcity of resources and the weak linkages among research centers, government, the private sector, and the general public, it is necessary to develop and fund national strategies for research and development.

Some promising initiatives have started recently, such as the Mohammad Bin Rashid Al Maktoum Foundation initiative to provide ten billion dollars for improving research in the Arab countries. The goal of the initiative is to bridge the knowledge gap between the Middle East countries and the more developed countries, improving the standard of education and research in the region, developing leadership programs for youth, and stimulating job creation (Mohammed bin Rashid Al Maktoum Foundation 2013). Another example is the Qatar Foundation for Education, Science and Community Development, which is a private non-profit organization that serves the people of Qatar by supporting and operating programs in three core mission areas of education, science and research, and community development (Qatar Foundation 2013).

Education

Education has been identified as a key factor for the training of manpower needed for the development and management of the Middle Eastern countries. Still, some countries such as Yemen and Libya are far from the success of other countries such as Turkey and Lebanon. Both Turkey and Lebanon, for instance, adopted a policy of early and intensive investment in education, accompanied by sustained and rapid improvement of its levels (UNDP 2009). Efforts to measure the quality of education in many countries of the region are limited (Akdere *et al.* 2006); in itself this is a crisis in education. Quantitative measurements show key deficiencies relevant to knowledge production. For example, in Yemen fewer than one in 20 university students are pursuing scientific disciplines, such as computer science, while in Lebanon the figure is one in five (UNDP 2009). Similarly, there are 142 universities in Turkey at present (International Colleges and Universities 2013); however, the lack of well-funded and well-attended business and management education has a direct impact on management technology achievement and transfer.

Some Middle Eastern countries also suffer from the accelerated emigration of their educated professionals, such as Egypt, Jordan, and Lebanon. It is no wonder then that the role played by some countries in the 1960s and 70s, such as Lebanon, has been assumed by other regional centers such as UAE. Paradoxically, the Lebanese themselves have helped to make this possible, by moving their knowledge base and expertise abroad (Nasser and Abouchedid 2003).

Information technology

Some efforts to build capacity and improve IT education have been made by most Middle Eastern governments, through the respective Ministries of Education, private centers for training and development, and with collaboration with experts from United Nations Agencies and other regional agencies. Statistics had shown a dim picture of the IT status quo (UNESCO 2013). For instance, Constantine (2005) reported that during the 2003–2004 school year, on average, 50 per cent of the private schools were teaching IT compared with 12 per cent in public schools (data compiled from seven countries in the region: Lebanon, Syria, Jordan, Egypt, UAE, Bahrain, and Qatar). Besides, Constantine found that many public schools were still unequipped with IT laboratories, some of them did not have a room for use as an IT laboratory, and many lacked specialized teachers (0.7 per cent IT teachers in public schools compared with 2.7 per cent in private schools).

There is a lack of vision in most countries that is critical in the implementation of technology in any training or academic program. Other barriers to IT advancement are lack of infrastructure, an unreliable network, economic stagnation, lack of familiarity with techniques and methods (know-how), and lack of regulatory policies that facilitate the use of IT, to name a few (Dirani 2007). Governments and organizations need to provide the strategies and clear visions of their future goals with respect to developing their human resources, and need to provide the systems to support these visions. People who do not change or do not accept such change are left behind or may become a stumbling block and a source of frustration for others who do.

Some countries, such as Turkey and UAE, have a global perspective on economic and management development and are generally more accustomed to dealing with other cultures in both business and social contexts. For example, English has become the common language of commerce in the multicultural, multilingual, Arab-speaking UAE (Dirani 2007). Foreign investment also has grown in the past decade and many large international high-technology companies have now established their global or Middle Eastern headquarters in UAE, particularly in Dubai. Contracting with expatriates for goods and services is the dominant mode of operation in the UAE.

Modern and technology-rich industries in UAE are based on imported machinery and management systems that have been parachuted in as "black boxes" (Dirani 2012). These technologies were neither adapted nor developed in the country. These interventions and models of practice were created within the context of the developed world, with most coming from the United States, United Kingdom, or mainland Europe (UNESCO 2012). From an international perspective, these interventions might be hard to implement in regions with different social and cultural backgrounds. This leaves the country at a disadvantage. As producers of such technologies and management continue to improve on them, UAE modern industries will turn obsolete in the absence of national research capabilities (UNDP 2009).

Final remarks

Because there is little research in the HRD area from the Middle East, the induction of categories and themes for competencies associated with HRD in the region is better suited to understanding the specific challenges related to the indigenous organizations and to country specific policies. This approach is more effective than imposing predetermined classifications and systems that were predominantly developed in the West and generalizing them to the whole region. By doing so, it will allow for deeper understanding and facilitation of HRD practices, rather than deciding whether HRD fits predetermined criteria, of which few exist.

To illustrate, words, symbols, and activities do hold different meanings for different people based on their cultural background. Thus, at the organizational level, it is very important for individuals to construct their own meaning about the situations and circumstances related to HRD activities in the workplace. As they share that knowledge with others, the recipients are also constructing their own personal meaning of what has been shared. Together the sharer and receiver may construct new knowledge and meaning. Therefore, studying how HRD is practiced in organizations could be labeled as interpretivism. Interpretivism looks at culturally derived interpretations of work-related management issues (Dirani 2007). This perspective will provide researchers and practitioners with insights to help understand the strengths and challenges associated with HRD functions.

Conventional wisdom as well as management practices have led us to form some assumptions about organizations and the way they conduct HRD. First, organizational leaders have the ability to facilitate or inhibit HRD practices among their employees in a number of ways, through both their actions and their attitudes. Second, the physical and social structure (organizational culture) of the organization impacts the opportunity of HRD to take place, or not. And third, informal dialogues and learning that emerge in an organization influence the ways that HRD is transferred as well as the types of management technologies that are transferred.

At the national level, governments need to support research in the field to include evaluation and monitoring programs to learn and improve HRD practice. Thus, education, capacity building, and utilizing technology should be priorities for these countries. It is worth mentioning that the rise of the Arab Spring in several of the Middle East countries has brought the winds of change to the region, and the HRD field will definitely be affected by this change, especially with capacity building and leadership development at the local and community levels (e.g. Lebanon's and Egypt's current situations). HRD scholars and practitioners are invited to learn from the changes and probably need to be involved in shaping the future of the region and not stand and watch from the sidelines.

References

Akdere, M. and Salem, J.M. (2013) Islamic perspectives on work-based learning. In Gibbs, P. (ed.) *Learning, Work and Practice: New understandings* (207–17). Dordrecht: Springer.

Akdere, M., Russ-Eft, D. and Eft, N. (2006) The Islamic worldview of adult learning in the workplace: Surrendering to God. *Advances in Human Resource Development* 8, 3: 355–63.

Aubert, J.E. and Reiffers, J.L. (eds) (2003) *Knowledge economies in the Middle East and North Africa: Toward new development strategies*. Washington, DC: International Bank for Reconstruction and Development/ World Bank.

Central Intelligence Agency (CIA) (2011) Country comparison: GDP (purchasing power parity). Retrieved on October 17, 2012 from https://www.cia.gov/library/publications/the-world-factbook/rankorder/ 2001rank.html.

Constantine, N. (2005) Technology and education: Pre-university education administration. *Technologies for Education for All: Possibilities and Prospects in the Arab Region* 1, 1: 49–54.

Cummings, T.G. and Worley, C.G. (2009) *Organization development and change* (9th edition). Mason, OH: South-Western Cengage Learning.

Dalacoura, K. (2012) The 2011 uprisings in the Arab Middle East: Political change and geopolitical implications. *International Affairs* 88, 1: 63–79.

Dirani, K.M. (2007) Individualism and collectivism as predictors for management and human resources development in the Lebanese context: An empirical study. *International Management* 7, 1: 45–68.

— (2012) Professional training as a strategy for staff development: A study in the learning transfer in the Lebanese context. *European Journal of Training and Development* 36, 2/3: 158–78.

Esposito, J. (2013) *Living in denial: US policy and Egypt's military coup*. Retrieved on August 4, 2013 from http://www.aljazeera.com/indepth/opinion/2013/07/2013715105014165446.html.

Garavan, T.N., Morley, M., Gunnigle, P. and McGuire, D. (2002) Human resource development and workplace learning: emerging theoretical perspectives and organisational practices. *Journal of European Industrial Training* 26(2/3/4): 60–71.

Hofstede, G. (1980) *Culture's consequences: International differences in work-related values*. London: SAGE.

International Colleges and Universities (2013) Retrieved on August 4, 2013 from http://www.4icu.org/tr/.

International Monetary Fund (IMF) (2013) *World economic outlook: Transitions and tensions*. Retrieved on April 3, 2013 from http://www.imf.org/external/pubs/ft/weo/2013/02/pdf/text.pdf.

Lewis, B. (2010) *Faith and power: Religion and politics in the Middle East*. New York: Oxford University Press.

McLagan, P.A. (1989) Models for HRD practice. *Training and Development Journal* 43, 9: 49–59.

McLean, G.N. and McLean, L. (2001) If we can't define HRD in one country, how can we define it in another? *Human Resource Development International* 4, 3: 313–26.

2012 Middle East Encyclopedia Britannica. *Britannica Concise Encyclopedia.* Retrieved on October 15, 2012 from http://www.britannica.com/EBchecked/topic/381192/Middle-East.

Miller, T. and Kim, A.B. (2013) Defining economic freedom. In Miller, T., Holmes, K.R., Feulner, E.J., Kim, A.B., Riley, B. and Roberts, J.M. (eds) *2013 Index of Economic Freedom.* Washington, DC: Heritage Foundation and Dow Jones and Company.

Mizzi, R. and Rocco, T.S. (2013) Deconstructing dominance: Towards a reconceptualization of the relationship between collective and individual identities, globalization and learning at work. *Human Resource Development Review* 12, 2: 1–19.

Mohammed bin Rashid Al Maktoum Foundation (2013) Retrieved on August 4, 2013 from http://www.mbrfoundation.ae/English/Pages/AboutUs.aspx.

Nasser, R. and Abouchedid, K. (2003) Occupational attainment through Lebanon's higher education: Using individual, societal, structural and gender factors as predictors. *Career Development International* 8, 7: 328–38.

Obst, D. and Kirk, D. (eds) (2010) *Innovation through education: Building the knowledge economy in the Middle East.* Washington, DC: Institute of International Education.

Qatar Foundation (2013) Retrevied on August 4, 2013 from http://www.qf.org.qa/about.

Rahme, J.G. (1999) Ethnocentric and stereotypical concepts in the study of Islamic and world history. *The History Teacher* 32, 4: 473–94.

Ronen, S. and Shenkar, O. (1985) Clustering countries on attitudinal dimensions: A review and synthesis. *Academy of Management Review* 10, 3: 435–54.

Swanson, R.A. and Holton III, E.F. (2009) *Foundations of human resource development* (2nd edition). San Francisco: Berrett-Koehler.

Swindell, G.S. (2013a) *World oil reserves.* Retrieved on August 4, 2013 from http://gswindell.com/temp28.gif.

— (2013b) *Gas reserve life index.* Retrieved on August 4, 2013 from http://gswindell.com/temp14.gif.

United Nations Development Program (UNDP) (2009) *Arab Human development report 2009: Challenges to human security in the Arab world.* New York: UN Publications.

UNESCO (2012) *ICT Survey – Arab states.* Retrieved on August 4, 2013 from http://www.uis.unesco.org/Communication/Pages/ict-survey-arab-states.aspx.

World Bank (2013) Retrieved on January 22, 2013 from http://data.worldbank.org/indicator/SP.POP.TOTL.

World Fact Book (2012) Retrieved on January 22, 2013, from https://www.cia.gov/library/publications/the-world-factbook/geos/we.html.

41
HRD IN JAPAN AND TAIWAN

Robert J. Schalkoff and Min-Hsun Christine Kuo

HRD is recognized as a strategy to ensure the competiveness of business enterprises and nations in an increasingly globalized economy (Xie and Huang 2010). The Japanese Ministry of Education, Culture, Sports, Science, and Technology (MEXT) has declared the development of global human resources, people who can function and excel in an increasingly globalized life and work environment, to be the most important challenge for Japan (MEXT 2012a). MEXT argues that lifelong learning and personal development skills will keep Japanese citizens and organizations competitive. In Taiwan, helping small and medium enterprises (SMEs) create competitive advantages and adapt to the demand for human resources in a global economy is a priority. The Taiwanese Ministry of Economic Affairs has joined together with related government agencies, research institutions, public and private enterprises, and civic organizations to establish guidance systems to provide HRD and related assistance to these SMEs (MEA 1999).

This chapter addresses two questions: How is HRD conceptualized and practiced in Japan and Taiwan? What can other nations learn from HRD in Japan and Taiwan? The review is divided into two major sections, one each for Japan and Taiwan. The following topics are addressed for each context: history of HRD; current trends and issues; national and cultural aspects; special characteristics; and future directions for HRD.

HRD in Japan

History

The history of HRD in Japan can be divided into four periods, each of which corresponds to historical or economic development.

HRD for modernization: 1853–1940

Over 200 years of a "closed door policy" to foreign relations rendered Japan nearly helpless against Western military technology and US demands for Japan to open itself for trade in 1853. After a period of initial turmoil, Japan responded with a national HRD initiative that eventually replaced the traditional apprentice style of HRD (Maekawa 2010). From 1860 to 1895, the national government and private industry employed approximately 3,000 foreign experts

(Uemura 2008) to train Japanese adults in academic, technical, administrative, and industrial sciences. Additionally, some 3,500 Japanese citizens were sent abroad between 1868 and 1940 for similar purposes (MEXT n.d.).

The late 1800s and early 1900s saw a growing blue and white collar work force in Japan (Sakamoto 1977). Industrial growth necessitated the development of strategies to retain employees (Odaka 1994); the primary objective of HRD became the creation of a disciplined workforce (Odaka 1994). Economic downturn in the early 1900s combined with a state of semi-war and growing emphasis on duty to the emperor led to the development of two unique aspects of Japanese HRD: lifelong employment and seniority/age-based pay (Sakamoto 1977).

HRD to rebuild Japan: 1945–1960

At the end of World War II, Japan had few human resources with managerial experience (Robinson and Stern 1995). Training Within Industries and the Management Training Program (MTP) were introduced into Japan by the US Air Force to fill this gap. MTP developed into a common national training platform for mid-level managers and contributed to the establishment of certain unique aspects of Japanese HRD: *kaizen* or "continuous improvement" (Robinson and Stern 1995: 138); a plan-do-study-check-act approach (Swanson and Holton 2009); and strong human relations (JITA 2008). MTP, in particular, led to the development of clear paths for information sharing within Japanese organizations (Robinson and Stern 1995).

HRD and the economic miracle: 1970–1980

In the 1970s and 1980s, the Japanese economic "miracle" brought worldwide attention to Japanese management and HRD practices. A number of characteristics were noted: 1) uniformly high levels of education prior to employment; 2) a culture that encouraged cooperation; 3) an extensive amount of time devoted to training; 4) lifelong employment; and 5) training in how to communicate and share information as well as how to teach fellow workers (Hashimoto 1994).

Emphasis on general academic skills rather than work specific skills in the recruitment process necessitated extensive orientation and on-the-job training (OJT) programs (Hashimoto 1994). New recruits trained with more senior employees, and activities focused on consensus-based decision making and team processes. Socialization outside of the workplace facilitated human relations (Nonaka 1991; Hashimoto 1994).

Formal off-the-job training (Off-JT) enhanced OJT, and a job rotation system developed "intrafirm general, though firm specific skills" (Hashimoto 1994: 126). These skills allowed employees to act resourcefully when faced with challenges and adapt quickly to new job requirements; moreover, they allowed employers to reposition rather than lay off employees when demand in one division declined. Nonaka *et al.* (2000) used the term "knowledge creation" to describe the processes leading to these types of skills. Knowledge creation consisted of three elements: a socialization, externalization, combination, and internalization (SECI) process; *ba* or shared context; and knowledge assets.

HRD in post-bubble Japan: 1990–2010

Economic stagnancy occurred in the late 1980s through the 1990s and into the first decade of the twenty-first century. Organizational cultures shifted from lifetime employment and seniority/age-based pay to long-term employment and performance-based practices (Harada 1999). Harada stressed the need for HRD to be more strategic and integrate career development, evaluative practices, organizational development, and performance-based incentives.

Current issues and trends

The current situation in Japan reflects trends noted by Harada (1999). The shift from lifelong employment to long-term and often short, contracted terms of employment has had major implications for HRD, particularly access to and participation in HRD. Moreover, differences in gender are present in HRD and career development.

Results from a 2011 survey (n = 7,000) on HRD by the Ministry of Health, Labor, and Welfare (MHLW) confirm what Hara (2010) and Sato (2010) noted in a similar survey from 2005 (n = 5,000): a large gap exists between full-time and short-term, contracted workers regarding participation in OJT, Off-JT, and self-development activities (MHLW 2012a). Although results from the 2011 survey did show some increase in the number of firms placing emphasis on HRD for all employees instead of just selected ones, the number of firms reporting "planned" OJT for full-time employees increased as did the percentage of firms offering Off-JT to full-time employees.

Two aspects identified in the MHLW survey (2012a) remained virtually unchanged in the last three years: 1) the number of employees engaged in self-development (approximately 40 per cent for full-time and 20 per cent for short-term, contracted employees), and 2) the barriers of time and money for participation in these activities. Although no data related to gender was available for the 2011 survey, Sato (2010) pointed to gender related differences in self-development activities in the 2005 survey: Women engaged in self-development activities for self-enrichment; whereas men focused on career development. Moreover, the participation of women in HRD was more likely to be influenced by the work environment than participation for men (Hara 2010).

Generally speaking, results from the 2011 and 2005 surveys indicated that larger corporations promoted work environments that encouraged learning at work. Hara (2010) attributed these findings to the likelihood that HRD and career development activities were regulated in these corporations. However, the 2005 survey revealed less formal career development activities than expected by analysts (Sato 2010).

Other current trends in Japan include new HRD platforms and organizations with diversified client bases that require more flexibility in HRD. Information and communication technology in professional development (Bayrakcı 2010) and virtual HRD (Watanuki 2006) are two new platforms for HRD. Non-traditional approaches to HRD for professionals in high risk fields such as corporate real estate and fund management are also needed (Tobita 2006).

A final trend in Japan is global HRD. The Ministry of Economy, Trade and Industry has repeatedly stated the need for human resources with international competencies (METI 2005; 2006; 2012). A 2010 survey (n = 280) revealed that the most pressing issues for corporations with both domestic and overseas operations were HRD to develop international competencies in current employees and the procurement of human resources with international competencies (MEXT 2012b).

National and cultural context

National government has played a key role in establishing HRD policies in Japan since the late nineteenth century. Human relations are also an important aspect of HRD in Japan. The importance of national government and human relations is likely the result of a collectivist culture where social relations take precedence over individuals' self-interests (Gheorghiu *et al.* 2009) and a society that places emphasis on hierarchy and seniority within organizations (Hashimoto 1994).

Ba plays an important role in the way Japanese organizations create and manage knowledge; OJT takes place in *ba* where senior members teach junior members of the team. Importance is placed on communication within teams; socialization reinforces these relationships. Moreover, the seniority system determines the type of HRD organizational members receive, the role they play in the HRD process, and the position in the organization they eventually obtain (Gamage and Ueyama 2005).

However, the work culture in Japan has changed (Harada 1999). Lessening importance of seniority and growing importance of performance have led to renewed emphasis on evaluative procedures. Changes from lifelong employment to long- or short-term employment have increased the necessity for career development.

Special characteristics and interventions

MTP and Training Within Industry (TWI) are two unique interventions in HRD in Japan (Japanese Industrial Trade Association 2008). Two other unique aspects are job rotation and recruitment based on general academic achievement rather than work-based skills.

A final unique characteristic of HRD in Japan relates to civil servants at the local, prefecture (similar to a US state), and national levels. Hiring practices are similar to the private sector; job rotation also plays a major role in OJT for civil servants (Nakamoto, personal communication November 2011). Off-JT for civil servants is provided at all levels. For example, Local Autonomy College provides HRD in public policy, law, leadership, and other areas for exceptional civil servants at either the prefecture or local levels (MIAC 2011).

Future challenges and directions

Sato (2010) lists a number of policy considerations for HRD in Japan: 1) opportunities for career development, particularly at mid-career level, need to be increased; 2) HRD activities at the middle management and line manager level need to focus on individual development as well as on helping managers develop HRD programs for less experienced employees; and 3) access to HRD activities for short-term, contracted employees needs to be improved in order to help them move into full-time positions.

Currently, the MHLW funds HRD centers at the prefecture and municipal levels to provide HRD to workers of all ages who are entering or re-entering the workforce. Labor regulations were revised in 2012 to protect Japan's approximately 12 million short-term, contracted workers (MHLW 2012b); new regulations allow contracted workers to petition employers for full-time employment after five years of contracted employment.

On a macro level, scholars are divided on the future of HRD in Japan. Mikami and Nishino (2004) stress that HRD that worked in the past cannot be expected to work in the present. They argue that strategy should dictate the type of human resources and HRD needed by organizations. Moreover, they advocate fair and equal HRD and assessment with a focus on career development. Collinson and Ono (2001) suggest that educators could benefit from a more research-based format similar to professional development in the US and the adoption of standards when planning and evaluating such programs.

Kawabata (2009), on the other hand, calls for a return to the "roots" of HRD in Japan. Kawabata argues that increased emphasis on results-oriented thinking, too much focus on short-term as opposed to long-term growth and development, and flatter management styles have created problems in quality control, compliance, and the ability of employees to engage in effective human relations and teamwork. Kawabata supports HRD policies more commensurate with Japanese culture and traditional management styles, for example, seniority based principals and lifetime employment.

HRD in Taiwan

History

The history of HRD in Taiwan can be divided into three periods, each of which is related to a shift in the focus of HRD.

Early recognition of the importance of HRD: 1912–1952

Dr Sun Yat-Sen, founder of the Republic of China, based the construction of the nation on the Three Principles of the People: Nationalism, Democracy, and People's Livelihood. People's Livelihood focused on enhancing the quality of human resources. Sun emphasized that "to strengthen and manage the nation, people must utilize their talents and skills. [Sun stressed that] if our nation wishes to regain its strength, we must focus on human resources" (Tsay 1989: 54). Implementing a new system to nurture and educate people was a prerequisite to attaining that goal.

HRD through education and vocational training: 1953–1986

Initially, this stage was characterized by disorganization, especially in in-service training sponsored by individual organizations. During this stage, most of the training was sponsored and conducted by various levels of government organizations. However, no official guidelines or policies were in place for an integrated system of vocational training in public or private organizations.

In 1961, Li Kuo-Ting, the Vice-Director of the US Aid Utilization Council, reinforced the idea that human resources were a requirement of a developing nation. Under Li, Taiwan began an initiative to reach full employment within the shortest possible time. Education and training related to the quality of workers were the main thrusts of the initiative.

Another development in 1961 was the Taiwanese government's decision to invite experts from Stanford Research Institute to undertake a research project entitled *The Role of Education Planning in Economic Development* (CEPD 1997a). The purpose of this project was to determine existing problems within Taiwan's educational system. This study introduced a new concept: education as investment. Since then, Taiwan has taken a proactive stance on vocational education, changing policy to meet national objectives (Land 1990).

Policies regarding the development of human resources and the purposes of HRD in restructuring the post-war economy were established in 1965 when the fourth Four-Year Economic Development Plan (EDP) was implemented. An additional chapter, entitled *Development of Human Resources*, was added to the fourth Four-Year EDP. With the establishment of the Statutes of the Vocational Training Fund, a variety of vocational training sponsorships emerged. This increased the share of training done by private business organizations and civic organizations.

In 1975, as the Taiwanese people started to grasp the concept of human resources and the government gained experience in planning human resources, Taiwan implemented the Manpower Development Special Plan (1976 to 1981) (CEPD 1997a). As part of this plan, more universities started industrial education programs to serve the need for developing vocational training.

The history of vocational education reached a turning point in 1976 with the approval of the new Vocational School Act, the first major legislation in Taiwan to support and strengthen vocational education (Land 1990). The positive relationship between economic growth and vocational education was evidence of the benefits of investing in human capital. In addition to an outstanding vocational education system, a number of universities in Taiwan implemented academic programs to educate and train HRD-related practitioners.

Vocational training after 1975 showed how the Taiwanese government integrated HRD with its national economic development policy. The supply of skilled laborers was crucial to the development of Taiwan. The Special Techniques and Vocational Training Committee began the Vocational Training Five-Year Plan in 1977 (CEPD 1997a). By the late 1970s, Taiwan's economic "miracle" received worldwide attention.

The final stage in this period saw a nearly fully employed unskilled labor force, rising wages, and a number of high school and college graduates that required additional training. The government established the Employment and Vocational Training Administration (EVTA) in 1981 in order to maintain full employment while fully utilizing human resources in production. The types of training programs provided by the EVTA were: 1) pre-employment training for new employees; 2) upgrading training for in-service employees; 3) second-expertise and job-transfer training; and 4) cooperative training. Through the efforts of EVTA, the Taiwanese government passed the Vocational Training Act in 1983. The EVTA played a significant role in promoting enterprise training in Taiwan.

Enterprise training in SMEs: 1990–2010

In the late 1980s, the concept of "enterprise" training became increasingly acceptable. Enterprise training can be defined as any training conducted in the workplace. However, Chu *et al.* (1992) reported the following contrast: Although most enterprises had proposals for education and training, the quality of training and the actual number of enterprises applying human resource planning was unsatisfactory.

Large corporations in Taiwan carried out HRD activities such as in-house training, joint training, outsourced training, and appointing employees for advanced education. SMEs, however, were not able to invest in HRD. The reasons for this included 1) a misunderstanding of the nature of employee training; 2) insufficient support from management; 3) over-emphasis on current and short-term profits; 4) emphasis on the quantity rather than quality of training; and 5) struggling with basic frameworks for HRD practice (Kuo 2002).

Through the Statute for Development of SMEs in 1991 (MOEA 1999), the Taiwanese government set forth a clear vision and list of objectives to guide SMEs. The Small and Medium Enterprise Administration (SMEA), established in the same year, created several projects designed specifically to enhance SMEs' competitive advantages. Ten individual guidance systems were used to strengthen SMEs, assist SMEs in individual or joint research and development of new products and technologies, and provide SMEs with technical assistance through immediate solution centers (MOEA 1999).

In addition to individual guidance systems, the SMEA established a variety of channels through which it provided education and training. For example, Research and Training Centers of SMEs were set up to use HRD in SMEs as a means to upgrade service quality and enhance the competitiveness of SMEs nationwide. These Centers coordinate various private and public training organizations contracted by the SMEA to provide seminars and training courses for utilizing limited resources more effectively. To meet long-term objectives, Centers not only conduct research related to management of SMEs, but also accumulate and disseminate the results of enterprise training.

Despite a dramatic increase in unemployment, the demand for skilled workers in the 1990s was greater than the number of skilled workers available (CEPD 1997b). The diverse needs and problems of a large population and work force became Taiwan's primary challenge. Taiwan had built a solid foundation for its labor-intensive industry by utilizing an abundant and relatively inexpensive labor force. However, with the shift to a knowledge-based economy, skilled human resources became a critical part of Taiwan maintaining its economic success.

Current issues and trends

Taiwan currently faces four major challenges brought about by economic growth and changes in society and the workplace. First, the underemployment rate has increased over the years. Second, the government no longer enjoys arbitrary power; many SMEs are shifting their operations abroad due to the appearance of strong environmental, labor, and consumer movements. Third, the policy on foreign workers in Taiwan continues to be one of supplementing the local workforce. Fourth, the trend in the employment market on the supply side is towards older workers; whereas on the demand side, the employment rate in service industries has increased continually and innovation in technology is needed in upgraded industries (CEPD 1997b).

Currently, training programs and research and development activities sponsored by the CEPD and the SMEA allow employees to update technical and professional levels. The SMEA also promotes specific policies to foster cooperation between firms. These include 1) inter-industry and intra-industry exchanges; 2) implementing cooperative projects; 3) assisting in the development of cooperative organizations; 4) and supporting the establishment of common facilities.

National and cultural context

Three perspectives provide lenses through which the functions for Taiwan's HRD system can be viewed. From a macro-economic point of view, HRD makes workers more employable, improves the quality of labor, decreases unemployment, and develops and utilizes human resources to accelerate economic growth. From a social point of view, HRD helps disadvantaged people develop the needed skills for jobs. In addition, the SMEA hopes that SMEs will make good use of external resources to enhance the quality of their employees and increase management efficiency of organizations. Ultimately, these activities should lead to the creation of a learning society in Taiwan. Finally, from a scientific and technological point of view, HRD improves workers' skill levels, upgrades their technological skills, increases their mobility, and prevents structural unemployment (Peng 1990).

The evolution of HRD in Taiwan is continuous at the government level. From the government's perspective, HRD is historically an intentional, innovative, long-term, and committed process of developing the work-related learning capabilities of individuals (Kuo 2002) achieved primarily through education and vocational training. There is also a minor emphasis on career development, "with the intention of contributing to individual, organizational, and national growth" (Kuo 2002: 215–16).

As noted, there has been a shift in policy towards enterprise training. Government policies now provide an infrastructure that enables HRD in a number of areas, including assisting enterprises to adapt to new technology, changing the attitudes of employees to ensure a high product quality, improving production efficiency, and strengthening competitiveness. Although there has yet to be an autonomous HRD system established at the provincial, municipal, and local levels (Kuo 2002), in-service training provided by vocational training centers under the jurisdiction of the EVTA, and the pragmatic mixture of government and private enterprise sponsored institutes seems successful.

Special characteristics and interventions

One of the most unique characteristics of HRD in Taiwan is the establishment of the SMEA. The nationwide network of Research and Training Centers set up by the SMEA to provide education and training is also unique to Taiwan. Efforts to train individuals and foster efforts for more cooperation between SMEs are two examples of the diverse interventions offered by these Centers.

The focus on vocational training throughout each historical period in the development of HRD in Taiwan is also a characteristic particular to the Taiwanese context. Although there is a need for a re-evaluation in order to meet demands for more skilled labor, there is little doubt that the strong focus on vocational training has greatly contributed to Taiwan's economic success.

Future challenges and directions

Adjusting training categories provided by the public Vocational Training Centers is essential to meet the demands for more skilled workers. Moreover, enterprises need to fill their own special training needs; the government needs to take an active role in advising enterprises about OJT training for employees. A regional HRD promotion council composed of representatives from business/industries, labor unions, educational institutions, and the local government could be established to help with this process. Finally, moving Taiwan towards its goal of becoming a learning society needs to become a goal of HRD.

Comparison of HRD in Japan and Taiwan

Table 41.1 shows a comparison of the similarities and differences between Japan and Taiwan as seen in literature on HRD in both contexts.

Similarities

Both Japan and Taiwan have successfully implemented HRD policy on a national scale. Nation building via HRD was an early goal for both nations. Recovery following WWII provided both Japan and Taiwan with unique opportunities for economic growth, and it is clear that HRD played a major role in the so-called economic "miracles" of both nations. Moreover, this economic growth made it possible for Japan and Taiwan to engage in HRD outside their borders through programs like Japan International Cooperation Agency (JICA) and Taiwan's International Cooperation and Development Fund (ICDF).

Currently, both nations are experiencing changes in labor conditions and increases in underemployed human resources. On the other hand, Japan and Taiwan have set goals to become lifelong learning societies. Flexibility and new types of HRD are needed to meet these challenges and achieve these goals.

Attention to individual needs is one area where both nations need to reconsider their approach to HRD. Although Taiwan has placed emphasis on helping citizens find employment commensurate with their talents, neither it nor Japan has placed great importance on individual satisfaction in HRD. Career development is one area where this deficiency might be met.

Differences

One difference between HRD in Japan and Taiwan is conceptual. Although both nations view HRD as work-based learning for adults, HRD in Japan currently includes undergraduate and graduate education. This difference is particularly true regarding so-called global HRD. In 2012, funding for programs to help college students develop international competencies exceeded 116 million US dollars (MEXT 2012b).

A second difference is the importance of the relationship between vocational education and economic policy. Parallel planning for economic growth and HRD is prominent in Taiwan. In order to create a large, skilled labor base following World War II, most education at the junior high school

Table 41.1 Similarities and differences between HRD in Japan and Taiwan

	Japan	*Taiwan*
Scope of HRD	Not limited to working adults. HRD includes undergraduate and graduate students; also includes handicapped adults, adults who are changing careers, and new graduates	Includes working adults, new graduates, handicapped/disadvantaged adults, adults who want to develop a second expertise, and adults who want to have a second career
Focus of HRD	1. Work-based knowledge, but evidence of discrepancies in access to and type of OJT, Off-JT between full-time employees and employees under contract 2. Expertise 3. Productivity as evidenced in MTP, TWI	1. Focus on work-based knowledge evidenced in CEPD and SMEA 2. Expertise 3. Productivity as evidenced in CPE, SMEA
Satisfaction with HRD	Not necessarily tied into satisfaction of individuals	Not necessarily tied into satisfaction of individuals. However, evidence of focus on realization of individual talent
Personal development	Self-development activities noted. Women more likely to pursue for self-gain; men for change of jobs or career development. Differences noted between full-time employees and short-term employees under contract	Personal gain in lifelong learning for new graduates, handicapped/disadvantaged people, people who want to develop a second expertise, people who want to have a second career, and working adults
Organizational development	Strong evidence of socialization and importance of human relations in group activities inside and outside of work environment	Particularly evidenced in CEPD, SMEA
Beneficiaries of HRD	Nation; organization; community via self-development activities; larger world-community via JICA; some evidence of larger benefit to society at the private level	Nation; organization; community via "Taiwan One Town One Product"; larger world-community via ICDF
Special characteristics and interventions	*Kaizen*; strong human relations; knowledge creation; *ba*; job rotation; MTP and TWI	SMEA sponsored Research and Training Centers; prominence of vocational training
Issues and future considerations	Movement away from lifetime employment and seniority-based advancement; need for career development, especially for contracted workers; need for global human resources	Demands for more skilled labor; more collaboration amongst stakeholders in HRD; movement toward becoming a learning society

level in Taiwan was vocational. Only recently with the emergence of Taiwan as a knowledge-based society have youth become more interested in university degrees over junior vocational degrees.

Japan, on the other hand, has traditionally placed vocational training at the high school or junior college level. Nonetheless, recent policies, particularly those related to global HRD, suggest that Japan sees the need to connect education to competiveness and economic growth. Hiring practices that emphasize general academic achievement over vocational skills, however, may make this type of connection very difficult.

Differences in HRD providers are present between Japan and Taiwan. Until recently, both HRD policy and practice have been the responsibility of the national government in Taiwan. In contrast, private corporations and enterprises play the largest role in HRD practice in Japan. This difference is particularly clear in Japan's push for global HRD. Policy has been established by the government, but implementation is the responsibility of the organizations engaged in HRD.

Division between policy and practice has resulted in the establishment of an autonomous HRD system in Japan. Taiwan lacks such a system. However, the existence of an autonomous system in Japan has not resulted in systematic training of HRD practitioners. Unlike Taiwan, graduate programs for future HRD practitioners are rare in Japan.

Finally, there are differences in the way Japan and Taiwan approach HRD in SMEs. Like Japan, large corporations in Taiwan provide more opportunities for HRD than SMEs. However, Taiwan appears to have a longer history of assisting SMEs with HRD. Nevertheless, Japan appears to be moving towards a more active stance on HRD in SMEs. Press releases by the Small and Medium Enterprise Agency in Japan reveal a shift in the last two years from human resource management to HRD policy and financial support for HRD in SMEs.

Conclusion

What can we learn from the histories of HRD in Japan and Taiwan? More specifically, what can other countries learn from both nations' policy experiences in shaping HRD? Of those experiences that are transferable, the first is the early recognition by the Japanese and Taiwanese governments of the importance of investing in human capital. Japan recognized this importance in its efforts to modernize; it undertook a similar stance following WWII. Taiwan recognized that the surest way to building a strong nation and economy was to focus on the development of its human resources. Strong leadership was influential in realizing this vision. Second, both Japan's and Taiwan's experiences show that deliberate government involvement, or intervention, in HRD can bring long-term material gain.

Although much can be learned from the study of HRD in Japan and Taiwan, cultural context must be emphasized. Strong national identity, collectivist cultural traditions, and tendencies to respect and follow government policy have contributed greatly to the successful implementation of HRD in Japan and Taiwan. Moreover, both nations are island nations with few natural resources. This factor may be the reason why both countries placed and continue to place so much importance on human resources. These important contextual factors must be considered when comparing HRD in Japan and Taiwan with that in other nations.

References

Notes

* References written in Chinese.

** References written in Japanese.

Bayrakcı, M. (2010) In-service teacher training in Japan and Turkey: a comparative analysis of institutions and practices, *Australian Journal of Teacher Education* 34, 1: 10–22.

CEPD (1997a) *The Evolution of Manpower Development Policies and Strategies in Taiwan for the Past 30 Years*, Taipei: Council for Economic Planning and Development.*

— (1997b) *Cross Century Manpower Development Plan 1997–2000*, Taipei: Council for Economic Planning and Development.*

Chu, C.M., Yang, C.C. and Chang, S.K.C. (1992) The analysis of applying human resources planning on Taiwanese enterprises, *Journal of HRD* 2, 1–15.*

Collinson, V. and Ono, Y. (2001) The professional development of teachers in the United States and Japan, *European Journal of Teacher Education* 24, 2: 223–48.

Gamage, D.T. and Ueyama, T. (2005) Professional development perspectives of principals in Australia and Japan, *Educational Forum* 69, 1: 65–78.

Gheorghiu, M.A., Vignoles, V.L. and Smith, P.B. (2009) Beyond the United States and Japan: testing Yamagichi's emancipation theory of trust across 31 nations, *Social Psychology Quarterly* 72, 4: 365–83.

Hara, H. (2010) HRD in private industries, in Sato, H. (ed.) *Working and Learning*, Kyoto: Minervashobo, 185–229.**

Harada, K. (1999) The changing Japanese human resource development system: two models that enhance prediction and reflection of dynamic changes, *Human Resource Development International* 2, 4: 355–68.

Hashimoto, M. (1994) Employment-based training in Japanese firms in Japan and in the United States: experiences of automobile manufacturers, in Lynch, L.M. (ed.) *Training in the Private Sector*, Chicago: University of Chicago Press, 109–48.

JITA (2008) *Frequently Asked Questions*, Tokyo: Japan Industrial Training Association.**

Kawabata, D. (2009) Rebuilding the Japanese model of human resource development, *Nippon Academy of Management* 60: 17–21.**

Kuo, M.C. (2002) *The History of Human Resource Development in Taiwan: 1950s–1990s*, PhD dissertation, University of Minnesota, US.

Land, M.H. (1990) A new era of vo-ed in Taiwan, *School Shop* 50, 1: 30–31.

Maekawa, H. (2010) Thoughts, actions: an historical look at the characteristics of HRD in Japan, *Works* 100, 7–10.**

MEA (1999) *The Republic of China Small and Medium Enterprises White Paper*, Taipei: Ministry of Economic Affairs.*

METI (2005) *Trade White Paper*, Tokyo: Ministry of Economy, Trade and Industry.**

— (2006) *Trade White Paper*, Tokyo: Ministry of Economy, Trade and Industry.**

— (2012) *Trade White Paper*, Tokyo: Ministry of Economy, Trade and Industry.**

MEXT (2012a) *Life-Long Learning in Times of Great Change: Towards a University System that Promotes Critical Thinking Skills* [online] Available at: http://www.mext.go.jp/a_menu/koutou/kaikaku/sekaitenkai/1323011.htm [Accessed 6 March 2012, University Council of Japan Interim Report, Ministry of Education, Culture, Sports, Science and Technology].**

— (2012b) *Summary of Budget for Internationalization of Higher Education* [online] Available at: http://www.mext.go.jp/a_menu/koutou/kaikaku/sekaitenkai/1323011.htm [Accessed 6 March 2012, University Council of Japan Interim Report, Ministry of Education, Culture, Sports, Science and Technology].**

— (n.d.) *History of Study and Research Abroad* [online] Available at: http://www.mext.go.jp/b_menu/hakusho/html/others/detail/1317724.htm [Accessed 3 January 2013, 100 years of education, Ministry of Education, Culture, Sports, Science and Technology].**

MHLW (2012a) *2011 Basic Survey on Human Resources Development* [online] Available at: http: //www.mhlw.go.jp/stf/houdou/2r98520000026dk1-att/2r98520000026dli. [Accessed 13 January 2013, Survey results, Ministry of Health, Labour and Welfare].**

— (2012b) *Labor Reform Act* [online] Available at: http://www.mhlw.go.jp/seisakunitsuite/bunya/koyou_roudou/roudoukijun/keiyaku/kaisei/dl/h240829-01.pdf [Accessed 29 January 2013, Pamphlet on labor reform for contracted workers, Ministry of Health, Labour and Welfare].**

MIAC (2011) *Local Autonomy College* [online] Available at: http://www.soumu.go.jp/jitidai/image/pdf/2011englishpamphlet. [Accessed 13 January 2013, Pamphlet on Local Autonomy College, Ministry of Internal Affairs and Communication].

Mikami, N. and Nishino, H. (2004) The ideal relationship between corporate strategy and HRD, *Operations Research Society of Japan* 10: 641–48.**

MOEA (1999) The Republic of China small and medium enterprises white paper. Taipei, Taiwan: Ministry of Economic Affairs, Small and Medium Enterprise Administration.*

Nonaka, I. (1991) The knowledge-creating company, *Harvard Business Review* 69, 6: 96–104.

Nonaka, I., Toyama, R. and Konno, N. (2000) SECI, *ba* and leadership: a unified model of dynamic knowledge creation, *Long Range Planning* 33: 5–34.

Odaka, K. (1994) *Era of HRD*, Tokyo: Iwanami Shoten.**

Peng, T.L. (1990) Socio-economical development and the HRD strategies, *Labor Relations* 8, 12: 6–17.

Robinson, A.G. and Stern, S. (1995) Strategic national HRD initiatives: lessons from the management training program of Japan, *Human Resource Development Quarterly* 6, 2: 123–47.

Sakamoto, F. (1977) *History of Employment in Japan*, Tokyo: Chuokeizaisha.**

Sato, H. (2010) Working and learning: present situation and challenges in HRD, in Sato, H. (ed.) *Working and Learning*, Kyoto: Minervashobo, 185–229.**

Swanson, R.A. and Holton, E.F. (2009) *Foundations of Human Resource Development* (2nd edition). San Francisco: Berrett-Koehler.

Tobita, M. (2006) HRD for professionals specializing in high risk management, in Koike, K. (ed.) *Human Resource Development in Japan*, Kyoto: Nakanishiya, 145–82.**

Tsay, J.Y. (1989) *The Doctrine of the People's Livelihood Human Resource Development Strategy: A Study of Taiwan's Experience*, Master's thesis, Chinese Culture University, Taipei, Taiwan.*

Uemura, S. (2008) Salaries of Oyatoi (Japan's foreign employees) in early Meiji, *Journal of University of Marketing and Distribution Sciences* 21, 1: 1–24.**

Watanuki, K. (2006) Knowledge acquisition and job training for advanced technical skills by using immersive virtual environments, *Japan Society for Precision Engineering* 72, 1: 46–51.

Xie, J. and Huang, E. (2010) Comparative analysis of human resource development between different countries under the vision of competition, *Frontiers of Education in China* 5, 3: 382–408.

42
HRD IN AUSTRALIA AND NEW ZEALAND

Kenneth R. Bartlett and Roger Harris

A problem often encountered within international HRD research is broad generalizations that overstate or over-simplify important context factors to describe HRD in areas of the world less familiar to Northern Hemisphere readers. All too frequently international publications lump Australia and New Zealand together for analysis. Yet, each nation is unique in many important ways despite the somewhat common location in the South Pacific thousands of miles away from North America and Europe. This vast distance from most other English-speaking developed nations, seemingly shared colonial origins and perceived common cultural traits often promote misunderstanding. This chapter provides a backdrop of the historical, cultural and socio-political contexts and regional traditions that influence HRD in Australia and New Zealand and reviews the current state of HRD in professional practice, research and academic study.

Australasia refers to the global region of Oceania that includes Australia, New Zealand, New Guinea, and the islands of the Pacific Ocean. However, geopolitically Australasia is most often used as a term for Australia and New Zealand together, and there are many organizations whose names are prefixed with Australasian that are limited to just Australia and New Zealand. This chapter focuses on HRD in Australia and New Zealand, as an overview of HRD in the Pacific Islands was previously published (Bartlett and Rodgers 2004).

HRD in Australia

HRD as a term is not prominent in Australia. There is no professional association with that term in its title, nor does it appear in the 2006 Australian and New Zealand Classification of Occupations, the 2008 Australian and New Zealand Standard Research Classification or the 2001 Australian Standard Classification of Education.

Yet the actual *practice* of what can be considered HRD is widespread. It is, in fact, "represented" by other labels: within human resource management (HRM), general management, organizational development, career development, vocational education and training, workplace learning, workforce development or simply HR. We therefore perceive the field of HRD in Australia as *an intertwined rope* comprising these various strands to varying degrees. It is a field whose activities are divided between two main disciplines, business/management and post-school education. Such lack of visibility and variations in emphasis result in Australian HRD being a field of study, research and practice that is fragmented – in focus, location, target membership, name and disciplinary emphasis. Some background is now outlined to provide context for understanding the positioning of HRD in Australia.

Context

Emergence of protectionist industry policies early in the twentieth century, as separate colonies became one nation in 1901, reinforced rigid and hierarchical work patterns and strong trade unions, and "resulted in training and development in Australia remaining largely fragmented and narrowly focused around basic occupational skills and managerial control" (McKeown and Teicher 2006: 26). As a consequence, reactive and inward-looking approaches characterized Australian industry, and training became *ad hoc* and crisis driven (McKeown and Teicher 2006, Hutchings and Holland 2007).

Australia remained a highly regulated economy until the 1980s. By the beginning of the twenty-first century, it had been transformed into one of the most deregulated through the use of centrally planned policies. This change was dramatic, underpinned by ideas in the *Australia Reconstructed* report (ACTU/TDC 1987). The significant turning point in the development of HRD and training came in 1987 when an Australian Tripartite Mission reported on trade skills in Europe. It recommended that "consideration be given to . . . the establishment of national competency standards for all skilled occupations and the introduction of nationally consistent final competency testing in such occupations" (ACTU/TDC 1987: 37).

The policy and funding climate of the late 1980s privileged vocational training. The National Training Reform Agenda commencing at that time was more fundamental than at any other period in history. Re-focusing on micro-economic reform was seen as the strategy to promote competitiveness and increase productivity. One of the key planks was the mandate for competency-based training, approved in 1989 and continuing today as the imperative for all accredited training. In addition, those associated with training were to be minimally qualified with a certificate in workplace training and assessment.

Embedded in this reform was renewed focus on skill enhancement. Major changes were made to the national training system to increase competitiveness and responsiveness to the needs of industry and to stimulate employers' investment in HRD. Hutchings and Holland (2007: 243) characterize Australian training and development as having been historically "fragmented and narrowly focused around occupational skills supported by waves of immigration and poaching of staff," where the nation, under such a focus on external labor markets, had stumbled from one skill shortage to the next. These reforms from the late 1980s, and the increasing pressures of globalization, led to the need for organizations to concentrate more on the development and utilization of *internal* labor resources.

The reform agenda shifted power away from training institutions (supply side) towards industry (demand side). Two important consequences have been greater pressure on industries to provide relevant, contextualized, job-specific learning opportunities, and a re-claiming of the workplace as an authentic site for learning (Harris 2001). The critical issue is to what extent those involved with HRD are ready, willing and able to meet this enhanced commitment in the Australian economy. Overall, this reform signified "a major shift in the nature of HRD in Australia over the past decade" (Peretz and McGraw 2011: 41).

So how is HRD viewed in contemporary Australia? Given that the multiple strands of HRD are intertwined in one developmental rope, and because of the relative invisibility and varying emphases leading to the fragmentation mentioned above, HRD is difficult to map. Nevertheless, these characteristics can be best illustrated by examining how HRD is depicted in research, how it is organized and where and what is taught about it.

How is HRD depicted in research?

In 1990, Swain *et al.* (1990) proclaimed that HRD was at the crossroads. However, by the later 1990s Elsey (1997) contended that, although HRD had had a long history of marginality in its evolution from limited notions of industrial training, it was now coming of age in Australia, with much of its thinking derived from American sources and adapted to suit Australian conditions.

In September 2007, the *Human Resource Development International* journal incorporated a special section, reporting it as the "first comprehensive collection of research to address key developments in HRD in Australia" (Hutchings and Holland 2007: 244). Tellingly, Holland *et al.* (2007) claimed in this issue that HRD was still not sufficiently recognized as a source of competitive advantage in Australian organizations. Moreover, Peretz and McGraw (2009: 7) found "an inconsistent pattern in the developmental trend of HRD in Australian organizations," with a significant increase in practices concerned with career development and performance appraisal, but a decreasing use of practices relating to training evaluation. Another survey of HR professionals found that employers were inconsistently allocating resources; issues concerned with attraction-recruitment and selection were being addressed but less attention and resources were being given to critical areas of retention and development. This was seen as a "major weakness in Australian organizations coming to terms with the importance of retention and development" (Holland *et al.* 2007: 259).

Literature analysis suggests that researchers in the workplace learning area view HRD more positively. Evidence that Australian employees were receiving more and better training than in the past was published by Smith (2003). Other research by Smith and Smith (2007: 278) concluded that "after years of relative organizational marginality, training is now coming to play an increasingly central role in the HRM strategies of many Australian organizations." Smith and Sadler-Smith (2006) maintained that HRD practitioners have a key role to play in fostering an organization's competitive advantage. The situated nature of knowledge and skill is critical, with HRD shifting from instruction and knowledge dissemination to creation of opportunities for knowledge sharing and interpretation.

A key problem in these differing perspectives lies in definition. Elsey (1997: 136) claimed that in Australia the HRD term inevitably "has a rather elastic meaning, which allows for some stretching without destroying the general sense of what it is intended to convey." In claiming that Australian HRD is hampered by an "identity crisis," O'Toole (2010: 420) believed that contemporary models of HRD perceive it as integrating learning and development, organization development and career development. For him, HRD was organized learning experiences provided by employers to improve performance and personal growth, and build work-related learning capacity at individual, group and organizational levels. He pleaded for a clearer identity so that deeper understanding of the intersection of all of these concepts might be promoted.

HRD in Australia was recognized relatively early as "a more comprehensive field than just training and development" (Cacioppe *et al.* 1990: 55), and that organization development, seen as an independent field, was becoming increasingly aligned with HRD activities. Cacioppe *et al.* believed also that career development was increasingly being integrated into HR systems as organizations realized the benefits of aligning organizational and individual goals. However, they found most organizations were only at the discussion and conceptual stage of a comprehensive approach to HRD.

In fact, a "huge gap" between HRD theory and practice was identified by Koornneef *et al.* (2005) in their study of HRD practitioners whose roles they found to be traditional in nature, focusing mainly on training delivery and needs analysis. They posed the question as to whether HRD practice is too conservative or HRD theory and professional ideals are too progressive, given the "large disconnect between normative ideas put forward in HRD literature and organizational practices in this area." Garrick (1998), too, drew attention to a gulf – between HRD practices being highly performance-based and strongly linked to market economics, and the backdrop of postmodern conditions against which they are set, such as globalization, discourses of market penetration, de-regulation, privatization, marketization, dispersal of authorities and the search for a new identity.

Certainly HR professionals have been encouraged for many years to make a greater strategic contribution to their organizations. Around the start of the reform agenda, Swain *et al.* (1990: 4) proclaimed that HRD had become "a major focal point of the current debate on labor market reform," yet a decade later, Tebbel (1999) was inquiring whether the HR function was dead in Australia or becoming obsolete. Subsequent moves towards more strategic HR galvanized Kramar (2006) to pronounce that by that time it was HRM that was at the crossroads. Dainty (2011) raised the crucial question of whether HR professionals have the range of skills needed, as his research suggested they were still not central to the strategy formulation process. This notion was supported by Andersen *et al.* (2007) who found only a moderate level of strategic HRM practiced within organizations and that the limited training offered to line managers greatly undermined their capacity to perform HR activities effectively. A more strategic positioning requires HR professionals "to examine their moral, economic and social responsibility to the broader community" (Sheehan *et al.* 2006), though it is recognized that their role is fraught with tensions because they serve a number of mistresses and masters (Kramar 2006: 130–31). Their role is also "well acknowledged [to be] potentially ambiguous and complex, given the inherent tensions associated with the reconciliation of organizational and individual interests" (Lowry 2006: 135). Given this ambiguity about HRD and its multiple strands, it is timely to examine how HRD is organized.

How is HRD organized?

At least 12 professional associations embrace human resource development activities in Australia. Some may be considered more integral to HRD, others focus on particular strands of the HRD rope, and still others are more tangential. A conceptualization of the field of HRD in Australia is presented in Figure 42.1.

Table 42.1 summarizes the key features and activities of these associations. They exhibit different purposes, histories and memberships. Some focus on managers, HR personnel, trainers and developers and workplace learning, others on more specific areas such as vocational education

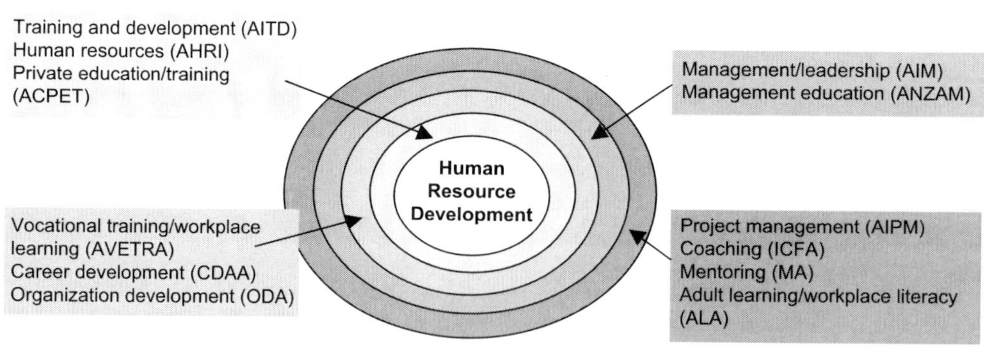

Figure 42.1 A conceptualization of the field of HRD in Australia by associations

Table 42.1 Features of the associations relating to HRD in Australia

Feature	*Australian Institute of Training and Development*	*Australian Human Resources Institute*	*Australian Council for Private Education and Training*	*Career Development Association of Australia*	*Australian Institute of Management*	*Australian and New Zealand Academy of Management*	*Australian Vocational Education and Training Research Association*
Formation	1971	1943 (started as Personnel Officers Association)	1992	1988 (started as Association of Career Counsellors)	1941 (started as Foremanship Association)	1987 (started as ANZ Academy of Management Educators)	1997
Purpose	Build capability of professionals who plan, develop and deliver learning activities to individuals and organizations	Provide research, education and representation to promote the standing of the profession and engender HRM best practice within workplaces	Promote and enhance the provision of private education/ training, through: representation, advocacy, services and promotion	Provide career services for people (re)entering the workforce, managing work/ life roles, seeking career information or changing careers	Promote the advancement of education and learning in the field of management and leadership	Advance scholarship and practice in management education and research	Further the contribution of VET research to the development of Australian VET policy and practice
Membership	Professionals in training, learning and development. Approx. 2,600 members	HR and people management professionals. Approx. 20,000 members	Private colleges, training consultants and product developers. Includes HE, VET, English for Overseas Students, foundation studies. 1,100 provider members	Career development professionals in industry, government, education, employment programs and community organizations	Managers and other professionals in commerce, industry and government. Over 25,000 managers and 5,000 businesses	Teachers, researchers and others in management education or research. Approx. 500 members	Researchers and stakeholders from VET, university, industry and government. Approx. 300 members

(*Continued*)

Table 42.1 (Continued)

Feature	*Australian Institute of Training and Development*	*Australian Human Resources Institute*	*Australian Council for Private Education and Training*	*Career Development Association of Australia*	*Australian Institute of Management*	*Australian and New Zealand Academy of Management*	*Australian Vocational Education and Training Research Association*
Main publications	*Training & Development in Australia* (Started 1972, 6 issues/year)	*Asia Pacific Journal of Human Resources* (started 1966, peer-reviewed, 4 issues/year). *HRmonthly*	*ACPET Journal for Private Higher Education* (started 2012, bi-annual, peer reviewed)	*Australian Career Practitioner* (started 1989, quarterly magazine). *National e-bulletin* (fortnightly)	*Management Today* (started 1955, monthly magazine – previously *Management Digests)*	*Journal of Management and Organization* (started 1987, peer-reviewed, 5–6 issues/year)	*International Journal of Training Research* (started 1985, peer-reviewed, 2–3 issues/year)
Conference	National (April)	National (August)	National (August) State Forums	National (May) State PD workshops	Regular events and network meetings	ANZAM conference (December)	National (April) State-based forums
Website	www.aitd.com.au/	www.ahri.com.au/	www.acpet.edu.au/	www.cdaa.org.au/	www.aim.com.au/	www.anzam.org/	www.avetra.org.au/

Note: Five other associations more tangential to the field of HRD are Organization Development Australia; Australian Institute of Project Management; The International Coach Federation Australasia; The National Mentoring Association of Australia; Adult Learning Australia.

and training, career development and organizational development, and yet others on areas where HRD may be only a component such as workplace literacy, coaching, mentoring and project management. Each has a different perspective, yet all embrace the field of HRD to varying degrees, building organizational capacity through individual and team development.

Apart from these 12 associations, Skills Australia was established in 2008, a national entity for workforce development. Rebadged the Australian Workforce and Productivity Agency in 2012, it is an independent statutory body that provides advice to the Australian Government on current, emerging and future workforce skills and needs. This agency has recommended a fundamental overhaul of the way the nation approaches and supports workforce development at all levels. Its charter clearly extends beyond skills training, as signaled by its name change, defining workforce development as:

> those policies and practices which support people to participate effectively in the workforce and to develop and apply skills in a workplace context, where learning translates into positive outcomes for enterprises, the wider community and for individuals throughout their working lives.
>
> *Skills Australia 2010: 67*

The sequencing of the three beneficiaries is noteworthy – the furnishing of organizational and societal benefits, before individual ones. The Agency has now published two National Workforce Development Strategies, and the influence of this body is likely to significantly affect future directions in HRD activity.

Where and what is taught about HRD?

Another way in which we can gain insights into how HRD is interpreted in Australia is through examining formal courses. Cacioppe *et al.* (1990: 68) wrote that in the early 1990s, only four higher education institutions offered higher degrees in HRD, training and development or organization development. Today, many more universities have programs with HRM in their titles: 28 offer postgraduate programs – four have doctorates, nine have MBAs, 24 have Masters, 11 have graduate diplomas and 13 have graduate certificates; and 32 offer undergraduate courses, mainly Bachelors of Business or Commerce.

Notably, however, no programs have HRD in the title. The study of HRD is subsumed within programs by other names, such as Human Resources and Organizational Development, Commerce (HRM) and, most commonly, Human Resource Management. It is also embedded within many subjects variously named, such as Introduction to HRM or Leading and Managing People. The majority of studies on HRD are postgraduate (i.e. beyond the baccalaureate), with only a few undergraduate courses. In the non-university (VET) sector, the study of HRD is subsumed within three government-accredited and nationally recognized qualifications: Certificate in Training and Assessment, Certificate in Human Resources and Diploma of HRM.

Having focused on the context and current state of HRD in Australia, the chapter now turns to the situation in New Zealand before concluding with some general observations on both countries.

HRD in *Aotearoa* New Zealand

New Zealand (*Aotearoa* is the Maori name for New Zealand) is a country of approximately 4.4 million people located in the south-western Pacific Ocean, with its closest neighbor, Australia, some 2,250 kilometers to the west. In length New Zealand is approximately equal to California or Japan and is slightly larger in land area than Great Britain. But, to highlight the size difference, New Zealand would fit into Australia 28.6 times. The isolated geographical location has greatly shaped the history of the nation, as well as the character and culture of the people.

The indigenous people of New Zealand are Maori, a Polynesian people who arrived around AD 800 after voyaging from islands in the South Pacific. The signing of the Treaty of Waitangi in 1840 saw the conceding of all Maori land and the establishment of British colonial government, an event regarded as the official founding of the nation. New Zealand, like Australia, is now a constitutional monarchy with a parliamentary democracy based on British institutions and legal concepts. Today New Zealand is described as a "sophisticated, predominantly urban, well-educated, bi-cultural and multi-cultural society" (Findsen 2012: 230–31).

The development of New Zealand's economy was largely driven by the export of agricultural products (especially lamb, meat, wool, and dairy products) to the UK, while an extensive system of import control and licensing was used to maintain foreign exchange reserves and protect domestic manufacturing. By 1953 New Zealand was one of the four wealthiest countries as measured by per capita Gross Domestic Product (GDP). Beginning in the mid-1970s, a broad restructuring of New Zealand began following changes in the historically strong trade relationship with the United Kingdom and the opening of new markets. The most significant shifts in public policy occurred between 1984 and 1999 as New Zealand became a classic case study for neo-liberal reforms (Larner 1997). Many other nations undertook a similar approach to political and economic reorientation, but the scale and speed of New Zealand's restructuring make it somewhat unique. These reforms are in many ways the defining recent historic event when examining social, political, economic, business, and education issues – and, we also argue, for the analysis of HRD in New Zealand.

In many ways the New Zealand labor market is similar to those in other English-speaking countries. However, the number of small businesses is considerably different as approximately 90 per cent of all organizations in New Zealand have 20 or fewer employees and less than 1.5 per cent of firms have 100 or more employees, although this group accounts for 48 per cent of all New Zealand employees (Bascand 2012). New Zealand has a mixed economy with considerable manufacturing, service and tourism activity in addition to a strong agricultural sector. Employment relations in New Zealand shifted from heavy protectionism and union influence to a highly de-regulated business environment with a strong culture of individualized employment relationships (Rasmussen and Lamm 2002). Indeed, prior to the restructuring reforms of the 1980s and 1990s, New Zealand and Australia were the only two countries in the world to have used a system of compulsory arbitration to regulate industrial conflict and determine the wages and conditions of employment (including training) for the majority of their workforce (Wailes 1999). More recent analysis has suggested a move towards "Europeanization" of New Zealand employment relations which is distinctly different from Australian employment relations reforms (Rasmussen *et al.* 2006). The role of government in New Zealand "is extremely important in fostering the "social capital" on which employers depend" (Boxall 2003: 246), and plays a key role in the education system that at all levels is largely publicly funded, supports industry-based training initiatives designed to improve skills, and manages immigration programs.

Current state of HRD

The term HRD is infrequently used in New Zealand, with training and development as a component of HRM dominating in academic literature, government reports and professional practice. Since the 1980s HRM replaced personnel management as the preferred scholarly and practitioner term (Macky and Johnson 2002), with a more recent move towards a strategic HRM role with greater awareness and influence of HR professionals on strategic decision making in organizations (Rasmussen *et al.* 2010). Yet the perception exists that there is "limited evidence that strategic and effective HRM is seen as important for the success of New Zealand organizations" (Macky 2008: 6). The adoption of a suite of HR practices known as high performance work systems which includes a high profile for employee training has increased over the last few years (Boxall and Macky 2011), with research showing strong links to organizational performance (Fabling and Grimes 2010).

However, HRD in the New Zealand context must also consider discourse and practice related to organization behavior, organization development, industrial and organizational psychology, adult education, vocational and technical education, lifelong learning, as well as workplace learning. These concepts are acknowledged as having multiple meanings and are enmeshed in the historical and cultural context of New Zealand (Findsen 2012). As McLean *et al.* (2003) noted, there has been a lack of effort in New Zealand to specifically define HRD as a component or as being distinctive from these other concepts – in part as a result of the multifaceted nature of fields of practice in which HRD is embedded and the absence of HRD as a standalone academic discipline in universities.

Some forms of HRD including industry training, apprenticeships and trade cadetships have a long history in New Zealand. As a component of broad-sweeping economic reforms, a new approach to labor market management was ushered in with the passage of the 1991 National Qualifications Framework and the 1992 Industry Training Act. This act repealed earlier and outdated apprenticeship legislation and established the creation of industry training organizations (ITO). The various industries that make up the New Zealand economy each have an ITO responsible for setting national skill standards for their industry, providing information and advice to trainees and employers, arranging delivery of on- and off-the-job training, assessing trainees and monitoring training quality. The funding system for industry training has changed four times since 1992 and the number of ITOs has been reduced with awareness of the need for greater flexibility, accountability and increased responsiveness to learning needs of employees. In early 2013, the government announced a further revision to the legislation to re-introduce a "re-booted" apprenticeship program and suggested further changes to the funding, operation and performance expectations for industry training programs (New Zealand Government 2013). The core element of New Zealand's industry training system remains, in that it is government-funded, market-focused, industry-driven and competency-based within a national qualifications standards framework.

The development of human resources in New Zealand organizations (that portion of HRD not considered initial vocational training [apprenticeships], foundation education, education to achieve occupational registration, as well as continuing vocational education) is harder to assess. Over a decade ago, Gray (2001) noted a paucity of research in the area of HRD, and this statement appears equally relevant today. A long line of studies have shown an ongoing concern that many New Zealand employees do not receive training to do their job, or prepare them for future employment (Elkin and Inkson 1995). As Mason *et al.* (2010: 1) commented, "information on why New Zealand employers do not train or train very few of their existing staff remains unclear and critical for policy-makers to design appropriate incentives to encourage firms to provide in-house training."

New Zealand's largest organizations tend to have in-house departments to provide HRD as well as relying on outsourced training programs from specialist consulting firms (Pio 2007). Research by Edgar and Geare (2005) identified training and development as an increasingly important issue for New Zealand workers to create healthy employment relationships, with the recommendation that employer investment in this area of HRM may have the greatest potential to contribute beneficially to organizational performance. A study of HRM in New Zealand's service industries (Browning *et al.* 2009) examined the contribution of training and development as a source of firm competitive advantage. More recent research has had a specific focus on skills training in various industry segments such as services (Browning *et al.* 2009) and small–medium sized firms (Dalziel 2010). Short and Harris (2010: 382) described how HRD professionals in New Zealand align workplace learning with business goals with the conclusion that many organizations fail "to exploit opportunities that could be available through an improved and systematic recognition of the employees' tacit knowledge and skills with job requirements."

Where and what is taught about HRD?

While HRD practice in New Zealand is consistent with or at least familiar to professional practice in many other western countries, HRD programs are absent in higher education institutions. All eight of New Zealand's universities offer programs in HRM, with five having specific degrees or majors related to human resources. A number of postgraduate degree programs (Masters and doctoral) also allow for advanced study of HRM and development. Many HR and training and development courses are offered by polytechnics and institutes of technology, often as part of certificate or Bachelor-level degree programs.

How is HRD depicted in research?

A noteworthy study by Gray and McGregor (2003) examined HRD and older workers by highlighting the impact of age stereotypes on training provision. This is one of only a handful of studies in New Zealand to specifically define the goal of HRD. Using a combination of well-known performance-oriented views from the United States, together with a strategic HRM perspective, the goal of HRD was described as to increase organizational performance through development of the organization's workforce and to become integral to an organization's strategic goals to show a contribution to organizational profitability.

For the past 15 years substantial government and media attention has been directed to macro-level changes that impact the New Zealand economy. The realities of global competition, shifting demographics, and the consequences of government policy have prompted discussion on how to realign existing education and training systems. In response, the literature related to HRD has increasingly been dominated by narratives related to human capability and skills development (Sloman and Malinen 2010). A specific context factor in New Zealand that has strategic HRD implications is the high turnover with a mobile labor market, especially in the largest cities (Short and Harris 2010). New Zealand's productivity compared with other OECD countries is low, with the nation ranking 22nd out of the 30 OECD countries in GDP per hour worked and GDP per capita (Kidd 2008). Additional challenges to the management and development of human resources in New Zealand organizations have been identified. These include managing organizational change (Du Plessis *et al.* 2006), shifts in the structure of the labor market (Brougham 2011), increased concern at the growing ethnic inequalities of wealth (Stewart-Harawira 2007), and new awareness of indigenous knowledge systems and ways of knowing (Papuni and Bartlett 2006).

Conclusion

While citizens from the two countries often highlight the various distinctions and differences from each other, both Australia and New Zealand share a number of important characteristics related to their history, culture, and recent economic development. Casey's (2006: 345) statement that "historical variations between them may be seen as variations of general patterns and themes more often than of divergence and contrast" also applies to the evolution and current status of HRD. Australia has a more complex system than New Zealand, mainly due to the interaction between state and federal governments. New Zealand continues to have heavy government influence, especially for entry-level and lower skilled occupations but overall adopts a free-market approach which may not encourage the necessary investment and activity level in HRD for sustained growth. Despite strong economic cooperation between Australia and New Zealand there are clear differences and diversity in the development and current application of HRD that need to be appreciated to avoid applying overly broad generalizations.

While the term HRD is little used in both Australia and New Zealand, both countries have adopted and continue to shape a broad, multifaceted approach to developing human resources that draws strength from related fields of study and practice. The first decade of the 2000s saw both countries stimulating debate on knowledge and innovation to shape public policy. The learning society/knowledge economy frame is contested by some, especially scholars and leaders concerned with inequalities continuing to be perpetuated against indigenous populations. The critical perspective to HRD remains an important component of the literature with selected topics including issues of career development for Maori (Reid 2011). Ashkanasy (1997) suggested that comparisons between similar cultures, such as Australia and New Zealand, are important as they go beyond the obvious to reveal subtle yet important cultural differences. This review of antipodean perspectives on HRD has highlighted some common characteristics as well as unique aspects that trace how approaches to developing human resources have evolved to fit the needs of individual learners, organizations, communities and the economy at both national and global levels.

References

ACTU/TDC (1987) *Australia Reconstructed: Report of the Mission to Western Europe*, Melbourne: Australian Council of Trade Unions/Trade Development Council.

Andersen, K.K., Cooper, B.K. and Zhu, C.J. (2007) 'The effect of SHRM practices on perceived firm financial performance: some initial evidence from Australia', *Asia Pacific Journal of Human Resources*, 45: 168–79.

Ashkanasy, N.M. (1997) 'A cross-cultural comparison of Australian and Canadian supervisors' attributional and evaluative response to subordinate performance', *Australian Psychologist*, 32: 29–36.

Bartlett, K.R. and Rodgers, J. (2004) 'HRD as national policy in the Pacific Islands', *Advances in Developing Human Resources*, 6: 307–14.

Bascand, G. (2012) *New Zealand Business Demography Statistics*. Online. Available HTTP: http://www.stats.govt.nz/browse_for_stats/businesses/business_characteristics/BusinessDemographyStatistics_HOTPFeb12.aspx (accessed 30 August 2013).

Boxall, P. (2003) 'New Zealand', in Zanko, M. and Ngui, M. (eds) *The Handbook of Human Resource Management Policies and Practices in Asia-Pacific Economies*, Volume 2, Cheltenham: Edward Elgar, 228–84.

Boxall, P. and Macky, K. (2011) 'High-involvement work processes in New Zealand: a briefing paper for HR practitioners', *New Zealand Journal of Human Resource Management*, 11: 40–44.

Brougham, D. (2011) 'When the minority becomes the majority: the implications of New Zealand's changing demographics', *New Zealand Journal of Human Resource Management*, 11: 78–89.

Browning, V., Edgar, F., Gray, B. and Garrett, T. (2009) 'Realizing competitive advantage through HRM in New Zealand service industries', *Service Industries Journal*, 29: 741–60.

Cacioppe, R., Warren-Langford, P. and Bell, L. (1990) 'Trends in human resource development and training', *Asia Pacific Journal of Human Resources*, 28: 55–72.

Casey, C. (2006) 'A knowledge economy and a learning society: a comparative analysis of New Zealand and Australian experiences', *Compare*, 36: 343–57.

Dainty, P. (2011) 'The strategic HR role: do Australian HR professionals have the required skills?', *Asia Pacific Journal of Human Resources*, 49: 55–70.

Dalziel, P. (2010) 'Levering training: skills development in SMEs – an analysis of Canterbury Region, New Zealand', *OECD local economic and employment (LEED) working papers* 2010/03. OECD Publishing. Available from http://dx.doi.org/10.1787/5km9d6g1nc8p-en.

Du Plessis, A.J., Beaver, B. and Nel, P.S. (2006) 'Closing the gap between current capabilities and future requirements in human resource management in New Zealand: some empirical evidence', *Journal of Global Business and Technology*, 2: 33–47.

Edgar, F. and Geare, A. (2005) 'Employee voice on human resource management', *Asia Pacific Journal of Human Resources*, 43: 361–80.

Elkin, G. and Inkson, K. (1995) 'Employee development', in Boxall, P. (ed.) *The Challenge of Human Resource Management: Directions and Debates in New Zealand*, Auckland: Longman Paul, 150–77.

Elsey, B. (1997) *Australian Graduate Human Resource Studies: The People Factor in Workplace Change Management*, Findon: Techpress.

Fabling, R. and Grimes, A. (2010) 'HR practices and New Zealand firm performance: what matters and who does it?', *International Journal of Human Resource Management*, 21: 488–508.

Findsen, B. (2012) 'New Zealand: lifelong learning and higher education in Aotearoa New Zealand', in Slowey, M. and Schuetze, H.G. (eds) *Global Perspectives on Higher Education and Lifelong Learners*, London: Routledge, 230–47.

Garrick, J. (1998) *Informal Learning in the Workplace: Unmasking Human Resource Development*, London: Routledge.

Gray, L. (2001) 'What do job advertisements reveal about HRD practitioners in New Zealand?', *New Zealand Journal of Human Resource Management*, 1: 1–12.

Gray, L. and McGregor, J. (2003) 'Human resource development and older workers: stereotypes in New Zealand', *Asia Pacific Journal of Human Resources*, 41: 338–53.

Harris, R. (2001) 'Training reform in Australia: implications of a shift from a supply to a demand-driven VET system', in Deissinger, T. (ed.) *Vocational Education and Training – Orientation and Adaptation: Analyses of the Model Character of VET Systems and Policy*, Baden-Baden: Nomos, 231–55.

Holland, P., Sheehan, C. and De Cieri, H. (2007) 'Attracting and retaining talent: exploring human resources development trends in Australia', *Human Resource Development International*, 10: 247–62.

Hutchings, K. and Holland, P. (2007) 'Recent advances in HRD in Australia: application and implications for international HRD', *Human Resource Development International*, 10: 243–46.

Kidd, N. (2008) *Putting Productivity First*, New Zealand Treasury. Online. Available HTTP: http://www.treasury.govt.nz/publications/research-policy/tprp/08-01/ (accessed 30 August 2013).

Koornneef, M., Oostvogel, K. and Poell, R.F. (2005) 'Between ideal and tradition: the roles of HRD practitioners in South Australian organizations', *Journal of European Industrial Training*, 29: 356–68.

Kramar, R. (2006) 'HRM at the crossroads: recent developments and ethics', *Asia Pacific Journal of Human Resources*, 44: 130–31.

Larner, W. (1997) 'A means to an end: neoliberalism and state processes in New Zealand', *Studies in Political Economy*, 52: 7–38.

Lowry, D. (2006) 'HR managers as ethical decision-makers: mapping the terrain', *Asia Pacific Journal of Human Resources*, 44: 171–83.

Macky, K. (ed.) (2008) *Managing Human Resources. Contemporary Perspectives in New Zealand*, Sydney: McGraw-Hill.

Macky, K. and Johnson, G. (2002) *Managing Human Resources in New Zealand*, Auckland: McGraw-Hill.

Mason, G., Mok, P., Nunns, P., Stevens, P. and Timmins, J. (2010) *The training's a-comin' in: an analysis of training decisions using microdata*, Paper presented at the New Zealand Association of Economists Conference. Online. Available HTTP: http://nzae.org.nz/wp-content/uploads/2011/08/Mason_et_al__The_Trainings_A-Comin_In.pdf (accessed 20 August 2013).

McKeown, T. and Teicher, J. (2006) 'Human resource management in a deregulated environment', in Holland, P. and De Cieri, H. (eds) *Contemporary Issues in Human Resource Development*, Sydney: Pearson Education, 25–54.

McLean, G.N., Bartlett, K.R. and Cho, E. (2003) 'Human resource development as national policy: Republic of Korea and New Zealand', *Pacific-Asian Education Journal*, 15: 41–59.

New Zealand Government (2013) *Increasing the number of apprenticeships in New Zealand and improving the quality of industry training*. Online. Available HTTP: http://www.minedu.govt.nz/NZEducation/EducationPolicies/TertiaryEducation/PolicyAndStrategy/ReviewIndustryTraining/FinalDecisions IndustryTrainingCabPaper.aspx (accessed 30 August 2013).

O'Toole, S. (2010) 'Training, OD, L&D, HRD: what's in a name?', *Australian Journal of Adult Learning*, 50: 419–26.

Papuni, H.T. and Bartlett, K.R. (2006) 'Maori and Pakeha perspectives of adult learning in Aotearoa/New Zealand workplaces', *Advances in Developing Human Resources*, 8: 400–7.

Peretz, M. and McGraw, P. (2009) 'The evolution of HRD in Australia: rhetoric or reality?', *International Employment Relations Review*, 15, 2: 1–13.

— (2011) 'Trends in Australian human resource development practice, 1996–2009', *Asia Pacific Journal of Human Resources*, 49: 36–54.

Pio, E. (2007) 'International briefing 17: Training and development in New Zealand', *International Journal of Training and Development*, 11: 71–83.

Rasmussen, E. and Lamm, F. (2002) *An Introduction to Employment Relations in New Zealand*, Auckland: Pearson Education.

Rasmussen, E., Hunt, V. and Lamm, F. (2006) 'Between individualism and social democracy', *Labour & Industry*, 17: 19–40.

Rasmussen, E., Andersen, T. and Haworth, N. (2010) 'Has the strategic role and professional status of human resource management peaked in New Zealand?', *Journal of Industrial Relations*, 52: 103–18.

Reid, L. (2011) 'Looking back to look forward: Maori cultural values and the impact on career', *International Journal for Educational and Vocational Guidance*, 11: 187–96.

Sheehan, C., Holland, P. and De Cieri, H. (2006) 'Current developments in HRM in Australian organizations', *Asia Pacific Journal of Human Resources*, 44: 132–52.

Short, T. and Harris, R. (2010) 'Challenges in aligning workplace learning with business goals: a perspective from HRD professionals in New Zealand', *Australian Journal of Adult Learning*, 50: 358–86.

Skills Australia (2010) *Australian Workforce Futures: A National Workforce Development Strategy*, Canberra: Commonwealth of Australia.

Sloman, M. and Malinen, S. (2010) 'One size doesn't fit all: the skills debate and the New Zealand economy', *New Zealand Journal of Human Resource Management*, 10: 83–98.

Smith, A. (2003) 'Recent trends in Australian training and development', *Asia Pacific Journal of Human Resources*, 41: 231–44.

Smith, A. and Smith, E. (2007) 'The role of training in the development of human resource management in Australian organizations', *Human Resource Development International*, 10: 263–79.

Smith, P.J. and Sadler-Smith, E. (2006) *Learning in Organizations: Complexities and Diversities*, London: Routledge.

Stewart-Harawira, M. (2007) 'Globalization, work and indigenous knowledge in the global marketplace. The New Zealand Experience', in Farrell, L. and Fenwick, T. (eds) *Educating the Global Workforce: Knowledge, Knowledge Work, and Knowledge Workers*, London: Routledge, 27–40.

Swain, P., Warren-Langford, P. and Francis, A. (1990) 'Australian HRD at the crossroads: a discussion of the current debate on labour market reform', *Asia Pacific Journal of Human Resources*, 28: 4–17.

Tebbel, C. (1999) 'Selling the concept of strategic HR', *HR Monthly*, 17–19 July.

Wailes, N. (1999) 'The importance of small difference: the effects of research design on the comparative study of industrial relations reform in Australia and New Zealand', *International Journal of Human Resource Management*, 10: 1006–30.

43

HRD IN HUNGARY AND POLAND

Maria Cseh, Andrzej Różański, Zsolt Nemeskéri and Béla Krisztián

Central and Eastern Europe (CEE) is a geopolitical region that includes the European countries which were under Soviet influence before 1990, formerly referred to as the Eastern Bloc. This region has witnessed unprecedented political and socio-economic changes in the past two decades that have had a major impact on adult learning, organization development and change and leadership. These vital components of the human resource development (HRD) field are concerned with enabling learning for all, facilitating change and ensuring that leaders understand the importance of learning and development. The increased understanding of the value of human capital and human resource management (HRM) and HRD for the wellbeing of the region led to national HRD initiatives and changes in higher education systems and organization practices. However, more than 20 years after the fall of the Berlin Wall differences still exist between CEE and the rest of Europe (Brewster *et al.* 2010), which are important to understand in order to address the HRD issues in this region.

A search and examination of the literature related to HRD in CEE suggest that HRD is not generally viewed in this region as separate from the broader and more established areas of human resources (HR) and human resource management (HRM), terms often used interchangeably. Instead, topics related to US and Western European conceptions of HRD such as workplace learning, training and development, employee development, career development, organizational learning and change (McGuire and Cseh 2006, Lee 2010) – are embedded within HR and HRM in CEE. For example, Horwitz (2011: 440) notes that talent management research indicates that high-skill workers in knowledge-intensive industries rate the following elements as critical to work motivation: effective utilization and retention; autonomy and opportunity to plan and control their own work; challenging and stimulating work; collegial peer and boss relations; career development and personal growth; competitive, flexible remuneration; an 'engaging' culture with direct, informal communications; work–life balance; and 'decent' work. However, in CEE nations, the concept of clear autonomy/decision-making powers received only 22 per cent support. Horwitz (2011: 441) further notes that, in terms of CEE HR strategy, the top three "most effective HR practices all revolved around personal growth: increased training was first; using a mentoring system, second; and personal-development road maps or plans, third." While these terms and concepts are couched in HR terms, they are also HRD practices. In this chapter, we will refer to HR, HRM and HRD as represented in the published research studies. Since in most of the cases, HRD is included under the umbrella of HR or HRM, we will focus our discussions on HRD.

The field of HRD has grown to prominence in the past four decades as an independent discipline in the USA and Western Europe. HRD higher education programs at the undergraduate, graduate and postgraduate levels, professional associations such as the Academy of Human Resource Development (AHRD) and the University Forum for Human Resource Development (UFHRD) and refereed journals such as the HRDQ, HRDI, ADHR and HRDR had a major impact in the development of HRD scholars and practitioners around the world and in Central and Eastern Europe. Alumni of US and Western European education programs returned to their home countries, or became members of diasporas in their host countries. Scholars from around the world participate in HRD international conferences held in Europe, the USA and Asia and publish in and read HRD journals – these individuals are becoming change agents in their own countries by integrating Western HRD concepts and processes into their historical, socio-cultural and economic-driven approaches to management and human resource development. HRD practices introduced by multinational corporations (MNCs) as part of their HRM strategies also contribute to this knowledge transfer (Aydinli 2010, Dobrai *et al.* 2012). To understand the continuum of convergence and divergence of Western HRD ideas in Central and Eastern Europe, as sifted through the fine meshes of cultures, this chapter will present the state of HRD practice, education and research in two countries in this region, Hungary and Poland.

Hungary and Poland have strong historical and economic ties to Western Europe. They maintained a private enterprise sector during their socialist/communist political and economic systems, experienced the liberalization of their economy earlier than other countries in the former Eastern Bloc, and had strong higher education histories with the first university in Hungary founded in Pécs in 1367 and the first university in Poland founded in Cracow in 1364. They are also ranked very closely as "very high development countries" (on the 37th and 39th place respectively) in the Human Development Index (HDI) calculated on estimates from 2012 in the 2013 Human Development Report by the United Nations Development Programme released on March 14, 2013. Despite the lack of systematic research in human resource management (HRM) (HRD is considered part of HRM in most of the research studies) in CEE, both countries are among the few in this region (joined by Slovenia and Russia) where academic research on HRM was conducted (Michailova *et al.* 2009). In the following three sections we will present the status of HRD in Hungary and Poland and will conclude with implications for research and practice.

HRD in Hungary

Located in the heart of Europe, Hungary is midsized in size and population among CEE countries with an area of 93,028 square kilometers and a (slowly shrinking) population of 10 million. It has several major industries – including mining, metallurgy, construction materials, processed foods, textiles, and chemicals – but services represent 69.1 per cent of its economy, with industry and agriculture accounting for 27.6 and 3.3 per cent respectively (CIA 2013, OECD 2013). In 2000, Hungary celebrated its 1,100 years of history. After the crowning of its first king, King Stephan, Hungary became closely linked with the Western Christian church and Western European culture. The historical and cultural legacy of Hungary is marked by wars and revolutions fueled by the opposition tradition of its people against occupation. In 1956, Hungary was the first country to rebel against the Soviet-ruled socialist system and economic reforms were introduced in Hungary as early as 1968 (Bakacsi *et al.* 2002). The gradual relaxation of central control and the development of private enterprise during the 1980s meant that the transition from a centrally planned to a market economy in early 1990s was less of a shock than in some other CEE countries. Hungary is a parliamentary democracy, and inaugurated a new constitution in 2012. It joined NATO in 2009 and entered the European Union in 2004. The nation's literacy rate is 99 per cent and its labor force is approximately 4.4 million (OECD 2013). At the time of this writing, Hungary is slowly recovering from the worldwide recession that began in 2007, and showed real GDP growth of 1.6 per cent in 2011 and a per-capita GDP of $21,547, the latter representing the highest to date (OECD 2013).

The first references to HRD in Hungary are related to training and specifically to management training and development. In 1991, Frank and Bennett (1991: 10) described Hungary's National Management Development Centre (part of the Ministry of Labor), as having the following HRD-related functions: offer courses to senior enterprise managers and its own faculty staff; conduct basic and applied research in management science and co-operate with state and municipal bodies, educational and research institutions; prepare and publish training materials (texts, manuals, guides, etc.); carry out pilot studies to test new management methods and consult practicing managers; provide up-to-date documentation and information services; and establish and operate a computer center with a view to promoting the application of computer-based management systems and mathematical techniques in management on a scale as wide as possible. This training function as related to HRD remains the most mentioned one in the literature, although its content became more encompassing to fit the changing needs of the market. Mezei and Fodor (2012: 145), discuss HRD training as containing the following components: digital communication and digital literacy skills development; public procurement procedural knowledge, development and supportive knowledge (e.g. PCM, development resources, regional and urban knowledge development, application techniques, etc.); financial and planning skills; and various training (negotiation, partnership building, conflict management and organization building).

The expanding role of HRD is captured by Lee (2010: 531). She notes that "In so far as HRD is a facilitative process then in a world of multiple shifting boundaries and different understandings it plays a crucial balancing role in enabling the needs of the organization and employees to be met." Lee gives meaning to her description by referring to the keynote speech of Ildiko Szűts, the then CEO of the Magyar Posta Zrt. [Hungarian Postal Services], on June 2, 2010, at the 11th International Conference on HRD Research and Practice across Europe, Pécs, Hungary, in the following way: "An excellent practical example of these issues was given by Szűts (2010), who was CEO of the Hungarian Postal Services, (Magyar Posta Zrt). She analyzed the HRD strategies that she put into place to manage the 'Borderless Postal Market' in Europe from a Hungarian Perspective. She talked about the challenges of managing such a large and complex organization within an increasingly borderless environment, and of the need for restructuring employment, motivational programs and labor force retention, reshaping competencies, training, knowledge management, career management, and issues around diversification. She concluded that the biggest dilemma was around liberalization vs. social dumping (the problematic side of migration), arguing that this was no longer just a business issue, but was also a regulatory and social issue – one that the government as well as HRD needs to take responsibility for."

Reflecting on the rapid development of the fields of management and human resources in Hungary since the 1990s, Krisztián (2013) noted that such changes could have not been possible without the accumulation of knowledge and experiences from the previous decades and the national policies that created the opportunities for them. The author highlights the main national policies and strategies that emerged since the late nineteenth century and the beginning of the twentieth century as a result of industrialization and the development of a civil society that required new approaches to management including the management and development of personnel/human resources. Despite the centralized economy that was characterized by a centralized approach to human resources driven by the political ideologies that ruled the society after 1945 (e.g. the selection and development of managers based on their party affiliation), the low productivity and efficiency of organizations and their negative impact on the country's economy, pushed to the forefront, by the end of 1964, the need for a critical review of the economic system and its mechanisms. This analysis led to the 1968 economic reforms that replaced the centralized directives bestowed upon organizations to market-driven strategies in the confines of the state's economic structure, in the so called "socialist market." These reforms allowed for the strengthening of professional and management development, thus expanding on the required political development of human resources. The follow-up decrees in 1974 and 1987 furthered conveyed strategic approaches to personnel development. The 1988 Company Act that allowed for the establishment of private companies and joint ventures triggered changes to personnel development previously regulated by the state. The 1990 Sole Proprietorship Law and the 1999 Small Business Act (Richbell *et al.* 2010) continued to shape the approaches to HRD in Hungary.

After joining the European Union (EU) in 2004, the Hungarian government prepared the National Development Plan (NDP) in order to improve the competitiveness of the economy and ensure maximum utilization of human resources. One of the NDP's five operational programs focused on HRD (European Commission 2009) and as Mezei and Fodor (2012) noted, training funding from the National Public Employment Foundation subsidized by the labor-market fund provided resources for HRD initiatives. According to the Human Resources Development Operational Programme (2004–2006: viii–ix), "The challenges of a knowledge-based society can only be met if knowledge, skills and adaptability are improved continuously by ensuring opportunities for life-long learning." The promotion of lifelong learning and adaptability was planned to be achieved by "supporting the following fields and activities: creating an appropriate methodological and pedagogical basis for the development of basic skills and competences, improving the system of vocational training so that it better responds to the needs of the economy, facilitating the adaptation of higher education to the requirements of the knowledge-based society and the changing demands of the economy, promoting adult training including, among others, in-company training and the development of entrepreneurial skills." The Programme (2004–2006: 5) highlights the role of HRD as "an essential tool in supporting economic growth and in responding to structural change. To this end, one of the purposes of this Programme is to promote the acquisition of skills and competencies required by the knowledge-based economy, and to make lifelong learning available to as many people as possible." The Social Renewal Operational Programme 2007–2013 further emphasized the importance of HRD for the prosperity of the nation and it is expected the next 2014–2020 Programme will continue to support HRD initiatives. Despite all these national strategies with specific references to HRD, research and higher education programs focused on HRD are scarce.

To understand the landscape of HR related higher educational programs, Bittner and Varga (2012) studied the representation of HR content in the curricula of universities and colleges that had specialization in HR. They sent out surveys to 19 state universities and 10 colleges and received 19 responses. They noted the difficulties in identifying these higher education programs and their faculty members given the plethora of titles/names associated with this topic. This issue was evidenced by the more than 10 program titles listed by the participants (e.g. HRM, HR and knowledge management, regional workforce management). They also realized that the titles of the programs were not necessarily related to their curriculum which could pose challenges to students selecting their majors or areas of concentration. In 12 participating institutions up to 30 per cent of the students were exposed to HRM concepts and in the other seven between 31 and 50 per cent of the students learned about HRM. It is not clear if these concepts included HRD related issues. The authors mentioned that with the spread of the idea that "people count," more and more students and leaders are learning about managing people and treating subordinates as colleagues, thus there is hope for the future (Bittner and Varga 2012: 124). Most of the HR related programs are embedded in management departments while a few of them are found in social sciences such as the ones offered by the Department of Adult Education and Human Resource Development at the University of Pécs, earlier called the Adult Education and Human Resource Development Institute, the first institute/department that used HRD in its name. Given the emphasis on HRD at the national level over the past decade, it is surprising that higher education institutions are not supported in the development of programs geared to the education of HRD professionals. Such individuals could understand the complexities of developing and studying HRD interventions at both the individual and collective (societal and organizational) levels. At the same time, although some of the main functions of HRD were described by Nemeskéri and Fruttus (2001), it is not clear if the evolving meaning of HRD used in the USA and Western Europe as a complex multidisciplinary field travels as such to this region, especially given the many references to HRD as training.

Although, at the organizational level, both the English and Hungarian language literature is rich in research focused on HR/HRM and other organizational and management issues where HRD-related functions are mentioned (Aydinli 2010, Benedek and Klekner 1997, Berde 2006, Berde and Piros 2006, Clement *et al.* 1994, Csath 1988, Cseh and Krisztián 2005, Cseh and Short 2000, 2006, Cseh *et al.* 2004, Fodor *et al.* 2011, Karoliny *et al.* 2010, Kuchinke *et al.* 2011, Mezei and Fodor 2012, Poór *et al.* 2010, Poór *et al.* 2011, Poór *et al.* 2012, Richbell *et al.* 2010, Simon and Davies 1996, Weiss 2003), research specifically focused on HRD is scarce. Dobrai *et al.* (2012: 155) studied knowledge transfer in multinational subsidiaries in Hungary. Noting that MCSs employ 20 per cent of people working in the private sector in Hungary, the authors examine knowledge transfer from MNC expatriates to Hungarian managers and employees in terms that align with HRD principles. They sought information related to (a) formal/informal learning, (b) the place where formal learning takes place, and (c) the possibilities to learn as a result of work-related mobility. In addition, the authors found that respondents in their study identified local training/development and informal learning on the job site as the most powerful learning methods.

In a comparison of how Hungary, Bulgaria, Slovakia, and Romania responded to the 2008 financial crisis, Fodor *et al.* (2011: 92) focused on company responses related to hiring/firing, wage freezes, cost reductions and organizational efficiency of workers and whether they were reactive or proactive in the crisis. In addition, however, they also examined the degree to which the four countries made changes in HR activities and investments. Hungarian companies were the least likely to make HR changes in every category. The categories related to HRD functions included workforce development, knowledge management, changes in organizational culture, competency management and career planning. These results may be explained by the Hungarians' relatively high level of uncertainty avoidance based on Hofstede and Hofstede's (2005) findings. Hungarians' low power distance and relatively high individualism (Aydinli 2010, Cseh *et al.* 2004, Fodor *et al.* 2011, Poór *et al.* 2011) among CEE countries may explain (1) the Hungarian entrepreneurial spirit, (2) their conduciveness to democratic principles in organizations such as equality in the workplace, (3) their less hierarchical organizations, and (4) their adoption of Western HRD practices. Conversely, their high level of uncertainty avoidance may explain divergence from some of these practices.

Several articles analyzed data gathered from the Cranfield Network on International Human Resource Management (Cranet), which conducts international comparative surveys of "organizational practices in comparative Human Resource Management across the world" (Cranet 2013). And while most of the Cranet data focus on HR and/or HRM and not HRD, the research includes country-by-country comparisons related to training and professional development. Two studies by Karoliny *et al.* (2009, 2010) use Cranet data to compare the proportion of annual payroll costs spent on training between Hungary, Eastern Europe, and all the countries examined. The findings show that Hungary in 2005 invested more in training than other Eastern European countries, and that "the Hungarian figure is the highest (3.54 per cent) of the sample averages of the training cost ratios found in our three samples, though it does not much exceed the average value of the total sample (3.36 per cent)" (2009: 31). The authors (2009: 31–32) note that (a) internal training was most common among all the three groups, that (b) "Hungarian employees receive more external or internal training than employees in the total sample" (2009: 31), and that (c) Hungarian management, professional, and clerical staff receive fewer training days per year than either their Eastern European or other international counterparts. Line managers have the most influence in defining training needs, and the role of the line managers in defining the training needs is higher in the Hungarian sample than for any other group. The authors also note that in the Hungarian sample – similarly to the other two samples, but with slightly stronger values – the most frequently used methods in managerial career development are participation in project team work, involvement in cross-organizational tasks and other special tasks to stimulate learning. In addition to these methods, the respondents of the CEE and the total samples reported a rather high use of networking (24 per cent). In contrast, Hungarian organizations hardly use this method.

In a follow-up article comparing 2005 and 2008 Cranet data, Karoliny *et al.* (2010: 742) report that the average Hungarian annual payroll cost/training cost ratio increased from 3.54–4.1 per cent from 2005–2008. Line managers solely made decisions about training development 43 per cent of the time in 2008, compared with 7 per cent of the time in 2005, and the number of annual training days for Hungarian managers (6.81) and professional/technical staff (6.63) rose to exceed the overall international averages (6.1, 6.1) and nearly match the CEE averages (7.2, 6.8). Poór *et al.* (2011: 439) also plumbed Cranet data to evaluate the importance of the HR function (which includes HRD components) in Hungary compared with other nations. Three of their findings shed light on HRD practice in Hungary. First, HR directors in Hungary are less likely (47 per cent compared with 55 per cent) to be on the board of directors or senior management of their companies than in other countries. Second, Hungary relies on other countries for their senior HR managers (49 per cent) more than do other CEE countries. Third, "nearly half of the Hungarian and other EE organizations turn to external providers when developing, running and managing pay and benefits systems." Along similar lines, Poór and Milovecz (2011: 310) found that "nearly half (48.9 per cent) of the respondents in Hungary claimed that they had increased the use of external service providers in the field of training and development in the past three years."

Richbell *et al.* (2010: 275) found that 56 per cent of SMEs in Hungary did not provide training for their employees, but appeared to compensate for this omission through informal training activities and opportunities. They speculate that the "overall low level of training, especially in small and micro firms, could be one of the reasons for the limited competitiveness of SMEs in Hungary." Other researchers also enfold the HRD components of training and professional development within HR or HRM functions. In a study comparing HRM practices and structures in Hungarian and Turkish banks, Aydinli (2010: 1506) analyzed a number of variables including career planning systems, performance-based pay, types of training and employee satisfaction. One significant difference between Hungarian and Turkish banks was that the majority of HR bank managers in Hungary were women, which the authors note was "not surprising considering that Hungary is one of the countries having the highest ranking for women in management" and a high representation (54 per cent) of women in the workforce (OECD 2013).

HRD in Poland

Poland is one of the biggest EU countries located in central Europe with a territory of 312,685 square kilometers and a population of 38 million. It has several major industries such as machine building, iron and steel, coal mining, chemicals, shipbuilding, food processing, glass, beverages, and textiles. However, services represent 63.8 per cent of its economy with industry and agriculture accounting for 32.3 per cent and 4 per cent respectively (CIA 2013). The year 966, when Polanian Prince Mieszko was baptized, is regarded as marking the origin of Poland as an independent, Christian, centralized state, following the model set up in Christian Europe. Poland is a pioneer of European constitutionalism. In 1791 the King and Parliament of the Republic of Poland and Lithuania passed the first constitution in the Old World, later called the 3rd of May Constitution. Labor turmoil in 1980 led to the formation of the independent trade union "Solidarity" that over time became a political force with over ten million members. The events in Poland precipitated the fall of the entire Communist bloc (http://en.poland.gov.pl). Free elections in 1989 and 1990 won Solidarity control of the parliament and the presidency, bringing the communist era to a close. A "shock therapy" program during the early 1990s enabled the country to transform its economy into one of the most robust in Central Europe. Poland is a parliamentary democracy and joined NATO in 1999 and the European Union in 2004 (CIA 2013). The nation's literacy rate is 99.7 per cent and its labor force is approximately 17.4 million (OECD 2013). Poland has pursued a policy of economic liberalization since 1990 and Poland's economy was the only one in the European Union to avoid a recession through the 2008–2009 economic downturn. Real growth rate was 2 per cent in 2012 and per-capita GDP $20,900 (CIA 2013). Although EU membership and access to EU structural funds have provided a major boost to the economy since 2004, GDP per capita remains significantly below the EU average while unemployment continues to exceed the EU average (CIA 2013).

Since the early 1990s, HRD in Poland has become a universal term for educational activities focused on the development of employee competencies based on the needs of the market economy. In broader social terms, HRD encompasses all activities related to the identification of the causes of social maladjustment, determining needs and planning interventions for selected professional areas, regions, states or social and professional groups (Różański 2008: 13). The practice of HRD started to develop with the emergence of modern training companies following Western and American models that replaced the old personnel development centers. During the past two decades, Poland witnessed a sharp increase in the number of companies providing training services. In 2011 the number of these companies operating in Poland ranged from 6,900–9,800, of which over 40 per cent were established after 2006 (Czernecka *et al.* 2011: 3). As a result, the availability of educational services to the business community increased and a growing scale of direct involvement of companies in the improvement of employee competencies was noticed. The increased activity in this area is bound to, *inter alia*, economic growth and to the increasing scale of use of EU funds under the Sector Operational Programme (SOP) after 2005 (Różański 2011: 87–94).

At the societal level, a national HRD plan started to unfold. The Council of Ministers adopted the Strategy for the Development of Human Capital 2020 (Resolution No. 104 of the Council of Ministers of 18 June 2013). The main goal of this plan is the development of human capital through human potential enhancement in such a way that people can fully participate in the social, political and economical life at all stages of their lives. One of the main objectives of the strategy is to raise the level of competence and skills of all citizens. This objective is to be achieved by expansion of adult learning opportunities at work and in social settings (e.g. informal learning, non-formal education such as short training courses), and the recognition of learning outcomes as a result of these forms of learning that will allow for the quick response to the development of the needed employee skills. This objective will also be achieved by the admittance to higher education of adults through a new system of accreditation of their competences acquired outside the higher education system (e.g. obtained in the process of self-improvement, professional work, through participation in courses and training, as well as through the recognition of qualifications acquired in vocational colleges functioning in the existing education system) (Strategy for the Development of Human Capital 2020, 2013: 60).

At the higher education level of HRD professionals, HRD in Poland is considered to be one of the elements of HRM, a subfield of study in faculty/department of economics. Thus, currently there are no undergraduate and graduate programs in the field of HRD. However, "HR" majors exist, mainly within management related programs (broadly defined HRM), and psychology based programs. In this case, the emphasis is on the processes of staff selection, recruitment and employee assessment. To a small extent, some majors referring to HRD issues can be found within faculties/departments of education (pedagogy), andragogy and career counselling programs with an emphasis on work education, adult education and counselling for education. Thus, due to the political and socio-economic changes in the last two decades, the 1970s and 1980s work pedagogic and continuous adult education programs deeply rooted in the old political and economic system were replaced with a more market oriented adult university system. Although the new system opened opportunities for the higher education of adults interested in HRD-related topics, given the interdisciplinary character of the HRD field rooted in andragogy, psychology, social economics and sociology there is no single paradigm for HRD education and research. The range of research issues focuses on educational activities and the opportunities and potentials for development of adults in the case of social trends, and system and organizational solutions in management related fields. This situation reflects the two paradigms impacting HRD research and education: learning or performance. The former is represented by social sciences and humanities researchers and educators, while the latter by management sciences researchers and educators. This situation results in difficulties in creating a uniform, in the professional sense, HRD profession.

This state of affairs is hindered by lack of specific professional standards for HRD specialists. The Decree of the Polish Ministry of Labour and Social Policy (2010) on the classification of professions and specialties for the needs of the labor market and the scope of its use, has specified a group (No. 24) of "Specialists on the economics and management" with the following subgroups: (2424) Specialists in professional training and staff development, including: (242401) Educational Broker, (242402) Professional Development Specialist, (242403) Training Specialist, and (242490) Other Specialists for Training and Staff Development. However, in accordance with the Regulation in relation to persons taking the position of the Training and Professional Development Specialist (242490), the professional requirements are limited only to the stipulation of the preferred, but not mandatory, type of education. For the above-mentioned positions professionals with higher education in the fields of, *inter alia*, education, psychology, sociology, are preferred. Although the Higher Education Law (Polish Ministry of Science and Higher Education 2011) gives universities the opportunity to create arbitrary training programs while maintaining the standards specified in the Act, the development of undergraduate and graduate programs in the field of HRD has not started. This issue is also related to the lack of professional standards, which are not recognized by the previously mentioned Regulation.

Due to the nature of the work of HRD professionals in the field of development and training the knowledge of economics, entrepreneurship and the basics of management and labor law are desirable for candidates. As this content in classic curricula of the previously mentioned programs is limited or does not exist at all, the graduates of these programs complement their knowledge deficiency with postgraduate studies. Therefore, for many years the main burden of HR (HRD) professional training has rested on postgraduate programs offered by universities and academic institutes: "postgraduate studies are a different form of education than MA and PhD studies for those who already hold a university diploma" (Polish Ministry of Science and Higher Education 2005: art. 2, point 11). They are intensive "training programs" taking around a year and offering

200–300 hours of classes. The goal of postgraduate studies is to help individuals and groups adapt their skills and qualifications to the changing socio-economic situation.

Thus, it seems that from a practical point of view, in order to build a strong position for HRD education and research the emphasis should be placed on developing international standards for HRD professional education and training. In this case, the context of the regulations concerning a particular profession is extremely important. Sanctioning this type of solution – the designation of the place of trained HRD specialists in the work environment – will help to clarify the directions of research and to develop a uniform education and research methodology.

At the organizational level, under the third edition of the project Bilans Kapitału Ludzkiego (Human Capital Comparison) (Szczucka *et al.* 2012) an analysis of the activity of adult Poles as well as the organizations' involvement in the development of employee competencies has been conducted. According to the authors, in 2011, 36 per cent of Poles aged 18–59/64 raised their competence by participating in various forms of training; 4.8 million customers benefited from the services of the training sector; and 3.6 million participated in courses other than safety training. According to the Diagnoza społeczna 2009 (Social Diagnosis 2009) report, in 2000–2007 in Poland the percentage of persons in all age groups benefiting from various forms of education steadily grew (Czapiński and Panek 2009: 89). In 2005–2008 in Poland primarily those who were best educated and skilled supplemented their education (Kałużyńska *et al.* 2009: 252). Thus, predominantly professionals and higher level managers raised their competence, as well as a group of technicians and middle level staff. According to Rakowska (2007: 187) the most popular forms of in-service professional training in addition to postgraduate studies were: longer forms of education, short training courses up to three days, seminars, conferences, training at the workplace, self-directed learning (reading), interviews with experienced colleagues, simulations, case studies of other companies, role-playing games, diagnostic questionnaires for getting to know each other, lectures and training, and computer-aided learning.

In 2011, over 70 per cent of employers financed or co-financed activities aimed at the development of competence and/or skills of their employees (Szczucka *et al.* 2012). The general trends remained constant, which indicate that the larger the enterprise or institution regardless of the business sector, the more activity is undertaken towards the development of employee competence and qualifications. In the case of micro-entities at least one activity of this kind was declared by 70 per cent of employers, in the case of small employers it was 80 per cent, and for medium-sized and large employers the numbers reached 93 per cent and 95 per cent, respectively. The dominant strategy was to use the services of an external training company with only 37 per cent of employers using a mixed strategy of internal and external training. Less than one in seven employers were developing the competence of employees by using exclusively their own resources. Large companies and corporations with human resources departments used a wide range of HR tools (Pocztowski 2004). Różański's (2012) study in the SME sector showed that most frequently employees are trained in health and safety (safety training) and in the skills and qualifications to perform specific technical activities (90 per cent) such as trainings in operating specialized service applications (equipment operation process control; approximately 50 per cent), IT systems operation (approximately 50 per cent) and customer service (40 per cent). Almost 50 per cent of managers employed in companies admitted that they did not have a plan of development of human resources in the organization. In most companies training plans were created primarily based on the current needs of the organization.

Bartkowiak's (1999) study on orientations aimed at development and learning found that employees with lower seniority (less than four years), presented significantly higher levels of orientation focused on development and learning, and demonstrated greater involvement in learning and developing their skills. In her study of executive training, Andrzejczak (1998) identified fifteen most highly rated skills such as good listening, motivating, asking effective questions, communicating orders and creative problem solving (Andrzejczak 1998: 43). Rakowska (2007) on the basis of her extensive research on improving management skills pointed to eleven mostly taught groups of skills: expertise, foreign languages, self-management, stress management, conceptual skills, communication, motivation, organization and control, exerting influence, conflict resolution, team work and change management (Rakowska 2007: 73).

Kwarcińska (2005: 127–29) presented interesting insights into the determinants of educational activity of line and middle level managers. Among the respondents nearly one third were women. Based on the survey it was found that women occupying managerial positions demonstrated higher educational activity. Różański (2011) in the study of educational orientations of managers noted that in the case of women pursuing managerial careers, the high self-esteem of their abilities, including their educational experience, is often a stimulating factor in taking actions relating to their own development and learning. Such a pattern was not revealed in men.

Comparative studies conducted among executives in 2000–2009, found that in the period of the growth of spending on training (financed by the SOP), educational activity of managers has more than doubled. In 2005–2009 high activity was observed in over 43 per cent of respondents, compared with 21 per cent in 2000–2004. Furthermore, nearly 37 per cent of managers with a high level of educational activity worked in companies that required the employees to systematically develop their skills, and only 28 per cent of those with identified high level of activity were employed by companies where such a requirement was not enforced (Różański 2011). The highest pro-development activity is demonstrated by employees who work for enterprises with a well developed HR(D) system requiring systematic skills improvement (Różański 2012). Therefore, it can be concluded that persons operating in favorable socio-economic conditions (work situation) show a greater willingness to take on new pro-development tasks.

Conclusions and implications for research and practice

As reflected in the reviewed literature, HRD, HRM and HR are intrinsically related in Hungary and Poland. Very few articles focused solely on HRD and only a handful of HRD academic/degree programs exist (while HRD-related topics are included in HRM programs and other related programs). This situation raises concerns about the professionalization of the field and specific educational programs and practices related to HRD as embedded in humanistic and constructivist paradigms. Since the practice of HRD relies on systems thinking and the ability to understand the interconnections among all parts of changing systems, the development of a set of competencies flexible enough to keep pace with the continuous changes experienced by HRD practitioners could be very beneficial both for formal educational and informal learning programs and environments and could contribute to the professionalization of the field. A comparative study in each of the countries of practices used by graduates of different HR/HRM/HRD programs to understand their philosophy and application of HRD values and principles could illuminate the strength and areas of development needed by existing formal educational programs.

Given that national HRD plans and strategies related to HRD education and practice were prominent in both countries, the study of their impact on HRD would allow the understanding of their strength. This understanding could shape the development of future policies that will continue to ensure the development of needed competencies and a global mindset that includes curiosity and openness to new ideas. These developments are conducive to creativity and innovation, while creating market conditions that will appreciate them.

Well-designed research agendas are needed in these two countries to understand the adaptation of Western HRD practices. These agendas need to consider the cultural and socio-economic contexts of Hungary and Poland (as well as those of other CEE countries) with their national HRD plans and institutional forms. Furthermore, the agendas should take into account the specific structures and organizational cultures of the many types of organizations such as MNC, large, medium and small entrepreneurial organizations. The proliferation of MNCs creates a tendency toward convergence in HRD values and practices around the world, given the complexities of national policies, organizational structures and diversity of the workforce in these two countries and in the CEE region. However, we expect a continuum on the convergence, cross-vergence and divergence of HRD values and practices and understanding their root causes is essential for the respect and understanding among cultures. Given the rate of change of knowledge and competencies in the developing global markets that have a direct impact on local markets, the study of the socio-economic and organizational conditions conducive to continuous learning would allow HRD professionals to create these environments.

Last, but not least, the meaning of HRD is continuously evolving in the Western world and its interpretation in CEE is also evolving. Keeping in mind the dynamic nature of this field, and the meaning making that occurs when the ideas that it represents travel to Hungary, Poland and other CEE countries, understanding the meaning attached to these ideas is essential for speaking the same professional language not just in words but in meaning (Cseh and Short 2000, 2006).

References

Andrzejczak, A. (1998) *Raport z Badań nad Szkoleniem Kadry Kierowniczej*, Poznań: Fundacja Kadry dla Wielkopolski.

Aydinli, F. (2010) 'Converging human resource management: a comparative analysis of Hungary and Turkey', *International Journal of Human Resource Management*, 21: 1490–511.

Bakacsi, G., Takács, S., Karácsonyi, A. and Imrek, V. (2002) 'Eastern European cluster: tradition and transition', *Journal of World Business*, 37: 69–80.

Bartkowiak, G. (1999) *Orientacja Nastawiona na Rozwój i Uczenie się Osób Zatrudnionych w Organizacji*, Poznań: Wydawnictwo Akademii Ekonomicznej.

Benedek, A. and Klekner, P. (1997) 'Managing economic transition: dimensions of human resource development in Hungary', *Industry and Higher Education*, 11: 182–88.

Berde, C. (2006) 'Human resource management in Hungarian agriculture', *Jahrbuch der Österreichischen Gesellschaft für Agrarökonomie*, 15: 157–64.

Berde, C. and Piros, M. (2006) 'A survey of human resource management and qualification levels in Hungarian agriculture', *Journal of Agricultural Education and Extension*, 12: 301–15.

Bittner, P. and Varga, R. (2012) '"Így tanítjuk mi!" – a HR oktatás módszertani kérdései', in Poór, J., Karoliny, Z., Berde, C. and Takács, S. (eds) *Átalakuló Emberi Erőforrás Menedzsment*, Budapest: Complex.

Brewster, C., Morley, M. and Buciuniene, I. (2010) 'The reality of human resource management in Central and Eastern Europe: a special issue to mark the 20th anniversary of Cranet', *Baltic Journal of Management*, 5: 145–55.

CIA (2013) *The World Fact Book: Hungary*. Online. Available HTTP: https://www.cia.gov/library/publications/the-world-factbook/index.html (accessed 2 December 2013).

Clement, R.W., Payne, W.F. and Brockway, G.R. (1994) 'Training central and eastern European managers: the Hungarian experience', *Journal of Management Development*, 13: 53–61.

Cranet (2013) *Cranet*. Online. Available HTTP: http://www.cranet.org/home/Pages/Default.aspx (accessed 2 April 2013).

Csath, M. (1988) 'The Hungarian economic reform problems of human resource management and corporate culture', *International Journal of Manpower*, 9: 21–27.

Cseh, M. and Krisztián, B. (2005) 'Magyar szervezeti kultúra típustan Hofstedétől – 2005-ben', *Humánpolitikai Szemle*, 16: 35–38.

Cseh, M. and Short, D. (2000) 'An intercultural training/consulting process and its implications on meaning making and organizational change: the case of a Hungarian organization', in Kuchinke, K.P. (ed.) *Proceedings of the 2000 Academy of Human Resource Development Annual Conference*, Baton Rouge, LA: AHRD.

— (2006) 'The challenges of training with interpreters and translators: the case study of a Hungarian organization', *Journal of European Industrial Training*, 30: 687–700.

Czapiński, J. and Panek, T. (eds) (2009) *Diagnoza Społeczna, Warunki i Jakość Zycia Polaków*, Warszawa: Rada Monitoringu Społecznego.

Czernecka, M., Milewska, J., Woszczyk, P. and Zawłocki, P. (eds) (2011) *End of Financial Support*, Łódź: Przyszłość Rynku Szkoleń w Polsce, HRP.

Dobrai, K., Farkas, F., Karoliny, Z. and Poór, J. (2012) 'Knowledge transfer in multinational companies – evidence from Hungary', *Acta Polytechnica Hungarica*, 9: 149–61.

European Commission (2009) *Hungarian SME Policy: Development after EU Accession*. Available HTTP: http://ec.europa.eu/enterprise/ebsn/policies/national/hungary/documents/pdf/hungarian_sme_policy. (accessed 15 October 2013).

Fodor, P., Kiss., T. and Poór, J. (2011) 'Focus on the impact of the economic and financial crisis on the human resource function: four Eastern European countries in the light of empirical research in 2009', *Acta Polytechnica Hungarica*, 8: 81–103.

Frank, E. and Bennett, R. (1991) 'HRD in Eastern Europe', *Journal of European Industrial Training*, 15: 1–35.

Hofstede, G. and Hofstede, G.J. (2005) *Cultures and Organizations: Software of the Mind*, New York: McGraw-Hill.

Horwitz, F.M. (2011) 'Future HRM challenges for multinational firms in Eastern and Central Europe', *Human Resource Management Journal*, 21: 432–43.

Karoliny, Z., Farkas, F. and Poór, J. (2009) 'In focus: Hungarian and Central Eastern European characteristics of human resource management – an international comparative survey', *Journal of East European Management Studies*, 1: 9–47.

— (2010) 'Sharpening profile of HRM in Central-Eastern Europe in reflection of its developments in Hungary', *Review of International Comparative Management*, 11: 733–47.

Kałużyńska, M., Smyk, K. and Wiśniewski, J. (eds) (2009) *5 Lat Polski w Unii Europejskiej*, Warszawa: Urząd Komitetu Integracji Europejskiej.

Krisztián, B. (2013) 'Az emberierőforrás-menedzsment hazai változásai', *Humánpolitikai Szemle*, 24(9–10): 3–12.

Kuchinke, K.P., Ardichvili, A., Borchert, M., Cornachione, E.B., Jr., Cseh, M., Kang, H.S., Oh, S.Y., Różański, A., Tynaliev, U. and Zavyalova, E. (2011) 'Work meaning among mid-level professional employees: a study of the importance of work centrality and extrinsic and intrinsic work goals in eight countries', *Asia Pacific Journal of Human Resources*, 49: 264–84.

Kwarcińska, B. (2005) *Doskonalenie Menedżerów w Gospodarce Opartej na Wiedzy*, Poznań: Garmond Oficyna Wydawnicza.

Lee, M. (2010) 'Shifting boundaries: the role of HRD in a changing world', *Advances in Developing Human Resources*, 12: 524–35.

McGuire, D. and Cseh, M. (2006) 'The development of the field of HRD: a Delphi study', *Journal of European Industrial Training*, 30: 653–67.

Mezei, Z. and Fodor, P. (2012) 'Human resources development in a lagging region', *International Journal of Business and Social Science*, 3: 144–53.

Michailova, S., Heraty, N. and Morley, M. (2009) 'Studying human resource management in the international context: the case of Central and Eastern Europe', in Morley, M., Heraty, N. and Michailova, S. (eds) *Managing Human Resources in Central and Eastern Europe*, London: Routledge.

Nemeskéri, G. and Fruttus, I.L. (2001) *Az emberi erőforrás fejlesztésének módszertana* [Methodology of the development of human resources], Budapest, Hungary: Ergofit.

OECD (2013) *Country Statistical Profile: Hungary. Country Statistical Profiles: Key Tables*, Online. Available HTTP: www.oecd-ilibrary.org/economics/country-statistical-profile-hungary_20752288-table-hun (accessed 2 December 2013).

Pocztowski, A. (ed.) (2004) *Najlepsze Praktyki Zarządzania Zasobami Ludzkimi w Polsce*, Kraków: Wolters Kluwer.

Polish Ministry of Labour and Social Policy (2010) *Rozporządzeniu Ministra Pracy i Polityki Społecznej z Dnia 27.04.2010 r. w Sprawie Klasyfikacji Zawodów i Specjalności na Potrzeby Rynku Pracy* [Regulation from the Minister of Labour and Social Policy, dated 27 April 2010, on the Classification of Occupations for Labour Market Needs], Warsaw: Ministry of Labor and Social Policy.

Polish Ministry of Science and Higher Education (2005) *Ustawa o Szkolnictwie Wyższym z Dnia 27 Lipca 2005* [Higher Education Law, bill of 27 July 2005], Warsaw: Ministry of Science and Higher Education.

— (2011) *Ustawa o Szkolnictwie Wyższym z Dnia 18 Marca 2011* [Higher Education Law, bill of 18 March 2011], *Journal of Laws* vol. 84 item 455, vol. 112 item 654, vol. 2012 item 1544, Warsaw: Ministry of Science and Higher Education.

Poór, J. and Milovecz, A. (2011) 'Management consulting in human resource management: Central and Eastern European perspectives in light of empirical experiences', *Journal of Service Science and Management*, 4: 300–14.

Poór, J., Engle, A. and Gross, A. (2010) 'Human resource management practices of large multinational firms in Hungary, 1988–2005', *Acta Oeconomica*, 60: 427–60.

Poór, J., Karoliny, Z., Alas, R. and Vatchkova, E.K. (2011) 'Comparative international human resource management (CIHRM) in the light of the Cranet regional research survey in transitional economies, *Employee Relations*, 33: 428–43.

Poór, J., Karoliny, Z., Berde, C. and Takács, S. (eds) (2012) *Átalakuló Emberi Erőforrás Menedzsment*, Budapest: Complex.

Rakowska, A. (2007) *Kompetencje Menedżerskie Kadry Kierowniczej we Współczesnych Organizacjach*, Lublin: Wydawnictwo UMCS.

Richbell, S., Szerb, L. and Vitai, Z. (2010) 'HRM in the Hungarian SME sector', *Employee Relations*, 32: 262–80.

Różański, A. (2008) 'The educational orientation of participants on post-graduate managerial study programs in Poland: the Lublin case', *Human Resource Development International*, 11: 91–99.

— (2011) *Orientacje Edukacyjne Menedżerów w Warunkach Gospodarki Posttransformacyjnej*, Lublin: Wydawnictwo UMCS.

— (2012) 'Dobór szkoleń pracowniczych w małych i średnich przedsiębiorstwach – analiza zjawiska', *E-mentor*, 5: 72–76.

Simon, L. and Davies, G. (1996) 'A contextual approach to management learning: the Hungarian case', *Organization Studies*, 17: 269–89.

Szczucka, A., Turek, K. and Worek, B. (eds) (2012) *III edycji projektu Bilans Kapitału Ludzkiego*, Warszawa: Polska Agencja Rozwoju Przedsiębiorczości (PARP).

Szűts, I. (2010, June 2–4) *HRD Strategies in a European Borderless Postal Market: A Hungarian Perspective*, Keynote speech at the 11th International Conference on HRD Research and Practice across Europe, held in Pécs, Hungary.

Weiss, C. (2003) 'Scientific and technological responses to structural adjustment: human resources and research issues in Hungary, Turkey, and Yugoslavia', *Technology in Society*, 15: 281–99.

44

HRD IN THE EUROPEAN UNION

Alexandra Dehmel and Jasper B. Van Loo

In the European context, Vocational Education and Training (VET) is understood as education and training which aims to equip people with knowledge, know-how, skills and/or competences required in particular occupations or more broadly on the labour market (Cedefop 2008). Initial VET (I-VET) is vocational education and training carried out in the initial education system, usually before entering working life. Continuing VET (C-VET) takes place after initial education and training – or after entry into working life – and is aimed at helping individuals to a) improve or update their knowledge and/or skills, b) acquire new skills for a career move or retraining, and/or c) continue their personal or professional development (Cedefop 2008).

VET and adult learning more generally are cornerstones of Europe's skills base and constitute a large part of Europe's HRD efforts. Similar to countries in other parts of the world, European countries face several challenges that increase the need for HRD and lifelong learning. Among those challenges are population ageing, skills upgrading, sustainability and globalization. An important feature of HRD in Europe is that, next to private investment in skills by organizations and individuals and public initiatives at the level of member states, the European Union (EU) shapes lifelong learning and skills investment through education, labour market and skill policies that support the ambitions of its strategic agenda Europe 2020 (European Commission 2010a). This is mainly a process of soft coordination, as the subsidiarity principle is dominant in the area of education policy. The subsidiarity principle implies that the EU's competences are strictly limited to areas in which the EU treaties explicitly authorize such actions and in which the intended aims cannot be attained sufficiently by member states independently (Ertl 2006: 11).

As HRD is an important mechanism developing human capital, it is a key determinant of innovation and economic development (OECD 2010, Cedefop 2012a). But there are also several other reasons why investing in HRD is important. Investment in HRD supports the inclusion of groups with low participation in lifelong learning, such as the low-skilled and ageing people (Cedefop 2012d, 2013). Investments in skills also counteract obsolescence, the outdating of human capital, which is a common feature in modern economies (Cedefop 2010b). A survey in four EU member states showed that skills obsolescence is a pervasive phenomenon: a quarter of workers aged 30–55 is at risk of skills obsolescence (Cedefop 2012c). The same survey showed that ageing workers, the low-skilled and those without learning opportunities are most affected by skills obsolescence. In addition, not being able to use skills in the workplace and working environments not supportive of learning are important risk factors (ibid.).

Focusing on the supranational level, this chapter gives an overview of the status of HRD in Europe from the perspective of adult learning and VET by considering several interrelated issues. Examining the relationships between learning and innovation performance, we will first make the case for investments in HRD. In this context, innovation refers to "the implementation of a new or significantly improved product (good or service) or process, a new marketing method, or a new organizational method in business practices, workplace organization or external relations" (Cedefop 2012a: 24). The innovation performance of a country can be understood holistically in terms of favourable conditions for innovation, investment and results.

The analysis of the relationship between learning and innovation performance is followed by a review of recent statistical evidence to highlight patterns in lifelong learning participation and C-VET in enterprises. This gives an impression of HRD efforts across the continent and helps in identifying differences between countries. In the next part of this chapter, we discuss the main priorities of EU policies in the fields of adult learning and VET and examine to what extent and in what ways countries have progressed towards them in recent years. This analysis is based on a review carried out by the European Centre for the Development of Vocational Training (Cedefop) of what European countries have done to implement common goals for VET agreed in 2010, in line with its mandate to support policy development and implementation, to report on progress towards priorities set for VET at the European level, and to provide evidence for policy-making in VET (Council of the European Union and European Commission 2010). The final section presents several conclusions that can help support future VET and adult learning policies.

Making the case for promoting HRD: learning and innovation

A better understanding of links between learning and innovation helps to further encourage HRD in Europe. Global competition in the fields of innovation and economic development is fierce. Calculated at country level, the Innovation Union Scoreboard (IUS) is a measure of innovation performance based on a synthesized index that combines 25 innovation indicators in three domains (innovation enablers, innovation activities by firms and innovation outputs). The IUS shows that the EU is facing a significant innovation gap compared with other world economies such as the USA and Japan (European Commission 2013). According to the IUS, these two countries achieve substantially higher levels of innovation performance compared with the average scores of the EU. However, the IUS also reveals that there are large differences between the EU member states. Some (e.g. Sweden) perform well above the EU-27 average, whereas others (e.g. Bulgaria) perform well below that level (ibid.). One of the eight dimensions used in the IUS to measure the innovative capacity and to monitor the progress in the EU is human resources, thus indicating the importance of a skilled workforce. At the European level, a broad approach to innovation policies has been taken to stimulate innovation and to address the innovation gap (Cedefop 2012a). The EU flagship initiative 'Innovation Union' outlines the EU's strategic approach to innovation, also emphasizing the role of education and training, and the need to raise skill levels to foster innovation (European Commission 2010b).

Generally, the importance of education and training and HRD for the innovation performance of countries is widely acknowledged, but many policies designed to promote innovation tend to focus on tertiary education (e.g. on raising educational attainment, attracting researchers and creating high quality PhD programmes), and neglect the crucial role of HRD and VET in a broad sense, i.e. including not only VET provision (e.g. continuing training courses), but also learning-conducive work organizations that enable or facilitate learning at the workplace (Dehmel 2014). A recent study on learning and innovation in enterprises (Cedefop 2012a) reveals that the potential of VET and HRD to foster innovation is not being fully exploited yet in Europe. It therefore calls for stronger links between VET, HRD and innovation policies. The study covers the EU member states (in 2007, i.e. excluding Croatia) plus Norway and uses quantitative and qualitative research methods. It investigates the relations between learning-conducive work organizations (using data from the European Working Conditions Survey – EWCS, see Eurofound 2007), learning in enterprises (using data from the CVTS; Eurostat 2006) and innovation performance (using data from the IUS; PRO INNO Europe 2012), with due account also being taken of previous studies in this field (e.g. OECD 2010, Lorenz and Lundvall 2006, Lorenz and Valeyre 2005).

The findings show that learning-intensive forms of work organization and learning at the workplace – besides other, more formal and organized modes of VET – have a positive impact on innovation performance, at least at the country level: Countries with a high percentage of enterprises that provide training (see Figure 44.1) and with a high percentage of enterprises with learning-conducive work organizations have a higher innovation performance (e.g. Denmark and Sweden) (Cedefop 2012a).

Particularly opportunities for learning at the workplace seem to constitute a major component of the innovative ability of enterprises. A closer inspection of the characteristics of learning-intensive forms of work organization shows that task complexity seems to have a stronger impact on innovation performance than the other characteristics (e.g. task autonomy). The learning-conduciveness of a working environment depends not only on factors such as high autonomy, team work, task variety and task complexity, but it is to a considerable extent also influenced by the wider HR and management practices of the organization (e.g. the performance management

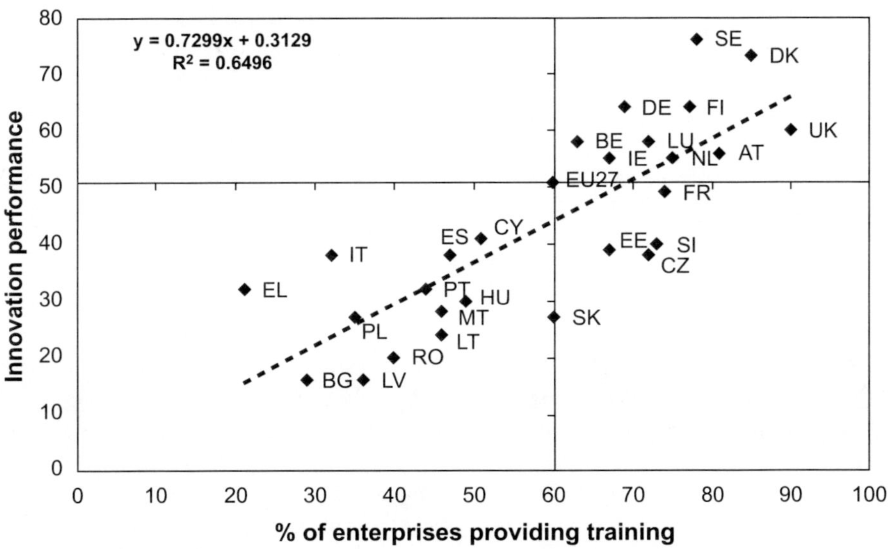

Figure 44.1 Relation between training enterprises and innovation performance

Source: Own calculations, data from CVTS3 (Eurostat 2006) and the European Innovation Index (MERIT 2006; see also Cedefop 2012a: 42). Country abbreviations: EU27 = European Union, BE = Belgium, BG = Bulgaria, CZ = Czech Republic, DK = Denmark, DE = Germany, EE = Estonia, IE = Ireland, EL = Greece, ES = Spain, FR = France, IT = Italy, CY = Cyprus, LV = Latvia, LT = Lithuania, LU = Luxembourg, HU = Hungary, MT = Malta, NL = Netherlands, AT = Austria, PL = Poland, PT = Portugal, RO = Romania, SI = Slovenia, SK = Slovakia, FI = Finland, SE = Sweden, UK = United Kingdom.

processes: systems which focus on improving performance and planning development rather than assessing and paying for performance might be more learning conducive; see Eraut and Hirsh 2007, Hirsh 2006).

Workplace organization and learning in enterprises appear to be at least equally important predictors of innovation performance compared with well-established indicators (e.g. attainment rates in tertiary education) that are used in national and supranational monitoring systems such as the IUS (Cedefop 2012a). But the role of HRD and VET (in a broad sense) is underrepresented and underestimated in current monitoring systems. There is a need for HRD and VET-related indicators to become firmly integrated in such systems alongside traditional indicators. If monitoring indicators cover relevant human capital (participation in formal, non-formal and informal C-VET) and structural capital (e.g. work organization) dimensions, enterprises and policy makers would become more aware of the importance of HRD and VET for innovation.

Although research confirms positive relations between learning at the workplace and innovation, an analysis of innovation policies and 1,030 publicly funded innovation programmes in the EU member states plus Norway – using the European database ERAWATCH – shows that the potential of learning is not yet fully exploited (Cedefop 2012a). Examples of the few programmes that promote innovative ability by targeting organizational structures and processes at the workplace level, aim at more learning-intensive forms of work organization and, thereby, encourage workplace learning, are the VINNOVA's 'Management and work organization renewal' programme in Sweden (Steiber and Alänge 2013) and the BMBF programme 'Working–Learning–Developing Competences' in Germany (BMBF 2007). In many European countries, however, such initiatives are completely absent from the programme portfolio (Cedefop 2012a).

In summary, the evidence suggests that the true benefits of VET, work organization and workplace learning in terms of innovation performance are underestimated in Europe. Other studies in this field confirm this. An example is the OECD, that also emphasizes the crucial role of VET and highlights that "the bottleneck to improving the innovative capabilities of European firms might not be low levels of R&D expenditures . . ., but the widespread presence of working environments that are unable to provide fertile grounds for innovation" (OECD 2010: 11). In other words: many workplaces are not yet conducive to learning. As a result, there is a strong case for expanding and further promoting HRD in Europe.

The state of HRD in Europe: recent evidence

If there are indications that the potential of learning in terms of innovation performance is not yet fully tapped, what does the learning landscape in Europe look like? There is no straightforward answer to this question as different forms of learning take place in various settings. While the more measurable types of learning are regularly monitored using surveys, other types of learning, such as e.g. learning-by-doing are processes that are difficult to measure and quantify. Examining lifelong learning participation by individuals and investments in C-VET by enterprises can, however, provide some initial insights. By presenting recent statistical evidence collected by Eurostat in these domains, this section gives a rough impression of HRD in Europe.

It is important to realize that many national education and training systems have for a long time mainly focused on the education and training of young people, with the consequence that only limited progress has been made in changing or adapting the systems to mirror the need for learning throughout the lifespan (cf. European Commission 2006: 2). There are, however, considerable country differences in the provision of adult learning and in the participation rates of adults in lifelong learning and C-VET. We present evidence on both below.

Participation in lifelong learning

Eurostat defines lifelong learning as "all purposeful learning activity, whether formal, non-formal or informal, undertaken on an ongoing basis with the aim of improving knowledge, skills and competence" (Eurostat 2013c). Figure 44.2 (horizontal axis) shows that adult participation in lifelong learning (age group 25–64) in 2012 ranged from under 3 per cent in some of the Eastern and Southern European countries (e.g. Croatia, Greece and Hungary) to more than 25 per cent in several Scandinavian countries (e.g. Sweden, Denmark and Finland) and Switzerland. The EU-27 average participation rate in 2012 was 9 per cent. This is still far from the 15 per cent target set for 2020 in the strategic framework for European cooperation in education and training ('ET 2020', Council of the European Union 2009). In order to reach the target, C-VET – as a crucial part of adult learning – plays an important role; its potential has not yet been fully exploited. Learning opportunities at the workplace should be expanded, and more learning-conducive working environments that encourage the development of knowledge, skills and competences need to be created.

To explore a core dimension of access to lifelong learning, Figure 44.2 (vertical axis) presents the inclusion of people in the 55–64 age cohort. Inclusion is defined as the share of 55–64 year olds engaged in lifelong learning as a percentage of total lifelong learning participation (in per cent) among adults. Two conclusions emerge. First, even in some countries where overall participation

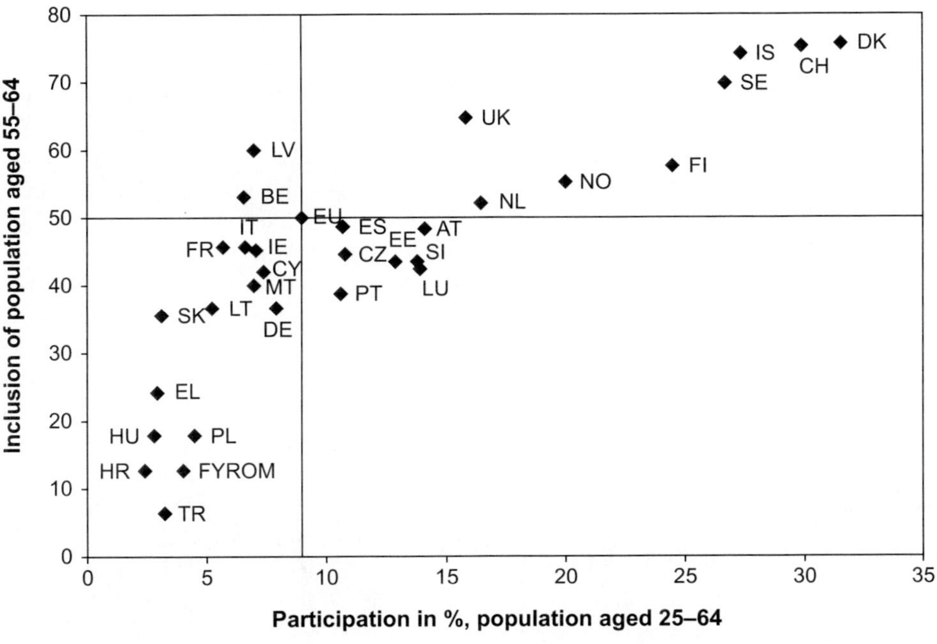

Figure 44.2 Participation in lifelong learning in European countries and inclusion of the 55–64 age cohort in lifelong learning in 2012

Notes: Participation in lifelong learning in percentages of the population aged 25–64.
Source: European Labour Force Survey (Eurostat 2012). Country abbreviations: EU = European Union, BE = Belgium, CZ = Czech Republic, DK = Denmark, DE = Germany, EE = Estonia, IE = Ireland, EL = Greece, ES = Spain, FR = France, IT = Italy, CY = Cyprus, LV = Latvia, LT = Lithuania, LU = Luxembourg, HU = Hungary, MT = Malta, NL = Netherlands, AT = Austria, PL = Poland, PT = Portugal, SI = Slovenia, SK = Slovakia, FI = Finland, SE = Sweden, UK = United Kingdom, IS = Iceland, NO = Norway, CH = Switzerland, FYROM = Former Yugoslav Republic of Macedonia, TR = Turkey.

in LLL is relatively high, there is a significant gap between overall participation and the participation in LLL of 55–64 year olds. Second, there is an obvious correlation between overall LLL participation and inclusion of 55–64 year olds. In countries with low overall participation, inclusion is also very low, while in countries with high overall LLL rates, inclusion of the older age cohorts is much higher.

Continuing vocational training in enterprises

The Continuing Vocational Training Survey (CVTS), which is carried out by Eurostat every five years, gives a unique insight into HRD in European enterprises with ten or more employees. The latest CVTS (CVTS4) refers to the year 2010, covers the 28 EU member states plus Norway and looks at learning and training provision during working-time or paid at least partially by the employer (Eurostat 2013a, 2013b). It reveals that in 2010, two thirds (66 per cent) of EU companies provided training to their employees, either through C-VET courses or other forms of training, compared with 60 per cent in 2005. The share of companies that trained their staff varied considerably between the countries, ranging from 23 per cent in Poland and 24 per cent in Romania to 87 per cent in Sweden and Austria.

Similar to previous years (Cedefop 2010a), enterprises generally preferred to provide training through C-VET courses (offered by external training providers or the enterprises themselves), rather than to use 'other forms of training' such as planned learning through job rotation, staff exchange, participation in learning or quality improvement groups, or self-directed learning. The use of other forms of training in European enterprises was rather stable between 1999 (EU-25 average 52 per cent), 2005 (EU-25 average 49 per cent) and 2010 (EU-27 average 53 per cent). This finding is interesting, especially taking into account that many researchers and policy makers have considered forms of non-formal and informal learning to be important or of an increasing importance in the future (European Commission 2000), arguing that 'traditional' forms of C-VET (i. e. courses) may increasingly be replaced by other forms of learning (see e.g. Bailey *et al.* 2004, Rohs 2002). This is not reflected in the CVTS results. When it comes to the forms of C-VET used and the proportion of 'traditional' and 'other' forms of training, there are, however, major differences between countries.

The CVTS4 shows that company size does not have a substantial impact on C-VET participation rates of employees, although the approach towards training might differ. In the EU-27, only a slightly higher proportion of employees in large enterprises (250 or more employees) participated in C-VET courses (49 per cent of employees), as compared with medium-sized (50–249 employees) and small companies (10–49 employees), which have participation rates of 45 and 46 per cent respectively (Eurostat 2013a, 2013b). However, the analysis of the previous CVTS (CVTS3) indicated that large enterprises have a much more formalized approach towards training than small ones (Cedefop 2010a).

Figure 44.3 combines two indicators of training intensity in EU countries based on CVTS4: the average hours of training per participant and the cost of training as a percentage of total labour cost. The average training cost in the EU is 0.8 per cent of total labour costs and the average duration of training is 25 hours. Overall, it appears that in countries in which enterprises spend more on training, average training duration is higher.

Although many studies show that C-VET has a positive impact on enterprise results such as productivity, profitability, competitiveness, innovative ability and job satisfaction of employees (e.g. Hansson *et al.* 2004, Bassanini 2004, De La Fuente and Ciccone 2003, Böheim and Schneeweis 2007, Cedefop 2012a), a substantial share of enterprises does not provide C-VET for their staff, i.e. do not use the potential that C-VET has to offer and waive possible returns. The

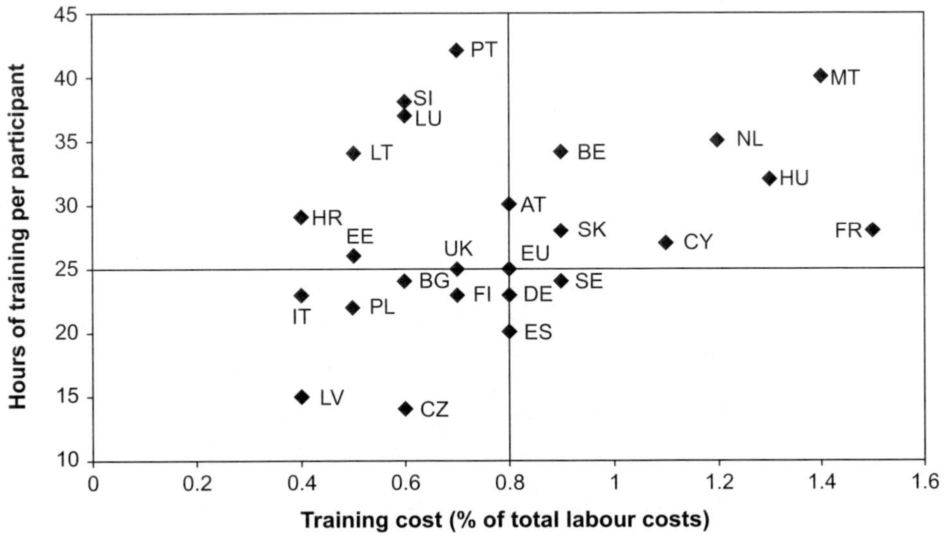

Figure 44.3 Average hours of training per participant and cost of training as a percentage of total labour cost of all enterprises in 2010

Source: CVTS4, see Eurostat (2013a). Country abbreviations: EU = European Union, BE = Belgium, BG = Bulgaria, CZ = Czech Republic, DE = Germany, EE = Estonia, ES = Spain, FR = France, IT = Italy, CY = Cyprus, LV = Latvia, LT = Lithuania, LU = Luxembourg, HU = Hungary, MT = Malta, NL = Netherlands, AT = Austria, PL = Poland, PT = Portugal, SI = Slovenia, SK = Slovakia, FI = Finland, SE = Sweden, UK = United Kingdom.

CVTS explores the reasons for not providing training, and reveals that training cost is not the main explanation, but comes only at the third place (Eurostat 2013b). The two main reasons that EU enterprises gave for not providing training were that there was no need for training, as "existing skills and competences matched current needs" (Eurostat 2013b), and that they "preferred to recruit individuals with the required skills and competencies" (ibid.). This should be a concern given the strong developments towards knowledge intensive economies and societies and the fact that shortages of personnel with specific skills and competences will be on the rise due to ageing populations in many European countries.

Core EU policies on adult learning and VET

The evidence on HRD patterns in Europe presented in the previous section shows that there are substantial differences between European countries and that countries with higher HRD investment also tend to be more inclusive towards people in the older age cohorts. In addition, a substantial share of enterprises in Europe does not provide C-VET to its staff. This indicates that in terms of lifelong learning and C-VET European countries are moving at different speeds and that there are several challenges, not only in terms of raising overall participation, but also in terms of ensuring that those with limited learning opportunities are included and in terms of using the full spectrum of learning provision. These concerns have been driving policy debates in adult learning and VET over the last decade.

Although adult learning has always been considered a vital component of lifelong learning and has thus been an integral part of the EU's lifelong learning policies since the very beginning, the European Commission has placed adult learning as such more explicitly on the political agenda since 2006. By adopting a Communication and an Action Plan on Adult Learning (European Commission 2006, 2007), it has called on the member states to promote adult learning. Building on this, a renewed European Agenda for Adult Learning defines the focus for European cooperation in adult learning policies for 2012–20 (Council of the European Union 2011). It emphasizes the key role of adult learning to the EU's economic and social development, and identifies the provision of learning opportunities for all adults, especially also for the disadvantaged groups (e.g. low-skilled), as a main challenge that has to be addressed in Europe with joint efforts of all EU member states. The policy priorities of the Agenda are listed below:

1. Making lifelong learning and mobility a reality.
2. Improving the quality and efficiency of education and training.
3. Promoting equity, social cohesion and active citizenship.
4. Enhancing the creativity and innovation of adults and their learning environments.
5. Improving the knowledge base on adult learning and monitoring the adult learning sector.

Policy priorities for VET highlight the cooperation between the EU's member states. In 2002, in Copenhagen, under the Lisbon strategy and as a parallel to the Bologna process for higher education, ministers responsible for VET in the EU, EEA-EFTA and candidate countries, the European Commission and social partners agreed on several common priorities. Since then, European countries have worked jointly on these priorities for VET in the 'Copenhagen process'. The core intentions were to improve lifelong learning opportunities and mobility between member states in a single European labour market. The process of coordination that followed has supported member state cooperation and has become a catalyst for modernizing VET systems across Europe (Cedefop 2012b).

The second phase of that process started in 2010 and supports the Europe 2020 agenda (European Commission 2010a). The Bruges communiqué in 2010 (Council of the European Union and European Commission 2010), in line with the Europe 2020 strategy and the policy priorities for VET, combines a long term perspective with short term measures. While the Bruges communiqué covers both initial VET and continuing VET, the focus in this chapter is on the latter. The long term perspective of the Bruges communiqué is reflected in its strategic objectives, which are listed below:

1. Making I-VET an attractive learning option.
2. Fostering the excellence, quality and relevance of both I-VET and C-VET.
3. Enabling flexible access to training and qualifications.
4. Developing a strategic approach to the internationalization of I-VET and C-VET and promoting international mobility.
5. Fostering innovation, creativity and entrepreneurship, as well as the use of ICT (in both I-VET and C-VET).
6. Realizing inclusive I-VET and C-VET.
7. Transversal objectives.

In addition to the strategic objectives, the Bruges communiqué features 22 short term deliverables. These are actions that countries have agreed to implement by 2014. The short term deliverables cover the whole spectrum of VET. Two of the 22 short term deliverables focus explicitly on lifelong learning and participation in C-VET: Participation in C-VET in line with the Education and Training 2020 15 per cent benchmark (#7), and Raising participation of low-skilled and other 'at-risk' groups in education and training (#17). By presenting an analysis of what countries have done to address these short term deliverables, the next part of this chapter gives a structured overview of recent trends in supporting participation in learning and improving access to it.

Recent trends in policies and practices in European countries

Given the diversity of skills and training systems, traditions and socio-economic contexts in European countries, it is a challenge to obtain a good understanding of what have been the most recent developments in policies and practices relating to adult learning and C-VET. A meaningful monitoring of progress towards the Bruges communiqué short term deliverables requires an approach that generates an overall impression of the types of actions the EU member states and other European countries have emphasized (Cedefop 2012b). After presenting the core elements of the approach to assess progress, we present the results of the monitoring for the two short term deliverables focused on lifelong learning and C-VET.

Approach

To assess progress towards short term deliverables, the European Centre for the Development of Vocational Training (Cedefop) developed an approach based on *policy options*. These policy options represent different ways a country can work towards achieving a short term deliverable. Working with policy options ensures some comparability across countries and at the same time addresses the issue that the short term deliverables specify broad aims, without going into the ways countries can achieve them (Cedefop 2012b). As many of the priorities agreed in Bruges are not new, the approach incorporates the possibility that some policy options could have been already in place before or in 2010, and recognizes that policies often develop dynamically.

For most of the 22 short term deliverables, several policy options were determined on the basis of a review of the most important policy documents at the EU level, literature analysis and consultation with the main stakeholders in VET. The policy options were the basis of a questionnaire distributed through Cedefop's ReferNet, which is a network of VET institutions in all EU member states and Norway and Iceland that delivers information on VET on a regular basis. The questionnaire that contained over 100 policy options relevant for one or more short term deliverables was completed by all ReferNet partners in 28 European Countries. It covered all EU member states except Ireland and Norway and Iceland, which have been part of the Copenhagen process from the outset. Five candidate countries (Croatia – still a candidate country at the time of the analysis, the Former Yugoslav Republic of Macedonia, Montenegro, Serbia and Turkey) were reviewed by the European Training Foundation (ETF) using the Cedefop questionnaire. Within EU member states, in some countries education and training policies are developed and implemented at regional levels. As no meaningful analysis is possible at the national level, the Flemish, French and German-speaking communities were analyzed separately for Belgium, as were England, Wales, Scotland and Northern Ireland for the UK.

Results

Fourteen policy options are relevant for the two Bruges communiqué short term deliverables closely related to lifelong learning and C-VET. By indicating the stage of development of these policy options, Figure 44.4 gives an overview of the state of play and recent trends in these fields in European countries (Cedefop 2012b). The policy options analyzed cover a wide range of

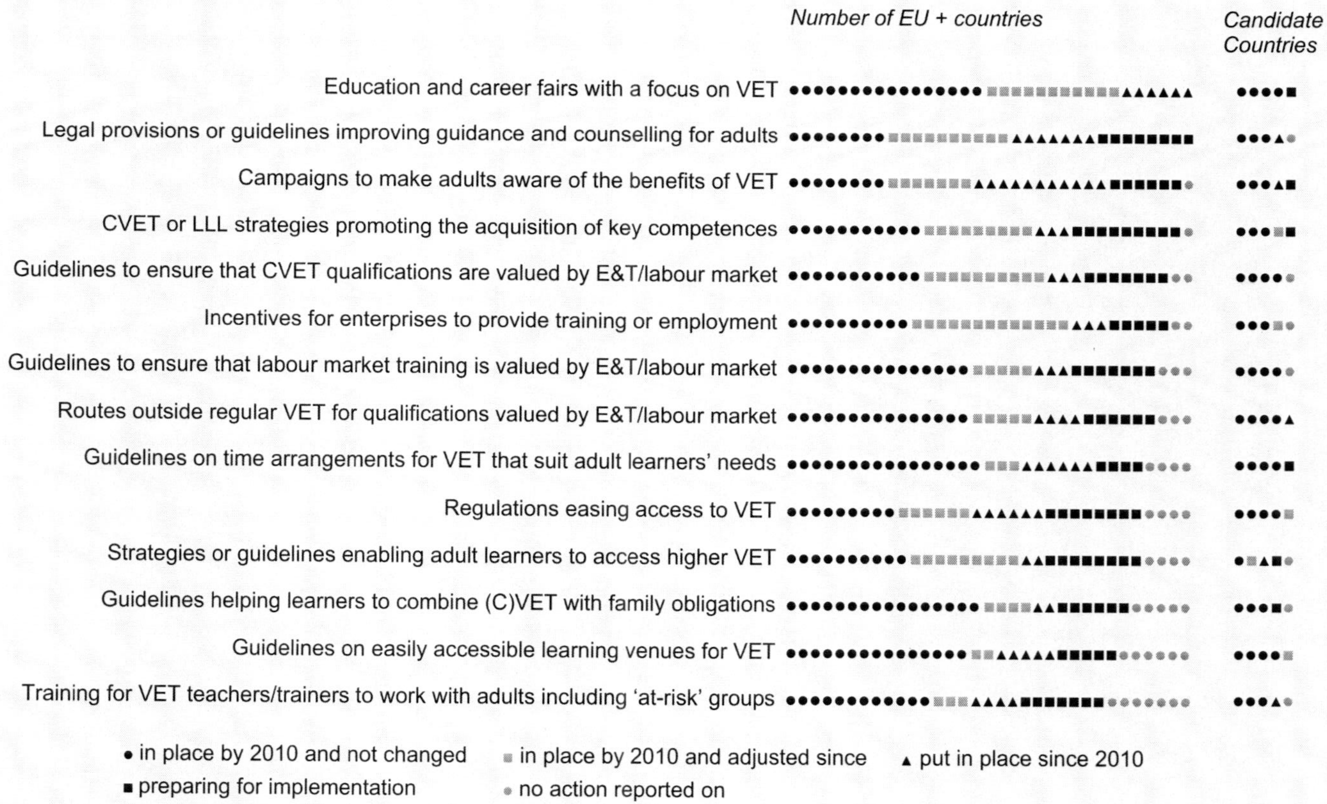

Figure 44.4 State of play and progress towards two short deliverables from the Bruges Communiqué

Notes: E&T = education and training; EU+ = EU Member states (excluding Ireland) and Norway and Iceland.
Source: Cedefop (2012b). Deliverables include participation in C-VET in line with ET 2020 15 per cent benchmark (#7) and raising participation of low-skilled and other 'at-risk' groups in education and training (#17).

possibilities to raise participation in C-VET and lifelong learning and to open up learning opportunities for adults. They include legislative/regulatory elements, strategies, promotion activities, incentives, and measures that facilitate adults in taking part in learning. Based on the replies to the questionnaire to ReferNet, for each policy option, Cedefop has characterized the stage of development as follows (Cedefop 2012b):

- in place before 2010 and not changed;
- in place before 2010 and adjusted since then (e.g. by expanding a measure);
- put in place since 2010;
- preparing for implementation (e.g. discussing, agreeing on, or piloting a measure);
- no action reported on.

Campaigns to make adults aware of the benefits of VET were in place in 2010 in about half of the countries. In 2012, education and career fairs to promote VET for adults existed in all countries and campaigns in most. C-VET or LLL strategies that promote the acquisition of key competences (which have a specific meaning in the EU context and according to the recommendation (European Parliament and Council 2006) comprise literacy and communication in mother tongue and (two) foreign languages, numeracy, basic competences in science and technology, digital skills as well as sense of initiative and entrepreneurship, cultural awareness, social and civic competences and learning to learn skills) are widespread. By 2010, 20 EU+ countries and four candidate countries already had such a strategy. Since then, three countries put a strategy in place and nine EU+ and one candidate country are preparing to do so. Good access to higher level VET helps adult learners further expand their skills and shape their careers. In 2010, 19 EU+ and two candidate countries already had strategies or guidelines in place that open up higher level VET for adult learners.

Stimulating participation in learning and training, legal provisions or guidelines to improve guidance and counseling for adults were in place in 18 EU+ and three candidate countries in 2010. Of these, more than half took action to change or complement existing initiatives.

Incentives for enterprises to provide training or employment evolve dynamically: 13 EU+ countries and one candidate country have made adjustments to measures already in place by 2010. Several measures have also been taken to facilitate adults to take part in learning and training. Since 2010, six EU+ countries have introduced guidelines on time arrangements to suit adult learner needs. Guidelines on accessible learning venues for VET were in place by 2012 in 22 countries while five were preparing to implement such guidelines.

Supporting inclusion in learning and training is on the agenda of many European countries. It is the aim of 24 EU+ and the five candidate countries to stimulate the participation of low-skilled and other at-risk groups through routes to qualification outside regular VET that are valued by education and training and on the labour market. In addition, since 2010, four EU+ countries and one candidate country introduced training for VET staff to work with adults and at-risk groups, and seven countries are preparing for this.

Considering the trends over the last years, one of the key messages is that despite significant progress, there is still work to be done in the coming years. For several policy options in Figure 44.4, several countries are still in the preparation phase. This is the case in particular for legal provisions or guidelines improving guidance for adults, regulations easing access to VET, and C-VET or lifelong learning strategies promoting the acquisition of key competences. Other priorities should be to make learning venues more accessible and to help VET teachers and trainers to work with adults and at-risk groups. These are areas for which several countries have not reported any action.

Conclusion

HRD does not only play a crucial role in making Europe more competitive and innovative, but also for making it more inclusive for groups with low participation in lifelong learning. In a unique way, the EU works together with its member states on improving HRD in Europe, and supports the further development of lifelong learning and of VET systems and practices. This chapter has provided an overview of the innovation potential of learning and the learning landscape in Europe. Exploring the common priorities in this field in Europe and presenting an analysis of recent developments, the chapter has shown that some progress has been made over the last years. Looking at the developments in the different countries, it becomes however evident that there is a need for further action in order to tap the full potential that HRD has to offer to individuals, enterprises and societies, and last but not least to Europe as a whole. Based on our analysis of key issues and the monitoring of progress, some directions for further action can be identified.

A lack of progress in VET and adult learning negatively affects Europe's innovative capacity. The crucial role that learning – in a broad sense – plays for innovation is not fully acknowledged. Stronger links between VET, HRD and innovation policies should be forged to better make use of the synergies between learning and innovation. Important tools in this respect are for example innovation programmes with a strong focus on work organization and workplace learning in enterprises. These should not only aim at immediate effects, but also include elements that increase awareness among political and industrial decision makers, industrial and trade associations and other stakeholders of the importance of learning-intensive forms of work organization and workplace learning for innovation. Especially in those countries where such awareness appears less well developed, accompanying measures (e.g. conferences) and the active involvement of the social partners and other stakeholders are crucial. Fostering learning-conducive work environments and expanding learning opportunities at the workplace could also have a positive effect on the learning of vulnerable groups and compensate at least to some extent their lower participation in formal and informal learning. Research shows that learning at the workplace, while working, seems to offer particular potential for ageing workers (Barabasch *et al.* 2012), and for the low-skilled (Cedefop 2013).

Recent developments show that supporting and encouraging investments in HRD are on the agenda across the continent, but more action is needed. Issues of concern are for example the inclusion of particular groups without sufficient opportunities to access training and learning. Measures to expand access to skills development and raise learning participation include for example the use of the full spectrum of learning options (amongst them workplace learning), adapting training and learning better to the needs of learners and expanding the offer of high quality career guidance and counseling services that help people to make learning and career choices.

EU policies on lifelong learning and VET and cooperation between European countries have made a difference, but a key challenge for the coming years is to keep up the momentum. Many actions taken in recent years are still in the preparation phase. In the current economic crisis and with increasing pressure on public finances, it is a challenge to implement initiatives so that they can help expanding Europe's skill base.

References

Bailey, T.R., Hughes, K.L. and Moore, D.T. (2004) *Working Knowledge: Work-Based Learning and Education Reform*, London: RoutledgeFalmer.

Barabasch, A., Dehmel, A. and Van Loo, J. (2012) 'Introduction: the value of investing in an ageing workforce', in Cedefop (ed.) *Working and Ageing: The Benefits of Investing in an Ageing Workforce*, Luxembourg: Publications Office of the European Union.

Bassanini, A. (2004) 'Improving skills for more and better jobs: does training make a difference?', in OECD (ed.) *Employment Outlook 2004*, Paris: Organisation for Economic Co-operation and Development.

BMBF (2007) *Arbeiten – Lernen – Kompetenzen Entwickeln. Innovationsfähigkeit in einer Modernen Arbeitswelt*, Berlin: BMBF. Online. Available HTTP: http://pt-ad.pt-dlr.de/_media/Broschuere_Arbeiten-Lernen-Kompetenzen-entwickeln. (accessed 1 December 2013).

Böheim, R. and Schneeweis, N. (2007) 'Renditen betrieblicher Weiterbildung in Österreich', in Kammer für Arbeiter und Angestellte für Wien (ed.) *Materialien zu Wirtschaft und Gesellschaft no 103*, Vienna: Abteilung Wirtschaftswissenschaft und Statistik der Kammer für Arbeiter und Angestellte für Wien.

Cedefop (2008) *Terminology of European Education and Training Policy: A Selection of 100 Key Terms*, Luxembourg: Publications Office of the European Union. Online. Available HTTP: http: //www.cedefop.europa.eu/EN/Files/4064_en. (accessed 15 December 2013).

Cedefop (2010a) *Employer-Provided Vocational Training in Europe: Evaluation and Interpretation of the Third Continuing Vocational Training Survey*, Luxembourg: Publications Office of the European Union. Online. Available HTTP: http://www.cedefop.europa.eu/EN/Files/5502_en. (accessed 30 November 2013).

Cedefop (2010b) *The Skill Matching Challenge: Analysing Skill Mismatch and Policy Implications*, Luxembourg: Publications Office of the European Union. Online. Available HTTP: http://www.cedefop.europa.eu/EN/Files/3056_en. (accessed 18 October 2013).

Cedefop (2012a) *Learning and Innovation in Enterprises*, Luxembourg: Publications Office of the European Union. Online. Available HTTP: http://www.cedefop.europa.eu/EN/Files/5527_en. (accessed 20 July 2013).

Cedefop (2012b) *Trends in VET Policy in Europe 2010–12: Progress towards the Bruges Communiqué*, Luxembourg: Publications Office of the European Union. Online. Available HTTP: http://www.cedefop.europa.eu/EN/Files/6116_en. (accessed 17 October 2013).

Cedefop (2012c) *Preventing Skill Obsolescence: Rapid Labour Market Changes Leave Too Many Workers at Risk of Losing Their Skills*, Luxembourg: Publications Office of the European Union. Online. Available HTTP: http://www.cedefop.europa.eu/EN/Files/9070_en. (accessed 10 December 2013).

Cedefop (2012d) *Working and Ageing: The Benefits of Investing in an Ageing Workforce*, Luxembourg: Publications Office of the European Union. Online. Available HTTP: http://www.cedefop.europa.eu/EN/Files/3064_en. (accessed 3 November 2013).

Cedefop (2013) *Return to Work: Work-Based Learning and the Reintegration of Unemployed Adults into the Labour Market*, Luxembourg: Publications Office of the European Union. Online. Available HTTP: http://www.cedefop.europa.eu/EN/Files/6121_en. (accessed 27 September 2013).

Council of the European Union (2009) 'Council conclusions – a strategic framework for European cooperation in education and training ("ET 2020")', *Official Journal of the European Union*, C 119, 28 May 2009.

Council of the European Union (2011) 'Council Resolution on a renewed European agenda for adult learning', *Official Journal of the European Union*, C 372, 20 December 2011. Online. Available HTPP: http://register.consilium.europa.eu/pdf/en/11/st16/st16743.en11. (accessed 21 September 2013).

Council of the European Union and European Commission (2010) *The Bruges Communiqué on Enhanced European Cooperation in Vocational Education and Training for the Period 2011–2020*. Online. Available HTTP: http://ec.europa.eu/education/lifelong-learning-policy/doc/vocational/bruges_en. (accessed 24 November 2013).

Dehmel, A. (2014) 'Die EU auf dem Weg zur "Innovationsunion": Berufliche Bildung als Schlüsselfaktor', in Jostmeier, M., Georg, A. and Jacobsen, H. (eds) *Sozialen Wandel Gestalten. Zum Gesellschaftlichen Innovationspotenzial von Arbeits- und Organisationsforschung*, Wiesbaden: Springer.

De La Fuente, A. and Ciccone, A. (2003) *Human Capital in a Global and Knowledge-Based Economy, Final Report*, Luxembourg: Publications Office of the European Union. Online. Available HTTP: http://www.antoniociccone.eu/wp-content/uploads/2007/07/humancapitalpolicy. (accessed 17 October 2013).

Eraut, M. and Hirsh, W. (2007) *The Significance of Workplace Learning for Individuals, Groups and Organizations*, Oxford: SKOPE. Online. Available HTTP: http://www.skope.ox.ac.uk/sites/default/files/Monogrpah%209.pdf (accessed 2 September 2013).

Ertl, H. (2006) 'European Union policies in education and training: the Lisbon agenda as a turning point?', *Comparative Education* 42: 1, 5–27.

Eurofound (2007) *Fourth European Working Conditions Survey*, Luxembourg: Publications Office of the European Union. Online. Available HTTP: http://www.eurofound.europa.eu/pubdocs/2006/98/en/2/ef0698en. (accessed 14 October 2013).

European Commission (2000) *A Memorandum on Lifelong Learning*, Brussels: European Commission. Online. Available HTTP: http://www.bologna-berlin2003.de/pdf/MemorandumEng. (accessed 15 November 2013).

European Commission (2006) *Adult Learning: It Is Never Too Late to Learn*, Brussels: European Commission. Online. Available HTTP: http://eur-lex.europa.eu/LexUriServ/site/en/com/2006/com2006_0614 en01. (accessed 15 November 2013).

European Commission (2007) *Action Plan on Adult Learning: It Is Always a Good Time to Learn*. Online. Available HTTP: http://eur-lex.europa.eu/legal-content/EN/TXT/PDF/?uri=CELEX:52007DC0558&from=EN (accessed 15 November 2013).

European Commission (2010a) Europe 2020: *A Strategy for Smart, Sustainable and Inclusive Growth*. Online. Available HTTP: http://eur-lex.europa.eu/LexUriServ/LexUriServ.do?uri=COM: 2010: 2020: FIN: EN: PDF (accessed 15 November 2013).

European Commission (2010b) *Europe 2020 Flagship Initiative Innovation Union: Communication from the Commission to the European Parliament, the Council, the European Economic and Social Committee and the Committee of the Regions*. Online. Available HTTP: http://ec.europa.eu/research/innovation-union/pdf/innovation-union-communication-brochure_en. (accessed 2 October 2013).

European Commission (2013) *Innovation Union Scoreboard 2013*. Online. Available HTTP: http://ec.europa.eu/enterprise/policies/innovation/files/ius-2013_en. (accessed 15 October 2013).

European Parliament and Council (2006) *Recommendation of the European Parliament and of the Council of 18 December 2006 on Key Competences for Lifelong Learning*, *Official Journal of the European Union*, L 394, 30 December 2006. Online. Available HTTP: http://eur-lex.europa.eu/LexUriServ/LexUriServ.do?uri=OJ: L: 2006: 394: 0010: 0018: EN: PDF (accessed 15 November 2013).

Eurostat (2006) *The 3rd Continuing Vocational Training Survey (CVTS3): European Union Manual*, Luxembourg: European Commission. Online. Available HTTP: http://www.cedefop.europa.eu/EN/Files/3d_Continuing_Vocational_Training_Survey_Manual.pdf (accessed 15 October 2013).

Eurostat (2012) *European Union Labour Force Survey*. Online. Available HTTP: http://epp.eurostat.ec.europa.eu/portal/page/portal/microdata/lfs (accessed 16 September 2013).

Eurostat (2013a) *Continuing Vocational Training: Two Thirds of Enterprises in the EU27 Provided Vocational Training in 2010*, Luxembourg: Eurostat. Online. Available HTTP: http://epp.eurostat.ec.europa.eu/cache/ITY_PUBLIC/3-11062013-AP/EN/3-11062013-AP-EN.PDF (accessed 2 December 2013).

Eurostat (2013b) *Continuing Vocational Training Statistics*. Online. Available HTTP: http://epp.eurostat.ec.europa.eu/statistics_explained/index.php/Continuing_vocational_training_statistics (accessed 14 December 2013).

Eurostat (2013c) *Lifelong Learning Statistics*. Online. Available HTTP: http://epp.eurostat.ec.europa.eu/statistics_explained/index.php/Lifelong_learning_statistics (accessed 14 December 2013).

Hansson, B., Johanson, U. and Leitner, K. (2004) 'The impact of human capital and human capital investments on company performance: Evidence from literature and European survey results', in Descy, P. and Tessaring, M. (eds) *Impact of Education and Training: Third Report on Vocational Training Research in Europe, Background Report*, Luxembourg: Publications Office of the European Union. Online. Available HTTP: http://www.cedefop.europa.eu/EN/Files/BgR3_Hansson. (accessed 12 October 2013).

Hirsh, W. (2006) *Improving Performance through Appraisal Dialogues*, London: Corporate Research Forum.

Lorenz, E. and Valeyre, A. (2005) 'Organizational innovation, HRM and labour market structure: a comparison of the EU 15', *Journal of Industrial Relations* 47, 4: 424–42.

Lorenz, E.H. and Lundvall, B.Å. (eds) (2006) *How Europe's Economies Learn: Coordinating Competing Models*, Oxford: Oxford University Press.

MERIT (2006) *European Innovation Index 2006: Comparative Analysis of Innovation Performance*, Maastricht: Maastricht Economic Research Institute on Innovation and Technology (MERIT) and the Joint Research Centre of the European Commission. Online. Available HTTP: http://www.madrimasd.org/Queesmadrimasd/Indicadores/Documentos/EuropeanInnovationScoreboard2006final.pdf (accessed 1 December 2013).

OECD (2010) *Innovative Workplaces: Making Better Use of Skills within Organizations*, Paris: OECD.

PRO INNO Europe (2012) *Innovation Union Scoreboard 2011: The Innovation Union's Performance Scoreboard for Research and Innovation*. Online. Available HTTP: http://www.proinno-europe.eu/sites/default/files/page/12/02/IUS_2011_final. (accessed 2 December 2013).

Rohs, M. (ed.) (2002) *Arbeitsprozessintegriertes Lernen: Neue Ansätze für Berufliche Bildung*, Münster: Waxmann.

Steiber, A. and Alänge, S. (2013) *Diffusion of Organizational Innovations: Learning from Selected Programmes*, Stockholm: Vinnova. Online. Available HTTP: http://www.vinnova.se/upload/EPiStorePDF/vr_13_07. (accessed 17 December 2013).

SECTION IX

Emerging topics and future trends

45

LINE MANAGERS AND HRD

David McGuire and Heather C. Kissack

In an age characterized by economic decline, environmental turbulence, redundancies and job and organizational instability, corporations are increasingly looking for ways to rationalize and streamline their systems and processes. Pressure has been placed on the Human Resource (HR) function to deliver more effective and cost-efficient solutions and both direct and develop organizational resources towards achieving greater strategic capabilities in an increasingly competitive market. This has led to the reorganization of the HR function and the reallocation of many operational HR responsibilities to line managers (Gilbert *et al.* 2011). Uniquely positioned on the organizational frontline, these managers have become the lynchpin through which HR solutions are channeled in the organization (Den Hartog *et al.* 2004). Such a dramatic transformation of the line manager's role however has raised important questions regarding whether or not, and how, these individuals are being prepared for these new enhanced responsibilities and whether they are becoming overloaded in their day-to-day role (Nehles *et al.* 2008). It has also posed important challenges for the HR function regarding the identity of HRD across the organization and whether the HR function is effectively responding to rapid changes in the external environment.

This chapter examines changes to the role of line managers in organizations, seeking to expose the tensions facing them in the exercise of their role. It proposes a theoretical model through which to explore environmental forces affecting line managers at the global, organizational and departmental levels. Such forces have repositioned the line manager role within organizations, restructuring and reshaping the nature of their HRD responsibilities.

A model of line manager HRD responsibilities

The role and responsibilities of line managers have changed radically in the last decade. Line managers are defined by Nehles *et al.* (2006: 257) as "the lowest managers at the operational level, who direct a team of employees on a day-to-day basis and are responsible for performing HR activities." Often promoted on the basis of their individual performance and contribution as employees, rather than demonstration of effective management and interpersonal skills, line managers have become "mini-general managers" charged with both production and staff responsibilities (Busch and Dooley 2011; Hales 2005).

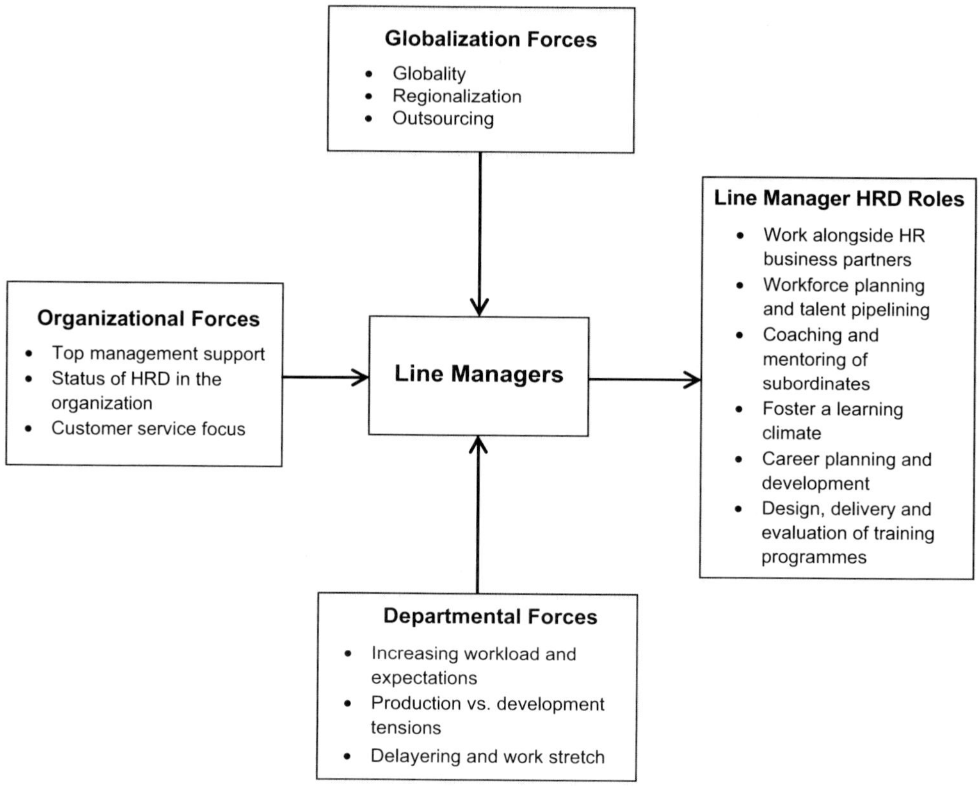

Figure 45.1 Environmental forces affecting line manager HRD roles

The model in Figure 45.1 depicts the environmental forces affecting line managers and how these impact specifically and have shaped line manager HRD roles and responsibilities. The remaining sections of this chapter will explore each of the constituent components of the model.

Globalization forces

Globalization is altering the way in which organizations operate and the nature and shape of HRD delivery. As organizations trade and compete cross-culturally, due to the removal of trade barriers and the increased potency of e-commerce, HRD has become a critical tool in helping employees learn new skills, cultures, languages and outlooks to perform effectively in a global environment (Hurn 2007). Sirkin *et al.* (2008: 1) coin the term globality to represent the "global reality in which we'll all be competing with everyone, from everywhere, for everything." Through globalization, work is increasingly completed cross-nationally mediated through technology and has become more uncertain, varied and complex. Such a dynamic changing environment requires organizations to act quickly and flexibly ensuring that they have appropriate systems, people and capabilities to adapt to environmental changes. Line managers are thus directly affected by globalization as it can alter dramatically work processes, people and systems. Through teleconferencing, e-mail and work division and specialization (Friedman 2006), line managers are interfacing with colleagues across the globe, working on specialist projects according to their unique core capabilities and reference knowledge. For this reason, Easterby-Smith *et al.* (1998) argue that learning is the most significant factor in the success of today's organizations – albeit in this case, the learning occurs cross-culturally. Similarly, Lee (2010) argues that organizations need to develop capacity for worldwide knowledge transfer to support transnational organizational learning.

Regionalization has become a key priority for many firms, with global markets divided into regional blocs such as EMEA – Europe, Middle East and Africa; the Americas and Asia Pacific. As Jackson *et al.* (2003) point out, a regionalization strategy enables organizations to identify customers' needs accurately and respond to local conditions. This approach also supports organizations in responding to language, cultural and ethnic differences and develops localized skillsets and competencies (Ghemawat 2008). Far from responding to converging or diverging forces, Mayrhofer *et al.* (2004) argue that many organizations are adopting a hybrid model towards operating in a European context. Such a model acknowledges a converging market, technological and institutional context, while recognizing diverging societal norms and values. This hybrid model acknowledges the complexity of businesses working in a European context. For line managers, the implications of regionalization may involve the increased use of e-learning; the rolling out of standardized training and development packages; the need to build cross-cultural teams and understand local cultural values and norms. Line managers are therefore required to be culturally competent, defined by Selvarajah (2006) as a learnt activity about a specific culture and the application of cultural knowledge in sensitive, creative and meaningful ways to individuals from diverse backgrounds.

A further globalization trend has been an increase in the use of outsourcing by organizations. Organizations are looking to reduce costs through restructuring their operations and delivering services through use of external providers. Not only is the HRD function not immune from outsourcing, but several researchers have identified outsourcing as a key trend affecting the future of HR (Adler 2003; Gurchiek 2005). Chaudhuri (2009) maintains that the outsourcing of the HRD function can have long-term disastrous consequences for organizations as it inhibits the development of future skills and competencies. As well as affecting the perceived importance of HRD, she argues that it can distance the HRD function from employees and erode trust and confidence. A newer form of outsourcing relates to the increasing use of development networks to deliver learning and development solutions. Bottrup (2005) argues that development networks support organizational learning and change through dissemination of knowledge and expertise across participating organizations in the network. Such networks offer members access to a wider knowledge base and informal learning opportunities through participation with other participating organizations. Going forward, line managers will thus have to liaise with a range of training providers to access development interventions; many of whom may have limited understanding of internal business operations.

Organizational forces

Gaining top management support is crucial in ensuring that HRD is valued in organizations. As Kirby *et al.* (2003: 32) put it, "learning in the workplace can only be successful if there is a commitment from employers." However, far too often, employees are regarded by organizations as costs, with HRD being viewed as an expensive, unnecessary luxury (Bassi and McMurrer 2007). In this regard, Garavan (2007) argues that the integrity and credibility of HR professionals and the HRD function are critical to ensuring that it is accepted within organizations and part of the "dominant coalition" driving change and strategic decision-making. Not only must top managers support the provision of HRD across the organization, they need to display an active commitment to new HRD delivery structures and to fostering a HRD culture across the organization.

Such top management support will empower line managers to more fully engage with and accept responsibility for HRD.

How HRD is perceived and viewed in an organization is critical to the respect and status it receives within the organization. In recessionary times, research indicates that many organizations are reducing investment in HRD activities or eliminating such investments entirely (Baird *et al.* 2011). Such actions increase pressure upon line managers to ensure employees are adequately skilled to perform their roles competently and effectively. Bing et al. (2003: 344) argue that HRD must be seen as consistently "ahead of the game" in order to be accepted as strategically relevant and capable of adding value. However, according to Visitchaichan (2010), the increasingly pressurized nature of the line manager role means that short-term business deliverables are often prioritized at the expense of value added strategic contributions. He argues that HR systems are often developed from a bottom-up ad-hoc basis, and therefore lack alignment with strategic objectives and priorities.

Line managers are increasingly required to implement a strong customer service ethic across their departments and the organization in general. Hamel and Prahalad (1994: 290) have long argued that managers have long been allowed to "to design their own jobs, fix their own processes, and do whatever it takes to satisfy a customer." Such increased level of autonomy and discretion in satisfying customer needs may have been sacrificed in this recessionary age of low profit margin and intense competition. That being said, line managers are being asked to work as coaches, mentors, role models and talent scouts in encouraging frontline employees to exhibit the highest standards of customer service behavior (Stahl *et al.* 2012).

Departmental forces

Line managers are increasingly being asked to achieve higher targets and take on greater responsibility with less access to resources. Key to the effectiveness of line managers is their desire to perform HRD roles as well as their skills to effectively discharge these responsibilities. In this regard, Purcell and Hutchinson (2007) argue that line managers need preparation, development and support from the HR function to undertake HRD activities with frontline employees. However, in many cases, line managers do not receive such training and MacNeil (2003) cautions against line managers learning their HR role experientially and advocates the provision of guidance, support and feedback from senior management and HR itself. Additionally, line managers need to be rewarded for engaging with HR issues. The lack of reward for line managers in delivering effective HR solutions is seen as problematic when positioned against business pressures and demands for which they are specifically rewarded and measured against (Hunter and Renwick 2009). Thus, in order for HR to be delivered effectively by line managers, senior management needs to recognize individual line managers who achieve HR targets.

The pressure for line managers to achieve higher targets and take on greater responsibility promulgates a greater priority on production initiatives than on development initiatives (Heraty and Morley 1995). In today's fast paced, global market with production occurring at a rapid rate, line managers turn their focus on immediate needs and concerns on a day-to-day basis rather than long-term developmental initiatives. Line managers' training and development activities are, thus, concerned with short-term objectives aimed at improving efficiency to meet production goals rather than with strategic, long-term development. Indeed, production and development goals often appear at odds with each other and competing against each other for time and focus. Lack of involvement in policy and planning activities (Heraty 1992), distrust between line managers and training and development specialists (Garavan *et al.* 1993), and a lack of HRD training (MacNeil 2003) further divide line managers' attention to short-term, production initiatives.

Delayering and increasing workloads are placing additional strain on line managers as they struggle to deliver upon operational targets and assume supplementary HR duties with fewer employees under their control. Zavyalova and Kosheleva (2009) comment that line managers are now performing their duties in an unfavorable environment for their growth and development as growing administrative duties affect their ability to deliver effective operational results. In a difficult recessionary climate, as Thornhill *et al.* (1997) argue, line managers need to be able to deal with difficult situations arising out of delayering, downsizing, and redundancies. They argue that the way in which employees who are being made redundant are treated will affect their perception of the organization as well as the resulting level of commitment of survivors to the organization. The authors argue that line managers will suffer high levels of stress in redundancy situations and will require support from colleagues, senior managers and perhaps, specialist counsellors.

The HRD roles of line managers

The model describes six specific HRD roles that should be devolved to line managers. This reshaping of their role firmly fixes line managers with responsibility for operational HR delivery as well as giving them a "linking" role, obliging them to work with business partners and the HR function to achieve organizational level goals – such as the creation of positive learning climate or contributing to succession planning and talent management approaches. Indeed, Harney and Jordan (2008) posit that line managers act as critical intermediaries in shaping the actual form of HR practices and ultimately determining the performance of specific departments and business units. The following subsections describe each of these roles and the wider implications for line managers.

Work alongside HR business partners

While the restructuring of the HR function following Ulrich and Brockbank's (2005) framework has devolved greater responsibility for HR to line managers and built closer relationships between line managers and the HR function through the activities of business partners, research has pointed to considerable tension among line managers in accepting the legitimacy of the business partner role (Higgins and Zhang 2008; Nickson *et al.* 2008). Indeed, many line managers see the actions of business partners as little more than an unwarranted imposition and interference with the authority and autonomy of line managers. Caldwell and Storey (2007) find that business partnering roles for HR staff can be complex, ambiguous and confusing – leading to conflict and disharmony for line managers. To this end, Visitchaichan (2010) advocates a reprioritization of HR at all levels of the organization. He maintains that line managers and HR business partners need to recognize and respect each other's skills and needs for mutual learning and jointly work to identify problems and solutions.

Workforce planning and talent pipelining

Finding, attracting, developing and retaining the best talent has become an important goal for most organizations. Kollasch (2009) argues that line managers have an important role in talent management in identifying future leaders as well as assessing skills gaps and development needs. Devolving issues related to talent management to line managers can be problematic as line managers may lack knowledge of how talent management interventions align with other HR policies and the degree to which the focus should be on internal or external talent (Harris and Foster

2010). Moreover, to be done effectively, line managers need to understand the organization's strategic priorities as well as being guided by the HR function and business partners in relation to future talent needs and areas for growth. To this end, Kesler (2002) argues that line managers need to own the outcomes of talent development, while the HR function safeguards and controls the overall process. As such, line managers have a critical role in talent pipelining and making sure that future development needs are identified and fulfilled. They need to ensure that opportunities for development are made available equitably across the team and that individual aspirations are understood and supported as far as possible.

Coaching and mentoring of subordinates

Coaching and mentoring of frontline employees is critical to ensuring optimal organizational performance. Line managers act as role models as well as valuable guides to employees on organizational processes, systems and standards. As well as coaches and mentors, Beattie (2006) views line managers as being an important source of technical and interpersonal information needed by employees and subordinates to perform well in their jobs. In this way, supervisors can play an important socialization role, helping employees adjust to new surroundings and giving them regular feedback on their performance (Reio and Callahan 2004). Park *et al.* (2008) go further and suggest that if line managers perform their coaching role well, this can lead to a genuine and lasting desire to learn for employees and as such, line managers must acquire adequate coaching skills to encourage growth and development through their everyday interactions with employees. However, Beattie *et al.* (2009) argue that to date, there has been limited development of line managers to enable them to engage effectively with their newly acquired mentoring and coaching roles. They argue that the HR function needs to play a stronger role as "guardian" of developmental practices and roles in ensuring that line managers are suitably equipped with the knowledge, skills and outlook to carry out their roles in a competent professional manner.

Foster a learning climate

Developing a positive engaging learning climate is a crucial task for line managers. MacNeil (2003) argues that line managers need to communicate a positive learning attitude and communicate and set expectations among team members. She argues that fostering a learning climate will also depend upon the organization's culture, values and priorities. Line managers must also provide practical support to employees in developing a learning climate within their department. Sambrook and Stewart (2000) maintain that line managers need to ensure employees have adequate time and space to pursue learning in line with their other responsibilities. This provision will ensure that employees develop a strong, lifelong commitment to their own professional development, which will enhance their own and the organization's productivity. Tseng and McLean (2008) argue that line managers play an important role in providing valuable advice, direction and counselling to subordinates, helping improve the effectiveness of organizational learning.

Career planning and development

In an age when employees are expected to take greater levels of responsibility for their own career development, line managers are expected to support staff ambitions through appropriate career planning and development. Yarnall (1998) argues that in engaging in career planning, line managers can sometimes face an inherent conflict in acting as both boss and career coach. For such arrangements to work, a high degree of trust and understanding is required between the employee and line manager. However, as Knies (2011) points out, line managers can provide both structural and instrumental assistance to employees which can help them progress their careers. However, according to Renwick and MacNeil (2002), a number of important issues have arisen regarding the involvement of line managers in employee career development. First, they argue that how line managers develop themselves in HR work and how they update their HR knowledge and skills are not fully understood. Second, they question whether line managers see their involvement in the career development of their staff as career-enhancing or career-inhibiting. Finally, they suggest that the precise nature of the line manager's role in today's turbulent economic environment needs clarification.

Design, delivery and evaluation of training programs

A key role of line managers within the new HR arrangements is the delivery of operational training and development. Heraty and Morley (1995) argue line managers need to be involved in the identification of training needs, deciding who should be trained and the undertaking of the training itself. For their part, Ellinger *et al.* (1999) argue that line managers have an important educative role in the workplace and are charged with teaching and training employees in positive organizational behaviors. However, they caution that adopting a training role has the potential to alter the relationship between line managers and their subordinates as well as possibly exposing their lack of technical expertise, knowledge and skills as trainers. The reallocation of training responsibilities from trainers to line managers has meant that line managers are now seen as mentors and facilitators who direct employees towards the best and most timely training solutions available (Zavyalova and Kosheleva 2009; Hutchinson and Purcell 2007; Sadler-Smith *et al.* 2000). Indeed, the nature of training is changing with much training now being delivered through e-learning or distance learning, rather than by face-to-face delivery (Garavan *et al.* 2002; Hallier and Butts 2000). Trainers are becoming increasingly separated from operational training delivery and have less presence across the business, as they are being tasked with formulating HRD strategy and supporting the design of distance learning programs (Raidén and Dainty 2006).

Conclusion

Line managers operate in an increasingly complex organizational environment. A range of globalization, organizational and departmental forces affect how line managers perform their duties in the workplace. Starved of resources, line managers have to work cross-nationally with a range of global and regional teams in a dynamic fast-changing business environment. Outsourcing is a contemporary reality in modern organizations and line managers are asked to interface with a number of automated self-service HR systems as well as external stakeholders and consultants in order to deliver upon devolved HRD responsibilities. Far from simply delivering upon production and operational targets, line managers are a critical lynchpin in delivering HRD at the organizational coalface. Line managers are being asked to create and maintain a positive customer service culture through acting as coaches, mentors and talent scouts to frontline employees. At a local level, line managers are asked to engage in career planning and development as well as designing and delivering operational training programs.

With seismic changes taking place to line manager roles and responsibilities, a substantial research agenda has emerged which seeks to understand the pressures, tensions and anxieties of line managers as well as exploring how line managers are coping with wide scale changes affecting the organizations they serve. Research questions to be considered could include:

- To what degree do line managers receive formal training regarding their HR responsibilities? What informal mechanisms do line managers employ to learn about their HR duties? To what degree can line managers access informal networks to receive advice and guidance on HR-related issues?
- With the intensification of the line manager role, how well are such managers coping with their new responsibilities? What mechanisms have line managers employed to resist HR devolution?
- In light of increasing devolution of HR responsibilities, how are HR business partners and the HR function viewed within organizations?
- How much autonomy and discretion is provided to line managers in HR program delivery and in the performance of their other responsibilities?
- What tensions have arisen from the introduction of automated self-service HR systems and have such systems assisted or hindered line managers in the performance of their duties?
- How well are line managers negotiating the plethora of workplace relationships in which they must engage (HR function, Virtual Teams, Outsourced Providers, External Consultants etc.)?

In conclusion, the role and responsibilities of line managers have changed beyond recognition in recent years. This development of the line manager role has undoubtedly led to tensions in how line managers can effectively deal with heavier workloads and how line managers can be upskilled to confidently perform their HRD responsibilities. Indeed, recent research has focused on the HR stressors affecting line managers with the authors concluding that appropriate support and training needs to be provided to ensure that line managers are well-equipped to discharge their new roles (Gilbert *et al.* 2011). Much work remains to be done to ensure that the status of HRD does not suffer at the hands of inexperienced line managers and lower workplace visibility of HRD staff.

References

Adler, P.S. (2003) Making the HR outsourcing decision. *Sloan Management Review* 45(1): 53–60.

Baird, M., Charlesworth, S., Cooper, R. and Heron, A. (2011) *Women, Work and the Global Economic Downturn.* Report produced for Department of Families, Housing, Community Services and Indigenous Affairs. Canberra: Australian Government.

Bassi, L. and McMurrer, D. (2007) Maximizing your return on people. *Harvard Business Review* 85(3): 115–23.

Beattie, R. (2006) Line managers and workplace learning: Learning from the voluntary sector. *Human Resource Development International* 9(1): 99–119.

Beattie, R.S., Hamlin, R.G., Ellinger, A.D. and Sage, L. (2009) *Leadership and Management: Mentoring and Coaching – Confusion, Conflict, Clarity . . . Does it Matter?* Paper presented at the Academy of Human Resource Development Conference in the Americas, held in Washington, DC, February 18–22.

Bing, J.W., Kehrhahn, M. and Short, D.C. (2003) Challenges to the field of human resource development. *Advances in Developing Human Resources* 5(3): 342–51.

Bottrup, P. (2005) Learning in a network: A "third way" between school learning and workplace learning? *Journal of Workplace Learning* 17(7): 508–20.

Busch, T.K. and Dooley, L.M. (2011) *Building a Competency Model for Business-to-Business Front-Line: Sales Managers in For-Profit Organizations.* Paper presented at the Academy of Human Resource Development Conference in the Americas, held in Schaumburg, IL, February 22–26.

Caldwell, R. and Storey, J. (2007) The HR function: Integration or fragmentation? In Storey, J. (ed.), *Human Resource Management: A Critical Text.* London: Thomson Learning.

Chaudhuri, S. (2009) *The Impact of Training Outsourcing on the Organizational Commitment of Employees.* Paper presented at the Academy of Human Resource Development Conference in the Americas, held in Washington, DC, February 18–22.

Den Hartog, D.N., Boselie, P. and Paauwe, J. (2004) Performance management: A model and research agenda. *Applied Psychology* 53(4): 556–69.

Easterby-Smith, M., Araujo, L. and Burgoyne, J. (1998) *Organizational Learning: Developments in Theory and Practice.* London: SAGE.

Ellinger, A.D., Watkins, K.E. and Barnas, C.M. (1999) Responding to new roles: A qualitative study of managers as instructors. *Management Learning* 30(4): 38–412.

Friedman, T.L. (2006) *The World is Flat.* New York: Penguin Books.

Garavan, T.N. (2007) A strategic perspective on human resource development. *Advances in Developing Human Resources* 9(1): 11–30.

Garavan, T.N., Barnicle, B. and Heraty, N. (1993) The training and development function: its search for power and influence in organizations. *Journal of European Industrial Training* 7(7): 22–32.

Garavan, T.N., Morley, M., Gunnigle, P. and McGuire, D. (2002) Human resource development and workplace learning: Emerging theoretical perspectives and organizational practices. *Journal of European Industrial Training* 26(2/3/4): 60–71.

Ghemawat, P. (2008) The globalization of business education: through the lens of semiglobalization. *Journal of Management Development* 27(4): 391–414.

Gilbert, C., De Winne, S. and Sels, L. (2011) Antecedents of front-line managers' perceptions of HR role stressors. *Personnel Review* 40(5): 549–69.

Gurchiek, K. (2005) Record growth: Outsourcing of HR functions. *HR Magazine* 50(6): 35–36.

Hales, C. (2005) Rooted in supervision, branching into management: Continuity and change in the role of first-line manager. *Journal of Management Studies* 42(3): 471–506.

Hallier, J. and Butts, S. (2000) Attempts to advance the role of training: process and context. *Employee Relations* 22(4): 375–402.

Hamel, G. and Prahalad, C.K. (1994) *Competing for the Future.* Boston: Harvard Business School Press.

Harney, B. and Jordan, C. (2008) Unlocking the black box: Line managers and HRM-performance in a call centre context. *Personnel Review* 57(4): 275–96.

Harris, L. and Foster, C. (2010) Aligning talent management with approaches to equality and diversity: Challenges for UK public sector managers. *Equality, Diversity and Inclusion: An International Journal* 29(5): 422–35.

Heraty, N. (1992) *Training and Development: A Study of Practices in Irish Based Companies.* Limerick: University of Limerick.

Heraty, N. and Morley, M. (1995) Line managers and human resource development. *Journal of European Industrial Training* 19(10): 31–37.

Higgins, P. and Zhang, L.F. (2008) *'Thinking performer' or 'automated bureaucrat': the thinking styles of human resource managers registered for CIPD-accredited HRM courses.* Chartered Institute of Personnel and Development Centres Conference, Nottingham, June 26–27. Retrieved July 24, 2008 from http://www.cipd.co.uk/NR/rdonlyres/659F8418-C0A5-4FE0-9906-F19E1B1D4A35/0/Centres_Conference-08seminarResearchHigginsetal.pdf.

Hunter, W. and Renwick, D. (2009) Involving British line managers in HRM in a small non-profit work organization. *Employee Relations* 31(4): 398–411.

Hurn, B.J. (2007) Pre-departure training for international business managers. *Industrial and Commercial Training* 39(1): 9–17.

Hutchinson, S. and Purcell, J. (2007) *Line Managers in Reward Learning and Development: Research into Practice.* London: Chartered Institute of Personnel and Development.

Jackson, S., Farndale, E. and Kakabadse, A. (2003) Executive development: Meeting the needs of top teams and boards. *Journal of Management Development* 22(3): 185–265.

Kesler, G. (2002) Why the leadership bench never gets deeper: Ten insights about executive talent development. *Human Resource Planning* 25(1): 32–44.

Kirby, J.R., Knapper, C.K., Evans, C.J., Carty, A.E. and Gadula, C. (2003) Approaches to learning at work and workplace climate. *International Journal of Training and Development* 7(1): 31–52.

Knies, E. (2011) When do supervisors support tailor-made work arrangements? An exploratory study. *Labour & Industry* 21(3): 621–43.

Kollasch, M. (2009) *Succession Planning for Managers and Executives: A Literature Review with Implications for HRD.* Paper presented at the Academy of Human Resource Development Conference in the Americas, held in Washington, DC, February 18–22.

Lee, C.Y. (2010) A theory of firm growth: Learning capability, knowledge threshold, and patterns of growth. *Research Policy* 39(2): 278–89.

MacNeil, C.M. (2003) Line managers: Facilitators of knowledge sharing in teams. *Employee Relations* 25(3): 294–307.

Mayrhofer, W., Muller-Camen, M., Ledolter, J., Strunk, G. and Erten, C. (2004) Devolving responsibilities for human resources to line management? An empirical study about convergence in Europe. *Journal for East European Management Studies* 9(2): 123–46.

Nehles, A.C., Van Riemsdijk, M., Kok, I. and Looise, J.C. (2006) Implementing human resource management successfully: A first-line management challenge. *Management Revue* 17(3): 256–73.

Nehles, A.C., Van Riemsdijk, M.J. and Looise, J.C. (2008) *Assessing the Constraints of HR Implementation: Development and Validation of a Research Instrument.* Paper presented at the Academy of Management Annual Meeting, Anaheim, CA, August, 8–13.

Nickson, D., Hurell, S., Warhurst, C., Newsome, K. and Preston, A. (2008) *'Employee Champion' or 'Business Partner'? The views of aspirant HR professionals.* Chartered Institute of Personnel and Development Centres Conference, Nottingham, June 26–27. Retrieved July 24, 2008 from http://www.cipd.co.uk/NR/rdonlyres/B227B99E-72CF-491A-B460-D4648F64E92B/0/Centres_Conference08seminarResearch-Nicksonetal.pdf.

Park, S., Yang, B. and McLean, G.N. (2008) *An Examination of Relationships between Managerial Coaching and Employee Development.* Paper presented at the Academy of Human Resource Development Conference in the Americas, held in Panama City, FL, February 20–24.

Purcell, J. and Hutchinson, S. (2007) Front-line managers as agents in the HRM-performance causal chain: theory, analysis and evidence. *Human Resource Management Journal* 17(1): 3–20.

Raidén, A.B. and Dainty, A.R.J. (2006) Human resource development in construction organizations: An example of a "chaordic" learning organization? *Learning Organization* 13(1): 63–79.

Reio, T.G, and Callahan, J. (2004) Affect, curiosity, and socialization-related learning: A path analysis of antecedents to job performance. *Journal of Business and Psychology* 19(1): 3–22.

Renwick, D. and MacNeil, C.M. (2002) Line manager involvement in careers. *Career Development International* 7(6): 407–14.

Sadler-Smith, E., Down, S. and Lean, J. (2000) "Modern" learning methods: Rhetoric and reality. *Personnel Review* 29(4): 474–90.

Sambrook, S. and Stewart, J. (2000) Factors influencing learning in European learning oriented organizations: issues for management. *Journal of European Industrial Training* 24(2/3/4): 209–19.

Selvarajah, C. (2006) Dimensions that relate to cross-cultural counselling: Perceptions of mental health professionals in Auckland, New Zealand. *Cross Cultural Management* 13(1): 54–68.

Sirkin, H., Hemerling, J. and Bhattacharya, A. (2008) *Globality: Competing with Everyone from Everywhere for Everything.* New York: Hachette Book Group.

Stahl, G.K., Björkman, I., Farndale, E., Shad, S.M., Paauwe, J. and Stiles, P. (2012) Six principles of effective global talent management. *Sloan Management Review* 53(2): 25–32.

Thornhill, A., Saunders, M.N.K. and Stead, J. (1997) Downsizing, delayering – but where's the commitment? The development of a diagnostic tool to help manage survivors. *Personnel Review* 26(1): 81–98.

Tseng, C.C. and McLean, G.N. (2008) Strategic HRD practices as key factors in organizational learning. *Journal of European Industrial Training* 32(6): 418–32.

Ulrich, D. and Brockbank, W. (2005) *The HR Value Proposition.* Boston: Harvard Business School Press.

Visitchaichan, S. (2010) *Human Resource Development and Human Resource Management Strategies and Practices in Thailand.* Paper presented at the Academy of Human Resource Development Conference in the Americas, held in Knoxville, TN, February 24–28.

Yarnall, J. (1998) Line managers as career developers: Rhetoric or reality? *Personnel Review* 27(5): 378–95.

Zavyalova, E.K. and Kosheleva, S.V. (2009) Assessment of labor behavior factors and selecting line managers' lines of development at Russian industrial enterprises. *Journal of European Industrial Training* 33(3): 271–96.

46

EMPLOYEE ENGAGEMENT AND HRD

Intersections of theory and practice

Brad Shuck and Sally Sambrook

Recently, scholars in human resource development (HRD) have contributed to the conversation around employee engagement and its application to workplace learning and performance. This literature stream however is young and the application of engagement within HRD has been gradual. Building toward further maturation and application, the purpose of this chapter is to provide a comprehensive and critical overview of the concept of employee engagement in HRD. This chapter unfolds in three main sections: (a) a critical review of current perspectives and theories of engagement research, (b) the current state of measuring engagement, and (c) implications for HRD practice and future research.

Critical review of current perspectives and theories of engagement research

The phenomenon of engagement has a relatively recent, yet rapidly maturing historical footing, from roots in *personal* engagement (Kahn 1990; Rich *et al.* 2010) and *work* engagement, both as antithesis to burnout (Maslach *et al.* 2001) and distinct construct (Schaufeli *et al.* 2002), to more recent notions of *employee* engagement (Saks 2006; Shuck 2011). From a disciplinary perspective, engagement has been heavily dominated by research in applied psychology (Bakker *et al.* 2011a) with deep philosophical roots in positive psychology (Seligman 1990). Further, as an application to practice, the construct has gained momentum in fields such as healthcare (Simpson 2009), management (Rich *et al.* 2010), human resource management (Alfes *et al.* 2010; Gruman and Saks 2011) and more recently HRD (Shuck and Wollard 2010).

However, several parallel streams of engagement literature are in tension, notably between individual (humanistic) and organizational (managerialist) foci. This tension is subtle, yet significant for informing and shaping HRD strategies and interventions. For example, Wefald and Downey (2009) observe that although there is some overlap in the definitions of engagement from both academic and industry sides, there remain distinct differences. Management's focus, fed by industry-led practitioner work (see, for example, Development Dimension International [DDI], Hewitt, Towers Perrin, Gallup and Mercer), addresses macro issues of team and organizational performance. Macey and Schneider (2008: 3) note, "the notion of employee engagement . . . has been heavily marketed by HR consulting firms who offer advice on how it can be created and leveraged." On the other hand, academic researchers tend to address individual differences such as state and trait, adopting a micro focus on the construct itself. Cascio (2007) talks of the split between these foci of concern as different "thought worlds" where well validated empirical research findings are not utilized by practitioners because results do not match industry perceptions of importance (i.e. being able to predict and increase employee performance). Wefald and Downey (2009) argue that this gap must be closed before both parties become entrenched.

Situating the construct globally, considerable research has been conducted in Europe, notably the United Kingdom (Robinson *et al.* 2004; Truss *et al.* 2006; MacLeod and Clarke 2009), the Netherlands (Schaufeli *et al.* 2002; Schaufeli *et al.* 2006a; Schaufeli and Bakker 2004, 2010; Schaufeli and Salanova 2011), Germany (Demerouti *et al.* 2001; Sonnentag 2003, 2011), Denmark (Engelbrecht 2006), and Spain (Salanova *et al.* 2005). Other non-European contexts have also been explored such as Australia (Albrecht 2010), North America (Kahn 1990; Macey and Schneider 2008), and Canada (Laschinger and Leiter 2006). Little research however has considered engagement in India (Bhatnagar 2007; Devi 2009), Africa (Cawe 2006; Stander and Rothmann 2010), Asia or Central and South America. There are some limited cross-national studies (see for example, Flade 2003; Schaufeli *et al.* 2006b) but there remains a considerable gap in the understanding of engagement across cultures or from emerging and diverse cultural perspectives.

Defining engagement

In attempting to define the construct, Simpson (2009) identified four categories of engagement research; *personal engagement*, *work engagement* in two forms (as antithesis to, and then independent of, burnout) and *employee engagement*, but did not include job engagement. This is similar to Shuck's (2011) four approaches that identified Kahn's (1990) *need-satisfying approach*, Maslach *et al.*'s (2001) *burnout-antithesis approach*, Harter *et al.*'s (2002) *satisfaction-engagement* approach, and Saks' (2006) *multidimensional approach*.

Personal engagement was the original focus of engagement (Kahn 1990), concentrating on the individual person and their roles (within and without work). Related to this are the constructs of work role (Rothbard 2001) and job engagement (Rich *et al.* 2010). *Work* engagement, a derivative term of personal engagement (Maslach and Leiter 1997; Maslach *et al.* 2001; Schaufeli *et al.* 2002) has been closely aligned with burnout. *Employee* engagement, a second derivative term, considers the individual's engagement not only in role and work but also with the organization (Harter *et al.* 2002), a subtle but important distinction. Related to this, Saks (2006) distinguishes between job and organization engagement, the CIPD operationalizes job engagement (CIPD 2006), and MacLeod and Clarke (2009) present the deficit model of employee engagement all in an attempt to better define the construct.

From a practitioner perspective, the *Gallup Organization* (Harter *et al.* 2002) arguably popularized employee engagement, followed by *DDI*, *Hewitt*, *Towers Perrin* and *Mercer*, all international consultancy firms. There is considerable overlap between these consultancy firms' definitions of engagement, and other constructs such as job involvement and job satisfaction, leading Schaufeli and Bakker (2010: 12) to deem these conceptualizations as "putting old wine in new bottles". While no universal definition yet exists, and any definition is highly dependent on context and approach, for HRD, employee engagement has been defined as the cognitive, emotional, and behavioral energy an employee directs toward positive organizational outcomes (Shuck and Wollard 2010).

Models and theories of engagement

Several theoretical and empirically tested models have been advanced. The first theoretical model of engagement was proposed by American psychologist Kahn (1990). His work differentiated engagement and psychological presence and focused toward authenticity. This work drew managerial attention toward the importance of handling employees with an ethos of care. Further, Schaufeli and Bakker (2004) presented an empirical *Job-Demands-Job-Resources* model, that later included *Personal Resources*. This very popular model emphasized the impact of engagement and burnout on wellness and absenteeism. Focusing toward employee engagement, Luthans and Peterson (2002) identified an association between manager self-efficacy and their team's engagement, again drawing attention to the important role (and development) of managers (Xu and Cooper-Thomas 2011). Still further, Macey and Schneider (2008) and with other colleagues (Macey *et al.* 2009) presented an overview model of the business case for employee engagement, which focused toward creating a climate of engagement.

Currently, many academic models are limited in their consideration of how engagement states vary amongst employees at any one time (cf. Bledlow *et al.* 2011). Practitioner and academic treatments of engagement appear static, failing to recognize the importance of understanding the transitions from different engagement states (e.g. from engagement to non-engagement for example, or from job to organization). While several practitioner models promote engagement, many lack even exploratory evidence.

Engagement typologies

The UK Institute of Employment Studies has produced a number of reports on employee engagement (Robinson *et al.* 2004; Robinson 2007; Robertson-Smith and Markwick 2009). They utilize Gallup's descriptions of three types of employee: *engaged*, *non-engaged* or *actively disengaged*. This typology presents engagement as fixed: an employee is either engaged or not engaged. Similarly, research for the Scottish Executive (ORC International 2009) identified five clusters of employees: *highly engaged*, *engaged*, *motivated non-advocates*, *on the fence and uninspired*, and *disengaged*. The report does not state which of these groups could and should be targeted to maintain high levels of engagement or how to increase engagement amongst lower level groups through HRD interventions. Although helpful in labelling employee groups, assumptions about the experience of engagement and a lack of fluidity between categories are major drawbacks to these typologies.

Still in the United Kingdom, the MacLeod and Clarke report to the UK government talks of an engagement *deficit* across the UK economy (MacLeod and Clarke 2009: 15). Reference is made to approximately three in ten employees across the UK being engaged in work (Truss *et al.* 2006). MacLeod and Clarke (2009: 15) opine, "*that overall levels of engagement in the UK are lower than they could be*". However, there does not appear to be any consideration by engagement scholars or practitioners of appropriate engagement benchmarks within an organization. Such claims are based on the predominance of survey evidence, although some practitioner-oriented literature (Vance 2006; MacLeod and Clarke 2009) relies heavily on case studies of organizations where engagement interventions have been successful.

The current state of measuring engagement

Few scholars have explored engagement from a critical measurement perspective with application to theory and practice. In the following, we examine the general reluctance to consider and measure engagement beyond the positivistic, psychological and quantitative orientations and highlight the few notable exceptions. In addition to highlighting the prevailing survey methodology we also consider several alternative approaches to understanding the experience of engagement.

Survey approaches to examining employee and work engagement

Survey methodology has primarily dominated the measurement of engagement, perhaps due in part to the ease with which surveys are deployable to large groups of people, within a reasonably short period of time. Schaufeli *et al.* (2002) published one of the more widely utilized survey measures of engagement, the *Utrecht Work Engagement Scale* (UWES). This ever-popular measure comes in several forms (long and short) and is widely cited in the literature as the operationalization of engagement. Other popular more established measures available for use in research include scales put forward by Rich *et al.* (2010) and May *et al.* (2004).

The focus on utilizing surveys to measure engagement perhaps revolves also around the ease at which multiple levels of variables and analysis can be conducted simultaneously. For example, within the HRD literature, Shuck *et al.* (2011) examined the linkages between a model of antecedents and outcomes in relation to engagement concurrently. Findings provided evidence of the likely climate for engagement as well as expected organizational performance outcomes of engagement all within the same research study. The efficiency and speed at which surveys are deployable clearly support their frequent use in organizational research. However, at times, survey approaches tell only one dimension of the engagement story.

Qualitative approaches to exploring employee and work engagement

Beyond the conventional survey methodology, few studies have examined engagement through a qualitative lens. Those of exception have used approaches such as grounded theory, single case study design, and diary studies to explore the rich narratives around employee engagement. For example, Kahn's (1990) seminal study of engagement employed an ethnographic-grounded theory approach considering the experience of workers from two divergent work-based samples. This work is often cited as a cornerstone study to the developing theory of engagement, yet it is ironic that most research since has adopted a mostly quantitative method. Kahn's early work (1990) as well as his more recent writing (2010) have provided context to the meaning of engagement and the emergent themes prevalent within contemporary streams of engagement research today (see Shuck 2011 for further discussion).

More recently and more closely aligned with HRD, Jones *et al.* (2011) also applied an ethnographic approach to capture the experience of engagement. Their collective work introduced a four-part model, illuminating the practice of engagement and its application as a movement within the Welsh public sector. As an innovative perspective to the engagement construct, the Jones *et al.* (2011) model highlighted for the first time the life cycle of engagement from an organizational perspective and further pointed to the challenges and opportunities that presently face the state of engagement in public service work. Developing this, in a highly innovative auto-ethnographic study, Jones (2012) identified tensions and contradictions between personal attempts at engagement (to enhance state) and organizational interventions (as a device to enhance performance). Using a slightly different qualitative focus, Shuck *et al.* (2011) employed a single case study methodology to examine the experiences of work with food service employees at a large multinational service corporation. This work proposed an emergent model of engagement and provided a descriptive framework of engagement from which to build HRD-related interventions that considered the contextual sensitivity of the individual and environment simultaneously. The insights gleaned from these three qualitative approaches (Jones *et al.* 2011; Jones 2012; Shuck *et al.* 2010) provide an intimate, personal account into the experience of engagement from both individual and organizational perspectives.

Notwithstanding, some scholars have taken an even deeper micro approach to engagement, employing a diary study methodology. The majority of research utilizing this method to study engagement originated from the Netherlands and Norway with scholars such as Petrou *et al.* (2012), Xanthopoulou *et al.* (2009), and Ouweneel *et al.* (2012). While rigorous and demanding from both a participant and researcher perspective, these methods are quasi-mixed method in approach, often pairing survey responses alongside frequent entries of narrative into personal journal diaries in response to a series of prompted questions.

Alternative approaches and innovative applications to consider

As an interlude to alternative approaches, Cooper-Thomas *et al.* (2010: 87) asked the critical question, "does engagement flourish, fade, or stay true" across time and context? From a critical measurement perspective, the experienced change of engagement and the potential for fluctuation could affect measurement accuracy across samples and contexts and therefore, skew statistical interpretation. Currently, most measurement approaches of engagement do not account for this. Thus, the question of a best approach for engagement has been something of a conversation piece building momentum over the past decade. In response, several scholars have undertaken unique approaches.

For example, one of the more interesting alternative approaches examined the short-term fluctuations of everyday life and their relation to measures of well-being (operationalized as a component of engagement; Xanthopoulou *et al.* 2012). Here, Xanthopoulou *et al.* (2012) proposed that even the most positive of people suffer from momentary losses of enthusiasm and fulfilment; a realistic depiction of everyday life. Subsequently, the measurement of actual fluctuation provides a context into the experienced phenomena of engagement, which can be lost when using typologies that connote either being engaged or disengaged as a general sentiment (i.e. the all or nothing phenomenon). The researchers went on to suggest that the appraisal context, domains of psychological capital (i.e. hope), and a healthy balance between challenge and skill can help explain momentary fluctuations of engagement operationalized through the broader concept of well-being. These domains offer leverage points for boosting short-term moments of individual well-being (Xanthopoulou *et al.* 2012).

Further, using self-regulation theory as a framework, Bledow *et al.* (2011) developed the affective shift model of work engagement. This affective shift model examined the dynamic interplay of positive and negative emotions in relation to work engagement. This research draws attention to the more dynamic and transitional status of engagement, rather than simply an on/off phenomenon, and presents leverage points for how organizations, supervisors, and individual employees can actively shape events that influence the extent of engagement. Ultimately, Bledow *et al.* (2011) provided an alternative approach for examining engagement using a longitudinal design strategy. This approach was more true-to-experience then other traditional snapshot survey methodologies. Moreover, recent theoretical work by Bakker *et al.* (2011b) extended empirical research around work engagement to consider Subjective Well Being (SWB) and advocated the use of the Day Reconstruction Method (Kahneman *et al.* 2004) as an innovative qualitative approach to longitudinal data collection.

Implications for HRD practice

Given the complexity of the employee engagement concept, there are several factors and foci associated with HRD (see Figure 46.1).

Figure 46.1 connects different factors and foci (e.g. levels) of engagement commonly found disparately in the literature with features of possible HRD interventions. Focus on the individual employee relates to Kahn's (1990) notion of personal engagement, with various influencing factors such as personal context and resources, roles and colleagues. Here, direct implications for

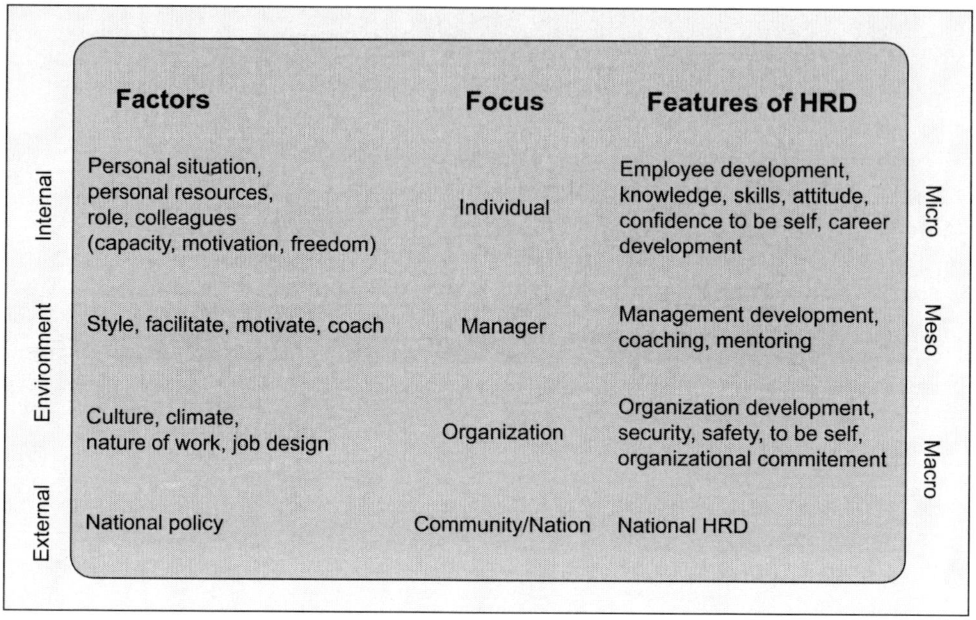

Figure 46.1 Intersections of HRD and engagement framework

HRD practice include attention to employee development, enabling the employee to have confidence to be their authentic self, and fulfilling personal career ambitions. Extant literature also considers the role of a manager in the development of engagement (Shuck *et al.* 2011). This focus recognizes the crucial role of managers in creating an engagement-supportive environment, resulting in specific HRD interventions to enhance managers' motivational, mentoring and coaching skills. Focus on the organization has implications for practice that highlight influential factors such as organizational culture, the environment of work climate, and job design which all lead to wider OD-system interventions. Moreover, as HRD is increasingly conceptualized as a national phenomenon (NHRD) (McLean 2004), engagement interventions could be more broadly defined and designed toward national policy levels that serve wider socioeconomic needs. We acknowledge there are not fixed boundaries between these factors, foci and features. Hence, we note that factors might exist within, and be influenced by, both the internal (individual and organizational) and external environment, as indicated on the left hand side. However, we suggest it is helpful to consider how HRD interventions might occur at micro, meso, and macro levels.

Building from the intersections of HRD and engagement framework, Figure 46.2 highlights the spheres of engagement and the permeable boundary between work and non-work.

We propose that four levels of engagement can be deducted from the previously reviewed literature: (a) micro (employee), (b) meso (colleagues and managers), (c) macro internal (organizational) and (d) macro external. At the *micro level*, the model represents a sense of experienced self within and beyond work, providing and/or constraining the availability of personal resources for engagement. This level represents overlapping and, at times, competing responsibilities depicting the imbalanced state of engagement that an employee can experience (being highly engaged in one area could decrease the potential for engagement in other areas) as a result of their experienced life, not just a focus of work. This level is personal to the employee and is influenced by the meso and macro levels. The *meso level* identifies a range of other individuals (within and beyond the organization) who can positively or negatively influence engagement. For example,

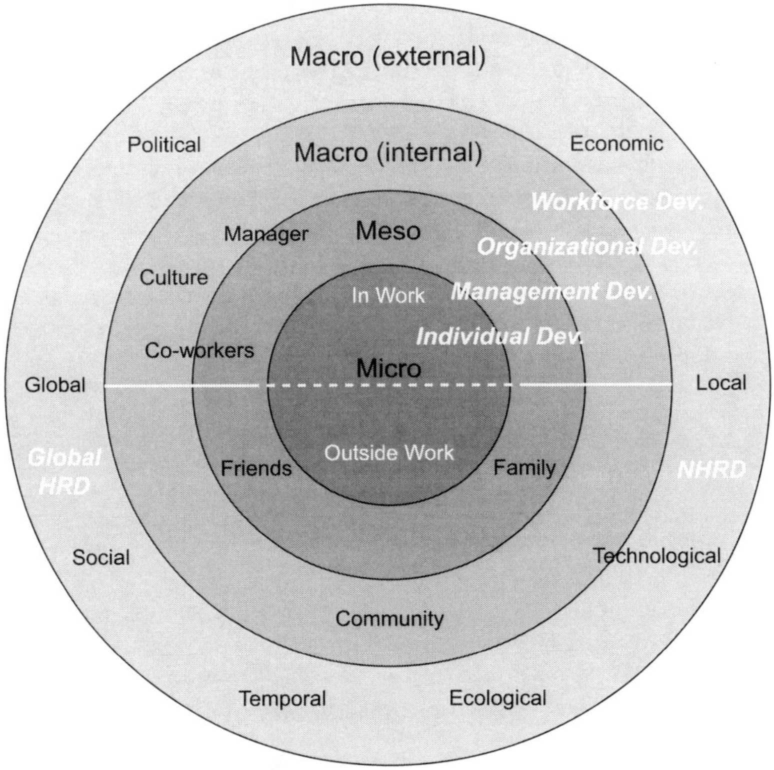

Figure 46.2 HRD and spheres of engagement influence

this could include other organizational actors internally, direct colleagues, and supervisors. These individuals impact the micro level and are influenced at varying levels by the macro levels. The first macro level, *internal macro*, depicts how organizational culture can shape attitudes toward and interventions around engagement development. This level represents unique culture norms and community relations that draw from, and push toward, the employee. The second macro level, *macro external*, suggests that wide ranging policy changes, political agendas, economic conditions, social values, ecological concerns and technological developments, both in a local (organizational) and global context can also affect engagement. This broadly connects with emerging areas of NHRD and the evolving boundaries of the HRD field. We further note that some categories within each of the levels overlap within the model to best highlight the shaping role they play (e.g. an employee's manager can effect engagement at both the meso and macro internal levels).

This conceptual model identifies various spheres in which engagement – and thus HRD interventions that are highlighted in white – might develop and be influenced, within and outside of work. As an HRD tool, Figure 46.2 provides a basic diagnostic framework with which to assess internal and external influencing factors and applies known HRD approaches to developing engagement. The model is not designed to be prescriptive, rather investigative and relational in nature. As designed, this can help better focus and bring attention to areas of opportunity to HRD scholars and practitioners within the temporal nature of engagement at each level of the model. For example, issues of poor workplace culture can be addressed through organizational development; however further, within the context of engagement, poor workplace culture also affects relationships between coworkers, managers, and internal organizational constituents as well as the individual.

Thus, a focus toward the development of a more positive culture is not enough; each level has been influenced accordingly and must be addressed.

In addition to these two frameworks for situating engagement within HRD, we further suggest that more expansive perspectives of engagement practice are equally important to consider. For example, tensions exist between the unitarist human resource management approach (i.e. engagement is good for both the individual and organization in the context of improving performance), the pluralist human resource management approach (i.e. the potentially competing interests of different stakeholders), and more critical perspectives of engagement (i.e. engagement as another form of worker exploitation that explicitly serves the needs of capitalism) (Thompson 2011). These tensions have implications for practice depending on perspective and viewpoint. Care should be taken to fully consider and understand these tensions as well as explore each in emerging directions for future research.

Directions for future research

There are several directions for future research, both theoretical and methodological. Theoretically, future research might consider emerging contexts of HRD and their application to engagement. For example, currently, engagement is applied to HRD; however, what if HRD was applied to engagement? Provided the espoused role of engagement is increasing individual and organizational performance, it is possible that there exists a framework of engagement within HRD, not just applied to HRD. For example, engagement is commonly utilized in research as an outcome variable; however, for HRD, employee engagement could be reoperationalized as a framework for understanding and explaining the behavior connected to performance no matter how it might be defined. In this context, HRD scholars and practitioners could better understand and influence employee behavior beyond the traditional unidimensional application of engagement as a task oriented performance outcome. This might also include exploring emerging boundaries that focus not only toward an organizational context, but also toward social, political, and economic challenges, and doing so through both theoretical and empirical lenses equally. Moreover, theoretical research might consider the biasing effect of cross-national studies employing an etic (Headland *et al.* 1990) Western-centric perspective. Since inception, the Western-centric perspective of engagement has dominated research, but not all countries share such a philosophy. For example, to what extent do current theories fit Eastern World and Asian cultures, or Islamic cultural contexts?

Further, we wonder if it is possible for engagement to be conceptualized through an Eastern-alternative orientation and what emic (Headland *et al.* 1990) studies might be needed to further explore this area. Research through this lens could open streams that more fully consider emerging research themes within HRD and NHRD especially as research expands to underrepresented countries and cultures (i.e. Eastern Europe, Asia, Africa and Central and South America). We also suggest cross-national collaborations that involve deep investigation into what it means to be engaged, what the application of engagement could be across cultural and national boundaries, and how engagement might be conceptualized differently in differing parts of the world (with language, the arts, and economies of community).

Methodologically, future researchers might employ designs that utilize qualitatively and quantitatively centred multi-year longitudinal approaches and advanced statistical techniques such as survival analysis to examine time to event data. For example, research has yet to consider a multi-year, multi-context study that examines the natural ebb and flow of engagement over several points in time and in differing circumstances. These studies could cover a multitude of position levels (staff, management, executive) and examine the intersection between work and personal life (i.e. relationships and the cost of engagement, health and wellness metrics), as well as objective, distal long-term performance indicators such as health indexes, life span, and cultural developments. This could directly connect with emerging contexts of NHRD and the future of the HRD field as well as promote cross and multidisciplinary methodologies and perspectives. Moreover, mixed-methods approaches that cover the nuances of experience as well as experimental design procedures would also be of great utility. Different approaches might be combined to consider the micro-, meso- and macro-dimensions of engagement as proposed in Figure 46.2 and to discuss and explore their interplay.

Pushing forward, future HRD researchers might consider what innovative philosophical approaches and methods are needed to better understand the complexities and emerging applications of employee engagement.

Conclusion

In sum, we have critically reviewed current perspectives, theories and measures of engagement, identified diverse implications for HRD practice in two conceptual figures, and highlighted new directions for future research, both theoretically and methodologically. To conclude, we are excited by the potential for HRD research and practice to enhance micro, meso and macro attempts at engagement and look forward to the discourse regarding the future application and intersection of employee engagement and HRD.

References

Albrecht, S.L. (ed) (2010) *Handbook of Employee Engagement Perspectives, Issues, Research and Practice.* Cheltenham: Edward Elgar.

Alfes, K., Truss, C., Soane, E.C., Rees, C. and Gatenby, M. (2010) *Creating an Engaged Workforce: Findings from the Kingston Employee Engagement Consortium Project.* London: Chartered Institute of Personnel and Development.

Bakker, A.B., Albrecht, S.L. and Leiter, M.P. (2011a) Key questions regarding work engagement. *European Journal of Work and Organizational Psychology* 20(1): 4–28.

Bakker, A.B., Albrecht, S.L. and Leiter, M.P. (2011b) Work engagement: Further reflections on the state of play. *European Journal of Work and Organizational Psychology* 20(1): 74–88.

Bhatnagar, J. (2007) Talent management strategy of employee engagement in Indian ITES employees: Key to retention. *Employee Relations* 29(6): 640–63.

Bledow, R., Schmitt, A., Frese, M. and Kuhnel, J. (2011) The affective shift model of work engagement. *Journal of Applied Psychology* 96(6): 1246–57.

Cascio, W.F. (2007) Evidence-based management and the marketplace for ideas. *Academy of Management Journal* 50(5): 1009–12.

Cawe, M. (2006) *Factors Contributing to Employee Engagement in South Africa.* Master's thesis Human Resources Management, University of the Witwatersrand, Johannesburg.

CIPD (Chartered Institute of Personnel and Development) (2006) *Working Life: Employee attitudes and engagement.* London: CIPD.

Cooper-Thomas, H.D., Leighton, N., Xu, J. and Knight-Turvey, N. (2010) Measuring change: Does engagement flourish, fade, or stay true? In Albrecht, S. (ed.). *Handbook of Employee Engagement: Perspectives, Issues, Research and Practice.* Northampton, MA: Edward Elgar, 87–97.

Demerouti, E., Nachreiner, F., Bakker, A.B. and Schaufeli, W.M. (2001) The job demands-resources model of burnout. *Journal of Applied Psychology* 86(3): 499–512.

Development Dimension International (2012) *Thought-Leadership White Papers and Monographs.* Available at: http://www.ddiworld.com/pdf/ddi_employeeengagement_mg. [Accessed March 17, 2012].

Devi, V.R. (2009) Employee engagement is a two-way street. *Human Resource Management International Digest* 17(2): 3–4.

Engelbrecht, S. (2006) *Motivation and burnout in human service work: The case of midwifery in Denmark.* Available at: http://www.arbejdsmiljoforskning.dk/~/media/boeger-og-rapporter/sen-phd. [Accessed August 01, 2010].

Flade, P. (2003) Great Britain's Workforce Lacks Inspiration, *Gallup Management Journal* [online]. Available at: http://businessjournal.gallup.com/content/9847/Great-Britains-Workforce-Lacks-Inspiration.aspx [Accessed December 03, 2012].

Gallup (2010) *Employee Engagement* [online]. Available at: http://www.gallup.com/consulting/52/Employee-Engagement.aspx [Accessed March 01, 2010].

Gruman, J. and Saks, A. (2011) Performance management and employee engagement. *Human Resource Management Review* 21(2): 123–36.

Harter, J.K., Schmidt, F.L. and Hayes, T.L. (2002) Business unit level relationship between employee satisfaction, employee engagement and business outcomes: A meta-analysis. *Journal of Applied Psychology* 87(2): 268–79.

Headland, T., Pike, K. and Harris, M. (eds) (1990) *Emics and Etics: The Insider/Outsider Debate.* London: SAGE.

Hewitt (2012) *Best Employers Studies* [online]. Available at: https://ceplb03.hewitt.com/bestemployers/pages/index.htm [Accessed March 17, 2012].

Jones, N. (2012) *Full Circle: Employee Engagement in the Welsh Public Service.* PhD dissertation, Bangor University.

Jones, N., Sambrook, S. and Doloriert, C. (2011) *Employee Engagement in the Welsh Public Service: An ethnographic approach.* Paper presented at the 15th International Research Society for Public Management, held at Dublin University, 11–15 April.

Kahn, W.A. (1990) Psychological conditions of personal engagement and disengagement at work. *Academy of Management Journal* 33(4): 692–724.

Kahneman, D., Krueger, A.B., Schkade, D., Schwartz, N. and Stone, A.A. (2004) A survey method for characterizing daily life experience: The day reconstruction method. *Science* 306(5702): 1776–80.

Laschinger, H.K. and Leiter, M.P. (2006) The impact of nursing work environments on patient safety outcomes: The mediating role of burnout engagement. *Journal of Nursing Administration* 36(5): 259–67.

Luthans, F. and Peterson, S.J. (2002) Employee engagement and manager self-efficacy. *Journal of Management Development* 21(5): 376–87.

Macey, W.H. and Schneider, B. (2008) The meaning of employee engagement. *Industrial and Organizational Psychology* 1(1): 3–30.

Macey, W.H., Schneider, B., Barbera, K.M. and Young, S.A. (2009) *Employee Engagement: Tools for analysis, practice, and competitive advantage.* Chichester: Wiley-Blackwell.

MacLeod, D. and Clarke, N. (2009) *Engaging for Success: Enhancing performance through employee engagement.* London: Department for Business, Innovation and Skills.

Maslach, C. and Leiter. M.P. (1997) *The Truth about Burnout: How organizations cause personal stress and what to do about it.* San Francisco: Jossey-Bass.

Maslach, C., Schaufeli, W.B. and Leiter, M.P. (2001) Job burnout. *Annual Review of Psychology* 52: 397–422.

May, D.R., Gilson, R.L. and Harter, L.M. (2004) The psychological conditions of meaningfulness, safety and availability and the engagement of the human spirit at work. *Journal of Occupational and Organizational Psychology* 77(1): 11–37.

McLean, G.N. (2004) National human resource development: What in the world is it? *Advances in Developing Human Resources* 6(3): 269–75.

Mercer (2012) *What's Working?* [online]. Available at: http://www.mercer.com/pages/1418255 [Accessed March 17, 2012].

ORC International (2009) *Scottish Government Employee Survey (2008 Results Report).* Edinburgh: Scottish Government Social Research. Available at: http://www.scotland.gov.uk/Publications/2009/03/19111703/0 [Accessed May 07, 2012].

Ouweneel, E., Le Blanc, P.M., Schaufeli, W.B. and Van Wijhe, C.I. (2012) Good morning, good day: A diary study on positive emotions, hope, and work engagement. *Human Relations* 65(9): 1129–54.

Petrou, P., Demerouti, E., Peeters, M.C., Schaufeli, W.B. and Hetland, J. (2012) Crafting a job on a daily basis: Contextual correlates and the link to work engagement. *Journal of Organizational Behavior* 33(8): 1120–41.

Rich, B.L., LePine, J.A. and Crawford, E.R. (2010) Job engagement: Antecedents and effects on job performance. *Academy of Management Journal* 53(3): 617–35.

Robertson-Smith, G. and Markwick, C. (2009) *Employee Engagement: A review of current thinking.* Brighton: Institute of Employment Studies.

Robinson, D. (2007) *Employee Engagement.* Brighton: Institute of Employment Studies. Available at: http://www.employment-studies.co.uk/pdflibrary/op11. [Accessed February 11, 2010].

Robinson, D., Perryman, S. and Hayday, S. (2004) *The Drivers of Employee Engagement.* Brighton: Institute of Employment Studies.

Rothbard, N.P. (2001) Enriching or depleting? The dynamics of engagement in work and family roles. *Administrative Science Quarterly* 46(4): 655–84.

Saks, A. (2006) Antecedents and consequences of employee engagement. *Journal of Managerial Psychology* 21(7): 600–19.

Salanova, M., Agut, S. and Peio, J.M. (2005) Linking organizational resources and work engagement to employee performance and customer loyalty: The mediation of service climate. *Journal of Applied Psychology* 90(6): 1217–27.

Schaufeli, W.B. and Bakker, A.B. (2004) Job demands, job resources and their relationship with burnout and engagement: A multi-sample study. *Journal of Organizational Behavior* 25(3): 293–315.

Schaufeli, W.B. and Bakker, A.B. (2010) Defining and measuring work engagement: Bringing clarity to the concept. In Bakker, A.B. and Leiter, M.P. (eds) *Work Engagement: A handbook of essential theory and research*. Hove: Psychology Press, 10–24.

Schaufeli, W. and Salanova, M. (2011) Work engagement: On how to better catch a slippery concept. *European Journal of Work and Organizational Psychology* 20(1): 39–46.

Schaufeli, W.B., Salanova, M., González-Romá, V. and Bakker A.B. (2002) The measurement of engagement and burnout: A two sample confirmatory factor analytic approach. *Journal of Happiness Studies* 3(1): 71–92.

Schaufeli, W.B., Taris, T. and Bakker, A.B. (2006a) Dr Jekyll or Mr Hyde: On the differences between work engagement and workaholism. In Burke, R. (ed.) *Work Hours and Work Addiction*. Northampton, MA: Edward Elgar, 193–217.

Schaufeli, W.B., Bakker, A.B. and Salanova, M. (2006b) The measurement of work engagement with a short questionnaire: A cross-national study. *Educational and Psychological Measurement* 66(4): 701–16.

Seligman, M. (1990) *Learned Optimism: How to change your mind and your life*. New York: Free Press.

Shuck, B. (2011) Four emerging perspectives of employee engagement: An integrative literature review. *Human Resource Development Review* 10(3): 304–28.

Shuck, B. and Wollard, K. (2010) Employee engagement and HRD: A seminal review of the foundations. *Human Resource Development Review* 9(1): 89–110.

Shuck, B., Rocco, T.S. and Albornoz, C.A. (2010) Exploring employee engagement from the employee perspective: Implications for HRD. *Journal of European Industrial Training* 35(4): 300–25.

Shuck, B., Reio, T.G. and Rocco, T.S. (2011) Employee engagement: An examination of antecedent and outcome variables. *Human Resource Development International* 14(4): 427–45.

Simpson, M. (2009) Engagement at work: A review of the literature. *International Journal of Nursing Studies* 46(7): 1012–24.

Sonnentag, S. (2003) Recovery, work engagement, and proactive behavior: A new look at the interface between nonwork and work. *Journal of Applied Psychology* 56(2): 518–28.

Sonnentag, S. (2011) Research on work engagement is well and alive. *European Journal of Work and Organizational Psychology* 20(1): 29–38.

Stander, M.W. and Rothmann, S. (2010) Psychological empowerment, job insecurity and employee engagement. *Journal of Industrial Psychology* 36(10): 1–8.

Thompson, P. (2011) The trouble with HRM. *Human Resource Management Journal* 21(4): 355–67.

Truss, C., Soane, E., Edwards, C., Wisdom, K., Croll, A. and Burnett, J. (2006) *How Engaged Are British Employees?* London: CIPD. Available at: http://www.cipd.co.uk/NR/rdonlyres/E6871F47-558A-466E-9A74-4DFB1E71304C/0/howengbritempssr. [Accessed May 07, 2012].

Vance, R. (2006) *Employee Engagement and Commitment*. Alexandria, VA: Society for Human Resource Development Foundation. Available at: http://www.vancerenz.com/researchimplementation/uploads/1006EmployeeEngagementOnlineReport. [Accessed May 07, 2012].

Wefald, A.J. and Downey, R.G. (2009) Job engagement in organizations: Fad, fashion or folderol? *Journal of Organizational Behaviour* 30(1): 141–45.

Xanthopoulou, D., Bakker, A.B., Demerouti, E. and Schaufeli, W.B. (2009) Work engagement and financial returns: A diary study on the role of job and personal resources. *Journal of Occupational and Organizational Psychology* 82(1): 183–200.

Xanthopoulou, D., Bakker, A.B. and Ilies, R. (2012) Everyday working life: Explaining within-person fluctuations in employee well-being. *Human Relations* 65(9): 1051–69.

Xu, J. and Cooper-Thomas, H.D. (2011) How can leaders achieve high employee engagement? *Leadership and Organization Development Journal* 32(4): 399–416.

47

NEW WAYS OF WORKING AND EMPLOYABILITY

Towards an agenda for HRD

Beatrice I. J. M. Van Der Heijden, Pascale Peters and Clare Kelliher

The past decade has seen a number of changes in the world of work across many economies, such as internationalization, individualization, informalization, informatization and intensification (see Schnabel 2000, for more details), each of which has implications for employability and HRD. The era when careers involved an upward trajectory within a long-term employment relationship appears to have passed (Arthur and Rousseau 1996; Briscoe *et al.* 2006; Sullivan 1999). Constant change, both in terms of the economic environment and required job qualifications, has made it hard to predict what knowledge and skills are needed in the (near) future. Therefore, a high level of employability, or career potential (Van Der Heijde and Van Der Heijden 2006; Van Der Heijden *et al.* 2009), and through this achieving flexibility in functioning, seem to be the key criteria that enable an employee to stay "in the race".

Workers' employability comprises their capabilities to maintain, nurture, and further develop their essential qualifications, according to Van Der Heijde and Van Der Heijden (2006). They refer to the permanent acquisition and fulfilment of employment within or outside of one's current organization, for one's current or future customer(s), and also with regard to future prospects (Forrier and Sels 2003; Fugate *et al.* 2004; Hillage and Pollard 1998; Rothwell and Arnold 2007). Following the so-called HRM-performance cycle (Guest 2002), we assume that employability, being an employee-level outcome, is a strong predictor for corporate performance. In view of rapidly changing, unpredictable, and global markets, organizations need to be increasingly flexible in order to achieve organizational success and competitive advantage. Workers that have obtained differentiating knowledge and skills that can be more flexibly deployed by organizations, and therefore can add value, are unique or scarce, are not imitable, and not substitutable (cf. Barney 1991). To achieve this, organizations may make use of employer-friendly flexible working arrangements (cf. Fleetwood 2007), such as involuntary part-time employment, temporal labor contracts, and unpredictable working hours.

However, employees may themselves want flexibility and may expect employers to offer employee-friendly forms of flexibility (cf. Fleetwood 2007), such as voluntary part-time work, flexible working hours, and teleworking (cf. Peters *et al.* 2009a). This implies that in the current economic context, reaching the requirement of "flexibility" goes beyond the traditional distinction between employer-friendly versus employee-friendly flexibility. In case of a *win-win situation*, flexibility may have positive consequences for both employers and employees (Rapoport *et al.* 2002). In fact, over the course of time, the concept of (time-spatial) flexibility has gained a much more positive connotation, being increasingly associated with the concept of "work–life balance" (Fleetwood 2007). However, when employees work under so-called "New Working Conditions", having higher levels of job autonomy, working in project teams, being managed by objectives, and facing strict deadlines, they may be vulnerable to negative side effects as well (Peters *et al.* 2009a), such as working longer hours and experiencing a poorer work–life balance.

In the current debate, flexibility and employability are interrelated concepts that play an increasingly important role in current labor market developments. In this chapter we advocate that, in order to enhance workers' employability and to strive for a vital and sustainable global economy, flexibility should take on a new meaning as an HR-strategic tool creating multiple values, both for the individual worker and for the work organization as a whole. There is a need for employers and other stakeholders to recognize their roles in providing support for employees, to develop their human resources, and to enhance employability and career potential, which in turn is likely to reduce the risks that we assume to be associated with the increasingly flexible world of work. The need for work organizations, and other stakeholders alike, to think more radically about the possible impact of New Ways of Working (NWW) in the light of employees' career potential, and the key role HRD plays in this regard, calls for new initiatives at all policy levels: a national, regional, industry, organizational (employer), and an individual worker level, stimulating workers to benefit equally from NWW.

The key imperative might be the mutual understanding and openness in communication in order to respond to the differences in expectations with regard to work and personal development, in line with the differences in individual aspirations and capabilities. The more diverse working population, the increasing acknowledgement of the importance of non-work areas of life, such as "quality time" with family and friends and leisure, urge us to avoid thinking in categories regarding career development and career success alone. We argue that HRD plays a central role in this regard by carefully fine-tuning, and even going beyond, employer- and employee-friendly forms of flexibility with individual workers' aspirations, needs and potential.

First, we will present an overview of current thinking on employability. Second, we will explore a number of recent contextual changes which create pressure for organizations to become more flexible and to stimulate workers' employability. Third, we will examine the concept of NWW and its relationship to employability, paying attention to both the "bright" and "dark" sides associated with this relationship. The chapter concludes by presenting a future research agenda.

Employability

Recent market developments have led to significant reorganizations of work structures, in terms of de-specialization and deregulation. As a result, the way work in organizations is divided into separate tasks and the way these are coordinated (cf. Mintzberg 1980) have changed, which may lead to job enrichment, empowering employees, giving them more job autonomy and accountability, while at the same time, paying more attention to team work (cf. Hales 1993) and to roles instead of jobs. The associated "transition from a job-based HRM system to a competence-based, person-related HR-system" (Van Der Heijde and Van Der Heijden 2006: 451) has had consequences for individual employees. This transition not only reflects a change in the type of competences needed by employees to perform their jobs or roles effectively; employees also need to add to their competences on an ongoing basis, in order to remain employable and to ensure life-long employment and personal career success (De Vos *et al.* 2011; Van Der Heijde and Van Der Heijden 2006). Presently, gaining labor market success requires workers, on the one hand, to invest seriously in enhancing their domain-specific expertise, and, on the other hand, to invest in competences that enable them to handle ambiguity, to be flexible, and to manage multiple tasks simultaneously (Friedman and Greenhaus 2000).

Van Der Heijde and Van Der Heijden's (2006) conceptualization of employability goes beyond training and education, as they may not be sufficient to ensure job and career success in the current labor market context, being generally focused only on domain-specific fields of expertise. Instead, their conceptualization of employability is defined as "the continuous fulfilling, acquiring or creating of work through the optimal use of competences" (Van Der Heijde and Van Der Heijden 2006: 143), which is consistent with more general definitions focusing on the individual's ability to get and retain a job, or to obtain a desired job (cf. Berntson and Marklund 2007; Fugate *et al.* 2004; Hillage and Pollard 1998; Rothwell and Arnold 2007). This definition refers to investment in human capital in a broader sense, which is needed to guarantee life-long employment and career success; both in economic (objective career success) and in non-economic terms (subjective career success).

Van Der Heijde and Van Der Heijden (2006) distinguished between five dimensions of employability. The first, *Occupational expertise*, is domain-specific, and is assumed to be a requirement for positive career outcomes for workers. Fundamentally, it comprises the set of knowledge and skills which are needed to perform a particular job in a particular field. The other four, more general dimensions of competences, are *Anticipation and optimization*, *Personal flexibility*, *Corporate sense*, and *Balance*. These dimensions, relate to both job-related matters and broader career development aspects, and these are outlined below (as per Van Der Heijde and Van Der Heijden 2006).

Anticipation and optimization is a self-initiating, proactive adaptation, where workers prepare themselves for future work changes, based on the knowledge they have about the labor market, by exploring it on an ongoing basis in order to find out what types of skills are currently being sought by employers. Furthermore, this enables them to better prepare themselves for areas outside their domain-specific field of expertise.

Personal flexibility is a more passive, reactive type of adaptation involving the ability to adapt to unforeseen changes, which employees have no control over in their work and labor market environment, such as shifts between jobs and/or organizations.

Corporate sense involves departmental and organizational sharing and collaboration, and encourages workers to participate in different work groups (employee involvement). In modern organizations, employees are required and expected to participate more as integrated team members, to identify with corporate goals, and to share responsibility for the decision-making process (Chapman and Martin 1995). Furthermore, corporate sense builds on an employee's social capital, social skills, and emotional intelligence, because continuously improving skills and being able to make their abilities known through a network may increase the chances of finding (alternative) employment; either with their current employer, an approach by another employer, or independent job search. This aspect of the employability concept links to Kanter's work (1995) who underlined the increasing importance of social capital, since social networks may help the individual to achieve more throughout their career, by making their knowledge and skills known on the (internal or external) labor market (see also Melamed 1996).

Finally, the fifth dimension *Balance* is the process of trying to find a middle ground between opposing work, career, and private interests of the individual employee, and between opposing interests of the employer and the employee. This process of negotiation aims to achieve a balance between the investments of and benefits for both parties. But this balance may not always be easy to achieve, since the demands of the two parties may conflict. For example, employers may wish for highly committed workers while, at the same time they want employees to be willing to be flexible and work on an irregular basis. Employees may also have opposing interests, at different levels – the work process level, career developmental level, and private level – that are difficult to reconcile.

To respond to ongoing labor market changes, employees are increasingly required to invest their own time, money and energy in the enhancement of their employability (Hall 1976; De Cuyper *et al.* 2011).

Contextual changes

In recent years, a number of changes to the world of work have had implications for the employability requirements of individual workers. First, increased competitive pressures for many businesses have affected the way in which work is organized, and have placed emphasis on the importance of enhanced flexibility, and employability. This set of circumstances has been further exacerbated by the Global Financial Crisis (GFC).

In an attempt to increase efficiency, employers may seek to reduce labor costs in several ways, for example by reducing the numbers of people employed, sourcing cheaper labor and/or seeking greater value from employees. This may involve using labor in more flexible ways to allow employers to match the supply and demand for labor more closely, for example, by using temporary agency staff, and by employing staff on annual hours contracts. Increased competitive pressure has been fuelled, at least in part, by greater global integration. Employers are able to scan the globe for the source of the most appropriately skilled and cheapest labor and utilize outsourcing and off-shoring (Oshri *et al.* 2007). Outsourcing may be utilized in order to reduce costs, particularly labor costs and/or may be used to access expertise not available internally in the organization. Off-shoring relocates business activity to another part of the world, normally where labor costs are lower. For example, much call center work has been off-shored to India and manufacturing activities have been off-shored to China, where appropriately qualified labor may be available at a significantly lower cost. These developments have implications for employability in the sense that employees need to anticipate such changes and to prepare themselves for alternative opportunities, such as self-employment.

Increased global integration can also lead to restructuring *inside* organizations, in order to move from a national or regional structure to a more global one. Restructuring along these lines may have significant implications for the nature and organization of work. For example, Kelliher *et al.* (2012) found that managers with country-level responsibilities experienced a reduction in discretion as a result of global restructuring. By being aware of these types of changes and by being prepared to adapt, employees may be able to seek out and/or shape roles for themselves which make better use of the skills and experience they possess, increasing their flexibility and their employability. Increased global integration also means that organizations need to operate in different ways. Rather than being co-located, work teams may be drawn together from across an organization's operations and may therefore be distributed across different locations. Working with colleagues or customers in different time zones often has implications for when work is carried out. For example, a team which is geographically distributed may have little or no opportunity for real time working inside the "normal working hours" of each location. As a result, there may be a need for personal flexibility on the part of the employee in relation to working time, in order to accommodate real time communication and co-ordination when it is needed (Collins and Kolb 2011). This may lead to the introduction of teleworking, even in uncertainty avoiding contexts with hierarchical relationships (Peters *et al.* 2009b). In addition, employees may need to acquire additional communication and co-ordination skills in order to be effective team members where teams are geographically distributed, either with or without the assistance of their employer.

Besides market pressures, institutional environments may also create pressures for organizations to become more flexible. In the Dutch context, for example, part-time work has been used to help employees, particularly women, achieve a better work–life balance. In view of the current economic situation, however, pressures to adopt flexible working, instead of part-time work, are strong. As of 2010, the Netherlands have seen various media campaigns, supported by the Dutch government, aimed at increasing employees' and employers' awareness, acceptance and use of flexible working in order to improve work–life balance and to stimulate participation of women in the labor market and, herewith, gender equality (Peters 2011).

Technology has also had important implications for the nature and organization of work inside organizations causing a significant increase in work which is technology-assisted in some sense. Information and Communication Technologies (ICT) allow work to be carried out remotely from the workplace. This, in turn, may allow employers to reduce workplace costs, by reducing the amount of workspace available, and by encouraging employees to become mobile workers (Anderson and Kelliher 2011; Peters 2011). Some employers may desire to reduce their carbon footprint and, as a result, they may wish to reduce the travel time of employees and may encourage them to work remotely, be that at home, or in other workplace facilities (Anderson and Kelliher 2011; Peters 2011). For the employee, working in a remote location is likely to involve different attributes and competences. For example, they may need to exercise greater self-discipline, be more self-sustaining and develop different communication skills to work effectively with colleagues they are not in face to face contact with (cf. Daniels *et al.* 2000). Furthermore, developments in wireless technology also mean that work can be done almost anywhere (Castells *et al.* 2007) and, as a result, employees may be expected to be available for work beyond "designated" working hours. The ability to communicate almost instantaneously changes expectations in relation to speed of response to communications. In order to work effectively in this context, while at the same time protecting their personal space, employees will need to develop connectivity norms (Collins and Kolb 2011), regarding when they will and will not be available for work activities. In a similar vein, Kossek *et al.* (2005) pointed out that employees, in the light of increased work flexibility leading to blurred boundaries, need to develop new boundary management skills to better free themselves from work (cf. Mirchandani 2000; Dikkers *et al.* 2004).

The growth in service work, and particularly "emotional" and "aesthetic" labor, has implications for what employers expect from their staff. Where employees are expected to engage in emotional labor as part of their employment, they are expected to manage their emotions in a prescribed and/or desired way (Hochschild 1983). This requirement in a job exercises different demands on employees, and may result in outcomes specifically associated with this element. For example, empirical research shows that where employees are required to display emotions which are not consistent with their authentic feelings, there are negative outcomes for employee well-being (Cote 2005; Kinman 2009). Aesthetic labor requires employees to look, sound, and/or present themselves in a particular way, in line with the brand or image of their employing organization (Warhurst *et al.* 2000). As with emotional labor, this may require a degree of misrepresentation of their selves, such as when an employee speaks with a particular accent or adopts a particular form of self-presentation. These growing elements of work require different behaviors from employees, which may not always be explicit. For employees involved in this kind of work there is a need to recognize these aspects of work, be prepared to adapt and prepared to carry out these elements effectively. As such, the service work labor market places high demands on workers' employability not only in terms of their domain-specific expertise, but more particularly, in terms of their generic competences, such as personal flexibility (Van Der Heijde and Van Der Heijden 2006).

New ways of working

In many countries, some forms of flexible work arrangements are now commonplace. However, there are clear cross-national differences in how these are implemented in organizations (Peters *et al.* 2009b), and in the extent to which they deliver positive outcomes. The trends towards flexible working arrangements are increasingly discussed under the more general heading of "New Ways of Working" (Peters 2011). This term may refer to a wide variety of flexible working arrangements where employees are able to exercise discretion over where, when, and how much they work. This may include (Peters 2011): *reduced working hours*, where employees are able to negotiate contractual working hours lower than the full-time norm; *flexi-time schemes*, where employees are allowed greater control over their working hours, normally allowing them to vary the start and finish of their working day; *individual scheduling*, where employees' physical presence in the workplace is important, but employees are not only given more control over the timing of their working hours (e.g. shifts), but also participate in and have responsibility regarding the work-scheduling process itself; *teleworking*, which may include mobile work and home-based working. Telework arrangements are often negotiated with the employees' line managers (Peters *et al.* 2010a) and can be associated with enhanced job autonomy (Gajendran and Harrison 2007). In some studies, self-employed workers are also included in the telework definition (cf. Peters 2011).

Currently, societal and academic discussions go beyond flexibility by referring to a fundamentally different work philosophy and related management practices, associated with a "flexible office", remote working (often from home), and intensified use of ICT to communicate and collaborate with colleagues, allowing employees to potentially work at any time and away from a centralized workplace. This trend implies that employers need to focus more on giving the employee – within certain limits – more job autonomy and flexibility regarding how, where, when and with whom work is done, and more responsibility for meeting targets and deadlines (cf. Peters *et al.* 2009a). Based on these trends, NWW can be taken to refer to HRM practices enhancing employee empowerment, teleworking and creating trust relationships among team members (Handy 1995; Peters *et al.* in press).

The relationship between NWW and employability

Flexibility concerning working time provides employees with greater control to schedule work to fit with the demands of their non-work lives (Gajendran and Harrison 2007). The opportunity to work remotely allows employees to work from home or another location, and assist them in avoiding a long or stressful commute to work. These two types of practices, combined, are referred to as time-spatial flexibility, implying that workers have a say in their working time and place (Peters *et al.* 2009a). Time-spatial flexibility is expected to enhance positive career outcomes and satisfaction, allowing workers to align work and family demands better, by resolving time and scheduling problems (Friedman and Greenhaus 2000), and to be physically able to spend more time and energy in other life domains. Workers may be able to fulfil their various life sphere demands more effectively (Powell and Greenhaus 2006), and with fewer conflicts and stress. In turn, they may be more creative, committed and flexible. Furthermore, they may be more productive away from the distractions of the workplace (Kelliher and Anderson 2010) and may consequently enhance their employability.

A trend towards seeing time spent at work, i.e. the so-called time bind, as signaling productivity and ambition (Hochschild 1997; Peters *et al.* 2010b) results in those employees seeking flexible working arrangements being seen as not working hard enough or being sufficiently committed (Clarke 2005) by important stakeholders, such as one's direct supervisor (Peters *et al.* 2010b). Although telecommuting is often offered on a part-time basis (Peters and Van Der Lippe 2007), the "face-time" employees spend at the workplace diminishes, which may lead to a misperception about the productivity of teleworkers, which may, subsequently, result in fewer advancement opportunities (Raines and Leathers 2001; Schmidt and Duenas 2002). Previous research has indicated that women are perceived to be most affected by such lack of advancement opportunities (Rogier and Padgett 2004).

Time-spatial flexibility may have the potential to allow both men and women to better fulfil their private-life responsibilities and, thereby, reduce the costs regarding caring tasks that arise from not being at home, which positively affects their social well-being. Geurts *et al.* (2009) argued that flextime is a potential means to help workers maintain a satisfactory work–family balance. This may apply particularly for women (Peters *et al.* 2009a). Employees granted the opportunity to telework, on a regular basis, experience an improved quality of work, social, and home life, provided by more flexible hours and schedules (Raines and Leathers 2001), which has the potential to reduce time pressure (Peters and Van Der Lippe 2007). Madsen (2003) found that teleworkers, especially those with childcare responsibilities, experienced a better work–life balance compared with regular workers: 54% stated that they worked the same or greater number of hours than they used to do when they were at the office, while still being able to attend to the personal and/or family responsibilities they had (Potter 2003).

The importance of "time-spatial flexibility" in the light of women's labor market participation is expected to enhance their employability and career success (cf. Crompton *et al.* 1996). Particularly women having young children may perceive time-spatial flexibility as an attractive tool to balance work and family life, while investing time and energy in their employability enhancement as well. Indeed, previous studies have reported on women's preferences for time-spatial flexibility (e.g. Keuzenkamp *et al.* 2009) and on its advantages for women's labor market and household positions, in terms of providing additional income, better work–life balance (Brewster *et al.* 2007), and career achievement and satisfaction. Peters and colleagues (in press) investigated the relationship between NWW and work-related flow (operationalized as work enjoyment, absorption, and intrinsic motivation) and found that employees need to feel empowered (operationalized as autonomy at work, teamwork, and output management) and supported by both the management team and their colleagues to align NWW with their personal preferences. Hence, a culture of trust forms the basis for success when NWW are to be implemented.

Future agenda: flexibility and employability

NWW lead to new forms of careers and HRD needs, particularly when NWW are accompanied by an increase in temporary employment contracts and outsourcing work to account workers, in addition to work performed by core workers. NWW also create specific opportunities for HRD activities and employability enhancement, such as the changing organizational environment that is constituted by new ICT (Gattiker and Coe 1986), which allows a more diverse workforce, such as women workers, working carers, partly disabled workers, and elderly workers, to participate in the labor market, and to enlarge their number of working hours (cf. Peters 2011).

Some promising areas for future research can be distinguished. First, given the demographic changes in the labor market, it might be helpful to understand the possible moderating role of gender, age, disabilities, and ethnicity in the relationship between NWW and employability, in order to provide management in work organizations with tailor-made advice for diversity-aware HRD activities.

A second area of research comprises a better understanding of the impact of NWW upon the psychological contract that employees experience (Rousseau 1995), preferably taking a lifespan perspective, given its established importance in the light of career outcomes, such as organizational commitment (Bal *et al.* 2013), life and job satisfaction, performance, and turnover intention (De Cuyper *et al.* 2011). Moreover, the increasingly temporary nature of relationships between employers and employees, coupled with flatter hierarchies, urges us to better understand how the psychological contract and idiosyncratic deals (that is "voluntary, personalized agreements of a nonstandard nature, negotiated between individual employees and their employers regarding terms that benefit each party"; Rousseau *et al.* 2006: 978) may help to sustain the relationship between employer and employee. When NWW are used as a strategic tool, serving the employer's agenda for enhancing flexibility for competitive advantage and organizational success, and the employee's individual needs and preferences to balance work and life demands, win-win outcomes may be within reach.

Third, despite the rapidly increasing globalization of business and industry, there is a lack of cross-national, cross-cultural, and cross-industry comparative career research aimed at the questions faced by working organizations and to provide guidance for HRD practice (Arnold 1997; Brewster *et al.* 1996). Future empirical research should compare contexts wherein norms and preferences regarding NWW may differ.

Hence, future research should be aimed at examining of the potential of NWW, and possible negative side effects. Both policy makers at a national, regional and industry level, and employers and employees, should place the issue of NWW, employability and employee well-being high on their agendas. Only when they carry the responsibility for designing healthy, prosperous, sustainable and challenging careers, can work–life be improved and life-long employability guaranteed.

References

Anderson, D. and Kelliher, C. (2011) Spatial aspects of professionals' work-life integration. In: Kaiser, S., Cunha, M. and Eikhof, D (eds) *Creating balance? International perspectives on the work-life integration of professionals.* New York: Springer, 303–49.

Arnold, J. (1997) *Managing careers into the 21st century.* London: SAGE.

Arthur, M.B. and Rousseau, D.M. (1996) (eds) *The boundaryless career.* New York: Oxford University Press.

Bal, P.M., De Lange, A.H., Zacher, H. and Van Der Heijden, B.I.J.M. (2013) A lifespan perspective on psychological contracts and their relations with organizational commitment. *European Journal of Work and Organizational Psychology*, 22(3): 279–92.

Barney, J. (1991) Firm resources and sustained competitive advantage. *Journal of Management* 17(1): 99–120.

Berntson, E. and Marklund, S. (2007) The relationship between employability and subsequent health. *Work and Stress* 21(3): 279–92.

Brewster, C., Tregaskis, O., Hegewich, A. and Mayne, L. (1996) Comparative research in human resource management: A review and example. *International Journal of Human Resource Management* 7(3): 585–604.

Brewster, C., Sparrow, P. and Vernon, G. (2007) *International Human Resource Management.* London: CIPD.

Briscoe, J.P., Hall, D.T. and Frautschy DeMuth, R.L. (2006) Protean and boundaryless careers: An empirical exploration. *Journal of Vocational Behavior* 69: 30–47.

Castells, M., Fernandez-Ardevol, M., Qui, J. and Sey, A. (2007) *Mobile communication and society.* Cambridge, MA: MIT.

Chapman, G.M. and Martin, J.F. (1995) Computerized business games in engineering education. *Computers & Education* 25(1/2): 67–73.

Clarke, R. (2005) *Flexible Working: Impact and Implementation and Employer Survey.* London: CIPD.

Collins, P. and Kolb, D. (2011) Innovation in distributed teams: The duality of connectivity norms and human agency. In: Kelliher, C. and Richardson, J. (eds) *New ways of organizing work: Developments, perspectives and experiences.* New York: Routledge, 140–59.

Cote, S. (2005) A social interaction model of the effects of emotion regulation on work strain. *Academy of Management Review* 30(3): 509–30.

Crompton, R., Gallie, D. and Purcell, L. (1996) *Changing forms of employment: Organizations, skills, and gender.* London: Routledge.

Daniels, K., Lamond, D.A. and Standen, P. (eds) (2000) *Managing telework: Perspectives from human resource management and work psychology.* London: Thomson Learning.

De Cuyper, N., Van Der Heijden, B.I.J.M. and De Witte, H. (2011) Associations between perceived employability, employee well-being, and its contributions to organizational success: A matter of psychological contracts? *International Journal of Human Resource Management* 22(7): 1486–503.

De Vos, A., De Hauw, S. and Van Der Heijden, B.I.J.M. (2011) Competency development and career success: The mediating role of employability. *Journal of Vocational Behavior* 79: 438–47.

Dikkers, J., Geurts, S., Den Dulk, L., Peper, B. and Kompier, M. (2004) Relations among work–home culture, the utilization of work–home arrangements, and work–home interference. *International Journal of Stress Management* 11(4): 323–45.

Fleetwood, S. (2007) Why work–life balance now? *International Journal of Human Resource Management* 18(3): 387–400.

Forrier, A. and Sels, L. (2003) The concept employability: A complex mosaic. *International Journal of Human Resources Development and Management* 3(2): 102–24.

Friedman, S.D. and Greenhaus, J.H. (2000) *Work and family – allies or enemies? What happens when business professionals confront life choices.* New York: Oxford University Press.

Fugate, M., Kinicki, A.J. and Ashforth, B.E. (2004) Employability: A psycho-social construct, its dimensions, and applications. *Journal of Vocational Behavior* 65: 14–38.

Gajendran, R.S. and Harrison, D.A. (2007) The good, the bad, and the unknown about telecommuting: Meta-analysis of psychological mediators and individual consequences. *Journal of Applied Psychology* 92: 1524–41.

Gattiker, U.E. and Coe, L. (1986) *Relationship of computer attitudes with perception of career success.* Proceedings of the 46th Annual Meeting of the Academy of Management, 294–8.

Geurts, S.A.E., Beckers, D.G.J., Taris, T.W., Kompier, M.A.J. and Smulders, P.G.W. (2009) Worktime demands and work–family interference: Does worktime control buffer the adverse effects of high demands? *Journal of Business Ethics* 84: 229–41.

Guest, D.E. (2002) Human Resource Management, corporate performance and employee well-being: Building the worker into HRM. *Journal of Industrial Relations* 44(3): 335–58.

Hales, C. (1993) *Managing through organization. The management process, forms of organization and the work of managers.* London: Routledge.

Hall, D.T. (1976) *Careers in organisations.* Pacific Palisades, CA: Goodyear.

Handy, C. (1995) Trust and the virtual organization. *Harvard Business Review* 73: 40–50.

Hillage, J. and Pollard, E. (1998) *Employability: Developing a framework for policy analysis.* Brighton: Institute for Employment Studies.

Hochschild, A.R. (1983) *The managed heart: Commercialization of human feeling.* Berkeley: University of California Press.

— (1997) *The time bind: When work becomes home and home becomes work.* New York: Metropolitan.

Kanter, R. (1995) *Nice work if you can get it: The software industry as a model of tomorrow's jobs. The American prospect.* Retrieved from http://prospect.org/article/nice-work-if-you-can-get-it-software-industry-model-tomorrows-jobs.

Kelliher, C. and Anderson, D. (2010) Doing more with less? Flexible working practices and the intensification of work. *Human Relations* 63: 83–106.

Kelliher, C., Clarke, C., Hope Hailey, V. and Farndale, E. (2012) Going global, feeling small: An examination of managers' reactions to global restructuring in a multinational organisation. *International Journal of Human Resource Management* 23(11): 2163–79.

Keuzenkamp, S., Hillebrink, C., Portegijs, W. and Pouwels, B. (2009) *Deeltijd (g)een problem* [Part-time (no) problem]. The Hague: SCP.

Kinman, G. (2009) Emotional labour and strain in "front-line" service employees. Does mode of delivery matter? *Journal of Managerial Psychology* 24(2): 118–35.

Kossek, E.E., Lautsch, B.A. and Eaton, S.C. (2005) Telecommuting, control, and boundary management: Correlates of policy use and practice, job control, and work–family effectiveness. *Journal of Vocational Behavior* 68: 347–67.

Madsen, S.R. (2003) The effects of home-based teleworking on work–family conflict. *Human Resource Development Quarterly* 14(1): 35–58.

Melamed, T. (1996) Career success: An assessment of a gender-specific model. *Journal of Occupational and Organizational Psychology* 69(3): 217–42.

Mintzberg, H. (1980) Structure in 5's: A synthesis of the research on organization design. *Management Science* 26(3): 322–41.

Mirchandani, K. (2000) "The best of both worlds" and "cutting my own throat": Contradictory images of home-based telework. *Qualitative Sociology* 23(4): 159–82.

Oshri, I., Kotlarsky, J. and Willcocks, L.P. (2007) Managing dispersed expertise in IT offshore outsoucing: Lessons from Tata consultancy services. *MIS Quarterly Executive* 6(2): 53–65.

Peters, P. (2011) *Flexible working time arrangements: Exchange of good practices on gender equality*. Retrieved from http://ec.europa.eu/justice/gender-equality/other-institutions/good-practices/review-seminars/seminars_2011/new_forms_of_work_en.htm.

Peters, P. and Van Der Lippe, T. (2007) The time pressure reducing potential of telehomeworking: The Dutch case. *International Journal of Human Resource Management* 18(3): 430–47.

Peters, P., Den Dulk, L. and Van Der Lippe, T. (2009a) The effects of time-spatial flexibility and new working conditions on employees' work–life balance: The Dutch case. *Community, Work & Family* 12(3): 279–98.

Peters, P., Bleijenbergh, I. and Oldenkamp, E. (2009b) Cultural sources of variance in telework adoption in two subsidiaries of an ICT-multinational. *International Journal of Employment Studies* 17(2): 66–101.

Peters, P., Den Dulk, L. and De Ruijter, J. (2010a) May I work from home? Views of the employment relationship reflected in line managers' telework attitudes in six financial-sector organizations. *Equality, Diversity and Inclusion* 29(5): 517–31.

Peters, P., Bleijenbergh, I., Pas, B. and Gremmen, I. (2010b) De deeltijdval [The part-time trap]. *Tijdschrift voor Genderstudies* 13(4): 21–32.

Peters, P., De Bruijn, T., Van Der Heijden, B.I.J.M., Poutsma, E. and Bakker, A.B. (in press) Enjoying new ways to work: A configurational approach to new organizational forms that stimulate work-related flow. *Human Resource Management*.

Potter, E.E. (2003) Telecommuting: The future of work, corporate culture, and American society. *Journal of Labor Research* 24(1): 73–84.

Powell, G.N. and Greenhaus, J.H. (2006) Is the opposite of positive negative? Untangling the complex relationship between WFE and conflict. *Career Development International* 11(7): 650–59.

Raines, J.P. and Leathers, C.G. (2001) Telecommuting: The new wave of workplace technology will create a flood of change in social institutions. *Journal of Economic Issues* 35(2): 307–13.

Rapoport, R., Bailyn, L., Fletcher, J.K. and Pruitt, B.H. (2002) *Beyond work–family balance. Advancing gender equity and workplace performance*. San Francisco: Jossey-Bass.

Rogier, S.A. and Padgett, M.Y. (2004) The impact of utilizing a flexible work schedule on the perceived career advancement potential of women. *Human Resource Development Quarterly* 15(1): 89–106.

Rothwell, A. and Arnold, J. (2007) Self-perceived employability: Development and validation of a scale. *Personnel Review* 36(1): 23–41.

Rousseau, D.M. (1995) *Psychological contracts in organizations: Understanding written and unwritten agreements*. London: SAGE.

Rousseau, D.M., Ho, V.T. and Greenberg, J. (2006) I-deals: Idiosyncratic terms in employment relationships. *Academy of Management Review* 31: 977–94.

Schmidt, D.E. and Duenas, G. (2002) Incentives to encourage worker-friendly organizations. *Public Personnel Management* 31(3): 293–308.

Schnabel, P. (2000) *Maatschappij in beweging* [Society on the move]. The Hague: SER.

Sullivan, S.E. (1999) The changing nature of careers: A review and research agenda. *Journal of Management* 25: 457–84.

Van Der Heijde, C. and Van Der Heijden, B.I.J.M. (2006) A competence-based and multidimensional operationalization and measurement of employability. *Human Resource Management* 45(3): 449–76.

Van Der Heijden, B.I.J.M., De Lange, A.H., Demerouti, E. and Van Der Heijde, C.M. (2009) Employability and career success across the life-span: Age effects on the employability–career success relationship. *Journal of Vocational Behavior* 74: 156–64.

Warhurst, C., Nickson, D., Witz, A. and Cullen, A.M. (2000) Aesthetic labour in interactive service work: Some case study evidence from the "New" Glasgow. *Service Industries Journal* 20(3): 1–18.

48

AN INTERNATIONAL PERSPECTIVE OF THE WORK–LIFE SYSTEM WITHIN HRD

Sunny L. Munn and Hae-Young Lee

The purpose of this chapter is to provide an international sampling of the work–life system within the field of HRD. Relevant to this conversation are the interactions of employees, organizations and governments as a means of developing and implementing initiatives and actions which impact the work–life balance of individuals (Munn 2013). Although work–life balance is most frequently discussed and internationally understood to indicate how individuals find agreement within their work and home life, it is not the only piece to the work–life system. The work–life system is comprised of three forces (employees, organizations and government), and three dimensions (work–life balance, work–life initiatives and work–life policy); all interdependent on the others (Munn 2013). Space requirements limit this chapter to a selection of research within a few countries rather than providing a comprehensive international review of the work–life system. Specifically, relevant theoretical perspectives, policy considerations, issues of practices and implications within the context of HRD will be identified and discussed.

Dimensions of the work–life system

Work–life balance is how individuals prioritize work, family, individual, and community responsibilities. How individuals prioritize work, family, individual and community responsibilities is influenced by the availability and knowledge of work–life initiatives. Organizational cultures influence whether or not employee use of these benefits is acceptable (Munn 2013). Work–life initiatives include: flexible/alternative work practices; paid and unpaid leave; dependent care services; and informational resources/services (Gray and Tudball 2003). Sometimes health insurance, retirement and educational benefits are also included (Perry-Smith and Blum 2000). Work–life initiatives exist to help employees achieve work–life balance with the intent of positively impacting organizational performance (Pitt-Catsouphes *et al.* 2007). Work–life policy is public policy which impacts individuals and organizations within the work–life system. In many countries the work–life agenda is impacted by work–life policies which specifically aim to shape the social care of women, children and families as a means to increase female labor participation. Although still limited, in many developed countries the work–life system is beginning to acknowledge and include the needs of men.

Situating the work–life system within the context of HRD: evidence from the United States

In the United States work–life research emerged because of changing workforce dynamics and family structures. Grounded in sociology, family studies, psychology and management, the study of work–life is approximately 40 years old and emerged in HRD within the last decade (Morris and Madsen 2007). Kanter (1977) originally identified the separation of work and family as a myth. She called for organizational and public policy to empower employees and their families by creating initiatives which transcended the ideal worker (i.e. long hours and prioritizes organizational commitment over family) by recognizing the integration of work and family. Kahnweiler (2008) later identified the need to better incorporate work–life as an essential component of HRD.

Integral to the study of work–life is how one achieves work–life balance. Although many definitions of work–life/work–family balance have been offered within and outside of HRD (Clark 2000, Crooker *et al.* 2002, Greenhaus *et al.* 2003, Grzywacz and Carlson 2007, Voydanoff 2005), a single agreeable definition has yet to be identified. Similarly, a common method of measurement is lacking (Chang *et al.* 2010, McMillan *et al.* 2011), resulting in the inability of HRD professionals, researchers and policy makers to effectively understand the impact of work–life initiatives on the work–life balance of employees. If in practice measurement is "to become a leverage point for HRD managers, valid measures are needed to monitor the effectiveness of programs targeting balance" (Grzywacz and Carlson 2007: 459).

The business case supporting the existence and implementation of work–life initiatives seems simple – that which helps employees will also help to advance organizational performance (Perry-Smith and Blum 2000). Work–life interventions improve: the quality of work–life for parents and non-parents (Galinsky and Stein 1990); productivity for both the employee and the employer; recruitment and retention of employees (Casper and Buffardi 2004, Lee 2004), including older workers, women and minorities. When work–life initiatives exist research indicates increased employee job satisfaction, morale, loyalty, commitment, motivation, organizational citizenship, volunteerism, and engagement, in addition to increased corporate social responsibility, investors, customer satisfaction and customer loyalty (Morris 2008). Companies with a majority female and professional employee population demonstrate a positive relationship between work–life programs and organizational performance (Konrad and Mangel 2000). Declining organizational performance due to costs, inequitable application of benefits, limited support for employee needs, and long-term organizational benefits have also been demonstrated (Galinsky *et al.* 1993). Often the language used to promote work–life initiatives is ineffective or inconsistent causing inequitable practices among different groups of employees such as sexual minorities (Hornsby and Munn 2009). Information regarding how employees use work–life initiatives and what personal characteristics influence their decisions to do so remains scarce.

Individuals, organizations and governments interact to produce work–life policy. Although national work–life policy in the US is limited, it does exist. The government's role in determining a work–life agenda is a contested issue; for example, public policies such as health insurance, the provision of sick leave or opportunities to use the Family and Medical Leave Act (FMLA) have implications for organizational development and performance. The role of public policy is unclear – often seen as support and interference at the same time. For example, the FMLA is useful only to families who can afford to take unpaid leave and is not required of organizations with fewer than 50 employees.

Identifying variations in the work–life system across cultures

Since the 1970s, governments across the globe have tried to respond to work–life/family issues by designing and implementing public interventions (Maitland and Thomson 2011). Research devoted to work–life issues has increased; however, most is conducted in Australia, Europe, and North America. This limitation could cause the uniqueness and variety of work–life issues to be overlooked creating an unintended generalization of Western concepts of work–life issues across the globe. Therefore, it is critical to recognize that socio-economic, cultural and political contexts might have an impact on relevant interventions on work–life issues (Joplin *et al.* 2003, Poelmans *et al.* 2003).

The Organization for Economic and Co-operation and Development (OECD) (2007: x) defines work–life balance or family-friendly workplace arrangements "as those practices that facilitate the reconciliation of work and family life, and which firms introduce to complement statutory requirements". Intergovernmental organizations such as the International Labour Organization (ILO), OECD, and United Nations Educational, Scientific and Cultural Organization (UNESCO) have addressed work–life issues by formulating policy recommendations. The ILO, for instance, specifies that the right to work implies that family responsibilities cannot constitute cause for discrimination or restrict access to employment thus creating a need for work–life initiatives. The measures also recommend that member states of ILO implement policies ensuring more equal distribution of care responsibilities (ILO 2011). Most OECD member states have experienced socio-economic and demographic changes including labor supply shortages (OECD 2007). For example, the declining number of children in some countries has implications for economic growth and the shape of future societies (Buchanan and Rotkirch 2013). This phenomenon forces governments to review an inefficient use of labor resources, due to limitations on economic growth. To address labor shortages, many countries have implemented diverse governmental interventions which encourage female participation in the labor market (OECD 2008). Raising children and fulfilling workforce commitments are not comprehensively orchestrated in many countries; thus, traditional public policies on family, labor, and social welfare become questionable.

How women work, when women work and how their work interferes with or contributes to family life is at the forefront of the work–life system in most cultures; these relationships are not the same for men. Block *et al.* (2013) provide the labor market trends of women in six industrialized nations. In 2008, 71 per cent of women in the US worked while in the European Union 60 per cent were employed. Japan, Korea, Canada and Australia all reported women's labor market participation as between 42 per cent and 45 per cent in 2007. While the US demonstrates the greatest increase of women in the workforce since 1975 when 47.4 per cent of women worked outside of the home, other nations also reported an increase. In many nations, such as those discussed here, work–life initiatives are largely irrelevant until women enter the workforce creating a need for government and organizational policy to consider the welfare of families and children.

The following sections identify work–life trends amongst various cultures based on the geographical demarcations provided by six of the seven continents. Whereas research on work–life is common in North America, Europe and Australia, it is emerging in South America, Africa and Asia. Vast differences exist across the countries within each continent which are far too great to detail here so only a select few will be discussed as examples. This section explores how socio-economic changes such as demographic and labor markets influence the development of work–life policies for both organizations and governments. Special attention will be given to emerging trends in public and organizational policy and the influence of changing family dynamics on traditional work climates as they might impact cross-cultural comparisons globally.

Europe

An ageing society, increased cultural diversity and the "feminization of the workforce" shape Europe's workforce (Khallash and Kruse 2012: 681) and greatly impact work–life policies and decisions. Increases in part-time work serve as a means to recruit and retain working mothers (Fleetwood 2007b). However, women's household and caregiving responsibilities remain unchanged causing women to assume a second shift at home. As female workforce participation increases in the European Union (EU), organizational recruitment and retention strategies focus more on "family-friendly" practices and those which support work–life balance (Khallash and Kruse 2012). Similar to the United States such practices focus on working and frequently married mothers, excluding the needs of those without children and men. Unlike the United States, great strides have been made recently to alleviate this issue by including men and women without children in the design of work–life initiatives. While working mothers in the US versus UK have markedly different work patterns, Tomlinson (2007) finds that both are limited by welfare systems, capitalism and gender inequities which continue to limit the ability of women to find work–life balance and opportunity for men to take more family responsibility.

In the UK, work–life initiatives like flexible working practices emerged in the 1980s in response to the need for flexible labor markets and to decrease unemployment (Fleetwood 2007b). Flexible work practices are thought to facilitate work–life balance but it is also possible that they limit one's ability to achieve work–life balance. Fleetwood (2007b) identifies three types of flexible work practices – those which are employee friendly/employer unfriendly, employer friendly/employee unfriendly and neutral. Employee friendly flexible practices include flex-time, job sharing and compressed work weeks. Employer friendly practices include annualized hours, split shifts or a mixture of nights and days. Not all work–life initiatives positively impact the worker nor do they all provide support for improved organizational performance. For example, employee earnings can be reduced due to the costs of work–life initiatives (Brough *et al.* 2008). Conversely, a typology of flexible work practices in nearly 21,000 EU firms indicated six profiles. Organizations in the two most flexible profiles indicate flexibility as support for employee work–life balance or support for the preferences of customers and firms. Results do not support the dichotomous relationship that flexibility practices can only support the needs of workers or the employer, but instead suggest that both groups' needs can be met simultaneously (Kerkhofs *et al.* 2008). Work–life balance is viewed as a luxury for those in privileged jobs; however, in instances of economic insecurity Europeans are less concerned with the availability of work–life benefits and more concerned with simply having a job.

Australia and New Zealand

Work–life research in Australia and New Zealand has been directed by a variety of stakeholders including the Australian Council of Trade Unions (ACTU) and the Equal Employment Opportunities Trust (EEOT) in New Zealand. Both have initiated programs supporting work–life balance including the ACTU Work and Family Campaign (Bardoel *et al.* 2008). Similar to the US and EU increased interest in work–life emerged from changing workforce dynamics, including an increase in female labor participation.

Seven prominent themes were identified in a review of work–life research in Australia and New Zealand including: organizations and the provision of work–life, the structure of work, occupation and industry, government investment in work–life, psychological health, the experience of family (structure and children) and gender (Bardoel *et al.* 2008). Barriers identified as obstacles to effectively implementing and using work–life initiatives include: organizational cultures that reward employees reflective of the traditional ideal worker, work environments hostile to non-work commitments, inadequate managerial support, managerial recruitment of those with similar characteristics and insufficient information regarding the existence and usability of work–life initiatives (De Cieri *et al.* 2005).

New Zealand is focused on improving organizational culture as a means of facilitating employee work–life balance and employer performance (Fleetwood 2007a). Organizational culture includes how the organization communicates information and how knowledge of practices is disseminated. Using work–life initiatives is impacted by the implications of what practices are acceptable or unacceptable to use (McDonald *et al.* 2007) and the relationship between employee knowledge of work–life initiatives and organizational commitment (Haar and Spell 2004).

Data from the Australian Work and Life Index 2010 indicates that 67 per cent of employees report satisfaction with their work–life balance, yet 25 per cent believe that work inhibits their ability to participate in non-work activities (Pocock *et al.* 2010). Work–life initiatives contribute to one's sense of balance and are frequently used to attract and retain employees. Organizations seeking market competitiveness are encouraged to create work–life practices which fulfill the needs of a diverse workforce including identifying and implementing effective recruitment and retention practices (De Cieri *et al.* 2005). Employees from over 1,500 Australian organizations identified an awareness of work–life initiatives including: part-time work, education, flex-time, working from home and job sharing (De Cieri *et al.* 2005). In Australia, telework has had positive implications for businesses including decreased costs and increased productivity, while also increasing the work–life balance of employees (Brough *et al.* 2008).

South America

The persistent and increasing entrance of women into the workforce is critical to recent developments in Latin American countries. In the last two decades, female labor participation has grown steadily, while male economic participation has remained stable (Chioda and De La Torre 2012). These trends are impacted by decreasing fertility rates, growing elderly populations, and increased numbers of single-parent and dual-earner households. The dominating social perception is that home is the core and natural space for the provision of care and this responsibility inevitably falls on women. However, women's workforce participation is not accompanied by a social care system and men's household participation has not changed enough to warrant modifications in workforce demands thus creating conflict.

Despite the lack of social care services to facilitate work–life balance the issue is emerging in the public policy arena. The Chile Grows with You Program, introduced in 2006 to support children's development and their mothers' participation in the labor market (Enriquez 2012), demonstrates the development of effective policies. In Uruguay, the newly designed social care system, National System of Care, was implemented. Additional progress is indicated by continued discussion around the system's design, need for social care, heightened social awareness and a distribution of responsibilities throughout society (Enriquez 2012).

Government interventions have lacked adequate regulation and provision of social care services including access because of socio-economic stratification where public social care services are poorly organized and private care services are expensive. Although the anti-egalitarian sentiment against socio-economic status, political participation, and the roles of females in the region has improved (Chioda 2011), governmental support for work-family balance remains weak (Enriquez 2012).

Africa

African countries have experienced rapid socio-economic growth in recent decades. However, the absolute poverty rate continues to force families to alter conventional roles making adaptation to social and economic changes difficult. Whereas the function and role of family was a fundamental unit of production, it is now a unit of labor supply chain and consumption creating conflicts between traditional social foundations and emerging issues.

Income generating activity is essential to a woman's responsibility in much of Africa; therefore, women's workforce participation and traditional home responsibilities compete in the context of multiple and inseparable roles, rather than complementary roles. Women are responsible for the home and children regardless of employment status often creating work–life conflict. Some assistance is in place such as overtime limitations for women, and statutory maternity leave. Paternity leave, however, is rarely available causing gaps between the needs of workers, families and existing legal establishments. However, women are most often employed in the informal labor market and employment is concentrated in a narrow range of activities with the lowest returns (Mokomane 2014).

South Africa adopts the Codes on the Protection of Employees (although not legislatively enforced) that provides employees with leave during pregnancy and after birth. The Code of Good Practice on the Integration of Employment Equity into Human Resource Policies and Practices adds that an employer should provide reasonable accommodation for pregnant women and parents with young children, including health and safety adjustments and post-natal care leave.

In Nigeria, employees desire jobs that provide flexible work schedules to allow for better work–life conflict management (Nwagbara and Akanji 2012). Work–life balance now surpasses job security as an employee priority. Employees of the Nigeria Local Government System want employers to introduce work–life initiatives to better enable them to attend to the demands of their personal life while maintaining an enhanced level of productivity in the workplace.

Asia

Countries in Asia, specifically Japan and Korea, share the common background of Confucian culture and societal norms which emphasize evident gender roles (Lee *et al.* 2011). They face emerging concerns about rapid demographic changes and family formation influencing societal and economic changes. Recently, the concept of work–life balance in these countries shifted from traditional work–life policies including fertility, gender gap, and labor force shortages to include social and political issues including childcare, children's development, education and poverty (Goodman and White 1998, Kim and Chang 2011).

In Korea, the foundational legislation of work-family policies is the Act on Equal Employment and Support for Work–Family Balance. This Act was reformed in 2007 from the Equal Employment Act, expanding the Act's goal from workplace gender equality to work–family balance. Introduced in 2008 for families that cannot afford the income loss due to using full-time parental leave and parents whose job duties are not conducive to extended leaves, employed parents eligible for parental leave can request reduced working hours instead of using parental leave (Koh 2012).

The Japanese government has implemented childcare policies such as Angel Plans (1994–1998), New Angel Plans (1999–2004), and the Child–Family Support Plan (2005–2009) in response to continuous low fertility rates. In 2000, the "Work–life Balance" campaign was initiated which encouraged firms to use flexible work practices resulting in improved managerial perceptions of such practices. Recently, the Japanese government shifted the focus to promote work–life balance among young couples with children. The new initiative intends to change the Japanese work-centered culture into a family-centered culture, encouraging men to spend more time at home and allowing mothers with young children to remain active in the workforce (Haub 2010). Agreement between employers and employees allows for more flexible working hours and practices (Goodman and Peng 1996).

The time a person spends at work is a critical factor to understanding and adequately addressing work–life balance issues in East Asian countries. Previously, Korean and Japanese governments targeted mostly housewives suffering from anxiety and stress because of childcare responsibilities. These governments are now shifting policies toward dual-income households and private sector actions. The goal is to change the social and cultural atmosphere in addition to managerial behavior within organizations. Efforts are underway to reform men's work styles and to change managerial behaviors within the private sector – the intent is to empower local government in issues related to work–life balance.

International implications of the work–life system on HRD research and practice

Industrialized nations around the world have taken action to create and implement effective work–life practices which serve to benefit both the employee and the employer. Facilitating a better integration of work and family/life is necessary to improve workforce dynamics and societal interactions as a whole. Improved support for working parents in an effort to influence family stability is a common theme. There is also support for firms to provide work–life initiatives as part of their recruitment tactics (Khallash and Kruse 2012). Yet, internationally the meaning and parameters of work–life initiatives are unclear. Questions remain regarding who is responsible for providing work–life initiatives, and creating and maintaining work–life balance – individuals, organizations or governments (Brough *et al.* 2008, Fleetwood 2007b).

In a review of statutory annual/vacation leave in five industrialized nations (EU, US, Canada, Australia, Japan and Korea), Block *et al.* (2013) found that all require a minimum of two weeks, but average four, except for the US (which has no requirement). US family leave policy, FMLA, allows for a yearly maximum of 12 weeks unpaid leave, while among the other countries the minimum entitlements allow 32 weeks with a maximum of 200. Though work–life initiatives may be on the organizational radar in the US, this enormous difference illuminates a wide social policy gap when it comes to public policy that could help individuals with work–life balance.

Developing countries in Africa and South America are better integrating women into their workforces and creating policies to ultimately enhance childcare and address education needs for families and children. However, given the varied types of labor, how the work–life system can benefit those who need the most help is yet to be determined.

Internationally, similarities and differences exist within the work–life system. *Family* in all parts of the world is critical to the work–life system. Caregiving versus work responsibilities frequently overlap and in general this overlap is endured by women resulting in the exclusion of men from responsibilities outside of work. *Cultural context* plays a significant role in shaping the policies and perceptions of the work–life system. Work–life initiatives "have been developed differently, depending on historical, religious and cultural influences, stage of economic development, and different government regimes" (Brough *et al.* 2008: 270). These factors impact the structure of firms, including organizational development and change. *Working patterns*, such as long working hours, vary by nation; in particular, less industrialized nations are most likely motivated by economic need, high inflation and unemployment rates. Individuals are more likely to prefer time reductions in paid work to accommodate family life in more economically developed countries. *Government involvement* and the extent to which public policy plays a role in the "reconciliation of work and non-work responsibilities" vary significantly across the globe (Brough *et al.* 2008: 269). In spite of cultural differences and state of economic development, governments are moving forward by endorsing the importance of work-family balance through the development and implementation of public policy. However, families in Latin America and Africa receive less government assistance (if any support at all) compared with families in East Asia, Australia, the EU and the US.

In 2003, Polach called for the incorporation of work–life integration into the practice of HRD professionals. The integration of HRD and work–life is limited because of unsupportive organizational cultures, inconsistent application of policies and practices, practices and programs which are designed to benefit employees but are actually restrictive and ineffective (Morris 2008, Fleetwood 2007b), and the potential mismatch between organizational and public work–life policy. It is the role of HRD professionals to foster the relationship between employees and employers, respond to the work and non-work needs of both, facilitate a healthier workplace and encourage employer responsiveness (Morris 2008). Whereas work–life policy is emergent in both public and organizational policy, efforts have been minimal to reorganize the workplace to ensure effective implementation, application and use of such policies (Brough *et al.* 2008). The integration of work–life initiatives by HRD professionals may be a key driver in organizational change across the globe; however, diversity in cultural compositions, variances in individual needs, and wide ranges in societal expectations create great challenges for crafting a single approach to the work–life system.

References

Bardoel, E.A., De Cieri, H. and Santos, C. (2008) 'A review of work–life research in Australia and New Zealand', *Asia Pacific Journal of Human Resources*, 46: 316–33.

Block, R.N., Park, J.Y. and Kang, Y.H. (2013) 'Statutory leave entitlements across developed countries: why US workers lose out on work–family balance', *International Labour Review*, 152: 125–43.

Brough, P., Holt, J., Bauld, R., Biggs, A. and Ryan, C. (2008) 'The ability of work–life balance policies to influence key social/organisational issues', *Asia Pacific Journal of Human Resources*, 46: 261–74.

Buchanan, A. and Rotkirch, A. (2013) *Fertility Rates and Population Decline: No Time for Children?*, Hampshire: Palgrave Macmillan.

Casper, W.J., and Buffardi, L.C. (2004) 'Work–life benefits and job pursuit intentions: The role of anticipated organizational support', *Journal of Vocational Behavior*, 65(3): 391–410.

Chang, A., McDonald, P. and Burton, P. (2010) 'Methodological choices in work–life balance research 1987 to 2006: a critical review', *International Journal of Human Resource Management*, 21: 2381–413.

Chioda, L. (2011) *Work and Family: Latin American Women in Search of a New Balance*, Washington, DC: World Bank.

Chioda, L. and De La Torre, A. (2012) *Women's Economic Empowerment in Latin America and the Caribbean. Policy Lessons from the World Bank Gender Action Plan*, Washington, DC: World Bank.

Clark, S.C. (2000) 'Work/family border theory: a new theory of work/family balance', *Human Relations*, 53: 747–70.

Crooker, K.J., Smith, F.L. and Tabak, F. (2002) 'Creating work–life balance: a model of pluralism across life domains', *Human Resource Development Review*, 1: 387–419.

De Cieri, H., Holmes, B., Abbott, J. and Pettit, T. (2005) 'Achievements and challenges for work/life balance strategies in Australian organizations', *International Journal of Human Resource Management*, 16: 90–103.

Enriquez, C.R. (2012) *Work-Family Balance Issues in Latin America: A Roadmap to National Care Systems*, Paper prepared for the expert group meeting on "Good practices in family policy making: Family policy development, monitoring and implementation: Lessons learnt", organized by the UN Department of Economic and Social Affairs, held in New York, 15-17 May 2012.

Fleetwood, S. (2007a) 'Re-thinking work–life balance: editor's introduction', *International Journal of Human Resource Management*, 18: 351–59.

— (2007b) 'Why work–life balance now?', *International Journal of Human Resource Management*, 18: 387–400.

Galinsky, E. and Stein, P.J. (1990) 'The impact of human resource policies on employees: balancing work/family life', *Journal of Family Issues*, 11: 368–83.

Galinsky, E., Bond, J.T., and Friedman, D.E. (1993) *The Changing Workforce: Highlights of the National Study*, New York: Families and Work Institute.

Goodman, R. and Peng, I. (1996) 'The East Asian welfare state: peripatetic learning, adaptive change, and national building', in Anderson, G.E. (ed.) *Welfare States in Transition: National Adaptation of Global Economies*, London: SAGE.

Goodman, R. and White, G. (1998) 'Welfare orientalism and the search for an East Asian welfare model', in Goodman, R., White, G. and Kwon, H.J. (eds) *The East Asian Welfare Model: Welfare Orientalism and the State*, London: Routledge.

Gray, M. and Tudball, J. (2003) 'Family-friendly work practices: differences within and between workplaces', *Journal of Industrial Relations*, 45: 269–91.

Greenhaus, J.H., Collins, K.M. and Shaw, J.D. (2003) 'The relation between work-family balance and quality of life', *Journal of Vocational Behavior*, 63: 510–31.

Grzywacz, J.G. and Carlson, D.S. (2007) 'Conceptualizing work-family balance: implications for practice and research', *Advances in Developing Human Resources*, 9: 455–71.

Haar, J.M. and Spell, C.S. (2004) 'Programme knowledge and value of work-family practices and organizational commitment', *International Journal of Human Resource Management*, 15: 1040–55.

Haub, C. (2010) *Japan's demographic future*, Population Reference Bureau Brief.

Hornsby, E.E. and Munn, S.L. (2009) 'University work–life benefits and same-sex couples', *Advances in Developing Human Resources*, 11: 67–81.

ILO (International Labour Organization) (2011) *Equality at Work: The Continuing Challenge. Global Report Under the Follow-Up to the ILO Declaration on Fundamental Principles and Rights at Work*, Geneva: ILO.

Joplin, J.R., Shaffer, M.A., Francesco, A.M. and Lau, T. (2003) 'The macro-environment and work-family conflict development of a cross cultural comparative framework', *International Journal of Cross Cultural Management*, 3: 305–28.

Kahnweiler, W.M. (2008) 'The work–life conundrum: will HRD become more involved?', *Human Resource Development Quarterly*, 19: 75–83.

Kanter, R.M. (1977) *Work and Family in the United States: A Critical Review and Agenda for Research and Policy*, New York: Russell Sage Foundation.

Kerkhofs, M., Chung, H. and Ester, P. (2008) 'Working time flexibility across Europe: a typology using firm-level data', *Industrial Relations Journal*, 39: 569–85.

Khallash, S. and Kruse, M. (2012) 'The future of work and work–life balance 2025', *Futures*, 44: 678–86.

Kim, E. and Chang, Y. (2011) 'The relationship between family-friendly organizational culture and job satisfaction: a comparative study of Korea and Japan', *Journal of Korean Japanese Economics and Management Association*, 50: 89–128.

Koh, S. (2012) *Family friendly workplace for work-family balance: family friendly workplace index and certification*, Paper presented at the conference of the Korean Home Economics Association, held in Seoul, South Korea.

Konrad, A.M. and Mangel, R. (2000) 'The impact of work–life programs on firm productivity', *Strategic Management Journal*, 21: 1225–37.

Lee, E.S., Chang, J.Y. and Kim, H. (2011) 'The work–family interface in Korea: can family life enrich work life?', *International Journal of Human Resource Management*, 22: 2032–53.

Lee, S. (2004) 'Women's work supports, job retention, and job mobility: child care and employer-provided health insurance help women stay on jobs', *Research-in-Brief.* Washington DC: Institute for Women's Policy Research.

Maitland, A. and Thomson, P. (2011) *Future Work: How Businesses Can Adapt and Thrive in the New World of Work*, Hampshire: Palgrave Macmillan.

McDonald, P., Pini, B. and Bradley, L. (2007) 'Freedom or fallout in local government? How work–life culture impacts employees using flexible work practices', *International Journal of Human Resource Management*, 18: 602–22.

McMillan, H.S., Morris, M.L., and Atchley, E.K. (2011) 'Constructs of the work/life interface: A synthesis of the literature and introduction of the concept of work/life harmony', *Human Resource Development Review*, 10(1): 6–25.

Mokomane, Z. (ed.) (2014) *Work-Family Interface in Sub-Saharan Africa: Challenges and Responses*, London: Springer.

Morris, M.L. (2008) 'Combating workplace stressors: using work–life initiatives as an OD intervention', *Human Resource Development Quarterly*, 19: 95–105.

Morris, M.L. and Madsen, S.R. (2007) 'Advancing work–life integration in individuals, organizations, and communities', *Advances in Developing Human Resources*, 9: 439–54.

Munn, S.L. (2013) 'Unveiling the work–life system: the influence of work–life balance on meaningful work', *Advances in Developing Human Resources*, 15: 401–17.

Nwagbara, U. and Akanji, B.O. (2012) 'The impact of work–life balance on the commitment and motivation of Nigerian women employees', *International Journal of Academic Research in Business and Social Sciences*, 2: 38–47.

OECD (Organisation for Economic Co-operation and Development) (2007) *Babies and Bosses – Reconciling Work and Family Life: A Synthesis of Findings for OECD Countries*, Paris: OECD.

— (2008) *Babies and Bosses: Balancing Work and Family Life, Policy Brief*, Paris: OECD.

Perry-Smith, J.E. and Blum, T.C. (2000) 'Work-family human resource bundles and perceived organizational performance', *Academy of Management Journal*, 43: 1107–17.

Pitt-Catsouphes, M., Matz-Costa, C. and MacDermid, S.M. (2007) 'HRD responses to work-family stressors', *Advances in Developing Human Resources*, 9: 527–43.

Pocock, B., Skinner, N. and Pisaniello, S.L. (2010) *How Much Should We Work?: Working Hours, Holidays and Working Life: The Participation Challenge*, Centre for Work + Life, Magill: University of South Australia.

Poelmans, S., Spector, P.E., Cooper, C.L., Allen, T.D., O'Driscoll, M. and Sanchez, J.I. (2003) 'A cross-national comparative study of work/family demands and resources', *International Journal of Cross Cultural Management*, 3: 275–88.

Polach, J. (2003) 'HRD's role in work–life integration issues: moving the workforce to a change in mindset', *Human Resource Development International*, 6: 57–68.

Tomlinson, J. (2007) 'Employment regulation, welfare and gender regimes: a comparative analysis of women's working-time patterns and work–life balance in the UK and the US', *International Journal of Human Resource Management*, 18: 401–15.

Voydanoff, P. (2005) 'Toward a conceptualization of perceived work-family fit and balance: a demands and resources approach', *Journal of Marriage and Family*, 67: 822–36.

49

EMOTIONS AND SELF-DEVELOPMENT

Paul L. Nesbit

In recent years emotions have come to be seen as playing an important role in the cognitive and motivational processes that influence learning (Baumeister *et al.* 2007, Dirkx 2008, Pekrun *et al.* 2002). Most of the research addressing emotion in learning has focused on traditional and formal learning approaches, especially within academic settings (Simpson and Marshall 2010, Zimmerman 2000, 2008). However, the growing complexity and dynamic nature of the contemporary work environment have stimulated considerable research attention to less formal and self-directed approaches to learning (Ellinger 2004).

Self-directed leadership development, or self-development, holds considerable appeal as an approach to deal with the need for leaders to continuously learn in the face of dynamic and changing environments (Nesbit 2012, Orvis and Leffler 2011). Furthermore, self-development helps organizations contain training and development costs (Boyce *et al.* 2010) in an era when management careers are more likely to include work across organizations and industries (Arthur and Rousseau 1996). Given the importance of self-development within the contemporary workplace and the relevance of emotions for learning, it is surprising that the relationship between emotion and self-development has been relatively unexplored. This exploration is particularly needed, because in self-development, the learner is both the subject of emotional reactions and the source of regulatory actions to ensure that emotions and motivational beliefs are generated and managed effectively. The growing recognition that emotions can either disrupt or support learning (Fineman 1997) suggests that emotions and their regulation are likely to play a significant role in the success or failure of managers' attempts at self-development.

This chapter seeks to provide an impetus for the ongoing exploration of emotion within self-development and thus advance learning theory in this increasingly important form of leadership development. For HRD practitioners, recognition of the role of emotion will also aid in constructing more appropriate interventions in supporting self-development. The chapter will first examine the nature of emotions and their role in learning generally. The processes involved in self-development will then be elaborated to guide an exploration of roles of emotions. Finally, given the recognition of cultural dimensions in emotion perception (Matsumoto 1989) and emotion regulation (Mesquita and Albert 2009), the chapter will conclude with a discussion of the cultural context of emotions and their implication for the self-development process.

Emotions and learning

Emotions are subjective feelings or inner states that reflect positive or negative affect. In addition emotions have characteristic behavioral expressions, such as facial expressions, which help to signal one's emotional state to others. Emotions are typically short-lived in nature in comparison to moods, which are more general, less intense and longer-lasting affective states (Plutchik 2001). Emotions originate in response to external or internal events and can arise relatively automatically (fear arising from seeing a snake) or after giving consideration to an event where meaning and interpretation take place[1] (Gross and Oliver 2002). Emotional responses help direct attention to important events in one's environment as well as prepare for future action in relation to one's goals (Pekrun *et al.* 2002).

Although emotions produce broad behavioral tendencies of approach (positive affect) and avoidance (negative affect), researchers generally do not ascribe a direct behavioral influence to emotions (Tice 2009). As argued by Baumeister *et al.* (2007: 168) "human conscious emotions operate mainly and best by means of its influence on cognitive processes, which in turn are input into decision and behaviour regulation processes." Thus experiences and events are interpreted and made meaningful through the cognitive processing that accompanies or is triggered by emotions. For example, test anxiety does not automatically undermine performance of exams, but is mediated by cognitive beliefs, such as efficacy beliefs and achievement goal orientation (Tyson *et al.* 2009). Similarly, cross-cultural differences in the way emotions are acted upon also highlight the cognitive mediation of emotions (Mesquita and Albert 2009).

In the field of learning, the relationship between emotion and cognition has traditionally been viewed as a negative one with emotions being seen as dysfunctional to rational thinking and information processing (Dirkx 2008). Reflecting this perspective, research on emotion in learning has been dominated by a focus on negative affective states such as the impact of anxiety on test performance. In a review of the literature on students' academic emotions, from 1974–2000, Pekrun *et al.* (2002) identified that the overwhelming majority of the studies has focused on test anxiety (over 1,200 studies). The next highest emotion studied was anger (64 studies) followed by joy (61 studies). Many emotions, such as hope – the opposite emotion to anxiety – were not studied at all. These data are in contrast to the emerging contemporary perspective on emotions as integral to learning and the recognition that people experience a rich diversity of emotions in their learning process (Dirkx 2008).

Fineman (1997: 13) has emphasized the interconnectedness of emotion and learning suggesting that "emotions should be considered not just as by-product or interference to the learning process, but also intrinsic to what is learned, how it is learned and the organizational context in which learning takes place." Educators are acknowledging the powerful roles of emotions and affect in both facilitating and hindering adult learning.

This capacity for emotions to produce either positive or negative effects on learning is evident in the move towards greater self-directedness within adult learning (Clardy 2000, Ellinger 2004). Self-directed learning has the potential to enhance engagement with learning material and contribute to deeper understanding and critical analysis of knowledge (Lord and Hall 2005); however, learners vary in their capacity to respond to teaching that requires them to be self-directing (Grow 1991). For some students self-directed learning raises anxiety, stress and resentment that can undermine the learning process. Grow (1991: 136) proposed that "teaching style should be governed not by subject matter but by the balance between teacher directiveness and student control, usually set by the student's ability to participate as a self-directed, self-motivated, responsible learner." Thus teaching style needs to recognize the potential for mismatches in the student's self-directed learning capabilities and the nature of the learning situations.

Anderson and Gilmore (2010) give a salutary example of this mismatch in discussing the emotional reactions of students to changes in curriculum of a university course that required them to work in small groups to research, design and deliver interactive sessions for their peers. The initial positive anticipation was quickly replaced by frustration because of the perceived lack of clarity around the task and insufficient guidance given by tutors. As presaged by Grow (1991: 764), opinions among students were polarized with some being positive about the learning experience while others were very negative and students reported feeling "scared, tearful, stressed and worried, unmotivated, bored."

In summary, emotions are feelings that arise within the learning process in response to the cognitive processing of events and experiences encountered. Emotions influence behavior by drawing attention to events and experiences and are accompanied by cognitions that mediate the nature of emotional responses and the behaviors enacted.

As will be seen in the discussion of self-development, a variety of emotions will likely occur as leaders engage in self-directed efforts to enhance their leadership capability. These emotional reactions have the potential to support self-development efforts or to unsettle and divert these efforts. Thus, the manner in which leaders regulate their emotions is likely to significantly influence the effectiveness of their self-directed learning effort. In the next section a brief overview of the nature of self-development is presented to provide a framework for the exploration of emotions and their regulation.

The self-development process

Self-development is a form of self-directed learning focused on addressing the development needs of leaders (Nesbit 2012). Development in this sense refers to learning that seeks growth of the individual not just acquisition of skills and knowledge; to maximizing potential rather than actual performance in a role; and to enhancing future and long-term capacities rather than short-term performance (Garavan 1997). Self-development, therefore, aims to expand leaders' "conceptual frame of meaning" (Boyce *et al.* 2010: 162) to enhance their capacity for behaving in cognitively and behaviorally more complex ways (Denison *et al.* 1995, Nesbit 2012). Self-development incorporates a set of learning stages similar to self-directed learning: identification of learning needs, formulating goals for one's learning, thinking about and determining appropriate strategies to address needs and strive for goal achievement, evaluating strategies relative to learning goals, and modifying strategies as required (Boyce *et al.* 2010, Nesbit 2012). Thus the distinctiveness of self-development arises in its focus on the aim of development rather than substantial differences with the broadly defined self-directed learning process.

Self-development requires leaders to develop self-awareness of competency strengths and deficits as a primary focus for ongoing development strategies. In formal learning situations, such as leadership development programs, learners are aided in this process. However, in self-development the individual must initiate analysis of development needs through self-assessing current performance and experiences. This analysis can be done through reflection on performance feedback from others, such as managers, peers, direct reports, customers, etc., or more commonly through reflection on one's ongoing leadership experiences (Nesbit 2012). Managers may also seek insight about their leadership style and characteristic preferences in behaviors through the use of psychological inventories, although this approach is more likely to occur as part of a formal institutional program. The self-reflection that occurs in this phase of self-development requires more than casual introspective thinking about events and experiences; rather, this reflection needs systematic thinking leading to deep-level analysis (Seibert and Daudelin 1999).

Following self-directed needs analysis, leaders need to design, initiate, sustain and evaluate learning and change activities to address their development needs. These strategies for development and ongoing maintenance of new behaviors must be built into self-constructed and self-initiated action plans. Ultimately this stage of self-development is determined by the leader's capacity for self-regulation to guide learning activities over time and to adapt to the demands across changing circumstances (Karoly 1993, Zimmerman 2000).

This brief overview of the self-development process highlights two important phases in self-development: that is, a phase focused on self-understanding and awareness of leadership strengths and deficits followed by a phase in which actions for self-change and learning are executed. Both of these phases involve self-reflective evaluations that highlight the potential for emotional reactions. A range of cognitions that impact on and influence emotions accompanies these evaluations. Indeed, the facility of individuals to self-regulate and self-direct the learning process, for example in reappraising events (Gross and John 2003), relies on their intentional capacity to influence their cognitions, which then indirectly influence emotions (Nesbit 2012, Zimmerman 2000). In the next section, the interconnections between emotions and cognitions that arise within the self-development process are explored.

Emotions within the self-development process

Reflective processes are central to the analysis of development needs and to the entire self-development learning process. A leader experiencing unanticipated outcomes or behaviors by others will typically respond with reflective thinking about events or experiences in order to extract meaningful understanding and insights about those experiences (Daudelin 1996). This reflective process is stimulated by the perplexity experienced and is accompanied by the emotion of curiosity that activates a sense of exploration to think reflectively (Kashdan *et al.* 2004). Thus an important contribution of emotions to the self-development learning process is to stimulate reflective thinking when leaders are confronted with novel and challenging experiences (Tice 2009). These reflections contribute to deepening the understanding of events and this deepened understanding can help leaders build more complex conceptual models. The enhanced conceptual models contribute to self-understanding and self-awareness of performance deficits (Daudelin 1996) that can lead to the development of greater complexity in future analysis and action (Denison *et al.* 1995, Lord and Hall 2005).

In order for insights to be effectively used in self-development, they need to be accurate in their nature and accepted by the person. Unfortunately, reflective processing of experiences can also elicit cognitive and affective responses that can reduce the accuracy and acceptance of insights, thus hindering the self-development process. People generally prefer to receive feedback that is positive and supportive of their self-concept (Cope and Watts 2000). However, given that in self-development leaders are pursuing understanding of their development needs it is likely that evaluations will have critical and negative overtones related to a leader's current performance. In these situations, motivational conflict may arise between providing information that guides self-improvement and threatens self-esteem (Trope *et al.* 2003). That is, feedback that has the potential to help leaders understand their development needs may also give rise to emotional reactions, such as anxiety, anger, frustration and disappointment.

According to Tracy and Robins (2004) self-conscious emotions are evoked when events bring salience to actual, ideal or hoped-for self-representations. Thus in reflecting on feedback, emotive reactions, such as guilt or shame, may arise if leaders compare feedback about their behaviors, achievements/outcomes with self-representations and appraise the situation as incongruent with their self-concept. In this case, thinking and behavior are directed to protection of the self-concept rather than to goal attainment. Consequently, feedback may be rejected or distorted (Kluger and DeNisi 1996), and future performance standards reduced (Ilies *et al.* 2010) or avoided by withdrawing from pursuit of the goal (Ilgen and Davis 2000). In such cases, the self-development efforts are terminated.

Emotions also play a role in the self-change phase of self-development when learners engage in self-regulation of learning behavior following analysis of development needs. Researchers taking a social cognitive perspective of self-regulation (Bandura 1991) have highlighted the affective-cognitive and behavioral dimensions of self-regulation and the cyclical and reciprocally deterministic processes associated with the pursuit of development goals (Karoly 1993, Lord *et al.* 2010, Porath and Bateman 2006). Zimmerman (2000) has outlined a model of the structure and function of these self-regulatory processes that views the process in terms of three cyclical phases: (1) a forethought phase that relates to processes and beliefs that occur before efforts to learn, (2) a performance phase which refers to processes that occur during the behavioral implementation of change efforts, and (3) a reflection phase that occurs after each learning effort. While emotions may arise at any time in the self-regulation process they are likely to be most salient within the self-reflection phase when managers evaluate the impact of learning strategies relative to development goals.

Emotional reactions arise relatively automatically in response to goal performance evaluations (Ilies *et al.* 2010). For example, emotions such as pride and happiness are associated with successful achievement of challenging goals and this achievement in turn reinforces the sequence of behaviors and their related cognitions associated with that goal attainment. In other words, emotions strengthen the link between actions and their rewarding or punishing consequences (Tice 2009, Tracy and Robins 2007). Furthermore, ongoing self-regulatory learning efforts such as self-directed exploration and cognitive engagement with learning material are facilitated by positive affective states such as curiosity (Kashdan *et al.* 2004).

Another way that emotional reactions may influence self-development processes is through the capacity of individuals to anticipate the emotional outcome of actions. For example, the potential for self-regulatory failure – not carrying out a behavior associated with a learning plan – is ever present in any self-development effort and is likely to produce negative affect such as the emotion of guilt (Tracy and Robins 2007) in not carrying out intended actions. This capacity to anticipate negative affect helps a person transcend the temptations of the immediate situation by increasing attention to the implications of this action for one's goals (Baumeister and Heatherton 1996). Thus emotions can aid in maintaining engagement with one's self-development goals and learning strategies.

The significant influence of emotions in self-development is not surprising given that emotions are integral to all human behavior (Bierema 2008). However, the discussion in this section leads to the conclusion that managers engaged in self-development need considerable skills in emotion regulation. Fortunately, while people are often presented as being at the mercy of their emotions, in reality people are flexible in dealing with emotions and actively seek to regulate and shape their emotions (Gross and Oliver 2002, Koole 2009). Given the relationship between cognitions and emotions (Baumeister *et al.* 2007) and the focus on development goals, the regulation of emotions through the strategy of cognitive reappraisal (Koole 2009) is one which holds great promise for self-development. In cognitive appraisal, an individual actively seeks to construe a situation to reduce the intensity of an emotion felt or influence the types of emotions that arise. As noted by Gross and Oliver (2002: 303), "the personal meaning you assign to the situation is crucial, because it powerfully influences which experiential, behavioral and physiological response tendencies will be generated in the particular situation." Thus how a leader interprets and reflects on development goal performance discrepancies may have substantial impact on the regulation of emotions. Of course managers are likely to vary in terms of their capability in emotion regulation. Recent attention to the concept of emotional intelligence (Salovey and Grewal 2005), which is increasingly seen as an important leadership competency (George 2000), highlights the variability around emotion-based leadership skills.

In summary, the discussion above has highlighted some of the ways that emotions and their regulation are involved in the self-development process. Emotional reactions tend to arise from evaluations, especially those associated with self-reflection throughout the self-development process. These emotional reactions influence cognitions and are themselves influenced by cognitive appraisals (Baumeister *et al.* 2007) such as causal attributions for events, efficacy beliefs about one's ability, etc. (Ilies *et al.* 2010). Thus emotions and their regulation play a critical function in the success of self-regulatory and learning behaviors associated with self-development.

Given the interconnectedness of cognitive and affective dimensions in the determination of self-development actions, culture-related cognitions are also likely to play an important role in the operation of self-development processes. In the next section a brief overview of the literature on culture and emotions is examined for insight into implications for self-development processes.

Cultural aspects of emotions in self-development

As noted by Mesquita and Albert (2009: 488), "cultural models importantly constitute a person's reality, because they focus attention, they guide perception, they end meaning, and they imbue emotional value. Therefore, a cultural model is decisive for what one's world is like . . . and reflects the cultural "answers" to existential questions, such as how to be a person and how to maintain relationships." Thus culture influences emotions because it shapes understanding and interpretation of social experiences and these cognitions in turn impact the emotions felt. Furthermore, emotional displays are governed by normative displays, so that people from different cultures will respond to emotions in different ways (Singelis and Sharkey 1995).

An influential perspective on the nature of cultural models is associated with the way people differ in the construal of the self and relationships with others (Markus and Kitayama 1991, Matsumoto 1989). According to Markus and Kitayama (1991) in Western cultures, an independent self-construal predominates and people are said to be motivated to become independent from others and to pursue the expression of one's unique configuration of needs, rights, and capacities and to stand out among their peers. In Eastern cultures, an interdependent self-construal predominates, and people tend to suppress and restrain inner attributes such as desire, personal goals and private emotions to fit in with significant others, and to meet social obligations as part of social networks.

One reason that differences in cultural models may need to be considered in self-development is the potential they have to influence the strategies adopted in response to goal performance discrepancy elicited emotions. For example interdependent and dependent cultural models have been associated with differences in the way people orient themselves towards goal accomplishment and the way they regulate their behavior (Higgins 1997, Lee *et al.* 2000). According to regulatory focus theory (Higgins 1997), promotion and prevention are the two fundamental self-regulatory orientations. Promotion regulatory focus involves people's desire for advancement, growth, and accomplishment, whereas a prevention regulatory focus involves people's concern for safety, obligation and responsibility. Lee *et al.* (2000) have argued that people from cultures with an independent self-construal are likely to focus on promotion focus goals given their normative values associated with developing one's unique potential through the pursuit of success and accomplishments. In contrast, people from cultures with a dominant interdependent self-construal are inclined to avoid social disapproval or failures that may disrupt their commitment to enhancing social relations, which is more consistent with a prevention regulatory focus. In a series of experimental studies Lee *et al.* (2000) provided evidence that US students who had a dominant independent self-construal perceived promotion-framed scenarios to be more important than prevention-framed scenarios. In contrast, students from Hong Kong with a dominant interdependent self-construal perceived prevention-focused scenarios to be more important than promotion focused scenarios.

In addition to implications for self-development actions, cultural models have implications for the direct experience of emotions. For example, Bagozzi *et al.* (2003) investigated how salespeople in the finance industry from the Philippines and the Netherlands experienced and responded to the emotion of shame. Filipino salespeople were considered to have interdependent self-construal and were inclined to maintain harmony and connections with others, and to fulfill their social obligations. In contrast, people from the Netherlands were considered to have independent self-construal, which is consistent with developing their unique potential through the pursuit of success and accomplishments (Markus and Kitayama 1991).

Sales staff were given scenarios to read and asked 15 shame-experience questions on which they indicated their level of agreement using a 7-point Likert-type scale. Results showed that the experience of shame was similar across salespersons in the two cultures. Both groups of salespeople felt threat to the core self, heightened self-focused attention, both characteristic of self-conscious emotions (Tracy and Robins 2007), physiological symptoms typically associated with shame, and sensed an urge to hide. However, differences were found in the way the salespersons responded to shame. Filipinos responded with adaptive reactions by approaching people who are the source of shame to repair damage to the relationship. Also Filipino salespersons were more likely to engage in prosocial behavior. Prosocial behavior refers to actions that are not formally required in terms of one's job responsibilities but support others and promote the organization's interests (Brief and Motowidlo 1986). In contrast, the salespersons from the Netherlands sought to protect their self-concept by adopting protective actions; for example, if they felt shame around certain people, they would avoid contact with them. They also exhibited reduced prosocial behaviors within their roles again due to their need to close off contact with others. The authors concluded that these differences were consistent with the differences in self-construal and what shame implies for the self. "Shame primarily serves as threat to their uniqueness and self-worth for Dutch salespeople, as it does for most Westerners who live in independent-based cultures. Shame for Filipinos functions largely as a threat to their social self and sense of connectedness and the need to fit in with others" (Bagozzi *et al.* 2003: 229). These different approaches to the way people respond to emotions highlight the need to consider cultural dimensions within the self-development process.

In summary, this brief exploration of cultural models highlights the potential importance culture has for self-development. Different cultural models are likely to reflect differences in the way emotions are experienced in the self-development process as well as differences in the way self-development is pursued. Thus given the emotional dimensions embedded in self-development as discussed in this chapter, cultural dimensions will need to be considered in the construction of theoretical models concerning self-development.

Conclusion: emotion and self-development

The increasingly dynamic and changing nature of contemporary work environments has contributed to the growing attraction for self-directed approaches for leadership development. This chapter has sought to advance the theory and practice of self-development by exploring the relationship of emotion in that process. Considering the role of emotions in self-directed learning situations is likely to assist in advancing theoretical understanding of the self-development process – a process that is still in its early stages of development. A better understanding of emotions within the self-development process will aid HRD professionals in supporting self-development practices.

Although emotions clearly arise in self-development processes, especially during self-reflective evaluations, it is unlikely that emotions directly influence learning behavior (Baumeister *et al.* 2007, Tice 2009). Rather, emotions matter because they have implications for ongoing cognitions, which in turn have direct implications for motivation and enactment of behavior associated with self-regulation. Thus in self-development leaders need to actively manage both the cognitive and affective aspects that arise during the ongoing and cyclic processes. The extensive literature surrounding emotion regulation (Koole 2009) as well as emotional intelligence (Salovey and Grewal 2005) presents opportunities for theoretical development of self-development literature as well as offering practical insights into the strategies that might be included in self-leadership learning processes. Specifically, by understanding the role of emotions to both support and undermine the learning process HRD professionals can better design learning opportunities to encourage self-development processes. Additionally, training in emotional intelligence may also have indirect benefits associated with enhancing self-development in organizations.

Note

1 Given the focus of the chapter on self-development – a form of self-directed learning – the chapter only discusses consciously attended emotions and their relationship to learning rather than automatic or primed emotions.

References

Anderson, V. and Gilmore, S. (2010) 'Learning, experienced emotions, relationships and innovation in HRD', *Journal of European Industrial Training*, 34: 753–71.

Arthur, M.B. and Rousseau, D.M. (1996) *The Boundaryless Career: A New Employment Principle for a New Organizational Era*, New York: Oxford University Press.

Bagozzi, R.P., Verbeke, W. and Gavino Jr, J.C. (2003) 'Culture moderates the self-regulation of shame and its effects on performance: the case of salespersons in the Netherlands and the Philippines', *Journal of Applied Psychology*, 88: 219–33.

Bandura, A. (1991) 'Social cognitive theory of self-regulation', *Organizational Behavior and Human Decision Processes*, 50: 248–87.

Baumeister, R.F. and Heatherton, T.F. (1996) 'Self-regulation failure: an overview', *Psychological Inquiry*, 7: 1–15.

Baumeister, R.F., Vohs, K.D., DeWall, C.N. and Zhang, L. (2007) 'How emotion shapes behavior: feedback, anticipation, and reflection, rather than direct causation', *Personality and Social Psychology Review*, 11: 167–203.

Bierema, L.L. (2008) 'Adult learning in the workplace: emotion work or emotion learning?' *New Directions for Adult and Continuing Education*, 120: 55–64.

Boyce, L.A., Zaccaro, S.J. and Wisecarver, M.Z. (2010) 'Propensity for self-development of leadership attributes: understanding, predicting, and supporting performance of leader self-development', *Leadership Quarterly*, 21: 159–78.

Brief, A.P. and Motowidlo, S.J. (1986) 'Prosocial organizational behaviors', *Academy of Management Review*, 11: 710–25.

Clardy, A. (2000) 'Learning on their own: vocationally oriented self-directed learning projects', *Human Resource Development Quarterly*, 11: 105–25.

Cope, J., and Watts, G. (2000) 'Learning by doing – an exploration of experience, critical incidents and reflection in entrepreneurial learning', *International Journal of Entrepreneurial Behaviour and Research*, 6: 104–24.

Daudelin, M.W. (1996). 'Learning from experience through reflection', *Organizational Dynamics*, 24: 36–48.

Denison, D.R., Hooijberg, R. and Quinn, R.E. (1995) 'Paradox and performance: toward a theory of behavioral complexity in managerial leadership', *Organization Science*, 6: 524–40.

Dirkx, J.M. (2008) 'The meaning and role of emotions in adult learning', *New Directions for Adult and Continuing Education*, 120: 7–18.

Ellinger, A.D. (2004) 'The concept of self-directed learning and its implications for human resource development', *Advances in Developing Human Resources*, 6: 158–77.

Fineman, S. (1997) 'Emotion and management learning', *Management Learning*, 28: 13–25.

Garavan, T.N. (1997) 'Training, development, education and learning: different or the same?', *Journal of European Industrial Training*, 21: 39–50.

George, J.M. (2000) 'Emotions and leadership: the role of emotional intelligence', *Human Relations*, 53: 1027–55.

Gross, J. and Oliver, P.J. (2002) 'Wise emotion regulation', in Barrett, L.F. and Salovey, P. (eds) *The Wisdom of Feelings: Psychological Processes in Emotional Intelligence*, New York: Guildford Press, 297–318.

Gross, J.J., and John, O.P. (2003) 'Individual differences in two emotion regulation processes: implications for affect, relationships, and well-being', *Journal of Personality and Social Psychology*, 85(2): 348.

Grow, G.O. (1991) 'Teaching learners to be self-directed', *Adult Education Quarterly*, 41: 125–49.

Higgins, E.T. (1997) 'Beyond pleasure and pain', *American Psychologist*, 52: 1280–300.

Ilgen, D. and Davis, C. (2000) 'Bearing bad news: reactions to negative performance feedback', *Applied Psychology*, 49: 550–65.

Ilies, R., Judge, T.A. and Wagner, D.T. (2010) 'The influence of cognitive and affective reactions to feedback on subsequent goals', *European Psychologist*, 15: 121–31.

Karoly, P. (1993) 'Mechanisms of self-regulation: a systems view', *Annual Review of Psychology*, 44: 23–52.

Kashdan, T.B., Rose, P. and Fincham, F.D. (2004) 'Curiosity and exploration: facilitating positive subjective experiences and personal growth opportunities', *Journal of Personality Assessment*, 82: 291–305.

Kluger, A. and DeNisi, A. (1996) 'Effects of feedback intervention on performance: a historical review, a meta-analysis, and a preliminary feedback intervention theory', *Psychological Bulletin*, 119: 254–84.

Koole, S.L. (2009) 'The psychology of emotion regulation: an integrative review', *Cognition and Emotion*, 23: 4–41.

Lee, A.Y., Aaker, J.L. and Gardner, W.L. (2000) 'The pleasures and pains of distinct self-construals: the role of interdependence in regulatory focus', *Journal of Personality and Social Psychology*, 78: 1122.

Lord, R.G. and Hall, R.J. (2005) 'Identity, deep structure and the development of leadership skill', *Leadership Quarterly*, 16: 591–615.

Lord, R.G., Diefendorff, J.M., Schmidt, A.M. and Hall, R.J. (2010) 'Self-regulation at work', *Annual Review of Psychology*, 61: 543–68.

Markus, H.R. and Kitayama, S. (1991) 'Culture and the self: implications for cognition, emotion, and motivation', *Psychological Review*, 98: 224.

Matsumoto, D. (1989) 'Cultural influences on the perception of emotion', *Journal of Cross-Cultural Psychology*, 20: 92–105.

Mesquita, B. and Albert, D. (2009) 'The cultural regulation of emotions', in Gross, J.J. (ed.) *Handbook of Emotion Regulation*, New York: Guildford Press, 486–503.

Nesbit, P.L. (2012) 'The role of self-reflection, emotional management of feedback, and self-regulation processes in self-directed leadership development', *Human Resource Development Review*, 11: 203–26.

Orvis, K.A. and Leffler, G.P. (2011) 'Individual and contextual factors: an interactionist approach to understanding employee self-development', *Personality and Individual Differences*, 51: 172–77.

Pekrun, R., Goetz, T., Titz, W. and Perry, R.P. (2002) 'Academic emotions in students' self-regulated learning and achievement: a program of qualitative and quantitative research', *Educational Psychologist*, 37: 91–105.

Plutchik, R. (2001) 'The nature of emotions', *American Scientist*, 89: 344–50.

Porath, C.L. and Bateman, T.S. (2006) 'Self-regulation: from goal orientation to job performance', *Journal of Applied Psychology*, 91: 185–92.

Salovey, P. and Grewal, D. (2005) 'The science of emotional intelligence', *Current Directions in Psychological Science*, 14: 281–85.

Seibert, K.W. and Daudelin, M.W. (1999) *The Role of Reflection in Managerial Learning: Theory, Research, and Practice*, Westport, CT: Quorum.

Simpson, B. and Marshall, N. (2010) 'The mutuality of emotions and learning in organizations', *Journal of Management Inquiry*, 19: 351–65.

Singelis, T.M. and Sharkey, W.F. (1995) 'Culture, self-construal, and embarrassability', *Journal of Cross-Cultural Psychology*, 26: 622–44.

Tice, D.M. (2009) 'How emotions affect self-regulation', in Forgas, J.P., Baumeister, R.F. and Tice, D.M. (eds) *Psychology of Self-Regulation*, New York: Psychology Press, 201–15.

Tracy, J.L. and Robins, R.W. (2004) 'Putting the self into self-conscious emotions: a theoretical model', *Psychological Inquiry*, 15: 103–25.

— (2007) 'The self in self-conscious emotions: a cognitive appraisal approach', in Tracy, J.L., Robins, R.W. and Tangney, J.P. (eds) *The Self-Conscious Emotions: Theory and Research*, New York: Guildford Press, 3–20.

Trope, Y., Gervey, B. and Bolger, N. (2003) 'The role of perceived control in overcoming defensive self-evaluations', *Journal of Experimental Social Psychology*, 39: 407–19.

Tyson, D.F., Linnenbrink-Garcia, D.F.T.L. and Hill, N.E. (2009) 'Regulating debilitating emotions in the context of performance: achievement goal orientations, achievement-elicited emotions, and socialization contexts', *Human Development*, 52: 329–56.

Zimmerman, B.J. (2000) 'Attaining self-regulation: a social cognitive perspective', in Boekaerts, M., Pintrich, P.R. and Zeidner, M. (eds) *Handbook of Self-Regulation*, San Diego: Academic Press, 13–41.

— (2008) 'Investigating self-regulation and motivation: historical background, methodological developments, and future prospects', *American Educational Research Journal*, 45: 166–83.

50

WORKPLACE INCIVILITY AS AN INTERNATIONAL ISSUE

The role of HRD

Thomas G. Reio, Jr.

HRD professionals need to be aware that incivility is prevalent in organizations, as it can be targeted towards coworkers, supervisors, supervisees, vendors and customers. In a US study of one healthcare and two manufacturing companies, Trudel and Reio (2011) found that roughly 86 per cent of the participants experienced incivility over the past year; 90 per cent admitted instigating it during the same time period. Moreover, incivility is not only prevalent, but on the rise. Porath and Pearson (2013) observed that as compared with their 1998 workplace research where one quarter of those surveyed had been treated rudely once a week or more, half of the respondents indicated being treated rudely at least once a week in their research conducted over a decade later. Rudeness at work has been shown to occur not only in US workplaces, but throughout the world (Power *et al.* 2013). In a large Asian study encompassing six countries and territories, for instance, the large majority of respondents reported experiencing incivility from either their coworkers or their superiors at least once in the previous year (Yeung and Griffin 2008). Thus, workplace incivility is not merely an oddity in select local settings; instead, it occurs all too frequently internationally to the detriment of all.

Organizational researchers continue to amass empirical evidence that rude, discourteous behavior has many negative outcomes. In a meta-analysis of workplace aggression that included incivility (interpersonal targeted aggression), Hershcovis *et al.* (2007) found that it was positively associated with trait anger, negative affectivity, being male, interpersonal conflict, job dissatisfaction, and distributive and procedural injustice. In their survey research with 800 managers from 17 industries, Porath and Pearson (2013) discovered that being treated uncivilly resulted in appreciable amounts of decreased work effort, work quality, job performance, and organizational commitment. Twenty-five per cent admitted taking their frustration out on customers and 12 per cent left their jobs because of being treated uncivilly. Likewise, in a study of 460 service workers in Spain, incivility was strongly linked to poorer job satisfaction and greater turnover intent (Moreno-Jiménez *et al.* 2012).

On the other hand, there may be a "silver lining" to being exposed to a deviant coworker (Markova and Folger 2012). Markova and Folger found that being exposed to a deviant coworker was linked to enhanced self-image (as compared with deviants) and better role clarity for those with more interdependent jobs. For organizational newcomers, demonstrating that we can learn from others' mistakes, mentors and experienced coworkers can draw attention to uncivil "norm breakers" whose behavior should not be emulated for risk of not fitting into one's job, team, or workgroup

(Reio and Wiswell 2000). Moreover, Anand *et al.* (2004) also suggested that incivility could be beneficial situationally, such as when breaking organizational norms to openly criticize an unethical supervisor. Although it seems clear that there can be conflicting instances where the positive effects of incivility can be seen, the vast majority of the research characterizes workplace incivility as being problematic at best. Thus, the need for additional incivility research to refine organizational theory and practice remains critical. The field needs to move forward with regards to understanding how best to reduce the prevalence of incivility and concomitantly dampen its negative consequences in any meaningful way (Cortina *et al.* 2001, Reio and Ghosh 2009).

Incivility is defined as rude verbal and non-verbal behaviors targeted towards another. This relatively mild form of aggressive behavior is characterized as being low intensity and ambiguous in intent, lacking in mutual respect, and violating organizational norms for acceptable behavior (Andersson and Pearson 1999). Incivility is based upon perceptions in that what a target might find rude and unacceptable behavior, the instigator or an onlooker might find just the opposite. In addition, these perceptions of what constitutes mutual respect and acceptable behavior can vary individually, situationally, and culturally (Hershcovis *et al.* 2007, Reio 2011). Examples of incivility include: answering a cellphone call during a meeting, blatantly disregarding wasting a supervisee's time, sending a "snippy" email, and ostracizing a team member (Porath and Pearson 2013). These apparently harmless behaviors can escalate through a tit-for-tat exchange (target-instigator-target) into patterns of intentional behavior (bullying) that can lead to physical violence if left unchecked (Andersson and Pearson 1999).

The aim of this chapter is to alert HRD professionals of incivility's insidious nature, prevalence, and demonstrated consequences in the organization. First, several theories are presented that help explain why one might behave uncivilly towards another, followed by seminal research regarding its consequences in organizational settings, a discussion of what HRD practitioners might do to reduce its likelihood, and some final thoughts.

Theoretical perspectives

Although organizational researchers worldwide have drawn upon a number of theories to understand the nature of incivility and guide research about its antecedents and outcomes, three have generated a notable amount of recent interest: incivility spiral theory (Andersson and Pearson 1999), social exchange theory (Homans 1958), and frustration–aggression theory (Dollard *et al.* 1939, Fox and Spector 1999).

Incivility spiral theory

Andersson and Pearson (1999) present a spiraling framework for assessing factors that may contribute to uncivil behavior and its escalation to more overt forms of aggression like bullying and physical violence. In general, from Andersson and Pearson's social interaction perspective, workplace incivility is an interactive event that is affected by a combination of the instigator, target, onlooker, and social context. Target perceptions of being treated disrespectfully can spiral into a tit-for-tat exchange of increasingly aggressive actions between the target and instigator. A supervisor sends a subordinate a snippy email; the subordinate responds tersely; the supervisor responds with an angry email; the subordinate responds in kind; angry words are exchanged in the hallway; someone gets pushed and things continue to spiral out of control until someone gets injured. In this example, what started as a rude, thoughtless act by a supervisor, ambiguous as to intent to harm, initiated a spiral of increasingly hostile behavior. The spiral continued until someone eventually perceived a personal or professional identity threat (i.e. they had reached a tipping point), motivating overt aggressive responses. There are many cases of such incivility spirals leading to physically harmful actions in organizations (Porath and Pearson 2013).

Incivility spiral theory encompasses a number of factors that may contribute to increasing or decreasing the likelihood of uncivil workplace behaviors and negative outcomes. Personality traits (e.g. thrill seeking), conflict management style (dominating), organizational climate (informal), socialization practices (e.g. negative mentoring experiences), demographics (e.g. male), and organizational support (e.g. inequitable access to professional development opportunities), among others have been associated with greater incivility instigation.

Social exchange theory

Homans (1958) and Blau (1964) posited the notion that human behavior was associated with social exchange in that it was not only for material goods, but also for symbolic ones that are socio-emotional in nature (e.g. self-esteem needs). Social exchange theory proposes that exchanges are predicated upon the rewarding actions of others. These mutually rewarding transactions over time can develop into longer-term relationships that influence positive work attitudes and behaviors (Blau 1964, Cropanzano and Mitchell 2005). Thus, interpersonal relationships at work (e.g. relationship between a supervisor and subordinate or mentor and protégé) follow certain rules of exchange that guide the development of trust, loyalty and mutual commitment.

Reciprocity is probably the most common and universal social exchange rule in the workplace (Homans 1958). However, norms for reciprocity vary by individual *and* culture. Some individuals and cultures favor a more quid pro quo orientation (return positive treatment for positive treatment or vice versa). Thus, everyone may not value reciprocity to the same degree (Cropanzano and Mitchell 2005).

Reciprocal exchange emphasizes interpersonal transactions that encourage mutual cooperation and interdependence. In the context of the supervisor–subordinate relationship, for example, the exchange of mutual respect fosters a productive partnership that aids trust building and learning. Clearly, a supervisor's uncivil behavior would be an example of violating the norms of reciprocal exchange, leading to a decline in mutual respect and trust. Social exchange theory predicts that supervisor-instigated incivility would obstruct mutually rewarding transactions and increase the likelihood of the subordinate's own uncivil response because of reciprocal exchange norm violations. These uncivil actions subsequently can have a negative bearing upon distal organizational outcomes like job satisfaction, organizational commitment, and job performance.

Frustration–aggression theory

Dollard *et al.*'s (1939) frustration–aggression theory hypothesizes that frustration arising from having one's goals delayed or thwarted causes aggressive behavior. In cases where the individual has no means to contest the source of frustration, aggressive behaviors are transferred onto innocents such as one's coworkers, customers or family. Building upon Dollard *et al.*'s theory, Fox and Spector (1999) proposed a new model of frustration–aggression that hypothesized that an emotional reaction mediates the relation between situational constraints and aggressing. The researchers found strong empirical evidence that frustration (i.e. an emotional reaction) mediated the relation between a situational constraint and an uncivil behavioral response. The upshot of this theoretical model is it predicts that when faced with situational constraints like the lack of resources to do one's job; frustration can *cause* aggressive behavior, including relatively milder forms such as incivility. Currently, the Fox–Spector model remains one of the few empirically tested models that link situational or environmental constraints to emotional reactions like frustration and workplace incivility.

Seminal studies about the consequences of workplace incivility

In this section, I present seven groundbreaking studies that offer empirical evidence linking incivility to negative organizational outcomes. These studies are not meant to be exhaustive, but rather illustrative of the rich array of incivility-related research being conducted internationally. In all but one case, the study is linked to one of the aforementioned theoretical frameworks.

Cortina *et al.* (2001) were among the first researchers to empirically link incivility to organizational outcomes, including job satisfaction, job withdrawal (turnover intent), career salience, and psychological distress. The researchers used incivility spiral theory (Andersson and Pearson 1999) and the results of a number of Scandinavian studies (e.g. Einarsen and Skogstad 1996) to support the proposed conceptual models. The sample consisted of 1,180 US public sector employees. Over 70 per cent experienced incivility at work over the past five years. Women tended to be incivility targets more frequently than males; however, incivility did not differ by ethnic group or marital status. Both men and women became more distressed as incivility experiences increased, but especially so for males. Increased incivility predicted also less job satisfaction and greater job withdrawal.

Yeung and Griffin (2008) examined workplace incivility in the context of six Asian countries/regions: China, Hong Kong, India, Japan, Korea, and Singapore. As a theoretical framework, they employed Andersson and Pearson's (1999) incivility spiral theory. With a sample of 116,986 participants, the researchers found that 77 per cent had experienced incivility in the past year, similar to Cortina *et al.* (2001). Twelve per cent had experienced such behavior weekly and 19 per cent monthly. Higher levels of incivility were experienced in India and Korea. They found too that moderate and high levels of incivility negatively affected employment engagement. Coworkers were the highest source of incivility, followed by managers and leaders. A surprising finding was that the higher the level of management, the greater the incivility. These findings strongly support the notion that being the target of incivility is not simply an isolated phenomenon, but consistent with previous research in the US and elsewhere.

Noting that the vast majority of incivility research concerned targets and not instigators, Reio and Ghosh (2009) conducted a survey study with a large, heterogeneous Midwestern USA sample. The researchers used Weiss and Cropanzano's (1996) affective events theory (closely linked to Dollard *et al.*'s [1939] frustration–aggression theory) to support predicting the affective link to incivility. Besides finding that roughly 50 per cent of the participants admitted to instigating interpersonal or organizational incivility, they found that the lack of workplace adaptation (i.e. establishing relationships with peers and supervisors is a prerequisite for adapting successfully to the workplace) and negative affect were strongly associated with interpersonal (instigated against a coworker or supervisor) and organizational incivility (instigated against teams, groups, and organization). This study supported Cortina *et al.*'s (2001) research about the prevalence of workplace incivility and extended it by adjusting Cortina *et al.*'s focus on asking participants to recall incivility from five years to one year to address possible recall effects.

In a nationally representative British study, Fevre *et al.* (2013) found 21 different types of ill-treatment among those with disabilities, including being gossiped about, humiliated, shouted at and ignored, each examples of incivility. Although the researchers did not use social exchange theory explicitly, they used a closely related social model of disability (Foster 2007) where environments and attitudes influence being productive workers rather than the impairment itself. In 20 of the 21 types of ill-treatment (including physical violence), those with a disability were much more likely to experience incivility versus those without a disability. They hypothesized that these findings may be a reflection of how coworkers' erroneous capability beliefs or attitudes regarding those with disability capabilities can affect social relations externalized as uncivil behavior. Overall, the study is among the few that links experiencing incivility to those with disabilities.

Power *et al.* (2013), in an interesting bullying study of participants from six continents, found that the acceptability of bullying varied by culture. Bullying differs from incivility in that the intention is clear rather than ambiguous, and it is a consistent pattern of instigated incivility, rather than being less frequent or intense. Still, the items of the measure used were almost identical to a number of incivility scale items currently in use. Confucian Asia (Singapore, Taiwan, Hong Kong) participants found work-related bullying more acceptable than Anglo (England, USA, Australia), Latin American (Columbia, Argentina, Mexico), and Sub-Saharan (Nigeria) country clusters. Participants from cultures with both a high future (e.g. China) and humane orientation (e.g. Latin America, Nigeria) found work-related bullying less acceptable versus those with a high performance culture (Confucian Asia). The study highlighted the advantage of studying cultural variations in uncivil behavior acceptance.

In one of the relatively rare group-level studies of incivility, Griffin (2010) used Bliese and Jex's (2002) multilevel theory to frame the study where incivility, a stressor, was considered both an individual- and group-level construct. The participants consisted of a sample of 179 organizations across Australia and New Zealand (N = 34,209). At the group level, incivility was averaged across all the group members. Griffin (2010) found that group-level or shared environmental incivility affected employees' intent to turn over above incivility experienced at the personal level. Interactional injustice climate also mediated the relation between incivility environment and turnover intent. The findings validated examining incivility from a multilevel lens because both group-level and individual-level incivility uniquely predicted turnover intent.

Finally, in a meta-analysis of 57 workplace aggression articles (incivility was one of the search terms), Hershcovis *et al.* (2007) reported that individual differences (e.g. traits – negative affect, thrill seeking) and situational variables (e.g. injustice, interpersonal conflict) combine to predict two forms of workplace aggression: interpersonal and organizational. Fox and Spector's (1999) model of frustration–aggression mediated by a situational constraint served as the theoretical lens for this work. For coworker targeted aggression, trait anger and interpersonal conflict were the strongest predictors of interpersonal aggression; interpersonal conflict, situational constraints, and job dissatisfaction were the strongest predictors of supervisor-targeted aggression. The researchers did not find differences by gender, concluding that this may be an artifact of including more indirect forms of aggression (e.g. incivility) in the study. This research supported the utility of examining both individual difference and situational variables when predicting workplace aggression.

The role of HRD in handling workplace incivility

Given that research has demonstrated that workplace incivility is present on six continents (see Power *et al.* 2013), a wide selection of HRD practices might work to curtail and correct uncivil behavior. Although a wide array of activities could be listed, the eight most promising are presented below.

Policies and procedures

At the macro-level, an organization might create a healthy organizational climate by establishing policies and procedures that discourage incivility. The organizational environment plays an important role in either encouraging or preventing workplace incivility (Porath and Pearson 2013). Policies and procedures communicate boundaries within which employees of the organization can operate. To highlight the uniqueness of workplace incivility, HRD practitioners could construct a written policy also that specifically addresses incivility instead of amending existing policies that address racial or sexual harassment to include incivility. By communicating the standards of behavior through written policies and by opening channels of communication for reporting a formal complaint against workplace incivility, uncivil acts at work can be reduced.

Orientation

Orientation is one of the primary organizational means for socializing newcomers or "outsiders" into becoming organizational "insiders" (Feldman 1981, Reio and Wiswell 2000, Schein 1988). Thus, it is a way for newcomers to begin learning how to fit in as a fully functioning member of the organization. Orientation sessions can be used to communicate the organization's written rules, codes of conduct, and policies and procedures related to workplace incivility (Porath and Pearson 2013). In addition, this would be the ideal time for setting zero-tolerance expectations for incivility, informed by the laws and customs of all countries where the organization conducts business. As part of presenting the zero-tolerance expectations, information about how uncivil behavior would be enforced should be introduced, along with its potential consequences. For managers, training aimed at modeling civil behavior and asking for feedback can be introduced at this time. Moreover, training during orientation could be used to help expatriates learn the nuances of acting appropriately civilly whenever they are transferred. Role playing, for example, would be an excellent means to demonstrate how to act and not act civilly in the new international setting (Reio and Ghosh 2009).

Mentoring and coaching

HRD professionals seem well suited for developing and implementing mentoring programs to improve interpersonal skills, particularly in management positions. Although the reciprocal benefits of formal mentoring relationships has garnered recent research attention (e.g. Ghosh and Reio 2013), the benefits of informal mentoring activities should not be overlooked. Appropriately matched mentor–protégé relationships, either formal or informal, can provide invaluable advice related to thinking and acting in a civil, respectful manner. Mentors can serve as role models for new, more appropriate ways to behaving on the job. An example might include how to convey feelings of mutual respect to even the most difficult colleague or customer. Organizationally acceptable attitudes and values can be modeled as well. This activity would be a useful follow-up to the role modeling introduced during orientation. Mentoring also could be in the form of coaching actions like providing feedback regarding a protégé's performance related to interacting with coworkers or clients from international locations.

Recruitment and selection

Porath and Pearson (2013) tout recruitment and selection activities as effective means of reducing incivility through preventing possible instigators from entering the organization in the first place. Hill, Callahan and Reio (2006) noted the power of "anticipatory socialization," where HRD professionals can present the organization's vision, mission, and goals through social media like the Internet to attract like-minded individuals to volunteer for or become an employee of an organization.

HRD professionals might also use extant research to identify personality trait predictors of incivility, bullying and other forms of aggressive behavior to inform recruitment practices. Hershcovis *et al.* (2007), for example, detected that negative affectivity and anger were traits associated with aggressing. Grant (2013) discovered that "ambiverts" at a call center (i.e. people who fall in the middle of the spectrum between being extraverted and introverted) demonstrated better sales performance than extraverts because they were less pushy and tended to strike the right balance between talking and listening. In a quasi-experimental study, Johnson *et al.*

(2008) found that managerial job applicant personality was linked to participants' attraction to simulated managerial jobs. In other words, job advertisements were written to successfully attract individuals with personalities aligned with certain types of managerial jobs. Thus, to recruit managerial applicants with the appropriate personality traits to fit a job, this research suggests that HRD professionals can create recruitment media to assure good person–job fit. For instance, to fill an expatriate managerial job, the advertisement might be written to attract those who possess an integrating conflict management style to lessen the likelihood of introducing someone into the organization not attuned to the win-win orientation arguably necessary to best engender civil behavior in international settings. Aligning advertisements to match known personality trait requirements for a job is a proactive means for reducing costs associated with recruiting and keeping aptly civil managers and workers.

Selection efforts can be strongly supported through detailed background checks where patterns of incivility can be traced to previous employment. Background checks can be problematic though because organizations can be hesitant to share work information beyond acknowledging the prospective employee actually worked there, and for how long because of legal purposes. When interviewing a prospective candidate, interviewees understandably tend to provide socially desirable information, making selection at best tricky. Reio and Ghosh (2009) advocated employing role plays during the interviewing process because it asks the applicant to do and act instead of merely discuss a topic. Provided a simulated situation (e.g. handling an employee who steadfastly denies he or she is not acting rudely towards coworkers), applicants are asked to act out how they would behave. This kind of behavioral screening can expose the applicant's characteristic attitudes and behaviors associated with the situation, which could uncover disconcerting behavioral tendencies related to incivility such as being impatient, anger prone, impulsive, and dogmatic.

Training and development

Researchers have identified a number of useful strategies to help reduce the likelihood of workplace incivility. As a preventative strategy to identify and manage incivility before it escalates, Trudel and Reio (2011) highlighted the use of mediation or conflict management training for supervisors, managers and other leaders. Specifically, they recommended training focused on reducing dominating conflict management styles (i.e. "win-lose" orientation) and increasing integrating styles (i.e. "win-win" orientation) to reduce the negative consequences of clashing conflict management styles, like job dissatisfaction and voluntary turnover. Discordant conflict styles can be especially problematic with expatriates operating in a new culture or unsocialized organizational newcomers because cultural expectations about acceptable attitudinal and behavioral norms can be decidedly unclear. Because civility is skills-based, Pearson and Porath (2005) advocated training designed to build interpersonal employee competencies like negotiating, managing stress, listening, and dealing with difficult people. Incivility training could also sensitize employees to the need for promoting civility and mutual respect in all phases of organizational life, from worker to manager to CEO (Reio and Ghosh 2009). Further, incivility sensitization could be linked to issues of diversity, including not only gender, ethnicity, and culture, but also physical (e.g. hearing impairment) and psychological/emotional disabilities and long-term illnesses (Fevre *et al.* 2013).

Career development

In light of the importance of training and development and organizational development to HRD professionals, career development is often overlooked (McDonald and Hite 2005). Inasmuch as organizational support can shape careers, career development is greatly influenced by the level of organizational support afforded to employees at all levels of the organization. Perceived lack of organizational support however can be a situational constraint that leads to employee frustration and uncivil behavior (Reio 2011). Three organizational support mechanisms are related to career development: fairness/equity, life–work balance, and environmental or situational (McDonald and Hite). Employees must perceive that criteria employed to determine the distribution of career development-related resources (e.g. access to training) are fair and equitable. Fairness perceptions must extend to life–work balance issues in that the minority gender or ethnic member of a team or workgroup needs satisfactory access to the social networks that can act as a form of socio-emotional support when experiencing life–work conflict. Fairness also is a germane part of environmental issues affecting career development, such as perceptions of equitable reward structures and supervisor support. Importantly, HRD professionals could facilitate ways to reduce the likelihood of uncivil behavior arising from perceptions of organizational support-related inequity. For instance, managers could be sensitized to the possible existence of inequity related to support and provided prevention and correction guidance.

At another level, one's career development could be thwarted by inappropriate, rude behavior in that instigators could be denied immediate financial reward (e.g. bonus) and promotional opportunities. Organizational policies might reflect this reality by specifying that developmental opportunities associated with advancement might be delayed or denied (e.g. fast-tracking managers) until appropriate civility skills have been mastered. This action might be even more salient in organizations where successful performance in overseas assignments is a prerequisite for advancement. Again, HRD professionals could assist managers and leaders in understanding what is and what is not civil behavior and how to set the tone for a positive organizational climate.

Feedback seeking and attending system

One of the best ways to learn and improve is through systematically seeking feedback (Reio and Wiswell 2000). HRD could design and implement a 360-degree feedback system to solicit anonymous feedback from all levels of the organization, including vendors and customers (Pearson and Porath 2005). Such a feedback system could not only identify patterns of incivility, but also solicit respondents' recommendations about how to improve incivility reduction efforts. Special emphasis could be placed on soliciting feedback regarding issues of mutual respect associated with operating in a multicultural and diverse work setting. An additional source of feedback could be through conducting post-departure interviews with employees who have recently left the organization and have settled comfortably at their new place of work (Pearson and Porath 2005).

After incivility has been identified, it must be attended to promptly for the purpose of correction before escalating into patterns of intentional, more troublesome behavior such as bullying and physical violence. For example, the organization could provide open channels for anonymously reporting possible violations of the organization's policies regarding uncivil behavior. An example of such a channel would be a telephone or Internet hotline where violations could be reported 24 hours a day, seven days a week.

Dealing with the consequences

Despite even the most systematic organizational efforts to dampen the likelihood of incivility through the aforementioned activities, acts of uncivil behavior will occur (Reio and Ghosh 2009). Incidents of incivility should be addressed promptly by the organization or risk being seen as condoning such behavior. A policy against retaliation must be included in such efforts. Incivility instigators should be educated about their actions and provided with tools to change erroneous ideas, beliefs and behaviors. HRD professionals would be able to provide training to deal effectively with problematic individuals, for example.

One important issue concerns how to best manage powerful instigators of incivility. Too many of us have been confronted with having to deal with "norm breakers" who happen to be the "top" salesperson, grant generator, fast-track manager, etc. that when left unchecked, became obnoxious self-aggrandizers who ostensibly forgot the importance of treating others civilly (Pearson and Porath 2005). Organizations understandably want to support the occasional star performer, but care should be taken to not permit rude behavior towards anyone from such individuals. In other words, star performers or influential managers who instigate rude behavior should be held accountable, regardless of the extent of their knowledge, international experience or political clout, just like anyone else. For example, it should not matter if the individual has a major role in a key project or can develop international business well; rude behavior is detrimental to not only the organizational commitment, job satisfaction, and workplace engagement of those who have experienced it (Reio 2011), but to the overall performance of the organization (Porath and Pearson 2013). Making excuses for such individuals only enables additional incivility.

Conclusion

Workplace incivility is a relatively mild form of aggression that occurs frequently and has been associated with a large number of negative organizational outcomes in every country it has been investigated. Its significance is international because it can lead to more troubling types of aggression like bullying and physical violence. Indeed, understanding the antecedents of incivility cannot be overemphasized because it has been shown to hamper individual-, team-, group-, and organizational-level performance. HRD researchers could lead efforts to locate and test new antecedent variables that might influence the instigation of incivility and its associated outcomes. For example, both formal and informal mentoring could be tested as socialization agents that might reduce the likelihood of uncivil behavior. Because personality traits like disinhibition, thrill seeking, and risk taking have been linked to more severe forms of aggression, investigation seems warranted too into the traits' association with milder forms of aggression like incivility. Untested moderator variables like organizational culture could be investigated as to the degree they dampen or strengthen the association between incivility and job performance, voluntary turnover, and other vital organizational outcomes. Moreover, HRD professionals could also play a leadership role in sensitizing organizations to its presence in the workplace and providing the guidance and training necessary to improve interpersonal skills for appropriate use in a wide variety of international settings.

References

Anand, V., Ashforth, B.E. and Joshi, M. (2004) 'Business as usual: the acceptance and perpetuation of corruption in organizations', *Academy of Management Executive*, 18: 39–53.

Andersson, L.M. and Pearson, C.M. (1999) 'Tit for tat? The spiraling effect of incivility in the workplace', *Academy of Management Review*, 24: 452–71.

Blau, P.M. (1964) *Exchange and Power in Social Life*, New York: John Wiley.

Bliese, P.D. and Jex, S.M. (2002) 'Incorporating a multilevel perspective into occupational stress research: theoretical, methodological, and practical implications', *Journal of Occupational Health Psychology*, 7: 265–76.

Cortina, L.M., Magley, V.J., Williams, J.H. and Langhout, R.D. (2001) 'Incivility in the workplace: incidence and impact', *Journal of Occupational Health Psychology*, 6: 64–80.

Cropanzano, R. and Mitchell, M.S. (2005) 'Social exchange theory: an interdisciplinary review', *Journal of Management*, 31: 874–900.

Dollard, J., Doob, L.W., Miller, N.E., Mowrer, O.H. and Sears, R.R. (1939) *Frustration and Aggression*, New Haven, CT: Yale University Press.

Einarsen, S. and Skogstad, A. (1996) 'Bullying at work: epidemiological findings in public and private organizations', *European Journal of Women and Organizational Psychology*, 5: 185–201.

Feldman, D.C. (1981) 'The multiple socialization of organization members', *Academy of Management Review*, 6: 309–18.

Fevre, R., Robinson, A., Lewis, D. and Jones, T. (2013) 'The ill-treatment of employees with disabilities in British workplaces', *Work, Employment & Society*, 27: 288–307.

Foster, D. (2007) 'Legal obligation or personal lottery? Employee experiences of disability and the negotiation of adjustments in the public sector workplace', *Work, Employment & Society*, 21: 67–84.

Fox, S. and Spector, P.E. (1999) 'A model of work frustration–aggression', *Journal of Organizational Behavior*, 20: 915–31.

Ghosh, R. and Reio, T.G., Jr. (2013) 'Career benefits associated with mentoring for mentors: a meta-analysis', *Journal of Vocational Behavior*, 83: 106–18.

Grant, A.M. (2013) 'Rethinking the extraverted sales ideal: the ambivert advantage', *Psychological Science*, 24: 1024–30.

Griffin, B. (2010) 'Multilevel relationships between organizational-level incivility, justice and intention to stay', *Work & Stress*, 24, 309–23.

Hershcovis, M.S., Turner, N., Barling, J., Arnold, K.A., Dupré, K.E., Inness, M. and Sivanathan, N. (2007) 'Predicting workplace aggression: a meta-analysis', *Journal of Applied Psychology*, 92: 228–38.

Hill, K.R., Callahan, J. and Reio, T.G., Jr. (November 2006) *The role of the internet in anticipatory socialization: a nethnography of concerned women for America*, Paper presented at the 2006 annual meeting of the National Communication Association, San Antonio, TX.

Homans, G.C. (1958) 'Social behavior as exchange', *American Journal of Sociology*, 63: 597–606.

Johnson, A., Winter, P.A., Reio, T.G., Jr., Thompson, H.L. and Petrosko, J.M. (2008) 'Managerial recruitment: the influence of personality and ideal candidate characteristics', *Journal of Management Development*, 27: 631–48.

Markova, G. and Folger, R. (2012) 'Every cloud has a silver lining: positive effects of deviant workers', *Journal of Social Psychology*, 152: 586–612.

McDonald, K.S. and Hite, L.M. (2005) 'Reviving the relevance of career development in human resource development', *Human Resource Development Review*, 4: 418–39.

Moreno-Jiménez, B., Díaz-Gracia, L. and Hernández, E.G. (2012) 'La aggresión laboral y la intención de abandono: evaluación del papel mediador de la satisfacción laboral', *Revista Mexicana De Psicología*, 29: 125–35.

Pearson, C.M. and Porath, C.L. (2005) 'On the nature, consequences and remedies of workplace incivility: no time for "Nice"? Think again', *Academy of Management Executive*, 19: 7–18.

Porath, C. and Pearson, C. (2013) 'The price of incivility: lack of respect hurts morale – and the bottom line', *Harvard Business Review*, 91: 115–21.

Power, J.L., Brotheridge, C.M., Blenkinsopp, J., Bowes-Sperry, L., Bozionelos, N., Buzády, Z. (. . .) and Nnedumm, A.U.O. (2013) 'Acceptability of workplace bullying: a comparative study on six continents', *Journal of Business Research*, 66: 374–80.

Reio, T.G., Jr. (2011) 'Supervisor and coworker incivility: testing the work frustration–aggression model', *Advances in Developing Human Resources*, 13: 54–68.

Reio, T.G., Jr. and Ghosh, R. (2009) 'Antecedents and outcomes of workplace incivility: implications for human resource development research and practice', *Human Resource Development Quarterly*, 20: 237–64.

Reio, T.G., Jr. and Wiswell, A.K. (2000) 'Field investigation of the relationship between adult curiosity, workplace learning, and job performance', *Human Resource Development Quarterly*, 11: 1–36.

Schein, E.H. (1988) 'Organizational socialization and the profession of management', *Sloan Management Review*, 30: 53–65.

Trudel, J. and Reio, T.G., Jr. (2011) 'Managing workplace incivility: the role of conflict management styles – antecedent or antidote?', *Human Resource Development Quarterly*, 22: 395–423.

Weiss, H.M. and Cropanzano, R. (1996) 'Affective events theory: a theoretical discussion of the structure, causes, and consequences of affective experiences at work', in Staw, B.M. and Cummings, L. (eds) *Research in Organizational Behavior*, Greenwich, CT: JAI Press, 1–74.

Yeung, A. and Griffin, B. (2008) 'Workplace incivility: does it matter in Asia?', *People and Strategy*, 31: 14–19.

51

CROSS-CULTURAL TRAINING AND ITS IMPLICATIONS FOR HRD[1]

Kyoung-Ah Nam, Yonjoo Cho and Mimi Miyoung Lee

With the rapid increase in global market exchanges, Asian multinational corporations (MNCs) have extended their subsidiaries beyond their national boundaries, expanding globally, and sending their employees to branches worldwide. The Cross-Cultural Training (CCT) literature, however, still revolves around the adjustment of Western expatriates while the experiences of Asian expatriates in non-Asian countries continue to be under-represented. Addressing the need to understand the support system of the Asian companies for their employees on an international assignment from an Asian perspective, we conducted an integrative literature review (Callahan 2010; Torraco 2005) and examined 42 studies on CCT research involving expatriates (Nam *et al.* 2014). Based on the review and analysis of the studies, we identify missing areas in current CCT research involving expatriates, address emerging issues, and provide implications for research and practice on human resources in the following sections.

Review of CCT Research

This section presents a review of major CCT research (Nam *et al.* 2014) to provide a platform on which we will argue the underrepresentation of Asian perspectives. Using content analysis, we have identified three main areas: adjustment issues, theories and conceptual frameworks, and CCT methods.

As shown in the work of Black *et al.* (1991), the issue of adjustment is multifaceted, encompassing factors concerning training (anticipatory adjustment) as well as in-country adjustment (work and non-work factors). Non-work factors such as spouse/family cross-cultural adjustment are critical factors and can have a "spillover effect" (Takeuchi *et al.* 2002: 655) on expatriates' adjustment. The term "spillover effect" refers to the influence that expatriate attitudes in a particular domain (work) have on the attitudes in other domains (non-work). Tung's (1981) pioneering work reports the inability of expatriates' spouses to adjust to the host culture as the number one reason for expatriate failure. On a similar note, Mesmer-Magnus and Viswesvaran (2008) examined five personality factors as predictors of expatriate success: agreeableness, conscientiousness, emotional stability, extraversion, and openness to experience. These authors indicated that although many organizations provide little formal preparation for expatriation, CCT is effective in developing trainees' cultural perceptions, facilitating adjustment to the host culture, and enhancing performance in international assignments. Caligiuri and Tarique's

(2006) work centred on selection and training that promotes cross-cultural effectiveness among expatriates. The authors argued that the key to expatriate success is to understand the interaction of selection and training to determine who benefits the most from training. Through surveys with international executives from three large MNCs, Caligiuri and Tarique (2011) indicated that a combination of selection and development (training) is critical for achieving key business goals to build a well-prepared pipeline of future global leaders (Nam *et al.* 2014).

Researchers have employed various theories and conceptual frameworks to investigate issues in CCT. Hofstede's six Dimensions of National Cultures (Hofstede *et al.* 2010) have been popular and continue to generate further studies (i.e. Black and Mendenhall 1990; Kirkman *et al.* 2006). Although Hofstede's dimensions have been criticized pertinently (McSweeney 2002), Minkov and Hofstede (2011) credit such criticism to misinterpretation of the dimensions or attempting to utilize the dimensions for anything other than their intended scope of national or organization – not individual – culture. Bandura's social learning theory (1977) has been used to explain training as a social learning process. Others have turned to Kolb's experiential learning (Kolb and Kolb 2009; Yamazaki and Kayes 2004) to emphasize the importance of experience for successful expatriate adaptation or sequential adjustment theory (Littrell *et al.* 2006; Ting-Toomey and Chung 2012) to explain various aspects of adjustments. Those who are interested in the relationships among cultural contexts have referred to social capital theory (Lengnick-Hall and Lengnick-Hall 2006; Gubbins and Garavan 2009).

As with any training, the method of delivery and its effectiveness proved to be one of the most important issues in the discussion of CCT. The researchers have argued for a contingency approach (Tung 1981) or proposed using cross-cultural competency clusters (Yamazaki and Kayes 2004). Some studies have focused on examining different types of CCT programs (Osman-Gani 2000; Holtbrügge and Schillo 2008; Shen and Lang 2009). Others also have emphasized the importance of comprehensiveness over the length of CCT (Moon *et al.* 2012) as well as the effectiveness of an integrated CCT program (Landis *et al.* 2004).

The effectiveness of CCT

CCT research has evaluated the effectiveness of CCT (Nam *et al.* 2014). Table 51.1 demonstrates some positive and negative results.

Table 51.1 The effectiveness of CCT

Positive Results	*Negative Results*
• Black and Mendenhall (1990): The impact of CCT on expats' adjustment • Deshpande and Viswesvaran (1992): CCT's positive effect • Caligiuri *et al.* (2001): The relevant pre-departure CCT • Waxin and Panaccio (2005): CCT, international experience, and cultural distance • Selmer (2005): CCT for work adjustment • Osman-Gani (2000): The role of self-efficacy in expatriate adjustment via CCT • Moon *et al.* (2012): Pre-departure CCT, cultural intelligence and cross-cultural adjustment	• Black and Gregersen (1991): Ineffective company-provided training • Puck *et al.* (2008): The impact of pre-departure CCT on adjustment • Morris and Robie (2001): The effectiveness of CCT • Hechanova *et al.* (2003): CCT related to adjustment • Kealey and Protheroe (1996): A lack of literature on the impact of CCT on expatriates • Mendenhall *et al.* (2004): A review of CCT evaluation studies

Positive results

Black and Mendenhall (1990) conducted the first study on the effectiveness of CCT on expatriates' cross-cultural skill development, adjustment, and performance by reviewing the previous 29 empirical studies. In their study, CCT had a positive impact on individuals' development of skills, adjustment to the cross-cultural situation, and job performance. This pioneering work served as a foundation for the subsequent empirical studies on CCT (Nam *et al.* 2014).

The following six studies have resulted in positive results indicating that CCT accelerates expatriate adjustment. Deshpande and Viswesvaran's (1992) meta-analysis of 21 studies provided evidence that CCT has a positive impact on cross-cultural skill development, cross-cultural adjustability, and job performance. Caligiuri *et al.* (2001) showed that the more contextually tailored pre-departure CCT is, the more expectations were positively met. Selmer (2005) found CCT had a weak positive association with work adjustment for expatriates in joint ventures in China. Waxin and Panaccio (2005) examined the effect of four types of CCT (conventional/experimental and general/specific to the host country) on expatriate adjustment and found that CCT, in all its forms, facilitated all three facets of expatriates' adjustment (work, interaction, and general). Osman-Gani (2000) demonstrated the positive effects of CCT on expat adjustment are due to an increase in self-efficacy as a result of training. Moon *et al.* (2012) showed pre-departure CCT is important for developing cultural intelligence as well as cross-cultural adjustment.

Negative results

Findings of six other studies have cast some doubts on the effectiveness of CCT. Black and Gregersen (1991) found most expatriates received little pre-departure training, and company-provided training was not significantly related to either work or general adjustment. Puck *et al.*'s (2008) analysis of 339 German expatriates did not provide empirical support for the assumed impact of pre-departure CCT on adjustment; rather, they found that language played a central role as a prerequisite for adjustment (Nam *et al.* 2014).

Morris and Robie (2001) identified 16 studies for expatriate adjustment and 25 studies for expatriate performance. The results of this meta-analysis revealed that CCT was somewhat less effective than expected. Their study supports the use of CCT for expatriates, but its effectiveness should be carefully evaluated. Hechanova *et al.*'s (2003) meta-analysis of 42 empirical studies demonstrated that CCT negatively relates to all three facets of expatriate adjustment (cross-cultural skill development, adjustment, and performance). Kealey and Protheroe (1996) also argued that the existing literature on the impact of intercultural training is seriously deficient; no study on intercultural training for expatriates has met the full criteria for rigorous experimental research (e.g. the use of multiple measures beyond self-reports). Additionally, based on 28 quantitative evaluation studies, Mendenhall *et al.* (2004) found most studies relied on self-reports, and most treatment groups were composed of university students.

A major criticism of the existing literature on the effectiveness of CCT revolves around its foundation on anecdotal evidences and broad theories and models (Caligiuri and Tarique 2006). Most CCT research has been theoretical; few empirical studies have assessed the relationship between CCT and expatriate performance (Littrell *et al.* 2006). CCT research needs to generate empirical studies with rigorous research designs such as longitudinal designs and multiple measures of adjustment and performance (Hippler 2009) beyond its reliance on quantitative methods. Qualitative means need to be developed for measuring expatriate performance and CCT effectiveness. Qualitative research methods such as ethnographies and case studies using prolonged engagement and in-depth interviews of not only the expatriates themselves but also their family members, peers, and host country counterparts could yield the necessary contextual information.

Working towards successful CCT

This section aims to provide a constructive critique and suggestions for successful CCT design and delivery. Based on the literature review as well as the interviews and observations from the authors' CCT experiences, key research streams and challenges proposed here include increasing needs for cross-cultural assessment instruments, the significant difference between domestic and international assignments, CCT methods, and issues relating to CCT trainers.

Cross-cultural assessment instruments

While the demands of using assessment instruments in CCT have been rapidly increasing, conducting a cross-cultural assessment requires careful analysis. Broadly classified, assessment instruments are used to measure individual and/or groups' intercultural competence, cultural difference, intercultural adaptability, and global leadership competency (Mendenhall *et al.* 2013). With the increasing demands, misusing assessments has become a growing concern. This concern includes Western bias of cross-cultural validity, translation lacking in-depth culture-specific knowledge, lack of predictive validity, and the self-reported nature of data.

Cross-cultural validity (Bennett 1993) with its in-built Western bias (Szkudlarek 2009) is one of the most critical issues in cross-cultural assessment because instruments currently used in CCT are mostly developed from US-American and/or European cultural perspectives. While most of these assessment instruments are well researched and some instruments claim to be cross-culturally valid, a majority of instrument samples are comprised of a mostly Western population, including at most a small number of non-Western samples. This situation leads to a serious question regarding the criteria of items valued in assessment. What is encouraged as competence in Western culture is often not readily applicable to non-Western contexts and sometimes even evaluated negatively. For example, although self-promotion is considered to be a positive competence in US workplaces, the same trait is often viewed negatively in many Asian countries (Stahl *et al.* 2012). On the other hand, modesty and self-humbling, regarded as an important virtue in Confucian cultures, are often perceived as a lack of participation or self-confidence in a US context (Nam *et al.* 2014). Considering unique sociocultural norms and their significant influence on business practices in many non-Western countries, these assessment results could be seriously inaccurate or misleading. Moreover, these assessments are simply translated into local languages, often without aptly translating cultural nuances, and used to assess non-Western local candidates' competencies for the selection and promotion process. Even when questionnaires are translated, the results and feedback are mostly provided in English. As a result, non-Western CCT participants are often puzzled over their assessment results.

The dependence of most assessments on self-reported data also raises questions in cross-cultural contexts. Employees' attitudes toward self-evaluation and modesty when reporting their accomplishments are culturally dependent. From one-on-one interviews with CCT participants over the last 15 years, we learned that individuals from various cultures respond very differently to the Likert scale questionnaires from many assessment instruments. In accordance with culturally valued humble attitudes, Asian participants tend to underestimate their competence when evaluating themselves on a Likert scale survey. Respondents from East Asia, for example, tend to use the middle point of Likert scales more (Tungli and Peiperl 2009), as a reflection of their cultural norms emphasizing balance and harmony (Nam *et al.* 2014). If organizations depend solely on CCT assessment results that rarely incorporate culturally specific norms and values, a quick summative assessment used for employees' selection and promotion may even raise ethical concerns (Romani and Szkudlarek 2013; Szkudlarek 2009).

The issues addressed above bring important questions to HRD practitioners. How accurate and applicable are these self-reported assessment results, especially when comparing cultures where self-promotion is encouraged versus discouraged? How do we decode the hidden values and assumptions with their pro-Western bias? How should we assess and interpret intercultural competence, when the very definition of effectiveness and appropriateness is culturally constructed? These are just a few pressing questions that beg further investigation.

Domestic versus international assignments

Another mistake is an assumption that if someone was successful in the domestic market, he/she will also be successful in international assignment. MNCs often assign high-potential employees in international assignment as part of global leadership pipeline programs, mistakenly equating potential for successful international performance with domestic success. Differences between domestic and international assignments vary significantly. The importance of contextual and situational approaches is well supported by CCT in the contingency leadership context. Traits that assist in effective leadership in one culture may be detrimental in another cultural context (Mendenhall *et al.* 2013). While Chinese managers approach employees with indirect communication and use metaphors to deliver their points, indirect communication is often not necessarily positively valued by US-American managers. The word *self* often has a negative connotation in many Asian countries where relationships and collectivism are the norm (Stahl *et al.* 2012). Further, these terms reflect the need to move beyond "*either–or*," the dichotomous mode of thinking more common in the Western framework, to that of "*both–and*" that is considered more characteristic of Asian thought patterns (Nisbett 2004).

It is important for organizations and HRD practitioners to understand why employees and leaders who are effective in a domestic context may not be effective in cross-cultural contexts. Work tasks that have even the slightest cultural aspects require cultural learning and adjustment (Black and Mendenhall 1990). HRD practitioners should consider personality characteristics, language fluency, cultural distance between home and host culture, and prior international experiences as factors for expatriate success. All of these contribute to an employee's ability to perceive, reflect upon, and reproduce novel cultural behaviors necessary to successful performance in cross-cultural workplaces (ibid.). Flexibility, curiosity for other cultures, tolerance with uncertainty, and ability to code-shift between cultural contexts are also important success factors for international expatriates in intercultural adjustment.

CCT methods

Issues related with CCT methods such as timing, length, purpose, audience, and the emphasis of intercultural competence building versus language training are pertinent when HRD practitioners plan CCT. Minimal CCT is provided, while the CCT currently delivered heavily focuses on pre-departure training for relocation. While pre-departure CCT is important, cultural shock and other overwhelming adjustment challenges usually arise after landing. On the ground, real-time CCT is needed for expatriates and their families. Further, re-entry culture shock is even more severe than the initial culture shock. CCT should be accompanied by the overall expatriate cycle beginning from selection, pre-departure, in-country, re-entry, and knowledge transfer processes. The timing, length, and methods of CCT need to be customized based on the needs of individual expatriates and their family members. HRD practitioners need a variety of means to ensure expatriate success. One suggestion is to invite repatriates to the company's CCT so participants can acquire culturally relevant, situated knowledge in the process of social learning.

Although many organizations emphasize language skills in the expatriate selection process, language competence does not necessarily guarantee intercultural competence. Expatriates have said in their interviews, "You can get by without knowing the language, but you can't get by without knowing the culture." Becoming *fluent fools* (Bennett 2008), those who are able to articulate linguistically yet fail to understand the culture, can cause more serious mistakes.

CCT trainers

CCT and its impact vary depending on who delivers a program. Interviews by the first author with HR managers from MNCs reveal that they are often hesitant to invest in CCT because trainers frequently fail to address the competitive complexities that MNCs face. CCT trainers "often engage participants in intense interpersonal interactions and/or deal with issues that are both highly emotional and controversial" (Weaver 2013: 92). Because of its unique nature of focusing on the *process* of learning rather than simply delivering cognitive knowledge, the quality and competency of a CCT trainer are important variables for successful CCT; however, these variables have not been fully examined.

Competent CCT trainers are aware of possible risk factors when planning and sequencing activities for a CCT program. These include the risk of participants' personal disclosure, failure, embarrassment, threat to one's cultural identity, and becoming culturally marginal and alienated (Paige 1993). Inexperienced CCT trainers, however, may perpetuate stereotypes. When CCT activities and simulations are executed without appropriate facilitation skills and mindful debriefing discussion afterwards, they can be unintentionally harmful or unethical, causing "psychological stress and perpetuating bigotry" (Weaver 2013: 92). Because CCT is an emerging field, the unethical behaviors of a CCT trainer could damage the CCT profession, if not the entire CCT field.

One of the key challenges is "there is no overall licensing or accrediting body which determines who is qualified to do training" (Weaver 2013: 93). Further, CCT trainers should be able to balance the depth and breadth of theoretical knowledge, practical implication, and organizational complexity illustrating how concepts and principles apply to expatriate adjustment processes in the real world rather than provide simple dos-and-don'ts. Simply memorizing different customs without understanding the values and norms behind them could cause even more serious miscommunication in cross-cultural encounters.

Implications for HRD

The past decade has witnessed an explosion of social networking technologies and a shift in world economic powers. Developing intercultural competence (Deardorff 2009) is no longer a recommendation but a means of survival for responding to the complexities of globalization. The need for organizations to prepare expatriates for global markets has become crucial and urgent. While intercultural competence is becoming a critical factor for success, the definitional and conceptual challenges have grown (Morley and Cerdin 2010) because the majority of CCT literature has heavily focused on Western perspectives. Considering the rapid rise to prominence of East Asian global companies in recent years, Western examples and perspectives can only provide a partial picture of CCT research and practice. While many values are shared universally, there are also some values, norms and customs that are culturally specific. In this sense, the field of CCT should encourage and generate more research on how Eastern companies' experiences inform their performance and assess its outcome. With such a goal in mind, we provide the following major practical implications and questions for HRD researchers and practitioners based on the key issues addressed earlier in this chapter.

In order to examine CCT from a new perspective, we need to pay less attention to the simple geographical distinction of East and West and focus more on how perspectives of cultural diversity are interpreted in culturally specific ways in CCT. Even the concept of *training*, for example, can be defined differently depending on cultural context. We learned over our CCT practice that in some cultures, participation in CCT training is seen as recognition and even a privilege – the participants are *selected* based on their high-potential value to the company. In other cases, participants hold negative attitudes assuming that they are being *penalized* for their lack of intercultural competence. In order to design and develop CCT that incorporates more diverse perspectives, more data and additional sources from non-Western companies should be collected and utilized. The first step for cross-cultural trainers is to understand that many definitions used in training are culturally dependent, not to mention the personal and organizational-specific values that participants and trainers bring with them. The notion of cultural diversity is also interpreted differently across cultures. While diversity is usually translated with reference to racial, ethnic, or gender differences in the US, other countries have their own categories through which people differ, depending upon their historical and linguistic heritages (Gundling and Zanchettin 2007).

Another example is the adaptation of family members, which has been a major factor determining expatriate success (Lee 2007; Rosenbusch and Cseh 2012). While the issue of family has been addressed in existing CCT literature and an increasing number of studies examines the importance of family roles in expatriate adjustment (Lee 2007; Rosenbusch and Cseh 2012), the meaning and significance of family factors in CCT needs to be examined in a more cultural/ context specific manner. For example, how is "success" defined in Confucian Asian societies? Is an individualized concept of success in many Western CCT adjustment models adequate to assess the collective notion of success in which a family is regarded as a unit? According to Hippler (2009), key motives of relocatees at German MNCs were centred around individual goals such as seeking professional or personal challenges. For many East Asian expatriates, on the other hand, an overseas assignment may serve as an opportunity for their children to learn and master English, the command of which serves a crucial role in notoriously competitive college entrance exams. The success of their overseas assignment is associated with the successful adjustment of their family members whose concerns qualitatively differ from those of many Western expatriates.

Incorporation of family into CCT needs more attention from HRD practitioners. The influence of family factors on expatriates' success varies from culture to culture. For example, a spouse's (un)willingness to live abroad (called "the expat dilemma") (Groysberg *et al.* 2011), marital status, physical conditions of elderly parents, and education of school-aged children are key determinants for expatriate success in some Asian countries that are often overlooked in CCT literature. Issues such as family adjustments and performance assessments cannot be fully understood without taking cultural components into consideration.

While the importance of CCT is increasingly recognized, measuring the immediate impact and effectiveness of CCT remains a challenge for many HRD practitioners. Two issues seem to be the primary contributors to this challenge. First, many MNCs and organizations are unwilling to share their CCT data, citing confidentiality. In the rare cases of shared information, the data are often limited to success stories that they are proud to present. Such hurdles in accessing companies' uncensored data have often discouraged researchers from attempting to carry out empirical studies in CCT.

The second issue involves how effectively CCT outcomes are measured. While various attempts have been made to measure the effectiveness of the CCT including expatriates' adjustments, productivity in the host country, and early return from the assignment, the tangible return-on-investment (ROI) of CCT has been the major concern of HRD practitioners. The assessment criteria used to measure CCT outcomes and expatriate performance may also differ. Because it is difficult to quantify the effectiveness of CCT and measure its immediate impact on expatriate performance, CCT has been one of the most vulnerable areas to budget cuts when organizations face financial difficulties. Conceding that the challenges imposed by ethical and research standards are growing stronger, Osborn (2012: 14) argued for the identification of "culture-specific career variables as a necessary step to allow for research-based statements of best practices for using cross-cultural assessments". In this regard, organizations should consider evaluating the impact of CCT in the long-term range beyond short-term return-on-investment (ROI) and need to incorporate more qualitative, culturally appropriate approaches to assessment.

Utilizing a stronger partnership with subsidiaries is another important consideration (Ananthram and Chan 2013). In order to minimize misunderstanding and enhance collaboration within a multicultural workplace, CCT should be designed and delivered to expatriates and their counterparts in the host country, including expatriates' supervisors, colleagues, and staff members. Although expatriates need help adjusting to their host countries, successful cross-cultural collaboration can be best achieved through effective communication between members of both cultures.

Culturally rooted pre-departure training, ongoing support while in the country, a realistic job preview for prospective employees and their families, and faculties such as a high degree of openness and adaptability point to the need for clearly defined cross-cultural assessment strategies. Closer attention should be given to determining which strategies could be universally applied and which need to be localized (Ananthram and Chan 2013).

Conclusion

We have identified major research themes in current CCT literature and suggested emerging issues that need to be addressed in the field. Based on our discussion, immediate research agendas call for further investigation on: (1) How do non-Western companies train their expatriates for successful performance in international contexts? (2) How do contextual variables (e.g. types of expatriates, gender and age, and length and timing of an assignment) influence expatriate adjustment and performance? And (3) what cultural issues in CCT should be addressed for expatriates and their families from non-Western companies? As CCT attempts to better prepare expatriates in the global economy, future research needs investigations on diversity across and within cultures, which extend beyond binary terms such as East and West (Nam *et al.* 2014).

Note

1. This chapter draws on Nam, K.A., *et al.* (2014) "West meets East? Identifying the gap in current cross-cultural training research" *Human Resource Development Review* 13, 1

References

Ananthram, S. and Chan, C. (2013) "Challenges and strategies for global human resource executives: Perspectives from Canada and the United States" *European Management Journal* 31, 3: 223–33.

Bandura, A. (1977) *Social learning theory*. Oxford: Prentice-Hall.

Bennett, J.M. (2008) "On becoming a global soul: A path to engagement during study abroad" In Savicki, V. (ed.) *Developing Intercultural Competence and Transformation* (13–31). Sterling, VA: Stylus.

Bennett, M.J. (1993) "Towards ethnorelativism: A developmental model of intercultural sensitivity" In Paige, R.M. (ed.) *Education for the intercultural experience* (2nd edition) (21–71). Yarmouth, ME: Intercultural Press.

Black, J.S. and Mendenhall, M. (1990) "Cross-cultural training effectiveness" *Academy of Management Review* 15, 1: 113–36.

Black, J.S. and Gregersen, H.B. (1991) "Antecedents to cross-cultural adjustment for expatriates in Pacific Rim Assignments" *Human Relations* 44, 5: 497–515.

Black, J.S., Mendenhall, M. and Oddou, G. (1991) "Toward a comprehensive model of international adjustment: An integration of multiple theoretical perspectives" *Academy of Management Review* 16, 2: 291–317.

Caligiuri, P. and Tarique, I. (2006) "International assignee selection and cross-cultural training and development" In Stahl, G.K. and Björkman, I. (eds) *Handbook of research in international human resource management* (302–22). Cheltenham: Edward Elgar.

Caligiuri, P. and Tarique, I. (2011) *Dynamic competencies and performance of global leaders: The role of personality and developmental experiences.* Alexandria, VA: SHRM Foundation.

Caligiuri, P., Phillips, J., Lazarova, M., Tarique, I. and Bürgi, P. (2001) "The theory of met expectations applied to expatriate adjustment: the role of cross-cultural training" *International Journal of Human Resource Management* 12, 3: 357–72.

Callahan, J.L. (2010) "Constructing a manuscript: Distinguishing integrative literature reviews and conceptual and theory articles" *Human Resource Development Review* 9, 3: 300–4.

Deardorff, D.K. (2009) *The SAGE handbook of intercultural competence.* Thousand Oaks, CA: SAGE.

Deshpande, S.P. and Viswesvaran, C. (1992) "Is cross-cultural training of expatriate managers effective: A meta-analysis" *International Journal of Intercultural Relations* 16, 3: 295–310.

Groysberg, B., Nohria, N. and Herman, K. (2011) "HBR case study: The expat dilemma" *Harvard Business Review* 89, 11: 150–53.

Gubbins, C. and Garavan, T.N. (2009)"Understanding the HRD role in MNCs: The imperatives of social capital and networking" *Human Resource Development Review* 8, 2: 245–75.

Gundling, E. and Zanchettin, A. (2007) *Global diversity: Winning customers and engaging employees within world markets.* Boston, MA: Nicholas Brealey International.

Hechanova, R., Beehr, T.A. and Christiansen, N.D. (2003) "Antecedents and consequences of employees' adjustment to overseas assignment: A meta-analytic review" *Applied Psychology* 52, 2: 213–36.

Hippler, T. (2009) "Why do they go? Empirical evidence of employees' motives for seeking or accepting relocation" *International Journal of Human Resource Management* 20, 6: 1381–401.

Hofstede, G., Hofstede, G.J. and Minkov, M. (2010) *Cultures and organizations: Software of the mind.* Maidenhead: McGraw-Hill.

Holtbrügge, D. and Schillo, K. (2008) "Intercultural training requirements for virtual assignments: Results of an explorative empirical study" *Human Resource Development International* 11, 3: 271–86.

Kealey, D.J. and Protheroe, D.R. (1996) "The effectiveness of cross-cultural training for expatriates" *International Journal of Intercultural Relations* 20, 2: 141–65.

Kirkman, B.L., Lowe, K.B. and Gibson, C.B. (2006) "A quarter century of 'culture's consequences': A review of empirical research incorporating Hofstede's cultural values framework" *Journal of International Business Studies* 37, 3: 285–320.

Kolb, A.Y. and Kolb, D.A. (2009) "Experiential learning theory" In Armstrong, S.J. and Fukami, C.V. (eds) *The SAGE handbook of management learning, education and development* (42–68). Thousand Oaks, CA: SAGE.

Landis, D., Bennett, J.M. and Bennett, M.J. (eds) (2004) *Handbook of intercultural training* (3rd edition). Thousand Oaks, CA: SAGE.

Lee, P.C. (2007) "Family support as a factor in cultural adjustment" *Journal of Business Systems, Governance and Ethics* 2, 2: 29–35.

Lengnick-Hall, M.L. and Lengnick-Hall, C.A. (2006) "International human resource management and social network/social capital theory" In Stahl, G.K. and Björkman, I. (eds) *Handbook of research in international human resource management* (475–87). Cheltenham: Edward Elgar.

Littrell, L.N., Salas, E., Hess, K.P., Paley, M. and Riedel, S. (2006) "Expatriate preparation: A critical analysis of 25 years of cross-cultural training research" *Human Resource Development Review* 5, 3: 355–88.

McSweeney, B. (2002) "Hostede's model of national cultural differences and their consequences: A triumph of faith – a failure of analysis" *Human Relations* 55, 1: 89–118.

Mendenhall, M.E., Stahl, G.K., Ehnert, I., Oddou, G., Osland, J.S. and Kühlmann, T.M. (2004) "Evaluation studies of cross-cultural training programs: A review of the literature from 1988 to 2000" In Landis, D. Bennett, J.M. and Bennett, M.J. (eds) *Handbook of intercultural training* (129–43). Thousand Oaks, CA: SAGE.

Mendenhall, M.E., Osland, J.S., Bird, A., Oddou, G., Maznevski, M.L., Stevens, M. and Stahl, G.K. (2013) *Global leadership: Research, practice, and development.* New York: Routledge.

Mesmer-Magnus, J.R. and Viswesvaran, C. (2008) "Expatriate management: A review and directions for research in expatriate selection, training, and repatriation" In Harris, M.M. (ed.) *Handbook of research in international human resource management* (183–206). New York: Lawrence Erlbaum.

Minkov, M. and Hofstede, G. (2011) "The evolution of Hofstede's doctrine" *Cross Cultural Management* 18, 1: 10–20.

Moon, H.K., Choi, B.K. and Jung, J.S. (2012) "Previous international experience, cross-cultural training, and expatriates' cross-cultural adjustment: Effects of cultural intelligence and goal orientation" *Human Resource Development Quarterly* 23, 3: 285–330.

Morley, M.J. and Cerdin, J.L. (2010) "Intercultural competence in the international business arena" *Journal of Managerial Psychology* 25, 8: 805–9.

Morris, M.A. and Robie, C. (2001) "A meta-analysis of the effects of cross-cultural training on expatriate performance and adjustment" *International Journal of Training and Development* 5, 2: 112–25.

Nam, K.A., Cho, Y. and Lee, M. (2014) "West meets East? Identifying the gap in current cross-cultural training research" *Human Resource Development Review* 13, 1.

Nisbett, R. (2004) *The geography of thought: How Asians and Westerners think differently . . . and why.* New York: Free Press.

Osborn, D.S. (2012) "An international discussion about cross-cultural career assessment" *International Journal for Educational and Vocational Guidance* 12, 1: 5–16.

Osman-Gani, A.M. (2000) "Developing expatriates for the Asia-Pacific region: A comparative analysis of multinational enterprise managers from five countries across three continents" *Human Resource Development Quarterly* 11, 3: 213–35.

Paige, R.M. (1993) "On the nature of intercultural experiences and intercultural education" In Paige, R.M. *Education for the intercultural experience* (2nd edition) (1–19). Yarmouth, ME: Intercultural Press.

Puck, J.F., Kittler, M.G. and Wright, C. (2008) "Does it really work? Re-assessing the impact of pre-departure cross-cultural training on expatriate adjustment" *International Journal of Human Resource Management* 19, 12: 2182–97.

Romani, L. and Szkudlarek, B. (2013) "The struggles of the interculturalists: Professional ethical identity and early stages of codes of ethics development" *Journal of Business Ethics* 112, 1: 1–19.

Rosenbusch, K. and Cseh, M. (2012) "The cross-cultural adjustment process of expatriate families in a multinational organization: A family system theory perspective" *Human Resource Development International* 15, 1: 61–77.

Selmer, J. (2005) "Cross-cultural training and expatriate adjustment in China: Western joint venture managers" *Personnel Review* 34, 1: 68–84.

Shen, J. and Lang, B. (2009) "Cross-cultural training and its impact on expatriate performance in Australian MNEs" *Human Resource Development International* 12, 4: 371–86.

Stahl, G.K., Mendenhall, M.E. and Oddou, G.R. (2012) *Readings and cases in international human resource management and organizational behavior.* New York: Routledge.

Szkudlarek, B. (2009) "Through Western eyes: Insights into the intercultural training field" *Organization Studies* 30, 9: 975–86.

Takeuchi, R., Yun, S., and Tesluk, P.E. (2002) "An examination of crossover and spillover effects of spousal and expatriate cross-cultural adjustment on expatriate outcomes", *Journal of Applied Psychology* 87,4: 655–66.

Ting-Toomey, S. and Chung, L.C. (2012) *Understanding intercultural communication.* New York: Oxford University Press.

Torraco, R.J. (2005) "Writing integrative literature reviews: Guidelines and examples" *Human Resource Development Review* 4, 3: 356–67.

Tung, R.L. (1981) "Selection and training of personnel for overseas assignments" *Columbia Journal of World Business* 16, 1: 69–78.

Tungli, Z. and Peiperl, M. (2009) "Expatriate practices in German, Japanese, U.K., and U.S. multinational companies: A comparative survey of changes" *Human Resource Management* 48, 1: 153–71.

Waxin, M.F. and Panaccio, A. (2005) "Cross-cultural training to facilitate expatriate adjustment" *Personnel Review* 34, 1: 51–67.

Weaver, G.R. (2013) *Intercultural relations: Communication, identity and conflict.* Boston, MA: Pearson.

Yamazaki, Y. and Kayes, D.C. (2004) "An experiential approach to cross-cultural learning" *Academy of Management Learning and Education* 3, 4: 362–79.

52
INTERCULTURAL COMPETENCE AND HRD

Katherine Rosenbusch

With the increase of globalization, everything is changing. International markets have become stronger, multinational companies have increased, international mobility has become essential for many employees, information technologies continue to grow and the multicultural environment has exploded. In this ever changing global environment, individuals are being challenged to work in complex cross-cultural arenas in which they may or may not have appropriate skills. They are thrown into new business opportunities and expected to be able to communicate, manage, and negotiate effectively in global settings. Studies show that the number of long, short, intraregional, and commuter assignments will surge with more expatriates exposed to cross-cultural situations (Brookfield Global Relocation Services 2010). Executives who operate across national boundaries will be challenged by complex business problems that are linked to the capacity of their people's mindsets and behaviors to operate in this new global domain (Pucik 2005). The need for individuals to possess intercultural competence is becoming essential to meet the demands of the business world (Yu 2012). This "boundaryless" business environment will continue to drive changes in where an organization does business and what it needs from its people to compete and thrive in both existing and emerging markets.

This chapter will examine the scope of intercultural competence by providing an overview of the various definitions and models, and highlighting the instruments available to measure this construct, and describing how human resource professionals can aid in the development of intercultural competence. The chapter concludes with the impact that intercultural competence can have on HRD practice for the future.

Defining intercultural competence

Intercultural competence is a multifaceted construct that encompasses many different disciplines (management, education, psychology, anthropology, and sociology). Although the term is used frequently, opinions vary as to what it encompasses. Researchers have used a wide range of terms to discuss intercultural competence. These include intercultural readiness, cultural intelligence, global mindset, cross-cultural competence, intercultural sensitivity, intercultural effectiveness, and intercultural communication. Cross-cultural competence was primarily utilized in domestic research including healthcare and education whereas intercultural competence was considered to be more global and spanned national boundaries. Fantini (2005), for example, states that intercultural competence can incorporate a variety of traits (flexibility, humor, patience, openness, interest, curiosity, empathy, tolerance for ambiguity and suspending judgment); numerous domains (ability to establish and maintain relationships, ability to communicate with minimal loss or distortion); several different dimensions (knowledge, attitudes/affect, skills, and awareness); and levels of attainment (Level I: Educational traveler; Level II: Sojourner; Level III: Professional; Level IV: Intercultural Specialist).

Several definitions have been formulated for intercultural competence over the years. Deardorff (2009: xiii) defines intercultural competence as "a cultural learning process in which one builds authentic relationships by observing, listening, and asking those who are from different backgrounds to teach, to share, to enter into dialogue together about relevant needs and issues". Fantini (2005: 1) describes intercultural competence as "the complex set of abilities needed to perform effectively and appropriately when interacting with others who are linguistically and culturally different from oneself". Hammer (2009; 2011) defines intercultural competence in more holistic terms, as the capability to shift cultural perspective and appropriately adapt or bridge behavior to cultural differences and commonalities. J.M. Bennett (2009) states that intercultural competence is a set of cognitive, affective and behavioral skills and characteristics that assists with effective interaction in various cultural settings. The European Council states:

> The basis of intercultural competence is in the attitudes of the person interacting with people of another culture. This means a willingness to suspend one's own values, beliefs and behaviours, not to assume that they are the only possible and naturally correct ones, and an ability to see how they might look from an outsider's perspective who has a different set of values, beliefs and behaviours. This can be called the ability to "decentre".
>
> *European Council 2009: 23*

A common element amongst all the interpretations of intercultural competence is the complex nature of interacting, engaging and learning from individuals of other cultures in order to develop particular skills and abilities.

Whether intercultural competence should be looked at from a specific cultural aspect or holistic point of view is a contested issue. Mazeikiene and Loher (2008: 49) stated that "defining intercultural competence can be problematic because there is no ultimate agreement whether culture is related to more traditional anthropological dimensions (nation, race, and ethos) or whether it is related to other categories of social differences (gender, age, social-economic status)". In most professional fields, including human resources, intercultural competence is referred to in a wider more holistic point of view that includes the social context. Onorati and Bednarz (2010: 56) describe intercultural competence from "a holistic perspective that considers the individual not as an isolated entity but as an integral part of a wider relational system". They believe that cross-cultural learning is an essential part to intercultural competence and that social context and culture are at the core of understanding and learning.

In the past 20 years, intercultural competence has primarily been examined from a Western point of view including United States, Canada and European nations. More Eastern researchers are beginning to study this concept including Panggabean *et al.* (2012) in Singapore and Australia but there is much to be learned from the Eastern interpretations of intercultural competence. Are the definitions above all encompassing of both a Western and Eastern point of view? This has yet to be determined. Nam, Cho and Lee provide a chapter (51) in this volume on cross-cultural training which begins to examine this perspective.

Models of intercultural competence

Several researchers have developed models for intercultural competence over the last 20 years. These include (see Spitzberg and Changnon 2009 for details of each model):

- compositional models (Howard-Hamilton *et al.* 1998; Ting-Toomey and Kurogi 1998; Deardorff 2006; Hunter *et al.* 2006)
- co-relational models (Fantini 1995; Byram 2003; Kupka 2008)
- developmental models (Bennett 1993; King and Baxter Magolda 2005; Ruben 1976)
- adaptational models (Kim 1988; Gallois *et al.* 1988; Berry *et al.* 1989)
- causal path models (Arasaratnam 2008; Griffith and Harvey 2000; Ting-Toomey 1999; Hammer *et al.* 1998; Imahori and Lanigan 1989).

For the purpose of this chapter we will focus on five models of intercultural competence that have become the most widely used in the field and provide a sound theoretical understanding for human resource professionals.

Ruben (1976) was one of the first to use a behavioral approach to intercultural competence. He linked aspects of knowing and doing; therefore, he examined what individuals know to be competent in an intercultural environment and what their actions should be in the intercultural situation. He identified seven dimensions of intercultural competence: display of respect, interaction posture, orientation to knowledge, empathy, self-oriented role behavior, interaction management, and tolerance for ambiguity. Ruben (1976) discovered that the more interaction one made with individuals unlike oneself the greater the self-awareness of one's own intercultural competence and the increase of change in one's behavior.

Byram (1997) theorized a multidimensional model of intercultural competence. He proposed a five-factor model of intercultural competence which included: attitude, knowledge and skills of interpreting/relating, skills of discovery/interaction, and critical cultural awareness. Knowledge refers to different understandings about social groups of one's own culture and others. It includes knowledge about practices, history, societal interaction and geography. Skills to interpret/relate refer to abilities to interpret events of another culture and relate them to one's own culture. These skills include recognition of one's own ethnocentrism and misunderstandings of the culture. Skills to discover and interact refer to the ability to obtain new knowledge about culture and practices and then apply it to one's own knowledge, skills and attitudes. Attitude includes cultural curiosity and openness. It refers to readiness to communicate and interact with people of different cultures. Lastly is cultural awareness which refers to critically interpreting one's own perspective in context of other cultures and ability to interact in intercultural exchanges (Mazeikiene and Loher 2008). In 2004, Byram added six elements in which intercultural competence could be evaluated. These included tolerance to uncertainty, flexibility of behavior, communicative awareness, knowledge acquisition, openness to other cultures and empathy. He made a point in stating that this list is not comprehensive and that the elements can and will change. Byram emphasized the developmental aspect of intercultural competence. He truly believed that over time and exposure people could increase their level of intercultural competence.

Bennett developed a framework entitled Developmental Model of Intercultural Sensitivity (DMIS) which suggests that "individuals and groups confront cultural differences in predictable ways as they develop or learn to become more competent intercultural communicators" (Bibby 2008: 6). He proposes that as an individual's experience of cultural differences becomes more diverse and complex, their competence increases. The DMIS points out seven developmental orientations including three ethnocentric dimensions (ethnocentrism/denial, defensiveness, and minimization of perceived differences) and three ethnorelative dimensions (acceptance, adaptation and integration). According to Bennett (1993: 35), the ethnocentric stages and ethnorelative stages characterize the learner's growing recognition of and adjustment to intercultural differences. The core of ethnocentrism is "the assumption that one's own world view is central to all reality" whereas in ethnorelativism "cultures can only be understood relative to one another and that a particular behavior can only be understood within a cultural context". Research by Hammer (2011; Hammer *et al.* 2003) confirms that individuals develop along the Intercultural Development Continuum. The recent work with the IDI (Hammer 2009; 2011; 2012) identified key modifications in the original DMIS model, the most notable of which are: (1) Defense and Reversal are sub-dimensions of Polarization, (2) Minimization is a transitional orientation, neither fully ethnocentric nor fully ethnorelative (intercultural), and (3) Integration is not a stage or orientation of intercultural competence but rather, a distinct experience not on the continuum, of identify re-formulation (see Figure 52.1).

Schaetti *et al.* (2009: 128) describe developing intercultural competence in terms of three spheres nested within one another, the first being culture specific followed by culture general and finally intercultural practice. The first sphere focuses on culture specific competence which provides generalizable information about particular cultural groups. This ideology to developing competence "emphasizes learning about specific cultural patterns exemplified by chosen group and analyzing the impact of those cultural patterns when members of that group are involved in intergroup relations". This approach alone cannot build intercultural competence. The second sphere looks at the culture general approach to intercultural competence. This approach examines general cultural contrasts. It allows individuals to assess the extent of difference amongst themselves and those they are working with in other groups. Finally, the sphere of practice recognizes that to be fully competent individuals must take the theories and knowledge and transform them into practice. Schaetti *et al.* (2009: 128) describe it as "a whole-person approach to building intercultural competence, for culture is as much emotional and physical as it is an intellectual one". Figure 52.2 shows the embedded nature of this model. It shows that in order for individuals to be interculturally competent they must build their skills, knowledge and abilities from the center out.

Finally we will conclude with Deardorff's intercultural competence model. Deardorff (2006) conducted a Delphi study in order to achieve consensus on intercultural competence from intercultural experts. She developed this framework to be a more comprehensive approach to include both internal and external outcomes of intercultural competence (see Figure 52.3).

She believes that intercultural competence is an ongoing process, thus it is vital that individuals be given opportunities to develop and reflect upon their own intercultural competence. She also states that critical-thinking skills remain a fundamental element in an individual's ability to

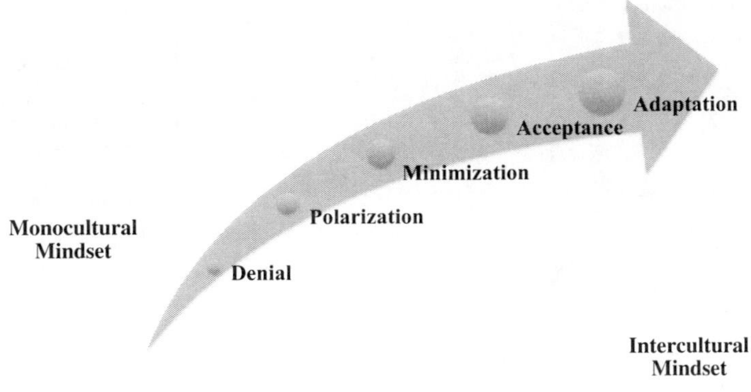

Figure 52.1 Intercultural development continuum (based on Hammer 2011)

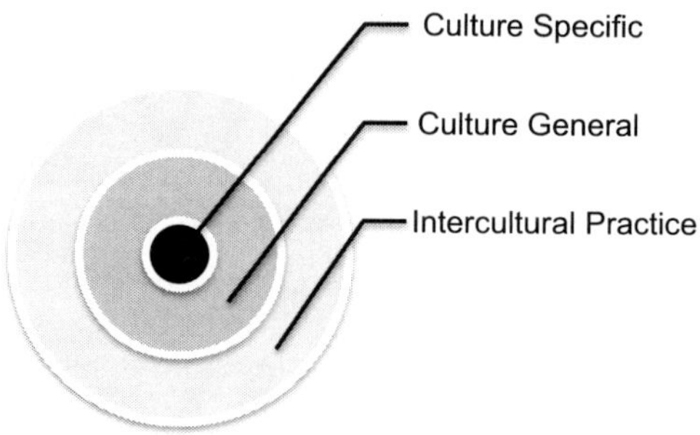

Figure 52.2 Embedded intercultural competence model

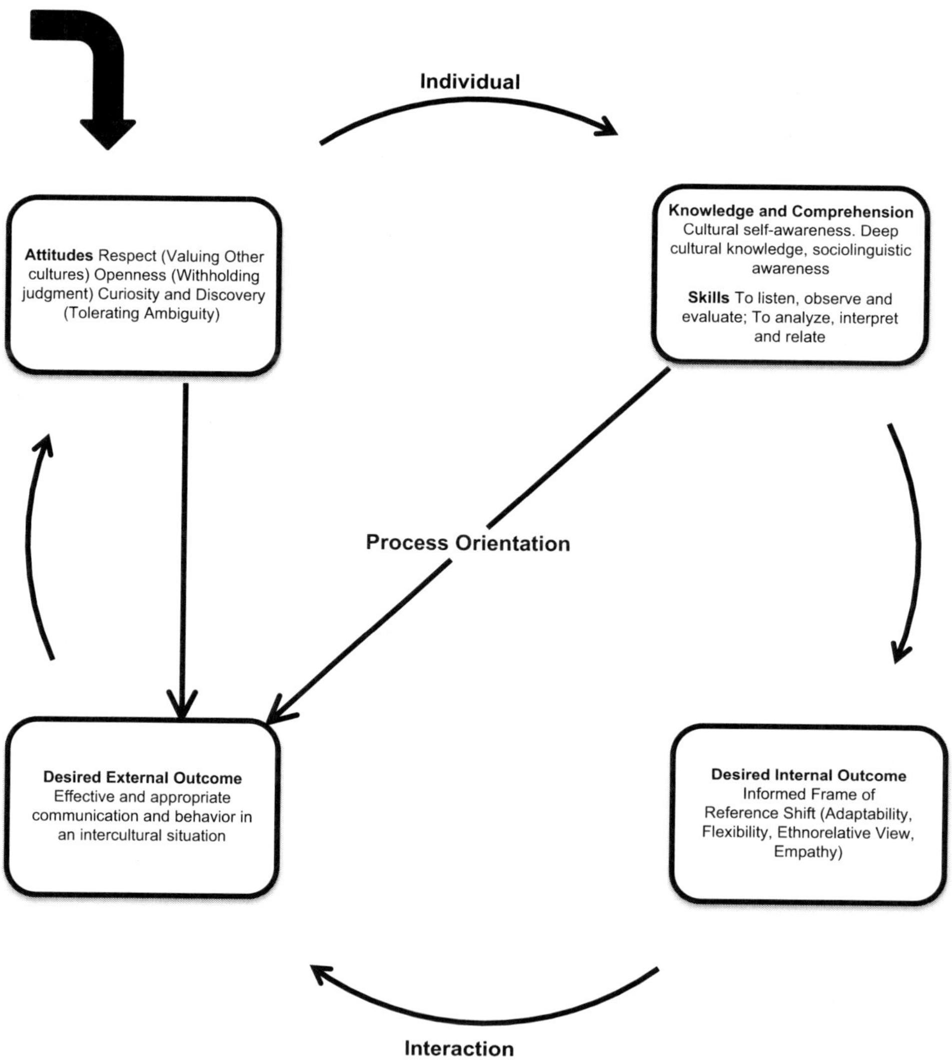

Figure 52.3 Process model of intercultural competence (Deardorff 2009)

acquire and evaluate knowledge. She, along with other researchers, believes that attitudes (especially respect, openness and curiosity) are essential and serve as the basis for intercultural competence. Finally she concludes that it is vital for individuals to be able to assess global perspectives and understand other worldviews. She states this foundational element is essential for development of intercultural competence.

Each of these models provides a lens to understand the many aspects that influence intercultural competence. The developmental and behavioral models are helpful frameworks for human resource professionals. Deardorff's processual model provides an important framework in that it highlights both the internal and external forces that may influence individuals. The researchers cited here agree that intercultural competence is built over time and experiences. It is a continuous process of learning and honing certain skills, attitudes and knowledge.

Measuring intercultural competence

Intercultural competence models/frameworks illustrate phases in cultural adaptation that show the interface of cultural awareness between declarative knowledge and procedural knowledge (Bibby 2008). Many of the models study cultural adaptation at various stages in the process looking at pre-departure, on assignment, and re-engagement. They are very useful in assessing the levels of intercultural competence and creating developmental programs for students and employees. Several formal and informal instruments have been developed from these frameworks. Eight assessments have been chosen and critiqued for this chapter (see Table 52.1).

Table 52.1 Intercultural competence assessments

Name of Assessment	*Author*	*Constructs/Variables*
Assessment of Intercultural Competence (AIC)	Fantini (2000; 2005)	Knowledge, attitude, skills and awareness
CernySmith Assessment (CSA)	Cerny and Smith (2007)	Cultural, behavioral, relational, organizational, psychological, personal
Cross-Cultural Adaptability Inventory (CCAI)	Kelley and Meyers (1995)	Emotional resistance, flexibility/openness, perceptual acuity, personal autonomy
Intercultural Development Inventory (IDI)	Hammer (2011)	Denial, polarization, minimization, acceptance, adaptation
Intercultural Sensitivity Index (ISI)	Olson and Kroeger (2001)	Denial, defense, minimization, acceptance, adaptation integration, substantive knowledge, perceptual understanding and intercultural communication
Intercultural Sensitivity Inventory (ICSI)	Bhawuk and Brislin (1992)	Expatriate living, flexibility, open-mindedness
Multicultural Personality Questionnaire (MPQ)	Van Der Zee and Van Oudenhoven (2001)	Cultural empathy, open-mindedness, emotional stability, social initiative and flexibility
Intercultural Competence Assessment (INCA)	Byram, Kühlmann, Müller-Jacquier and Budin (2004)	*Assessor:* tolerance for ambiguity, behavioral flexibility, communicative awareness, knowledge discovery, respect for otherness, and empathy *Examiner:* openness, knowledge and adaptability

The *Assessment of Intercultural Competence (AIC)* by Fantini (2005) measures the intercultural competence of individuals. The instrument studies four dimensions: knowledge, skills, attitude and awareness. The instrument is quite lengthy with seven sections and 211 items. Each question is evaluated on a five-point Likert-type scale ranging from 0 = none/not at all to 5 = extremely high. Fantini (2005) found that the reliability was .70 and after a factor analysis all dimensions loaded at .60 or higher. He has plans for further development of this instrument including expanding its use in multiple cross-cultural contexts. This instrument is quite in-depth covering several important dimensions which makes it long and tedious to administer. It was primarily used in a government funded project and therefore needs further analysis on its usefulness in the field of human resources – especially short-term and long-term global assignments.

The *CernySmith Assessment (CSA)* measures the level of cross-cultural adjustment for an individual or group during an in-field experience. The instrument contains 97 questions measured on a five-point rating scale ranging from "Not at all" to "Extremely". There are five dimensions including: cultural, personal, relational, psychological, and organizational domains. The Cronbach alpha for the CSA was .96. The factor analysis for the 20 statistically significant factors yielded a Cronbach alpha of .68 or above (Cerny *et al.* 2008). During the development phases of the CSA face validity was checked through the cross-cultural stress and adjustment literature and from the clinical files of the lead authors. Content validity was measured by ten open-ended items and rated by each participant. The ratings were then placed in a factor analysis and found to have a reliability of .94 (Cerny *et al.* 2008). This instrument is best used for longer term assignments and semester long study abroad programs. It provides valuable feedback to the individual which is best communicated through a certified cross-cultural coach. The report provides the individuals with useful analysis of the areas of strengths and opportunities to allow for further development of their cross-cultural skills.

The *Cross-Cultural Adaptability Inventory (CCAI)* measures an individual's ability to adapt to different cultures. It looks at four dimensions: emotional resilience, flexibility/openness, perceptual acuity and personal autonomy. This instrument has 50 items and uses a six-point Likert-type scale ranging from 1 = definitely not true to 6 = definitely true. The instrument was developed by Kelley and Meyers in 1987 based on a need from cross-cultural trainers. Several studies have utilized this instrument and the reliability has varied greatly ranging from .54 to .84 (Cronbach alpha). Davis and Finney (2006) found that the four-dimension model described by CCAI does not fit the data gathered by the instrument. They suggest that further research should be conducted to clarify these issues. This instrument is used quite frequently due to the cost and ease of administration. Since it is rather short in nature it provides a brief understanding for individuals to gauge their intercultural competence. The publisher provides materials useful for cross-cultural training and further explanation of the dimensions.

The *Intercultural Sensitivity Index (ISI)* measures global intercultural competency. The instrument was built from the DMIS framework by Bennett. It looks at the six stages of the DMIS (denial, defense, minimization, acceptance, adaptation, and integration) and three dimensions of global competency (substantive knowledge, perceptual understanding, and intercultural communication). The number of items for each dimension and the scale point descriptors were not reported. Each item utilizes a five-point Likert-type scale. Minimal research exists on the overall outcomes of this assessment.

The *Intercultural Sensitivity Inventory (ICIS)* was developed by Bhawuk and Brislin in 1992. It measured an individual's ability to modify behavior in culturally appropriate ways when moving between cultures. The self-report instrument was made up of 46 questions on a seven-point Likert-type scale. The instrument has two parts. The first section asks participants to imagine living in the US and Japan, and to respond to 16 questions while the second section has the participant respond to 14 questions on flexibility and open-mindedness. This instrument has a definite business orientation. Bhawuk and Brislin administered their instrument to graduate students in business disciplines. They found that students with three or more years of cross-cultural experience exhibited greater intercultural sensitivity. Cronbach alpha was not reported for this instrument; therefore more research needs to be done to validate this tool. This assessment seems to work well for academic programs and to assist students in gauging their baseline for intercultural sensitivity.

The *Intercultural Development Inventory (IDI)* is built off Bennett's DMIS framework. Many studies have utilized this instrument to measure intercultural competence (Straffon 2003; Engle and Engle 2004; Altshuler *et al.* 2003; Jackson 2009; Medina-López-Portillo and Salonen 2012). The IDI is a self-report instrument with 50 items. It has a five-point Likert-type scale ranging from 1 = disagree to 5 = agree. The creators of IDI have reported reliability for the six stage DMIS to be from .74 to .91 with four of the six scales to be above .80 (Cronbach alpha). Hammer *et al.* (2003) conducted a study in order to examine the instrument's content and construct validity and found that participants' responses were comparable and categorized participants in similar ways in relation to two other scales. Additional validation studies were conducted and demonstrated strong confirmatory factor analysis substantiating the basic orientations toward cultural difference originally discovered by Bennett (1986; 1993) in the Developmental Model of Intercultural Sensitivity (DMIS) and strong support for an overall Developmental Orientation (DO) scale and an overall Perceived Orientation (PO) scale. The criterion validity of the IDI indicated that the IDI has strong predictive validity toward bottom line goals within organizations including the achievement of diversity and inclusion goals. The IDI also incorporates systematic qualitative assessment protocols to identify individual and group cross-cultural goals and challenges. This instrument has proven predictive value in studies including one business study which indicated that overall team level of intercultural competence is related to team effectiveness in meeting diversity and inclusion staffing goals as well as in the field of education through study abroad programs where there was an increase in the knowledge of the host culture, intercultural anxiety, intercultural friendships, and satisfaction with the study abroad experience (Hammer 2011). This assessment is the most widely used instrument and definitely has the research to support it. In order to maintain quality control a trained facilitator must administer the instrument.

Byram, Kühlmann, Müller-Jacquier and Budin created an assessment tool entitled *Intercultural Competence Assessment (INCA)* to measure the level of intercultural competency built off the multidimensional model. The model examines two sets of dimensions (assessor and examiner's point of view). The assessor looks at tolerance for ambiguity, behavioral flexibility, communicative awareness, knowledge discovery, respect for otherness, and empathy, while the examiner's point of view studies openness, knowledge, and adaptability. The combination of both the assessor's and examiner's analysis enables individuals to see both their strengths and weaknesses when working with those of other cultures. It allows the individual then to develop a plan for continuous improvement and development. Because this instrument is primarily used as a developmental tool there are no psychometric properties to be found for this assessment.

The *Multicultural Personality Questionnaire (MPQ)* was developed by Van Der Zee and Van Oudenhoven. It measures five dimensions of cross-cultural competence. These dimensions include cultural empathy, openmindnesses, emotional stability, social initiative, and flexibility. The instrument has a total of 91 items based on a five-point Likert scale. The MPQ has shown internal consistencies from which the Cronbach alpha has ranged from .70 to .89 (De Beuckelaer *et al.* 2012). Leong (2007) found the MPQ to have stable psychometric properties in various cultural settings.

The instrument has been found to be predictive of students' success in various cultural settings (Leong 2007; Mol *et al.* 2001) and in diverse groups of people including job applicants and employees (Van Der Zee and Brinkmann 2004; Van Der Zee *et al.* 2003). There is a growing trend in the field of education to utilize this instrument for research.

Each of these instruments has extreme value in gauging individual intercultural competence. Table 52.2 provides the psychometric properties of each assessment and indicates the intended audience. Some of these instruments are more conducive for educational programs while others were designed for the humanitarian or business sector. Assessing objectives should occur before determining the value and selecting an instrument to apply in a particular context.

Although instruments are useful and practical they do have some drawbacks. Behrnd and Porzelt (2012) stated that because there is no common definition and it is difficult to measure the attitudes and awareness through surveys there really is no true measure that can comprehend intercultural competence. Intercultural scholars are beginning to recommend case studies and

Table 52.2 Instruments' psychometric properties and intended audience

Name of Instrument	*Validity and Reliability*	*Intended Audience*
Assessment of Intercultural Competence (AIC)	211 items–7 dimensions Reliability: .70 Factor analysis: .60 or higher	Short Term Study Abroad (Education) Short-Term Assignments (Business)
CernySmith Assessment (CSA)	97 items–5 dimensions Reliability: .96 Factor analysis: .68 or higher	Long-Term Assignments (Business, Humanitarian) Semester Long Study Abroad (Education) Best Used After 4 Months On Assignment
Cross-Cultural Adaptability Inventory (CCAI)	50 items–4 dimensions Reliability: range .54–.84 Factor analysis: .06–.78	Pre-Post Assignments/Study Abroad (Education, Business, Humanitarian)
Intercultural Development Inventory (IDI)	50 items–6 dimensions Reliability: .83; Developmental Score Confirmatory Factor Analysis: GFI = .91; RMR = .05; RMSEA = 04	Business, Government, Not-For-Profit, Education; Domestic Diversity And Inclusion, Global Leadership, Overseas Assignments, Study Abroad (Education, Business)
Intercultural Sensitivity Index (ISI)	48 items–9 dimensions Reliability: not reported	Short-Term Study Abroad (Education)
Intercultural Sensitivity Inventory (ICSI)	46 items–4 variables Reliability: range .63–.88	Pre-Assignment/Study Abroad (Education, Business) Primarily Used With MBA Grads
Multicultural Personality Questionnaire (MPQ)	91 items–5 variables Reliability: range .70–.89	Short-Term Study Abroad (Education) Short/Long-Term Assignments (Business)
Intercultural Competence Assessment (INCA)	9 variables Reliability: not reported	Long-Term Study Abroad (Education) Long-Term Assignments (Humanitarian)

interviews in order to gain the best understanding and assessment of intercultural competence (Deardorff 2006). Deardorff (2006) and Fantini (2009) recommend that intercultural competence be assessed through multiple measures on multiple dimensions using both quantitative and qualitative methods. Instruments and assessment tools can be an excellent source to create awareness of current intercultural mindsets but must be followed by developmental and enrichment opportunities.

Developing intercultural competence

Developing intercultural competence is extremely complicated. Multiple layers (Schaetti *et al.* 2009) of knowledge, skills, and abilities need to be developed to successfully manage and work in an intercultural environment. Trimble *et al.* (2009: 501) state that becoming interculturally competent can occur in a variety of ways (readings, conferences, workshops, and courses) but in order for the full acquisition of competency and knowledge individuals must immerse themselves in the culture. They go on to say that intercultural competence is a "lifelong endeavor". Development really comes from a combination of education/training, immersion, and reflection to understand oneself and know both one's strengths and areas of improvement.

The most common approach to developing intercultural competence by human resource professionals is cross-cultural training. Littrell *et al.* (2006: 356) define such training as an "educative process used to improve intercultural learning via the development of cognitive, affective and behavioral competencies needed for successful interactions in diverse cultures". Approaches to intercultural competence training vary from culture general to culture specific programs. Culture general training is superior to culture specific training because many intercultural topics are not limited to a specific culture (Triandis 2004). Graf (2004) reviewed intercultural training programs and found that only 6 of 27 dimensions of intercultural competence (i.e. intercultural sensitivity, social problem-solving capacity, and self-monitoring) were culture specific. Therefore it is more effective to engage in culture-generic training which is more applicable and a better investment of organizational resources. Wilderman *et al.* (2011) discuss various training approaches including didactic (cultural assimilator), experiential (role playing and behavior modeling), and mixed training (language training, relational ideology training). After researching training interventions they could not uncover which trainings were most practically applied to organizations or the extent of their effectiveness on real-world settings. However, they did find an abundance of empirical work that measured the outcomes of various training interventions. Cultural assimilators were found to increase rote knowledge, intercultural adjustment, and job performance. Behavioral modeling and relational ideology emerged as the most promising training interventions that positively impacted on performance and adjustment.

The field of intercultural and cross-cultural training has changed over the years. One of the greatest changes is that cross-cultural training has "gone domestic" (Storti 2009). No longer is the training just for expatriates or people who live and work abroad. It is now being used to understand the migration of people across borders. Six different European countries developed an intensive international learning program aimed at developing intercultural competence through three professional fields: education, social work, and healthcare. They designed the program to encompass a holistic viewpoint of intercultural competence in which transformative learning took place. The program focused on building a solid theoretical foundation which supported the higher education priorities started by the Bologna Process (Onorati and Bednarz 2010). The ultimate outcome was to help individuals become intercultural practitioners. Programs like this are increasing worldwide. Organizations both large and small are seeing the value of creating this sense of openness and dialogue across cultures not only to improve their bottom line but also to increase the diverse thought that inspires creativity and innovation.

Impact of intercultural competence on HRD practice

A common belief found globally is that intercultural competence is crucial to our changing environment whether that be business, education, or humanitarian work. Intercultural competence is often not brought up until individuals are confronted with change and dissonance of their own worldview. Once challenged, individuals begin to realize the differences that exist in their own ability to work with those that have a different perspective.

Training is the first step in developing intercultural competence but human resource professionals need to take it a step further. Organizations should be encouraged to conduct stretch assignments that push employees to new cultural experiences both short and long term. These immersion programs will bring benefit not only to the company but also to the individual. Individuals can begin to explore their own knowledge and attitudes towards other cultures through these experiences. According to Ng *et al.* (2009) intercultural competence is the key to helping global leaders grow from international assignments. Immersion programs provide experiential learning opportunities to connect learning outcomes of flexibility, self-efficacy and leadership across cultures. In order to build competitive advantage organizations must now focus on their global talent development. Global leaders with strong intercultural competence can be the competitive advantage for many organizations. Further research needs to be conducted as to how global leaders develop their intercultural competence. The exact tools, techniques and reflection components could assist organizations in fine tuning their development programs and justify that it is more than training that will increase the capacity to work with other cultures.

For the most part the focus on intercultural competence places onus on individuals and their ability to gain required skills, knowledge, and attitudes. While this focus is understandable more responsibility needs to be put on the cultural and structural levels within organizations. Human resource professionals are responsible for providing the tools and encouraging opportunities for growth and learning. Hoskins and Sallah (2011: 120) assert that "cultural/intercultural competence is conceptualized as a moral imperative, the need to do the right thing". This perspective conceptualizes interpersonal competence as a humane initiative not just skill development. Future research needs to examine the organization's role in building interculturally competent employees. Many employees will agree that they are the ones who must take the initiative to hone these skills. However, why not embed into an organization's mindset that all people should be treated fairly regardless of their locale? Researching organizations that have already embedded this cross-cultural mindset will provide solid frameworks for other companies to follow.

This chapter has focused on the critical issue of intercultural competence. As the world begins to get flatter, this issue will become more central to success of organizations. As interactions between individuals from different cultures increase, the complexity of workforces will intensify. Organizations need to examine and act on how they develop and grow their people to work in dynamic and culturally diverse societies.

References

Altshuler, L., Sussman, N.M. and Kachur, E. (2003) Assessing changes in intercultural sensitivity among physician trainees using the Intercultural Development Inventory. In Paige, R.M. (guest ed.) Special Issue on the intercultural development inventory. *international Journal of intercultural Relations* 227, 4: 387–401.

Arasaratnam, L.A. (2008) *Further testing of a new model of intercultural communication competence.* Paper presented at the annual meeting of the International Communication Association, New York, NY.

Bennett, J.M. (2009) Transformative training: Designing programs for culture learning. In Moodian, M.A. (ed.) *Contemporary Leadership and Intercultural competence: Exploring the Cross-Cultural Dynamics within Organizations* (95–110). London: SAGE.

Bennett, M.J. (1986) Towards ethnorelativism: a developmental approach to training for intercultural sensitivity. *International Journal of Intercultural Relations* 10, 2: 179–196.

— (1993) Toward ethnorelativism: A developmental model of intercultural sensitivity. In Paige, R.M. (ed.) *Education for the Intercultural Experience* (21–71). Yarmouth, ME: Intercultural.

— (2009) Defining, measuring, and facilitating intercultural learning. *Intercultural Education* 20: S1–2, S1–13.

Berry, J.W., Kim, U., Power, S., Young, M. and Bujaki, M. (1989) Acculturation in plural societies. *Applied Psychology: An International Review* 38: 185–206.

Behrnd, V. and Porzelt, S. (2012) Intercultural competence and training outcomes of students with experiences abroad. *International Journal of Intercultural Relations* 36, 2: 213–223.

Bhawuk, D.P.S. and Brislin, R. (1992) The measurement of intercultural sensitivity using the concepts of individualism and collectivism. *International Journal of Intercultural Relations* 16, 4: 413–436.

Byram, M., Kühlmann, T., Müller-Jacquier, B. and Budin, G. (2004) *INCA: Inter Cultural Competence Assessment.* Retrieved 10 March 2012 from http://www.incaproject.org/index.htm.

Bibby, F. (2008) *Cultural intelligence/intercultural competence.* Retrieved 5 March 2012 from http://www.verlegjegrenzen.eu/CMS/uitnodig/UsersFBLINK7DocumentsINTENTOverview_knowledge_cultural_intelligence_(module_4).pdf.

Brookfield Global Relocation Services (2010) *Global Relocation Trends 2009–2010.* Woodridge, IL: Brookfield Global Relocation Services.

Byram, M. (1997) *Teaching and Assessing Intercultural Communicative Competence.* Philadelphia, PA: Multilingual Matters.

— (2003) On being 'bicultural' and 'intercultural.' In Alfred, G., Byram, M. and Fleming, M. (eds), *Intercultural experience and education* (50–66). Tonowanda, NY: Multilingual Matters.

Cerny, L.J. and Smith, D.S. (2007) *CernySmith Adjustment Index (CSAI) Manual* (2nd edition), Orange, CA: Cerny Smith Assessments.

Cerny, L.J., Smith, D.S., Ritschard, H. and Dodd, C.H. (2008) *Development of the CernySmith Adjustment Index (CSAI) as an Integrative Cross-Cultural Adjustment Assessment.* Orange, CA: CernySmith Assessments.

Davis, S.L. and Finney, S.J. (2006) A factor analytic study of the cross-cultural adaptability inventory. *Educational and Psychological Measurement* 66, 2: 318–30.

Deardorff, D.K. (2006) Identification and assessment of intercultural competence as a student outcome of internationalization. *Journal of Studies in Intercultural Education* 10: 241–66.

— (2009) Preface. In Deardorff, D.K. (ed.) *The SAGE Handbook of Intercultural Competence.* Los Angeles: SAGE.

— (2011) Assessing intercultural competence. *New Directions for Institutional Research* 149: 65–79.

De Beuckelaer, A., Lievens, F. and Bucker, J. (2012) The role of faculty members' cross-cultural competencies in their perceived teaching quality: Evidence from culturally diverse classes in four European countries. *Journal of Higher Education* 83, 2: 217–48.

Engle, L. and Engle, J. (2004) Assessing language acquisition and intercultural sensitivity development in relation to study abroad program design. *Frontiers: The Interdisciplinary Journal of Study Abroad* 10: 219–36.

European Council (2009) *Autobiography of Intercultural Encounters: Context, Concepts and Theories.* Strasbourg: European Council.

Fantini, A.E. (1995) Language, culture, and worldview: Exploring the nexus. *International Journal of Intercultural Relations* 19: 143–53.

— (2000) *A Central Concern: Developing Intercultural Competence.* SIT Occasional Papers Series: Addressing Intercultural Education, Training & Service, 25–43.

— (2005) *Exploring and Assessing Intercultural Competence.* Retrieved 10 March 2012 from http://digitalcollections.sit.edu/cgi/viewcontent.cgi?article=1001&context=worldlearning_publications.

— (2009) Assessing intercultural competence: Issues and tools. In Deardorff, D. (ed.) *The SAGE Handbook of Intercultural Competence* (Chap. 27, 456–76). Washington, DC: SAGE.

Gallois, C., Franklyn-Stokes, A., Giles, H. and Coupland, N. (1988) Communication accommodation in intercultural encounters. In Kim, Y.Y. (ed.) *Theories in Intercultural Communication* (157–85). Newbury Park, CA: SAGE.

Graf, A. (2004) Screening and training intercultural competencies: Evaluating the impact of national culture on intercultural competencies. *International Journal of Human Resource Management* 15, 6: 1124–48.

Griffith, D.A. and Harvey, M.G. (2000) An intercultural communication model for use in global interorganizational networks. *Journal of International Marketing* 9, 3: 87–103.

Hammer, M.R. (2005) *Assessment of the Impact of the AFS Study Abroad Experience: Executive Summary & Final Report.* New York: AFS, International.

— (2009) The Intercultural Development Inventory: An approach for assessing and building intercultural competence. In Moodian, M.A. (ed.) *Contemporary Leadership and Intercultural Competence: Exploring the Cross-Cultural Dynamics within Organizations* (203–217). Thousand Oaks, CA: SAGE.

— (2011) Additional cross-cultural validity testing of the Intercultural Development Inventory. *International Journal of Intercultural Relations* 35, 4: 474–87.

— (2012) The Intercultural Development Inventory (IDI): A new frontier in assessment and development of intercultural competence. In Van de Berg, M., Paige, R.M. and Lou, K. (eds) *Student learning abroad: What our students are learning, what they're not, and what we can do about it* (Ch. 5, 115–36). Sterling, VA: Stylus.

Hammer, M.R. and Bennett, M.J. (1998) *The Intercultural Development Inventory (IDI) Manual.* Portland, OR: The Intercultural Communication Institute.

Hammer, M.R., Wiseman, R.L., Rasmussen, J.L. and Bruschke, J.C. (1998) A test of anxiety/uncertainty management theory: The intercultural adaptation context. *Communication Quarterly* 46: 309–26.

Hammer, M.R., Bennett, M.J. and Wiseman, R. (2003) Measuring intercultural sensitivity: The Intercultural Development Inventory. *International Journal of Intercultural Relations* 27, 4: 421–43.

Hofstede, G. (2001) *Culture's Consequences: Comparing Values, Behaviors, Institutions and Organizations across Nations* (2nd edition). Thousand Oaks, CA: SAGE.

Hoskins, B. and Sallah, M. (2011) Developing intercultural competence in Europe: The challenges. *Language and International Communications* 11, 2: 113–25.

Howard-Hamilton, M.F., Richardson, B.J. and Shuford, B. (1998) Promoting multicultural education: A holistic approach. *College Student Affairs Journal* 18: 5–17.

Hunter, W., White, G. and Godbey, G. (2006) What does it mean to be globally competent? *Journal of Studies in International Education* 10, 3: 267–85.

Imahori, T.T. and Lanigan, M.L. (1989) Relational model of intercultural communication competence. *Intercultural Communication Competence* 13: 269–86.

Jackson, J. (2009) Globalization, internationalization, and short-term stays abroad. *International Journal of Intercultural Relations* 32, 4: 349–58.

Kelley, C. and Meyers, J. (1995) *The Cross-Cultural Adaptability Inventory.* Minneapolis, MN: Vangent.

Kim, Y.Y. (1988) *Communication and Cross-Cultural Adaptation: An Integrative Theory.* Philadelphia: Multilingual Matters.

King, P.M. and Baxter Magolda, M.B. (2005) A developmental model of intercultural maturity. *Journal of College Student Development* 46: 571–92.

Kupka, B. (2008) *Creation of an instrument to assess intercultural communication competence for strategic international human resource management.* Unpublished doctoral dissertation, University of Otago, Otago, New Zealand.

Leong, C. (2007) Predictive validity of the Multicultural Personality Questionnaire: A longitudinal study on the sociopsychological adaptation of Asian undergraduates who took part in a study abroad program. *International Journal of Intercultural Relations* 31, 5: 545–59.

Littrell, L.N., Salas, E., Hess, K.P., Paley, M. and Riedel, S. (2006) Expatriate preparation: A critical analysis of 25 years of cross-cultural training research. *Human Resource Management* 5, 3: 355–88.

Mazeikiene, N. and Loher, D. (2008) Competence of university teachers and graduate students for international cooperation. *Social Sciences* 2, 60: 48–65.

Medina-López-Portillo, A. and Salonen, R. (2012) Developing a global learning and living community: A case study of intercultural experiences on The Scholar Ship. In Vande Berg, M., Paige, R.M., and Lou, K.H. (eds) *Student Learning Abroad: What Our Students Are Learning, What They're Not, and What We Can Do About It.* (Ch.15, 360–82). Sterling, VA: Stylus.

Mol, S.T., Van Oudenhoven, J.P. and Van Der Zee, K.I. (2001) Validation of the Multicultural Personality Questionnaire among an internationally oriented student population in Taiwan. In Salili, F. and Hoosain, R. (eds) *Multicultural Education: Issues, Policies and Practices* (167–86). Greenwich, CT: Information Age.

Ng, K., Van Dyne, L. and Ang, S. (2009) From experience to experiential learning: Cultural intelligence as a learning capability for global leader development. *Academy of Management Learning and Education* 8, 4: 511–26.

Olson, C.L. and Kroeger, K.R. (2001) Global competency and intercultural sensitivity. *Journal of Studies in International Education* 5, 2: 116–37.

Onorati, M.G. and Bednarz, F. (2010) Learning to become an intercultural practitioner: The case of lifelong learning intensive programme interdisciplinary course of intercultural competences. *US–China Education Review* 7, 6: 54–62.

Panggabean, H., Murniati, J. and Tjitra, H. (2012) Profiling intercultural competence of Indonesians in Asian workgroups. *International Journal of Intercultural Relations* 37, 1: 86–98.

Pucik, V. (2005) Global HR as competitive advantage: Are we ready? In Losey, M., Meisinger, S. and Ulrich, D. (eds) *The Future of Human Resource Management: 64 Thought Leaders Explore Critical HR Issues of Today and Tomorrow* (370–77). Hoboken, NJ: Wiley.

Ruben, B.D. (1976) Assessing communication competency for intercultural adaptation. *Group and Organization Studies* 1, 3: 334–54.

Schaetti, B.F., Ramsey, S.J. and Watanabe, G.C. (2009) From intercultural knowledge to intercultural competence: Developing an intercultural practice. In Moodian, M. (ed.) *Contemporary Leadership and Intercultural Competence: Exploring the Cross-Cultural Dynamics within Organizations.* Los Angeles: SAGE.

Spitzberg, B.H. and Changnon, G. (2009) Conceptualizing intercultural competence. In Deardorff, D.K. (ed.) *The SAGE Handbook of Intercultural Competence.* Los Angeles: SAGE.

Storti, C. (2009) Intercultural competence in human resources. In Deardorff, D. (ed.) *The SAGE Handbook of Intercultural Competence* (Chap. 15, 272–86). Washington, DC: SAGE.

Straffon, D.A. (2003) Assessing the intercultural sensitivity of high school students attending an international school. *International Journal of Intercultural Relations* 27, 4: 487–501.

Ting-Toomey, S. (1999) *Communicating Across Cultures.* New York: Guilford.

Ting-Toomey, S. and Kurogi, A. (1998) Facework competence in intercultural conflict: An unpdated face-negotiation theory. *International Journal of Intercultural Relations* 22: 187–225.

Triandis, H.C. (2004) The many dimensions of culture. *Academy of Management Executive* 18, 1: 88–93.

Trimble, J.E., Pedersen, P.B. and Rodela, E.S. (2009) The real cost of intercultural incompetence. In Deardorff, D.K. (ed.) *The SAGE Handbook of Intercultural Competence.* Los Angeles: SAGE.

Van Der Zee, K.I. and Brinkmann, U. (2004) Construct validity evidence for the intercultural readiness check against the multicultural personality questionnaire. *International Journal of Selection and Assessment* 12, 3: 285–90.

Van Der Zee, K.I. and Van Oudenhoven, J. P. (2001) The multicultural personality questionnaire: reliability and validity of self- and other ratings of multicultural effectiveness. *Journal of Research in Personality* 35, 3: 278–288.

Van Der Zee, K.I., Zaal, J.N. and Piekstra, J. (2003) Validation of the multicultural personality questionnaire in the context of personnel selection. *European Journal of Personality* 17, S1: S77–S100.

Wilderman, J.L., Xavier, L.F., Tindall, M. and Salas, E. (2011) Best practices for training intercultural competence in global organizations. In Lundby, K. and Jolton, J. (eds) *Going Global.* Hoboken, NJ: Wiley.

Yu, H. (2012) Intercultural competence in technical communication: A working definition and review of assessment methods. *Technical Communication Quarterly* 21, 2: 168–86.

53
VIRTUAL HRD (VHRD)

Simone C.O. Conceição and Kristopher J. Thomas

Today, in order to survive and thrive in the workforce, lifelong learning is necessary to acquire twenty-first century skills like problem solving, knowledge management, information technology management, and collaboration. These skills can drive success in a solution-driven environment, assist in the management of knowledge, motivate the development of creative solutions, provide the ability to analytically look at communication technology to interpret messages, and prepare virtual teams for collaboration. Human Resource Development (HRD) needs to react to these changes. Virtual HRD is an emerging field within HRD that has been responding to these changes.

Scholarship on VHRD has emerged in recent years (Bennett 2009, 2010; Bennett and Bierema 2010; McWhorter 2010). Likewise, the steady evolution of increasingly more powerful and more mobile technologies has brought with it a commensurate expansion of technology-based HRD applications (Bada and Madon 2010). This proliferation of VHRD tools and applications will only increase in the years ahead.

The purposes of this chapter are to provide a definition of VHRD, identify technologies employed in VHRD contexts, address the skills needed to survive and thrive in the twenty-first century, present the current state of VHRD literature, detail the benefits of twenty-first century skills and VHRD, and discuss future trends for VHRD scholars and practitioners.

Definition of VHRD

The use of technology within the field of HRD is certainly not a new phenomenon. The growth of VHRD as an operational construct, however, can largely be attributed to the connectivity made possible through the Internet and through the growing ubiquity of information and communication technologies (ICT). Bennett (2009: 365) defines VHRD as "a media-rich and culturally relevant web environment that strategically improves expertise, performance, innovation, and community building through formal and informal learning". Leaders within organizations are well served to recognize that the way in which we work together is a process and not an event; adaptation to new environments and new technologies is requisite in this new economy (Holton 2001). Short (2010) offers that to remain effective, HRD professionals will not only need to be comfortable with and understand technology but also have to champion the use of technology for learning in organizations.

Accordingly, the importance of VHRD in the context of both HRD research and practice will continue to increase (Mancuso *et al.* 2010). Nafukho *et al.* (2010) argue that the success of organizations rides on their ability to leverage their human capital in a virtual workplace by generating new knowledge that is applicable in both traditional and virtual work environments. Bennett (2010: 729) notes the importance of recognizing the complementary nature of traditional HRD and VHRD in "that VHRD does not unseat the traditional purposes of HRD but rather shifts perspective on the paradigm in which HRD operates" by making the development of people within organizations easier, more flexible, more cost efficient.

The leveraging of technology is intended to increase the speed of communication and the efficiency of work. Technology does not replace human interaction; technology changes and enhances the way(s) in which we interact. Brandenburg and Ellinger (2003) caution HRD professionals against focusing too much on technological tools and infrastructure. Instead, we must look at the human aspects and the more social components of learning and choose and implement technology wisely. Technology should be transparent, a medium to connect learners, rather than the center of the interactions. An additional challenge for HRD professionals will be staying abreast of the various and growing available technologies (Conley and Zheng 2009).

Technologies employed in VHRD contexts

The pace at which technology changes can be staggering. Only recently, Blackberry was the dominant smartphone, laptops were the common form of portable computing, video and web conferencing were a relative novelty. Today, in business, school, and personal settings, a broad selection of similar smartphones have gained prominence, the iPad and comparable tablets are overtaking laptops as the preferred form of portable computing, video conferencing applications like Skype, and web conferencing applications like Adobe Connect or WebEx, are commonplace (Spielman and Windfeld 2003). The recent emergence of cloud computing has simplified the remote access and storage of data and knowledge. Though these new technologies may have appeared novel at first, it did not take long for their utility in the VHRD context to be discovered and exploited. The iPad and similar tablets, for example, were initially thought to be little more than smartphones with larger screens. However, the number of applications for these tools has grown prolifically so that tablets now can be used for word processing, presenting, calculating, reading books, and watching videos (Nafukho *et al.* 2010). Concomitantly, the use of tablets in the training environment has grown dramatically. Training products that are materially and visually rich are now portable and can be consumed by employees when and where it is convenient to do so.

It is increasingly important that HRD professionals recognize the impact of these technologies and design HRD materials that best take advantage of the inherent affordances of powerful, portable media. As the millennial cohort that has grown up with smartphones, tablets, iPods, and texting enters the workplace, they will expect the workplace to mirror the technological environment to which they are accustomed (Fazarro *et al.* 2011). Work-centered social media, chat rooms, blogs, and wikis not only allow for the sharing of work-related knowledge, but they provide motivation and foster creativity by keeping employees involved and engaged (Bennett 2010).

The challenge for VHRD in the years ahead will be to design and deliver training "that engages the virtual learners, meets both the learners' and business' needs, and fosters collaboration in research and development" (Nafukho *et al.* 2010: 660). HRD professionals must ensure that organizations select tools that are appropriate for achieving desired organizational objectives

(Bennett 2009; Short 2010). Yet, the use of technology for HRD professionals will continue to be *one* possible solution – not *the* solution for each HRD effort. At times, a low-tech intervention may still provide the best HRD support in a given situation (Bennett and Bierema 2010). Thus, HRD professionals must not rush to jump on the technology bandwagon for its own sake. Rather, VHRD interventions need to be thoughtfully conceived, designed and delivered without losing sight of the primary goals of improving the effectiveness of the learning, performance and development of employees (Yoon and Lim 2010). Before designing training environments for HRD professionals, it is important to understand the skills required to survive and thrive in the twenty-first century.

Skills needed to survive and thrive in the twenty-first century

With the emergence of digital technologies in the workplace, certain skills are needed to survive and thrive in the twenty-first century. According to Jukes *et al.* (2010), amongst these skills are problem solving, knowledge management, development of creative solutions, information technology management and collaboration.

Problem solving

Problem solving is related to whole-brain thinking and it can be applied in "just-in-time" learning. When interacting with others in real time meetings using technology, HRD professionals must clearly define a problem, design a solution, apply the solution and evaluate the process and the outcome (Jukes *et al.* 2010). Problem solving skills are essential for HRD professionals to be effective and efficient when using technology.

Knowledge management

Knowledge management involves two subsets of skills: (1) access to digital information sources and (2) assessment and management of information. Accessing information means retrieving data from searches or the content of messages being received. HRD professionals must know not only from where to retrieve information in text, images, sound and video formats, but also how to critically evaluate the data being retrieved (Jukes *et al.* 2010). Cloud computing has made such access easier and more efficient. Technology still requires that we conduct research using a systematic approach for gathering data and determining the accuracy of the data. Today information can be easily found in social media, wikis and the web; however, finding data is not enough. HRD professionals must have the ability to critically assess the data in digital environments.

Development of creative solutions

According to Jukes *et al.* (2010: 66), creativity "is the process by which artistic proficiency adds meaning through design, art and storytelling. It regards form in addition to function, and the principles of innovative design combined with a quality functioning product". Easy access to information demands a more creative mind. Creative minds lead to creative solutions. In the workplace, regurgitation of others' ideas without innovation is less appreciated. HRD professionals must expand on what is already available. In this case, technology can be a threat and at the same time a powerful tool to create innovative solutions.

Information technology management

Information technology management goes along with what Jukes *et al.* (2010: 66) call media fluency, "the ability to look analytically at any communication media to interpret the real message, determine how the chosen media [are] being used to shape thinking and evaluate the efficacy of the message". In this instance, the management of technology is how HRD professionals use information technology to understand, create and publish products. This skill allows for using and managing technology to effectively interpret the message and create environments to communicate with others. It can be overwhelming with the amount of interactions HRD professionals engage in daily in the workplace when using technology. Managing information for learning, developing processes and products and disseminating information and products is a premier skill in the twenty-first century.

Collaboration

Collaboration in the workplace is a skill needed to communicate, interact and do business at a global level. Jukes *et al.* (2010) state that collaboration allows for teamwork proficiency – the ability to work with others with virtual and real colleagues in the online environments. People interact with each other globally as if everyone is in the same room. It has created the death of distance for many companies, saving both travel costs and time for employees.

The current state of VHRD literature

Bennett and Bierema (2010: 633) offer that "VHRD produces something new and value added for organizations when it is viewed as a virtual space interconnected with people and various organizational systems". The benefits of utilizing VHRD interventions are not confined to the increased connectivity, speed and efficiency. For example, when deciding between a traditional HRD or a VHRD intervention, organizations can also consider the reduction in travel that is enabled by technology which not only allows for reduced expenses, but also takes much less of a toll on the environment (Fazarro *et al.* 2011). A look at the current VHRD literature tends to focus on five primary areas: (1) communication, (2) learning and training, (3) knowledge management, (4) team building and maintenance, and (5) organization development and planning. The literature reviewed for this chapter provided only one example of empirical research related to VHRD (Mancuso *et al.* 2010); the need for additional empirical research should be noted.

Communication

Most literature concerning VHRD thus far tends to center on the West and Western organizations. Yet, technology creates global interconnectivity that was unimaginable a decade ago (McWhorter 2010). VHRD can have impact for those people who are not highly skilled or who work in modern, technologically advanced workplaces. Noting that VHRD tools can help those in developing countries, Bada and Madon (2010: 179) offer that the primary goal of HRD "involves increasing the knowledge, skills and capacities of all the people in a society as well as the promotion of their well-being through economic growth and development". By utilizing VHRD tools, HRD professionals can play a significant role in the training and development of employees around the globe.

Many of the newer jobs that are created globally require low-level skills for which simple technology-based training is best suited (Benson *et al.* 2002). As organizations grow and become increasingly global, HRD professionals will be tasked with assuring that employee training and development in all parts of the world is consistent and effective. An advantage of VHRD is that it has "the potential to foster multimodal, multidimensional growth and development of individuals, groups, organizations, and, potentially, organizational alliances" (Bennett and Bierema 2010: 633) worldwide. VHRD will allow HRD professionals to be at the fore of organizational growth and development by mitigating tremendously the constraints of time and geography.

Learning and training

As Bingham and Conner (2010) note, new technologies allow for an organization to be better connected while raising its cumulative IQ. However, organizations must be willing to evolve along with these technologies. To that end, Thomas and Akdere (2013) advocate the use of the term *collaborative media* to represent the use of social media tools as a means to communicate, learn and collaborate in the workplace. Several authors elaborate on different approaches specific to training and learning in virtual environments. Schmidt and Kunzmann (2006: 1070) discuss *technology-enhanced workplace learning*, the focus of which is "learning activities integrated into work processes, merging e-learning, knowledge management, and performance support". The implementation of VHRD initiatives must not be viewed in isolation as HRD needs arrive but rather as a comprehensive, integrative effort.

Yoon and Lim (2010) favor *strategic blended learning*, a mix of face-to-face learning and web-based media technologies that improve learning and integrate it with organizational performance goals. They caution that the focus of technology-based HRD initiatives should not be the training itself, but it should be learning and the acquisition of knowledge. The mode of training should be appropriate for the learning need. Technology should not get in the way of learning; technology should enhance learning.

As with all adult learning situations, the focus should remain on the learner (Mancuso *et al.* 2010). Technology also enables *just-in-time (JIT) learning*, which is "predicated on a framework that attempts to anticipate learning and performance requirements as opposed to being responsive to them" (Brandenburg and Ellinger 2003: 309). Driven by the learner, a JIT approach allows for learners to create their own learning agendas at a place and pace that is most appropriate for them and which is dynamic and adaptive enough to meet that user's specific and changing needs.

Nafukho *et al.* (2010) cite four challenges that HRD professionals face concerning the implementation of VHRD initiatives: (1) the varying learning preferences inherent to the different generations in the workplace, (2) overloading learners with too much training (since technology so significantly eases its production and distribution), (3) not all efforts at collaboration may be suitable for a virtual environment, and (4) the assessment of learners in a virtual classroom. These challenges must be taken into consideration when developing virtual learning and training in organizations.

Knowledge management

The tools necessary to gain organizational commitment to ensure successful knowledge management efforts are directly related to HRD in the form of "challenging work, collaboration and teamwork, work culture, communication, concern from people and training and development" (Cho *et al.* 2009: 268). Because it more easily enables communication and collaboration, VHRD is uniquely qualified to play an important role in the implementation and continued success of an organization's knowledge management efforts.

For example, at the Mayo Clinic, radiologists use a Twitter-like *microsharing* tool to share x-rays and solicit diagnosis opinions from other physicians (Bingham and Conner 2010). The capture and sharing of collective organizational knowledge through microsharing demonstrates how technology can be leveraged to increase organizational expertise and the informal learning that takes place as a result. Technologies like electronic performance support systems (EPSS), electronically published materials (blogs, wikis) and human performance technology are used "to capture and manage existing institutional knowledge, support job performance by providing electronic performance support, and facilitate the exchange of work-related information through networked communication systems" (Benson *et al.* 2002: 398). On a very basic level, VHRD technology can help employees throughout an organization get their job done – anytime, anywhere – by providing unfettered access to organizational knowledge.

As the emphasis on an organization's technology infrastructure shifts from a focus on the collection and sharing of knowledge to the enabling of personal connections amongst employees, HRD professionals will be called upon to facilitate the efficient flow of knowledge throughout their organizations (Conley and Zheng 2009). Further, HRD professionals can leverage VHRD tools and their expertise in training and development to identify the needs of employees surrounding the organization's knowledge management efforts; to provide employees with the training and resources necessary to utilize technologies and systems related to knowledge management; and to ensure the employees stay continually engaged in the organization's knowledge management efforts.

Team building and maintenance

In addition to changing the ways in which we communicate and learn, technology has impacted how we define, form and maintain teams in the work setting. Technologies like instant messaging, video conferencing and web conferencing now allow virtual teams to work together without being physically present with each other in the same workplace (Benson *et al.* 2002). Munkvold and Zigurs (2007: 288) define a *virtual team* as "a collection of geographically and/or organizationally dispersed individuals who communicate via computer-based technology to accomplish a defined task". A virtual team relies on ICT to interact across various geographic locations while being bound by "the pursuit of interdependent tasks and a common purpose" (Soule and Applegate 2009: 2).

Not all members of a virtual team may prefer to work in such an environment. Team members may be pulled off task by competing priorities, particularly those physically present to them (Holton 2001). Munkvold and Zigurs (2007) identify as potential issues with virtual teams a lack of integration of the final team product; a lack of ownership of the project; issues of trust and collaboration; and a lack of team bonding. They suggest that many of these issues can be avoided by an initial face-to-face meeting at the inception of the team. Because social cues may be hampered by electronic media and disagreements may be hard to resolve when factoring in conflicts of time and place, Johnson *et al.* (2002) offer three recommendations for creating and maintaining virtual teams:

- *Select appropriate virtual learning team tasks.* The accomplishment of a given assignment should be possible in and, at the very least, not hampered by a virtual setting.
- *Provide team building and collaboration training.* Particularly for newer virtual teams, allow time for a technology learning curve and for the team to get accustomed to collaborating in the virtual setting.
- *Develop appropriate project timelines.* Work done virtually may take a longer (or shorter) amount of time for completion. Learn to adapt as you complete more projects virtually.

Holton (2001) further suggests allowing for enough time for substantive conversations and meaningful interactions that will lead to the development of trust and comfort in the virtual environment.

Development planning

The aforementioned benefits of technology can afford HRD professionals additional opportunities to implement career or organization development initiatives. Bennett (2010) notes that organizations already use webcasts for town hall forums, for example, to communicate consistent messages. Applicant tracking systems, virtual job boards, virtual job fairs and succession planning tools are already commonplace in organizations. Online tools allow for job analyses and their resulting competencies to be stored virtually in talent management systems that are accessible by managers and employees alike. Such systems help create an HRD professional that "swiftly and effectively locates, places, enhances, and rewards experts and expertise in environments" (Yoon and Lim 2010: 722) for which they are best suited and in which they can prosper and grow while allowing organizations to grow from within rather than recruit from the outside.

Benefits of twenty-first century skills and VHRD

Problem solving, knowledge management, development of creative solutions, information technology management and collaboration are all essential skills to keep up with the demands of a digital workplace. These twenty-first century skills provide opportunities for organizations and can be turned into benefits for HRD professionals. Some of the benefits that VHRD provides are better access, convenience, flexibility, efficiency, community building, connection with others without boundaries and a green environment (Conceição and Lehman 2011; Fazarro *et al.* 2011).

HRD professionals living in a country where there is not a training center for the organization can have better access to training through audio, video, or web conferencing. VHRD can be convenient for those whose work tasks and time demand that they stay in a specific physical location. This way HRD professionals do not need to travel and can attend training around their schedule.

With the proliferation of technologies, HRD professionals can attend training anytime, anywhere and at their own pace, which provides flexibility. Training is in the palm of their hands and at the tips of their fingers through the use of multiple technologies. Just-in-time knowledge can be obtained using a smartphone, a tablet, a computer, a Personal Digital Assistant (PDA) and so on. This provides multiple opportunities for HRD professionals to learn and manage knowledge.

Not only does VHRD provide the opportunity to expand knowledge and extend the reach to people and places globally, it can save time, travel and costs as well. HRD professionals can avoid the need to take risks in going to other locations. It also allows opportunities to learn through new modes of instruction. Participating in virtual teams using audio, video, or web conferencing, HRD professionals can connect to a diverse group of co-workers globally through virtual communities no longer limited to physical places. Video and web conferencing also make easier the processes of team and culture building by allowing for more efficient and inexpensive communication to wider audiences. Such communication can be recorded for retrieval at a later time.

Finally, VHRD can be a benefit for a green environment. HRD professionals can store information and knowledge in digital devices and carry them anywhere. Though not inclusive, these are some of the benefits of VHRD. To better understand the differences between traditional HRD and VHRD, we offer a comparative table. Table 53.1 provides examples of traditional and VHRD workplace instances related to twenty-first century skills and the benefits of a digital workplace. These examples serve as a starting point for HRD professionals to consider the current state of VHRD and future trends.

Table 53.1 Traditional HRD and virtual HRD examples related to twenty-first century skills and benefits of a digital workplace

Twenty-First Century Skills	*Traditional HRD*	*Virtual HRD*	*Benefits of a Digital Workplace*
Problem solving	Face-to-face sessions scheduled at a specific location, formal learning	Just-in-time learning, learning online, independent learning	VHRD allows for a more accessible, efficient, and autonomous workforce
Knowledge management	Knowledge managed using databases or data warehouses located in a computer drive	Knowledge managed in the palm of our hands and tips of our fingers through the use of smartphones and tablets. Just-in-time knowledge	VHRD allows for a more flexible, effective, efficient, and less place-bound knowledge management
Development of creative solutions	Innovation through the creation of products using print books, magazines, business libraries situated within the organization at a specific location	Virtual innovation through the creation of technology-based products through using information or materials available globally through digital means	VHRD promotes more cutting edge products and meets global needs
Information technology management	Information management through the use of singular static technology	Information management through cloud computing and multiple mobile technologies anywhere, anytime	VHRD allows for more effective, efficient, and less place-bound information management. It also saves the environment
Collaboration	Face-to-face meetings with teams at a specific location and time	Virtual teams meet from anywhere in the globe through audio, video, or web conferencing	VHRD saves costs on travel, engages HRD professionals in global community building. It creates connections with other HRD professionals without boundaries

Future trends for scholars and practitioners

As HRD scholars and practitioners look at the current state of VHRD and how it is being used in the workplace, they must look at the direction in which the field is moving. In our examination of the current literature on VHRD, we found a dearth of empirical studies involving VHRD. Given the speed at which technology evolves, there is a need for just-in-time research to match the speed of change prevalent in both technology and the global economy. Just-in-time research means an efficient review process of investigation and publication. Otherwise, HRD practitioners and scholars will fall behind as research is being published. With the multiple opportunities to engage in just-in-time learning through emerging technologies, HRD scholars must take advantage of the opportunity to research virtual teams and their interactions at the global level. This research can feed into technology courses in HRD curricula.

One important aspect to consider is how to best position HRD scholars and practitioners within the digital workplace. What is the role of HRD professionals in this new technological context? We must be proactive as scholars and practitioners to prepare the workforce as well as ourselves. At the same time that technology is changing our work environment, we cannot neglect the human side of VHRD. We believe that developing people is still the ultimate goal of HRD. Technology should be transparent and used as a support for managing knowledge and competencies, developing creative solutions, accessing information, communicating with others and collaborating globally.

A primary concern regarding the use of technology in the workplace is that it has blurred the lines between work and personal life (Thomas 2013). Whereas technology can provide for flexibility and increased access to work, such tools can also create environments in which people feel obligated to work constantly and add hours to their workweek. As technology increases in prevalence, it will be important to set boundaries by setting aside time for personal obligations in order to maintain a healthy work–life balance (Conceição and Lehman 2011). On the other hand, some people will not be comfortable using technology of any sort (Davis 1989); therefore, they may not utilize VHRD. Basic technology training will need to be made available to reluctant or late adapters so that they can remain engaged and productive employees.

Conclusion

This chapter serves as a call for HRD scholars and practitioners to recognize the rapid and significant technological changes that have affected the field. There is no other time and no other context for which the concept of lifelong learning has been more applicable for HRD professionals. For scholars, just-in-time research can allow the field to keep in step with the speed of change. Producing cutting edge research that is published expeditiously will help inform practitioners with relevant and useful knowledge. Additionally, empirical research that clarifies and validates the impact of VHRD is needed. For HRD practitioners, just-in-time learning using VHRD can help meet the needs of twenty-first century learners and employers.

The trend is that technological changes will continue to proliferate and impact the global workplace. The future success of HRD lies in the hands of HRD scholars and practitioners to educate themselves about current technologies and select the appropriate tool for a given intervention. Staying current empowers HRD professionals to choose interventions that satisfy the needs of the workforce. In the application of VHRD, professionals must keep at the fore the human element of *human resource development*, while technology should be used as a tool to learn new knowledge; create products; and connect, communicate and collaborate with others. While VHRD tools will be great for their flexibility and accessibility, it is important to keep in mind that work–life balance must be considered in the context of technology and that not everyone will accept and use technology. Lastly, while technology enhances lives professionally and personally, it is not necessarily the solution for every problem.

References

Bada, A.O. and Madon, S. (2010) Enhancing human resource development through information and communications technology. *Information Technology for Development* 12, 3: 179–83.

Bennett, E.E. (2009) Virtual HRD: The intersection of knowledge management, culture, and intranets. *Advances in Developing Human Resources* 11, 3: 362–74.

— (2010) The coming paradigm shift: Synthesis and future directions for virtual HRD. *Advances in Developing Human Resources* 12, 6: 728–41.

Bennett, E.E. and Bierema, L.L. (2010) The ecology of virtual human resource development. *Advances in Developing Human Resources* 12, 6: 632–47.

Benson, A.D., Johnson, S.D. and Kuchinke, K.P. (2002) The use of technology in the digital workplace: A framework for human resource development. *Advances in Developing Human Resources* 4, 4: 392–404.

Bingham, T. and Conner, M. (2010) *The new social learning: A guide to transforming organizations through social media*. San Francisco: Berrett-Koehler.

Brandenburg, D.C. and Ellinger, A.D. (2003) The future: Just-in-time learning expectations and potential implications for human resource development. *Advances in Developing Human Resources* 5, 3: 308–20.

Cho, Y., Cho, E. and McLean, G.N. (2009) HRD's role in knowledge management. *Advances in Developing Human Resources* 11, 3: 263–72.

Conceição, S.C.O. and Lehman, R.M. (2011) *Managing online instructor workload: Strategies for finding balance and success*. San Francisco: Jossey-Bass.

Conley, C.A. and Zheng, W. (2009) Factors critical to knowledge management success. *Advances in Developing Human Resources* 11, 3: 334–48.

Davis, F.D. (1989) Perceived usefulness, perceived ease of use, and user acceptance. *MIS Quarterly* 13, 3: 319–40.

Fazarro, D.E. and McWhorter, R.R. (2011) Leveraging green computing for increased viability and sustainability. *Journal of Technology Studies* 37, 2: 116–29.

Fazarro, D.E., Lawrence, H.M. and McWhorter, R.R. (2011) Going virtual: Delivering nanotechnology safety education on the web. *JSTE Teacher Education* 48, 2: 38–62.

Holton, J.A. (2001) Building trust in a virtual environment. *Team Performance Management* 7, 3/4: 36–47.

Johnson, S.D., Suriya, C., Yoon, S.W., Berrett, J.V. and La Fleur, J. (2002) Team development and group processes of virtual learning teams. *Computers and Education* 39, 4: 379–93.

Jukes, I., McCain, T. and Crockett, L. (2010) *Understanding the digital generation: Teaching and learning in the new digital landscape*. Thousand Oaks, CA: SAGE.

Mancuso, D.S., Chlup, D.T. and McWhorter, R.R. (2010) A study of adult learning in a virtual world. *Advances in Developing Human Resources* 12, 6: 681–99.

McWhorter, R.R. (2010) Exploring the emergence of virtual human resource development. *Advances in Developing Human Resources* 12, 6: 623–31.

Munkvold, B.E. and Zigurs, I. (2007) Process and technology challenges in swift-starting virtual teams. *Information and Management* 44, 287–99.

Nafukho, F.M., Graham, C.M. and Muyia, H.M.A. (2010) Harnessing and optimal utilization of human capital in virtual workplace environments. *Advances in Developing Human Resources* 12, 6: 648–64.

Schmidt, A. and Kunzmann, C. (2006) Towards a human resource development ontology for combining competence management and technology-enhanced workplace learning. *On the Move to Meaningful Internet Learning Systems* 4278: 1078–87.

Short, D. (2010) Foreword: Reflections on virtual HRD from a scholar-practitioner. *Advances in Developing Human Resources* 12, 6: 619–22.

Soule, D.L. and Applegate, L.M. (2009) *Virtual team learning: Reflecting and acting, alone or with others*. Retrieved from http://www.hbs.edu/research/pdf/09-084.

Spielman, S. and Windfeld, L. (2003) *The web conferencing book: Understand the technology, choose the right vendors, software, and equipment, and start saving time and money today!* New York: AMACOM.

Thomas, K.J. (2013) Workplace technology and the creation of boundaries: The role of HRD in a 24/7 work environment. *Proceedings of the Academy of HRD International Research Conference in the Americas*. Washington, DC: Academy of Human Resource Development.

Thomas, K.J. and Akdere, M. (2013) Social media as collaborative media in workplace learning. *Human Resource Development Review* 12: 329–344.

Yoon, S.W. and Lim, D.H. (2010) Systemizing virtual learning and technologies by managing organizational competency and talents. *Advances in Developing Human Resources* 12: 715–27.

EPILOGUE

A synopsis of the present, future and intrigue of HRD

Gene L. Roth, Tonette S. Rocco and Rob F. Poell

The chapter authors of this book have taken us on an incredible journey. Through their eyes we have explored the many facets of HRD, and we have used their lenses to view HRD across cultures, disciplinary boundaries, and ideological expanses. Because of their efforts, we believe this *Routledge Companion to HRD* will serve as an invaluable resource for HRD practitioners and researchers.

This final chapter consists of summative comments by the authors on their respective chapter topics. Chapter authors were asked to provide responses to the following three questions:

1. The first question addresses key issues that pertain to the status of the chapter topic or what is going on right now; that is, what is the current state of affairs with the topic?
2. The second question is futuristic. What is important to the chapter topic down the road? What should we be concerned about?
3. And third, what is an intriguing research question related to the chapter topic that the author(s) would like to see addressed? That is, what research question should be pursued that could really move the chapter topic forward?

A conceptual matrix was formed for each section of this book, and the authors' responses to these questions were organized in tabular form. The responses to the questions are in the authors' own words – and we chose not to trim back responses, even if they exceeded our requested length. We believe these tables provide wonderful insights for emerging scholars who are seeking direction for their research agendas. Additionally, we have provided introductory paragraphs for each conceptual matrix, in which we have tried to identify a few common threads from select authors.

Section I: origins of the field

The conceptual matrix of this section begins with Lee reminding us of the evolving and changing nature of HRD. It is a moving phenomenon, and "we make sense of it based on our own context and our own prior experiences" (Lee 2013).[1] This viewpoint applies to the broad concept of HRD, but it also applies to the movement that is experienced by the various fields forming the roots from which HRD originated. For example, Illeris (2013) acknowledges how our understanding of adult learning has shifted over time. Kessels (2013) makes similar observations about the turbulent history of andragogy as one of the fields upon which HRD draws. Perhaps this is why Billett points to "the importance of interdependence – the ability to interact with and utilize the contributions of others, artifacts, technologies" (Billett 2013). In an organizational world that changes continually, HRD evolves with it and the interdependence of learners is crucial for them to be able to make sense of a transforming world.

Section II: adjacent and related fields

Although Werner (2013) specifically addresses the relationship of HRD and HRM, his observation fits many of the chapter topics; that is, common ground exists among many components of HRD, yet inertia exists because of separate academies, different research traditions and different publication outlets. Authors of this section provided another convincing layer to the argument that HRD scholars need to go beyond their comfort zone if HRD is going to be relevant in helping to solve complex global issues. For example, McDonald and Hite noted the impact on careers of globalization, advances in technology, and fiscal crises. Spencer and Kelly (2013) suggest that these complex global conditions should be the impetus for workers around the world to seek out sustainable co-operative solutions for the workplace and for society. They make the case "for the new structures of ownership and control that could benefit workers and communities." Will HRD have anything to offer in such transitions? Egan (2013) has a hopeful response. He asserts that organizational development (OD) can be used to take on myriad problems facing organizations, communities and societies of the world.

Table E.1 Origins of the field

Current State of Affairs	*Future of Topic*	*Intriguing Questions*
1. Monica Lee – The history, status and future of HRD		
HRD practice and research has moved from 'just training' to being seen as integral to the development of individuals, organizations and nations. We cannot say what HRD really is, but as we work within it we co-create an understanding of it. It is our humanity, our motivations, desires and ethics that make HRD what it is, and delineate our workplaces.	Similarly, it is our aspirations that help build the future. Political, economic and geographical boundaries are dissolving, creating complex work environments that we have to negotiate. I believe the nature and focus of HRD will reflect (or lead?) that of the changing world and expand to incorporate a larger focus on conflict resolution, multiculturalism, the ageing workforce, alternative organizational forms including not-for-profit, and ethical issues.	There is enormous scope for research into this – we are heading into uncharted waters! Globally, we know relatively little about HRD in places other than in the privileged West – there is much to find out about alternative types of organizations and how they develop – what can the West learn from them? What about our traditional organizations – how can HRD help them cope with a changing future? What is the comparative picture? We can also ask similar questions with a more individual focus – what skills will people need to be able to cope? How does this affect the qualifications and the profession? What sort of society are we trying to foster locally? Nationally? Globally? And, of course, what methods should we use, and how do we understand/interpret our data? So many questions – so little time!

(*Continued*)

Table E.1 (Continued)

Current State of Affairs	*Future of Topic*	*Intriguing Questions*
2. Joseph W. M. Kessels – Andragogy		
Andragogy has a turbulent history when it comes to the specific attention for helping adults to learn and develop. This domain of study not only marked the shift from teaching of children towards helping adults in their learning, it also promoted self-directedness, autonomy and emancipation of adults in the wider context of their work and living. Due to a lack of official academic recognition of andragogy these important aspects of human resource development seem to get lost.	Does andragogy still have a role to play in the further advancement of HRD and Adult Education? The focus on supporting adults in their professional development and personal growth has been shared by HRD. The critical awareness associated with andragogy can also be found in the critical perspectives in HRD. In some countries andragogy claimed a broad domain of study, beyond the primary focus of the world of work as it is studied in HRD. Does andragogy inspire HRD to broaden its horizon of inquiry or is it a potential pitfall?	When we consider the current economic crisis, often ascribed to the perverse financial performance triggers of corporations, financial institutions and even government agencies, what new perspectives does an andragogical lens offer when examining this current context in view of human development and growth?
3. Knud Illeris – Adult learning		
There seems from about the middle of the 1990s to have been a strong tendency in relation to adult education to change focus from general enlightenment and interest-based education towards qualification for the labor market.	This aforementioned tendency needs to be balanced by activities aiming at personal development, engagement, and identification – for example by encouraging transformative learning and even questions of identity.	How can adult education be practiced in ways in which professional knowledge and skills are learned as integrated elements of a more general personal development?
4. Stephen Billett – Technical and vocational learning		
One of the most important developments in this area of research has come about through the recent contributions of neuro- and cognitive science which is beginning, for the first time, perhaps, to understand more about intra-psychological processes; that is, how humans engage with experiences "beyond the skin" and come to represent, utilize and develop further the knowledge arising from what has been experienced. Increasingly, human cognition and how we represent knowledge is seen as being a multimodal (i.e., sensory, neural, cognitive, haptic) process. Consequently the kind of experiences we have in the circumstances of those experiences have become even more central	The key emerging issue is the one of the learner interdependence. It has been realized that although given the need to engage with the social and brute world beyond the individual, it is not sufficient to see the learner independence as being a key goal for initial and ongoing occupational development. Instead, the importance of interdependence – the ability to interact with and utilize the contributions of others, artifacts, technologies – is emerging as a key consideration for educational provisions at all levels, and the initial and ongoing education for occupations is no exception here.	In what ways can learner interdependence be best understood and developed in novice workers?

to our understanding of the potency of particular experiences and the likelihood of what is experienced being represented in ways which can then be utilized elsewhere. This takes us somewhere beyond earlier accounts of what is referred to as transfer, largely seen as a cognitive process.		
5. Barbara J. Daley and Ron M. Cervero – Continuing professional education, development, and learning		
Movement is occurring towards developing systems of lifelong professional development and learning.	The foci of CPD and learning are shifting away from time spent in educational activities to the demonstration of learning outcomes and competencies achieved. CPE providers will need to develop programs that rely on evidence from research in learning, program planning, evaluation, and translation to practice.	The manner in which professionals learn is an area that needs research within systems of CPD.

Table E.2 Adjacent and related fields

Current State of Affairs	*Future of Topic*	*Intriguing Questions*
6. Toby Egan – Organization development		
The current state of affairs in OD is a strengthening of understanding by many in organizations and large systems about the importance of systems level consideration beyond the simple direction of positional leaders/executives in the organization – OD adds value. Within academia, there is broad acceptance of the general tenets of OD across several fields of study, especially management, industrial/organizational psychology, organizational behavior, education, public administration and, of course, HRD. OD is largely framed as action research as a primary orientation or implementation model – whereby a combination of established field-based assumptions (often provided by empirically oriented researchers; quantitative, qualitative or critical) and extant research results are combined with	Like any applied social science, OD (like HRD) is vulnerable to calls for evidence-based support for OD and OD-related practices and, therefore, OD practitioners and scholars must continue to record, research, and assess the effectiveness of OD interventions in a variety of contexts. This type of evidence-based orientation must embrace research-to-practice oriented praxis in a manner that is accessible to OD and research *insiders* and *outsiders*. It must also include multiple methods and be epistemologically inclusive.	There are three overarching questions covering three broad areas of inquiry (quantitative empirical, qualitative empirical, and critical), accompanied by sub-questions, including: **Quantitative empirical** (1) What does multinational, multi-organizational, longitudinal OD-related data collection look like? And how can meaningful large data sets be created? To more adequately explore new research questions, such as: • What is the current state of the global economy in terms of wealth, health and participation in family, community and government? And, how can these data be utilized in forming a needs assessment?

(*Continued*)

Table E.2 (Continued)

Current State of Affairs	*Future of Topic*	*Intriguing Questions*
current data and information gathered through a multi-method, tailored, organization-specific assessment and feedback process. Within OD practice, there has been a steady rejection of any specific, overt philosophical orientation to OD in favor of atheoretical or eclectic approaches. Although other systems and perspectives, such as six-sigma, executive coaching, appreciative inquiry and technology-based learning and development have emerged, those engaged in these practices are less inclined to delve into needed philosophical or values-based considerations. The emergence of OD as a more broadly participative practice in terms of women and non-Whites should be viewed as a positive. If we think of OD in terms of gendered participation, OD is only in the second "generation" of broad-based women's involvement and, in many contexts, OD (like HRD) has become a female dominated profession. OD has the capacity to address some of the most pressing issues faced by organizations, communities and the world.	Key areas for evidence-based research, action and reflection include: • Aligning executive strategies that address organizational mission, financial goals and core values • Refining approaches to understanding and influencing organizational culture, particularly during major transitions • Clarifying organizational purpose in a manner that inspires and retains the workforce and stakeholders • Using technology in new and effective ways • Addressing organizational, community and global problems systematically • Engaging individuals from diverse backgrounds and cultures in collaborative action and reflection • Building present and future leadership capacity • Inspiring ethical, self-regulating, and accountable organizations, communities and nations • Extending whole system global and multicultural vantage points • Transforming workplaces to outstanding learning and performance cultures • Exploring the potential for new assumptions about people and the natural environment – ontological, epistemological and phenomenological • Forming more natural synergies between work, family, community and national systems, and identities	• What data/metrics can be used, collected, and/or developed to better understand individual, community, national and global readiness for global system change(s)? • What processes and policies are cost effective, efficient, and align with mission goals while emphasizing clear, measurable outcomes? • What is an adequate amount of assets to accomplish organizational and programmatic objectives – including financial, physical, environmental and human resources? • What are key characteristics of effective, ethical and visionary leaders and how can they be developed and advanced? **Qualitative empirical** (2) What does large-scale/multi-study phenomenologically oriented qualitative data collection, synthesis, and inquiry involve? And how can meaningful themes and insights be formed? To more adequately explore new research questions, such as: • What is the experience of OD practitioners? • What is the experience of organizational collaborators on OD implementation? • What profound change has OD influenced? • What are the limitations of OD for practitioners, leaders and stakeholders? • What can be learned from large system/community/national OD interventions? And, how can this knowledge be applied?

- Addressing inequity, poverty and the ways OD can contribute to sustainable organizations, communities, nations and global interconnectivity

- How can we collectively form truly sustainable human relationships? Organizations? Communities? Nations? Global systems?

Critical action research

(3) What would a large-scale multi-organizational/ multinational OD-focused critical action research undertaking entail? And how can greater human awareness be formed? To more adequately explore new research questions, such as:

- What is the array of human biases in organizations and human systems? And, what is their impact?
- What is the nature of bias perpetuating systems?
- What are the limitations of scientifically rationally oriented systems and cultures? How can these limitations be addressed?
- How best can OD address the growing socio-economic divides in communities and nations?
- What is the current state of human myth/religion worldwide? How can human belief and action systems be transformed to better include (1) sustainability; (2) global environment; and (3) collective human dignity?
- How can OD help individuals gain a constructive, positive orientation to their life situations and to engage in action toward sustainable families and communities?
- What does truly inclusive OD look like and how can capacity for it be formed?

(*Continued*)

Table E.2 (Continued)

Current State of Affairs	*Future of Topic*	*Intriguing Questions*
7. Kimberly S. McDonald and Linda M. Hite – Career development		
Two key issues dominate current career development: economics and demographics. Globalization, advances in technology, and fiscal crises are some of the major economic issues influencing careers. The resulting worldwide competition, outsourcing, knowledge economy, unemployment and underemployment strongly affect career development. Demographics play out on multiple other levels. A more diverse labor pool has resulted in an influx of employees from previously under-represented groups; mixed generations of employees pose different career development challenges; part-time and temporary employees add another dimension. These factors combine to create new challenges regarding how we conceptualize and implement initiatives to develop careers. HRD can be instrumental in assisting both organizations and individuals in this unsettled environment.	Indications suggest that careers will continue to change due to the aforementioned factors, and others not yet on the horizon. Both organizations and individuals need to develop adaptive strategies to survive. We are most concerned about the widening gaps occurring in workplaces around the globe – between skilled and unskilled workers, between part-time and/or contingent employees and full-time employees, and between high-wage and low-wage workers – and the impact these schisms have on individuals' careers. These gaps will continue to grow unless individuals and groups advocate for disadvantaged workers and create change. HRD must adapt to become a leader in these efforts.	What constitutes successful adaptability and employability throughout a career? What HRD interventions and initiatives can help individuals develop these skills (adaptability and employability)?
8. Bruce Spencer and Jennifer Kelly – Workers and union HRD		
The major problems facing workers (whether or not they are union members) result from uncertain economic times – job and income insecurity is not compatible with imaginative proposals for greater worker empowerment. However, the continuing economic malaise should be the spur for workers everywhere to argue for a greater voice at work and to push for sustainable cooperative solutions at work and in society: for the new structures of ownership and control that could benefit workers and communities.	The impetus behind employee development is too often the narrow concerns of management and the belief that focusing on those will lead to increased productivity – what practitioners and scholars should be looking for is more generic training and skill development, and for employees to have an opportunity to develop more broadly by taking advantage of employee development which is not specifically work-related. The next five to ten years needs to mark such a change if the ground is to be laid for even greater worker empowerment in the future.	There needs to be renewed attempts to survey and document such schemes in the USA and Canada combined with case studies of the more imaginative schemes that can then become benchmarks for other employers, unions and workers to emulate. It is without doubt an obvious truism but in this field progressive change can feed off good "progressive" examples.

9. Jon M. Werner – Human resource management

The general public often makes little distinction between HRD and human resource management (HRM). For many employees, "It's all HR" (both for better, and for worse). In the US, HRD academics are more likely to be found in Colleges of Education, whereas HRM academics are more likely to be housed in Colleges of Business. There is greater breadth of research methodology used in top research publications in HRD, than in HRM. The areas of greatest overlap concern learning, training and development, career development, and organization development.

How can we better "connect the dots" between HRD and HRM research? There is common ground between the disciplines, yet the inertia of separate academies and research traditions and publication outlets makes this challenging. Joint publications, attending one another's conferences, and seeking to ensure that top HRD and HRM journals are viewed as valuable and relevant to both audiences are good starts.

Building on Mankin (2001): Do organizations with greater alignment between strategy/ structure, culture, and HRM practices also have higher levels of HRD practices? If so, does this impact important organizational outcomes? The theoretical argument is that, as the "overlap" is greater amongst strategy/ structure, organizational culture, and HRM practices, this should lead to a more significant role for HRD. The research question is whether this is true, and if so, what difference does this make for organizational performance?

10. Seung Won Yoon, Doo Hun Lim and Pedro A. Willging – Performance improvement

Despite the benefits that performance technology frameworks provide, especially in analyzing performance focus, clarifying drivers and barriers, and designing an environment-fitting mix of instructional and non-instructional solutions, recent HRD curricular studies indicate that it is not a part of core courses in most HRD academic programs. At present, performance technology is more frequently offered as a graduate-level course by instructional technology programs where HRD is introduced as one of the cognate fields. Early exposure to performance technology in academic or professional HRD work is necessary.

The pervasive use of and rapid changes in technologies in the workplace continuously change organizational members' behaviors, cognition, and affects. As technologies create and archive more digital trails, new opportunities and challenges will constantly arise and coexist in conducting performance technology projects. Leveraging technologies, especially (big) data analytics will become very important in implementing performance technology processes. Data analytics tools can help HRD professionals identify and predict patterns of employee behaviors and correlate findings to important business decision making promptly, but issues of privacy and misuse of data need more attention.

As six key technologies were identified as significant drivers for workplace learning (mobile apps, learning analytics, games, gesture-based learning, tablet computing, and the Internet of Things), future research needs to investigate how these technologies will shape workplace learning and performance practices. HRD research has been keen on factors affecting successful technology adoption. Future research should investigate holistic pictures including culture and environments, user readiness and skills, laws and policy, technology standards and utilization, and cost and benefits.

Section III: theoretical approaches

As Lee (2013) alluded to in her opening chapter of the book, the movement and transitioning of HRD occurs amongst ongoing tensions. Poell and Van Der Krogt (2013) explain that HRD is purposeful, but it is used differently by organizational actors who have competing interests. These competing interests are playing out within complex work environments amidst dissolving political, economic and geographical boundaries (Lee 2013). Given this morass, Fenwick and Torraco offer suggestions for negotiating some of the field's wicked problems. Fenwick (2013) is hopeful that HRD can move forward with critical development in ways that can lead to maturity as a scholarly field. And Torraco (2013) urges HRD practitioners and scholars to walk the talk; he points out that, "while proclaiming a broad systems viewpoint, we often overlook variables and concepts outside our interest or discipline, or dismiss unfamiliar factors as irrelevant." Given these tendencies, he ponders, "Are human tendencies for linear and short-term thinking innate or learned?"

Table E.3 Theoretical approaches

Current State of Affairs	*Future of Topic*	*Intriguing Questions*
11. Tara Fenwick – Critical HRD		
It is fair to say that critical theoretical development is in its infancy in the HRD field. Unlike other related fields of practice (education, management studies, etc.), HRD seems to have been surprisingly slow to recognize, debate and integrate leading social science theories and methodological approaches. My chapter is, first, an attempt to signal where HRD is now (and how far it has come in the past decade) in beginning to ask questions informed by critical and feminist sociology. Second, I hope to point out terrain that beckons: issues and perspectives that HRD could engage to move forward its critical development – which of course will move it towards maturity as a scholarly field.	In the broader social sciences, the issues now being debated in critical circles have to do with materiality, ontological politics, spatiality, and many related concerns that decenter the individual human and rethinking the "social". These will have potentially profound and illuminating effects in HRD thinking and practice. Further afield are issues of race, faith and sexuality that extend beyond identity politics to fundamentally challenge the practices of existing institutions (such as work organizations and HRD) with questions emanating from postcolonial and queer locations. Finally, online engagements and virtualities are engendering important critical fields of scholarship in digital cultures, with attendant new digital methodologies. These don't yet have serious visibility in HRD, and should. Everything from critical questions regarding big data assembling and mining in organizations to social media issues – and questions about who owns online information and who benefits from digital engagements – require strong critical thinkers in HRD who are educated to help organizations work through these issues.	How can HRD develop a unique critical scholarship that can transform the field of practice and contribute to broader social science debates, while maintaining continuity with its own best historical traditions?

12. Claire Gubbins and Russell Korte – Social capital theory		
It is recognized within management, organizational behavior and HRM literatures that the *relational* component or specifically social capital is key to understanding individual, collective and societal behavior and practice. The HRD field also recognizes the importance of relationships for HRD research and practice. In particular Harrison and Kessels (2004) highlight that emerging challenges facing HRD include developing, not only the human capital of organizations, but also the social capital. However, the extent of HRD research from the social capital perspective is still limited.	In recognition of the tensions inherent in the two competing views of social capital, the economic and the sociological, further research is required to investigate how to enable social capital which balances both the economic and social or community needs of organizations. One way forward is recognizing that enabling the *relations between* individuals is likely to improve collaborative working arrangements and environments and consequently individual, collective and organizational performance. Equally, while a human capital perspective focuses at the individual level on development of expertise, a social capital perspective illustrates the opportunity to get higher returns on that human capital.	Derived from recognition of the broader social context in which organizational work and HRD practices occur, this chapter suggests a need for more multilevel and socially oriented approaches to HRD research and practice. Valuable future research questions are two-fold: • What is the influence of the social context, or more specifically the intra-organizational social capital/network, on HRD practices such as individual learning and performance in organizations? • What are the influences of HRD strategy and practices on social capital structure, content, and evolution; and the implications of this?
13. Rob F. Poell and Ferd J. Van Der Krogt – Learning-Network Theory		
Organizing HRD processes in practice is a difficult task for two major reasons. First, the dualistic nature of HRD means that both work experiences and explicit learning experiences form its basis; however, combining the two is a key challenge. Second, the strategic nature of HRD means that all actors (not just managers) attempt to use it as an instrument to further their own interests; strategies that are often not aligned. The traditional (structure) approach to organizing HRD cannot deal with these issues satisfactorily anymore. We propose a broader perspective, based on the Learning-Network Theory: the dynamic-network approach, which does more justice to the dualistic and strategic nature of organizing HRD.	Every employee organizes his or her own HRD processes in the form of a learning path. A learning path is a more or less coherent set of (work-based) learning activities that are meaningful to the employee. Other actors can have an impact on employees' learning paths through organizing learning programs, reorganizing work processes, offering career development opportunities, and so forth. The influence of HRM and work organization on learning paths needs much better understanding.	How do employees create learning paths that are meaningful to them? What do these learning paths look like? How do they develop over time? How do they differ among employees, professions, departments, organizational types, sectors, and countries? How do HRD, HRM, and the organization of work influence employees' learning paths? How do employees use the opportunities offered by HRD, HRM, and the organization of work to create their learning paths?

(*Continued*)

Table E.3 (Continued)

Current State of Affairs	*Future of Topic*	*Intriguing Questions*
14. Richard J. Torraco – Systems theory		
Even though HRD may value systems theory, we often engage in subsystems thinking. While proclaiming a broad systems viewpoint, we often overlook variables and concepts outside our interest or discipline, or dismiss unfamiliar factors as irrelevant. We find comfort in the relative certainty which this creates. However, our research likely presents only part of the potential knowledge offered because we have taken a partial systems view. Despite its promise, the current state of affairs is that systems theory remains underutilized in research and practice. Systems theory cannot coexist with subsystems thinking.	One of the most recent applications of systems theory is to social network analysis. As we look over the horizon, what is next? How can systems theory support HRD research and practice to develop the workforce needed for a technology-rich, globalized economy? How can systems theory help us navigate a complex and uncertain future?	Are human tendencies for linear and short-term thinking innate or learned? If learned, what types of experience and education facilitate the development of system thinking capabilities? What does systems theory tell us about the mental models people use to make decisions in complex, dynamic situations? Can systems thinking be taught?
15. Judy Yi. Sun and Greg G. Wang – Human capital theory		
HRD as a field of research and practice is still in the course of embracing and applying human capital theory in the process of forming its own unique identity.	While HCT's application at individual and organizational levels in relation to HRD requires finer-grained treatment, its domain appears to be less disputable. Yet the embracement of HCT at the national level is likely to either unite or disengage the field in relation to the uniqueness of HRD's identity.	Critical questions to explore may include: • How to understand the uniqueness of HRD as a field of research and practice in international settings in applying HCT? • What is the relevance and rigor for HRD to become an all-inclusive field to engage in not only change, learning, and performance based on HCT, but also in all aspects of human development? • Is it feasible for HRD to address the concern of the "whole of humanity" and in what ways? How would this mindset foster or prohibit a healthy course for HRD to become mature as a relevant and rigorous field?

Section IV: policy perspectives

Our authors within this section outlined some of the contextual tensions related to their topics, and how these tensions affect HRD. Hawley (2013) describes how the status of a region's workforce can be either a driver of economic creativity or a burden of workforce deficiencies. He explains that needs of countries can vary greatly based on their levels of maturity and wealth. He stresses the need for systemically examining the effectiveness of workforce interventions. With regard to national HRD, McLean and Osman-Gani believe that the number of cross-country case comparisons is increasing. However, in line with Hawley's observation, they wonder about the feasibility of suggesting and/or testing models or theories about national human resource development, given the variances that can be found across countries. Stewart (2013) uses the phrase "uncertain status" to describe the theory and practice of strategic HRD. It is a phrase that many of the authors could have used. His comments are parallel to the aforementioned responses of Spencer and Kelly; that is, he is concerned with who is served by strategic HRD and how strategic HRD might be applied to reconcile competing interests.

Table E.4 Policy perspectives

Current State of Affairs	*Future of Topic*	*Intriguing Questions*
16. Gary N. McLean and AAhad M. Osman-Gani – National HRD		
Rather than seeing a continuation of single country case studies (though they are continuing), we are beginning to see more interest in cross-country case comparisons.	Is it possible to suggest and test models or theories about NHRD, especially given the huge variations between countries?	Can we provide evidence of the value added to a country from NHRD in concrete ways, beyond anecdotal evidence that is currently used today?
17. Joshua D. Hawley – Workforce development		
The workforce development area is increasingly important for developed and developing nations as governments try to make sure education systems produce individuals who are employable. The workforce development field is in transition from fragmented social and economic interventions such as "unemployment assistance" and vocational training, to general strategies that are place-based or involve sector-specific strategies. Therefore, while workforce development as a term is used widely, the programmatic focuses of specific interventions vary widely.	The workforce more generally will continue to be a primary driver of economic creativity, as well as a burden on nations that can't adjust the workforce to gaps in skills and knowledge quickly. Mature nations differ in their needs from emerging countries and underdeveloped nations. Europe and to an extent Japan are facing a demographic trap, where countries must deal with immigration as a way to address workforce gaps because there are too few young people. In contrast, nations in the Global South vary significantly from highly skilled countries with excess labor to nations with significant disparities in skills. India is an interesting contrast, with high numbers of skilled technical workers and among the highest illiteracy rates for the whole globe.	My wish would be to focus on documenting effective programs and policies in workforce development. There are too few empirical studies in any area that touches HRD. Practitioners worry too much about defending their funding or pet programs, and too little about systematically studying and assessing the effectiveness of workforce interventions. Power to the evaluators!

(*Continued*)

Table E.4 (Continued)

Current State of Affairs	*Future of Topic*	*Intriguing Questions*
18. Paul Bélanger – Lifelong learning		
A key issue is the recognition of the dual constituent of any work-related learning demand, that is the learning requirements of organization and employers, but also the needs and aspirations of individuals who seek in their work not only exchange but also use value. Such recognition implies the creation of mechanisms to facilitate both the expression and mediation of these two essential components.	What is at stake for the future is the continuing enhancement of the capacity of initiative of individuals throughout their life, their evolving capacity to pilot their life transitions and hence to develop their autonomy of action. This competence is becoming more and more essential in all areas of human activity. However, people cannot enhance their capacity of action unless there is recognition of their individual and collective demand for a type of learning that has personal meaning for them, not just now in their workplaces, but also throughout their lives.	I hope that researchers will explore, in all areas of lifelong learning, the dialectic relation between life-large and life-deep learning. I wish that decision-makers will discover and enliven this crucial dynamic between the sociality and the intimacy of learning biographies.
19. Jim Stewart – Strategic HRD		
Strategic HRD seems to experience a continuing crisis of identity. Arguments and debates about what exactly strategic HRD is and if and how it differs from HRD occupy both scholars and professionals alike. The recent work by the UK Chartered Institute of Personnel and Development (CIPD) in establishing what they term the HR Profession Map argues that strategy and being strategic is essential at all levels of HR practice. This suggests that there is no single strategic level and that HR practice is of itself strategic. But many scholars and professionals argue distinctions between strategic and non-strategic practice in HRD. So, it seems clear that Strategic HRD has an uncertain status in the theory and practice of our field.	The main future concern is not settling debates on meaning and definitions but questioning and establishing what exactly Strategic HRD is for. Recent sessions at the Critical Management Studies conferences have examined the role of HRD in the recent financial crisis, posing questions such as that implied in part of the title of the Critical HRD stream in 2013; HRD as co-conspirator, disinterested profession or facilitator of resistance? In other words, does Strategic HRD always and exclusively serve the interests of owners and managers of corporations or can and should other interests such as those of employees and citizens take equal focus or even precedence?	How does strategic HRD reconcile competing interests in formulating and implementing development based strategies in employing organizations?

20. Paul Iles – Talent management and leadership development

Talent management and leadership development are moving from infancy to adolescence and are being increasingly recognized as key areas bringing HRD and strategic management together in making a positive contribution to organizational performance. However, questions remain over conceptual boundaries, efficacy, ethics and practice.	There is a need for greater clarity over their definition, theoretical underpinnings, conceptual boundaries, impacts and effective practices, as well as recognition of diversity in conceptualization and practice in different national, cultural and strategic contexts and the ethical issues involved here, especially in "exclusive" and individualistic conceptualizations of talent management and leadership development and their impact on the motivation and performance of those included and excluded from talent pools.	What is the impact of different talent management and leadership development practices in different national, cultural and strategic contexts on individual and organizational performance? How do they add value, and what methodologies will best address this question?

Section V: interventions

Authors within this section describe contextual issues and other challenges that face HRD interventions. For example, Marsick and Watkins observe that informal and incidental learning are "organic and nearly ubiquitous in the workplace." They believe that although these forms of learning can be encouraged and supported, they cannot be rigidly structured or mandated in organizations. Perhaps similar statements can be made about mentoring in the workplace. Ellinger (2013) cites studies indicating that two-thirds of employees have been involved in some form of mentoring relationship. Yet, as she explains in her chapter, varying degrees of success can be found across formal and informal mentoring approaches. Kohut and Roth (2013) contend that a voice missing from the literature is from the individual worker who must contend with and adapt to change. These authors are interested in aspects of organizational politics that affect survivorship in organizations. De Laat, Schreurs and Nijland offer a hopeful view of the recent developments in technology and society. They contend that these changes have resulted in increased openness in organizational processes and practices, and that these developments have reduced impediments to knowledge sharing. They wonder what might be the best approaches to open practices for integrating work, learning and innovation.

Table E.5 Interventions

Current State of Affairs	*Future of Topic*	*Intriguing Questions*
21. Ann Kohut and Gene L. Roth – Change management		
In the change management literature, change theories and issues surrounding change management convey the perspectives of the organization, manager, or change agent. The voice of the individual who must adapt to change is missing from this literature base.	When it comes to successfully managing change HRD practitioners must (1) be attentive to the unique characteristics of the context and (2) develop and refine their political and communication skills with strategic insight as a means of preparing for and dealing with change. These two constructs are important considerations for future research that links HRD and change management.	What are the elements of organizational politics that affect survivorship in organizations? The intersection of organizational culture and organizational politics is an area for future study. Specifically, what is the role of organizational culture in organizational politics and organizational members' perceptions of organizational politics? Does organizational culture dictate organizational politics or vice versa? What is the organization's perspective of organizational politics and how can improving employees' political skill contribute to organizational learning and better business results? Further, what is the organization's ethical responsibility as it relates to organizational politics?
22. Victoria J. Marsick and Karen E. Watkins – Informal learning in learning organizations		
Currently, many organizations are trying to understand how to best conceptualize, support, and measure informal learning. Informal and incidental learning are organic and nearly ubiquitous: they can be encouraged and supported, but not rigidly structured or mandated.	Informal and incidental learning place significant stress on the learner who must evaluate often disparate information, especially digital information, and make meaning of that information and apply it to their work situation. Informal and incidental learning also place stress on managers who must often identify resources and opportunities to guide the development of their employees in a context where information is overwhelmingly available, but nonspecifically targeted to the needs of their mentee(s).	What are the system-level leverage points in organizations that catalyze and sustain high levels of organically occurring, productive informal and incidental learning at the individual, group and organizational levels?
23. Maarten de Laat, Bieke Schreurs and Femke Nijland – Communities of practice and value creation in networks		
The growing significance of human capital development and value creation in open practices in our knowledge and network society has major implications for understanding how organizations manage	Although learning in open practices could be highly valuable for professionals, the ad hoc and fluid nature of these practices makes it difficult for professionals and organizations to establish its value and apply the outcomes of such practices.	What is the architecture behind productive open practices (integrating work, learning, and innovation) and what is its impact on value creation and the development and utilization of human capital?

their knowledge and how professional development activities are organized to strengthen the knowledge of professionals. While the traditionally controlled organizational approach tends to focus on individual skills and knowledge acquisition, the ideas developed around CoPs opened the debate to focus more on professional development through participation in the midst of practice. Recent developments in technology and society have given rise to more openness in organizational processes and practices making employees less constrained by boundaries that otherwise would impede knowledge sharing. These ideas continue to have a big influence on research and professional practices investigating how professional development needs to be organized.

Open practices are characterized by "fluidity", implying that membership, interests, social relations and aims are constantly fluctuating depending on the resources available. This raises tensions for professionals and organizations in the ability to monitor, utilize, and integrate the knowledge created in such practices. The tension between openness and utilization of knowledge will be magnified when these open practices emerge predominantly from professionals' learning needs independent of organizational involvement. When participation in open practices is dynamic and evolving based on needs and desires it will become harder for these practices to demonstrate their value and to sustain over a longer period of time. As such these practices are constantly negotiating openness with focus, while participants come and go. Being able to deal with these fluctuations will challenge researchers and practitioners to find ways to capture and protect potential knowledge within organizations.

24. Andrea D. Ellinger – Coaching and mentoring

The pervasive growth of coaching and mentoring as powerful developmental interventions can be witnessed by the estimates that coaching has grown to a 2 million USD industry with over 47,000 professional coaches practicing worldwide. Further, it has been reported that more than one third of major US corporations offer formal mentoring programs, and estimates from mentoring participation studies suggest that two thirds

The literature base on coaching and mentoring continues to expand with scholars calling for more research that examines the benefits of coaching and mentoring for coaches and mentors, the negative consequences of such developmental interventions, the notions of upward coaching and reverse mentoring, along with studies that examine virtual forms of coaching and mentoring, and explorations of both constructs in diverse global contexts since these concepts tend to be Western in their origin and orientation.

Scholars have noted that multiple definitions, conceptualizations, and operationalizations exist in terms of coaching and mentoring in research studies which can create considerable confusion. Therefore, precision in defining terms, clarity in explicating the nature of the relationships being examined, and the use of robust and previously tested research instruments are recommended pathways for further researching these developmental interventions.

(*Continued*)

Table E.5 (Continued)

Current State of Affairs	*Future of Topic*	*Intriguing Questions*
of employees have been involved in some form of mentoring relationship. Accordingly, coaching and mentoring represent important research and practice domains for the field of HRD.		
25. Ronald L. Jacobs – Structured on-the-job training		
S-OJT continues to be implemented in organizations, across business sectors, types of organizations, and types of training content. The majority of S-OJT programs continue to focus on technical training and in conjunction with quality management systems.	How technology might be integrated into the use of S-OJT continues to be a question in many organizations. Technology is primarily used now to manage the S-OJT modules. That is, making them available upon demand and providing a way to revise the documents as necessary. Of importance for the future would be to use technology as a means to connect trainers and trainees, who might be at different locations, but still need to be in contact during the training.	An important set of research questions revolves around the cross-cultural aspects of S-OJT. S-OJT requires that trainers and trainees come into close contact with each other. What that means in terms of time on task, question asking, retention, and other learning issues has not been fully investigated.

Section VI: core issues and concerns

Kuchinke opens this section with a critical look at one of the key issues underlying HRD: the meaning of work. In line with several authors in this volume who have emphasized the active nature of organizing learning and work, he concludes that the "meaning of work . . . is not so much 'found' as it is created; it is a dynamic process rather than a static phenomenon" (Kuchinke 2013). Hutchins and Leberman take this observation to the domain of learning transfer and suggest that since "mobile learning is increasingly becoming the preferred method (by which) individuals access information and learning content . . . a focus on leveraging this technology would be helpful in advancing . . . research" (Hutchins and Leberman 2013). Echoing Garavan and MacKenzie's critical look at HRD's role in the global financial crisis, Ardichvili stresses that managers and employees need education and training that feature culture change, ethics and social responsibility. Kormanik and Nwaoma pose a couple of fascinating questions related to diversity and inclusion advocacy – the first relates to economic challenges, and the second pertains to the future relevance of national citizenship. Ismail and Wahat (2013) explain the need for research that includes the voices of two specific groups – child labor and migrant workers – voices that are more or less missing from mainstream HRD literature.

Table E.6 Core issues and concerns

Current State of Affairs	*Future of Topic*	*Intriguing Questions*
26. K. Peter Kuchinke – Work and its personal, social, and cross-cultural meanings		
We see the concern over the meaning of work crop up in many levels of analysis. In the public policy arena, there are important questions over this topic as it relates to the current discussion about low-wage work; immigration reform and the need to integrate new citizens into our communities and the economy; the question how more young people can be attracted to careers in scientific, technical, engineering, and math related fields; and how countries can rebuild their competitiveness based on adults' work-based knowledge, skills, and abilities. Employers in countries around the world continue to struggle with issues of employee relations: how to attract, retain, and motivate the best and brightest, how to assure adequate leadership talent pipelines, and how to build workplaces that are high performing, inclusive, and capture the energy and passion of their employees. Finally, at the individual level, the topic is critical in the aftermath of the great recession that has caused such high levels of unemployment and underemployment, has increased the level of youth unemployment in many countries, and extends the need for work into old age. In all these contexts, the core question remains: how to navigate the economic, social, and global opportunities, tensions, and trade-offs to form a life that is productive, satisfying, energetic, and worth living. Work, as a central personal, social, and economic commitment remains a process of adaptation, movement, and change. The meaning of work, thus, is not so much "found" as it is created; it is a dynamic process rather than a static phenomenon; and it is a complex array of factors rather than a single dimension.	As an HRD scholar, I am concerned with individual, organizational, and societal aspects of work and working. In my research and my practice, I encounter many individuals for whom work is characterized as toil and trouble, and who have resigned themselves to the fact that the workplace has little more to offer than drudgery and unpleasantness. In turn, many organizations with which I consult have little insight into the potential for performance, innovation, and change that a changed work culture might have to offer. Societies, be they in the developed or developing world, suffer from youth unemployment and underemployed human resources despite the fact that every country has a huge backlog of societal work that needs to be attended to. Examples are the building and rebuilding of communities, cleaning up the environment, providing services to the elderly and homebound, and caring for the economically disadvantaged. A central goal for the future will be to connect the creative energies of individuals and groups, to create organizational structures that encourage innovation and new thinking about old problems, and focus the creative energy of individuals and organizations on the central task of community, nation, and global well-being and progress.	The research program on the meaning of work touches many areas, as outlined above. A central question for research and practice is how to connect the various social sciences related to work and working and develop a central force to improve the experience of work, the institutional context in which work takes place, and the objectives of meaningful work in terms of contributions to the common good.

(*Continued*)

Table E.6 (Continued)

Current State of Affairs	*Future of Topic*	*Intriguing Questions*
27. Alexandre Ardichvili – Organizational sustainability, corporate social responsibility and business ethics		
In this chapter I argue that CSR, sustainability, and ethics in business organizations can be viewed as parts of a larger system that is shaped by a complex interaction between individual knowledge and moral development, group and organizational practices, power relationships, and organizational and societal culture. I argue that HRD should play a key role in shaping organizational cultures of ethics, sustainability, and responsibility. Related activities should include culture change efforts and ethics and social responsibility-related education and training for managers and employees. HRD practitioners are the most visible carriers and promoters of organizational values and, therefore, must act as role models of ethical behavior. Furthermore, they need to take into account issues of organizational power differentials, and question and critically re-examine not only organizational, but also their own habits and practices.	Thinking about crucial issues for future research and practice I would like to focus on the impact of globalization on CSR, sustainability, business ethics, and HRD. For example, there is a growing realization that the recent global economic crisis was triggered, to a large extent, by ethics violations at large multinational financial corporations, and that, while the negative impact of business activity on the global ecosystem and communities is rapidly escalating, corporations governed by questionable cultures of ethics tend to behave in irresponsible and unsustainable ways.	A question I plan to address in my research is related to the impact of multinational expansion of companies from emerging economies on global business cultures: Will norms that shape currently acceptable business behavior be challenged by the growing importance of MNCs from the emerging market countries? What competing values and norms will business executives and HRD practitioners have to take into account as they conduct business with emerging market MNCs?
28. Martin B. Kormanik and Peter Chikwendu Nwaoma – Diversity and inclusion initiatives		
Diversity and inclusion (D&I) is an expanding area of focus for HRD, with organizations worldwide pursuing D&I initiatives. Operationalizing D&I has expanded from narrowly focused rhetoric on race and gender to a broader, more inclusive definition. D&I theory, research, and practice have moved from a moral-ethical dimension to a business-economic perspective, with D&I initiatives progressing from compliance to systemic action to organizational transformation.	Although some D&I initiatives focus on transformation, most are limited to compliance. D&I initiatives require forethought and careful implementation. Lack of understanding of D&I can be stressful, distracting, create misunderstandings and tension, and can lead to allegations of unfair treatment and hostile work environments. D&I goals and strategy need to be clearly articulated, communicated routinely, woven into all HRD activities, and institutionalized into organizational culture. HRD practitioners' professional development must prepare them to support and often lead D&I initiatives.	What are appropriate measures for assessing D&I progress? What are the correlations between D&I support and job opportunities, organizational or national life cycle, and organizational or national health? What is the cost-benefit of D&I initiatives? What are the economic profiles of organizations that have formalized their D&I policies? How can D&I be used to reposition world economic outlook, given pervasive global economic downturn and widespread unemployment?

		How can citizens facing severe economic challenges change their fortunes through D&I advocacy? Will national citizenship remain relevant as the global community addresses D&I?
29. Maimunah Ismail and Nor Wahiza Abdul Wahat – Working conditions of child labor and migrant workers		
This analysis shows that child labor issues are almost absent from most developed countries but they increase in countries with low HDI ranks. The opposite is observed for migrant workers in which the number is higher in the developed and fast industrializing countries compared with the under-developed countries. The occurrence of child labor and migrant workers, however, seems to be unstoppable due to increased pace of globalization, growing demographic and socio-economic disparities, the effects of environmental change, technological revolution, and the emergence of new forms of social networks resulting from the spread of MNCs in the globalized economy.	A futuristic issue concerning child labor and migrant workers is their status on working conditions and the impact on sustainable development because working conditions have far reaching implications to workers and employers. There have been debates among the stakeholders on their working conditions; however, relevant information is often not well shared and understood.	More detailed studies are needed based on voices of individual child labor and migrant workers at the grass roots level in terms of needs and aspiration in relation to their participation in the workforce. These voices should be understood and taken up by responsible stakeholders to improve their strategies and commitment involving child labor and migrant workers. Further comparative analyses on the occurrence of child labor and migrant workers across countries should be conducted periodically to see changes over the years because they are considered among the dynamic segment of the workforce due to their unstable status.
30. Holly M. Hutchins and Sarah Leberman – Transfer of learning		
Organizations are seeking low cost yet high impact options for transfer of learning, and many (at least, from a UK perspective) are looking at in-house options. In New Zealand, action learning approaches are being used by several organizations. From a US perspective, transfer of learning appears to be more in the purview of independent consulting firms	The challenges of the transfer of learning will always be present, particularly where leadership development (one of the more costly and high profile learning and development interventions) is concerned. Increasingly, organizations will be seeking customized solutions that are easier to embed in their training systems,	What are the critical success factors for long-term transfer of learning to both the individual and the organization from leadership development programs? That is, what is the best way(s) to assess, support, and

(*Continued*)

Table E.6 (Continued)

Current State of Affairs	*Future of Topic*	*Intriguing Questions*
(e.g. Bersin, Fort Hill, LTS Global, Wilson Learning) offering assessment and targeted intervention solutions rather than organizations focusing on the issue from an internal perspective.	and are routinely reported and used in performance evaluations. Making transfer of learning accountable in manager and employee performance evaluations will be critical. This is not "new", Mary Broad and other transfer of learning researchers have been saying this for two decades now; however, it continues to be a difficult expectation to realize.	demonstrate transfer of learning from (executive) leadership development programs given the significant program investment? Also, how can technology help cue, capture and assist in transfer of learning? Mobile learning is increasingly becoming the preferred method for individuals to access information and learning content, so a focus on leveraging this technology would be helpful in advancing transfer of learning research.

Section VII: HRD as a profession

Echoing Lee's earlier remarks, Garavan and MacKenzie (2013) sum up this section neatly by simply asking us, "If HRD really existed, what would it look like?" Carliner and Hamlin (2013) may have thought the same thing when they took on the humongous task of describing HRD certification efforts across the globe. Seeing the highly diverse picture that ensues, they ask "how the HRD domain should progress towards becoming recognized and accepted as a 'true' profession and as a 'true' academic discipline." They go even further by suggesting that the currently distinct 'HRD', 'OD' and 'Coaching/Mentoring' communities of practice could look into making "a concerted effort . . . to forge a single all-embracing 'People and Organization Development' profession underpinned by one unique/distinctive body of knowledge that may ultimately become a discrete academic discipline." The debate is perennial and Carliner and Hamlin offer some fresh ideas for the HRD profession to ponder over. This small section in the volume is completed by the results of another rather enormous task, taken on by Roberts, Walton and Lim, to present an overview of university programs in HRD worldwide. The fuzzy boundaries of the field are echoed in the great diversity of program titles that universities use for their 'HRD' degrees.

Table E.7 HRD as a profession

Current State of Affairs	*Future of Topic*	*Intriguing Questions*
31. Saul Carliner and Robert G. Hamlin – Certification of HRD professionals		
Certification is active. Most of the major organizations have changed the competency model – that is, the conceptual model on which they base certification – in the past couple of years. I've been doing research to determine whether one of the competency models is complete. The question, however, is the extent to which certification is subscribed to outside the US. It has hit critical mass in the UK and some European countries, and it is close to critical mass in Canada. But, as is noted in the chapter, with competing certifications in the US, that has not yet happened in the US. Furthermore, it's unclear where it's heading right now, absent of other indicators. ASTD support for its certification is steadfast; I'm not sure the other organizations offering certification to US-based HRD practitioners have the resources to compete against it long term.	As is mentioned in the chapter, a combination of the competency-based approach mixed with the availability of free MOOCs could cause certifications to offer an alternative to university degrees as credentials for HRD professionals.	How will the availability of MOOCs and certification affect university-based programs, including degree and continuing education programs? A key issue that HRD scholars and practitioners will need to address as part of future deliberations is how the HRD domain should progress towards becoming recognized and accepted as a "true" profession and as a "true" academic discipline. Another key issue is the current "fragmented" identity of professionals concerned with people and organization development, which includes all those who perceive themselves as belonging to either the HRD, OD or Coaching and Mentoring communities of practice. A provocative question could be as follows: "Should a concerted effort be made by all three extant domains to forge a single all-embracing 'People and Organization Development' profession underpinned by one unique/distinctive body of knowledge that may ultimately become a discrete academic discipline?"
32. Paul B. Roberts, John Walton and Doo Hun Lim – University programmes in HRD		
Roberts – Programs in HRD continue to evolve and in the absence of a bounded definition, the programs take many different directions, such as training and development, organizational development and change, HRM, instructional design, and e-learning. **Walton –** Although HRD themes are apparent across a range of UK and mainland European Masters programs, there is an absence of consensus on program titles.	**Roberts –** What will HRD look like in 2025? Will HRD still be the title we live within? Does the absence of a single unifying definition keep us from growing and gaining greater acceptance or does it give us the agility to change and adapt with society? **Walton –** So long as HRD continues to be seen as a significant subject area within the curriculum this may not be a matter	**Roberts –** In the US we are faced with two fundamental questions: first "is HRD a discipline?" There are several good articles written from many perspectives. Second, the absence of a single agreed upon definition has created a box with such fuzzy edges that it is difficult to examine HRD programs. **Walton –** Program directors who are members of the AHRD/UFHRD should be asked, "What factors govern the titles of HRD-related programs in their institution and why?"

(*Continued*)

Table E.7 (Continued)

Current State of Affairs	*Future of Topic*	*Intriguing Questions*
	of concern in terms of academic careers and research activity. Of greater concern is the lack of understanding within university faculties over what HRD as a subject area consists of, which over time will affect its credibility.	
33. Thomas S. Garavan and Clíodhna A. MacKenzie – HRD and the global financial crisis		
In the years since Lehman Brothers filed for bankruptcy on September 15, 2008 and subsequent public inquiry hearings and official reports indicating that a "failure to account for human weakness" had led to "an erosion of standards of responsibility and ethics . . . that stretched from the ground level to the corporate suites" (Financial Crisis Inquiry Commission 2010) there has been a deafening silence from within the HRD field. Having reviewed *Human Resource Development Review*, *Human Resource Development International* and *Human Resource Development Quarterly* from early 2009 [allowing for a financial crisis time lag] to Summer 2013 there were fewer than 12 articles that referenced the financial crisis. Ardichvili (2011), Poell (2012), MacKenzie (2012), Scully-Russ (2012) and Elliott (2013) all attempted to advance an exploration of HRD's contribution in the crisis – but alas, the field did not respond.	What should we be concerned about? Overpromising, under-delivering and not challenging whether HRD is fit for purpose. McLean (2010: 320) argued that "we need to find ways to encourage thinking that is outside the box . . . so that it may help us to keep HRD dynamic, growing, and barrier busting" but in an editorial in the same journal, Wang (2011: 3) argued that "rebelling research takes more than courage and research expertise; it also requires constant reflection and being mindful of ongoing research". Fine, no disagreement here; however, this sounds very much like pouring water on a fire to extinguish it before it spreads – this [rebellious research] is a fire that needs to spread. And this is the problem. How can we truly begin to unpack and rebuild a profession and scholarly endeavor if we are afraid of what we might find?	If HRD really existed – what would it look like? Discuss.

In short, the current state of affairs reflects an academic community unwilling to addresses the elephant in the room – people and organizational failures are HRD failures.

Dynamic, growing and barrier busting may as well be sluggish, static and status quo. When you oversell, sooner or later you get found out – the financial crisis found us out, only problem: we haven't realized it yet.

Section VIII: HRD around the world

Although the authors of this section represent several different countries, common threads can be found in their descriptions of the status of HRD. Harris and Bartlett (2013) offer a perspective that can probably be used in many parts of the world. They explain that the "term HRD is not prominent in Australia or New Zealand although the practice of HRD is widespread." Commenting on HRD in China, Huang, Ouyang and Li (2013) call for research on topics such as disciplinary boundaries and the essence of HRD.

Brown, Delgado and Cass (2013) note, "cultural diversity is one of the inescapable influences of human resource development (HRD)." They also explain a barrier that affects scholars and practitioners in bilingual countries; that is, HRD findings in one language may not be accessible to others in the country who do not share that language. Ghosh and Barman (2013) share a concern that is voiced by several authors about their respective regions. The context of HRD in India is influenced by a "complex interplay of political, social, and cultural changes." One of the concerns that they mention is bridging the academia–industry–government disconnect.

Aligned with the perspectives of Ghosh and Barman, Akdere and Dirani (2013) explain that in the Middle East "country specific cultures play a strong role in determining every aspect of HRD activities in the region." They stress the importance of considering the specific HRD challenges relative to the indigenous organizations and to country specific policies. Conversely, they caution against using interventions and systems developed in the West and generalizing them to the Middle East region.

Several of the authors characterize the workforces of their respective countries in ways that impact on the types of services needed from HRD. For example, Schalkoff and Kuo (2013) characterize Japan and Taiwan, respectively, as countries that are becoming increasingly diversified as birthrates continue to decrease. Kraak (2013) describes the unemployed youth crisis of South Africa and how it is purported to be "the greatest threat to South Africa's young democracy." Similar to social concerns expressed by Stewart and Ardichvili in their respective responses, he ponders how a social compact might be put forth that benefits the economic conditions for all in South Africa. Alagaraja and Arthur-Mensah (2013) pose a similar request. In the context of the stable and fast-rising economy of the African country of Ghana, they urge the development of positive work environments in which "fair and ethical HRD policies are implemented."

Table E.8 HRD around the world

Current State of Affairs	*Future of Topic*	*Intriguing Questions*
34. Meera Alagaraja and Nana K. Arthur-Mensah – HRD in Ghana		
Currently, policy makers and organization leaders are recognizing the need to develop human capacity and capability as a critical driver for holistic social, political, cultural and economic development. With Ghana's economic growth and status as a stable and fast rising African country, there is huge potential for HRD to support learning and development of the workforce both within and outside the organizational contexts.	HRD initiatives in Ghana must be more than just providing access to training and development for employees. What is critical is fostering positive work environments within organizational settings so that fair and ethical HRD practices are implemented. Furthermore, enabling sociocultural contexts in which individuals can thrive and grow through the inclusion and integration of different ethnicities, maintaining regional and gender balance in the workplace, developing communities and organizations through learning and performance can drive positive change and impact all areas of the Ghanaian economy and society.	How do HRD managers design HRD policies and practices that are transferable to different country contexts? How do organizations evaluate the effectiveness of HRD practices and policies in cross-cultural contexts and their impact on organizational performance?
35. Andre Kraak – HRD in South Africa		
Reform of the further college system has not yet taken place, largely because the state does not have the capacity to manage change and has been consumed by crises of legitimacy (corruption) and popular protest – so the chapter's criticisms still hold. Core features of the failing system include: supply-side dominance, lack of employer buy-in, poor progression from vocational to other forms of post-school education, and lack of partnerships with industry.	The post-school education and training system is malfunctioning and the unemployed youth crisis in South Africa is growing – a crisis which is said to be the greatest threat to South Africa's young democracy. An effective college system has to be part of the solution, equipping young people with skills that the economy requires (demand-led) with meaningful pathways to further and higher learning.	In the early part of South Africa's young democracy, the idea of a social compact to bring employers, unions and the state together to forge a new South Africa was the central political platform for change. In the current period, this has been abandoned as politics has become more adversarial (and corrupted). The intriguing question of the day is what would it take to bring about such a social compact that advanced economic progress for all in a South Africa of tomorrow and what would it look like in terms of education and training? Or do adversarial relations continue into the future with no gains for any side?

36. Rod P. Githens, Carlos Albornoz, Librado Enrique Gonzalez, Tonette S. Rocco and Christine Wiggins-Romesburg – HRD in Central and South America

Our chapter is a description of two national HRD systems, Chile and Panama. Both Chile and Panama have growing economies and democratically elected governments. Chile recently held elections with the more socialist party winning. Panama is a country in transition both economically and politically. Its changed relationship with the US opened the doors to the current economic and political transformation. However, possible threats to an independent judiciary cause uncertainty politically. Economically, the massive construction boom has spurred the economy, along with the expansion of the Panama canal and increasing presence of international firms. Both countries have workforce development needs like raising the literacy levels and training more technical and knowledge workers. Both countries' economies are focused somewhat narrowly on one or two sectors. The workforce development policies of both countries are items on the government's agenda. Specifically in Panama, there is a strong need for enhancement of the overall public education system. The chapter is an effort to open the scholarly debate of ideas for developing human resources in Central and South America.

The relevance of our chapter is primarily in the lack of information and research that exists on Central and South America related to HRD. Considering the little academic work available about the region, a future goal should be to work with South American scholars to document the workforce development and NHRD changes occurring in the different countries. HRD does not exist as a formal training or field of study in either of the countries profiled. The fact is that colleges and universities do not offer a degree in HRD and few people know/understand what HRD is.

The economies of Central and South America are diverse and in various stages of development. However, as they continue evolving and modernizing, it will be important to watch if the quality of domestic education levels improves in many countries and if organic economic growth can be built and sustained. For example, the impressive growth in Panama has relied primarily on foreign management and investment and has had somewhat limited effects for large masses of the domestic population.

The types of national HRD systems that could work in Central and South American countries have little emphasis on the technology industry and are highly dependent on the technology produced in the US and Europe. For example, the literature discusses the importance of developing knowledge workers, but is that true for Chile, given its historic reliance on natural resources? Or Panama, given its reliance on jobs supported by the canal? How can the economies of Central and South America successfully transition from a historic reliance on those natural resources as economic drivers?

37. Travor C. Brown, José Ernesto Rangel Delgado and Bronwyn Cass – HRD in North America

Mexico – First consider that in the case of Canada and Mexico, cultural diversity is one of the inescapable influences on HRD. I suggest this topic also be considered for the USA. In the case of Mexico there have been attempts to standardize education surrounding the Spanish language, without definitive results. Mexico's companies still require technological modernization of administrative processes, particularly micro and small ones.

Mexico – Mexico requires a public policy to meet modern economic conditions, one that does not leave business development by the wayside. Mexico requires a policy that creates greater competitiveness and better performance, one that avoids corruption and promotes a receptive attitude to new global conditions that direct the country's economy.

Mexico – Unequal conditions refer to regional differences. Not all can be planned from the central government's perspective. It is necessary for the State to consider both local and global aspects or in other words follow the premise encapsulated by "thinking globally and acting locally", to develop HRD policies "glocally".

(*Continued*)

Table E.8 (Continued)

Current State of Affairs	*Future of Topic*	*Intriguing Questions*
Canada – While Canada borders the US, a country with a rich HRD history, several important trends are evident. First, Canada lacks a distinct HRD community; there are limited educational programs that focus solely on HRD. Rather the focus is on the more generic HRM and Adult Education fields. Second, as a bilingual country, there may be HRD findings in one language that are inaccessible to those who cannot speak that language. Third, Canada's strength in the HRD arena tends to be in the training field.	**Canada –** The primary challenge for Canada will be the movement to a comprehensive HRD community. It will be interesting to see if Canada, down the road, moves to a distinct HRD community or whether the field becomes absorbed into HRM and/ or Adult Education. Failure to create a vibrant HRD community may result in the Canadian discipline being focused narrowly on training and development.	**Canada –** To move HRD forward in Canada in a comprehensive way, the discipline must be more comprehensive and its uniqueness from HRM and Adult Education understood. A research question that could aid in that matter would be a comprehensive, comparative study of HRD practices/communities in Canada vs the US (or the UK). The goal of that study would be to compare perspectives of practitioners and scholars in those countries in an attempt to see why HRD in Canada has largely remained embedded in HRM and Adult Education.
38. Rajashi Ghosh and Arup Barman – HRD in India		
The long term focus on employee development as represented by the concept of HRD has gained much traction in organizations in India in the last decade. Due to a newly emerged market-oriented economy, the HRD function has begun receiving greater recognition and importance. At the micro level, all private, public, and multinational organizations in India have started focusing more on how to develop and engage their employees to reduce attrition. At the macro level, the Government of India has started initiating partnerships with different nongovernmental organizations for planning towards promoting national skill development. However, the full scope and potential for human capital development in India has been tempered by the complex interplay of political, social, and cultural changes.	Although the field of HRD in India has advanced in the last decade, the HRD function is still not well structured at both the organizational and national levels. Some key challenges confronting the field of HRD in India include managing diversity (especially pertaining to integration of women into the workforce), linking operational HRD activities to strategic HRD relevant to the organization's business, acknowledging and addressing cultural influences, and bridging the academia–industry–government disconnect.	How can we prepare an industry-ready skilled workforce? How can we ensure equitable workforce education and development? How can we integrate women in all levels of the workforce? How can we prepare the Indian workforce to embrace globalization in all sectors and industries? How can we align both rural and urban educational institutions in India with industry and government needs and vice versa?

39. Jian Huang, Zhongming Ouyang and Jessica Li – HRD in China

The development of HRD as a research field in China derived from the great demand China had for HRD professionals and knowledge systems since the 1990s. The first HRD program was born in East China Normal University in 2007. Yet it has been operated in few other universities so far. The systematic and specialized research on HRD is based on the springing up and deep-going of HRD programs, which amount to a small number. Moreover, there have been considerable disputes over the boundary of the field. Scholars from related disciplines such as education, psychology, and management all started to build their HRD circles, resulting in the emergence of HRD studies from interdisciplinary perspectives in large numbers.	With the rapid development of HRD practice and policy in China and influence from the international HRD academic world, future hot issues of HRD may increasingly cover: training management and tapping into intellectual resources within organizations, e-learning, competence models, coaching, tutoring and action learning, and performance improvement.	Future HRD research in China should be concerned with basic problems of the discipline, like the connotation and essence of HRD, disciplinary boundaries, and main research interests. On the other hand, the major issues of HRD practice areas should receive monographic studies from multidisciplinary perspectives, for instance, study on the learning and ability development of various groups, innovative learning methods and techniques, transformation of training achievements and assessment of training effectiveness, blended learning and mobile learning, organizational development and performance improvement, and others.

40. Mesut Akdere and Khalil M. Dirani – HRD in the Middle East

The field of HRD in the region traditionally existed in the form of personnel training (mainly formal) and apprenticeship. The apprenticeship model in the Middle East often involved sending young boys (never girls) to work with a master in a given occupation such as bakery, metal works, and woodshops. To this date, this practice exists particularly in the countries that are not industrialized. As for management and leadership development, the main focus is on helping natives develop a skill set to become effective managers and successful leaders. Little emphasis is given to continuing education and lifelong learning. Furthermore, although many countries in the region have a comprehensive national HRD plan or strategy, the educational and technological prerequisites for HRD are not in place. It is important to note that country-specific cultures play a strong role in determining every aspect of HRD activities in the region.	Thus HRD can play a role at the national level by helping with eliminating illiteracy, improving education and ensuring active participation of women in the society in general and in the workplace specifically.	Because there is little study on the Middle East in the HRD area, the main research question evolves from understanding the specific HRD challenges related to the indigenous organizations and to country-specific policies rather than imposing predetermined classifications, and systems that were predominantly developed in the West, and generalizing them to the whole region. This will allow for deeper understanding and facilitation of HRD practices, rather than deciding whether HRD fits predetermined criteria, of which few exist.

(*Continued*)

Table E.8 (Continued)

Current State of Affairs	*Future of Topic*	*Intriguing Questions*
41. Robert J. Schalkoff and Min-Hsun Christine Kuo – HRD in Japan and Taiwan		
Japan – Development of international competencies continues to be an issue. New MEXT programs at the secondary education level focus on linguistic, critical thinking, and cross-disciplinary competencies aimed at helping Japan regain its competitive edge. Government has also called for HRD programs to help women re-enter the workforce after childbirth and to enable them to work while raising families. Work–life balance is an issue for males; HRD initiatives focus on sharing family responsibilities. **Taiwan –** HRD continues to be important for large companies and MNCs. Focus is on developing competency models and strategic partnerships with HR staff. Government continues to play a role in providing HRD assistance for SMEs. Programs to enhance human capital projects are increasingly popular; new systems to assist enterprises in developing well-organized T&D have been introduced. Public, private, and academic resources are being combined to provide central, diversified subsidies for SMEs.	**Japan –** As birthrates continue to decrease, workforce diversity will increase. HRD will need to address language and cultural training. The government may not be able to continue steering policy in this environment. Lack of economic growth may cause issues in funding for NHRD initiatives. **Taiwan –** The workforce is becoming increasingly diversified as the birthrate continues to decrease. The government may not be able to resolve emerging issues by providing subsidies. Enterprises, especially SMEs, continue to deal with small profits; issues of overtime and work–life imbalance are severe. Labor-management controversy is also increasing.	**Japan –** What role can HRD practitioners play in setting policy at the national and organizational level? What, if any, are the barriers to establishing undergraduate and graduate level programs to train HRD professionals? **Taiwan –** How can the government help SMEs develop competence in T&D; in the face of lack of funds and HRD practitioners, how can enterprises resolve issues of overtime and labor management conflict through organizational development?
42. Kenneth R. Bartlett and Roger Harris – HRD in Australia and New Zealand		
All too frequently international publications lump Australia and New Zealand together, yet analysis of historical, cultural and sociopolitical contexts and regional traditions shows both common themes and unique aspects of the current state of HRD in professional practice, research and academic study. Australia has a more complex HRD system than New Zealand, mainly due to the interaction between state and federal governments; whereas New Zealand continues to have heavy government influence, especially for entry-level and lower skilled occupations, but overall adopts a free-market approach raising future concerns over needed HRD investment for sustained growth.	The term HRD is not prominent in Australia or New Zealand although the practice of HRD is widespread. Both countries have an approach to HRD that could be represented by an *intertwined rope* with several strands, including business/management and post-secondary/adult education, which has resulted in a lack of visibility for HRD as a field of study. The current approach may bring new perspectives to HRD research and practice, or it may result in a fragmented focus, location, target membership and disciplinary emphasis.	In both Australia and New Zealand there is an absence of HRD as a standalone academic discipline in universities. The multifaceted nature of fields of practice in which HRD is embedded and the involvement of government at various levels has not translated into a need for specific HRD university programs or degrees. With increasing concerns about the need for HRD innovation and investment, should HRD academic programs be established?

HRD, HRM and HR are intrinsically related in Hungary and Poland. There are very few articles focused solely on HRD and only a handful of HRD academic/degree programs (while some HRD-related topics are included in HRM programs and other related programs). The research points to the range of HRD practices in different organizations with MNCs using mostly practices based on Western HRD values and principles and SME using the least of these practices. National development plans and strategies that include HRD such as Hungary's 2004–2006 Human Resource Development Operational Program and the 2007–2013 Social Renewal Operational Program and Poland's National Strategy for the Development of Human Capital 2020, are evidence of the vital role of HRD in the health and well-being of these countries.

The treatment of HRD as an appendix to HR/HRM raises concerns about the professionalization of the HRD field and its needed educational programs and practices embedded in humanistic and constructivist paradigms. Since the practice of HRD relies on systems thinking and the ability to understand the interconnections among all parts of changing systems, the development of a set of competencies flexible enough to keep pace with the continuous changes experienced by HRD practitioners could be very beneficial both for formal educational and informal learning programs and environments and could contribute to the professionalization of the field.

The tendencies toward convergence of HRD values and practices promoted by MNCs could be a concern given the complexities of national policies, organizational structures and diversity of the workforce in these two countries and in the CEE region. A continuum on the convergence, crossvergence and divergence scale of HRD values and practices is to be expected.

A comparative study in each of the countries of practices used by graduates of different HR/HRM/HRD programs to understand their philosophy and application of HRD values and principles could illuminate the strength and areas of development needed by existing formal educational programs.

Since NHRD plans and strategies related to HRD education and practice were prominent in both countries, the study of their impact on HRD would allow the understanding of their strength and could shape the development of future policies that will continue to ensure the development of needed competencies including a global mindset that includes curiosity and openness to new ideas conducive to creativity and innovation, while creating the market conditions that will appreciate them.

A well designed research agenda to understand the needed adaptation of Western HRD practices to (1) the cultural and socio-economic contexts of Hungary and Poland (as well as those of other CEE countries) with their NHRD plans and institutional forms, and (2) the specific structures and organizational cultures of the many types of organizations such as MNC, large, medium and small entrepreneurial organizations will allow for the understanding of the potential convergence, crossvergence and divergence tendencies of HRD values and practices.

Given the rate of change of knowledge and competencies in the developing global markets that have a direct impact on local markets, the study of the socio-economic and organizational conditions conducive to continuous learning would allow HRD professionals to create these environments.

(*Continued*)

Table E.8 (Continued)

Current State of Affairs	*Future of Topic*	*Intriguing Questions*
	Another concern is the lack of or limited use of HRD practices in SMEs that in both countries account for a large percentage of jobs and of the national GDPs. Thus, their competitiveness relies on continuous learning and change to adapt to the changing markets is crucial.	Last, but not least, the meaning of HRD is continuously evolving in the Western world and its interpretation in CEE is also evolving. Keeping in mind the dynamic nature of this field, and the meaning making that occurs when the ideas that it represents travel to Hungary, Poland and other CEE countries, understanding the meaning attached to these ideas is essential for speaking the same professional language not just in words but in meaning.
44. Alexandra Dehmel and Jasper B. Van Loo – HRD in the European Union		
In Europe, HRD policies at the supranational level have had an impact on what is happening in Europe, but the true innovation potential of learning has not been fully tapped into. Important challenges today are to open up learning opportunities to all, to ensure that enterprises see the true benefits of investing in their staff and to make more workplaces learning places.	Labor market forecasts show increasing demand for highly skilled people but people with medium level skills remain an important and stable base of Europe's economies. Competing effectively in the global marketplace requires much more attention for learning as a core driver of innovation and skills policies that recognise that HRD should be inclusive in terms of age and skill level. The megatrends of population ageing and skills upgrading in virtually all jobs could lead to skills shortages down the road when adult learning and vocational training opportunities are insufficient.	Considering that European countries work towards common priorities set at the EU level, how can HRD research and practice contribute to ensuring that the specific adult learning and vocational education and training policies countries pursue and implement maximise learning opportunities and innovation potential in their unique socio-economic context?

Section IX: emerging topics and future trends

Authors of this section describe common threads that are aligned with key points from the preceding sections. Van Der Heijden, Peters and Kelliher (2013) seek to examine stratifications within the workforce, such as core versus flexible workers, and workers from different age categories. Additionally, they are intrigued by current trends and their impact on social cohesion across workforce categories within and outside of organizations. McGuire and Kissack (2013) wonder about such trends and muse as to whether or not globalization and technology innovations enable or inhibit the line manager's role in organizations. Rosenbusch (2013) brings to our attention that people are engaged in cross-cultural work settings whether they have the needed skills or not. She stresses that HRD can play an important role in helping workers and leaders develop intercultural competence. However, Nam, Cho and Lee explain that challenges await this worthy goal. To them, a significant challenge is determining meaningful ways to measure cross-cultural competency while embracing cultural diversity. Finally, Conceição and Thomas (2013) "caution the 'human' element of HRD risks being lost amid all of the technological development and adaptation."

Table E.9 Emerging topics and future trends

Current State of Affairs	*Future of Topic*	*Intriguing Questions*
45. David McGuire and Heather C. Kissack – Line managers		
Globalization, technology and changes to organizational and work structures have significantly changed the role and function of line managers in organizations. Changes to HR delivery structures have also placed added responsibility on line managers to not only ensure production and service schedules are adhered to, but also to guarantee the effective training and development of front-line staff. With little research being conducted into the changing nature of the role of line managers, this chapter sheds light on the burgeoning workload of line managers; the lack of preparation and support given to line managers to deliver upon an ever-increasing list of priorities and the widening range of stakeholders that line managers must interact with in order to discharge their responsibilities effectively.	This chapter calls on HR academics, industry leaders and business commentators to reflect upon the intensification of the line manager role in organizations. In the absence of proper training and development as well as adequate support and resources, line managers are facing an ever-more stressful working environment, leading to greater levels of staff burnout and ill-health. Moreover, it appears that levels of autonomy and discretion afforded to line managers have diminished, casting doubt over how truly effective line managers can be in their role. While the role of line managers has expanded exponentially, their status in the organization appears weakened. The future success of organizations depends not only on the skills and effectiveness of senior management, but also more crucially on the ability of line managers to inspire and motivate front-line employees. Organizations are thus challenged to ensure line managers are given the space and freedom to nurture, develop and grow the best employees and, through their role as motivators and departmental/divisional leaders, help improve customer service and performance levels.	Are globalization and technology innovations enablers or inhibitors of the line manager's role in organizations?

(*Continued*)

Table E.9 (Continued)

46. Brad Shuck and Sally Sambrook – Employee engagement		
Engagement is at a critical point in empirical and theoretical maturation. While scholarship on the topic is robust in places, agreement on what it is and how it is experienced remains elusive. Notwithstanding, within a mostly positivist perspective, there is agreement emerging around the idea that engagement is a positive psychological state.	The universal aspect and the applicability of engagement across human dynamics is the future of the engagement field. As we explore the international, cultural, and national issues of engagement, we uncover the applicability of engagement as a human phenomenon experienced by many people in many situations and in many countries.	Connected to the future of engagement, there are three lines of work to be passionately pursued. The first is a unifying theory of engagement that explores the psychological phenomenon as it relates to the whole person. The second is a beginning understanding of the disengagement phenomenon and its process.
In terms of outcomes, the research is gaining some clarity – we know for example that employees who experience high levels of engagement in their work report experiencing life, both inside and outside of work, more robustly.	As we have carried out our own research, we have been excited by the appeal of engagement as a positively experienced phenomenon in many different contexts.	We know very little about disengagement, how it is experienced and at what levels it exists. Third is a more critical examination of engagement in contrast to the dominant positivist, unitarist, managerialist perspective. If pursued, these three lines will substantially move the field forward as well as positively influence the way we all experience a new era of work and the employee–work relationship.
47. Beatrice I. J. M. Van Der Heijden, Pascale Peters and Clare Kelliher – New ways of working and employability		
Recent changes in the world of work have meant that the relevance and currency of the knowledge, skills and attributes (so-called employability or career potential) of employees have become increasingly important. In a similar way, employees' willingness to be deployed on a basis which meets organizational needs to be more flexible and responsive is more relevant than ever too. At the same time, we have seen a changing profile of employees seeking greater flexibility in order to balance the needs of their work and family lives more effectively.	As global competition increases and the profile of the workforce changes, it is likely that these trends will intensify and that potential tensions may emerge. Therefore, it is urgent that policy makers address these issues at national, organizational and individual levels.	Given the changing workforce, the moderating role of workforce characteristics in the relationship between employability and flexibility needs to be examined. It might be especially interesting to study possible differences between core and flexible workers, and between workers from different age categories. Also, differences between workers across different levels of educational or occupational sectors are assumed to be valuable. Moreover, a fruitful research question would be to study how current trends regarding flexibility and employability affect social cohesion between workforce categories within and outside organizations.

Stakeholders need to examine the ways in which these concepts are interrelated, the potential impact different ways of working may have on employees' careers, and the role HRM/HRD may play to reconcile organizational and individual needs.	Further, there needs to be a better understanding of the implications of NWW for the psychological contract and associated outcomes such as commitment and satisfaction at work, as well as in the light of workers' employability. The "darker side" of NWW should be explored as well, and the possible (negative) link it may have with employee well-being. Cross-national research on careers would help inform this debate in a globalized world and provide guidance for HRM and HRD practice across the globe. In the newspapers, there is a lot of reporting about the younger generations not being able to have a permanent job anymore. Will that also be true when the labor market becomes tighter in the future? Issues to be studied at the organizational level: What problems do employers who want and need to take these trends into account in their HRM policy encounter? And what factors determine the success of an employability policy in an organization (contingency approach)? How can organizations enhance their workers' employability using a regional level (network) approach? At an individual and job level: What problems do direct line managers who want and need to take these trends into account in their HRM policy and practices encounter? And what factors determine the success of employability policy and practices?

(*Continued*)

48. Sunny L. Munn and Hae-Young Lee – Work–life system		
The study of work–life is an important issue for individuals, organizations and governments, not only in industrialized but also emerging nations. Regardless of location four key themes emerged relevant to the work–life system: family, cultural context, working patterns and government. However, diversity in cultural compositions, variances in individual needs, wide ranges in societal expectations and differences in government create great challenges for crafting a single approach to the work–life system.	The accurate study of the work–life system across the globe is impacted by several issues including measurement, unique populations such as farming or tribal communities, the needs of men and individuals without children, policy development at organizational and governmental levels and finally data collection which allows for the hierarchical study of individuals, organizations and government within the context of the work–life system.	Across countries and cultures how are the needs of men – fathers and non-fathers – being impacted within the work–life system?
49. Paul L. Nesbit – Emotions and self-development		
In the field of emotion and learning contemporary research is focusing more and more on the role of emotions in online learning. Given that self-directed learning is likely to incorporate increasing use of technology and Internet learning strategies this research direction has considerable relevance. As noted in the chapter learners vary in their capacity to respond to teaching that requires them to be self-directing and the greater use of Internet based learning will increasingly challenge the self-directed capacities of learners.	Within the area of emotion and learning, it is necessary to understand in greater depth the role of emotion in the learning process, especially self-development approaches, and how it may be considered both in the research sense and in the applied sense by HRD professionals.	The difficulty in moving the topic of emotion and self-development forward lies in part on the agreement of a valid measure of self-directed learning within organizations. At present a variety of approaches have been developed but none of these are focused on learning in the workplace. A secondary issue relates to assessing how people feel throughout their learning experience. Moving the topic forward will require innovative approaches to research that include both qualitative and qualitative methods.
50. Thomas G. Reio, Jr. – Workplace incivility		
The current state of affairs related to workplace incivility is such that the frequency of workplace incivility is increasing worldwide to the detriment of all. Business	What I find important to the chapter topic (incivility) is that we still lack sufficient hard-hitting empirical evidence that uncivil behavior is truly costly to organizations (that is, causal data).	Based on Porter's theory of competitive advantage (4 building blocks), the research question would be as follows: What is the relationship between workplace

leaders must be made aware of incivility's insidious nature and how it can lead to more serious types of aggression. We must find ways to reduce the instigation of uncivil behavior because it is quite costly to organizations (it increases turnover and reduces productivity). HRD can play a leading role in reducing incivility's likelihood through training and development (e.g. learn conflict management skills), recruitment and selection, orientation, and mentoring programs activities.

What evidence we do have is limited mostly to North American contexts or select countries in Europe. We need more research in a wider variety of settings; settings that include not only heretofore unexamined countries, but also different types of workplaces (e.g. manufacturing and service; male dominated versus female dominated), samples of expatriates, etc.

incivility and an organization's competitive advantage?

H1: Workplace incivility has a negative impact on organizational efficiency.

H2: Workplace incivility has a negative impact on organizational quality.

H3: Workplace incivility has a negative impact on organizational innovativeness.

H4: Workplace incivility has a negative impact on organizational customer responsiveness.

51. Kyoung-Ah Nam, Yonjoo Cho and Mimi Miyoung Lee – Cross-cultural training

Current Cross-Cultural Training (CCT) research is heavily focused on Western expatriates' experiences and Western cultural perspectives, revealing only a partial picture. We identified gaps in CCT research, addressed emerging issues, and provided implications for future research and practice. Current streams and challenges include issues relating to cross-cultural assessment, CCT methods, CCT trainers, and differences between domestic and international assignments.

We suggest that future CCT research and practice be expanded to consider alternative perspectives including that of non-Western expatriates. To minimize misunderstanding and enhance collaboration within a multicultural workplace, CCT should be designed and delivered not only to expatriates, but also to their host country counterparts; CCT should utilize a stronger partnership with subsidiaries. Further, a more systematic, long-term approach to CCT is needed, including in-depth pre-departure training with realistic job previews for employees and their families, ongoing in-country support, and thoughtful re-entry preparation.

What unique issues arise with the increasing complexity of expatriate movements beyond between West and East? (E.g. Korean expatriates working in India, Chinese-American expatriates working in Taiwan.)

While there is an increasing demand for cross-cultural assessment instruments measuring cross-cultural competencies, current instruments are mostly developed from Western perspectives. What is the best way to measure cross-cultural competency while embracing cultural diversity?

How do contextual variables (e.g. types of expatriates, gender, age, length of assignment) influence expatriates' adjustment to new environments and job performance?

What cultural issues in CCT should be addressed for non-Western expatriates and their families?

How do non-Western companies train their expatriates for successful performance in global contexts?

(*Continued*)

Table E.9 (Continued)

52. *Katherine Rosenbusch – Intercultural competence*		
With the increase of globalization, everything is changing. International markets have become stronger, multinational companies have increased, international mobility has become essential, information technologies continue to grow and the multicultural environment has exploded. Individuals are being challenged to work in complex cross-cultural arenas with or without the skills. It is imperative for employees to possess intercultural competence to be effective and thrive.	In order to build competitive advantage, organizations must now focus on their global talent development. HRD needs to focus on how to develop global leaders and build intercultural competence. What potential career derailers may affect their global talent pool (dual-career couples, global mobility fatigue, and reintegration)?	Further research needs to be conducted as to how global leaders develop their intercultural competence. What exact tools, techniques and reflection components could assist organizations in fine tuning their development programs in order to justify that it is more than training that will increase the capacity to work with other cultures?
53. *Simone C. O. Conceição and Kristopher J. Thomas – Virtual HRD*		
The speed of technological development and adaptation continues to accelerate. Organizations are continually challenged to incorporate new technologies and novel ways of adapting those technologies into their learning and development efforts. Blended course environments with shorter, more frequent periods of engagement have become more prevalent. Employees are increasingly expected to engage in self-directed virtual learning at their place in their own time. This virtual learning is frequently augmented by traditional face-to-face learning.	We caution the "human" element of HRD risks being lost amid all of the technological development and adaptation. Though the reach, scalability, and flexibility afforded by VHRD are important elements to ensure that learning and development efforts are both attainable and sustainable, there should always be a place for face-to-face classroom interaction. There is a strong risk that technology becomes the answer to every question related to HRD. In our view, VHRD should complement traditional HRD, not replace it.	Given that VHRD is a burgeoning field that is changing at a staggering pace, there is not yet a body of literature that studies the longitudinal impact of VHRD interventions. Using a constructivist framework, we would like to see asked "What is the long-term impact of VHRD on employees' cognitive development and, ultimately, their ability to translate learning gained via VHRD into results in the workplace?"

Note

1 All references pertain to email communications from our chapter authors in response to the three questions we sent them; they were returned to us between October and December of 2013.

References

Ardichvili, A. 2011. Sustainability of nations, communities, organizations and individuals: the role of HRD. *Human Resource Development International*, 14, 371–74.

Elliott, C. 2013. Critically thinking. *Human Resource Development International*, 16, 133–34.

FCIC Report. 2011. *The Finanical Crisis Inquiry Report: Final Report of the National Commission on the Causes of the Financial and Economic Crisis in the United States [full report]* [Online]. New York. Available: http://fcic.law.stanford.edu/ [accessed October 2011].

MacKenzie, C. A., Garavan, T. N. and Carbery, R. 2012. Through the looking glass: challenges for human resource development (HRD) post the global financial crisis – business as usual? *Human Resource Development International*, 15, 353–64.

Poell, R.F. 2012. The future of human resource development: from a management tool to an employee tool as well. *Human Resource Development International*, 15, 1–3.

Scully-Russ, E. 2012. Human resource development and sustainability: beyond sustainable organizations. *Human Resource Development International*, 15, 399–415.

INDEX OF TERMS

H

I

T

U

V

INDEX OF NAMES

L